Paul Watkins Medieval Studies
Anglo-Saxon Writs

PAUL WATKINS MEDIEVAL STUDIES

General Editor: Shaun Tyas

---

1. ANDERSON, Alan Orr, *Early Sources of Scottish History, A.D. 500 to 1286*; a new edition with corrections, in two volumes. *Available 1989.*

2. HARMER, Florence E., *Anglo-Saxon Writs*; a new edition comprising the original work together with her later essay, 'A Bromfield and a Coventry Writ of King Edward the Confessor'.

ANGLO-SAXON WRITS

By

Florence E. Harmer

A Second Edition
PAUL WATKINS
STAMFORD
1989

ISBN 1 871615 02 X

This new edition is a combination of two works: the original 1952 *Anglo-Saxon Writs*, reprinted with the permission of Manchester University Press; and Florence Harmer's essay 'A Bromfield and a Coventry Writ of King Edward the Confessor' from *The Anglo-Saxons: Studies in Some Aspects of Their History and Culture Presented to Bruce Dickins*, ed. Peter Clemoes (published Bowes and Bowes, London, 1959) and reprinted with the permission of The Bodley Head, London.

Paul Watkins
45 St Leonard's Street, Stamford, Lincolnshire PE9 2HN

Printed (on long-life paper) and bound by Woolnoughs of Irthingborough.

CONTENTS

ANGLO-SAXON WRITS

THE WARD BEQUEST

The late Sir Adolphus William Ward, successively Professor of History and English, Principal of Owens College and Vice-Chancellor of the University of Manchester, bequeathed one thousand pounds to the University. By the decision of the Council of the University, the income from this sum is to be devoted to the advancement of research in History and in English. It will normally be used to assist the publication by the University Press of approved works of scholarship, and all works of which the cost of publication has been wholly or partially defrayed from the fund will be issued with the imprint of ' The Ward Bequest '.

This is the tenth volume published under the terms of the fund.

PLATE I (*Frontispiece*)

Authentic writ for Christ Church, Canterbury, of King Edward the Confessor, wi⸱
authentic seal appended. The change of handwriting after ' beon ' marks the work ⸱
a forger. See No. 33, pp. 103, 173 and 451–2. The writ is here reduced to about tw⸱
thirds of its actual maximum dimensions, $7\frac{2}{5}'' \times 3\frac{3}{5}''$.

THE WARD BEQUEST

ANGLO-SAXON WRITS

By

F. E. HARMER

MANCHESTER UNIVERSITY PRESS

Published by the University of Manchester
at the University Press
316–324, Oxford Road
Manchester, 13
1952

PREFACE

Of the 120 Anglo-Saxon writs printed here (to which has been added the letter of the monk Edwin, no. 113), ranging (ostensibly) in date from King Æthelred II to King Harold II (or possibly later with nos. 6, 72), and comprising writs of non-royal persons as well as of kings and queens, three at least, nos. 33 (in part), 55 and 96 (P), are probably on all grounds actual products of the royal clerks, with the royal seal; one or two others, without a seal, probably no. 115, possibly no. 11, might be added to this select group. My purpose has been to bring together here all the Anglo-Saxon writs that have survived; among these the undoubtedly authentic nos. 46, 120, and the dubious or spurious nos. 31, 32, 34 (Anglo-Saxon version printed only in facsimile), 89, have remained, so far as I can discover, unprinted hitherto.

A strict application of the definition of the Anglo-Saxon writ as it is given on p. 1 has led to the exclusion of documents merely approximating to the type, so that it is unfortunately not yet possible to say (in spite of modern editions of the charters and wills of the Anglo-Saxon period) that all the surviving business documents of the period in the vernacular have now appeared in annotated editions. While I have included here as Appendix I a spurious Ripon writ, it did not seem worth while to include a spurious Crowland letter in Latin of Edward the Confessor (p. 578). I have omitted spurious Latin charters with address and greeting clause. I have also omitted the two undoubtedly genuine Proclamations of King Cnut, and two wills of private persons; though all these have the same kind of protocol, they do not in other respects conform to the pattern of writs printed here.

All the manuscripts given under ' Authorities ' in the Notes have been inspected (either directly or by photographs) with only one or two exceptions, in order that a proper choice might be made for printing; that copy (not necessarily the earliest) has been selected (unless for special reasons some other was to be preferred) which seems to reproduce most closely the (presumed) Anglo-Saxon original. No attempt has been made to print the innumerable spelling variants arising from unconscious or deliberate scribal alteration (see p. 153); only those variants which seemed to be significant have been printed. Since the defects of Kemble's texts

v

are now sufficiently well recognised, it has not seemed necessary (except in special cases) to record his errors. In discussing the texts I have, when it seemed appropriate, given the passage in question in its correct Old English form, and not as it may appear in the manuscript.

The spelling and punctuation of texts in the vernacular have been preserved, except that I have made myself responsible for capital letters, and that while retaining the ordinary Old English abbreviations (see p. xix), I have expanded in italics the other abbreviations and contractions in the texts. For convenience in printing I have not indicated the different kinds of punctuation marks used, a stop merely indicating the existence of a mark of punctuation there. I have joined together without notice parts of words written separately by copyists. Interlineations in the manuscript have been inclosed in ' ', supplied readings between square brackets. Variations in spacing in the texts from one writ to another are merely typographical. When punctuation is lacking in the manuscript, I have usually supplied it.

Latin versions appearing in the manuscripts have been included here (but not those known to have been composed by scholars such as Joscelin, Somner and Hickes), because although they rarely help to elucidate difficulties in the corresponding English texts, they may on occasion provide material for the criticism of those fourteen writs which are extant only in Latin. In the Latin versions printed here, as also in the Latin headings and other notes, the punctuation and use of capitals have been modernised, and abbreviations (except in the case of stock abbreviations or forms that are indeterminate) have been extended without notice. Even in Latin versions the symbol 7 (' and ') is printed when this, or something like it, appears in the manuscript.

As work on this edition proceeded, it became clear that (in spite of obvious difficulties) it would be desirable to mark out in some rough-and-ready way those writs which for a variety of considerations could not in their entirety be taken at their face-value ; I have not however included in this category no. 50, with errors of translation. The purpose of the bracket round the date at the head of such writs, i.e. (1053–57), is merely to direct the reader to the discussion of the authenticity of the individual text. Writs which are probably fabrications are left undated.

The debts I owe for help of various kinds in the production of this book are too numerous to be acknowledged here in full detail, but are in many cases referred to in the text itself. But I should like to express my special gratitude to Dr. C. E. Wright for invaluable assistance with the manuscripts, and in other ways, and to

Professor V. H. Galbraith for constant help and encouragement. Like all workers in this field I owe much to the printed works of Professor Sir Frank Stenton, to whom I am indebted for the first suggestion of this book, for kind advice and help, and for the brilliant new interpretation of *scypgesceot* as ' ship-scot '. To Professors E. Vinaver and R. Fawtier I owe thanks for supplying me with photographs and a cast of the Taynton documents and seal. The late Professor Wilhelm Levison, through the kind mediation of Mr. B. Colgrave, with characteristic generosity read this book in typescript, and from his vast store of learning supplied me with information and references. I offer my best thanks for their criticisms and suggestions to those others who have read the book in typescript or in proof, in whole or in part,—to Professors H. M. Cam, C. R. Cheney, M. Deanesly, and especially to Miss D. Whitelock, to whom I am particularly and gratefully indebted. For what errors may still remain, in spite of the help of many friends, I alone am responsible.

I wish also to thank those owners and custodians of records who have given me access to their archives and permission to publish from them ; especially the Archbishop of Canterbury and the Librarian and Sub-librarian at Lambeth Palace, the Deans and Chapters of Canterbury, Ely, St. Paul's, Wells, Westminster, Winchester, Worcester and York, as well as the Librarians and Keepers of the Muniments (*or* Archives) ; the custodians of the Diocesan Registry at Worcester and of the muniments of the Corporation of King's Lynn ; also the University of Glasgow, the Master and Fellows of Corpus Christi College, Cambridge, the Council of Trinity College, and the Librarian, University Library, Cambridge ; also Bodley's Librarian, the Deputy Keeper of the Public Records, the Director of the Bibliothèque Nationale and the Librarian of the Guildhall, London. The authorities at the British Museum and the Director of the Archives Nationales have also kindly permitted the printing of texts and the reproduction of the photographs published here. I owe thanks for photographs and photostats kindly made available to me of no. 44 to Lord Vestey and the Reverend F. W. Potto Hicks, and of no. 121 to the late Lord Lonsdale, Miss S. E. Bailey, and Miss A. M. Armstrong, and to the owners of these manuscripts for permission to publish. I am also indebted to Messrs. Longmans, Green and Co. Ltd. for permission to reprint texts and use material from my article in *Eng. Hist. Rev.* vol. li (1936) ; and to the Governors of the John Rylands Library and the late Dr. Henry Guppy for permission to use material from my article in *The Bulletin of the John Rylands Library*, vol. xxii (1938). Finally, I am grateful to the Manchester

University Press for undertaking the publication of this book and
to the Committee of the Ward Bequest for their handsome contribution towards the cost of publication.

FLORENCE ELIZABETH HARMER.

1951

TABLE OF CONTENTS

LIST OF PLATES

CHRONOLOGICAL LIST OF WRITS

The fact that few writs can be assigned to a definite year makes it impossible to compile an exactly dated chronological table. The following list gives the extreme chronological limits of writs printed here, and also gives the names of non-royal senders of writs. With writs which should not be taken at their face value, the dates are enclosed within brackets. No. 36, a forgery in Cnut's name, has not been included. For the spurious writ of King Æthelstan, see Appendix I.

Years	No.	Sender	Reign
(978–1016)	52	King Æthelred II	Æthelred II
(984–1001)	107	,,	,,
995–1002	108	Queen Ælfthryth	,,
1001/2–1009/12	63	Bishop Æthelric	,,
1017–20	26	King Cnut	Cnut
(1017–30)	48	,,	,,
1020	27	Archbishop Wulfstan	,,
1020	28	King Cnut	,,
(1027–35)	37	,,	,,
(1033–35)	53	,,	,,
1035	29	,,	,,
1035	30	,,	,,
1040–42	56	King Harthacnut	Harthacnut
1040–42	57	King Harthacnut and Queen Ælfgifu	,,
1042–5 Jan. 1066 *passim*		King Edward	Edward
1041–64	121	Gospatric	Edward (probably)
1045–48	3	Bishop Siward	Edward
1061–66	70	Queen Edith	,,
1061–82	6	Abbot Wulfwold	Edward to William I
1066	71	King Harold	Harold
1066–75	72	Queen Edith	Harold *or* William I

NUMERICAL LIST OF WRITS

ABBOTSBURY
   1. King Edward   concerning   Urk's shore
   2.   ,,   ,,   ,,   Tole's lands

ABINGDON
   3. Bishop Siward   ,,   Leckhampstead
   4. King Edward   ,,   rights
   5.   ,,   ,,   ,,   Hormer hundred

BATH
   6. Abbot Wulfwold   ,,   Evesty and Ashwick

BEVERLEY
   7. King Edward   ,,   St. John's, Beverley

BURY
   8. King Edward   ,,   Abbot Ufi
   9.   ,,   ,,   ,,   Mildenhall and the Thingoe sokes
  10.   ,,   ,,   ,,   the Thingoe sokes
  11.   ,,   ,,   ,,   rights
  12.   ,,   ,,   ,,   rights
  13.   ,,   ,,   ,,   rights
  14.   ,,   ,,   ,,   Pakenham
  15.   ,,   ,,   ,,   exemption from heregeld
  16.   ,,   ,,   ,,   Kirby
  17.   ,,   ,,   ,,   Kirby
  18.   ,,   ,,   ,,   Thingoe sokes
  19.   ,,   ,,   ,,   soke
  20.   ,,   ,,   ,,   Coney Weston
  21.   ,,   ,,   ,,   Ælfric Modercope
  22.   ,,   ,,   ,,   Ælfric Modercope
  23.   ,,   ,,   ,,   Abbot Baldwine
  24.   ,,   ,,   ,,   Thingoe sokes
  25.   ,,   ,,   ,,   a moneyer

CHRIST CHURCH, CANTERBURY
  26. King Cnut   ,,   Christ Church
  27. Archbishop Wulfstan   ,,   Æthelnoth
  28. King Cnut   ,,   Æthelnoth
  29.   ,,   ,,   ,,   assessment of lands
  30.   ,,   ,,   ,,   Ælfmær's property
  31. King Edward   ,,   lands and rights
  32.   ,,   ,,   ,,   hunting
  33.   ,,   ,,   ,,   rights
  34.   ,,   ,,   ,,   lands and rights
  35.   ,,   ,,   ,,   Mersham

ST. AUGUSTINE'S, CANTERBURY
  36. King Cnut   ,,   rights
  37.   ,,   ,,   ,,   St. Mildred
  38. King Edward   ,,   rights
  39.   ,,   ,,   ,,   Fordwich

WESTMINSTER
77. King Edward concerning Chalkhill
78. ,, ,, ,, Aldenham
79. ,, ,, ,, Datchworth and Watton
80. ,, ,, ,, Ickworth
81. ,, ,, ,, rights
82. ,, ,, ,, rights
83. ,, ,, ,, rights
84. ,, ,, ,, Moulsham
85. ,, ,, ,, Eversley
86. ,, ,, ,, Shepperton
87. ,, ,, ,, Teinfrith
88. ,, ,, ,, Greenford
89. ,, ,, ,, Greenford
90. ,, ,, ,, Wormley
91. ,, ,, ,, Ayot
92. ,, ,, ,, Tooting
93. ,, ,, ,, Claygate
94. ,, ,, ,, Rutland
95. ,, ,, ,, Launton
96. ,, ,, ,, Perton
97. ,, ,, ,, Windsor and Staines
98. ,, ,, ,, Staines and *Stæningahaga*
99. ,, ,, ,, Pershore and Deerhurst
100. ,, ,, ,, Pershore and Deerhurst
101. ,, ,, ,, Pershore and Deerhurst
102. ,, ,, ,, Pershore and Deerhurst
103. ,, ,, ,, Islip and Marston
104. ,, ,, ,, Islip and Marston
105. ,, ,, ,, London rights
106. ,, ,, ,, London rights

WINCHESTER
107. King Æthelred ,, assessment of Chilcomb
108. Queen Ælfthryth ,, Ruishton
109. King Edward ,, Bishop Ælfwine
110. ,, ,, ,, Bishop Ælfwine
111. ,, ,, ,, a Winchester messuage
112. ,, ,, ,, Portland
113. Edwin's Letter ,, a Winchester concordat

WOLVERHAMPTON
114. King Edward ,, priests at Wolverhampton

WORCESTER
115. King Edward ,, Bishop Wulfstan
116. ,, ,, ,, Prior Ælfstan
117. ,, ,, ,, market rights

YORK
118. King Edward ,, rights
119. ,, ,, ,, rights
120. ,, ,, ,, Axminster

GOSPATRIC'S WRIT
121. Gospatric ,, rights

B

ABBREVIATIONS

abb	abbud	OHG	Old High German
7	and	OIcel	Old Icelandic
arceb	arcebisceop	OIr	Old Irish
b	bisceop	OLG	Old Low German
bes, b'es	bisceopes	ON	Old Norse
ME	Middle English	OS	Old Saxon
OBret	Old Breton	OScand	Old Scandinavian
OBrit	Old British	OSwed	Old Swedish
ODan	Old Danish	OW	Old Welsh
OE	Old English	OWScand	Old West Scandinavian
OEScand	Old East Scandinavian	Sce	Sancte
OFr	Old French	þ	þæt
OFris	Old Frisian	T.R.E.	Tempore Regis Edwardi
OG	Old German	WS	West Saxon
OGaul	Old Gaulish		

Archiv f. Urk. . . .	*Archiv für Urkundenforschung.*
Attenborough . . .	F. L. Attenborough, *Laws of the Earliest English Kings* (Cambridge, 1922).
B.	W. de Gray Birch, *Cartularium Saxonicum* (London, 1885–93), quoted by number of document.
Birch, *Cat.* . . .	Birch, *Catalogue of Seals in the Brit. Mus.* (1887–1900).
Bond	E. A. Bond, *Facsimiles of Ancient Charters in the British Museum* (London, 1873–78).
BT	J. Bosworth and T. N. Toller, *Anglo-Saxon Dictionary* (Oxford, 1882–98).
BT Suppt. . . .	Supplement to the above (Oxford, 1908–21).
Brunner . . .	K. Brunner, *Altenglische Grammatik nach der Angelsächsischen Grammatik von Eduard Sievers* (Halle, 1942).
Bresslau, *Archiv f. Urk.*	*Archiv für Urkundenforschung*, vi (1918).
Bresslau, *Urkundenlehre* .	*Handbuch der Urkundenlehre*, see p. 2, n. 1.

Goebel	Julius Goebel Jr., *Felony and Misdemeanor* (New York, The Commonwealth Fund, 1937).
Harmer, *Chipping and Market*	For full reference, see p. 78.
Harmer, *Eng. Hist. Docs.* .	F. E. Harmer, *Select English Historical Documents of the Ninth and Tenth Centuries* (Cambridge, 1914).
Harmer, *Rylands Bulletin* .	*Bulletin of the John Rylands Library*, xxii (1938), 339–67.
Harmer, *Saga-Book* . .	*Saga-Book of the Viking Society*, xiii, pt. 3 (1950), 115–55.
Harmer, *Westminster Writs* .	*Eng. Hist. Rev.*, li (1936), 97–103.
Hickes	G. Hickes, *Linguarum Vett. Septentrionalium Thesaurus* (Oxford, 1705).
K.	J. M. Kemble, *Codex Diplomaticus Aevi Saxonici* (London, 1839–48), quoted by number of document.
Liebermann	F. Liebermann, *Gesetze der Angelsachsen* (Halle, 1903–16).
Mon. Angl.	Dugdale's *Monasticon Anglicanum*, ed. J. Caley, H. Ellis, and B. Bandinel (London, 1846).
Mon. Germ. Hist. . . .	*Monumenta Germaniae Historica*, ed. Pertz etc.
NED	*A New English Dictionary*, ed. Sir James Murray etc. (Oxford, 1884–1928).
Ord. Surv. Facs. . . .	Ordnance Survey, *Facsimiles of Anglo-Saxon Manuscripts* (1878–84).
Robertson	A. J. Robertson, *Anglo-Saxon Charters* (Cambridge, 1939).
Robertson, *Laws* . . .	A. J. Robertson, *The Laws of the Kings of England from Edmund to Henry I* (Cambridge, 1925).
R.S.	Rolls Series.
Searle, *Onomasticon* . .	W. G. Searle, *Onomasticon Anglo-Saxonicum* (Cambridge, 1897).
Searle, *Anglo-Saxon Bishops* .	W. G. Searle, *Anglo-Saxon Bishops, Kings and Nobles* (Cambridge, 1899).
Sievers-Cook	E. Sievers, *Angelsächsische Grammatik* (3rd ed. 1898), trans. A. S. Cook, *Old English Grammar* (3rd ed., Boston and London, 1903).

Stratmann-Bradley . . F. H. Stratmann and H. Bradley, *Middle English Dictionary* (Oxford, 1891).

Stubbs, *Reg. Sac. Angl.* . . W. Stubbs, *Registrum Sacrum Anglicanum* (2nd ed. 1897).

Tengvik . . . . G. Tengvik, *Old English Bynames* (Nomina Germanica 4, Upsala, 1938).

Thorpe . . . . . B. Thorpe, *Diplomatarium Anglicum Ævi Saxonici* (London, 1865).

VCH . . . . . *Victoria History of the Counties of England.*

Wanley . . . . . H. Wanley, *Antiquæ Literaturæ Septentrionalis Liber Alter* (Oxford, 1705), vol. ii of Hickes' *Thesaurus.*

Whitelock . . . . D. Whitelock, *Anglo-Saxon Wills* (Cambridge, 1930).

Wm. Malmes, *G.P.* . . William of Malmesbury, *Gesta Pontificum*, ed. N. E. S. A. Hamilton, R.S.

Wm. Malmes, *G.R.* . . William of Malmesbury, *Gesta Regum*, ed. W. Stubbs, R.S

Wyon . . . . . A. and A. B. Wyon, *The Great Seals of England* (London 1887)

PART I

GENERAL INTRODUCTION

The ' Anglo-Saxon writ ' was a letter on administrative business to which a seal was appended, and the protocol (or opening clauses) of which named the sender of the letter and the person or persons to whom it was addressed, and contained a greeting.[1] This definition, in which the form of the protocol is included, has the merit of isolating that particular form of Anglo-Saxon document which was borrowed from their predecessors by the Anglo-Norman kings, and which forms the basis of the royal writ which has been continuously employed, though not of course always with the same formulas, down to the present day. More than one type of royal writ now current contains an address and greeting and is given under the king's seal. And a form of greeting employed in the middle ages in Letters Patent (lineally descended from the Anglo-Saxon writ) may be employed by modern heads of states in their international relations.[2] Diplomatically the Anglo-Saxon royal writ is a development of the letter, and it is possible to be too definite in relegating the king's writ to a special category. Consequently the existing writs (by the definition suggested above) of non-royal persons have been printed here. An attempt will be made in this general introduction to ' place ' the Anglo-Saxon writ in its proper background, and in so far as the evidence exists, to investigate its origin and use. The formulas that compose it will be analysed and attention will moreover be given to the two-faced seal of wax appended to the document. We shall find the Anglo-Saxon king in the late tenth century conveying his instructions to his subjects by means of *gewrit* [3] and *insegel*. And *ærendgewrit* [4] (where *ærend* means

[1] No. 113, the spurious letter of the monk Edwin, stands outside this definition, for there is no reason to suppose that it was sealed—the seal being the distinctive mark of the writ.

[2] In the ' Manchester Guardian ' of 22 August 1945, reference was made to the credentials presented by Lieutenant-General Kawabe, leader of the Japanese surrender delegation, to General MacArthur, beginning : ' Hirohito, by the grace of Heaven Emperor of Japan, seated on the throne occupied by the same dynasty changeless through the ages eternal, to all to whom these presents shall come, greeting '. Compare the formula : ' Omnibus ad quos presentes litterae pervenerint ', of the English Letters Patent.

[3] For *gewrit* (writing, document, *in pl.*, books) in the sense of letter, compare BT Suppt. s.v. *gewrit*, II (2), (c) : ' Sigewulf frequently questioned him from afar concerning every knotty point by means of letters ' (*mid gewritum*).

[4] See BT and Suppt. ; *ærendgewrit* is used to render *epistola*, and it is also glossed by *commonitorium* (from its contents), and by *pitaciolum, membranula*, ' small strip of parchment ', from its form (see *Medieval Latin Word-List*, ed. Baxter and Johnson).

' message ') and *insegel* are used together by King Alfred to designate a document with a seal whereby a subordinate might recognise his lord's will and pleasure. Criteria will be suggested for determining (so far as this is possible) the authenticity of existing writs. From the time when we first encounter it, and probably from the time of its earliest use in this country, the Anglo-Saxon writ is written in English and not in Latin.

The use of the letter as an administrative instrument is of high antiquity. In Anglo-Saxon England in the latter part of the ninth century, and no doubt even before this, a sealed letter was employed for administrative purposes either as a spontaneous native development or as an imitation in whole or in part of foreign diplomatic usage. The Anglo-Saxons through their contact with the papacy and with the countries of western Europe entered into such of the heritage of the later Roman Empire as had survived. Roman emperors and provincial governors employed *epistulae* and rescripts for purposes of government, and the diplomas and mandates of the early Frankish kings were drawn up in epistolary form. So likewise were papal privileges, whether under the influence of the official, or of the private letter of the Roman Empire.[1] And further, the use of a seal, a characteristic feature of the Anglo-Saxon writ, goes back to Roman times. But since the impulse to use letters for administrative orders arose elsewhere long before there was any question of papal or Frankish influence,[2] the conclusion that in

[1] On these documents in general, see H. Bresslau, *Handbuch der Urkundenlehre für Deutschland und Italien*, 2nd ed. vol. i (Leipzig, 1912), vol. ii, pt. i (Leipzig, 1915), vol. ii, pt. ii (Berlin and Leipzig, 1931, ed. Hans-Walter Klewitz) ; ' Internationale Beziehungen im Urkundenwesen des Mittelalters ', *Archiv für Urkundenforschung*, vi (1918), 19–76 ; A. Giry, *Manuel de Diplomatique* (Paris, 1894, reprinted 1925) ; R. Lane Poole, *Lectures on the History of the Papal Chancery* (Cambridge, 1915) ; Paul Kirn, ' Zum Problem der Kontinuität zwischen Altertum und Mittelalter ', *Archiv f. Urk*, x (1928), 128–44.

[2] There are for example documents preserved in the Book of Ezra which contain royal rescripts in the form of letters ; see Ezra ch. 5, 6, 7. Compare also the Aramaic papyrus sent by an official to the Jewish colony in Elephantine in 419 B.C. (*Aramaic Papyri of the Fifth Century B.C.*, ed. A. Cowley (Oxford, 1923), p. 62, no. 21. This letter contains an edict of Darius II, king of Persia, ordering an observance of the feast of Unleavened Bread, and, if the proposed restoration of the text is right, the Passover. The rendering of the text given by Cowley (with conjectural emendations) runs : ' To my brethren, Yedoniah and his colleagues the Jewish garrison, your brother Hananiah. The welfare of my brethren may the gods seek. Now this year, the fifth year of King Darius, word was sent from the king to Arsames saying ' etc. An interesting feature of this opening is the parallel that it presents to the protocol of the Anglo-Saxon writ, that is to say, the opening clauses up to and including the greeting. Going back still further, letters have come down to us from early in the second millennium B.C. in which Hammurabi, king of Babylon,

Anglo-Saxon England the employment of the letter for purposes of internal administration was due simply to imitation of papal or of Frankish practice, does not seem to be inevitable. The use of a token to identify the sender of a message was moreover known among the Germanic peoples [1] before the time when seals were generally used, so that the employment of a seal in England for the purpose of authenticating a letter may have been in part at any rate a development of Germanic practice as well as, indirectly, a development of Roman usage. The sealed letter (*ærendgewrit and insegel*), spoken of by King Alfred, is often overlooked, as also is his rendering of a New Testament *ærendgewrit*; so that conclusions regarding the characteristics of the writ form in Anglo-Saxon England have so far been based almost entirely upon the surviving writs of the closing years of the tenth, and of the eleventh, century. At this time a sealed letter or writ, drawn up in the vernacular tongue as it had been perhaps from the beginning, was being used by Anglo-Saxon kings for administrative purposes side by side with the solemn royal diploma, a document constructed on entirely different lines, used for different purposes, and destined to be superseded by the writ in course of time. The writ form, at first in English, and then prevailingly in Latin, was adopted by the early Norman kings. It was developed by their successors, until in time the writ became in England the 'keystone' of the 'system of centralised justice'; and it has survived as a judicial and administrative instrument until the present day.[2]

sends orders to his officials. See the letter in *Cuneiform Parallels to the Old Testament*, ed. R. W. Rogers (New York, 1912), p. 248, no. 3, also p. 249. No seals are mentioned in connection with these letters, but seals were used to certify documents in early times by the Babylonians and the Persians, as by other peoples. See the seal cylinders illustrated in Rogers, *op. cit.*, Plates 14, 17, 18; see also Cowley, *op. cit.* p. 10, no. 5. I am indebted for the above references to Professor H. H. Rowley.

[1] On the use among the Germanic peoples of tokens (*jartegn, jarteikn*) employed as a means of recognition, see Bresslau, *Urkundenlehre*, i (1912), 686–7, and references. On the use of seals in antiquity and in the Middle Ages, see Erben–Schmitz–Redlich, *Urkundenlehre*, iii (Munich and Berlin, 1911 = von Below and Meinecke's *Handbuch der Mittelalterlichen und Neueren Geschichte*, iv), 104 ff.; R. Lane Poole, 'Seals and Documents', first published in 1919, reprinted in *Studies in Chronology and History* (Oxford, 1934), 90–111.

[2] For the development of the writ in the later Middle Ages, and for the position occupied by the writ in English Law, see P. H. Winfield, *The Chief Sources of English Legal History* (Harvard, 1925), *passim*; *Encyclopædia Britannica* (11th and 14th ed.) s.v. 'Writ'; T. F. T. Plucknett, *Concise History of the Common Law* (3rd ed., London, 1940), *passim*; Pollock and Maitland, *History of English Law* (2nd ed. Cambridge, 1898), *passim*; Sir W. S. Holdsworth, *History of English Law* (London, revised edition, 1937–45), *passim*. For the semantic development of the word 'writ' as a term of law, see NED.

The Anglo-Saxon writ was also imitated abroad. The oldest known Norwegian royal charters (of the thirteenth century), unlike those of Denmark and of Sweden, but like those of Anglo-Saxon England, are composed in the vernacular.[1] Their protocols resemble in all essential points those of Anglo-Saxon writs. There are also resemblances between the earliest (well-preserved) Norwegian royal seal (of 1250) and the seal of King Edward the Confessor (which may possibly have been modelled on the seal of King Cnut) ; [2] the Norwegian and Icelandic term *innsigli*, ' seal ', seems indeed to be derived from Old English *insigle, insegel*, itself a loan-word from Latin *insigillum*.[3] Comparison between the writs printed here and a grant of King Hakon of Norway, of 1226–54, will illustrate the resemblances between the protocol of such documents and that of Anglo-Saxon writs :—

' King Hakon, son of King Hakon, sends to Sir Askatl, bishop of Stavanger, N. the archdeacon, and all the canons, learned men and landed men, franklins and freeholders, present and future, to all God's friends and his own, who may see or hear this letter (*bréf*), God's greeting and his own '.[4]

The ' present and future ' and the ' may see or hear this letter ' of this protocol, are later features, not found in Anglo-Saxon writs ; but in other respects the resemblance is close. And although the form ' God's greeting and his own ' (' quidio guðs oc sina ') does not appear in the Anglo-Saxon writs in this book, it was in use in this country in the Anglo-Saxon period, and appears, for instance, in a writ now known only at second-hand of King Harold Harefoot (see p. 18). A still earlier instance of the writ protocol appears in a letter (*bréf*) sent by King Ingi of Norway in 1139 to his brother Sigurðr and his adherents, and handed down in the *Heimskringla* of Snorri Sturluson :—

' King Ingi, son of King Harald, sends to his brother King Sigurðr, to Sáða-Gyrðr . . . to all the landed men, bodyguards and housecarls, and to all the common people, rich and poor, young and old, God's greeting (*kveðju*) and his own '.[5]

---

[1] See Bresslau, *Archiv f. Urk.* vi (1918), 59 f. and references. Exceptions, as Bresslau observes, are texts in Latin for foreign recipients.

[2] See further Bresslau, *Archiv f. Urk.* vi. 60, and p. 99 below. For the Norwegian seal, see Harmer, *Saga-Book*, Plate 5.

[3] See M. S. Serjeantson, *A History of Foreign Words in English* (London, 1935), 30, 271, 277. The form *insigle* seems to be the earlier borrowing of the two.

[4] For the text and for a Modern German rendering, see Bresslau, *Archiv f. Urk.* vi. 61 ; see also L. M. Larson, *The King's Household in England before the Norman Conquest* (Madison, Wisconsin, 1904), 198.

[5] Bresslau, *ut supra*, 62 ; Larson, 199 ; *Heimskringla*, ed. F. Jónsson (Copenhagen, 1911), 576 ; Mod. Eng. rendering, *Heimskringla*, E. Monsen (Cambridge, Heffer, 1932), 670.

Bresslau observes that the letter concludes with the words : ' *Lif i guðs fridi* ' (' Live in God's peace '), which is nearer to the *God eow gehealde*, ' God keep you ', of Anglo-Saxon writs than to the common Latin valediction *Valete*. The resemblances between these Norwegian documents and Anglo-Saxon writs are too great to be due to coincidence ; they must be due to the imitation in Norway of the Anglo-Saxon writ, perhaps as early as the late tenth or early eleventh century. Bresslau suggests the possibility that the adoption of this form in Norway is to be attributed to the bishops and priests (some of whom are mentioned by name) who, according to Adam of Bremen, were brought into the country from England by St. Olaf ; [1] but English influence may have begun even earlier. There was also intercourse at other times between English ecclesiastics and Scandinavian rulers and their peoples in the tenth and the eleventh centuries.[2] The writ form in Latin was moreover adopted by the kings of Scotland, but whether it was modelled on the Anglo-Norman writ, or whether it was borrowed from England before the Norman Conquest is uncertain, since no documents from Scotland of this type have survived of earlier date than the late eleventh century.[3] Further, the two-faced pendent seal which is to be observed on writs associated with the Confessor—but which was probably not an invention of his reign—has had a long line of descendants. Not only was the method of sealing *sur simple queue* [4] employed in Anglo-Saxon writs imitated abroad, but the two-faced seal itself became the model for the seals of other rulers.[5] And further, the representation of the king in majesty which appears on the Great Seal of King Edward the Confessor (and which had already in his time a long history behind it) came to be widely used. It was employed on English seals by his successors ; and it has appeared, with variations in attire, insignia, and background, on the seals of all the kings and queens of England down to the present day.[6]

[1] Adam of Bremen, *Gesta Hammaburgensis Ecclesiae Pontificum* (ed. J. M. Lappenberg, 2nd ed. Hanover, 1876), ii. 35, 55. For comments on Adam of Bremen's statement, and a suggestion that it should not be taken at its face value, see Stenton, *Anglo-Saxon England*, 456–7, where it is observed that the tradition was recorded within a half-century after St. Olaf's death, but that of the four ecclesiastics named as being the most eminent, two bore names which were not of English origin. But foreign priests may have sought service here. And missionaries from England, even if of foreign descent, may have carried with them to Scandinavia the epistolary usages of the English court. [2] Stenton, *ut supra*, Harmer, *ut supra*.
[3] For texts, see *Early Scottish Charters*, ed. A. C. Lawrie (Glasgow, 1905)..
[4] See p. 92. [5] Bresslau, *Archiv f. Urk.* vi. 63 ff. and p. 93 below.
[6] For these seals, see W. de Gray Birch, *Catalogue of Seals in the Department of Manuscripts in the British Museum*, 6 vols. (1887–1900) ; A. and A. B. Wyon, *The Great Seals of England* (London, 1887).

It has indeed been observed that the writ and the seal pendent
which authenticated it are 'contributions to the civilisation of
western Europe scarcely less important than the Era of the Incarna-
tion' which was popularised by Englishmen of Bede's age.[1]

THE INTELLECTUAL BACKGROUND

The issue in Anglo-Saxon England of administrative orders in the
vernacular contrasts strongly with usage on the Continent, where
Latin was invariably used for diplomas and for mandates until a
much later date ; but it is in line with other developments in this
country.   This is a matter of such importance for the development
of the writ form and for the maintenance of its use that the background of writing in Anglo-Saxon England must be made clear.
Anglo-Saxon was being employed in this country for the promulga-
tion of laws in writing (which have however been preserved only in
one manuscript of much later date) soon after the arrival of St.
Augustine in 597 and the acceptance of Christianity in the kingdom
of Kent ; the Laws of King Æthelberht of Kent are the earliest
document written in the English language.[2]   Before the close of the
seventh century, the earliest Anglo-Saxon poetry that can be dated
on external evidence, the poetry of the unlearned Cædmon (of which
little now remains) was being composed in Northumbria, and it is
to be noted that Aldhelm and Bede, the most learned Englishmen
of their age, did not disdain poetry in the mother tongue.[3]   Of
Anglo-Saxon poetry four famous codices have been preserved, not
copied until the time of the monastic revival of the second half of
the tenth century, but containing poems of much earlier date : a few
pieces have also come down to us from other sources.   Of prose in
English (except for what may be incorporated in the Anglo-Saxon
Chronicle) there is little now extant dating from before the time of
King Alfred,[4] and it is greatly to be regretted that Bede's translations have perished.   He translated from Latin into English, ' for
the profit of the Church of God ', ' some extracts from the works of

[1] R. Lane Poole, *Chronicles and Annals* (Oxford, 1926), 26 ; R. R. Darlington,
' The last phase of Anglo-Saxon History ', *History*, N.S. xxii (1937–38), 9.

[2] F. L. Attenborough, *The Laws of the Earliest English Kings* (Cambridge,
1922), 3. Æthelberht's Laws are dated by Liebermann, *Gesetze der Angelsachsen*, iii. 2, A.D. 602–03, but the dating is merely a matter of inference, and
may be only approximately correct.   The language of this code and of the two
other Kentish codes has been modernised, though not consistently, in the only
surviving manuscript, the twelfth-century Textus Roffensis.

[3] Wm. of Malmesbury, *Gest. Pont.* R.S. 335 f. (Aldhelm) ;   *Venerabilis
Baedae Opera Historica*, ed. Plummer, i. clxi.   Five lines of vernacular poetry
recited by Bede upon his deathbed have been preserved.

[4] See H. Sweet, *The Oldest English Texts*, E.E.T.S. 1885.

Bishop Isidore ', and the Gospel of St. John (on which, we are told, he was engaged upon his deathbed).[1] But charters are being drawn up in English from the beginning of the ninth century, if not earlier ; the earliest wills appear soon after A.D. 800. The earliest royal diploma in English now extant is a grant of Berhtwulf, king of the Mercians, dating from A.D. 845.[2] The earliest piece of English narrative prose known is the well-known annal in the Anglo-Saxon *Chronicle* for the year 755 (inserted out of its proper place, see p. 27, n. 6), which recounts the death of Cynewulf and Cyneheard and their followers in 786, and which has been brought forward as evidence for the cultivation of prose saga in Anglo-Saxon England.[3] It is entirely probable that the story itself was in circulation soon after the event, though the narrative in its written form cannot be traced back beyond the *Chronicle*, in which alone it is preserved. The *Chronicle* assumed its present form in the reign of King Alfred, and it was subsequently kept up in the vernacular tongue until the middle of the twelfth century. Although, as we learn from King Alfred's well-known Preface to the *Cura Pastoralis*,[4] Latin learning in the ninth century had decayed, many, as he tells us in the following passage, could read English writing :—

Ða ic ða gemunde hu sio lar Lædengeðiodes ær ðissum afeallen wæs giond Angelcynn ond ðeah monige cuðon Englisc gewrit arædan ' etc., (' When I remembered how the knowledge of Latin had formerly decayed throughout England, and yet many could read English writing ' etc.),

and for these King Alfred provided translations into English of Latin works then standard. Prominent among his projects was the plan for securing that ' all the youth now in England of free men, who have the means to devote themselves to it, be set to learning, as long as they are not capable of other employment, until they are able to read English writing well '. Further instruction in the Latin language was to be given to those who were to continue in learning

---

[1] Plummer i. lxxv, clxii. On the works of Isidore of Seville, and their great popularity throughout the Middle Ages, see M. L. W. Laistner, *Thought and Letters in Western Europe*, A.D. 500 to 900 (London, 1931), 89 ff.

[2] Harmer, *English Historical Documents*, no. 3, Sweet, *ut supra*, no. 48, K. 243, B. 452. For other early charters see A. J. Robertson, *Anglo-Saxon Charters* (Cambridge, 1939).

[3] R. H. Hodgkin, *History of the Anglo-Saxons* (1939), ii. 393–5 ; C. E. Wright, *The Cultivation of Saga in Anglo-Saxon England* (Edinburgh, 1939) ; C. L. Wrenn, ' A Saga of the Anglo-Saxons ', *History*, xxv (1940), 208–15.

[4] *King Alfred's West-Saxon Version of Gregory's Pastoral Care*, ed. H. Sweet, E.E.T.S. (1871), 3 ; Sweet's *Anglo-Saxon Reader*, 10th ed. no. 2. The Preface is of course King Alfred's circular letter on the state of learning in England. For details of editions and full commentary on the text, see F. Klaeber, *Anglia*, 47 (1923), 53–65 ; and F. P. Magoun, Jr., *Mediaeval Studies* (Toronto), x (1948), 93–107, xi (1949), 113–22.

and be promoted to ecclesiastical orders.[1] In the age that followed
his own King Alfred's literary and educational enterprises found no
imitators. Little Anglo-Saxon prose has come down to us from this
period save for the annals of the *Chronicle*, themselves comparatively meagre. In Latin however a new departure seems to have
been made in the elaborate and impressive royal diplomas of King
Æthelstan, and of his successors up to the time of King Edgar, in the
formulas of which the influence of Aldhelm is strongly marked ; [2]
whilst the growing importance of Anglo-Saxon for purposes of
business is indicated by its increasing use throughout the tenth
century and up to the time of the Conquest, for charters, wills, and
other documents, both royal and private. That knowledge of Latin
was widespread at this time among English ecclesiastics is demonstrated by the letters that have come down to us from leading figures
of the second half of the tenth and of the early eleventh centuries.[3]
This period was moreover distinguished by the appearance of the
first Latin grammar in a vernacular in medieval Europe,[4] and of
a Colloquy written to aid the teacher of Latin,[5] both of them the
work of Abbot Ælfric of Eynsham, the outstanding literary figure of
this time.[6] For the benefit of those ignorant of Latin there

[1] In Asser's *Life of King Alfred* we find a description of a court school. It
is there stated that the young nobles and some few others of humbler birth
who were educated in company with the youngest of the king's sons were made
to read books in both languages, Latin and Anglo-Saxon, and that there was
also time for writing. Elsewhere in the same text we read how in consequence
of the king's reforming zeal, almost all the ealdormen and reeves and thegns
(*ministri*) who had been illiterate from infancy applied themselves to study,
preferring rather to acquire laboriously the unaccustomed learning than to
give up their posts ; and if anyone was too old or too stupid to learn, he would
order his son, or a kinsman, or if necessary a servant, to read to him by day
and by night, whenever he found leisure, ' Saxon books '—which, from the
context, would no doubt have included the Anglo-Saxon legal codes. See
Asser's Life of King Alfred, ed. W. H. Stevenson (1904), cap. 75, 102, 106.
[2] These diplomas are analysed and discussed by R. Drögereit, ' Gab es eine
angelsächsische Königskanzlei ? ', *Archiv f. Urk.* xiii (1935), 335–436 ; see also
F. M. Stenton, *Anglo-Saxon England* (Oxford, 1943), 348–9.
[3] Printed by Stubbs, *Memorials of Saint Dunstan*, R.S. *passim*.
[4] *Ælfrics Grammatik und Glossar*, ed. J. Zupitza, i (Text und Varianten),
Berlin, 1880.
[5] *Ælfric's Colloquy*, ed. G. N. Garmonsway (London, 1939).
[6] On Ælfric, see E. Dietrich, *Abt Ælfrik, Zur Literaturgeschichte der angel-
sächsischen Kirche* (Z. f. hist. Theol. 1855–56) ; C. L. White, *Ælfric, A New
Study of his Life and Writings* (Yale Studies in English, 1898), closely based
on Dietrich ; K. Sisam, *Review of English Studies*, vii (1931), 7–22, viii (1932),
51–68, ix (1933), 1–12, and for a bibliography, *ibid.* vii. 15 ; M.-M. Dubois,
Ælfric, Sermonnaire, Docteur et Grammairien (Paris, 1943). The date of
Ælfric's birth is unknown. In 987 he was sent to the newly-founded
monastery at Cerne to instruct the brethren in the Benedictine Rule. In 1005
he was appointed abbot of the newly-founded monastery at Eynsham. Miss

developed in this period a new religious literature in Anglo-Saxon which was an outstanding feature of the new ' efflorescence of culture ' which resulted from and accompanied the monastic revival associated with the names of Edgar, Dunstan, Oswald and Æthelwold. In the literary revival of the close of the tenth century and the early part of the eleventh, Abbot Ælfric of Eynsham played a leading part as the greatest prose-writer of the Anglo-Saxon period. But Ælfric did not stand alone. Archbishop Wulfstan of York (the writer of the *Sermo Lupi ad Anglos* and of other works), the anonymous writers of the Blickling Homilies, Byrhtferth of Ramsey (the author of the scientific treatise known as *Byrhtferth's Manual*), all in their various ways ministered to the edification of their contemporaries, and contributed to what has been called the ' Golden Age ' of Anglo-Saxon prose. The fact that the themes of several of his works were suggested to Ælfric by prominent laymen and others less well known clearly indicates that culture in this age was not confined to ecclesiastical circles. Outstanding in this group were the ealdorman Æthelweard, and his son the ealdorman Æthelmær (the founder of the monasteries at Cerne and at Eynsham in which Abbot Ælfric spent his literary career). It was observed by the late Robin Flower that the evidence of Abbot Ælfric makes it clear that Ealdorman Æthelweard was active in the promotion of literary enterprise in the vernacular, that books were written in the monasteries of the west on his commission, and that there is nothing inherently improbable in the suggestion that the famous Exeter Book of Anglo-Saxon poetry may have been written for him [1] in the same way as a special copy of Ælfric's Catholic Homilies was later to be prepared to his order. [2] Ealdorman Æthelweard had suggested to Ælfric, or commissioned from him, the composition of portions of his Catholic Homilies, as also of the Lives of the Saints, and of the Anglo-Saxon rendering of part of the book of Genesis. Among those many people who had urged him to undertake the second of these works, Ælfric in his Latin Preface to the Lives of the Saints, also includes Æthelweard's son Æthelmær (' quia arguet me praecatus multorum fidelium et maxime Æþelwerdi ducis et Æðelmeri nostri '), whilst other works were composed at the request of, or in the interests of, other individual laymen. In an epistolary preface addressed to Wulfgeat of Ilming-

Whitelock has argued (*Mod. Lang. Rev.* xxxviii. (1943), 122 ff) that Ælfric may have died many years before 1020–25, the date assigned to his death by Dietrich.

[1] See further, Introd. to *The Exeter Book*, by R. W. Chambers, Max Förster and Robin Flower (1933), 83 ff., and R. R. Darlington, *History*, xxii (1937–38), 10.

[2] Introd. to *The Exeter Book*, 90. The approximate date of 970–90 is suggested for the writing of the Exeter Book, *ibid.* p. 89.

ton, for instance, Ælfric refers to English writings which he had lent to Wulfgeat and to his promise to send him more.[1] Ælfric's patron, Ealdorman Æthelweard, himself undertook the task of rendering into Latin the annals of the Anglo-Saxon *Chronicle*, and though his success was limited, for his Latin is highly obscure, his attempt provides further evidence of the intellectual interests of this circle. It is in the background of a continuous tradition in the use of the vernacular tongue for literary and business purposes that the development of the Anglo-Saxon writ must be studied. But it must be emphasised that the Anglo-Saxon writ is not to be regarded primarily as a literary product; it is a business document or administrative instrument.

THE SEALED LETTER IN KING ALFRED'S TIME

Of the origin and early history of the Anglo-Saxon writ nothing certain is known, but already in King Alfred's time the employment of an *ærendgewrit* [2] authenticated by an *insegel* for administrative business was a commonplace :—

' Consider now ', says Reason, in a passage inserted by King Alfred into a translation of St. *Augustine's Soliloquies*, intended for general reading, ' if your lord's letter and his seal comes to you, whether you can say that you cannot understand him thereby or recognise his will therein.' (' Geþenc nu gyf ðines hlafordes ærendgewrit and hys insegel to þe cymð, hwæðer þu mæge cweðan þæt ðu hine be ðam ongytan ne mæge ne hys willan þæron gecnawan ne mæge.') [3]

No vernacular letter of this time with the writ protocol has survived, and although signet rings of his father and his sister are in existence (see p. 13, n. 1), no seal of King Alfred is now known to exist. But since an essential feature of the writ protocol as it has been defined above is the greeting, it is significant that the ninth-century translator (if indeed the translator was not King Alfred himself), rendering into English the opening clauses of the dedication of Bede's *Historia Ecclesiastica* to King Ceolwulf :—

' Gloriosissimo regi Ceoluulfo Baeda famulus Christi et presbyter ',

employs a protocol which we must suppose to have been current, into which he introduces a clause *sende gretan*, ' send to greet ', absent from his original :—

---

[1] See p. 23, n. 4.
[2] See p. 1, n. 4, for this compound.
[3] See King Alfred's *Old English Version of St. Augustine's Soliloquies*, ed. H. L. Hargrove (Yale Studies in English, no. xiii, 1902), 23 ; W. Endter (Grein-Wülker-Hecht, *Bibl. der Angelsächs. Prosa*, xi, 1922), 24. The passage is cited (not quite accurately) in BT s.v. *insegel*.

' Ic Beda Cristes þeow and mæssepreost *sende gretan* ðone leofastan cyning Ceolwulf '.[1]

But for the early history of the writ form in English it is even more significant that the writ protocol of later times appears already, substantially, in the opening words of the well-known Preface provided by King Alfred himself for the Old English rendering of Pope Gregory's *Cura Pastoralis* :—

' Ælfred kyning hateð gretan Wærferð biscep his wordum luflice ond freondlice, ond ðe cyðan hate [2]ðæt me com swiðe oft on gemynd ' etc.   ' King Alfred bids greet Bishop Werferth with his words in loving and friendly wise, and I would have you informed that it has very often come into my remembrance ' etc.)

A variant of this form, namely, *hælo eow wyscað*, ' wish you health ', rendering the *salutem* of the Vulgate version, appears in the translation into the vernacular of the *ærendgewrit* (as Alfred calls it) in Acts of the Apostles, 15, 23 ff., which is inserted into the introduction to Alfred's Laws, 49, 3 ff. (Liebermann i. 42 f.).   Incidentally there is an indication here that the notification of later days already formed a normal part of an *ærendgewrit* in the fact that in Alfred's translation the address is followed by : ' we eow cyðað þæt we geascodon ', which is not in the Vulgate text, which reads ' *quoniam audiuimus* '.   The notification is a constant feature of the writs printed here.   Further the connotations of the term *ærendgewrit* are indicated by the fact that it glosses or is glossed by *commonitorium*, presumably ' admonition ', and by *pitaciolum, membranula*, ' small piece of parchment ' (see p. 1, n. 4).

The conclusion that the sealed letter was in use in King Alfred's time was also arrived at by W. H. Stevenson (who does not mention this passage from King Alfred's Preface) on the evidence of a letter written after King Alfred's death in 899, by a contemporary of his, to Alfred's son and successor, King Edward the Elder.[3]   But Stevenson arrives at this conclusion only by a conjunction of terms which cannot be accepted as it stands :—

' The writ ', says Stevenson, ' is clearly older than Cnut's time, for we hear of Alfred delivering his " hondseten " as testimony of his confirmation of a private grant and this document is described as an " insegel " or " seal " '.[4]

---

[1] Latin text, *Baedae Opera Historica*, ed. Plummer, i. 5, Anglo-Saxon, *The Old English Version of Bede's Ecclesiastical History*, ed. T. Miller, E.E.T.S. Pt. i (1890), 2.   Both together, Grein-Wülker, *Bibl. der angelsächs. Prosa*, iv (1899), ed. Schipper, i.

[2] On *hateð gretan* and *cyðan hate*, see G. V. Smithers, *Engl. and Germanic Stud.* (Birmingham, 1947–8), 109 ff.   The *ond eowic gretan het* of *Beowulf* 3095b, from its formulaic ring, is ancient (suggested to me by Prof. Magoun).

[3] K. 328, B. 591, Thorpe p. 169, Harmer, *English Historical Documents*, no. 18.   [4] *Eng. Hist. Rev.* xxvii (1912), 5.

But Stevenson's interpretation of this letter cannot be justified. King Alfred's *hondseten*, ' signature ', and the *insegel*, ' seal ', in this letter, belong to different episodes in the history of an estate, and there is no justification for bringing them together. As to the *hondseten*, we learn from this letter that when a certain Oswulf had bought an estate at Fonthill,

' King Alfred had given him his signature (*hondseten*) that the sale should hold good, and so had Edward and Æthelnoth and Deormod and all those men whose signatures they then wished to have ' ; and that when later the possession of the land was disputed and the charter was produced and read, ' then all the signatures were to be found there '.

The reference is of course to the list of witnesses at the end of a charter, each accompanied by a phrase signifying consent and by the sign of the Cross. This production of the charter with its signatures was regarded as decisive at the stage then reached in the matter in dispute, and the suit regarding the estate at Fonthill was in the end settled in favour of a certain Helmstan. The document on which the *hondseten* of King Alfred and other witnesses was found was clearly a private charter (it is described in the document as a *boc*) ; it was not a writ. The episode of the *insegel* [1] took place ' a year and a half, or perhaps two years ', later, in the reign of King Alfred's son, Edward the Elder :—

The Helmstan who had been involved in the earlier episode, when his estate at Fonthill had been claimed by other persons, after he had committed the crime of stealing a belt, now ' utterly ruined himself ' by stealing some oxen. He was caught, and when he wished to deny the charge, the fact that ' a bramble scratched him all over the face ' as he fled, was brought as evidence against him. His property as that of a thief was confiscated to the king ' because he was the king's man ', and the king declared him an outlaw.

The *insegel* was the means whereby Helmstan secured the revocation of the sentence of outlawry pronounced against him and the restoration of his property :—

' Then thou didst declare him an outlaw. Then he made his way to thy father's (i.e. King Alfred's) body,[2] and brought an *insegel* to me, and I was at Chippenham with thee. Then I gave the *insegel* to thee. And thou didst give him back his home and the estates to which he has now returned '(' Þu hine hete ða flyman. Ða gesohte he ðines fæder lic 7 brohte *insigle* to me 7 ic wæs æt Cippanhomme mit te. Ða ageaf ic ðæt *insigle* ðe. 7 ðu him forgeafe his eard 7 ða are ðe he get on gebogen hæfð ').[3]

---

[1] The spelling *insigle* in the letter is for the sake of uniformity replaced here by the more usual *insegel*, which I have adopted throughout. On the two forms, see p. 4, n. 3.

[2] King Alfred's remains, buried first at Old Minster, Winchester, were transferred by his son, Edward the Elder, to New Minster.

[3] The interpretation of the last clause is somewhat doubtful.

The writer of this letter, addressing the king, who knew the circumstances of the case, had no need to explain his allusion ; but to us the clue to the interpretation of the *insegel* episode seems to be lost. The meaning of *insegel* in this context is uncertain, but it cannot be, as Stevenson supposed, the document with the *hondseten* of King Alfred and others relating to Oswulf's purchase of the land at Fonthill. The *insegel* of the episode relating to the revocation of Helmstan's outlawry has been explained to mean a signet ring,[1] by means of which presumably the king, on receiving it, would recognise the sender and carry out his wishes. But at a later date we hear of King Æthelred II sending his *insegel* to a shire court, greeting ' all the witan who were there assembled ' (see p. 47), and it seems likely that this stands for *gewrit and insegel*, ' sealed letter '. The same interpretation may be the right one for the *insegel* brought back by Helmstan from King Alfred's burial place at Winchester.[2] Helmstan may have taken sanctuary there and the *insegel* brought back by him, and handed to the king, may have been a sealed letter, by whomsoever issued, which fulfilled the requirements for his restoration to the favour of King Edward the Elder.[3] But this interpretation is clouded with uncertainty, and it is fortunate that King Alfred's own allusion to the *ærendgewrit and insegel* as a familiar institution is so clear that no testimony from any other source is needed to establish the fact.

THE WRIT IN THE TENTH AND ELEVENTH CENTURIES

The history of the writ during the first eighty years or so of the tenth century is obscure. The reference to the *insegel* in the letter of the reign of King Edward the Elder has been explained in more than one way, whilst the authenticity in its existing form of a reputed

[1] Thorpe (*Diplomatarium Anglicum*, p. 173. Earle, *Hand-Book to Land-Charters*, Glossarial Index, s.v. *insigle*, ' seal in a ring ; writ '. Bresslau, *Archiv*, vi. 48, n. 4 : ' perhaps a signet ring (Siegelring) '. For a coloured plate illustrating signet rings of King Æthelwulf, King Alfred's father, and of Queen Æthelswith, wife of Burhred, king of the Mercians, King Alfred's sister, see R. H. Hodgkin, *A History of the Anglo-Saxons*, ii. Plate iv, facing p. 671, in the edition of 1939. Bresslau's statement (*loc. cit.*) that there is no reliable evidence for the use of royal writs before the time of Æthelred II must be qualified ; he was evidently not aware of the allusion to the *ærendgewrit and insegel* in King Alfred's Preface.

[2] Writs are extant of four late eleventh- and twelfth-century abbots of Westminster (*Mon. Angl.* i. 310, *Gilbert Crispin*, J. Armitage Robinson (1911), 37), each certifying that a person named, in one of them a thief, has taken sanctuary at the shrine of King Edward the Confessor (not yet canonised), and praying the sheriff that the accused may be pardoned.

[3] A suggestion mentioned (among others) by Liebermann, *Gesetze*, ii. 650, s.v. ' Siegel '.

writ of King Æthelstan for the church and chapter of Ripon cannot be sustained.[1]

The documentary records that have come down to us from the first half of the tenth century are not numerous, the literary remains are few, and the entries in the Anglo-Saxon *Chronicle* are comparatively meagre.[2] Of sealed letters with the writ protocol used for administrative business there seems to be no trace among the eighty or more charters that have come down to us in the vernacular —in addition to a number in Latin—from the first three-quarters of the tenth century. Was there a real break in continuity in the use of the sealed letter for administrative purposes, or is the apparent break to be attributed merely to the loss of the relevant records ? And was the characteristic writ protocol as we find it in all essential details in King Alfred's well-known Preface, in continuous use from the time of Alfred to the time of Æthelred II, or did it fall into disuse, to be revived again in the latter part of the century ? These are difficult problems. But it is not easy to believe that so convenient a device as the sealed letter would have been discarded when once it was established in use. That it was normal for a lord to communicate with his thegns by means of a letter is manifest from a passage in an unpublished homily of the Ælfrician type, kindly communicated to me by Miss Whitelock, in which the homilist answers those who refuse to listen to preaching in order to be able to plead ignorance at the Last Judgment. He cites as a warning the thegn who, when his lord sends him a letter (*gewrit*), incurs his lord's displeasure by refusing to listen to it (*gehyran*) or to look at it. Again, the fact that the protocol of the Anglo-Saxon writ, and some other formulas, exhibit few variations from the early eleventh century onwards, favours the supposition that the forms employed

---

[1] For this text, see Appendix I. The writ begins with a verbal invocation not found in writs of the pre-Conquest period, and employs phraseology which belongs to post-Conquest legal language. At the minster at Ripon, as at York and Beverley Minsters, King Æthelstan was regarded as the donor of various privileges ; these he was supposed to have conferred on them on a journey to the north. The writ represents a later conception of what a writ of Æthelstan should have contained. The text is printed and annotated in *Memorials of the Church of SS. Peter and Wilfrid, Ripon*, ed. J. T. Fowler, vol. i, Publications of the Surtees Society, lxxiv (1881), 89–90 ; also printed in *Mon. Angl.*, ii. 133, K. 358 (from *Mon. Angl.*), Thorpe, 179 (from *Mon. Angl.*), and elsewhere (see Fowler, *loc. cit.*). For discussion, see *Bede Commemoration Essays*, ed. A. Hamilton Thompson (Oxford, 1935), 97 f. ; VCH *Yorkshire*, iii. 367.

[2] On the literary conditions of this period, see R. W. Chambers' essay on ' The Continuity of English Prose ', in Harpsfield's *Life and Death of Sir Thomas Moore*, ed. Hitchcock, E.E.T.S. 1932, lx ff. The essay was also printed separately (Oxford, 1932).

had become fixed by long and continuous usage. Instances of the use of the writ protocol between King Alfred's time and that of Æthelred II seem however to be lacking in extant texts. A form current in the tenth century, and probably later, is the notification to individuals or the declaration addressed generally, without the greeting of the writ. King Edward the Elder in his first code of laws addresses reeves in this form :—

' Eadwerd cyning byt ðam gerefum eallum ðæt ge deman swa rihte domas swa ge rihtoste cunnon' etc. ('King Edward commands all reeves that ye pronounce such legal decisions as ye know to be most just' etc.) [1]

A similar form was employed by King Æthelstan :—

' Æðelstan cyng cyþ þæt ic hæbbe geahsod ' etc. (' King Æthelstan declares that I have learned ' etc.) [2]

and also by King Edmund in his second code :—

' Eadmund cyning cyð eallum folce, ge yldrum ge gingrum, ðe on his anwealde synd ' etc. (' King Edmund informs all people, both high and low, who are under his authority ' etc.) [3]

The same form was employed c. 960 by Queen Eadgifu when informing the archbishop and the monks of Christ Church how a certain estate had come into her possession :—

' Eadgifu cyþ þam arcebiscope 7 Cristes cyrcean hyrede hu hire land com æt Culingon '. (' Eadgifu informs the archbishop and the community at Christ Church how her estate at Cooling came to her '.) [4]

Other instances can be cited :—

' Æþelweard cyð Ceolbrehte þæt ic wille þæt þu ' etc. ('Æthelweard informs Ceolberht that it is my wish that you ' etc.) [5]

and

' Æðelmær ealdorman cyð on ðisum gewrite his cynehlaforde and eallum his freondum ' etc. (' Ealdorman Æthelmær in this document informs his royal lord and all his friends ' etc.) [6]

---

[1] Liebermann, Gesetze, i. 138, Attenborough, Laws of the Earliest English Kings, 114. I have not succeeded in finding any basis for Mr. J. E. A. Jolliffe's statement (Constit. Hist. of Med. England (1937), 133) that ' Ælfric speaks familiarly in the Homilies of the king's writ and seal '.

[2] Liebermann i. 166, Attenborough, 152. See also Liebermann i. 146, Attenborough, 122. In the manuscripts the texts vary between the first and the third person : ' Æðelstan cyng . . . cyð ', and ' Ic Æþelstan cyng . . . cyðe '.

[3] Liebermann i. 186, Robertson, Laws of the Kings of England, 8.

[4] Harmer, English Historical Documents, no. 23.

[5] Of uncertain date. Max Förster, Der Flussname Themse (for full reference see p. 266, n. 2), 793 ; H. Meritt in Journal of English and Germanic Philology, xxxiii (1934), 344. For the change of person, see Harmer, ut supra, 117.

[6] Of 971–82/3. D. Whitelock, Anglo-Saxon Wills, no. 10.

But it is doubtful whether this opening continued to be employed in royal circles in the eleventh century, for the authenticity of the texts in which it appears is not certain.[1] Other varieties of epistolary openings were also current. Letters to a superior frequently begin with *Leof!* (lit. ' beloved ')—which appears in the interior of Archbishop Wulfstan's writ (no. 27)—as, for example, the Fonthill letter to King Edward the Elder which has been discussed above (pp. 11 ff.) :—

' Leof, ic ðe cyðe hu hit wæs ymb ðæt lond ' etc. (' Beloved, I will inform thee what has taken place with regard to the land ' etc.) [2]

though this was not the only other epistolary opening employed.[3]

Through allusions in contemporary charters to the *gewrit and insegel* and the (probably equivalent) *insegel* of King Æthelred, and through the survival of actual texts, the sealed letter comes again into view in the reign of King Æthelred II (978–1016).   From that time onward there is no break in its history ; writs are printed here of all the successors of Æthelred II up to the Norman Conquest, with the one exception of King Harold Harefoot, the successor of Cnut, whose writ for Christ Church, Canterbury, is known only from a contemporary abstract (see p. 18).   And further, in the earliest protocol printed here (dating from A.D. 984–1001) of a writ of an Anglo-Saxon king (no. 107),[4] the formula is the same as in King Alfred's Preface to the *Cura Pastoralis*, except that the *hate* of the earlier text is now absent.   The authenticity of the writ in the name of Æthelred II for St. Paul's, no. 52, is too doubtful for this document to be brought into account here.   But the wording of the *Chronicle* suggests that it was by writ that King Æthelred II communicated with his subjects during the negotiations for his return which took place after the death of King Swein ; see Appendix IV, no. 3. There has also been preserved from this period, a writ of King Æthelred's mother, Queen Ælfthryth, addressed to an archbishop and an ealdorman, in which she gives an account of the history of an estate.   We have then clear evidence that the writ protocol was

---

[1] On a (Winchester) notification in this form attributed to Cnut (K. 753), see pp. 382, 551 below. On some Bury texts, see p. 141 and n. 2. The authenticity of the declaration in the name of the Confessor in this form that he has granted the land at Steyning to the monastery at Fécamp (K. 890) is not beyond doubt.

[2] Harmer, *English Historical Documents*, no. 18. Compare also the letter extant only in Latin, beginning ' Karissime ', of the bishops and thegns of Kent to King Æthelstan (Liebermann i. 170, Attenborough, 142, B. 1341) ; see also Whitelock, no. 3, Harmer, *ut supra*, no. 20.

[3] See, for example, *Crawford Charters*, ed. Napier and Stevenson, no. 7 ; B. 1136.

[4] The authenticity of the remainder of the text is not certain ; see pp. 377–80 below.

employed for sealed letters issued by the clerks of the royal secretariat in the reign of King Æthelred II, and it continued to be employed in the scriptorium of Æthelred II's successor, Cnut, who issued not long after his accession, between 1017 and 12 June 1020, a writ, no. 26, announcing his confirmation of the liberties of Christ Church, Canterbury. The writ protocol was also employed in the long Proclamation issued between February and June 1020, outlining his policy past and present, as also in the Proclamation of 1027, now extant only in Latin, sent by Cnut to inform his subjects of his visit to Rome and the success that had attended his negotiations on their behalf with the pope, the Emperor Conrad II, and other rulers, and of other matters.[1] Seven other writs of Cnut, of which four or five are in all probability authentic, are printed here. No seal of Cnut is now known to exist, but there is evidence for his use of a seal from more than one quarter. The native evidence is not quite conclusive. Thomas of Elmham writing in the early fifteenth century a history of the abbey of St. Augustine's, Canterbury (see p. 192), says :—

' Non enim usque post conquestum a tempore fundationis huius monasterii, *excepta carta regis Knuti*, qui fuit alienigena et conquestor, aliqua in munimentis reperimus sigilla cerea, sed solummodo crucis signa ';[2]

the last two words refer of course to the sign of the Cross accompanying the names of witnesses to charters. But although the monastery may have possessed a seal attributed to Cnut, it does not follow that it was authentic. It seems very likely that the seal to which Elmham refers was the seal which is mentioned on the *Cartæ Antiquæ* Roll, with reference to the St. Mildred's writ of St. Augustine's (see p. 195). But this text as it stands bears evident signs of post-Conquest origin, and it is therefore impossible for an authentic seal of Cnut to have been appended to it by the clerks of Cnut's secretariat. More satisfactory evidence is cited by W. H. Stevenson.[3] He observes that the Saga of St. Olaf ascribes a seal to Cnut, and that in the *Fagrskinna* version of this saga we are told that Queen Emma got hold of Cnut's seal and caused a letter (*bréf*) to be sealed with it, ordering the Danes to make her son Harthacnut king of Denmark, and that this letter was read before the ' thing ' at Viborg—incidentally by the chaplain of Jarl Ulf, the brother-in-law

[1] For these Proclamations see Liebermann, *Gesetze*, i. 273–5, 276–7 ; Robertson, *Laws of the Kings of England* (Cambridge, 1925), 140–5, 146–53 (text and Mod. Eng. rendering) ; Mod. Eng. rendering without text, L. M. Larson, *Canute the Great* (New York and London, 1912), 341–7 ; Mod. Eng. rendering of Proclamation of 1020, Stubbs, *Select Charters*, 9th ed., 1913, 90–2. The 1020 Proclamation (the other being in Latin) differs from the common form of writs printed here by the use of *his* for *my* : ' King Cnut sends friendly greetings to *his* archbishops ' etc.   [2] *Hist. Mon. S. Augustini*, R.S. 118.
[3] *Eng. Hist. Rev.* xxvii (1912), 6, n. 17.

of Earl Godwine.[1]   One is the more inclined to believe this story
from the fact that the letter (so we are told) was addressed in the
manner of writs printed here to definite persons who were named in it
(' and there were named there all the greatest chiefs in Denmark '),
and that Cnut in the letter was made to send his ' greetings ' to them
and to all Danes.   Of the seal of Cnut, restored by Harthacnut to
his father when he made his submission, we are told only that it had
the king's name on it.[2]   It was conjectured by Bresslau (see p. 101)
that Cnut's seal was made on the model of a wax seal employed by
the Emperor Conrad II, but that unlike the German seals, Cnut's
seal was two-faced to denote his two-fold lordship, of England and of
Denmark, and there is much to recommend this hypothesis.   Reference to ' letters and seals ' of Cnut is also made elsewhere in the
Saga of St. Olaf in *Heimskringla* :—

' Cnut the Mighty sent men east from England to Norway . . . they had
letters and seals (*bréf ok innsigli*) of Cnut ' etc.[3]

Of seals employed by Cnut's successors on the throne of England,
Harold Harefoot, and the Harthacnut mentioned above, no trace
now remains, but both these kings employed the writ form.   Reference to a writ now lost of Harold Harefoot appears in a contemporary
charter which tells how the king, between c. 1037 and 1040, communicated, evidently by writ, with the archbishop of Canterbury
and the monks of Christ Church, and in which not only the greeting
(' He greeted them all *with God's greeting and his own* '), but also
other characteristic writ formulas are unmistakably employed.[4]
The two writs extant of King Harthacnut (nos. 56, 57) have come
down to us only in Latin versions preserved in cartulary copies.
The sole Anglo-Saxon king represented by any letter with a seal still
attached is King Edward the Confessor, and to him, as is well-
known, the great majority of pre-Conquest writs belong.   Two writs
of his wife Queen Edith are preserved in later copies, and a writ of

---

[1] *Fagrskinna*, ed. F. Jónsson (Copenhagen, 1902–03), 187.   The story also
appears in *Heimskringla*, ed. Jónsson (Copenhagen, 1911), 341.   Mod. Eng.
rendering, Monsen, 390.   See also *Flateyjarbók*, ed. G. Vigfússon and C. R.
Unger (Christiania, 1860, 1859–68), ii. c. 210.   Stevenson observes that Walter
Map's story (*De Nugis Curialium*, ed. M. R. James (Anec. Oxon. Med. and
Mod. Ser. xiv, 1914), 216 ff.) of Earl Godwine's breaking Cnut's seal and
substituting another message, ' a remarkable parallel to Saxo's story of
Hamlet ', ' need not detain us '.   [2] *Fagrskinna*, 187.

[3] Ed. Jónsson, p. 308, Mod. Eng. rendering, Monsen, 356.   See also
Flateyjarbók, ii. 253.   *Bréf ok innsigli* is rendered : ' letters and the seal ',
by M. Ashdown, *English and Norse Documents*, p. 171 ; but with the comment
(p. 228) that the *innsigli* may refer to a seal ring sent in addition to the letter,
or to the seal on the letter, and that, since *bréf* is mentioned alone in another
passage, the latter explanation is more probable.

[4] See Appendix IV, no. 5.

King Harold, son of Earl Godwine, King Edward's successor, is also preserved in the same sources. Many more royal writs must have been issued than have survived. To some of these we find allusions elsewhere. Besides the two writs of Æthelred II which give orders that disputes shall be settled in shire courts (Appendix IV, nos. 1, 2), and the writ of Harold Harefoot restoring Sandwich with full privileges to the archbishop of Canterbury and the monks of Christ Church (see above), we hear in the *Chronicle* of a writ ordering the consecration of a bishop (*ibid.* no. 6). References in Domesday illustrate the purposes for which the king's writ and seal were employed before the Conquest. Some relate, as do the great majority of writs printed here, to the tenure of land, and/or rights of jurisdiction. In one case a man of standing is transferred with all his land from the king's jurisdiction to that of the bishop of Lincoln (*ibid.* no. 15). One writ gives permission to the commended freemen of the outlawed Edric of Laxfield to return to him after his reconciliation with the king (*ibid.* no. 17). A statement that ' they have not seen a writ and seal of King Edward ' (*ibid.* nos. 20, 21) in a given case is valuable testimony as to the circumstances in which the issue of a writ would have been considered appropriate. Side by side with the writ used for general administrative business, the issue of large numbers of administrative orders in the form of writs would have been necessitated by the intricate system adopted for the collection of the geld by Anglo-Saxon kings ; of such writs four at any rate are extant ; nos. 15, 29, 66, 107 (no. 67 is spurious).

WRITS AND LETTERS OF NON-ROYAL PERSONS

But among the existing Anglo-Saxon writs, there are writs not only of kings and queens, but also of non-royal persons. Although in England no letter with seal attached of a non-royal person appears to have survived from the pre-Conquest period, a few seal matrices and impressions have come down to us. A list of such seals given by W. H. Stevenson [1] includes among others the matrix of the seal of Bishop Æthelwald (Ethiluuald) of Dunwich [2] (845–70), the matrix of thĕ double seal of Godwine *minister* and Godgyth *monacha*, which has been dated in the late tenth or early eleventh century,[3] and also the matrix of the seal of one Ælfric [4] (but the identification of this person with Ælfric, ealdorman of Mercia 983–1003, is not certain,

---

[1] *Eng. Hist. Rev.* xxvii (1912), 6, n. 18.

[2] Birch, *Catalogue of Seals in the British Museum*, i. 1488.

[3] O. M. Dalton, *Cat. of the Ivory Carvings of the Christian Era in the British Museum* (1909), no. 31, Plate xxxiv ; M. H. Longhurst, *English Ivories* (London, 1926), p. 10, Plate 17, no. 11.   [4] Birch i. no. 4.

for the name is a common one). Two seals, known only from impressions, of religious houses, are also included in Stevenson's list, one of Durham Cathedral, the other of Wilton Abbey, and both from matrices of the tenth or the eleventh century.[1] Moreover, though there is no seal attached, a private charter of 860–66 at Canterbury,[2] bears marks of sealing. There is then no difficulty in supposing that the letters printed here, nos. 3, 6, 27, 63, 121, of persons of superior consequence, whether ecclesiastical or lay, outside the royal circle, would have been authenticated by a seal. It is worth noting that in a statement in Latin attributed to Bishop Lyfing of Worcester (K. 941), the bishop declares that he had at the command of the Confessor confirmed by a document (? a writ) with a seal, *cum meo breui et sigillo*, given to the abbot of Evesham in the presence of the witan (' testibus sapientibus hominibus '), who were with the king, the liberties granted or confirmed by King Edward to Evesham Abbey. The statement in which we read this is also called a *breve* (' Ego Liuingus episcopus manifesto *in isto breui* ') but this is a declaration not a letter.[3] Whatever this sealed *breve* may have been, this statement, if it were authentic, would provide further evidence for the use of seals by bishops. There is then evidence for the use of seals by non-royal persons at least as early as the ninth century, whilst the private charter at Canterbury mentioned above provides clear evidence that seals were affixed to documents. To the survival—or revival—of the use of the sealed letter in the latter part of the tenth century, usages both administrative and literary may have contributed. The leading laymen in the circle in which the writ protocol is found to be extensively employed, by persons outside the royal circle, in letters and epistolary prefaces surviving from this period, Ealdorman Æthelweard, and his son, Ealdorman Æthelmær, were not only conspicuous for their literary interests, as has been shown above (p. 9), but were also of royal descent, for they could trace back their line to King Æthelred I, an elder brother of King Alfred. In no other family outside immediate royal circles (in which the writ with its characteristic protocol was also now employed) were the administrative usages and the epistolary traditions of the court of King Alfred more likely to have survived than in that of Æthelweard and Æthelmær. No letter sent by either of these magnates seems to have survived, though Æthelweard is addressed in no. 108, Æthelmær in no. 63, and Æthelweard is also

[1] Birch i. nos. 2511, 4335.

[2] R. Lane Poole, *Studies in Chronology and History*, 106, and Plate. But Poole uses the term *sur simple queue* in a different sense from that employed in this book.

[3] The same term *breve* is used of a closely-related text, an (? authentic) declaration of King Edward (K. 911).

addressed in letters of Abbot Ælfric with the writ protocol. An inscription : ' + Æþel + Æþelweord gret ', written in an eleventh-century hand on the last leaf of Lambeth MS. 149, seems to refer to another Æthelweard *dux*, who according to an inscription elsewhere in the same manuscript, gave the manuscript in 1018 to a religious house, and who is identified by Robin Flower with the Ealdorman Æthelweard who was Ealdorman Æthelmær's son-in-law, and succeeded him in office.[1] Whether the characteristic writ protocol was used in royal letters throughout the tenth century we have no means of telling ; evidence on this point is lacking. The influence of Abbot Ælfric himself in continuing the tradition of the character-istic writ protocol as it appears (substantially) in King Alfred's well-known Preface to the Anglo-Saxon version of the *Cura Pastoralis*, must certainly be taken into account. The works of King Alfred were familiar to him, and indeed he seems to be re-echoing the words of Alfred's famous Preface in his own complaint (possibly exaggerated) of the illiteracy and indifference to learning of the age which preceded that of the monastic reform :—

' . . . þæt seo halige lar on urum dagum ne acolige oððe ateorige, swa swa hit wæs gedon on Angelcynne nu for anum feawum gearum, swa þæt nan Englisc preost ne cuðe dihtan oððe asmeagean anne pistol on Leden oðþæt Dunstan arcebisceop and Aðelwold bisceop eft þa lare on munuclifum arærdon '. (' That holy learning may not in our days grow cold or fail, as it had done in England a few years ago, so that no English priest could compose or understand a letter in Latin, until Archbishop Dunstan and Bishop Æthelwold re-introduced learning into monasteries '.) [2]

Contemporary with the writs of King Æthelred II and Queen Ælfthryth (see pp. 16 f.) are the First Latin Letter and the Second Latin Letter (both addressed to Archbishop Sigeric) prefixed by Ælfric to his Catholic Homilies, completed 991–92,[3] in which Ælfric employs, as he does elsewhere, a variation of the ancient *salutem*-formula which had been used by Aldhelm :—

' Ego Ælfricus alumnus Adelwoldi, benevoli et venerabilis presulis, *salutem exopto* domno Archiepiscopo Sigerico *in Domino* ',

and

' Ælfricus humilis servulus Christi, honorabili et amando Archiepiscopo Sigerico *perpetuam sospitatem optat in Domino* '.[4]

---

[1] Introd. to *The Exeter Book*, 87 f. It should however be noted that the elder Ealdorman Æthelweard, the Chronicler, prefixed to his Chronicle a Latin epistolary preface with an elaborate protocol of this type (Sir Henry Savile, *Rer. Anglicar. Script.* 1596, 473).

[2] *Ælfrics Grammatik und Glossar*, ed. J. Zupitza (Berlin, 1880), 3.

[3] For this dating see K. Sisam, *Review of English Studies*, vii (1931), 17.

[4] B. Thorpe, *Homilies of the Anglo-Saxon Church* (Ælfric Society, 1844–46), i. 1, ii. 1 ; Mod. Eng. rendering, S. H. Gem, *An Anglo-Saxon Abbot* (Edin-

Further, the influence of the works of Alcuin in the carrying-on of the tradition of the *salutem*-formula cannot be ignored. Lingard observed [1] that a considerable part of a letter written between 993 and 1001 by an archbishop [2] to Bishop Wulfsige of Sherborne, is copied directly or indirectly, from one written by Alcuin to Eanbald II, archbishop of York, in 796 [3]; and although the opening clauses of Alcuin's letter are not copied exactly, we find in both letters the characteristic protocol, containing the name of the writer, that of the person addressed, and a greeting. Moreover the same traditional opening, with variations, appears in Latin letters of other ecclesiastics corresponding with one another, of which a few have come down to us from the late tenth century, written at much the same time as Ælfric's Prefaces, and sometimes to the same correspondent or to members of the same circle.[4] Such forms, it is interesting to observe, were also being employed in letters written on the Continent. The interest of these letters and epistolary prefaces resides in the fact that they provide evidence for the use in England in the tenth century of the well-known protocol ' X to Y *salutem* ', which frequently appears, not only in documents of earlier times, but also in later versions of Anglo-Saxon writs. Ælfric uses the simple *salutem*-formula (with the addition of *in Christo*) in the Preface to his life of St. Æthelwold, of 1005–06 :—

' Alfricus abbas, Wintoniensis alumnus, honorabili episcopo Kenulfo et fratribus Uuintoniensibus *salutem in Christo* ',

and he also employs other unelaborated forms of this in Latin epistolary prefaces to other works of his.[5]

burgh, 1912), 112–14, 198. For another instance of *salutem exoptat*, see B. Fehr, *Die Hirtenbriefe Ælfrics* (Grein-Wülker, *Bibl. der angelsächs. Prosa*, ix, 1914), 222. For the formulas : *optabilem in Domino salutem*, *optabilem sospitatem*, employed by Aldhelm and his imitator Boniface, see W. Levison, *England and the Continent in the Eighth Century* (Oxford, 1946), 286. Ælfric's prefaces are in C. L. White, *Ælfric*, 164–82.

¹ *History and Antiquities of the Anglo-Saxon Church* (London, 1845), ii. 309, n. 1.

² Stubbs, who prints the letter, *Memorials of Saint Dunstan*, 406, gives reasons for supposing that the archbishop whose name is no longer legible in the letter, was Archbishop Ælfric of Canterbury.

³ For text, see *Mon. Germ. Hist. Epist. Kar. Aevi*, ii (1895), no. 114.

⁴ To Archbishop Sigeric of Canterbury, to whom Ælfric dedicated his Catholic Homilies, Abbot Ælfweard writes, 990–4, as follows : ' Dilectissimo in Christo patri Sigerico misteriarchæ, humilis vestræ paternitati abbas Elfwardus æternæ beatitudinis et perpetuæ prosperitatis salutem ' ; (Stubbs, *ut supra*, 400). See also *ibid*. 408, an encyclical letter of 993–1001 of Bishop Wulfsige of Sherborne ; *ibid*. 409, a letter of 1000–04 of Abbot Wulfric of St. Augustine's, Canterbury, to Abbot Abbo of Fleury.

⁵ *Chron. Mon. Abingdon*, R.S. ii. 255, White, 181, Gem, 166. Also B. Fehr, *Die Hirtenbriefe Ælfrics*, 1 (*salutem in Domino*), 68 (*salutem in Christo*),

Of more immediate interest for the history of the writ protocol in the vernacular are the epistolary Prefaces in Old English prefixed by the Abbot Ælfric to other religious and literary works. The earliest of these, contemporary (it must again be emphasised) with the writs of King Æthelred II and Queen Ælfthryth (pp. 16 f.), are the epistolary Prefaces in the vernacular addressed by Ælfric to Ealdorman Æthelweard. The Preface to the *Lives of the Saints* begins :—

' Ælfric gret eadmodlice Æðelwerd ealdorman and ic secge þe, leof ' etc., (' Ælfric sends humble greetings to Ealdorman Æthelweard, and I tell thee beloved ' etc.) [1]

and the Preface to the translation of the Book of Genesis begins :—

' Ælfric munuc gret Æðelwærd ealdormann eadmodlice. þu bæde me, leof ' etc. (' Ælfric the monk sends humble greetings to Ealdorman Æthelweard. Thou didst request me, beloved ' etc.) [2]

Ælfric employed the same protocol, but with *freondlice* instead of the adverb *eadmodlice* used above—which also appears in writs nos. 27, 108—in prefaces of this same period (before 1020) addressed to other persons. One of these begins :—

' Ælfric abbod gret Sigefyrð freondlice. Me is gesæd ' etc. (' Abbot Ælfric sends friendly greetings to Sigeferth. I have been told ' etc.) [3]

Whereas in these epistolary prefaces the protocol is that appearing in the vast majority of writs printed here, the use in the greeting in another of Ælfric's prefaces of the pronoun ' I ' with the verb in the first person (instead of the name unaccompanied by ' I ' and a verb in the third person) affords a useful parallel for two writs, nos. 53, 113, where this same usage with the first person appears, and where its authenticity might otherwise have appeared doubtful :—

' Ic Ælfric abbod on ðisum Engliscum gewrite freondlice grete mid Godes gretinge Wulfget æt Ylmandune.' (' I Abbot Ælfric in this English letter greet as a friend with God's greeting Wulfgeat of Ilmington '.) [4]

It also provides another instance of the ' with God's greeting ' formula, which is mentioned elsewhere (p. 62, n. 2). From Ælfric's contemporary Archbishop Wulfstan of York there has come down to us not only a writ, no. 27, informing the king and queen that

---

White, 180, 181. See also E. Breck, *Fragment of Ælfric's Translation of Æthelwold's De Consuetudine Monachorum* (Leipzig, 1887), 37 (*salutem in Christo*), White, 181.

[1] *Ælfric's Lives of the Saints*, ed. W. W. Skeat, E.E.T.S. lxxvi (1881), 4 ; White, 173, Gem, 143.

[2] Grein-Wülker i. 22, White, 176.

[3] B. Assmann, *Angelsächsische Homilien und Heiligenleben* (Grein-Wülker iii), 13, White, 175. For another instance see Grein-Wülker i. 1, White, 177.

[4] Assmann, *loc. cit.*, 1, White, 175.

Æthelnoth has been consecrated to the see of Canterbury, but also the so-called Pastoral Letter. This has, in MS. C, an epistolary opening employing the same protocol :—

'Wulfstan arcebisceop greteð freondlice þegnas on ðeode, gehadode and læwede, ealle gemænelice, þa ðe him betæhte sindon for Gode to wissianne'. ('Archbishop Wulfstan sends friendly greetings to thegns in the nation, ecclesiastical and lay, all without exception, who have been entrusted to his guidance in spiritual things'.) [1]

Among the non-royal writs that have survived, an early instance of a letter with the writ protocol, dealing with administrative business, and authenticated no doubt in its original form (it is now extant only in a copy) by a seal, is Bishop Æthelric's letter (no. 63) to Æthelmær, who was in all probability the ealdorman of that name to whom reference has frequently been made. Can we conclude on the existing evidence that in the late tenth and early eleventh centuries the writ protocol was in general use outside the royal scriptorium, and that it was employed for general epistolary purposes, as well as for letters on administrative business authenticated by a seal ? It seems impossible to answer this question, for the relevant texts have come down to us, as is evident, from a comparatively small circle.[2] But the writ form in the reign of the Confessor is not confined, any more than it had been before, to the use of royal personages. Writs were addressed to a shire court by a bishop and an abbot respectively (nos. 3, 6), and the writ form was also employed by the northern magnate Gospatric (no. 121), murdered at the court of the Confessor in 1064.

ORIGIN AND EARLY USE OF WRIT PROTOCOL

The use of the sealed letter or writ as an administrative instrument in this country can then, as we have seen, be carried back by King

---

[1] *Wulfstan : Sammlung der ihm zugeschriebenen Homilien*, ed. A. [S.] Napier, i (Berlin, 1883), 108, n. 2. Napier considered the epistolary opening of the Pastoral Letter to be spurious on the ground that this opening is absent in the other manuscripts ; see *Über die Werke des altenglischen Erzbischofs Wulfstan* (Weimar, 1882), 7. But this scepticism seems unfounded. Miss Whitelock kindly informs me that Miss D. Bethurum has suggested to her the possibility that the Pastoral Letter may have been first composed for oral delivery to an audience, and may then have been sent out to the thegns—a theory which, as Miss Whitelock remarks, gives a reasonable explanation for the survival of the letter with and without the greeting formula. It is perhaps worth noting that the opening clauses with their alliteration and balance (*þegnas on ðeode, gehadode and læwede*) seem to have the authentic ' ring ' of Wulfstan's writings. MS. C is considered by experts to have had access to good materials.

[2] ' To the writs mentioned here should be added two wills with a writ protocol ; ' Mantat ancer Godes wrǣcca *greteð* Cnut cing 7 Emma hlǣfdie *swiðe bliþelike mid Godes blisse*' (Whitelock, *Anglo-Saxon Wills*, no. 23) ; and : ' Leofgiue *gret* hyre leuedi *Godes gretinge*' (*ibid*. no. 29).

Alfred's own allusion to the *ærendgewrit and insegel* to the latter part of the ninth century, whilst in a document composed by him, we find for the first time in English a protocol containing in all essential points the address and greeting formula which was to become ' common form ' for the Anglo-Saxon writ ; and further, a Biblical *ærendgewrit*, as translated by the king, closely resembles in structure the writ of later days. But is it likely that an institution, so familiar as King Alfred's casual allusion to the lord's *ærendgewrit and insegel* implies this to have been, can have been an innovation of King Alfred's own time ? The letter dealing with business matters, authenticated by some token or by a seal, could in theory at any rate have been a spontaneous native development at any time during the Anglo-Saxon period : all that would be required would be some person, whether the sender or some one acting on his behalf, who could write and seal a letter, whether in the vernacular tongue or in Latin, and at the other end a recipient who could read it, or else could find someone capable of reading it to him. It is however important to observe that the Anglo-Saxon writ exhibits certain diplomatic and literary usages which are not likely to have arisen spontaneously. The sign of the Cross with which the writ sometimes begins, the protocol (or opening clauses up to and including the greeting), the prohibition, the benediction and the anathema (or punitive or penal clause), the valediction, in so far as these appear in Anglo-Saxon writs, all reflect in some degree older diplomatic or literary usage. But the clearest evidence of a settled literary tradition is to be found in the protocol ; the valediction, which is by no means a constant feature of Anglo-Saxon writs as they have come down to us, can be left out of consideration here. There can be little doubt that the protocol of the Anglo-Saxon writ, containing as it does the name of the sender and (except when the address is a more general one) the name of the person or persons addressed, together with a greeting, originated in an imitation or adaptation to the vernacular, of a conventional Latin epistolary opening in the form : ' X to Y *salutem* ', which can be traced back to antiquity, and which appears in the Latin versions of writs printed here. This protocol appears in letters of Roman emperors and provincial governors.[1]

---

[1] Compare, for instance, the *epistula* of Vespasian to the Vanacini preserved as a bronze inscription discovered in Corsica : ' Imp. Caesar Vespasianus Augustus magistratibus et senatoribus Vanacinorum salutem dicit ' (P. F. Girard, *Textes de Droit Romain* (Paris, 1890), 149) ; compare also H. Dessau, *Inscriptiones Latinae Selectae* (Berlin, 1892–1916), i. no. 2948 : ' Nicomacho Flaviano cons. Sicil., vicar Afric., quaest. aulae divi Theodosi, praef. praet. Ital. Illyr. etc. Imperatores Caess. Fl. Theodosius et Fl. Placidus Valentinianus semper Augg. senatui suo salutem ' etc.

It appears in letters of Cicero ; it appears in the New Testament. It was used in papal letters.[1] It was employed in the land of the Franks ; compare the letter of Charlemagne to Offa, king of Mercia, beginning :—

' Karolus gratia Dei rex Francorum et Longobardorum et patricius Romanorum viro venerando et fratri karissimo Offæ regi Merciorum salutem '.[2]

It must have become known in England at all events after the arrival here of St. Augustine and his Roman mission in 597. A letter employing the protocol with *salutem* sent by Pope Honorius to Edwin, king of Northumbria, in 634, and inserted by Bede into the *Historia Ecclesiastica*, begins as follows :—

' Domino excellentissimo atque praecellentissimo filio Æduino regi Anglorum, Honorius episcopus seruus seruorum Dei salutem ',[3]

and other letters employing the *salutem*-formula were inserted by Bede into his works.[4] We may take as another instance the letter written by Bede himself to Albinus, abbot of St. Augustine's, prefixed to the *Historia Ecclesiastica*, and beginning :—

' Desiderantissimo et reuerentissimo patri Albino, Baeda Christi famulus salutem '.[5]

Papal decretals, some of which must have been known in England, sometimes employ the ' X to Y *salutem* ' formula.[6] The letters of

[1] On the usages of the papal chancery, see R. Lane Poole, *Lectures on the History of the Papal Chancery* (Cambridge, 1915), 22, 41–2. In the fourth century some popes employed the greeting *in Domino salutem*, or *in Domino aeternam salutem*. Pope Adeodatus (672–76) wrote *salutem a Deo et benedictionem nostram*, and the greeting formula becomes more frequent from the time of his pontificate, though it was not a constant feature. *Salutem et apostolicam benedictionem* appears in the tenth century, and gradually becomes fixed, though varieties may appear. This is the greeting which has persisted till modern times. For specimens of formulas employed in the papal chancery, see the *Liber Diurnus*, ed. Th. Sickel (Vienna, 1889), and for the texts of extant papal letters sent to this country, see W. Holtzmann, *Papsturkunden in England* (Berlin, 1930 etc.).

[2] B. 270 ; cf. also Haddan and Stubbs, *Councils and Ecclesiastical Documents*, iii, 486, another letter of Charlemagne to Offa with a similar protocol. For a letter of St. Boniface to King Pippin, of 753–55, in the same tradition, see *Mon. Germ. Hist. Epist. Mer. et Kar. Aevi*, i (1892), 394.

[3] *Venerabilis Baedae Opera Historica*, ed. Plummer (Oxford, 1896), i. 118.

[4] *Ibid.* i. 333, 383 = 399. Cf. also i. clx, 405.

[5] *Ibid.* i. clxxix.

[6] It was suggested by J. D. A. Ogilvy, *Books known to Anglo-Latin writers from Aldhelm to Alcuin*, 670–804 (The Mediaeval Academy of America, Studies and Documents, no. 2, 1936), p. 47, that the ' Collectio Decretorum ' of Dionysius Exiguus (Migne, *Patrologia Latina*, lxvii) may have been the source from which Bishop Daniel of Winchester (705–44), and Bede, derived the papal decretals cited by them. On the collection of Dionysius Exiguus, see F. M. Powicke, *History*, N.S. xviii (1933–34), 15, and references.

Aldhelm,[1] of Boniface, of Alcuin, and of other Englishmen, and of their correspondents in this country and on the Continent, are sufficient to establish the fact that in the first few centuries after the conversion of the Anglo-Saxons to Christianity and the reintroduction of Latin culture into England, this letter opening must have been widely known and used.[2] Of special interest is the letter of Bishop Waldhere of London to Archbishop Berhtwald of Canterbury, in Latin, written in 704 or 705, 'the first letter known to have been written by one Englishman to another'[3]; this also employs the *salutem*-formula. The same formula was employed in royal letters in England. It was used, for instance, in letters sent to Boniface, archbishop of Mainz, by King Ælfwald of East Anglia, and King Æthelberht of Kent,[4] before 755, as also in letters sent to Boniface's successor Lull by King Alhred of Northumbria and his wife,[5] and by King Cynewulf of Wessex, in the second half of the eighth century. The letter addressed to Lull by King Cynewulf, his bishops, and his *satrapae* (ealdormen and thegns), renewing an agreement for mutual prayer made with his predecessor St. Boniface, employs a variant of the *salutem*-formula, of which there are other instances (see p. 21) :—

'Domino beatissimo et speciali amore venerando Lullo episcopo, ego Cynewulf rex occidentalium Saxonum una cum episcopis meis necnon cum caterva satraparum, *æternam sospitatis in domino salutem*'.[6]

---

[1] It was pointed out to me by the late Wilhelm Levison that Aldhelm was studying c. 671 (among other subjects) unidentified 'Roman laws', possibly the *Lex Romana Visigothorum* (or *Breviarium Alarici*), which contains constitutions of later Roman emperors in the form of letters, with the *salutem*-protocol ; see *Lex Romana Visigothorum*, ed. G. Haenel (Leipzig, 1849), pp. 160, 282. See further, W. Levison, *Neues Archiv*, xxxv (1910), 373 f., A. S. Cook, 'Aldhelm's Legal Studies', *Journal of English and Germanic Philology*, xxiii (1924), 105–13, and M. R. James, *Two Ancient English Scholars : St. Aldhelm and William of Malmesbury* (Glasgow University Publications xxii, 1931), and for other references, Ogilvy, *op. cit.* But it is not suggested that this is the only source from which Aldhelm could have become acquainted with the *salutem*-formula.

[2] See, for instance, *Mon. Germ. Hist.*, *Aldhelmi Opera*, ed. Ehwald (Berlin, 1919), 475–503, 13 letters from, or to, Aldhelm, ranging from A.D. 671 to 705/9, in all of which some variant of this protocol is employed. Also *Epist. Mer. et Kar. Aevi*, i (1892), 231 ff., *Kar. Aevi*, ii (1895), 18 ff., where letters of Englishmen are included. Also Haddan and Stubbs, iii. *passim*. For letters of Alcuin, see *Epist. Kar. Aevi*, ii (1895), *passim*.

[3] Stenton, *Anglo-Saxon England*, 142. Facsimile in *Facs. of Anc. Chart. in the Brit. Mus.*, ed. Bond, pt. i, no. 5. Text, B. 115.

[4] *Epist. Mer. et Kar. Aevi*, i. 361, 391.

[5] *Ibid.* i. 410.

[6] This moving letter, B. 249 (written perhaps by one of the bishops), exhibits in a new light the Cynewulf whose death in 786 at the hands of his enemies is recounted in one of the best-known annals of the *Chronicle* (s.a. 755, actually

The same convention is observed in a letter sent by King Coenwulf of Mercia to Pope Leo III in 798 :—

'Domino beatissimo et vere amantissimo Leoni sanctæ et apostolicæ sedis Romanæ pontifici, Kenulfus gratia Dei rex Merciorum cum episcopis, ducibus et omni sub nostra ditione dignitatis gradu *sincerissimæ dilectionis in Christo salutem* '.[1]

With these letters of Anglo-Saxon kings we seem to come within sight of the Anglo-Saxon writ. That the letters in question were authenticated by seals or by some other token is entirely probable. It is at all events significant that a leaden *bulla*, or coin-seal, bearing the name of Coenwulf, king of Mercia, the last king mentioned here, is still preserved.[2]

POSSIBILITIES OF FOREIGN INFLUENCE

Whence did the impulse come to employ the sealed letter for purposes of internal administration ? The practice of using letters, accompanied no doubt by a seal or other means of identifying the sender or certifying the document, for conveying administrative

the year of Cynewulf's accession); and whose followers (like those of the ætheling Cyneheard) exhibited the loyalty to their lord, even at the cost of life, which was prescribed by the heroic code going back to pre-Christian times. See also on this annal p. 7. In 786, the year of Cynewulf's death, a council was held in Offa's hall by Offa, king of Mercia, in conjunction with Cynewulf, to receive the two legates sent by the pope to propose for the acceptance of the kings, their bishops and nobles, a body of canons relating to questions of faith and ecclesiastical order, and the reform of abuses current among the laity : see Haddan and Stubbs, iii. 447 ff., where it is suggested that the 12th canon, on the honour due to kings, may possibly have reference to the death of Cynewulf, the legates' report of the proceedings of the council having been drawn up a little later ; see also Stenton, *Anglo-Saxon England*, 214 ff. Charters issued by Cynewulf are to be found in Birch, vol. i.

[1] B. 287.

[2] In the Department of Mediæval Antiquities in the British Museum ; see Birch, *Catalogue of Seals*, i (1887), p. 1, no. 2, where it is stated that there is on the obverse a small cross moline, joined at the ends, as appears also on the coins of this king, and on the reverse the same design. On the obverse the words COENVVLFI REGIS appear, on the reverse MERCIORVM. See also Wyon, *The Great Seals of England*, Plate I, nos. 2, 3. According to a note in *Archæologia*, xxxii (1847), 449, the seal had been in Italian collections before it was brought to this country. It ' appears to have been attached to some instrument in the manner of the seals appended both in early and later times to the Papal Bulls.' But since it is not attached to any document it is difficult to form any conclusions as to its use. The seal is discussed by R. Lane Poole, *Studies in Chronology and History*, 106, where it is suggested that ' the idea of using a leaden bull comes from Rome, but that the engravers fell back upon a coin for a model of the lettering '. The genuineness of Coenwulf's *bulla* is, however, questioned by Bresslau (*Archiv f. Urk.* vi (1918), 47, n. 2), on the ground that evidence of its authenticity is lacking.

orders, is so ancient and so widespread that, theoretically at any rate, it does not seem impossible that the practice might have arisen spontaneously in this country quite apart from any foreign influence. And further it does not seem justifiable to assume that the use in England of the sealed letter for administrative purposes necessarily arose at only one time or in one particular region or that it originated with only one individual. In so far as the sealed letter was employed in England for transmitting administrative orders before the closing years of the ninth century, when King Alfred casually alludes to it, the impulse which gave rise to its employment may have been of different origin at different times and in different parts of the country. The possibility of foreign influence must be considered, but it must be remembered that similar circumstances may produce similar results. Can there have been a connection between the Anglo-Saxon writ and the Frankish royal mandate—not amounting to any real imitation or copying on the English side—but merely the adoption of a similar structure based on the general idea of the Frankish mandate ? The possibility that another type of Frankish document, namely, the solemn royal diploma of Frankish kings and their successors relating to grants of lands and privileges, had any influence on the development of the Anglo-Saxon writ,[1] seems remote. Although in early times the protocol of the Merovingian royal diploma (like that of the Anglo-Saxon writ) contained the name of the sender (that is the grantor), and an address to individuals or categories of people—the greeting however being generally absent—this kind of address was from about the time of Charlemagne replaced by a general address (sometimes to all the *fideles* of the church or emperor), or else disappeared altogether. Moreover the formulas of the Frankish diploma are different from those of the Anglo-Saxon writ as we know it. In fact the resemblance between the Frankish diploma and the Anglo-Saxon writ is more apparent than real. There is no indication, so far as I can ascertain, that the

---

[1] The suggestion of J. Goebe, Jr. (*Felony and Misdemeanor*, 379, n. 149) that 'the Anglo-Saxon writ is due to foreigners, Lotharingian or Norman, in the Chancery' (of the Confessor) is to be rejected. The writ as an administrative instrument is far older than Goebel realised, and moreover, to whatever extent priests of foreign origin may have been employed by the Confessor in his scriptorium, there is no indication that they made any contribution to its formulas in the form of phrases of Frankish or other foreign origin. The *cum omnibus pertinentibus* clause is too constantly recurring a feature of charters of the Anglo-Saxon period (see Kemble, i. xl) for the appearance of its equivalent : ' with everything belonging thereto ', in Anglo-Saxon writs, to be regarded as an imitation of Frankish formulas. Again, exclusionary clauses which appear both in Frankish diplomas and in Anglo-Saxon writs have their origin no doubt in comparable circumstances in religious houses in England and in Frankish territory.

Frankish documents in question were intended to be read, as were the Anglo-Saxon writs, at a public assembly. The resemblances are merely resemblances of form—both are letters and both are sealed. It seems unlikely that the Frankish royal diploma can have contributed to the employment of the sealed letter in Anglo-Saxon England.

But from the chancery of the Frankish kings and emperors there issued not only the solemn royal diplomas which have been mentioned above, but also much more informal and unpretentious documents in epistolary form, which, like the diplomas, however, were invariably in Latin. These letters of a simpler (and different) type, which are sometimes but not always sealed, are called by German scholars, ' Mandate ', ' Reskripte ',[1] when they transmit the instructions of a ruler to his subordinates. Bresslau found in such documents a resemblance to the Anglo-Saxon writs [2] :—

' Zuerst am Ausgang des 10. Jahrhunderts tritt nun neben diesen Diplomen ' (i.e. the solemn royal diplomas of the Anglo-Saxon kings) ' eine neue Art von Königsurkunden auf, die wir mit den Indiculi der merovingischen Kanzlei, mit den festländischen Mandaten des folgenden Jahrhunderts vergleichen müssen '.

Bresslau does not develop his comparison, and he puts the origin of the Anglo-Saxon writ too late. That the Merovingian indiculus had any influence on the development of the Anglo-Saxon writ form seems most improbable.[3] The Frankish mandates, like Anglo-Saxon writs, are addressed to individuals or categories of people ; this special address, which is sometimes in the mandates accompanied by a greeting, becomes indeed a distinguishing mark of the mandate, when, about the time of Charlemagne, the special address to individuals or categories of people which had at one time appeared in Frankish royal diplomas, became a general one, or was omitted altogether. Both by their form and by their function the Frankish mandates were distinguished from the Frankish royal

[1] C. Erdmann (*Archiv f. Urk.* xxi (1939), 184 ff.) uses 'mandate' differently, for letters with the seal impressed (as with a royal diploma), unlike the ' closed letter ', the opening of which destroyed the seal.

[2] *Archiv f. Urk.* vi, 48.

[3] On the meaning of the term *indiculum, indiculus,* appearing in the formula books, see Ducange. For examples see Zeumer, *Mon. Germ. Hist. Legum sectio v : Formulae Merowingici et Karolini Aevi* (1886), 46 ff. ; e.g. 46, ' Indecolum regis ad episcopum, ut alium benedicat ' ; 60, ' Indecolum ad laicum '. The *indiculus* was a form used in the procedure of Merovingian episcopal elections. It was a letter rather than a writ, and being informal, had a protocol running, e.g., ' Sulpicio episcopo Dagobertus Rex '. For the close parallels between the *indiculi regales* of later Frankish kings and certain Anglo-Norman types of writ, see H. Brunner, *Die Entstehung der Schwurgerichte* (Berlin, 1872), 76–83 (' Excurs über die gerichtlichen Indiculi Regales ').

diploma.[1] They are used to transmit orders to a subordinate or to issue general instructions. For example, a mandate of Charlemagne, of 772–74, commands that property belonging to the *ecclesia Scotorum* on the island of Honau, which had been alienated, be restored.[2] In a later mandate of probably 1029–34, but not in Charlemagne's mandates, we find a greeting clause parallel to that of the Anglo-Saxon writ :—

' Chuonradus Dei gratia Romanorum imperator augustus Berenhardo duci, Sigifrido comiti, Bernhardo marchioni, salutem et gratiam '.[3]

By this time, however, the Anglo-Saxon writ was already in being. More interesting, therefore, in view of the possibility of an (? unconscious) affinity between the Frankish mandate and the Anglo-Saxon writ, is a ninth-century document in which we find not only a greeting but a notification in the form *sciatis*, to be compared with the *ic cyðe eow* of the writ), namely a mandate addressed to the people of Barcelona, by Charles the Bald, king of France and emperor of Germany, the father-in-law of King Alfred's father King Æthelwulf, by Æthelwulf's second marriage, to Charles's daughter Judith.[4] It begins :—

' In nomine Sanctae et Individuae Trinitatis, Karolus ejusdem Dei Omni-

---

[1] Bresslau (*Urkundenlehre*, i (1912), 53, 64) supposes that the Frankish mandate had only a transitory value which ended as soon as the measures which it directed had been carried out. Sickel suggests that in Frankish territory every grant (' concessione ') was probably accompanied by a notification of some sort, a letter or a mandate, written to the local authority, which it would be the duty of the count to read publicly to his subordinates, in order to secure for the contents of the royal diploma which had been secured by the beneficiary the publicity desired. Sickel observes that the phraseology of the mandates is more informal than that of the diplomas (nearly all the mandates being devoid of recognition formula and date), the mandates are shorter, the parchment on which they are written is smaller, the style of writing is not the same. See Th. Sickel, *Notizie e Trascrizioni dei diplomi imperiali e reali delle cancellerie d' Italia* (Rome, 1892), 22 f. Erdmann conjectures (*loc. cit.* 194) that ' open mandates ' (in his sense) were less often issued than ' closed letters ', and does not think that large numbers of ' open mandates ' have been lost.

[2] *Mon. Germ. Hist., Die Urkunden der Karolinger*, ed. Mühlbacher (Hanover, 1906), no. 77 ; see also *ibid.* 172, a mandate of Charlemagne of 791 commanding the official who has been entrusted with the legal business of the monastery of Farfa, diligently to support the monastery in every legal action. For other instances see Sybel and Sickel, *Kaiserurkunden in Abbildungen* (Berlin, Text, 1891, Plates, 1880–91), Text, p. 4, nos. 7a, 7b, and corresponding plates.

[3] Sybel and Sickel, Text, p. 19, no. 4a, and plate.

[4] J. Calmette, ' Une lettre close originale de Charles le Chauve ', *Mélanges d' archéologie et d' histoire* de l' École française de Rome, xxii (1902), 135–9. Plates iv, v ; also *Bibl. de l' École des Chartes*, lxiii, lxiv (1902–03), 696–9, 329–34. Compare Bresslau, *Urkundenlehre*, i (1912), 66, n. 4. On Judith see P. Grierson, *Trans. R. Hist. Soc.* 4th ser. xxiii (1941), 83, n. 5, and the references there.

potentis misericordia Imperator Augustus omnibus Barchinonensibus peculiaribus nostris salutem. Sciatis quoniam ' etc.[1]

But in spite of the existence of these parallels, it does not seem probable that the Anglo-Saxon writ was merely an imitation of the Frankish mandate. All that is suggested here is that there were resemblances between the writ form and some mandates, but no actual copying on the English side. The Anglo-Saxon writ developed on its own characteristic lines, and apart from the parallels that have been traced, there is no real resemblance between the formulas of the writ and those of the extant mandates. There was, however, some similarity in function. Although many of the surviving writs have acquired a different function, that of announcing grants of lands and privileges to the appropriate authorities, writs employed, like the Frankish mandates, to convey administrative orders still survive ; cf. nos. 15, 29, 66, and, in part, nos. 72, 80, 100, 104, and for lost writs of this type compare Appendix IV, nos. 1, 2, 6, etc. Whether the employment of the sealed letter in Anglo-Saxon England for conveying administrative orders was at any time or in any degree due to imitation of Frankish practice, remains, however, uncertain, though opportunities for such imitation existed. When after the Danish onslaught King Alfred attempted to restore Latin learning in England, he called to his aid, together with ecclesiastics from Mercia, Grimbald of St. Bertin's and John the Old Saxon.[2] But the sealed letter used for administrative

[1] Compare *Mon. Germ. Hist., Die Urkunden der deutschen Karolinger*, ed. P. Kehr, i (1932), p. 101, no. 71, an original mandate of probably 854, undated, with the salutation, *in domino salvatore salutem* ; p. 203, no. 146, an original mandate of 873, dated, with *perpetuam in domino Iesu Christo salutem* ; ii (1936), no. 40, of probably 881, with *in domino salutem*. I have not found any surviving mandates in the volumes published so far of *Chartes et Diplômes relatifs à l' histoire de France* (Paris, 1908 ff.). But it was pointed out to me by the late Wilhelm Levison that among the charters of King Philip I of France (1059–1108), there are extant seven ' mandements ' or ' lettres missives ' which have, following the name and title of the king and the address, *salutem*, or *salutem et gratiam (nostram)* ; see *Recueil des Actes de Philippe I[er], roi de France*, ed. M. Prou (Paris, 1908), nos. 119, 137, 148, 150, 160, 169, 171, and pp. ccv–ccvii. The question was raised by Levison whether the same formulas may not have been used in earlier French mandates now no longer extant. The occurrence of *salutem* (in various forms) in some of the capitularies seemed to Levison to point in this direction. See *Mon. Germ. Hist., Legum sectio ii* (Capitularia), ii (1897), pp. 283 f. (A.D. 856 :—' Mandat vobis senior noster *salutes*), 286 (857 :—*salutem*), 329 (865 :—*salutem*). Professor C. R. Cheney has pointed out to me that a charter of Baldwine V, count of Flanders, of cent. mid. xi, has the *salutem*-formula (A. Teulet, *Layettes du Trésor des Chartes, Archives de l' Empire*, i (1863), p. 21, no. 17.) The editor describes this document, a diploma, not a mandate, as a ' copie authentique scellée ' ; it is not the original diploma.

[2] Stevenson, *Asser's Life of King Alfred*, 307, 311 ; P. Grierson, *loc. cit.* 84, and also *Eng. Hist. Rev.* lv (1940), 528 ff.

business was already a familiar institution in his time, and a connection between England and the land of the Franks had existed long before.[1] King Alfred's father, King Æthelwulf of Wessex (839–58), stayed for a year in Frankish territory, marrying during his sojourn there (as has been said above) the daughter of Charles the Bald. King Æthelwulf also at one time employed a Frankish secretary named Felix to write his letters.[2] But King Æthelwulf was not the first of his family to visit the land of the Franks. His father, Egbert, afterwards King of Wessex, spent some years in exile in Frankish territory under the protection of Charlemagne.[3] William of Malmesbury,[4] writing four centuries later, surmised that Egbert turned his exile to good account, that he made use of it ' to rub off the rust of indolence, to quicken the energy of his mind, and to adopt foreign customs, far differing from his native barbarism '. Whether Malmesbury had in mind anything more than the military success by which Egbert's reign was distinguished, is not clear. He attributes to ' the counsels of God ' the circumstance that Egbert, having lost the protection of King Offa of Mercia, went overseas to France, ' that a man destined to rule so great a kingdom might learn the art of government from the Franks (' regnandi disciplinam a Francis acciperet '), for this people has no competitor among all the western nations in military skill or polished manners ' (' et exercitatione virium et

---

[1] See W. Levison, *England and the Continent in the Eighth Century* ; and also P. Kletler, *Nordwesteuropas Verkehr, Handel und Gewerbe im frühen Mittelalter* (Vienna, 1924).

[2] About the middle of the ninth century Abbot Lupus of Ferrières (on whom see Laistner, *Thought and Letters in Western Europe*, 205 ff.) writes to King Æthelwulf asking for lead for the roofing of a church ; he hopes for the fulfilment of his request ' postquam vestrum in Dei cultu fervorem ex Felice didici, qui epistolarum vestrarum officio fungebatur '. See W. H. Stevenson, *Asser's Life of King Alfred*, 225–6, and the references there given ; also *Mon. Germ. Hist., Epist.* vi (*Kar. Aevi*, iv, 1925), 22, no. 13. The import of these words of Lupus is illustrated by two other letters of his ; in the one he describes Ludwig, the chancellor of Charles the Bald, as *epistolare in palatio gerens officium*, in the other he speaks of a run-away monk, whom the emperor Lothar sent back to his monastery, but wished to employ *in officio condendarum epistolarum* (*ibid.* p. 33, no. 28, p. 93, no. 108) ; see also H. Bresslau, *Archiv f. Urk.* vi (1918), 51, n. 1. Lupus had become acquainted with Felix in the monastery of Faremoutiers-en-Brie (Seine-et-Marne, France) a few years earlier. Stevenson suggests that Felix may have left King Æthelwulf's service before the letter of Lupus was written. Incidentally it is worth noting that Lupus's letter to King Æthelwulf has an elaborate protocol built round the words : . . . Aedilulfo . . . Lupus abbas . . . salutem.

[3] *Chron.* 836. Plummer's suggestion (ii. 75) that the ' three years ' of the *Chronicle* has been rightly corrected by historians to ' thirteen ' is controverted by Stenton, *Anglo-Saxon England*, 218, n. 4.

[4] *Gesta Regum*, ed. Stubbs, R.S. i. 105 f. ; transl. J. A. Giles, 95.

comitate morum '). Egbert returned from exile and succeeded to
the throne of Wessex in A.D. 802. The possibility that in the
kingdom of Wessex at all events Frankish influence may have played
some part in the development of the writ cannot be excluded. But
neither in outward appearance nor in formulas, with the exception
of the epistolary opening of a particular type which is employed in
both documents, is any significant resemblance to be traced between
Anglo-Saxon writ and Frankish mandate. The Frankish mandates
which have survived in their original form are strikingly unlike the
Anglo-Saxon writ in their outward appearance ; their dimensions
are dissimilar ; their methods of sealing (where sealing exists in the
mandates) are different. The resemblances between the Anglo-
Saxon and the Frankish documents—both being employed to give
administrative orders—may have arisen out of similar circumstances
on both sides of the Channel. That Anglo-Saxon in this respect
owed a debt to continental practice cannot be proved. So close
however and so constant was the intercourse both personal and
epistolary between England and the Continent throughout almost
the whole of the Anglo-Saxon period, that borrowing would have
been easy. At almost any time during that period, the sealed letter
used for administrative purposes might (in theory) have been
introduced from abroad, either by foreign scholars or scribes or in
imitation of foreign practice ; or if the writ was already employed
in England, its use might have been reinforced from foreign sources.

WRIT AND DIPLOMA

The Anglo-Saxon royal writ was totally different in its structure
and in its formulas from the charter, diploma, or landbook (as this
type of document is variously called, but with the same signification),
employed by Anglo-Saxon kings for grants of land.[1] Characteristic
features of the diploma (not to be found in the writ) are the verbal
invocation ; the preamble setting out according to convention, the
consideration, or supposed consideration, religious or otherwise,
which had led to the making of the grant—for example, the duty of
almsgiving, the necessity of laying up treasure in heaven, the
transitoriness of earthly things, the desirability of committing grants
to writing ;[2] the recitation of the boundaries of the estate ; the
dating clause ; the list of witnesses, the name of each being accompanied by the sign of the Cross, and by a clause signifying consent
to the grant. The differences in the Anglo-Saxon period, between

[1] For analysis and discussion of the diploma, see Kemble, *Codex Diplomaticus*, Introduction to vol. i, etc. ; Hall, *ut supra*, 177 ff. ; Maitland, *Domesday Book and Beyond*, 261 ff. ; Bresslau, *Archiv f. Urk.* vi. 45 ff.

[2] Examples will be found in Kemble i. x ff.

diploma and writ, are not however merely differences of form and style. The writ, being a letter, was authenticated by the seal of the sender, whereas the diploma was not sealed.[1] But the essential difference between landbook and writ was one of function. The distinction between the writ addressed to the shire court or other authorities, and the diploma, the function of which was to provide for the grant ' testimony more permanent than that of mortal witnesses ',[2] must have been clearly present to the mind of King Edward the Confessor when in three writs printed here (nos. 7, 55, 68) he gave permission, or directions, that a landbook or a *privilegium* (see pp. 129 f.) should be drawn up with reference to his grant. Something approaching this is also to be found in the writ for Christ Church (no. 26), where King Cnut states that he gave Archbishop Lyfing permission to draw up a new *freols*, or ' charter of freedom ', for Christ Church ; this *freols* may possibly be represented by a Christ Church diploma in the name of Cnut (K. 727, see p. 169), which though it is not authentic as it stands, may incorporate authentic material. In his writ for Archbishop Ealdred fixing the status of the minster of St. John at Beverley (no. 7), King Edward announces that the archbishop has his consent and full permission to draw up a *privilegium* for the lands belonging to the minster. In his writ for Bishop Giso of Wells (no. 68) relating to his grant of Wedmore to the bishop, the king announces that he has given to Bishop Giso the land at Wedmore and all things lawfully belonging thereto with sake and with soke as fully and completely as he himself possessed it, and he declares that it is his will that the bishop draw up a *privilegium* concerning this ' with his full permission '. In neither of these cases has the *privilegium* been preserved. But there still exist both the writ (no. 55) in which King Edward commands ' the bishop ' to draw

[1] There seems no reason for dissenting from Bresslau's statements (*Archiv f. Urk.* vi (1918), 45, n. 2, 54, n. 4) that royal diplomas of the Anglo-Saxon period did not have seals affixed, and that the few documents brought forward by W. H. Stevenson (*Eng. Hist. Rev.* xxvii (1912), 8) cannot prove the contrary against the mass of unsealed diplomas that we possess. On the seal now fastened to the diploma of the Confessor for St. Denis, but probably originally affixed in the usual way to the St. Denis writ (no. 55), there are indications of former sealing (see p. 470). See further for the differences between the writ and the diploma, V. H. Galbraith, *An Introduction to the Use of the Public Records* (Oxford, 1934), 15 ff. ; ' Monastic Foundation Charters of the Eleventh and Twelfth Centuries ', *Cambridge Historical Journal*, iv, no.3 (1934), 205–22 ; and *The Literacy of the Medieval English Kings* (British Academy, 1935), 18 ff.

[2] See F. M. Stenton, *Transcripts of Charters relating to Gilbertine Houses* (Lincoln Record Society, xviii), xvii ; H. D. Hazeltine's General Preface to D. Whitelock's *Anglo-Saxon Wills*, xxix ; V. H. Galbraith, ' Monastic Foundation Charters ', *ut supra*, 206.

up a landbook (*boc*) concerning his grant of land at Taynton to St. Denis, and a diploma in Latin referring to this grant, which, if it is authentic, may have been the *boc* drawn up by 'the bishop' (see p. 39). The diploma,[1] preserved together with the Taynton writ in the Archives Nationales at Paris, is copied on a large sheet of parchment in a hand of c. 1100, which may or may not have been an English hand. It is dated A.D. 1059, and the dates of the witnesses indicate a date of 1058–60. The document gives the impression of a later copy of an authentic diploma—though the preamble is not in the tradition of the English preamble—with a note added at the end which (as Prof. Wormald has kindly pointed out to me) may have been originally an endorsement, associating Baldwine with this grant. Leaving out of account the note (which is discussed below, p. 41), as forming no essential part of the diploma, the diploma itself seems to be unexceptionable. The seal now attached to it must have been attached by someone ignorant of the fact that diplomas of King Edward the Confessor were not sealed, and may indeed have been taken from the Taynton writ, where there are indications of former sealing (see p. 470). In this diploma the king, after a lengthy preamble, declares that he has given the vill of Taynton to St. Denis with everything pertaining thereto, with freedom from all obligations except military service and the construction of bridges and fortifications. There follows an anathema, and this is followed by the recitation of the boundaries of the estate in Anglo-Saxon, the date (1059), a long list of witnesses, and the above-mentioned note associating Baldwine with the grant. The style, formulas and content of the Taynton writ in Old English (no. 55), which is typical of its class, are quite different ; the two do not in any way overlap, except for the statement of the grant of Taynton itself. Leaving out of account the customary differences of form and style between diploma and writ, there is no mention in the writ of the *trinoda* (*trimoda*) *necessitas* (the three-fold burden incumbent on all landowners who were not specially exempted), nor is there any mention in the diploma of sake and soke. It is rightly observed by Goebel [2] that diplomas attributed to King Edward which contain

---

[1] Text, Appendix II. Printed : J. Doublet, *Histoire de l'Abbaye de S. Denys* (Paris, 1625), 831 ; *Mon. Angl.* vi. 1077, from a cartulary copy, omitting boundaries ; other printed copies as for the Taynton writ. For other references see W. H. Stevenson, *Eng. Hist. Rev.* vi (1891), 736–42, where it is mentioned but not discussed. For further references to St. Denis charters, see W. Levison, *England and the Continent in the Eighth Century*, 8, n. 1. The diploma in question was considered genuine by Bresslau (*Archiv f. Urk.* vi (1918), 54, n. 4) : ' dessen Echtheit nicht wohl angefochten werden kann '. He does not however consider the question in detail.

[2] *Felony and Misdemeanor*, 362, n. 88.

a clause 'with sake and with soke' (K. 808, 813, 817, 907, 916), all bear marks of suspicion. The evidence suggests that grants of sake and soke were notified by writ to the appropriate authorities, and that they are not matters that find a place in a landbook. Many writs printed here relate to the king's grant of sake and soke (and often other rights) in cases where land has been granted away by himself or by some other person ; indeed several writs announce grants of judicial and financial rights by the Confessor to religious foundations in respect of lands that had long been theirs ; we may compare the grant of King Edward of the hundred (court) of Hormer to the abbey of Abingdon, and a similar grant of the hundred (court) of Godley to Chertsey Abbey (see nos. 5, 41, 42, and discussion in the relevant places). We may also compare two charters (K. 938, 941), which are extant only in early thirteenth-century copies, relating to Earl Leofric's grant of Hampton to Evesham Abbey; from which it would appear that Leofric's own grant of this estate :—

'cum uictu et hominibus et omnibus rebus et consuetudinibus ad eandem pertinentibus, ita sicuti ego ipse unquam melius illam in manu mea tenui et possedi ',

was confirmed by the Confessor himself with a grant of sake and soke *et cum omnibus in quibus constat mandatum regis.*[1]

It would seem that from the time of Cnut [2] at all events, the sealed letter used originally for transmitting simple administrative orders was employed by the king (among other purposes) for notifying to the appropriate authorities the grant of land and of judicial and financial rights, and the mere mandate was thereby raised to a higher power. Those writs which have survived assume (with few exceptions) the function of the diploma, and provide enduring testimony to the grants of land and privileges announced in them. Many writs must owe their preservation to the fact that they served as title-deeds ; and it is worthy of note that in Domesday Book the appeal is not to the landbook or the *privilegium*, but to the *brevis et sigillum* of King Edward.[3] Whether the Anglo-Saxon writ

[1] The second of these charters, K. 941, in particular however is not free from suspicion, claiming as it does for Evesham Abbey freedom from outside interference, and especially from the authority of the bishop, and relating as it does to Hampton, the rights over which (together with those over Benge-worth) were a matter of dispute between Evesham and Worcester (see p. 465). K. 938 and 941 may both be spurious as they stand, but there seems to be at least a possibility that no. 938 had an authentic basis.

[2] See no. 28. The writ of King Æthelred II announcing the grant of sake and soke to the priests of St. Paul's (no. 52) is too doubtfully authentic to be brought into account here.

[3] See Appendix IV. The above statement should not be taken to imply that charters were never produced as evidence ; cf. DB i. 101b.

was merely evidentiary or whether it was a dispositive instrument, has been disputed.[1] But there is some slight evidence—though not in texts of high repute—that it was supposed, at all events by the authors of those texts, that a grant of privileges, like a grant of land, might be made verbally before witnesses. In the writ of King Cnut for St. Paul's (no. 53)—on which see pp. 239 ff.—the names are given of those persons who witnessed the king's grant to the priests of St. Paul's of sake and soke, toll and team,[2] within festival season and without, as fully and completely as ever they had them, within borough and without, in the days of any king. Again, Bishop Lyfing testified in a dubious Charter (K. 941) that Edward the Confessor gave his consent to Earl Leofric's grant of Hampton to Evesham Abbey (K. 938, 941, p. 37, n. 1), which Leofric himself gave to the abbey ' with its produce and its men ', *cum saca et cum socne et cum omnibus in quibus constat mandatum regis* ; and granted to the abbey other liberties ; and the text adds : *Istud totum factum est ad uillam nomine Bedewinde in camera regis*. It is stated that the bishop's own confirmation of the liberties of the abbey, made apparently on the same occasion by means of a sealed declaration handed to the abbot, was witnessed by the witan who were with the king (*testibus sapientibus hominibus qui cum rege fuerunt*), and who, it would seem, also witnessed the grant of privileges by the Confessor. But, as I have said above, the sources from which the evidence comes may not be worthy of credence.

DIPLOMAS DRAWN UP BY INTERESTED ECCLESIASTICS

The question whether the solemn royal diplomas of Anglo-Saxon kings were the products of a royal ' chancery ' (a term not actually employed in Anglo-Saxon sources), or whether on the other hand such charters were generally drawn up by the recipients, has long been debated. The literature of the subject from the time of Hickes's *Dissertatio Epistolaris* (1703) has been described and summarised by R. Drögereit.[3] Among the many scholars who have interested themselves in this question was W. H. Stevenson, who is reported by Drögereit (*loc. cit.* p. 340) to have summed up the matter in a letter of about 1916 :—

---

[1] Maitland, *Domesday Book and Beyond*, 262 ; H. Hall, *Studies in English Official Documents*, 203 ; H. D. Hazeltine's General Preface to D. Whitelock's *Anglo-Saxon Wills* ; Goebel, *Felony and Misdemeanor*, 362. For references to other, and more recent writings on the subject, see T. F. T. Plucknett in *Trans. R. Hist. Soc.* 4th ser. xxxii (1950), 143, n. 1.

[2] This clause may possibly be due to interpolation.

[3] ' Gab es eine angelsächsische Königskanzlei ' ? *Archiv f. Urk.* xiii (1935), 335–436.

' It is quite clear that after the union of the kingdom under Aethelstan the royal chancery (if we may use the term) was in possession of fixed formulas and methods of drawing up charters. This favours the view that the actual scribes of the charters would be royal clerks . . . Already in Aethelstan's time we find charters in the hand of one and the same scribe in different parts of England. In this case the inference seems unavoidable that the writer was a royal clerk '.[1]

The suggestion that in the early tenth century the Anglo-Saxon royal charters were produced by royal clerks was endorsed, elaborated, and extended, by Drögereit, whose researches ended however with the reign of Edgar, and who observed : ' Nach 963 können wir kein individuelles Diktat mit mehreren Urkunden feststellen ' (loc. cit. p. 402). Stevenson too had observed that the charters of King Æthelred II ' do not employ stereotyped proems, and hence they present great variety '.[2] This subject is outside my sphere. But it seems strange that the four writs (nos. 7, 26, 55, 68, see p. 35) which refer to the drawing up of charters by Archbishop Ealdred, Archbishop Lyfing, Bishop Wulfwig, and Bishop Giso, respectively, should never (so far as I can discover) have been brought into account in a discussion which has engaged the attention of so many scholars over so long a period. The simple inference from these four texts is that from the time of Cnut onward the boc, privilegium, or freols (' charter of freedom '), was being produced not by royal clerks, but by interested ecclesiastics. Only in the case of Bishop Wulfwig of Dorchester (see no. 55), is there a possibility of a connection with the royal scriptorium ; a late and spurious text gives the title of cancellarius to one Wulfwius (see p. 60). But this conjunction may be illusory, or the Confessor's precept may have been addressed to Wulfwig simply in his capacity of bishop of the diocese. Again, Bishop Giso of Wells, who in no. 68 is directed to draw up a privilegium with reference to a grant of which he was the beneficiary, had been a ' king's priest ', and was probably employed in the royal scriptorium before his promotion to the bishopric, but there is no evidence, so far as I am aware, that Giso had any connection afterwards with the king's writing office.[3] Neither Archbishop Lyfing in Cnut's reign, nor Archbishop Ealdred in the Confessor's, are mentioned (so far as I can ascertain) in connection with the

[1] For other pronouncements of Stevenson on this subject, see Crawford Charters, passim ; Eng. Hist. Rev. xi (1896), 731 ff. ; and the notes to Asser's Life of King Alfred.

[2] Crawford Charters, 110.

[3] K. 816, containing a statement that the document was scripta by Bishop Giso at the king's command, is not authentic in its present form ; similarly the authenticity of K. 817, said to have been drawn up by Abbot Brihtric of Malmesbury, is more than doubtful. Again, the statement that Giso drew up the Ashwick charter (K. 811, see p. 430) is not to be relied upon.

royal scriptorium. Of the instances that have already been cited of charters drawn up by interested ecclesiastics, one belongs to Cnut's reign, the others to the Confessor's. But already in the reign of Cnut's predecessor Æthelred II, Archbishop Wulfstan was entrusted by the king with the drawing up of a landbook (*boc*), according to a statement which seems to have been overlooked by students of diplomatic. We read in a charter [1] (the top portion of a chirograph) which gives an account of a lawsuit of (probably) A.D. 1023 concerning an estate at Inkberrow in Worcestershire, that some years earlier the land in question had been bought by Bishop Æthelstan of Hereford from a certain Leofric of Blackwell ' with King Æthelred's leave and the cognisance of Archbishop Ælfheah and Archbishop Wulfstan and all the witan who were alive at the time in England '; and following a statement giving the terms, that ' the king commanded Archbishop Wulfstan to draw up a land-book about this ' (*þærto boc settan*), and ' gladly hand over land-book and land to Bishop Æthelstan ' (*Æpelstane bisceope boc 7 land betæcan unnendere heortan*, lit. with willing, *or* glad, heart).[2] That the estate at Inkberrow was land of the bishopric of Worcester is rendered certain by the plain statement at the end of the chiro-graph : ' There are three of these documents ; one is in Worcester at St. Mary's (i.e. Worcester Cathedral) to which the estate belongs '. That it was in his capacity of bishop of Worcester (which was held with the archbishopric of York from 1002 to 1016) that Archbishop Wulfstan was called up to draw up the *boc* relating to Bishop Æthelstan of Hereford's purchase of the estate is indicated by the king's instruction (mentioned above) that Wulfstan should hand over (landbook and) land to Bishop Æthelstan. It is entirely probable that Leofric of Blackwell, the vendor of the five hides at Inkberrow, was one of those tenants who could sell their land. The five hides purchased by Bishop Æthelstan of Hereford in Æthelred's reign may indeed have been identical with the five hides at Inkberrow held T.R.E. by the bishop of Hereford of the bishop of Worcester.[3] Land at Inkberrow had been bequeathed to the bishopric of Worcester towards the close of the eighth century, and leases of land there were made two centuries later by Bishop Oswald of Worcester.[4] The interest of Wulfstan as bishop of Worcester in

---

[1] Robertson no. 83 = K. 898.

[2] The chronological difficulty involved in the conjunction here of Bishop Æthelstan of Hereford, appointed in 1012 (if K. 719, dated 1012, and witnessed by his predecessor is authentic), and Archbishop Ælfheah (captured by the Danes before Michaelmas 1011, and murdered by them the following April) need not affect the credibility of the statement in the charter about Archbishop Wulfstan.

[3] DB i. 173, VCH *Worcs.* i. 289.   [4] Robertson pp. 264, 322.

this purchase of Worcester land by Bishop Æthelstan of Hereford is then clear, and there is no need to suppose that any other reason—such as the part taken by Wulfstan in the composition and writing of the codes of laws, or the literary skill manifested by him in other directions—was responsible for the king's choice. It is interesting to observe that the king's instruction to Wulfstan to hand over the landbook and the land to the purchaser affords support to the statement attributed to Baldwine at the end of the Taynton diploma (p. 539) : *de manu eiusdem regis et scriptum et donum suscepi.* Was King Æthelred following or was he breaking with tradition in thus entrusting the drawing up of the landbook to an interested ecclesiastic ? This is not the place to continue these enquiries, but it is evident that the whole matter of the circumstances in which charters were produced in the Anglo-Saxon period needs still further detailed investigation.[1] It is unfortunate that with few exceptions the royal diplomas of the Anglo-Saxon kings from 975 (when Birch's *Cartularium Saxonicum* ends) have not been printed since Kemble's time, and that the royal diplomas of the whole pre-Conquest period still await a competent editor.

MISTAKEN THEORIES REGARDING THE EVOLUTION OF THE WRIT

The fact that the Confessor himself makes a distinction between the writ and the diploma when in his writs he directs that a landbook or *privilegium* be drawn up makes it all the more difficult to accept the theory of the evolution of the writ form propounded by Sir Percy Winfield.[2] According to this theory the starting-point for the evolution of the writ is to be found in the Anglo-Saxon diploma itself. Such royal diplomas or landbooks were issued as early as the seventh century, and they continued to be issued throughout the Anglo-Saxon period, most frequently in Latin, occasionally in Anglo-Saxon. It is suggested by Winfield that by a gradual course

---

[1] Miss M. P. Parsons has discussed the significance of scribal memoranda found as dorsal notes on certain authentic charters of the eighth and ninth centuries, and from the study of about 40 charters of this period has concluded that with few exceptions they were drawn up by or for the recipients, and not in the royal scriptorium ; see *Mitteil. d. Österreich. Instit. f. Geschichtsf.* xiv Ergänzungsb. (1939), 13–32. Drögereit (*ut supra*) on the other hand has brought forward evidence which makes it probable that in the tenth century, up to the time of Edgar, royal charters were being drawn up by a body of scribes, presumably the king's clerical staff. Were the directions given by Æthelred, Cnut and Edward to archbishops and bishops for the drawing up of diplomas exceptional measures, or were they merely matters of ordinary routine ?

[2] See *The Chief Sources of English Legal History*, 290 ff., and also the article ' Writ ' in the *Encyclopædia Britannica*, 14th ed.

of change the diploma form was transformed into the writ form by the substitution of the writ proem [1] for the proem characteristic of the diploma, and by the discarding of the religious element that pervaded the diploma ; and further, that in this evolution a type of document called by Winfield the ' epistolary charter—the cross-bred between the letter and the charter ', played a part. He asserts that ' there is some indication that in Alfred's time, kings employed what may be called the " epistolary charter " ' ; that ' the differentiation ' of this cross-bred document from the charter ' is beginning to become marked in Cnut's reign ', when we find Cnut's proclamation of 1020 (see p. 17) beginning with a proem which ' at once puts us in mind of the *Rex vicecomiti salutem* of a later age ', and in which, ' though religious feeling permeates it, it does not predominate, as in the old charters '. Again, in the article ' Writ ' in the *Encyclopædia Britannica*, Winfield asserts that ' these documents cross-bred between charter and writ show progress, but fall far short of the pure (post-Conquest) writ, which was concise, secular, practical, and implicit with power ', and that the distinction between writ and charter ' is known to have existed as early as 1071 '. This theory of the evolution of the Anglo-Saxon writ cannot be accepted. The evidence brought forward by Winfield is not sufficient to establish the existence in the Anglo-Saxon period of a document ' cross-bred between the letter and the charter ' to which he gives the name of ' epistolary charter '. Winfield finds the business-like proem of the writ in a grant of Cnut (K. 753), but this document does not prove his point, for it is a declaration (see p. 382) which has been provided (perhaps by the monks of Winchester, in whose cartulary it appears) with a dating clause and a list of witnesses, and with a Latin version. The declaration, whether authentic or not, has not in any case the characteristic writ proem or protocol as it is defined above (p. 1), for it lacks the greeting clause. Further, the text which Winfield cites as containing ' a blend of the writ proem and the religious proem ' (K. 785) is of doubtful authenticity, and it is not at all unlikely that it was produced after the Norman Conquest :

It is a charter of St. Benet, Holme, which begins : ' Eadwardus rex Anglorum omnibus Deum timentibus et fidelibus suis totius Angliae salutem ' ; sets out the religious considerations which have induced the king to make the grant, and enumerates the vills, churches, lands and privileges, with which the grant is concerned. There is no dating clause, but there is a list of witnesses. The mention in the text of a seal (' sigilli mei protestationem ') is one suspicious feature ; another is the description of Bishop Æthelmær as *Theth-*

---

[1] Where Winfield employs the term ' proem' for the ' protocol ', I have retained his term.

fordensis episcopus, although the see of Elmham was not moved to Thetford until 1078.[1]

Further, it would appear, from the reference that he gives, that Winfield derives the conception of the 'epistolary charter' from W. H. Stevenson, whose use of the term in the context in which it occurs is perhaps unfortunate, since it has been misunderstood. Stevenson speaks in one place [2] of the 'writ-charter' with special reference to Cnut's Proclamation of 1020. This he describes as the 'direct lineal ancestor of the Anglo-Norman charter of liberties, and, in consequence, of Magna Charta', since (as he explains) these documents 'are developments of the Anglo-Norman writ-charter, and that in its turn is . . . merely the Anglo-Saxon writ translated into Latin'. But the type of document to which the term 'writ-charter' is properly applied is a development of the Anglo-Norman period,[3] although it was applied by Stevenson to Cnut's Proclamation of 1020 in order to show the continuity of development from the Anglo-Saxon to the post-Conquest period at a time when the fact of this continuity was denied. But in another passage in the same article Stevenson speaks of 'the writ *or* (the italics are mine) epistolary charter'. He says that the writ gradually 'ousted entirely the formal charter or diploma, of which we can still trace some use in Norman times', and that 'the writ or epistolary charter had the great merit of adaptability to all purposes, and thus its great progeny in the later middle ages is intelligible'. It seems clear to me that to Stevenson 'writ' and 'epistolary charter' meant one and the same thing, namely, the sealed letter employed by Anglo-Saxon kings for administrative business, with which this book is concerned, and that the 'writ-charter', the term which he applies to the Proclamation of King Cnut, meant something

---

[1] For other suspicious features, see *The Eleventh and Twelfth Century Sections of Cotton MS. Galba E ii* (the Register of the Abbey of St. Benet of Holme), ed. J. R. West (Publications of the Norfolk Record Society, nos. 2, 3, 1932), i. 5, ii. 199.

[2] *Eng. Hist. Rev.* xxvii (1912), 4.

[3] The evolution of the post-Conquest writ-charter can be plainly seen in the long series of post-Conquest documents of the abbey of Bury St. Edmunds. The Anglo-Saxon writ style persists after the Conquest in writs written at first in the vernacular, then in Latin, which preserve the address to individuals and some of the formulas of the Anglo-Saxon writ; these documents are undated, and without witnesses. But there develops in the Anglo-Norman period a type of document which differs both from the Anglo-Saxon writ and from the Anglo-Saxon royal diploma, a form which had not yet, in the early Anglo-Norman period, become entirely obsolete. The writ-charter is addressed generally, not to individuals, and it concludes with the names of witnesses. See further, D. C. Douglas, *Feudal Documents from the Abbey of Bury St. Edmunds* (British Academy, 1932), xxix ff.

E

different. Everything encourages the belief that the Anglo-Saxon royal diploma and the writ developed independently ; there is no evidence that the one formed the starting-point for the other.[1] And further, the ' distinction between writ and charter ' which Winfield says, ' is known to have existed as early as 1071 ',[2] is in reality far more ancient, and must in fact go back to the earliest period of the use of landbook and writ in Anglo-Saxon England. As for the statements made by Giry [3] concerning the history of the writ form in England—statements which appear again in the *Encyclopædia Britannica* [4]—in the opinion of Bresslau, they must simply be reversed.[5] They were controverted many years ago by W. H. Stevenson.[6] Giry had said that the documents of the Anglo-Saxon kings did not serve as models for those of the ensuing epoch, and that

*les actes de Guillaume Ier, roi d' Angleterre, depuis 1066, ne diffèrent de ceux du duc de Normandie antérieurs à cette date que par l'addition du titre de *rex Anglorum* dans la suscription '.

But it was shown by Stevenson, with direct reference to Giry's misconceptions, that the writs of the Norman kings of England composed in the vernacular follow the lines of the vernacular writs of Cnut and the Confessor, and that it was only necessary to translate these Anglo-Saxon writs into Latin to obtain the brief charter or writ that eventually ousted the diploma from the chancery of the twelfth century. Stevenson remarked that if the Latin portion of the writ of Henry II for Christ Church, Canterbury, stood alone, we

[1] It would be difficult to substantiate the statement in the *Encyclopædia Britannica* s. ' Writ ', that the ' diffuse royal charters ' of the Anglo-Saxon period were used to ' express the king's commands or wishes '. The Anglo-Saxon royal diplomas are concerned with grants of land, hence the term *landboc* ; they are not otherwise used to express the king's commands or wishes. Further, it is impossible to accept Winfield's theory that the ' common form commencement of the writ ' is merely the witnessing clause of the royal diploma transferred to the head of the document.

[2] The dating here seems to be based on an Abingdon writ of William I of c. 1071 (Davis, *Regesta*, no. 49), announcing the grant to the abbot of Abingdon of all the ' customs ' over his lands that he can prove by writ or charter (*per breve vel cartam*) to have been possessed by the church of St. Mary and his predecessor by the gift of King Edward (see p. 124). For other instances of terminological distinctions made by chancery clerks between the writ (*breve*) and the charter (*carta*), see Douglas, *Feudal Documents*, xxviii f. ; see also 130 below.

[3] *Manuel de Diplomatique*, 795.

[4] Article ' Diplomatic ', by Sir E. Maunde Thompson, 11th and 14th ed.

[5] *Archiv f. Urk.* vi (1918), 44.

[6] *Eng. Hist. Rev.* xi (1896), 735. Stevenson pointed out (*ibid.* xii (1897), 108, n. 3) that Giry's views were largely derived from the *Nouveau Traité de Diplomatique*, Toustain and Tassin, (Paris, 1750–65).

should say that it was drawn up in the characteristic language of the twelfth-century chancery, but that we can see by means of the English version that it is merely a Latin translation of an Old English writ that was in use at least as early as the time of Cnut.[1]

PERSONS ADDRESSED IN ANGLO-SAXON WRITS

In a highly important study of the Anglo-Saxon writ, it was stated by W. H. Stevenson that the Anglo-Saxon writ ' was in its origin a letter from the king to a shire-moot '.[2] The inclusion in this generalisation from a few writs of the time of Æthelred II and Edward the Confessor (mentioned by Stevenson), of the words ' in its origin ' is unfortunate, for the origin of the use of the Anglo-Saxon sealed letter used for administrative business is lost in obscurity. It is moreover to be noted that in King Alfred's allusion to the lord's *ærendgewrit and insegel* (which had escaped Stevenson's notice), we are free to suppose that the writ was addressed to an individual (see Introduction, p. 10). Besides the writs addressed to shire courts of the close of the tenth and the eleventh centuries which have been preserved because they serve the purpose of title-deeds, a much larger number must have been destroyed because they had no enduring value, at a time when it had become normal for the king to send a letter to one of his thegns (see p. 14). And further the writs of Archbishop Wulfstan and of Bishop Æthelric (nos. 27, 63) clearly indicate that this form of document was in more general use than Stevenson had realised. But in point of fact the majority of royal writs extant are addressed to the officers and suitors of shire courts [3] and of other courts, at a meeting of which it was

---

[1] For these Christ Church writs, see no. 28 below, and the relevant discussion and notes ; see also 173–5.

[2] *Eng. Hist. Rev.* xxvii (1912), 5. The term ' writ ' was also used by Stevenson (*Eng. Hist. Rev.* xi (1896), 732, note) of the spurious Wargrave charter, Cotton Charter x. 17, which does not come within his definition, or mine ; on this document, a Winchester fabrication which has been given the outward appearance of a writ, see F. E. Harmer, *Bulletin of the John Rylands Library*, xxii (1938), 349–51.

[3] On the shire court, its functions, officers and suitors, see Liebermann, *Gesetze*, ii. 479 ff. s.v. ' Grafschaft ', ' Grafschaftsgericht ' ; F. Zinkeisen, ' The Anglo-Saxon Courts of Law ', *Political Science Quarterly*, x (1895), 132 ff. ; Stenton, *Anglo-Saxon England*, 539 ff. For references on the early Curia Regis Rolls to the county court, the hundred court, and other local courts, see C. T. Flower, *Introduction to the Curia Regis Rolls*, A.D. 1199–1230 (Selden Society, 1944), 61–91. For records of the county court of the thirteenth and fourteenth centuries, which sometimes throw light on conditions in the Anglo-Saxon period, see W. A. Morris, *The Early English County Court* (University of California Press, 1926). See also H. M. Cam, ' From Witness of the Shire to Full Parliament ', *Trans. R. Hist. Soc.* 4th ser. xxvi. 13–35.

intended that the king's writ should be read. A command that an estate be transferred to the king as soon as the writ is read appears in no. 80, which is spurious as it stands, but in which this direction may well have been derived from an authentic writ.[1]

Disputes concerning the ownership of land were normally settled in the shire court, to which writs announcing changes in the ownership of land would therefore be addressed. Similarly it was necessary that the king's financial agent, the sheriff, should be informed of grants to the king's subjects of judicial and financial rights, whereby the king's revenue would be diminished. According to an ordinance of King Edgar (III Edgar 5, 1, 2), in which we find the earliest specific mention of borough court or shire court, the borough court was to meet thrice, and the shire court twice, a year, and the bishop of the shire and the ealdorman were to be present, and were to expound (or direct the observance of) both ecclesiastical and secular law (' habbe man þriwa on geare burhgemot 7 tuwa scirgemot 7 þær beo on ðære scire biscop 7 se ealdorman 7 þær ægðer tæcan ge Godes riht ge woruldriht '.)[2] This ordinance was re-enacted by Cnut (II Cnut 18), on penalty of a fine, with the additional direction that if necessity arose these courts might meet more frequently.[3] Some information is available in charters regarding actual meetings of shire courts. A Kentish shire court held at Erith, Kent, c. 964–88, at which Archbishop Dunstan formally established proof of ownership of an estate by an oath taken with supporters, was attended by

' Ælfstan, bishop of London, and all the community (i.e. the priests of St. Paul's Cathedral), and that at Christ Church (Canterbury), and Ælfstan, bishop of Rochester, and the sheriff, Wulfsige the priest, and Brihtwold of Mereworth, and all the men of East Kent and West Kent '.[4]

At a meeting of a Herefordshire court in the reign of Cnut,

' there were present Bishop Æthelstan and Hrani (Ranig) the ealdorman, and Edwin, the ealdorman's son, and Leofwine, Wulfsige's son, and Thurkil the White, and Tofi the Proud came there on the king's business ; and Bryning the sheriff was present, and Æthelweard of Frome and Leofwine of Frome and Godric of Stoke and all the thegns of Herefordshire '.[5]

Another such meeting (whether an ordinary meeting or an extra-

---

[1] For post-Conquest instances, see pp. 504 f. We may compare the : ' Quarum recitatio literarum in Berkescire ' etc. of *Chron. Mon. de Abingdon*, R.S. ii. 1.

[2] Liebermann, *Gesetze*, i. 202, Robertson, *Laws*, 26, Stubbs, *Select Charters*, 9th ed. 1913, 83. It was not of course the rule for the shire to have an earl or a bishop to itself as it might have its own sheriff (though the sheriff sometimes held office in more than one shire), but each shire was under an earl and a bishop. [3] Liebermann i. 320, Robertson, 182.

[4] Robertson, *Anglo-Saxon Charters*, no. 41, B. 1097.

[5] *Ibid.* no. 78 = K. 755. For other instances cf. *ibid.* nos. 83, 99, 103, 112, 114 = K. 898, 802, 789, 923, 1337.

ordinary session) is described in a charter of the reign of Æthelred II.[1] The king sent a writ (*gewrit and his insegel*) to the archbishop of Canterbury, directing that he and his thegns in East Kent and West Kent should settle a disputed claim of the bishop of Rochester to land at Snodland in Kent ; the seal attached to the letter would demonstrate to the recipient without possibility of doubt that the letter came from the king himself. Thereupon a meeting of the shire court was held at Canterbury, attended by the archbishop, the sheriff, two abbots, and the thegns in question—' all the leading men '. When the bishop had produced his evidence, the suitors of the court—who were the judges—decided how the differences between the rival claimants should be adjusted, and suggested a compromise ; and this was accepted by the bishop and his opponent. A few years earlier in the same reign, some time between 990 and 992, the king sent his seal (*insegel*) by Abbot Ælfhere to a Berkshire shire court, which dealt with another dispute about land, the proceedings at which, with reference to this particular dispute, are described in some detail.[2] The phraseology of the charter strongly suggests that *insegel* stands here for *gewrit and insegel*, ' sealed letter ' or ' writ '. It is stated that the king

' *greeted* all the witan who were there assembled, namely, Bishop Æthelsige and Bishop Æscwig and Abbot Ælfric and the whole shire, and prayed and commanded them to settle the case . . . as justly as they could ',

and it seems very probable that we have here a summary of the protocol and content of a writ.

The BISHOP or ARCHBISHOP is addressed in royal writs to the shire court, but not (except in nos. 26, 35) in those concerned with his affairs (see nos. 7, 50, 64–71, 107, 115, 117, 119) ; Eadsige, then bishop at St. Martin's, is addressed in two writs (nos. 29, 30) concerning the interests of Archbishop Æthelnoth of Canterbury. An archbishop and a bishop are addressed in nos. 26, 61, 76 (perhaps spurious) ; and an archbishop and two bishops in no. 102. Two bishops are addressed in no. 60 (see pp. 246 ff.). Reference to the Latin version will show that the Alred ' earl ' of no. 49 is a mistake for Aldred ' bishop '. The bishop's name appears in writs addressed to the borough court of London and of Winchester (for references see p. 53), but not in that addressed to the borough court of Thetford (no. 56) nor in the writ addressed to the hundred [court] at Wedmore (no. 72).

In a few writs ABBOTS are included in the address. The prominence accorded to Abbot Æthelnoth of Glastonbury in Wells writs

---

[1] Robertson, *Anglo-Saxon Charters*, no. 69 = K. 929. For text see Appendix IV, no. 2.

[2] *Ibid.* no. 66 = K. 693. For text, see Appendix IV, no. 1.

(nos. 64–8, 71), as also in no. 6, is striking ; but a parallel can be found in the mention of Ælfmær, Ælfstan, and Wulfric, abbots of St. Augustine's, in nos. 26, 29, 30, 35. Abbot Leofstan of Bury is addressed in no. 80, a spurious Westminster writ with an address most probably authentic. Abbot Wulfwold of Chertsey appears in no. 93, a spurious writ ; the authenticity of the address is doubtful. ' Abbots ' appear among those addressed in nos. 4, 36, 37, 45, 101, all addressed generally, and all dubious as they stand ; they come from different houses, and it seems possible that the Confessor may on occasion have included abbots collectively in the address of an authentic writ, but no indubitably authentic instance seems to exist.

The EALDORMAN, or EARL, who ' in the exercise of his functions, both military and administrative . . . was a public official ',[1] is usually addressed in royal writs to the shire court. In the two earliest writ protocols extant, nos. 107, 108 (no. 52 being of too uncertain authenticity to be considered here), both of the reign of Æthelred II, the term *ealdorman* is used, but elsewhere in Anglo-Saxon writs its place is taken by *eorl*. In general *ealdorman* gives way to *eorl* in the first half of the eleventh century ; it is still used occasionally in the Laws of Cnut, but not in his surviving writs. The absence of the earl in the address is sometimes to be explained by the circumstances of the time. In nos. 8, 9, the absence of the earl no doubt indicates that these writs were issued before the appointment of Harold in 1044/5 to the earldom of East Anglia, and the same explanation may be valid for nos. 73, 74 (? address authentic) ; for no. 71 the explanation is no doubt that no successor had been appointed to Harold's former earldom of Wessex ; and for no. 94, that Tostig had been expelled from his earldom (which included Northamptonshire) ; no. 6 may have been issued in Harold's reign (cf. no. 71), or even after the Conquest. No earl is named in Cnut's writs for Christ Church (nos. 26, 29, 30). The use of ' headmen ' (*heafedmen*, cf. BT and Suppt.) in no. 102, in the place of ' earls ', is remarkable.

The SHERIFF [2] does not always appear in the address of royal writs

[1] R. R. Darlington, *History*, N.S. xxii (1937–38), 6. See also Chadwick, *Anglo-Saxon Institutions*, 160 ff. ; Liebermann ii. 359 ff., 388 f. ; Hoops, *Reallexikon der germanischen Altertumskunde*, i (1911–13), 497 ; Stenton, *Anglo-Saxon England*, 408 ff.

[2] On the office of sheriff, in its various functions, judicial, fiscal, and police, and the degree to which the sheriff was the representative of the king and the ealdorman (earl) respectively, see Liebermann ii. 648 ff., s.v. ' sheriff ' ; W. A. Morris, ' The Office of Sheriff in the Anglo-Saxon Period,' *Eng. Hist. Rev.* xxxi (1916), 20–40, and *The Medieval English Sheriff to 1300* (Manchester, 1927), incorporating some of the material in the above article ; Hoops, *Reallexikon*, iv. 151 ; Stenton, *Anglo-Saxon England*, 540 ff.

addressed to the shire courts. Where the sheriff's name is absent,
it is argued by Morris [1] that since the matters which were brought
forward in the shire court ' largely concerned financial administration, it can hardly be supposed that the sheriff was absent when his
name is not specifically mentioned ' in the king's writ, and ' that in
assuming that he was absent, Zinkeisen seems to go further than the
evidence justifies '. The sheriff is addressed by name with the style
of sheriff (or *vicecomes*) in nos. 1, 6, 26 (*scirman*), 48, 59, 61 and 62
(? address authentic), 64, 66, 67 (spurious), 68–9, 73, 74 (? address
authentic), 77, 86, 87, 94. ' My sheriffs ' collectively appear in
nos. 44, 47, both authentic ; also in nos. 34, 45, 102, and as *vicecomites* in nos. 31–2, 36–7, all doubtful or spurious ; ' my sheriff '
in nos. 41–2 (dubious). The *Toli* of six Bury writs, the *Godwine*
of no. 65, and the *Touid* of nos. 70, 71—all named without the title
of sheriff—are styled sheriff in other Anglo-Saxon writs. The
Osweard of nos. 35, 39, is rightly styled *vicecomes* in the Latin
version of no. 35. The term *vicecomes*, however, used in Domesday
Book as the Latin equivalent for sheriff, and used as the equivalent
of ' sheriff ' in Latin versions of Anglo-Saxon writs, was borrowed
from Normandy [2]; it was not current in England before the
Norman Conquest. The *Godric* of no. 5, and the *Æthelwig of
Thetford* of no. 56, who appear without any title, were probably
or certainly sheriffs. The *Æthelric* of nos. 26, 29, 30, is probably
the (king's) reeve [3] of that name, mentioned in another place in
no. 29 (line 4), who was evidently the king's fiscal agent. Liebermann [4] takes him to have been sheriff of Kent, perhaps rightly
(though Æthelwine was *scirman* in 1017–20, see no. 26) ; but it
does not seem certain that the differentiation between the sheriff
and the other reeves of the king which was taking place in the
late tenth and early eleventh centuries was at this time complete.[5]
It is true that, when in Cnut's Proclamation of 1027, § 12,[6] ' all
the sheriffs and reeves throughout my kingdom ' are addressed
(the *vicecomitibus et praepositis* of the Latin version, the only one
extant, standing no doubt for *scirgerefum and gerefum*), the distinction
is clearly made. On the other hand, when in Cnut's writ of 1020,

---

[1] *Eng. Hist. Rev., ut supra*, 28 ; *Med. Eng. Sheriff*, 25.

[2] On the functions of the Norman *vicecomes*, see C. H. Haskins, ' Normandy
under William the Conqueror ', *American Historical Review*, xiv (1908–09),
469 ; *Norman Institutions* (Harvard Historical Studies, xxiv), 1918, 46.

[3] On the king's reeve, see Chadwick, *Anglo-Saxon Institutions*, 228 f. ;
Liebermann ii. 718, s.v. ' Vogt ' ; Hoops, *Reallexikon*, ii. 159 ; Morris, *Eng.
Hist. Rev. loc. cit.* 21 ff., *Med. Eng. Sheriff*, 9 ff.

[4] *Op. cit.* ii. 649, 1 (e) ; see also Morris, *Eng. Hist. Rev., ut supra*, 26.

[5] On this see Morris, *Eng. Hist. Rev., loc. cit.* 25, *Med. Eng. Sheriff*, 15 ff.

[6] For references see p. 17, n. 1.

no. 28, the king's reeves appear in the address, it is not certain that the term ' reeves ' is confined merely to sheriffs, and that it does not also include other royal reeves. The appearance of reeves (and not sheriffs) in a writ of the Confessor, no. 33 (where the address is authentic), is perhaps to be explained on the supposition that in its original form this writ was modelled on a writ of Cnut. Other types of reeve are also addressed. The Æthelweard of no. 107 may have been the ' king's high-reeve '.[1]   In nos. 43, 51, a *portreeve* appears, in nos. 105, 106, two portreeves. The portreeve was the reeve of a market town or trading centre, and therefore the chief town officer ; the portreeves in these writs belong to London.[2]   On the basis of two writs of William I, it was demonstrated by Round [3] that under the Conqueror, the portreeve of London and the sheriff of Middlesex were one, and that the official head of the Londoners could be addressed by either style.   There is no reason to doubt that under the Confessor also the two offices were sometimes combined, and that Ulf the portreeve (of London) of no. 75, was Ulf the sheriff (of Middlesex) of no. 77.   There does not however seem to be any evidence that Wulfgar, portreeve of London at the beginning (no. 51), or Leofstan and Ælfsige, who appear together in nos. 105, 106, as portreeves of London towards the end of the Confessor's reign, ever held the office of sheriff of Middlesex,[4] and evidence is also lacking as to whether Ælfgæt, the sheriff (of Middlesex) addressed in nos. 86, 87, was portreeve of London.

In nos. 75, 84-5, 91, 93, 98, a STALLERE is named, in no. 76 (spurious) two ' stallers ', a term rendered by Stenton,[5] ' placeman ', and explained by him as a term ' which could be applied to anyone with a permanent and recognised position in the king's company '. The earliest datable appearance in English sources of the *stallere* (supposed to be a loan-word from ON *stallari* [6]) is possibly the

[1] On the *heahgerefa*, see Chadwick, 231–2, Liebermann ii. 498–9, s.v. *heahgerefa*.

[2] For other references to portreeves, see Robertson nos. 69, 103, 116 ; A. Ballard, *The Domesday Boroughs* (Oxford, 1904), 110–12 ; Tengvik, 265. For the decree of Edward the Elder that no one should buy or sell except in a *port*, or market town, and that every transaction should be witnessed by the portreeve or by other trustworthy witnesses, see I Edward 1 (Liebermann i. 138, Attenborough, *Laws*, 114).   On the portreeve, see Liebermann ii. 573, 45a.

[3] *Geoffrey de Mandeville*, 353 f.

[4] For two portreeves acting jointly at Exeter, see Earle, p. 256.

[5] *Anglo-Saxon England*, 420, 632.   For a list of stallers, see Kemble, *Saxons in England*, ii. 108, Larson, 151 f.   For stallers in Domesday, see Tengvik, 270–1.

[6] On the *stallari* in Scandinavian sources (from the early eleventh century), see Larson, *King's Household in England*, 147 f. and Hoops, *Reallexikon*, ii. 543–6, s.v. ' Hofämte ' (Larson).

'Esgar the staller' of no. 75, to be dated, if the writ is authentic, between the accession of the Confessor in ? June 1042, and the death of Bishop Ælfweard on 25 July 1044. It must however be observed that stallers are mentioned in writs with their name and style, only in those of Westminster Abbey, and that although there is no reason why the king should not have addressed his stallers—and indeed the Osgod Clapa of no. 77 (see Biographical Notes) may be addressed there in that capacity—we cannot be sure that the introduction of the staller into any one of these texts is not due to a Westminster hand.[1] But if the appearance of Esgar the staller in no. 75 is not authentic, then the earliest authentic mention of a staller seems to be the 'Ælfstan the staller' of an undated Christ Church charter, Cott. Aug. ii. 70,[2] which cannot be earlier than 26 December 1045, the date when Abbot Wulfric of St. Augustine's, one of the witnesses, received as abbot the episcopal benediction (see Biographical Notes).[3]

Kemble observed [4] that 'in some of the writs addressed to the shires, the place properly filled by the scirgerefa is given to noblemen of the king's household'; and he believed 'these persons (namely Eadnoth, Esgar, and Robert) to have been really the sheriffs, but to have been named by their familiar, and in their own view, higher designations, as officers of the court'. This suggestion was adopted by Freeman, Round, and Morris.[5] There is however no clear evidence that any of the three stallers Esgar, Eadnoth, and Robert, whose introduction singly, into the address of nos. 75, 84, 85, at all events, is probably authentic, held the office of sheriff in the Confessor's reign; no one of them is ever described as sheriff in contemporary sources, so far as I am aware. Round, from evidence which I find unconvincing, deduced that Esgar the staller was portreeve of London (and sheriff of Middlesex).[6] But it is to be observed

---

[1] The mention most likely to be authentic (in spite of *holde frend* in the address, which may be due to interpolation) is Eadnoth in no. 85, since he appears only once in surviving writs; nos. 75, 84 may also be authentic. Nos. 91, 98 come under suspicion, if only for evidence that the text has probably been tampered with in the appearance here of *holde freond* (not found in writs of the highest class). The address of no. 93 has certainly been tampered with, if it is not entirely spurious. The address of no. 76 cannot be authentic as it stands.

[2] Robertson no. 101 = K. 773.

[3] A spurious charter of Cnut, Robertson no. 85 = K. 1327, from which Larson, 147, deduced that the staller appears for the first time in English sources in 1032, is unfortunately useless for dating purposes owing to a chronological dislocation in the list of witnesses; see F. E. Harmer, *Bull. of John Rylands Library*, xxii (1938), 353–6.

[4] *Saxons in England*, ii. 165, n. 2; see also *ibid.* 167 f.

[5] For references see Morris, *Med. Eng. Sheriff*, 37, n. 164.

[6] *Geoffrey de Mandeville*, 353. Round refers to a story in the *Foundation of Waltham Abbey*, ed. Stubbs, p. 13, that 'the Conqueror placed Geoffrey de

that in the London writ, no. 75, where Esgar appears as staller, there is a portreeve of London named Ulf (no doubt Ulf, the sheriff (of Middlesex), of no. 77), and there is also at about the same time a portreeve of London named Wulfgar (no. 51) ; whilst at the close of the Confessor's reign, not long before Esgar is represented as entering into negotiations with William concerning the submission of London (see Biographical Notes), there were two portreeves of London named Leofstan and Ælfsige (nos. 105–6). Again, the probability of Freeman's assumption (ii. 345, and n. 3, iv. 755)—which was adopted by Round—that Robert fitz Wimarch, sheriff of Essex after the Conquest, held this office T.R.E., and similarly that Eadnoth the staller was sheriff of Hampshire, on the ground that these two stallers appear in writs between the earl and the thegns of the shire—a position which, according to Freeman, ' generally belongs to the sheriff '—is reduced by the fact that the Richard (without any title) of no. 117, appears in no. 116 as Richard, ' my housecarl '. This fact also diminishes the inevitability of Freeman's conclusions (ii. 345, n. 3), that the Osbern of no. 50 was sheriff of Herefordshire. Some names which appear in the address of writs between the earl and the thegns of the shire may of course be those of hitherto un-recorded sheriffs ; but some may be those of royal officials, or of reeves of royal estates, or of persons of local importance, or of persons addressed because they were interested in the transactions which the writ announces. To one or other of these or similar categories may belong those persons of whom nothing seems otherwise to be known ; e.g. *Cyneweard* in no. 3, *Cyneric* in nos. 57–8.

Royal writs to shire courts also mention the THEGNS OF THE SHIRE. In the eleventh century thegns were persons of high rank, some under the immediate lordship of the king, some under the lordship of other persons. F. M. Stenton observes that, on the eve of the Con-quest, men of this rank ' played an essential part in the maintenance of public order ' ; that they ' administered law in the courts of shire and hundred ', and ' as lords of what we can only call manors ' they ' governed innumerable villages ' ; that they were ' responsible for the military service, as for the other public burdens due by custom from the men of their estates ', and that in addition ' they were

Mandeville in the shoes of Esgar the staller ', and remarks that ' the special interest of the story lies in the official connection of Esgar the staller with London and Middlesex, combined with the fact that Geoffrey occupied the same position '. But it seems to me that in the passage in question the *hereditas* of Esgar, which came into the possession of Geoffrey de Mandeville, need not necessarily have comprised anything more than his lands (some of which belonged to his stallership). Stubbs observed that the statement that Geoffrey de Mandeville received Esgar's estates from the Conqueror is borne out fully by Domesday Book.

themselves required to serve in the army when summoned by the king or their immediate lord '.[1] The thegns of the shire are sometimes mentioned as acting collectively as witnesses to legal transactions ; see Robertson, nos. 87, 94, 106, 107 (= Earle, p. 238, 242, K. 820, 949). They were the principal suitors to the shire court. On the ' burhthegns ' of London, see below.

Other public assemblies as well as shire courts are addressed in writs. Queen Edith in no. 72 addressed the HUNDRED (COURT) [2] at Wedmore.[3] Other writs are addressed to the BOROUGH COURT [4] of London, Winchester and Thetford (nos. 43, 51, 56, 111).

In London writs, nos. 43, 51, the term *burhware* [5] appears in the address [6] ; in no. 56 the *burgenses* of Thetford ; in no. 111 the *burhmen* of Winchester. The equivalent in each case is *citizens*. Some of these in London, of higher rank, are styled *burhþegnas* [7], see nos. 75, 105, 106. When the Confessor addressed writs in favour of Westminster ' to the " burhthegns " in London ', he was, in the words of F. M. Stenton, ' recognising a civic patriciate of birth '.

No. 112, a writ of doubtful authenticity, is addressed to all the king's WITAN (lit. ' wise men ', i.e. counsellors, advisers),[8] ecclesiastical and lay ; and the *witan* appear again in the address of two Ramsey texts (nos. 61, 62) which are not in their present form authentic.

---

[1] F. M. Stenton, *The First Century of English Feudalism* (Oxford, 1932), 115 ; see also Vinogradoff, *English Society in the Eleventh Century* (Oxford, 1908) *passim* ; Liebermann ii. 680 ff. s.v. ' Thegn ' ; Stenton, *Anglo-Saxon England*, 481 ff.

[2] On the police and judicial powers of the hundred court, see Morris, *Medieval English Sheriff*, 20, Liebermann, *Gesetze*, ii. 516 f. s.v. ' Hundred ' ; Vinogradoff, *English Society in the Eleventh Century*, 97 ff. The meeting of the hundred court was held every four weeks : see the piece headed by Liebermann (i. 192) ' Hundredgemot ', and compare II Edward 8. On the controversy concerning the origin of the hundred, see Liebermann ii. 516 f., and H. M. Cam, *Eng. Hist. Rev.* xlvii (1932), 370 f. ; see also p. 125, n. 3, and the references there. [3] See p. 491.

[4] On the *burhgemot* or borough court, which met three times a year (see p. 46, n. 2), see James Tait, *The Medieval English Borough*, 38 f. ; Carl Stephenson, *Borough and Town* (1933), 64–70.

[5] *Burhware* is either the accus. of the collective noun *burhwaru*, or a noun in the plural. The meaning is the same in either case.

[6] On the legal status of the *burhware* of London, see Liebermann ii. 571, s.v. ' London ', 9 ff., Hoops, *Reallexikon*, i. 354 ff. (Ballard). See also on eleventh-century London, F. M. Stenton, *Norman London* (Historical Association Leaflets, nos. 93, 94, London, 1934), and *Anglo-Saxon England*, 531–3.

[7] On these see James Tait, *The Medieval English Borough*, pp. 80, 122, 257, and the references there ; also Stenton, *Norman London*, p. 19.

[8] On the powers and functions of the witan, which have been the subject of controversy, see Chadwick, *Anglo-Saxon Institutions*, ch. ix, Liebermann, *National Assembly in the Anglo-Saxon Period* (Halle, 1913), *Gesetze*, ii. 737 f. s.v. ' witan ' ; see also Stenton, *Anglo-Saxon England*, 542 ff.

But the inclusion of the *witan* in the address of a writ is not necessarily of itself a suspicious feature, for the term *witan* is used in a
charter of the time of King Æthelred II to describe those present at a
Berkshire shire court.[1]   The authenticity of the term HOLDAN (-en),
'loyal, faithful' (rarely, if ever, recorded in the Anglo-Saxon
dictionaries as a noun, 'lieges'), in *ealle mine holde freond* (no. 102),
mine holde freond (nos. 77, 85, 91, 98), *ealle mine (his) holden* (nos.
45, 62), seems much more doubtful.   It appears only in dubious
texts, and moreover these are texts of Coventry, Ramsey and
Westminster, three houses between whose dubious charters and
writs a connection has been traced (p. 256).   It is difficult to avoid
the suspicion that these phrases may represent an attempt to
supply something corresponding to the address to the king's *fideles*
in post-Conquest writs.   A writ of William I for Regenbald is
addressed to *ealle mine holde frynde*; see p. 62, n. 1.

Common form demands in the address the possessive 'my' ('all my
bishops, all my earls' etc.).   There are a few exceptions ('our' in
no. 70, 'the' in nos. 107, 115).   'His' in the address of a vernacular
writ (as in nos. 4, 5, 61, 62) is sufficient to arouse suspicion as to its
authenticity.   In Latin texts, nos. 58, 59, 60, 119, the *suis* is probably to be attributed to a translator rendering *ealle mine ðegnas*.
The clause *ceteris suis fidelibus* appears in nos. 31, 32, both dubious,
but also in the Latin version of no. 47.   The *all his undurlynges*
of no. 49 is no doubt a rendering of *ealle mine ðegnas*, and need
not be regarded with suspicion.

THE RECIPIENTS OF ANGLO-SAXON WRITS

Who were the recipients of the writs of Anglo-Saxon kings?   It
was asserted by H. W. C. Davis [2] that

' from the earliest years of Cnut it was the practice to notify appointments,
gifts, and judicial decisions by means of these official circulars to all the shire
courts and all the magnates affected.'

Davis observes that only a small number of these writs has been
preserved, but, he asserts,

' we may infer, from the salutations which they contain, that each of them
was issued at least in duplicate or triplicate.'

And, he continues,

' it is significant that we possess no less than four different writs relating to
such a simple matter as the appointment of a new bishop of Wells.'

---

[1] Robertson no. 66 = K. 693 : ' se cyning . . . grette *ealle þa witan* þe
þær gesomnode wæron, þæt wæs Æþelsige biscop 7 Æscwig biscop 7 Ælfric
abbud 7 eal sio scir ' (App. IV, no. 1).   [2] *Regesta*, p. xi f.

These statements obviously call for further discussion. The view expressed here by Davis, that writs were ' official circulars ' of which two or three copies at least were issued and dispatched to the persons named in the address from the king's writing office, was opposed by Bresslau,[1] who points out that evidence for this view is lacking, and his correction of Davis's statement seems justified.   Bresslau suggests that the writs, when they referred to a grant of office, of privileges, of land, or other matters of that kind, were handed over to the person for whose benefit they were issued, and that it was for the beneficiary himself to lay the writ—presumably in most cases at a meeting of the shire court or borough court or other public assembly —before the persons to whom the document was addressed.   The fact that the beneficiary himself received and kept the writ is indicated by those passages in Domesday Book where the Confessor's writs are produced as evidence of title (see App. IV).   Even in those cases where we hear of the sending by the king of a writ not now extant to the shire court (see pp. 46 f.), we may suspect that a similar procedure was followed, that is to say, that the process was set in motion by the person for whose benefit the writ was expedited. Further, Bresslau rightly observes, as against Davis, that there is no evidence that more than one copy of any individual writ was issued by the clerks of the royal secretariat ; and that although the four writs of Wells (nos. 64–67) mentioned by Davis are indeed connected by the mention in each of them of Giso, bishop of Wells, their contents are not identical.[2]   All the extant writs which refer to the granting of land or privilege or office by the king have, as Bresslau remarks, come down to us in the archives of those religious houses that benefited from the grants.   The exceptions to this rule are only apparent for, so far as the writs now extant are concerned, even when the beneficiaries were private individuals, their possessions passed subsequently into the possession of a religious house, among whose records the writ recording the grant to the original beneficiary is preserved.   In the first writ printed here King Edward declares that he has granted the foreshore to his housecarl Urk, and in the second that he gives permission to Urk's widow to leave the joint property of herself and her husband to St. Peter's, Abbotsbury. Clearly the monastery would succeed to any grants that had been made to Urk, and these writs were preserved among its records. Similarly the writ announcing that King Edward has granted land at Shepperton to his church-wright Teinfrith (no. 87) is preserved only in a cartulary of Westminster Abbey, and that announcing his grant to the English Cnihtengild (no. 51) is preserved in the cartulary

[1] *Archiv f. Urk.* vi (1918), 50, n. 4.
[2] One, no. 67, is not authentic.

of the religious house which ultimately came into possession of the property of the gild. It would then seem that the beneficiary was the recipient of the writ issued in his favour, and that Davis was mistaken in regarding Anglo-Saxon writs notifying grants of lands and privileges to individuals and to religious houses as ' official circulars '. Everything encourages the belief that these writs of Anglo-Saxon kings were documents of great weight and of considerable cost to the recipient. We must not suppose that these writs, like the judicial writs of a later age, were writs-of-course (*brevia de cursu*).

But in the passage under discussion here, Davis speaks not only of ' appointments ' and ' gifts ' as having been announced by writ to the shire courts and magnates affected, but also of ' judicial decisions '. What had he in mind ? Was he thinking of the judgments pronounced by thegns in the shire courts (where the suitors themselves were the judges) ? Such decisions are twice referred to in writs (nos. 35, 79), but no information as to their tenor is given, and it is assumed that the persons addressed in the writ will be familiar with them. Of writs communicating such decisions to the shire courts there are none extant. But the fact that Davis prefixes his statement with the words ' from the earliest days of Cnut ' rather suggests that he may have had in mind Cnut's two Proclamations, of 1020 and 1027 (see p. 7). These two lengthy documents, which are in epistolary form, and employ the writ protocol, are addressed generally. The earlier begins :—

' Cnut cyning gret his arcebiscopas and his leodbiscopas and þurcyl eorl and ealle his eorlas and ealne his þeodscype, twelfhynde and twyhynde, gehadode and læwede, on Englalande freondlice ', (' King Cnut sends friendly greetings to his archbishops and his diocesan bishops and Earl Thurkil and all his earls and all his subjects in England, nobles and commoners, ecclesiastics and laymen ').

The second of this pair of texts has come down to us only in a Latin version, but the same epistolary form is adopted. These Proclamations in which the king outlines his policy, announces the success of some of his endeavours, instructs his officers to maintain justice and to further the rights of the church, issues injunctions against such offences as the harbouring of thieves, marriage with a professed nun, and breaking the sabbath, may well have been sent round to the shire courts.[1] But the matters with which they are concerned are scarcely ' judicial decisions '. Nor did Davis by ' judicial decisions ' mean simply ' legal codes ', for though he supposes (on

---

[1] On the publication of Great Charters by English kings after the Conquest, see R. Lane Poole, *Studies in Chronology and History*, 308–18.

_b_ and _c_. Obverse and reverse of authentic St. Denis seal of King Edward the Confessor. See No. 55, pp. 103, 470.

_a._ Authentic writ for St. Denis of King Edward the Confessor. See No. 55, p. 470.

rather slight evidence) that 'a copy of every new law was trans-
mitted' to each shire court, he does not suggest that this was done
by writ. Stubbs on the other hand does convey this suggestion, by
an erroneous rendering of a passage in a code of Edgar as: 'let
many writs be written, giving these laws'.[1] What is at fault here
is the rendering of Old English *gewrita*, 'writings' (the exact sense
of 'writings' being determined by the context) as 'writs'. The
document in question, Edgar's Fourth Code, is itself described in the
opening clauses as a *gewrit* (' Her is geswutelod on þisum *gewrite* ').
A better rendering of the whole context would be :—

'Let many copies of this ordinance be made and sent to both the ealdormen',
Ælfhere and Æthelwine, and they shall distribute them in all directions, so
that this measure shall be known both to poor and rich.'[2]

THE CLERKS OF THE ROYAL SECRETARIAT

The Anglo-Saxon royal writs were produced by the clerks of the
royal secretariat. From the beginning the writs of Anglo-Saxon
kings now extant exhibit so strong a similarity both in their inner,
and also, in so far as this can be tested, in their outer characteristics,
that it cannot be doubted that they had a common origin. The
formulas of Anglo-Saxon writs will be discussed a little later. Writs
of the same period, issued on similar occasions, sometimes resemble
one another. The writ, for instance, announcing the appointment
of Walter as bishop of Hereford (no. 50) must, in the Anglo-Saxon
text (now lost) from which the extant Latin version was derived,
have been drawn up in much the same terms as the writ issued about
the same time (no. 64) to announce the appointment of Giso to the
see of Wells. Again, there are marked resemblances between the
writ of 1042–44 issued in favour of the English Cnihtengild of London
(no. 51), and the writ issued about the same time for the priests
of St. Paul's Cathedral (no. 54), which is not however authentic
in its entirety. On the other hand, the family resemblance which
can frequently be traced between writs of the same house, indicates
that the content of a writ would be varied according to the requirements of the beneficiary, or might be suggested by precedents.
For example, the three (unquestionably authentic) writs which
relate to the eight and a half hundreds of St. Edmund's Bury (nos. 9,
18, 24) are all constructed on the same lines. Similarly with the writs
of Wells Cathedral and with the writs of Westminster Abbey that are
authentic. The name of one of the clerks of King Æthelred has
come down to us through a grant made to him in 984 as Ælfwine

[1] *Select Charters*, 9th ed. (1913), 84.
[2] Liebermann i. 214, Robertson, *Laws*, 39. IV Edgar 15, 1.

' my faithful writer '. [1] The name is not uncommon at this time ; there seems to be no evidence either for or against the identification of this Ælfwine with the person of that name who became bishop of Wells in 997, or with any of the other persons of the same name who were appointed to bishoprics a little later.[2] There was, however, a close connection between the royal scriptorium and the king's chapel, and some of those persons described in contemporary records as ' king's priest ' were no doubt occupied in the king's writing office. This would be a legitimate inference from the analogy of Frankish practice and of later English usage ; and moreover, evidence has recently been brought forward by Professor V. H. Galbraith which indicates ' the close association of the activity represented by the word Chancery with the Sanctuary and the Chapel of Anglo-Saxon kings '.[3] And further, an instance of the combination of the two offices of scribe and priest in the time of Cnut is provided by William, afterwards bishop of Roskilde in Denmark, whom Saxo Grammaticus, recording his appointment to this see, describes as follows :—

' Wilhelmus, quo Kanutus Maior et scriba et sacerdote usus fuerat, genere quidem Anglus, sed omnibus virtutis partibus ac numeris abunde instructus idemque pontificalium sacrorum apprime peritus '.[4]

The fact that William was appointed to the see of Roskilde in 1044, prevents us from supposing that this promotion was given him by Cnut (who died in 1035) as a reward for his secretarial services. But some of the ecclesiastics who had served in the royal scriptorium, may have been rewarded by Anglo-Saxon kings by promotion to bishoprics. It was indeed conjectured by Davis that the office of

[1] F. M. Stenton, *Anglo-Saxon England*, 349, with date ' 993 ', which should, however, as Mr. Eric Barker has kindly demonstrated to me from a photostat of the manuscript, be corrected to 984. The grant of land is to ' dilecto fidelique ministro videlicet meo scriptori qui a notis noto Ælfwine nuncupatur vocabulo pro eius amabili humilique obsequio '.

[2] Searle, *Anglo-Saxon Bishops, Kings, and Nobles*, 226. Charters of Cnut of 1024–32 (K. 741, 745 (= Robertson no. 86), 746) are attested by Ælfwine *presbyter* ; see further Larson, 141. It seems reasonable to suppose that Ælfwine was an ecclesiastic.

[3] *Studies in the Public Records* (London, 1948), 36 ff. See also on the relations of chancery and chapel on the Continent, H.-W. Klewitz, ' Cancellaria ', *Deutsches Archiv für Geschichte des Mittelalters* i (1937), 44–79.

[4] *Saxonis Gesta Danorum*, ed. J. Olrik and H. Ræder (Copenhagen, 1931), i. 304. William (an Englishman in spite of his Norman name) may have accompanied Cnut on his journeys, as secretary and chaplain. In a later reign he became a member of the *familia* of Archbishop Adalbert of Bremen (1043–72), who consecrated him to the see of Roskilde *de suis clericis*. William had a successful career in Denmark as bishop. He died in 1074, and was subsequently canonised. For references see Harmer, *Saga-Book*, p. 126.

head of the royal 'chancery' was held successively by Stigand, Leofric, Ulf, Cynesige, and Giso,[1] all of whom became bishops. Of these conjectures Bresslau remarked : ' Zu gutem Teil scheinen sie mir ganz in der Luft zu schweben ',[2] a comment which seems fully justified. When Klewitz (*ut supra*) objects that Bresslau brings no evidence in support of this view, it seems clear that Klewitz has not observed that Davis's conjectures are not supported by evidence.

Although the title of *cancellarius* [3] is assigned in some sources to ecclesiastics of the Confessor's time, to Regenbald, Leofric and Wulfwig, the relevant passages are unsatisfactory as evidence for the use of this term in England before the Conquest, being either too late, or of doubtful authenticity.[4] Bresslau reminds us that Norman influence in this direction cannot be assumed, since it is still doubtful whether the Norman dukes had before 1066 an organised chancery.[5] Further, Davis's statement that the headship of the king's scriptorium was called the chancellorship ' after 1061 ' seems to be based on the appearance of Regenbald as *regis cancellarius* in the spurious Waltham charter dated 1062 (K. 813). The confirmation of a long series of estates in a set form of words, as in this charter, was not the usual practice of English charter writers, and raises of itself the suspicion that this text is spurious ; and although the list of witnesses here is a possible one for the time, the ascription of the title *princeps* to a long list of witnesses of the second or third rank suggests the possibility that a genuine list of witnesses has been ' improved ' in the post-Conquest period, and the style given in the list to Regenbald may have the same origin. Whether Regenbald was ever officially accorded the style of *cancellarius* before the Conquest remains uncertain. In Domesday he is several times called *presbyter*, and once, in an inter-lineation, but in a hand which may be contemporary, *canceler*

---

[1] See *Regesta*, p. xv. Incidentally Davis identifies the Ulf who became bishop of Dorchester in 1050, and fled the country in 1052, with the Wulfwius *cancellarius* of a spurious Westminster charter (K. 779). But it is much more likely that this Wulfwius *cancellarius* (supposing him to have existed) was Ulf's successor Wulfwig, who became bishop of Dorchester in 1053 ; see p. 60.

[2] *Archiv f. Urk.* vi (1918), 52, n. 9.

[3] On the title *cancellarius* elsewhere in the early Middle Ages, and the history of the office, see Erben–Schmitz–Kallenberg, *Urkundenlehre*, i. 41 ff. ; Bresslau, *Urkundenlehre*, i (1912), 184 ff.

[4] See W. H. Stevenson, *Eng. Hist. Rev.* xi (1896), 732, note ; H. Hall, *Studies in English Official Documents*, 163–8 ; R. Lane Poole, *The Exchequer in the Twelfth Century* (Oxford, 1912), 25, n. 2 ; and on two frequently cited charters, nevertheless spurious or inconclusive, Robertson no. 118 (Cotton Charter x. 17) and the Portland Writ printed here (no. 112), see F. E. Harmer, *Bulletin of the John Rylands Library*, xxii (1938), 349–53.

[5] *Archiv f. Urk.* vi. 52 ; C. H. Haskins, *American Historical Review*, xiv, 471 f., *Norman Institutions*, 52.

F

(DB i. 180b). He attests as *presbyter* charters dating from 1050 to 1054 (K. 791 (considered genuine by W. H. Stevenson, in spite of Kemble's asterisk), 792, 796, 800) ; but the charters in which he is styled *cancellarius* are spurious (K. 809, on which see p. 473), 824, 825 (on these see pp. 289 f.), and also K. 813 (mentioned above). The Portland writ (no. 112) in which he appears as *cancheler* among other witnesses, whose names conclude the document, and may therefore have been a later addition in the cartulary, is itself of doubtful authenticity. Further, Bresslau's statement (*ut supra*) that ' when Edward confers on Regenbald ' in a writ issued in his favour (no. 44) the privileges which his predecessors have had in the days of Cnut, this is a new proof that the Danish Conqueror also had a ' kanzleimässige Organisation ' at his court, rests on a mistaken rendering of the word *forgengan*. The natural interpretation of *forgengan* in this writ is not ' predecessors in office ', but predecessors in the possession of the rights over lands and men, the grant of which is announced in the Confessor's writ for Regenbald, in which (it is to be noted) he is described by King Edward as ' my priest '. But whether Regenbald held the title of *cancellarius* in the Confessor's time, or whether it was ascribed to him only after he had entered the service of William I, his services to the Confessor were sufficiently important for him to be granted a status equivalent to that of a diocesan bishop (see pp. 211 f.). The first person however who can be proved to have held the office of chancellor in England is Herfast, appointed in or before 1068 by the Conqueror.[1] The title of *regis cancellarius* is given by Florence of Worcester (s.a. 1046) to Leofric, a royal chaplain who had been promoted to the see of Crediton in that year ; but this evidence is not contemporary. On the other hand, the *Wulfwius regie dignitatis cancellarius* who appears among the witnesses of a spurious Westminster charter (K. 779, with date 1045), which must have been compiled at a later date than the Confessor's reign, was dismissed (without discussion) by W. H. Stevenson as ' an invention of the Westminster school of forgers ',[2] a condemnation which seems to me too sweeping. Though the title of *cancellarius* is not given to Wulfwig elsewhere, and the evidence of K. 779 is in any case not contemporary, the Taynton writ for St. Denis (no. 55) directs ' the bishop ' to draw up a *boc* (charter) with regard to this grant ; the bishop of the diocese named in the address was Wulfwig of Dorchester, and it may be that he is the *Wulfwius* of the spurious Westminster charter, and that he served at one period or another in the king's scriptorium. Whether in that case he was directed by King Edward to draw up the Taynton

---

[1] Stenton, *Anglo-Saxon England*, 634.
[2] *Eng. Hist. Rev.* xi. 732, note.

diploma because of his secretarial experience, or whether he comes into the category of the ' interested ecclesiastic ' (see p. 39) remains uncertain.

Of any organisation of the king's writing office from the time of Edgar to the Norman Conquest nothing has been recorded. There is however evidence in Anglo-Saxon writs not only of the use of the same formulas at the same period in writs for different people and different institutions (see p. 57), but also of continuity in the use of formulas from one reign to another. A writ of Cnut relating to assessment for taxation (no. 29) for Christ Church, Canterbury, is drawn up in terms similar to those of a writ of the Confessor for Bishop Giso of Wells (no. 66), and the same term *werige*, employed in both of these, is already being employed at an earlier date in a writ of Æthelred II (no. 107), supposing this latter writ to be authentic. Similarly, a close resemblance can be traced between a writ of Cnut for Christ Church, Canterbury (no. 28), and a writ of the Confessor for St. Augustine's (no. 38). It has been pointed out above (p. 11) that the protocol of writs of the time of Æthelred II can be traced back (substantially) to the time of King Alfred.

CONVENTIONS AND FORMULAS OF ANGLO-SAXON ROYAL WRITS

Anglo-Saxon royal writs, which are highly developed documents, are linked together by similar conventions and similar formulas. Many, even in late copies, begin with the sign of the Cross, but it is uncertain whether the omission of this sign can safely be used to distinguish original writs from those which are merely copies, when the text is written in what appears to be a contemporary hand. It is unlikely that the copyist (or the forger) would have omitted the sign if he had considered it to be the criterion of an authentic writ. The sign of the Cross appears generally in Anglo-Saxon charters, royal and private. Many charters have a verbal invocation of the name of Christ which in writs is never found.[1] In the protocol, the verb in the third person *grett*, frequently spelt *gret*, is used with only two exceptions in writs in the vernacular ; in nos. 53, 113, the verb is in the first person : *Ic Cnut . . . grete, Ic Eadwine . . . grete*, but one cannot positively say that this usage is non-authentic since the verb *grete* in the first person appears in a Preface

---

[1] On the origin and development of the *Invocatio*, whether verbal or not, see Giry, 531-3, R. Lane Poole, *The Papal Chancery*, 41-2. Erben etc., *Urkundenlehre*, i. 140-43. In papal bulls the *Invocatio* is seldom expressed in words ; if it appears at all, it takes the form of a chrismon or of the sign of the Cross. Merovingian charters usually employ a chrismon (i.e. the Greek form of R, within a X), or a cross.

of Ælfric (see p. 23). With the verb *gret*, in the third person, the change later in the protocol to the first person with ' my ' (' *my* bishops, *my* earls, *my* thegns ') is not an irregularity but the accepted form ; the same change appears in declarations, e.g. ' Æþelwold ealdarman *cyþ his* leofan cynehlaforde . . . hu *ic* wille ymbe þa landare þe *ic* æt *mine* hlaforde geearnode ' (lit. ' Ealdorman Æthelwold *informs his* dear royal lord . . . how *I* wish about the land which *I* acquired from *my* lord ') ; for other examples see p. 15 above. The adverb usually employed is *freondlice*, ' in a friendly manner or spirit '. In two writs (nos. 27, 108) we find instead : *eadmodlice*, ' humbly '. Some Westminster writs and a Ramsey writ (nos. 62, 81–3, 88–9, 90, 97 (F), 101) employ in addition the adverb *wel*, ' well ' ; but *wel* is also used alone in the greeting in some post-Conquest writs,[1] and it may be of post-Conquest origin in some of the writs enumerated. The formula : ' with God's greeting and his own ', which appeared in the lost writ of Harold Harefoot does not appear in extant writs, though it must have been current [2] ; nor does the greeting, 'with God's bliss ', appear there, which is to be found in a will in epistolary form, which may have been tampered with by later copyists.[3] It seems impossible to arrive at an entirely satisfactory Modern English rendering of the protocol of Anglo-Saxon writs. *Freondlice* in this context is variously rendered by scholars : ' amicably ', ' in friendship ', ' in friendly wise ' etc. But the real difficulty in Modern English is of course the change of construction in the protocol from the first person to the third. I have rendered the formula : ' *Cnut cyng gret . . . freondlice . . . mine eorlas,*' lit. ' King Cnut greets in friendly

[1] Compare, for instance, a writ of William I for Regenbald, calendared Davis, *Regesta*, no. 19 : ' Willelm kyng gret wel ealle mine holde frynde ' (' King William greets well all my loyal friends '). With the *eadmodlice* of Queen Ælfthryth in no. 108, compare the *Ælfgyfu regina humillima* of a small group of (western) charters ; see A. Campbell, *Encomium Emmae Reginae* (1949), 59–60. See also p. 23 above.

[2] For reference, see p. 71, n. 3. For another instance, but without the ' and his own ', see the Will of Leofgifu (Whitelock no. 29) : ' Leofgifu greets her lady with God's greeting '. For post-Conquest instances, see the writs in English of Abbot Gilbert Crispin of Westminster (who died in 1114), addressed in similar terms to the sheriffs of Essex and Surrey with regard to offenders who had taken sanctuary at the Confessor's shrine at Westminster Abbey (J. Armitage Robinson, *Gilbert Crispin, Abbot of Westminster* (1911), 37 ; *Mon. Angl.* i. 310) : ' G. Abbod and alle tha brodera on Westmynstr' gretith N. schirerefan on Estsex' Godes gretyng' and owr ' (' Abbot G. and all the brethren at Westminster greet N. the sheriff of Essex with God's greeting and ours '). It was also employed in a form which became stereotyped in a protocol derived from Anglo-Saxon writs, in grants of the kings of Norway ; see p. 4.

[3] Whitelock no. 23.

fashion my earls ', as ' Cnut sends friendly greetings to my earls ', because this breaks the shock to modern ears of the change from ' Cnut greets ' to ' my earls '. Others may prefer to insert an initial pronoun ' I ', and to change the person to the first : ' I Cnut greet ', a device frequently adopted by post-Conquest translators of Old English writs (' Ego . . . saluto '). With few exceptions (nos. 3, 32 (possibly spurious), 114 (spurious)) there is a notification in the form *ic cyðe eow* (or *ðe* or *inc*), from *cyðan*, ' to make known to, to inform '.

A constantly recurring formula in the terms of grant in writs is : *swa full 7 swa forð swa*, lit. ' as fully and to the same extent as '. Since a freer rendering : ' with as full rights as ', ' with all the rights with which ', raises difficulties in some contexts, I have adopted the rendering : ' as fully and as completely as '. The formula is frequently enlarged by the addition of *fyrmest* (occasionally, *best*), adv. ' to the fullest extent ', ' to the furthest degree '. *Swa forð swa fyrmest*, means ' as far as ever possible ' ; cf. BT Suppt. s.v. *fyrmest*, adv. III, where *Chron.* 1052 : ' man sealde Godwine his earldom *swa full 7 swa forð swa he fyrmest ahte* ', is rendered ' they gave Godwine his earldom with all the rights that he had ever possessed '. Retaining the rendering ' as fully and as completely ', I have rendered *fyrmest* in this formula as ' ever ', i.e. ' to the highest degree ', and so ' as fully and as completely as ever he possessed it '. In post-Conquest copies of writs in Wells and Westminster and other cartularies, *formest* replaces *fyrmest* ; this in two cases was wrongly supposed by medieval translators to be an adverb of time (cf. NED ' former ', ' foremost ', for earlier *formest*), and so is rendered by the translator of no. 46 as *primitus*, of no. 49 as *prius*. A constantly recurring feature of the technical language of the writs is the use of *þæs þe*, ' according as ', ' in so far as ' (BT s.v. *se*, v. 2(c)), often best translated simply as ' which ', ' that ' ; cf. no. 55, ' ælc þæra þinga *þæs þe* þær inn mid richte to gebyraþ '.

So far as the MAIN ANNOUNCEMENT is concerned, the surviving writs of Æthelred II, Cnut, Harthacnut, Edward the Confessor, Harold II, Ælfthryth and Edith fall into the following groups :—

(1) In a large number of authentic writs and others of dubious authenticity, an announcement appears in the form : ' I inform you that *I have granted*, or *given* (in no. 112, *bequeathed*) ' such and such an estate, privilege, or office, to X, or to a religious house, ' as fully and completely as ' etc. In no. 48 alone the verb, *concedo*, is in the present tense. In nos. 69, 90, the announcement is that X or Y ' has sold ', ' has given ' an estate. This is the largest group of writs.

(2) Here the announcement appears in the form : ' I inform you

that my will is that X shall be "*worthy of*" i.e. shall be entitled to, shall legally possess, such and such an estate, privilege, or office,[1] ' as fully and completely as ' etc. In no. 69 the ' worthy of ' clause follows the main announcement. In two authentic writs (nos. 28, 38), one doubtful one (no. 34), and one only partially authentic (no. 33), the announcement appears in the form : ' I inform you that I have granted him (them) that he (they) be worthy of such and such a thing ' etc. Here also belongs no. 80, in which the king announces that he himself wishes to be ' worthy of ' an estate. The *liberi* of no. 49 is most probably a mis-translation of *wyrðe* in the lost Anglo-Saxon text ; but the Middle English version has ' that they have ' (see group 4 below).

(3) Writs of this group follow more or less closely in individual texts the pattern : ' I inform you that my will is that the land (*or* the sokes) at X *shall belong to* (*licgan in to*) such and such a religious house as fully and completely as ' etc. There can be little doubt that the *pertineat* of no. 60 is a rendering of *licge in to*. Five Westminster writs (nos. 73, 74, 76, 84, 93) also belong to this group ; of these the most likely to be authentic is no. 84, while nos. 74, 76, are probably spurious. Although they conform in the main to this pattern, these Westminster writs are distinguished by greater length and by greater elaboration of detail. Further, the simple ' with sake and soke ' of other writs of this group becomes here a separate grant : while several have the additional clause : ' and I fully consented to that ' ; see further pp. 297 ff., 307. In no. 39 the announcement that the king is aware that he had already granted land to a monastery is followed by : ' It is now my will that it shall belong to (*licgan in to*) the holy monastery exactly as I granted it to them previously '.

(4) The pattern of the writs of this group—' my will is that he *shall have* such and such a thing as fully and completely as ' etc.— appears most clearly in the Latin version of a Ramsey writ (no. 56) : ' uolo et precipio ut abbas Æthelstanus de Ramesia *habeat* mansum suum in Tedfordia ita plene et ita libere sicut habuit in diebus Cnutonis regis patris mei '. It also appears in no. 58, another Latin version of a Ramsey text, and in no. 49, a rendering into later English of a Hereford text. Writs in Old English of this pattern appear elsewhere only among the writs of Westminster Abbey (nos. 75, 77, 85, 91, 92, 98, 102), and of these no one is of unquestionable authenticity as it stands. It is to be observed that in these Westminster writs the normal *ic wille* is expanded by the addition of *ic ann*.

---

[1] For further instances of ' worthy of ' used in this technical sense, see pp. 475 f.

(5) The announcements in writs of this group, which vary in subject matter, are characterised by the appearance in each case of the words ' *my permission* ', ' *my leave* ', ' *my command* '. Two or three types can be distinguished : (i) Here the pattern is represented by no. 1 : ' Ic cyðe eow þæt Urk . . . habbe his strand . . . be minum fullan bebode ' ; compare also no. 5 (not of unquestionable authenticity), no. 15, and also nos. 88–9, which refer to a transaction in the past. (ii) Here the pattern is represented by no. 7 : ' ic cyðe eow þæt hit is min unna 7 min fulle leafe þæt Ealdred þæt he dihte ' etc. (iii) Here the two constructions are combined ; compare nos. 2 and 21. In the Coventry writ (no. 45) the construction is peculiar, and arouses suspicion as to the authenticity of the text : ' ic ann mid fulre unne þæt þa ilcæ gyue þæ Leofric eorl 7 Godgyue habbeð gegiuen Criste . . . swa icc hit festlice getyþie '.

(6) This group comprises four writs, nos. 29, 66, 67, 107, of which no. 67 can be disregarded as spurious, while nos. 29 and 66 afford evidence of continuity in the formulas employed by the clerks of King Cnut and those of the Confessor. In both the pattern runs : ' I inform you that my will is that X shall now discharge the obligations on his land (*werige his land(are)*) at the same rate as he (his predecessor) did ' etc. In both these cases the prohibition is also in the same form. The authenticity of the other writ of this group (no. 107), the Chilcomb writ of King Æthelred II, which has been doubted, receives support from the existence of these two writs on a similar theme.

(7) In nos. 22, 108, the king (queen) announces that he (she) bears witness that a grant has been made. In no. 39 the king declares that he is aware that he has made a previous grant of an estate.

A few writs stand outside these groups. No. 26 is (except for its anathema) wholly narrative ; so also is no. 107, the Chilcomb writ, of group 6. No. 62 also contains a narrative element, but the authenticity of this text, made up of material probably drawn from more than one source, is more than doubtful.

The main announcement is followed frequently but not invariably by additional clauses ; the object of the additional clauses may be to ensure the carrying out of the king's grant, to amplify its provisions, to prohibit its violation. In a number of writs for ecclesiastics and religious houses the king calls upon the persons to whom the writ is addressed to help the beneficiaries to obtain their lawful rights (nos. 23–4, 49, 60, 64–5, 71) ; in nos. 50, 64–5, 69, 70 he orders the restitution of anything that has been alienated from the persons in whose favour the writ is issued ; in no. 60 he appeals to the persons addressed not to allow the community to be deprived of any of the things that are recognised to belong to them. In nos. 7, 55, 68, the king instructs in his writ that a *privilegium* or a *boc* (landbook) be drawn up by a person who is named. Reference to the texts themselves will show that these additional clauses exhibit considerable variety.

The PROHIBITION CLAUSES, usually introduced by *and*, occasionally by *for ðan (ðe)*, forbidding alteration or diminution or other interference with the king's grant, conform to certain well-marked patterns :—

(1) 'Ic nelle geþafian þæt heom ænig man *misbeode*', no. 51, etc. ; 'mid ænigum þinge *misbeode*', nos. 53, 54, 87, etc. ; *unlage beode*, nos. 29, 71, 116 ; *woh beode*, no. 11 ; *unriht beode*, no. 12. Here and in the categories below the references to writs are not necessarily exhaustive ; nor have small variations in spelling or phraseology been noted unless significant.

(2) 'Ic nelle nanum men geþafian þæt him *fram hande teo* ænig þara þinga', nos. 23, 43, etc., and in Latin no. 50 ; 'him *to honde teo*', no. 41 ; *of handa ateo*, no. 47 ; 'him þær *on ateo*', no. 8 ; 'þær nan þing *on ne teo*', no. 7 ; 'aht þær *on teo* buton he and his wicneras', nos. 28, 38, both authentic, and nos. 31, 33, 34, 36, all doubtful or spurious. For a parallel to the content of this latter clause, see no. 111 : 'nan minra wicnera *nane socne habbe*'. For the meaning of *teo* in these passages, see note on pp. 432 f. The clauses above specifically excluding the sheriff in no. 41, and the bishop in no. 8, inevitably excite suspicion for various reasons, as does also the exclusion (employing other phraseology) of the sheriff and the *motgerefa* in no. 5. For a discussion of these clauses see the relevant passages in the Introductions to the writs of the religious houses concerned.

(3) 'Ic nelle geþafian þæt hem ænig man *ætbrede* ænig þara þinga', nos. 9, 10 (spurious).

(4) 'Ic nelle geþafian þæt þær *geutige* ænig þæra þinga', nos. 2, 84, 96, '*geutige* ænig þing', nos. 13, 19, 39.

(5) In a closely linked group of Westminster writs, nos. 75, 77, 85, 91, 98, 102, none of them of indubitable authenticity (see pp. 306 ff.), the verbs *ætbrede* and *geutige* of the two preceding groups are combined.

(6) 'Ic nelle geþafian þæt ænig man ænigne *onsting* hæbbe ofer his land ne ofer his men . . . buton se abbod to þæs mynstres neode' appears in nos. 81–3, 95, 97, Westminster writs of good repute, and also in more dubious Westminster writs. In nos. 73, 74, the *onsting* formula is combined with an injunction that no one 'undo' the king's grant. In the Westminster writs of group 5 above (nos. 75,

77 etc.), and in no. 45 (spurious, Coventry), the *onsting* formula is combined with the *æthrede and geutige* clause (no. 92 being an exception).

(7) ' Ic nelle nanum men geþafian þæt him ænig þæra þinga *of anime* ', no. 4 only.

In some writs the prohibition clause is followed by a STATEMENT OF THE RELIGIOUS MOTIVE for the grant, e.g. ' for the salvation of my soul ', which may also appear elsewhere in the text. Such statements appear in great variety in Anglo-Saxon charters generally ; some were brought together by Kemble.[1] But in authentic Anglo-Saxon writs such statements are actually rare. In nos. 28, 38, ' for the (eternal) salvation of my soul ' is no doubt authentic, as is also the similar phrase (employing a different substantive) in no. 55, and the ' for my soul and for my father's soul and for the souls of all my ancestors ' in no. 68. The ' pro anima Cnutonis regis domini nostri 7 nostra amborum ', of no. 57 may likewise be authentic, but there is no parallel elsewhere for the ' in nomine Sče Trinitatis ' which in this writ precedes the ' dedimus et concessimus ' in this sentence ; since however only one other writ of Harthacnut (no. 56) is extant (in a Latin version) there is not sufficient material from Harthacnut's time for comparison. In the Chertsey writs, nos. 40, 41, the clause ' for the help of my soul ' may not be authentic, for it is evident that these two texts, even if they are founded on one or more authentic writs of the Confessor, have undergone a certain amount of rehandling, and the statement in question may have been an addition of a period later than the Confessor's time. The same is true of similar passages in nos. 74, 93, both spurious Westminster writs, where to the statement ' for my soul and for their souls ' is added the highly suspicious ' for alle quiken and for alle dede to helpe (to alesennesse) '. One's doubts as to the authenticity of this additional clause are increased by the fact that it occurs only in these two writs, which must be rejected as spurious on other grounds. In the spurious Coventry writ, no. 45, ' for the help of their souls ', appears in a highly dubious background, whether or not it is ultimately derived from an authentic writ of King Edward the Confessor for Coventry Minster. But in no. 72 ' for the soul of King Edward and for my soul ', is probably authentic.

In a small number of writs a SANCTION, or a PENAL CLAUSE, appears. The king enjoins that the action he forbids be refrained from ' for love of me ', ' for the love of God and of me ' (nos. 23, 24, 49, 60, 71). In others (nos. 28, 38, both authentic texts, the one of Cnut, the other of the Confessor), the offender is threatened with the loss of the king's friendship—a threat which is no doubt to be

---

[1] *Codex Diplomaticus*, i. xvii f.

interpreted in the positive sense, that the offender will incur the king's enmity.[1] ' I will know that man's name ', says the Confessor in no. 19, ' who shall wish to rob God and St. Edmund and me.' But in a number of texts the offender is threatened with spiritual penalties, in accordance with a widespread usage which can be traced back to much earlier times. Grants of land and privileges were safeguarded, or the enforcement of an order or a judgment secured, by means of an ' anathema ', that is to say, a ' penal ' or ' punitive ' clause, threatening the offender with punishment in the spiritual sphere. Punitive clauses of the kind appearing in Anglo-Saxon writs appear also not only in Anglo-Saxon charters, but in papal documents, in Lombard diplomas, in ecclesiastical and private charters everywhere ; they have a long history behind them.[2] Occasionally, but much more rarely, a benediction appears, promising a blessing on those carrying out the will of the donor or augmenting his grant. We may compare for instance the following passage (where anathema is followed by benediction) from the papal formula-book, the *Liber Diurnus*, from which is ultimately derived the *temerario ausu* of no. 31 (spurious) :

' Si quis autem temerario ausu magna parvaque persona contra hunc nostrum apostolicum [preceptum] agere presumpserit, sciat se anathematis vinculo esse innodatum et a regno Dei alienum et cum omnibus impiis aeterni incendii supplicio condemnandum ; at vero qui observator extiterit precepti, gratiam atque misericordiam vitamque aeternam a misericordissimo domino Deo nostro consequi mereatur '.[3]

A ' sanctio ' proper, similar to the prohibition clause of papal documents, which according to one form forbad under pain of excommunication that anyone should presume to do injury to a monastery taken under the pope's protection or to alienate its goods or possessions,[4] appears in some Anglo-Saxon writs, as also in Anglo-Saxon charters, where punitive clauses of this nature are widely

[1] For illustrative passages in the Laws, see II Edward 5, 1 ; II Æthelstan 20, 7, and 25, 2 ; II Edmund 1, 3 ; IV Edgar 1, 5 ; compare, for instance, Cnut's proclamation of 1020 § 11 : ' under pain of forfeiting my friendship and all that they possess and their own lives '. See also Goebel *op. cit.* 420, n. 289. For Frankish parallels, see Erben–Schmitz–Redlich, *Urkundenlehre*, i. 361–3.

[2] See F. Boye, ' Über die Poenformeln in den Urkunden des früheren Mittelalters,' *Archiv f. Urk.* vi (1918), 77–148 ; H. Voltelini, ' Die Fluch- und Strafklauseln mittelalterlicher Urkunden und ihre antiken Vorläufer,' *Mitteilungen des österreichischen Instituts für Geschichtsforschung*, xi Ergänzungsband (1929), 64–75 ; J. Studtmaun, ' Die Pönformel der mittelalterlichen Urkunden ', *Archiv f. Urk.* xii (1932), 251–374. In these studies the term ' Poenformeln ' covers not only punitive clauses threatening spiritual penalties, but also clauses relating to financial penalties.

[3] Ed. Sickel, 118.

[4] See Poole, *op. cit.* 45 f.

used. Further, for the *nisi satisfecerit, nisi emendaverit,* of papal documents, we find in nos. 6, 26, 104, 105, *buton he hit þe stiðlicor gebete,* lit. ' unless he make amends for it the more stringently ' *or* ' as stringently as possible '. Nos. 62, 109–10 omit *þe stiðlicor.*[1] In an authentic Beverley writ (no. 7) the offender is warned that he will incur the anger of God and of St. John and of all the saints to whom the minster is dedicated. In two spurious texts of St. Augustine's (nos. 36, 37) the offender is threatened with excommunication : ' a Deo omnipotente et omni sancta ecclesia excommunicatus sit '. ' Let him account for it with God ' (' wite he wið God '), says the Confessor in no. 55, an excellent text. But expressions such as these frequently shade off in writs into an anathema ; compare no. 112 (a dubious text) : ' Lo, whosoever shall wish to undo this bequest, may he have to account for it with God on the Day of Judgment ' (' hæbbe he wið God gemæne on domes dæg '), and no. 48 (also dubious), with a Latin equivalent. ' May he be accursed of God who shall alter this ', appears as the conclusion of the writ of St. Paul's Cathedral in the name of Cnut (no. 53), known, since the disappearance of the cartulary, only from Dugdale's printed version, and therefore only doubtfully forming part of the writ itself. Such final clauses as these could of course easily be added by a copyist, in order to provide an additional safeguard for the grant. It is to be observed that the more elaborate of such penal clauses appear only in writs which have come down to us in later copies. But the anathema is so constant a feature of Anglo-Saxon charters both royal and private, that there is at least a possibility that some of those appearing in writs may be authentic, and each case must be considered, so far as that is possible, on its merits. The anathema, accompanied by a benediction, which appears in the Islip writ of Westminster Abbey (no. 104), announcing the Confessor's grant to the abbey of the place where he was born, seems to support, and to receive support from, the anathema in the Wedmore writ of Wells Cathedral (no. 68), announcing the Confessor's grant to the bishop and community of an ancient possession of his house for his own soul, and for his father's soul, and for the souls of all his ancestors who established the episcopal see.[2] If the principle be admitted that a grant made for religious or personal reasons might be protected by the insertion of an anathema into a writ, then the anathema in a Ramsey writ of King Harthacnut

---

[1] In the Anglo-Saxon period the Latin charters no doubt provided the model for such formulas, which appear also in vernacular charters.

[2] With the anathema of this writ (' may God remove him from his sight ' etc.), compare similar expressions in Robertson, 142, 146, Whitelock, 74, 78, 92, 94. A common formula is : ' May God turn away his face from him ! ' See also BT Suppt. s.v. *ansin.*

(no. 57) is probably authentic, if this text rightly records that the grant was made for the souls of King Cnut and of the donor himself and his mother. This principle is widely observed : Giry [1] speaks of :—

' L'usage de menacer de peines spirituelles, à défaut d'autre sanction, ceux qui contreviendraient à une volonté exprimée par un acte, surtout lorsque l'auteur avait agi dans une vue pieuse '.

Can this principle be extended to cover the anathema in the Broughton writ of the Confessor for Ramsey Abbey (no. 59), recording a grant made to the abbot in return for a service done to the king ' in Saxony ' ; or does it seem more probable that in this case the anathema was an addition made by the monks of Ramsey to a genuine writ issued in their favour ? In the writ for Christ Church (no. 26) in which Cnut confirms the liberties of that house, it would seem that it is hoped that the anathema will be effective when other means of protecting its liberties have proved to be ineffective. The authenticity of the anathema seems more than doubtful in the two Ramsey writs (nos. 61, 62), compiled from material drawn from more than one source. Further, the anathema in two Winchester writs (nos. 109, 110) is not indubitably authentic, for there is evidence in this pair of parallel texts of rehandling of the material. Two other dubious texts, nos. 31, 34, also conclude with the same ancient and widely-used anathema consigning the offender to the company of Judas Iscariot ; this appears in Marculf in the form :—

' Si quis vero . . . obvius vel repetitor extiterit, a conventu omnium christianorum vel limitibus ecclesiarum extraneus habeatur, et Iudae, traditoris domini nostri Iesu Christi, perfruatur consortium.' [2]

A very few writs have both anathema and benediction : authentic in no. 6 (a non-royal writ, where the anathema is of a constantly-recurring type, cf. nos. 26, 105) ; possibly authentic in no. 104 ; doubtfully authentic in no. 105 ; probably spurious in no. 45.

The VALEDICTION : *God eow (ealle) gehealde*, which appears in about twenty writs, also reflects ancient usage. The imperial rescripts of ancient Rome conclude with *Bene vale, Bene valeas*, or *Bene valete*, the last of which becomes constant in papal letters in the seventh and eighth centuries.[3] But the Anglo-Saxon : *God eow*

[1] *Manuel de Diplomatique*, 562.

[2] Ed. Zeumer (for full ref. see p. 30, n. 3). *Marculfi Formulae*, p. 76. See also *Liber Diurnus* (ed. Sickel), 113, 127, 129, 135. See also K. Brandi, *Urkunden und Akten* (Berlin, 1932), no. 16, a charter at Rome of cent. vii or viii. For instances elsewhere in Anglo-Saxon texts, see for instance, Whitelock, p. 66, Robertson, pp. 94, 96, K. 260, 632, 715, 972, 1119, 1335.

[3] R. Lane Poole, *Papal Chancery*, 23 f. Since the authenticity of no. 48 is not certain, it is doubtful whether the *valete* is a rendering of a valediction in an Anglo-Saxon version.

(*ealle*) *gehealde*, comes nearer to the valediction of earlier papal usage : *Deus te incolumem custodiat*, which appears for instance in a letter of Pope Boniface to Archbishop Justus which is quoted by Bede, and was in general use at all events from the seventh century onwards.[1] The valediction in a few Westminster writs, nos. 75, 77, 82–3, 91, 106, is followed by *Amen*, but in no one of these texts is the authenticity of the *Amen* unquestionable.[2] Difficult questions are raised by the longer valedictions which conclude some of the Westminster writs, for the texts in which these appear are in no case of indubitable authenticity, and on the other hand little evidence is available for the form of valedictions in the Anglo-Saxon period. The document which has been referred to above as containing in *oratio obliqua* some clauses from a lost writ of King Harold Harefoot,[3] concludes with : ' *Godes bletsung si* mid us eallon a on ecnysse. Amen ' (' God's blessing be with us all to all eternity. Amen '). The document in question is a statement, not a letter, written at Christ Church possibly in King Harold Harefoot's reign, but the content of this aspiration affords some support to the valediction of no. 101 : ' *Godes bletsunga syo* mid ælc þara manna þe seo hold into þam halgan mynstre '. The misspelling *bletsunga* in no. 101 prevents one, however, from supposing that the valediction was written as it stands in the time of King Edward the Confessor,[4] and moreover, there is evidence in a Beverley writ of William I, extant in later copies (which seems to be authentic), that a similar formula was in use in his time : ' *Godes bletsunge beo* mid eallum cristenum mannum ðe filstað to þes halgan weorscipe. Amen.' (' God's blessing be with all Christian men who promote the honour of the saint. Amen.') [5] In writs of William I for St. Edmund's Bury we find : ' God sy eower ealra freond ' (' God be the friend of you all '), and ' God be mid ihu (eow) ', (' God be with you ').[6] Of these the first at any rate may also have been employed in the Confessor's writing office, for *God seo eow alre freond*, appears in

---

[1] *Opera Historica*, ed. Plummer, i. 97. Compare *Mon. Germ. Hist.*, *Epist. Mer. et Kar. Aevi*, i. 57, 58, 60, etc. The valediction often appears in highly elaborated forms, as for instance, in the letter of King Cynewulf of Wessex to Lull (B. 249, see p. 27 above) : ' Omnipotens Deus qui dispersa congregat et congregata custodit, ipse vos sua gratia protegat et vestri laboris fructum in æterna patria nos videre concedat '. Cf. Isaiah (Vulg.), 56, 8 ; C. Plummer, *Devotions from Ancient and Mediæval Sources* (1916), 141.

[2] On *Amen* in papal documents see Poole, *op. cit.* 47. In Frankish documents : ' In Dei nomine feliciter. *Amen*,' is frequent.

[3] Robertson no. 91 ; see p. 542.   [4] See p. 332.

[5] Thorpe, p. 439, Farrer, *Early Yorkshire Charters*, i. 88. Calendared, *Regesta*, no. 31.

[6] Douglas, *Feudal Documents*, charters nos. 3, 5. For another Bury valediction see Robertson no. 119.

no. 25, a Bury writ, which has however been preserved only in later copies.

In writs of the Conqueror for Westminster Abbey [1] the valediction is in the form : ' God eow (e)alle gehealde ', as it is also in a number of Anglo-Saxon writs of good repute (nos. 38, 47, 72, etc.), and the elaborate forms appearing in Westminster writs attributed to the Confessor find no place there. In addition to the normal form : ' God eow (ealle) gehealde ', and the ' Godes bletsunga syo etc.' valediction of no. 101 (which has been discussed above), the following (dubious) valedictions appear in Westminster writs :—

(1) ' God eow gehealde, Sce Petres holde ', nos. 78, 80, 93, and, with the certainly spurious (possibly scribal) insertion of ' and ' (' God eow gehealde 7 Sce Petres holde '), which would exclude those addressed from the category of St. Peter's lieges (holde), nos. 73, 76, 104.

(2) ' God eow gehealde 7 ealle þa ðe beoð (or sind) holde into þære halegan stowe ', nos. 74, 84, 91 (which adds Amen).

(3) ' God eow ealle gehealde 7 gife eow ece gesælþe. Amen ', no. 75.

It is difficult to avoid the suspicion that these enlarged valedictions in the Westminster texts, which do not appear in writs extant in contemporary copies, were the contribution of the monks of Westminster. But it would be difficult to prove it, and all that can be said is that the evidence is insufficient to determine whether the longer valedictions found in Westminster writs, and there alone, were ever employed in royal writs by the clerks of the Confessor's writing office. Similar doubts arise when one considers the passages approximating to the following which appear in a small number of Westminster texts (nos. 77, 85, 98, 102), and nowhere else in Anglo-Saxon writs : ' Ic wille and fæstlice bebeode ' (' be fulre wite ' is added in no. 77) ' þæt þeos mundbyrdnesse beo strang and staþelfæst into ðære halgan stowe a on ece erfe. Amen.' Until further evidence is forthcoming, it would not be safe to assume that these passages had their origin in the Confessor's scriptorium.

A few points remain to be dealt with here. Unlike Frankish charters and papal bulls, Anglo-Saxon writs bear no ' subscription ' of the sender or of any of his officials ; nor were any of the written devices employed which were used by the popes to authenticate their letters. The sole means of authentication employed in their writs by Anglo-Saxon kings was the seal. The Anglo-Saxon writs are not dated : the only exceptions are two spurious Ramsey texts (nos. 61, 62) which give a date of time but not of year, and also the

[1] E. Neufeldt, *Zur Sprache des Urkundenbuches von Westminster*, Diss. Rostock, 1907, nos. 28, 32, 34.

names of the persons supposed to have been present when the documents were made.[1] There can be no doubt that these details too are spurious (see pp. 248–50). On the other hand there seems no reason for doubting the authenticity of the names given as those of persons witnessing transactions referred to in the relevant writ in nos. 26, 62 (ll. 19–21, 34–6), 69, 79 ; on no. 112, see p. 386 ; nos. 2, 3, 78, mention unnamed witnesses. In no other writ however in the name of an Anglo-Saxon king do we find a list of witnesses included in the manner of the alleged writ of Cnut for St. Paul's Cathedral (no. 53) ; but it would probably be carrying scepticism too far to reject this writ on that account, and the authenticity of the list receives support from the fact that the dates of the persons named in the list, so far as they are known, are consistent with one another (see p. 239).

JUDICIAL AND FINANCIAL RIGHTS

Judicial and financial rights, the grant of which to a subject is announced in many royal writs, are denoted by technical terms. Those most frequently granted are *sacu and socn*, often accompanied by *toll and team*, and often by *infangenetheof*. The formula ' *sake and soke, toll, team and infangenetheof* ', is first recorded in the reign of Edward the Confessor.[2] The rights granted away in Anglo-Saxon writs may also include *hamsocn, grithbryce* or *mundbryce, foresteall, fihtwite, fyrdwite, flymenafyrmth*, or any of these ; but these rights are much less frequently mentioned in the writs, and grants of *fihtwite* and *fyrdwite*, in particular, are rare. Other rights, such as *morthsliht, blodwite*, and some others, appear as the subject of grant only in doubtful or spurious texts, and it may not be possible to prove that these were in fact ever the subject of a royal grant before the Conquest. All these terms regarded collectively, with the exception of *toll* (self-explanatory), stand for profits of justice which might be granted away by the king to a subject. Some scholars believe that the grant of ' jurisdiction ', or of these separate profits of justice, carried with it the right to hold a private court, to compel tenants to attend, and to take from it the profits in question.[3] Others maintain that the grantee would merely

---

[1] On the dating of early papal documents, see A. Menzer, ' Die Jahresmerkmale in den Datierungen der Papsturkunden bis zum Ausgang des xi Jhs,' in *Römische Quartalschrift*, xl (1932), 27–99 ; and on the dating of Frankish and German mandates, seldom dated before the second half of the twelfth century, see Bresslau, *Urkundenlehre*, ii (1931), 394.

[2] Stenton, *Anglo-Saxon England*, p. 490.

[3] F. M. Stenton, *Types of Manorial Structure in the Northern Danelaw* (1910), 78–81 ; Introduction, pp. ix–xxviii, to *The Lincolnshire Domesday*, ed. C. W.

become entitled to receive the fines and other profits of justice arising out of the matters that are the subject of the grant, and that the penalties would be imposed in a public court.[1] Without entering into a discussion which is beyond my scope, I have adopted the terminology ' judicial and financial rights '.

The sources of profit granted by the king to subjects in Anglo-Saxon writs are as follows :—

(1) SACU AND SOCN, ' cause and suit ', ' jurisdiction ', ' sake and soke ', the most common and vaguest of these rights. The formula stands probably for the right to hold a private court to deal with offences committed by persons to whom the grant relates, but at all events for the right to receive the profits of justice arising from cases in which the persons to whom the grant relates were involved.

Sacu, ' dispute, cause at law, crime ', is used in writs in the plural as well as the singular. Instances of the plural in writs extant in hands of the middle of the eleventh century or earlier : no. 28, *his saca* (gen. pl.) ; no. 81, *saca* (acc. pl.) ; instances of the singular : nos. 55, 115. In NED s.v. ' sac ', 1, the first word of the formula is given only as representing Old English *saca*, accus, and gen. pl. ; in BT as sing. only.

On the (difficult) question of the original meaning in the formula *sacu and socn* of *socn*, lit. ' seeking ' (cf. *secan*, ' to seek '), see Liebermann, *Gesetze*, ii. 454 ff. s.v. ' Gerichtsbarkeit '. *Socn* in this context is explained by F. M. Stenton [2] as the act of ' seeking ' a lord, or a formal assembly. But when *socn* is joined with *sacu* in the formula *sacu and socn* the two terms in combination stand for ' jurisdiction '.

Socn standing alone has in nos. 5, 9, 10, 18–19, 24, 60–1, 98, 102, 111, the same meaning, ' jurisdiction ', as the formula *sacu and socn*. In the derived sense of ' district over which *socn* (" jurisdiction ", " soke ") is exercised ', it has survived in Modern English place-names ; e.g. the *Soke* of Peterborough, Thorpe-le-*Soken*. The earliest clear instance of *socn* used as a descriptive term for

Foster and T. Longley (Lincoln Record Society, xix, 1924) ; *Anglo-Saxon England*, 485–92. Also Maitland, *Domesday Book and Beyond*, 97 ; J. E. A. Jolliffe, *Constit. Hist. of Med. England* (1937), 70. See also N. D. Hurnard, *Eng. Hist. Rev.* lxiv (1949), 292, n. 1.

[1] Adams, *Essays in Anglo-Saxon Law* (Boston, 1876), 44 ; Julius Goebel, Jr., *Felony and Misdemeanor* (New York, The Commonwealth Fund, 1937), i. 339 ff. For discussion of Professor Goebel's views, see reviews by Professors H. M. Cam and Plucknett respectively, in *Amer. Hist. Rev.* 1938, and *Law Quart. Rev.* 1938.

[2] *Anglo-Saxon England*, 487. We can safely reject the rendering ' the power of *seeking* or levying fines ' in BT s.v. *socn*, VIII, as being derived merely from Hickes's Latin translation of no. 77, which was printed by Kemble without any warning that it had no manuscript authority.

the lands over which ' jurisdiction ' is exercised is, in the opinion of W. H. Stevenson, the charter (dated by him c. 1030) beginning : ' Ðis is seo socn into Scyreburna ', ' This is the soke which belongs to Sherburn ', and continuing with the enumeration of a large number of vills.[1] Socn was no doubt used in this sense in the (hypothetical) vernacular text, reading no doubt on mine socne, from which the : infra meam sacam et socam of no. 119, extant only in Latin, was derived (see further p. 414).

The earliest known use of the formula sacu and socn occurs, according to Sir Frank Stenton,[2] in a charter of 956 (B. 1029), by which King Eadwig granted Southwell in Nottinghamshire to Archbishop Osketel of York ; after which the formula was used again three years later in a charter of 959 (B. 1052) with reference to eight dependent villages attached to Howden in south Yorkshire. A different view is taken by Liebermann ii. 460. Here the first appearance of the formula is assigned to the early eleventh century. In Liebermann's opinion the formula first appears in documents (' Urkunden ') from 1020, namely two writs of Cnut, nos. 28, 53 (authenticity not indubitable), and a charter of Cnut, K. 1327 (not authentic in its present form).[3] Liebermann rejects as ' spurious or wrongly dated ' charters ostensibly of ' c. 958/9 ' in which the formula ' sake and soke ', according to him, appears. His statement that the charters in question are ' falsch oder falsch datiert ' is, however, too loosely phrased,[4] and there seems to be little or no justification for Liebermann's rejection as spurious of the two charters, namely B. 1029 (= B. 1348), and B. 1052, recently cited by Sir Frank Stenton (ut supra) for the first appearance of the formula sacu and socn. In B. 1029 (= B. 1348), extant only in a later form, the date of 958 must be corrected to 956 if it is to agree with the Indiction (14), but the charter seems otherwise to be unexceptionable. Here it is stated that : ' These are the villages (tunes) that belong to Southwell with sake and with soke '. In B. 1052, dated 959, and free from suspicious features, it is stated that eight (named) villages ' belong to Howden with sake and with soke '. The term socn on the other hand, in the sense

---

[1] Eng. Hist. Rev. xxvii (1912), 20. Reprinted W. Farrer, Early Yorkshire Charters, i (1914), 21, Robertson no. 84 (not in Kemble or Birch). All with Modern English rendering and notes.

[2] Anglo-Saxon England, 487 f.

[3] See Bull. of the John Rylands Library, xxii (1938), 353–6.

[4] B. 1013, 1018 (= Robertson 73, 93) are not dated at all, and cannot be dated on internal evidence. On external evidence they may belong to the early eleventh century ; see Robertson ut supra. B. 1058, 1080, both spurious, cannot affect the issue, for the existence of the formula is established (ut supra) by B. 1029, 1052.

of ' jurisdiction ', appears a little later in a statement of 972–92 in which Archbishop Oswald of York declares that his estate at Sherburn had lost half the ' soke ' which had once belonged to it.[1] In writs, the earliest appearance of the formula *sacu and socn* in a text of reasonable authority is in Cnut's writ of 1020 for Christ Church (no. 28).

The formula *sacu and socn* has been spelt in various ways since the Anglo-Saxon period ; a variety of spellings appears indeed in later copies of Anglo-Saxon writs printed here. ' Sac and soc ', ' sac and soke ', are both current (see NED s.v. ' sac ', 1). But from the time of F. W. Maitland the spelling ' sake and soke ' has been widely used, and for the sake of uniformity it has been adopted here.

(2) TOLL AND TEAM. In this formula *toll* stands for the right to take toll on the sale of cattle and other goods within an estate. No contemporary statement is available to determine whether a grant of *toll* also included the right of taking toll on goods in transit during the Anglo-Saxon period. According to a twelfth-century statement, *toll* (*theloneum*) is *libertas vendendi et emendi in terra sua*.[2] *Team* stands for the right to take the profits, and perhaps to hold the procedure,[3] in a case of ' vouching to warranty ', whereby a person accused of the unlawful possession of cattle or other goods could ' vouch his warrantor ', that is, pass on the charge to the person from whom he had acquired the disputed property. Stenton has observed [4] that the connection between *toll* and *team*, is one of sense as well as alliteration, for the best proof of honesty ' was the open testimony of witnesses who had seen the payment of toll when the disputed chattels were acquired '. It was enacted by Cnut [5] that no one might take advantage of the process unless he had trustworthy witnesses to his purchase, and that no purchase of livestock or other property should be made to the value of more than four pence, either in a borough (*burh*) or in the country (*upp on lande*), unless four men were present as trustworthy witnesses. Stenton has pointed out [6] that these passages from Cnut's code ' are particularly interesting, because they prove the existence of

---

[1] Robertson no. 54 = B. 1278. On this and other early passages in which *socn* appears, see Stenton, *ut supra*, 488 f.

[2] In the so-called Leges Edwardi Confessoris § 22, 2 (Liebermann i. 647 ; for comment, see *ibid.* ii. 753, s.v. ' Zollabgabe ', 5).

[3] Goebel *op. cit.* i. 370 denies that a grant of *team* involved the right to hold the warranty procedure. He supposes that only ' the mulcts of such a proceeding ' was conveyed by a grant of *team*. For a criticism of this view, see Hurnard, *ut supra*, 292, n. 1.

[4] *Anglo-Saxon England*, p. 491.

[5] II Cnut 23–24, 2 (Liebermann i. 326, Robertson, *Laws*, p. 186).

[6] *First Century of English Feudalism* (Oxford, 1932), p. 100, n. 2.

trade in cattle and goods outside borough markets, as to which there is very little direct evidence in the Old English period ', and that ' the definite reference to purchases made " upp on lande " makes intelligible the inclusion of *team* among the jurisdictional rights which the greater Anglo-Saxon lords of the eleventh century normally possessed '. A grant of *team* as a profitable right would involve the right to receive the fees for the *team* procedure, together with other profits which might arise in a case, for instance, when pledges and surety were forfeited because the person accused failed to produce his warrantor ; compare II Æthelred 8 : ' He shall give pledges and furnish security that he will produce his warrantor '. For the rules of the ' vouching to warranty ' procedure, see II Æthelred 8–9, 4, Leis Willelme, 21–21, 5,[1] and Holdsworth, *History of English Law*, ii. 100 f. ; and for an instance of ' vouching to warranty ' in actual practice, see Robertson, *Anglo-Saxon Charters*, no. 44 = B. 1063, where the wergeld of a person vouched to warranty who let the case go by default was demanded by the ealdorman on the king's behalf (the forfeiture of the wergeld in a case of the kind being characteristic, as Miss Robertson observes (*ibid.* p. 337), of Mercia and the Danelaw). For alternative forms of the oaths employed by plaintiff and defendant, see Liebermann, i. 396 (' Swerian ', 2–4).

In BT s.v. *team*, p. 973, following an exposition of the ' vouching to warranty ' procedure, reference is made to the meaning given mistakenly to *team* in Hickes's Latin rendering of no. 77 (not printed here, since it has no manuscript authority) : ' privilegium habendi totam suorum seruorum propaginem '. This rendering was no doubt derived by Hickes from one or other of the later lists of definitions in Latin or in French of Anglo-Saxon legal terms, frequently to be found in medieval cartularies. For such lists see *The Red Book of the Exchequer*, R.S. iii. 1032 ff., and for other such lists, see *Festgabe für Wendelin Foerster* (Beiträge zur romanischen und englischen Philologie, 1902), 205 ff. For a definition somewhat resembling Hickes's rendering, see *Les Termes de la Ley* (printed without name of author c. 1520, and reprinted in later editions), s.v. ' Them '. For comments on these glossaries of Anglo-Saxon legal terms, see Pollock and Maitland, *Hist. of Eng. Law*, i. 577, n. 2.

The earliest authentic instance of the combination of *toll* with *team* as a source of profits appears in a lease of a small estate, dating from the time of Cnut, and granted between 1017 and 1023 [2]; it was agreed that the church-tax and tithes were to be paid to the abbot and monks of Evesham, the owners of the land, and that

---

[1] Liebermann i. 224–7, 506 ; Robertson, *Laws*, 60–3, 264–5.

[2] Robertson no. 81 = Earle p. 235.

toll and team were also to be paid to them unless the lessee could acquire them from whoever was in control of the monastery at the time. There is no mention of *toll and team* in the earliest writ of Cnut (no. 28), dating from 1020, announcing a grant to Christ Church of sake and soke, grithbreach, hamsocn, foresteall, and infangenetheof. The formula *toll and team* appears, however, in a writ of Cnut for St. Paul's (no. 53) which if it is authentic (as is not certain), must have been issued 1033–35.

Besides the grants of toll covered by the formula *toll and team*, a toll specifically called *ceaptoln* (*toln* = 'toll'), 'toll on buying and selling,' is granted away by the Confessor as to one third, no doubt with reference to the market at Worcester (no. 117) ; in the same writ we hear of *seamtoln*, 'toll on the pack-horse load '. See also no. 61, and p. 477, for toll on goods brought in, and carried out. For further references to tolls in the Anglo-Saxon period, see Hoops, *Reallexikon*, iv. 392, s.v. 'Zoll' (Vinogradoff), and F. E. Harmer, ' *Chipping* and *Market* ; a lexicographical investigation ', in *The Early Cultures of North-West Europe* (H. M. Chadwick Memorial Studies), Cambridge, 1950, pp. 337 ff.

(3) INFANGENETHEOF, lit, ' thief captured within ' (the privileged area), composed of the adverb *in*, + *fangen* (past participle of *fon*, ' to take '), + ' thief ',[1] stands for the right to try a thief taken on the property and to take the profits.[2] The hanging of a thief was accompanied by the forfeiture of his chattels. For references, see Liebermann, ii. 523, s.v. ' Infangenþeof ', and for the extensive legislation regarding theft in the Anglo-Saxon period, see Liebermann ii. 349–52.

Æbærepeof, appearing in nos. 18, 24, is lit. ' manifest thief ', i.e. a thief whose guilt cannot be denied. On *æbære*, see BT Suppt. and Liebermann ii. 5. For the distinction between manifest and non-manifest theft—the former being much more heavily punished than the latter—see Pollock and Maitland, *Hist. of Eng. Law*, ii. 495. In III Edgar 7, 3,[3] it is declared of *se æbæra þeof*, as of the man discovered in treason against his lord, that ' he shall never be able to save his life, unless the king grant that it be spared '.

---

[1] The term is sometimes used in writs in oblique cases : *infangenne þeof*, accus., *infangenes þeofes*, gen., *infangenum þeofe*, dat., all in the sing. In this book I have used the post-Conquest *infangenetheof*.

[2] For a different interpretation, namely that a grant of ' infangenetheof ' gave to the grantee no more than the right to half the thief's chattels, see Goebel i. 367–8. For a criticism of this view see Hurnard, 292, n. 1.

[3] Liebermann i. 204 (D), Robertson, *Laws*, 26. Compare also II Cnut 26.

THE KING'S DUES

'Sake and soke', 'toll and team', and 'infangenetheof', are terms which frequently appear as the subject of grant in Anglo-Saxon writs. More rarely in Anglo-Saxon times the king grants away to a specially-favoured subject royal dues (*gerihta*) normally reserved to himself alone. When ' he wishes to do special honour ' to someone, as we learn from II Cnut 12–15,[1] the king may grant to him, exceptionally, the receipt of these payments. According to this code, the king enjoyed over all men in Wessex and Mercia—except when any of these rights were granted away by him to a subject as a special mark of honour—the payment for *mundbryce*, ' breach of *mund* ', for *hamsocn*, ' forcible entry, or an assault in a house ', for *foresteall*, ' obstruction ', ' waylaying ' etc., together with *fyrdwite*, ' the fine for neglect of military service ' ; and everywhere he had the payment for *flymena fyrmth*, ' the harbouring of fugitives '. Similarly the king enjoyed in the Danelaw, unless he granted any of them away as a special favour, *fihtwite*, ' the fine for fighting ', *fyrdwite* (explained above), the payment for *grithbryce*, ' breach of a special peace ', and *hamsocn* (explained above). The penalties imposed for these offences might vary at different times and at different places ; the fine is in some cases stated to have been 5 pounds. In Domesday Book sometimes three, sometimes more, of these forfeitures (*forisfacturae*) are stated to belong to the king's special prerogative ; for references see Pollock and Maitland, *Hist. of Eng. Law*, ii. 453–5, Vinogradoff, *English Society in the Eleventh Century*, 111 ff. The earliest writ of reasonable authenticity relating to the grant of any of these special royal rights is Cnut's writ for Christ Church of 1020 (no. 28).

(4) HAMSOCN, ' forcible entry, or an assault on a person in a house ' (where *socn* means ' attack, assault '), first appears in the Laws in conjunction with *mundbryce*, in II Edmund 6.[2] It was then enacted that the offender in either case ' must forfeit all that he has, and it shall be for the king to decide whether his life shall be preserved '. The *Leges Henrici* (1114–18) emphasise the element of forcible entry, or pursuit, into a building to commit the assault ; see also Liebermann ii. 504, s.v. ' Heimsuchung '. According to the customs of Oxfordshire given in Domesday Book : ' Si quis alicujus curiam vel domum violenter effregerit vel intraverit, ut

---

[1] II Cnut, 12–15 (Liebermann i. 316–18, Robertson, *Laws*, 180, Stubbs, *Select Charters*, 9th ed. 1913, 86.
[2] Liebermann i. 188, Robertson, *Laws*, 10.

hominem occidat vel vulneret vel assaliat, c. solidis regi emendat '; [1] and the same penalty may have been imposed T.R.E. In II Cnut 62 the compensation is stated to have been 5 pounds in districts under English law.

(5) GRITHBRYCE, ' breach of *grith* '. *Grith*, a Scandinavian loanword, stands here for the king's special peace or protection given to particular persons, whether by the king's own hand, by writ and seal, or by the king's deputy. We read in the Domesday entry relating to Chester : ' Pax data manu regis uel suo breui uel per suum legatum, si ab aliquo fuisset infracta, inde rex .c. solidos habebat '.[2] In the same place we read, among other additional details, that when the offence was aggravated by homicide the penalty was outlawry, and the forfeiture to the king of all the offender's goods and chattels. We have perhaps instances of such special protections given to individuals or to religious houses in Anglo-Saxon writs, where the king forbids that anyone should do the grantee any wrong ; see nos. 11, 12, 29, 46, 51, 54, 71, 87, 114. Post-Conquest instances are given by Goebel, i. 430, n. 339. See also Stubbs, *Select Charters*, 107 ; Liebermann ii. 494, s.v. ' Handfrieden ' ; Hurnard, 303 ff.

(6) MUNDBRYCE, ' breach of *mund*, or special protection '. *Mund* seems to have been more general in scope than *grith*, but the distinction between *mund* and *grith* is not always kept in the sources, and the difference does not ever seem to be defined in contemporary texts. In authentic writs and charters of the pre-Conquest period *mundbryce* and *grithbryce* do not stand together. For discussion see Liebermann ii. 551 s.v. ' Königsfrieden '. In nos. 2, 7, 74, a religious foundation is said to have been taken under the king's *mund*, ' guardianship, protection ', and violation of this would have been punished ; see also no. 26 for the *mund* of Christ Church, extended to those within its walls, and note on p. 447. The king's *mund*, which originally surrounded his residence and wherever he happened to be (I Æthelberht 3, 5), could be extended by custom or at the king's pleasure. The establishment of the king's *mund* is spoken of in II Edmund 7, 3, and in the piece called by Liebermann ' Wergeldzahlung ' (*Gesetze*, i. 392-3, dated by Liebermann 944–1060) as one stage in the procedure for the payment to his kindred, of the wergeld for the slaying of a man. Again a fine to his lord or to the king for the breach of his *mund* must be paid if a man in holy orders was bound or beaten or deeply insulted (II Cnut 42), or again, payment must be made for the violation of *mund* if a warship of the

---

[1] DB i. 154 b, VCH *Oxon*. i. 401 ; Stubbs, *Select Charters*, 107.

[2] DB i. 262b, *The Domesday Survey of Cheshire*, ed. James Tait (Chetham Society, lxxv, N.S. 1916, 78.

nation ('folces fyrdscip') was damaged (VI Æthelred 34). At one period at any rate the compensation paid for *mundbryce* was 5 pounds. See also Chadwick, *Anglo-Saxon Institutions*, 115 ff.

(7) FORESTEALL, explained, probably rightly, in NED s.v. 'forestall', sb., as 'position taken up in front of', from *fore*, 'before', and *steall* (apparently) 'position taken up'. The term may have covered several offences in the eleventh century : obstruction, waylaying, ambush. A different explanation, 'assault', is given in BT and Suppt, on the supposition that in the compound *foresteall*, *steall* means 'leap, spring'; but this interpretation is probably incorrect. In the Anglo-Saxon Laws *foresteall* is used in the sense of 'obstruction', that is, resisting officials tracking stolen cattle (III Edmund 6), and also for resisting the law of Christ or of the king (V Æthelred 31, VI Æthelred 38). For the various senses developed by the word see Liebermann ii. 285, s.v. 'Angriff', ii. 627, s.v. 'Rechtssperrung', and NED s.v. 'forestall', sb. and vb. See also Hurnard, 306. As with *hamsocn* and *mundbryce*, the penalty for *foresteall* is stated to have been 5 pounds (but might vary).

(8) FIHTWITE, the fine (*wite*) imposed for fighting. If a man was slain in a fight, the *fihtwite* had to be paid to the king, over and above the *manbot* (the compensation to the slain man's lord), and the wergeld to his kin. See further Liebermann i. 392–3, 'Wergeldzahlung', and ii. 318, s.v. 'blutig fechten'.

(9) FYRDWITE, the fine (*wite*) imposed for neglect of military service. In 1016 King Æthelred summoned out the fyrd, *be fullum wite*, 'on penalty of the full fine for failure to attend' (*Chron.* C, D, E). In Ine's code a penalty of 120 shillings and the forfeiture of his land, was exacted as *fyrdwite* from a nobleman holding land, 60 shillings from a nobleman holding no land, and 30 shillings from a commoner (Ine 51).[1] Penalties for neglect of military service are mentioned in Domesday ; in Berkshire the offender forfeited all his land to the king ; in Oxfordshire he paid a fine of 100 shillings.[2] See further Liebermann ii. 499, s.v. 'Heer', and Vinogradoff, *English Society in the Eleventh Century*, 110 f.

(10) FLYMENAFYRMTH, lit. 'the harbouring of fugitives'. It was enacted by Cnut (II Cnut 13) that if anyone did a deed which would legally involve outlawry, 'the king alone shall have power to grant him security', and that 'whoever feeds or harbours the fugitive shall pay 5 pounds to the king, unless he clear himself by

---

[1] Liebermann i. 112, Attenborough, *Laws*, 53.
[2] DB i. 56b, 154b ; cited Stubbs, *Select Charters*, 107.

a declaration that he did not know he was a fugitive '.[1] But the principle was an ancient one. Æthelstan decreed (II Æthelstan 2) concerning the lordless man who had been declared an outlaw, that anyone encountering him might assume him to be a thief and kill him ; and that anyone harbouring him after he had been declared an outlaw, should pay for the offence to the amount of the outlaw's wergeld, or clear himself with an oath of equivalent value.[2] See further Liebermann ii. 302, s.v. ' Begünstigung '. On outlawry, see Goebel i. 419, n. 289.

DOUBTFUL CASES

Other privileges mentioned in Anglo-Saxon writs as the subject of royal grants appear in more dubious contexts, and their occurrence in these texts may be anachronistic :—

(11) MISKENNING (a later spelling for normal Old English *miscenning*, from *cennan*, ' to declare '), lit. ' wrong declaration ', means ' a mistake in pleading ', and when the subject of a royal grant, stands for the right to take the fines incurred when mistakes in pleading were made in legal procedure. See Liebermann ii. 585, s.v. ' Missesprechen '. The statement in BT Suppt. that *miscenning* is ' often ' the subject of grant by the king is inexact for the Anglo-Saxon period ; the only references cited there are nos. 105, 106 (both dubious). It is in fact doubtful whether *miskenning* was ever the subject of grant by the Confessor. The term appears only in nos. 85, 91, 98, 102, 105, 106, all Westminster writs of doubtful authenticity, or spurious. It also occurs in three charters in the name of the Confessor, K. 771, 809, 825, where besides ordinary rights such as *hamsocn* and *foresteall*, others are granted ; in K. 771 *miskenning, weardwite, blodwite, sceawung*, etc., in K. 809 *miskenning, feardwite* (? for *weardwite* or *fyrdwite*), *blodwite*, etc., in K. 825 *miskenning, weardwite, sceawung*, etc. K. 771, an ostensible charter of the Confessor for St. Peter's, Ghent, cannot be authentic as it stands, for though it is dated A.D. 1044 with the correct Indiction, it is attested by Abbot Edwin of Westminster, who was not appointed to office until 1049. On K. 809, a spurious Ramsey charter, see p. 473, note on l. 3 ; and on K. 825, a spurious Westminster charter, see p. 290, n. 1. One cannot help suspecting that the appearance of *miskenning* in the dubious or spurious Westminster writs is in some way connected with its appearance in three writs attributed to the Conqueror (no one of them of undoubted

---

[1] Liebermann i. 316, Robertson, *Laws*, 180.
[2] Liebermann i. 152, Attenborough, 128 ; Stubbs, 74.

authenticity), which are closely linked in various ways to certain of this group of Westminster writs; see Davis, *Regesta*, nos. 216, 233, 234, and pp. 329, 334. For *miskenning* in the period after the Conquest, see M. Bateson, *Borough Customs* (Selden Society, 1906), pp. cxlix ff., 1–4.

(12) SCEAWING, 'showing', a technical term of which the Latin equivalent is *ostensio*, signifies a duty or toll payable for the privilege of displaying goods for sale. See BT s.v. *sceawung*, and NED s.v. 'showing', 3. At a later date 'shewage', 'scavage', and other forms were current; on these see NED. *Ostensio* appears in IV Æthelred 2, 6 and 7,[1] a code dealing with the payment of toll and the trading rights of foreigners in London. We learn that 'men from Flanders and Ponthieu and Normandy and the Isle of France exhibited (*monstrabant*) their goods and paid toll. Men from Huy and Liége and Nivelles who were passing through (London) paid a sum for exhibition (*ostensionem*) and toll'. See further Liebermann ii. 168, s.v. *ostensio*, and Ducange. *Sceawing* appears as a subject of a royal grant in nos. 105, 106, both dubious Westminster writs, and in two spurious charters of the Confessor, nos. 771, 825, which have been mentioned above under *miskenning*. But it will be suggested below (p. 334) that the appearance in London writs of the right to receive the dues for 'showing' may well be derived from an authentic source, even though the writs in question are in their present form probably not authentic.

(13) BLODWITE, the fine (*wite*) incurred by the shedding of blood. See further Liebermann ii. 318–20, and also NED s.v. 'blood-wite'. The term *blodwite* does not occur in the Anglo-Saxon codes of law. Its first appearance in the Laws is in the *Leges Henrici* of 1114–18.[2] On the evidence of the interlinear gloss in the Lambeth Psalter the term was current c. 1025. In this text *blodwitum* appears with *blodum* in the meaning 'blood', *of blodum oððe of blodwitum* glossing: 'Non congregabo conventicula eorum *de sanguinibus*'.[3] Whether or not *blodwitum* (where *wite* is 'punishment', if not 'fine') could be regarded as exactly equivalent to *blodum*, the term is clearly not used here in its technical sense, and it is not recorded in the Anglo-Saxon dictionaries as appearing elsewhere. But *blodwite* appears in the technical sense of 'fine for the shedding of blood' in Domesday Book. Sokemen on the Ramsey manor of Broughton (see no. 59) had *blodewitam*.[4] At Wallingford ten house-

---

[1] Liebermann i. 232, Robertson, *Laws*, 72.

[2] For references, see Liebermann ii. 25, s.v. *blodwite*.

[3] Psalm 15, 4, in the Authorised Version 16, 4. See U. Lindelöf, *Der Lambeth-Psalter* (Acta Societatis Scientiarum Fennicæ, Helsingfors, 1909, tom. xxxv, no. 1), 19. [4] DB i. 204.

holders had *sanguinem*, i.e. *blodwite*, in certain circumstances.[1]
The problem is to determine whether *blodwite* was ever the subject
of grant by the Confessor. The term appears in nos. 45, 93, both
spurious, and in the dubious no. 105 ; also in spurious charters of
the Confessor, K. 771, 809 (on both of which see under *miskenning*,
above), K. 785, 813 (see p. 59). Liebermann, who cites three of
these spurious charters as well as no. 105, had not apparently considered the unsatisfactory character of these sources for evidence
of grants of *blodwite* by King Edward. He is particularly concerned
(ii. 319, 11 ff.) to draw a (difficult) distinction between *blodwite* and
fihtwite, and makes a differentiation which cannot be sustained
between the spurious Ramsey charter, K. 809, in which *blodwite*
and *fihtwite* appear together and the spurious Ramsey writ, no. 61,
in which *fihtwite* appears alone. Liebermann described the writ as
' echt ' and the charter as ' unecht ', but in fact both are spurious as
they stand. *Blodwite* also appears with *fihtwite* in the spurious no. 45,
not noticed by Liebermann. The existing evidence is not sufficient
to prove that *blodwite* was ever the subject of grant by the Confessor.

(14) WEARDWITE, on the analogy of *fyrdwite*, the fine (*wite*) paid
for neglecting to keep guard, but not recorded in the Anglo-Saxon
dictionaries. It appears here in nos. 45, 93, both spurious, 104,
dubious, and also in the spurious charters K. 771, 825, and possibly
(as *feardwite*) in K. 809 ; on these spurious charters see above.
Liebermann ii. 726, s.v. ' Wache ', takes no. 104, and K. 771, 825,
at their face value, but it would be hazardous to assume on this
evidence, uncorroborated elsewhere, that *weardwite* was ever the
subject of grant by the Confessor. There is however no obvious
reason why the term should not have been current before the
Conquest, for various types of ' guard ' T.R.E. are on record.
The term *weardwite* (*wardwite* etc.) appears with varying definitions
after the Conquest in lists of later definitions of Anglo-Saxon legal
terms ; for such lists see p. 77. *Inward* and *custodia* appear in
Domesday. At Hereford T.R.E. when the king was in the city,
men who had not whole burgages provided guards (*ineuuardos*) for
the hall.[2] At Fulbourn, Cambs., the men of the manor paid
nothing to the sheriff T.R.E. except carrying-services and watch
and ward (*inguardos*), or 12s. 8d. ; whilst at Litlington in the same
county, held T.R.E. by Earl Ælfgar, the sheriff collected *weardpenig*
in lieu thereof if the guard were not performed (' homines hujus
manerii reddebant *warpennam* uicecomiti regis aut *custodiam
faciebant*').[3] See further Liebermann, *ut supra*, and ii. 569, s.v.

---

[1] DB i. 56b. For discussion see Maitland, *Domesday Book and Beyond*, 193,
VCH *Berks.* i. 317.　　　　　　　[2] DB i. 179, VCH *Hereford*, i. 309.
[3] For both the Cambridgeshire instances, see DB i. 190, VCH *Cambs.* i. 362.

' Leibwache ', where other types of ' guard ' are also mentioned.
See also NED s.v. ' wardwite ' ; Morris, *Medieval English Sheriff*,
33 ; and the forthcoming *P.-N. Cumberland*, vol. iii.

(15) MORTHSLECHT (normally spelt *morthsliht*) stands in two
Chertsey writs, nos. 40, 41, for the *murdrum*-fine of the early Norman
period, and its appearance in these texts is no doubt connected with
the appearance of the *murdrum*-fine in Chertsey writs attributed to
Anglo-Norman kings (on which see p. 207). In no other Anglo-
Saxon writ does the term *morthsliht* occur, and all the evidence
suggests that the appearance of this term in nos. 40, 41, is an
anachronism. This fine, probably introduced into England by
William I for the protection of the lives of Frenchmen (see Liebermann ii. 593, s.v. *murdrum*), was imposed on the hundred in which
the body was found, if a man who was not of English birth was slain,
and his slayer was unknown, or if known, not apprehended within
a given period. For an account of the procedure see the *Leges
Henrici* § 13, 2, and 92,[1] where a fine of 46 marks is imposed if the
slayer is not apprehended within seven days. See further on the
murdrum-fine, Liebermann ii. 587, s.v. ' Mord ' ; F. C. Hamil,
' Presentment of Englishry and the Murder Fine ', *Speculum*, xii
(1937), 285–98 ; S. Painter, *Studies in the History of the English
Feudal Barony* (Baltimore, 1943), 79 ff.

ALLITERATION, RHYME OR ASSONANCE, AND PARALLELISM IN FORMULAS

It is then evident that a number of factors have contributed to the
shaping of the form of the Anglo-Saxon writ. The formulas commonly used have already been discussed, as have also the technical
legal terms employed. Since the royal writ announcing a grant of
land and privileges was intended to be read in the shire court or
other public assembly, it was necessary that it should be readily
understood, and its contents easily remembered. This was facilitated by the strongly-marked rhythm of the clauses which relate to
the actual grant, and by the alliteration, the assonance or rhyme,
and the parallelism, which link the words together. The extent to
which these devices were used can best be realised by breaking up
into their component parts passages from Anglo-Saxon writs and
other prose passages used here as illustrations :—

> . . . his sace weorðe 7 his socne
> 7 tolles 7 teames
> ofer his land 7 ofer his men
> binnan porte 7 buton,

[1] Liebermann i. 558, 607 f., dated 1114–18 by Liebermann.

or,

> . . . on wuda 7 on felde
> mid sace 7 mid socne
> swa full 7 swa forþ
> swa hit me sylfan on hande stod
> on dæge 7 æfter,

or,

> . . . heora saca weorðe 7 heora socne
> 7 griðbryces
> 7 hamsocne
> 7 forstealles
> 7 infangenes þeofes
> 7 flymena fyrmðe
> ofer heora agene menn
> binnan burh 7 butan
> tolles 7 teames
> on strande 7 on streame,

or,

> . . . scotfreo 7 gafolfreo
> on scire 7 on hundrede.

Anglo-Saxon writs have their own characteristic vocabulary and formulas, but this material belongs of course to the common Anglo-Saxon stock, and it appears not only in writs but also in charters and in wills.   Formulas such as

> . . . swa ful 7 swa forð
> swa he hit me to handa let,

or,

> . . . swa ful 7 swa forð
> swa ic hit fyrmest ahte,

or,

> . . . ær dæg 7 æfter dæge,

or,

> . . . binnan byrig 7 butan,

and many others, were evidently in common use.[1]   Anglo-Saxon charters frequently record the actual terms of business agreements of all kinds—sales and leases and exchanges of land, grants in reversion, marriage settlements, and the like, and it is to be observed

---

[1] It is worth noting that *mid mete 7 mid mannum*, common in business documents in the late Old English period, appears only in Ælfthryth's writ (no. 108), though in charters of cent. xi, it sometimes appears in conjunction with the ' sake and soke ' formula ; cf. Robertson, nos. 73, 93.

that these terms often fall into the same kinds of linguistic patterns as the formulas employed in writs. With the terms of the Confessor's charter of which Abbot Wulfwold speaks in no. 6 :—

> . . . to gyfanne 7 to syllanne
> ær dæge 7 æfter dæge
> loc hwam me leofast is,

we may compare the very similar terms of a Worcester marriage settlement, and of a Worcester land-purchase (both of the time of Archbishop Wulfstan, who was interested in both transactions) :—

> . . . to gyfene 7 to syllenne
> ðam ðe hire leofest wære
> on dæge 7 æfter dæge
> ðær hire leofest wære,[1]

and

> . . . to geofene 7 to syllenne
> ær dæge 7 æfter dæge
> sibban oððe fremdan
> þær him leofost wære.[1]

It is reasonable to suppose that in such cases we have a record of the actual words spoken when the agreement in question was made verbally before witnesses. The names of the witnesses are recorded in the charters, and their recollection of the terms would be facilitated by the stylistic devices employed.

The use of ' alliterative jingles '[2] and similar devices is undoubtedly ancient. It is entirely probable that before the laws were committed to writing, legal forms were arranged for remembrance among the Germanic peoples in rhythmical and alliterative patterns.[3] The use of such devices to assist the ear and guide the memory is to be remarked, for instance, in the legal ritual of oath-making among the Anglo-Saxons.[4] The formal oaths employed in Anglo-Saxon times have come down to us in Christian garb, but Liebermann and others have pointed out that the appearance in the oaths of material common to other Germanic peoples favours the supposition that some portions of these oaths go back to pre-

[1] Robertson, nos. 76, 83. For other documents from different centres employing similar formulas, cf. Robertson, nos. 92, 98, 114, 117, and *ibid*, nos. 93, 97, 100.

[2] For the term, see Hall, *Studies in English Official Historical Documents*, 204.

[3] Palgrave, *Rise of the English Commonwealth* (London, 1832), i. 42, ii. cxxxiii. Also O. Hoffmann, *Reimformeln im Westgermanischen* (Leipzig, 1886), where alliterative, rhyming, and balanced, formulas are brought together from a number of Anglo-Saxon works in verse and prose, including many charters, and many parallels are cited from Old Saxon, Frisian, and Old High German sources. There is a copy of this (rare) work in the British Museum.

[4] See Liebermann, *Gesetze*, i. 396–9, ' Swerian ' ; discussion, iii. 233–6. Mod. Eng. rendering, C. Stephenson and F. G. Marcham, *Sources of English Constitutional History* (London, 1938), 25. See also Palgrave ii. cxxxv.

Christian Germanic antiquity. But the same parallelism, the same alliteration, assonance or rhyme, were also employed in formulas composed in Christian times. The oath to be employed when cattle were stolen will illustrate the use of such devices in oath-making :—

> On ðone Drihten
> næs ic æt ræde ne æt dæde
> ne gewita ne gewyrhta
> ðær man mid unrihte
> N. orf ætferede.[1]

The terms employed in the claims and counter-claims recited in an action concerning a claim to property in some respects present close parallels, and sometimes identical words, to those appearing in writs :—

> Ic agnian wylle
> to agenre æhte
> ðæt ðæt ic hæbbe
> and næfre ðe myntan
> ne plot ne ploh
> ne turf ne toft
> ne furh ne fotmel
> *ne land ne læse*
> ne fersc ne mersc
> ne ruh ne rum
> *wudes ne feldes*
> *landes ne strandes*
> wealtes ne wæteres
> butan ðæt læste
> ða hwile ðe ic libbe.

and

> . . . ne gyrne ic ðines
> ne læðes ne landes
> *ne sace ne socne.*[2]

But alliteration and parallelism were also used as stylistic devices by the homilists of the late tenth and early eleventh centuries—most conspicuously by Archbishop Wulfstan of York, whose famous *Sermo Lupi ad Anglos* exhibits a strongly marked rhythm combined with alliteration : for instance :—

> . . . Ac soð is þæt ic secge,
> þearf is þære bote,
> forþam Godes gerihta
> wanedan nu lange
> innan þysse þeode
> on æghwylcum ende.[3]

---

[1] Liebermann i. 396 ; for another instance see Stubbs, *Select Charters* 9th ed. (1913), 73.

[2] Liebermann i. 400, ' Hit becwæð ', dated in text heading, c. 1020–c. 1060, but in iii. 236, apparently a little earlier. Evidence for exact dating is lacking.

[3] *Wulfstan : Homilien*, ed. Napier, i. 158 ; *Sermo Lupi ad Anglos*, ed. D. Whitelock, 16. On this aspect of Wulfstan's style, see E. Einenkel, ' Der Sermo Lupi ad Anglos ein Gedicht ', *Anglia*, vii, *Anzeiger*, 200 ff.

Professor Angus McIntosh has recently observed that Wulfstan's prose is characterised by ' a continuous chain of phrases of certain permitted rhythmical patterns each containing two main stresses, no more, no less ' ; and that ' such alliteration and rhyme as Wulfstan has . . . serves . . . to join more intimately the two important elements within a single phrase '. The style of late Old English prose has not yet been fully examined, though some attention has been given to the style of Ælfric and of Wulfstan. But indeed the two-stress pattern, with alliteration, rhyme and assonance, runs through the technical formulas of the writs, though the texture is not identical.[1]

Other preachers also employed the same devices of alliteration and parallelism to catch the attention of their hearers : one of the Blickling Homilies (which treats of the near approach of the end of the world) begins :—

> Men þa leofostan hwæt!
> Nu anra manna gehwylcne
> ic myngie and lære
> ge weras ge wife
> ge geonge ge ealde
> ge snottre ge unwise
> ge þa welegan ge þa þearfan
> þæt anra gehwylc hine sylfne
> sceawige and ongyte. [2]

The same devices are employed in the Anglo-Saxon legal codes, but it is to be observed that only a few instances appear in the earliest laws.[3] The most conspicuous instances are to be found in the codes of Æthelred II and of Cnut, between which and Wulfstan's homilies there is a close connection.[4] A very short passage will suffice to illustrate the use of alliteration and parallelism in these codes :—

> . . . Mannslagan 7 manswaran,
> hadbrecan 7 æwbrecan
> gebugan 7 gebetan
> oððe of cyððan mid synnan gewitan.[5]

---

[1] *Wulfstan's Prose* (Proc. Brit. Acad. xxxiv, 1948), 9 ff. See also D. Bethurum, *ut infra*, *Wulfstanstudien*, K. Jost (Bern, 1950).

[2] *The Blickling Homilies*, ed. Morris, E.E.T.S. (1874–80), 107 ; *An Anglo-Saxon Reader*, ed. J. W. Bright (London, 1909), 67.

[3] See D. Bethurum, *Modern Language Review*, 27 (1932), 263–79. There are a few in the code of Wihtred, dated by Liebermann 695–96 (Liebermann i. 12–14, Attenborough, *Laws of the Earliest English Kings*, 24–30) ; þæt *wite* and ðæt *weorc* ; gif man his heowum in *fæsten flæsc gefe*, *frigne* ge *þeowne* halsfang alyse ; oððe hine man *cwelle* oþþe ofer sæ *selle* (Wihtræd 11, 14, 26). For other instances in the Laws, see Liebermann ii. 11–12, 62, s.v. ' Alliteration ', ' Endreim '.

[4] On Wulfstan's authorship of legal codes, see Whitelock, *Eng. Hist. Rev.* lvi (1941), 1 ff., *ibid.* lxiii (1948), 433 ff.

[5] II Cnut 6 (Liebermann i. 312, Robertson, *Laws*, p. 178) ; cf. V Æthelred 25.

That the tendency to employ alliterative and balanced phrases must have been widespread in the tenth and eleventh centuries is manifest from a passage employing such phrases in the prose treatise ' Gerefa ', expounding the duties of the manorial reeve :—

> . . . Gyf he wel aginnan wile
> ne mæg he sleac beon
> ne to oferhydig
> ac he mot ægðer witan
> ge læsse ge mare
> ge betere ge mætre
> ðæs ðe to tune belimpð
> ge on tune ge on dune
> ge on wuda ge on wætere
> ge on felda ge on falde
> ge inne ge ute.[1]

The arrangement of the matter relating to the grant in Anglo-Saxon writs, as in other legal documents, in balanced phrases, often with alliteration, assonance, or rhyme, follows then a usage which can be traced back to Germanic antiquity ; but it is at the same time in harmony with a tendency to use the same devices which is to be plainly seen in some types of prose in the tenth and eleventh centuries.

The framework of alliteration, sometimes rhyme or assonance, and parallelism, which appears elsewhere in formulas of great antiquity such as *ne að ne ordal,* or *wer and wite,*[2] is to be found in some apparently ancient formulas which appear in Anglo-Saxon writs.[3] But it is also employed in writ formulas which are composed of elements which may not have been brought together until times comparatively recent, as for instance : *mid þære cyrice 7 mid þære cyricsocne* in no. 73. The formula *sacu and socn* may already have been long in use when it appeared in an early writ of Cnut (no. 28) ; on this see pp. 75 ff. above. But there is some reason to believe that the combination of *toll* with *team* may have been made, if not in Cnut's time, at any rate not very long before (see p. 77). Their meaning remained discrete, whereas in *sacu and socn* the two elements are fused together (see p. 74).

[1] Liebermann i. 453 ff. Liebermann dates the piece 960–1060, probably c. 1025–60. Mod. Eng. rendering by W. W. Skeat in W. Cunningham's *Growth of English Industry and Commerce* (5th ed. 1922), 573–6.

[2] On these, see Bethurum, *op. cit.* 272.

[3] See Hoffmann *op. cit.* on Anglo-Saxon *binnan and butan* ; parallels are cited by him from Frisian (*binna ieftha buta*), and German (*binnen und buszen*). Compare also : *oððe on ceapstowe oððe on stræte, ge binnan byrg ge butan* in a charter of 884–901 (Harmer, *Eng. Hist. Docs.* no. 13 = B. 579), *ge ner tune ge fyr* in K. 617, *mid were and mid mylene* in K. 667, both leases of Bishop Oswald of Worcester (961–92). For other instances see Hoffmann *ut supra.*

The various elements which compose the alliterative or balanced formula may be linked together in several ways :—

(1) The formula contains two different words linked by alliteration. This seems to be the largest class : e.g. *sacu* and *socn*, *toll* and *team*, mid *lande* and mid *læse*, mid *lande* and mid *loge*, on *strande* and on *streame*, on *weren* and on *wætere*, on *wæterum* and *werum*, *weorc* and *waru*, *scer* and *sacleas*, *abrece* and *awansige*, swa *deorf* ne swa *dyrstig*.

(2) The formula contains two contrasted words linked by alliteration : e.g. *ær* dæg and *æfter* dæge, *binnan* byrig and *butan*, mid *inlade* and *utlade*.

(3) The second element is identical in both words : fiht*wite* and fyrd*wite*, of sem*tolne* and chyp*tolne*, wið *borene* 7 wið un*borene*.

(4) The elements are connected by rhyme : be *lande* and be *strande*, be *strande* ne be *lande*.

(5) The elements are connected by assonance : mid *mæde* and mid *læse*, mid *læse* and mid *hæðe*.

(6) The connection is one of parallelism or antithesis : be *wuda* and be *felda*, *mæde* and *eitum*, ofer heora *land* and ofer heora *men*, sy þær *mare* landes sy þær *læsse*.

The number of alliterative and balanced formulas is particularly large in Westminster writs of doubtful authenticity ; but in Westminster writs of the highest repute such phrases are not more numerous than in the reputable writs of other houses. Some at any rate of those appearing in dubious Westminster writs may have originated as mere embellishments ; it is however to be observed that they are not merely conventional sequences like the ancient and widely-used formulas : *cum campis, pratis, pascuis* etc. which appear in Anglo-Saxon charters.[1] They bear some relation to the actual physical features of an estate ; the *mid morum*, for instance, of the Eversley writ (no. 85) must have been the contribution of some one familiar with the surrounding countryside. That in the eleventh century (or later) the ordinary material of business transactions might be arranged in such balanced and alliterative formulas is illustrated by the

        ' wercstan æt Bernace and
         walstan æt Burh '

of no. 61 (spurious). But speech-patterns such as these are not of course confined to the older periods of our language. Alliteration, employed from early times as a mnemonic and rhythmical device, appears in phrases such as ' kith and kin ', ' chick or child ', ' hearth and home ' ; whilst the two-stress phrase, as has been

---

[1] Some of these formulas are collected by Kemble, *Codex Diplomaticus*, i, xxxvii. They are common in Frankish charters ; see Giry *op. cit.* 551, n. 3.

recently demonstrated by Miss Marjorie Daunt,[1] forms at all periods a dominant feature of English speech.

THE SEALING OF WRITS

A small number of writs in the name of King Edward the Confessor have come down to us in the form of texts copied on small pieces of parchment, to which in some cases a seal is attached. The writ which best illustrates the method of sealing employed, that is, the ' sceau pendant sur simple queue ', as it is called by French scholars, is the Christ Church writ, a photograph of which forms the Frontispiece. It will be observed that two very narrow strips of parchment have been cut horizontally parallel to the lower edge to within a short distance of the left-hand edge. The wax of the seal has been placed on both sides of the upper strip, the king's image being stamped on both sides ; a short end of the parchment is left free. When the document was folded, the narrow lower strip, intended as a tie, was placed round it, and fastened in such a way that it could be opened and re-closed at pleasure, without breaking or removing the seal.[2] In some cases either seal tag or wrapping tag or both are absent, but their former existence may be indicated by a ' step ' at the lower left-hand corner of the parchment. The existence of the wrapping tag or of a ' step ' indicating its former existence with writs of the Confessor seems to have escaped the notice of R. Lane Poole, who discusses the method of sealing *sur simple queue*.[3] Hall rightly observes (*ut supra*, p. 218) that it will not infrequently be found that later forgeries of Anglo-Saxon and Anglo-Norman writs, while indicating in some way the attachment of a seal, usually fail to reproduce the wrapping tag. An instance of such omission appears in the spurious Cotton Charter x. 17.[4] The appending of a wax seal *sur simple queue* is generally considered to have been a discovery of the Anglo-Saxons, for not only was a pendent seal of wax first employed in England (so far as north-west Europe is concerned), but the special method of its attachment is an innovation for which no earlier model is known to have existed.[5] Wax seals had long been employed upon the Continent, but there they were

---

[1] ' Old English Verse and English Speech Rhythm ', *Trans. Philological Society* (1946), 56–72.

[2] H. Hall, *Studies in English Official Documents*, 218 ; H. C. Maxwell-Lyte, *Historical Notes on the use of the Great Seal of England* (London, 1926), 300.

[3] *Studies in Chronology and History*, 109.

[4] *Facs. of Anc. Chart. in the British Museum*, ed. Bond, pt. iv, no. 37. Charter discussed, F. E. Harmer, *Bull. of the John Rylands Library* xxii (1938), 349–51.

[5] *Archiv f. Urk.* vi (1918), 55 f.

single-faced, the wax for the seal being placed directly on the face of the document over an incision, that is to say, *plaqué*, or attached *en placard*.[1] Further the hanging of a leaden *bulla* or coin-seal to papal documents has been traced to the beginning of the seventh century (or even a little earlier),[2] and metal seals were also in some degree employed in Frankish territory.[3] These were appended to the lower edge of the document by a strip of parchment or by strings of hemp or silk. Documents sealed in this way would of course have become known in England.

The affixing, with Anglo-Saxon writs, of a two-faced seal to a strip of parchment cut from the document itself, was a new device in sealing, which may have been employed as soon as writs were sealed. A glance at the writs reproduced here (Plates 1, 2) will show that on these small strips of parchment there is room neither for a seal impressed upon the document, nor for the fold and incisions customary when a seal was suspended at the base of the parchment.

As has been said above, hanging seals of wax originated in this country and from this country extended to the Continent.[4] We find the hanging wax seal employed in Capetian royal charters in the last years of Philip I (1059–1108), but only in the mandates,[5] which correspond to the Anglo-Saxon writs, and not in the diplomas, where this method was employed later. It was then, according to Bresslau, in all probability, borrowed from France into Germany, where it appears in the twelfth century; while in Sicily, in his opinion, either the French or the English model may have provided the pattern. And further the special method of attachment *sur simple queue* was imitated in other countries, in France, and in the later Middle Ages, also in Germany. In England sealing *sur simple queue* continued after the Norman Conquest, and was the normal form of sealing for the overwhelming bulk of letters issued patent all through the Middle Ages.

---

[1] On this and other methods of sealing, see Bresslau, *Urkundenlehre*, ii, part ii (1931), 584 ff.; and also R. Lane Poole, *Studies in Chronology and History*, 103.

[2] Poole, *Studies in Chronology and History*, 97 ff. For an example, see Steffens, *Lateinische Palãographie* (2nd ed. Berlin and Leipzig, 1929), no. 58, a privilege of Pope Leo IV of A.D. 850.

[3] For metal seals in Frankish territory see Bresslau, 'Zur Lehre von den Siegeln der Karolinger und Ottonen', *Archiv f. Urk.* i (1908), 355–70; and for reproductions of actual examples, see O. Posse, *Die Siegel der Deutschen Kaiser und Könige*, 751–1806 (5 vols. Dresden, 1909–13), i, Plate 2, etc.

[4] On Scand. seals, see Harmer, *Saga-Book*, 128 ff. But I do not now consider the seal of St. Cnut of Denmark (see p. 100, n. 3, below) to be authentic.

[5] See M. Prou, *Receueil des Actes de Phillipe I*, ccvi f. and nos. 137, 169.

THE ORIGIN OF THE GREAT SEAL

The figure of King Edward the Confessor appears on both sides of his seal, which is approximately 3 inches in diameter. The king, with beard and moustache, is represented crowned, seated in frontal pose on a stool or backless throne ; he is clothed in an undertunic reaching nearly to his feet, which are covered with shoes or low buskins ; over the tunic is worn a mantle fastened on the shoulder with a brooch. There are differences in detail between the representation of the king on the obverse, and on the reverse, of his seal, but in their main outlines these closely resemble each other. In his hands the king bears the symbols of power : on the obverse of the seal he bears in his right hand a sceptre topped with a trefoil, and in his left hand an orb (also called a globe or a mound) : on the reverse, he bears in his right hand a long sceptre topped with a bird, whilst his left hand holds a sword which rests against his left shoulder. The legend running round the rim of the seal on both sides is : + SIGILLVM EADVVARDI ANGLORVM [1] BASILEI. What is the origin of this representation on the Confessor's seal—the first Great Seal of England in existence—of the king enthroned in majesty bearing the insignia of power ? No authentic wax seals of earlier English kings have come down to us,[2] but this portrait of a king in majesty did not originate with the Confessor. Many of its features appear to be traditional.[3] Representations of a ruler in majesty, called *majestas*-portraits, in which he is shown seated upon a throne or chair of state in formal posture, in a rigidly frontal

---

[1] Abbreviated to ANGLORV on the obverse of the First Seal.

[2] On the use of seals by kings and other persons in the Anglo-Saxon period, see W. H. Stevenson, *Eng. Hist. Rev.* xxvii. 6, n. 17, 18. He rejects as not issued by Offa and Edgar wax seals affixed to spurious charters of those kings for the abbey of St. Denis near Paris. For these see B. 259, 1057, with representations of the seals ; the seals are also in Birch's *Catalogue*, nos. 1, 3, reproduced in Wyon, Plate I, nos. 1, 4, and also in *The Archæological Journal*, xiii (1856), opposite p. 366. Stevenson's arguments regarding the origin of these seals are reinforced by Bresslau, *Archiv f. Urk.* vi (1918), 47, n. 1. The seal matrices were antique gems. In Bresslau's opinion the seals were taken from genuine diplomas and attached to the spurious charters of Offa and Edgar, fabrications, according to Bresslau, of c. 1100, and demonstrated to be spurious by Stevenson long before (*Eng. Hist. Rev.* vi (1891), 736 ff.). On the leaden coin-seal of Coenwulf, see p. 28, n. 2 above.

[3] See, for instance, P. E. Schramm, ' Das Herrscherbild in der Kunst des frühen Mittelalters ', *Vorträge der Bibliothek Warburg*, ed. F. Saxl, vol. ii (*Vorträge*, 1922–23), part i (Leipzig and Berlin, 1924), 145–226 ; Schramm, *Die deutschen Kaiser und Könige in Bildern ihrer Zeit*, 751–1152 (Leipzig and Berlin, 1928). For representations on seals of German emperors and kings, see also Posse, *Die Siegel der deutschen Kaiser und Könige*.

pose, and bearing the symbols of power, have been traced back to the early fourth century.[1] The Carolingian rulers and their successors are frequently depicted in portraits of the *majestas*-type.[2] But the *majestas*-type of portrait did not for some time appear upon their seals of wax. The early Carolingian rulers used antique gems or gems modelled on the antique to stamp their wax seals, usually with a head in profile ; in a later type of wax seal, spear and shield were added. The change to a frontal representation of the head and upper part of the body is to be seen on the first wax seal of Otto I as emperor, in 962, and it appears on a wax seal at about the same time (997) in France. This seal of Otto I shows the bearded head of the emperor, wearing a crown. His right hand holds a sceptre headed with a trefoil, as does that of the Confessor on the obverse of his seal ; his left hand, as does the left hand of the Confessor, holds an orb.[3] But this seal of Otto I is not a seal of the *majestas*-type, for the emperor is not represented as enthroned in majesty.

Giry[4] finds the earliest instance of the wax *majestas*-seal in the supposed seal of Count Arnulf of Flanders (918–65), the grandson of King Alfred, affixed to a diploma of 8 July 941 of St. Peter's, Ghent ; but the authenticity of this seal is more than doubtful.[5]

---

[1] H. Bresslau, *Archiv f. Urk.* vi (1918), 26–7 ; Schramm, *Das Herrscherbild*, 189 ff., and corresponding Plates. See for instance the representation of a ruler by the Chronographer of A.D. 354 (J. Strzygowski, *Die Calendarbilder des Chronographen vom Jahre 354* (Berlin, 1888), Plate xxxiv), and portraits of Valentinianus II and Arcadius (R. Delbrueck, *Spätantike Kaiserporträts* (Berlin and Leipzig, 1933), Plates 96, 97). For numerous representations of Roman consuls, see Delbrueck, *Die Consular-Diptychen und verwandte Denkmäler* (Berlin and Leipzig, 1929). See also Harmer, *Saga-Book*, pp. 134 ff.

[2] See Schramm, *Die deutschen Kaiser* etc., and *Das Herrscherbild*, *passim*.

[3] On these developments, see Schramm, *Die deutschen Kaiser*, 63 ff., *Das Herrscherbild*, 184 ff. ; Bresslau, *Urkundenlehre*, ii, part ii (1931), 600 ff. ; Posse, i, Plates 1–7 ; J. Roman, *Manuel de Sigillographie Française* (Paris, 1912), 70 ff. and the corresponding plates. Erben–Schmitz–Redlich, *Urkundenlehre*, i. 174 ff.

[4] *Manuel de Diplomatique*, 639.

[5] On this diploma, see G. Des Marez, ' Notice sur un diplôme d'Arnulf le Vieux, comte de Flandre ', *Bulletin de la Commission Royale d'histoire de Belgique*, 5th series, vi (1896), 219–42, text 243–52. For facsimile, see *L'Album belge de diplomatique* (1909), ed. H. Pirenne, Plates ii, iii. The authenticity of Arnulf's diploma has been effectively demonstrated by E. Sabbe in two articles : ' Deux points concernant l'histoire de l'abbaye de Saint-Pierre du Mont-Blandin ' (*Revue Bénédictine*, xlvii (1935), 52–71), and ' Étude critique sur le diplôme d'Arnoul Ier comte de Flandre, pour l'abbaye de Saint-Pierre à Gand ' (*Études d'histoire dédiées à la mémoire de Henri Pirenne* (Brussels, 1937), 299–330). In the second of these Sabbe attempts to vindicate the authenticity of the seal attached to Arnulf's diploma. This seal was considered spurious by O. Oppermann, ' Die älteren Urkunden des Klosters Blandinium und die Anfänge der Stadt Gent ' (*Bijdragen van het Instituut voor Middeleeuwsche Geschiedenis der Rijks-Universiteit te Utrecht* (1928), i. 39 ;

If, as seems probable, Arnulf's seal is not authentic, the first ruler in western Europe to have been represented full-length in the posture of the *majestas*-portrait, seated upon a throne, and bearing the insignia of power, will have been the Emperor Otto III (983–1002), who is depicted after this fashion on the wax seal that he adopted in 997 and employed until the spring of the following year.[1] On a wax seal about three inches in diameter, the emperor is depicted crowned and seated upon the throne, holding in his right hand a sceptre with trefoil top, and in his left a globe, on the surface of which a cross is depicted.[2] It would be difficult to exaggerate the importance for the subsequent history of royal seals of this new development, in which, instead of the portrait of only the head, or head and upper part of the body, of the monarch, or, in the case of two earlier wax seals of Otto III, the standing figure, there now appears the full-length portrait of the monarch seated in majesty upon his throne, crowned and bearing his insignia in his hands. The inscription runs : OTTO DI GRACIA ROMANORV IMP AUG. Although for the remaining four years of his reign the *majestas*-seal of wax was no longer employed by the Emperor Otto III, this new type of wax seal was adopted by his successor Henry II (1002–24), who used it for wax seals both for his second seal as king, and also for his seal as emperor, from 1014 to 1023.[3] It was adopted for wax seals by Conrad II (King 1024, Emperor 1027–39),[4] and by Henry III (1039–56), Henry IV (1054–1105), and by their successors. But not only did the German emperors and kings for centuries to come in imitation of the seal of Otto III have themselves depicted enthroned in majesty with the symbols of power upon their seals,[5] but other rulers followed suit. The *majestas*-portrait came indeed to be regarded as the proper way to represent a western monarch upon his seal : ' nur auf dem Thron mit Szepter und Reichsapfel kann man sich einen mittelalterlichen König verstellen.'[6] On the widespread

also by Erben in Erben–Schmitz–Redlich, *Urkundenlehre*, i. (1907), 176, n. 4, and by Bresslau, *Urkundenlehre*, i. (1912), 707, n. 2, *Archiv f. Urk.* vi (1918), 26, n. 5. I am kindly allowed by Professor F. L. Ganshof to quote the opinion of Dr. Ramackers, conveyed to him personally, that the supposed seal of Arnulf was not issued by Arnulf, and was affixed to the diploma at a later date.

[1] For a reproduction of this seal, see Posse, vol. i, Plate 10, no. 1, and for a description, vol. v, p. 15, no. 5. Schramm, *Die deutschen Kaiser*, 193 and Plate 68 e. See also Harmer, *Saga-Book*, Plate 1.

[2] For details of the seal, see D. L. Galbreath, *Inventaire des Sceaux Vaudois* (Lausanne, 1937), no. 2, Plate I, 1.

[3] See Posse, i, Plate 11, nos. 2, 3 ; v, p. 16, no. 2, and p. 17, no. 3 ; Schramm, *Die deutschen Kaiser*, 196 and Plates 79 b, 79 c.

[4] Posse, i, Plates 12, 13 ; v. 18–19 ; also iv, Plate 73, no. 11. Schramm, *Die deutschen Kaiser*, 201, and references.

[5] See Posse and Schramm.   [6] Schramm, *Das Herrscherbild*, 206.

imitation of the new seal-picture of Otto III, ' das nun seinen Siegeszug durch die Welt nahm ', Bresslau speaks as follows [1] :—

' Es blieb im deutschen Reiche herrschend bis zu dessen Ausgang, es wurde noch in der ersten Hälfte des 11 Jahrhunderts in England und in Frankreich rezipiert, es findet sich auf den ältesten Siegeln dänischer und skandinavischer Könige, die wir kennen, es wurde in Sizilien schon von dem Grossgrafen Roger I angenommen, und man sieht es auf den Majestätssiegeln der Könige von Spanien und Portugal, von Böhmen, Ungarn und Polen, in dem letzteren Reiche freilich erst am Ende des 13 Jahrhunderts, als Przemysl II den Königstitel annahm.'

The representation of King Edward the Confessor on his seals follows the model of the seal of majesty of the Emperor Otto III and of his immediate successors, and in the whole sequence of the Great Seals of English kings and queens since the Confessor's time the sovereign has always been depicted on one side of the Great Seal enthroned in majesty and crowned, and bearing the royal insignia.[2] In the representation of King Edward the Confessor upon his seals, the general features of the posture and the attire of the monarch, as also of the insignia he bears (with the exception of the sword), are essentially the same as those appearing on the seals of Otto III and his three immediate successors—the only seals, for reasons of date, of the German emperors and kings, with which we are concerned here. There are of course some differences in detail ; the youthful Otto is beardless ; others, including the Confessor, are depicted with beards.[3] There are differences in the insignia borne by the monarchs, in which uniformity is lacking even on the emperors' seals.[4] But the insignia displayed on the seal of King Edward the Confessor, the sceptres headed respectively with trefoil and with bird, the orb, the sword, can all be found depicted on one or other of these continental seals, or in earlier representations of rulers. Only in one respect do the Confessor's seals differ in any essential point from the Carolingian and Ottonian seals and those of their immediate successors ; unlike all these other seals of wax, the Confessor's seals are two-faced.

[1] *Archiv f. Urk.* vi. 26.

[2] H. S. Kingsford, *Seals* (Helps for Students of History, no. 30), London, 1920, 32. For reproductions of the Great Seals of England, see Birch, and Wyon, *loc. cit.*

[3] With the representation of the Confessor on his seals, his representation on the Bayeux Tapestry may be compared. On the problem of the value as likenesses of portraits of medieval rulers on coins, seals, and in manuscripts, (but without any reference to portraits of the Confessor), see N. de Wailly, *Éléments de Paléographie* (1838), ii. 104 ; Schramm, *Das Herrscherbild*, 146–50 ; *Die deutschen Kaiser*, 4 ff. ; Bresslau, *Urkundenlehre*, ii, part ii (1931), 599.

[4] On the insignia of rulers, see Schramm, *Herrscherbild*, 158, 203, *Die deutschen Kaiser*, 119 f. ; Hoops, *Reallexikon*, ii. 597, s.v. ' Insignien des Königtums ' ; Harmer, *Saga-Book*, 129, n. 46.

The origin of the appearance of the *majestas*-portrait on royal seals in England has been variously derived, and its occasion variously dated. The ' facile conclusion ' that King Edward derived his seal from the Normans was controverted by W. H. Stevenson [1] in an article explaining the errors in the views expressed by Giry.[2] Stevenson's arguments were supported by Bresslau, who had undertaken a further examination of certain Norman charters, in which he had the help of C. H. Haskins.[3] Bresslau observes that since it is still doubtful, on the existing evidence, whether the dukes of Normandy before the Norman Conquest employed a seal, the conclusion that the Confessor's seal was modelled on theirs cannot be maintained, and there are indeed other arguments against it. Another theory, that the Confessor derived the representation of the king in majesty from France, appears (somewhat strangely) in the last edition of the last volume of Bresslau's *Handbuch der Urkundenlehre*.[4] There we read :—

' Zweifellos nach deutschem Muster hat man dann unter Heinrich I (1031–60) in Frankreich den Typus des Thronsiegels angenommen und aus Frankreich hat ihn Eduard der Bekenner nach England mitgebracht.'

But the differences between the seal of Henry I of France [5] and the Confessor's seal make it difficult to accept this theory. The insignia borne on his (single-faced) seal by King Henry I of France are different. He bears in his left hand, not an orb, but a staff which rests upon his throne ; in his right hand he grasps a fleur-de-lis or trefoil with a very short stem—much shorter than the trefoil-headed sceptre of the Confessor's seal and of the German Emperors'. And further, whilst the flat-topped backless stool or throne of the Confessor's seal is of the traditional form going back to antiquity, that on which Henry I of France is depicted, seated, is of a different, triangular, shape. It is to be noted that the writer of this part of the *Urkundenlehre*, probably not Bresslau himself—for the book was not completed until after Bresslau's death [6]—makes no comment on the divergence between this theory and that of Bresslau. Both in

[1] *Eng. Hist. Rev.* xxvii (1912), 4, n. 11.

[2] *Manuel de Diplomatique*, 795.

[3] *Archiv f. Urk.* vi, 55, n. 1 ; cf. Haskins, *Norman Institutions*, 53.

[4] Vol. ii, part ii (1931), 602, n. 4.

[5] The seal of Henry I of France is attached to a diploma dated 1035 (F. Soehnée, *Cat. des Actes d'Henri Iᵉʳ, roi de France* (Biblio. de l'École des Hautes Études, Fasc. 161, Paris, 1907), no. 46). For a facsimile, see Mabillon, *De re diplomatica* (Paris, 1681–1704), 423 ; Wailly, *Éléments de Paléographie*, ii. Plate B, no. 6, and 379, xvii ; Roman, *Manuel de Sigillographie Française*, 75, Plate iv, no. 1. The inscription runs : HEINRIC DI GRA FRANCORV REX.

[6] See Titlepage and Preface, p. iii. This part was edited by H.-W. Klewitz ' aus dem Nachlass '.

the *Urkundenlehre* and in his article, often referred to, in the *Archiv für Urkundenforschung*, Bresslau expressed the view that the Confessor in his use of the two-faced seal, and in the representation on it of the king in majesty, was following as a model a seal of Cnut, who was king both of England and of Denmark.[1] Another possibility is suggested by R. Lane Poole,[2] who does not seem to have been acquainted with this hypothesis of Bresslau's. Poole observes that the seals of Conrad II bear, as Bresslau had also remarked, a remarkable resemblance to that of the Confessor. He continues : ' It cannot be forgotten that Edward's half-sister Gunhild married the son of Conrad, the future Emperor Henry III. There were frequent relations between England and the Empire about 1050, and Edward's seal appears to have been in use not much later than 1051.' But this theory of direct borrowing from the Germans fails to account for the fact that the Confessor's seal is two-faced, and it seems therefore less acceptable than that of Bresslau. Bresslau suggests that in employing a two-faced seal Edward the Confessor was merely copying a seal (now no longer existing) of Cnut (the evidence for whose use of a seal has been given above, pp. 17–18), and that although there was nothing in Edward's position to justify the use of a double seal, in the case of Cnut the seal would have expressed his two-fold lordship, the one side of England, the other of Denmark.[3] It must be made clear that this is no more than a hypothesis. But it has the merit of explaining a feature of King Edward's seal which is difficult to account for—the fact that the two sides of the seal differ only in small details. In the case of Cnut, according to this theory, the two sides would have borne different images and inscriptions. Bresslau's view was based in part on the fact that the two-faced seal which accompanies a diploma supposedly issued in 1085 by King Cnut IV (the Saint) for the cathedral at Lund, of which an apparently reliable representation has been preserved,[4] shows on the one side the king seated in majesty, on the other the king

---

[1] The writer of the sentence quoted above gives a reference to p. 26 f. of Bresslau's article in the *Archiv f. Urk.* vi. But what Bresslau says there is as follows : he observes that the ' Siegelbild ' (of the king in majesty) ' blieb im deutschen Reiche herrschend bis zu dessen Ausgang, es wurde noch in der ersten Hälfte des 11 Jahrhunderts in England und in Frankreich rezipiert ' etc. Further a reference to the theory of imitation from the seal of Cnut appears in the *Urkundenlehre*, i (1912), 686–7 ; and there is no indication that Bresslau himself altered his view.

[2] *Studies in Chronology and History*, 108.

[3] *Archiv f. Urk.* vi (1918), 56 ff.

[4] The original was burnt in 1692. It is depicted in Thorkelin, *Diplomatarium Arnamagnæanum* (Copenhagen, 1786), vol. 1, Plate 1, no. 1. See also Harmer, *Saga-Book*, Plate 3.

seated on horseback. The inscription in hexameters on the one side runs : + PRESENTI REGEM SIGNO COGNOSCE CNUTONEM, and on the other : HIC NATUM REGIS MAGNI SUB NOMINE CERNIS. Bresslau points out that there is an obvious resemblance between this seal and the seals of King William the Conqueror.[1] These also represent the king on one side seated in majesty, on the other on horseback. They bear on the rider-side the inscription in hexameters : HOC NORMANNORUM WILLELMUM NOSCE PATRONUM SI, and on the other : HOC ANGLIS REGEM SIGNO FATEARIS EUNDEM.[2] Bresslau finds it difficult to believe that the Danes would have imitated the seal of the Normans, against whom they had fought. He suggests that it is much easier to suppose that the resemblance between the Danish and the Norman seals which have been described above, is to be explained by the imitation of a model common to both, namely, the (presumed) seal of Cnut, a predecessor in Denmark of Cnut the Saint, and in England of William the Conqueror.[3] Bresslau then concludes that Cnut, king of England and Denmark, had also a two-faced seal, and that this was the pattern followed in the two-faced seal of King Edward the Confessor.[4] This hypothesis is rendered the more easy of acceptance by the close correspondence (to which Bresslau drew attention)

[1] See Birch, *Catalogue*, nos. 15–21, Plate 1, no. 17 ; Wyon, Plate II, nos. 11–14 ; F. M. Stenton, *William the Conqueror*, Frontispiece.

[2] R. Lane Poole (*loc. cit.* 108) follows Bresslau in printing SI at the end of the line, but makes no comment. The SI has been variously explained. Bresslau, *Archiv* vi. 57, expands it to SIGNO or SIGILLO. For a different arrangement, see Birch, *Trans. R. Soc. Lit.* x. 152, where SI is placed at the beginning of the second line.

[3] But actually, as Mr. P. Grierson has pointed out to me, certain thirteenth-century features in the iconography of the supposed seal of St. Cnut raise doubts as to its authenticity which prevent the acceptance *in toto* of Bresslau's theory. The rider-with-falcon motif on the reverse of St. Cnut's seal, appears, for example, on seals of Henry III and John I of Brabant, as also on some Brandenburg coins ; seated figures with feet crossed, as on the obverse, are found at the same period. See F. Philippi, *Siegel* (1914), 14, and Pl. iv. 8 ; also Pl. v, 4, 5 ; Ewald, *Siegelkunde* (1914), 204, Pl. 29, 1, 32, 2.

[4] Hexametric inscriptions appear on Norwegian royal seals of the late twelfth and thirteenth centuries (Harmer, *Saga-Book*, 131, 132), but not on the remaining Danish, or on Swedish, seals. Professor W. Holtzmann has observed to me that the hexameters on English seals could have been derived from the famous verse : ROMA CAPUT MUNDI REGIT ORBIS FRENA ROTUNDI on the reverse of the small two-sided metal bulla (not issued before 1033) of the Emperor Conrad II (Posse, i, Pl. 13, 7, 8, v. 19). But this metal bulla, with an obverse with two standing figures, of Conrad II and Henry III, could not have provided the model for the *majestas*-portrait on English seals. This, according to Bresslau's hypothesis (see following page) was derived from the single-sided wax seal of Conrad II (without verse inscription). The matter is less simple than Bresslau implies.

between the insignia borne by King Edward the Confessor on the obverse of his seal—a sceptre topped with the fleur-de-lis or trefoil and an orb, and those depicted on the first imperial seal of the Emperor Conrad II ; the insignia borne on their seals by the Confessor's contemporaries, the Emperors Henry III and IV, are differently distributed. The easiest way to account for this correspondence is, in Bresslau's opinion, to suppose that the connecting link was to be found in the (lost) seal of King Cnut, who was present at the coronation of Conrad II in Rome in 1027 ; that Cnut's seal, in fact, imitated this seal of Conrad II, and served in its turn as the model for the seal of King Edward the Confessor. The inscription employed on wax seals by Conrad after his coronation as emperor, which runs : + CHVONRADVS DI GRA ROMANORV IMP AVG, was not however closely imitated on the Confessor's seal.

But if this hypothesis of Bresslau's should prove unacceptable, we are of course at liberty to suppose that the Anglo-Saxon two-faced seal was adopted from a coin, or from the leaden *bullae* of popes or of emperors. There is however another feature (besides those mentioned above) which links the Confessor's seals with those of Otto III and his successors, namely, the dimensions of the seals. They are all approximately of the same diameter, about three inches, more or less.

SEALS OF KING EDWARD THE CONFESSOR

The seals, or reputed seals, of King Edward the Confessor were described by Birch and Wyon [1] who subdivide the seals of the Confessor into three types, taken from three different matrices. With them the question of the authenticity of any given seal as a product of the Confessor's writing office is scarcely raised at all—not even in the case of the so-called First Charter of Edward the Confessor at Westminster which they admit to be spurious. We cannot escape the conclusion that if a text is spurious, the seal appended to that document cannot have been appended to it in its existing form by the clerks of the Confessor's secretariat ; and that unless the seal bears clear signs of having been detached from some other document and re-affixed to the one under examination, the seal in question cannot be an authentic seal of the Confessor. Again, if a seemingly authentic text is copied in a later

---

[1] Birch, ' On the three Great Seals of King Edward the Confessor ', *Trans. R. Soc. Lit.* 2nd ser. x (1874), 136–48, and Plates ; also *Cat. of Seals in the Dept. of Manuscripts in the British Museum*, i (1887), nos. 5–14, and Plate 1, no. 9. A. and A. B. Wyon, *The Great Seals of England* (1887), p. 3 ff., Plate 1, no. 7.

handwriting, with linguistic forms within the text indicating a date of origin later than King Edward's reign, the seal now appended to the document cannot have been appended to it by the clerks of the Confessor's secretariat, but must have been appended to it by a later hand. In such a case a genuine seal might again (in theory) have been detached from a writ extant in a contemporary form and appended to the new document—as seems indeed to have been done with the writ (without a seal) and the (sealed) diploma relating to Taynton (see p. 36) ; but there is no obvious instance among extant writs of a seal appended to a writ having been taken from another document. What the evidence suggests is that a genuine or forged matrix of a seal of the Confessor was being used at Westminster Abbey after his death, and that seals made from this matrix were being appended there to later copies of writs (both authentic and spurious). These seals thus affixed at a later date cannot be regarded as authentic seals of the Confessor, and products of his writing office. The case of Campbell Charter xxi. 5, a Christ Church writ (no. 33), is exceptional ; here the parchment and the seal seem to be those of an original writ of the Confessor issued by the royal clerks, but after the first few lines the text has been washed out and replaced by something in a later hand. Birch and Wyon did not concern themselves with these considerations ; their business was simply to enumerate seals and casts of seals with which they were acquainted. The First Seal is the only one generally known.

On the FIRST SEAL (according to Birch's classification) of King Edward the Confessor, the king's features are strongly marked. No complete and undamaged specimen of this seal is known anywhere to exist, the representation given by Birch in his *Catalogue* being taken from a cast apparently of unknown provenance. In an earlier discussion of the Confessor's seals (*Trans. R. Soc. Lit.* 1874) Birch reproduced the seal of the spurious Ickworth writ (no. 80), but with no comment on its authenticity. Nor is any specimen of this seal now appended to an authentic writ of King Edward the Confessor extant in its original form. All the existing specimens of the seal known to me are in fact associated with Westminster Abbey, where this seal was being impressed on documents as late as 1100 or even later ; an account of these seals is given below, Items 3 and 4. The same seal was appended to the so-called Third Charter of King Edward at Westminster Abbey, fabricated about 1100 or later ; and the seal appended to the First Charter of King Edward, which I have not seen, would seem to be of the same type and date (see p. 289, n. 3, p. 290, n. 1). In none of these cases does the seal appear to have been removed from another (genuine) document and then affixed to the writ or charter. This was of course easily done by making an incision in the edge of the seal with a piece of hot metal and placing the new seal tag in the incision—a method actually employed (as it would seem) when the seal (of the Second Type) illustrated in Plate 2 was removed from the St. Denis writ and appended to the St. Denis diploma. Until a seal of the First Type is actually forthcoming which can be accepted as an authentic seal appended to a writ by the royal clerks, the following possibilities in my opinion lie open :—

(a) The monks of Westminster got hold of a genuine matrix of a seal of King Edward the Confessor and used it in the reign of his successors to make impressions on copies of authentic and spurious writs and of spurious charters made in Westminster Abbey itself. Could it have been originally shown as a relic ?

(b) The monks of Westminster made for themselves or had made for them a matrix bearing a portrait of King Edward and the inscription employed on his authentic seals, and employed this matrix for making impressions on the documents named above.

On the SECOND SEAL, well authenticated by two specimens, one from Christ Church, the other from St. Denis (Plates 1 and 2, and Items 1 and 2 below) the king's features are not so strongly marked, and the figure is more vigorous ; and moreover this seal is differentiated from the First, not only by small differences of posture (summarised by Wyon), but also by the unabbreviated ANGLORVM on both sides of the seal. Authentic writs issued by the Confessor for Westminster Abbey among other houses would presumably have had affixed to them a seal of this type or of any other authentic type issued by the king. But the evidence for this sealing of Westminster writs is now lost, except that Birch and Wyon placed here the fragmentary seal appended to the earlier Perton writ (Item 6 below). Further, Doublet, who in 1625 described the St. Denis seal as ' sain et entier ', observed that the orb in the king's left hand was surmounted by ' le signe de la Croix '—a statement which seems to have escaped notice hitherto. Although in the imperfect state of the surviving specimens no trace of this cross remains, the possibility that the Second Seal did indeed exhibit a ' globus cruciger ' is increased by the fact that the Confessor holds an orb surmounted by a cross on coins of the so-called ' sovereign ' type,[1] where he is depicted enthroned in majesty with details closely resembling those of the *majestas*-portrait, except that his head is turned to one side. Furthermore, King Harold holds a ' globus

[1] See for instance Grueber and Keary, *Cat. of Engl. Coins*, Anglo-Sax. Ser. ii (1893), Plate xxiii, 2, Plate xxiv, 10, etc.

cruciger' on the Bayeux Tapestry. So that the existing Second Seal of the Confessor may well have been in this respect the proto-type of all the seals of English sovereigns on which a ' globus cruciger' is depicted from William I onwards (no seal of King Harold being now extant). The second seal can be dated 1052–66 (see below).

The THIRD SEAL, as distinguished by Birch and Wyon (see Item 5 below), is merely a fragment.

The existing evidence for the sealing of writs authentic or not of the Confessor is summarised here :—

(1) A probably authentic seal of King Edward, imperfect and repaired, and with blurred outlines, is still appended *sur simple queue* to Campbell Charter xxi. 5, no. 33. The seal can be dated 1052–66, the date indicated by the (authentic) address of the writ, the greater part of the text of which is spurious.

(2) A probably authentic seal of King Edward, attached now to the Taynton diploma of the abbey of St. Denis (see Appendix II), was probably once appended to the Taynton writ (no. 55). If this hypothesis is correct, the seal can be dated 1053–57, the date of the writ.

(3) Seals of red wax, in the three existing specimens broken and defective, are or were formerly appended to nos. 73, 76, 93, 94 ; of the seal of no. 73 we know only from Madox's statement. The handwriting of nos. 76, 93, 94, is of the latter part of the eleventh century. Further, seals are described by Hickes as being in his time appended to nos. 77, 97, both again in late copies. Disregarding here the question of the texts, these seals affixed to copies of a later date cannot have been affixed by the clerks of the royal secretariat, and are therefore not authentic seals. They must have been taken from a forged or a genuine matrix after the Confessor's death.

(4) The seal of reddish-brown substance, twisted and bent, appended upside-down to the spurious Ickworth writ (no. 80), cannot since the writ is spurious itself be authentic.

(5) A small and indistinct fragment of a seal of white wax, the so-called Third Seal of Birch and Wyon, attached to no. 101, exhibits differences (summarised by Wyon) in the angle at which the insignia are held and other small points.

(6) The remains of the seal of white wax attached to the earlier copy of the Perton writ (no. 96) were assigned by Birch and Wyon to the Second Type.

(7) A small fragment of seal attached to no. 82 when it was photo-graphed for the Ordnance Survey Facsimiles, has now vanished.

(8) The spurious Coventry writ, no. 45, with its strands of twisted silk drawn through incisions (but with no seal appended), exhibits

a method of sealing employed in the Anglo-Norman period, but not in the Confessor's time.

(9) Nothing can be said with any certainty regarding the seal depicted by Charles (see pp. 469 f.) in connection with a St. Paul's writ, no. 54.

(10) The seal once appended to a Hereford writ (no. 49) bore the inscription customary on writs of the Confessor, but beyond the inscription no further information concerning it is given.

(11) No. 81 has two tags, the upper of which has broken away, perhaps through the weight of a seal.

Seven other writs of varying degrees of authenticity are copied on single pieces of parchment. In nos. 34, 96 (R), 115, a 'step' may indicate former sealing. In nos. 11, 24, 90, 98, there is no direct indication of the existence of earlier sealing.

THE AUTHENTICITY OF WRITS

The number of Anglo-Saxon writs without any substantial basis of fact is in all probability small, but the possibility that a text may not be authentic in all its parts must be constantly borne in mind. That a writ of Westminster Abbey was already in 1086 alleged to have been forged is known from an entry in Domesday Book itself (DB ii. 14). The manor of *Phantuna* in Essex (the name of which survives in Great Fanton Hall) is entered under the land of St. Peter of Westminster, but with the statement that this land is claimed for the king's use on the ground that it came to the church by a forged writ :—

'Phantunam tenuit Alestan Stric T.R.E. Hac terra calumpniata est ad opus regis quod *per falsum breuem* uenerit ad ecclesiam '.[1]

The writs of Anglo-Saxon kings that have survived are mainly concerned with grants of lands and liberties to ecclesiastics and religious houses. It is known that many religious houses in Norman England did in truth possess estates and rights that they asserted to have been conferred upon them by kings such as Cnut and Edward the Confessor, who were famed for their liberality to the church. In some cases they possessed these lands and privileges until the Dissolution. That Cnut and Edward the Confessor at all events, among the later Anglo-Saxon kings, made throughout their reigns extensive grants to monasteries, and that such grants were notified by writ to the appropriate authorities, is quite beyond doubt. But the conditions in which the documents were preserved and handed down afforded, at every stage, opportunities for alteration of the text. Writs in

[1] The spurious Great Charter of Edgar for Westminster (see p. 338) purports to confirm this grant of Fanton to the abbey. For further references to Fanton see *Crawford Charters*, 96.

their favour issued by the clerks of the royal secretariat were preserved in the monasteries themselves, and they were copied and re-copied into the monastic registers. The temptation to tamper with the text of an existing writ, or even, on occasion, to construct a new one, must have been great. These writs purport to notify the conferment of possessions and rights of the most important and lucrative kind ; and the documents safeguarding these rights were jealously preserved. The evidence of writs of King Edward is sometimes appealed to in Domesday (see App. IV). From time to time after the Conquest the writs and charters of a monastery were confirmed. Kern has pointed out that besides the ' ancient charters which guaranteed the venerable age and high quality of the rights concerned ', it was useful to possess new charters granting the same rights [1]; and there is, for instance, a reference on the Memoranda Roll of I John to a sum of 300 marks due from Ramsey Abbey ' pro renovatione cartarum suarum tempore regis Ricardi ', and for quittance from other debts due at the Exchequer. [2] On some occasions the renewal of charters was ordered by the crown. In 1198 Richard I for instance ordered all clerics and laymen who had charters or confirmations under the old seal to bring them in for renewal under the new seal, without which renewal they would be held to be void. [3] The well-known *Placita de Quo Warranto* proceedings provided other occasions for the production of ancient writs and charters. It is not hard to imagine that a community might take steps by the interpolation of an existing writ or by the fabrication of a new one to strengthen their claim to a right that they were known to possess. The fact that a writ has come down to us under the royal *inspeximus* is no guarantee that it is authentic. Mr. H. G. Richardson has observed that : ' if the primary concern of the chancery clerks in instituting the Charter Roll was, as seems to have been the case, the collection of fees, then we should not expect them to be greatly concerned with the validity of the documents enrolled '.[4] It is

---

[1] F. Kern, *Recht und Verfassung im Mittelalter* (1919). Trans. S. B. Chrimes, *Kingship and Law* (Studies in Mediaeval History, Oxford, 1939), 170 ff. The mental and moral attitude of the medieval forger is convincingly analysed by Kern. It is tempting to suggest that the benediction sometimes invoked on those augmenting the grant (see p. 70) may in some cases have provided an additional motive for fabrication.

[2] *Memoranda Roll I John*, ed. Pipe Roll Society, 1943, p. xxxvi, n. 6, 12, 13.

[3] *Itinerary of Richard I*, ed. L. Landon (Pipe Roll Society, 1935), 179, with a reference to the *Chronica Rogeri de Houeden*, R.S. iv. 66. See also Matthew Paris, R.S. iii. 122, with reference to the cancellation by Henry III when in 1227 he came out of his minority of all charters *de libertatibus forestae* (cited by Stubbs, *Select Charters*, 9th ed. 1913, 323.).

[4] *Memoranda Roll I John*, p. xlj ; on the *Cartæ Antiquæ* and *Patent Rolls*, see *ibid*. liv ff., xliii.

certain that of the pre-Conquest writs enrolled not only on Charter Rolls but also on the *Cartæ Antiquæ*, Patent and Confirmation Rolls, some are spurious. Or again, a writ which is not authentic as it stands may possibly have had its origin, in whole or in part, in the desire to assert a claim to land or privileges which were in danger of being lost to the community because of the encroachments of Norman lords on the rights of individual monasteries after the Conquest, and may perhaps have been composed in the course of the litigation to which such encroachments may have given rise. Or again, a spurious text may have been devised to meet the claim by some rival foundation to possess jurisdiction or other rights within a particular liberty or over certain persons. In other cases the mention in the writ or charter of a post-Conquest king of a (supposed) grant by King Edward the Confessor which was at this later date being confirmed, may have been the occasion for the provision of evidence for such a grant in the shape of a writ in the name of King Edward which was at any rate in some degree spurious. In some cases a writ may have had its origin in a desire to provide evidence for a lost or existing right ; in others to provide a substitute for a lost or damaged text. In such cases the compiler may have had access to authentic models or to collections of ancient formulas. Again, on some occasions, a copy of an authentic writ may have been made and even provided with a seal, for production to royal officials, in order that the original sealed writ issued for the grantee by the clerks of the royal secretariat might be protected from damage. The new copy made for this purpose may or may not have been embellished or improved or in some way altered in the process. But in no case are we ever given any warning that a document is a copy. Since the original may have been closely imitated, it will often prove difficult to determine the nature of the document, that is to say, whether it is the original writ produced and sealed in the king's scriptorium or whether it is a copy made perhaps only a short time after in the monastery for the benefit of which the original writ was issued. ' La question d'authenticité ', observes Giry, ' demeure toujours la première et la plus délicate qui se doive poser en présence d'un acte quelconque '. [1]

CRITICISM OF WRITS

Generally speaking, little has been done hitherto to determine the authenticity of Anglo-Saxon writs as a class, or of individual

[1] *Manuel de Diplomatique*, 4.

texts.[1] Sir Roger Twysden writes in 1658 to William Dugdale, who had brought out the first volume of the *Monasticon Anglicanum* (the earliest systematic collection of charters—including a few writs—to be printed in this country) in 1655 conjointly with Roger Dodsworth (who had died in 1654) :—

'I have sometimes told you, I did wish in the preface to your second edition of the *Monasticon*, you would express somewhat as if you did not answer for the truth of every Bull or Charter you have related, otherwise than that you found them faithfully you hope in bookes belonging to some Abbies or other, out of which you have tooke them, but doe not, nor can not, affirme, they all came, totidem verbis, eyther from Prince or Pope, as they are by you recorded '.[2]

Twysden gives reasons for this wish of his, demonstrating that a charter of King Edgar, and a bull of Pope Agatho, among other documents printed in the *Monasticon*, cannot be authentic, and adducing as evidence anachronistic formulas, impossible ' styles ', and erroneous dating. Dugdale did not however accede to his request.[3] About forty years later Dr. Thomas Smith, the compiler of the catalogue of Sir Robert Cotton's Library (1696), in letters written 1695–97 to Humphrey Wanley, praises Mabillon's *De Re Diplomatica*, and several times refers to the difficulty of distinguishing between authentic and forged charters in cases where the signs of forgery are not obvious.[4] But the foundations of diplomatic study in this country were laid by that great scholar George Hickes, in his detailed examination of Anglo-Saxon charters in his *Dissertatio Epistolaris* (Oxford, 1703), where a number of forged charters in Latin are critically examined, and reasons for their rejection are given. Some of the criteria applied by Hickes, such as anachronisms in language or in content, are applicable to documents of all kinds ;

[1] For a discussion of the general principles, and an investigation of the authenticity of nos. 34, 61, 112, see F. E. Harmer, *Bull. of the John Rylands Library*, xxii (1938), 339–67. For some valuable suggestions by J. H. Round in his review of H. W. C. Davis's *Regesta Regum Anglo-Normannorum*, see *Eng. Hist. Rev.* xxix (1914), 348 ff. Round pointed out that the compilers of that work had not distinguished precisely enough between the various ways in which an original text may have been tampered with, such as interpolation (additions to the original text), the reconstruction of an existing genuine text or of a lost text, and embellishment (inflation). For the outlines of the history of diplomatic criticism in this country, see R. Lane Poole, ' The teaching of Palaeography and Diplomatic ', *Essays on the Teaching of History* (Cambridge, 1901), 17 f.

[2] *The Life, Diary, and Correspondence of Sir William Dugdale*, ed. W. Hamper (London, 1827), 335 ff.

[3] Comments on the authenticity of charters appear in the 1846 edition of the *Monasticon* ; cf. the remarks on the Westminster forged charters, i. 266–9.

[4] *Original Letters of Eminent Literary Men of the sixteenth, seventeenth, and eighteenth centuries*, ed. Sir Henry Ellis, Camden Society, xxiii (1843), 238–57.

but Hickes confined his critical investigations mainly to royal diplomas. On the use of seals in the pre-Conquest period Hickes's views are unsound ; he unjustifiably rejects (*op. cit.* p. 72) the evidence for the use of a seal by Æthelred II and by Cnut. Richard Widmore's condemnation of some of the Westminster Abbey charters as forgeries,[1] and the rejection as later fabrications of other charters by other editors of this time, John Lewis, for example,[2] show that in the eighteenth century criticism was on the alert. But no other scholar followed Hickes in formulating general principles of criticism for charters purporting to belong to the Anglo-Saxon period, until the task was taken up again by J. M. Kemble in the Introductions prefixed to several of the volumes of the *Codex Diplomaticus* (London, 1839–48). Later investigation has in some cases of course modified or even reversed Kemble's judgments,[3] the reason for which is not often given in the *Codex Diplomaticus.* Kemble rightly affixed his ' critical asterisk ' to the Ripon writ in Latin attributed to King Æthelstan (Appendix I), and with less justification to the Evesham writ in Latin attributed to King Cnut (no. 48), but without giving reasons for assigning either of these to the category of texts ' which were ascertained forgeries or which appeared suspicious '. In the fourth volume of his *Codex Diplomaticus* in which most of the Anglo-Saxon writs printed by him appear (there are a few in the sixth volume) and which extends from c. 1018 to the eve of the Norman Conquest, Kemble abandoned in part his system of discrimination, safeguarding himself by the statement that he does not ' mean to pledge himself to the authenticity of every charter which he prints here without an asterisk '.[4] Reference to the *Codex Diplomaticus* will show that none of the writs in the vernacular of Anglo-Saxon kings were marked by him as spurious, and none were marked spurious by Benjamin Thorpe in his *Diplomatarium Anglicum Ævi Saxonici* (London, 1865). Nor was much progress made in the matter of distinguishing the authentic from the unauthentic in John Earle's *Handbook to the Land-Charters and other Saxonic Documents* (Oxford, 1888) or in Birch's *Cartularium Saxonicum* (London, 1885–93) which ends at A.D. 975. Earle's plan, whereby in its first design, his book ' was to have been just a few specimens of land-charters, so grouped as to exhibit roughly the contrast of genuine and spurious ' was afterwards abandoned, and the book now presents a false contrast

[1] *Enquiry into the First Foundation of Westminster Abbey* (1743), 10.
[2] See p. 456.
[3] See for instance Haddan and Stubbs, *Councils*, iii. 644, n. a, *Crawford Charters*, 121, n. 3. Other instances will be found among the documents discussed below. [4] See vol. iv, p. vi.

between ' Genuine ' documents, dated or undated, and ' Secondary '
documents, which are not, as one might have expected, spurious
documents, but documents which have come down to us in later
copies.[1] Earle's book is of little or no value for the criticism of
writs. His description of no. 28 printed here as ' a document which
seems to be quite above suspicion ' can be accepted ; but his sweeping condemnation of no. 26 as a document ' not available as historical
material ' cannot be sustained (see p. 169). On the genuineness of
nos. 4, 61, 68, 102, documents of varying degrees of authenticity,
he makes no comment ; and though they are printed together in
his Group V (pp. 339 ff.) of ' Secondary Documents ', as belonging to
the twelfth century, and as having been ' copied with little attention
to the English of the originals or of the time purported ', these texts,
which are actually derived from sources ranging in date from the
thirteenth to the seventeenth century, are not only wrongly dated
by Earle, but they are printed by him, not from the manuscripts, but
straight from Kemble's normalised texts, even to the reproduction
of Kemble's ' eccentric accentuation '.

The work of W. H. Stevenson on the charters is to be found
scattered in footnotes in many places, and has never been brought
together as a whole. In his article, ' Trinoda Necessitas ',[2] for
example, Stevenson discusses in footnotes the authenticity of many
texts. Similarly many charters come under review in the edition
of the *Crawford Charters* which he produced in conjunction with
A. S. Napier, as also in his edition of *Asser's Life of King Alfred*, and
in the portion of *Two Cartularies of the Abbeys of Muchelney and
Athelney* [3] which is from his hand. On the Anglo-Saxon writ
Stevenson's pioneer work is of outstanding importance.[4] He gave
instances of its use, described its method of sealing, and placed it in
its proper setting as a document which survived the Conquest and
was adopted as the model for the writs of Anglo-Norman kings.
On the question of authenticity Stevenson touched only by implication, except in the case of a few documents, his opinion of which has
been quoted here in the appropriate places ; but by his emphasis
on the fact that some writs have been preserved in contemporary
form, and by his remarks on the seals and methods of sealing, he
placed the study of the writ on its right footing. At the end of one
of his articles Stevenson had drawn attention to the imitation of

---

[1] The confusion arising from this divided aim is analysed still further by
Max Förster, *Der Flussname Themse* (for full ref. see p. 266), 203. See also
W. H. Stevenson's review, *Eng. Hist. Rev.* iv (1889), 353 ff.

[2] *Eng. Hist. Rev.* xxix (1914), 689 ff.

[3] For full reference, see p. 144, n. 1.

[4] *Eng. Hist. Rev.* xi (1896), 731 ff. ; xxvii (1912), i ff.

the Anglo-Saxon writ form in Scotland and in Scandinavia. His investigations were carried still further by H. Bresslau in a highly important article, ' Internationale Beziehungen im Urkundenwesen des Mittelalters ',[1] which I have often had occasion to cite ; Bresslau however, like Stevenson, is naturally more concerned with general considerations than with the authenticity of the individual text. Bresslau's conclusions scarcely ever run counter to those of Stevenson, the soundness of whose arguments further investigation has with few exceptions confirmed. The significance of the Anglo-Saxon writ in its historical background, and its importance as the *fons et origo* of later diplomatic forms, have frequently been emphasised by Professor V. H. Galbraith. For Anglo-Saxon historical studies the long series of books and articles by Sir Frank Stenton, in which Anglo-Saxon charters are critically examined, are indispensable, whilst the late Professor Wilhelm Levison in his Ford Lectures threw fresh light upon the descent of these documents.

CRITERIA OF AUTHENTICITY

Two main questions need to be considered in any attempt to determine the authenticity of a writ which purports to announce a grant of land or privileges. Was the grant which the writ purports to announce actually made ? Is the existing text the actual text produced by the clerks of the king's writing office, or if the copy is a later one, is it an unaltered copy of an authentic writ produced by the royal clerks ? [2] To deal first with the question whether the grant was actually made—in nearly every case it can be shown that the religious foundation in question did at one time possess land in the places named in the writs purporting to have been issued in its favour, sometimes until the Dissolution. But on the other hand, although an estate owned by a religious house may at one period or another have been identical with the land alleged to have been granted to it by an Anglo-Saxon king, there can obviously be no certainty that this was the case. The land originally acquired may have been increased or diminished by purchase, sale, gift or exchange, and there are so many gaps in manorial history that it would be hazardous to assume without some corroboration that a manor held by a religious foundation at any subsequent period was identical with the land supposed to have been granted to it by an Anglo-Saxon king. But bearing this consideration in mind, a straight-

---

[1] *Archiv f. Urk.* vi (1918), 19–76.

[2] I use ' authentic, authenticity ' in the sense recorded in the NED s.v. ' authentic ', 6 : ' really proceeding from its reputed source or author ; genuine opp. to counterfeit, forged, etc.) '.

forward statement in Domesday Book regarding the tenure of an
estate can be accepted as good evidence of the fact : it implies that
the claim to hold the estate passed unchallenged. Similarly a
statement in Domesday that a monastery held an estate *ex dono
Regis Edwardi* can be accepted ; it implies that the grant was
uncontested. But the value of Domesday in this connection is not
confined to its testimony to the tenure of an estate. A Domesday
entry implying that a monastery had not come into possession at the
time of his death, of land supposed to have been granted to it by
King Edward, may supply a reason for the existence of suspicious
features in the relevant writ ; the writ may have originated in an
attempt to establish a claim. The value of the information derived
from Domesday will in fact vary from one writ to another. But
where there is a conflict of evidence the testimony of Domesday Book
may be indecisive. During the period that had elapsed between the
death of the Confessor in 1066 and the taking of the Survey twenty
years later, many estates had undergone changes of ownership, and
in some cases an interval of more than forty years may have elapsed
between the mention of an estate in a writ of the Confessor and the
appearance of its name in a Domesday entry. During the interven-
ing period the persons for whom grants of land recorded in writs were
made may have sold or exchanged or otherwise disposed of it.
Cases occur of illegal transference of ownership and of forcible
appropriation of estates. In other cases the beneficiaries named in
writs may have had difficulty in making good their claim, and the
arrangement recorded in a writ may have been frustrated ; or the
grant may have been revoked. In some cases the donor of an estate
may have remained as tenant for life of an abbey, on the under-
standing that the land should revert to the abbey at his death ; but
in the end the abbey's claim to the reversion may have been disregarded.[1] Moreover, the history of a number of estates during the
early Norman period is obscure, sometimes because information is
lacking, sometimes because the evidence is conflicting. For these
reasons it may be impossible after examining all the evidence to
prove that a grant of land was actually made. Again, an attempt
to prove that judicial and financial rights were actually conferred
upon a bishop or abbot or religious foundation by an Anglo-Saxon
king may encounter difficulties. One way however of assessing the
authenticity of a claim to have received a grant of privileges is to

---

[1] Attention was drawn to J. H. Round (VCH *Berks.* i. 298) to the fact that
' Domesday bears frequent witness to the disastrous effect for religious houses
of their leasing their manors for lives with the result that, after the Conquest,
the new-comers who found themselves in the shoes of the lessees refused to
admit the reversion.'

compare the relevant writ with later grants (if such exist), where the privileges said to have been granted in the time of the Confessor are enumerated and confirmed. When more is claimed in the alleged writ of King Edward than writs of later kings give grounds for supposing to have been actually granted in his time, there is reason for suspicion, if not of fabrication, at all events of alteration and improvement of the text.

There now remain for discussion those tests of authenticity which may be applied in an attempt to determine whether the existing text of a writ—in those cases where it seems probable that a grant was actually made—was issued by the clerks of the king's secretariat, or if the copy is a later one, whether it is an unaltered copy of an authentic writ so issued. The value of seals as a criterion of authenticity is limited, for seals could be forged ; on the other hand, in the case of Campbell Charter xxi. 5 (no. 33), a perfectly genuine seal still remains attached to a document which has evidently been tampered with, and which is not in its existing form authentic. The general appearance of a writ produced in the king's writing office could be, and was, on occasion, imitated in such details as the size and shape of the parchment and the method of appending the seal. When the matter of handwriting is considered, a number of difficulties may arise. It is clear from the reference in Domesday Book to a writ alleged to be forged (see p. 105) that the alteration or fabrication of a writ may have taken place before 1086 ; and further, from the existence of two copies of the (authentic) Perton writ (no. 96) of Westminster Abbey (with slight differences in handwriting and in linguistic forms), it is evident (as other considerations also indicate) that writs of the Confessor were being worked over not long after their date of issue.[1] But when one is attempting to discover whether a given writ was produced in the king's writing office before the death of the Confessor on 5 January 1066, or in some other place a few days, or a few weeks, or a few months, or a few years later, difficulties are likely to arise from the fact that in so limited a period there is no likelihood of the development of strongly marked differences in handwriting. Again, attempts to date the hands of comparatively short periods, like the reigns of Cnut and the Confessor, are rendered difficult by the fact that hands of the same date may vary in the degree of development attained. And further, the person whose handwriting may have been taken as a basis for comparison may have been for a long period engaged

---

[1] The majority of the writs which have come down to us written on strips of parchment seem, if normal conditions are assumed, to have been written before the end of the eleventh century ; some are of earlier date, but none of these texts (from its content) is of earlier date than the reign of the Confessor.

on the writing of texts, and conclusions based on the evidence of the handwriting may therefore be in some degree illusory. If writs in identical handwriting for different recipients had been preserved, it would have been reasonable to conclude that the documents were probably authentic products of the royal scriptorium ; but no such case exists. For these reasons the criterion of handwriting cannot be decisive on points of authenticity, and although the apparent date of the handwriting has been given for writs printed here, other factors must also be taken into consideration. Cases arise for instance where the linguistic evidence corroborates that of the handwriting. Both combine to show that the Rutland writ (no. 94) belongs to a period later than King Edward's reign in spite of the fact that a seal taken from a genuine or a forged matrix of the Confessor is appended *sur simple queue* to the writ. F. Liebermann is reported by Neufeldt [1] to have expressed the view that the Ickworth writ, no. 80, was an ' original ' rather than a copy, ' on account of the old seal ' (' wegen des alten Siegels '), a dangerous assumption, since seals could be forged. The Ickworth writ is in fact spurious, and the seal cannot therefore have been appended to it by the clerks of the Confessor's secretariat. But Liebermann's view that the second text of the Perton writ (no. 96) is a copy of the first can be accepted. Three texts were con- sidered by Liebermann to be copies on the assumption of scribal errors : the Lessness writ, no. 76, because of the appearance in the text of ' mid eallum *ðæra* (for *ðæm*) ðingum ' ; the Chalkhill writ, no. 77, because of Liebermann's mistaken notion that in this text *Cealchylle*, ' Chalkhill ', is an error for *Cealchyðe*, ' Chelsea ' (see p. 497), and also because of the supposed ' Fehler ' ' be *fulre* (for *fullan*) wite ' ; the Wormley writ, no. 90, because of the occurrence of ' be *minre* geleafan and be *minre* unnan ', where *minum* might in both cases have been expected. But in these three cases the conclusion that the texts are copies and not ' originals ' can be arrived at on the dating of the handwriting, which belongs to the latter part of the eleventh century, or more probably, in the case of no. 77, to the early twelfth century. The important question of authenticity does not seem to have been considered by Liebermann. Of these three writs only the Wormley writ, no. 90, is probably a later copy of an authentic writ of King Edward.

With the great majority of writs such questions do not arise, for the texts are obviously copies. Some have been entered in blank spaces in manuscripts, some have been copied into cartularies. A large number are inscribed on the *Cartæ Antiquæ*, Charter, Patent,

[1] *Zur Sprache des Urkundenbuches von Westminster* (Diss. Rostock, 1907), 4.

and Confirmation Rolls. The earliest of these copies date from the early eleventh century ; the copy of no. 63 was probably made in the time of King Æthelred II, but copies of writs were being made by antiquaries and others as late as the eighteenth century. To these documents the considerations of outward appearance which have been discussed in connection with the writs on single strips of parchment cannot of course apply. In the opinion of Kemble (who left out of account such matters as sealing, handwriting, and orthography), almost the only test of authenticity which can be successfully applied to texts in the vernacular,[1] is that of ' anachronism '.[2] The most obvious case of anachronism would be the introduction into a text of some person whose dates were incompatible with the supposed date of the document. An instance of such a chronological dislocation appears in no. 10, where Ælfgar, who did not become earl of East Anglia till 1051 at the earliest, is brought into conjunction with Grimketel, who held the East Anglian see for a short time within the period 1043–44. An anachronism of a different kind is the appearance in a list of privileges alleged to have been granted to Chertsey Abbey by the Confessor of *morthsliht*, the *murdrum*-fine for the secret slaying of a Frenchman, which was not introduced into England until after the Norman Conquest. The value of this criterion is obvious, and other cases of anachronism in writs will be discussed below.

Another criterion on which stress was laid by Kemble was that of ' genuine forms ', by which he obviously means the characteristic features of Anglo-Saxon accidence and syntax. ' Instruments in the vernacular tongue,' he says, ' bear along with themselves the surest test of authenticity '. ' The language,' he continues, is ' of very various degrees of impurity, but the genuine forms are not to be mistaken, and cannot be unrecognized, in spite of the careless transcribers of monastic chartularies.' This statement, although in general valid, ignores the fact that documents might be tampered with or even fabricated within the Anglo-Saxon period itself, or during that period subsequent to the Norman Conquest till late in the twelfth century (at Winchester), during which Anglo-Saxon was still a familiar form of writing. In such cases there might be little or nothing in the syntax or accidence of a text to bear witness to interpolation or fabrication. But cases do occur where suspicion is aroused by some clear departure from normal usage, as for example in the Wolverhampton writ (no. 114) in the name of the Confessor. And instances illustrating the importance of ' genuine

---

[1] For the (different) criteria which can be applied to Latin charters, see *Crawford Charters*, Preface, viii.

[2] *Codex Diplomaticus*, iv, p. vi.

forms ' as a criterion of authenticity are also readily forthcoming, as in the case of a writ of St. Edmund's Bury (no. 9), the authenticity of which has been doubted, but which receives support from the appearance in the text of ' genuine forms ' which have not been smoothed out by the transcriber.

Of all the criteria that can be applied to test the authenticity of an Anglo-Saxon writ, the most valuable is probably that of conformity to a general pattern. By the eleventh century the writ, an instrument of immemorial antiquity, had become formalised and so in a sense artificial. The writs of Edward the Confessor are in general cut-and-dried products, more or less in common form, or at least conforming to definite types. Not only in content, but also in phraseology and structure, the writs of Anglo-Saxon kings, with the exception of those that are purely narrative, follow certain clearly marked patterns, and are, with few exceptions, constructed by the use of constantly-recurring formulas. Information as to the history of an estate may be lacking, the background of a grant may be obscure, the evidence may be conflicting ; extensive modernisation of linguistic forms may have taken place ; or the writ may be extant only in a Latin version. But by applying this test, it is often possible to distinguish between those writs that are probably authentic, and those that are not. The awkward transitions and clumsy constructions of a Ramsey writ (no. 61), for instance, mark it out as a forgery when it is brought into comparison with other writs. Even in Latin versions the characteristic phraseology of the Edwardian writ frequently shines through ; we may take as examples the Latin version of a Hereford writ (no. 50), or of a Coventry writ (no. 46), the phraseology of both of which is testimony to the fact that they are translations from authentic Anglo-Saxon writs. The writs that are not royal writs are of course wider in their range, and freer in construction, and to them this criterion does not in the same degree apply.

Difficult problems arise when one is confronted with two or more closely-related writs constructed on the same pattern, in favour of the same recipient, differing perhaps only in their length, or exhibiting only apparently insignificant variations in linguistic forms, spelling, and the like. Did it often happen—did it indeed ever happen—that the same text was issued by an Anglo-Saxon king more than once with only minor differences ? Such closely-related writs have in fact come down to us from only three houses : Chertsey (nos. 40–1), Westminster (nos. 81–3, 88–9, 99–101, 105–6, and possibly 103–4), and Winchester (nos. 109–10). No general rules can be laid down for the consideration of these texts and each will be considered on its merits. Differences arising in the text in the course of transmission through careless mistakes and omissions, capricious and irresponsible interpolations, trivial embellishments— these are possibilities which will have to be considered, but will only rarely meet the case. The general conclusion would seem to be that in some, if not the majority of these writs, the ' improved ' version of the text, in cases where one is more advantageous than another, has probably been deliberately produced by or for the community for the benefit of which the writ purports to have been issued.

AUTHENTIC AND NON-AUTHENTIC WRITS

When those texts have been eliminated the authenticity of which is not virtually certain, how many authentic writs remain which can with reasonable certainty be considered to have been written in their earliest extant form before the close of the eleventh century ? Such texts, which of course afford material for the study of the language of the time, can be divided (normal conditions being assumed) into the following classes :—

(1) Writs of the reign of Æthelred II and of Cnut in handwriting which may be contemporary or almost contemporary with their contents : nos. 27, 28, 29, 30, 63.

(2) Writs of the Confessor's reign in handwriting which may be contemporary with their contents : nos. 11, 24, 33 (up to *beon*), 55, 96 (P), 115. No. 81 may possibly belong here, but more probably it belongs to the following group.

(3) Writs in handwriting of the second half of the eleventh century : nos. 82, 96 (R).

(4) Writs in handwriting of the late eleventh century : nos. 35, 90, 94, 97. The authenticity of no. 26 is probably sufficiently well assured for it to be placed in this group.

A rough-and-ready classification of the remaining writs will now be attempted, but it must of course be realised that such a classification can be no more than tentative :—

(5) Writs, written on single pieces of parchment in hands ranging (normal conditions being assumed) from the second half of the eleventh century to the early twelfth, which should not in my opinion be taken at their face value : nos. 45, 77, 93, 98, 101.

(6) Writs in my opinion probably authentic, but extant in handwriting dating from c. 1100 onwards :—

(*a*) In *English* of various periods with a greater or smaller degree of modification (' modernisation ') of linguistic forms at the hands of transcribers : nos. 1, 2, 6, 7, 9, 12, 13, 14, 15, 16, 17, 18, 19, 20, 21, 22, 23, 25, 38, 39, 43, 44, 47, 49 (in ' lingua Anglicana '), 51, 64, 65, 66, 68, 69, 70, 71, 72, 83, 87, 88, 95, 99, 103 (or perhaps belonging to Group 7a below), 107 (or perhaps belonging to Group 7a below), 108, 116, 117, 118, 120, 121.

(b) In *Latin* : nos. 3, 46, 48 (or perhaps belonging to Group 7b below), 50 (although mistranslated), 56, 57, 58, 60, 119.

(7) Writs which in my opinion should not be taken at their face value (though they may nevertheless be based on authentic writs on the relevant theme), extant in handwriting dating from c. 1100 onwards.

(a) In *English* of various periods with a greater or smaller degree of modification (' modernisation ') of linguistic forms at the hands of transcribers : nos. 4, 5, 8, 34, 40, 41, 42, 52, 53, 54, 59, 61, 62, 73, 75, 78, 79, 84, 85, 86, 89, 91, 92, 100, 102, 103 (or perhaps belonging to Group 6a above), 104, 105, 106, 107 (or perhaps belonging to Group 6a above), 109, 110, 111, 112.

(b) In *Latin* : nos. 31, 32, 37, 48 (or perhaps belonging to Group 6b above), 59.

(8) Texts which cannot be accepted as evidence of the issue of independent writs on the main subject with which they are respectively concerned, and which constitute fabrications of various kinds :—

(a) In *English* : nos. 10, 33 (after *beon*), 67, 74, 76, 80, 114. Edwin's letter (no. 113) can be conveniently placed here but stands of course outside the normal categories.

(b) In *Latin* : no. 36.

PART II

DISCUSSION AND TEXTS

ABBOTSBURY

Everything encourages the belief that the two writs of King Edward the Confessor which have come down to us in an *inspeximus* charter in favour of the monastery of St. Peter at Abbotsbury,[1] Dorset, are copies of authentic writs of that king, the orthography of which has been only slightly altered in the course of transmission ; e.g. *þegenes, cipe, egen* in no. 1, *ehta, gewrhte, geforewird, elcan,* in no. 2. So far as the main announcement is concerned, both belong to Group 5 of the Confessor's writs (see Introduction, p. 65). No. 1 announces a grant by the Confessor to his housecarl Urk of the SHORE OVER AGAINST HIS LAND (presumably at Abbotsbury, where the shore is now part of the formidable shingle ridge known as Chesil Bank). No. 2 announces that King Edward has given leave to his ' man ' [2] Tole, Urk's widow—who would seem to have been in the position of those persons of whom Domesday Book records that they could not give or sell their land without their lord's permission—TO BEQUEATH HER LAND AND POSSESSIONS to the monastery at Abbotsbury that she and her husband had founded. The king declares in this writ that he himself will be the protector and guardian of the monastery and its property, and that none of the things granted to it by Urk and Tole are to be alienated from it. The protection thus extended to the monastery was continued to it by William I, according to a vernacular writ, dated by Davis 1066–78, in which the Conqueror declares that the abbot of Abbotsbury and

---

[1] For this foundation, see *Monasticon Anglicanum,* iii, 52–61, VCH *Dorset,* ii, 48–53. The only register of the monastery known to have existed is said to have been destroyed with the house of the Strangeways in the Civil War. Urk and his wife (see nos. 1, 2) are traditionally supposed to have founded the monastery, but in the absence of contemporary documents, the circumstances are obscure, and it is uncertain whether monks were introduced there in the reign of Cnut, or of Edward the Confessor ; see *Mon. Angl., ut supra,* for the surviving sources. To M. R. James (*Abbeys* (London, 1925), 71) the records seemed to indicate that in 1026 Urk put in secular canons and in 1044 substituted Benedictine monks from Cerne, and that Urk was the real founder, ' whatever may be the probability of some earlier ill-defined community having existed on this site '.

[2] OE *mann* means primarily a human being, irrespective of age or sex. OE *mann* in the sense of a person (of either sex) who is under the authority of another, is used in a specialised sense. For instances of women tenants described as *homo* in Domesday, see p. 427 below.

the community and their lands and men and everything pertaining to St. Peter's, Abbotsbury, are all under his own guardianship and full protection under God (*on minre munde 7 on minan fullan gehealde under God*), with as full rights as the abbey possessed in King Edward's time ; grants to the abbot his sake and soke within town and without, toll and team and infangenetheof, and forbids any man to do them wrong.[1] But in spite of the extension of the royal protection to the abbey by the Confessor and William I, the monks complained in 1086 (DB i. 78) that a hide of land belonging to the manor of Abbotsbury (assessed for the payment of geld at 21 hides), which had been assigned to their sustenance (*ad victum monachorum*) in the time of King Edward, had been taken from them by the Norman sheriff Hugo fitzGrip, and that they had also been deprived by the same sheriff of a virgate of land in Portisham, and these lands his widow still retained.[2]

(1)

King Edward declares that his housecarl Urk is to have his shore over against his land and everything driven to his shore.   1053–58

(Ch. R. 8 Edw. II, m. 3, no. 5)

1   + Eadward kingc gret Alfwold .b. 7 Harold eorl. 7 Alfred scyrgereuan 7 ealle mine þegenes on Dorsætan freondlice. 7 ic ciþe eow. þ Urk min huskarl habbe his strand eall forn egen hys age land ouer eall wel 7 freo[l]slic[e] . upp of sæ. 7 ut on sæ.
5 7 eall þ to hys strande gedryuen hys be minum fullan bebode.

The ' thorn ' (þ) and ' wyn ' (= w) of Anglo-Saxon script are reproduced in the MS., but the letters are indistinguishable in form. Several representations of earlier ʒ, arising out of (earlier) confusion with forms of s.   1. kyng M.
2. myne M.   3. cyþe M.   4. MS *probably* age, *with twisted* g (*or* s) *on line* ; ase M.   4. freolslice M ; *in MS final* e *invisible at edge of roll.*

---

[1] Davis, *Regesta*, no. 108.   The text (printed in *Mon. Angl.* iii, 56, no. vi) is possibly corrupt.   It is tempting to suggest that *furþ Orc* (? ' (in the) life (of) Orc ') in the sentence :   *swa full 7 swa forð swa hit þeder in furð Orc leg on Eadwardes dæge kyncges mines meges* is an interpolation, for the syntax is complete without it ; for the phrase *þeder* (*þider*) *inne leg,* cf. no. 8.   Moreover it seems unlikely that the rights confirmed to the abbey by the Conqueror would be limited to those possessed by the abbey in Urk's lifetime, for the Confessor's writ printed here makes it clear that it was only after the death of Urk and Tole that the abbey was to come into full possession of their lands and property.
[2] For the property of the abbey, see further, p. 427.

Translation

King Edward sends friendly greetings to Bishop Ælfwold and Earl Harold and Alfred the sheriff and all my thegns in Dorset. And I inform you that Urk my housecarl is to have his shore, all that is over against his own land, everywhere completely and freely, up from the sea and out into the sea, and all that is driven to his shore, by my full command.

(2)

King Edward declares that Tole his ' man ', Urk's widow, has his full permission to bequeath her lands and possessions to St. Peter's, Abbotsbury.   1058–66

(Ch. R. 8 Edw. II, m. 3, no. 5)

+ Eadwar[d] kyng gret Heremann .ꝥ. 7 Harold eorl 7 ealle 1
mine þegenas on Dorsætan freondlice. 7 ic cyðe eow ꝥ hit is min
fulla unna ꝥ Tole min mann Urkes lafe ꝥ heo becweðe hire land
7 ehta in to Sēe Petre æt Abbodesbyrig swa swa hire leofest sy be
minan fullan geleafan swa full 7 swa forð swa þa forewirda ær 5
gewrhte wæran ꝥ hit sceolde æfter heora begra dage hire 7 Urkes
hire hlafordes for heora sawle gan in to þam haligan mynstre. Nu
wille ic ꝥ heora cwide stande swa swa hit geforewird wes. on godre
manna gewitnesse þe þar wið weran. 7 ic wille ꝥ swilc freols beo
in to þam mynstre swilce is in to elcan oðre þær þe best is on eallan 10
þingan. 7 ic me sylf wille beon geheald. 7 mund þer ofer. 7 ofer
þa are þe þar inn to hirð. 7 ic nelle nanan menn geþafian ꝥ þar
geutige ænig þæra þinga þæs þe hig þider inn gedon habbað.

See *no. 1* for *note on script.*   2. ys M.   3. hyre M.
6. geworhte M.   9. wið] wid MS, M ; *but cf. also nos. 62, 69, which*
have mid(e).   12. hyrð M.   12. ꝥ] þe MS, M.

Translation

King Edward sends friendly greetings to Bishop Herman and Earl Harold and all my thegns in Dorset.   And I inform you that Tole, my ' man ', Urk's widow, has my full permission to bequeath her land and possessions to St. Peter's at Abbotsbury, as best pleases her, with my full consent, as fully and completely as it was arranged by the agreements previously made, that it should after the death of both of them—her death and that of Urk her lord—pass into the possession of the holy monastery for [the benefit of] their souls. Now my will is that their bequest shall remain in force in accordance with the agreement(s) made with the cognisance of good men who were present. And my will is that the monastery shall enjoy as much freedom as is enjoyed by any other where such freedom is enjoyed to the fullest extent in all things. And I myself will be protector and guardian over it and over the property that belongs to it. And I will not permit anyone to alienate from it any of the things that they (Urk and Tole) have bestowed upon it.

ABINGDON

The Latin writ of Siward, formerly abbot of Abingdon, and the two Anglo-Saxon writs attributed to King Edward the Confessor, that have come down to us in the thirteenth-century cartularies [1] of the Abbey of Abingdon [2] in Berkshire, appear to be of varying degrees of authenticity. The state of affairs disclosed by BISHOP SIWARD'S WRIT (no. 3) is cited by J. H. Round [3] as an illustration of the difficulty that might be encountered by a monastery wishing, after the prescribed term, to recover lands leased out for several lives. The Abingdon chronicler informs us that King Edmund in 943 granted 10 *mansas* at Leckhampstead to his faithful *minister* Eadric, who bequeathed the estate to the abbey.[4] Then in the time of Cnut one Brihtmund obtained from the abbot of Abingdon a lease of this estate for three lives (of which his widow and his son Brihtnoth were the second and third), on condition that after this time it should be freely restored to the monks. But on the death of Brihtnoth,

[1] F. M. Stenton (*The Early History of the Abbey of Abingdon*, Reading, 1913), 4 ff., has shown that MS. Cotton Claudius C. ix (from which the vernacular texts printed here are taken) is an early thirteenth-century transcript of a manuscript written before 1170 (and perhaps before 1164) by a monk who was an inmate of the abbey of Abingdon before 1117. The other cartulary, MS. Cotton Claudius B. vi, is 'a revised and improved copy' made about fifty years later.

[2] For the foundation and early history of this house, see Stenton, *ut supra*. King Eadred is said to have granted the monastery, then destitute and deserted, to St. Æthelwold, the monastic reformer, who introduced there the Benedictine Rule. The monastery was endowed with lands, and a church built, dedicated to St. Mary. See the ' Vita S. Æthelwoldi ', printed in the *Chronicon Monasterii de Abingdon* (hereafter referred to as the *Chron. Abingdon*), ed. J. Stevenson, R.S. ii. 255 ff. ; Modern English rendering, S. H. Gem, *An Anglo-Saxon Abbot, Ælfric of Eynsham* (Edinburgh, 1912), 166–80.

[3] VCH *Berks.* i. 298.

[4] *Chron. Abingdon*, i. 103, 477, K. 1147. A grant in similar terms by King Eadwig (*ibid.* i. 476, K. 1217) is incomplete and without witnesses.

the third life, his brother, Brihtwine, obtained from Siward, then abbot, before 1043, an extension of the lease for his own life, and subsequently claimed that Siward had given him the land in inheritance (*protestando sibi suisque de terra ipsa jus hereditarium concessum*). On hearing of this claim, Siward, no longer abbot of Abingdon but coadjutor to Archbishop Eadsige, set out in the letter printed here his version of these transactions.[1]   But the matter was not settled until some years later, when Abbot Ordric, having with the help of Earl Harold compelled Brihtwine to give up the titledeed (*landboc*) of the estate, brought a suit for the recovery of the land at a meeting of the witan and won his case ; and Bishop Herman, visiting Abingdon not long after, pronounced sentence of excommunication against those who should henceforth deprive the monks of Abingdon of the land at Leckhampstead.[2]   The moderation of the tone of Siward's letter and the modest nature of its claims are arguments in favour of its authenticity.   It is a reasonable assumption that the Latin version that has come down to us was translated from a writ in English addressed by Siward to the shirecourt.

The first of the two writs for Abbot Ordric, relating to a grant of SAKE AND SOKE AND OTHER RIGHTS (no. 4), is not authentic as it stands ; like the writ following (no. 5) it departs from ' common form ' in the use in the address of ' his ' (' his bishops and his abbots and his earls ') in place of the customary ' my ', and moreover it omits the customary *freondlice*.   In no. 5 the alteration may have originated with the copyist of MS. Cott. Claud. C. ix : in his text *mine* has been erased, and *his* written over the erasure.   Moreover the fact that in no. 4 the sign for *and* before ' his abbots ' is similar to the sign employed in the Latin version, but different from that employed elsewhere in the Anglo-Saxon text of this writ, seems to suggest the possibility that the text has been tampered with.   But the real problem here is to determine whether this text, which purports to announce a grant by the Confessor of sake and soke, toll, team and infangenetheof, hamsocn, grithbreach, and foresteall, to Abbot Ordric, over his own land, is in all other respects an authentic copy of a writ of King Edward.   There is nothing in this list of privileges to excite suspicion as to its authenticity, on general grounds ; we may compare no. 38 (certainly authentic) where these privileges and more are said to have been granted to St. Augustine's. But if we accept the testimony of a statement in the historical

---

[1] *Ibid.* i. 457–9.   The chronicler adds : Hæc quamquam ab episcopo sint testimonio prolata, vir ille tamen tanto calluit ingenio, ut ad Ordrici abbatis . . . illius inde dominatus excuti nequiverit tempora.

[2] *Ibid.* i. 475.

account of the abbots of Abingdon (headed *De Abbatibus Abbendoniæ*) [1] in Cott. Vitell. A. xiii, we shall have to suppose that the list of privileges enumerated in no. 4 has been enlarged to the advantage of this house—over and above what was actually granted to the abbey by the Confessor. This history tells us that the Confessor exempted the abbey of Abingdon from toll, [2] and granted to it sake and soke, team and infangenetheof. The history of the abbots is a late authority, and the author of this passage has interpreted these terms in his own way :—

' Confirmavit rex Eduuardus monasterio Abbendoniæ ut nemo per totam Angliam in omni mercatu vel in nundinis quicquid ipsi [emerint *supplied by editor*] teloneum ab eis exquirat. Concessit etiam et confirmavit Sake (id est, conflictus) et Socne (id est assaltus) et Them (id est compellationem) et Infangethof (id est fur in dominio suo captus).'

It would not be safe to accept as authentic the interpretations of these terms given in this passage ; but it seems reasonable to assume that the customary formula : ' sake and soke, toll, team and infangenetheof ' lies behind it, and was to be found in the source from which it was derived. And it is on the whole easier to believe that the privileges which he does not include in his list, namely hamsocn, grithbreach and foresteall, have been added in the reputed writ of the Confessor, than it is to suppose that they were omitted by the compiler of this passage cited from the Abingdon history. The fact that these three forfeitures of hamsocn, grithbreach and foresteall, are not explicitly mentioned in the extant Abingdon writs of the early Norman kings, is not decisive on this point, for these texts are rarely specific : they often grant to the abbot and monastery their *consuetudines* [3] (' customs ') as in the time of King Edward (and in later grants, of King William I and II). For instance, in a writ of c. 1071 of William I in favour of Abbot Æthelhelm of Abingdon, a grant is announced of :—

' omnes consuetudines terrarum suarum, quæcunque jacent in ecclesia prædicta, ubicumque eas habeat, in burgo vel extra burgum, secundum quod abbas iste Athelellmus poterit demonstrare, per breve vel cartam, ecclesiam Sanctæ Mariæ de Abbendona et prædecessorem suum, eas consuetudines habuisse dono regis Eadwardi.' [4]

---

[1] *Chron. Abingdon*, ii. 281. On this text, see Stenton, *ut supra*, 1 f., where it is stated that the text is written in a hand of cent. xiii, and apparently for the use of the Abingdon cell of Colne in Essex.

[2] On such exemptions, see p. 252.

[3] On *consuetudines*, see p. 451.

[4] *Ibid.* ii. 1–2 ; Davis, *Regesta*, no. 49. On Abbot Æthelhelm's predecessor Ealdred, who incurred the enmity of the Conqueror and died in custody, see *Chron. Abingdon*, i. 485 f., ii. 283. Also D. Knowles, *The Monastic Order*, 104.

But it is noteworthy that in the writ-charter of Henry I—seemingly the first surviving post-Conquest grant for Abingdon in which these three forfeitures appear—hamsocn, grithbreach, and foresteall stand apart from sake and soke, toll, team and infangenetheof.

In this charter addressed generally in which the king announces the appointment of Vincentius (1121–30) as abbot of Abingdon, after the passage: ' Sciatis me dedisse et concessisse Vincentio abbati abbatiam de Abbendona cum omnibus rebus abbatiæ ipsi pertinentibus, et volo et firmiter præcipio ut bene et in pace et quiete et honorifice et libere teneat *cum saca et soca et tol et team et infangenethef* in burgo et extra burgum,' the text continues: ' *hamsocnam vero et grithbriche et forestal* super propriam terram abbatiæ ei concedo sicut aliquis antecessorum suorum unquam melius et quietius et honorificentius et liberius tenuit cum omnibus aliis consuetudinibus suis '.[1]

One cannot help suspecting that the appearance of the three forfeitures in the reputed writ of the Confessor is in some way connected with their mention in the text of Henry I. But in any case, on the combined evidence of these passages it seems at least doubtful whether the three forfeitures of hamsocn, grithbreach, and foresteall, were granted to the abbey of Abingdon by King Edward the Confessor, and the possibility must be considered that the writ in the name of the Confessor in which they appear may represent the alteration and interpolation of a genuine writ issued by him for the abbey of Abingdon, which on other grounds also would appear to have been tampered with.[2] It is less likely that it is in its entirety a post-Conquest fabrication, for its linguistic colouring is that of late West Saxon, and the phraseology is similar to that of writs which we have reason to believe authentic.

There is also reason for doubting the authenticity in its present form of the second writ for Abbot Ordric (no. 5), which purports to grant to the abbot and community the HUNDRED OF HORMER, that is to say, the hundred court and the profits of justice arising therefrom. The hundred court was the ordinary criminal court in the pre-Conquest period.[3] In Maitland's view the grant of a hundred involved the right to hold the hundred court, to take the profits of

---

[1] *Chron. Abingdon*, ii. 162.

[2] See above, p. 123.

[3] On the territorial divisions called hundreds, which formed the basis of the administration of justice, see Liebermann, *Gesetze*, ii. 516, s.v. ' Hundred ', and the references there, and H. M. Cam, *Liberties and Communities in Medieval England* (Cambridge, 1944), *passim*. For *hundred* used interchangeably with *hundredes gemot*, see II Cnut, 17: *Sece man his hundred. Sece man hundredes gemot* etc.' ' Everyone shall attend his hundred (court). Everyone shall attend the hundred court ', etc. See also on the hundred, Chadwick, *Anglo-Saxon Institutions*, 239 ff. For a different view of the hundred's jurisdiction from that expressed here, see Hurnard, *Eng. Hist. Rev.* lxiv (1949), 444 ff. See also p. 53, n. 2, above.

jurisdiction within the hundred, and to demand the attendance at the hundred court of residents within the hundred.[1]   The grant of hundredal soke was explained by W. J. Corbett to mean that the king's rights within the hundred were transferred to the grantees, who would thenceforth be entitled to receive the fines due from persons convicted of committing crimes within the area.   Corbett supposed this to mean that such persons when charged with any crime would have to appear before officials appointed by the grantees.[2]   In Liebermann's opinion the grant of the hundred court involved the right to appoint the presiding officer and to take the profits.[3]   Dr. J. Goebel, while accepting Liebermann's view, is reluctant to suppose that ' the control and direction of procedure is a matter of private command '.[4]   Dr. Cam has observed to me that in so far as routine matters were concerned, the effect of a grant of hundredal jurisdiction would be to put the grantee in the place of the king.   The grant of a hundred did not of course involve the grant of all the land within the hundred, only of the royal rights, especially of the profits of justice.   The lands of the hundred of Hormer had come previously into the possession of the abbey of Abingdon, but it was not until the Confessor's time that the abbey was granted hundredal jurisdiction.

The hundred of Hormer had long been associated with the abbey of Abingdon ; the several villages of the district had almost all come into the possession of the abbey in the second half of the tenth century ; and in 1086 all the land in the hundred belonged to the abbey.[5]   That the grant of the hundred court of Hormer and of the profits of jurisdiction was actually made to the abbey of Abingdon by King Edward the Confessor, there seems no reason to doubt. He was not the first English king to delegate a hundred for judicial purposes to a religious house ; a number of these traced back their claim to private hundreds to grants by Edward the Elder, Eadred, Eadwig, or Edgar.[6]   Nor is the alleged grant of the hundred of Hormer by Edward the Confessor to the abbey of Abingdon an

---

[1] See *Domesday Book and Beyond*, especially 84–97.

[2] *Cambridge Medieval History*, iii. 376–7.

[3] *Gesetze* ii. 461, s.v. ' Gerichtsbarkeit '.

[4] *Felony and Misdemeanor* (1937), i. 342–3.   For a discussion of Goebel's position see H. M. Cam, *American Historical Review*, xliii (1938), 583–7. Dr. Cam has pointed out to me that there can be little doubt that in some, if not all, cases the grant of a hundred involved the right to receive certain customary dues in addition to the profits of justice ; on these see Carl Stephenson, *Eng. Hist. Rev.* xxxix (1924), 161–74 ; N. Neilson, ' Customary Rents ', *Oxford Studies in Social and Legal History*, ch. v, vi ; E. B. Demarest, *Eng. Hist. Rev.* xxxiii (1918), 62 ff., xxxv (1920), 78 ff., xxxviii (1923), 161 ff.

[5] Stenton, *op. cit.* 47–8 ; see also pp. 129, 429 below.

[6] See Cam, *Liberties and Communities*, 59, n. 2, 3.

isolated one.   Other religious houses were granted by him hundredal jurisdiction in other shires.   Undoubted instances recorded in Anglo-Saxon writs are the grant of the eight and a half Suffolk hundreds to Bury (nos. 9, 10 (spurious), 18, 24), and of Clackclose hundred or hundred and a half to Ramsey Abbey (nos. 60, 61 (spurious in existing form)).   The grant of Godley hundred to Chertsey Abbey is recorded only in writs of dubious authenticity (nos. 41, 42), but the grant may none the less have been made. Other sources record pre-Conquest grants of hundredal jurisdiction elsewhere.[1]   There is therefore no difficulty on general grounds in supposing that Hormer hundred was actually granted to the abbey of Abingdon by King Edward the Confessor.   But is the writ under discussion relating to the Confessor's grant of Hormer hundred an authentic writ of that king ?   It is not improbable that the main body of the text, from *ic cyðe eow* to *andwealde* (ll. 2–5) is derived from an authentic writ of the Confessor, for the vocabulary employed is in several respects similar to that of the reputed writ of the Confessor concerning the hundred of Godley (no. 42).[2]   But the writ concludes with a precept that no sheriff or *motgerefa* shall have there any jurisdiction or court without the abbot's own command and permission.   This passage is rejected by Goebel[3] as ' undoubtedly a forgery ', on the ground that, as far as can be ascertained, neither William nor Rufus gave the abbey of Abingdon a grant or confirmation with a *ne intromittat* clause or anything approaching it, and that the first *ne intromittat* clause for Abingdon

[1] On the combined evidence of charters and Domesday Book the three Malmesbury hundreds were granted to Malmesbury Abbey by the Confessor (K. 817, not authentic as it stands, but possibly founded on genuine material, cf. Davis, *Regesta*, no. 136, DB i. 66–7).   Dr. Cam has suggested to me that in some cases where charters are suspicious or non-existent, Domesday proves the actual exercise of hundredal jurisdiction in 1066.   She computes (*loc. cit.* n. 5) that in 1066 there were private hundreds in twenty counties of England, and that there is strong presumption of the existence of at least 130 private hundreds by 1086.

[2] Compare *andweald* and *onweald*, *frigelice* and *freo*, *freost*.   The spelling *frigelice* for *freolice* in the former writ does not seem to be recorded in the dictionaries, though *frig-* appears of course in the oblique cases of *freo*, and forms like *frigscipe* (*Eng. Hist. Rev.* xi (1896), 735) in late texts.   Parallels can be found in Westminster writs (see p. 114) for the unusual genders of *hired* (l. 3), usually masculine, but here provided with a neuter definite article, and *andweald* (l. 5), usually masculine or neuter, but here qualified by *agenre*, with a feminine ending *-re* (but the *-re* might be due to the neighbouring *hire* and *agenre*).   But these Westminster texts are extant only in post-Conquest copies.   On the whole, the words which nos. 5 and 42 have in common are probably not numerous enough or rare enough to prove the theory of a common origin in the king's scriptorium.   I find it difficult to believe that ' in perpetuity ' is authentic (line 5).

[3] See *loc. cit.* i. 355, n. 62.

is in a charter of Henry I.[1] That is not to say that exclusionary clauses do not appear elsewhere already in the Anglo-Saxon period. Already in the time of Cnut we find the clause, in an authentic writ (no. 28) : (' I forbid) anyone to take anything therefrom except himself and his officers '. The same clause appears also in nos. 31, 33, 34, 36, in Anglo-Saxon and Latin, but these are doubtful or spurious. A fuller exclusionary clause appears in no. 111, a probably authentic writ of the Confessor : ' none of my officers shall have any jurisdiction over those who dwell therein, nor anyone in any matter, except the community and those whom they appoint as their officers '.[2] But the background of the passage in the writ in the name of the Confessor purporting to exclude from the hundred of Hormer sheriff and *motgerefa* is a dubious one. Goebel rightly observes that there is no such clause in Abingdon writs of William I and II.[3] Further, the passage itself as it appears in the Confessor's Hormer writ for Abingdon seems to differ linguistically from the remainder of the text. The absence of termination in *æni* (for *ænige*), if not attributable to scribal carelessness, and still more markedly in *agen* (for *agenum*), stands in strong contrast to the full terminations in *ealle his þegenas*, in the address. Moreover the transition, made by *and swa þæt*, between this passage and what precedes it, is awkwardly contrived. Whether the occasion for the confection of the exclusionary clause (if as seems probable it is not

[1] The *ne intromittat* clause prohibits outside interference in the privileged area. Goebel (i. 355) cites as a parallel the *absque introitu* clause of Frankish charters. An exclusionary clause (' to be free from every due both to king and ealdorman and reeve, from every service small or great ') appearing in a late ninth-century charter of Ealdorman Æthelred of Mercia (B. 551 = Harmer, *English Historical Documents of the Ninth and Tenth Centuries*, 21), and cited by H. M. Cam, *Local Government in Francia and England*, 115, as possibly corresponding with the Frankish *absque introitu*, is in Goebel's opinion ' too rare to form any sort of precedent '. But compare B. 432, 436, 487, 509.

[2] Goebel suggests that ' a first tentative employment of the *absque introitu* occurs in a few precepts of the Confessor '. Rejecting the Abingdon writ of the Confessor under discussion, he cites the Latin version of the spurious writ no. 34, and K. 907. The latter is an Ely diploma of the Confessor, drawn up in the form of a general confirmation, without date and witnesses. It contains the clauses : ' sine aliqua exceptione saecularis uel aecclesticae iusticiae ' ; and ' neque episcopus neque comes neque alicuius exactionis minister sine licentia uel aduocatione abbatis et fratrum ullo modo se praesumat intromittere '. Whatever may be the source of these passages, it seems unlikely that this Ely diploma is authentic.

[3] For William I, see p. 124 above. For William II, see *Chron. Abingdon*, ii. 17 = Davis, *Regesta*, no. 289. There is no exclusionary clause in two short writs of Henry I relating to Hormer hundred (*Chron. Abingdon*, ii. 115). On the bearing of *ne intromittat* clauses in the Norman period, see Goebel i. 393 f., S. Painter, *Studies in the History of the English Feudal Barony* (1943), 109 ff.

authentic) arose in the reign of Henry I, or at some earlier date,[1] it seems likely that the clause in question was in some way connected with attempts made after the Conquest to deprive the abbot of his rights in Hormer hundred, of which we learn from the Abingdon chronicler. Some such attempts seem to have been frustrated without difficulty, ' nunc regiis litteris (i.e. royal writs), nunc qualibet alia cautela '. Among such royal writs were two short writs of Henry I, issued seemingly in consequence of attempts to gain possession of the hundred frequently (*multoties*) made by persons described as ' regis homines de Suttona juxta Abbendonam '.[2] Encroachments, not unfortunately specified—whether in the hundred of Hormer or elsewhere—upon the rights of the monks of Abingdon, had at an earlier date led to the issue of a writ addressed by William II to Peter, sheriff of Oxford, declaring that the abbot of Abingdon and his monks are to have their ' customs ' as in the days of the Confessor and William I ; a postscript adds that the sheriff is to do full right to the abbot in the matter of the sheriff's reeve and his other servants who have done wrong to the monks.[3] An attempt made at a later date to induce King Henry I to deprive Abbot Vincentius of Abingdon (1121-30) of Hormer hundred and of market rights at Abingdon led to the issue by the king of a writ-charter containing an exclusionary clause not unlike that in the Confessor's reputed Hormer writ, after the abbot, producing the *privilegium* of King Edward which was read before the king, had successfully petitioned King Henry that he would confirm it under his own seal, and had promised to pay the king the sum of 300 marks for the undisturbed and undisputed possession of Hormer hundred and of market rights at Abingdon.[4] Was this alleged *privilegium* of the abbey of Abingdon read before Henry I a diploma in the name of the Confessor, or was it a writ, possibly even the writ under discussion here ? The terminology employed does not unfortunately permit of a definite answer to this question. *Privilegium* refers to the content of the document, not its form ; the term is defined elsewhere as ' a special

[1] There is no direct evidence to support or to controvert Goebel's conjecture (i. 355, n. 62) that ' the occasion for this Saxon confection was very likely ' the writ of William I (see p. 124, n. 4), confirming customs as of Edward the Confessor. But on the whole a later date seems more probable. Grants as in the time of the Confessor are still being announced in Abingdon writs of Henry I and Henry II.

[2] *Chron. Abingdon*, ii. 114-15. In one of these writs of Henry I the hundred of Hormer is granted to the abbot : ' sicut melius habuerunt et tenuerunt in tempore Eaduuardi regis et Willielmi patris et Willielmi fratris mei ' ; in the other : ' sicut unquam antecessores sui melius habuerunt tempore patris mei et fratris mei et meo '.

[3] *Ibid.* ii. 41 = Davis, *Regesta*, no. 390, there dated 1087-97.

[4] *Chron. Abingdon*, ii. 163.

honour or peculiar freedom '.[1] King Henry I, confirming (as has been said above) the reputed *privilegium* of the Confessor for Abingdon, speaks of it as the *carta* of King Edward (as also of the *carta* of King William). No diplomas of these kings relating to Hormer hundred seem to have survived, and none may ever have been issued. The term *carta* was indeed employed after the Norman Conquest both for diploma and for writ,[2] though a distinction was made between the two in such clauses as : *per breve vel cartam*, ' by writ or charter '.[3] But verbal resemblances between Henry I's writ-charter and the alleged writ of the Confessor strongly suggest that the writ formed the basis of Henry's text. In his own writ-charter confirming the grants of his predecessors, King Henry announces that he has granted to the abbey of Abingdon, to the abbot and all his successors, and to the monks, the hundred of Hormer, just as it was granted to the abbey by King Edward and confirmed by William I ; and he declares that the abbot and the monks, present and to come, are to hold the hundred with all the *consuetudines* and quittances with which they ever held it in the days of King Edward and King William :—

' scilicet, quod nullus vicecomes vel eorum ministri inde se quicquam intromittant, sed ipsi libere justitiam suam habeant et faciant.' [4]

It is in this background that the reputed writ of the Confessor relating to Hormer hundred must be considered, and it seems entirely probable that the passage excluding the sheriff and the *motgerefa* from the hundred had its origin, if not in the dispute concerning the abbot's possession of the hundred in the time of Abbot Vincentius, at all events in some post-Conquest dispute. How much of the reputed Hormer writ of King Edward the Confessor was in existence in his lifetime is a matter for conjecture. But since the linguistic forms of the address of the writ (in spite of the irregular ' his ' in its opening clauses, written by the copyist over the erasure of *mine*, which has been noted above) [5] are those normal in late West Saxon, and since there is nothing improbable in the conjunction of the persons named in the address, it seems likely that although the existing Hormer writ is probably not

[1] See p. 432.
[2] See Stevenson, *Eng. Hist. Rev.* xi (1896), 733.
[3] For this clause in an Abingdon text, see the writ of the Conqueror, p. 124, n. 4. Further instances of the use of *breve* and *carta* are given by D. C. Douglas, *Feudal Documents from the Abbey of St. Edmunds*, p. xxix. See also Liebermann, *Gesetze*, ii. 329, s.v. *breve*.
[4] *Chron. Abingdon*, ii. 164. For a writ of Stephen in similar terms, see *ibid.* ii. 178, and for other post-Conquest writs concerning Hormer hundred, see ii. 182, 217, 220, 246.
[5] See p. 123.

authentic as it stands, it may have been based upon an authentic writ of King Edward the Confessor in favour of the abbey of Abingdon.

The Latin versions of nos. 4 and 5 have no independent value. They are each headed in the cartulary : ' Interpretatio in Latinum ', and their rendering of ' thegn ' by *baro* and ' sheriff ' by *uicecomes* is an indication that they were not composed until after the Conquest.

(3)

Bishop Siward makes a statement concerning Brihtwine's claim to Leckhampstead.　1045-48

(Cott. Claud. C. ix, f. 128 b)

Siwardus episcopus Godwino comiti & Hermanno episcopo & 1 Kinewardo & ceteris omnibus nobilibus de Bearrucscira salutem. Audiui Brithwinum terram de Lechamstede sibi omnino appropriare, sed iniuste id agit, nam me permittente ea potitus est eo tenore, ut post suum decessum monachorum libere in manum redeat ; quod 5 conuentione dispositum est illustrium uirorum plurimorum presentia, eo die quo Brithnodus eius frater defunctus Abbendonie sepultus fuit, qui tercius a patre (nam mater eius inter se & patrem media) eiusdem terre possessione functus est, quibus tantummodo, Cnutonis regis tempore, trino uite spacio hominum possessores fieri, 10 inde a monachis Abbendonensibus concessum fuerat. Hęc haud aliter haberi, fide quam Deo & regi meo domino debeo interposita iuro ; sed & si adhuc his quis discrederit, iudicio quo censura uestra potuerit iure definiri, in ueritate que protestatus sum, ero paratus.

3. Brihtwinum B.　　　7. Brihtnodus B.　　　7. MS *repeats* eius *after* frater.

(4)

King Edward declares that he has granted to Abbot Ordric for St. Mary's monastery judicial and financial rights over his own land. (1052-66)

(Cott. Claud. C. ix, f. 130)

Eadward king gret his bisceopas & his abbodas 7 his heorlas. 1 7 þeignas þe on þam scyran syndon þe Ordric abbud hæf land inne. 7 ic kyþe eow ꝥ ic hæbbe geunnon him into Sča Mariam mynstre sace. 7 socne. toll. 7 team. 7 infangeneþeof. binnan burgon 7 butan burgon. hamsocne. 7 griðbrice. 7 foresteal. ofer his agen 5

land.   And ic nelle nanu[m] men geþafian Þ him ænig þara þinga
of anime þe ic him geunnen hebbe.

Latin Version
(Ibid.)

Eadwardus rex salutat suos episcopos & suos abbates & suos
comites & barones qui in illis uicecomitatibus sunt ubi Ordricus
10 abbas habet terram infra.   Et ego ostendo uobis quia ego habeo
permissum sibi ad Sancte Marie monasterium litigium, exquisi-
tionem, teloneum & appropriationem & infra captum latronem,
infra burgum et extra burgum, domus assaltum & pacis infractionem,
obuiationem, super suam propriam terram.   Et ego nolo ulli
15 homini permittere ut ei aliqua harum rerum auferat que ego sibi
concessi habere.

Heading : Carta Regis Eadwardi anglice.   2. heafð B.   3. hic B.
4. *The numbers i–viii interlined above* sace, socne *etc. and over the corresponding words in Latin text, in same ink as main text.*   5. -bryce B.
7. hæbbe B.   *Heading of Latin version :* Interpretatio in Latinum.

Translation

King Edward sends friendly greetings to his bishops and his abbots
and his earls and thegns who are in the shires in which Abbot Ordric
has land.   And I inform you that I have granted to him for St.
Mary's monastery sake and soke, toll and team and infangenetheof,
within boroughs and without, hamsocn and grithbreach and foresteall
over his own land.   And I will not permit anyone to take away
from him any of the things that I have granted him.

(5)

King Edward declares that Abbot Ordric and all the community in
the monastery of Abingdon are to possess the hundred of Hormer
in perpetuity.   (1053–55, or 1058–66)

(Cott. Claud. C. ix. f. 130)

1   Eadward cyningc gret Hereman bisceop 7 Harold eorl.   7 Godric.
7 ealle his þegenas on Bearrucscyre freondlic.   7 ic cyðe eow Þ
Ordric abbud 7 eal Þ hired on Abbendunes mynstre be minre unne
7 gife frigelice habban 7 wealdan Hornemeres hundred . on hyre
5 agenre andwealde on ecere worulde.   7 swa Þ nan scyrgerefe oððe
motgerefe þar habban æni socne oððe gemot, buton þes abbudes
agen hæse 7 unne.

Latin Version

(Ibid.)

Eadwardus rex salutat Hermannum episcopum & Haroldum comitem & Godricum & omnes suos barones de Bearrucscira amicabiliter. Et ego ostendo uobis quod Ordricus abbas & omnis [10] congregatio Abbendonensis monasterii meo concessu & dono libere 'h'abeant & possideant hundredum de Hornemere in sua propria potestate in sempiterna secula, & sic ut nullus uicecomes uel prepositus ibi habeant aliquam appropriationem seu placitum sine abbatis proprio iussu & concessu.   [15]

Heading : Carta Regis Eadwardi de hundredo de Hornimere.   2. his *over* mine *erased* C ; his *without erasure* B.   6. mot B. *Heading of Latin version :* Interpretatio in Latinum.   8. *the* -at *of* salutat, *and* suos, *over erasures.*

Translation

King Edward sends friendly greetings to Bishop Herman and Earl Harold and Godric and all his thegns in Berkshire. And I inform you that, by my grant and gift, Abbot Ordric and all the community in the monastery at Abingdon shall freely possess and have in their own power in perpetuity the hundred of Hormer, and in such wise that no sheriff or moot-reeve shall have there any jurisdiction or court without the abbot's own command and permission.

BATH

The writ of Abbot Wulfwold (addressed to the bishop, the sheriff and the thegns of the shire, and to the abbot of a neighbouring monastery) [1] announces a grant made by Wulfwold of land at Evesty and Ashwick to the abbey of St. Peter at Bath [2] over which

[1] On the absence of the earl among the persons addressed, see p. 48, and on the presence here of Abbot Æthelnoth of Glastonbury, see pp. 47–8.

[2] Little is known of the early history of the abbey of Bath. It seems to have been founded first as a nunnery but appears later as a house of monks. In the tenth century the monastery appears to have been in the king's hand with only a few clerks to serve the church. It was probably restored or reformed during the monastic revival of the reign of Edgar who was crowned at Bath in 973, and it became famous afterwards on account of St. Ælfheah (see Biographical

he presided, for the provision of clothing and food for the monks, the estates in question having been given him by his lord, King Edward, with full freedom to grant them to whomsoever he pleased. There is no reason to question the authenticity of this letter. Not only is it free from suspicious features, but the letter of Bishop Siward to the shire court (no. 3) provides further testimony, if such is needed, that letters were addressed to shire courts by non-royal persons. The outside limits of date are 1061 to 1082, but the letter may have been written in the early years of this period. The few late forms and mis-spellings which it contains (e.g. *heafde*, *elmihtig*) may be due to the twelfth-century transcriber, to whom the definite article *þe* (for *se*) in l. 11 should in all probability be attributed (see p. 393 below). But except for these few linguistic forms the writ, as it has come down to us in the Bath cartulary, probably differs scarcely at all from the text issued by Abbot Wulfwold.

(6)

Abbot Wulfwold announces that he has given to St. Peter's minster at Bath land at Evesty and Ashwick. 1061–82, possibly 1061–66.

(C.C.C.C. MS. 111, p. 92)

1 Uulfwold abbod gret Gisa bisceop. 7 Ægelnoð aƀƀ. 7 Tofig sciregerefan. 7 ealle þa þegenas on Sumersæton freondlice. And ic cyðe eow. ꝥ Eadweard cingc min hlaford geaf me ꝥ land æt Eofestige. ꝥ min fæder ahte. And þa feowwer worðias æt Æscwican.
5 And þa ækeras mæde þe þarto gebyriað. And on wuda. 7 on felda. swa micel swa ꝥ ic heafde læs minan orfe. 7 minra manna orfe. And eall swa freols on eallan þingan . eall swa þæs cinges agen innland. to gyfanne. 7 to syllanne. ær dæge. 7 æfter dæge. loc hwam me leofast is. Nu kyðe ic eow eallan. ꝥ ic habbe gifen
10 ꝥ land. in to Scs Petres mynstre in to Baðan. þam munecan to scrudfultume. 7 to fodan. eall swa full. 7 swa forð swa þe cingc hit me geúðe on eallan þingan. And se ðe mine gyfe geéce. þe ic habbe gyfen in to Scs Petres mynstre. geéce God ælmihtig his lif her on worulde. And þonne hé heonan fare. gyfe him Crist heofona

Notes), who had lived there as a hermit. The present dedication of Bath Abbey is to St. Peter and St. Paul ; but the church is described in Domesday Book, as in this letter, as the church of St. Peter of Bath (see further on this dedication, W. Levison, *England and the Continent in the Eighth Century*, 31, 260). See VCH *Somerset*, ii. 69 ff. ; J. Armitage Robinson, *The Times of St. Dunstan* (Oxford, 1923), 61 ff. ; W. Hunt, *Two Chartularies of the Priory of St. Peter at Bath*, Somerset Record Society, vol. 7 (1893).

rice to medes. And se þe hit þence to litlianne. gelitlige hine God 15
elmihtig her on worulde. 7 þonne hc heonan faran sceal. si his
wunung on helle grunde. buton he hit ær his ende þe stiðlicor gebete.

Heading : De Euestia et Æscwica.   11. fodan] foðan MS.

Translation

Abbot Wulfwold sends friendly greetings to Bishop Giso and
Abbot Æthelnoth and Tofi the sheriff and all the thegns in Somerset.
And I inform you that King Edward my lord gave me the land at
Evesty that my father owned, and the four homesteads at Ashwick
and the acres of meadowland pertaining to them, and in woodland
and in open land sufficient for me to have pasture for my cattle and
my men's cattle, and it [was to be] just as free in all things as the
king's own inland, to give and to grant before my death and after
it (*or ?* in perpetuity) to whomsoever I please. Now I inform you
all that I have given the land to St. Peter's monastery at Bath
for the provision of clothing and food for the monks, just as fully and
completely as the king granted it to me in all things. And if anyone shall increase my gift, that I have given to St. Peter's monastery,
may God Almighty increase his life in this world, and when he
departs hence may Christ give him as a reward the kingdom of
heaven. And if anyone shall purpose to diminish it, may God
Almighty bring him low in this world, and when he must depart
hence, may his dwelling be in the abyss of hell, unless before his end
he make amends for it as stringently as possible.

BEVERLEY

There is every reason to accept as authentic the writ, no. 7,
which announces that King Edward has given Archbishop Ealdred
of York permission to draw up a *privilegium* with regard to the lands
pertaining to St. John's minster at Beverley,[1] declares that the

---

[1] The minster at Beverley is dedicated to St. John of Beverley (died 721),
who is said to have established at Beverley a double monastery, a house of
monks dedicated to St. John the Evangelist, and a nunnery dedicated to St.
Martin (*Dict. Christ. Biog.* s.n. Joannes of Beverley). King Æthelstan is
traditionally reputed to have been the re-founder of the church and to have
established at Beverley a college of secular canons which he endowed with
lands. For the early history of these religious foundations at Beverley, see

minster and its property shall be as free in all things as any other minster, and subjects the minster to the bishop of the diocese (the archbishop of York). This writ is of great interest as an indication of the fact, hitherto generally disregarded, that in King Edward's time a *privilegium* might be drawn up not by the royal clerks but by an interested ecclesiastic ; see further, Introduction, pp. 38 ff. Archbishop Ealdred's interest in the minster of St. John at Beverley was manifested by his endowment of the chapter with new grants of land, the building for them of a presbytery, and the decoration of their church with painting and splendid furniture. It was at his suggestion that the first Life of St. John of Beverley, by Folcard, was written.[1] To protect the liberties and endowments of the canons (who seem at this time to have been placed on the footing of a corporate body endowed with landed property), and to ensure that they should be protected from encroachment from outside, Ealdred during his occupancy of the see of York obtained on their behalf three writs, one from King Edward printed here, two others from the Conqueror. In one of these,[2] dated by Davis 1066–69, King William announces that he has granted to St. John of Beverley sake and soke over all the lands which were given to the minster in King Edward's day, and also over the lands acquired by Archbishop Ealdred for the minster during the Conqueror's own reign,[3] with the precept (which also appears in no. 7, the Confessor's writ) that minster-life shall be maintained there in perpetuity. In another Beverley writ of 1066–69 King William announces (as King Edward announces) that he has granted to Ealdred permission to draw up (*dictare*) a *privilegium* regarding all the lands pertaining to the church of St. John of Beverley ; and King William adds that all that land shall be free as against himself and as against his officers (*prepositi*) and as against all men save the archbishop and the priests of the minster.[4] The idiomatic nature of the language of King Edward's Beverley writ, no. 7, and its freedom from any

VCH *Yorkshire*, iii. 353. See also the *Beverley Chapter Act Book*, ed. A. F. Leach, Surtees Society, vol. 98 (1898), vol. 108 (1903). See also G. Oliver, *History and Antiquities of the Town and Minster of Beverley* (Beverley, 1829), and G. Poulson, *Beverlac* (London, 1829).

[1] *Historians of the Church of York*, ed. J. Raine, R.S. i. 239.

[2] Davis, *Regesta*, no. 31, Farrer, *Early Yorkshire Charters*, i. no. 89.

[3] This is the natural rendering of the Old English : ' ic cyðe eow þ ic hæbbe gegyfen Sċe Johanne æt Beuerlic sac 7 socna ofer eallum þam landum þe wæron gyfene on Ædwærdes dæg cynges innto Sċe Iohannes mynstre 7 eac ofer þam landum ðe Ealdred ærcebiscop hæfð siðþan begitan on minan dagan þider inn.' Davis's rendering is somewhat misleading : sake and soke ' over all his lands *where he had these rights* in Edward's day, and over all the lands that Archbishop Aldred has since *given* '.

[4] Farrer, *op. cit.* i. no. 88 (not in the *Regesta*). See p. 432 below.

suspicious feature, are evidence of its authenticity. Its linguistic forms are in the main those normal in late West Saxon. There is no obstacle to the belief that this is an (only slightly modernised) copy of an authentic writ of King Edward.

(7)

King Edward declares that Archbishop Ealdred has his permission to draw up a *privilegium* for the lands pertaining to St. John's minster at Beverley ; and that the minster and its property shall be as free as any other minster ; and that the bishop of the diocese to whom it shall be subject shall be the guardian and protector of the minster under King Edward himself.   Christmas 1060–65

(Ch. R. 4 Edw. II, m. 20)

+ Eadweard cyngc gret Tostig eorl 7 ealle mine þegenas on 1
Eoferwicscire freondlice.   7 ic cyðe eow ꝥ hit is min unna 7 min
fulle leafe ꝥ Ealdred arceb̄. ꝥ he dihte priuilegium to þam landan
þe ligcað innto Sc̄e Iohannes mynstre æt Beferlicc.   7 ic wille ꝥ ꝥ
mynster 7 seo are þe þider innto hirð. ꝥ hit beo swa freols swa ænig 5
oþer mynster is æt eallan þingan.   7 loc hwilc b̄p þær ofer byð ꝥ
hit beo him underþeod.   7 ꝥ he beo þær to geheald 7 mund under
me. ꝥ þær nan mann nan þing on ne teo butan he.   7 ꝥ he na
geþafige ꝥ man þanon ut do ænig þæra þinga. þæs þe þær mid
rihte to gebyrað. swa swa he wille beon wið Godd geborgen 7 Sc̄s 10
Iohannes.   7 eallra þæra halgena þe seo halige stoww is fore
gehalgod.   7 ic wille ꝥ þær æfre beo mynsterlif 7 samnung þa hwile
þe ænig mann leofað.

4. ligcað] ligead MS., S, M ; lygead N.   5. *Not* circ, *as all edd.* ;
MS. *probably* cire, *but possibly* are, *with very square* a ; S *rubbed, but looks*
like o.re ; M *and* N *probably copying text with* are.   5. herð M. N.

Translation

King Edward sends friendly greetings to Earl Tostig and all my thegns in Yorkshire.   And I inform you that Archbishop Ealdred has my consent and full permission to draw up a *privilegium* for the lands that belong to St. John's minster at Beverley.   And my will is that the minster and the property belonging thereto shall be as free as any other minster is in all things : and whatever bishop shall be over it, that it be subject to him, and that he be its protector and guardian under me, so that no one but he shall take anything from it and so that he shall not permit to be alienated any of the things that lawfully pertain thereto, in so far as he wishes to be secure from [incurring the anger of] God and St. John and all the saints in whose honour the holy foundation is consecrated. And my will is that minster-life and assembly shall be always maintained there as long as any man shall live.

BURY ST. EDMUNDS

The writs of the monastery of Bury St. Edmunds,[1] of which eighteen are now extant, are exceeded in number only by those of Westminster Abbey. From the point of view of authenticity, the Bury writs stand high. Two, nos. 11, 24, have come down to us in a form of the period to which their contents relate, and it is not at all impossible that no. 11 may be an original writ written and sealed (though no trace of sealing now remains) by the clerks of King Edward the Confessor's secretariat. The others have survived only in later copies,[2] but while their linguistic forms have in many cases undergone alteration, their form and content is that of the normal Edwardian writ. One only of their number (no. 10)

---

[1] For the early history of the monastery, see T. Arnold, *Memorials of St. Edmund's Abbey*, R.S. 1890–96, 3 vols. ; VCH *Suffolk*, ii. 56 ff. : M. D. Lobel, *The Borough of Bury St. Edmund's* (Oxford, 1935). See also V. H. Galbraith, ' The East Anglian See and the Abbey of Bury St. Edmunds ', *Eng. Hist. Rev.* xl (1925), 222–8. For a critical note on the extensive literature dealing with the history of the monastery, see D. C. Douglas, *Feudal Documents from the Abbey of Bury St. Edmunds* (London, British Academy, 1932), xvi. The history of the monastery begins with the transference, in 903 or later, of the relics of St. Edmund, king of East Anglia, slain by the Danes, to Beadricesweorth, afterwards known as St. Edmund's Bury. In 1020 the seculars who were in charge of the shrine were replaced by monks from Ely and from St. Benet's at Holme, and Ufi, the prior from Holme, was consecrated first abbot of Bury. A new stone church, begun by order of Cnut, was dedicated in 1032 in honour of Christ, St. Mary and St. Edmund.

[2] For some of these writs a number of copies have been preserved, dating, for the most part, from the late thirteenth, the fourteenth, and the fifteenth centuries. Some of the originals may possibly have perished in a fire at Bury in 1140 or 1150 ; see Lambeth MS. 448, f. 94 : *Nota quod anno domini* 1140 *factum est incendium magnum apud Bury Sancti Edmundi, Annales S. Edmundi,* s.a. 1150 ; Liebermann, *Ungedruckte Anglo Normannische Geschichtsquellen* (Strassburg, 1879), 133. Others may have been destroyed in the Bury riots of 1327, when the abbey was plundered, and documents were carried off by the rioters.

is in its present form definitely spurious ; another (no. 8) contains a final clause, the authenticity of which demands discussion.[1]

THE OFFICE OF ABBOT AND THE RIGHTS OF THE MONASTERY

The first of the three groups into which it is convenient to divide the Bury writs comprises those writs (of a type to be found among the writs of other houses) that concern the office of abbot, or notify the grant or confirmation to the abbot and his house of judicial and financial rights.[2]   Three abbots, Ufi, Leofstan, and Baldwine, ruled in succession over St. Edmund's Bury in the Confessor's reign.   Ufi (who had been appointed abbot in the reign of Cnut) was confirmed in his office and privileges by King Edward in the earliest Bury writ (no. 8).   The grant of sake and soke over their own men to Abbot Leofstan and the community is announced in another writ (no. 11), while still another (no. 12) announces the Confessor's grant to the same abbot and the community, of sake and soke over lands bequeathed to the monastery, as fully and completely as these privileges were possessed in each case by the previous owner.   The privileges of the monastery were still further safeguarded by the issue, within a year or two of the appointment of Abbot Leofstan, of a writ (no. 13) declaring that all things lawfully pertaining to the property of St. Edmund should be the uncontested possession of the monastery.   Another writ (no. 15) records the exemption from taxation of the inland of St. Edmund ; an exemption confirmed by William I according to a writ [3] in which the king declares that the *dominia* (demesne lands) of St. Edmund are to be : ' quieta ab omnibus scottis et geldis sicuti melius fuerunt tempore regis Ædwardi '.   A few years later, and still during the time of Leofstan, the Confessor declared that the monastery was ' now ' to have possession of the soke already granted by him to St. Edmund's as fully and completely as he himself possessed it.   This writ (no. 19) does not however state clearly whether the grant of soke referred to is one of sake and soke over all their own men, and over the lands bequeathed to them (nos. 11, 12), or whether the reference is to the sokes over the eight and a half Suffolk hundreds, the grant of which had been notified in yet another writ (no. 9).   The appointment

---

[1] Some scepticism might legitimately be felt concerning the genuineness of a group of Bury charters attributed to Cnut and the Confessor, discussed below, p. 141 and n. 2.

[2] For later confirmations of grants announced in the Confessor's writs for St. Edmund's Bury, see Douglas, *Feudal Documents*, where the texts are given. These confirmations will not generally be referred to here, except in special circumstances.

[3] Douglas, *Feudal Documents*, Charter no. 4, issued 1066–70.

L

(only a few months before the Confessor's death) of Baldwine as abbot of Bury was signalised by the issue of a writ, no. 23, notifying his appointment, declaring that the king had granted him everything pertaining to his office as fully and completely as it was ever held by Abbot Leofstan or any abbot before him, and requesting, as was done in other cases (see Introduction, p. 65), that the abbot might be assisted, if need arose, to obtain his lawful rights. Writs in Baldwine's favour relating to the eight and a half hundreds, and to the grant of a moneyer (nos. 24, 25), are also still extant ; of the existence of other writs now lost, we learn from other sources.[1]

With one exception, namely the writ in favour of Abbot Ufi (no. 8), the Bury writs just mentioned do not differ in essentials from those of other houses, and there is no need to question their authenticity. But this particular writ is outstanding by reason of the king's precept that the freedom (*freols*)[2] granted to the monastery first by King Cnut and then by King Harthacnut shall abide with it unaltered, and that no bishop whatsoever shall appropriate to himself anything therein.[3] The various histories connected with the monastery of St. Edmund claim that from the time of its re-establishment by Cnut it had been exempt from episcopal control. We may take as an example the following statement :—

' Concessit idem præsul Ayelwinus (i.e. Bishop Ælfwine) in ingressu monachorum præfato monasterio omne jus suum ac jurisdictionem et episcopalia sacramenta intra idem monasterium et oppidum, et in circuitu ejusdem oppidi, per ambitum unius stadii, ad augmentum gloriæ et loci dignitatem, et contemplationem sanctissimi regis et martyris Edmundi . . . Statuta fuit et annotata hujusmodi dimissio præsulis Alwini (Ælfwine) pro se et successoribus suis in perpetuum anno regis Canuti quinto '.[4]

This is obviously a partisan statement, which leaves unexplained the readiness with which Bishop Ælfwine is supposed to have

---

[1] See Appendix IV, nos. 18, 19.

[2] For *freols* used elsewhere with reference to a monastery, see no. 26.

[3] In his study of monastic privilege, M. Lemarignier observes that the question of the relation of the monasteries to the diocesan bishop arose as soon as monasteries came into existence ; that the Council of Chalcedon in A.D. 451 decreed that they should be subject to episcopal authority, but that, four years later, in consequence of a dispute between the bishop of Fréjus and the abbot of Lérins, the Council of Arles set limits to the authority of the bishop. See J.-F. Lemarignier, *Étude sur les privilèges d'exemption et de juridiction ecclési-astique des abbayes normandes depuis les origines jusqu'en 1140* (Archives de la France monastique, xliv (1937), 1). A too favourable attitude to Bury and Coventry charters claiming exemption from episcopal control is taken by W. H. Frere in his study of monastic exemption (*Visitation Articles and Injunctions*, i (Alcuin Club Collections, xiv), 59 ff.

[4] Arnold, *Memorials*, i. 359–60, from Bodley MS. 240 ; also *ibid*. i. 341.

divested himself voluntarily of jurisdiction over the abbey.[1] Bury charters in the name of Cnut and Harthacnut also purport to grant to and confirm to the monastery freedom in perpetuity from the domination of all bishops of the shire. But the charter of Cnut (K. 735) is of most dubious authenticity (see pp. 433 f.), and the charter of Harthacnut (K. 761) is spurious (see pp. 434 f.), whilst the authenticity of two charters in the name of the Confessor, covering much the same ground as the charter attributed to Cnut, is more than doubtful.[2] The problem is to determine whether the passage under discussion in the writ in favour of Abbot Ufican be accepted as genuine and contemporary, and it must be placed in its proper background.

The dispute between the abbot of St. Edmund's Bury and the bishop of the diocese took place, not in the reign of the Confessor, but in the latter years of the eleventh century.[3] Bishop Arfast

[1] See further V. H. Galbraith, *loc. cit.* 225. Also M. D. Lobel in *Oxford Essays in Med. Hist. presented to H. E. Salter* (1934), 122 ff. ; N. D. Hurnard, *Eng. Hist. Rev.* lxiv (1949), 319.

[2] K. 895, with Latin version K. 910, Thorpe p. 347 ; K. 1346, with Latin version K. 915, Thorpe p. 417. It should be noted that Kemble's text of K. 910 is incomplete, and that copies of K. 895 far superior to his text are P.R.O. Cartæ Antiquæ P (no. 15) no. 1 (where the scribe imitates Anglo-Saxon script) and B.M. Harley MS. 638, f. 25 b. These two charters are not starred as spurious by Kemble, and they are accepted as genuine without discussion by H. W. C. Davis (*Eng. Hist. Rev.* xxiv (1909), 418, and by Lemarignier (*op. cit.* 112, n. 107) ; they are included in a list of spurious charters by W. H. Stevenson ; see p. 144, note 1 ; their form is unusual : they are not to be classed as writs since they lack the customary writ address and greeting. Like the vernacular charter appended to the dubious Latin charter of Cnut (K. 735), they are declarations addressed ' to all men ' (' to all believers '). The first of the pair (K. 895) declares that the monastery of St. Edmund and the town in which it is situated shall for ever be in the same freedom as King Cnut and King Hardacnut granted to it ; forbids that the place shall ever be inhabited by men of any order but monks ; declares that no bishop in Norfolk or Suffolk shall ever have any authority in the monastery or within the boundaries of the town, marked out with crosses ; grants to the monks freedom in electing their abbot ; and confirms the Confessor's own grant to them of sake and soke over their own land. The English version of the second charter (K. 1346) so closely resembles in structure and phraseology the English version (summarised pp. 433–4 below) appended to Cnut's doubtful charter (K. 735) that the two versions cannot be independent. These two alleged charters of the Confessor are in dubious company, and their authenticity in their present form is more than doubtful.

[3] For a detailed account of the struggle between Abbot Baldwine and Bishop Arfast, which extended over a number of years, see the *Miracula Sancti Eadmundi*, written late in the eleventh century, of Hermann the archdeacon, printed Arnold, *Memorials* i. 60 ff. and Liebermann, *Ungedruckte Geschichtsquellen*, 248 ff. Also D. Knowles, ' The Growth of Exemption ', *Downside Review*, N.S. xxxi (1932), 200–31, 396–436 ; Lemarignier, *ut supra*, 146–52. For a narrative by a Norwich writer, purporting to have been

(Herfast) made an attempt (which was in the end unsuccessful) to move the seat of the bishopric of East Anglia from Thetford to Bury —a measure which was strenuously resisted by the abbot of Bury, for it would have involved the subjection of the abbey and town to the bishop. The matter was tried in 1081 before King William and his council, and a Latin writ of William I announces briefly that the claims of Abbot Baldwine were accepted and those of Bishop Arfast rejected :—

' Assenserunt unanimiter quod Arfastus episcopus predictam ecclesiam et villam iniuste requirebat. Et abbas ea iuste habere debebat. Et quod Arfastus episcopus neque successor eius de prefata ecclesia et uilla nichil reclamare debebat. Quod sic stare et firmiter inuiolatum manere precipio '. [1]

Another charter, a formal diploma in Latin and English, with a list of witnesses and the date A.D. 1081, attributed to William I, relates in full the episodes of the trial.[2] We are told that Bishop Arfast's pleading at the trial was not successful, for he had neither documents nor witnesses to support his case ; but Abbot Baldwine, for his part, related how Cnut had established monks at Bury ; how the church had been dedicated by the archbishop of Canterbury ; how the first two abbots who ruled there in succession had received the episcopal benediction as abbot [3] from the bishop of London and the bishop of Winchester, respectively, and he himself, the third abbot, from the archbishop of Canterbury ; and how for fifty-three years the monks of that house, without protest from any of Arfast's predecessors, had received orders (' ordines susceperint ', ' underfengon had ') from whatsoever bishop they would. Baldwine then produced the *precepta* of King Cnut and of the most glorious King Edward, in which these kings granted that that church should be completely free in perpetuity from all domination of all the bishops of the shire. Thereupon the verdict was given in his favour : ' tanti loci tantam auctoritatem inuiolatam usque in finem saeculi debere permanere ' ; and the king, at Baldwine's request, confirmed by his own *preceptum* the *precepta* granted to the monastery by Edmund, Cnut, Harthacnut, and Edward, and granted that the church and the vill in which it was situated should be free from the domination of Bishop Arfast and his successors. This account of the trial is based on the Latin version of the charter, but it should be noted that the written 1103–19, and setting forth the substance of the bishop's ' case ' in this dispute, see V. H. Galbraith, *ut supra*.

[1] For text see Douglas, Charter no. 8.

[2] Douglas, Charter no. 7. For a parallel account, not identical in every detail, see Hermann's *Miracula Sancti Eadmundi* (Arnold, i. 65 f., Liebermann, 254 ff.).

[3] In Latin version, *sacrauerit*, in Anglo-Saxon version, *hadode, halgode* (of the bishop).

vernacular version has a number of details not to be found in the Latin ; it is more partisan and more favourable to Bury. For instance, whereas the Latin version narrates that Bishop Arfast at the trial made his claim eloquently (' satis facunde fecit clamorem '), the English version has the acid comment : ' if it had been true ' (' gif hit soð wære ') ; and for the Latin : ' sed scriptis et testimoniis omnimodo vacuum ', the English version has : ' ac heo wæs eallum mannum geþuht idel 7 unnyt forþi þe he næfde naþor ne gewritu ne gewitnesse ' (' but it (his claim) seemed to all men vain and useless for he had neither documents nor witness '). Again, to the statement in the Latin version that Cnut and Edward freed the holy foundation from the domination of all bishops, the English version adds : ' and of all laymen ' (' ealra woruldmanna '). It would be a reasonable conjecture that the English version, at any rate, was written in the monastery itself.

The authenticity of this alleged charter of the Conqueror, which purports to show that the success of Abbot Baldwine's pleading was due in part to his production of documentary evidence appearing to substantiate it, was called in question by H. W. C. Davis,[1] who remarked that ' the style shows all the marks of a forgery '. In a detailed examination of the charter [2] Professor Douglas expresses doubts as to whether ' style ' can of itself be a reliable guide to the genuineness of any early charter. He points out that opinions unfavourable to the charter have been based only on the incomplete or imperfect printed versions, and while not arguing ' that the charter is genuine in toto ', remarks that the handwriting of a copy of the Latin version is of a date hardly later than 1100, and indeed that the handwriting of the pretended original (which he is inclined to regard as a copy of an original now lost) ' suggests a date contemporary with the date given in the charter itself '. Discussing the attestations of the charter, Professor Douglas makes the point that since none of the bishops' titles occur in the pretended original, arguments founded on apparent errors in the names of their sees have no weight ; and further, that ' the attestations in the pretended original and in the earliest copy of this deed ' are in keeping with the date in the charter. He notes, however, the possibility of a chronological difficulty in connection with the attestation of Abbot Ægelnoth (Æthel-), who also attests a suspicious Westminster charter [3] also dated 1081, with a list of witnesses strikingly similar to this Bury list. M. Lemarignier,[4] without any discussion of the problem, pronounces rather more favourably than does Professor Douglas on the authenticity of this charter : ' cet acte qui, tout au

[1] *Regesta*, no. 137.   [2] *Feudal Documents*, xxxii–xxxix.
[3] Davis, *Regesta*, no. 144.   [4] *Op. cit.* p. 152, note 74.

plus, nous est peut-être parvenu avec quelques remaniements de forme n'altérant pas le fond '.

In his examination of the alleged charter of the Conqueror which is under discussion, Professor Douglas observes that ' it is hard to see what motive can have inspired an elaborate fabrication, since the abbey was already possessed of a genuine document (the Latin writ referred to above, p. 142), which conferred on the abbot the same privileges '. But the alleged charter of the Conqueror must be considered in its relationship to other Bury charters. This document specifically mentions charters of Edmund, Cnut, Hartha-cnut, and Edward. It would then if it were genuine, or accepted as such, serve the valuable purpose of helping to authenticate charters (whether genuine or not) purporting to have been granted to Bury by these kings. This, if it is not authentic, may have been the reason for its fabrication. The monks of Bury laid stress on their possession of charters purporting to exempt them from episcopal control from the time of the re-establishment of their house by Cnut. It is not difficult to imagine that the abbey's successfully-asserted claim (which is not supported by any inde-pendent authority) may have given rise to documentary fabrication, and indeed, of the alleged charters of Edmund, Cnut, Harthacnut, and Edward, which bear upon this dispute, not one is above suspicion.[1] Whether the writ of the Confessor for Abbot Ufi, no. 8, is, unlike these other documents, authentic in all its details, it is difficult to say. There is no reason for doubting the authenticity of ll. 1–5 of the text, down to *þider inne lay*, and the next sentence, as far as *Hardcnut kyng mine brother*, may well be authentic. It is the last sentence of all that arouses suspicion. Unfortunately the only vernacular copies of this writ have come down to us in two cartularies in which alterations of the linguistic forms of earlier copies have been systematically made, so that any differences which might originally have existed between the linguistic colouring of the passage : *7 ic nelle . . . þer on ateo*, and the remainder of the text of the writ are not now perceptible. In other writs, nos. 5, 41,

---

[1] For an alleged charter of Edmund to Bury, generally considered spurious, dated A.D. 945, and purporting to confirm the abbey's special jurisdiction over the vill and the surrounding land, the boundaries of which are given in one version, see B. 808. For the charters of Cnut, Harthacnut, and Edward, see p. 141, n. 2, and pp. 433–4. We cannot tell whether these were the *precepta* to which the alleged charter of the Conqueror refers, and whether the Confessor's writ in favour of Abbot Ufi, which is under discussion, was pro-duced by Abbot Baldwine in the course of the suit. A list of charters of other houses purporting to grant exemption from the authority of the bishop is given by W. H. Stevenson (*Two Cartularies of the Abbeys of Muchelney and Athelney*, ed. E. H. Bates, Somerset Record Society, xiv (1899), 41). In Stevenson's opinion no one of these is genuine.

passages which on other grounds excite suspicion exhibit differences of spelling, terminations and the like, which distinguish them from the remaining text. The authenticity of the final passage in the writ must remain an open question. When all the evidence is weighed it still remains uncertain whether the passage asserting the monastery's freedom from episcopal authority formed part of the Confessor's writ for Abbot Ufi when it was first issued.

THE SOKES OF THE EIGHT AND A HALF HUNDREDS

The second group of Bury writs comprises the four writs (nos. 9, 10 (spurious), 18, 24) relating to the sokes of the eight and a half Suffolk hundreds [1] annexed to the vill of Beadricesweorth, afterwards St. Edmund's Bury, where the body of the saint lay. In this context *socn* is used in the sense of jurisdiction, and appears in the plural, as it does elsewhere ; compare : ' ealla þa socna ofer þæt fennland into þam twam hundredum ', ' all the sokes, *or* jurisdiction, over the fenland belonging to the two hundreds '.[2] It is perhaps worth noting that the sokes of the eight and a half hundreds seem sometimes to have been regarded collectively ; reference to the texts will show that in nos. 9 and 24 a verb in the singular is employed ; not much, if any, weight is to be attached to the isolated plural *ligcne* of R in no. 24 (for which see textual variants). It is unfortunate that the original text of no. 18 has been obscured by the copyists who have modernised the forms relating to these sokes into *it liggen, it stoden*, employing a common Middle English construction, *it* with a plural verb. In the writ of William I relating to these sokes we find *þa socne*, plural, with a verb in the plural in some texts, in the singular in others.[3]

To these sokes of the eight and a half hundreds which in all probability had been the dowry of his mother Ælfgifu Emma, and which had presumably come into his hands when she forfeited her lands on her disgrace,[4] King Edward added, on his first grant of them to St. Edmund's Bury (no. 9), the royal vill of Mildenhall, which however afterwards passed out of the possession of the monastery. Hermann, the archdeacon, writing at the end of the eleventh century, tells us that this grant of the sokes of the eight and a half hundreds and of the *regia mansio* of Mildenhall was made

[1] On the hundred, and on grants of hundreds, see pp. 125 ff.

[2] Robertson, *Anglo-Saxon Charters*, p. 100.   On *soke* used in this sense, see Introduction, p. 74.

[3] Douglas, *Feudal Documents*, Charter no. 3.

[4] See p. 547 below, and compare *Chron.* C. 1043 : ' se cing let geridan ealle þa land þe his moder ahte him to handa '.

(seemingly in the time of Abbot Ufi) for the sustenance of the community.[1] This grant, made first in 1043 or 1044, was confirmed with full privileges during the rule of Abbot Leofstan (no. 18), and again confirmed shortly after the appointment to office in 1065 of Abbot Baldwine (no. 24).

The authenticity of the first of these writs (no. 9) which is addressed to Bishop Grimketel, among other persons, seems virtually certain. The principal arguments in its favour are its conformity with the common form of the Edwardian writ, and the occurrence even in the fourteenth-century copy printed here, of linguistic forms which are almost without exception those of late West Saxon, contemporary with the transactions which the writ records : for instance, the vowel change in the dative case, *minre meder*, and the idiomatic : *þæs þe ic . . . geuðe*. Forms and constructions such as these are frequently levelled out in later versions, as they are in Kemble's text of this writ, which is greatly inferior to the text printed here. It is true that the dates given by Florence of Worcester for Bishop Grimketel raise a difficulty. Miss Whitelock,[2] discussing the succession of the bishops of East Anglia, and accepting the statement of Florence of Worcester, s.a. 1038, that Grimketel became bishop of East Anglia in 1038, adds that ' it seems most probable that he relinquished ' the see ' when he became bishop of Selsey in 1039 '. The serious implications of this dating of Grimketel's tenure of the see of East Anglia for the authenticity of the writ under discussion (where Grimketel is addressed in his capacity of bishop of that see) will be obvious. If Grimketel ceased to be bishop of East Anglia in 1039, a writ in which he is addressed in that capacity by the Confessor after his accession in 1042, cannot be authentic. But there is reason to believe that the dating of Florence of Worcester is incorrect. There were, in fact, two bishops of East Anglia named Ælfric in succession. Both Florence of Worcester (i. 233) and William of Malmesbury (*Gesta Pontificum*, 150) include both these Ælfrics in their lists of bishops of East Anglia ; but in his chronicle, s.a. 1038, Florence has ignored the existence of the second Ælfric, and has in consequence brought into his annal dated 1038 the events that followed on the death of the second Ælfric, in

[1] See the *Miracula Sancti Eadmundi*, in Arnold, *Memorials*, i. 48. For a fuller development of this story see *Mon. Angl.* iii. 154, no. xxi, and H. M. Cam, *Liberties and Communities*, 186. In this latter (fifteenth-century) version the grant of Mildenhall and the eight and a half hundreds is made by the Confessor to the (better-known) Abbot Baldwine, who asks for the grant of'them in response to the king's offer to give him whatsoever he shall ask, so that his young monks may be the better fed, and may take their part in the divine service with greater alacrity and vigour.

[2] *Anglo-Saxon Wills*, 182.

1043, namely, the appointment of Stigand in place of the second
Ælfric, the ejection of Stigand, the appointment and the ejection
of Grimketel, and the restoration of Stigand.[1] There is then no
obstacle to the belief that we have in the present text of no. 9 a
good copy of an authentic writ of King Edward the Confessor.

No such claim can be made for no. 10, a text which in its phraseology closely resembles the preceding writ, but does not mention
Mildenhall. This document cannot be authentic. The mention
of Earl Ælfgar in conjunction with Bishop Grimketel is an
anachronism, for Ælfgar did not become earl of East Anglia till 1051,
seven or eight years after Grimketel had relinquished the see of East
Anglia, and four years after Grimketel's death. This writ is to be
found, as far as I am aware, only in B.M. Add. MS. 14847, a cartulary in which I have not succeeded in discovering any copy of writ
no. 9. Preceding the texts of the writs in this cartulary is a list
(f. 29 b) of the *cartæ* granted by King Edward to St. Edmund. The
second item in this list : ' Collacio viii hundredorum 7 dimidii cum
omnibus libertatibus ad ea spectantibus una cum manerio de
Mildenhale ', should correspond with the contents of the writ under
discussion. Nevertheless this writ (i) omits all mention of Mildenhall, (ii) contains the names of Earl Ælfgar and Toly, a pair of names
constantly recurring elsewhere, in place of the Ælfwine and Ælfric
of no. 9, and (iii) inserts after *sokne* in l. 3, a relative, *þe*, which
destroys the syntax. This document cannot therefore be accepted
as a copy of a genuine and independent writ of the Confessor. Its
immediate source, which cannot be exactly determined, was not
perhaps any one of the extant versions of no. 9, for no. 10 employs
the phrase : *half nigende hundred*, whereas the order of the words
in the known versions of no. 9 is : *nigen half hundreda*.

Another Bury writ (no. 18), issued in the time of Abbot Ufi's
successor Leofstan (1044–65), contains a more detailed account of
the earlier history of the eight and a half hundreds granted to the
abbey by King Edward the Confessor in 1043 or 1044 (no. 9), and
enumerates among the rights conferred upon the monastery,
hamsocn, grithbreach, foresteall, fihtwite and æberetheof.[2] In a
writ issued in favour of Abbot Baldwine (no. 24), the rights of the
abbot are still further protected by the royal injunction that the
officers and suitors of the shire court are to help the abbot to secure
his lawful rights, and by an even more emphatic expression than in
no. 18 of the king's conviction that he has not granted to any other

[1] See Biographical Notes.
[2] On the absence from this list of *fyrdwite*, frequently included among the
six forfeitures, see p. 161. On the other legal terms, see Introduction,
pp. 79 ff.

person any of the sokes previously granted to the abbot. The authenticity of this writ for Baldwine (no. 24) can scarcely be in doubt ; and a claim to be accepted as a copy of an authentic writ of the Confessor can also be made for no. 18, though the existing texts of this writ have been extensively modernised. No. 24 has come down to us in a hand which seems to be contemporary with its contents. But if, as seems virtually certain, writs produced by the clerks of the royal secretariat were handed over to the bene-ficiary, then the absence in this (apparently contemporary) copy of the word *þinga*, which the sense requires, and which appears in other, later, copies, prevents us from supposing that this earliest copy was in its existing form a product of the royal scriptorium, for the later copies must have been derived from a text in which *þinga* had not been omitted.

MISCELLANEOUS GRANTS

The third group of Bury writs comprises writs notifying grants of land or dealing with the affairs of individuals ; to this section must also be assigned the Confessor's grant to the abbot of a moneyer. Pakenham, Kirby, Coney Weston and Loddon, which in varying circumstances (as these writs declare) were granted to the abbey, were all in the possession of this house before the Conquest, and they are entered among the lands of the abbot of Bury in the Domesday Survey. Everything encourages the belief that the PAKENHAM writ (no. 14), notifying the Confessor's grant to Bury of the estate at Pakenham, with all the rights that Osgot had had when it was in his possession, records an authentic grant, and that it is a copy of an authentic writ of King Edward. If Osgot, the former owner of Pakenham, is rightly identified with Osgot Clapa (see Biographical Notes) it would be, as has been suggested below, a natural inference that the estate had come into the king's hands in consequence of Osgot's outlawry in 1046. Again, the estate at KIRBY had at an earlier date belonged to Leofstan, a retainer of Queen Ælfgifu Emma, and she, with her son's sanction (announced in the first of the two Kirby writs, no. 16, which was issued not long before her death), became possessed of the estate and the rights that Leofstan had had there. She bequeathed them to St. Edmund's Bury. In the second of the Kirby writs (no. 17), the king declares that St. Edmund's shall have possession of the estate at Kirby with all the rights of the former owners. The illegal encroach-ments of Semer, of which the king complains, were presumably brought to an end, for in 1086 Rafridus held of the abbot of Bury *Kercheby*, ' which St. Edmund held ' in King Edward's time (see

p. 440. There seems no reason to doubt that the two Kirby writs are modernised copies of writs of the Confessor. The writ (no. 20) relating to CONEY WESTON likewise appears to be authentic. This writ is of a usual type (see Introduction, p. 64), and everything encourages the belief that what we have here is a modernised copy of a writ of King Edward.

Two other writs (nos. 21, 22), whose claims to be considered authentic stand equally high, are concerned with the affairs of ÆLFRIC MODERCOPE. ' Before he went over the sea ', and probably in 1042 or 1043, Ælfric made a will (Whitelock no. 28), in which he made bequests to certain East Anglian monasteries. To Bury he gave land at Loddon, woodland, open land, and fen, with all the rights with which he himself had owned it. To Ely he gave land at Bergh (Apton), with all the rights with which he acquired it, both woodland and open land. His sheep were to be divided into two portions, half for Loddon, half for Bergh Apton. Other bequests were made to Ramsey Abbey and to St. Benet's, Holme. To Bishop Ælfric he bequeathed his tent and his bedclothing, ' the best that I had out on my journey with me '. He made provision for the payment of his heriot, and appointed as his executors Bishop Ælfric and two other persons. In one of the two writs which relate to his affairs (no. 21), both of which are to be dated somewhat later than this will, the king states that Ælfric Modercope has his full per-mission to ' bow to ' the two abbots, at Bury and at Ely, that is, to ' submit himself to ', to ' commend himself to ', to ' become the man of ', these two great magnates. Miss Whitelock observes [1] that it would appear from this that Ælfric was originally a king's man and in the position of those men of whom Domesday states that they could not ' go where they would ' without permission.[2] The case of Ælfric Modercope is of special interest as an instance of a man commending himself simultaneously to two lords ; other cases are however on record of a man being commended to two, or even more, lords, in some cases no doubt because the commendation had descended to co-heirs.[3] In the second writ relating to Ælfric Modercope's affairs (no. 22), King Edward testifies that Ælfric

---

[1] *Anglo-Saxon Wills*, 186.

[2] For references, see Carl Stephenson, ' Commendation and Related Problems in Domesday ', *Eng. Hist. Rev.* lix (1944), 289–310, and the refer-ences there. See also Maitland, *Domesday Book and Beyond*, 66–74 ; Stenton, *Anglo-Saxon England*, 483–4. Commendation involved in the case of a man submitting himself to the lordship of another, the doing of homage and in some cases the payment of a yearly sum as a recognition of lordship, in return for which he would receive from his lord protection and support. See further B. Dodwell, *Eng. Hist. Rev.* lxiii (1948), 289 ff.

[3] See Maitland *op. cit.* 74.

Modercope had granted Loddon after his death to St. Edmund's Bury. Professor Douglas is unquestionably right, in his discussion of these texts, in saying that ' these documents must certainly be taken together '.[1] His interpretation of these transactions is that Ælfric ' bequeaths land to the church and at the same time performs some sort of homage to two of the abbots to whom his possessions were assigned ' ; and that ' presumably, like so many other of the great men of the land, he held his " bequeathed " estates from his ecclesiastical superiors.' He observes that in Domesday Loddon is held by St. Edmund (of Bury), and has been granted to Frodo, who, like Ælfric, is also a tenant of the abbot of Ely, and that Bergh Apton is in the possession of the abbot of Ely, who has granted it to Godric Dapifer, whilst ' even the sheep-farming, conspicuously mentioned ' in Ælfric Modercope's will, is referred to in the Domesday account of Loddon.[2] Professor Douglas's phrase : ' at the same time ', needs however further consideration. The writ (no. 21) in which the king announces that Ælfric has his permission to commend himself—in the present tense—dates from 1051–52 or 1053–57. The second writ (no. 22) announcing that Ælfric *had*—in the past tense—granted Loddon, was in all probability issued later than the ' commendation ' writ, but within the same limits of time. Ælfric's will, setting out his assignment of his estates, dates from 1042–43, but that is not to say that further arrangements concerning estates named in it were not made subsequently. One might hazard the conjecture that Ælfric at a later date may have made arrangements for a life-tenancy of Loddon and other estates, and that his act of commendation was in some way connected with such arrangements. The Confessor's writ relating to Loddon (no. 22) may have been issued in consequence of some enquiry or some dispute which had arisen, possibly after Ælfric Modercope's death. It must be added that a highly unusual feature of the protocol of the Loddon writ is the employment of the preposition *into* before ' Norfolk ' in the place of the *on* which is common form. The only other instance is in the spurious Ickworth writ of Westminster Abbey (no. 80). BT Suppt, s.v. *into*, VII, gives two instances of *into* ' marking position, *in* ' ; *Chron.* 1015, ' þa yldestan þegnas *into* Seofon Burgum ', E 1048, ' to þan þet he hine hadian sceolde to biscope *into* Lundene '. But does it not seem likely that in all these instances *into* has the sense, not of ' marking position, *in* ' but of ' pertaining to, *of* ' ? However this may be the employment in nos. 22 and 80 of *into* instead of *on* need not be regarded as a suspicious feature.

As for the writ (no. 25) notifying the Confessor's grant of

[1] *Feudal Documents*, cxi f.
[2] For references, see Douglas, *ut supra*, and p. 443.

A MONEYER to the abbot, it is unfortunate that the text printed by Kemble should be corrupt (and Thorpe's translation inaccurate),[1] for on this basis an interpretation of the implications of this grant which it would be difficult to justify was made by H. W. C. Davis, and accepted by Mrs. Lobel. Davis remarked that ' the Bury mint had been important at the close of the ninth century and under Edward the Martyr ', that the Confessor's grant ' is worded as though he had previously maintained moneyers in the vill ',[2] and that ' the grant, therefore, is in effect a transference of a royal mint to private hands '. But in fact the writ is not worded as though the king had previously maintained moneyers at Bury. A literal translation would read : ' as freely in all things to have as to me mine stand in (my) hand anywhere in any of my boroughs (burge) most freely of all ', that is, that Abbot Baldwine is to have mintage rights with the same freedom from restriction as the king himself has in respect of his own royal mints in any of those boroughs where he maintains them. Although this is the only example known of the announcement by writ of a grant by the Confessor of a moneyer, there is nothing in the form or content of this writ to excite suspicion as to its authenticity. A code of Æthelstan (II Æthelstan 14) speaks of moneyers of the archbishop of Canterbury, of the abbot of St. Augustine's, Canterbury, and of the bishop of Rochester ; and although Æthelred II declared (III Æthelred 8, 1) that no one should have a moneyer except the king, a Domesday entry (DB i. 179) states that the bishop of Hereford in the time of the Confessor had a moneyer who, when the king's moneyers paid fees to the king on the issue of new dies, paid the same fees to the bishop (see p. 445). The idiomatic language of the writ is a point in its favour, and it can be confidently accepted as a modernised copy of an authentic writ of King Edward the Confessor, issued in the last few months of his reign.[3]

[1] See p. 445 below.
[2] Davis, *Eng. Hist. Rev.* xxiv (1909), p. 420, M. D. Lobel, *op. cit.* 11. Evidence (not mentioned by Davis, but see p. 444) for the existence of a mint at Bury T.R.E. is to be found in the coins struck there ; but no conclusions as to the existence of a mint at Bury can be drawn from the wording of the writ. In G. C. Brooke's *English Coins* (2nd ed. London, 1942) the earliest Bury coins are of Harold Harefoot (1035–40).
[3] For particulars of the mint at St. Edmund's after the Norman Conquest, see VCH *Suffolk* ii. 58, n. 8, and the references there ; it is stated that the privilege of a moneyer was confirmed to the abbot of Bury by William I, William II, Henry I, Richard I, John and Henry III. For a writ of William I, issued 1066–70, and referring to an earlier grant by the Confessor, see Douglas, *op. cit.*, Charter no. 5. See also G. C. Brooke, *A Catalogue of English Coins in the British Museum* (1916), i. clxiv.

BURY CARTULARIES

The numerous cartularies and registers of the abbey of Bury St. Edmunds have in recent years been systematically examined and described.[1] The modernised orthography of the ten writs taken from the Sacrist's Register (C.U.L. MS. Ff. 2.33), copied at the end of the thirteenth or the beginning of the fourteenth century, and of the one (spurious) writ (no. 10) from the roughly contemporary Registrum Album (B.M. Add. MS. 14847), differentiates them from texts derived from other sources ; but they have some affinities with the four writs in the register of Walter Pinchbeck (on which see p. 435). The texts in the Sacrist's Register and the Registrum Album (neither of which is a copy of the other) have their own constantly recurring individual peculiarities of spelling. Some words regularly follow the normal pattern of late West Saxon spelling ; e.g. *ic, wille, freols, þider* ; others have a characteristically Middle English form : e.g. *erl, þeynes* ; others have a form characteristic in Middle English of the East Midland dialect area to which Bury St. Edmunds belonged : e.g. *biri, bireth (bureð, ibered), kithe, minstre,* and the Scandinavianised *frendlike* and *swilk.* A peculiar usage is the spelling *ih-, yh-,* for initial *g-* or *ge-.* The pronouns *ge, gu, gure* of the Middle English poem *Genesis and Exodus* sometimes appear in these texts as *ihe, ihu, ihure* ; e.g. *ihu,* nos. 8, 13, etc. ; the Pinchbeck Register f. 126 b has *yhu* for the same word. Similarly the Registrum Album ff. 30, 30 b has *ihiuen* for *giuen, ihuthe* for *geuthe.* A comparison between the texts of nos. 11, 24, in contemporary copies, and in copies in the Sacrist's Register, shows that these later copies are in the main trustworthy (though this should not be taken to imply that the Sacrist Register copies are derived directly from the contemporary copies of nos. 11, 24, now extant). While orthographical alterations, and alterations in accidence are frequent, omissions of words and phrases are rare, and for this reason copies in the Sacrist's Register have been preferred to those in the Registrum Album, where omissions frequently occur, and misunderstandings of the text sometimes appear ; for instances, see p. 157, no. 13, note on l. 2 (omission), l. 3 (misunderstanding). But other sources have been preferred here to the Sacrist's Register whenever a text has been available approaching more nearly to Old English orthography, or preserving some essential feature of the Old English text. The Registrum Werketon (Harley

---

[1] See VCH *Suffolk,* ii. 56, n. 2, and VCH *Guide to Materials,* 103–4 ; M. R. James, ' On the Abbey of St. Edmund at Bury ', *Cambridge Antiquarian Society, Octavo Publications,* xxviii (1895), 95–9, and *Eng. Hist. Rev.* xli (1926), 251–60 ; and especially D. C. Douglas, *Feudal Documents,* xix ff.

MS. 638) is notable for its preservation of many Old English forms in nos. 9, 15. A copy of no. 19 preserving an essential word (' now ') omitted in other copies is to be found in the register of John of Lakenheath (Harley MS. 743), compiled a year or two before the Peasants' Revolt. One writ (no. 12) has been taken from the Registrum Nigrum (C.U.L. MS. Mm. 4. 19, on which see Douglas, *op. cit.* pp. xx–xxii). One (no. 25) has been taken from the Cartæ Antiquæ Roll. The fifteenth-century Registrum Cellerarii (C.U.L. Gg. 4.4) has Latin versions of nos. 8, 18. As has been stated in the Preface, it has not been considered desirable to record the innumerable spelling variants in post-Conquest copies. Some idea of the number of these variants in Bury texts may be gained from the fact that when these are printed in full, for one vernacular Bury writ of the Conqueror preserved in six manuscripts, 89 footnotes of textual variants are required, and for another surviving in F and A, 20 footnotes.[1] It would be easy to find similar instances among the writs printed here.

The Latin versions of Bury writs (nos. 8, 12, 18)—headed in several cases : ' Interpretacio istius carte ' (i.e. of the Old English text)—present in general a fairly close rendering, though in no. 12 *bequepeth*, present (used also for future) has been rendered *dederunt*, and in no. 18 the final phrase : *be fullen wite* has been expanded into a full sentence. The use of the term *barones* in nos. 12, 18, and the expansion of the king's style in no. 8 into : *gratia Dei Anglorum rex*, indicate that these Latin versions were not made until after the Norman Conquest. It should be noted that *vendicet*, ' claim ', in the Latin version of no. 8, is not an exact rendering of the Old English *ateo*.

(8)

King Edward declares that Abbot Ufi is to be entitled to the monastery at St. Edmund's Bury and to everything pertaining thereto, and that the monastery is to retain unaltered the freedom granted to it by Cnut and Harthacnut. (1042–43)

(Ff. 2. 33, f. 22 b)

Eadward king gret Alfric biscop and alle mine þeynes on Norf' 1
7 on Suff' frendlike. And ic kithe ihu þat ic wille þat Vui abbot
be þet minstres wirðe at Seynt Eadmundes biri. and alle þinge þe þer
to bireth on lande 7 on sake and on sokne. and 'on' alle þinge so ful
and so forth so it firmest þider inne lay. 7 ic wille þat se freols 5

---

[1] See Douglas, *Feudal Documents*, Charters nos. 1, 3.

stonde into þat minstre unawent þe Cnut king þider inne uthe.
7 sithen Hardcnut kyng mine brother. 7 ic nelle þat efre ani
bisscop ani þing him þer on ateó.

Latin Version

(*Ibid.*)

Eduuardus gratia Dei Anglorum rex Alfrico episcopo cun[c]tisque
10 primatibus australibus 7 aquilonaribus salutem. Notum vobis esse
volo quod Vuy abbati monasterium Sancti Edmundi cum omnibus ad illud pertinentibus annui siue in terris siue in iure regali ita
pleniter sicut unquam plenius habuit. Ac libertatem quam Cnut
rex 7 postea Hardacnut rex frater meus eidem monasterio
15 [annuerunt] semper immutatam esse volo, illud quod penitus
prohibeo ut nullus episcoporum monasterium Sancti Edmundi ullo
modo sibi vendicet.

In Margin, in paler ink, in somewhat later hand : Prima carta Sancti
Eduuardi, *which is repeated with the Latin version at foot of page, copied in same
later hand. Latin version headed :* Interpretacio istius carte. 3. wirðe]
wirde MS. 13. libertates quas G. 15. annuerunt *from* G.
15. immutatas G. 15. illud que MS.

Translation

King Edward sends friendly greetings to Bishop Ælfric and all
my thegns in Norfolk and Suffolk. And I inform you that my will
is that Abbot Ufi shall be entitled to possess the monastery at St.
Edmund's Bury and everything pertaining thereto in land and in
sake and in soke and in all things as fully and as completely as ever
they pertained to that house. And my will is that the freedom
shall abide with the monastery unaltered which King Cnut granted
to it, and afterwards King Harthacnut, my brother. And I forbid
that any bishop whatsoever appropriate to himself anything therein.

(9)

King Edward declares that the land at Mildenhall and the sokes of
the eight and a half Thingoe hundreds are to belong to St. Edmund's
as fully and completely as his mother possessed them. 1043–44

(Harley MS. 638, f. 26)

1   + Eædward cyng gret Grymkytel .ᛒ. 7 Ælfwine 7 Ælfric.
7 ealle mine þegenas on Suðfolce freondlice. 7 ic cyðe eou þ ic
wille þ þ land æt Mildenhale 7 þa nigen half hundreda socne in to

þinghogy licgce in to Sc̄e Eædmunde. mid sace. 7 mid socne. swa
ful 7 swa forð swa hit minre meder on hande stod. 7 ic nelle **5**
geðafian þ̄ heom ænig mann ætbrede ænig þare þinga þæs þe ic
heom ær geuðe.

1. L grett, *the rest* gret.   3. *none read :* healf nygoðe hundreda
(*cf. no. 24, a contemporary copy*) ; nigend F ; *the rest some form of* nigen (nygen,
neghen, nighen).   4. þinghowe F, E ; Thynghowe L ; Thinghogi S, T.
4. *all have a verb in sing.* ; lige F ; ligge, E, L, S, T.   5. istod F.

Translation

King Edward sends friendly greetings to Bishop Grimketel and
Ælfwine and Ælfric and all my thegns in Suffolk.   And I inform
you that my will is that the land at Mildenhall and the sokes of the
eight and a half hundreds pertaining to Thingoe shall belong to
St. Edmund's with sake and with soke as fully and as completely
as my mother possessed it.   And I will not permit anyone to
take away from them any of the things that I have already granted
to them.

(10)

King Edward declares that the sokes of the eight and a half Thingoe
hundreds are to belong to St. Edmund's.

(Add. MS. 14847, f. 30)

Edward king gret Grimketel biscop and Alfger eerl.   7 Toly. and **1**
alle mine theines on Suthfolk frendlike.   And ic kithe ihu þat ic
wille þat þe half nigende hundred sokne þe *in* to þinghowe lige *in* to
Seint Ædmunde mid sake and mid sokne so ful and so forth so it
mine moder on hande istod. 7 ic nelle thafien that hem oni man **5**
abrede ani þere þinge þat ic her uthe.

3. *On intrusive* þe *in line 3 see p. 147.*

Translation

King Edward sends friendly greetings to Bishop Grimketel and
Earl Ælfgar and Toli and all my thegns in Suffolk.   And I inform
you that my will is that the sokes of the eight and a half hundreds
—which—pertaining to Thingoe shall belong to St. Edmund's with
sake and with soke as fully and as completely as my mother possessed it.   And I will not permit anyone to take away from them
any of the things that I have already granted to them.

M

(11)

King Edward declares that Abbot Leofstan and the brethren in
St. Edmund's Bury are to have sake and soke over all their own men
both within borough and without. 1044–65

(Cott. Aug. ii. 80)

1 + Eadweard cyngc gret mine bisceopas. 7 mine eorlas. 7 ealle
mine þegnas on þam sciren þær Sc̄e Eadmund hafað land inne
freondlice 7 ic cyðe eow þ̄ ic wylle þ̄ Leofstan abƀ. 7 ealle þa
gebroðra on Eadmundes byrig. beon heora sake 7 heora socne
5 wurðe ofer ealle heora agene menn. ægðer ge binnan burh ge butan.
7 ic nelle geðafian þ̄ heom ænig man ænig woh beode.

6. þat ani man ani woch em bede F, A.
Endorsed in a hand of cent. xii : . . . Ædmundus habet sacam et socam
in ciuitate et extra ; *and in a hand of cent. late xiv :* Sancti Edwardi.

Translation

King Edward sends friendly greetings to my bishops and my earls
and all my thegns in the shires in which St. Edmund has land.   And
I inform you that my will is that Abbot Leofstan and all the brethren
in Edmund's Bury shall be legally entitled to their sake and their
soke over all their own men, both within borough and without.
And I will not permit anyone to do them any wrong.

(12)

King Edward declares that Abbot Leofstan and the brethren
are to have sake and soke over the lands bequeathed to them
as fully and completely as this right was enjoyed by the previous
owner. 1044–65

(Mm. 4. 19, f. 105 b)

1 Eadward king gret mine .ƀes. 7 mine earles 7 alle mine þeignes
on þam schiran þer þe lond inne liggeð freondlike. 7 ic kithe eow
þat ic wille þat Leofstan abbot 7 þa brothere þat he ben here sake
7 here socne wrthe ofer þa land þe man in to þer halgen minstre
5 bequeþeth so ful 7 so forth so he hauede þe hig her ahte. 7 ic nille
þafien þat men hem ani unricht bede.

Latin Version

(Ibid.)

Eadwardus rex omnibus episcopis, comitibus, 7 baronibus, de uniuersis prouinciis ubicumque Sanctus Ædmundus habet aliquam terram salutem amicabiliter. Notum uobis sit quod ego iubeo ut Leofstanus abbas et fratres habeant sacam suam 7 socam in omnibus 10 terris quas homines illi sancto monasterio dederunt tam plenarie 7 perfecte sicuti illi habuerunt qui ante easdem terras possederunt, et nolo pati quod aliquis eis aliquam iniuriam faciat.

Heading : De Saca 7 Soca.   1. biscopes F, A.   2. ligge inne A.
4. þat halege stowe, F, A ; *original reading may have been* þære haligan stowe, *cf. the* þer *of* MS.   12. illi *omitted before* habuerunt, F, A.

Translation

King Edward sends friendly greetings to my bishops and my earls and all my thegns in the shires in which the lands are situated. And I inform you that my will is that Abbot Leofstan and the brethren shall be legally entitled to their sake and their soke over the lands which are bequeathed to the holy monastery as fully and as completely as he had them who was their former owner. And I will not permit that any wrong be done to them.

(13)

King Edward declares that all things lawfully pertaining to the property of St. Edmund are to be the uncontested possession of that house. 1044/5–47

(Ff. 2. 33, f. 23)

Eadward kyng gret Stigand bisscop 7 Harald erl and alle mine 1 þeynes on Estangle frendlike.   And ic kithe ihu þat ic wille þat alle þinge þe mid rithte bireð into Seynt Eadmundes are mine meyes 7 gode men þider inne uthen lige þider in unbesaken.   And ic ne[lle] þafien þat ani man uttige ani þing þat hem mid rithte to bireð 5 neither ne on londe ne oþere þingan.

2. A *omits* ic wille þat.   3. richte A ; MS *probably* rithte *rather than* richte *here, and throughout texts printed from* F.   3. Edmundes minister are A.

Translation

King Edward sends friendly greetings to Bishop Stigand and Earl Harold and all my thegns in East Anglia.   And I inform you that my will is that all things lawfully pertaining to the property of my kinsman St. Edmund, and granted by good men to that house, shall belong to it without dispute. And I will not permit anyone to alienate anything that lawfully pertains to them, either in land or in other things.

(14)

King Edward announces that he has granted the land at Pakenham to St. Edmund as fully and completely as Osgot had it. 1044/5–47, possibly 1046–47

(Ff. 2. 33, f. 23)

1   Eadward kyng gret Stigand bisscop and Haroᵛl'd erl and alle mine þeynes on Estangle frendlike. And ic kithe ou þat ic habbe unnen Seynt Eadmund mine meye þat lond at Pakenham so ful and so forth so it Osgote on honde stod.

Heading : Pakenham.   4. Osgothe A.

Translation

King Edward sends friendly greetings to Bishop Stigand and Earl Harold and all my thegns in East Anglia. And I inform you that I have granted to St. Edmund my kinsman the land at Pakenham as fully and as completely as Osgot possessed it.

(15)

King Edward declares that St. Edmund's inland is to be exempt from payment of heregeld and from every other render. c. 1051

(Harley MS. 638, f. 26)

1   + Eadward cyningc gret Ægelmer .ᵬ. 7 Ælfgar eorl 7 ealle mine ðegenas 7 sciregerefan on Suthfolce 7 on Norðfolce 7 swa hwer swa Sᴄ̄e Eadmund ænig land hafeþ freondlice. 7 ic cyða eou þ hic gehate be fullan hæse þ Sᴄ̄e Eadmundes inland sy scotfreo fram 5 heregelde. 7 fram eghwilc oðer gaful.

2. Q *omits* sciregerefan.   2. Q (*wrongly*) *inserts* freondlice *after* Norðfolce.   3. cyðe eow þ ic Q.   4. F, A, E, *insert* ihu (' you ') *before* gehate.

Translation

King Edward sends friendly greetings to Bishop Æthelmær and Earl Ælfgar and all my thegns and sheriffs in Suffolk and Norfolk

and wheresoever St. Edmund has any land.   And I inform you that
I expressly command that the inland of St. Edmund be exempt from
payment of heregeld and from every other render.

(16)

King Edward declares that his mother is to have the estate at
Kirby as fully and completely as ever her retainer Leofstan had it.
September 1051–March 1052

(Ff. 2. 33, f. 23 b)

Eadward kyng gret Aylmer bisscop and Aelfger erl. 7 alle mine   1
þeynes on Norf' frendlike.   And ic kithe ou þat ic wille þat mine
moder be þes londes wrthe at Kirkeby. and alle þinge þat þer to mid
rithte bireð so ful and so forth so Lefstan hire knyth it firmest
hauede.   5

Heading: Kirkeby.   3. worthe A.   3. A *omits* mid rithte.

Translation

King Edward sends friendly greetings to Bishop Æthelmær and
Earl Ælfgar and all my thegns in Norfolk.   And I inform you that
my will is that my mother be entitled to the land at Kirby and
everything lawfully pertaining thereto as fully and completely as
ever Leofstan her retainer had it.

(17)

King Edward declares that the monastery at St. Edmund's is to
possess Kirby with all the rights of the former owners.   Probably
March–September 1052

(Ff. 2. 33, f. 23)

Eadward kyng gret Aylmer bisscop 7 Aelfger erl 7 alle mine   1
þeynes on Norf' frendlike.   And ic kithe ihu þat ic wille þat þat
lond at Kirkeby 7 alle þinge þat þer to mid rithte bireð lige into
þan halege minstre at Seynt Eadmund mid sake 7 mid socne so fol
and so forth so it ani man firmest hauˑeˈde.   7 mine moder it þider 5
inne byquath.   And ic bidde ihu alle þat ge deme me swilc dom of
Semere þat haueð þider inne faren mid unlage swilk ge for Gode
witen þat me mid rithte to bireð.

3. richte A.   3. A *omits* lige.   4. Edmundes A.   4. ful A.
7. Kemble *reads* sende *for* Semere.   *But* MS *has* sem'e *with the same mark
of contraction above the line as in* Aylm' = Aylmer *and* Aelfg' = Aelfger
in line 1.   7. inne þider, *with dashes at each side of* inne MS.; þyder
inne A.

Translation

King Edward sends friendly greetings to Bishop Æthelmær and Earl Ælfgar and all my thegns in Norfolk. And I inform you that my will is that the land at Kirby and all things lawfully pertaining thereto shall belong to the holy monastery at St. Edmund's with sake and with soke as fully and as completely as ever any man had it, and my mother bequeathed it to that house. And I pray you all that you pronounce for me a judgement concerning Semer, who has illegally occupied it, such as you, in the sight of God, know to be my lawful right.

(18)

King Edward declares that the monastery at St. Edmund's Bury is to possess the sokes of the eight and a half hundreds which he has given to that house, as fully and completely as ever his mother had them, and he himself possessed them. 1052, or 1053–57

(Ff. 2. 33, f. 22)

1 Eadward kyng gret Aylmer bisscop 7 Alfger erl 7 Toly. and alle mine theynes on Suff' frendlike. And ic kithe ihu þat ic wille þat þe half nigende hundred sokne þe ic habbe ihiuen God and Seynt Eadmunde mine mey þat it liggen into þat halegen minstre at 5 Eadmundes biri so ful and so forth so mine moder it fermist aihte. and it Alfrich Withgares sune hire to hande biwiste. and it sithen me seluen on honde stoden. 7 ic ne am becnowe þat ic ani man uthe þenen ut neyther ne hamsokne ne grithbreche ne forstal ne fichtwite ne hebberethef ne non þere rithte þa thider in mid rithte ibereð be 10 fullen wite.

Latin Version

(Ibid.)

Ego Eadwardus rex saluto Aylmerum episcopum 7 Algarum comitem 7 Toli 7 omnes meos barones de Suff' amicabiliter. Notifico vobis quod ego volo ut viii hundredorum 7 dimidii soka quam Deo 7 Sancto Eadmundo meo cognato dedi, adiacent 15 monasterio predicti martiris ita plene 7 perfecte sicuti mea mater ea primitus habuit, et sicut Aelfricus Withagari filius ad manum matris mee custodivit, et sicut ea postea michimet in manu fuerunt. Nec ego cognosco me dedisse alicui nisi predicto monasterio istas rectitudines, videlicet, hamsokne 7 grithbreche 7 forstal 7 ferdwite 20 7 hebberethef 7 fithwite nec aliquam rectitudinem quam Sancto

Eadmundo prius dederam. Nec volo pati ut aliquis ullam harum rectitudinum que ad prefatum monasterium pertinent extra mutat per plenariam forisfacturam.

3. nigende *in* A *also*. 5. authe A (OE ahte) 6. *Kemble omits from* and it sithen *to* stoden. 7. standen A. 8. fyrdwite *absent in* MS. *and* A ; *cf. Lat. ver. and no.* 26. *Heading in Latin version :* Interpretacio carte eiusdem. 14. Deo *omitted* A. 21. *Cole, Mon. Angl. and* K. *omit last sentence :* Nec volo . . . forisfacturam.

Translation

King Edward sends friendly greetings to Bishop Æthelmær and Earl Ælfgar and Toli and all my thegns in Suffolk. And I inform you that my will is that the sokes of the eight and a half hundreds that I have given to God and to my kinsman, St. Edmund, shall belong to the holy monastery at Edmund's Bury as fully and as completely as ever my mother owned it, and Ælfric, Wihtgar's son, administered it on her behalf, and it was afterwards in my own possession. And I am not aware that I have granted away from it to anyone either hamsocn or grithbreach or foresteall or fihtwite or æbæretheof or any of the rights that lawfully pertain to it with payment of the penalty at the full rate.

(19)

King Edward declares that the soke previously granted by him to St. Edmund's is now to belong to that house as fully and completely as he himself possessed it. 1051–52, or 1053–57

(Harley MS. 743, f. 59 b)

Edward kyng greth Aegelmare bischop 7 Aelf[g]ar eorl 7 aelle mine   1 þeinas on Sudfolke frendliche.   And ich kiðe eou þatt ich wille þat se sokne ligge nou in to Saynt Edmunde þe ich aer þider inn geuðe. swa ful 7 swa forð swa hit me seolfan on handa stod.   And ich nelle geþafian þat hit aenyng man geouthtyge ne gehaddod ne gelaewede.   5 and ich wille gewytan þaes mannes nama þe wyle God refian and Sayntt Edmond and me.

1. gret F, A. 2. kiðe] kide MS. 3. F, A, *omit* nou. 5. uttige F, A. 5. gelaewede *for* OE læwed ; *cf. no.* 26, *l.* 5.

Translation

King Edward sends friendly greetings to Bishop Æthelmær and Earl Ælfgar and all my thegns in Suffolk. And I inform you that my will is that the soke shall belong now to St. Edmund's which I formerly granted thereto as fully and as completely as I myself possessed it. And I will not permit anyone, ecclesiastic or layman, to alienate it. And I will know that man's name who shall wish to rob God and St. Edmund and me.

(20)

King Edward declares that the land at Coney Weston is to belong to St. Edmund's monastery with everything which is known to pertain lawfully to that house. 1051–52, or 1053–57

(Ff. 2. 33, f. 23)

1   Eadward kyng gret Aylmer bisscop 7 Aelfger erl and Toly and alle mine þeynes on Suff' and on Norf' frendlike. And ic kithe ou þat ic wille þat þat lond at Cunegestone lige into Seynt Eadmundes minstre and alle þe þinge þat þer to mid rithte bireð mid sake and 5 mid sokne so ful and so forth so ihe alle for Gode witen þat it mid rithte in bureð.

Heading : Cunegeston'.   3. Conuestune (*or possibly* Connestune) A.
4. richte A.   4. inibireð A.

Translation

King Edward sends friendly greetings to Bishop Æthelmær and Earl Ælfgar and Toli and all my thegns in Suffolk and Norfolk. And I inform you that my will is that the land at Coney Weston and everything lawfully pertaining thereto shall belong to St. Edmund's monastery with sake and with soke as fully and as completely as you all, in the sight of God, know it lawfully to pertain to that house.

(21)

King Edward declares that Ælfric Modercope has his full permission to commend himself to the abbots of Bury and of Ely. 1051–52, or 1053–57

(Ff. 2. 33, f. 23)

1   Eadward kyng gret Aylmer bisscop 7 Aelfger erl 7 alle mine þeynes on Suff' and on Norf' frendlike. And ic kithe ou þat ic wille þat it is min fulle unna þat Alfrich Modercope mot bugan to þo tueyen abboten at Seynt Eadmunde 7 at Sce Aetheldrede be Godes leue and 5 be mine.

Heading : Confirmacio 7 ratificacio collacionis Alfrici Modercope. 2. *Thorpe inserts* ' and ' *after* wille.   4. F, A, *wrongly* loue ; *cf. no. 23,* for mine loue (*with* for, *not* be), *similarly no.* 24.

Translation

King Edward sends friendly greetings to Bishop Æthelmær and Earl Ælfgar and all my thegns in Suffolk and in Norfolk. And I inform you that my will is that Ælfric Modercope with my full permission may submit himself to the two abbots at St. Edmund's and at St. Æthelthryth's by God's leave and by mine.

(22)

King Edward testifies to Ælfric Modercope's grant of Loddon after his death to the monastery at St. Edmund's Bury. 1051–52, or 1053–57

(Ff. 2. 33, f. 22 b)

Eadward kyng gret Aylmer bisscop 7 Alfger earl. and alle mine 1
þeynes into Norf' frendlike. And ic kithe ihu þat ic am to withnesse
þat Alfric Modercop hauede unnen after his day þat land at Lodne
into þat halegen minstre at Eadmundes biri and alle þe þinge þat þer
to bireð mid sake and mid sokene so ful and so forth so it him 5
seluen on hande stod.

2. into (Northf') A *also*.

Translation

King Edward sends friendly greetings to Bishop Æthelmær and Earl Ælfgar and all my thegns of Norfolk. And I inform you that I bear witness that Ælfric Modercope had granted after his death to the holy monastery at Edmund's Bury, the land at Loddon and everything pertaining thereto with sake and with soke as fully and as completely as he himself possessed it.

(23)

King Edward announces the appointment of Baldwine as abbot of Bury. 1 August 1065–5 January 1066

(Ff. 3. 33, f. 22 b)

Eadward kyng gret Aylmer biscop 7 Girth earl 7 Toly and alle 1
mine þeynes on Estangl' frendlike. 7 ic kithe ihu þat ic habbe
unnen Baldewine abbot þe abbotriche into Seint Eadmundes biri
7 alkere þinge þe þer into bireth mid sake and mid sokne so ful
7 so forth so Lefston abbot oþer ani abbot it toforen him firmest 5

haude. Nu bidde ic alle þe manne þe ben Godes frend and min þat him filste to lage 7 to rithte loc wer him ned beth. 7 he ihure fultumes beþurfe for mine loue. And ic nelle nane men þafien þat him fro hande teo ani þing þat 'ic' him gifen habbe oþer get þinke to done 10 no swither þan he min brother were.

    2. ihu kythe A.   7. loc wer] loc þer MS.   8. beþurfe]
bewrfe MS.

Translation

King Edward sends friendly greetings to Bishop Æthelmær and Earl Gyrth and Toli and all my thegns in East Anglia. And I inform you that I have granted to Abbot Baldwine the abbacy at St. Edmund's Bury, and everything pertaining thereto with sake and with soke as fully and completely as ever Abbot Leofstan or any abbot before him had it. Now I pray all the men who are God's friends and mine that they, for love of me, help him to obtain what is lawful and right wherever the need shall arise for him, and he may require your help. And I will not permit anyone to take away from him anything that I have given him or still intend to give, any more than I would [permit it] if he (the abbot) were my brother.

(24)

King Edward confirms to the monastery at St. Edmund's Bury the sokes of the eight and a half hundreds (after the appointment of Baldwine as abbot of Bury). 1 August 1065–5 January 1066

(Cott. Aug. ii. 49)

1   + Eadweard cyningc gret Ægelmær ᛒ. 7 Gyrð eorl. 7 Tolig. 7 ealle mine þegenas. on Suðfollce. freondlice 7 ic cyðe eow ꝧ ic wylle ꝧ þa healf nygoðe hundreda sócne ligce innto þam halgan mynstre innto Sce Eadmundes byrig mines mæges. swa full. 7 swa forð.
5 swa Ælfric Wihtgares sunu hig minre meder to hánda bewiste. 7 heo syððan me sylfan on hánda stod. on eallan þingan. 7 ic hig þider inn geuðe mid ælc þæra [þinga] þæs þe þær mid rihte to gebyrað. mid fyrdwite. 7 fyhtwíte. 7 æbære þeof. 7 griðbryce. 7 foresteall. 7 hamsócne. 7 ic bidde eow eallan ꝧ ge beon Baldewine 10 abbe on fultume. ꝧ he mote beon ælc þæra gerihta wurðe. þæs þe he ah þær of rihtlice to habbene. for minan lufan. 7 ic ne eom gecnáwe ꝧ ic ænigean menn geafe þa sócne þanon ut þe ic hig ær þider inn geofrode. 7 gyf ænig mann sy ꝧ wylle ænig þæra sócna him to hánda drægen. 7 segce ꝧ ic hig ær him geunnan sceolde.

ic wylle ꝥ he cume beforan me mid his sweotelunge. 7 do me 15
gecnawe hwær ic hig him ær geuðe. ꝥ nan oþer ne sy.

3. nigende F, A, niggende E.   3. MS. *probably* ligce, *the reading
of* W ; *but* K. *prints* ligæ, *the reading of* Q ; F, E, A, *and* Ch. R. *copies (except*
R) ligge ; ligcne R.   7. MS *alone omits* þinga ; ælc þære þinga Q ;
alkere þinge F, A.   13. W, Ch. R., Conf. R. *end at* geofrode ; *spelling*
geoffrode, W, R.   14. dragen Q, F.

Translation

   King Edward sends friendly greetings to Bishop Æthelmær and
Earl Gyrth and Toli and all my thegns in Suffolk.   And I inform
you that my will is that the sokes of the eight and a half hundreds
shall belong to the holy monastery at the Bury of St. Edmund
my kinsman, as fully and as completely in every respect as Ælfric,
Wihtgar's son, administered it on my mother's behalf, and it was
afterwards in my possession, and I granted it to that house with
all the things that lawfully pertain thereto, with fyrdwite and fihtwite and æbæretheof and grithbreach and foresteall and hamsocn.
And I pray you all that you will for love of me assist Abbot Baldwine so that he may legally possess all the rights that he ought
justly to have therefrom.   And I am not aware that I have granted
away from it to anyone the sokes that I had formerly devoted to
that house.   And if there be anyone who shall wish to take into
his own possession any of the sokes, and shall say that I had
already granted them to him, my will is that he come before me
with his evidence [substantiating his claim] and demonstrate to
me where I had previously granted it to him, so that the matter
may be settled.

(25)

King Edward declares that he has granted to Abbot Baldwine a
moneyer within St. Edmund's Bury.   1 August 1065–5 January 1066

(Cartæ Antiquæ Roll P, no. 4)

   + Eadward cyng gret Æigelmer ƀ. 7 Georð eorl [7 Tolig] 7 ealle   1
mine þegenas on Æstengle freondlice.   7 ic cyðe éou ꝥ ic habbe
geunnen Baldwine aƀƀe onne menetere wið inne Seint Eadmundes
byrig. al swa freolice on ealle þing to habben. al swa me mine on
hande stonden ower on enig minre burge alre freolukeost.   God seo   5
eow alre freond.

1. Ægelmer W.   Girth F, E.   7 Tolig *in all except* MS.   3. onne
meonetere W, R ; one munetere F, A ; on munetere E ; on(e) monetere
S, T.   5. stoden ower S, T, M ; stoden. oþer W, R ; stoden oðer
in K. *is still further removed from the original reading* (*in* MS.).

Translation

King Edward sends friendly greetings to Bishop Æthelmær and Earl Gyrth and Toli and all my thegns in East Anglia. And I inform you that I have granted to Abbot Baldwine a (*or* one) moneyer within St. Edmund's Bury, to have with the same freedom from restriction as I have my own anywhere in any of my boroughs where I have them more freely than anywhere else. May God be the friend of all of you.

CHRIST CHURCH, CANTERBURY

Of the ten surviving writs of Christ Church, Canterbury,[1] the four writs of Cnut and the writ of Archbishop Wulfstan, all of which are entered in the margins or in blank spaces in manuscripts, appear to be authentic. But the same cannot be said of the five writs in the name of King Edward the Confessor ; of these only one, no. 35, seems to be of reasonably certain authenticity. In another writ bearing the name of King Edward (no. 33) we can actually detect the work of two hands : the first has written the address and salutation and the opening words of the king's declaration, while the second has written the remainder over an erasure. It is not often that the process of alteration of a writ is so plainly manifest as it is here (see Frontispiece). We need not doubt that the Confessor did in actual fact grant to the two archbishops appointed in his reign and to the community at Christ Church the customary judicial and financial rights, as he did in other cases. Domesday Book, the Domesday Monachorum [2] and other records bear witness

[1] Christ Church, Canterbury (Canterbury Cathedral) was founded by St. Augustine, the church being consecrated ' in nomine sancti Saluatoris Dei et Domini nostri Jesu Christi ' (Bede, *Hist. Eccles.* i. cap. 33, ed. Plummer, i. 70). Not much is known of the early history of this foundation, for which see *Mon. Angl.* i. 81 ff. and VCH *Kent*, ii. 113 ff. The house was known during the Middle Ages as the priory of the Holy Trinity. The registers of Christ Church, some of which contain copies of the writs printed here, are described in the Appendices to the Reports of the Historical MSS. Commission (1876–83) ; *Fifth Report*, Part i, Appendix, 426 ff. ; *Eighth Report*, Part i, Appendix, 315–55 ; *Ninth Report*, Part i, Appendix, 72–121. See also M. R. James and C. Jenkins, *Catalogue of Manuscripts at Lambeth Palace* (Cambridge, 1930), 316–20, W. Holtzmann, *Papsturkunden in England*, ii (1935), 8 ff.

[2] See *The Domesday Monachorum of Christ Church, Canterbury*, ed. D. C. Douglas (R. Hist. Soc., 1944).

to their privileges. But no unquestionably genuine writs in the Confessor's name notifying such grants are now known to exist, though everything encourages the belief that the opening lines and the seal of a genuine writ in favour of Archbishop Stigand are preserved in no. 33, mentioned above. The absence of genuine writs announcing grants to Archbishops Eadsige and Stigand of such privileges as had been conferred on Archbishop Æthelnoth by King Cnut (no. 28) is perhaps to be explained by the disastrous fire at Christ Church in 1067, in which many manuscripts are said to have been destroyed.[1] But it is to be noted that it would have been highly desirable in their own interests for the archbishop and the monks of Christ Church to have been able after the Conquest to produce writs supporting their claims to lands and privileges, for the changes brought about by the Norman Conquest led to a long period of litigation in Kent. In consequence of the encroachments of the Conqueror's half-brother, Odo, bishop of Bayeux and earl of Kent, Lanfranc, the newly-appointed archbishop of Canterbury, determined to vindicate the possessions and rights of his see. The matter was tried at a great shire court lasting three days at Penenden Heath,[2] to which were summoned all the men of the shire, French and English, especially those of English birth who were expert in ancient laws and customs. There Lanfranc, we are told, successfully proved his claim not only to numerous estates, but also to the privileges and ' customs ' of his church, and these are enumerated in terminology which is customary in the writs :—

' Et in eodem placito non solum istas prænominatas et alias terras, sed et omnes libertates ecclesiæ suæ et omnes consuetudines suas renovavit, et renovatas ibi diratiocinavit, soca, saca, toll, team, flymena fyrmthe, grithbrece, foresteal, heimfare (hamsocn *in the Christ Church writs*), infangennetheof, cum omnibus aliis consuetudinibus paribus istis vel minoribus istis, in terris et in aquis, in sylvis, in viis, et in pratis, et in omnibus aliis rebus infra civitatem et extra, infra burgum et extra, et in omnibus aliis locis.' [3]

---

[1] *Chronicle* A 1066, D, E, 1067. Plummer considers 1067 to be the correct date. For references to the fire and to the destruction of documents, including a reference by Lanfranc himself, see Plummer ii. 260. There was another fire at Christ Church in 1174 ; see the tractate concerning the burning and repair of Christ Church in Gervase of Canterbury, *Opera*, R.S. i. 3–29.

[2] For an account of this litigation see Wharton's *Anglia Sacra*, i. 334–6 ; A. J. Macdonald, *Lanfranc* (Oxford, 1926), 126–9. There is no certainty as to the date of the trial. J. H. Le Patourel, ' The date of the trial on Penenden Heath ', *Eng. Hist. Rev.* lxi (1946), 378–88, adopts the generally accepted date of 1072 ' because the weight of the published evidence seems in favour of it ', whilst admitting the possibility that the date of 1076 may be correct.

[3] *Anglia Sacra*, i. 335. Similarly, with some verbal variations, in the text printed by W. Levison, ' A Report on the Penenden Trial ', *Eng. Hist. Rev.* xxvii (1912), 717–20. For other texts see D. C. Douglas, ' Odo, Lanfranc,

Further litigation followed, in which Lanfranc was again successful. One cannot help suspecting that the fabrication at Christ Church, by the alteration of a genuine writ, of the writ (no. 33) purporting to announce a grant by the Confessor to Archbishop Stigand and the community of privileges similar to these, was in some way connected with the vindication in the early Norman period of the rights and privileges of the archbishop. The other Christ Church writ in favour of Stigand (no. 34), in spite of individual peculiarities, appears to be closely related to the bilingual writs with similar content attributed to Henry I and Henry II, and it seems unlikely that it is authentic in its present form. As for the two writs in favour of Archbishop Eadsige (nos. 31, 32), these have come down to us in copies of much later date preserved only in a Christ Church cartulary at Lambeth Palace (Lambeth MS. 1212), and their resemblance to other Christ Church documents of the same type is so close that they cannot be accepted as independent evidence of actual grants by the Confessor. The only one of the Christ Church writs attributed to the Confessor that is of reasonably certain authenticity is in fact the Mersham writ (no. 35), in its Anglo-Saxon form. And it should be noted that this authentic writ, like the authentic Christ Church writs of Cnut, and the authentic writ of Archbishop Wulfstan, is preserved as a copy in a Gospel Book.

WRITS OF KING CNUT

King Cnut is reputed to have been a benefactor of Christ Church, and to have given to that house the arm of St. Bartholomew the Apostle, and the haven of Sandwich, and the golden crown from his own head.[1] In the first Christ Church writ printed here, no. 26, Cnut is stated to have visited Christ Church. On one such visit Cnut and his brother Harold with some other persons were admitted to confraternity, an event commemorated by an entry on the page preceding the text of this writ in the copy of the Latin Gospels in which it has come down to us.[2] In this first writ we learn that Cnut gave permission to Archbishop Lyfing to draw up a new *freols*, or charter of freedom, for Christ Church in the king's name, and that the king himself took the monastery's charters of freedom and, in the

and the Domesday Survey', *Historical Essays in Honour of James Tait* (Manchester, 1933), 47–58. And see especially Le Patourel, *Stud. in Med. Hist. presented to F. M. Powicke* (Oxford, 1948), 15–26.

[1] MS. Cott. Galba E. iii, f. 33 b. See also K. 1328 (an entry in the MacDurnan Gospels), and the entry in the late list of Christ Church benefactors printed in *Mon. Angl.* i. 97. For the grant of the haven of Sandwich see *Chron.* A 1031, *Crawford Charters*, no. xii, and Robertson no. 82.

[2] Text in Wanley ; for reference see p. 446.

presence of witnesses, laid them upon the altar, using the same terms as King Æthelberht had used in freeing it, and all the king's predecessors. The importance of this writ must be stressed. It provides further evidence of the drawing up of a charter of freedom at the king's command by an interested ecclesiastic (see Introduction, p. 39). The terms of the *freols* are not given in the writ, but it is possible that they are preserved in a charter dated 1018 (K. 727) which has come down to us in one of the Christ Church registers. This charter can scarcely be independent of King Cnut's writ. It states that Cnut, hearing the *beneficia* or *regalia privilegia* of his royal predecessors, and perceiving the freedom (*libertatem*) of the monasteries in Kent, has, at the suggestion of Archbishop Lyfing, decided to make firm the present charter (*præsentam chartulam corroborare*) : that is to say, that Christ Church with everything pertaining to it, is to be free (*libera*),

' nec quisquam hominum in ea et rebus suis aliquid iuris uel consuetudinis praeter archiepiscopum et monachos ibidem Deo famulantes exigat uel obtineat ' ;

and it concludes with the king's precept that his inviolable decree shall stand firm for ever. There is no obvious reason for supposing the charter to be devoid of any substantial basis of fact, though its present form is irregular, and there is some slight doubt concerning two of the witnesses.[1] But whether the charter does or does not represent a genuine diploma of King Cnut, the authenticity of the writ relating to the *freols* of Christ Church seems on the whole to be reasonably certain.

Doubt was however cast on the authenticity of the Christ Church writ under discussion (no. 26) by Earle. ' When . . . Cnut is made to address his thanes as " twelfhynde and twihynde " ', says Earle, ' as we have no other example of " twihynde " thanes and as this document bears other suspicious marks, it is not available as historical material.' [2] This unqualified condemnation of the document seems quite unjustifiable. In spite of the sharp line of

---

[1] This charter, if it is authentic, can hardly in its present form be complete, the customary preamble being absent ; but there is nothing remarkable about this, for scribes copying charters into the Christ Church registers frequently took liberties with their texts. The dates of the witnesses—in so far as they are known—seem to be consistent with one another, except that Ælfgar who here attests as bishop (presumably of Elmham) is by some authorities said to have resigned his see before 1016 (Searle, *Anglo-Saxon Bishops, Kings and Nobles*, 51), though he did not die till 1021. But the *Leofricus* who attests as bishop does not appear in the usual lists ; it is not impossible that this name may have been substituted at one stage or another in the transmission of the text for that of *Leofsige*, who became bishop of Worcester in 1016. And further the witness list has been Latinised and possibly altered.

[2] Earle, *Land-Charters*, xlii.

cleavage generally drawn between the king's thegn, the person whose wergeld amounted to 1200 shillings, here and elsewhere described as *twelfhynde*, and the peasant or commoner, whose wergeld amounted to 200 shillings, here and elsewhere described as *twihynde*, there is other evidence to indicate that in Kent the word ' thegn ' might be used to include commoners as well as nobles. In the opening clauses of a letter sent from Kent c. 928–c. 938 to King Æthelstan,[1] the word *thaini* includes both *comites* and *villani* [2] :—

' Karissime ! Episcopi tui de Kantia et omnes Cantescyre Thaini, Comites et Villani, tibi, domino karissimo suo, gratias agunt quod nobis de pace nostra præcipere voluisti etc.'

This use of *thaini* in conjunction with *comites* et *villani* provides a close parallel for the : *þegnas twelfhynde and twihynde*, of Cnut's writ.   The fact that Cnut's writ is addressed to the archbishop of Canterbury, the bishop of Rochester, the abbot of St. Augustine's, Canterbury, and the sheriff Æthelwine, and Æthelric (both of whom are elsewhere associated with Kent), makes it probable that the writ was addressed to a Kentish shire court, though the words ' in Kent ' do not actually occur in the address.   This supposition would explain the inclusion in the address of Archbishop Lyfing, who would already of course have been familiar with the proceedings described in the writ.   No other ' suspicious marks ' except the conjunction of *twihynde* with *þegnas* are brought forward by Earle, and there are none that are obvious.   It is hard to see what Christ Church would have gained by the fabrication there of a writ drawn up in such general terms.   Parallels are forthcoming for the placing of the *freolsas* of Christ Church on the altar by Cnut in the presence of many witnesses.   In a Christ Church charter of c. 960 we read :—

' Then Eadgifu, with the leave and cognisance of the king and all his bishops, took the title-deeds (*bec*) and gave the estates to Christ Church, and with her own hands laid them upon the altar '.

And again in a charter of King Æthelberht of Wessex (860–65) for Sherborne, we read :—

' King Æthelberht on Friday two days before Easter with joyful heart laid this *freols* with his own hand upon the high altar at the monastery in Sherborne, in the presence of all the assembled brethren . . . and also of his

---

[1] The letter is now known only from a Latin version made c. 1114 in the Quadripartitus.   See Liebermann, *Gesetze*, i. 170–1, F. L. Attenborough, *Laws of the Earliest English Kings*, 142–6 ; Stubbs, *Select Charters*, 9th ed. (1913), 75.

[2] For comments on this use of the term ' thegn ', see Kemble, *Saxons in England*, ii. 234 ; Stubbs, *Constitutional History*, 5th ed. I. 128 ; Larson, *King's Household in England*, 102 ; Liebermann ii. 481, iii. 111 ; Attenborough, 209 ; Stenton, 481.   On the term ' thegn ' in general, see H. M. Chadwick, *Anglo-Saxon Institutions*, 79–87.   Attenborough suggests that this use of ' thegn ' is Scandinavian rather than English.

kinsmen Æthelred and Alfred, and of his other counsellors who were there with him '.[1]

Again, the anathema which protects the liberties of Christ Church is a feature not infrequently found in Anglo-Saxon writs, and in this text it may well be authentic (see Introduction, pp. 67 ff.). That the archbishop of Canterbury and the community at Christ Church should have enjoyed liberties going back to King Æthelberht of Kent, the founder of the see, does not seem improbable. Nor is there anything in the phraseology or in the linguistic forms of this writ to excite suspicion. Taken all together, the evidence favours the supposition that we have in this text a slightly later copy of an authentic writ of King Cnut.

The writ (no. 28) of A.D. 1020 in which King Cnut announces that he has granted to Archbishop Æthelnoth of Canterbury sake and soke, foresteall, grithbreach, hamsocn, infangenetheof and flymenafyrmth over his own men within borough and without, is probably the earliest example extant of a writ announcing the grant of judicial and financial rights to a prelate or a religious foundation, since the authenticity of the writ of King Æthelred II for the priests of St. Paul's (no. 52) seems unfortunately too doubtful for it to be considered here. That we have in the writ of Cnut for Archbishop Æthelnoth a slightly later copy of an authentic writ of that king seems quite beyond doubt ; both in form and in content this text appears to be above suspicion. It is evident that King Cnut had acceded to the request expressed by Archbishop Wulfstan of York in his writ to the king and queen (no. 27), announcing the consecration, in accordance with a declaration received by him from the king, of Æthelnoth to the see of Canterbury, and petitioning that the archbishop be granted the same privileges as his ancestors. Everything encourages the belief that Wulfstan's writ is authentic. The other two writs of Cnut for Christ Church, nos. 29, 30, both in favour of Archbishop Æthelnoth, seem also to be above suspicion. There is nothing improbable in the content of no. 29, issued perhaps in consequence of attempts by the reeve Æthelric [2] to increase the amount paid to

[1] For Eadgifu, see Harmer, *English Historical Documents*, p. 38 ; for Æthelberht, Robertson, *Anglo-Saxon Charters*, p. 20. For other instances and for comments, see H. Brunner, *Zur Rechtsgeschichte der römischen und germanischen Urkunde* (Berlin, 1880), 156 f.

[2] For instances of complaints regarding the unjust exactions of reeves, see Morris, *Medieval English Sheriff*, 11-14 ; and note particularly Cnut's Proclamation of 1027, § 12, where the king says, addressing sheriffs and reeves : ' I have no need that money should be collected for me by any unjust exactions.' See also II Cnut 69 (Liebermann i. 356, Robertson, *Laws*, 209) announcing measures by which the oppression of the people by reeves might be mitigated.

N

the king from the land belonging to the archbishopric, in money and in kind and services, and declaring that the land of the archbishopric shall be assessed at the same amount as it had been hitherto, both before and after Æthelric's appointment ; whilst the use of the term *werige* (see p. 450) provides an interesting instance of continuity in the employment of formulas in the king's writing office, appearing as it does in no. 66 (no. 67 is spurious), and also in no. 107 (supposing this to be authentic). The other writ of Cnut, no. 30, is concerned with a Christ Church estate formerly held by a certain Ælfmær, which Cnut now grants to the archbishop. Nothing is known of Ælfmær or of the estate that he had held. Earle (pp. 237–8) supposes that the purpose of the writ was the restoration to the archbishop of an estate that had been wrongly alienated, and remarks : ' If the Ælmær here dispossessed is that Ælmær Dyrling whose name is coupled A.D. 1016 in the Abingdon Chronicle with that of the traitor Eadric, as aiding the invaders, it might follow that Cnut was not restrained from doing justice by his sense of obligation to disloyal aid '. But in fact there is nothing to connect the Ælfmær of this writ with the person of that name who fought on the Danish side at Sherston in 1016 (*Chron.* D, E), and the name is of frequent occurrence. A possibility that might be considered is that the land was a Christ Church estate that had been leased to Ælfmær or to some predecessor of his, and that when the time came for it to be restored to Christ Church its possession was disputed. There is nothing in any of these writs of Cnut to cause one to question their authenticity. They are short, business-like documents, they make no extravagant claims, and from the point of view of linguistic forms and phraseology they may well have been produced in Cnut's reign. They have been carefully copied in hands that are almost contemporary. These writs fit in well with what is known from other sources of Cnut's benevolence towards the English church.[1]

WRITS OF KING EDWARD

Of the five Christ Church writs attributed to King Edward the Confessor, three are concerned with grants of judicial and financial rights to Archbishops Eadsige and Stigand respectively, and to the community at Christ Church. As has been said above, it is doubtful whether any one of these three documents is in its present form an authentic copy of a genuine writ of King Edward, though we need not doubt that such rights as these were given to the archbishop

---

[1] Stenton, *Anglo-Saxon England*, 390–1.

and the community.[1] The writ in favour of Archbishop Stigand preserved in the Campbell Collection (no. 33) is written on a single piece of parchment with a seal of yellowish-brown wax (see Frontispiece). There can be little doubt that the first three lines of the writ and the seal belong to an authentic writ of the Confessor for Archbishop Stigand produced by the clerks of the king's secretariat. But the remainder of the original text has been expunged, and the existing text has been written over it in a different handwriting, which is in all probability not earlier than of the late eleventh century. A similar tampering with the text is to be observed in a writ in English purporting to have been issued by William I for Archbishop Lanfranc, where a second handwriting begins after the first line ; and moreover the second handwriting of this document is in the same style as that of Campbell Charter xxi. 5, if indeed it is not by the same hand.[2] Further the two writs, the one in the name of Edward, the other in the name of William, closely resemble each other in every respect.[3] It does not however follow that that part of the Campbell Charter that is written by the second hand bears no relation to any genuine writ of the Confessor. This matter may well have been derived from a genuine writ, for a seemingly authentic writ of the Confessor for the monastery of St. Augustine at Canterbury (no. 38) is drawn up in very similar terms. The use in both Cnut's writ for Æthelnoth (no. 28), and in this writ of the Confessor for St. Augustine's of the characteristic formula : *ofer swa fela þegena swa ic heom to gelæten hæbbe* (also found in the Campbell Charter), is evidence of a continuity of formulas between King Edward's staff of writers and King Cnut's. Moreover the resemblance, not amounting to identity, between the phraseology of the Campbell Charter and that of the writ issued by Cnut for

[1] For the privileges of the archbishop, see the *Domesday Monachorum*, ed. D. C. Douglas, 98 : ' Through all the city of Canterbury the king has sake and soke, the land of the Holy Trinity (Christ Church) and St. Augustine excepted. The archbishop claims the forfeiture in ways outside the city where his land lies, on both sides of the ways. In case of adultery, through all Kent, the king has the man, the archbishop the woman ; but in the land of the Holy Trinity the king has neither '. See also the relevant passages in the Exchequer Domesday (DB i. 1, VCH *Kent*, iii. 203–4).

[2] Davis, *Regesta*, no. 38, from a copy on the Patent Rolls. The above remarks refer to a copy on a single piece of parchment (C. 4) in the Dean and Chapter Library, Canterbury ; other copies, Roll C. 204, no. ii, Register A, f. 158 b, Register E, f. 53 b, Register I, f. 59.

[3] C. 4 is slightly longer than Campbell Charter xxi. 5 : (i) it inserts after *scolden* in l. 8, *7 ouer Cristes cyrican* ; (ii) it adds before *forgeuene* in l. 11, *Criste* ; (iii) it adds the valediction, *God eow gehealde*. Beside the difference in the king's name, it has the variation *eal swa Eadward king mi mæi (ær dyde)* ; cf. l. 12. Otherwise, except for orthographical variations in about a score of words in the whole of the two texts, the two are identical.

Archbishop Æthelnoth, suggests that this writ of Cnut may possibly have been used by the clerks of the royal secretariat as the basis of a genuine writ of the Confessor for one of Æthelnoth's successors. Whatever may have been the motive for its confection—and the change of hand is so obvious that it can scarcely have been even intended to deceive—the authorities of Christ Church by tampering with this text produced in Campbell Charter xxi. 5 a document which purported to afford evidence of a grant of judicial and financial rights to them by Edward the Confessor. They also by the same means provided themselves (as has been said above) with a similar document purporting to have been issued for them by William I. And these two documents are closely connected on the one hand with Cnut's writ for Archbishop Æthelnoth, and on the other hand with a series of royal writs in which the grant to the archbishop of judicial and financial rights is combined with a confirmation to Christ Church of its lands,[1] purporting to have been issued for successive archbishops of Canterbury and the monks of Christ Church [2] by Henry I,[3] Henry II,[4] and Richard I,[5] all with the same

[1] In some such form as : ' þæt hi beon ælc þæra landa wurðe þe hi hæfdon on Eadweardes dæge mines mæges and on Willelmes kynges dæge mines fæder '.

[2] In the Latin writ for Archbishop Anselm (Davis, *Regesta*, no. 336) in the name of William II, the confirmation of privileges is combined with the grant of the harbour of Sandwich, and although this text employs some of the same formulas, it is constructed on somewhat different lines, and does not belong to this group of writs.

[3] For writs of Henry I in Latin and in English, in identical terms, for Archbishops Anselm (1093–1114), and William of Corbeuil (1123–39), see *Facsimiles of Royal and other Charters in the British Museum*, ed. G. F. Warner and H. J. Ellis (London, 1903), i. no. 6 (with a facsimile of the writ for Archbishop William), Joseph Hall, *Selections from Early Middle English* (Oxford, 1920), ii. 264–5, and the references there. To these should be added the writ in Latin and in English in identical terms for Archbishop Raulf (1114–23), W. Somner, *A Treatise of Gavelkind* (London, 1660), 205. See also W. H. Stevenson, *Eng. Hist. Rev.* xi (1896), 735, n. 11. The whole series of Christ Church writs in these terms, including nos. 33, 34, is entered on the Patent Roll 12 Henry VI, p. 2, m. 9 ff. ; the texts are printed in full in *Cal. of Patent Rolls*, 1429–36, 415 ff.

[4] For the English text of the writ in Latin and in English attributed to Henry II in favour of Archbishop Theobald (1139–62), see Hall, i. no. iv. Another version of this writ also exists in which ' swa fele þeinas swa ich heom to leten habban (*sic*) ', is replaced by : ' swa fela þegena swa Willelm kyng min ealde ealdefæder 7 Henri kyng min ealdefæder heom geteiðet hædde ', with a corresponding change in the Latin version ; see Dean and Chapter Library, C. 14, Reg. A, f. 159, Reg. E, f. 54, and other copies. See also for writs of Henry I and Henry II, Hickes, *Thesaurus*.

[5] In Latin only, purporting to have been issued for Archbishop Baldwine (1185–93) ; Roll C. 204, Register A, f. 158 b, Register E, f. 53 b, Register I, f. 75, Register O, f. 186 b.

characteristic matter and phraseology.[1] The authenticity of these post-Conquest writs in their existing forms has however been doubted. The editors of the *Facsimiles of Royal and other Charters in the British Museum* [2] observe that if genuine these confirmations of rights granted by earlier kings·were probably copied in the monastery from precedents with the necessary changes of name, and then submitted to the king for his seal. But they do not exclude the possibility that these documents may be later copies (or actual forgeries) to which seals were fraudulently attached.[3]

Standing a little apart from this group of writs is a writ in Anglo-Saxon and in Latin in the name of the Confessor (no. 34), which, like the Christ Church writs of Henry I and Henry II and Richard I mentioned above, combines the confirmation of privileges with the confirmation of lands. But two important variations differentiate it from other Christ Church writs : In the first place, whereas these employ the formula : *ofer swa fela þegena swa ic heom to gelæten hæbbe*,[4] this writ has *ofer swa fela þegena swa hi habbað*. In the second place this writ concludes with an ancient anathema not found elsewhere in Christ Church writs of Cnut or the Confessor, but one for which a source must have been ready at hand, since it appears again in a Christ Church charter attributed to the Confessor.[5] Similarities of phraseology, including the use of the word *cwide*, suggest that these passages were borrowed by no. 34 from this Christ Church charter or more probably perhaps from a source common to both ; the resemblances can scarcely be accidental.

[1] The writs of Henry I, Henry II, and Richard I, make the alterations necessitated by the different names and relationships, add the words ' French and English ', and confirm to Christ Church the possession of its lands (see p. 174, n. 1), but otherwise the differences between these writs and Campbell Charter xxi. 5 (and the closely-related writ in the name of William I) are negligible.

[2] See p. 174, n. 3.

[3] See also Hall, ii. 265.

[4] A variation (with *geteiðet*) in the second version of the writ attributed to Henry II has been remarked on.

[5] See Robertson no. 95 = K. 896. This charter is a composite document. It comprises a grant by Edward the Confessor of land at Chartham, Kent, to Christ Church, and a statement that the king is the guardian and upholder of the monastery and will not permit the alienation of any of its lands ; a precept that gifts of estates which in his father's day belonged to Christ Church shall remain in force ; an anathema introducing the name of Judas ; a second anathema. To this is added a list beginning : ' These are the names of the estates ', followed by the names in question. The main document is written in two hands of the late eleventh century of approximately the same date, with a change to the second (rougher) hand at the eighth line. The list of estates is in yet a third hand, with a number of names erased. The charter is not in its present form authentic, though it may contain authentic material. On the list of estates, see Kissan, *Eng. Hist. Rev.* liv (1939), 287.

The words of the charter are as follows : *7 gif ænig mann si swa dyrstig oþþe þærto gepwærlæce . . . si he Iudas gefera þe Crist belæwade, 7 þe þisne cwyde æfre awende . . . drihten fordo hine á on ecnesse. Amen.* With this we may compare the anathema in no. 34 : *7 gif ænig man sy swa dirstig þ þisne cwide æfre awænde oððe þær to gepwærlæce sy he Iudas gefere þe Crist belæwde 7 drihten fordo hine a on ecnysse. Amen.* The inappropriateness of the term *cwide* in no. 34 (however its use in the Christ Church charter may be regarded) [1] seems decisive for the supposition that this term was not to be found in any actual writ of the Confessor for Christ Church with the contents of no. 34, and that *cwide* and the anathema introduced by it were derived, as has been suggested above, from another source. The earliest version of no. 34 now known to exist is a copy on a single piece of parchment (C. 3) in the Dean and Chapter Library, in a hand of c. 1100. Its closest affinities (except for the features mentioned, not found elsewhere in Christ Church writs) are with the Christ Church writs (in Anglo-Saxon and in Latin) attributed to Henry I and Henry II mentioned above, with which except for some necessary alterations of names and relationships, it is virtually identical. Like them the Anglo-Saxon text of this writ reads : *þurh Godes geuu Ænglelandes kining,* the Latin text merely inverting the order and reading : *gratia Dei rex Anglorum,* for the *Dei gratia rex Anglorum,* of the other group.[2] In the Anglo-Saxon writ the addition of ' by the grace of God ', and ' of England ' to the king's name and title (Æthelred *cyning,* Cnut *cyning,* Eadweard *cyning,* Harold *cyning*) is highly irregular, but such clauses are frequently found in the Anglo-Saxon royal diploma, and moreover *gratia Dei* is often added to the style of bishops.[3] The presence of ' by the grace of God ' and ' of England ' in the protocol of the writ attributed to the Confessor is undoubtedly a suspicious feature. It seems likely that it is to be attributed to imitation of usages followed in royal or episcopal charters, and that the protocol was composed in its existing form after the Norman

---

[1] For instances of *cwide*, ' bequest ', see nos. 2, 111, 112. The term *cwide* is not appropriate to any of the clauses of the composite charter (see preceding note). The passage has probably been taken from some other context.

[2] It is perhaps worth noting that the writ attributed to the Confessor reads : *ealra* (' all ') *þare lande wurðe,* instead of the idiomatic *ælc* (each) *þare lande wurðe* of the other group.

[3] On the *gratia Dei* formula in Anglo-Saxon charters, laws, etc. see Liebermann, *Gesetze,* ii. 479, s.v. ' von Gottes Gnaden ', and W. Levison, *England and the Continent in the Eighth Century,* 119–21. Some instances are collected by Kemble, *Codex Diplomaticus,* i. xxvii. For a fuller discussion of its use from early Christian times, and also by secular rulers of the Middle Ages, see K. Schmitz, *Ursprung und Geschichte der Devotionsformeln, bis zu ihrer Aufnahme in die fränkische Königsurkunde* (Stuttgart, 1913).

Conquest.[1]   Again, the *grete* in the greeting, in place of the normal *gret(t)*—which, however this is to be explained, actually appears in one copy, in Register E—is a deviation from the common form of the Edwardian writ which might have been introduced by a later copyist.   There is no means of determining whether the basis of this text was an authentic writ of King Edward for Archbishop Stigand—altered perhaps and enlarged—or whether this text is a post-Conquest fabrication.   The text printed here as its Latin version resembles it in the use of the phrase *super tot thegnes quot habent*, and in its anathema, or punitive clause.   But it is not in every respect a close rendering into Latin of the text of the Anglo-Saxon writ.   Where the Anglo-Saxon text reads : ' in the time of all my predecessors and in mine ', the Latin reads : ' in the time of my father and all my predecessors '.   Further the address is fuller in the Latin text, and resembles closely the address of the Henrician writs, except that in the writ in the name of the Confessor *dux* and *comes* both appear.   For a parallel to *procer* (in the Latin text) as a rendering for ' thegn ', see II Cnut 22, 2, and the corresponding Latin versions [2] ; here both *tainus* and *procer* render OE *þegn*.   That the protocol of the Latin version of the writ of the Confessor under discussion dates from a period subsequent to the Norman Conquest is indicated by the appearance of *vicecomes* for ' sheriff ' (see Introduction, p. 49).   The Latin text seems indeed to bear to the Anglo-Saxon text a similar relation to that which exists between the Latin versions of the Henrician writs of this series and their respective

[1] The style *þurh Godes geuu Ænglelandes kining* appears in the Anglo-Saxon version of the Sandwich charter of Christ Church, Canterbury (Robertson, p. 158), which is attributed to Cnut, but which from its linguistic forms is of later date than Cnut's reign and the authenticity of which is not certain. For another charter attributed to Cnut with the *þurh Godes gyfe* formula, see p. 382.   The Latin version of this charter reads : ' *diuina fauente gratia Anglorum ceterarumque adiacentium insularum basileus* ' (*Crawford Charters*, no. xii).   On the style *Dei gratia rex Anglorum* in charters of Henry I, where it is rare in original charters, see Charles Johnson, ' Some charters of Henry I ', in *Historical Essays in honour of James Tait* (Manchester, 1933), 139 ff.   In original charters of Henry II the *Dei gratia* formula does not become normal until the latter part of the reign ; see L. Delisle, *Bibliothèque de l'École des Chartes*, lxvii (1906), 361–401, lxviii (1907), 272–314 ; R. Lane Poole, ' The dates of Henry II's charters ' (1908) in *Studies in Chronology and History*, 302–7 ; and *Memoranda Roll I John* (Pipe Roll Society, 1943), xii, n. 7, where H. G. Richardson cites a charter which ' appears to fix the introduction of the *Dei gratia* into the royal style at least as early as May 1172 '.   But there is evidence that the series of texts relating to grants of privileges to Christ Church, Canterbury, was worked over by a number of hands, and the authenticity of the charters in this series attributed to Henry I and Henry II is not beyond doubt ; see p. 175.   In copies the style *Dei gratia* might have been introduced by the copyist at any date.

[2] Liebermann, *Gesetze*, i. 325.

vernacular versions.   The Latin text of the writ attributed to King
Edward the Confessor has indeed close affinities with these Henrician
writs ; like them the Latin version of the Confessor's writ reads :
nolo ut aliquis hominum se intromittat, where the corresponding
vernacular versions have : *ic nelle þæt ænig mann ænig þing þær on
teo*.[1]

Two other writs in the name of the Confessor (nos. 31, 32) remain
for discussion here.   In the Christ Church cartulary at Lambeth
Palace known as Lambeth MS. 1212 there has come down to us a
Latin writ in favour of Archbishop Eadsige of Canterbury which is
drawn up in terms identical with the Latin version of the writ in
the name of the Confessor for Archbishop Stigand (no. 34), which
has just been discussed above.   We have no clue to the date of
composition of the text in favour of Eadsige.   The only known
copy is copied in a fifteenth-century handwriting on a piece of parchment which has been tacked into Lambeth MS. 1212.   In the
absence of an Anglo-Saxon version this text in favour of Eadsige
cannot be accepted as evidence of an actual grant of the Confessor
to Archbishop Eadsige with these contents, or of a writ issued to
announce such a grant.   The writ in question may be no more than
a copy of the writ in favour of Stigand in which the name of Stigand
has been replaced by that of Eadsige.   It might be tentatively
suggested that the reason for the fabrication of the writ for Eadsige
was a desire to have a writ for each archbishop of the Confessor's
reign ; but this is no more than a conjecture.

The other writ in favour of Archbishop Eadsige (no. 32), extant
only in Latin, is also of dubious authenticity.   It appears in a
section of Lambeth MS. 1212 (pp. 304–39) headed : ' Transcripta
de veteri libro Cantuar.   Memoranda cartarum et conciliorum Arch.
et ecclesie Cant.', probably written in the late twelfth century.[2]
This text is one of a group of Christ Church writs, in very similar
terms, which purport to restrict the right of hunting stags, hinds,
and roe-deer (to which some texts add hares) in the woods and
lands of the archbishop, to those to whom the archbishop has given
his command or licence.   It is in fact in every way identical,
except for a change in the name of the king and archbishop, with
a writ of William I in Lambeth MS. 1212, p. 15, which, so far as
I can discover, has not been printed hitherto (it is not noticed by
Davis in the *Regesta*) :—

' Willelmus rex Anglorum episcopis comitibus uicecomitibus 7 ceteris
fidelibus suis salutem.   Mando et precipio uobis ne in siluis uel terris

---

[1] On the *ne intromittat* clause, see note on p. 128.
[2] See E. G. Box, *Archæologia Cantiana*, xliv (1932), 103 ff.

Lanfranci archiepiscopi ceruos uel ceruas nec capreolos nec lepores capiatis nec omnino aliquam uenationem faciatis preter eos quibus ipse Lanfrancus preceperit uel licentiam dederit.   Et hoc preceptum meo tempore 7 successorum in omnibus terris que ad archiepiscopatum eius pertinent semper conseruetur.   Idem in Anglico ibidem——'

but the English text has not unfortunately been copied into the manuscript.   The relation of these two closely-linked texts, the one in the name of William, the other of Edward, to a Christ Church writ of Henry II [1] in similar terms, which like them is generally addressed, is doubtful.   So also is their relation to an (apparently genuine) Christ Church writ of William I, in English and Latin, addressed to Geoffrey (Gosfregth, Goisfred) the sheriff and all the citizens (*burhwaru*) in London, in the English text (for which the Latin text substitutes 'ceteris Lundoniensibus fidelibus suis'), forbidding them to take stag or hind or roe-deer in the land of Archbishop Lanfranc which pertains to Harrow, and forbidding anyone to hunt there without the archbishop's command or licence.[2]   Differences between this Harrow writ and the two closely-linked writs in Latin in the names of William I, and of Edward are : (i) The Harrow writ reads : *on Lanfrances lande arcebisceopes þe gebyrað into Hergan*, Lat. : *in terris Lanfranci archiepiscopi quæ ad Hergam suum manerium pertinent* ; the other two read : *in siluis uel terris Eadsini (Lanfranci) archiepiscopi* ; (ii) to the beasts named in the Harrow writ, the other two writs add *lepores* ; (iii) the Harrow writ lacks the concluding passage in the other two, enjoining that the king's precept shall be observed for ever in all the lands of the archbishopric.

That the 'prescriptive sporting rights' of the citizens of London had at some time been impaired by restrictions is apparent from the last article in the London charter of Henry I :—

'Et ciues habeant fugationes suas ad fugandum sicut melius et plenius habuerunt antecessores eorum, scilicet in Chiltre et Middelsexe et Sureie,' [3]

as was pointed out by J. H. Round.[4]   If the writ in the name of the Conqueror, with which the writ in the name of the Confessor is so closely linked, is authentic, then it would seem that the restriction of the right of hunting stags, hinds, and roe-deer, had been extended from the Harrow woodlands to all the woods and lands of the

---

[1] Printed, Rymer, *Foedera*, i. 40, *Cartæ Antiquæ*, Rolls 1–10, ed. Landon, no. 205.

[2] Calendared, Davis, *Regesta*, no. 265 ;   printed in full, Hickes, *Thesaurus*, Præfatio, xvi, *Mon. Angl.* i. 111, no. xxxix.

[3] Liebermann, *Gesetze*, i. 526, Robertson, *Laws*, 293.

[4] *The Athenæum*, 30 June, 1894, 838.

archbishop. The reason for the fabrication of the writ attributed to the Confessor, if, as seems probable, it is not authentic, may have been the desirability of providing a pre-Conquest prohibition.[1] The appearance in the opening clauses of this text of the clause : *rex Anglorum*,[1] suggests that the text has at the least undergone interpolation, if indeed it is not a fabrication on the model of the closely-linked writ of William, whilst the use of the Norman *vicecomes* as an equivalent for ' sheriff ' indicates that the text was not produced until after the Conquest. In the absence of an Anglo-Saxon version, this text cannot be accepted as evidence of the issue of a writ in these terms by King Edward the Confessor.

In the last of the Christ Church writs printed here (no. 35) King Edward declares that the land at Mersham and everything pertaining to it, is to belong to Christ Church with sake and soke as fully and completely as Sigweard and his wife granted it to that house ; for his will is that the judgment pronounced by his thegns shall be upheld (*stande*). The Latin versions of this writ appearing in several Christ Church sources, which differ from one another in length and in content (see textual variants), do not give an exact translation of the writ in Anglo-Saxon, and moreover none of these Latin versions contains the passage which concludes the Anglo-Saxon text, referring to the judgment given by King Edward's thegns. The fact that the earliest extant version of this Latin writ (that in the ' Evidentiæ Ecclesiæ Christi Cant.') is the shortest (except for a seventeenth-century abridged copy), rather favours the supposition that the Latin versions may be ultimately based on the Anglo-Saxon text, but that they have undergone a good deal of re-handling. The appearance in the address of the Norman term *vicecomes*, for ' sheriff ', is an indication that they were not composed until after the Conquest,[3] as is also the remarkable *dilectoribus*, corresponding to ' thegns '. The chief interest of these Latin versions, which they share with the Canterbury lists of benefactors and grants to Christ Church,[4] is that they provide us with the name Matildis, of the wife of Sigweard. This name does not appear in the Anglo-Saxon text. In the Christ

---

[1] For hunting rights during the Anglo-Saxon period and after, see Liebermann, *Über Pseudo-Cnut's Constitutiones de Foresta* (Halle, 1894), and *Gesetze*, ii. 403, 525 f., s.v. ' Forst ', ' Jagd ', Stubbs, *Select Charters*, 9th ed. 1913, 185–6, and the references. It had been enacted by Cnut that every man should be entitled to hunt in woodland and in open country on his own property, but that everyone should avoid hunting on the king's preserves, wherever they should be ; see II Cnut, 80.

[2] See p. 176.

[3] See Introduction, p. 49.

[4] See *Mon. Angl.* i. 97 ; for other versions of this list, see E. G. Box, *Archæologia Cantiana*, xliv (1932), 103 ff.

Church obituaries [1] on the other hand the name of Matildis stands alone as the donor of Mersham to Christ Church. [2]

One might conjecture that after their gift of Mersham to Christ Church had been made, and confirmed by the Confessor, Sigweard and Matildis continued to hold the estate as tenants for life, and that Sigweard dying first, Matildis continued to hold Mersham, relinquishing it to Christ Church at her death. [3]   In that case the monk who first entered her name in the obituary may well have regarded her as the donor of Mersham.   There is nothing here to suggest that the Anglo-Saxon writ of the Confessor to Mersham is not authentic.   The writ is of a common type (see Introduction, p. 64), its forms are those of the Confessor's day, and its content appears to be unexceptional.   What we have here is evidently a close copy of an authentic writ of the Confessor for Christ Church.

(26)

King Cnut declares that he has confirmed, at the request of Archbishop Lyfing, the liberties of Christ Church.   1017–20

(MS. Royal I D. ix, f. 44 b)

+ Cnut cing gret Lyfing arceb. 7 Godwine b. 7 Ælmær abb.   1
7 Æþelwine scírman. 7 Æþelric. 7 ealle mine þegnas. twelfhynde. 7 twihynde freondlice. 7 ic cyðe eow þ se arceb spæc to mé ymbe Cristes cyrcean freols. þ heo hæfð nu læsse munde þonne hio hwilan ǽr hæfde.   þa lyfde ic him þ he moste níwne freols settan on minan   5

---

[1] For these obituaries, which record the anniversaries of archbishops and abbots, monks and benefactors, see John Dart, *History and Antiquities of the Cathedral Church of Canterbury* (London, 1726), Appendix, pp. xxiii–xxvi, xxxii–xlii, and also A. Boutemy, *Eng. Hist. Rev.* l (1935), 292–9.   Boutemy suggests that one of the obituaries printed by Dart may have been written between 1087 and 1122, possibly about 1100, another between 1225 and 1240.

[2] Dart, p. xxiv: 8 kal. Oct. ' Obiit Matildis quæ dedit Meresham Ecclesiæ Christi & Hayene ', similarly, *ibid.* p. xxxvii ; see also *Eng. Hist. Rev. ut supra*, p. 297, n. 12.

[3] The statement in the Latin version of the Mersham writ of the Confessor that Mersham was given to Christ Church *ad opus monachorum* is in accordance with the statement of the Domesday Monachorum f. 4 : *Merseham est manerium monachorum Sancte Trinitatis* (i.e. Christ Church) *et de cibo eorum*, and also with the statement (*et est de cibo eorum*) in the late list of grants to Christ Church printed in *Mon. Angl.* ; see p. 180 above.   In the Exchequer Domesday (i. 3 b) under the heading : *Terra Archiepiscopi Cantuariensis*, it is stated that *ipse archiepiscopus tenet in dominio Merseham*.   On the division of lands between the archbishop and the community at Christ Church, see B. W. Kissan, *Eng. Hist. Rev.* liv (1939), 285 ff., *The Domesday Monachorum*, ed. Douglas, p. 16, n. 9.

naman. Þa cwæð he to me ꝥ he freolsas genoge hæfde gyf hi aht
forstodan. Þa nam ic me sylf þa freolsas 7 geléde hi uppan Cristes
agen weofod on þæs arceð gewitnysse. 7 on Þurkilles eorles. 7 on
manegra goddra manna þe me mid wæron to ðan ylcan foreweardan
10 þe hit Æþelbyrht cing gefreode. 7 ealle mine foregencgan. ꝥ næfre
nan man ne sy swa dyrsti. sy he gehádod. sy he læwode ꝥ ænig þara
þinga gelytlie þe on ðam freolse stænt. Gyf hit hwa þænne dó.
sy his lif her gescert. 7 his wunung on helle grúnde butan he hit þe
stiðlicor gebéte ær his ænde be þæs arcebisceopes tæcincge.

Translation

King Cnut sends friendly greetings to Archbishop Lyfing and
Bishop Godwine and Abbot Ælfmær and Æthelwine the sheriff and
Æthelric and all my thegns, nobles and commoners. And I inform
you that the archbishop spoke to me about the freedom of Christ
Church—that it now has less *mund* than it once had. Then I gave
him permission to draw up a new charter of freedom in my name.
Then he told me that he had charters of freedom in plenty if only
they were good for anything. Then I myself took the charters of
freedom and laid them on Christ's own altar, with the cognisance
of the archbishop and of Earl Thurkill and of many good men who
were with me—in the same terms as King Æthelberht freed it and
all my predecessors : that no man, be he ecclesiastic or be he
layman, shall ever be so presumptuous as to diminish any of the
things that stand in that charter of freedom. And if any one do
so, may his life here be shortened and his dwelling in the abyss of
hell, unless before his end he make reparation for it as stringently as
possible, as the archbishop shall direct him.

(27)

Archbishop Wulfstan informs King Cnut and Queen Ælfgifu Emma
that Æthelnoth has been consecrated to the see of Canterbury.
1020

(Gospels of MacDurnan, f. 69 b)

1 + Wulfstan arceð gret Cnut cyning his hlaford. 7 Ælfgyfe þa
hlæfdian eadmodlice. 7 ic cyþe inc leof ꝥ we habbað gedon swa swa
us swutelung fram eow com æt þam ꝧ Æþelnoþe. ꝥ we habbað hine
nu gebletsod. Nu bidde ic for Godes lufon. 7 for eallan Godes
5 halgan ꝥ ge witan on Gode þa mæþe. 7 on þam halgan hade. ꝥ he
mote beon þære þinga wyrþe þe oþre beforan wæron Dunstan þe god

wæs 7 mænig oþer þ þes mote beon eall swa rihta 7 gerysna wyrðe.
þ inc byð bam þearflic for Gode.   7 eac gerysenlic for worolde.

Translation

Archbishop Wulfstan sends humble greetings to his lord King
Cnut and to the Lady Ælfgifu.   And, beloved ! I inform you both
that we have done to Bishop Æthelnoth as notice came to us from
you : that we have now consecrated him.   Now I pray, for the love
of God and for all God's saints, that you will show respect to God
and to the holy order : that he may be entitled to the things that
others had before—Dunstan the Good and many another ; that this
man likewise may be entitled to rights and honours.   That will be
profitable to both of you in the sight of God, and also fitting in the
sight of men.

(28)

King Cnut declares that he has granted to Archbishop Æthelnoth
judicial and financial rights over his own men, and over Christ
Church, and over as many thegns as the king has granted him to
have.   1020

(Gospels of MacDurnan, f. 114 b)

+ Cnut cyncg gret ealle mine. ꝺ 7 mine eorlas 7 mine gerefan on   1
ælcere scire þe Æþelnoð arceꝺ.   7 se hired æt Cristes cyrcean land
inne habbað freondlice.   7 ic cyðe eow þ ic hæbbe geunnen him þ he
beo his saca 7 socne wyrðe. 7 griðbryces 7 hamsocne 7 forstealles
7 infangenes þeofes 7 flymena fyrmðe ofer his agene menn binnan   5
byrig 7 butan 7 ofer Cristes cyrcean 7 ofer swa feala þegna swa ic him
to lætan hæbbe 7 ic nelle þ ænig mann aht þær on teo buton he 7 his
wicneras for þam ic hæbbe Criste þas gerihta forgyfen minre sawle
to ecere alysendnesse 7 ic nelle þ æfre ænig mann þis abrece be
minum freondscipe.   10

Translation

King Cnut sends friendly greetings to all my bishops and my earls
and my reeves in every shire in which Archbishop Æthelnoth and the
community at Christ Church have lands.   And I inform you that
I have granted him that he be entitled to his sake and soke, and to
grithbreach and hamsocn and foresteall and infangenetheof and
flymenafyrmth over his own men within borough and without, and
over Christ Church, and over as many thegns as I have granted him
to have.   And I forbid anyone to take anything therefrom except

himself and his officers, because I have given these rights to Christ
for the eternal redemption of my soul. And I forbid that anyone
ever violate this, on [pain of losing] my friendship.

(29)

King Cnut declares that Archbishop Æthelnoth is to discharge the
obligations on the lands belonging to his archbishopric at the same
rate now as he did both before and after the appointment of
Æthelric as reeve up till now. 1035

(Cott. Tib. B. iv, f. 87 b)

1   + Cnut cyngc gret Eadsige ᵬ. 7 Ælfstan abᵬ. 7 Ægelric.
7 ealle mine þegnas on Cent freondlice 7 ic cyþe eow þ̄ ic wylle þ̄
Æþelnoð arceᵬ. werige his landare into his bisceoprice nu eal swa
he dyde ær Ægelric wære gerefa. 7 siððan he gerefa wæs forð oð
5 þis. 7 ic nelle na geþafian þ̄ man þam bisceope ænige unlage beode
beo gerefa se þe beo.

Translation

King Cnut sends friendly greetings to Bishop Eadsige and Abbot
Ælfstan and Æthelric and all my thegns in Kent. And I inform
you that my will is that Archbishop Æthelnoth shall discharge the
obligations on his landed property belonging to his episcopal see
now at the same rate as he did before Æthelric was reeve and after
he was reeve up to the present day. And I will not permit that
any wrong be done to the (arch)bishop, whoever may be reeve.

(30)

King Cnut declares that he has granted to Archbishop Æthelnoth
all the landed property that Ælfmær had. 1035

(Cott. Tib. B. iv. f. 87)

1   + Cnut cyngc gret Eadsige ᵬ. 7 Ælfstan abᵬ. 7 Ægelric. 7 ealle
mine þegenas on Cent freondlice. 7 ic cyðe eow þ̄ ic hæbbe geunnan
Æþelnoðe arcebisceope. ealre þare landare þe Ælfmær hæfde. 7 mid
rihte into Cristes cyricean gebyrað. binnan birig 7 butan. on wuda
5 7 on felda. swa full 7 swa forð swa Ælfric arceᵬ hyre weold oþþe
ænig his forgengena.

Translation

King Cnut sends friendly greetings to Bishop Eadsige and Abbot
Ælfstan and Æthelric and all my thegns in Kent. And I inform

you that I have granted to Archbishop Æthelnoth all the landed
property which Ælfmær had, and which lawfully pertains to Christ
Church, within borough and without, in woodland and in open
country, as fully and as completely as Archbishop Ælfric owned
it or any of his predecessors.

(31)

King Edward declares that he has granted to Archbishop Eadsige
and the monks of Christ Church all the lands that they had in the
time of the king's father and of all his predecessors, and judicial and
financial rights over their own men, and over as many thegns as they
have. (1042–44 or 1048–50)

(Lambeth MS. 1212, p. 16)

Ego Edwardus gratia Dei rex Anglorum omnibus episcopis, 1
ducibus, comitibus, proceribus, vicecomitibus, ceterisque suis
fidelibus in omnibus comitatibus in quibus Eadsinus archiepiscopus
7 monachi ecclesie Christi Cantuar' terras habent amicabiliter
salutem. Notum vobis facio me concessisse Eadsino archiepiscopo 5
7 monachis ecclesie Christi omnes terras quas habuerunt tempore
patris mei et omnium antecessorum meorum, saca 7 socne on strande
7 streame, on wode 7 ffelde, tolnes 7 theames, grit[h]breche 7
hamsocne, forestealles, infangenes theofes 7 flemene fermthe super
suos homines infra urbes 7 extra, in tantum 7 tam pleniter sicud 10
proprii ministri mei exquirere deberent, 7 super tot thegnes quot
habent. Et nolo ut aliquis hominum se intromittat nisi ipsi 7
ministri eorum quibus ipsi committere voluerint propterea quia ego
concessi Christo has consuetudines pro eterna redempcione anime
mee sicud pater meus 7 antecessores mei fecerunt. Et nolo pati 15
ut aliquis eas frangat si non vult perdere amiciciam meam. Si
quis autem huius donacionis aliquid fregerit temerario ausu faciendo
aut consenciendo socius sit Jude qui tradidit Christum 7 ab omnipotente Deo imperpetuum dampnetur.

Endorsed in a hand of cent. xv : Copia litterarum patencium Sancti Edwardi.

(32)

King Edward forbids hunting in the woods or lands of Archbishop
Eadsige except by the archbishop's command or licence. (1042–44
or 1048–50)

(Lambeth MS. 1212, p. 332)

Eaduuardus rex Anglorum episcopis, comitibus, uicecomitibus, 1
7 ceteris fidelibus suis salutem. Mando 7 precipio uobis ne in siluis

uel terris Eadsini archiepiscopi ceruos uel ceruas nec capreolos nec
lepores capiatis, nec omnino aliquam venationem faciatis, preter
5 eos quibus ipse Eadsinus archiepiscopus preceperit, uel licenciam
dederit. Et hoc preceptum meo tempore 7 successorum meorum
in omnibus terris que ad archiepiscopatum eius pertinent semper
conseruetur.

In margin : lxxxvii . . . De warenna.

(33)

King Edward declares that he has granted to Archbishop Stigand
and the community at Christ Church judicial and financial rights
over their own men, and over as many thegns as he has granted
them to have.

(Campbell Charter xxi. 5)

1   + Eadweard cyngc gret ealle mine ƀes. 7 mine eorlas. 7 mine
gerefan. 7 ealle mine þegenas on þam sciran þær Stigande arceð.
7 se hired æt Cristes cyrcean on Cantwarabyrig habbað land inne
freondlice. 7 ic cyðe eow ꝥ ic habbe him geunnan ꝥ hi beon heora
5 saca 7 socne wurþe. on strande 7 on streame. on wudan 7 on feldan.
tolnes 7 teames. griþbrices 7 hamsocne. forestealles 7 infangenes
þeoues. 7 flemena fermþe ouer hera agene menn binnan burgan 7
butan. swa full 7 swa forþ swa mine agene wicneras hit secan scoldan.
7 ouer swa fela þegena swa ic heom to gelæten hæbbe. 7 ic nelle ꝥ
10 æni man æni þing þær on teo butan hy 7 heora wicneras þe hi hit
betæcan wyllaþ. for þan þingan þe ic habbe þas gerihta forgiuen
minre sawle to ecere alysednesse. swa Cnut cyng ær dyde. 7 ic
nelle geþauian ꝥ æni man þis tobrece be mina freondscipe.

4. *Change of hand after* beon.   *Endorsed in a hand of cent. xii :*
Carta Edwardi Regis de saca 7 socna 7 libertatibus ecclesie Christi ; *and in
another hand :* Ed. Confess.

Translation

King Edward sends friendly greetings to all my bishops and my
earls and my reeves and all my thegns in the shires in which
Archbishop Stigand and the community at Christ Church have
land. And I inform you that I have granted them that they be
legally entitled to their sake and soke, on strand and in stream,
in woodland and in open country, to toll and to team, to grithbreach and to hamsocn, to foresteall and to infangenetheof and
to flymenafyrmth, over their own men within boroughs and without as fully and as completely as my own officers would exercise

it, and over as many thegns as I have granted them to have. And I forbid that any one take anything therefrom except themselves and their officers to whom they wish to commit it, because I have given these rights for the eternal redemption of my soul, as King Cnut did previously. And I will not permit any one to violate this on [pain of losing] my friendship.

(34)

King Edward declares that he has granted to Archbishop Stigand and the community at Christ Church all the lands that they had in the time of his predecessors and in his own time (Lat. version : all the lands that they had in the time of his father, and of all his predecessors) ; and judicial and financial rights over their own men, and over as many thegns as they have. (1052-66)

(Confirmation Roll I Henry VIII, p. 3, m. 9)

Eadward þurh Godes geuu Ænglelandes kining grete ealle mine 1
bisceopes 7 ealle mine eorles 7 ealle mine scirgereuan 7 ealle mine
þegenes on þam sciran þe Stigand ærceð 7 se hyred æt Cristes
ciricean on Cantwarebyrig habbað land inne freondlice.   7 ic kyðe
eow ꝥ ic habbe heom geunnon ꝥ hy byon ealra þare lande wurðe 5
þe hi hæfdon on ealre minre foregænla timan 7 on minan, 7 saca
7 socne, on strande 7 on stræme, on wudan 7 on feldan, tolnes 7
theames, griðbrices 7 hamsocne, forstealles 7 infangenes þiofes [7]
flamene feormðe, ofer hire agene mænn binnan burgan 7 butan, swa
full 7 swa forð swa mine agene wicneres hit secan scoldan, 7 ofre swa 10
fela þegena swa hi habbað. 7 ic nelle ꝥ ænig man ænig þing þær on
tyo buton hi 7 hiore wicnaeres þe hi hyt betæcan willað, for þan
þingan þe ic habbe Criste þas gerihte forgeuen minre sawle to ecere
alysednesse. 7 ic nelle geþafian ꝥ ænig man þis tobrece be minan
fullan freondscipe. 7 gif ænig man sy swa dirstig ꝥ þisne cwide æfre 15
awænde oððe þær to geþwærlæce, sy he Iudas gefere þe Crist belæwde
7 drihten fordo hine a on ecnysse. Amen.

Latin Version

(D. and C. Library, Canterbury, C. 204)

Ego Eadwardus gratia Dei rex Anglorum omnibus episcopis,
ducibus, comitibus, proceribus, vicecomitibus, ceterisque suis
fidelibus in omnibus comitatibus in quibus Stigandus archiepiscopus
7 monachi ecclesie Christi Cantuar' terras habent amicabiliter 20
salutem.   Notum vobis facio me concessisse Stigando archiepiscopo
7 monachis ecclesie Christi Cant' omnes terras quas habuerunt

tempore patris mei 7 omnium antecessorum meorum. Et saca
25 7 socne on stronde 7 streame, on wde, on felde, tolles an[d] teames,
griðbreche 7 hamsocne 7 forstalles 7 infangeneþefes 7 flemen-
fremthe supra suos homines infra urbes 7 extra, in tantum 7 tam
plenarie sicuti proprii ministri mei exquirere deberent, et etiam
super tot thegnes quot habent. Et nolo ut aliquis hominum se
30 intromittat nisi ipsi 7 ministri eorum quibus ipsi committere
uoluerint propterea quia ego concessi has consuetudines Christo
pro eterna redemptione anime mee. 7 nolo pati ut aliquis frangat
eas si non uult perdere amicitiam meam. Si quis autem huius
donationis aliquid fregerit temerario ausu faciendo aut consentiendo
35 socius sit Jude qui tradidit Christum 7 ab omnipotenti Deo in
perpetuum dampnetur.

   1. gret E, *the rest* grete.   4. kyde I, keþe D, G, *missing in* C]
keyde MS.   5. *Omission of stroke through* þ *(to render* þæt) *corrected
here and elsewhere in this text without further comment.*   5. heom]
heon MS.   5. wurðe] furde MS.   6. forgengle D, G, foregænla C, MS.
6. saca] saco MS.   8. grið-] grid- MS.   10. wicneres] wicnreres MS.
12. hi 7 hyore C] him hiore MS.   13. þe ic] þa ic MS.   13. gerihte]
gerehte MS.   14. ænig man] ængenan MS.   15. cwide] ciwde MS.
15. æfre] æfere MS.   16. þær] þære MS.   16. geþwærlæce] -læse MS.
Heading to Latin version : Carta Sancti Eadwardi.   26. grið-] grid- MS.
28. pleniter L, Th.   31. preterea quia G.

Translation

Edward by the grace of God king of England send(s) friendly
greetings to all my bishops and all my earls and all my sheriffs and
all my thegns in the shires in which Archbishop Stigand and the
community at Christ Church in Canterbury have land. And I
inform you that I have granted them that they be entitled to all
the lands that they had in the time of all my predecessors and in
my time, and to sake and soke, on strand and in stream, in woodland and in open country, to toll and to team, to grithbreach and
to hamsocn, to foresteall and to infangenetheof and to flymenafyrmth, over their own men within boroughs and without, as fully
and as completely as my own officers would exercise it, and over
as many thegns as they have. And I forbid that anyone take
anything therefrom except themselves and their officers to whom
they wish to commit it, because I have given these rights to Christ
for the eternal redemption of my soul. And I will not permit
anyone to violate this on [pain of losing] my full friendship. And
if anyone is so presumptuous as ever to alter this bequest or to
consent to its being altered, may he be the companion of Judas
who betrayed Christ, and may the Lord destroy him for ever to
all eternity. Amen.

(35)

King Edward declares that the land at Mersham is to belong to Christ Church with sake and soke, as fully and completely as Sigweard and his wife granted it to that house. 1053–61

(Cott. Claud. A. iii. f. 5 b)

+ Eadweard cyngc gret Stigande ærce.ƀ. 7 Harold eorl. 7 1 Wulfric aƀƀ. 7 Osweard. 7 ealle mine þegenas on Cent freondlice. 7 ic cyðe eow þ ic wille þ þ land æt Merseha*m* 7 ælc þæra ðinga þæs þe ðær mid rihte to gebyrað ligce into Cristes circean on Cantwarabyrig mid sace 7 mid sócne swa full 7 swa forð swa Sigweard 7 his 5 wíf hit þider inn geuðan. for ða*m* þe ic wille þ se dóm stande þe mine ðegenas gedémdan.

Latin Version

(Reg. C, f. 237)

Ego Eadwardus rex Stigando archiepiscopo 7 Wlfrico abbati Sͨi Augustini 7 Oswardo vicecomiti ceterisque dilectoribus suis in Kancia salutem. Notifico uobis quod ego concedo donacionem 10 Siuuardi 7 Matildis uxoris illius quam dederunt ecclesie Christi in Dorobernia ad opus monachorum ibi in eadem ecclesia Deo seruiencium, uillam scilicet que nominatur Merseham cum omnibus rite pertinentibus ad eam, pratis, siluis, marascis, sicut idem Siuuardus 7 Mahthildis unquam melius 7 plenius habuerunt, 15 7 eidem ecclesie pro salute anime sue contulerunt. Si quis illam uillam a iure predicte ecclesie aliquo modo auferre conatus fuerit, sociatus Beelzebub principi demoniorum commendetur.

Heading of Latin version : Donacio manerii de Merseham. *Note :* Dat' codicelli istius est anno domini m.lj. tempore Sancti Edwardi Regis suprascripti.   11. uxoris ejus Th.   12. S *ends with* ad opus monachorum.   12. ibidem in ecclesia P.   12. Th *omits :* ad opus . . . Deo seruiencium.   13. nomine *for* que nominatur Th.   14. ad eam *after* omnibus, *and next three words omitted* Th.   15. Th *ends with* unquam melius tenuerunt (*omitting* 7 plenius).   16. P *omits* sue.

Translation

King Edward sends friendly greetings to Archbishop Stigand and Earl Harold and Abbot Wulfric and Osweard and all my thegns in Kent. And I inform you that my will is that the land at Mersham and everything lawfully pertaining thereto shall belong

to Christ Church at Canterbury with sake and with soke as fully
and as completely as Sigweard and his wife granted it to that house,
for my will is that the judgment given by my thegns shall be upheld.

ST. AUGUSTINE'S, CANTERBURY

Of the four surviving writs of the monastery of St. Augustine at
Canterbury [1] the two of King Edward, in Anglo-Saxon, are of reasonably certain authenticity ; the two in Latin, of Cnut, are in all
probability spurious. No. 36, in Latin, which purports to announce
that Cnut has granted to the brethren of St. Augustine's JUDICIAL
AND FINANCIAL RIGHTS over their own men and over all the alodiaries
whom he has granted them to have, appears in only one cartulary,
and was apparently unknown to the chroniclers who inserted in
their works other writs of Cnut and Edward (p. 192, n. 1, 2). The
material of which it is composed is to be found in two other writs :—
(i) the opening clauses, ll. 1 to 3, in the St. Mildred's writ, no. 37.
(ii) ll. 3 to 12, in the Latin version of Edward's grant of sake and
soke, no. 38, ll. 15 to 24. (iii) the conclusion in the St. Mildred's
writ, no. 37, l. 9 to the end.

In the cartulary this writ heads a series of grants and confirmations of sake and soke and other privileges to the abbot and monks
of St. Augustine's by kings of England from Edward the Confessor
to Henry III. One cannot help suspecting that it was compiled
in order to round off the list. In the absence of an Anglo-Saxon
version this writ cannot be accepted as evidence of an authentic
grant by Cnut to St. Augustine's of judicial and financial rights.
It seems altogether likely that the suggestion for its composition
may have come from a phrase in a writ of the Confessor, no. 38 :

[1] This monastery was founded at the end of the sixth century at Canterbury,
to the east of the town, by St. Augustine and King Æthelberht of Kent, and
its church was dedicated to St. Peter and St. Paul. Archbishop Dunstan,
re-dedicating the church in 978, added the name of St. Augustine to those of
its original patrons. For the history of the monastery, see VCH *Kent*, ii.
126 ff., and the historians and chroniclers mentioned below. On its manuscripts see M. R. James, *The Ancient Libraries of Canterbury and Dover*, 531–4.
See also G. J. Turner and H. E. Salter, *The Register of St. Augustine's Abbey,
Canterbury, commonly called the Black Book* (British Academy, 1915–24). On
registers and rolls containing writs preserved among the muniments of Christ
Church, see the references among the 'Authorities' for Christ Church writs
above.

'as fully and completely as ever they had it in the days of King Cnut ', or from the corresponding phrase in the Latin version.[1]

The second of the Latin charters in the name of Cnut (no. 37) recalls a controversy regarding the relics of ST. MILDRED which was to linger on for many years. There is ample evidence in the monastic chronicles and lives of saints of the tenth and eleventh centuries (the period with which we are here concerned) of the veneration paid to the bodies of the saints and of the cult of relics.[2] The possession of relics of the saints was eagerly desired, and was sometimes a subject of dispute between rival monasteries. During the reign of Cnut the relics of certain English saints were moved to other resting-places. The remains of St. Alphege (Ælfheah), murdered by the Danes in 1012, were in 1023 removed by Cnut's permission with great ceremony from London to Canterbury (Chron. C, D, E, 1023). The relics of St. Felix were taken to Ramsey ; the remains of St. Wigstan were removed to Evesham ; the bodies of St. Botolph and St. Jurmin were translated to St. Edmund's Bury.[3] There is then no inherent improbability in the contents of the writ (no. 37) purporting to announce a grant by Cnut to St. Augustine's of the body of St. Mildred with all her land within the island of Thanet and without, with all the consuetudines belonging to her church, and with all the rights which the king himself had there, on land, in sea, and on shore, when it was in his own hands. The medieval hagiographers and chroniclers of St. Augustine's, Goscelin,[4] and the author of the ' Vitæ

---

[1] See Placita de Quo Warranto (Rec. Comm.), p. 341, 7 Edward II, for an occasion when the abbot of St. Augustine's cited a charter of Cnut and another of Edward as the warrant for his liberties (prout carta Regis Knutty et carta Regis Edwardi testantur).

[2] See J. Armitage Robinson, The Times of St. Dunstan (Oxford, 1923), pp. 71 ff. See also Max Förster, Zur Geschichte des Reliquienkultus in Altengland (Munich, 1943) and E. W. Kemp (see p. 560, below).

[3] Cart. Mon. de Rameseia, R.S. iii. 174 ; Chron. Abbat. de Evesham, R.S. p. 83 ; Arnold, Memorials of St. Edmund's Bury, R.S. i. 361.

[4] Goscelin, formerly a monk of St. Bertin's, came to England in 1058 (or possibly in 1050) under the protection of Bishop Herman (see Biog. Notes), stayed in several monasteries, and among other eulogies of saints honoured in the English church, wrote : ' Historia Major de Miraculis S. Augustini ' ; ' Textus translationis beatæ Mildrethæ, cum miraculorum attestatione ' ; ' Libellus contra inanes Sanctæ Mildredæ usurpatores '. For these see Hardy, Cat. of Materials, R.S., i. nos. 539, 881, 882. See also Bibliotheca Hagiographica Latina, ii (Brussels, 1900–01), nos. 5960–64. On the life and writings of Goscelin, see A. Wilmart, Analecta Bollandiana, lvi (1938), 5–101, 265–307, Revue Bénédictine, xlvi (1934), 414–38, l (1938), 42–83, and W. Levison, England and the Continent in the Eighth Century (1946), 200. To Goscelin's works above should be added : ' Vita Deo dilectae Virginis Mildrethae ' (Hardy i. 879).

Abbatum ',[1] and Thorne,[2] and Elmham [3] either refer to or narrate in detail the circumstances in which the grant of St. Mildred's [4] body to St. Augustine's, and the translation of her relics to the church of the abbey, were traditionally supposed to have taken place. Goscelin (writing some seventy years later), and following him, Thorne,[5] deal first with Abbot Ælfstan's attempt to secure the lands of St. Mildred's and with the exchange of estates whereby he obtained possession of half the property of the derelict nunnery, before approaching the king with a request for permission to translate to his own monastery the relics of the saint, then lying at Minster. The story, it will be observed, is related to a journey of Cnut to Rome which actually took place, but the complicated chronology of Cnut's journeys round about the year 1027 is, as might be expected, over-simplified in this narrative :—

[1] The 'Vitæ Abbatum S. Augustini Cantuariæ, ad annum 1252 ' (Hardy, iii. no. 225, and p. 457 below) (a) gives s.a. 1027 a summary of no. 37, (b) mentions s.a. 1043 the Confessor's grant of Minster (K. 900), (c) gives without date Latin text of no. 38, (d) mentions s.a. 1055 the Confessor's grant of Fordwich (no. 39). See, on the treatise, G. J. Turner and H. E. Salter, *The Register of St. Augustine's Abbey, Canterbury, commonly called the Black Book*, xiv.

[2] William Thorne wrote the history of the abbey from its foundation to 1397, *Chron. Guill. Thorne de rebus gestis Abbatum S. Augustini Cantuariæ*, ed. R. Twysden, *Scriptores X* (London, 1652) ; Mod. Eng. rendering, A. H. Davis, *William Thorne's Chronicle of St. Augustine's Abbey, Canterbury, rendered into English* (Blackwell, 1934), with an Introduction discussing among other matters the historians of St. Augustine's. Thorne gives the text of nos. 37, 39.

[3] Thomas of Elmham wrote before 1414 *Historia Monasterii S. Augustini Cantuariensis*, R.S., a chronicle fuller than Thorne's, with texts of charters and papal bulls, which ceases at 806 except for a few later entries.

[4] For St. Mildred, see Biographical Notes. Little is known of the nunnery over which she ruled, and which was afterwards called by her name. It was still in existence in the first part of the ninth century (Thorne col. 1775–76). In the chronicle of Thomas of Elmham (which was never completed) the history of the nunnery ceases (p. 222) with its destruction by the Danes and the subsequent disappearance of the nuns c. 840. It may have been re-established : Thorne records (col. 1780,1908) the burning of the nunnery in a raid on Thanet in 980, and assigns to A.D. 1011 its final destruction. But it is not certain that the nunnery was still in existence at that time. For a suggestion that the nunnery of St. Mildred presided over by the abbess Leofrun who was captured at the siege of Canterbury in 1011 (*Chron.* C, D, 1011, but E wrongly calls her Leofwine ; Fl. Wig. s.a. 1011) was at the time of this inroad established not at Minster but at Canterbury, see C. Cotton, *The Saxon Cathedral at Canterbury* (Manchester, 1929), 76. For another theory, namely, that the captured abbess may have been an abbess of Reading visiting Canterbury, see Gordon Ward, *Archæologia Cantiana*, xlix (1937), 242. After the final destruction of the nunnery the church is said to have been served only by two or three *clerici* (Thorne col. 1908, Elmham p. 222).

[5] Goscelin, *Text. Trans.* cap. 6–9. Thorne, col. 1909.

We learn that Abbot Ælfstan, whose wish to secure the relics of St. Mildred had been strengthened by a vision, was graciously received by Cnut, who gave to St. Augustine's the remaining portion of the possessions of the saint, but deferred the translation of her body till a more opportune time. A journey to Rome having been decided upon, the king vowed that if by the help of St. Augustine his patron he should be brought back in safety, he would permit the body of St. Mildred to be translated to St. Augustine's. When on his return journey he was in danger of shipwreck Cnut successfully invoked the name of St. Augustine, and therefore on his return home, in conformity with his vow, gave to Abbot Ælfstan the desired permission. The abbot received the ' royal letter ' [1] from the king authorising the translation, on the Saturday before Pentecost, and went immediately to his house at Minster, where he held a feast on Whit Sunday. That night, with three or four companions, he secretly entered the nunnery church, and after some delay, succeeded in removing the body of St. Mildred from her tomb. The people of Thanet, discovering their loss, tried unsuccessfully to intercept him, and the abbot, having crossed by the ferry to the mainland, was able, escorted by a rejoicing crowd, to convey the relics in safety to his church, where they were enshrined before the high altar. The narrative concludes with an account of the miracles of St. Mildred up to the time of the writer.

The claim of the monks of St. Augustine's to possess the relics of St. Mildred was none the less disputed, and by the end of the eleventh century a curious controversy had arisen. The canons of the new foundation dedicated to St. Gregory at Canterbury [2] asserted that the monks of St. Augustine's did not possess, and never had possessed, the relics of the saint—that St. Mildred's body was in fact in their own church, having been given to them by their founder Archbishop Lanfranc. The dispute seems to have arisen not long after the foundation of St. Gregory's at Canterbury by Lanfranc c. 1085. In the opinion of Stubbs [3] it was the immunities which accompanied the grant of the relics which led to the dispute. But the evidence available clearly indicates that what was coveted by both sides was the possession of the relics themselves and the benefits which would accrue to the religious house in which they rested. The claim of the Gregorian canons involved certain confusions and chronological difficulties, but it was difficult to refute ; our knowledge of its basis depends solely on the arguments put forward at St. Augustine's to refute it. It would appear that when Archbishop Lanfranc granted to his new foundation the relics of St. Æthelburh or Eadburh (the two were confused), then resting at Liminge, there was found next to the body of that saint another body to which was assigned by popular repute the name of St. Mildred, and that both bodies were translated to the church of

---

[1] See Appendix IV, no. 4.

[2] See D. Knowles, *Religious Houses of Medieval England* (1940), 92 ; VCH *Kent*, ii. 157–9.

[3] *Dict. Christ. Biog.* (1882), i. 914, s. ' Mildred '.

St. Gregory's.   The confusion between Æthelburh and Eadburh and
the chronological difficulties involved were discussed by Goscelin in
his *Libellus* (cap. 2–4) and by Thomas of Elmham (p. 224).[1]   The
exasperation of the monks of St. Augustine's at the pretentions of
their opponents, the ' usurpatores ' of St. Mildred's body, is reflected
in those passages in which Goscelin, Thorne and Elmham argue in
favour of the claims of their own monastery.   William of Malmesbury (in the early twelfth century), who cannot have been ignorant
of the controversy, speaks unhesitatingly of the presence of St.
Mildred's relics at St. Augustine's.[2]   John of Tynemouth (in the
fourteenth century) comments on the Gregorian claim, but does not
profess to be able to settle the rights of the matter :—

' Inueni enim scriptum in cenobio Sancti Gregorii Cantuarie quod anno
domini millesimo octuagesimo quinto Lamfrancus archiepiscopus corpora
sanctarum uirginum Mildrede et Edburge, in Thaneto insula sepulta, de terra
leuauit et in ecclesia beati Gregorii Cantuarie, quam ad pauperum solamen
paulo ante de rebus ecclesie cui presidebat, ditauerat, cum magno honore
transferens collocauit.   Ibi reuera scrinium satis preciosum aduentantibus
ostenditur ; sed et altercationem inter monachos et canonicos pro corpore
Sancte Mildrede nondum tempore nostro sedatam, peritioribus discutiendam
relinquo, qui quod in utroque loco scriptum repperi, ad futurorum noticiam
venire volui.' [3]

The feud was still alive at the beginning of the fifteenth century
(and even later), and the champions of St. Augustine's still feared
lest the members of the rival foundation should after all make good
their claim to possess the relics of the saint.   As far as one can judge
from the existing evidence, the monks of St. Augustine's supported
their claim in this singular controversy not by documentary evidence
but by stories of miracles and supernatural visions testifying to the
presence of the saint's relics in their church.   This was one of the
lines of argument adopted by Goscelin in his *Libellus* (cap. 19), and
Thorne (col. 1911) repeats from Goscelin the story of a ' miraculum '
which took place on the eve of the removal of the saint's body in
Abbot Scotland's time to a new place in the church, whilst Elmham
attempts (*loc. cit.* pp. 224–6) to refute the ' temerarious ' claims of
the canons by another story of the miraculous virtues of the saint's
relics.   It was of course an argument which might have been
expected to prove effective.   A similar proof was accepted in the
story told by Eadmer of the four *clerici* who came to the court of

[1] The evidence, in so far as it exists, was discussed by R. C. Jenkins, ' St.
Mary's Minster in Thanet, and St. Mildred ', *Archæologia Cantiana*, xii (1878),
177 ff.

[2] *Gesta Regum*, R.S. i. 267 ; Mod. Eng. rendering, Giles, 243.

[3] ' De Sancta Mildreda ', in *Nova Legenda Anglie*, ed. Horstman (Oxford,
1901), ii. 197.

King Edgar, bringing with them, so they said, the relics of St. Audoenus (Ouen). Their story was not believed until Archbishop Odo (942–58) had performed miracles by healing by means of the relics, which were then accepted as those of the saint and placed in Christ Church.[1]

On the balance of probabilities, and on the available evidence, the claim of the monks of St. Augustine's to possess the relics of St. Mildred seems superior to that of the canons of St. Gregory's. Was their claim well-founded to have been granted by King Cnut, with the body of the saint, all the lands of the nunnery of St. Mildred within the isle of Thanet and without, with all the ' customs ' belonging to her church, and with all the rights which the king himself had there, on land, in sea and on shore, when it was in his own hand ? For this claim there seems to be no contemporary corroboration. The Latin charter of the Confessor purporting to confer on the monastery a portion of the isle of Thanet and confirming all previous grants of the kings his predecessors is not authentic.[2]

The charter incorporates the romantic story of the grant by an early king of Kent to Queen Domneva, the mother of St. Mildred, as compensation for the murder at the king's command of her two brothers, of part of the isle of Thanet, that is to say, of as much land there as the queen's tame hind could encompass in a single course.

The value of such a writ as no. 37 to the monks of St. Augustine's will be obvious. It purported to announce the grant to them of the relics of a saint, together with lands and valuable ' customs '.

Whether it represents an actual writ of Cnut is uncertain. The spuriousness of the Confessor's Thanet charter (K. 900) and that of many other charters and bulls of St. Augustine's has recently been demonstrated by Wilhelm Levison.[3] This writ may also be a fabrication without any substantial basis of fact. One of the earliest copies of the writ is a copy of the early thirteenth century entered on the Cartæ Antiquæ Roll. One's confidence in its authenticity is not increased by the description of it, in a heading on that roll, as a *carta* of the monks of St. Augustine's *cum sigillo*. Although there is good evidence for the use of a seal by Cnut (see Introduction, pp. 17 f.), the seal accompanying this writ, the post-

[1] Eadmer's *De reliquiis Sancti Audoeni . . . quae Cantuariae in aecclesia domini Salvatoris habentur*, ed. A. Wilmart, *Revue des sciences religieuses*, xv (1935), 362–70 ; also in John of Tyn mouth, *Nova Legenda* i. 72–3. On the cult of St. Ouen, see Levison, *England and the Continent in the Eighth Century*, 211.

[2] K. 900. On the charter see W. Levison, *England and the Continent in the Eighth Century*, 182 ff. On the story, see F. M. Stenton, *Trans. R. Hist. Soc.* xxiii (1941), 18.

[3] *Ut supra*, Appendix i.

Conquest date of composition of which is betrayed by its use of the term *vicecomes*, cannot have been a genuine seal of Cnut, unless a genuine seal had been detached from some other writ and attached to this one. But a comparison of the Latin version of another writ, no. 38, with its Old English equivalent, induces caution. In the Latin version of this authentic writ the initial *Ego*, and the style *Dei gratia rex Anglorum* (see p. 176), are evidently the contribution of the translator who translated this writ after the Norman Conquest, as his use of the term *baro* for ' thegn ' indicates. The initial *Ego* in the St. Mildred's writ, the style *per Dei misericordiam*, and the phrase *salutem et amicitiam* (for *gret* . . . *freondlice*) might equally well have been introduced into the St. Mildred's writ by a translator rendering into Latin a (hypothetical) St. Mildred's writ in English. But there is in the phraseology of this text a link with the spurious charters of St. Augustine's which have been discussed by Wilhelm Levison. The anathema which we find in the St. Mildred's writ :—

' Et qui *hanc donationem* meam infringere uel *irritam facere temptauerit*, a Deo omnipotente et *omni sancta ecclesia excommunicatus sit* ',

closely resembles the anathemas employed in the spurious charter (B. 4, 5), in which King Æthelberht grants lands for the foundation of a monastery (later to be called St. Augustine's) in 605 :—

' Si quis vero de *hac donacione* nostra aliquid minuere aut *irritum facere temptaverit, sit* in præsenti separatus a *sancta communione* corporis et sanguinis Christi, et in dei judicii ob meritum malitiæ suæ a consortio sanctorum omnium segregatus ',

and in the second of the two charters attributed to Æthelberht, with different phrasing of the final passage :—

' . . . *sit* hic segregatus ab *omni sanctæ ecclesiæ communione* et in dei judicii ab omni electorum societate '.[1]

It is worth remarking that the spurious charter of the Confessor (K. 900) purporting to record the grant to St. Augustine's of the isle of Thanet (see above) belongs to this group of spurious charters of St. Augustine's, for Levison has remarked [2] upon the connection and interdependence between the eleven charters of this group (he does not include the St. Mildred's writ). And further it should be noted that there are verbal resemblances between the protocol of the St. Mildred's writ and that of other (spurious) charters of St. Augustine's discussed by Levison. With the ' Knut *per Dei misericordiam* basileus . . . *salutem et amicitiam* ', of the writ, we may compare the ' rex Anglorum Aethilbertus *misericordia omnipotentis Dei* . . . *salutem vitæque æternæ beatitudinem*' of

---

[1] Levison, 181, nos. 1, 2.   [2] Levison, 182.

another spurious charter of Æthelberht (B. 6), and the *pacem et salutem* of the spurious privilege of St. Augustine (B. 7).[1]   On the other hand, the features of no. 37 which arouse suspicion, might have been due to the ignorance of someone attempting to reconstruct a (possibly genuine) writ of Cnut which had been lost or destroyed. In the disastrous fire at Canterbury in 1168 many ancient documents perished (Thorne col. 1815), and it may not be without significance that the church at Minster (' ecclesia de Menstre ') was one of three churches assigned by Pope Alexande to the monks of St. Augustine's for the repair of the damage that their church had sustained.   The St. Mildred's writ as we have it is not a literal rendering of an authentic writ of Cnut.   We cannot absolutely exclude the possibility that an authentic writ of Cnut may lie behind it.

The two remaining writs (nos. 38, 39) are of a very different character.   Their subject-matter is unexceptionable, and their phraseology that of the Confessor's time.   Their linguistic forms have been in some degree modernised, but there is nothing here to excite suspicion.   For the *gecnawe* clause of no. 39 we have a parallel (as an expression employed by the royal clerks) in no. 24, and parallels also exist elsewhere for the *licgan in to* clause (see Introduction, p. 64).   Information regarding the Confessor's grant of FORDWICH appears in Domesday (see p. 458).   Similarly the authenticity of the writ in which Edward announces his grant to the abbey of JUDICIAL AND FINANCIAL RIGHTS (no. 38) is rendered still more certain by its striking resemblance to Cnut's writ for Archbishop Æthelnoth (no. 28), even to the appearance in each text of the clause : *swa feola þegna swa ic him to gelæten hæbbe* (see p. 173).[2] Everything encourages the belief that nos. 38, 39, are authentic copies of genuine writs of the Confessor.   With regard to the Latin version of no. 38, it has been pointed out above that the initial *Ego*, and the style : *Dei gratia rex Anglorum*, are the contribution of the translator ; while his use of the term *baro* indicates a post-Conquest date for this translation.[3]

(36)

King Cnut declares that he has granted to the brethren of St. Augustine's judicial and financial rights over their own men, and over all the alodiaries whom he has given to them.

[1] Levison, 181, nos. 3, 4.
[2] Maitland, *Domesday Book and Beyond*, 153, n. 7, remarked upon the occurrence of this clause in its two versions, Eng. and Lat., in a series of post-Conquest charters for St. Augustine's from two of William I to one of John. Its appearance in the charters of Christ Church has been remarked on above (p. 176).   [3] See p. 428.

(Cott. Claud. D. x, f. 57)

1   Ego Knut per Dei misericordiam basileus Ægelnodo archiepiscopo et omnibus episcopis, abbatibus, comitibus, vicecomitibus, et omnibus fidelibus totius Anglie salutem et amicitiam. Sciatis me dedisse Deo ac Sancto Augustino et fratribus ut habeant eorum saca et socna
5 et pacis fracturam et pugnam in domo factam et uie assaltus et latrones in terra sua captos latronumque susceptionem uel pastionem super illorum proprios homines, infra ciuitatem et extra, theloneumque suum in terra et in aqua, atque consuetudinem que dicitur theames, et super omnes allodiarios quos eis habeo datos. Nec uolo
10 consentire ut aliquis in aliqua re de hiis se intromittat nisi eorum prepositi quibus ipsi hec commendauerint, quia habeo has consuetudines Deo datas et Sancto Augustino pro redemptione anime mee et successorum meorum, ita ut eas libere et pleniter habeant et possideant inperpetuum. Et qui hanc donationem meam infringere
15 uel irritam facere temptauerit, a Deo omnipotente et omni sancta ecclesia excommunicatus sit. Amen.

Heading : Rex Cnutus de libertate ecclesie Sancti Augustini Cantuar '. *In margin :* Rex Knutus d[e saca] et socna.

(37)

King Cnut declares that he has given to St. Augustine the body of St. Mildred with all her land and with all the ' customs ' belonging to her church. (1027–35.)

(Cott. Jul. D. ii, f. 85 b)

1   Ego Knut per Dei misericordiam basileus Ægelnodo archiepiscopo 7 omnibus episcopis, abbatibus, comitibus, uicecomitibus, 7 omnibus fidelibus totius Anglie salutem 7 amicitiam. Notum sit uobis omnibus me dedisse Sancto Augustino patrono meo corpus Sancte
5 Mildriþe gloriose uirginis cum tota terra sua infra insulam de Tenet 7 extra cum omnibus consuetudinibus ad suam ecclesiam pertinentibus. Hec omnia ita libera 7 quieta reddo Deo 7 abbati Ælfstano 7 fratribus loci sicut ego ea unquam melius habui tam in terra quam in mari 7 in litore, ut habeant, possideant, inperpetuum. Et qui
10 hanc donationem meam infringere uel ir[r]itam facere temptauerit, a Deo omnipotente 7 omni sancta ecclesia excommunicatus sit. Amen.

Heading : Donatio Regis Knuti de Taneto. *Heading in* Q : Carta eorundem (sc. monachorum Sancti Augustini Cantuar.) cum sigillo.   1. Ægelnoðo Q.   7. Athelstano (*wrongly*) Ed, Cl.   9. 7 (' and ') *between* habeant, possideant, Q, Th ; *the rest omit.*

(38)

King Edward declares that he has granted to St. Augustine's judicial and financial rights over their own men, and over as many thegns as he has granted them to have.   1042–50

(Patent Roll 2 Henry VI, p. 3, m. 3)

+ Eadward king gret Eadsige arceƀ. 7 Godwine eorl 7 ealle 1
mine þegnas on Kent frendlice 7 ic kyðe eow ꝥ ic hæbbe geunnen
Sce Augustine 7 þam gebroðran þe þær to hyrað ꝥ hi beon heora
saca wurðe 7 heore socna 7 griðbrices 7 hamsocne 7 forstealles
7 infangenes þiofes 7 flymaene fyrmðe ofer heore agene menn binnan 5
burh 7 butan tolles 7 teames on strande 7 on str[e]ama 7 ofer swa
feole þegna swa ic hiom habba to gelæten 7 ic nelle ꝥ æni mann æni
þing þær on teo buton heom 7 heore wicneres þe hi hit betæcen
willan for þam ic habbe forgefen Sancte Augustine þas gerihte minre
sawle to alesednysse swa full 7 swa forð swa hi hit fyrmest hæfdan 10
on Cnudes dægge cinges.   7 ic nelle geþafian ꝥ æni mann þis abrece
be minan freon[d]scipe.   God eow gehealde.

Latin Version

(Cott. Claud. D. x, f. 57)

Ego Eaduuardus Dei gratia rex Anglorum Eadsio archiepiscopo
et God[w]ino comiti et omnibus suis baronibus Cantie salutem.
Sciatis me dedisse Deo ac Sancto Augustino et fratribus ut habeant 15
eorum saca et socna et pacis fracturam et pugnam in domo factam
et uie assaltus et latrones in terra sua captos latronumque susceptionem uel pastionem super illorum proprios homines, infra ciuitatem
et extra, theloneumque suum in terra et in aqua, atque consuetudinem que dicitur teames, et super omnes allodiarios quos eis 20
habeo datos.   Nec volo consentire ut aliquis in aliqua re de hiis
se intermittat nisi eorum prepositi quibus ipsi hec commendauerint,
quia habeo has consuetudines Deo datas et Sancto Augustino pro
redemptione anime mee ita pleniter et libere sicut melius habuerunt
tempore predecessoris mei Knuti regis, et nolo consentire ut aliquis 25
hec infringat sicuti meam amicitiam vult habere.

Heading : Carta eorundem (sc. monachorum Sancti Augustini Cantuar.) de
Libertatibus.   3. hyrað] hyrad MS.   4. grið-] grid- MS.
8. wicners F, wicnefer MS.   11. geþafian] geeþafian MS.   *Heading of*
Latin version : Eaduuardus rex de libertate.   *In margin :* Eaduuardus
re[x de] saca et socna.   18. burgum F, ciuitatem MS.   22. intromittat F, J, intermittat B, O.   22. commendauerint F, commendauerunt
J, commodauerint B, O.

Translation

King Edward sends friendly greetings to Archbishop Eadsige and Earl Godwine and all my thegns in Kent. And I inform you that I have granted to St. Augustine and the brethren belonging thereto that they be entitled to their sake and their soke and to grithbreach and hamsocn and foresteall and infangenetheof and flymenafyrmth over their own men within borough and without, to toll and team on strand and in stream, and over as many thegns as I have granted them to have. And I forbid that anyone take anything therefrom except themselves and their officers to whom they wish to commit it, because I have given these rights to St. Augustine for the redemption of my soul as fully and as completely as ever they had them (lit. it) in the days of King Cnut. And I will not permit anyone to violate this on [pain of losing] my friendship. God keep you.

(39)

King Edward declares that the land at Fordwich previously granted by him to St. Augustine's is now to belong to the monastery with all the rights with which he had granted it to that house. 1053–66

(Cott. Claud D. x, f. 177)

1 Eadward cyng gret Stigande arceƀ 7 Harold eorl. 7 Osweard. 7 ealle mine þegenas on Cent fren[d]lice. 7 ic cyðe eow ƥ ic eom þæs gecnawe ƥ ic geuðe Criste 7 S̄c̄e Augustine 7 þan halgan þaer binnan. sua micel landes binnan Fordwic for minre saule swa ic me sylf þer
5 hafde. swa full 7 swa forð swa it me sylfan on honde stod on eallan þingan. Nu wille ic þat hit licge into þan halgan minstre. eall swa ic hit aer [þider] in geuðe. 7 ic nelle geþafian þat aenig man mine gyefe geutige. 7 ic wille habban fullne dom of þam menn þe mine swutelinge awaengnian wolde þe ic þer to gegyefen hafde.

Heading : Donatio Domini Eadwardi Regis de Fordwico. *In margin :* Sanctus Edwardus.   4. for] ford MS.   5. it] ic MS.   7. þider in geuðe F.   7. soffre R, W, X, Y, Z, geþafian F, MS.   9. swute-linge F] swatel- MS.   9. awemman (en) R, W, X, Y, Z ; *illegible in F except for* -men.

Translation

King Edward sends friendly greetings to Archbishop Stigand and Earl Harold and Osweard and all my thegns in Kent. And I inform you that I am aware that I granted to Christ and St. Augustine and the saints therein as much land within Fordwich, for the good of my soul, as I myself had there, as fully and as completely in every respect as I myself possessed it. It is now my will that it shall belong to the holy monastery exactly as I granted it to them previously. And I will not permit anyone to alienate my gift. And I will exact the full penalty from the man who would annul my declaration that I had given with regard to it.

CHERTSEY

Of the four writs of St. Peter's Abbey at Chertsey [1] only no. 43 can be confidently accepted as a reasonably accurate, but modernised, copy of an authentic writ. The authenticity of the three others (nos. 40-2), which are closely interlinked by content and phraseology, is much less certain, and there is some reason for thinking that no. 41 at all events does not represent a separate writ of King Edward the Confessor separately issued. Linguistic forms indicating a date later than the Confessor's time abound in the extant copies of these texts.

The LONDON writ (no. 43) which announces Edward's grant to Abbot Wulfwold of sake and soke over his own lands in London and over his own men, is of a usual type, and there are no grounds for doubting its authenticity. The words *hagan land* were however explained by A. Ballard [2] in such a way as to make this phrasing appear to be exceptional. He rendered *hagan land* by ' haws ', which he explained as ' urban tenements ', ' the town houses which were appurtenant to rural manors ', and he referred to the Confessor's Staines-*Stæningahaga* writ in favour of Westminster Abbey (no. 98), where -*haga* is rightly interpreted in this sense. But *haga* is not there compounded with *land*, and indeed the compound *haganland* (not apparently recorded elsewhere) seems on the face of it an unlikely one. If this passage does actually refer to the abbot of Chertsey's urban tenements in London,[3] there is no difficulty in

---

[1] For the early history of Chertsey Abbey, founded by St. Erkenwald in the seventh century, destroyed by the Danes in the ninth, and restored by St. Æthelwold (for whom see Biog. Notes), see VCH *Surrey*, ii. 55-64. See also *Chertsey Cartularies* (Surrey Record Society, vol. xii, 1933), on Cott. Vitellius A, xiii, and other registers of the abbey.

[2] *British Borough Charters* (Cambridge, 1913), i. lvii.

[3] Ballard remarked that Domesday Book does not record that Chertsey Abbey owned any manors with appurtenant houses or burgesses in London.

supposing that either *hagan* or *land* was originally an interlinear gloss which has been taken into the text. But, on the other hand, *hagan* may be a misspelling : the rhythm of the sentence suggests that *ofer his hagan land* ' over his own lands ', and *ofer his agene man* are parallel. The *h* of *hagan* would in that case be an unetymological *h* prefixed to the word ; cf. *hic* for *ic* in the Vitellius text of this writ, and *heorlas* for *eorlas* in no. 4.[1] *Land* could be sing. here or plural, since *land* is uninflected in the accus. plur. ; I have translated it as plural. Other instances of similar formulas occur in nos. 42, 49, 51, 116, 118. The form *man*, ' men ' here (*ofer his agene* man) and in no. 42 (*ofer ealle his* man 7 *ofer his lande*), is no doubt a form of the Middle English dialect of Surrey, where OE *en* (*æn*) appears as *an* in place-names such as *Handon, Wandsworth* ' and in most derivatives of *fenn* '.[2] Support for the rendering adopted here of *hagan land* as ' own land ' is to be found in the Latin rendering of this writ in an *inspeximus* charter of Henry III :—

' quod prædicti abbas et monachi habeant sacham et socham in civitate Londoniarum *de omnibus hominibus et terris suis* sicut aliqui predecessorum dictorum abbatis et monachorum plenius et liberius habuerunt '.[3]

GODLEY HUNDRED AND THE FOUR MANORS

The other three Chertsey writs are linked together by their subject-matter. They purport to announce that Edward has granted to Chertsey Abbey the hundred (court) of Godley, the vills of Chertsey, Egham, Thorpe, and Chobham (which together form a compact block of territory in that hundred), with judicial and financial rights, and has surrendered to the abbey other rights, *gescot, weorc, waru*, not named in other writs. There is reason to believe that lands at Chertsey, Egham, Thorpe, and Chobham, were among the earliest possessions of this monastery, and that they had come to it through a gift (made before A.D. 675) of Frithuwald, *subregulus* of Surrey, whose charter was confirmed by Wulfhere, king of the Mercians.[4] They receive special mention in an alleged diploma of King Edward the Confessor declaring that the king has restored to Chertsey Abbey the liberty conferred on it of old, in that he is

---

[1] On such spellings see Bülbring, *Altenglisches Elementarbuch*, § 480 note, Luick, *Hist. Gramm. der Engl. Sprache*, § 657.

[2] *Place-Names of Surrey* (E.P.-N.S.), xxiii ; Jordan-Matthes, *Handbuch der Mittelenglischen Grammatik* (1934), 53 ; Wyld, *Short History of English*, 113.

[3] *Mon. Angl.* i. 432, no. xxi.

[4] B. 34. F. M. Stenton has observed (*Historical Essays in honour of James Tait*, Manchester, 1933, 313, n. 2) that the foundation charter of Chertsey Abbey, now extant only in a late copy, seems to represent a text composed between 673 and 675. For Chertsey charters attributed to later kings confirming the possessions of the monastery, see VCH *Surrey*, ii. 55.

freeing from all royal tribute 5 *mansas* at Chertsey *in situ eiusdem monasterii*, 10 at Thorpe, 15 at Egham, and 10 at Chobham, the usual reservation being made of the *trimoda necessitas*. This long diploma (K. 812), dated 1062, has no witnesses in the copy in the Chertsey cartulary, and it seems unlikely that this document is in its present form an authentic diploma of the Confessor. But King Edward may well have 'granted' the four manors to Chertsey, though in view of the earlier connection between the four manors and the abbey, it may be that his grant involved no more than the transfer to the abbot of the royal rights over them. The four manors were in the possession of the abbot of Chertsey in 1086 [1]; they were included in subsequent confirmations to the abbey of its lands; and they are said to have been held by Chertsey Abbey till the Dissolution.[2]

It has been remarked above that the four vills of Chertsey, Egham, Thorpe, and Chobham, lay in Godley hundred. In one of the two writs printed here relating to GODLEY HUNDRED (no. 42) King Edward announces that he has given the hundred to the abbey and to Abbot Wulfwold 'freely', and with everything belonging to himself in woodland and in open country. Here, as in the Abingdon writ relating to the hundred of Hormer (no. 5), the grant of the hundred is to be interpreted to mean the grant of the hundred court and of the profits of justice accruing therefrom.[3] As far as I can discover, no writ of the immediate successors of King Edward now exists explicitly referring to, or confirming, this or any other grant of Godley hundred to Chertsey Abbey, but there is of course no inherent improbability in the making of such a grant by the Confessor.[4] Further, King Edward in the Godley writ (no. 42) declares that the abbot is to be entitled to his sake and his soke, and toll and team and infangenetheof, and grithbreach, foresteall, hamsocn and

---

[1] DB i. 32b, VCH *Surrey*, i. 309–10.

[2] VCH *Surrey*, iii. 406, 414, 421.

[3] See pp. 125 f. Chertsey Abbey was not the owner of all the land in Godley hundred in the Confessor's reign or subsequently. In King Edward's time Pyrford was held by Earl Harold, and was afterwards given by William I to Westminster Abbey (DB i. 32, VCH *Surrey*, i. 306).

[4] No importance of course is to be attached to the fact that in the *Quo Warranto* proceedings the abbot of Chertsey claimed to have the hundred by King Edward's gift; see *Placita de Quo Warranto* (Record Commission), 744. For reference to the hundred of Godley in Chertsey writs of Henry I and II, see a grant by Henry II in Cott. Vitell. A. xiii, f. 59b, of the 4 manors, *cum hundredo suo de Godelye*, and a grant of the same by Henry I summarised in an *inspeximus* charter of Henry III (*Mon. Angl.* i. 432 ff.). Richard I grants to the monks of Chertsey the hundred of Godley free and quit with everything belonging to the king from the hundred; see *Cal. of Ch. Rolls*, ii. 306.

P

flymenafyrmth. Of these the first five find a place in a writ in
English of William I, but the four forfeitures, grithbreach, foresteall,
hamsocn, and flymenafyrmth, are not mentioned there.[1] It seems
then likely that in claiming in the Godley writ, as in two other
closely related writs (nos. 40, 41) relating to Godley and the four
manors, that the Confessor had granted them grithbreach, foresteall,
hamsocn, and flymenafyrmth, the monks of Chertsey were making
a claim that exceeded the content of the Confessor's actual grant ;
and if that was the case, the texts purporting to record such grants
are not unaltered copies of authentic writs of the Confessor.[2] Two
other features of the writ under discussion excite misgivings. Is the
inclusion of ' my sheriff ' in the address authentic, or is it due to
interpolation ? Only in nos. 41 and 42 does ' my sheriff ' (sing.)
appear, without a name. Is the passage : *swa freo 7 swa forð swa
ænig is freost* authentic or is it the contribution of a later hand ?
It is not unlikely that this passage, for which there is no exact
parallel in the writs printed here, has arisen out of the mingling of
two formulas : *swa freo swa ænig is freost* (cf. the phrase in no. 25,
an excellent text), and *swa full 7 swa forð*, the formula generally
employed in writs (compare nos. 8, 9, 12, 14, etc.). *Swa full 7 swa
forð 7 swa freo* appears in no. 104, a text of dubious authenticity.

---

[1] Text in *Mon. Angl.* i. 431, no. x ; calendared and dated c. 1067 in Davis,
Regesta, no. 14. King William declares that his will is that Abbot Wulfwold
be entitled to possess his land as fully and completely as he ever had it in
King Edward's day ; and all the things which King William has subsequently
granted him ; and his sake and his soke, toll and team and infangenetheof,
over his lands and over his men, within borough and without, by land and by
strand, as fully in all respects as ever the abbot had them previously ; and
the king forbids anyone to deprive the abbot of any of the things that he has
granted him.

[2] Since the authenticity of the post-Conquest writs of Chertsey Abbey has
not yet been fully investigated, it is difficult to determine at what date the four
forfeitures of grithbreach, foresteall, hamsocn, and flymenafyrmth, mentioned
above, first appear in a genuine Chertsey writ. Two writs attributed to
William I in which they appear are not authentic. (i) Davis, *Regesta*,·
no. 224, and Charter no. xxxiii, dated 1066–86 by Davis ; and *Cartæ Antiquæ*,
ed. Landon, no. 110 : ' quietas ab omni geldo et consuetudinibus que ad me
pertinent, scilicet, *soc et sac, tol et tem et infangenetheof et gridbrich et foresteal
et hamsocne et flemenefornith et murdro in festo et sine festo* et cum aliis consuetudinibus que habuerunt tempore regis Eadwardi '. (ii) Davis, *Regesta*,
no. 51, dated 1066–71 by Davis ; and *Cartæ Antiquæ*, no. 109 : ' et habeant
*socam et sacam, tol et tem et infangenetheof et gridbrich et foresteal et flemene-
fornith et hamsocne* per totam suam terram '. For comments on the
authenticity of these two texts in the name of William I, see J. H. Round,
Eng. Hist. Rev. xxix (1914), 348 ff. The four forfeitures in question appear
in Chertsey writs of later kings, and they were claimed by the abbot of Chertsey
in the Quo Warranto proceedings (*Plac. de Quo Warranto*, p. 744). For a writ
of William II confirming their privileges see Davis, *Regesta*, no. 439.

Swa freo appears in no. III. Again, the customary ' in Surrey ' is absent from l. 2. The evidence favours the supposition that no. 42 is not an unaltered copy of an authentic writ of the Confessor, but one that has been retouched and improved by a later hand.

The relation the one to the other of the two remaining Chertsey writs (nos. 40, 41) is not easy to determine. Both purport to announce a grant by Edward to Chertsey Abbey of the four vills of CHERTSEY, EGHAM, THORPE, AND CHOBHAM, and of judicial and financial rights ; to which the longer writ (no. 41) adds, among other matter, ' with the HUNDRED OF GODLEY '. Looking at the protocols of these two texts, there can be little doubt that the authentic form is that of no. 40, and that : *ofer Engle þeode*, and : ' and my sheriff ', are due to interpolation.[1] *On wude 7 on felde*, if no. 41 is not based on a separate writ of the Confessor issued independently of no. 40, may possibly have been taken from no. 42. Further, besides the words ' with the hundred of Godley ', we find in no. 41 an additional passage : lit. ' and I will not permit that any sheriff take to himself—of—any of the things that belong in the hundred of Godley, without the abbot '. One cannot help suspecting that this passage as it stands was composed in the post-Conquest period. The objections to it are stylistic. It seems improbable that the peculiarities of : *teo of ænig þarre þing þe beolimpað inne þan hundrede of Goddelie wiðuten þan abbode*, can be due merely to careless copying. Leaving out of account the eccentric spelling *þarre* for *þare* (*þæra*), which appears only in one text, it is impossible to translate in this context the *of* before *ænig*, and the *to* which should come between *inne* and *þan hundrede* (*inne to þan hundrede*) is missing. For the normal preposition *butan*, ' without ', of Old English we find here *wiðutan* (*wiðuten*), of which the first and only instance recorded in BT is in the *Chronicle* s.a. 1086 ; the preposition ' without ' is assigned in NED to the Middle English period onwards (not the Old English). What would have been the consequences of the inclusion of a prohibition of this nature in an authentic pre-Conquest writ— supposing a writ with these contents to have been issued ? Dr. H. M. Cam pointed out to me that even if the right of holding the hundred court and of taking the profits of justice accruing therefrom were granted to the abbot, other rights pertaining to the king would still remain within the hundred unless they had been expressly

---

[1] *Eduuard king ofer Engle þeode* is the opening clause of a Chertsey charter (K. 844) in which the Confessor is represented as informing Archbishop Stigand and Earl Harold and all his thegns that he restores to Chertsey Abbey the 10 hides at (White) Waltham and the church there and two woods and 20 acres of pasture at Cookham ; there is no greeting clause. This text may ultimately be based on an authentic writ or charter of the Confessor for Chertsey, but it can hardly be accepted as authentic in its present form.

granted away. In no. 42, the writ purporting to announce the royal grant of Godley hundred, the hundred is said to have been granted ' freely ', and ' with all things that belong to me in woodland and in open country '. It does not seem clear, in the absence of a direct statement, whether the king is here relinquishing royal rights such as the right to entertainment, or to the provision of an escort, or to the payment of geld, the levying of which would involve the entry of the sheriff into the geographical area of the hundred. Again, other rights might accrue to the sheriff within the hundred ; in the thirteenth century certain ' customary rents ' were the perquisite of the sheriff, and it seems more than probable that these were of ancient origin.[1] Dr. Cam has suggested to me that the precept forbidding the sheriff to take anything from the hundred ' without the abbot ' suggests the arrangements of a post-Conquest period, when the view of frankpledge might be held by the lord in the presence of a representative of the sheriff ; so that although the passage referring to the sheriff may have been appropriate to conditions before the Norman Conquest, it would certainly have been appropriate to post-Conquest conditions, when there was every degree of collaboration and sharing of profits between the lord of a hundred and the sheriff. It is suggestive that the clause : ' prohibeo ne quis vicecomes ibi (i.e. in Godley hundred) placitet *nisi per abbatem* ', and another : ' neque se intromittat infra quatuor maneria sua . . . *nisi per abbatem* ', appear in Chertsey writ-charters and writs of Henry I and II and Richard I.[2] One cannot help suspecting that the passage relating to the sheriff in this writ was the work of a post-Conquest hand. But when this dubious passage and the other passages which have been remarked on above are abstracted from the longer writ (no. 41), it becomes identical with the shorter (no. 40) except for orthographical variants.[3] The fact that only the improved and augmented form (no. 41) was entered with nos. 42 and 43 on the Cartæ Antiquæ Roll, and in a Latin form confirmed with them in the *inspeximus* charter of Henry III (the shorter form, no. 40, being ignored), favours the supposition that the longer writ, no. 41, is merely an improved and embellished

---

[1] See further on the duties of the sheriff in connection with the peace, and with police, and with the enforcement of services due to the crown, Morris, ' The office of Sheriff in the Anglo-Saxon period ', *Eng. Hist. Rev.* xxxi (1916), 30 ff. ; *Medieval English Sheriff*, 32 ff., 38.

[2] *Cartæ Antiquæ*, ed. Landon, nos. 112, 113, 115, 117. The antecedent of the second of these clauses is however : ' nullus justiciarorum et ministrorum uel forestariorum ' ; but cf. *ibid.* no. 109, ' ne aliquis vicecomes uel forestarius aut minister meus '.

[3] There is one insignificant variation : no. 40, Cott. Vitellius, *wið eche gescot* ; no. 41, Cartæ Antiquæ, *wið ælc gescot* ; *ibid.* Cott. Vitellius, *wið alle gescot*.

version of the shorter, no. 40, and that no. 41 does not represent a separate writ of the Confessor independently issued.

Can we then accept the shorter writ (no. 40) as a (modernised) copy of an authentic writ of King Edward ?   Although at first sight it resembles in its general outline writs of the Confessor, and may indeed have been based on one, closer examination of its contents reveals certain suspicious features, which are indeed found also in the longer version (no. 41).   In the first place both these texts purport to announce the grant to the monks of Chertsey of the four forfeitures, grithbreach, foresteall, hamsocn, and flymenafyrmth, which may not actually, as we have seen above (p. 204), have been granted to them in the Confessor's reign.   Further, these two texts in the clause : *morthslechte inne freols 7 ut of freols*, resemble one of the spurious charters of William I (p. 204, n. 2) with a clause : *murdro in festo et sine festo*.   Since on this evidence *morthslecht* stands for *murdrum*, *morthslecht* must in the reputed writs of the Confessor have been included in the matters supposed to have been granted to Chertsey Abbey, by some person familiar with the *murdrum*-fine of the early Norman period ; it is improbable that this fine was in existence in the time of King Edward.[1]   Further the *wiþ* of *wiþ alle þe þinge þe to me beolimpeþ*, in place of the *mid* which is normal in Old English, may, if it is not a copyist's substitution, betray the hand of a compiler in the Middle English period ; the normal *mid* appears in the corresponding passage of no. 42.   From the appearance of *gescot*, *weorc*, and *waru* (*ware*) in nos. 40 and 41, no certain conclusions can be drawn, for these are matters which, although they are not explicitly mentioned in writs of other houses, would not in texts otherwise unexceptionable excite suspicion.   The same consideration applies to the passage referring to the king's religious motive in making the grant ; it cannot be said with certainty that it is not authentic (see Introduction, pp. 67–70).   But when one examines the structure of nos. 40 and 41, the two texts under discussion, one observes that they seem to have been put together without proper regard for the syntax of the several parts.   The list of privileges beginning with : ' and saca and socha and tol and taem ' and continuing as far as ' ut of freols ', gives the impression of having been taken from some other context.   One would have expected that it would begin with the preposition ' with ' ; ' *with* (*mid*) sake

---

[1] See Introduction, p. 85.   *Murdrum* appears in other spurious Chertsey charters of William I, as also in Chertsey charters of Henry I and II and Richard I already referred to above, p. 203, n. 4.   See also *Cartæ Antiquæ*, Rolls 1–10, ed. Landon, nos. 109–10, 112, 115, 117.   Liebermann (*Gesetze*, ii. 587, s.v. ' Mord ') attributed the appearance of *morthslecht* in the writs of the Confessor under discussion to a twelfth-century forger.

and soke and toll and team etc.' and not as it does with ' and ' :
' *and* sake and soke and toll and team etc.' That the preposition
' with ' is really necessary is indicated by the ' and *with* all the
things that pertain to me ' that follows this passage. That King
Edward the Confessor issued a writ announcing a grant to Chertsey
Abbey of the four vills named in these Chertsey writs seems entirely
probable ; but it seems clear that the interest maintained at Chertsey
in the *carte* of the Confessor manifested itself after the Norman
Conquest in at the very least, the re-handling of older material, if
not in downright fabrication. As late as the reign of Richard I
reference is being made to the *carte* of King Edward and his successors, as for instance in a charter of Richard I confirming to Chertsey
Abbey among other matters the four manors with sake and soke,
toll, team and infangenetheof etc., ' sicut carte Sancti Eadwardi
regis et W. regis et alterius W. et H. regis proaui nostri et H. regis
patris nostri quas inde habent testantur '.[1] To what extent these
processes may have been responsible for determining the present
form and content of nos. 40, 41, can be scarcely more than a matter
of conjecture.

(40)

King Edward declares that he has granted to Chertsey Abbey,
Chertsey, Egham, Thorpe, and Chobham, with judicial and financial
rights. (1053–66)

(Cott. Vitell. A. xiii, f. 50 b)

1 [E]duuard king gret Stigand archeƀ and Harold eorl and alle mine
þegenas on Suþþereie frondliche. and ich kuþe geu þat ich habbe
geunnen Criste and Seinte Petre in to Cherteseye þane selue tun. and
Egeham and Þorpe and Chabbeham freo wið eche gescot and werc
5 and ware and saca and socha and tol and taem. and infangeneþef.
and grit[h]bruche and forestel homsocne and flemnesfremthe and
morthslechte inne freols. and ut of freols. and wiþ alle þe þinge [þe]
to me beolimpeþ. and be Godes bletsunge þis nan man ne awende
for þan þe ich hit beo minre witene rade for muchelere neode Gode
10 geuþe mine saule to helpene.

Heading : [C]arta eiusdem regis de quatuor Maneriis.   7. *first* freols
over erasure.

Translation

King Edward sends friendly greetings to Archbishop Stigand and
Earl Harold and all my thegns in Surrey. And I inform you that

[1] *Cartæ Antiquæ*, ed. Landon, no. 117.

I have granted to Chertsey, to Christ and to St. Peter, the vill itself and Egham and Thorpe and Chobham, exempt in respect of every contribution and work and service, and sake and soke and toll and team and infangenetheof and grithbreach and foresteall, hamsocn and flymenafyrmth and morthsliht in festival time and outside it, and with all the things that belong to me. And on [pain of forfeiting] God's blessing let no man turn this aside, since by the advice of my counsellors, I, because of great need, have granted it to God for the good of my soul.

(41)

King Edward declares that he has granted to Chertsey Abbey, Chertsey, Egham, Thorpe, and Chobham, with the hundred of Godley, with judicial and financial rights. (1053–66)

(Cartæ Antiquæ Roll D, no. 7)

+ Eadward cing ofer Engle þeode gret Stigand arceb. 7 Harold 1
eorl. 7 mine sirrefen 7 ealle mine þeines on Suðrége freon[d]lice.
7 ic kiðe éow ꝥ ic habbe geunnen Criste 7 Sce Petre into Certeseige
þone sylfa tun. 7 Eggeham 7 Torp. 7 Cebbeham mid þan hundrede
of Goddelie. fréó wið ælc gescot. 7 weorc. 7 ware. 7 saca. 7 soca. 5
7 tol. 7 team. 7 infangenetheof. 7 griðbruche. 7 forestel. hamsoca.
7 flemeneformth. 7 morthslehte. inne freols. 7 ut of freols. 7 wið
ealle þo þinge þe to me bilimpað on wude 7 on felde. 7 ic nelle
geþafian ꝥ ænig sirrefe him to honde téo of ænig þarre þing þe
beolimpað inne þan hundrede of Goddelie wiðuten þan abbode. 10
7 beo Godes bletsunge þis nan man ne awende for þan þe ic hit
beo minre witena rade for micelra neode Gode geuþe minre sawle to
helpene.

2. Suð-] Sud- MS.   3. kuþe V.   4. Chabbeham V.
5. wið alle gescot V.   6. hamsocne V.   9. of ani þare þing þe
belimpeð V.   11. hit *followed by* habbe *crossed through.*

Translation

Edward, king over the English people, sends friendly greetings to Archbishop Stigand and Earl Harold and my sheriff and all my thegns in Surrey.   And I inform you that I have granted to Chertsey, to Christ and to St. Peter, the vill itself and Egham and Thorpe and Chobham, with the hundred of Godley, exempt in respect of every contribution and work and service, and sake and soke and toll and team and infangenetheof and grithbreach and foresteall, hamsocn and flymenafyrmth and morthsliht in festival time and outside it, and with all the things that belong to me in woodland and in open country. And I will not permit that any sheriff take to himself—of—any of the things that belong in the hundred of Godley, without the abbot. And on [pain of forfeiting] God's blessing, let no man turn this aside, since by the advice of my counsellors, I, because of great need, have granted it to God for the good of my soul.

(42)

King Edward declares that he has granted to Chertsey Abbey and to Abbot Wulfwold the hundred of Godley, and that the abbot is to have judicial and financial rights over all his men, and over his lands. (1058–66)

(Cartæ Antiquæ Roll D, no. 8)

1 ✠ Eadward cing gret Stigand arceƀ 7 Harold eorl. 7 mine sirrefen
7 ealle mine þeines freondlice. 7 ic kiðe eow ꝥ ic habƀe geunnen
Criste 7 Sc̄e Petre into Certeseige 7 þan abƀ Wlwolde ꝥ hundred of
Goddelie. swo freo 7 swo forð swo ænig is freost þe beoð on mine
5 onwealde mid ealle þinge þe to me beolimpað on wde 7 on felde.
7 ic wille ꝥ se abbod beo his saca wurðe. 7 his soca. 7 tol. 7 tem.
7 infangenetheof. 7 griðbruche. 7 forestel. 7 hamsoca. 7 flemene-
formthe. binne porte. 7 buten. beo lande 7 beo strande. ofer ealle his
man 7 ofer his lande.

| 2. cuþe V. | 4. ꝥ beod V. | 4. beoð] beod MS. | 7. grið-] |
| grid- MS. | 7. homsokne V. | 9. mannen V. | |

Translation

King Edward sends friendly greetings to Archbishop Stigand and Earl Harold and my sheriff and all my thegns. And I inform you that I have granted to Chertsey, to Christ and to St. Peter and to Abbot Wulfwold, the hundred of Godley as freely and as completely as any that is under my control is most free, with all things that belong to me in woodland and in open country. And my will is that the abbot be entitled to his sake and his soke, and toll and team and infangenetheof, grithbreach and foresteall and hamsocn and flymenafyrmth, within town and without, by land and by strand, over all his men and over his lands.

(43)

King Edward declares that he has granted to Wulfwold, abbot of Chertsey, sake and soke over his own lands in London and over his own men. 1058–66

(Cartæ Antiquæ Roll D, no. 9)

+ Eadw*ard* cing gret Will*elm*. ƀ. 7 Swetman minne portgerefe   1
7 ealle mine buruhware on Lunden*e* freon[d]lic*e*. 7 ic kiðe eow ꝥ ic
wille ꝥ Wlwold aƀƀ at Certes*eige* beo his saca wurðe. 7 his socna. ofer
his hagan land her binnan. 7 ofer his agene man. swa ful. 7 swa forð
swa hit anig his forgengea toforen hi*m* fyrmest heuede *i*nto þa*n*   5
halga*n* minstre on ealle þi*n*ge. 7 ic nelle geþafian ꝥ hi*m* anig man
fra*m* hande teo anig þare gerihte þes þe he mid richte to hab*b*ene ah.
7 ic hi*m* geunnen habbe.

2. þe burhware V.   2. kuþe V.   5. hauede V.   6. munstre V.
8. hic V.

Translation

King Edward sends friendly greetings to Bishop William and
Swetman my portreeve and all my citizens in London.   And I
inform you that my will is that Wulfwold, abbot of Chertsey, shall
be entitled to his sake and his soke over his own lands herein, and
over his own men, as fully and as completely in all things as ever
any of his predecessors had it for the holy monastery.   And I will
not permit that anyone take away from him any of the rights
which he ought lawfully to have and I have granted him.

CIRENCESTER

The authenticity of the writ in favour of the Confessor's priest
Regenbald [1] seems certain.   The text printed here adds a new fact
to the biography of Regenbald, whose position has often been discussed (see Biog. Notes) ; he may have borne before the Conquest
the title *cancellarius* (see pp. 59 f.).   Regenbald appears in Domesday
as a wealthy landowner holding lands and churches in several
shires, but although he stood high in the favour of Edward and
of William I—both of whom issued writs in his favour—he was
never raised to the episcopate as were other king's priests.   Can
we suppose that his services in the king's writing office were too
valuable to be dispensed with ?   Or did some obstacle stand in

[1] On the spelling *Regenbald*, now used generally by historians, and appearing
in a writ of William I for Regenbald, see p. 570 below.

the way of his advancement ? The writ of the Confessor printed
here, addressed to the authorities of the shires in which Regenbald his priest has lands and men, announces a grant to Regenbald
of sake and soke over his land and over his men, and toll and
team and infangenetheof both within borough and without, and
also declares that the *wite*, or fine payable to him by offenders,
shall be equivalent to that paid to a diocesan bishop, the status
of whom in the reign of Alfred was equated with that of the
ealdorman (Alfred 40). The bearing of the concession made to
Regenbald by King Edward in granting him this exalted status
has been obscured hitherto. The unintelligible misreading: *swa
þ leod beþ*, for the manuscript: *swa þ leod biscopes* ('like, i.e.
equivalent to, that of a diocesan bishop'), stands in the text in
Archæologia. After the Conquest Regenbald entered the service
of King William who issued two writs in his favour, dated by
Davis in 1067.[1] In the first William declares that he has granted
to Reinbold his priest the lands at Eisey and at Latton (both in
Wiltshire) and everything pertaining thereto within town and
without, with sake and with soke, as fully and completely as
ever King Harold held them, to dispose of at his pleasure (' to
atheonne swa swa ealra lefest ys ') ; and forbids anyone to deprive
Reinbold of any of the things that he has granted him, on pain of
losing his friendship. In the other writ King William announces
that he has granted to his priest Regenbald all his land as fully and
completely in every respect with sake and with soke as he held it
under King Edward, and forbids anyone to impair his position
(*lytlian*, lit, ' to lessen '), on pain of losing the king's friendship.
One Domesday entry (DB i. 63) styles Regenbald : *Reimbaldus de
Cirecestre, Reinbaldi (gen.) de Cirecestre.* There was at Cirencester
before the Conquest a college of secular canons which was poorly
endowed and of which little is known. The possessions of the canons
in King Edward's time and in 1086 amounted to no more than two
hides of land in Cirencester hundred with 6 acres of meadow, except
that King William gave them a vill in *Wiche* and a portion of
wood.[2] Later tradition magnified this foundation into ' a fair and
riche college of Prebendaries ' of which Regenbald was supposed to
have been dean.[3] Leland says (v. 62) that in the body of the church
at Cirencester ' in a sepulchre Crosse of White Marble ' there was
this inscription : ' Hic jacet Rembaldus presbyter, quondam hujus
ecclesiæ decanus, [et tempore Edwardi regis Angliæ cancellarius] '.
However that may have been, when Henry I founded at Cirencester

---

[1] *Regesta*, nos. 9, 19 ; also in *Archæologia*, xxvi. 256.
[2] DB i. 166 b, VCH *Glouc.* ii. 79 ff. *Wiche*, i.e. Painswick, Glouc.
[3] J. Leland, *Itinerary*, ed. T. Hearne, editio altera, Oxford, 1744, ii. 22.

a new church of St. Mary served by Augustinian canons he endowed it with all the estate in lands, churches and other things, of Regenbald the priest, and conferred on it throughout all its possessions sake and soke, toll, team and infangenetheof, and all other liberties, immunities, customs and privileges as freely as the said church had held the same in the reign of the Confessor or in the reign of his father or brother, and in his own time.[1] It is for this reason that the writ of Edward and the two writs of William have come down to us as copies in the Cirencester cartulary. Everything encourages the belief that the writ in favour of Regenbald is a copy of an authentic writ of King Edward. In structure it resembles no. 46, a Latin version of a writ of King Edward the authenticity of which in its (presumed) Anglo-Saxon form there is no reason to doubt. Side by side with spellings characteristic of Old English there are others, e.g. *schyrreuen*, which denote a later date, and which are no doubt due to modernisation, unconscious or deliberate.

(44)

King Edward declares that Regenbald his priest is to have judicial and financial rights over his land and over his men, as fully and completely as any of his predecessors in the days of King Cnut. 1042–66

(Cirencester Cartulary, p. 26)

Edward king gret mine bissopes and mine eorles 7 mine schyr-   1
reuen. 7 alle mine þeigenes on þam schyren þær Reinbold min
preost hæfeð lond 7 men inne. freondliche. 7 ic cuþe eow þ ic wolle þ
he beo his saca wurð. 7 his socnes. ofer his lond 7 ofer his men.
7 tolnes wrth. 7 theames. 7 infangeneþeofes eægþar ge binne buruh.   5
ge buten. swa full 7 swa forð. swa ænig his forgengena toforen him
formest weren on Cnutes kinges daie. 7 þ his wite beo eall swa muchell
swa þ leodbes. æt ællan þingan. 7 ic nelle nenne man geþauian þ him
from hond teo ænig þære þinga þæs þe ic him geunne habbe.

Mr. N. R. Ker kindly points out that the 'thorn' (þ) and 'wyn' (= w) of Anglo-Saxon script are used throughout with two exceptions.   *Heading :* Carta Regis Edwardi confirmantis Reinbaldo Capellano omnes tenuras antecessorum suorum, *in red, in main hand.*   4. lond] lonð MS.

[1] *Mon. Angl.* vi. 177 ; the charter is dated 1133.   Round, *Feudal England*, 426, suggested that the king's phrase *dedi et concessi* might be taken to imply that he was not only confirming an endowment made by Regenbald, but also granting lands that had escheated to himself, and that this conclusion was confirmed by the fact that the king, while granting them, especially reserved the life-interest of the bishop of Salisbury and of two others who must have acquired their rights since Regenbald's death.

Translation

King Edward sends friendly greetings to my bishops and my earls and my sheriffs and all my thegns in the shires in which Regenbald my priest has lands and men. And I inform you that my will is that he be entitled to his sake and his soke over his land and over his men, to toll and team and infangenetheof both within borough and without, as fully and as completely as ever any of his predecessors before him were in the days of King Cnut ; and that the fine payable to him be equivalent to that of a diocesan bishop in all things. And I will not permit any one to deprive him of any of the things that I have granted him.

COVENTRY

Of the two writs extant in favour of the monastery of St. Mary at Coventry,[1] both in the name of the Confessor, one (no. 45) is well known, while the other (no. 46) appears to have escaped notice hitherto, and has not, so far as I am aware, been printed before.[2] The Anglo-Saxon writ recording the foundation and endowment of the monastery by Earl Leofric and his wife Godgifu (Godiva), frequently cited in histories of the city of Coventry, can hardly be accepted as an authentic writ of the Confessor. But although Latin charters relating to the foundation of the monastery have been subjected to critical examination by the editors of the *Crawford Charters* (pp. 94, 100) and by the late James Tait,[3] no such detailed

---

[1] For the early history of this house, see W. Dugdale, *Antiquities of Warwickshire* (Coventry, 1765), pp. 91 f., 104 ff., *Mon. Angl.* iii. 177 f., and VCH *Warwick* ii. 52 ff.

[2] My attention was drawn to B.M. Add. MS. 32100, in which it is copied, by a reference in the VCH *Warwick*, ii. 52, n. 4.

[3] ' An Alleged Charter of William the Conqueror ', in *Essays in History presented to R. Lane Poole* (ed. H. W. C. Davis, Oxford, 1927), pp. 151–67. This writ (B.M. Add. Charter 11205) purports to confirm to the monastery at Coventry all the gifts of land and other things made to it by Earl Leofric. Tait shows that the dates of the persons to whom the charter is addressed are inconsistent with one another, and that there are features in the form and contents of the charter which are not free from suspicion. See further G. L. Haskins, ' A Forged Charter of William the Conqueror ', *Speculum*, vol. xviii (1943), 497–8, where it is suggested that though the seal is genuine, its attachment is fraudulent.

examination of the Anglo-Saxon writ, no. 45, has to my knowledge appeared in print. The verdicts pronounced upon the Latin
charters of Coventry have been uniformly unfavourable. Not only
is the confirmation charter attributed to the Confessor spurious, but
the alleged foundation charter of Leofric (in its two versions)
contains anachronisms which, as Tait pointed out,[1] are fatal to any
claim to authenticity.

This Latin charter (beginning : *Ego Leofricus comes* in one version, *comes
Cestriae* in the other) states that Leofric with the consent of King Edward and
of Pope Alexander and with the sign and testimony of other religious men,
ecclesiastical and lay, has caused the church of Coventry to be dedicated in
honour of God and St. Mary and St. Peter, and St. Osburg, and all Saints. He
has assigned to the service of God and to the food and clothing of the abbot
and monks a large number of vills (23 or 24, the names of which are given in
the text), and half the vill of Coventry, with sake and soke, toll and team, with
liberty and all customs, as he himself held them of King Edward. Names of
witnesses follow. The abbot is to be subject to the king of England alone.
A curse is invoked on anyone who shall deprive the monastery of its liberty or
of Leofric's gift. There follows a letter of Pope Alexander (omitted in some
sources) granting privileges to the monastery.[2]

Again, the elaborate confirmation charter of Edward the Confessor, purporting to confirm Leofric's gifts to the monastery, is
a later fabrication :

In this solemn diploma (after a preamble) King Edward notifies all future
kings, archbishops, bishops, abbots, earls and all the faithful, that Earl Leofric
founded the monastery at Coventry, endowed it with liberal gifts, and for the
maintenance of the abbot and monks, granted to the monastery half the vill
of Coventry and the vills named in Leofric's charter. After which the king
on his own behalf grants to Abbot Leofwine and his successors, throughout all
the possessions of the monastery, sake and soke and toll and all laws and
customs with which Leofric held these estates of the king. Moreover the king
grants to the monastery still further privileges and immunities, and for the
warning of those who shall violate the rights of the abbey refers to the letter of
Pope Alexander which is to be found in the longer version of Leofric's alleged
foundation charter, and which some copies of this diploma recite in full.[3]

Tait describes the charter as ' an arrant forgery '. He points out
(*loc. cit.* p. 162) that although dated 1043 (in several copies, which
also include a list of witnesses) this document incorporates a letter
of Pope Alexander, 1061–73,[4] and that it is witnessed *inter alios* by
Queen Edith before her marriage and by Abbot Manni of Evesham
who was not elected till 1044.

That the Benedictine monastery of St. Mary at Coventry was

---

[1] *Ut supra*, 164.

[2] *Mon. Angl.* iii. 190, no. ii, 191, no. iv ; K. 939.

[3] *Mon. Angl.* iii. 191, no. iii ; K. 916 ; Thorpe p. 351. The contents of the
charter are not identical in all the sources.

[4] On this, see *Crawford Charters*, 94 ; Holtzmann, *Papsturkunden*, i. 42.

founded by Leofric (with whom Godgifu (Godiva) is associated by some authorities) [1] there can be no doubt. But like the alleged foundation charter of Leofric and the alleged confirmation charter of the Confessor, the document printed here as no. 45 is spurious. [2] After the protocol the writ continues with a consideration of the religious motives which have led the king to confirm the grants made to Coventry Minster by Earl Leofric and Godgifu. Then with an introductory clause, 7 *icc ann heom eft ealswa,* which appears elsewhere only in certain Westminster writs (see p. 64) he is represented as granting to the minster on his own behalf a long list of judicial and financial rights, and as declaring that the minster is always to be inhabited by monks living according to the rule of St. Benedict. There follows a two-fold prohibition such as is found elsewhere only in Westminster writs (see p. 66), and a conclusion where a blessing is invoked on those increasing the pious gifts made to the minster, and a curse on those setting them aside or impairing its position. In the form in which it has come down to us, copied in a hand of the end of the eleventh century on a large rectangular piece of parchment, with strands of silk for appending a seal threaded through the base, turned back in a fold, this document resembles in its appearance not the Edwardian writ form but the Anglo-Norman charter form of the end of the eleventh century. And further the linguistic colouring of the writ, with its numerous later spellings, e.g. *Ædsiæ, Couæntréé,* forbids one to regard it as a product of the Confessor's time.

Nor is it possible to regard no. 45 as an authentic but later copy of a genuine writ of King Edward. A comparison of its form and structure with those of other writs indicates that in this text the outlines of the writ form have been blurred through the insertion of other matter not usually found in these documents. The section beginning: ' Ælce mannum gebyreð ', and continuing to ' wunnungæ mid ænglum ', with its lengthy development of the religious motive, is the kind of preamble which we find normally not in the

---

[1] Leofric alone is mentioned in his alleged foundation charter ; in the Confessor's alleged charter of confirmation ; in the spurious letter of Pope Alexander ; in the Latin writ (no. 46) of Coventry ; in the alleged writs of William I discussed by Tait, *ut supra* ; and in *Chronicle* E 1066. But the writ under discussion attributes the foundation of Coventry to Leofric and Godgifu. So also do Florence of Worcester, s.a. 1057, and William of Malmesbury, *Gesta Pontificum,* p. 309, *Gesta Regum,* i. 237, ii. 388. The tradition is apparently confused in Ordericus Vitalis (*Historia Ecclesiastica,* ed. Le Prevost, ii. 183) where the construction of the abbey is attributed to Leofric's son, Earl Ælfgar.

[2] The late Professor James Tait informed me verbally that in stating that this document ' appears to be genuine ' (*ut supra,* 163), he accepted the view of W. H. Stevenson, an acknowledged authority, with whom he had corresponded on the matter of its authenticity.

writ but in the solemn royal diploma (see Introduction, p. 34). It is true that we have not from any other source a royal writ of a precisely similar kind, confirming grants made to a monastery at its foundation by its founders. But to make an obvious comparison, the religious consideration is not mentioned at all in the Westminster writs, nos. 94-106 (not all authentic as they stand), which relate to grants made by the Confessor to Westminster Abbey seemingly at the time of the dedication of the church that he had built. Then again in the Coventry writ the transition from the religious preamble to the notification of the grant is very awkwardly contrived by means of a phrase : ' for hwilcæ neodlicum þingan ', which is probably intended to go with ' ic ann ' (' for which pressing reasons . . . I grant with full permission ') rather than with ' icc kyþe ' (' I inform '). It is not easy, later on in the text, to find a proper antecedent for *hit* in the clause : ' swa icc *hit* festlice getyþie ' (' so I firmly grant it '). What one would expect to find here is some clause with *licgan in to*, ' belong to ', and *nu*, ' now ' (see Introduction, p. 64). The clumsiness exhibited in the construction of this document is so unusual that it is difficult to avoid the conclusion that the text has undergone extensive interpolation or possibly reconstruction, if indeed it is not in its entirety a post-Conquest fabrication. It is instructive to compare it with no. 46, the Latin version of a writ the authenticity of which in its Anglo-Saxon form can scarcely be in doubt, and which in its plainness and succinctness seems to represent the norm. A notable feature of no. 45 is its resemblance, in some points already commented on, to a group of dubious Westminster writs, discussed pp. 306 ff. below. It also resembles certain writs of this group in the employment in the address of the doubtfully authentic term *holden* (see Introduction, p. 54). Equally striking is the appearance in the Coventry writ of the phrase : *on lande 7 on loga*, recorded elsewhere (with *mid*) only in Westminster texts (see p. 462). Links between spurious Coventry charters and spurious Westminster charters were pointed out by the editors of the *Crawford Charters* (*ut supra*, pp. 94 f., 100) who demonstrated that the alleged confirmation charter of King Edward for Coventry (see p. 215 above) is closely connected with the spurious Great Charter of King Edgar for Westminster Abbey (see p. 338), certain portions of which the Coventry charter incorporates. It was suggested by Tait (*loc. cit.*) that we owe the spurious confirmation charter of the Confessor for Coventry to ' the desire of the monks after the Conquest to possess a solemn diploma with a preamble, a papal bull after the Westminster fashion, and a long string of witnesses '. In the same way the monks of Coventry may have desired to provide for their house an impressive and elaborate writ in English employing the phraseology of the more elaborate writs of Westminster. But their ignorance betrayed them. ' Those who drew it up ', says Tait of Edward's spurious confirmation charter, ' had an imperfect idea of what an Old English diploma should contain and introduced features ' (such as the general address) ' which were only appropriate to the writ '. The compiler of the Coventry writ must also have had an imperfect idea of the structure and content of the normal Edwardian writ when he foisted into his text phrases elaborating the religious motive which were appropriate only to the diploma. And further he went much too far when he drew up the comprehensive list of privileges supposed to have been conferred on the minster by King Edward : ' sake and soke, toll and team, hamsocn, foresteall, blodwite, fihtwite, weardwite and mund-breach '. Leaving out of account blodwite and weardwite (of which there is no mention in writs of reasonably certain authenticity, see Introduction, pp. 83–5), nowhere even in the spurious Coventry charters relating to the foundation do we find a list like this. Leofric's spurious foundation charter mentions specifically sake and soke, toll and team, King Edward's spurious confirmation charter mentions sake and soke and toll. A spurious writ of William I (which refers to these alleged grants of Leofric and King Edward) mentions sake and soke and toll and team ; a doubtful writ of William mentions toll and team.[1] No. 46, a Latin version of a probably authentic writ, mentions sake and soke, toll and team ; and there seems no reason to doubt that these were the privileges actually granted to the abbey at Coventry by King Edward. The inflated list in no. 45 is then spurious. No list of privileges claimed in Westminster writs, however, resembles it exactly ; the one in the Islip writ, no. 104 (a list not authentic in its present form), comes closest to it.

In contrast to the writ in English which has just been discussed (no. 45), the writ in Latin (no. 46), hitherto unprinted, can safely be regarded as a rendering of an authentic writ of King Edward the Confessor. In this text the king declares that Abbot Leofwine is to have sake and soke, toll and team, over his land and over his men, within city and without, as fully and completely as Earl Leofric had them. There is every reason to suppose that the Latin version was made after the Norman Conquest, possibly for entry on the roll from which it was transcribed into Add. MS. 32100. The fact that the Latin version of no. 45 transcribed into the same manuscript from the same roll begins with : *Ego Eadwardus rex saluto*, whereas the English version of no. 45 begins : *Eadward kyngc gret*, encourages the belief that the *Ego Eadwardus rex saluto* of no. 46 stands for the

[1] Davis, *Regesta*, nos. 57, 244.

normal *Eadweard cyng gret* (however spelt) of writs of the Confessor.
The plural in *infra ciuitates 7 extra* may represent post-Conquest
usage in the same way as the *infra urbes 7 extra* of no. 31, and
since a parallel formula with plural forms appears (seemingly) in
some vernacular writs (see p. 428), the use of the plural is not to
be regarded in no. 46 as a suspicious feature. Again the *primitus*
of l. 6 arises no doubt out of a misunderstanding of the *fyrmest*,
' to the highest degree ', frequently found in Edwardian writs (see
Introduction, p. 63), whilst *satisfaciat* (l. 7) is no doubt used in
error for *forisfaciat*. But behind the Latin form appears the characteristic structure and phraseology of an authentic writ of the
Confessor. A close parallel appears in the Cirencester writ (no. 44)
the authenticity of which seems to be beyond doubt. The final :
Et ego nolo pati etc. in no. 46 stands for a prohibition clause of
a familiar type (see p. 66). Everything encourages the belief that
the text under discussion is a Latin rendering of an authentic writ
of King Edward.

(45)

King Edward declares that he confirms the gifts made by Earl
Leofric and Godgifu (Godiva) to Abbot Leofwine and the brethren
at Coventry Minster, and that he grants them judicial and financial
rights.

(B.M. Add. Charter 28657)

+ Eadward kyngc gret Ædsiæ arceb. 7 ealle mine biscopes. 1
abbudes. 7 eorles. þeignes. 7 scírgeréfan. 7 ealle mine holden freondlice. Ælce mannum gebyreð swyðe rihte úre drihten Gód luuien.
7 hehlice weorðien. 7 geornlice Godes lagum 7 anrǽdlice filgean.
7 ælmesdæden georne befellen. þurh hwan þ he of synbænden hine 5
selfne mote alýnian. For úræ drihten on larspelle þúss cweð.
Gestrynað éow syluum mid ælmesdædum. madme hord on heofonan.
and wunnungæ mid ænglum. For hwilcæ neodlicum þingan ícc
kyþe eow eallum. þ ícc ánn mid fulre unne þ þa ilcæ gyue þæ Leofric
eorl. 7 Godgyuę habbeð gegiuen Criste. 7 his leoue moder. 7 Leofwine 10
abbyde. 7 þam gebroðran innan þam munstre æt Couæntréé. for
hiere saule to helpe. ón lande. 7 on lóga. on golde. 7 on seolfre. on
mádmen. 7 on oðre eallum þingum. swá fúll 7 swá forð. swá hit héom
sylfan on handen stod. 7 swa hie þer mide þæne ilcan mynster
wurðlice habbeð gegoded. swá ícc hit festlice getyþie. 7 ícc ánn 15
heom eft ealswa for minre saule. þ híe habben þer to fullne freodom.
sáca. 7 sócna. tóll. 7 téam. hamsocne. forsteall. blodwíte. fihtwíte.
weardwíte. 7 mundbryce. Nu willic henenforð þ hit sýe á muneca

Q

wunungc. and standen hiéo on Godes griðe 7 Sce Marían 7 on minre.
20 æfter Sce Benedictes régel. on þære abbuden wealdunge. 7 ícc nelle
nateshwon geþafian. ꝥ ænig mann ætbréde oððe géútige heora gýue
7 heora ælmessæ. oððe ꝥ þær ænig mann ænignę onstýngc habbe on
ænigum þingum. oððe on ænigum timan. buton sé abbud. 7 þa
gebroðran. to þæs mynstres neodan. 7 hwá sǽ þas elmessæ mid
25 ænige gode geéce. ece him drihten heofona blissan. 7 hwá sé hiéo
ætbréde oððe þane mynster on ænigum þingum. on ænigen tíman
awersie. stande hé on Godes ungriðe. 7 his leoue moder. 7 minre.
God eow ealle gehealde.

19. wunungc] wunuúgc MS.   *Endorsed in a hand of cent. xiii :* Carta
regis Eadwardi ; *and in a hand of cent. xiv :* Carta beati Edwardi Regis super
confirmatione et ecclesie fundacione.

Latin Version

(Add. MS. 32100, f. 115 b)

Ego Eadwardus rex saluto Edsium archiepiscopum et omnes meos
30 episcopos, abbates et comites, ministros et vicecomites [et] omnes
meos fideles amicabiliter. Unumquenque hominem decet nimis
recte dominum Deum nostrum diligere et sublimiter honorare,
diligenter legem Dei et constanter sequi, et eleemosynam diligenter
persequi, propter quod possit seipsum a peccati vinculo absoluere.
35 Nam dominus noster in Euangelio ita ait, Thesaurizate vobis cum
eleemosina thesaurum in celo et habitationem cum ang'e'lis. Pro
qua necessaria re, ego notum facio vobis omnibus quod ego annuo
cum plena concessione ut illud donum quod Leofricus comes et
Godiua dederint Christo, dilecte matri eius et Leofuuino Abbati et
40 fratribus in monasterio apud Couentriam pro salute animarum
suarum, in terris, in pascuis, in auro et in argento, in thesauro et in
alijs omnibus rebus ita plene et ita plenarie sicut sibimetipsis in
manibus stetit, et sicut ipsi monasterium illud honorabiliter cum eo
meliorauerint, ita ego firmiter illud annuo. Ego iterum eis annuo
45 scilicet pro anima mea ut ipsi plenariam libertatem ad hoc habeant,
sacam et socnam, theloneum, et team, hamsocne, forestall, blotwite,
fithwite, wardwite et mun[d]bruch. Modo volo ut amodo illud sit
semper monachorum habitatio et stent ipsi in Dei pace et Sancte
Marie et mea. Et secundum Sancti Benedicti regulam in abbatis
50 potestate. Et ego nihilominus nolo sustinere ut aliquis homo
distrahat vel alienet illorum donum et illorum eleemosynam vel
quod aliquis homo aliquam administrationem habeat in aliqua re
vel in aliquo tempore, nisi ipse abbas et fratres ad ipsíus monasterii
necessitatem. Et qui hanc eleemosinam cum aliquo bono adauxerit,
55 adaugeat ei dominus celi gaudium. Et qui illam vel illud monas-

terium in aliqua re in aliquo tempore deteriorauerit, stet ipse in inquietudine Dei et eius dilecte matris et in mea. Deus vos omnes conseruet.

In margin : Carta 'Sancti' Regis Edweardi.

Translation

King Edward sends friendly greetings to Archbishop Eadsige and all my bishops, abbots and earls, thegns and sheriffs, and all my lieges. It very rightly behoves every man to love and highly honour our Lord God and diligently and resolutely to obey God's laws and zealously to set about almsgiving, whereby he may deliver himself from the bonds of sin. For Our Lord in a sermon said as follows : ' Lay up for yourselves by almsgiving a treasure-hoard in heaven and a dwelling with angels.' For which pressing reasons I inform you all that I grant with full permission that those same gifts that Earl Leofric and Godgifu have given to Christ and his dear Mother and Abbot Leofwine and to the brethren in the minster at Coventry for the good of their souls, in land and in (? produce ? stock), in gold and in silver, in treasures and in all other things, as fully and as completely as they themselves possessed them, and as they therewith have munificently endowed the same minster—so I firmly grant it. And again I likewise grant them for my soul that they have with it full freedom, sake and soke, toll and team, hamsocn, foresteall, blodwite, fihtwite, weardwite and mundbreach. It is now my will that it shall be for ever henceforward the dwelling-place of monks, and may they be under the protection of God and St. Mary and under mine, (living) according to the rule of St. Benedict, under the authority of the abbots. And I will not on any account permit that any man set aside or alienate their gifts and their pious benefactions, or that any man have any authority there in any matter or at any time except the abbot and the brethren for the necessities of the minster. And whosoever shall increase these charitable gifts with any benefaction, may the Lord increase to him the bliss of heaven ; and whosoever shall set them aside or do harm to the minster in any respect at any time, may he incur the enmity of God, and of his dear Mother, and mine. God keep you all.

(46)

King Edward declares that Abbot Leofwine of Coventry is to have judicial and financial rights over his land and over his men, as fully and completely as Earl Leofric had. 1043-53.

(B.M. Add. MS. 32100, f. 115 b)

1　　Ego Eadwardus rex saluto meos episcopos et meos comites et
omnes meos ministros in illis comitatibus ubi Leofwinus abbas in
Couentria habet terras intus amicabiliter. Et ego demonstro vobis
quod ego volo quod ipse sit sua saca et sua socna dignus et theloneo
5　et themo super suam terram et super suos homines infra ciuitates
et extra ita plene et plenarie sicuti Leofricus comes primitus habuit.
Et ego nolo pati quod homo illi in aliqua re forisfaciat etc.

　　7. forisfaciat] satisfaciat, *with long initial s*, MS.

ELY

The authenticity of the Ely [1] writ of King Edward the Confessor
can scarcely be in doubt.   The king's connexion with Ely had begun
very early in life, when he was presented in a cradle by his parents
upon the altar, *palla involutus orbiculata brevibus circulis non plene
viridi coloris*.   The older monks were accustomed to relate how
Edward was reared there with the boys in the monastery (where the
cloth in which he was wrapped at his presentation was still shown),
and how he learnt with his companions psalms and *ymnos dominicos*.
It was believed that he never forgot the benefits that he had received
as a boy in the monastery, and that his gratitude was manifested
in an elaborate charter of privileges. [2]   On the death of Abbot
Leofsige, the king's kinsman Wulfric was appointed abbot of Ely,
and his appointment was announced in the writ printed here.   There
is nothing in the structure, phraseology, or linguistic forms, of this
writ to make one hesitate to accept it as a copy of a genuine writ of
King Edward.   It is however in one respect peculiar : in none of the
extant copies, English or Latin, that I have examined, is there any
direct mention of sake and soke among the privileges conferred upon

　　[1] The abbey of Ely was founded by St. Æthelthryth (Etheldreda) in 673
(Bede, *Hist. Eccles.*, iv. cap. 19), and was restored by King Edgar and Bishop
Æthelwold.   For the history of the abbey of Ely, see the *Liber Eliensis*,
published in part by D. J. Stewart (London, 1848), J. Bentham, *History and
Antiquities of the Conventual and Cathedral Church of Ely* (2nd ed. Norwich,
1812–17), *Mon. Angl.* i, 457 ff., J. Armitage Robinson, *The Times of St.
Dunstan* (Oxford, 1923), 118 ff.
　　[2] *Liber Eliensis*, ii. cap. 91–2. This charter (K. 907) which is without date
or witnesses can hardly be authentic in its present form.

Abbot Wulfric. That sake and soke were conferred on him can scarcely be doubted. Sake and soke head the list of ' customs ' which King William declares that the abbey of Ely shall have, in a writ issued in connection with the plea held at Kentford[1] on one or more occasions subsequent to 1066, to enquire into the losses in lands and liberties that the abbey had sustained since the Conquest. In this writ King William declares to all his lieges and sheriffs in whose shires the abbey of Ely has lands, that the abbey shall have all its ' customs ', namely, sake and soke, toll and team and infangenetheof, hamsocn and grithbreach, fihtwite and fyrd-wite, within borough and without, and all other emendable for-feitures over its own men in its own land, as it possessed them on the day of King Edward's death, and its right to them was proved at Kentford by the king's command by (the testimony of) several shires before his barons.[2]   The list given here is identical, with the addition of sake and soke, with that in Edward's writ. Again, in two later writs of William I it is made plain that the abbot of Ely had been possessed of sake and soke in the Con-fessor's reign. In one, William declares that the abbot of Ely shall have sake and soke and other ' customs ' as his predecessor held them on the day of King Edward's death,[3] while in the other he declares that the abbot of Ely shall have soke and sake of (*de*) five hundreds of Suffolk and from (*ab*) all the men holding lands in those hundreds, as his predecessor had in the time of King Edward.[4] The abbot of Ely appears to have continued in uninter-rupted possession of his rights and liberties, and when Henry I founded the bishopric of Ely he gave to the church of Ely all its customs, within borough and without, in land and in water and in marshes and in open country and in woodland, namely, sake and soke and toll and team and infangenetheof and hamsocn and grith-breach and fihtwite and fyrdwite and all other emendable forfeitures, as it possessed them on the day of King Edward's death, and as its claim to them was proved at Kentford.[5] How then is the absence of any mention of sake and soke in the Confessor's Ely writ to be

[1] For this plea, see *Liber Eliensis*, ii. cap. 116 ; *Inquisitio Comitatus Canta-brigiensis*, ed. N. E. S. A. Hamilton (London, 1876), xvii ff. ; Bentham, i. 106 f. ; Round, *Feudal England*, 457 ff. ; J. H. Le Patourel, *Eng. Hist. Rev.* lix (1944), 159–61 ; F. M. Stenton, *Anglo-Saxon England*, 640 ; E. Miller, *Eng. Hist. Rev.* lxii (1947), 438 ff.

[2] *Liber Eliensis*, ii. cap. 117, Bentham, Appendix, no. v (i), p. 9*, Davis, *Regesta*, no. 129, dated by the editor c. 1080, but see Le Patourel, *ut supra*.

[3] *Liber Eliensis*, ii. cap. 122, Bentham, Appendix, no. v (4), p. 10*, Davis, *Regesta*, no. 156, with date 1082.

[4] *Liber Eliensis*, ii. cap. 123, Bentham, Appendix, no. v (5), p. 10*, Davis, *Regesta*, no. 157, with date 1082.

[5] *Liber Eliensis*, iii. cap. 7, Bentham, Appendix, no. ix, p. 17*.

explained ? It is true that the rights of jurisdiction of the abbey of
Ely in the Isle and in Suffolk were supposed to have been conferred
on the abbey by King Edgar long before ; [1] but since the appointment of an abbot is in other cases followed by a grant to him of
sake and soke (frequently with other rights), even though these
rights may have been enjoyed by his predecessors, [2] it does not seem
probable that this would account for the absence of any mention of
sake and soke in the Confessor's writ. But reference to the dubious
Ely charter attributed to the Confessor which has been referred to
above, [3] suggests an explanation which may be the true one. In this
text sake and soke alone are mentioned by name among the sources
of profit conferred by the king. It does not therefore seem unreason-
able to suppose that sake and soke may actually have formed the
subject of an independent grant of the Confessor, but that the writ
notifying that grant is lost.

It must have been lost at an early date, for no trace of it is to be
found in the sources in which the writ under discussion appears. We
may then with some confidence infer that the two writs at least were
issued by the Confessor in favour of Abbot Wulfric, and that the
writ under discussion is a reasonably accurate copy of an authentic
writ of the king.[4] The Latin version, avowedly of later date (see
textual footnote), fails to render the idiomatic *sitte his man* . . .
wyrce, and substitutes a clause which is more commonplace.

(47)

King Edward announces that he has appointed Wulfric to the office
of abbot of Ely with full privileges. 1055–66, possibly 1045–66

(Cott. Tib. A. vi, f. 102 b)

1 Eadward kyng gret ealle mine biscopes 7 mine eorlas 7 mine
scirgereuan 7 ealle mine þegenas on þam sciran þer þa lande to
liggað into Ely. freondlice. 7 ic kyþe eow. þ̵ ic habbe geunnen.
Wlfrice þ̵ abbodrice *in* Hely. on eallan þingan. binnan burgan 7
5 butan. toll. 7 team. 7 infangenþeof. fyhtwiᵗ'e. 7 fyrdwite. hamsocne.
7 gryþbryce. sitte. his man þer þar he sitte. wyrce. þæt he wyrce.

---

[1] See the reputed charter of Edgar to Ely, in Latin and English, B. 1266,
1267, Robertson no. 48. For a suggestion that the English version may be
the work of Abbot Ælfric, see A. McIntosh, *Wulfstan's Prose* (Brit. Acad.
1948), 22, n. 8.

[2] Compare nos. 4, 11, 23, 81, and also no. 8.

[3] K. 907, see p. 222, n. 2.

[4] Two words omitted by a copyist at an early stage and absent in all the
texts, have been supplied by me in the printed text.

7 nelle ic geþauian þat ænig man [him] of handa ateo nan þæra þinge. þæs [þe] ic him geunnen hæbbe. God eow gehælde.

Latin Version

(MS. O. 2. 1, f. 79, no. 86)

Ædwardus rex Anglorum episcopis, baronibus 7 uicecomitibus 7 omnibus fidelibus suis in quorum comitatu abbatia de Ely terras 10 habet salutes. Notum sit uobis quod donaui Wlfrico abbatiam de Ely cum omnibus rebus ad eam pertinentibus infra burgum 7 extra, toll 7 team 7 infanganþeof, fihtwite 7 ferdwite, hamsochne 7 griðbrice, 7 omnes alias forisfacturas que emendabiles sunt in terra sua super homines suos. 7 nolo ut aliquis subtrahat ex his omnibus 15 quæ illic concessi. Deus uos conseruet.

Heading : Epistola Ædwardi Regis.   1. biscopas E.   2. land. O, E.   3. to liggað] toliccat MS., E, O ; -liggat L. ; -liggað T, 7. *all omit* him.   8. *all omit* þe.   8. gehealde O, T, E. *Introduction to Latin version :* Hanc quippe epistolam in Latinum duxi commutandum, 7 sic in hystoriam redigere.   14. grið-] greð- MS.

Translation

King Edward sends friendly greetings to all my bishops and my earls and my sheriffs and all my thegns in the shires in which the lands belonging to Ely are situated. And I inform you that I have granted to Wulfric the abbacy at Ely with everything within boroughs and without, toll and team and infangenetheof, fihtwite and fyrd-wite, hamsocn and grithbreach, wherever his man may dwell, what-ever he may do. And I will not permit anyone to take from him any of the things that I have granted him. God keep you.

EVESHAM

The Latin writ in the name of King Cnut which announces the king's grant to a certain Brihtwine for his lifetime of ' those five hides ' at Bengeworth that had become forfeit to the king, with the proviso that after Brihtwine's death they should go to the abbey of

Evesham,[1] was marked spurious by Kemble. His reasons for the rejection of this writ are nowhere given. It is true that land at Bengeworth was for a long time a subject of dispute between the abbey of Evesham and the cathedral priory of Worcester. According to Evesham tradition, the abbey had held land at Bengeworth (a ten-hide manor, with two halves, often held separately, of five hides each) from the time of Ecgwine, its founder,[2] though the monks of Evesham admitted that this land (together with the closely-adjacent estate of Hampton, which they said had, with Bengeworth and with other lands, been forcibly taken from the abbey) remained in other hands from the time of King Edmund to that of Cnut.[3] We are told that five hides of land at Hampton which had been held for many years as a gift from King Æthelred II by Northman, who was slain by Cnut in the first year of his reign, were subsequently given by Cnut to Northman's brother, Earl Leofric, and that Leofric, in recognition of the fact that this land formed part of the ancient endowment of Evesham, after some years restored Hampton to the abbey of which he and his wife Godgifu were benefactors.[4] But the Evesham Chronicle is at this point strangely silent concerning Bengeworth, and has nothing to say of any Bengeworth writ in the name of Cnut. Nothing is known of the circumstances in which the land became forfeit to the king, though we might conjecture that its forfeiture may have been in some way connected with the slaying of Northman and others by Cnut's orders in 1017 at the time when Eadric Streona was slain (*Chron.* D, E, 1017). Nor is anything known of Brihtwine or of his tenure of the estate. It is not even known whether Cnut's precept (supposing it to be authentic) set out in this writ, that the estate should after the death of Brihtwine go to the abbey of Evesham, ever became effective. There is no evidence that any appeal was ever made in the course of the struggle between the abbot of Evesham and the

---

[1] According to tradition the monastery at Evesham was in the beginning founded by Ecgwine, bishop of Worcester, early in the eighth century. In the tenth and early eleventh century the monastery was for some time under lay control and only obtained its independence with the appointment as abbot in 1014 of Ælfweard, afterwards bishop of London, who recovered certain of the abbey lands. For the history of Evesham Abbey see *Mon. Angl.* ii. 1 ff., *Chronicon Abbatiæ de Evesham*, R.S., and VCH *Worcs.* ii. 112 ff.

[2] *Chron. Abbat. de Evesham*, 72 and 84. There is no contemporary evidence to support this claim ; nor is there any to support the Worcester claim that Bengeworth was included in the grant of Cropthorne made to Worcester by Offa, king of Mercia, in 780 : see VCH *Worcs.* ii. 397. J. H. Round (*ibid.* i. 255) suspected the Cropthorne charter to be an eleventh-century forgery. See also B. 616.

[3] *Chron. Abbat. de Evesham*, 84.

[4] *Ibid.* 84–5.

bishop of Worcester for the possession of the land at Bengeworth,[1] to the writ under discussion here ; nor have we any reason to suppose that it was fabricated for the benefit of the abbey. In favour of the supposition that it may have been translated from a genuine Anglo-Saxon writ of King Cnut, it might be urged that there is nothing unusual in its structure or improbable in its content. The dates of the persons named in the address are (in so far as they are known) consistent with one another. The phraseology is of a kind frequently found in post-Conquest Latin versions of writs which may be genuine.[2] In fact, the only suspicious feature of the document is the tense of the verb denoting the grant : *concedo* where one would have expected *concessi*. But whether this is enough to stamp the text as a fabrication must remain an open question.

(48)

King Cnut declares that he grants to Brihtwine five hides of land at Bengeworth for his lifetime, with the proviso that the land shall go to Evesham Abbey after his death. (1017–30)

(Cott. Vesp. B. xxiv, f. 34)

Cnut rex salutat Leofsium episcopum et Hacun comitem et 1
Leouricum uicecomitem et omnes barones in Wireceastrescire
amicabiliter. Et ego manifesto uobis quod ipse concedo Briht'wino
meo baroni illas quinque hidas apud Beningwurðe in suis diebus,
propterea quod ipsa terra ad meam manum fuit forisfacta. Nunc 5
habet ipse meam amicitiam adquisitam sicut nos concordauimus,
ea conuentione ut post suos dies eat ipsa terra in sancto monasterio
de Eouesham illis Dei seruis ad uictum semper imperpetuum.
Et si quis hoc peruerterit, habeat sibi cum Deo iudicium et cum
Sancta Maria et cum omnibus sanctis ante Deum in die iudicii. Valete. 10

In margin : Beningwurðe.

HEREFORD

There is no reason to doubt that the two Hereford [3] writs printed here are translations from Anglo-Saxon of authentic writs of King

---

[1] For the subsequent history of the estate, see pp. 464 f. below.

[2] *baro = þegn*, see note on p. 428.

[3] For the early history of the see of Hereford, see *Mon. Angl.* vi. 1210 ; and F. M. Stenton, ' Pre-Conquest Herefordshire ', in *Royal Commission on*

Edward the Confessor. The earlier of the two belongs to the difficult period that followed the death in battle on 16 June 1056, of the martial Bishop Leofgar, of whom it is recorded (*Chron.* C, D, 1056) that 'he abandoned his holy oil and his cross and his spiritual weapons, and took up his spear and his sword, and went thus on an expedition against Gruffydd the Welsh king and was slain there and his priests with him, and Ælfnoth the sheriff and many other good men '. In the previous year Gruffydd had joined with the outlawed Earl Ælfgar, who had sought his aid, in burning the town of Hereford, and sacking the famous minster of Bishop Æthelstan, stripping it of its relics and vestments and of all its contents, and slaying the priests within the minster.[1] The aged bishop did not long survive the disaster [2]; and after the death of his successor Leofgar, who was bishop only eleven weeks and four days, the see was administered for four years (1056–60) by Ealdred, bishop of Worcester, who joined with Earl Leofric and Earl Harold in negotiations which resulted in Gruffydd's submission to King Edward.

Bishop Ealdred and Earl Harold are both addressed in no. 49, which announces that THE PRIESTS of St. Ethelbert's minster ARE TO HAVE SAKE AND SOKE over all their men and over all their lands as fully and completely in all respects as ever they had it. A division had evidently been made at Hereford, as it had at York [3] and some other places, between the property belonging to the episcopal see and that belonging to the collegiate body serving the church. This text is of special interest as being avowedly (see p. 230, footnote) a translation into Middle English (*lingua Anglicana*) of an original in Anglo-Saxon (*lingua Saxonica*), the translation having seemingly been made for insertion in the cartulary in the fifteenth century. Behind the Middle English version and the Latin version which accompanies it, appears the familiar structure of the Edwardian

---

Historical Monuments, Herefordshire (1934), iii. lv ff. The patron saint of the see of Hereford was (and is) King Ethelbert (Æthelberht) of the East Angles, who was beheaded in 794 at the command of Offa, king of Mercia (*Chron.* 792, to be corrected to 794), and buried at some place in the neighbourhood of Hereford, probably at Sutton Walls, 4 miles from the city. Before the end of the tenth century the body of Ethelbert was transferred to Hereford Cathedral, where he was honoured as a saint and a martyr. The church was rebuilt by Bishop Æthelstan (1012–56).

[1] *Chronicle*, C, D, 1055. Florence of Worcester s.a. 1055 informs us that seven of the canons who defended the doors of the principal church (*valvas principalis basilicæ*) were slain, and that the relics of St. Æthelberht and other saints in the minster were burnt.

[2] Bishop Æthelstan died on 10 February 1056, and was buried in his church.

[3] For York, see no. 120. In Domesday a distinction is made between the lands of the bishop and those of the canons (DB i. 181 b, VCH *Hereford*, i. 320 ff.).

writ, in spite of blunders (such as Alred *Eurl*, for ' bishop ', in the address) and mistranslations.   It is a reasonable conjecture that the *where that they haue to doone* of the English version, and the *ubicumque sicubi ipsi depauperantur* of the Latin, are attempts to render some such clause as the *lock huer hyt neod sy* (OE *loc hwær hit neod sy*) of no. 64.   Similarly the *liberi* in l. 13 seems to stand for OE *wyrðe*, ' entitled to ', a constantly recurring technical term in writs (see Introduction, pp. 63 f.) ; in the Middle English the difficulty of finding a rendering for *wyrðe* has been evaded.   The *prius* in l. 14 of the Latin text, and again in no. 50, l. 6, must be a misrendering of OE *fyrmest* (*formest* in the Middle English version) arising out of the mistaken notion that this is an adverb of time ; see Introduction, p. 63.   In the address *gret . . . his undurlynges, saluto . . . meos ministros* (the latter also in no. 50) are no doubt renderings of *gret . . . mine þegnas*.   But the mistakes made by the translator of no. 49 are no obstacle to the belief that he was rendering an authentic writ, one moreover which, as he tells us (p. 230, footnote), was accompanied by a seal which bore the inscription which appears elsewhere on seals attributed to the Confessor (see p. 94) ; *Edwardi* is no doubt due to scribal substitution for *Eadwardi*.

The close resemblance to be observed between no. 50 (which announces WALTER'S APPOINTMENT TO THE SEE OF HEREFORD), and nos. 64, 65 (which announce Giso's appointment to the see of Wells), is fortunate, since it helps to elucidate a passage in no. 50 which would otherwise be unintelligible.   No. 64 has already been utilised above in the discussion of no. 49.   Giso and Walter were appointed at about the same time (*Chron.* D, 1060), and they were consecrated together at Rome by Pope Nicholas II on 15 April 1061 ; the writs announcing their appointment belong to the same period.[1] Like no. 49, no. 50 contains mistranslations ; the *prius* for *fyrmest* of no. 49 (see above) appears again in no. 50.   In no. 64 the clause beginning : *other þæt man hit ofgo*, represents an OE : *oððe þæt man hit ofgo on his gemode swa man wið him hit findan mage*, ' or that one (*man*) hold it by his favour (*hit ofgo*) according to his pleasure (*on his gemode*) as one (*man*) can devise (*findan*) it with him '.   The same clause must have appeared in the Anglo-Saxon writ which the Hereford translator is translating in no. 50.   But he has rendered the conjunction *þæt* by the demonstrative *ille*, translated *findan*, ' devise ', by *invenire*, and rendered *ofgo* (from *ofgan*, ' hold by another's favour ') as *dimittat* ; he did not know the uncommon word *gemod*, and has rendered it *precio*.   But there is nothing in this

---

[1] For the suggestion that a difference in the date of beginning the year would account for the fact that *Chronicle* E places Walter's appointment in 1060, and Giso's in 1061, see Plummer, ii. 249.

text to suggest that the *Carta Regis Edwardi in lingua Saxonica* which is being rendered here was not authentic. In every respect the general pattern is that of authentic writs of King Edward.

(49)

King Edward declares that the priests of St. Ethelbert's, Hereford, are to have sake and soke over all their men and all their lands as fully and completely as ever they had it. 1057–60

(MS. Rawlinson B. 329, f. 104)

1 Edward kyng gret Alred Eurl. and Harald Eurl. and all his undurlynges in Herefordshire ffrendelich.   And I do yowe to understonden that I woll that the Prestes in Hereford at Seint Ethelb*ert* ministre that they haue eu*ere* Soke and Sake ou*ere* alle heor*e* men
5 and alle heor*e* londes withynne bourgh and w*t*oute so full and so forth so they formest hadde ynne alle thynges.   And iche bidde yowe alle that ge ben to hem fauerable and helpyng ou*ere* alle. wher*e* that they haue to doone. for Goddes loue and for myn.

Latin Version

(Ibid.)

Edwardus rex saluto Aldredum episcopum et Haroldum comitem
10 et omnes meos ministros in Herefordensi comitatu amicabiliter.   Et ego notifico vobis quod ego volo quod presbiteri Herefordenses apud Sancti Ethelberti monasterium quod ipsi sint de eorum Saca et eorum Soca liberi supra eorum terras et supra eorum homines infra burgum et extra tam plene et tam plane sicut ipsi prius
15 habuerunt in omnibus rebus.   Et ego precipio vobis omnibus quod vos sitis eis in adiutorium ubicumque sicubi ipsi depauperantur, pro Dei amore et pro meo.

Heading in red : Hec est translacio Carte Regis Edwardi in lingua Saxonica translata in linguam Anglicanam de diuersis priuilegiis et libertatibus Ecclesie Cath. Hereford. per prefatum Regem concessis, scilicet de Sock et Sack, cuius Sigillum coopertum est cum panno serico diuersi coloris.   Et hec est scriptura Sigilli Sancti Edwardi ∴ Sigillum Edwardi Anglorum Basiley ∴ *(the last four words in black).*   1. *A small e- is inserted here and in the Lat. version in a large space left for the initial capital of* Edward, *and over it, in red, in the main hand* ; .i. Ego.
Heading to Latin version : Hec est translacio carte supradicte in lingua Saxonica translata in Latinum [de] prefatis priuilegiis et libertatibus dicte ecclesie Cath. Hereford per dictum Regem Edwardum concessis.
17. *over last word,* meo, *in red* ; .s. amore.

(50)

King Edward declares that he has granted to Bishop Walter the bishopric of Hereford and everything belonging thereto, with sake and with soke, as fully and completely as ever it was held by any bishop before him. 1061–66, probably 1061

(MS. Rawlinson B. 329, f. 104 b)

Edwardus rex saluto Haroldum comitem et Osebarnum et omnes 1
meos ministros in Herefordensi comitatu amicabiliter. Et ego
notifico uobis quod ego concessi Waltero episcopo istum episcopatum
hic uobiscum et omnia uniuersa illa que ad ipsum cum iusticia
pertinent infra portum et extra cum saka et cum socna tam plene et 5
tam plane sicut ipsum aliquis episcopus ante ipsum prius habuit
in omnibus rebus. Et si illic sit aliqua terra extra dimissa que illuc
intus cum iusticia pertinet, ego uolo quod ipsa reueniat in ipsum
episcopatum uel ille homo ipsam dimittat eidem in suo precio, si
quis ipsam cum eo inuenire possit. Et ego nolo ullum hominem 10
licenciare quod ei de manibus rapiat aliquam suam rem quam ipse
iuste habere debet, et ego ei sic concessi.

Heading : Hec est translacio Carte Regis Edwardi in lingua Saxonica
translata in Latinum de collacione Episcopatus Herefordensis cuidam Waltero
facta, et de diuersis priuilegiis et libertatibus, scilicet Sok et Sak et aliis
libertatibus eidem Waltero 7 Episcopatui Herefordensi concessis. The text
is interlined with explanatory words in red ink in the main hand.   1. *A
small* e *inserted in a large space left for the initial capital of* Edwardus, *and
over it,* .i. Ego.   4. *over* ipsum, episcopatum.   6. *over* ipsum,
episcopatum.   6. *over* ipsum, episcopum.   7. *over* illuc, ad
episcopum.   8. *over* ipsa, terra.   9. *over* ipsam, terram.
9. *over* eidem, episcopo.   10. *over* ipsam, terram.   11. *over* ei,
episcopo. *A note follows in the main hand :* Sequitur expositio illorum
terminorum Soka et Saka. Soka hoc est secta de hominibus in curia vestra
secundum consuetudinem regni. Saka hoc est placitum et emenda de
transgressionibus hominum in curia vestra.   10. nolo] volo MS.

LONDON, THE ENGLISH CNIHTENGILD

Almost all that is known of the association now generally called
the English Cnihtengild [1] of London (in whose favour a writ was
issued early in his reign by King Edward the Confessor) is derived

---

[1] The advantage of using the term ' Cnihtengild ' is that it avoids the
military associations now bound up with the word ' knight '. There is
however no reason to suppose that this compound was in use in the pre-
Conquest period. The text of the writ printed here reads *on Ænglisce cnihte*

from the muniments of the Priory of the Holy Trinity (or Christ-church), Aldgate, in the city of London,[1] on which the lands and privileges were, in 1125, bestowed. In that year fifteen burgesses of London (whose names are given), assembling in the chapter-house of the priory (which was situated within the walls of the city near Aldgate), gave to that church and to the canons serving God therein all the land and soke which was called *de Anglisshe cnihtegildam*, adjoining the wall of the city, outside Aldgate, and extending to the Thames ; and in return for their gift, they and their predecessors in the gild were received by Prior Norman into the fraternity of that house and into participation in its spiritual benefits.[2] In order that their gift should remain valid and unimpaired, the members of the gild offered upon the altar the charter of St. Edward—no doubt the original, or a copy, of the writ printed here—and other charters relating to their donation, and gave the prior seisin of the land by (per) the church of St. Botolph which was built upon, and was head of, the land (' et deinde super ipsam terram seisiuerunt pre-dictum priorem per ecclesiam Sancti Botulphi que edificata est super eam et est ut aiunt caput ipsius terre '). Their grant was confirmed by Henry I at the request of one of their number Ordgar le Prude, who had been chosen as their representative, and the king sent his sheriffs Alberic de Ver and Roger, *nepos* of Hubert, to invest the church of Holy Trinity, on his behalf, with the land and soke ; which they did in the presence of many witnesses.[3]

gilde, where *cnihte* represents OE *cnihta*, the normal genitive plural of OE *cniht*. On the meaning of *cniht* in this context, see p. 234 below. The same form appears again in the phrase *de Anglisshe cnihtegildam* in the cartulary of the Priory of the Holy Trinity (Hunterian MS. U.2.6), f. 149 b, and in the phrase *de englische Cnithegilde* in a copy of a bull of Pope Innocent III in the same fifteenth-century cartulary (f. 150). But in transcripts in this cartulary of charters of William II, Henry I, and Henry II (ff. 149b–50) the word *cniht* has been given the weak genitive plural ending -*en*(*e*) (OE -*ena*) : *de cnihtene-gilda*, *de Anglica cnihtengilda*. Since these transcripts are not contemporary with the events recorded in the texts, it is not easy to determine at what precise date the form *cnihten*(*e*)*gild* came into being.

[1] The foundation of this priory for canons regular of the order of St. Augustine by Queen Matilda, wife of Henry I, in 1108, is recorded in the only surviving cartulary of the priory, U (for the letters given to the sources see p. 466 below) f. 149b ; G iv. p. 2 ; C f. 135 ; D f. 79. For the later history of the priory, see *Mon. Angl.*, vi. 150 ff. and VCH *London* i. 465 ff.

[2] For other instances of the admission of benefactors into fraternity and to a share in the spiritual benefits of a religious house, see J. H. Round, *Commune of London*, 104, n. 5 ; W. G. Clark-Maxwell, *Archæologia*, 2nd series, xxv (1926), 19–60. For much earlier instances (during the Old English period) see F. E. Harmer, *English Historical Documents*, 72.

[3] See U f. 149b–50 ; G iv. p. 2 ; C f. 135 (printed Sharpe, 220). See also Stow, *Survey of London*, ed. C. L. Kingsford, Oxford, 1908, i. 122. The *Albertus* (for *Alberic*) in U and G is most probably a transcriber's error.

The soke which thus came into the possession of the canons of the Holy Trinity, and which was confirmed to them by later kings, becoming united with the soke of Aldgate, was afterwards called the soke of the Port or Portsoken, and in virtue of its possession the prior for the time being of the Holy Trinity ranked as an alderman of the City of London until the dissolution of the priory in 1531.[1]

The writ bearing the name of the Confessor is the earliest document extant relating to the Cnihtengild, but allusions in its text carry back the existence of the gild at any rate to the reigns of Cnut, Æthelred II, and Edgar. We can however dismiss as a later fabrication the legend that

> in the days of King Edgar (or King Cnut) there were thirteen ' cnihts ' very dear to the king and the kingdom who desired of the king that he would grant them land in London and the liberty of a gild, and to whom the king made the desired grant on condition that each should victoriously accomplish three combats, one above ground, another under it, a third in water, and afterwards on a certain day should run with lance against all comers in the field called East Smithfield.   The condition, it is said, was gloriously fulfilled, and the same day the king declared them a ' Knyttegildam ' and defined by boundaries the limits of their land.[2]

The constitution of the Cnihtengild has frequently been discussed, but unfortunately there is no direct evidence as to the actions and character of the gild before the early twelfth century, and the nature of its membership may have changed during its long history.[3] Any explanation of the name *cnihta gild* must (as has been pointed out by Sir Frank Stenton) take into account not only the meaning (' servant, retainer ') of the word *cniht* before the Conquest, but also the fact that the members of the London gild of English *cnihtas* in the eleventh and early twelfth centuries were important persons. But this association of London *cnihtas* does not stand alone—other gilds of *cnihtas* are known to have existed [4]—and Stenton has

[1] Sharpe, Introduction, p. xv.   For the position of the Portsoken, a large area outside the east wall of the city, see the sketch map of London under Henry II by Miss M. B. Honeybourne appended to Historical Association Leaflets nos. 93, 94 (London 1934), containing *inter alia* F. M. Stenton's essay *Norman London*.

[2] See U f. 149 ; G iv. p. 2 ; C f. 134b (Sharpe pp. 216 ff.), D f. 78b ; also Trinity College Library, Cambridge, MS. O. 2, 20, f. 91 ff.   See also Stow, *Survey of London*, i. 120 ;   Gross, *The Gild Merchant* (1890), i. 187.

[3] Gross, *ut supra*, i. Appendix B ;   J. H. Round, *Commune of London*, 97–105 ;   F. M. Stenton, *Norman London*, 13 f. ;   James Tait, *The Medieval English Borough* (Manchester, 1936), 119–22.

[4] References to associations of *cnihtas* mentioned from time to time in historical records are collected by Gross, *Gild Merchant*, i. 183–8.   They are discussed by James Tait, *Medieval English Borough*, 119–23.   The Winton Domesday, for instance, mentions an association of *cnihtas* at Winchester

suggested that the most satisfactory way of reconciling these facts is to regard the original *cnihtas* who gave their name to such gilds as ' the ministers of rural landowners, set in charge of their lords' burghal properties, and forming a link between their lords' upland estates and the borough market '. The original *cnihtas* of the London gild would then have been ' responsible servants of magnates owning property in London, appointed to supply their lords with goods coming to the London market ', but in course of time ' independent traders entering the association changed the character of its membership while enrolling under its ancient name ', so that in the very last years of its existence the London Cnihtengild, whatever its origin, was ' a wealthy association of prominent London citizens '.[1]

The authenticity of the Confessor's writ (no. 51) can scarcely be in doubt. In structure and phraseology it closely resembles another London writ, the writ of Edward for the priests of St. Paul's, no. 54, which has however undergone interpolation. The linguistic forms of the Cnihtengild writ are in the main those of Edward's day, except that the termination *-a* in words like *cnihte, godre, heore*, has been replaced by *-e*, a later change, and that the scribe has omitted the final *-n* in *portgerefa* and the *d* in *freonlice*. But except for these insignificant linguistic alterations the writ is most probably a close copy of an authentic writ of King Edward the Confessor.

(51)

King Edward declares that his men in the gild of English *cnihtas* are to have their sake and their soke within borough and without over their land and over their men, and as good laws as they had in the days of King Edgar and of the king's father and of Cnut. 1042-44

(Hunterian MS. U. 2. 6, f. 149)

1   [E]adward cyncg gret Ælfward biscop 7 Wulfgar minne portgerefa 7 ealle þa burhware on Lundene freon[d]lice 7 ic cyþe eow þ ic wille þ mine men on Ænglisce cnihte gilde beon heore sace 7 heore

in the day of the Confessor : *Chenictes tenebant la chenictahalla libere de rege Edwardo* (DB iv. 533) ; *chenictehalla ubi chenictes potabant gildam suam et eam libere tenebant de rege Edwardo* (*ibid.* 531).

[1] *Norman London*, 13-14, and *The First Century of English Feudalism*, 133 f. But for a somewhat different view, see Tait, *ut supra*, 122. In the interval between the issue of this writ and their relinquishment of their property to the Priory of the Holy Trinity, the men of the Cnihtengild received from William II and Henry I confirmation of their gild and the land belonging to it, with all its privileges, as they had enjoyed them in the time of King Edward and the Conqueror ; see *Mon. Angl.* vi. 156, Sharpe, 218.

socne wurðe binnan burh 7 butan ofer heora land 7 ofer heora men
7 ic wille ꝥ heo beon swa godre lage wurðe swa heo wæron on 5
Eadgares dæge cynges 7 on mines fæder 7 swa on Cnudes 7 ic wille
eac hit mid gode geeacnian 7 ic nelle geþafian þæt heom ænig man
misbeode ac beon heo ealle gesunde 7 God eow ealle gehealde.

Heading in red : Carta Sancti Edwardi, *the initial* C *in blue.*

Translation

King Edward sends friendly greetings to Bishop Ælfweard and
Wulfgar my portreeve and all the citizens in London. And I inform
you that my will is that my men in the gild of English *cnihtas* shall
be entitled to their sake and their soke within borough and without
over their lands and over their men. And my will is that they
shall enjoy as good laws as they enjoyed in the days of King Edgar
and in my father's days and similarly in Cnut's. And I will moreover augment its benefits. And I will not permit anyone to do
them any wrong, but [on the contrary] may they all prosper !
And God keep you all.

LONDON, ST. PAUL'S

The three writs extant in favour of the priests of St. Paul's minster
in London (St. Paul's Cathedral),[1] present a number of problems.
Of special interest is the writ in the name of King Æthelred II, for
only one other writ, no. 107, attributed to that king is extant. This
writ of Æthelred, no. 52, has come down to us in only one copy,
and the question of the trustworthiness of its transcriber is therefore
important. It was copied in the early years of the seventeenth
century by the Reverend Richard James (1592–1638), Fellow of
Corpus Christi College, Oxford, nephew of Dr. Thomas James, the
first Keeper of the Bodleian Library, and himself librarian to Sir

[1] For the early history of the church of St. Paul in London, said to have
been founded in A.D. 604 by King Æthelberht of Kent when Mellitus had been
consecrated by Augustine as bishop of London (Bede, *Historia Ecclesiastica*,
ii. cap. 3, ed. Plummer, i. 85), see W. Dugdale, *A History of St. Paul's Cathedral
in London* (London, 1658, 1716, 1818), VCH *London*, i. 409 ff. and the references
there. See further for the early history and for the cartularies of St. Paul's
Early Charters of St. Paul's, ed. Marion Gibbs (Camden Society, Third Series,
vol. lviii, 1939).

R

Robert Cotton and his son Sir Thomas.[1] A number of volumes of extracts made by Richard James from various sources, in some cases from Old English manuscripts, were after his death purchased for the Bodleian Library, where they are still preserved. James's purpose in making his extracts was polemical rather than anti-quarian. His collections contain for the most part ' notes from ancient manuscripts (sometimes from printed authors) relating to history and antiquity and anything that could be found against St. Thomas of Canterbury, the greatness and corruption of popes, cardinals, bishops, abbots, priors, monks, friers, and the clergy ' before the reformation. And when he thought that the matter itself from the authors, whence he made his collections, was not ' sufficient to make them bad, his notes in the margin pointing to those matters, would do it to the purpose, arguing thereby an inveterate hatred he had to the said persons, as indeed he had, being a severe Calvinist, if not worse '.[2] James had acquired a knowledge of Anglo-Saxon : ' he was noted by all those that knew him to be a very good Grecian, poet, an excellent critic, antiquary, divine, and admirably well skill'd in the Saxon and Gothic languages '.[3] Where his copies of Anglo-Saxon writs can be tested, they appear as accurate, though sometimes abridged. But his writ of King Æthelred is a puzzling document. Nothing is known from other sources of the ' Rotulus Antiquus Ecclesiæ Sci Pauli ' tran-scribed by James,[4] in which this writ appears, and the date of the compilation of the roll is no more than a matter of conjecture. There is evidence for the use of the royal writ as an administrative instrument in the reign of Æthelred II (see Introduction, pp. 16 f.), but it remains doubtful whether James's text represents an actual writ of that king. The main obstacle to its acceptance is the close resemblance that it bears to no. 54, a writ of King Edward for the same community. Except for the difference in length—and James may not have copied the text in full—the two texts, no. 52 and no. 54, would be identical were it not for one small variant (*of* for *on* in l. 2), and some differences of spelling of no significance. The suggestion has been made by Miss Gibbs [5] that the name of King

---

[1] On Richard James, see Anthony à Wood, *Athenæ Oxonienses*, ed. P. Bliss (London, 1815), ii. 629–32 ; and Thomas Corser's edition (Chetham Society, 1845) of James's poem *Iter Lancastrense* ; also DNB. See also references on p. 428.

[2] *Athenæ Oxonienses*, ii. 632.

[3] *Ibid.* ii. 629. The DNB includes among James's manuscripts acquired by the Bodleian Library in 1676 an Anglo-Saxon dictionary.

[4] What James transcribed from the roll is printed in full in *Early Charters of St. Paul's*, ed. M. Gibbs.

[5] *Op. cit.* 2, J. 4, and note.

Edgar must have been substituted for that of King Æthelred of
Wessex in another charter copied by James from the same ancient
roll of St. Paul's, and one is tempted to suggest that the name of
Æthelred might in the writ under discussion have been substituted
for that of Edward. Such a substitution, whether conscious or not,
if it was actually made, must have been made at some earlier stage,
and not by James himself, for his comment (see p. 241) : ' similiter
in privilegio Cnuti et Edwardi ', shows that he had compared his
text with the St. Paul's writs of those kings. Another way of
accounting for the virtual identity of nos. 52 and 54 would be to
suppose that when in King Edward's reign it was decided to issue
a writ for the priests of St. Paul's, the writ of Æthelred (supposing
it to have existed) formed the basis of the new writ composed by the
clerks of the Confessor's secretariat, but there are, as will be seen,
serious objections to this hypothesis.

In the writ, no. 54, attributed to Edward the Confessor, two
constructions are confused. The resemblance of the writ to no. 51,
the Cnihtengild writ, is striking. But if we accept the Cnihtengild
writ as the norm, and compare its text with that of the writ of St.
Paul's, the difficulties which arise in attempting to translate the
St. Paul's writ as it stands are explained. In the Cnihtengild writ
we find, giving a literal rendering ' worthy of ' (on which see
Introduction, pp. 63 f.) :

Ic wille þæt heo beon swa godre lage wurðe swa heo wæron on Eadgares
dæge cynges ' (' My will is that they be worthy of as good laws as they were
[worthy of] in the days of King Edgar ').

In the St. Paul's writ we find :

' Ic wille þæt hig beon . . . swa godera lagana wurðe nu *swa full and swa
forð* swa hig best wæron on æniges cynges dæge (' My will is that they be
worthy of as good laws now *as fully and as completely* as they were [worthy of]
to the highest degree (best) in the days of any king '.)

If we abstract from the passage in the St. Paul's writ the formula
in italics, then we have an exact parallel to the passage in the
Cnihtengild writ. And indeed it is not possible to translate the St.
Paul's writ as it stands, for two constructions have been confused :

(i) ' worthy of *as* good laws as they were ' etc.,
(ii) ' worthy of good laws *as fully and as completely* as they were '
etc. ; as a result of which we have in the St. Paul's text :
(iii) ' worthy of *as* good laws *as fully and completely* as they were '
etc., in which either the *as*, or the *as fully and completely
as*, is redundant.

Has the St. Paul's writ undergone interpolation by a later hand, or
is this confused construction a product of the clerks of the Confessor's

secretariat ?   That the text of an authentic writ of the Confessor
may have been tampered with, is suggested by the fact that there
are indications in the writ attributed to Cnut (no. 53), to be discussed
below, of alterations to the text.   It is significant that in BT s.v.
lagu, where this passage is cited, the editor avoids the difficulty of
the confused construction by omitting *nu swa full 7 swa forð* from
his text (a fact that I had not observed until after I wrote the above
passage), and by giving *hig beon* and *hig wæron* a different reference,
which can scarcely be right, arrives at : ' that they be entitled
to as good laws as there ever have been in any king's day'.

In other respects the St. Paul's writ of the Confessor, no. 54,
which is under discussion seems unexceptionable.   The precept of
the king concerning the right of the canons to refuse admittance to
persons seeking admission to their community may have been
merely the affirmation of an ancient right ; but it would have been
particularly appropriate to conditions at St. Paul's Cathedral in
the early years of King Edward's reign.   The king declares that
the priests of St. Paul's shall not receive into their community
' any more priests than their estates can bear and they themselves
desire '.   Attention has been drawn by Sir Frank Stenton to the
fact that between c. 971 and 984, in Bishop Ælfstan's time, the
cathedral clergy had acted with their bishop in refusing admission
to a candidate whose past history may well have disqualified him
from acceptance.[1]   But it can readily be imagined that in the conditions of the Confessor's reign the cathedral clergy would have been
the more anxious to safeguard themselves against the entrance into
their community, and the consequent participation in their revenues,
of persons whom they had not themselves chosen to admit, for
both Robert of Jumièges, who became bishop of London in 1040,
and his successor William, were Normans.   It is not unlikely that
the bishops may have wished to introduce their own nominees,
possibly foreign ecclesiastics, into membership of the cathedral
chapter.[2]   It is in this sense that this passage is interpreted by
Miss Gibbs (*op. cit.* p. xxi), namely, that the priests of St. Paul's
claimed the right of rejecting from entrance into their community
(and consequently from provision with a prebend) at least episcopal
nominees.   She suggests that the writ may have been issued ' when
the first clash between Saxon and Norman had taken place early in
the Confessor's reign ' ; and she remarks that ' the passage in
question, although expressing a well-known canonical principle, was

---

[1] See M. Gibbs, xxxviii ff., where reference is made to *Liber Eliensis*, ii. 31,
and the passage in question is quoted and discussed.

[2] Several of the canons of St. Paul's mentioned in Domesday bear foreign
names ; e.g. Durand, Radulf (DB i. 127 b, 128).

yet eloquent of the attitude of a wealthy corporation whose interests lay in exclusiveness '. There is no reason for doubting that the passage formed part of an authentic writ of Edward the Confessor ; but the authenticity of the text as it stands, in view of the confused construction which has been discussed above, remains doubtful. If the writ in the name of Æthelred had been in existence, and if it had been taken as a model in composing a new writ in the time of King Edward, it is difficult to believe that this same confused construction, which appears also in the writ of Æthelred II, would not have been remedied.

The authenticity of no. 53, in which CNUT declares that HIS PRIESTS in St. Paul's minster ARE TO HAVE JUDICIAL AND FINANCIAL RIGHTS as fully and completely as ever they had in any king's day, is by no means certain, but F. Zinkeisen goes too far when he asserts that this writ ' ist offenbar eine Fälschung '.[1] If this should be a genuine writ, or based upon one, it would be of interest as one of two writs of Cnut announcing grants of judicial and financial rights, the other, no. 28, being of reasonably certain authenticity. The Folkestone charter [2] sometimes cited as another instance of such a grant by Cnut, which contains the clause : *mid sake and mid socne and mid eallon þam þingon þe þær fyrmest to læg* (' with sake and with soke and with all the things that ever pertained thereto '), cannot be accepted as genuine in its present form owing to a chronological dislocation in the list of witnesses,[3] and Zinkeisen rightly calls its authenticity in question. But there are three things in Cnut's writ, no. 53, which need to be accounted for before it can be accepted as authentic ; the form of the greeting, the appearance of *toll and team* in the list of judicial and financial rights enumerated here, the appearance in the text of a list of witnesses. For the greeting in the first person : *Ic Cnud grete*, parallels are available in the late ninth-century rendering of the Preface of Bede's *Historia Ecclesiastica*, which begins: *Ic Beda . . . sende gretan* (see Introduction, p. 11), in an epistolary Preface of Ælfric (p. 23), and in the letter of the monk Edwin (no. 113), which, though spurious, may be evidence that the greeting in the first person was in use in the twelfth century. Though this form of greeting does not appear elsewhere in royal writs, it cannot be condemned outright as spurious in the reputed writ of Cnut. The list of witnesses incorporated in the text (before the anathema) is free from chronological discrepancies and there seems no reason for doubting its authenticity. Other writs, e.g. nos. 26, 69, both reputable texts, give names of

---

[1] *Die Anfänge der Lehngerichtsbarkeit in England* (Diss. Berlin, 1893), p. 6.
[2] Robertson no. 85 = K. 1327.
[3] F. E. Harmer, *Bull. John Rylands Library*, xxii (1938), 353 ff.

persons present at the transaction which the writ announces (see further, Introduction, p. 73). The inclusion of *toll and team* in the list of rights granted by Cnut enumerated in this writ offers a more serious difficulty, for in King Edward's writ (no. 54) relating to sake and soke and as 'good laws' etc., there is specific mention only of sake and soke, though *toll and team* appears again in post-Conquest writs for St. Paul's.[1] But the broken construction of the text as it is represented in the printed copies of no. 53 (the manuscript having unfortunately been lost) does suggest that the text may have been tampered with. The sequence : *hig beon heora sace here 7 socna weorðe*, probably stands for *hig beon heora sace 7 here socna weorðe*, and the order of the words in the printed text may be due to careless copying or editing ; but on the other hand it may indicate that the text has been altered. Similarly the 7 ('and') in l. 5, between *tid* and *swa full*, seems to be intrusive. Further, the possibility might be suggested that a pronoun ('it' or 'them') required to form the object of *hig hæfdon*[2] in l. 5, is lacking. One cannot help wondering whether the hand responsible for the abnormal features of this text, or some other hand not that of a clerk in King Cnut's scriptorium, may not have been responsible for the inclusion in this writ of *toll and team*. No arguments as to the authenticity of the writ can safely be based on the anathema : 'God hine aweorge[3] þe þis awænde', since an anathema is a constantly-occurring feature of Anglo-Saxon writs, and in some instances at least may be authentic (see Introduction, p. 69) ; in any case, this anathema appears at the end of the text and could easily have been added to it. But when one looks at this text as a whole, and compares it closely with no. 54, it is evident that its phraseology has not simply been borrowed from the writ of the Confessor by some forger. It seems to me that there is just sufficient evidence of independence in its formulas and in their disposition to favour the supposition that this text may actually represent an authentic writ of Cnut. To what extent it may have been altered and tampered with cannot now be determined.

(52)

King Æthelred declares that his priests in St. Paul's minster are to have their sake and their soke within borough and without, and as

---

[1] See Gibbs, *op. cit.* nos. 2, 3, 6, 9.

[2] There is a parallel for the sequence : '*weorðe beon . . . swa hig hæfdon*', in no. 34, where : '*ealra þare lande wurðe þe hi hæfdon*', shows that *weorðe beon* is not necessarily followed in the qualifying clause by the same construction.

[3] For the verb *aweorge*, see BT Suppt. s.v. *awirg(e)an*.

good laws as ever they had in the days of any king or any bishop. (978–1016)

(Bodleian Library, MS. James 23, p. 32)

Æþelred kinc grete mine [beres] 7 mine eorles. 7 ealla mine þeinas 1
of þam sciram þær mine preostas on Pales mynstre habbað land inne
freondlice. 7 ic cyþe eow ꝥ ic wille ꝥ hig beon heora saca 7 heora
socna weorða æiþer ge binnan burh 7 butan. 7 swa godera laga
wyrþe nu swa ful 7 swa forð swa hig betste wæron on æniges kinges 5
dæge. oþþe on æniges beres on eallum þingan.

1. beres *omitted from text, written in margin. A mistaken extension of* MS.
bes = biscopes, *for other instances of which see l.* 6, *nos.* 44, 115. *James's note
shows that the form was unintelligible to him :* Similiter in privilegio Cnuti
et Edwardi. Quære ergo quid sit beres.   5. forð] ford MS.

Translation

King Æthelred sends friendly greetings to my bishops and my
earls and all my thegns of the shires in which my priests in Paul's
minster have land. And I inform you that it is my will that they
be entitled to their sake and their soke both within borough and
without, and entitled now to as good laws—as fully and as completely—as ever they were in all things in the days of any king
or of any bishop.

(53)

King Cnut declares that his priests in St. Paul's minster shall be
entitled to judicial and financial rights as fully and completely in
all things as ever they had them in any king's day. (1033–35)

(Dugdale, *Hist. of St. Paul's* (1716), Appendix, p. 13)

Ic Cnud cyng grete mine biscopes 7 mine eorles 7 ealle mine 1
þegenas on ðan sciran ðær mine preostas on S. Paules mynstre
habbað land inne freondlice 7 ic ciþe eow ꝥ ic wylle ꝥ hig beon heora
sace here 7 socna weorðe, tolles 7 teames binnan tid 7 buton tid
7 swa full 7 swa forþ swa hig hæfdon on æniges cynges deage fyrmest 5
on ællan ðingan, binnan burh 7 butan. 7 ic nelle geþafian ꝥ nan man
æt ænigum þingan heom misbeode. 7 þyses is to gewitnesse Ægelnoð
arcebiscop 7 Ælfric arcebiscop 7 Ælwi biscop 7 Ælfwine biscop
7 Duduce biscop 7 Godwine eorl 7 Leofric eorl 7 Osgod Clape 7
Thored 7 oþre genoge. God hine aweorge þe þis awænde.   10

Heading : Alia carta ejusdem Regis Canuti de quibusdam immunitatibus
eidem ecclesiæ per ipsum concessis, Saxonice.   3. ? *for* heora sace 7
here socna. *All edd. have the order* heora sace here 7 socna ; *Mon. Angl.*
1673 saca, *Thorpe* sacc.   9. Clape K.] clawe, *with Anglo-Saxon ' wyn '*
(= w), *Dugdale.*

Translation

I, King Cnut, send friendly greetings to my bishops and my earls and all my thegns in the shires in which my priests in St. Paul's minster have lands. And I inform you that it is my will that they be entitled to their sake and [their] soke, to toll and to team, in festival season and outside it—and—as fully and as completely as ever they had in the days of any king, in all things, within borough and without, And I will not permit anyone to do them any wrong in any matter. And the witnesses of this are Archbishop Æthelnoth and Archbishop Ælfric and Bishop Ælfwig and Bishop Ælfwine and Bishop Duduc and Earl Godwine and Earl Leofric and Osgot Clapa and Thored and numerous others. May he be accursed of God who shall alter this !

(54)

King Edward declares that his priests in St. Paul's minster shall be entitled to sake and soke within borough and without, and to as good laws as they ever had in the time of any king or any bishop ; and they shall not receive into their community any more priests than their estates can bear and they themselves desire. (1042–66)

(Dugdale, *Hist. of St. Paul's* (1716), Appendix, p. 14)

1   Eadward cyng gret mine biscopas 7 mine eorlas and ealle mine þegenas on þan sciran þar mine preostas on Paules mynstre habbað land inne freondliche. And ic cyðe eow ꝥ ic wille ꝥ hig beon heora saca and heora socne wurðe ægþer ge binnan burh ge buton 5 7 swa godera lagana wurðe nu swa full and swa forð swa hig best wæron on æniges cynges dæge oððe on æniges biscopes on eallan þingan : 7 ic nelle ꝥ hig underfon ani ma preostas into heora mynstre þonne heora landare aberan mage 7 hig sylfe willan. 7 ic nelle geþafian ꝥ heom ænig man æt ænigan þingan misbeode.

Heading : Alia carta ejusdem Regis Edwardi Saxonice.   1. Eadweard *preceded by a cross* P.   2. þegenas C, P.   2. þær C.   5. betste C, P.   7. *Dugdale, 1716 ed., reads* preostas ; *the MSS. (perhaps correctly)* preosta *(gen. pl. after* ma).   8. landare C, P] lande *are* Dugdale.

Translation

King Edward sends friendly greetings to my bishops and my earls and all my thegns in the shires in which my priests in Paul's minster have land. And I inform you that it is my will that they be entitled to their sake and their soke both within borough and without, and entitled now to as good laws—as fully and as completely—as ever they were in all things in the days of any king or of any bishop. And I forbid them to receive into their minster any more priests than their estates can bear and they themselves desire. And I will not permit any one to do them any wrong in any matter.

ST. DENIS, PARIS

The authenticity of the writ, no. 55 (Plate 2, announcing King Edward's grant of land at Taynton, Oxon., to the abbey of St. Denis,[1] near Paris, can scarcely be in doubt. Everything encourages the belief that the writ once preserved in the archives of the abbey of St. Denis, and now to be found in the Archives Nationales, accompanied by a diploma of King Edward relating to the grant (see p. 36), and by a seal which may be an authentic seal of the Confessor, is the original writ written and sealed by the clerks of King Edward's secretariat. The structure of the writ is unexceptionable and there is nothing in its content to excite suspicion. It provides us with a verb, *wītan* (*wīte he wið God*, l. 7), 'let him account for it with God', used in a sense apparently unrecorded hitherto in Anglo-Saxon dictionaries, but strongly supported by the noun *wīte*, 'punishment, fine'. The passage in the writ in which the king gives ' the bishop ' permission to draw up a charter (*boc*) relating to his grant is of considerable interest, as providing further evidence for the fact generally disregarded hitherto, that in the Confessor's time an Anglo-Saxon land-book

---

[1] The early records of the church of St. Denis (Dionysius) near Paris, supposed to have been built over the tomb of the holy martyr Dionysius, were critically examined by M. Léon Levillain (*Bibliothèque de L'École des Chartes* (tome 82 (1921), 5–116, tome 86 (1925), 5–99, tome 87 (1926), 20–97 and 245–346) ; and by M. Georges Tessier, *Le Moyen Âge*, 2ᵉ Série, tome 30 (1929), 36–77 (references for which I am indebted to Professor M. Deanesly). See also S. M. Crosby, *The Abbey of Saint Denis*, 475–1122, vol. i (Yale Historical Publications), 1942. Already in the sixth century the church of St. Denis, probably founded at the close of the fifth, enjoyed royal favour. King Dagobert I (623–39) enriched the church with gifts. In the reign of his son Clovis II a monastic rule was introduced there. Both Dagobert I and his wife were buried at St. Denis, which became the usual burying-place of the kings of France.

might be drawn up by an (interested) ecclesiastic instead of by the royal clerks ; this and other instances are discussed in the Introduction, pp. 35–41. It has been suggested by F. M. Stenton[1] that Taynton had (like the church at Deerhurst, see p. 293) originally been granted to Baldwine, the king's physician, himself a monk of St. Denis, and subsequently abbot of St. Edmund's Bury (see Biographical Notes). Nothing is said of Baldwine in the Taynton writ under discussion. But the records of St. Denis preserve a tradition (in existence about A.D. 1100) that Baldwine was concerned with King Edward's gift. The list of witnesses to the Latin diploma which accompanies the Taynton writ in the Archives Nationales (see Introduction, p. 36 and Appendix II) is followed by a note in the same hand of c. 1100 as the diploma itself, stating that Baldwine had received from the hand of King Edward *et scriptum* (i.e. the diploma recording the grant), *et donum* (see p. 41).

Although Domesday speaks (DB i. 157) of Taynton as a gift made by the Confessor to the church of St. Denis (' Ecclesia Sancti Dyonisii Parisii tenet de rege Teigtone. *Rex E. dedit ei* '), and although in a charter of William I, confirming King Edward's grant of Taynton, this is spoken of as a grant made by the Confessor to the church of St. Denis, there is evidence elsewhere to connect Baldwine with this grant. It has been pointed out [2] that in a list of persons holding property in the borough of Oxford (DB i. 154), ' the abbot of St. Edmund's ', that is, Baldwine himself, appears in possession of a dwelling belonging to Taynton, and that it would therefore seem that Taynton (as has already been suggested above) had originally been granted to Baldwine, ' and that after his election as abbot of Bury, he had annexed the property in Oxford which had belonged to Taynton to the possessions of the house of which he had become the head '. In the same way Abbot Baldwine is represented in Domesday (see p. 293) as holding a half-hide of land on the Westminster manor at Deerhurst.

(55)

King Edward declares that he has granted to the monastery of St. Denis beyond the sea the land at Taynton and everything lawfully pertaining thereto with sake and with soke as fully and as completely as he himself possessed it, and the bishop is to draw up a charter (*boc*) concerning it with his full permission. 1053–57

---

[1] VCH *Oxon.* i. 381. Davis, *Regesta*, no. 26. The grant would have been made by King Edward himself.

[2] F. M. Stenton, VCH *Oxon. ut supra.*

(Paris, Arch. Nat., Cartons des rois, K. 19, no. 6)

Eadward cingc grett Wulfwig biscop. 7 Raulf eorl. 7 ealle mine 1
þegenas on Oxnafordescire. freondlice. 7 ic cyðe eow Þ ic hæbbe
geunnan. Criste. 7 Sče Dionisie. into his halgan mynstre begeondan
sæ. þæt land æt Tengctune. 7 ælc þæra þinga þæs þe þær inn mid
rihte to gebyraþ. on wude. 7 on felde. mi'd' sace. 7 mid socne. swa 5
full 7 swa forð. swa hitt me sylfan on hánde stod. on dæge. 7 æfter.
for minre sawle hǽle. 7 wite he wið God. se þe hitt of þære haligan
stowe geútige. 7 ic wille Þ se biscop dihte bóc þær to. be minan
fullan geleafan.

Translation

King Edward sends friendly greetings to Bishop Wulfwig and Earl
Raulf and all my thegns in Oxfordshire. And I inform you that I
have granted to Christ and to the holy monastery of St. Denis
beyond the sea the land at Taynton, and everything lawfully pertaining thereto in woodland and in open country with sake and with
soke as fully and as completely as I myself possessed it, during my
lifetime and after it, for the salvation of my soul. And let him
who shall alienate it from the holy foundation account for it with
God. And my will is that the bishop draw up a charter concerning
it with my full permission.

RAMSEY

The writs of Ramsey Abbey in Huntingdonshire, all of which were
translated into Latin from English for insertion into the Ramsey
Chronicle, fall into two groups.[1] The authenticity of the writs of
the first group, nos. 56–60, seems on the whole reasonably certain—

[1] This monastery, dedicated to Our Lady, St. Benedict, and all holy Virgins,
is said to have been founded c. 968–70 by St. Oswald, bishop of Worcester,
and afterwards archbishop of York, with the help of Æthelwine, earl of East
Anglia, foster-brother of King Edgar, and to have been munificently endowed
by its founders and by other benefactors. For its records see the Ramsey
Chronicle (*Chron. Abbat. Rames.* ed. Macray, R.S.) written in a hand of
cent. xiii, but compiled, as is generally supposed, c. 1170 ; and the Ramsey
Cartulary (*Cart. Mon. de Rames.* ed. Hart and Lyons, R.S.) written c. 1350.
See also *Mon. Angl.* ii. 546. ff., VCH *Hunts.* i. 377 ff., and the anonymous life of
St. Oswald in *Historians of the Church of York*, ed. Raine, R.S. i. 399–475.
For a definite statement that because after the Conquest English was less

as translations into Latin of authentic writs of Harthacnut and King Edward. The two of Harthacnut (and, in no. 57, his mother Queen Ælfgifu) are the only writs of that reign known to exist. Of the abbot of Ramsey's *mansus* at THETFORD, the subject of no. 56, nothing seems to be known, but there is no apparent reason for doubting the authenticity of this writ since it bears a general resemblance to writs of other houses. The writ of King Edward, no. 58, confirming an earlier grant by Harthacnut and his mother (no. 57) of the 'east' land at HEMINGFORD, is also probably authentic ; the *suis*, for *meis*, in the clause *omnibus ministris suis*, here and in nos. 59, 60, is no doubt the contribution of a translator rendering *ealle mine pegnas*. On the principle that an anathema is in place where a grant stated to have been made with a religious motive (see Introduction, pp. 69 f.), the anathema in no. 57 may have formed part of the original writ of Harthacnut represented by this Latin version, which is probably in other respects authentic. But in discussing penal clauses in writs (p. 70) I have raised the question whether the motive of gratitude for the service rendered to King Edward by Abbot Ælfwine (see p. 472) is sufficient to account for the anathema which concludes the BROUGHTON writ, no. 59, a writ which in other respects (up to and including *immutare permitto*) seems to be above suspicion. Since there is a possibility that this anathema may have been added to the text in Ramsey Abbey, it is perhaps safer to regard the authenticity of the writ in its existing form as doubtful. On the ground of common form the remaining writ of this group, the short and businesslike writ relating to the soke within *Bichamdic* (no. 60), can also be regarded as authentic. The only abnormal feature of this text is the inclusion in the address, not of an archbishop and a bishop, of which there are instances elsewhere (Introduction, p. 47), but of two bishops. This is a feature which obviously demands discussion.

The two bishops addressed in THE SHORT *Bichamdic* WRIT (no. 60) are Stigand and Æthelmær (Ailmarus) his brother, both of whom appear in a number of writs, as do also the other persons to be mentioned here (see Biographical Notes). The mention of Earl Ælfgar, addressed here as earl of East Anglia, limits the date of the writ to between September 1051 and 1057 ; moreover from September 1052 to April 1053 Harold resumed possession of the earldom, and in 1055 Ælfgar was outlawed for a short period.

known and used, ' cartas et cyrographa quæ in tempore ejusdem regis ' (sc. Edward the Confessor) nobis facta sunt, de Anglico in Latinum ad posterorum notitiam curavimus transmutare ', see *Chron. Abbat. Rames.* 161 ; see also *ibid.* 176 : ' universis itaque cartis et cyrographis quæ in archivis nostris Anglica barbarie exarata invenimus non sine difficultate et tædio in Latinos apices transmutatis ' ; see also *ibid.* 65, 111, 112, 151.

During all this time the bishop of East Anglia was Æthelmær, included in the address of no. 60 in the normal way as bishop of the diocese ; the inclusion of Stigand (who had in 1047 been translated from the see of East Anglia to that of Winchester) being accounted for on the supposition that during his own tenure, between 1043 and 1047, of the East Anglian see (in which he was succeeded by Æthelmær), he had himself acquired some interest in the soke within *Bichamdic*, which forms the subject of no. 60. But it is hardly conceivable that Stigand would have been given precedence over Æthelmær in the latter's own diocese unless he had been regarded as the ecclesiastical superior of the diocesan bishop, and it seems reasonable therefore to suppose that the promotion of Stigand to the see of Canterbury (after 14 September 1052) had already taken place at the time when the writ was issued. How then is the ascription to Stigand of the title *episcopus* in this writ to be explained ?

The obvious explanations, such as omission of the prefix *archi-* by copyist or translator, or casual reference to an archbishop by the title of ' bishop ',[1] do not exhaust the possibilities here, for the case of Stigand was exceptional (see Biographical Notes). Since he had taken possession of the see of Canterbury during the lifetime of Archbishop Robert, his position was regarded as irregular. It would be of interest to discover what title, whether ' archbishop ', or ' bishop ', was used in referring to him during the interval between his appointment in 1052/3 and his reception of the pallium in 1058, and again, during the period 1059–66, when he was virtually suspended. The evidence is however inconclusive. There does not seem to be any authentic dated charter attested by Stigand as *episcopus* between 1052/3 and 1058 ; while in undated charters of varying degrees of authenticity he is sometimes styled bishop, sometimes archbishop.[2] The earliest dated charter of reasonably

---

[1] Archbishop Æthelnoth is referred to as ' bishop ' in nos. 27, 29. Other instances are given by Miss Whitelock, *Eng. Hist. Rev.* xli (1937), 461, n. 2, 3. An archbishop is referred to as ' bishop ' in Whitelock, *Anglo-Saxon Wills*, 94, and in Robertson, *Anglo-Saxon Charters*, 148. Dunstan is referred to sometimes as ' archbishop ', sometimes as ' bishop ', in a late tenth-century charter (Robertson, 84).

[2] Stigand is styled bishop in Robertson no. 114 = K. 1337, issued probably about 1053, but as this is concerned with Winchester affairs, he is no doubt addressed here as bishop of Winchester, which see he continued to hold in plurality after his appointment to Canterbury. K. 798, dated 1053, where he attests as bishop, is indecisive, for the authenticity of this text is suspect. See further on texts attested by Stigand, Robertson, 463. To her instances should be added K. 800, dated 1054, attested by Stigand as bishop, but attested as archbishop of Canterbury by Eadsige, who died in 1050. Stigand appears as archbishop in Robertson no. 115 = K. 956, undated but recording transactions of 1053–55, and probably drawn up not long after the event.

certain authenticity in which Stigand is styled archbishop is dated 1059 (Earle, 300). Nor are the writs of the Confessor decisive on this point. Except for a Winchester writ, no. III, in which he is addressed no doubt as bishop of Winchester, there is no instance of a writ with an authentic address issued after 1052 in which Stigand is styled bishop, whilst authentic writs in which he is styled archbishop could have been issued after his reception of the pallium in 1058. No useful conclusions can therefore be drawn from this evidence. Turning again to no. 60, it is to be observed that there is nothing to excite suspicion in its form or content. *Pertineat* (*ad*) in l. 4 no doubt renders *licge in to* in the (supposed) Anglo-Saxon text; and the structure of the text conforms to the pattern of the *licgan in to* writs (see Introduction, p. 64). There is nothing unusual in the king's request that the persons addressed shall help the abbot and monks of Ramsey to obtain ' justice ' (see Introduction, p. 65) ; nor in the appeal to them not to allow the community to be deprived of any of the things which are known to belong to them. However the ' Bishop ' Stigand of the address is to be explained, it is difficult to believe that this writ is not authentic.

NOS. 61 AND 62, COMPANION PIECES

King Edward's grant to Ramsey Abbey of the soke which lay within *Bichamdic*, otherwise the hundred and a half of Clackclose, and many rights there, appears again in no. 61, a writ which, though it may contain authentic material, is spurious as it stands. This long document and its companion piece, no. 62, have come down to us in two versions, English and Latin. They are linked together by their length (in comparison with that of other Anglo-Saxon writs), by the variety of their subject-matter, in particular by their dating and attesting clauses, for which there are no parallels in other writs printed here. They have in common the rare verb *awansige* (a derivative of *wansian*, recorded in BT only for no. 62, the example in no. 61 having been silently altered to *awunige* by Kemble) and their linguistic colouring is similar. The linguistic features of the best copies now extant, those copied on Charter Roll 8 Edward III, are characteristic of a period rather later than that of the Confessor, but two texts with this content must have been in existence well before the end of the twelfth century, for these documents are inserted in Latin form by the compiler of the *Chron. Abbat. Rames.* into his narrative, compiled, as is generally supposed, c. 1170. Since Kemble prints a ' normalised ' text, the texts printed here differ considerably from his.

RIGHTS IN CLACKCLOSE HUNDRED

The first of these two writs, no, 61, purports to announce that King Edward has given to Ramsey Abbey RIGHTS IN CLACKCLOSE HUNDRED. These comprise sake and soke and other judicial and financial rights at Brancaster and Ringstead, including what is cast up by the sea there, as well and as freely as he himself has it by the sea coast anywhere in England, and all the rights that he himself had there. Moreover, the abbey is to have the soke within *Bichamdic* in all things as fully and completely as he himself had it ; and all the rights that any king can have ; and in respect of the men who are ' moot-worthy ', ' fyrd-worthy ' and ' fold-worthy ' in the hundred and a half which comprises that soke, whoever may ' own ' the men (that is to say, whoever may have their commendation), the abbot and the community are to have the soke in all things over them ; and the market at Downham with all the rights that the king ever had. Further, in every shire in which St. Benedict has land, the saint is to have his sake and his soke, toll and team and infangenetheof, and in every place, whoever may own the soke, St. Benedict is to have his freedom in all things as well and as freely as the king has anywhere in England ; and all the offences that pertain to his crown in Yule and at Easter and in the holy week at the Rogation days, in all things as the king himself has ; and freedom from toll throughout all England, within borough and without, at the annual market and in every place by water and by land. The Ramsey chronicler tells us that it was at the request of Withman, a former abbot of Ramsey, that King Edward gave to the abbey ' Ringstede cum libertate adjacente et omni maris ejectu qui wrech dicitur ', and that it was at the request of the monk Oswald.[1] that he gave them Wimbotsham with the hundred and a half (of Clackclose, i.e. the soke within *Bichamdic*), and with 64 sokemen of that hundred, and the market of Downham with its liberties ; and he says that Abbot Ælfwine persuaded the king to set out these grants in ' litteris Anglicis regiæ suæ imaginis impressione roboratis '.[2] That the king's grants to the abbey should in this way be announced by sealed letters, that is, royal writs, would of course be in accordance with the customary practice. One of these writs can be traced in a list of Ramsey charters of which only the contents or titles are given in the Ramsey cartulary : *Sancti Edwardi de libertatibus in Norfolcia Brancestre et hundredo*

---

[1] For Oswald, nephew of St. Oswald (on whom see p. 245 above), see *Chron. Abbat. Rames.* pp. 112, 159–60, and DNB.

[2] *Chron. Abbat. Rames.* pp. 159 ff. Appendix IV, no. 7.

Clak[*eclose*] *in Anglico ; signum omnino fractum.*[1]   Another writ, issued on this, or on a later, occasion is no doubt the short *Bichamdic* writ (no. 60) already discussed above.   But there are good reasons for hesitating to accept the document under discussion (no. 61) as an authentic copy of a writ issued by the clerks of King Edward's secretariat, for it differs from the common form of the Edwardian writ in several important respects.   In the first place its construction is imperfect : its various parts are joined together without the use of the customary transition phrases and its syntax presents certain difficulties that have been smoothed out in the Latin version.   For instance, the section beginning with the phrase : *And in ælcer scire þær Scs Benedictus hafð land inne his saca 7 his socne* (ll. 19 f.) has the appearance of having been violently torn from its context for insertion here—there is no introductory clause.   The Latin version supplies the words : *concedo eis,* and the connective *quoque.*   Similarly some connecting word other than 7 ('and') is required before : *þ market æt Dunham bi waetere 7 bi lande* (preceded in the Latin version by : *concedo eis etiam*) ; and again before : *ealle þa gyltes þa belimpeð to mine kinehelme* (where the Latin version inserts : *habeant etiam*) ; and again before : *tolfreo ofer ealle Engleland* (where the Latin version supplies a verb and translates : *ab omni thelonei exactione liberi sint*).   Further, the attesting and dating clause of this document is highly abnormal : a clause of this sort is in fact to be found only in the other long Ramsey charter, no. 62, its companion piece.   This attesting and dating clause, it should be noted, is not a list of witnesses to the transaction that the writ records, such as is to be found in some of the documents printed in this book (see Introduction, p. 73), but a statement that ' This document was made at Windsor on the fourth day of Easter with the witness of Queen Edith and of Earl Godwine and of Earl Harold.'   This clause cannot be authentic, for the making of a writ was not in itself in the Old English period a transaction that required witnesses : a writ merely gave information and/or issued instructions.   And, moreover, it is impossible to harmonise the dates of the persons named in the attesting clause with the dates of the persons named in the address.   Those in the address indicate the period 1057/8–66, those in the attesting clause 1045–53.   The address may possibly have been taken from an authentic writ (though in that case the ' my thegns ' etc. of the

---

[1] *Cart. Mon. de Rames.* i. 85, no. 108.   The abbreviated and contracted forms of the manuscript are extended here as in the printed text of the Ramsey cartulary.   The editors assume that the manuscript *oīa* stands for *oĩo,* i.e. *omnino.*   As to the manuscript *sig^m,* which the editors expand to *signum,* the form *sigillum* ' seal ', which is equally possible, seems preferable.

original has here (as in no. 62) been changed to ' his ') ; but the
compiler, in adding a dating and attesting clause, has betrayed his
ignorance of the common form of the Edwardian writ.

Leaving aside the dating and attesting clause, it is difficult indeed
to believe that a document so clumsily constructed can have been
issued by the clerks of the king's secretariat, and its authenticity in
its present form must be regarded as in the highest degree doubtful.
The impression left by the whole structure of the document is that
it has been unskilfully compiled by the utilisation of material drawn
from more than one source.   The phrase : *ealle þa gyltes þa belimpeð
to mine kinehelme* (l. 25) is not found elsewhere in the writs printed
here, and we may well doubt whether this phrase was in use during
the pre-Conquest period.   One cannot help suspecting that when he
uses this phrase the compiler is translating back from Latin into
English.   The phrase *omnia placita ad coronam meam pertinentia*
appears in a charter of Henry I inserted into the same *Chron. Abbat.
Rames.* (p. 222, no. 215), a charter which itself deals with the same
privileges as those that the reputed writ of King Edward purports
to grant ; in Henry's charter we find : ' socam et sacam et thol et
theam et infangenethef et hamsokne et gritbriche et forestal et
blodwite et murdre et wrec maris et omnes libertates et *omnia
placita ad coronam meam* pertinentia apud Brauncestre et Ringstede
et apud Claclöshundred et dimidium '.   A similar phrase appears
in another charter of Henry I inserted into the same Ramsey
Chronicle (p. 214, no. 198) : *omnia alia placita coronæ meæ
pertinentia*.   It is difficult to resist the conclusion that the compiler
of this text derived the phrase : *ealle þa gyltes þa belimpeð to mine
kinehelme*, from one of these, or from a similar source.   Similarly
a parallel, if not a possible source, for the clause in l. 12 : *ealle þa
gerihte þa æni king mæi ahen* (which does not appear in other Anglo-
Saxon writs) is to be found in a writ of William I relating to Brancaster and Ringstead [1] : *omnes consuetudines quas rex habere potest.*
Again, there is a general resemblance, though not of so striking a
character, between the two following passages, the first from the
Conqueror's writ :

' Et præcipio ut ubicunque Sanctus Benedictus habet terras *infra civitatem
et extra*, habeat omnes consuetudines suas *ita bene et libere ut ego ipse habeo* ' ;

the second from the writ of King Edward (l. 19) :

' And in ælcer scire þær Sanctus Benedictus hafð land inne his saca 7 his
socne, tol 7 team 7 infangenþeof *wiðinne burhe 7 wiðuten* . . . *swa wel 7 swa
freolice swa ic hit me seolf betst ahe.*'

Again, this writ (no. 61) purports to announce the Confessor's

---

[1] *Cart. Mon. de Rames.* i. 233.   Davis, *Regesta*, no. 177.

grant to the monks of Ramsey that they shall be ' toll-free through-out all England within borough and without, at *geares ceping* and in every place by water and by land '. Neither ' toll-free ' nor *geares ceping*, ' yearly marketing, fair ', has been noticed as occur-ring elsewhere in Old English, but the terms may well have been current in Anglo-Saxon England. Exemption from toll was granted in various forms to religious houses in Kent by eighth-century kings, and such grants were frequently made after the Norman Conquest. But the casual reference in this text to the *geares ceping* or ' fair ' as an established and familiar institution seems to reflect post-Conquest rather than pre-Conquest conditions, and strongly suggests that this passage, clumsily introduced by ' and ', may have been taken by the compiler from some post-Conquest source, possibly from a grant of freedom from toll made to Ramsey Abbey by one of the post-Conquest kings.[1] Further King Edward is made to announce in no. 61 his grant to this abbey of ' the market at Downham by water and by land ', with certain tolls, namely *inlad*, and *utlad*, and with all the rights pertaining thereto as well and as freely as ever I myself possessed it '. This claim of the monks of Ramsey may again have had a substantial basis of fact, though corroboration from other sources seems to be lacking.[2] But taking the writ as a whole it is impossible to believe that it can be an unaltered copy of an authentic writ of King Edward. The evidence favours the supposition that this reputed writ of the Confessor was compiled in the Anglo-Norman period, on the basis perhaps of one or more authentic writs of Edward in favour of Ramsey Abbey, and with the addition of material derived from post-Conquest sources.

THE AFFAIRS OF FENLAND ABBEYS

To the second (no. 62), as to the first, of this pair of Ramsey charters, the test of ' common form ' can be applied, and with the same result : this document dealing with THE AFFAIRS OF FENLAND ABBEYS cannot in its present form be accepted as an unaltered copy of an authentic writ of King Edward. In this text the king is made to declare that he has given his consent to two separate trans-actions : the one, an exchange of land and an arrangement made for the supply to Ramsey of stone from quarries belonging to the abbey of Peterborough, and of eels to Peterborough ; the other, an early demarcation of the boundary between the property of the

---

[1] See, for example, *Chron. Abbat. Rames.* nos. 318, 343, 368.

[2] These alleged grants of the Confessor are discussed by me more fully in ' *Chipping* and *Market* : a lexicographical investigation ', in *Early Cultures of North-West Europe* (see p. 78).

abbeys of Ramsey and of Thorney in the fen later known as 'King's Delph' which lay between Ramsey and the Thorney manor of Whittlesey.[1] In length, and in abundance of minor detail, this text resembles its companion piece; and it shares with it, and with it alone, the highly abnormal feature of a dating and attesting clause. That is not to say that the document may not be true in substance and founded upon genuine material; but the evidence suggests that it has been compounded of material from more than one source. There is no difficulty in supposing that King Edward may have notified his approval of the terms agreed upon by the abbots named in this text in the matters that had arisen between them, but reference to the other texts printed here will show that the elaboration into which this text enters is highly unusual; moreover, one would hardly have expected the royal consent to two different transactions to have been announced in one single writ. A charter bearing on this second transaction, namely the demarcation of the boundary in the fen between the holdings of Ramsey and of Thorney, may indeed indicate the kind of material that may have been available to the compiler. It is a memorandum in English (of which two copies are entered in the *Cart. Mon. de Rames.* i. 188, iii. 38) giving the names of the persons present on the occasion when Abbot Ælfwine of Ramsey proved his right to the boundary of his land, and

[1] The boundary between the holdings of the abbey of Ramsey and the abbey of Thorney came to be a constant cause of dispute between the two houses. The fenland monasteries, Thorney, Ramsey, Peterborough, Crowland and Ely, were constantly contending with each other and with the neighbouring villagers and lords for the rights of pasture and of cutting turves, wood and rushes, and for other fen rights and profits; see Miss N. Neilson, *A Terrier of Fleet, Lincolnshire*, London, British Academy, 1920, pp. xxxiii ff. Miss Neilson points out that for the monasteries and villages on the small islands, where the space of arable land was often very restricted, the maintenance of such rights as they had in the adjacent fen was of the utmost importance. Disputes are recorded over several centuries. In 1224, for example, both Ramsey and Thorney demanded common pasture in Ramsey fen. A dike was made common to both from King's Delph to Whittlesey Mere, the part of the fen on the Ramsey side being assigned to Ramsey, that on the Yaxley-Farcet side to Thorney (*Cart. Mon. de Rames.* ii. 364 ff.). In 1281 the abbot of Ramsey laid claim to 3,800 acres of fen, his possession of which was disputed by the abbot of Thorney, the prior of Ely and others. The jurors declared that the boundaries of this holding ran from *Gangestede* to *Schirmere* and from *Schirmere* to *Hundelake* (*sic*), and that the abbot of Ramsey and his predecessors had had possession from time immemorial (*ibid.* iii. 40). In the middle of the fourteenth century there were still difficulties between the abbot of Ramsey and the abbot of Thorney and his men and tenants of Whittlesey with regard to 'drives' of cattle in King's Delph (*ibid.* i. 77). What the document under discussion purports to record is an early division of the fen, the effect of which was to give two-thirds to Ramsey and one-third to Thorney; see the memorandum cited on p. 254. For further references to these fenland disputes, see H. C. Darby, *The Medieval Fenland* (1940), 73 ff.

its authenticity as a record of fact is supported by the preservation of yet another copy in the Red Book of Thorney Abbey (C.U.L. Add. MS. 3021, f. 372), the other party to these negotiations. Except for a few variations in phraseology, many differences in spelling of no significance, and a substitution of the place-name *Witlesmere* in the Thorney copy, for the *Wendlesmere* (see p. 481) of the Ramsey copy, the two are identical. The opening words of the memorandum : *Þeise men waren þer Alwine abbot betealde þe marke and þe mere after Kyngesdelf bitwenen Rameseye and Þorneiye*, recall the phraseology of the text under discussion, ll. 30–32 : *þæt þæt ilce mærke and mære æfter Cnutes delfe kinges stande alswa Ælfwine abbod of Ramesege hit bitalde.* We are told in the memorandum that there appeared for Ramsey in these negotiations Abbot Ælfwine, his monks Alfwold and Ethelwold, and his retainers (*knittes*) Toki of Shillington, Leofwine Cloche, Brithman Balehorn, Osbern, Wlwine, and Leiwulf ; Thorney being represented by Leofric, abbot of Peterborough, ' for he then had Thorney in his charge ', and Siward, provost of Thorney, ' with him, who was afterwards abbot there '. The ecclesiastics present as witnesses were Lefsine (Leofsige), abbot of Ely, and his monk Sirik the provost, together with Wulfget, abbot of Crowland, Brixtan, his monk, and three other monks, namely, Ailsige, Leofwine the Long [1] of Peterborough, and Alfwold of Thorney—the name of Siward the provost of Thorney, afterwards abbot, repeated here, concluding the list. There were also present laymen, who when Abbot Ælfwine had proved his claim to (*betold*) the boundary, against the abbey of Thorney, swore that two parts of the fen belonged to Ramsey, the third part to Thorney (' hit sworen . . . þe two del into Sancte Benedicte into Rameseye and þe þridden del Sancte Botulfe into Þorneiye '). These laymen, Thurulf the fisherman of Farcet, and Lefstan Herlepic of Whittlesey, for Thorney, and Lefsi Crevleta, Ailmer Hogg of *Wellen*, and Wlfgeit the fisherman of Hepmangrove were no doubt the ' ancient men ' (*homines antiqui*) referred to in the rubric of the Thorney copy of this memorandum : ' De bundis marisci de Kingesdelf inter abbates de Rames' 7 de Thorn' ab antiquis limitatis per homines antiquos ' ; Wulfgeat of Hepmangrove is indeed stated in the Ramsey copy to have been concerned in a miracle reputed to have taken place at the foundation of the abbey in King Edgar's reign eighty years before. There seems on general grounds no reason to doubt the substantial accuracy of the

---

[1] Could this have been Leofwine *Lange*, a monk of Peterborough, who, when the Danes made the attack upon Peterborough Abbey described in *Chron.* E 1070, was lying sick in the infirmary and alone remained behind after the other monks had scattered ?

details given in this memorandum, though they are set out in rather a confused way. But the suggestion that the reputed writ under discussion and the memorandum are in every respect based on authentic records does in fact involve a chronological difficulty : Leofsige, abbot of Ely, who is supposed to have died in 1045, is mentioned in both in conjunction with Leofric, abbot of Peterborough, whose appointment to that office is supposed to have taken place in 1052.[1] Further, a fellow-witness named in both the transactions described in the reputed writ and also in the demarcation of boundaries described in the memorandum, is Wulfgeat, abbot of Crowland, whose appointment as abbot of that house would seem to have taken place not earlier than 1053 (see Biographical Notes). More than one possibility presents itself : the compilers of the reputed Ramsey writ and of the closely related memorandum may have been mistaken in bringing together at the same time and place Leofsige of Ely, Leofric of Peterborough and Wulfgeat of Crowland ; on the other hand, the apparently incompatible dates of these abbots as they are given above may be incorrect, and all three abbots may actually have been present at the transactions that the reputed writ and the memorandum purport to record. The situation is complicated by the fact that there were two abbots named Leofsige alive about this time ; two are named in a charter of 1053–55 (Robertson no. 115), and one of them may have been Leofsige, abbot of Ely. But there can be no certainty in the matter, for the reputed Ramsey writ and the memorandum are the only charters in which an abbot named Leofsige is given the title of abbot of Ely. On the other hand it is not difficult to imagine that an x may have been dropped from the date of 1045 given in the *Liber Eliensis* for Leofsige's death, and the abbot may actually have died not in 1045 but in 1055 (see further Biographical Notes). Both the writ and the memorandum may then have been based on authentic material.

But supposing this to be the case, the relation of the memorandum to the writ cannot be determined on the evidence now available. It is not suggested that the memorandum was the direct source of the writ attributed to the Confessor. In the first place the two documents differ in a few details. Whereas the writ calls Siward abbot of Thorney, and puts Abbot Leofric of Peterborough among the witnesses, the memorandum says that Siward was then provost of Thorney, but afterwards became abbot, and makes Abbot Leofric of Peterborough responsible for putting Thorney's case. Then the

---

[1] The date of 1045 for Leofsige's death is derived from the Anglo-Norman compilation known as the *Liber Eliensis*, ii. cap. 94, while the date of 1052 for Leofric's appointment comes from the post-Conquest insertion for 1052 in the Peterborough text of the *Chronicle*.

linguistic forms of the memorandum as it stands might be taken to rule out an eleventh-century date of composition, but it is of course entirely probable that it has been considerably modified in transmission. But the preservation of the memorandum does provide evidence of documents recording in detail the negotiations between the two houses, and it is likely that the agreement between Ramsey and Peterborough may also have been recorded in a charter. Material from such sources as these may have been combined with an address and greeting taken from a writ of the Confessor in which the ' my ' was altered by the compiler to ' his ', and provided with an attesting and dating clause. Everything favours the supposition that this writ (no. 62) is not authentic as it stands. But there is no difficulty here, as there is in no. 61, in reconciling the dates of the persons named in the address with those named in the attesting and dating clause, the statement in this latter clause that the document was made at Westminster being given plausibility by the inclusion of the name of Abbot Edwin of Westminster. If, as may well have been the case, authentic agreements between Ramsey and Peterborough, and Ramsey and Thorney, were actually submitted to the king for his approval, this may well have been done at Westminster, and the attestations in the writ, no. 62, may have been derived by the compiler from charters recording these transactions. Instances exist elsewhere of the king attesting an exchange of land (Robertson nos. 31, 53), and attesting an agreement (*ibid.* nos. 7, 101). But the hypothesis that these negotiations may actually have been approved at Westminster may be illusory, for since a link has been established between the forged charters of Westminster, Coventry, and Ramsey,[1] Westminster material may have been available there, and in that case the resemblance between the spurious Westminster and the spurious Ramsey diplomas might have arisen either through direct imitation on one side or the other, or through fabrication by the same hand. But whatever may have been the source of the material it is impossible to accept this Ramsey document as an authentic copy of a writ issued by the clerks of Edward's secretariat, and it is entirely probable that no. 62, like its companion piece, no. 61, was compiled in the Anglo-Norman period, and perhaps by the same person.

(56)

King Harthacnut declares that Abbot Æthelstan of Ramsey is to have his *mansus* in Thetford as fully and freely as he had it in the days of King Cnut. 1040–42

---

[1] W. H. Stevenson, *Eng. Hist. Rev.* xi (1896) 731 ; *Crawford Charters*, 94, 100 : James Tait, *Essays in History presented to R. Lane Poole*, 163.

(Rawlinson MS. B. 333, f. 19 b)

Hardecnut rex Agelwino 7 omnibus burgensibus de Tedfordia 1 salutem. Notum uobis sit quod ego uolo 7 precipio ut abbas Æthestanus de Ramesia habeat mansum suum in Tedfordia ita plene 7 ita libere sicut habuit in diebus Cnutonis regis patris mei.

Heading : Item carta eiusdem qua confirmauit nobis mansionem nostram apud Tedfordiam. 3. Æthelstanus B.

(57)

King Harthacnut and his mother Queen Ælfgifu declare that they have given to the church of Ramsey the ' east ' land at Hemingford with sake and soke, as fully as they themselves possessed it. 1040–42

(Rawlinson MS. B. 333, f. 19 b)

Hardecnut rex 7 Alfgiua mater eiusdem regina Ædnotho episcopo 1 7 Turi comiti 7 Kinrico 7 omnibus ministris [suis] de comitatu Huntendonie salutem. Notificamus uobis quod nos in nomine Sancte Trinitatis dedimus 7 concessimus ecclesie Ramesie pro anima Cnutonis regis domini nostri 7 nostra amborum terram 5 orientalem de Hemmingeforde 7 omnia que ad illam pertinent cum saca 7 soca ita plene 7 honorifice sicut nobis in manu stetit. Quicunque ergo hanc donacionem nostram ab eadem ecclesia alienare temptauerit alienetur ille in die iudicii a gaudio celesti 7 penas inferni cum demonibus sorciatur. 10

Heading : Carta eiusdem. A *and* B *seem to be independent versions ;* C *resembles* A. 1. eius B, C. 2. Turico B ; Turri C. 2. ministris suis B. 4. Ramesensi ecclesie B. 5. nostra utriusque salute B. 6. cum omnibus que B. 7. nobis stetit in manu B.

(58)

King Edward declares that St. Benedict of Ramsey is to have the land at Hemingford with everything pertaining thereto as fully and completely as King Harthacnut and Queen Ælfgifu Emma granted it to that church. 1043–49

(Rawlinson MS. B. 333, f. 21 b)

Eadwardus rex Ædnotho episcopo, Turi comiti, Kinrico 7 omnibus 1 ministris suis de comitatu Huntendonie salutem. Notum uobis sit

quod ego uolo ut Sanctus Benedictus de Ramesia habeat terram de
Hemmingfordia cum omnibus pertinenciis suis ita plene 7 perfecte
5 sicut rex Hardecnut frater meus 7 Alfgiua mater mea eam eidem
ecclesie concesserunt 7 nullum omnino nec Anglicum nec Danum
hanc donacionem mutare permitto.

Heading : Carta eiusdem regis de Hemmingfordia.   1. *Kemble*
(*wrongly*) Tuli *for* Turi.   1. [vicecom.] *after* Kinrico, *Gale, Kemble.*

(59)

King Edward declares that he has given to Ramsey Abbey the
land at Broughton which he himself possessed, with sake and soke.
(1050–52)

(Rawlinson MS. B. 333, f. 21 b)

1   Eadwardus rex Ulf episcopo, Siwardo comiti, Alfrico vicecomiti
7 omnibus ministris suis de Huntendone schire salutem. Notum
uobis sit me dedisse Deo 7 Sancto Benedicto 7 Alfwino abbati de
Ramesia terram de Broctona quam egomet ibi habui cum saca
5 7 soca in omnibus, 7 nulli homini hanc donacionem immutare
permitto. Quod si quis post dies meos hoc minuere uel mutare
ausus fuerit siue clericus sit siue laicus, segregetur ille a Christo
7 a Sancti Benedicti 7 omnium sanctorum consorcio 7 nisi hic
emendauerit quod temere deliquit penas infernales cum demonibus
10 sorciatur.

Heading : Item carta ipsius de terra 7 soca quam dedit apud Broctonam.
1. *Gale, Kemble* (*wrongly*) Ulfsio *for* Ulf.

(60)

King Edward declares that the soke within *Bichamdic* is to belong
to Ramsey Abbey as fully and completely as it was first given to
that church. 1053–57

(Rawlinson MS. B. 333, f. 21)

1   Eadwardus rex Stigando episcopo, Ailmaro episcopo, Alfgaro
comiti 7 omnibus ministris suis de Nortfolc salutem. Notum sit
uobis quod ego uolo ut soca infra Bichamdich in omnibus rebus ad
Sanctum Benedictum Ramesie pertineat ita integre 7 plene sicut
5 primo eidem ecclesie data fuit, 7 prohibeo ne aliquis eam in aliquo
minuat qui amiciciam meam diligit. Rogo igitur uos ut Alfwinum
abbatem 7 fratres Ramesie ubicunque opus habuerint omnes unani-

miter ad iusticiam adiuuetis, 7 pro amore meo nullum permittatis
eis auferre quicquam eorum que ad eos dinoscuntur pertinere.

Heading : Item carta regis Ædwardi de soca qua est infra Bichamdich.
3. saca (*for* soca) C.   8. aufferre MS.

(61)

King Edward declares that he has granted to Ramsey Abbey
judicial and financial rights and shipwreck and what is cast up by
the sea at Brancaster and Ringstead, the soke within *Bichamdic*, the
market at Downham, and judicial and financial rights in every shire
in which St. Benedict of Ramsey has land.

(Ch. R. 8 Edw. III, m. 13)

Eadward cyng gret Stigand erceb̄. 7 Ægelmær b̄. 7 Gyrð eorl 7 Toli 1
scirreue. 7 ealle his þeines inne Norðfolce 7 inne Suðfolce. 7 ealle his
oðre witen ofer eall Ængleland hadede 7 leawede. freondlice. 7 ic
cyðe eow þ̄ ic habbe gegeofen Criste 7 Sc̄e Marie. 7 Sc̄e Benedicte.
7 Ælfwine abb̄ in to Ramesege saca 7 socna. tol 7 team. 7 infangen- 5
þeof fihtwite 7 ferdwite. forestall 7 hamsocne. griðbryce. 7 scipbryce
7 þa sæupwarp on eallan þingen æt Bramcæstre. 7 æt Ringstyde
swa wel 7 swa freolice swa ic hit me seolf betst habbe bi ða særime
ahwær in Engelande. 7 ealle þa gerihte þa ic me seolf þær ahte.
7 ic wylle þ̄ seo socne wiðinnen Bicchamdic ligce in to Ramesege to 10
Sc̄e Benedihte on eallen þingen swa full. 7 swa forð swa ic heo me
seolf ahte. 7 ealle þa gerihte þa æni king mæi ahen. 7 ealle þa
men þa beon motwurði ferdwurði. 7 faldwurði in þæt oðer healfe
hundred swa hwilc man swa þa men ahe Sc̄e Marie. 7 Sc̄s Benedictus.
7 se abb̄. 7 þa gebroðra in to Ramesege habben þa socne on eallen 15
þingen ofer heom. 7 þ̄ market æt Dunham bi waetere 7 bi lande mid
inlade. 7 mid utlade. 7 mid eallen þan gerihte þe þær to hereð swa
wel 7 swa freolice swa ic hit me seolf betst ahte. 7 ic nelle geþafien þ̄
æniman þis gelytlige mid ænige þinge. 7 in ælcer scire þær Sc̄s
Benedictus hafð land inne his saca 7 his socne. tol 7 team. 7 infangen- 20
þeof wiðinne burhe 7 wiðuten. 7 on ælce styde be lande. 7 be strande.
be wude 7 be felde swa hwylc man swa þa socne ahe Sc̄s Benedictus
habbe his freodom on eallen þingen swa wel 7 swa freolice swa ic hit
me seolf betst ahe ahwær in Engelande. 7 ealle þa gyltes þa belimpeð
to mine kinehelme inne Iol. 7 inne Easterne. 7 inne þa hali wuca 25
æt gangdagas. on ealle þingan al swa ic heo me seolf ahe. 7 tolfreo
ofer ealle Engleland wiðinne burhe. 7 wiðutan. æt gæres cepinge.
7 on æfrice styde be wætere. 7 be lande. 7 ic forbeode Godes forbode
7 min þ̄ nan man þis geofe ne lytlige ne awende. 7 gif æni man hit

30 awansi mid æfrænige þinge. of þan þe ic habbe her geunnen on
þeosen gewrite. si he gesyndred fram Criste. 7 fram eallen his halgan.
Am*en*. Þis writ wæs gemaced æt Windlesoren on feorðe Easterdæi
on Eadgiðe gewitnysse þære cwene. 7 Godwines eorles. 7 Haroldes
eorles.

Heading : Inspeximus insuper quandam aliam cartam ipsius Sancti Edwardi
in hec verba.   1. cyng gret] cying gtret MS.   13. ferd- P, M, A
(*Lat. vers.*), *and cf.* ferdwite l. 6] forðwurði MS.   18. freolice] fredlice
MS.   27. wið] wid MS.

Latin Version
(Rawlinson MS. B. 333, f. 21)

35   Eadwardus rex Anglorum Stigando archiepiscopo, Ailmaro
episcopo, Girth comiti, Toli vicecomiti 7 omnibus ministris suis de
Nortfolc 7 de Suthfolc 7 uniuersis aliis fidelibus suis per totam
Angliam constitutis tam clericis quam laicis salutem.   Notifico uobis
me concessisse Deo 7 Sancte Marie 7 Sancto Benedicto 7 Alfwino
40 abbati de Ramesia sacam 7 socam, tol 7 team 7 infangenethef,
fihtwite 7 ferdwite, forestal 7 hamsokne, grithbriche 7 schipbriche 7
seupwerp in omnibus rebus apud Bramcestre 7 apud Ringstede ita
bene 7 libere sicut ipse ea melius 7 liberius habeo in littore marino
alicubi in Anglia omnesque rectitudines 7 iura que ibi ego ipse
45 unquam habui.   Volo etiam ut soca que est infra Bichamdich in
omnibus ad Sanctum Benedictum Ramesie pertineat ita plene 7
perfecte sicut eam ipse habui, 7 omnes rectitudines quas rex ibi
potest habere.   Volo preterea ut Sancta Maria 7 Sanctus Benedictus
7 abbas 7 fratres Ramesie habeant socam in omnibus super omnes
50 homines qui sunt motwrthi, ferdwrthi 7 faldwrthi in illo hundredo
7 dimidio cuiuscunque homines sint.   Concedo eis etiam mercatum
de Dunham per aquam 7 terram cum inductione 7 eductione 7 cum
omnibus rectitudinibus que ad illud pertinent ita bene 7 libere sicut
illud ipse unquam melius habui, 7 nolo pati ut aliquis hoc in aliquo
55 imminuat.   In omni quoque comitatu ubi Sanctus Benedictus
habet terram concedo eis sacam 7 socam suam, tol 7 team 7
infangenethef infra burgum 7 extra, 7 ubique in terra 7 aqua, in
bosco 7 plano, cuiuscunque fuerit soca, habeat Sanctus Benedictus
libertatem suam in omnibus, ita bene 7 plene sicut ego ipse alicubi
60 habeo in tota Anglia. Habeant etiam omnes forefacturas que
pertinent ad regiam coronam meam in Natali Dominico, in Pascha
7 in sancta ebdomada Rogacionum in omnibus rebus sicut ipse
habeo ; 7 per totam Angliam infra ciuitatem 7 extra in omni foro 7
annuis nundinis 7 in omnibus omnino locis per aquam 7 terram ab
65 omni thelonei exactione liberi sint.   Prohibeo itaque Dei pro-

hibicione 7 mea ne aliquis hanc concessionem meam mutet aut minuat. Si quis uero aliquid horum que in hoc scripto continentur temerare presumpserit, segregatus sit ille a Christo 7 ab omni sanctorum eius consorcio. Hec carta facta fuit apud Windleshoram in .iiii⁰. die ebdomade paschalis sub testimonio Ædgithe regine, 70 Godwini 7 Haroldi comitum.

Heading : Carta Regis Ædwardi.   41. fihtwite] fithwite MS.
57. C *inserts* uel ciuitatem.

Translation

King Edward sends friendly greetings to Archbishop Stigand, and Bishop Æthelmær, and Earl Gyrth, and Toli the sheriff, and all his thegns in Norfolk and in Suffolk, and all his other counsellors throughout all England, ecclesiastics and laymen. And I inform you that I have given to Ramsey, to Christ and St. Mary and St. Benedict, and Abbot Ælfwine, sake and soke, toll and team and infangenetheof, fihtwite and fyrdwite, foresteall and hamsocn, grithbreach and shipwreck and what is cast up by the sea in all things at Brancaster and at Ringstead, as well and as freely as I myself have it to the fullest extent by the seacoast anywhere in England, and all the rights which I myself had there. And it is my will that the soke within *Bichamdic* shall belong to St. Benedict at Ramsey in all things as fully and as completely as I myself possessed it, and all the rights that any king can have ; and all the men who are ' moot-worthy ', ' fyrd-worthy ' and ' fold-worthy ', in the hundred and a half, whosoever may own the men, St. Mary and St. Benedict and the abbot and the brethren at Ramsey are to have the soke in all things over them ; and the market at Downham by water and by land, with [toll on] what is carried in and carried out, and with all the rights that belong thereto as well and as freely as ever I myself possessed it ; and I will not permit any man to diminish this by any means. And in every shire where St. Benedict has land, his sake and his soke, toll and team and infangenetheof, within borough and without, and in every place, by land and by strand, in woodland and in open country, whosoever may own the soke, St. Benedict is to have his freedom in all things as well and as freely as I myself have it to the fullest extent anywhere in England. And all the offences that pertain to my crown in Yule and at Easter and in the holy week at the Rogation Days, in all things just as I myself possess them. And toll-free throughout all England within borough and without, at the annual market (*or* fair) and in every place by water and by land. And I forbid, in God's name and my own, that any man diminish or alter this gift ; and if any man by any means impair it, in respect of what I have granted here in this document, may he be cut off from Christ and from all his saints. Amen. This document was made at Windsor on the fourth day of Easter with the cognisance of Queen Edith and of Earl Godwine and of Earl Harold.

(62)

King Edward declares that he has confirmed the exchange and the agreement made between Ælfwine, abbot of Ramsey, and Leofric, abbot of Peterborough ; and also the boundaries along King Cnut's Delph as Ælfwine, abbot of Ramsey, proved his claim to them against Siward, abbot of Thorney.

(Ch. R. 8 Edw. III, m. 13)

1   + Eadward cing gret wel Wulfwi biscop 7 Tosti eorl. 7 Norðman scirrefe 7 ealle his witen 7 ealle his holden inne Hamtunescire hadede 7 leawede freondlice. 7 ic cyðe eow þ Æ[l]fwine abbod of Ramesege 7 Leofric abbod of Burh habben me gecyd of þ hwærf 7 of þa fore-
5 warde þe heo habben gespeken 7 gedon heom betweonan. 7 ic wylle þ ge understanden þ Ælfwine abbod of Ramesege on þas wise hafð gehwærfd æt Leofrice abbod of Burh nigen gerde landes æt Ludintúne of Scs Petrus socnelande of Burh. Huntinges hide be name 7 Godrices twa gerde þe Densce. 7 Brandes gerde. 7 Leofgares gerde 7 Ælfwines
10 gerde þe Blace scer 7 sacleas to fulle hwærfe wið æfric man ær dæige 7 æfter dæige. 7 hafð gifen him þær fore þ land æt Mærham al ðæt Scs Bendictus þær ahte. scer. 7 sacleas wið æfric man to fulle hwærfe. 7 toæken þis þe abb 7 þa gebroðra of Ramesege sculen gifan ælce gere feower þusend æl inne lenten to cariteð þon abbode 7 þam
15 gebroðre in to Burh to þære forwarde þ þe abb 7 þa gebroðra of Ramesege sculen habben of Scs Petrus landare wercstan æt Bernace. 7 walstan æt Burh. alswa mycel swa heom behofeð to fulle foreware scer 7 sacleas wið toll 7 wið ealle þing be wætere 7 be lande in to Ramesege æfre mare. 7 heo habben me gecyd þ þis forewarde wæs
20 imaked on Leofsies abbodes iwitnesse of Eli. 7 Wulfgeates abbodes of Crulande. 7 on þære manne þe heom mide wæren. Nu cyðe ic eow þ Ælfwine abb hafð swa wið me gespeken 7 of his me igefen þ ic habbe þis ilce forewarde igeated. 7 ic wille þ hit stande al swa heo hit gespeken habbeð Gode to lofe. 7 Sca Maria. 7 Sce Benedihte æfre
25 mare wið borene 7 wið unborene. 7 ic hate 7 beode þ nan man ne wurðe swa deorf ne swa dyrsti þ þis ilce hwærf 7 þis ilce forwarde breke. haded ne leawed. 7 ic forbeode be fulle wite þæt nan man ne wurðe swa dyrsti. þ Scs Benedihtus men ne heore þing nahwær ne

derie. ac Godes grið. 7 min habben heo 7 heore þing be wætere 7 be
lande. 7 ic hæte 7 beode mid þis ilce writ. þ̇ þæt ilce mærke 7 mære 30
æfter Cnutes delfe kinges stande alswa Ælfwine abb of Ramesege
hit betalde wið Siwarð abbod of Þornege æl beo þe Gangestyde be
east halfe þam dælue. 7 be west halfe be Hyndelake swa anan to
Wendelesmere 7 healf Ragereholt in to Ramesege on Leofsies
abbodes iwitnesse of Eli. 7 on Leofrices abb of Burh. 7 Wulfgeates. 35
abb of Crulande. 7 þare manne þa heom mide wæren. 7 gif æniman
þis ilce forewarde mid ænige þinge abreke. 7 awansige. si he
gesyndred fram heofener[i]ces myrhðe butan he hit ibete ær he
heonan gewite. Amen. Þis writ wæs imaked æt Westmunstre on
Sc̄s Petrus mæssedæi on Stigandes iwitnesse erceb. 7 Edwines abb. 40
7 Haroldes eorles. 7 Esegares stalres. 7 Hugelines burðeines.

Heading : Inspeximus etiam quandam aliam cartam eiusdem Sancti
Edwardi in hec verba.   11. ðæt] dæt MS.   18. wið (twice)]
wid MS.   29. derie] (*probably*) derian MS. *but the vowel before* n *is*
indistinct.

Latin Version

(Rawlinson MS. B. 333, f. 21 b)

Eadwardus rex Wlfwio episcopo, Tosti comiti, Normanno vicecomiti 7 omnibus fidelibus suis 7 ministris, clericis 7 laycis, de
comitatu Hamtonie salutem. Notum uobis facio quod Alfwinus
abbas de Ramesia 7 Leofricus abbas de Burgo notificauerunt mihi 45
pactionem 7 commutacionem quam habita collocucione inter se
fecerunt. Volo itaque ut uos intelligatis quod Alfwinus abbas de
Ramesia hoc modo accepit de Leofrico abbate Burgi nouem virgatas
terre apud Lodintonam de soca Sancti Petri, nominatim, scilicet,
hidam Huntingi, duas virgatas Godrici Dani, virgatam Brandi, 50
virgatam Leofgari, 7 virgatam Alfwini Nigri, in plenam commutacionem contra omnes homines nunc et perpetuo liberas 7
quietas ; 7 pro his dedit prefato abbati de Burch totam terram quam
Sanctus Benedictus habuit apud Marham liberam ab omni calumpnia
7 quietam in plenam commutacionem. Ipse insuper abbas 7 fratres 55
Ramesie singulis annis dabunt de caritate abbati 7 fratribus Burgi
quatuor milia anguillarum in Quadragesima, sub tali videlicet
condicione, quod abbas 7 fratres de Ramesia habebunt in territorio
Sancti Petri de Burch quantum sibi opus fuerit de lapidibus
quadratilibus apud Bernech 7 de petris muralibus apud Burch, in 60
plena cambicione ; eruntque omni tempore liberi a thelonei et
omnium exactionum vexacione per aquam 7 per terram. Notificauerunt quoque mihi quod hec composicio facta fuit inter eos
sub testimonio Lefsii abbatis de Ely 7 Wlfgeti abbatis Croilandie

65 7 eorum qui cum ipsis presentes affuerunt. Itaque uolo uos scire quod Alfwinus abbas ita mecum locutus est 7 tantum mihi de suo dedit quod ego hanc conuencionem concessi ; 7 uolo ut firmiter stet semper sicut inter se prolocuti sunt, ad laudem 7 honorem Dei 7 Sancte Marie Sanctique Benedicti, tam moderno tempore 70 quam futuro. Mando igitur 7 precipio ut nullus omnino nec clericus nec laycus hanc commutacionem 7 pactionem infringere audeat. Prohibeo quoque super plenam forisfacturam meam ne ullus homo tam audax sit ut aliquod grauamen aut iniuriam inferat hominibus Sancti Benedicti neque rebus eorum, sed pacem Dei 7 meam habeant 75 ipsi 7 omnia que ipsorum sunt aut erunt, ubique in aqua 7 terra. Mando preterea 7 precipio per hoc scriptum meum ut termini 7 mete in Kingesdelf ita permaneant sicut abbas Alfwinus Ramesie eas diracionauit contra Siwardum abbatem Thorneie sub testimonio Lefsii abbatis de Ely 7 Leofrici abbatis de Burch 7 Wlfgeti abbatis 80 Crolandie 7 eorum qui cum ipsis placito interfuerunt : ex parte, scilicet, orientali ipsius lade usque ad locum qui dicitur Gangstede 7 exinde in parte occidentali ab Hindelake usque ad Witlesmere 7 medietas de Rowereholt. Quicunque ergo hanc conuencionem eorum in aliqua re temerare uel imminuere presumpserit, separatus 85 sit ille a gaudio celesti nisi antequam hinc moriens recedat delictum suum congrue emendauerit. Amen. Hec carta facta fuit apud Westmonasterium in festo Sancti Petri. Teste Stigando archi-episcopo. Ædwino abbate, Haroldo comite, Esegaro stalre, 7 Hugelino cubiculario.

Heading : Hec est carta ejusdem regis de prefate condicione pactionis quam de Anglico in ydioma Latinum mutauimus.

81. nauigii uel lade C.   82. Hundeslake C.   83. Wenlesmere C.

Translation

King Edward sends kind and friendly greetings to Bishop Wulfwig and Earl Tostig and Northman the sheriff and all his counsellors and all his lieges in Northamptonshire, ecclesiastics and laymen. And I inform you that Ælfwine, abbot of Ramsey, and Leofric, abbot of Peterborough, have informed me of the exchange and of the agreement that they have agreed to and carried out between them. And I would have you take note that Ælfwine, abbot of Ramsey, has in the following circumstances taken in exchange from Leofric, abbot of Peterborough, nine virgates of land at Lutton of the soke-land of St. Peter of Peterborough : what is called *Huntinges hide*, and the two virgates of Godric the Dane, and Brand's virgate, and Leofgar's virgate, and the virgate of Ælfwine the Black, clear and undisputed in full exchange as regards every man for ever ; and has given him in exchange for this the land at Marholm, all that St. Benedict had there, clear and undisputed as regards every man in full exchange ; and in addition to this the abbot and brethren of Ramsey are to give every year four thousand eels in Lent as a voluntary gift to the abbot and brethren at Peterborough, on condition that the abbot and the brethren of Ramsey shall have ever afterwards for Ramsey from the property of St. Peter building-stone at Barnack and wall-stone at Peterborough, as much as they require, in full exchange, clear and undisputed as regards toll and everything by water and by land. And they have informed me that this agreement was made with the cognisance of Leofsige, abbot of Ely, and of Wulfgeat, abbot of Crowland, and of the men who were with them. Now I inform you that Abbot Ælfwine has so conferred with me, and given me a present, that I have given my consent to this same agreement, and my will is that it shall remain in force for ever, for those living and those yet to come, according to the terms that they have agreed upon, to the praise of God and St. Mary and St. Benedict. And I command and enjoin that no one, ecclesiastical or lay, be so bold or so audacious as to violate this same exchange and this same agreement. And I forbid, on pain of the full penalty, that any one be so audacious as anywhere to harm St. Benedict's men or their possessions ; but they and their possessions are to have God's protection and mine by water and by land. And I command and enjoin by this same document that the same boundary and division along King Cnut's Delph remain fixed just as Ælfwine, abbot of Ramsey, proved his claim to it against Siwarth, abbot of Thorney ; all by the *Gangstede* on the east side of the delph, and on the west side by Hindlake, (and) so on to *Wendelesmere*, and half Rawerholt, to Ramsey, with the cognisance of Leofsige, abbot of Ely, and of Leofric, abbot of Peterborough, and of Wulfgeat, abbot of Crowland, and of the men who were with them. And if any one by any means violate or diminish this same agreement, may he be cut off from the joy of the heavenly kingdom, unless he make amends for it before he goes hence. Amen. This document was made at Westminster on St. Peter's Day with the cognisance of Archbishop Stigand and of Abbot Edwin and of Earl Harold and of Esgar the staller and of Hugelin the chamberlain.

SHERBORNE

This is no reason for doubting the authenticity of the writ, no. 63, addressed by Bishop Æthelric of Sherborne [1] to a certain Æthelmær, who has with much probability been identified [2] with the well-known Æthelmær, earl of the Western Provinces from 1002 to 1017. The bishop complains that some of the lands which should have helped him to meet the charge of a ship [3] on his episcopal estate have been withdrawn from him, and he appeals to Æthelmær to use his influence so that they may be restored to him. Förster cites in this connection a (slightly later) injunction in Cnut's Proclamation of 1020, § 8 (see p. 17) : ' I enjoin upon my ealdormen to support the bishops in furthering the rights of the church ' (though the letter may have been sent to Æthelmær before his appointment) ; and we may also compare the injunctions sometimes given by the Confessor to the persons addressed in his writs, to help the bishop in cases where he may require their aid (see Introduction, p. 65). The immediate occasion of the writing of the letter may have been the levy of ships imposed in 1008 upon the country as a whole, on inland as well as coastal shires, for the purpose of building up a new fleet of warships to protect the country from the disastrous invasions of the Danes, or some earlier levy. And in the fifth code of King Æthelred II (V Æthelred 27), supposed by Liebermann to have been promulgated in 1008, it is enacted that the fitting-out of ships shall be carried out as diligently as possible (*geornost*), so that in every year all be equipped immediately after Easter [4] (when Danish invasions generally began). According to the *Chronicle*, C, E, F, 1008, the country was to be divided into districts of 310 hides, each of which was to provide a warship (called a *scegth*, of approximately 60 oars), and in addition every 8 hides throughout the country were

---

[1] The see of Sherborne was established in 705 as the bishopric of Wessex ' to the west of Selwood ', but was limited to Dorset when King Edward the Elder subdivided the two West Saxon sees. The foundation of the cathedral monastery seems to have taken place at or about the time of the establishment of the bishopric. In King Æthelred's time, soon after 992, the clerks serving the cathedral were replaced by monks. See *Mon. Angl.* i. 331 ff., VCH *Dorset*, ii. 62.

[2] See R. Brotanek, *Texte und Untersuchungen zur Altenglischen Literatur und Kirkengeschichte* (Halle, 1913), 33–49 ; Max Förster, *Englische Studien*, lxi (1927), 116–29, and *Der Flussname Themse und seine Sippe* (Sitzungsberichte der Bayerischen Akademie der Wissenschaften, Phil. Hist. Abteilung, Band I, Munich, 1941), Appendix, 776 ff.

[3] For other interpretations of the term *scypgesceot*, see p. 483. Everything encourages the belief that the one adopted here, for which I am indebted to Sir Frank Stenton, is correct.

[4] Liebermann, *Gesetze*, i. 242, iii. 167, Robertson, *Laws*, 86.

to provide a helmet and a coat of mail. The curious figure 310 appears in *Chronicle* C, E, F, and in sources derived from it ; D, which is corrupt, has sometimes been emended to give a different meaning.[1]   But an association of hundreds in groups of three for the provision of ships which is to be traced here and there seems to indicate another unit of assessment, namely 300, the unit which appears in the letter under discussion.[2]   There is reason to believe that the arrangements officially made for the supply of ships in 1008 were not an innovation.   In 1003 or 1004 Archbishop Ælfric made a bequest of ships : he bequeathed his best ship and the sailing tackle with it to the king, and 60 helmets and 60 coats of mail ; and further, a ship to the people of Kent, and another to Wiltshire.[3] This strongly suggests that the ship levy was known before A.D. 1008, as is also suggested by the associations of hundreds in groups of three referred to above (for some of these may be ancient), and by the general tenor of Æthelric's letter.   Bequests of ships appear elsewhere at about this time.   Between 975 and 1016 a testator bequeathed a *scegth* to Ramsey Abbey, half for the abbot, half for the monks, perhaps to help them to contribute to such a levy.[4] Between 988 and 1008/12 the bishop of Crediton bequeathed to the king a *scegth* of 64 oars.[5]   In his letter to Æthelmær Bishop Æthelric complains that of the 300 hides which had contributed to the ' ship- scot ' in the days of his predecessors, 33 hides are now lost to the bishopric.   If the vills which he names in his letter had been with- drawn from his lordship, it would mean that the royal dues payable for the 33 hides that they comprised would have been withdrawn as far as he was concerned ; but he did not necessarily own them. Furthermore, complains the bishop, his property is exposed to a new danger.   There is a possibility that what they had owned at

---

[1] See Plummer ii. 185 ; and also Liebermann ii. 638, s.v. ' Schiff '.

[2] On the association of hundreds in groups of three for the provision of ships see H. M. Cam, ' Early Groups of Hundreds ', *Historical Essays in Honour of James Tait*, 14 f.   In a twelfth-century copy of an alleged charter of King Edgar for Worcester (B. 1135), which may be founded on authentic material, Edgar is made to declare that the three hundreds of Oswaldslow shall con- stitute a *naucupletionem, scypfylleð* or *scypsocne*.   Traces of a similar grouping for the provision of ships appear in the twelfth century in the ' ship-sokes ' of Warwickshire.   An arrangement of hundreds in groups of three is also to be found in Buckinghamshire and apparently in Cambridgeshire.   See further, *The Place-Names of Warwickshire* (E.P.-N.S.), xix–xx ; *ibid. Cambridgeshire*, lix, 138 ; and O. S. Anderson, *The English Hundred-Names*, i. xix, 131–8, iii. i.   Dr. Cam has kindly pointed out to me that in the thirteenth century the bishop of Salisbury (the successor of Sherborne as the diocesan see) held three hundreds in Dorset, namely Sherborne, Yetminster, and Beaminster.

[3] Whitelock, *Anglo-Saxon Wills*, 52.

[4] *Ibid.* p. 32.

[5] *Crawford Charters*, 23.

Holcombe may be taken from them. In that case, reckoning all together, he will have been wrongfully deprived of 42 hides.

The reference here becomes clear if Bishop Æthelric's letter is taken in conjunction with a Sherborne charter (Robertson no. 74 = K. 1302) which records an agreement made between 1007 and 1012, or possibly in 1012, between the monks of Sherborne Cathedral and Edmund the Ætheling, afterwards King Edmund Ironside.[1] When the Ætheling asked the monks for permission to hold the estate at Holcombe the community did not dare to refuse him this request, ' but said that they would certainly grant it if the king and the bishop who was their superior gave their consent '. But when they had come to an agreement, and the Ætheling and the prior and the chief monks came to the king to ask for his consent, King Æthelred said that he did not wish the estate to be given away completely, but that an arrangement should be made by which the land should be restored to the holy foundation at a time agreed upon by all of them. It was then agreed that in return for a payment of 20 pounds the Ætheling should enjoy the estate for his lifetime, and that at his death it should revert to the holy foundation. The anxiety expressed by the bishop in his letter is likely to have arisen at a time before this agreement was made ; for although anxiety as to the disposition of the estate would have been natural at the time of King Edmund Ironside's death on 30 November 1016, when the estate should have reverted to Sherborne, at that date Bishop Æthelric himself was no longer alive. We may therefore conclude that Æthelric's letter was written before this agreement concerning Holcombe was made ; this was attested by Bishop Æthelric, the sender of the letter, and by other persons, including the ealdorman Æthelmær, in all probability the person to whom the letter is addressed. Brotanek calls the copy of the letter that has come down to us a ' first draft ' (Briefentwurf), a supposition for which there is no evidence one way or the other. But there can be little doubt on the grounds of general probability that the copying of the letter into the manuscript was contemporary with the letter

---

[1] Förster, *Themse*, 779, dates this agreement 1007–12, the limits being the date of the appointment of the ealdorman Eadric, a witness, as ealdorman of Mercia, namely, 1007, and the latest possible date for the death of Bishop Æthelric of Sherborne, the writer of the letter, namely 1012. It is however suggested by Brotanek (*loc. cit.*) and by A. J. Robertson that the name *Æthelsie* among the bishops attesting the charter may stand for Ælfsige II of Winchester (as it does apparently in K. 746). The first signature of Ælfsige II of Winchester in a dated charter appears in 1013 (K. 1308), but he may have been appointed in 1012. The only possible year for Æthelric of Sherborne and Ælfsige of Winchester to appear together as witnesses would be 1012, and if *Æthelsie* stands for *Ælfsige* this must be the date of the Holcombe charter.

itself, and there can be no doubt at all as to its authenticity. It is entirely free from any suspicious feature.

(63)

Bishop Æthelric complains of losses sustained by the bishopric of Sherborne in respect of lands which contributed to the ship-scot, and appeals to Æthelmær so that they may be restored. 1001/2–1009/12

(MS. Fonds latins 943, f. 170 b)

+ Æþelric ƀ gret Æþelmær freondlice. 7 ic cyþe þæt me ys 1
wana æt þam scypgesce[ote] þus micelys þe mine foregengan on
ealles folces gewitnysse æt Niw[antune hæfdon] ; an æt Bubbancumbe, 7 twa æt Awultune, .vii. æt Upcerl[e], .vi. æt Cliftun[e], æt
Hiwis[ce fif], æt Tril twa, æt Wyllon an, æt Buchæmatune .v., æt 5
Dibberwurðe þreo, æt Peder[...] þære abbuddyssan an. Þises ys ealles
wana þreo 7 þritig hida of ðam þrim hund hidun þe oðre bisceopas
ær hæfdon into hyra scy[re]. 7 gif hyt þin willa wære þu mihtest eaðe
gedon ƀ ic hyt eal swa hæfde. Git us man s[ege]ð ƀ we ne moton
þæs wurðe beon æt Holancumbe þe we hwilon ær hæfdon. Þonne 10
þolie ic þus miceles ealles 7 eall[es] þæs þe mine foregengan hæfdon,
ƀ syndon twa 7 feowertig hida.

1. ys F[örster] ; is K[emble] ; [me y]s B[rotanek].   2. scypgesceote, *see p. 483 below.*   3. folces K, F ; [fol]ces B.   3. Niw
[antune hæfdon] :: B; F :::: ; K *puts* hæfdon *after* foregengan.
4. .vi. æt Cliftun[e] F ; .v. K, B ; *but F considers that a tiny stroke almost
level with the top of the* v *is not a stop, but a trace of* i.   5. Hiwis[ce fif]
F ; Hiwisc.... K ; Hiwis[cbeorge] :: B. *Space at end of line after* Hiwis *for
only 5 or 6 letters. F supplies* fif (*or* .v.), *the number needed to make up the total
of 33 hides (see l. 7).*   6. Ped....... K ; Ped[ridun] :: B ; Ped[::::] F,
with the comment that after Ped *there is room for 4 or 5 letters. The above reading
has been kindly supplied to me by Mr. N. R. Ker.*   7. [hund] K ; [hun]d
B. F *observes : ' Das ganze Wort ist stark verblasst, aber dennoch deutlich
erkennbar.'*   8. scy[re] F ; scyre.. K ; scy[rum] B.   8. wære
þu F ; wær[e ðu] K ; wær[e þu] B.   9. F *reads* s[ege]ð, *and gives a
reference to Sievers* § 416, n. 3 (*Sievers-Cook,* Old English Grammar (*1903*),
*p. 339) for this late Old English form, with comment that there is room for
three letters ;* s[ecg]ð K ; s[æg]ð B.   10. F *observes '* wurðe beon *ist verblasst, aber deutlich lesbar '.*   11. miceles K, F ; micel[ys] B.   11. eall[es]
B, F ; ealles K.   12. feowertig K, F ; f[eow]ertig B.

Translation

Bishop Æthelric sends friendly greetings to Æthelmær. And I declare that I am no longer receiving the following amount of the ship-scot which my predecessors had by the testimony of the whole people at Newton ; one (hide) at *Bubbancumbe*, and two at Alton, seven at Up Cerne, six at Clifton, at Hewish (*or* Huish) five, at Trill two, at *Wyllon* one, at *Buchæmatune* five, at Dibberford three, at Peder[] (?) of (*or* with) the abbess one. This amounts in all to thirty-three hides which are lacking from the three hundred hides that other bishops had for their diocese. And if thou wert willing, thou couldst easily bring it about that I had it in the same way. Moreover we are told that we shall not be allowed to possess at Holcombe what we had in times past. In that case, reckoning all together, I shall be wrongfully deprived of the following amount of what my predecessors had, namely, forty-two hides.

WELLS

Besides writs of King Edward, the writs, nos. 64–72, at Wells Cathedral, all issued in favour of Bishop Giso of Wells, include writs of Queen Edith (one issued during her husband's lifetime, the other during her widowhood), and a writ of her brother King Harold II, the only one known to have survived from his short reign. The early history of St. Andrew's, Wells (now Wells Cathedral) is obscure.[1] In the eleventh century it was ruled by foreign bishops, of whom the first was Duduc (see Biographical Notes), appointed to the see in 1033 by King Cnut. His successor was Giso (see Biographical Notes), who had been a royal chaplain, and who used his influence with the king and queen to increase the endowment of his see. Returning to England from Rome after his consecration by Pope Nicholas on 15 April 1061, Giso procured from the pope a bull confirming him in the bishopric, with all its possessions.[2] The lands of the bishopric were greatly augmented by Giso, both through gifts

---

[1] Tradition attributes its foundation to King Ine of Wessex. A bishopric was first established there c. 909, on the subdivision of the diocese of Sherborne, but little is known of the internal history of the diocese or of the cathedral church. See J. Armitage Robinson, *The Saxon Bishops of Wells* (British Academy, Supplemental Papers, iv, 1918), and VCH *Somerset*, ii. 5 ff.

[2] Wells Cathedral Charters no. 2, Holtzmann, *Papsturkunden*, ii, pp. 131 f., no. 1. On the ancient endowment of the see of Wells see Armitage Robinson, *ut supra*, 52 ff. ; but the (probably spurious) charter (K. 816) cited by him as showing the extent of the property of the see bears the name of King Edward and not (as he states) of King William.

and by purchase, so that by 1086 the ' terra Gisonis ' amounted to 280 hides.[1] Giso's own account of his activities as bishop of Wells is preserved in an autobiographical fragment inserted in the *Historiola de Primordiis Episcopatus Somersetensis*.[2] On his arrival at Wells, his cathedral church appeared small to him, and it was served by only four or five *clerici* who lived in their own houses without a cloister or refectory. The bishop took measures to relieve the poverty of the community by applying to the king, who gave him land at Wedmore for the increase and support of the brethren ; to this Queen Edith, after her husband's death, added Mark and Mudgley, both members of Wedmore (see nos. 68 and 72). The estate at Winsham in Somerset which had been granted out for a term of years by one of his predecessors but for which no service had been paid, he vainly endeavoured to recover, first by an appeal to the shire court, and then by sentence of excommunication against the offender.[3] Remonstrances with Earl Harold for having seized what Giso regarded as the property of the church were fruitless, for although the earl on succeeding to the throne promised to restore what he had taken away, he died before he could carry out his promises. Some estates Giso purchased, among them Combe (see p. 274) and Litton (no. 69). Another was granted him by Abbot Æthelnoth of Glastonbury, but he was unable to retain it. Having obtained revenues for their support Giso increased the number of the canons at Wells and brought them under stricter discipline. He induced them to adopt a communal life of canonical obedience, and provided them with a cloister, refectory and dormitory. All this he tells us in the autobiographical fragment referred to above, and he concludes his preamble with an appeal to his successors to increase the properties of the church and not to allow the possessions that he had set aside for the use of the canons to be transferred to other purposes. His intention was to treat of all the lands belonging to the see, in order that it might be known ' what belongs peculiarly to the use of the canons and what to the demesne and disposal of the bishop ', so that, in the future, neither should encroach upon the rights of the other ; but this part of his narrative is now no longer extant. The determination of Giso to retain all the rights that his predecessors had had, and to defend his lands from spoliation, while increasing their extent wherever possible, is reflected in the writs printed here.

[1] VCH *Somerset*, ii. 10.

[2] This text, compiled in the twelfth century, was edited and translated by Joseph Hunter, *Ecclesiastical Documents*, Camden Society, 1840.

[3] This estate was granted him by King William at a later date (Davis, *Regesta*, no. 160).

THE TEXTS OF WELLS WRITS

The registers of the Dean and Chapter of Wells, the source of the Wells writs, have been described and calendared in the *Calendar of the MSS. of the Dean and Chapter of Wells*, Hist. MSS. Comm. 2 vols. 1907–14. The relevant details for the texts are given below under the heading ' Authorities ', before the notes. The texts of all the Wells writs have undergone considerable scribal alteration in transmission. Taking no. 64 as typical, the text exhibits a mixture of old and new. Some words retain their Anglo-Saxon forms, e.g. *cyðe eow, gebyrað, binnan porte 7 butan, þ man hit ofgo* ; others have been given a later spelling : *erl, schyrereuen, peynes,* and terminations have been reduced : *finde* for *findan. Vram* is a form from the local south-western dialect of Middle English. But there is nothing here to prevent one from regarding this and the other Wells texts in the Liber Albus I (our source for all these texts except no. 67) as (partially modernised) copies of authentic writs of King Edward. No. 67, which has come down to us from another source, the Liber Fuscus, has been badly copied, but it could not be rejected as spurious on linguistic grounds : its form *suppen* could be explained as a garbled form of *gepafian.* The grounds for its rejection lie in a significant omission (see p. 273).

KING EDWARD'S WRITS

There can be no hesitation in accepting as modernised copies of authentic writs nos. 64, 65, both announcing GISO'S APPOINTMENT AS BISHOP. A remarkable feature of no. 64 is its close resemblance to no. 50 (see p. 229), a writ extant only in Latin announcing Walter's appointment as bishop of Hereford. Walter and Giso— both foreigners, and (before they were both raised to the episcopate in 1060) in attendance on the king and queen, Walter as the queen's priest, and Giso as a priest of her husband—journeyed together to Rome and were both consecrated by Pope Nicholas II on 15 April 1061 ; the two writs belong to the same period. The precept in Giso's writ (but not in Walter's) enjoining that the persons addressed in the writ shall help the bishop to further the rights of the church, and the similar precept in no. 65, the writ issued after Giso's consecration, and in no. 71, the writ secured by him from Harold, may reflect particular difficulties in the diocese of Wells, and Giso's fear lest he should be deprived of rights that were his due.

The authenticity of no. 66, the writ declaring that Giso is to discharge the obligations on his land at CHEW at the same rate as his predecessor had done, is rendered even more certain by its resemblance to no. 29, a Christ Church writ of Cnut in similar terms ; reference may also be made to the less certainly authentic no. 107, of Æthelred II. No. 67 on the other hand is probably spurious. What it lacks is a defining and limiting clause indicating the territorial area to which the bishop's obligations relate : *his land æt Chyw*, no. 66, *his landare into his bisceoprice*, no. 29. No. 67 was at all events not recognised as a separate writ by the compiler of the Liber Albus in the thirteenth century, and the earliest known copy is of the fourteenth. It is difficult to escape the conclusion that it came into existence as a copy of the text now represented by no. 66, and that the feature in which it differs from no. 66 arose from deliberate omission of the words *æt Chyw*.

The two remaining writs of Edward for Giso, nos. 68, 69, relate to individual estates. It seems fitting that land at WEDMORE should be granted to Giso for the canons of Wells ' for my soul, and for my father's soul, and for the souls of all my ancestors who established the episcopal see ' ; for Wedmore formed part of the ancient royal demesne, having been bequeathed by King Alfred to his son King Edward the Elder.[1] This, the first gift of the Confessor to Giso for the canons of his cathedral, was made at the bishop's own request, with the ' assistance and suggestion ' of Queen Edith, who subsequently, after her husband's death, ' increased the gift with faithful benevolence by giving the part of the said lands belonging to herself, called by the inhabitants Mark and Mudgley '.[2] According to the terms of the Wedmore writ the land was to be assigned to the maintenance of the canons (*inne to his clerken bileua*), to which the autobiographical fragment in the *Historiola* adds : ' to the increase and support of the brethren ' (*in augmentum et sustentationem fratrum ibidem Deo servientium*). But in 1086 the manor was in Giso's own hands, as it had been in King Edward's time (see p. 489). This and other evidence suggests that Giso made a redistribution of the Wells manors, as between the bishop and the canons. Litton, for instance, which according to Edward's writ, no. 69, had been intended for the purposes of the bishopric of Wells, was held in 1086 by the canons (see p. 490) and is included in Giso's narrative in the *Historiola* among the estates which he assigned to the increase of the number of the canons and their support. Only one passage in the Wedmore writ (no. 68) presents any difficulty. No parallel has been found elsewhere for the passage : ' with all the offences that shall fall to me or to my successors in all things for my soul etc.' ; but in a writ announcing a grant of ancestral land for the souls of the king and his ancestors it does not seem inappropriate that he should

---

[1] See Harmer, *English Historical Documents*, no. 11 = K. 314.

[2] *Historiola*, 17 ; cf. no. 72.

also look forward to his successors and grant to the canons of Wells Cathedral the forfeitures which shall accrue to himself and to them. An argument in favour of the authenticity of the passage is the fact that it does not appear in the (later) Latin version—it may not have been understood. The authenticity of the clause in this writ directing Giso to draw up a *privilegium* for this gift, in almost the same terms as a similar precept in the Taynton writ, no. 55, can scarcely be in doubt. Nor need one hesitate to accept as authentic the penal clause, since a grant made with a religious motive is likely to be protected by an anathema (see Introduction, p. 69). Everything encourages the belief that the Wedmore writ is a modernised copy of an authentic writ of Edward the Confessor.

The LITTON writ, no. 69, which records the sale of land at Litton by one Alfred to Bishop Giso in the presence of the king and queen and many other persons, is free from suspicious features. For the mention of the presence of witnesses at a purchase of land a parallel is to be found in the Anglo-Saxon charter recording Giso's purchase for his see of land at Combe (St. Nicholas) from a certain Ætsere, agreed upon in the presence of Queen Edith and her retinue ' on the upper floor in the stone church at Wilton ' on Ember Wednesday in Lent 1072 [1] ; for the mention of witnesses in writs see Introduction, p. 73. There is no reason for doubting that no. 69 is a modernised copy of an authentic writ of King Edward.

WRITS OF QUEEN EDITH AND KING HAROLD

The authenticity of the two writs in the name of Queen Edith (nos. 70, 72) is also reasonably certain ; their structure and content are unexceptionable. The transfer to Giso of the manor of Milverton, the subject of the first of these two writs (no. 70), did in fact take place, for the Somerset Domesday records that the bishop held a manor here in King Edward's time ; but at some period it passed out of Giso's hands, and it was held in 1086 by King William (see p. 490). It may well be that the manor was only leased to Giso for a term of years and not granted to him outright, for the writ speaks of ' the terms that we have agreed upon ' ; what these were is not known. The other writ of Queen Edith, announcing her grant of land at Mark (see p. 491), is of special interest as the only Anglo-Saxon writ addressed to the hundred court (at Wedmore, to which Mark belonged). Nothing is known of Wudumann con-

---

[1] Text in *Som. Arch. and Nat. Hist. Soc. Proc.* xxii (1876), 106 ; calendared, *Cal. of the MSS. of the Dean and Chapter of Wells*, i. 434. Not printed by Kemble or by Miss Robertson.

cerning whose withholding of the rent due to her, the queen prays the hundred court to pronounce a just judgement.

There seems no reason for doubting the authenticity of no. 71, King Harold's writ for Giso. Its moderation is in its favour : there is nothing here which is not to be found in King Edward's writs for Giso, except that to the sake and soke of nos. 64, 65 are added the frequently-granted toll, team and infangenetheof. It is difficult to see what purpose could have been served by a fabrication of a writ of Harold in these terms, and it can readily be imagined that Giso would have been the more anxious to obtain from the new king a confirmation of his rights because he regarded Harold as one of the chief despoilers of his see. In the narrative in the *Historiola* (p. 16) Giso declares himself to have been deprived by Harold, when earl of Wessex, of two estates, Banwell and Congresbury. He also accuses Harold of having appropriated priestly vestments, relics, altar vessels, many books, and other possessions which (like Banwell and Congresbury) had been bequeathed or given to the see by his predecessor Bishop Duduc.

Giso's narrative (which in later times was transformed into a highly-coloured story of the banishment of Giso, brought about by Harold) was analysed by J. R. Green.[1] With a view to clearing Harold of the charge of sacrilege, Green and Freeman argue that what Harold is accused by Giso of having seized had never formed any part of the property of the see of Wells, that Harold had merely hindered the carrying out of Duduc's bequests, and that what lay between the bishop and the earl was simply a disputed claim to lands and goods. In any event, Giso, so he tells us in the fragment in the *Historiola*, did not give up his claim, but remonstrated with Harold, and even contemplated excommunicating him. But after he became king, Harold, he says, not only promised to restore what he had taken, but also to make ampler gifts. His intention was frustrated by his death, which appeared to the Lotharingian Giso in the light of divine vengeance (*præoccupante autem illum judicio divinæ ultionis*). Some support for Giso's claim to Banwell and to Congresbury is to be found in the fact that both estates are associated with the see of Wells at a later date. Congresbury passed after the death of Harold into the hands of King William, Bishop Giso and some other persons holding portions of the manor of him in 1086 (DB i. 87), and it remained with the Crown until it was granted to the see of Wells by King John.[2] Banwell (held like Congresbury by

[1] J. R. Green, ' Earl Harold and Bishop Giso ', *Som. Arch. and Nat. Hist. Soc. Proc.* xii (1863–64), 148 ff. (with comments on, and Mod. Eng. renderings of, some of the Wells writs printed here), and (following Green), Freeman, ii, note QQ.   [2] *Cal. of the MSS. of the D. and C. of Wells*, i. 147.

Earl Harold on the day of King Edward's death) appears in the possession of Bishop Giso in Domesday (DB i. 89 b), and remained subsequently with the bishopric of Wells. According to a Latin charter attributed to King William the king restores (the verb employed is *restituo*) to the episcopal see of Wells, at the petition of Bishop Giso, for the increase of the dignity of the church, and for the maintenance of the brethren of the church of Wells, 30 hides at Banwell which Bishop Duduc had given to God for his soul, and which King Harold had appropriated[1] ; but if this charter is authentic, it is singular, as Freeman remarked, that Giso in his narrative should say nothing of the grant. The writ of Harold for Giso (no. 71) seems to show (as Freeman observed) either that Harold was unconscious of wrong, or that, if he was conscious of wrong, he was anxious to make amends. There may be some significance in the fact that this is the only writ that has come down to us from Harold's short reign. Perhaps Freeman was right in his suggestion that, at a time when it was to his interest to be conciliatory to all, Harold was particularly anxious to conciliate Giso by a general confirmation of his privileges, and that ' those further gifts would have followed of which Giso speaks if the king's life had not been cut short '. There seems no reason for doubting that this writ is a modernised copy of an authentic writ of King Harold.

The inclusion in the register of Latin versions for the first four writs seems indeed to have been an afterthought, for the English texts follow each other uninterruptedly, the Latin versions coming later, each with a corresponding reference mark. Each of the four writs entered on a later page is however immediately followed by a Latin version. Mistranslations and omissions in the Latin versions indicate that they are not contemporary with the texts in the vernacular : e.g. in no. 68, ' quod episcopus isto *gaudeat* priuilegio ' is a mistranslation of ' þæt se biscop *dichte* (*draw up*) priuilegium '. In nos. 70, 72, matter which would have been of no importance at a later period has been omitted. The rendering *ballivi*[2] found in these Latin versions as an equivalent to ' thegns ',

---

[1] The text of this charter is printed, and its authenticity discussed by Freeman in 'The Banwell Charters', by F. H. Dickinson, *Som. Arch. and Nat. Hist. Soc. Proc.* xxiii (1877), 49 ff. ; see also C. S. Taylor, ' Banwell ', *ibid.* li (1905), 45–50 ; Davis, *Regesta*, no. 23. Davis, following Freeman, argues for 1068 as the date of the charter. For the text see also Earle, *Land-Charters*, pp. 431 ff.

[2] For the functions in the thirteenth century of the *ballivus*, ' bailiff ', sometimes the officer in charge, under the sheriff, of a hundred, or in charge of the administration of a liberty, a borough, or the like, sometimes the officer who on the instructions of the sheriff conveyed and executed writs, levied distresses, collected dues, and so on, see H. M. Cam, *The Hundred and the Hundred Rolls* (London, 1930), *passim*.

helps to date these Latin versions. Dr. H. M. Cam has observed
to me that *ballivus* indicates the idea of official, as against the idea
of social, status (a stage which '·thegn ' had seemingly reached by
1086) and that the use of this term suggests that the translation was
made by the thirteenth-century compiler of the Liber Albus I.   It
would seem that he was ignorant of the meaning of ' thegn ', and
therefore used the term *ballivus*, a natural rendering in the thirteenth
century.   If he had met the term *minister* as a rendering of ' thegn '
(as, for instance, in nos. 46, 49, 50 etc.) he might have taken this to
be the equivalent of *ballivus*, where an earlier translator might have
used *fideles, barones,* or one of the other renderings to be found in the
Latin versions of other writs printed here.

(64)

King Edward declares that he has granted to his priest Giso the
bishopric at Wells and everything pertaining thereto, with sake and
with soke, as fully and completely as ever it was held by Bishop
Duduc or any bishop before him.   1060–61

(Liber Albus I, f. 14)

Eadward king gret Harold erl. 7 Aylnoð abbot. 7 Godwine 1
schyrereuen 7 alle mine þeynes on Sum*er*seten frendliche.   And
ich cyðe eow þa[t] ich habb*e* geunnan Gisan minan p*r*esteo þes
bissopriche her mid eow. and alre þare þinge. þas þe þær mid
richte to gebyrað. on wode and on felde. mid saca. 7 mid sokna. 5
binnan porte. 7 butan. swo ful 7 swo forth swo Duduc' bissop o*þer*
any bissop hit formest him toforen hauede on ælle*n* þingan.   And
gif her ani lond sy out of þan bissopriche gedon. ich wille ꝥ hit cume
in ongeæn. other ꝥ man hit ofgo. on hise gemod*e* swo man with
him hit finde mage.   And ich bidde eou allen þat ge him fulstan to 10
driuan Godes gerichte lock huer hyt neod sy. and heo eowwer
fultumes biþurfe.   And ich nelle nanne man geþefien. þat him vram
honde teo anige þare þinge. þas þe ich him unnen habben.

Latin Version

(*Ibid.* f. 14 b)

Edwardus rex Haroldo comiti, Ailnodo abbati, Godwino vicecomiti 7 omnibus balliuis suis Sumerset' salutem.   Sciatis nos 15
dedisse Gisoni presbytero nostro episcopatum hunc apud uos cum
omnibus pertinentiis in bosco 7 plano 7 saca 7 socna in uillis 7 extra,
ita plene 7 libere in omnibus sicut episcopus Dudocus aut aliqui

predecessorum suorum habuerunt. Et si quid inde contra iusticiam
20 fuerit sublatum, uolumus quod reuocetur uel quod aliter ei satisfiat.
Rogamus etiam uos ut auxiliari eidem uelitis ad Christianitatem
sustinendam si necesse habuerit. Nolumus autem ut 'ullus'
hominum ei auferat aliquid eorum que ei contulimus. Valete.

3. geunnan] geumnan. 9. gemoð MS., *stroke through* d *denoting*
abbreviation. Hickes (wrongly) in footnote : ' Sax. gemot '. 10. MS
possibly hit, *but if* bit, *must be emended to* hit. 12. *For* geþafian.
Heading to Latin version : De donacione episcopatus Well' facta Gisoni
episcopo per Regem Edwardum. 20. satisfiat MS. ; satisfaciat
Hickes and the rest.

Translation

King Edward sends friendly greetings to Earl Harold and Abbot
Æthelnoth and Godwine the sheriff and all my thegns in Somerset.
And I inform you that I have granted to Giso, my priest, the
bishopric here with you, and all the things that lawfully pertain
thereto, in woodland and in open country, with sake and with soke,
within town and without, as fully and as completely as ever
Bishop Duduc or any bishop had it before him, in all things. And
if any land here has been taken away from the bishopric, it is my
will that it be restored or that it be held on such conditions as may
be agreeable to him, according to such arrangements with him as
can be devised. And I pray you all that you will help him to
further the rights of the church wherever it may be needful and
he may require your aid. And I will not permit anyone to take
away from him any of the things which I have granted him.

(65)

King Edward declares that Bishop Giso is to have the bishopric
at Wells and everything lawfully belonging thereto as fully and
completely as any of his predecessors. 1061–66, probably 1061

(Liber Albus I, f. 14)

1   Edward king gret Harold erl. 7 Aylnod abbot. 7 Godwine. 7 ealle
mine þeynes on Sumerseten frendliche. Ich queþe eou þ ich wille
þ Gyse bissop beo þisses bissopriches wrthe heer inne mid eou.
and alch þare þinge. þas þe þar mid richte to gebyrað binnan porte
5 7 butan. mid saca. 7 mid socna. swo uol 7 swo vorð swo hit eni
bissop him touoren formest hauede on ealle þing. And ich bidde
eou alle þat ge him beon on fultome Cristendom to spekene loc whar
hit þarf sy. 7 eower fultumes beþurfe eal swo ich getrowwen to eow

habben þat ge him on fultume beon willen.   And gif what sy mid
unlage out of þan bissopriche geydon. sy hit on londe oþer an oðð*er* 10
þinge þat fulstan him vor minan luuen þ̄ hit in ongeyn cume swo swo
ge for Gode witen þat hit richt sy.   God eu ealle gehealde.

Latin Version

(*Ibid.*)

Edwardus rex Haroldo comiti, Ailnodo abbati, Godwino 7 omnibus
balliuis suis Sumerset' salutem.   Significamus uobis nos uelle quod
episcopus Giso episcopatum apud uos possideat cum omnibus dictum 15
episcopatum in uillis 7 extra de iure contingentibus, cum saca 7
socna adeo plene 7 libere per omnia sicut ullus episcoporum predecessorum suorum unquam habebat.   Rogamus etiam uos ut coadiutores ipsius esse uelitis ad fidem predicandam 7 Christiani͘t'atem
sustinendam pro loco et tempore sicut de uobis fideliter confidimus 20
uos uelle id ipsum.   Et si quid de dicto episcopatu siue in terris siue
in aliis rebus contra iusticiam fuerit sublatum, adiuuetis eum pro
amore nostro ad restitutionem prout iustum fuerit habendam.
Conseruet uos Dominus.

Heading : Hec quattuor carte in anglico infra sunt translata in latinum ubi
similia signa inveniuntur.   *Heading to Latin version at foot of page with
corresponding reference marks :* Concessio Edwardi Regis facta Gisoni episcopo
de episcopatu Well.   1. erl] erld MS.   2. queþe ('*say*') *must go
back ultimately to the customary* cyþe.   *Interlined in later hand :* significo.
In margin : queth, significo.   4. þas þe þar] þe þas þar MS.   7. to
spekene] te spekene MS.   8. to eow] tho eow MS.   *The* quattuor carte
of the heading include no. 64.

Translation

King Edward sends friendly greetings to Earl Harold and Abbot
Æthelnoth and Godwine and all my thegns in Somerset.   I inform
you that my will is that Bishop Giso shall legally possess this
bishopric in this place with you, and all the things that lawfully
pertain thereto within town and without, with sake and with soke,
as fully and as completely as ever any bishop had it before him in
all things.   And I pray you all that you will help him to declare
the rights of the bishop wherever it may be needful and he may
require your aid, even as I have confidence in you that you will be
willing to help him.   And if anything has been taken illegally away
from the bishopric, whether it be in land or in other things, that
[you] will help him, for love of me, that it may be restored, as you
know, before God, is right.   God keep you all.

(66)

King Edward declares that Bishop Giso is to discharge the obligations on his land at Chew now at the same rate as his predecessor had done. 1061–66

(Liber Albus i, f. 17 b)

1   Edward king gret Harold [erl]. 7 Ægelnoð aƀƀd. 7 Godwyne scyregerefan. 7 alle mine þegenas on Sumerseten freondliche. 7 ic cyðe eow ꝥ ic wylle ꝥ Giso ƀp. weryge nu his land æt Chyw æl swo hys foregenga ætforen hym ær dyde. 7 ic nelle geþafian þat man hym 5 anige unlage beode.

Latin Version

(*Ibid.* f. 18)

Eadwardus rex Haroldo comiti, Aelnodo abbati, Godwino uice-comiti 7 omnibus balliuis suis Sumerset' salutem.   Sciatis me uelle quod Gyso episcopus possideat terram suam apud Chyw sicut fecerunt predecessores sui.   Nec autem inpune feram quod aliquis 10 ei iniuriam inferat aut molestiam.

1. king] ging MS.

Translation

King Edward sends friendly greetings to Earl Harold and Abbot Æthelnoth and Godwine the sheriff and all my thegns in Somerset. And I inform you that my will is that Bishop Giso shall discharge the obligations on his land at Chew now at the same rate as his predecessor did before him.   And I will not permit that any wrong be done to him.

(67)

King Edward declares that Bishop Giso is to discharge the obligations on his land now at the same rate as his predecessor had done.

(Liber Fuscus, f. 14)

1   Edward kynge gret Harold eorl 7 Egelnold abbod 7 Godwyne scherreue 7 alle mynes þoegenes on Somerset' froendlych 7 ich cuþe hou þᵗ ich wolle þat Gyso bisschop werie now his lond also his

forgenge aforen hym er dude.   'And' ich nelle suþþen þat man hym
eny unlawe boede.   5

In margin in same hand : Carta Regis Edwardi concessa Gisoni Episcopo
quod adeo libere teneat omnes terras suas prout etc.   3. how R ; *but*
cf. no. 66, eow.   4. suþþen MS. ; *but cf. no. 66,* geþafian.

Translation

King Edward sends friendly greetings to Earl Harold and Abbot
Æthelnoth and Godwine the sheriff and all my thegns in Somerset.
And I inform you that my will is that Bishop Giso shall discharge
the obligations on his land now at the same rate as his predecessor
did before him.   And I will not permit that any wrong be done
to him.

(68)

King Edward declares that he has given to Bishop Giso for the
maintenance of his canons at St. Andrew's, Wells, the land at
Wedmore and everything belonging thereto with sake and with
soke, as fully and completely as he himself possessed it ; and the
bishop is to draw up a *privilegium* concerning this.   1061–66

(Liber Albus I, f. 17 b)

Edward king gret Harold erl. 7 Ailnod abbot. 7 Touid schirereue. 1
7 alle mine þeines on Sumerseten frendliche.   And ich kyðe eow ꝥ ich
habbe gegefen Gyso ꝺpe þæt land æt Weodmor 7 ælch þære þinga
þæs þe þær inne mid richte to hyreð. inne to his clerken bileua æt
Sc̄e Andrea æt Wyllan. mid saca 7 mid socna swo full 7 swo forð 5
swo hit me sylfen on honde stod. mid eallon þam forwyrhtan þe me
oþer minon æftergengan to honda begon wyllen on eallen þingan for
mine sawle. 7 for mines fader. 7 for allra minna yldrena sawlan.
þe þone ꝺpstol gestaðelodon.   And gyf anig man syg þat mine
gyfe awendan wyllen. awende hine God almihgti fram his ansyne 10
7 fram ælre cristenne manna.   7 ich wylle ꝥ se ꝺ. dichte priuilegium
þær to bi minon fullan gelifan.

Latin Version

(*Ibid.*)

Edwardus rex Haroldo comiti, Ealnodo abbati, 7 omnibus
balliuis suis Sumerset' salutem.   Sciatis me dedisse Gysoni episcopo
ad sustentationem cleri ecclesie beati Andree in Well' terram de 15
Wedmor' cum omnibus pertinentiis suis, adeo plene 7 libere sicut

unquam plenius mihi ipsi manustetit, aut alicui predecessorum
meorum per omnia, pro anima patris mei 7 animabus antecessorum
meorum qui dictam sedem episcopi statuerunt. Si quis autem hanc
20 meam donationem presumpserit euertere, auertat eum Dominus
a conspectu suo, 7 a conspectu omnium fidelium. Volo etiam quod
idem episcopus isto gaudeat priuilegio, 7 uos amici mei ipsius sitis
coadiutores.

Interlined in later hand over relevant words : saluto . . . balliuis . . . et
ego etc.   2. kyðe] kyde MS.   4. hyreð] hyred MS ; *Hickes and
the rest (wrongly)* byreð.   5. forð] ford MS.   7. *Above* bogen,
in slightly later hand, begon.   11. dichte] ðichte MS.   13. MS.
omits Touid vicecomiti.

Translation

King Edward sends friendly greetings to Earl Harold and Abbot
Æthelnoth and Tofig the sheriff and all my thegns in Somerset.
And I inform you that I have given to Bishop Giso the land at
Wedmore and everything that lawfully belongs thereto, for the
sustenance of his clerks at St. Andrew's at Wells, with sake and
with soke as fully and as completely as I myself possessed it, with
all the offences that shall fall to me or to my successors in all
things, for my soul and for my father's soul, and for the souls of
all my ancestors who established the episcopal see. And if there
be anyone who shall wish to alter my gift, may God Almighty
remove him from his sight and from that of all Christian men.
And my will is that the bishop draw up a *privilegium* concerning
this, with my full permission.

(69)

King Edward declares that Alfred has sold to Bishop Giso his land
at Litton ; and declares that the bishop is now to have the land for
his bishopric and everything belonging thereto, with sake and with
soke, as fully and completely as any bishop ever had it. 1061–66

(Liber Albus I, f. 14)

1   Edward king gret Harold erl. 7 Touid minne schyrerefen 7 alle
mine þeynes inne Sumersæten frendliche. And ich keþe eu þat
Ælfred hauet yseld Gise bissop his land æt Hlytton'. sacleas and
clane toforan me siluen æt Peddredan. on mine iwetnesse 7 on
5 Eadithe mine ibedden. 7 on Haroldes ærles. 7 on manegra oþra
manna þe mid me þar waren. Nu wil ich þat se bissop beo þas
londes worthe into his bissopriche þe he under honde hauet. and alch
þare þinge þæs þe þær to mid richte gebyrað. mid saca 7 mid socna.

swo ful 7 so furth. swo hit ænige bissoppe formest on honde stod on
ællen þingan. And gyf þar sy anni þing. out gedon þas þe þar into 10
hyrð. ich beode þat man 'hit lete' in ongean comen. ϸ non oþer ne sy.

Latin Version
(*Ibid.*, 14 b)

Edwardus rex Haroldo comiti, Touid vicecomiti 7 omnibus
balliuis suis Sumerset' salutem. Sciatis quod Aluredus vendidit
Gisoni episcopo terram suam de Lutton' pacifice 7 quiete, teste me
ipso coram nobis apud Perret, 7 testibus Edith' coniuge nostra, 15
Haroldo comite, 7 multis aliis qui una nobiscum illic aderant.
Volumus igitur quod idem episcopus terram illam cum omnibus
pertinentiis habeat cum episcopatu quem possidet 7 saca 7 socna
ita plene sicut unquam aliquis episcoporum predecessorum suorum
in omnibus habuit. Et si quid inde contra iusticiam fuerit sublatum, 20
rogamus ut reuertetur, nec aliter fiat.

Interlined above relevant words in modern hand : notifico vobis quod . . .
5. B *and Hickes's shorter copy ends at* ærles.   9. furth] furht MS.
Heading of Latin version : Testimonium Regis Edwardi de terra vendita
Gisoni episcopo.   17. *In MS* igitur *is represented by* g *with* i *above* ;
Hickes *and the rest* quoque.

Translation

King Edward sends friendly greetings to Earl Harold and Tofig
my sheriff and all my thegns in Somerset. And I inform you that
Alfred has sold to Bishop Giso his land at Litton, with undisputed
title and free from obligations, in my presence at Perrott, with my
cognisance, and with that of Edith, my consort, and of Earl Harold,
and of many other persons who were there with me. Now it is my
will that the bishop shall legally possess the land for the bishopric
that he rules over, and everything that lawfully pertains thereto,
with sake and with soke, as fully and as completely as ever any
bishop held it in all things. And if any thing there has been
alienated that belongs to it, I command that it be caused to be
restored, that the transaction may be complete.

(70)

Queen Edith declares that Bishop Giso is to have the land at
Milverton as fully and completely as she herself possessed it.
1061-66

(Liber Albus I, f. 18)

Eadgyð se hlauedige gret Harold erl mine broðar. 7 Touid 7 ealle   1
ure þeyena on Sumerseatan. freondliche. 7 ic cyðe eow ϸ ic wylle

U

ꝥ Gyso .ᛒ. beo þaes londes wurðe æt Milferton'. swo full 7 swo forð. swo hit me selfen æn honde stod. to þan forewarden þæt weo
5 geworht habbað. 7 gyf þær hwa ænig land habbe hut biridan oððe geboht of þan þe þar mid richte into gehyrað. ic wylle þat man hyt læte in ongean cuman. 7 spece se mann wið þone mann þe him ær land sealde.

Latin Version

(Ibid.)

Eaditha domina Haroldo comiti fratri suo 7 Toui 7 omnibus
10 balliuis Sumerset' salutem. Sciatis me uelle quod Gyso episcopus habeat terram de Miluertone ita plene 7 libere sicut mihi plenius manustetit. Si qua autem terra ipsam iure contingens sublata uel quoquo modo distracta fuerit, uolo quod reuocetur.

3. B *ends at* forð.   6. into] inte MS.   6. gehyrað] -ad MS.
13. fuerint MS. *with deletion marks under* n.

Translation

The Lady Edith sends friendly greetings to Earl Harold my brother and Tofig and all our thegns in Somerset. And I inform you that my will is that Bishop Giso be entitled to the land at Milverton as fully and completely as I myself possessed it, on the terms that we have agreed upon. And if anyone there has seized or bought any of the land that lawfully belongs to this estate, my will is that it be caused to be restored ; and the man (aggrieved by this) is to speak with the man who gave him the land (of which he is now to be deprived).

(71)

King Harold declares that Bishop Giso is to have judicial and financial rights as fully and as completely as ever he did in King Edward's time.   6 January 1066–14 October 1066

(Liber Albus I, f. 14)

1   Harold king greet Ayllnoð abbot. 7 Touid 7 alle mine þeynes on Sumerseten frendliche.   And ich cweð eou ꝥ ich wille ꝥ Gyso .ᛒ. beo his saca werð. 7 his socna ofer his lond. 7 ouer his mannen. 7 tolles werð. 7 temes. 7 infangenes þefes, binnan burekh. 7 butan. swo ful.
5 7 swo forth. swo he furmest was on Edward' kinges dage. on alle þingan.   And ich bidde eou alle ꝥ ge bien hym on fultume at þys cristendome. Godes yerichtten for to setten 7 to driuen. loc war hym

ned sy. 7 heo eowres fultumes bithurfe. swo swo ich yetruwan to ew
habbe þ ye wyllan for mina luuen. And ich nelle yeþefien þ man
him æt anie þingan anye unlag' beode.   10

Latin Version

(*Ibid.*, 14 b)

Haroldus rex Ailnodo abbati, Toui 7 omnibus balliuis suis
Sumerset' salutem. Sciatis nos uelle quod episcopus Gyso habeat
saca 7 socna de terris suis 7 hominibus 7 toll 7 team 7 infangenethef
in villis 7 extra, ita plene 7 libere in omnibus sicut unquam habuit
tempore regis Edwardi. Rogamus etiam uos quatinus eidem si 15
necesse fuerit auxiliari uelitis ad Christianitatem sustinendam, sicut
de uobis confidimus id ipsum uelle. Nolumus autem ut ullus
hominum ei in aliquo inferat iniuriam. Valete.

2. *On* cweð *see no. 65.*   8. ned] noð MS.   10. beode] beoðe
MS.   10. *Hickes and the rest add* God eow gehealde, not in MS.   *Heading
to Latin version :* Confirmatio Haraldi Regis de libertatibus episcopatus Well.

Translation

King Harold sends friendly greetings to Abbot Æthelnoth and
Tofig and all my thegns in Somerset. And I inform you that my
will is that Bishop Giso shall be entitled to his sake and his soke
over his lands and over his men, and to toll and team and infangenetheof, within borough and without, as fully and as completely
as ever he was in King Edward's time in all things. And I pray
you all that you will help him with regard to these rights of
the bishop in order to establish and vigorously to promote the
rights of the church wherever it may be needful for him and he
may require your aid—even as I have confidence in you that you
will be willing to do for love of me. And I will not permit that
any wrong be done to him in any matter.

(72)

Queen Edith declares that she has given to Bishop Giso for his
canons at St. Andrew's, Wells, the land at Mark and everything
belonging thereto, with sake and with soke, as fully and completely
as she herself possessed it.   6 January 1066–19 December 1075

(Liber Albus I, f. 17 b)

Eadgyþ seo hlauedi Eadwardes kynges lefe gret al þat hundred at 1
Wedmore frendliche.   And ich cyþe eow þat ic habbe gegefen Gyso
.ƀ. þat land at Merkerun. 7 alch þare þinga þæs þe þar mid richte

to hireð. into his canonican æt Sce Andrea æt Wyllan mid saca 7 mid
5 socna swo full 7 swo forð swo hit me sylfen on honde stod. for
Eadwardes kynges sawle. 7 for mine sawle. And ic bidde eow þat
ge deme me richtne dom of Wudemann þe ic min hors bitachte 7 mi
gauel haueð ofhealden six gear eiðer ge hunig 7 eac feoch. God ew
gehealde.

Latin Version

(Ibid.)

10 Editha domina regis Edwardi relicta hundredo de Wedmore
salutem. Sciatis me dedisse Gisoni episcopo ad sustentationem
canonicorum ecclesie Sancti Andree in Well' terram de Merke cum
omnibus ipsam iure contingentibus cum soke 7 sake, ita plene 7
libere sicut mihi plenius manustetit pro anima regis Edwardi 7
15 anima mea.

8. haueð] haued MS. 8. Hickes and the rest add after feoch, and eac
feoth, not in MS.

Translation

The Lady Edith, relict of King Edward, sends friendly greetings
to all the hundred at Wedmore. And I inform you that I have
given to Bishop Giso the land at Mark and everything that lawfully
belongs thereto for his canons at St. Andrew's at Wells with sake
and with soke as fully and completely as I myself possessed it, for
the soul of King Edward and for my soul. And I pray you that you
will pronounce for me a just judgement concerning Wudumann to
whom I entrusted my horse(s) and who has for six years withheld
my rent—both honey and money also. God keep you.

WESTMINSTER

The thirty-four writs of the abbey of St. Peter at Westminster
(Westminster Abbey) record grants by King Edward the Confessor,
or confirmations by him of the grants of other persons, to the abbey
with which his name is inseparably connected, and in which his
shrine is still to be seen. Outside the walls of London, to the west,
on what was then an island, at one time called Thorney from the
dense thickets with which it was once covered, there stood a
monastery, the foundation of which came later to be assigned by

tradition to the seventh century.[1] Among its benefactors was accounted Offa, king of Mercia, to whom was attributed a grant in A.D. 785 of 10 *cassates* of land at Aldenham in Hertfordshire (see p. 501). The monastery is supposed to have been re-founded by King Edgar and Archbishop Dunstan, and in 998, at a period in its history of which little is known, bequests were made to it by a certain Leofwine ;[2] but the so-called Telligraphus of King Æthelred II[3] confirming grants to the abbey is not authentic. In 1040 King Harold Harefoot was buried there (*Chron.* E, F), his body being subsequently taken up. The monastery was restored by King Edward the Confessor, who greatly increased its endowment, and built for the monks a new church which was consecrated on 28 December 1065. A very brief account of the restoration of the monastery is given in what appears to be the most ancient of the existing lives of the Confessor, the *Vita Æduuardi Regis qui apud Westmonasterium requiescit*.[4] Here we are merely told (p. 417) that King Edward determined, because of his special devotion to St. Peter, to restore the monastery dedicated to that apostle which stood outside the walls of London (' parvo quidem opere et numero, paucioribus ibi congregatis monachis sub abbate in servitio Christi '), and to devote to this undertaking the tenth part of his revenue. The account given by Sulcard, a monk of Westminster, writing 1076-82,[5] is more detailed. Sulcard informs us that when King

[1] The date of the foundation of the monastery is not known ; see further *An Enquiry into the Time of the First Foundation of Westminster Abbey* (London, 1743) and *An History of the Church of St. Peter, Westminster* (1751) by Richard Widmore, M.A., Librarian to the Dean and Chapter of Westminster. For the legends of its early history see VCH *London*, i. 433 ff., and the introduction to J. Armitage Robinson's edition of *Flete's History of Westminster Abbey* (Cambridge, 1909). See also H. F. Westlake, *Westminster Abbey* (London, 1923).

[2] *Crawford Charters*, no. ix. See also Whitelock, *Wills*, no. 13, for a bequest of land at Brickendon, Herts., made to the abbey 975-1016 by a Cambridgeshire man. This shows that the abbey's fame was not merely local.

[3] Thorpe pp. 296-8.

[4] Ed. H. R. Luard, *Lives of Edward the Confessor*, R.S. 389-435. The date of this work, formerly dated between 1066 and 1075, has recently been under discussion. It was referred to the early part of the twelfth century by M. Bloch, *Analecta Bollandiana*, xli (1923), 17-44 ; see also F. M. Stenton, *Anglo-Saxon England*, 686. The older dating is defended by R. W. Southern, *Eng. Hist. Rev.* lviii (1943), 385-400, who suggests that the work was written 1066-76, perhaps in 1066. A similar position is taken up by E. K. Heningham, *Speculum*, xxi (1946), 419-56, who argues that the work was completed before the death of Queen Edith, 19 December 1075.

[5] For these dates see the *Crawford Charters*, p. 93. For the relevant section of Sulcard's *Prologus de prima constructione ecclesie Westmonasterii et de dedicacione loci eiusdem per Sanctum Petrum Apostolorum principem*, see Bloch, *Analecta Bollandiana* xli. 5, 132, Appendix ii.

Edward, desirous of rendering thanks to God and St. Peter for his peaceful accession to the throne, announced his intention of going on pilgrimage to Rome, the magnates of his kingdom, fearing lest during his absence the kingdom to which peace had only recently been restored should be troubled by fresh warfare, advised the king to remain at home, but to devote the money which would have been expended on his journey to the repair of some religious foundation in honour of St. Peter. Thereupon the king decided to restore the monastery dedicated to St. Peter at Westminster. But a much more developed account of the re-foundation of Westminster Abbey is given by Osbert of Clare, prior of Westminster, who, writing in 1138, is the earliest biographer of the Confessor to give details which have become traditional.[1] In Osbert's narrative the king consents to abandon his pilgrimage only if the pope grants him a dispensation from his vow. The king's envoys, Ealdred, then bishop of Worcester, and Herman, bishop of Ramsbury, bring back from Pope Leo IX a bull dispensing him from his vow on condition that he re-founds or restores a monastery in honour of St. Peter.[2] Thereupon in consequence of a revelation made to him by a hermit, the king determines to restore the monastery at Westminster. Some years later fresh scruples (we are told) cause King Edward to send to Rome a second embassy consisting of Ealdred, now archbishop of York, Giso, bishop of Wells, and Walter, bishop of Hereford, who take to the reigning pope, Nicholas II, a letter from King Edward, and return with a new papal bull.[3] This repeats the dispensation previously granted by Pope Leo IX, and furthermore grants certain privileges to the monks of Westminster and the kings of England. Bloch observes that if the two popes were in actual fact so closely concerned in the restoration of Westminster, it is strange that Sulcard, a monk of Westminster, should know nothing of it, or if he did, should pass over the matter in silence. He suggests (as had already been suggested by Widmore)[4] that this part of the Westminster story may have been derived from spurious Westminster charters, the so-called First Charter and Third Charter of King

[1] For the text of Osbert of Clare, see Bloch, *loc. cit.*, where it is critically examined. Bloch considered Osbert's narrative to be of little value as an independent historical source.

[2] For the (spurious) bull of Pope Leo IX, incorporated in the so-called First Charter and in the so-called Telligraphus of King Edward (for which see pp. 289 f. below), and also in the text of Osbert of Clare, see Bloch, 79, and W. Holtzmann, *Papsturkunden in England*, i. 217–19, no. 2.

[3] For King Edward's (spurious) letter and for the (spurious) bull of Pope Nicholas II, both incorporated in the so-called Third Charter of King Edward (for which see p. 290), and also in the text of Osbert of Clare, see Bloch, *loc. cit.* 88, 89.

[4] *History of Westminster Abbey*, 10.

Edward, which had been fabricated at the end of the eleventh century or the beginning of the twelfth. It is at all events a working hypothesis that in these charters the restoration of the monastery by King Edward was for the first time connected with journeys actually made to Rome by Ealdred, Herman, Giso and Walter. Bishop Ealdred's journey to Rome with Bishop Herman of Ramsbury is recorded in the *Chronicle* C 1049, D 1051, E 1047, and by Florence of Worcester s.a. 1050, but the phrase ' on the king's errand ' used in *Chronicle* C with reference to this journey does not seem to be elucidated in any contemporary source.[1] In 1061 Ealdred, now archbishop of York, went to Rome with Earl Tostig to secure the pallium, and in the same year Giso and Walter went to Rome for consecration to the sees of Wells and Hereford respectively.[2] It is evident, as Bloch observes, that the prestige of the monastery would have been enhanced and its claim to exceptional privileges strengthened if it had been believed that the four prelates named had actually collaborated in the royal foundation.

SPURIOUS DIPLOMAS

The (spurious) First Charter of King Edward (these titles being given to these charters in Westminster sources, as for instance in the cartularies in which they are entered), is, like certain other Westminster charters, indispensable for the criticism of Westminster writs. These texts preserve traditions which may well be authentic concerning the estates granted to the abbey by King Edward and his predecessors and also by other, non-royal, benefactors :

In the First Charter,[3] ostensibly dated 28 December 1065, the king is represented as narrating the circumstances outlined above in which he was led in return for his dispensation from a vow of pilgrimage to Rome (the bull

---

[1] On this see Bloch *ut supra*. He suggests that the real object of the mission may have been to represent the English church at the synod of April 1050. But see also Holtzmann, i. 218.

[2] See further Plummer ii. 249-50, and Biographical Notes.

[3] Text : *Mon. Angl.* i. 293, no. iv ; K. 824 ; Thorpe pp. 400 ff. Analysed : *Twenty-Ninth Report of the Deputy Keeper*, Appendix, pp. 24 f. Comment : *Mon. Angl.* i. 268 ; W. H. Stevenson, *Eng. Hist. Rev.* xi (1896), 732 ; *Crawford Charters*, 92 ; Armitage Robinson, *Flete*, 13-14. On the seal of the Confessor suspended by strands of silk to the reputed original ' in the Hatton Collection ', see Sir F. Madden's comments in *Archæological Journal*, xix (1862), 176. On authentic documents silk laces are not employed until *temp.* Henry I. The seal must have been taken from a genuine or forged matrix of the Confessor's seal, but diplomas were not sealed in the Confessor's time, nor was this method of sealing employed then for writs. Facs., *Eng. Studies*, xxi (1939), facing p. 154. Copy without seal, Cotton Charter vi. 2. The Second Charter (K. 779), largely concerned with episcopal intrusion, can be disregarded here.

of Pope Leo referred to above being incorporated in his narrative) to restore the ancient monastery at Westminster at that time decayed, to devote to this purpose a tenth part of his revenue, and destroying the old church, to build from the foundations a new church to which he gave many relics and granted the right of sanctuary. He is made to declare that on the day of the dedication of the church he has renewed and confirmed the privileges granted to the monastery by Edgar, Edward the Martyr, Archbishop Dunstan, and Æthelred II. He is made to confirm to the monastery the numerous estates (named) granted by earlier kings, together with those granted to it by his own *optimates* : and further to confer on them other estates, among them Launton, Islip, Staines, Windsor, Perton, Rutland (after the death of Queen Edith), Pershore and Deerhurst, exempting all the estates confirmed or granted to the monastery from all royal and episcopal services and dues. He is represented as reciting in detail the judicial and financial rights which he has granted to Abbot Edwin, and as invoking a blessing on those who shall augment his gifts and a curse on those who shall diminish or alienate them. A long list of witnesses is appended to this charter, the spuriousness of which seems to be beyond doubt.

Another form of this charter also exists, the so-called Telligraphus of King Edward, the text of which (Westminster Domesday f. 43 b ff., and Cott. Faust. A. iii, f. 114 ff.) does not seem to have been printed. In it the names of Westminster estates and of their donors are given with some differences ; this form too is spurious. The so-called Third Charter [1] continues the story of the First Charter, tells of the second embassy to Rome, and incorporates in the text the spurious letter of King Edward to the pope and the spurious bull of Nicholas II in reply. It is concerned mainly with the grant and confirmation of immunities and privileges. Like the First Charter it is dated 28 December 1065. It is attested by a long list of witnesses which is not identical with that of the First Charter. The editors of the *Crawford Charters* (pp. 89, 92), condemn both First and Third Charters as fabrications of the late eleventh or early twelfth century. J. Armitage Robinson suggests [2] that a bull of Pope Paschal II (1099–1118) addressed to Henry I may have furnished much of the phraseology of the Third Charter and that this charter in its turn supplied part of the phraseology of the spurious Great Charter of King Edgar (see p. 338). Bloch suggested that both the First Charter and the Third Charter (which may have been the work of the same man) were fabricated c. 1115.

Still another spurious Westminster charter in the name of the

[1] Facsimile in *Ordnance Survey Facsimiles*, pt. ii, Westminster, no. 18, with representation of seal. A (broken) seal taken from a genuine or forged matrix of the Confessor is suspended by strands of silk or hemp from the lower edge of the parchment ; see further the preceding note. Text: *Mon. Angl.* i. 295, no. vi ; K. 825. Analysed: *Twenty-Ninth Report of the Deputy Keeper*, Appendix, 25. Comment: Stevenson as in preceding note ; Armitage Robinson, *Flete*, 14.

[2] *Ibid.* 15.

Confessor (not mentioned by Bloch) helps to fill in the background in which the reputed writs of King Edward the Confessor in favour of Westminster Abbey must be considered. Here the story outlined in the so-called First and Third Charters of the circumstances in which the abbey was said to have been re-founded finds no place. In this charter, printed by Widmore [1] but not in Kemble's *Codex Diplomaticus*, the opening clauses are identical with those of a spurious Ramsey charter (K. 809) :—

The king, after the preamble, is made to speak of having renewed the laws and decrees of his ancestors. He has taken thought how he could restore the sacred places which since their time have been laid waste. As for Westminster, its ' pristina libertas ' was renewed by Edgar and Dunstan and by Æthelred. The king has therefore for his own part ordered this ' privilegium ' to be drawn up for the protection of the community at Westminster, fearing that after his death litigation will become frequent and all evils increase. He has granted to Abbot Edwin exemptions and privileges which are enumerated. The charter then gives a list of lands that belonged to the monastery before the king re-founded it, the list being similar to, but not identical with, the list of lands granted to the abbey by the king's predecessors which is given in K. 824, the spurious First Charter. Another list follows, of lands given to the abbey by *milites* of the king in his presence, this list being similar to, but not identical with, the list of lands given by the king's *optimates* in the First Charter. Next the king is made to declare, more explicitly than in the First Charter, that he has granted to the abbey certain estates *posteaquam ædificata erat et Deo dedicata illa sancta Ecclesia*. These estates are Staines, with everything belonging to it, Windsor with everything belonging to it, and similarly Wheathampstead, Stevenage, Ashwell, Deene, Sudborough, Islip, Launton, and Perton, Rutland (after the death of Queen Edith), Pershore and Deerhurst. The charter is dated A.D. 1065, Indiction 3. The list of witnesses is shorter than that of the First Charter, but contains no name that is not to be found there. Widmore remarked (*loc. cit.* p. 4) that in this charter ' the Marks of Fraud are not so obvious ' (as in certain other Westminster charters) ' but yet I do not believe it genuine '. There is no reason to dissent from his verdict.

The value of the charter for our purposes lies in the information which in some cases it supplies regarding Westminster estates. Both Widmore's charter attributed to King Edward and the First Charter (and the Telligraphus), but not the Second and the Third Charter, inform us that certain (named) estates were granted to Westminster Abbey by King Edward the Confessor on the day of the dedication of the church ; but in the discussion of the Westminster writs below it will make for economy of reference to refer usually to Widmore's charter and to its explicit statement that these grants were made after the church built by the Confessor had been

[1] *Enquiry into the Time of the First Foundation of Westminster Abbey*, Appendix, no. 11. Widmore states (*ibid.* 4) that the date of the transcript, ' in a Book belonging to the Church ', is ' about the Time of Queen Mary '.

dedicated. The tradition is probably well founded, the spurious charters in which it has come down to us are not independent the one of the other, and it is less cumbrous simply to refer to Widmore's charter (though without the implication that the same information does not exist elsewhere).

In the writs themselves references to the Confessor's new church at Westminster Abbey are rare. In no. 106, a writ of dubious authenticity, there is a reference to the consecration of the church. In no. 87 we hear of a grant by the king to his ' church-wright ' Teinfrith, a person otherwise unknown. From other sources we learn that the Leofsi Duddesunu who gave Wormley to the Abbey (no. 90), was a master-mason (see Biographical Notes) ; and that another master-mason called Godwine Gretsith was likewise a benefactor.[1] The building and the consecration of the church (the first church in England to be built in the Norman Romanesque style) are described by Sulcard, and the church itself (which, according to William of Malmesbury,[2] King Edward ' first in England had erected in that kind of style which now almost all attempt to rival at vast expense ') is described in the *Vita Æduuardi*.[3] King Edward was unable through illness to be present at the dedication ceremony, his place being taken by Queen Edith. He died eight days or so later, on 5 January 1066,[4] and was buried in the church that he had built. The church is represented in the Bayeux Tapestry, where its newness at the time of the king's funeral ' is symbolised by the man climbing to set the weathercock in place, its holiness by the Hand of God in the sky '.[5]

' EXTRACTA DE TESTAMENTO SANCTI EADWARDI REGIS '

The cartulary known as Westminster Domesday (see pp. 295 f.) contains what purport to be : ' Extracta de Testamento Sancti Eadwardi Regis ' ; see Appendix III. In the first item the grants made to Westminster Abbey by the Confessor are represented as being confirmed. In the next the king is made to enjoin that after Queen Edith's death, Rutland shall be given to the abbey and handed over to the monks without delay. But although King Edward granted to the abbey the reversion of Rutland after the

---

[1] See F. E. Harmer, *Eng. Hist. Rev.* li (1936), 98, n. 2.

[2] *Gesta Regum*, i. 280. See further on the church L. E. Tanner and A. W. Clapham, *Archæologia* lxxxiii (1933) ; Clapham, *Romanesque Architecture in Western Europe* (1936).

[3] Ed. Luard, 417 f.

[4] For another dating, 6 January 1066, see references in Biographical Notes s. ' Edward, King '.

[5] *The Bayeux Tapestry*, ed. E. Maclagan, King Penguin Books, 1943, p. 11, Plates nos. 30, 31.

death of the queen (no. 94), the monks of Westminster did not gain possession of it when she died, but there is evidence to suggest that it was recognised that they had some claim to it (see p. 324). The third item concerns the king's *locus religiosus* at Deerhurst, that is the church, and the monastery there, though it is uncertain whether the monastery was in existence in King Edward's time.[1] The king is represented as declaring that if this shall ever be alienated from the abbey of St. Denis at Paris, it shall be the property of Westminster Abbey in perpetuity. Whether this reference to the king's alleged grant of Deerhurst church to St. Denis represents the belief of a later time, when the true circumstances in which this church passed to St. Denis had been forgotten, is doubtful. From a charter of William I[2] of 1069, recording that the king and his wife have given to the abbey of St. Denis the church (*ecclesiam*) of Deerhurst, we learn that this church had been given by King Edward to their faithful subject Baldwine (see Biographical Notes), a monk of St. Denis, before he became abbot of St. Edmund's Bury ; King William and his wife had also, after their accession, confirmed Baldwine's grant. Baldwine may have enjoyed these grants under the lordship of St. Denis.[3] There is no mention of Deerhurst church in Domesday Book, but it is probably significant that in 1086 Abbot Baldwine held a half-hide of land on the Westminster manor there ; in addition to this the abbey of St. Denis held a number of vills in Deerhurst (DB i. 166).[4] The writ of King Edward relating to Pershore and Deerhurst which is most likely to be authentic, no. 99, makes no specific mention of the church ; but another writ, no. 102, which has probably been altered and enlarged, has additional clauses : ' with church and with mill ', etc., where reference to Deerhurst church can scarcely in the circumstances be authentic. The so-called extracts from King Edward's testament appear to represent a claim to property which never actually came into the possession of the monks of Westminster.[5] This document seems then to be a fabrication. Not only are its contents suspect, but its penal clauses : ' ne pace terrena priuetur ', and : ' ut possint euadere eternam dampnacionem et ut regnum meum et reges

---

[1] On the monastery at Deerhurst, see VCH *Glouc.* ii. 103.

[2] Davis, *Regesta*, no. 26. Text, *Mon. Angl.* iv. 665.

[3] Douglas, *Feudal Documents from Bury St. Edmunds*, lxi.

[4] Davis is mistaken when he states (*Regesta*, p. 8) that the manor of Deerhurst appears in DB i. 166 as the property of St. Denis and held from the crown. It was Westminster land.

[5] It is stated in the *Monasticon Anglicanum* (iv. 665) that the abbot and convent of St. Denis in 1250 with papal approbation sold the priory of Deerhurst to Richard, earl of Cornwall, but that the priory continued to exist.

successores mei habeant pacem temporalem ', are very unlike penal clauses employed elsewhere during the Anglo-Saxon period (see Introduction pp. 67 ff.). It names as the king's executors Archbishop Ealdred, Bishops Leofric and Godwine, Rodbert ' capellanus ', and Earls Edwin and Leofwine ; but there seems to be a chronological dislocation here. Ealdred, Archbishop of York, was elected to that office on 25 December 1060. Leofric held the sees of Cornwall and Devon between 1046 and 1072. Earl Leofwine was probably appointed to an earldom in 1057. Robert ' capellanus ' (who attests the spurious Third Charter, K. 825) became bishop of Lichfield, 1085. But Godwine, bishop at St. Martin's, if this is the bishop named here, died on 9 March 1061 (*Chron.* D, E) at which date Edwin had not yet been appointed to the earldom of Mercia, for his father, Earl Ælfgar, whom he succeeded, was still alive in the spring or summer of 1062, or even later ; no bishop named Godwine is known to have been alive at this date. On all these grounds the document must be rejected as spurious.

THE CONFESSOR'S WRITS

A number of Westminster writs of the Confessor record—if they are taken at their face value—royal confirmations, at various dates throughout the reign, of grants made to the abbey by other persons. The earliest of these, nos. 73–5, purport to belong to the first two years of Edward's reign. Between 1053 and 1057, on the evidence of writs, the Confessor gave to the abbey Eversley and Shepperton (nos. 85, 86). At the dedication of the church on 28 December 1065, he gave to the abbey Rutland, Launton, Perton, Windsor and Staines, Pershore and Deerhurst, and Islip (nos. 94–104). Besides this he is represented in five writs, nos. 81–3, 105–6, as conferring on the abbey judicial and financial rights. Some Westminster writs have almost certainly been lost, but reference to the spurious charters suggests that about half the grants recorded there as having been made by the Confessor and his nobles are represented by extant writs. Two writs, nos. 78, 79, referring respectively to Aldenham, and to Datchworth and Watton, can scarcely be classified, the former ownership not having been made clear. In no. 80 (not authentic as it stands) the king announces that he wishes to have handed over to him the land at Ickworth. In an authentic writ, no. 87, he deals with a grant of land to his ' church-wright' Teinfrith. The order in which the Westminster writs is printed here is only approximately chronological. In so far as nos. 73–9 as a group represent authentic writs, such writs must have been issued not later than 1051, and some considerably earlier.

The writ represented by no. 80 (spurious) must (on its address) have been issued not later than 1 August 1065. All the rest, nos. 81–106, could have been issued up to the time of Edward's death, 5 January 1066, but some may be as early in date as 1042. Rarely is it possible to assign to the individual writ narrower limits of date than the period of office of the bishop named in the address. When more than one writ refers to the same estate, or to similar privileges, the relevant texts have been grouped together here for the sake of convenience of reference. Similarly writs are discussed here with others of the group to which they belong even if this entails taking them out of their chronological order ; a reference to the pages where it is discussed is given in the notes to each individual writ. In discussing the Westminster writs the possibility will have to be considered that King Edward may actually have conferred upon the abbot and monks of Westminster judicial and financial rights more numerous than those conferred by him on other houses, and that the writs announcing these grants may have been more elaborate and detailed than those surviving elsewhere. But allowance will also have to be made for the probability that the hand of the forger has been at work upon the Westminster writs, and that even writs with a substantial basis of fact may have been altered and 'improved' to the advantage of the abbey. It has been observed above (Introduction, p. 105) that already in 1086 Fanton (*Phantuna*) was alleged to have come to the abbey by a forged writ and was therefore claimed for the king's use. Twelve writs of Westminster Abbey (nos. 76, 77, 80–2, 90, 93, 94, 96–8, 101, of which no. 96 is extant in two copies), as against seven of other houses, have come down to us written on single pieces of parchment to some of which a seal is, or has been, attached. Their authenticity will be discussed below.

CARTULARIES

The Westminster writs are preserved in four cartularies, which have been described by J. Armitage Robinson and M. R. James, *The Manuscripts of Westminster Abbey* (Cambridge, 1909).

The LIBER NIGER QUATERNUS (N) of the Abbey (Robinson and James, 95–8) compiled late in cent. xv, and another copy of this (H) at the College of Arms (*ibid.* pp. 101 f.) contain texts of nos. 97, 98, copied either from Westminster Domesday or from a common source.

WESTMINSTER DOMESDAY (D), a cartulary written early in cent. xiv (Robinson and James, 93–5) is the source from which most of the texts printed here have been taken ; only no. 73 is absent there, no. 74 is imperfect. In the writs in this cartulary the

spelling of large numbers of Old English words is preserved unchanged ; other words are modernised ; there is also a small number
of spelling aberrations and of insignificant omissions.   Exceptional
in their confusions of spelling (noted in the footnotes) are nos. 89,
105.   From the fact that letters of Anglo-Saxon script are frequently
imitated in Westminster Domesday texts, one would infer that the
transcriber (or a predecessor) had before him in such cases texts in
Anglo-Saxon script.   This cartulary has not hitherto been used
(with few exceptions) for printing Westminster writs.   The texts
of nos. 75, 104, may have been used at second hand by Thorpe in his
Diplomatarium, although he does not mention Westminster Domesday as a source in his Table of Contents.   He gives instead the
curious reference :   ' Nig. Quat. Westm.'—which cannot be the
Liber Niger Quaternus.   But reference to the Petrie Transcripts at
the P.R.O., where some of the Westminster Domesday texts have
a copyist's heading : ' Nig. Quat. Westm.', indicates the probable
source of Thorpe's error.   His text of no. 104 is however a conflate
or ' normalised ' text.   Neufeldt (see below) gives for nos. 75, 104,
the meaningless reference : ' Aut. Nig. Quat. Westm.', but his texts
here are taken from Cott. Faust. A, iii.

    COTT. FAUST. A, III (F), a Westminster cartulary into which the
Confessor's writs are copied in handwriting belonging, according to
G. F. Warner (*The Manuscripts of Westminster Abbey*, 99), to the
late cent. xiii.   The texts in this cartulary, independently derived,
have been systematically modernised.   Some spellings tend to be
preferred (though they are not invariably employed) ;   e.g. *pegnes*,
bebidde (as a substitute for OE *bebeode*).   Certain formulas are
employed in writs in this cartulary even when one may suspect that
they were not employed in the original ;   e.g. *formest on hande* is
preferred to the simple *on hande* in nos. 83, 95, 97, 100.   Scandinavianised forms occasionally appear in F :   e.g. *kirk-*, nos. 73, 85,
98, 102, 106 ;   other forms with *k* are not infrequent :   e.g. *frendlik*,
nos. 80, 88, *mikel*, no. 102, *heuenrik*, no. 105.   Possibly the *lis*
(*lið* D) and *hauez* (*hæf* D) of no. 77 are northernisms.   Such forms as
these occur only rarely in D :   e.g. *stiðliker*, *stilliker*, nos. 104, 105,
kirk-, 106.   Important for the investigation of the authenticity of
Westminster writs is the evidence in F (to which attention is drawn
in the footnotes) that transcribers did not confine themselves to a
mere reproduction of their exemplars.   Doubts as to the authenticity of nos. 105, 106, are increased when one observes that the
text of no. 105 in F contains additional passages.   The probability
that the absence of these in D is not due to simple omission in the
latter, is increased by the appearance in no. 82 of an obvious
alteration, where F substitutes *Crist and Sainte* [*Petre*] for the *hym*

in T. Again in nos. 78, 80, F inserts *and* in the formula : *God eow gehealde* (and) *Sancte Petres holde* ; the *and* here is obviously merely scribal.

Writs of King Edward and King William I in Cott. Faust. A. iii, were printed by E. Neufeldt, *Zur Sprache des Urkundenbuches von Westminster* (Berlin, 1907), together with most of the texts copied on single pieces of parchment (see p. 105). His interests were mainly linguistic. Neufeldt had not himself seen F—he depended on a copy made by another person—and a collation of his printed text with the manuscript reveals small inaccuracies which reduce its value for statistical purposes. He omits the writs which are not in Kemble's *Codex*. His table of references is useful, but his identifications of persons and places should be used with caution.

THE ' LICGAN IN TO ' GROUP

The five writs relating respectively to WENNINGTON, KELVEDON, LESSNESS, MOULSHAM, and CLAYGATE, nos. 73, 74, 76, 84, 93, form a group of closely-related texts in which much the same phraseology is employed ; their characteristic feature is the term *licgan in to*, lit. ' to lie in to, to belong to ', a technical expression which also appears in the writs of other houses (see Introduction, p. 64, Group 3). In these Westminster writs the king announces that the lands previously granted to Westminster by certain of his subjects are to belong to (*licgan in to*) the abbey as fully and completely as the donors possessed them and granted them to the abbey ; and he himself consented to this : and for his own part he grants to the abbey judicial and financial rights. In the Bury and the Christ Church writs of this type relating to grants of land (nos. 9, 17, 20, 35), the king declares simply that the land is to ' belong to ' the monastery with sake and soke ' as fully and completely as my mother possessed it ' ; *or* ' as ever any man possessed it and she bequeathed it to that house ' ; *or* ' as A and B granted it to that house '. But in the Westminster writs of this group, with the exception of no. 84, which in this respect stands apart from the others, and with the addition of nos. 77, 92, writs belonging to another group, we find after the statement that the land was granted or bequeathed to Westminster by A or B, the clause : ' and I fully consented to that ' (*and ic ðæs fullice geuðe*). Since this clause does not appear elsewhere among the writs attributed to the Confessor, and since not one of these texts is of high repute, one would be inclined to dismiss this clause as spurious, and to regard it as the contribution of a Westminster hand. But the fact that the same clause (with the omission of *fullice*) appears in what seems to be an authentic writ of William I, induces caution. This is the Marston writ of the Conqueror,[1] and there is no obvious reason for supposing that it is not authentic. It is addressed to Bondi the staller and Sawold the sheriff and all the king's thegns in Oxfordshire, and it continues :

' Icc kiþe eow þat se half hide at Mersctune and alc þare þinga þe þarto gebiraõ ligge into Westminstre swa full and swa forõ swa Wedet it formest hahte and þider inne bequaõ and ic þas geuþe ' (' I inform you that the half-hide at Marston and everything pertaining thereto shall belong to Westminster as fully and as completely as ever Weodet had it, and bequeathed it to that house, and I consented to that ').

The same *licgan in to* pattern appears in other writs of William I,[2] but not in contexts exactly parallel to this ; only with reference to grants of William himself or of the Confessor, and here the clause ' and I consented to that ' is not of course appropriate. There may then have been authentic writs of King Edward with the *ic õæs (fullice) geuõe* clause, and the pattern of such writs may have been followed by the royal clerks in composing the Marston writ of William I. Another possibility, of course, is that the Marston writ of William I was itself taken as a pattern by a forger remodelling, or even fabricating, writs in the name of King Edward the Confessor. It seems impossible to determine whether the clause is authentic in the writs of this group, since the only other instance of its post-Conquest use is in another writ of the same house. Further in all five Westminster writs, including no. 84, the simple ' with sake and soke ' of the Bury and the Christ Church writs becomes a separate grant. In no. 84 we find : ' And I grant that St. Peter have thereover sake and soke, toll, team, and infangenetheof . . . as fully and completely as ever he had in any place where he has other land ' ; while in nos. 73-4, 76, 93 we find : ' I grant that St. Peter have thereover sake and soke, toll, team and infangenetheof . . . and all other rights that belong to me.' The same separate grant appears in one of the two Greenford writs (no. 89) where its authenticity is in the highest degree suspect (see p. 121). It also appears in another group of Westminster writs (nos. 75, 77, 85, 91, 92, 98, 102, see pp. 306 ff.), which have a different conclusion. The Bury and the Christ Church writs support each other, and there can be no question as to the authenticity of their formulas. But although the Westminster examples are numerous, the Westminster writs stand alone, except for the closely-related (spurious) Coventry writ (no. 45).[3] Here, as

[1] See p. 335 for references.

[2] See Neufeldt nos. 31, 33, 34, Davis, *Regesta*, nos. 87, 25 (mis-translated by Davis ; see p. 325, n. 1), 32.

[3] No. 109, a (dubious) Winchester writ, has a *geann* clause, but only as an explanation or extension of what precedes ; it does not constitute an additional grant.

elsewhere, with writs of this house, the question arises whether the clauses peculiar to the Westminster writs and the Coventry writ are authentic, or whether they are not in some degree the contribution of the monks of Westminster themselves. A further link between this group of writs is that in each case the normal valediction *God eow (ealle) gehealde* is replaced by a fuller form in which the word *holde*, ' loyal ' (as adjective), ' lieges ' (as noun) appears ; on the use of this term (which is suspect) see Introduction, p. 54.

In the writs of the *licgan in to* group relating to LESSNESS and to MOULSHAM (nos. 76, 84) the king announces that it is his will that the estates bequeathed to them by benefactors shall ' now ' belong to them for the provision of food. If we can suppose that in the case of writs for Westminster Abbey the pattern followed in the *licgan in to* writs of other houses was replaced by other formulas, then on general grounds the Moulsham writ may be authentic. But it awakens suspicion to find among the judicial and financial rights enumerated in this writ, *flymenafyrmth*, a privilege which was not claimed by the monks of Westminster in the Moulsham writ extant in the name of the Conqueror (see p. 507), and which though not exceptional, is by no means always mentioned in Edward's Westminster writs. Further, as has been said above, the lack of parallels in other than Westminster writs makes one doubt whether (i) the passage : *icc an þæt Sainte Petre habbe þær ofer sake and socne . . . þar he oþer land haueð*, and (ii) the enlarged valediction, ever formed part of any authentic writ of King Edward the Confessor. A manor at Moulsham was held by Westminster Abbey in 1086, as it had been T.R.E. (see p. 507), and although according to a writ of William II the monks of Westminster claimed that a dependent estate of Moulsham held of them by a certain Wulfmær (Vlmarus) had been illegally seized by an officer of the bishop of Bayeux, there is no ground for thinking that their possession of Moulsham itself was disputed. But a doubt still lingers as to whether the Confessor did actually issue *licgan in to* writs of this elaborate type. All that can be said is that if any of the five Westminster writs of this group are authentic, then of the five the Moulsham writ is most likely to represent a (possibly improved and modernised copy of) a writ of King Edward.

The writ relating to LESSNESS (no. 76), a *cotlif* said to have been bequeathed to the abbey by one Ætsere, has a more dubious background. In the reign of Henry I [1] Lessness appears to have been held of the monks of Westminster by Robert, bishop of Lincoln, but how this manor came into the possession of the abbey, and whether it is to be identified with the Lessness of the writ in the

---

[1] See J. Armitage Robinson, *Gilbert Crispin*, 157, no. 42.

Confessor's name is not known. It is true that Domesday names a certain Azor (doubtless the Ætsere of this writ) as the holder of Lessness in King Edward's reign. But Domesday says nothing of any grant of Lessness to the abbey, though not only the writ of the Confessor but also a writ of the Conqueror assert that it was granted to the abbey in King Edward's time. King William is made to declare that Abbot Vitalis and the monks of Westminster are to have in perpetuity the manor of Lessness and the church in the same vill, as Adserus gave it to St. Peter and the brethren of that church for the salvation of his soul, and as King Edward granted it ; the writ has however been proved to be a forgery.[1] By 1086 the manor had passed into the hands of Odo, bishop of Bayeux, and it was held of him by Robert *Latinus*. The manor may however have been illegally appropriated by Bishop Odo, and the monks of Westminster may have needed documentary evidence to support their claim. Is the writ in the name of the Confessor authentic ? In its earliest form it has come down to us as a copy on a single piece of parchment with part of a seal attached, in a handwriting of the end of the eleventh century. Although it is constructed on much the same lines as the Moulsham writ which has been discussed above (no. 84), yet in a few points it resembles more closely the (dubious) writs relating to Wennington, Kelvedon, and Claygate (nos. 73, 74, 93), or one or other of these. Like them it contains the phrase *ic ðes fullice geuðe*, which has been mentioned above. Its valediction, identical with that of no. 73 ; ' God keep you *and* St. Peter's lieges ' can scarcely be correct, since it would exclude the persons addressed from the category of ' St. Peter's lieges ' (for the correct form see Introduction, p. 72), but the introduction of *and* here may be merely scribal. Further the Lessness writ is closely linked with the Claygate writ (no. 93) by the appearance in the address of territorial designations : ' of Rochester ', ' of Kent '. These are so unusual—though they might of course be explained as interpolations—that they bring the whole writ under suspicion. Another obstacle to the acceptance of this writ as authentic is the fact that Leofwine is addressed as earl in this writ purporting to have been issued in the lifetime of Archbishop Eadsige. Eadsige died in 1050, but the chroniclers narrating the events of this period, and particularly the course of the quarrel and the reconciliation between King Edward on the one hand, and Earl Godwine and his sons on the other, in the years 1051–52, never speak of Leofwine with the title of earl, though they give that title to his father, and to his two elder brothers Swein and Harold. It is then difficult to escape the conclusion that

[1] Davis, *Regesta*, no. 54, James Tait, *Essays in History presented to R. Lane Poole*, ed. H. W. C. Davis (Oxford, 1927), 158.

the writ as we have it is not a copy of an authentic writ of King Edward, and that it is probably a fabrication compiled at Westminster Abbey for the purpose of strengthening the claims of the abbey to the land at Lessness.

Of the three writs relating respectively to Wennington, Kelvedon, and Claygate (nos. 73, 74, 93) the WENNINGTON writ is typical. Here King Edward declares that the *burh* at Wennington and 4 hides of land, together with the church and the church soke and everything belonging thereto and the land ' at the lea ', shall belong to (' lie in to ') Westminster for the sustenance of the monks as fully and completely as ever Ætsere Swearte and his wife owned them and gave them to the abbey, and he consented to it ; for his own part he grants to the abbey judicial and financial rights. The seal of red wax of which Madox speaks in printing this writ (no. 73) seems to link the Wennington writ to the writs relating to Lessness, Claygate, and Rutland (nos. 76, 93, 94), all with red seals, and all written in hands of the late eleventh century. There is in my opinion nothing in the linguistic features of the Wennington writ which would render it unlikely that the text from which Madox was printing was also of late eleventh-century date. The possibility that he was printing from an original writ of King Edward, written by the clerks of the royal secretariat, seems to be ruled out (if we suppose his copy to be accurate) by the intrusive ' and ' in ' God keep you *and* St. Peter's lieges ' (on which see Introduction, p. 72). The greater length and more abundant detail of the Wennington writ as compared with writs of other houses, say, Bury or Worcester, might be due to differences of drafting in the king's scriptorium ; or again these features might be the contributions of a Westminster hand, working perhaps on the basis of an authentic writ of King Edward relating to Wennington. The historical background of the Wennington writ is not clear. The traditions relating to the grant of land to the abbey are confused, and the existence of a doubtful or spurious Wennington writ of William I closely related to Edward's writ (see p. 493), renders the hypothesis that the writ in the name of Edward has been worked over even more likely. One cannot positively say that the Wennington writ is not authentic, but while the doubt remains as to the authenticity of the *licgan in to* writs as a class, the authenticity of this writ in its existing form must remain open.

The KELVEDON writ, no. 74, announcing that King Edward has confirmed to Westminster Abbey the land at Kelvedon bequeathed to Westminster by a certain Ailhre and his wife Gode, presents a number of problems. This manor was held by Westminster in 1086, but it is not easy to reconcile the Domesday account of its earlier history with the details given in this writ. Domesday tells us [1] that one Ailricus had held *Keluenduna* as a manor T.R.E.

' This Ailricus went to take part in a naval battle (*abiit in navale prælium*) against King William, and when he returned he fell ill (*cecidit in infirmitate*). He then gave to St. Peter this manor, but none of the men from the county knows this save one (*sed nullus hominum ex comitatu scit hoc nisi unus*). And St. Peter has held the manor in this way till now, and the monks have had neither writ nor officer from the king (*neque brevem neque famulum regis ex parte*) since the king came into this land ', that is to say, so far as they knew, the gift had never received King William's sanction.

Freeman's assumption (iii. 728) is probably correct, namely, that the naval battle was a naval expedition against William in Harold's short reign recorded in the *Chronicle* s.a. 1066 E : ' He (Harold) for ut mid sciphere togeanes Willelme.' The identity of the Ailricus of Domesday with the Ailhre of this writ is made virtually certain by the fact that the name of the donor of *Kylewendun* to the abbey is given as the unambiguous *Ægelricus* in the spurious First Charter of the Confessor (p. 289 above). Domesday however says nothing of any grant of this land to Westminster Abbey by Ailric at an earlier date, that is, in the time of the Confessor, and the monks evidently knew nothing of the Confessor's writ. Can we in view of these discrepancies accept the writ as evidence of an actual grant of Kelvedon to the abbey in the Confessor's reign ? We might conjecture that the grant of Kelvedon to the abbey was actually made in the reign of King Edward, but that the donors' intention having been for some reason frustrated, the grant was made again by Ailric on his sickbed. Or as another possibility, that the grant having been made to the abbey, an arrangement was made whereby Ailric continued to hold the estate as life tenant, but falling ill relinquished it altogether to the abbot and community. Or as another possibility, that the memory of the single individual responsible for the Domesday account of the history of the estate was at fault concerning events which had taken place about the time of the Conquest. But a further complication arises, Domesday states that the monks had had no writ from the king concerning the estate at Kelvedon, whereas a Kelvedon writ in the name of William I (resembling the Wennington writ, see p. 493) appears in the Westminster cartularies purporting to confirm the gift and grant of Ailricus and of Edward (see p. 494). But on examination of this text it is evident that it cannot be authentic. Like the Chalkhill writ attributed to William I (see p. 497) it brings together Bishop William of London, who died in 1075, and Bishop William of Durham, who was not nominated till 1080. One might of course argue that William of

[1] DB ii. 14 b, VCH *Essex*, i. 445.

Durham was an error for Walcher of Durham, a possible witness at the time ; but in view of the Domesday statement that the monks had had no writ it seems likely that this writ of William I is spurious. We have then evidence of fabrication in relation to Ailric's grant of Kelvedon to Westminster which the writ in the name of William purports to confirm. What arguments are there in favour of the authenticity of Edward's Kelvedon writ (no. 74) ? There is no evidence that the abbey's claim to Kelvedon was disputed, and no reason is known for the fabrication of evidence, for confirmation of a bequest of Kelvedon to the abbey, made not long after the Confessor succeeded to the throne. One passage in the text for which there is no parallel in other Westminster writs gives an impression, which may be illusory, of having been derived from a genuine writ : ' for þam þe þæt minstre is on minen munde and al þat þar unto (*for* into) herð on allen þingan '. The idea that the king's *mund* or protection is extended to certain religious houses is expressed elsewhere (see note on no. 2). But otherwise there is scarcely anything to suggest that this text represents an authentic writ of King Edward, and there are arguments against it. One's confidence in the authenticity of the clause : ' for minre saule 7 for here saule 7 for alle quiken 7 for alle dede to helpe ', is not increased by the fact that the only close parallel in writs attributed to the Confessor (see Introduction, p. 67) appears in the more than dubious Claygate writ (no. 93). But indeed the whole tenor of the Kelvedon writ of the Confessor seems to betray the hand of the forger. A *licgan in to* writ of Edward of any period would be inappropriate for the notification of Ailric's grant of Kelvedon as it is described in Domesday, if *beqwað* has in this text its customary sense of ' bequeathed ' (see p. 495), and if it was intended that the bequest should take effect after his death, for Ailric outlived King Edward. It seems unlikely that an authentic writ of King Edward lies behind this text.

The family resemblance which has been traced in the writs relating to Wennington and to Kelvedon can also be observed in the writ relating to CLAYGATE (no. 93). The authenticity of this writ is more than doubtful. Its most remarkable feature is its mention of an Earl Tostig, whose wife Leofrun, associated with him in this text in the grant of Claygate to Westminster Abbey, is described as the foster-mother of King Edward. This Earl Tostig (see Biographical Notes) can scarcely be Tostig, the son of Earl Godwine, for his wife was Judith, half-sister of Count Baldwine V of Flanders, and there seems to be no mention elsewhere of any other wife of Tostig's.[1] But the mention of Leofrun as the Confessor's

---

[1] Judith was married to Tostig in 1051, had two children, and re-married after his death in 1066. See further P. Grierson, *Trans. R. Hist. Soc.* 4th ser. xxiii (1941), 109 ff.

foster-mother seems too remarkable a detail for one to dismiss this pair as a deliberate invention. Is it conceivable that there was actually some historical basis for the existence of the semi-legendary Tostig, earl of Huntingdon, who is said to have been slain by Earl Siward of Northumbria ? Or is it not more likely that the ' Earl ' before Tostig in the Claygate writ is really intrusive and added by a copyist, who had heard of an Earl Tostig, in order to distinguish this Tostig from the housecarl called Tostig who is named in the address ? In the spurious First Charter of the Confessor (see p. 289) the Tostig who gave Claygate to Westminster is classed among the king's *optimates*, and in the corresponding passage in the spurious charter printed by Widmore (see p. 291) among the king's *milites*, without any distinguishing title. The Claygate writ in its earliest extant form is preserved as a copy in a handwriting of c. 1100 on a piece of parchment to which a large red seal is attached in the manner customary with writs of the Confessor ; so too is the Lessness writ (no. 76, discussed above) which in some other respects the Claygate writ under discussion resembles. Like the Lessness writ and unlike the other writs printed here, the Claygate writ has a territorial designation after two names in the address : *on Wintanceastre, on Cyrteseiæ*. One cannot help suspecting that the same Westminster hand may have been responsible for these expanded forms in the Claygate and the Lessness writs, or else that the one may have been imitated from the other. On the other hand, the appearance of Stigand here as ' bishop ', in conjunction with Abbot Wulfwold of Chertsey, probably appointed in 1058, is not necessarily a suspicious feature, for Stigand retained the see of Winchester even after his promotion to the archbishopric of Canterbury in 1052. But the Claygate writ contains a further clause peculiar to itself, so far as writs in the name of the Confessor are concerned, namely, *symle ða ðe beoð to cumene ealsæ ða ðe nu synd*. This may represent an attempt to render into Anglo-Saxon the clause *presentibus et futuris* which appears, for instance, in the spurious Great Charter of King Edgar in favour of Westminster Abbey (see p. 338) : ' Ego Eadgarus Dei gratia Anglorum rex omnibus episcopis, abbatibus, comitibus, uicecomitibus, centenariis ceterisque agentibus nostris *presentibus scilicet et futuris salutem.*' It is not improbable that the appearance of the passage in question in the Claygate writ is in some way connected with this Latin equivalent in this spurious Westminster charter attributed to King Edgar.[1] But it is not absolutely necessary to suppose that the

---

[1] The editors of the *Crawford Charters* suggest (p. 91) that the forger of the alleged charter of King Edgar was a former inmate of St. Denis, and cite as the origin of this passage a similar passage in a spurious charter of King Dagobert I for the abbey of St. Denis.

person responsible for the appearance of this clause in the Claygate writ was acquainted with the forged charter of King Edgar (supposedly compiled in Norman times). Not only was the formula *presentibus et futuris* widely used in charters of the Frankish kings and their successors,[1] its equivalent in forms such as : ' Noverint omnes *tam futuri quam presentes* ', was in use in England after the Conquest. A somewhat similar expression also appears in a privilege in English of Bishop Osbern of Exeter, of June 1096–June 1102, which begins : ' Wite ða þe nu beoð and ða te cumene sy ' etc. (' Know those who now are and those who are to come ' etc.).[2] But no such phrase as this appears in any other Anglo-Saxon writ. Other features in this writ which excite suspicion are : (i) the term *dænegeld* (l. 11), the use of which in the Confessor's time is not certain, though the term was in use at a later date ; (ii) the mention as subjects of a royal grant of *blodwite* and *weardwite* (l. 16), appearing elsewhere as the subject of grant by the Confessor only in dubious or spurious texts (see Introduction, pp. 83–5) ; (iii) the religious consideration : ' for minre saule ' etc., in a form appearing elsewhere in these writs only in the dubious or spurious Kelvedon writ, no. 74 (see Introduction, p. 67). The valediction on the other hand may be ultimately derived from a text produced in the Confessor's scriptorium. But it is impossible to believe that this text as it stands is an authentic copy of a writ of King Edward.

The abbey of Westminster held Claygate in 1086, and there is no evidence that their right to possess it was disputed. But the monks provided themselves not only with a writ in the name of the Confessor, but also with one in the name of William I.[3] Here the king is made to declare that he has granted to the abbot and monks of Westminster the ' maneriolum ' of Claygate with everything pertaining thereto, namely, the third oak in his wood at Ditton, and the third acre if the grove die out, and the third part of every source of profit (*cum tertia utilitate*) of the vill of Ditton, in woodland and open country, in pannage and in pasture, in meadows and in fisheries, and in all other things, free from plaints and shires and hundreds and aids and *occasionibus* and *murdris*, and from the tax called in English geld and Danegeld ; as freely as ' comes Tostius et Leofruna comitissa ' gave it to St. Peter for their souls, and as King Edward granted and confirmed it by his charter ; with sake and soke, toll and team, and *latro*, and with all other matters belonging to the king

---

[1] See Erben–Schmitz–Redlich, *Urkundenlehre*, i. 342 f. ; Marculf, i. 2 ; Zeumer (for full reference, see p. 30, n. 3), *passim*.

[2] Thorpe p. 437, Earle p. 260 ; for date, Introd. to *The Exeter Book*, ed. Chamber, Förster and Flower, 49.

[3] Davis, *Regesta*, no. 237 ; full text, Armitage Robinson, *Flete*, 141.

himself. This writ, closely connected in content with the writ in the name of the Confessor, is marked spurious by Davis. It is not easy to see what purpose could have been served by its fabrication (since Claygate was in the possession of the monks of Westminster in 1086), unless perhaps it was confected to provide them with a continuous record of their title to Claygate, and to rights at Ditton. That this may have been the purpose of the fabrication of the writ of William I is suggested by the fact that Claygate and the wood of Ditton occur again in three writs of Henry I, two of Stephen and one of Henry II, all entered in Westminster Domesday (f. 458) under the heading ' Writings of the Almonry '. These documents relate to the freedom from pleas and scots and aids and disputes and all other ' customs ' of the lands assigned to the Almonry, namely the lands of Padding-ton and Fanton and Claygate, and to ' whatsoever the Almonry had in the time of King Edward in the wood of Ditton and in all other places '.[1] The interest of these documents as a group lies in the fact that they trace back the rights of the Almonry at Claygate and at Ditton to the time of King Edward, they mention the charters of King Edward and King William, and they are closely linked in phraseology to the spurious Latin writ of William, which itself contains in a Latin form many of the phrases of the writ in the name of King Edward. The writ attributed to the Confessor may possibly be ultimately based on an authentic writ recording the grant of Claygate and rights at Ditton to Westminster Abbey by the Con-fessor ; but in that case it has at the least been extensively inter-polated, while it is impossible to dismiss the suspicion that the docu-ment in its present form may be in its entirety a post-Conquest fabrication.

THE ' SHALL HAVE ' GROUP

Seven Westminster writs, nos. 75, 77, 85, 91, 92, 98, 102, relating respectively to Ulf's London land and wharf, Chalkhill, Eversley, Ayot, Tooting, Staines-*Stæningahaga*, and Pershore-Deerhurst, and belonging by the form of the main announcement to Group 4 (see Introduction, p. 64), are closely linked together by their structure. This is a matter of such importance for the criticism of these texts that the pattern is shown here (insignificant variations being dis-regarded) :—

(A) I inform you that I grant and I desire (*or* desire and grant) that St. Peter and the brethren at Westminster shall have (all seven writs)

---

[1] For the reputed originals of these texts see Westminster Abbey Muniments xxix, xxx, xxxvii : Armitage Robinson, *Crispin*, 143, no. 23, 144, no. 24. On Fanton see p. 105.

(B) the land (nos. 75, 77, 92), *or*

(B1) the *cotlif* (nos. 85, 91, 98, 102),

(C) which X and Y gave to the holy place as fully and completely as ever they had it (no. 75), *or*

(C1) as fully and completely as ever Z held it of me and gave it to the holy place (nos. 77, 92), *or*

(C2) as fully and completely as ever I myself, or M and N, possessed it (nos. 85, 91), *or*

(C3) as fully and completely as they were assigned in olden times to the soke of O or ever I myself possessed them (nos. 98, 102),

(D) and I fully consented to that (nos. 77, 92).

(E) And again I likewise grant them (all seven writs)

(F) that they have full freedom *on eallum þingum þe þær up aspringað* (no. 75), *or*

(F1) that they have sake and soke, toll and team, infangenetheof and flymenafyrmth, and all other rights *on eallum þingum þe þær up aspringað* (nos. 77, 92 ; 85 and 91 add miskenning ; 98 and 102 add grithbreach, hamsocn, foresteall and miskenning)

(G) and (or *forþan*) I will not permit (all seven writs), followed in all except no. 92 by a two-fold prohibition :

(H) *þæt ænig mann ætbrede oððe geutige* etc. (all except no. 92),

(J) (*oððe*) *þæt þær ænig mann ænigne onstyng hæbbe* (all seven writs),

(K) *and ic wille . . . stapolfæst* (nos. 77, 85, 98, 102).

Specially noteworthy here is the clause : *on eallum þingum þe þær up aspringað*, for it occurs here and nowhere else in Anglo-Saxon writs. Similarly the two-fold ' grant and desire ' *or* ' desire and grant ' following ' I inform you ' is peculiar to these texts. Again, the two-fold prohibition, H and J above, appears elsewhere in the close-linked Coventry writ, no. 45, but nowhere else as a two-fold prohibition in Anglo-Saxon writs.[1] The general pattern of this group : ' my will is that X shall have such and such a thing as fully and completely etc.,' appears among surviving Anglo-Saxon writs in three very much simpler writs of other houses (see Introduction, p. 64). It is entirely probable that it was also employed in writs for Westminster Abbey. But it can hardly be doubted that the simple pattern was enlarged and embroidered in the Westminster scriptorium. And indeed it would not have been difficult to confect a new writ by stringing together one or other of the clauses set out in the scheme outlined above.

In no. 75 (referring to ULF'S LONDON LAND AND WHARF), a writ less elaborate in structure and phraseology than some others of this group, the king announces that the monks of Westminster ' shall

[1] On these prohibition clauses see Introduction, pp. 66 f.

have ' the land and the wharf belonging to it which had been granted to them by Ulf the portreeve of London and his wife, as fully and completely as ever the donors possessed it. This type of writ is to be found in a shorter form elsewhere (see Introduction, p. 64, Group 4). In fact if one subtracts from this Westminster writ the passage : ' and ic ann heom eft ealswa þæt hy habben þær to fulne freodom on eallun þingun þe þer upp aspringað be lande 7 be strande ' (E, F, in the pattern above) ; if one reduces the two-fold prohibition clause to one ; and if one omits the second clause of the valediction ('and gife eow ece gesælþe. Amen '), what then remains bears some resemblance to writs of other houses, namely, nos. 49, 56, 58. This Westminster writ relating to Ulf's land and wharf raises in an acute form the question (which of course also arises elsewhere) whether the clerks of the king's secretariat did in fact issue on behalf of Westminster Abbey writs which though they resemble in their main structure those of other houses, are yet fuller and more elaborate than these. Since nothing seems to be known from other sources of the grant in question (which is not mentioned in the spurious Westminster charters), material for criticising the document is lacking. It is entirely probable that the writ is true in substance and that it does indeed represent an authentic writ of King Edward the Confessor. It may possibly be a close copy of such a writ—allowing of course for a few misspellings and a few later forms. But it seems equally probable that the text in question owes some part of its contents to the monks of Westminster— working probably on the basis of a writ on the same subject actually issued in their favour by King Edward the Confessor.

It is to be observed that in the writ (no. 75) that has just been discussed the privileges with which the king augments the grant that he announces are not enumerated ; the monks of Westminster are simply granted ' full freedom in everything that shall arise there '. In other writs of this group, these privileges are enumerated in great detail. The CHALKHILL writ (no. 77) is typical. The text is copied on a single piece of parchment in a handwriting which may be as late as the early twelfth century. A seal, now vanished, was affixed to it in Hickes's time, by a tie or strings of silk, a manner of sealing not employed for writs in the time of King Edward the Confessor, but employed, for instance, in the closely-allied spurious Coventry writ (no. 45), to which however no seal is now attached. The linguistic forms of this document are in the main those characteristic of late West Saxon, but some (e.g. *þeigenes*, *furmest*, *geburad*) seem to indicate a later date of origin than the Confessor's time. If then this is not a writ produced in its existing form in the Confessor's scriptorium, can we accept it as an unaltered copy, so far as its contents are concerned, of such a writ ? There seems no reason to doubt that the text records an actual grant, but in fact nothing is known of the estate at Chalkhill from any but a Westminster source. The chief difference between this writ and those of other houses consists in the additional matter which it contains, and which can quite easily be subtracted from it. This comprises (among others) (i) the passage beginning : ' And icc wille 7 fæstlice bebeode ' (l. 19), for which there are parallels only in other Westminster writs of this group (nos. 85, 98, 102, see Introduction, p. 72) ; (ii) the phrase (ealle) *mine holdan freond*, which also appears in the address of nos. 85, 91, 98, 102 of this group, and which may be no more than an embellishment (see Introduction, p. 54). But if the possibility of interpolation and embellishment is admitted for the Chalkhill writ as for other writs of this group, it becomes difficult to know where to draw the line between authentic and spurious. Not only has the Chalkhill writ come down to us in a copy dating probably from the early twelfth century, but a reference in a Chalkhill writ attributed to William I [1] to King Edward's confirmation *per cartas privilegii sui* of Thurstan's grant to the abbey is further evidence, whether William's writ is genuine or not, that the grant of Chalkhill to the abbey was under discussion in the reign of William I and later. Everything points to the conclusion that whether or not the writ under discussion had a substantial basis in an authentic writ of the Confessor, the writ in the form in which it has come down to us has been embellished and enlarged.

The EVERSLEY writ (no. 85), another elaborately-composed writ of the same group, is remarkable for the king's admonition to his four ' free sokemen ', namely Payn his ' mead-wright ', Wulfnoth his housecarl, Ælfric Hort (?), and Freborn, that ' they henceforth with land and with pasture, each of them with his part, be in the power of St. Peter and obey and be subject to the community of the monastery '. It is hard to believe that this passage is not authentic. In this preservation of the names of his tenants and the mention of their new obligations, as in the directions given in no. 104 to Wigod of Wallingford, we can imagine that we hear King Edward speaking. From Domesday we learn that four *liberi homines* held Eversley *in alodium* of the king, and since in Domesday Eversley is entered among the lands of Westminster Abbey, it is entirely probable that it was indeed conferred upon Westminster Abbey by King Edward. But it is hard to accept as authentic some other details of this writ. *Miskenning* (Introduction,

---

[1] Davis, *Regesta*, no. 89, charter no. xii, with an erroneous textual reading which led Davis to identify the place with Chelsea. On William's writ, see p. 497.

p. 82) appears in several writs of William I which accompany other writs of this group, but one is inclined to believe that its appearance in the Confessor's Eversley writ is anachronistic, and one cannot help suspecting that an authentic writ of King Edward relating to Eversley has been embellished and improved at a later date. Like the Chalkhill writ (no. 77) which in many respects it resembles, the Eversley writ is accompanied by one of William I dated 1080–81 by Davis.[1] Here King William declares that the monks of Westminster are to have the manor of Eversley with all the liberties which King Edward gave them, and that no one is to do them wrong on pain of a forfeiture of ten pounds. To what extent the process of tampering with a (presumed) writ of King Edward relating to Eversley may have gone is now no more than a matter of conjecture.

With the writs relating to Ayot and to Tooting, which also belong to this group, we are still on uncertain ground. The inclusion of *miskenning* among the privileges named in the AYOT writ (no. 91) seems as dubious as it does elsewhere in writs of this group (see Introduction, p. 82). Further there is no instance in writs of unquestionable authenticity of an elaboration of the normal valediction *God eow gehealde* into *God eow gehealde and ealle þa þe sind holde into þæm halgan stede. Amen* (see Introduction, p. 72). Moreover, the history of the manor of Ayot is by no means clear. Of the 3 manors at Ayot in 1086 one of $2\frac{1}{2}$ hides is entered under the lands of the abbot of Westminster, the abbot claiming that King William had conceded it to him. The Aluuinus of the Domesday entry, ' a thegn of King Edward ', the holder T.R.E. of this manor, which he could sell, can be confidently identified with the Ælfwine Gottone of the Confessor's writ. Domesday says nothing of any grant of this land to the abbey by Aluuinus, but the suggestion made in the VCH *Hertfordshire*, iii. 59, may very well be correct : that Ælfwine after making his grant continued to hold Ayot as sub-tenant of the abbey during King Edward's reign. That some agreement with the abbey had been made is clear from a (possibly authentic) tradition preserved in the spurious Telligraphus of William I (see p. 337) confirming earlier grants to Westminster Abbey : ' Ælfwynus Gottun duas hidas et dimidiam in fundo Ægeatte dicto cum campis et pascuis et silvis et pratis et aquis et molendino et omnibus ad illas pertinentibus *facta conventione sua cum abbate Eaduino et monachis coram Rege Eadwardo* eidem sancto dederat '. It is reasonable to suppose that King William would not have conceded Ayot to the abbot of Westminster, as the abbot claimed that he had done, unless he had been able to produce some such evidence of his claim as would be afforded by a writ (whether genuine or not)

[1] *Regesta*, no. 143.

of the Confessor. But is the extant Ayot an authentic copy of a writ of King Edward? It is to be observed that a Latin writ of William I referring to this estate does not go so far as to bestow (specifically) upon the monks of Westminster either *flymenafyrmth*, or *miskenning*—the latter being a right which (as has been observed above) may well be anachronistic when it appears in writs in the name of the Confessor. King William in his writ declares that the monks of Westminster are to have the manor called *Ægate* with church and wood, mills, meadow, and everything belonging to it, as it was given to the abbey by Alfwinus Gottun (Davis's spelling *Cottun* is a misreading) and his wife, for their souls, and conceded by King Edward, with sake and soke, toll, team, *latro*, ' et cum omnibus rebus et consuetudinibus et legibus '.[1] The abbot may well have had from King Edward a writ relating to his Ayot estate ; but it seems probable that the extant Ayot writ of the Confessor, even if it had a substantial basis of fact, has been improved, embellished and perhaps enlarged.

The details of the history of Tooting, to which another writ of the same group relates (no. 92), are conflicting ; so much so that in the opinion of J. H. Round, the Domesday entry ' throws doubt on the abbey's charter '.[2] But the exact bearing of the writ must be made clear. The statement of the writ that the donor Swein was (like the housecarl Thurstan of no. 77) a tenant of the king was overlooked by Round when he says : ' This entry throws doubt on the abbey's charter recording the gift to it of the 4 hides at Tooting by King Edward himself, as those which Swein his kinsman had held '. It would seem from the writs that Swein and Thurstan were supposed to belong to that class of tenants who could sell or otherwise alienate their land. What the writ records is that Swein gave to the abbey the land at Tooting that he held of the king, that the king consented to the grant, and that the king on his own behalf gave to the abbey judicial and financial rights and forbade that anyone save the abbot and community should have any authority there. Domesday records that Swein had held Tooting of King Edward (' Suen tenuit de rege Edwardo,' DB i. 32), but says nothing of any grant of this land by Swein to Westminster Abbey. According to Domesday, on the contrary, the abbey acquired Tooting only after the Conquest as the gift of a certain Alnod of London who ' granted it to St. Peter's (Westminster) for his soul '. Alnod (according to Domesday) had acquired the manor from Earl Waltheof, who had mortgaged it to him for 2 marks of gold ; and Earl Waltheof had ' received this land of Swein after the death of King Edward '

[1] Davis, *ibid*. no. 235, and charter no. 38, dated 1080–86 by Davis.
[2] VCH *Surrey*, i. 306.

('Hanc terram accepit Wallef comes de Suan post mortem R.E. et invadiavit pro ii markis auri Alnodo Lundoniensi qui concessit Sancto Petro pro sua anima scilicet quod ibi habebat.').[1] But it is worth noting that Domesday does not tell us whether Swein relinquished his land voluntarily to Earl Waltheof. Further, certain spurious Westminster charters have preserved a (possibly authentic) tradition that the Alnod (Ælfnoth) of London who (according to Domesday) gave the 4 hides at Tooting to Westminster Abbey, was a kinsman of Swein, that he made other benefactions to the abbey, and himself became a monk there.[2] The family connection with Tooting represented by the grant alleged to have been made to the abbey in the Confessor's reputed writ may then have been preserved. Swein, if he did actually grant Tooting to Westminster Abbey in the Confessor's reign, may, as was not unusual, have continued to hold his land of the abbey as tenant for life. He may—if he was Swein 'of Essex '—have been still living in 1086. His intention that the abbey should ultimately have possession of his Tooting estate, frustrated when it passed into the hands of Earl Waltheof, would have been fulfilled when the estate ultimately came to the abbey through the gift of Swein's *nepos* Ælfnoth.[3] On this hypothesis it would be possible to reconcile the apparent discrepancies between the Tooting writ attributed to the Confessor, and the Domesday entry relating to Tooting. On the other hand, if Swein did actually give Tooting to the abbey in the Confessor's time, it is strange that there should be no mention of the grant in the spurious Westminster charters which purport to confirm so many pre-Conquest grants to the abbey (but the grant of Greenford by Æthelric (nos. 88, 89) is also absent there). The conjunction

---

[1] DB i. 32, VCH *Surrey*, i. 302.

[2] A doubtful writ of William I (Davis, *Regesta*, no. 181, J. Armitage Robinson, *Crispin*, 128, no. 2, purports to confirm to the abbot and monks of Westminster those 4 hides in Tooting which Swein gave them and which Ailnoth of London his *nepos* now holds of St. Peter and the monks of that church, and also the land in London and the mill of Stratford with which the said Ailnoth endowed them. In the spurious First Charter of William I (for which see p. 337) Ælfnoth is said to have granted to the abbey when he was made a monk there houses and lands in London, and to have granted also a hide of land near Walthamstow and a certain mill at Stratford with the houses etc. belonging thereto. Further the spurious Telligraphus of William I (see p. 337) mentions: ' in regione Suthregena in villa Tottinge cognomine iiii hidas terre quas Alfnothus ciuis Londoniensis qui ibidem monachus effectus fuit ', gave to the abbey together with other gifts of lands.

[3] The claim of the monks of Westminster to Tooting was recognised in a writ of Henry I (Armitage Robinson, *Gilbert Crispin*, 142, no. 21, 1100–16), announcing a grant to the abbot and monks of Westminster of 4 hides in Tooting, ' ut eas ita bene et plenarie et honorifice teneant et habeant sicut habuerunt tempore patris mei et antecessorum meorum '.

in the address of this Surrey writ of Stigand as ' bishop ' with Leofwine, probably appointed to an earldom in 1057, is not necessarily a suspicious feature, for although Stigand had become archbishop of Canterbury in 1052, he is probably addressed here as bishop of Winchester, since he did not relinquish this see on his promotion.   But when we examine the structure of the Tooting writ we find that although its comparative simplicity, its single prohibition clause, and its normal valediction, might be considered arguments in its favour, it is actually composed solely of what might be called Westminster material, that is to say, the material which has been analysed on pp. 306-7.   When all the evidence is weighed, it is difficult to determine whether this writ is or is not authentic.

The two remaining writs of this group, namely the writs relating to Staines-*Stæningahaga* (no. 98) and to Pershore-Deerhurst (no. 102) will be discussed below (pp. 328 ff).   In each of these texts the address gives an impression of authenticity, and may represent the address of an authentic writ issued by the Confessor towards the end of his life.   But it is entirely probable that the text has in each case undergone improvement and embellishment at the hands of the monks of Westminster, for some of the formulas employed here appear only in other writs of this group.   These two writs are not authentic in their extant form.

ALDENHAM AND DATCHWORTH-WATTON

An investigation into the later history of the Westminster estates sometimes brings to light evidence which can be brought into account in an enquiry into the problem of the authenticity of Westminster writs, as in the case of those relating to ALDENHAM (no. 78) and to Datchworth-Watton (no. 79).   In many cases the monks remained in possession of their lands, and there is no reason to suppose that they had any difficulty in establishing their rights when these were challenged.   In the case of their Aldenham manor, however, a great dispute arose (apparently not long after the Conquest) between the abbot of Westminster and the abbot of St. Albans, who claimed rights of jurisdiction over this land, and this dispute lasted for several centuries.[1]   It is at least a working hypothesis that the reason for the unusual form of the Aldenham writ is to be found in this dispute.   Its opening phrases are on the lines of those Westminster writs in which the king announces his grant to the abbey of property that had formerly been in his own hands : ' I inform you that I have given to Westminster Abbey the land at Aldenham with sake and soke and toll and team and

---

[1] See VCH *Hertfordshire*, ii. 150 ff., and also pp. 499 f. below.

infangenetheof '. But in this writ it is not made clear, as it is elsewhere, by the use of the phrase *swa ful 7 swa forð swa hit mesilfon*, etc., that the grant that is being made is one of land and rights that had formerly belonged to the king himself. The Aldenham writ glances back instead over the former history of the estate, and the king is made to declare that the abbey is to have the land (i) as fully and completely as Earl Sihtric held of the monastery and before witnesses gave it up unequivocally to Abbot Ælfric and the brethren ; the use of *þiowlice* in connection with Earl Sihtric's tenure being itself a suspicious feature for this highly unusual term (see p. 500) is not part of the normal legal phraseology of the Anglo-Saxon period ; (ii) and as Abbot Ordbriht held it for the abbey in the days of King Offa (if this is the right interpretation of this clause) and King Cenwulf ; (iii) and as King Edgar in his charter confirmed it to the abbey. There may be a historical basis for any or all of these statements, but if the abbot of whom Earl Sihtric held Aldenham is here correctly named Ælfric, he belongs to that period of Westminster history of which virtually nothing is known. For the possibility that *Ælfric* is a mistake for *Ælfwig*, abbot of Westminster in the early eleventh century, see p. 548, s. *Ælfric, Abbot*. Abbot Ordbriht is the abbot of the Aldenham charter,[1] in which he is said to have purchased the grant of Aldenham from King Offa. To King Edgar is attributed a spurious charter known as the Great Charter of King Edgar (see p. 338 below) in which Aldenham is confirmed to the abbey together with many other estates. But it is hard to believe that this writ in its present form can be a copy of an authentic writ of the Confessor. The accumulation in it of a series of references to reputed former holders of the estate has the appearance of a piece of antiquarianism, not unconnected with the necessity under which the monks of Westminster may have found themselves of supporting their claim to Aldenham by documentary evidence of the antiquity of their possession of this estate. The antiquity of their possession of Aldenham is emphasised again in the Aldenham writ attributed to the Conqueror : ' sicut tenuerunt tempore regis Edwardi cognati mei et antecessorum meorum et *sicut tempore meo juratum est eos antiquitus illud habuisse* '.[2] We ought therefore to consider the possibility that the Aldenham writ may represent the reconstruction for the benefit of the monks of Westminster of an already existing writ of King Edward relating to Aldenham, or else perhaps the fabrication of a new one to serve their purpose in a particular emergency. Dr. Cam kindly informs me that this writ is exactly what would have been needed by the abbot of Westminster

[1] K. 149, B. 245, see p. 501.
[2] Davis, *Regesta*, no. 53, charter no. ix.

to establish his right to withdraw the Aldenham men from the jurisdiction of the abbot of St. Albans ; she has observed to me that in the dispute with St. Albans it was hundredal, public, jurisdiction that was in question, and that the statements in the VCH *Herts.* ii. 150 which imply that it was a question of feudal tenure need revision (see further p. 499 below).

The DATCHWORTH-WATTON writ (no. 79) must also be considered here. The first part of the writ follows the same general lines as the Aldenham writ ; the persons named in the address are identical, and the king declares in the same phraseology as in the Aldenham writ that he has given to Westminster Abbey Datchworth and Watton, with sake and soke, toll, team and infangenetheof. This similarity might of course be due to the issue by the Confessor of genuine writs relating to Aldenham and to Datchworth-Watton respectively, in the same terms ; or it might be due to borrowing on the one side or the other ; or to the use of the same source. The writ glances back, as does the Aldenham writ, over the past history of the estates. But the Aldenham writ refers to episodes the most recent of which may perhaps have taken place twenty years before— if the possibility be accepted that the Sihtric-Ælfric/Ælfwig episode belongs to the first quarter of the eleventh century (see Biographical Notes, s. Ælfric Abbot) ; otherwise this episode must belong to the first half of the tenth century, or possibly a few years later. The other two episodes referred to in the Aldenham writ belong to the remote past. In contrast to this the Datchworth-Watton writ refers to an episode—the surrender of the estates to Abbot Edwin, in the presence of Queen Edith—which must have taken place not more than a few months previously, if it was not a matter of weeks. There seems no reason for doubting that the surrender of the estates to Abbot Edwin actually took place ; and the surrender of the estates and the issue of the writ must both have taken place in 1049, after the appointment of Abbot Edwin to office at some date later than 19 October in that year, and before the death in the same year of Bishop Eadnoth, one of the persons to whom the writ is addressed. The award of Datchworth and Watton to the abbey in the assembly of the ' nine shires at *Wendelbury* ' cannot unfortunately be dated, but there is no reason for supposing that it did not take place. But the reference in this writ to a grant of these estates to the abbey by King Edgar is of a more dubious character, and it is impossible to feel certain of its authenticity. It is tempting to suggest that here, as in the Aldenham writ, the references to the (supposed) grant by King Edgar may have been introduced into the text in order to strengthen the abbot's claim to the possession of these lands at a time when he may have been in danger of losing

Y

them. A great part of the land at Datchworth and at Watton was actually lost to Westminster Abbey by 1086, and the dispute over Aldenham with the abbot of St. Albans dragged on for many years. It was still thought worth while at the end of the eleventh century, or in the twelfth, to fabricate the spurious Great Charter of King Edgar (on which see p. 338), purporting to recount the benefactions of Edgar to Westminster, in which the names of Aldenham, Datchworth and Watton occur, in the list of estates said in the charter to have been confirmed or granted by that king.[1] We ought to consider the possibility that the inclusion in the writs relating to Aldenham, and to Datchworth and Watton, of references to the (supposed) earlier history of these estates may have been in some way connected with the appearance of a reference to a (supposed) earlier grant by St. Dunstan in the writ in which King Edward announces his own grant to Westminster of land at Shepperton (no. 86). It must remain an open question whether the reference to St. Dunstan in the Shepperton writ is authentic.

ICKWORTH

The ICKWORTH writ, no. 80, has at first glance the appearance of an original writ of King Edward the Confessor, written and sealed by the clerks of the royal secretariat. The hand looks like a contemporary hand. The seal is of the First type, with the king's figure and inscription complete ; it is however badly twisted and bent, and appended upside down to the seal tag. Lines drawn with a sharp instrument on the back of the parchment, which has an appearance of great age, suggest, as Prof. Wormald has pointed out to me, that the parchment was cut from a book. The writ can be divided into three parts :

(1) The protocol and what follows, as far as : *swa full 7 swa forð*. The *into* which appears here before ' Suffolk ', in the place of the normal *on*, links this protocol with that of no. 22, an undoubtedly authentic writ, which also has *into*. The appearance of both Harold and Gyrth in the address might indicate that both were interested in these transactions, or again, that Gyrth was acting in a subordinate capacity to Harold. It is not unlikely that this Ickworth writ was a Bury writ originally, adapted by a Westminster forger to his own purposes. King Edward, addressing the Suffolk shire court announces that he intends to be ' worthy of' (see Introduction, p. 64) the land at Ickworth as fully and completely as . . .

[1] Wennington, among other estates, is also named in Edgar's charter, but the name of Edgar does not appear in the Wennington writ, which is constructed on different lines.

(2) A claim to Ickworth on the part of Westminster Abbey, in the words : *Crist 7 Sče Peter 7 ic hit mid rihte agan into þære haligan stowwe æt Westmunstre*, with what seems to be the 3rd pers. plur. pres. indic. of *agan*, ' to possess ', and with the meaning : ' Christ and St. Peter and I lawfully possess it for the holy place at Westminster '. Though ' Christ and St. Peter ' appear in Westminster writ as the recipient of grants (as for instance in no. 76), and ' Christ and St. Peter and St. Paul ' appear in the same capacity of recipients in Winchester writs (nos. 109, 110),[1] this conjunction of the king with ' Christ and St. Peter ' seems to be quite unparalleled. Extravagant claims were however not unknown at Westminster Abbey, the monks of which claimed for their abbey a miraculous dedication by St. Peter in person, as for instance in the treatise of Sulcard referred to above.[2] The evidence suggests that the text of a (probably authentic) writ of King Edward the Confessor has been manipulated so as to appear to support a claim of Westminster Abbey to the estate. Whether the clause : (*swa forð*) *swa gewitnesse hæfð to geboran*, formed part of the original writ seems doubtful.

(3) The remainder of the writ is undoubtedly authentic, and formed presumably part of the writ to which the protocol belonged. The king desires that the land at Ickworth be brought under his control as soon as the present letter has been read (in the shire court), and if anyone shall afterwards wish to lay claim to it, he will answer for it in such a manner as shall appear to people to be in accordance with the law. The valediction which stands here : *God eow ealle gehealde, Sče Petres holde*, appears in several other Westminster writs, but not in those of the highest repute, where the simple : *God eow (ealle) gehealde*, is employed. The additional clause : *Sče Petres holde*, could of course easily have been added at Westminster.

The Ickworth writ in its earlier form, the Sloane Charter, is not then an original writ of King Edward, but a copy of a forged text, to which a seal has been appended. The historical background of the writ is altogether obscure. In Widmore's spurious charter of King Edward (see p. 291), Ickworth (' Icceweorthe cum omnibus ad se pertinentibus ') is said to have been granted to Westminster Abbey by one of King Edward's *milites* named Byrhtsige (*Bricsige*), in the king's presence (like some other estates). But nothing appears to be known from any pre-Conquest source of a connection between Ickworth and Westminster Abbey. Ickworth is usually

---

[1] For a discussion of the principle, whereby the saints, or Christ and the saints, appear in this capacity, see Pollock and Maitland, *History of English Law*, i. 499. There are of course many other instances in Anglo-Saxon writs.

[2] See p. 287. For a paraphrase of Sulcard's narrative, and its literary relations, see Armitage Robinson, *Flete*, 4 ff.

associated with St. Edmund's Bury (see p. 504) and Abbot Leofstan
(of Bury) appears in the address of the writ. But towards the end
of the eleventh century Westminster had land at Ickworth, for
Westminster land there was leased out by Abbot Vitalis. A Latin
entry in Westminster Domesday f. 129, headed : ' These are the
feefarms of manors lands and tenements . . . leased after the
arrival of King William the Conqueror ', contains the item : ' Abbot
Vitalis (c. 1076–85) and the convent leased (*dimiserunt*) the manor of
Ickworth and Twyng in Suffolk for 60s. a year '. All the evidence
suggests that the Ickworth writ, Sloane Charter xxxiv. 1, represents
an attempt by the monks of Westminster to provide by means of a
spurious writ a record of a connection between Ickworth and
Westminster Abbey.

JUDICIAL AND FINANCIAL RIGHTS

The relations between the three writs (nos. 81–3) announcing the
king's grant to Westminster Abbey of JUDICIAL AND FINANCIAL
RIGHTS are difficult to determine. Comparing nos. 81 and 82 one
notes that the beneficiary named in one case is Abbot Edwin, in
the other St. Peter (for which the Faustina copy substitutes ' Christ
and St. [Peter])'. For the naming of St. Peter as beneficiary we can
find a parallel in, for instance, those Bury writs (*passim*) where the
beneficiary is St. Edmund ; see also p. 317 above. Although the
longer of the two writs, no. 82, could have been made out of the
shorter, no. 81 (except for the differences in the names of the
beneficiaries) merely by the insertion of additional matter which
could be removed without damage to the syntax (*on eallum
hys lande, infangenepeof 7 flymenefyrmpe, 7 ealle oðre gerihtu, on
stræte 7 of stræte, fyrmest, ne on wuda ne on felda, 7 þa gebroðru,
ealle. Amen*) there is perhaps sufficient independence in the character of the linguistic forms to suggest that the longer writ may have
been derived from an independent source. Each may be a writ of
King Edward independently issued ; one would conjecture that
no. 81 may have been issued not long after Abbot Edwin's
appointment to office, but the other writ cannot be more closely
dated than 1042–66. Although on palæographical grounds it is
not impossible that no. 81 in its earliest form is an original writ
of the Confessor, the probability that the handwriting belongs to
a date in the eleventh century rather later than that of the Confessor's time combines with the linguistic evidence (*æni, ænine* (for
ænig, ænigne) and the *-es* of ' bishops ') to suggest that this is not
an original writ but a slightly later copy of an original writ. The
same may be true of no. 82, copied in the same period, and with

similar linguistic forms : *binna, handan, socna, infangene-*. But if we accept no. 82 as authentic, there seems to be no real reason for rejecting no. 83, a writ in very similar terms to the two preceding, in which St. Peter is again named as beneficiary. Beside the orthographical variants easily accounted for by the difference in date of the two texts (the one of the eleventh, the other of the fourteenth century) no. 83 differs from no. 82 in the absence of the phrases : *on eallum his lande*; of : *7 ealle oðre gerihtu* ; of : *fyrmest* before *on handa* ; of : *ne on wudu ne on felda*, and of : *7 þa gebroðru* ; and in variations in the placing of the phrases : *binnan burh 7 butan burh* and of : *on stræte 7 of stræte* ; and also in a variation in one phrase (*hit . . . stod, hi . . . stodan*) between singular and plural. Can one with confidence assert that this is a copy of an independent writ of King Edward ? If it was not issued at a different date it is difficult to see what purpose could have been served by its fabrication, unless one regards it simply as an exercise in ringing the changes on familiar themes. There is abundant evidence that Westminster writs were ' worked over ' from time to time, but this particular text seems to be free from suspicious features.

The grant to Westminster Abbey by King Edward of rights belonging to himself (see Introduction, pp. 79 ff.) is noted in Domesday at the beginning of the Worcestershire Survey.[1] Domesday names the penalties for breach of the peace given by the king with his own hand, punishable with outlawry : for breach of the peace given by the sheriff, punishable by a fine of 100 shillings : for *forestellum*, punishable by a fine of 100 shillings ; for *heinfaram* (which, like *hamsocn*, was forcible entry into a man's house), punishable by a fine of 100 shillings : for rape, for which there was no amends except mutilation. It then continues : ' These forfeitures the king has in this county except (in) the land of St. Peter of Westminster, to whom King Edward gave whatever he had there, says the county (court) '. It is to be observed that of these offences, grith-breach, foresteall, and hamsocn (heinfare) are mentioned in the three writs which have just been discussed (nos. 81–3).

SHEPPERTON

The two SHEPPERTON writs, nos. 86, 87, must be discussed together, so far as their authenticity is concerned. The authenticity of no. 87, announcing the grant of land at Shepperton by the Confessor to Teinfrith, his ' church-wright ', can scarcely be in doubt. The text has been rather badly copied, and/or modernised, but its structure and phraseology are normal. With *ic nelle gepafian þ him*

[1] DB i. 172, VCH *Worcs.* i. 282.

ani man mid anigne þinga misbeode ac habbe he etc. we may compare in no. 51 the very similar : *ic nelle geþafian þæt heom ænig man misbeode ac beon heo* etc. ; for other prohibition clauses with *misbeode*, see Introduction, p. 66. The fact that this writ for Teinfrith is addressed to the abbot of Westminster and the sheriff is explicable on the supposition that the grant to Teinfrith represented some private arrangement regarding land at Shepperton already granted to the abbey ; and possibly the land there which formed the subject of a grant to Westminster Abbey recorded in the writ (no. 86) which precedes the Teinfrith writ in the Westminster Domesday cartulary. The two writs were evidently not regarded as conflicting. Teinfrith does not appear in Domesday and nothing is known of him from other sources. It was perhaps intended that he should hold the land as tenant for life, but the grant may never have become effective, or he may have held the land for only a short period. We learn from Domesday Book that the manor of Shepperton, rated at eight hides, was held in demesne by Westminster Abbey in 1086 as it had been in the time of King Edward (see p. 509). But the writ, no. 86, announcing the Confessor's grant of Shepperton to West-minster Abbey, is characterised by a feature, namely the omission in the address of the thegns of the shire, which is less easily explicable here than it is in Teinfrith's writ. This omission in no. 86 may of course have been made unconsciously or deliberately by a tran-scriber. But taken in conjunction with the reference in line 5 to St. Dunstan, this omission does arouse a doubt as to whether the Shepperton writ in favour of the abbey, no. 86, is actually an unaltered copy of an authentic writ of King Edward. In Anglo-Saxon writs references to the remote history of estates are rare. Such references appear only in two dubious Westminster writs, nos. 78, 79, and not in those of other houses. One cannot help suspecting that the Shepperton writ in favour of the abbey, no. 86, if it is founded on an authentic writ of the Confessor—and this there seems no reason to doubt—may have been altered, and that the reference to St. Dunstan's purchase of the land and his grant of it to Abbot Wulfsige and the brethren, may be due to interpolation. The peculiar form *herdet* (for *herð*) in line 3 is certainly the con-tribution of a later hand.

GREENFORD

Of the GREENFORD writ (nos. 88, 89) a shorter version is preserved in one cartulary and a longer version in the other. Both texts have passed through the hands of one or more copyists by whom a *g* in the exemplar was on occasion confused with *s* : this is not unusual in

Middle English copies of Anglo-Saxon writs, but the number of instances in the longer Greenford text is high ; and this suggests that the text before the copyist, where these confusions occur, was not written in Anglo-Saxon, but in a later, script. In the shorter version (no. 88) we have simply an announcement that Ailric's grant of Greenford to Westminster Abbey has been made with the king's consent ; in the longer version (no. 89) the king also for his own part grants to the monks of Westminster judicial and financial rights. The estate in question may or may not have constituted the whole or a part of the manor at Greenford rated at 11½ hides, which was held both in King Edward's time and in 1086 by the abbot of Westminster (see p. 510). Nothing is known of Ailric or of the circumstances in which he made his grant to the abbey, but there is no apparent reason for doubting that Greenford was granted by him to the monks of Westminster. The problem is, to discover which of these two texts (differing only in the presence or absence of a clause purporting to announce a grant by the king of certain other rights) preserves unaltered, except for orthographical changes, the text of the original writ of the Confessor announcing the grant. If we apply to these two documents the test of ' common form ', we can find for the shorter of the two a fairly close parallel in the (probably authentic) writ in which King Edward announces the grant of Wormley to Westminster Abbey by Leofsi Duddesunu with his consent (no. 90). It is then entirely probable that we have in the shorter form of the Greenford writ (no. 88) a (later) copy of an authentic writ of King Edward. The additional passage in the longer Greenford writ (no. 89), which forms its conclusion, and which can without difficulty be detached from it, purports to grant to the abbey sake and soke, toll and team, infangenetheof, and *alle pase rithe pe to me belunged*. The passage is suspect in itself, occurring elsewhere as it does only in three Westminster writs, nos. 74, 93, 104, not one of which is authentic as it stands, where we find it in the form : ' sake and soke, toll and team, infangenetheof, *and ealle (ða) (oðre) gerihte ðe to me belimpað* '. And one's suspicions as to the authenticity of the passage as it appears as the conclusion of the Greenford writ are not lessened by the appearance in it of the word *belunged*, in the sense ' belong' (? present tense or past). The *belunged* of no. 89 may have had its origin in a misreading of the word *belimpað* ; or *belunged* may have been deliberately substituted for *belimpað*. The verb ' belong ' in its modern sense appears in early fourteenth-century (and later) copies, on the Charter and other Rolls, of the ' Goodbegot ' writ of the Confessor (no. 111), in place of the form *belimpoð* of the text of the ' Goodbegot ' writ which is printed in this book.[1] It seems on the whole improbable that the additional clause in no. 89 ever formed part of an authentic Greenford writ of the Confessor, and much more likely that the monks of Westminster themselves made this addition to a writ issued by the Confessor in their favour.

WORMLEY

In the WORMLEY writ (no. 90) King Edward declares that it is with his consent that Leofsi *Duddesunu* has given to Westminster Abbey 2½ hides at Wormley. It would appear that the grant did not become effective, or else the land for some reason passed out of the possession of the monks of Westminster, for Domesday says nothing of any Westminster land at Wormley, either before or after the Conquest. A connection between this manor and the family of Dudde (Dode) seems however to have been maintained, for in 1086 one of the three Wormley manors, of 2½ hides, was held by Alwin *Dodesone* of the king. This manor, according to the Domesday entry, had been held in King Edward's time by Wlward, a man of Asgar (Esgar) the staller, who could sell it, and it ' was sold for 3 marks of gold after King William came ' (see p. 511). This does not of course preclude the possibility that Leofsi Duddesunu was an earlier owner, for the Confessor's writ may have been issued as early as 1053/57. What is difficult is to reconcile the absence of any mention in Domesday of a connection between Westminster and any of the Wormley manors with the existence of a Wormley writ in Latin attributed to William I.[2] In this document, dated 1066–87 by Davis, the king declares that he grants to Westminster Abbey the land at *Wermelea* which Lefsinus de Lundon' (presumably the Leofsige of the writ under discussion) gave to that church, and that it is his wish that St. Peter shall have it with all the rights with which he ever possessed it, and as King Edward granted it to that church, and as that church was seised of it, and as he himself afterwards granted it to the abbey. It seems distinctly possible that this writ is not authentic, but there are evidently gaps in the recorded history of this Wormley manor, and it seems therefore safer to criticise the Confessor's writ on internal grounds. For the form of the announcement there is a parallel in no. 69. The hand-

[1] See p. 399, n. 6. Dr. Kenneth Sisam (*Modern Language Review*, vol. 18 (1923) 263) has drawn attention to an Old English instance of the verb *belangað*, with a meaning equivalent to Latin *interest* (*Ac hwæt belangað þæs þonne to eow?*). The verb ' belong ' is not recorded in NED until the fourteenth century.

[2] Davis, *Regesta*, no. 250, charter no. 43. Its authenticity is not questioned by Davis.

writing belongs to the late eleventh century, but there is nothing in the contents of the writ which would forbid one to suppose that we have here a close copy, with only slight alterations in linguistic forms, of an authentic writ of King Edward the Confessor. The simplicity and straightforwardness of this writ, and the moderation of its statements, are points in its favour.

RUTLAND, LAUNTON, PERTON

The writs relating to Rutland, Launton and Perton have reasonable claims to be considered authentic. The RUTLAND writ has come down to us (no. 94) in a hand of the late eleventh century on a single piece of parchment to which part of a seal of red wax is still attached. This can be confidently accepted as a later copy of an authentic writ of King Edward, the linguistic forms of which have been only very slightly altered in transmission. In this document King Edward announces that he has given to Westminster Abbey Rutland and everything belonging to it with judicial and financial rights as fully and completely as he himself possessed it ; and that Queen Edith is to have it as long as she shall live and annually enrich the monastery therefrom. It is true that that part of present-day Rutland to which the writ refers was not in the possession of Westminster Abbey in 1086. It had indeed come into the hands of King William, apparently without any intermediate tenure (see pp. 514 f.). It would seem then that the grant of the reversion of this vast estate to Westminster after Queen Edith's death was frustrated perhaps (as Sir Frank Stenton has suggested) [1] because its exceptional value deterred the king from surrendering it outright. But that the claim of the monks of Westminster to Rutland was in some degree recognised may be indicated by the occurrence in Domesday of the word ' cherchesoch ' after the name of each of the three manors of Oakham, Hambleton, and Ridlington, which with their respective berewicks constituted the wapentake of Martinsley, Queen Edith's holding. Sir Frank Stenton comments on the difficulty of determining in what sense the term ' church soke(land) ' could be applied to these lands. He suggests that its appearance here may not be unconnected with the Westminster claim, and that the abbey may possibly have been reconciled to the postponement of its possession by a grant of dues to be paid by the estate, that ' such dues would undoubtedly be regarded as a form of soke in 1066 ' but that ' we have no evidence on the point and it must be left open '.[2] Moreover the monks of

---

[1] VCH *Rutland*, i. 132.

[2] For *cyricsocn* in Westminster writs, see nos. 73, 104.

Westminster in the reign of William II, if not of William I, were given rights over some at any rate of the churches of Rutland.[1] We may then with some confidence conclude that although his intention was eventually frustrated, the Confessor did actually confer upon the monks of Westminster the privileges referred to in the Rutland writ, and we need not hesitate to accept this writ in its earliest form as a very slightly modernised copy of a writ of that king.

The authenticity of the LAUNTON writ, no. 95, can scarcely be in doubt. Here the king announces the grant of Launton to Westminster Abbey as fully and completely as he himself possessed it. Everything encourages the belief that this writ, which is free from suspicious features, is, in the cartulary copy in which it has come down to us in Westminster Domesday, an only very slightly modernised copy of a writ of King Edward.

Two copies—the one a slightly later copy of the other—have been preserved of the PERTON writ (no. 96), written on two single pieces of parchment, the earlier in a contemporary hand. The authenticity of the writ seems certain. The king announces his grant to Westminster Abbey of land at Perton with sake and soke as fully and completely as he himself possessed it. The text implies that the land at Perton had previously been in the king's own hand, a tradition preserved in the spurious First Charter (pp. 289 f.), which includes Perton among the lands granted to the abbey by King Edward himself. In another spurious charter, the Telligraphus of King Edward (see p. 290), the king's chamberlain Hugelin (see Biographical Notes) is associated with a grant to the abbey among other lands of Perton with everything pertaining to it. But it is not certain that the two estates were identical, and if so, what was the relation of Hugelin's grant to that made by the king. The possibility that some part of the land had been given to Westminster by Hugelin need not be rejected, if only for the fact that in another case, that of Marston (see p. 335), an estate granted to the abbey by the king's chamberlain Weodet appears in the relevant writs (nos. 103, 104) as being granted by the king himself. In the Telligraphus the king is made to confirm Hugelin's grant together with those of other benefactors of the abbey, and the two traditions need not be regarded as conflicting. According to Widmore's charter (p. 291), the grant of Perton was one of those made after the dedication of the church on 28 December 1065.

---

[1] *Mon. Angl.*, i. 301, nos. 42–4 ; Davis, *Regesta*, nos. 381, 382, 420 ; J. Armitage Robinson, *Crispin*, 139. For comments see F. M. Stenton, VCH *Rutland*, i. 132, where it is stated that in 1268 Westminster possessed the advowson of Oakham, Hambleton and Ridlington, and received dues from seven other villages in the neighbourhood.

Not long after this the monks of Westminster secured from William I a writ in English addressed to the same persons as are addressed in King Edward's writ, declaring that Perton should belong to Westminster, to the property of St. Peter (*ligge into Westminstre to Petres are*) as fully and completely as King Edward, the king's kinsman, granted it to that house ; directing that Abbot Æthelwig (of Evesham) and Thurkill the king's reeve should be protectors and guardians (*mund and weard*) of the land under the king himself ; and declaring that the king would not allow anyone to do them wrong ; and if anyone did do them wrong they were to inform the king of it, and to fix a very good compensation for the offence [1] (*sette ful gode bote fore*).

Is the earlier of the two copies of the Perton writ, no. 96, an original writ, written and sealed by the clerks of the royal secretariat, or is it a contemporary copy made in the abbey scriptorium ? The question of handwriting is indecisive, for there can have been no difference between the handwriting of an original writ issued in the last few days of the Confessor's life, and that of a copy made a little later, after his death. Linguistic forms afford little help, for in a contemporary copy the forms, except for the chance variant, will be those of the original. Two linguistic forms in this writ do however invite comment. The form *herð*, 'belongs' in line 4, stands in this text side by side with *hyrð*, line 8, the form normal in late West Saxon. But *herð* also appears in other writs of the Confessor preserved in eleventh-century copies, nos. 94, 97, and such forms with -*e*- are also found occasionally in other late West Saxon texts,[2] where they would normally be regarded as non-West Saxon (Anglian or Kentish). There is, so far as I am aware, no reason to suppose that the two forms *herð* and *hyrð* could not have stood side by side in an original writ of King Edward. Dr. Kenneth Sisam has pointed out a similar well-marked deviation from standard Late West Saxon in Wynfrith's Letter in MS. Otho C, i, where Anglian (or Kentish) *ungehersumnes* appears side by side with *ungehyrsum*.[3] Rather more difficult to account for at first sight is the *nane* of the passage : ' Ic nylle *nane men* geþafian ' (l. 7), for which the only exact parallel in these texts is the ' ic nelle *nane men* þafien ', of one of the two extant copies of no. 23, preserved in an early-fourteenth century cartulary.[4] The *nanum men* for the dative singular, which

---

[1] Dated 1066–68 by Davis, *Regesta*, no. 25 ; Neufeldt no. 33. Davis's rendering of OE *are*, ' property ', as ' altar ' is erroneous.

[2] Sievers-Cook, *Old English Grammar* (1903), § 97 ; K. Brunner, *Altenglische Grammatik* (1942), § 104. *Herð, hereð* appear sporadically in later copies of writs of other houses.

[3] *Mod. Lang. Rev.* xviii (1923), 253–72.

[4] The only other copy of no. 23 has the misspelling *mane men*.

we should expect to find here, appears indeed in no. 4, and it is also represented by other forms, whose relation to *nanum* is easily explained, in nos. 2, 63, 85.[1] More than one explanation is possible here. *Nane* for *nanum* may be instrumental, instead of dative case. Or the form may be explained as an instance of that interchange between *-e* and *-um* (at least as early as the mid-tenth century) of which there is evidence elsewhere ; we may compare the *ælce mannum* of no. 45 (spurious). Both usages may have combined in a clause in an early eleventh-century will (Whitelock, p. 56) : ' *cyð þis mine hlaforde 7 ealle mine freondum* '. Such forms as these may have been employed in documents written in the royal scriptorium.[2] There is, so far as I can see, nothing in the Perton writ in its earliest form to forbid us to suppose that this is an original writ of King Edward. But in such a case as this the appearance of the document itself may be decisive, and it is in my opinion probable that we have here the original Perton writ of King Edward the Confessor, written and sealed by the royal clerks. And this conclusion is reinforced by the fact that the fragmentary seal attached to this writ is assigned by Birch and Wyon to the Second type (see p. 103), of which the two other specimens known are probably authentic.

OTHER GRANTS AFTER DEDICATION OF CHURCH

The fact that Staines, Windsor, Pershore, Deerhurst, and Islip, are included in Widmore's spurious charter (p. 291) among the estates granted by the Confessor to Westminster Abbey after the dedication on 28 December 1065 of the church which he had built, and so only some eight days before his death on 5 January 1066, raises difficult problems. The short writs relating respectively to Windsor-Staines, Pershore-Deerhurst, and Islip-Marston, nos. 97, 99, 103, are each accompanied by a longer writ of an entirely different type, nos. 98, 102, 104, and moreover there are two other short writs, nos. 100, 101, relating to Pershore-Deerhurst. If we accept the statement relating to these estates in Widmore's charter, and if we accept both sets of writs, the longer and the shorter, as authentic, we shall have to suppose that both sets of writs were issued in the eight days or so that elapsed between the dedication of the church, and the death of the Confessor. It is not easy to accept this conclusion. The statement in Widmore's charter can of course be

---

[1] *Geþafian* with the accusative appears in no. 44 : ' *nenne man geþauian* '. The *nanne men* of no. 54, and also of the Faustina text of the writ under discussion, no. 96, are inconclusive in the matter, combining as they do (in later copies), the accusative *nanne* with the dative *men*.

[2] *Curme Volume of Linguistic Studies*, Northwestern University Publication, 1930, 110–18, an article by Professor Kemp Malone.

rejected, but no reason is known for its fabrication, and moreover it receives some corroboration from the fact that the monks of Westminster had not come into possession of Pershore, of Deerhurst, or of Staines, at the time of King Edward's death.   In strict law these estates were therefore at King William's disposal, and it is not surprising to find that Islip, another of these estates, came into the possession of the monks of Westminster only after long delay.   To explain the existence of the two sets of writs relating respectively to Pershore-Deerhurst, Islip-Marston, and for the third group, writs relating to Windsor-Staines and Staines-*Stæningahaga*, it might of course be argued that King Edward may have given lands and rights at some of these places to the monks of Westminster at an earlier date, and that the grants made by him after the dedication of the church were either grants of additional rights, or else in the nature of confirmations.   Another possibility is that some of the writs referring to these estates that have been enumerated above, may have been composed after King Edward's death, presumably at Westminster Abbey.   It is unfortunate that since nos. 97 and 99, seemingly the most reputable of these texts, are addressed generally, they contain no evidence as to their date of issue.

STAINES and WINDSOR, with everything belonging thereto, are (as has been said above) included in Widmore's charter (p. 291) among the estates granted by the Confessor to the abbey after the dedication of the church (eight days or so before the king's death). By 1086 (Old) Windsor had passed into the hands of King William. We learn from Domesday that King William gave the manor of Battersea to Westminster Abbey in exchange for (Old) Windsor, and in another passage that King William then held (Old) Windsor in demesne and that King Edward had held it (p. 517).   Although nothing is said in Domesday as to any grant of Windsor to the abbey by King Edward, it can scarcely be doubted that the grant was made.   The history of Staines was different.   Although the abbey held Staines in 1086, it is clear from the Domesday entry (see p. 518) that Staines had come to the abbey only after King Edward's death : ' Valet xxxv libras. *Quando receperunt similiter.* T.R.E. xl libras '.   Of the two writs now extant relating to the Confessor's grant of Windsor and of Staines to Westminster Abbey, the shorter (no. 97) has come down to us as a text copied in its earliest form on a single piece of parchment in a handwriting of the late eleventh century.   Unlike the writs relating to Rutland, Launton, and Perton (nos. 94, 95, 96)—three other estates said in Widmore's charter to have been conferred upon the abbey on the same occasion—the Windsor-Staines writ (no. 97) is generally addressed.   Its greater length is due to the inclusion of additional clauses, the authenticity of which there is on general grounds no reason to doubt ; and in other respects this writ does not differ markedly from the (authentic) Rutland, Launton and Perton writs (nos. 94, 95, 96). One cannot however lightly disregard the condemnation pronounced upon this writ by Humphrey Wanley,[1] who associated it with the undoubtedly spurious writs relating to Chalkhill and to Ickworth (nos. 76, 80), and declared : ' Has tres cartas suspectæ fidei esse censeo.' The Windsor-Staines writ (no. 97) under discussion cannot of course in its earliest form be regarded as a writ issued and sealed by the royal clerks. Although the seal, now vanished, as described by Hickes, and the method of sealing, resembled those of writs of the Confessor, this seal cannot have been affixed to the writ in the royal scriptorium, for the date of the handwriting combines with that of the linguistic forms [2] to suggest that this writ, as it stands, is a product of the late eleventh century. On the other hand the form *monekas* in the Westminster Domesday copy rather suggests that the unusual spelling *mynekas* (OE *munecas*) [3] in the Cotton Charter may be merely the contribution of a transcriber. Wanley's adverse comment seems then to be justified in so far as the outward form of the writ is concerned. But there are in my opinion no obvious reasons (such as exist for nos. 76, 80) for holding the contents of the writ in suspicion, and it seems to me entirely probable that we have in the Windsor-Staines writ (no. 97) under discussion a later copy of an authentic writ of King Edward.

The short Windsor-Staines writ (no. 97) which has just been discussed is accompanied by a much longer writ of a different type (no. 98) dealing with the Staines portion of the Confessor's grant to Westminster Abbey. This text, which relates to the estate at STAINES and to the land in London called STÆNINGAHAGA, closely resembles a long writ (no. 102) relating to Pershore and Deerhurst, two more of the estates included in Widmore's charter among the lands granted to the abbey by the Confessor after the dedication of the church. That these estates of Pershore and of Deerhurst had not come into the possession of the abbey by the time of the death eight days or so later of King Edward is evident from a writ of William I (which seems to be authentic) enjoining that the estates of Pershore and Deerhurst which King Edward granted to Westminster Abbey shall *now* come into the possessio*n*s of the monks of

---

[1] Wanley, *Ant. Lit. Liber Alter*, 265.

[2] The linguistic evidence is of the same order as that observed in nos. 81, 82. The terminations in *-es*, the final *-e* in *wude, felde*, the forms *æni, ænine*, taken together, seem to indicate a date of origin in the second half of the eleventh century.

[3] Possibly a miscopying as *y* of a *u* with long final stroke, possibly an ' inverted ' spelling.

Westminster, and forbidding the alienation of anything belonging thereto on penalty of losing the king's friendship.[1] That Staines had not passed to Westminster Abbey by the time of King Edward's death is evident from the passage from Domesday that has been cited above (p. 327). At what period the extant writs came into existence we do not know. The earliest copy of the Staines-*Stæningahaga* writ belongs to the end of the eleventh century ; the Pershore-Deerhurst writ has come down to us only in a much later cartulary copy. These two texts are linked together by close similarities in form and phraseology. Indeed, except for the variations in the protocol and in the descriptions of the estates, the differences between them are slight. The orthographical variants are easily explicable in copies of different dates ; there are some small differences in syntax, and the first and last clauses are fuller in the Pershore-Deerhurst writ. A further link between these two texts appears in two virtually identical writs in Latin in the name of the Conqueror (differing the one from the other only in some insignificant variations in spelling), the one relating to Staines, the other to Pershore and Deerhurst.[2] In the Staines writ King William announces his grant to Westminster Abbey *ad victuale subsidium* of the manor of Staines, with sake and soke, toll, team, *latro, emissio,* hamsocn, foresteall, *pacis fractura,* flymenafyrmth, and miskenning, and with the laws and customs pertaining to the king, as it was given to the abbey by King Edward and granted and confirmed *per cartas privilegii sui.* In the Pershore-Deerhurst writ King William announces his grant of these estates to the abbey in the same terms, with the same witnesses, on the same occasion. These two writs of the Conqueror however, dated 1080–86 by Davis, may not be authentic. Is the authenticity of the two related writs of King Edward reasonably certain ? These two texts in the name of the Confessor may well have had some substantial basis of fact. They are not addressed generally, but in the one case to the shire court of Middlesex, in the other to those of Worcestershire, Gloucestershire, and Oxfordshire. The dates of the persons addressed, so far as they are known, are consistent with one another, and moreover, they fall without any difficulty within the period

[1] Davis, *Regesta*, no. 32 ; dated by Davis 1066–69. Davis's remark (*ibid.* no. 234) that ' Edward's grant (i.e. of Pershore and Deerhurst) was to take effect after Queen Edith's death ' was founded on a misapprehension. The phrase : *post mortem Edgithe regine conjugis mee,* in the text of the spurious First charter of the Confessor (see p. 290) as printed by Kemble (no. 824), and Thorpe p. 404, really belongs to the preceding clause, and refers to King Edward the Confessor's grant of Rutland to Westminster Abbey (no. 94).

[2] Davis, *Regesta,* nos. 233, 234 : with full text of Staines writ, charter no. 37. The virtual identity of the two texts is however obscured in Davis's summary.

28 December 1065–6 January 1066. But it seems improbable that these two texts are unaltered copies of authentic writs of King Edward. They bear a family resemblance to the (dubious) writs nos. 75, 77, 85, 91, 92 relating respectively to Ulf's London land and wharf, Chalkhill, Eversley, Ayot, and Tooting (pp. 306 ff.), but they are more elaborate than any of these. They do not however cover precisely the same ground as the shorter writs relating to the same estates by which they are accompanied, and it is not inconceivable that both a Windsor-Staines writ (no. 97), and a Staines-*Stæningahaga* writ (no. 98), should have been issued, though not in the latter case precisely in the existing form, within the same eight days or so. The Windsor-Staines writ says : ' I inform you that I have given Windsor and Staines to Westminster Abbey as fully and completely as I myself possessed it '. The Staines-*Stæningahaga* writ says : ' I inform you that the monks of Westminster are to have Staines and *Stæningahaga* with the following privileges '. There seems therefore to be room for both. But it is altogether likely that if the existing long Pershore-Deerhurst and Staines-*Stæningahaga* writs represent authentic writs issued by King Edward, those writs were enlarged and improved and embellished within the abbey. How far this process may have gone we can only speculate. But to take one definite point the appearance of *miskenning* here is probably anachronistic, as it seems to be in other Anglo-Saxon writs (p. 82).

The existence of three short writs relating to PERSHORE AND DEERHURST (nos. 99–101) is more difficult to account for, for these texts are closely related the one to the other. They are all generally addressed and cannot therefore be dated closely, but (as has been said above) Widmore's spurious charter (p. 291) includes these estates among those conferred upon the abbey by King Edward after the dedication of the church, on 28 December 1065. In much the same terms as the Windsor-Staines writ (no. 97) which has been discussed above, these texts announce that the Confessor has given Pershore and Deerhurst to the monks of Westminster as fully and completely as he himself possessed them. The one of these three texts which most closely resembles the (authentic) writs relating respectively to Rutland, Launton, and Perton (nos. 94, 95, 96), issued supposedly within the same period of eight days or so before King Edward's death, is no. 99, the shortest of the three. There is no apparent reason for doubting that this text, although it is preserved in only one of the cartularies, is a (modernised) copy of an authentic writ of the Confessor. But when this text is compared with no. 100, another of this group of Pershore-Deerhurst texts, it is apparent that the only difference between the two is one of length. In addition to the sake and soke, toll and team, of no. 99, no. 100 purports to grant to the monks of Westminster the frequently-granted infangenetheof. But furthermore the longer of the pair, no. 100, contains a precept for all the (king's) thegns on the estates in question : they are henceforth to be subject to the monastery, to the abbot and monks, and they are to pay to the monastery all the dues and the recognition of lordship that belong to the king. It is not of course inconceivable that in the short time that elapsed between the dedication of the church and the death of King Edward, this second writ might have been issued, in addition to the first. But it seems equally possible that the second writ (no. 100) may have been produced in the abbey after the Conquest to meet some emergency which had not been foreseen at the time when the first writ (no. 99) was issued. A possible indication of a date of origin later than the Confessor's reign is perhaps to be detected in the *for*, conjunction, for Old English *for ðan*, in line 10, a form appearing in the long Islip writ (no. 104), and in the spurious Coventry writ (no. 45), which is generally considered to have originated in the Middle English period. It is hard to believe that no. 100 is a writ issued independently of no. 99, for in a number of points the two texts resemble each other closely, notably in the use of *birð, byreð*, as against the different verb, *herð*, of no. 101. On the balance of probabilities one is inclined to think that no. 100 may not have been an independent writ of the Confessor separately issued. But there is of course no inherent improbability in the directions concerning the thegns on the estate, and in the Eversley writ (no. 85) the king declares that his four free sokemen who hold the estate shall each of them henceforth be subject to the monks and obey them.

The third of the short Pershore-Deerhurst writs (no. 101) also presents problems. Whereas nos. 99 and 100 are addressed to ' my bishops, my earls and all my thegns in Worcestershire and Gloucestershire ', the writ under discussion substitutes ' abbots ' for ' earls '. Instances of writs addressed to ' abbots ' at large are given in the Introduction, p. 48. Was this writ specially issued to announce the king's grant to Westminster Abbey of the vast estates of Pershore and of Deerhurst to the abbots of Worcestershire and Gloucestershire, and in particular to the abbot of Pershore, who himself had a manor at Pershore, and in 1086 had rights over the Westminster lands there ? The earlier history of these estates and of the claims over them of Pershore Abbey was discussed by J. H. Round,[1] who observes that there is no real evidence for the statement sometimes made, that King Edward robbed Pershore Abbey of the lands that he bestowed upon Westminster, and of which Pershore Abbey

[1] VCH *Worcs.* i. 257 ff. See also pp. 519 f. below.

had, according to William of Malmesbury,[1] been formerly the owner. Round suggests that the real despoiler of Pershore was Earl Ælfhere of Mercia (died 983), the leader of the anti-monastic reaction, whose heir was Earl Odda, and that on Odda's death in 1056 without an heir, King Edward may have seized all his lands,[2] which the king would then have been in a position to bestow on Westminster Abbey. However that may have been, it is at all events clear that the abbot of Pershore would have had a special interest in this grant. But is the existing writ an original writ of the Confessor ? The text is written in a handwriting which may or may not date from the Confessor's time on a single piece of parchment which in its dimensions and in the manner of sealing, *sur simple queue*, resembles writs of King Edward. The absence of a wrapping tag may or may not be significant. The seal, however, now only fragmentary, is of an unusual type ; it is the only specimen listed by Birch and Wyon of the so-called Third Seal of King Edward ; it is not certain that it is authentic. In the text itself two forms excite misgivings. Would a clerk of King Edward's secretariat have used the form *fyrþmest*, apparently formed on the analogy of *forþ*, and not recorded elsewhere, in place of the usual *fyrmest* ? Would he have written *bletsunga*, which is probably a mistake, for the normal *bletsung* ?[3] *Fyrþmest* and *bletsunga* are abnormal forms, not merely late, or non-West Saxon forms, like the *herð* (l. 4), which occurs sporadically as a variant for *hyrð* (see p. 325), or like the *syo*, *seo*, of the valediction (for the usual late West Saxon *sie*, *si*, *sy*), of which another instance appears in the *syo he Judas gefere* in a thirteenth-century copy (D) of no. 34. It seems unlikely that the valediction in its present form was produced in the king's scriptorium. One way of explaining the abnormal features of this writ would be to suppose that a copy of an authentic writ of the Confessor was made in Westminster Abbey, where it underwent in the process of copying some degree of alteration and enlargement. In that case the original writ from which the existing text was derived may have been the original writ of the Confessor of which no. 99 is probably a close copy.

LONDON

The same difficulty—that of distinguishing between what formed part of an original writ and what may have been added later—

---

[1] *Gesta Pontificum*, 298.   [2] On Odda, see Robertson, 456 ff.

[3] On the content of the valediction, see p. 71, where a somewhat similar formula is cited from Robertson, no. 91. Brunner, § 255, 1, says that *-unge* is common in such nouns in the nom. sing., in the eleventh century. He does not mention *-unga*.

arises when one considers the TWO LONDON WRITS, nos. 105, 106 (now extant only in cartulary copies), in which King Edward announces to the authorities of London that he has granted to Westminster Abbey full freedom upon all the lands which belonged to the abbey, and judicial and financial rights as fully as ever he himself possessed them. The statement in the shorter version (no. 106) that the grant was made ' at the dedication of the church ' is probably well-founded, and the details of the royal grant may be true in the main. The Scandinavianised form *kirk* (*kirk-haleginge*) in both the cartulary copies of no. 105, which is not a normal Old English form, was probably introduced by the copyist responsible for similar forms occurring sporadically in the Faustina texts, and very occasionally in the Westminster Domesday versions (see p. 296). Looking at these two texts as a whole, the chief difference between them is the elaborate conclusion of no. 105, a conclusion of the same general character (though differing in details) as that which rounds off the longer Islip-Marston writ (no. 104) ; this writ relates to another royal grant made, we are told, on the same occasion, the dedication of the church. But does it seem likely that two London writs differing mainly in the elaborate conclusion of no. 105, would have been issued in the eight days or so which elapsed between the dedication of the church on 28 December 1065 and the Confessor's death ? One could of course argue that the longer writ in which the reference to the dedication of the church is lacking, was issued at some earlier date ; but this does not seem very probable. An alternative would be to suppose that one or more hands had worked over a writ announcing these grants to Westminster Abbey and so produced a second writ. Definitely due to scribal alteration are the pronoun *his* in *geafe se ðe his geafe*, in no. 106, found as an equivalent for ' them ' in Middle English texts, but not in Anglo-Saxon,[1] and the Middle English verb *longen*[2] which replaces *lagon* in the Faustina copy of no. 105. The additional phrase ' the holy apostle ', which follows the name of St. Peter in no. 105, has the appearance of an ' embellishment '. Can we then suppose that the shorter writ, no. 106, is a copy of an authentic writ of King Edward ? There is no justification for denying this writ any substantial basis of fact, but it seems likely that its form has undergone some degree of alteration ; the omission of this text to supply the words customary in Westminster writs : ' except the abbot and the brethren for the needs of the monastery '—if it is not simply a copyist's omission—needs to be accounted for. It is worth noting that the

---

[1] See *Anglia*, Beiblatt, vii, 331, xi. 302, and J. Hall, *Selections from Early Middle English*, ii. 274.

[2] On *long*, now replaced by *belong*, see NED ' long ' v.[2].

writs in the name of William I which purport to confirm the privileges enumerated in nos. 105, 106, are of dubious authenticity.[1]
Further neither *miskenning* (p. 82) nor *showing* (p. 83), both
occurring in nos. 105, 106, appear in Westminster writs of the
Confessor which are of reasonably certain authenticity. But the
Confessor may possibly have granted to Westminster Abbey
privileges that he did not concede to less-favoured houses, and
though the mention of *miskenning* here is in all probability
anachronistic, it seems only natural that *showing*, a commercial
liberty known to have existed before the Conquest, should be
emphasised in writs purporting to relate to the rights of Westminster Abbey in London. These two texts seem then to contain
authentic material, but it is likely that they have been ' worked
over ', and it is even possible that this process has resulted in the
production from one original writ of King Edward of two very
similar texts.

ISLIP AND MARSTON

Two writs (nos. 103, 104) are extant relating to King Edward's
grant to Westminster Abbey of his estate of ISLIP in Oxfordshire,
together with a half-hide at MARSTON. From the longer we learn
that Islip was his birthplace, and that on the day of his birth his
mother had assigned it to him as his heritage. Further in a writ
dated 1067–71 by Davis, King William declares that Abbot Edwin
and the monks of Westminster are to have their manor of Islip in
which the king's kinsman King Edward was born, with everything
belonging thereto, with all the rights with which it was granted them
by King Edward at the dedication of the church ; and he grants
them sake and soke, toll, team and *latro*, with all the laws and
' customs ' pertaining to his royal dignity, and freedom from plaints
and shires and hundreds, scot and geld and Danegeld.[2] This writ
is marked ' ? spurious ' by Davis. He remarks that Remigius,
addressed here as bishop of Lincoln, did not remove to that see
before 1072, whereas Abbot Edwin, in whose favour the writ purports to have been issued, died in 1071 ; but the word ' Linc '
which accompanies the name of Remigius, might have been inserted by a copyist. Davis observes that in Domesday Islip is
not mentioned as belonging to Westminster Abbey. Islip is entered
there as being held of the king by the wife of Roger d'Ivry. Her
estate (in which Oddington was also included) is said in Domesday

---

[1] Davis, *Regesta*, nos. 215, 216 (= Armitage Robinson, *Gilbert Crispin*, 129).
[2] *Regesta*, no. 52, charter no. 10.

to have been held *in commendatione*, a term taken by F. M. Stenton[1] to imply that she was regarded as its temporary holder pending a further investigation of the claims of the monks of Westminster. If the writ of William I mentioned above confirming Islip to the monks of Westminster is authentic, then we must suppose that the confirmation was subsequently revoked, and that the manor was otherwise disposed of through some sequence of events of which nothing is now known. In both the Islip writs (nos. 103, 104) the grant of Islip by King Edward is coupled with that of a half-hide of land *æt Mersce*, which, as we learn from another source, had been bequeathed to the abbey by King Edward the Confessor's chamberlain Weodet (see p. 522). We can with confidence infer that this is the half-hide at *Mersctun* (Marston) which, according to a writ of William I (in English) had been bequeathed by Weodet to Westminster Abbey with the king's consent. This writ of William I[2] implies that the abbey had not yet obtained possession of the land at Marston, for the king directs that the half-hide at *Mersctun* and everything pertaining thereto shall belong to Westminster (' ligge in to Westminstre ') as fully and completely as ever Weodet held it and bequeathed it to that house and the king consented thereto (' Wedet it formest hahte 7 þider inne bequað 7 ic þas geuþe '). That its possession had been disputed is implied by King William's direction that everything belonging to this estate which had been alienated from it shall be restored within a week from the day on which this letter (*gewritt*) comes to the persons to whom it is addressed (' to eow comþ '), ' because ', says the king, ' I will not permit anyone to " undo " the gift which I have granted to this house '. Nevertheless the half-hide at Marston came to be lost to the abbey. No later reference to Marston than that in William's writ is to be found, so far as I have been able to ascertain, among the Westminster muniments.

The relation of the shorter ISLIP-MARSTON writ (no. 103) to the longer (no. 104) cannot be determined with any degree of certainty, though the fact that the address of the one is identical with that of the other, and that the phraseology employed is similar, indicates that the two texts must be in some way connected. On the test of ' common form ' the shorter writ (although it is briefer than the Rutland and the Launton writs (nos. 94, 95), the texts that it

[1] VCH *Oxfordshire*, i. 386–7. It was conjectured by Dunkin (*Oxfordshire ; Bullington and Ploughley*, i. 291) that the Conqueror seized Islip and gave it to Hugh de Grentemesnil, and that Hugh gave Islip (and Oddington) to his daughter Adeline on her marriage to Roger d'Ivry. See further, note on no. 103.

[2] Davis, *Regesta*, no. 18, dated c. 1067 by Davis ; text in *Mon. Angl.* i. 301, no. xxxiv, Neufeldt no. 28.

resembles most closely) seems to be unexceptionable in all respects save one, namely, the omission of *freondlice* in the address. Is this an independent writ of the Confessor, in which the absence of *freondlice* is due to scribal omission ? Or is it a summary or abridgement of a longer writ, made perhaps after the Confessor's day ? It is worthy of note that in the shorter writ Islip is said to have been given merely *mid saca 7 mid socna 7 on eallan þingan*, and that there is no specific mention of the privileges named in the longer writ, and this moderation commands respect. If it were not for the omission of *freondlice* in the address one would have little hesitation in accepting the shorter writ as a copy of an authentic writ of the Confessor, but in view of this omission—which need not be merely a transcriber's error—the question of its authenticity must remain open.

It is not at all unlikely that in the longer Islip-Marston writ (no. 104) authentic and spurious material have been blended. In the list of privileges granted *blodwite* and *weardwite*, which are rarely mentioned in writs, and never in writs of the highest class (see Introduction, pp. 83 ff.), appear in company with the normal ' sake and soke, toll, team, infangenetheof, grithbreach, hamsocn, and foresteall ' ; and further the conjunction in this list of *grithbreach* and *mundbreach* awakes suspicion (see pp. 81 f.). Further it seems more than doubtful whether the clause *swa full 7 swa forð*, was ever used in authentic writs in combination, as it is here, with the clause *swa freo* (*swa full 7 swa forð 7 swa freo*). Although in an excellent Bury text (no. 25) *swa freolice* appears, and in an excellent Abbotsbury text (no. 1), *wel 7 freolslice*, only in a Chertsey writ, no. 42, which comes under suspicion on other grounds, is there a combination of the *forð* formula with the *freo* formula ; here we find *swa freo 7 swa forð swa ænig is freost*. Again, the ' and ' in the valediction (' *and* Sce Petres holde ') must be a mistake of the compiler, or possibly of the transcriber (see Introduction, p. 72). And further *for*, conjunction, in line 13, where *for ðan*, or *for ðan ðe*, would be normal in a writ of the Confessor, is most easily explained as the contribution of a later hand (see p. 331). All these things taken together seem to indicate the likelihood of the alteration and ' improvement ' of a (probably authentic) Islip-Marston writ of King Edward. There is no obvious reason for doubting the authenticity of the remainder of the document. There would be no point in inventing the instructions to Wigod of Wallingford at any later date ; and the benediction and anathema which protect the grant do not appear inappropriate in a text recording a grant by the Confessor to Westminster of the place where he was born (see Introduction, p. 69). It seems then probable that the longer Islip-

Marston writ (no. 104) represents the working over and improvement of an authentic writ of King Edward by a later hand. Whether the writ has undergone really extensive remodelling, it is difficult to say. But it is significant that only in dubious Westminster writs (and not in writs of other houses) do we find passages parallel to the one appearing here : ' and ic an heom þer ofer saca 7 socne . . . 7 ealle ða gerihte þe to me belimpað ' (see pp. 298 ff.).

LATIN DIPLOMAS

The long and elaborate Latin charters in favour of Westminster Abbey which bear the names of King Edward the Confessor and of King William have frequently been cited above. It has long been recognised that these charters cannot in their existing form be accepted as documents contemporary with the kings whose names they bear. Their interest lies in their presentation of the traditions current in the abbey at the time when they were composed. The details of lands and estates granted and confirmed to Westminster Abbey by King Edward in the so-called First Charter and in the spurious charter printed by Widmore [1] add little to the information given in the writs ; but the so-called Telligraphus of King Edward [2] adds information as to the conditions in which certain estates were given. The so-called Second Charter [3] and Third Charter [4] of King Edward give no list of properties, and like the Second, Third and Fourth Charters of King William I (all likewise spurious), they are mainly concerned with the privileges claimed by the abbey, and more particularly with its claim to freedom from episcopal and lay control.[5] Of greater interest for the history of the Westminster estates are the spurious First Charter and Telligraphus attributed to William I,[6] which give an even more detailed account of some of the grants made to the abbey in the Confessor's time than do the First

[1] For the First Charter see p. 289 above, and for the charter printed by Widmore see p. 291. These charters give the number of hides granted in each case. In some cases the information given differs from that given in writs, and the two charters are not in every detail consistent with each other.

[2] For this see p. 290 above.

[3] For the Second Charter see K. 779, *Mon. Angl.* i. 295 ; comment, Armitage Robinson, *Flete*, 14 ; Stevenson, *loc. cit.*

[4] For this see p. 290 above.

[5] Calendared by Davis, *Regesta*, nos. 34, 90, 144. See also Armitage Robinson, *Flete*, 15 f.

[6] Printed in full, *Cal. of Ch. Rolls*, iv. 330–6 ; calendared, Davis, *Regesta*, no. 11, but without the list of properties ; analysed, *Twenty-Ninth Report of the Deputy Keeper*, 34 f. ; for comment, see Armitage Robinson, *Flete*, 15, *Crispin*, 158. Telligraphus (apparently unprinted), calendared, Davis, *Regesta*, no. 251 ; comment, *Flete*, 15.

Charter and Telligraphus of King Edward, and the charter printed by Widmore (see p. 291). Further, the spurious Great Charter of King Edgar [1] and the spurious Great Charter of Archbishop Dunstan (B. 1050), two charters compiled much later than the time of those whose names they bear,[2] give details of the earlier history of certain Westminster estates said to have formed part of the endowment granted to the abbey by Edgar and Dunstan ; some of these estates appear in writs in the name of King Edward.

The so-called Great Charter of Edgar confirms to the abbey certain gifts of land, some as grants of land made by earlier kings and other benefactors, some as purchases made by Dunstan, and given by him to the abbey ; among the estates named, those which appear in alleged writs of the Confessor are : Wennington, Aldenham, Datchworth, Watton, and (the monastery at) Staines and everything pertaining to it. It is to be noted that Fanton, which according to an entry in Domesday had come to the abbey by a false writ (see p. 105) appears in this list. King Offa and King Coenwulf appear here as benefactors of the abbey ; they are named again, with King Alfred and King Edgar, in the spurious Great Charter of Dunstan, which is concerned mainly with the liberties and privileges of the abbey, but also mentions estates (among them Shepperton) purchased by Dunstan and given by him to Westminster.

It is unfortunately impossible to determine the relationship between the Westminster writs attributed to the Confessor and these spurious Latin charters, or to discover to what extent, if any, the writs were used by their compilers. The view taken by Armitage Robinson [3] seems a reasonable one ; he suggests that though these charters are not genuine as they now stand, they incorporate a great deal of valuable tradition, and that the monks of Westminster remodelled 'their short Saxon documents, which were unintelligible to the Normans, into the impressive Latin charters which presented their interpretation of the privileges given them by their founder '. The same line of argument appears in the

[1] Text, *Mon. Angl.* i. 291, no. iii, B. 1264 ; printed and critically examined, *Crawford Charters*, vi ; analysed, *Flete*, 12. The edd. of the *Crawford Charters* trace the origin of Edgar's Great Charter to an expanded version of a short charter of Edgar granting to the abbey land at Westminster granted by Offa (B. 1048), and suggest that 'instead of the Westminster estate the names of numerous other abbey estates, concerning which there were, presumably, no charters in existence, were inserted '.

[2] The editors of the *Crawford Charters*, 89, suggest that the date of Edgar's Great Charter must be later than 1082, and that the text they print, purporting to be the original, was written shortly before or after 1100. Armitage Robinson, *Flete*, 12, argues for an even later date (not much earlier than 1140) but gives no obvious indication of having seen the *Crawford Charters* text and discussion. See also Hickes, *Dissertatio Epistolaris* (1703), 66, 82, *Mon. Angl.* i. 266.

[3] *Flete*, 14, *Crispin*, 40.

Monasticon Anglicanum,[1] ' the monks to secure their property probably preferred forging charters in a language that the Normans could read to the production of instruments in the vulgar tongue, which however genuine, would be despised '. [2] The line of English abbots of Westminster came to an end with the death of Edwin in 1071, and there is reason to suppose that the compilation of these Latin charters was undertaken during the rule of one or other of their Norman successors. But it is abundantly evident that the Anglo-Saxon writs were after the Norman Conquest by no means ignored, and that interpolation, alteration, and fabrication, of these texts was proceeding until at any rate the early years of the twelfth century (if not later). By this time the fabrication of charters in Latin at Westminster had probably already begun, and it was the Latin charters and not the writs in English which were brought out for enrolment at a later date. For example the spurious First Charter (see p. 289) alone among the charters and writs attributed to the Confessor is entered with many other Westminster charters on the Patent Roll in the reign of Henry VI.[3] But however the Westminster forgeries (and those of other houses) may be regarded, the judgment pronounced by Widmore [4] on the forgeries of the monks of Westminster still holds good : ' When Persons give themselves Leave to defend even a good Title by undue means, they seldom know where to stop, and the Success at first emboldens them to enlarge beyond all Reason. And tho' I do not think that in this Practice the whole was Fiction and Invention, they only added what they imagined would more especially serve their Purpose ; yet by this means they have destroyed the Certainty of History, and left those who come after them no better Help, in separating the Truth from Fables, than Conjecture and not altogether improbable Supposition '.

(73)

King Edward declares that the *burh* at Wennington and 4 hides of land, together with the church and the church-soke, and everything pertaining thereto, and with the land at the lea, are to belong to Westminster Abbey as fully and as completely as ever Ætsere Swearte and his wife Ælfgyth owned them and gave them to the abbey with his consent : and he grants to St. Peter judicial and financial rights. (1042–44)

---

[1] i. 268.   [2] See also Widmore, *Enquiry*, 11.
[3] See *Cal. of Patent Rolls*, 1422–29, 119 ; there are other instances on the Patent Rolls.
[4] *Enquiry*, 11.

(Madox, *Formulare Anglicanum*, p. 36, no. lx)

1　+ Eadward kyng gret Ælfward biscop. 7 Leofcild scirgerefan.
7 ealle mine þeignas on Eastsexan frendlice.　Ic cyðe eow þ̄ ic
wille [þ̄ se] byrig æt Winintune. 7 feower hidan landes þær to. mid
þære cyrice. [7] mid þære cyricsocne. 7 mid ælce ðære [þin]ga þe þær
5 to gebyrað. 7 mid ðam lande æt þære lea liggen into Westmynstre
to ðære muneka bigleofan. swa full 7 swa forð swa Ætsere Swearte
7 his wif Ælfið hy fyrmest ahten. 7 ðider inn gefon 7 ic ðes fullice
geuðe.　And ic ann þæt Sc̄e Peter habbe þær ofer saca. 7 socna. toll.
7 team. infangeneþeof. 7 fulne freodom on eallum ðingum. swa full
10 7 forð swa he fyrmest hæfoð on ænigum stede þær he oðer land hefð.
for ðam ic nelle geðafian þ̄ ænig mann undo ða gyfe þe ic ðider inn
geunnen habbe oððe þ̄ ðer ænig mann ænigne onstyng habbe on
ænigum ðingum. oððe on ænigne timan buton se abbud 7 þa gebroðra
to ðes mynstres nytþærflicre neode.　God eow gehealde. 7 Sc̄es
15 Petres holde.

*Words in brackets supplied from F ;　Madox indicates by dots lacunæ in his
MS.　　　　2. freondlice F.　　　　3. hide F.　　　　15. F adds Amen.*

Translation

King Edward sends friendly greetings to Bishop Ælfweard and
Leofcild the sheriff and all my thegns in Essex.　I inform you that
my will is that the (defensible) house at Wennington and four hides
of land [belonging] thereto, with the church and with the church-
soke, and with everything pertaining thereto, and with the land at
the lea, shall belong to Westminster for the sustenance of the monks
as fully and as completely as ever Ætsere Swearte and his wife
Ælfgyth possessed them, and gave them to that foundation : and
I gave my full consent to that.　And I grant that St. Peter have
thereover sake and soke, toll and team, infangenetheof, and full
freedom in all matters, as fully and as completely as ever he has
in any place where he has other land.　Therefore I will not permit
that anyone undo the grant that I have made to that house, or
that anyone have any authority there in any matter or at any
time except the abbot and the brethren for the uses and necessities
of the monastery.　God keep you and St. Peter's lieges.

(74)

King Edward declares that the land at Kelvedon and everything
pertaining thereto is to belong to Westminster Abbey as fully and as
completely as ever Æthelric the chamberlain and his wife Gode

owned it and bequeathed it to the abbey with his consent ; and he grants to St. Peter judicial and financial rights.

(Cott. Faust. A. iii, f. 107)

Edward king gret Elfward ƀ. 7 Leofcild sirefan 7 alle mine þegnes ı on Estsexen freondlice. Ic kiþe eow þat ic wille ꝥ þaet land at Killeuendun' 7 alc þare þinga ꝥ þarto gebira ̌ligge into Sainte Petre at Westminstre swa full 7 swa forth swa Ailhre burthein 7 Gode hiis wif it formest hauchten 7 þider inne beqwa ̌. on allen þingen. 7 icc 5 þas fullice geuþe for minre saule 7 for here saule 7 for alle quiken 7 for alle dede to helpe. 7 icc an ꝥ Sainte Petre habbe þar ofer sace 7 socne toll 7 theam infangeneþef 7 alle o ̌ere rihte ꝥ to me bilimpa ̌. 7 ic nelle geþafian natheswon ꝥ it any man undo þa gife ꝥ ic þider inne geunnen habbe. o ̌ ̌e þat þar anig man any onsting habbe on 10 any þare þingen þas þe mid richte into þare halagen stowe gebire ̌. for þam þe ꝥ minstre is on minen munde 7 al þat þar into her ̌ on allen þingan. God eow gehealde 7 alle þa ̌e beo ̌ holde into þare halagen stowe.

Heading : Killeuedene. cap. cxij.   1. *D preserves earlier forms :*
Eadward, Ælfward, scirgerefan, Eastsexan.   3. Kylewenduna D.
3. þing- *written in* MS. *throughout these texts as* þng- *with no sign of contraction, expanded without further comment*; *similarly with* þider, MS. þder.
3. gebira ̌] -ad MS.   8. bilimpa ̌] -ad MS.   9. geþafian natheswon Neufeldt] gagifian natherwon MS.   10. þar anig] þas anig MS.   12. into] unto MS.   13. þa ̌e beo ̌] ꝥ þat ̌e beo ̌ MS.

Translation

King Edward sends friendly greetings to Bishop Ælfweard and Leofcild the sheriff and all my thegns in Essex. I inform you that my will is that the land at Kelvedon and everything pertaining thereto shall belong to St. Peter's, Westminster, as fully and as completely as ever Æthelric the chamberlain and his wife Gode possessed it and bequeathed it to that foundation in all things. And I gave my full consent to that for (the good of) my soul, and for their souls, and for the help of all the living and all the dead. And I grant that St. Peter have over it sake and soke, toll and team, infangenetheof, and all other rights that belong to me. And I will not on any consideration consent that anyone undo the grant that I have made to that house, or that anyone have any authority there in any of the things that lawfully pertain to the holy foundation, because the minster is under my protection, and all that belongs to it in all things. God keep you and all those who shall be well-disposed towards the holy foundation.

(75)

King Edward declares that the monks of Westminster are to have the land and the wharf which Ulf the portreeve and his wife Cynegyth gave to Westminster Abbey, as fully and as completely as ever the donors possessed it ; and he grants them full freedom in everything that shall arise there on land and on strand. (1042–44)

(Westm. Do. f. 506)

1   Edward king gret Alfword biscop 7 Easgar stallere 7 ealle mine burgþeingnes on Lundone freondlice.   Ic kiþe eow þat icc anne 7 icc wille þat Sčē Peter 7 þa gebroþera on Westminstre habben þat land 7 þane wearf þarto þe Ulf portegerefa 7 his wif Kinegið for here 5 sawle alesednisse into þare halgan stowe gæfon swa full 7 swa forð. swa hi best hit ahton.   And icc ann heom eft ealswa. ꝥ hy habben þer to fulne freodom on eallun þingun þe þer upp aspringað be lande 7 be strande. for þan icc nelle nateswon geþafian þat anig mann atbrede oððe geutige heora geofa 7 heore almesse oþþe þat þer anig 10 mann aningne onstinge habbe on ænigun þingun oððe on ænigun timan butan se abbod 7 þa 'ge'broðera to þæs minstres neoda. God eow ealle gehealde. 7 gife eow ece gesælþe.   Amen.

Folio heading : Camer'.   *Writ heading :* Confirmacio beati Regis Edwardi super kaio quem Ulphus et uxor sua dederunt Sancto Petro.   *In margin :* Lond'.   1. stallere F] stellare MS.   F *writes* Esgar.   2. icc ann 7 ꝥ ic wille F.   4. Kinegið] -gid MS.   7. aspringað] asprungað MS.

Translation

King Edward sends friendly greetings to Bishop Ælfweard and Esgar the staller and all my *burhthegns* in London.   I inform you that I grant and I will that St. Peter and the brethren at Westminster shall have the land and the wharf with it which Ulf the portreeve and his wife Cynegyth gave to the holy foundation, for the redemption of their souls, as fully and as completely as ever they possessed it.   And again I likewise grant them that they have with it full freedom in all matters that shall arise there, by land and by strand.   Therefore I will not on any consideration permit that anyone set aside or alienate their gift and their pious benefaction ; or that anyone have any authority there in any matter or at any time except the abbot and the brethren for the needs of the monastery. God keep you all and give you eternal happiness.   Amen.

(76)

King Edward declares that the estate of Lessness which Ætsere owned and bequeathed to Westminster Abbey is now to belong to the abbey with everything belonging thereto as fully and as completely as Ætsere bequeathed it to the abbey with his consent; and he grants to St. Peter judicial and financial rights.

(Westminster Abbey Muniments xi)

+ Eadward kyng gret. Ædsi arceƀ 7 Godwine .ƀ. on Rouancestre. 1
7 Leofwine eorll on Kent. 7 Esgar stallere. 7 Rodbert Wimarche sunu
stallere. 7 ealle mine þeignas on Kent frendlice.   Ic cyðe eow ꝥ íc
wille ꝥ þæt cotlif Leosne þe Ætsere ahte. 7 becwæð Criste 7 Sc̄e
Petre into Westmynstre. ligge nu ðider ínn. to ðæra muneca fodan. 5
mid eallum ðæra ðingum þe þær to hyreð. ón wude. 7 on felde. on
mæde. 7 on wætere. 7 on ealle oðre þingum. scótfréo 7 gáfolfréo. on
scíre. 7 on hundrede. swá fúl. 7 swá forð. swá he hít Sc̄e Petre
becwæð. 7 íc ðes fullice géuðe.   7 íc nelle nateshwon geðafian ꝥ þær
ænig mánn ænigne onstyng habbe on ænigum þingum. oððe on 10
ænigum timan. buton sé aƀƀ. 7 ða gebroðra to ðes mynstres
nytwurðlicre þearfe. 7 ic ánn ꝥ Sc̄e Peter habbe ofer ðam saca.
7 socna. tóll. 7 teám. infangeneþéof. 7 ealle oðre gerihte þe to me
belimpað.   God eów gehealde. 7 Sc̄e Petres holde.

Endorsed : Leosne.   1. Rowcestr' F.   2. Wymarche F.
3. freondlice D.   8. swa full fre 7 swa forth F.   12. ofer D,
F ; MS. *rubbed here.* *Birch reads* ouer.

Translation

King Edward sends friendly greetings to Archbishop Eadsige and Godwine, bishop of Rochester, and Leofwine, earl of Kent, and Esgar the staller and Robert fitz Wimarch the staller, and all my thegns in Kent.   I inform you that my will is that the estate of Lessness which Ætsere owned and bequeathed to Westminster, to Christ and to St. Peter, shall now belong to that foundation, for the food of the monks, with all the things belonging to it, in woodland and in open country, in meadow and in water, and in all other things, exempt from scot and tax in shire and in hundred, as fully and as completely as he bequeathed it to St. Peter; and I gave my full consent to that.   And I will not on any consideration consent that anyone have any authority there in any thing or at any time except the abbot and the brethren for the use and advantage of the monastery.   And I grant that St. Peter have over it sake and soke, toll and team, infangenetheof and all other rights that belong to me.   God keep you (and) St. Peter's lieges.

(77)

King Edward declares that the monks of Westminster Abbey are to
have the land at Chalkhill and everything lawfully pertaining thereto
as fully and as completely as ever Thurstan his housecarl held it
of him and gave it to the abbey with his consent ; and he grants
them judicial and financial rights and other privileges. (1044–51,
probably 1044–46)

(Cotton Charter vii. 6)

1 † Eadward kyngc gret Rodberd biscop. 7 Osgod Clapa. 7 Ulf
scirgereuan. 7 ealla mine þeigenes. 7 mine holdan freond on Middelsexan. freondlice. Íc kyþe eow þ ic wylle. 7 þ ic ánn þ Sc̄e PETER
7 þa gebroþra on Westmynstre habben to heora bileouen þ land æt
5 Cealchylle 7 ealc þare þinga. þe þær to mid riˋhˊte geburað. mid
lande 7 mid loge. mid wude 7 mid felde. mid mæde 7 mid læse. mid
mæste 7 mid æuesan. 7 mid eallum þingum. swa full 7 swa forð swa
Þurstan min huskarll hit furmest of me heold. 7 into þære halgan
stowwe geaf. 7 ic þæs fullice geúþe. And ic an heom eoft ealswa þ
10 hy habben þærófer saca 7 socna. tóll 7 team. infangæneþeof. 7
flemenefyrmðe. 7 ealle oðre gerihtu on eallum þingum þe þar úpp
aspringað. 7 æac swylce to þeosum lande mid fullan freodome ic ánn
þ þridde treow 7 þ þridde swíin. óf æuesan þæs nextan wudes þe lið
to Kyngesbyrig. se is gemæne swa he onn ældum timum gelegd
15 wæs. 7 for þánn ic nelle nateshwon geþafian þ æniman ætbrede oððe
geutige an æker landes of wude oððe of felde. þe he hæf þyder inn
gegyfan. oððe þ þær æniman ænine onstyngc habbe on æningum
þingum. oððe on ænige timan. buten se abbod 7 þa gebroþra to þæs
mynstres neode. And ícc wille 7 fæstlice bebeode be fulre wite.
20 þ þeos mundbyrdnesse beo stráng 7 staþelfæst. ínn to þære halgan
stowwe á on éce erfe. Amen.

3. kiþe eow þ ic an F.   5. geburað] -ad MS.   6. mid lase
7 mid mede F.   12. æac D, ec F.   13. swíin D, swun F.
16. hæf D ; hauez F. *Endorsed in hand of early cent. xii* Cealchylle.

Translation

King Edward sends friendly greetings to Bishop Robert and
Osgod Clapa and Ulf the sheriff and all my thegns and my loyal
friends in Middlesex. I inform you that I will and I grant that
St. Peter and the brethren at Westminster shall have for their
sustenance the land at Chalkhill and everything lawfully pertaining
thereto, with land and with (? produce ? stock), with woodland
and with open country, with meadow and with pasture, with mast
and with pannage, and with all things as fully and as completely

as ever Thurstan my housecarl held it of me, and gave it to the holy foundation ; and I gave my full consent to that. And again I likewise grant them that they have over it sake and soke, toll and team and infangenetheof and flymenafyrmth, and all other rights in all matters that shall arise there. And also with this land I likewise grant with full freedom the third tree and the third pig of the pannage of the nearest wood, which belongs to Kingsbury, which is held in common as it was constituted in olden times. And therefore I will not on any consideration permit that anyone set aside or alienate one acre of land, of woodland or of open country, that he has given to that foundation ; or that anyone have any authority there in any matter or at any time except the abbot and the brethren for the needs of the monastery. And I desire and firmly enjoin on pain of the full penalty that this protection of their rights remain firm and unshaken for the holy foundation ever in perpetuity. Amen.

(78)

King Edward declares that he has given to Westminster Abbey the land at Aldenham with judicial and financial rights as fully and as completely as Earl Sihtric held it of the monastery and committed it to Abbot Ælfric and the community, and as Abbot Ordbriht held it for the monastery in the days of King Offa and King Coenwulf, and as King Edgar in his charter confirmed it to the abbey. (1045–49)

(Westm. Do. f. 185 b)

Eadward cingc gret Eadnoð. ꝺ. 7 Beorn eorl. 7 alle mine þeignas 1
on Hertfordscire freondlice. 7 ic cyðe eow ꝥ ic habbe gegiuen Criste
7 Sꞇe Peter into Westmunstre ꝥ land æt Ældenham. mid saca. 7 mid
socna. mid tolle. 7 mid teame. 7 infangeneþeofe. swa full 7 swa forð
swa Sihtric eorl of þan munstre þiowlice hit hyold. 7 ætforen 5
gewitnesse mid halra tunge Ælfrice þam abb. 7 þam gebroðran up
betæhte. 7 swa swa hit stod Ordbrihte abb. on hande into þam
minstre. be'o' Offie. 7 be Cenwulfes cinges dagum. 7 swa swa
Æ'd'gar cinge on his gewrite þider in hit gefestnode. 7 ic nella
nateswan geþafian ꝥ þar ænig mann ænine onstynge þær ofer habbe 10
on ænige þingan oðer on ænige timan. buton se abb 7 þa munecas
to Sꞇe Petres neode. God eow gehealde. Sꞇe Petres holde.

Heading : Carta beati Regis Edwardi de tota terra de Aldenham cum omnibus libertatibus 7 pertinentibus suis.   3. Westminstre F. 5. minstre F.   5. þeowlic it heold F.   7. into þan minstre behoue 7 be Kenwlfes kinges dagen F ; a new folio begins at 7.   12. F *inserts* 7 *after* gehealde.

Translation

King Edward sends friendly greetings to Bishop Eadnoth and Earl Beorn and all my thegns in Hertfordshire. And I inform you that I have given to Westminster, to Christ and to St. Peter, the land at Aldenham with sake and with soke, with toll and with team and infangenetheof, as fully and as completely as Earl Sihtric held it humbly (?) of the monastery and before witnesses unequivocally (or *viva voce*) committed it to Abbot Ælfric and the brethren ; and as Abbot Ordbriht held it for the monastery, in the days of Offa and of King Coenwulf ; and as King Edgar in his charter confirmed it to the monastery. And I will not on any consideration permit that anyone have there any authority over it in any matter or any time except the abbot and the monks for the needs of St. Peter. God keep you, St. Peter's lieges.

(79)

King Edward declares that he has given to Westminster Abbey the estates of Datchworth and Watton with judicial and financial rights as fully and as completely as Ælfwynn the nun held them of the monastery and committed them to Abbot Edwin and the monks, and as King Edgar granted them to the monasteɪy, and as they were adjudged in (the assembly of) the nine shires at Wendlebury. (1049)

(Westm. Do. f. 227)

1 Edward kingc gret Eadnoþ .ƀ. 7 Beorn eorl 7 alle mine þegnes on Hertfordscire frendlice. 7 ic cyþe eow þat ic habbe gegifen Criste 7 Sc̄e Petre into Westmenstre þa land Deceswrþe 7 Wattune. mid sace 7 mid socne mid tolle 7 mid teame. 7 mid infangeneþeofe swa
5 full 7 swa forð swa Alwunn si nunne hit heold of þam minstre. 7 at[foren] Ædiðe þaire hlafdie Æadwine abbyde 7 þam monecan up hyo betehte. 7 al swa Æadgar cingc [in] to þam minstre hyo geuuþe. 7 eac alswa hyo gedemde waron on þam nigon sciran on Wendelbury. 7 ic nelle non oþer. God eow gehealde.

Folio heading : Hertford'. Dacesurþe 7 Wattune. *Writ heading :* Carta beati Regis Edwardi de terra de Dackewrþe 7 Wattune. *In margin, in a different hand :* dupl' : *and in later hand :* celer' xv s'.   2. freondlice F. 3. Westminstre F.   3. Daccewrth' 7 Wattone F.   5. Alfwin sy F. 6. foren *from* F.   7. in *from* F.   7. hy F, hyo MS.   9. Wendlesbiri F.   9. wille F, nelle MS.

Translation

King Edward sends friendly greetings to Bishop Eadnoth and Earl Beorn and all my thegns in Hertfordshire. And I inform you that I have given to Westminster, to Christ and to St. Peter, the lands Datchworth and Watton, with sake and with soke, with toll and with team and with infangenetheof, as fully and as completely as Ælfwynn the nun held it (? them) of the monastery and in the presence of Queen Edith committed them to Abbot Edwin and the monks ; and as King Edgar granted them to the monastery ; and also in full accordance with the judgment which was given concerning them in (the assembly of) the nine shires at *Wendelbury*. And I forbid that it be otherwise. God keep you.

(80)

King Edward declares that he intends to have legal possession of the land at Ickworth as fully and completely as etc. (spurious Westminster claim to this estate) ; and that it is to be transferred to him as soon as the present writ is read.

(Sloane Charter xxxiv. 1)

Eadward kyng gret Ægelmær ƀ. 7 Harold eorl. 7 Gyrð eorl. 7   1
Leofstan abƀ. 7 ealle mine þeignas. in to Suðfolce freo[ndl]ice.
7 íc cyðe eów ꝥ íc wille beon þæs landes wurðe æt Iccawurðe. swá
full. 7 swá forð swa gewitnesse hæfð to geboran. ꝥ Crist. 7 Sc̄e Peter.
7 íc hit mid rihte agan into þære haligan stowwe æt Westmunstre.   5
7 ic wille ꝥ man hit geride me to handa swa hraðe swa þis gewrit
her nu geræpp beo. ꝥ nan oðer ne sy. 7 syððan gif þær hwa on specan
wille. ic wille swa andswarian fore. swá swá mannan þincð ꝥ riht
lage sy. God eow ealle gehealde. Sc̄e Petres holde.

2. þegnas F.   5. agan MS. (*under ultra-violet rays*) ;   agan D ;
agen F.   5. Westminstre F, D.   9. F *inserts* 7 *after* gehealde.
Endorsed in later hand : Iccawurðe, *and in a hand of cent. xiv*, Suffolk.

Translation

King Edward sends friendly greetings to Bishop Æþelmær and Earl Harold and Earl Gyrth and Abbot Leofstan and all my thegns in Suffolk. And I inform you that it is my will that I have legal possession of the land at Ickworth as fully and as completely as it has been testified that Christ and St. Peter and I lawfully possess it for the holy foundation at Westminster. And I will that it be brought under my control as soon as this present letter has been read, so that the matter may be settled. And if anyone there shall afterwards wish to make claim to it, I will answer for it in such manner as shall appear to people to be in accordance with the law. God keep you all, St. Peter's lieges.

(81)

King Edward declares that he has given to Abbot Edwin judicial and financial rights as fully and as completely as he himself possessed them. 1049–66

(Westminster Abbey Muniments xviii)

1   + Eadward cingc grett wel mine .ƀes. 7 mine eorlas. 7 ealle mine þegnas on þam sciran ðær Sancte Peter hafaþ land inne 7 Eadwine aƀƀ. freondlice. 7 ic kyþe eow ꝥ ic habbe gegifen him sáca 7 sócne. toll 7 team. griþbryce 7 hamsocne. 7 foresteal. inne tíd 7 ut of tíd. 5 binnan burh 7 butan. swa full 7 swa forð swa hit mesyluan on handa stod. 7 ic nelle geðafian þæt æni man habbe ænine onstync. ofer his land ne ofer his men. be strande ne be lande butan se aƀƀ. to þæs mynstres neode. God eow gehealde.

Translation

King Edward sends cordial and friendly greetings to my bishops, and my earls and all my thegns in the shires in which St. Peter has land, and Abbot Edwin. And I inform you that I have given him sake and soke, toll and team, grithbreach and hamsocn, and foresteall, in festive season and outside it, within borough and without, as fully and as completely as I myself possessed it. And I will not permit that anyone have any authority over his land or over his men, by strand or by land, except the abbot for the needs of the monastery. God keep you.

(82)

King Edward declares that he has given to St. Peter of Westminster on all his land judicial and financial rights as fully and as completely as ever he himself possessed them. 1042–66

(Westminster Abbey Muniments xix)

1   + Eadward kyng gret [wel min]e biscopas. 7 mine eorlas. 7 ealle mine ðegnas on þam scyrum þær Sce Peter into Westmynstre hafa[ð land] inne. 7 menn. freondlice. 7 ic kyðe eow ꝥ ic hæbbe gegyfen hym on eallum hys lande. saca. 7 socna. toll. 7 team. infangeneþeof.

7 flymenefyrmþe. griðbrice. 7 hamsocne. 7 foresteall. 7 ealle oðre 5
gerihtu. inne tíd 7 ut of tíd. binna burh 7 butan burh. on stræte
7 of stræte. swa full 7 swa forð swa hi me sylfon fyrmest on handan
stodon. 7 ic nelle geþafian. ꝧ ænig mann hæbbe ænigne onsting
ofer hys land ne ofer hys menn be strande ne be lande ne on wuda
ne on felda. buton se abbod 7 þa gebroðru to ðæs mynstres neode. 10
God eow ealle gehealde. Amen.

Letters in brackets supplied from D, F.   4. F *substitutes for* hym,
Crist 7 Sainte, *the word* Petre *being omitted on turning the page.*

Translation

King Edward sends cordial and friendly greetings to my bishops
and my earls and all my thegns in the shires in which St. Peter of
Westminster has land and men. And I inform you that I have
given him on all his land sake and soke, toll and team, infangenetheof
and flymenafyrmth, grithbreach and hamsocn and foresteall and all
other rights, in festival season and outside it, within borough and
without, on street and off street, as fully and as completely as
ever I myself possessed them. And I will not permit that anyone
have any authority over his land or over his men, by strand or by
land, nor in woodland or in open country, except the abbot and the
brethren for the needs of the monastery. God keep you all. Amen.

(83)

King Edward declares that he has given to St. Peter of Westminster judicial and financial rights as fully and as completely as he
himself possessed them. 1042–66

(Westm. Do. f. 46)

Edward kincg gret wel mine .ᵬ. 7 mine eorles 7 ealle mine þeignes 1
on þan sciren þar Seinte Petre into Westminstre haueð land inne
7 men frendlice. 7 ic kiþe eow þat ic habbe gegifen him sace 7
socne. toll. 7 theam. infangeneþeof. 7 flemenesfirmth grithbrice 7
hamsocne. 7 foresteal. inne tid. 7 ut of tid. on stræte 7 of stræte 5
binnan burh 7 butan swa ful 7 swa forð swa hit me silfan on handa
stod. 7 ic nelle geþafian þat anig man anig onsting habbe ofer his
land ne ofer his men be strande. ne be lande. butan se abbod to þæs
minstres neode. God eow ealle gehealde. Amen.

Heading : Item carta eiusdem sancti de eodem (*this writ being copied
between nos. 81 and 82.*   2. þar F] þat MS. ; *cf. no. 82.*   4. grith-]
griht- MS.   6. buten burh F.   6. me silfen formest F ; *but*
formest *not adopted here, as absent in nos. 82, 95, 96, 97, 100.*   9. F
omits Amen.

Translation

King Edward sends cordial and friendly greetings to my bishops and my earls and all my thegns in the shires in which St. Peter of Westminster has land and men. And I inform you that I have given him sake and soke, toll and team, infangenetheof and flymenafyrmth, grithbreach and hamsocn and foresteall, in festival season and outside it, on street and off street, within borough and without, as fully and as completely as I myself possessed it. And I will not permit that anyone have any authority over his land or over his men, by strand or by land, except the abbot for the needs of the monastery. God keep you all. Amen.

(84)

King Edward declares that the estate of Moulsham which Leofcild owned and bequeathed to Westminster Abbey is now to belong to the abbey just as he granted it, with everything belonging thereto ; and he grants to St. Peter judicial and financial rights as fully and as completely as ever he had them in any place where he has other land. (1052–53)

(Cott. Faust. A. iii, f. 107 b)

1   Edward king gret wel Willem .b̄. 7 Harold eorll 7 Rodberd stallere 7 alle mine þegnes on Estsex' freondlice. Icc kyþe eow ꝥ ic wille ꝥ þaet cotlif Molesham þe Leofcild ahte 7 bequað Crist 7 Sainte Petre into Westminstre ligge nu þider in to þare munece
5 fodan ellswa he it geuþe on wode 7 on felde on made 7 on watere 7 on allen þingen ꝥ þarto hearð. 7 icc an ꝥ Sainte Petre habbe þaer ofer sake 7 socne toll 7 theam 7 infangeneþef 7 flimenesfirmth swa full 7 swa forth swa he firmest hauede on anigen stede þar he oþer land hafeð. And ic nelle nanun men geþafian ꝥ geutyge any
10 þare þinge þe þidere into gebireð oððe ꝥ þar any man any onsting habbe on any þingen oððe on any timen buton se abbod 7 þa gebroþra to þas minstres nitwirðelicre þearfe. God eow gehealde 7 alle þe ꝥ be holde into þare halagen stowe.

Heading : Confirmacio Molesham. cap. cxiij.   1. stallere] stellere MS.   9. geþafian] gegafian MS.   10. into] unto MS.   11. þa gebroþra] þase broþra MS.   12. nit-] mit- MS.

Translation

King Edward sends cordial and friendly greetings to Bishop William and Earl Harold and Robert the staller and all my thegns in Essex. I inform you that my will is that the estate of Moulsham which Leofcild owned and bequeathed to Westminster, to Christ and to St. Peter, shall now belong to that foundation, for the food of the monks, just as he granted it, in woodland and in open country, in meadow and in water, and in all things belonging thereto. And I grant that St. Peter have over it sake and soke, toll and team and infangenetheof and flymenafyrmth as fully and completely as ever he had in any place where he has other land. And I will not permit anyone to alienate any of the things that pertain thereto, or that anyone have any authority there in any matter or at any time except the abbot and the brethren for the uses and necessities of the monastery. God keep you and all those who are well-disposed towards the holy foundation.

(85)

King Edward declares that the monks of Westminster are to have the estate of Eversley and everything lawfully pertaining thereto as fully and as completely as ever he himself possessed it ; and he also grants them judicial and financial rights. His four free sokemen who hold the manor are henceforward to be in the power of St. Peter and to obey the monks and be subject to them. (1053–66)

(Westm. Do. f. 647 b)

Eadward cing gret Stigand arceð 7 Harold eorl 7 Eadnoð stallere 1
7 ealle mine þeingnas 7 mine holde frend on Suthamptunascire.
freondlice. 7 ic kiþe eow þat ic wille 7 þat ic anne þat Sce Peter
7 þa gebroðera on Westminstre habben þa[t] cotlif Eouereslea 7 alc
þare þinga þe þar to mid rihte gebirað mid circe 7 mid milne mid 5
wude 7 mid felde mid læse 7 mid hæþe. mid waterun and mid moren,
7 mid þare maed þat lið at Stratfelde wit[h] þare lange brigge 7
on eallun þingun swa full 7 swa forð swa hit me selfan firmest on
handa stod. And ic anne hem eft al swa þat hi habben þer to saka
7 socne tol 7 team infangeneþeof. 7 flemenesfirmth. 7 miskenninge 10
7 ealle oðere gerihtu. on eallun þingun þe þer up aspringeð. And
ic wille 7 fastlice bebeode þat Payn min medwrihte. 7 Wulnoð min
huskerall. 7 Alfric Hort(?) 7 Frebeorn mine fre socne men þe þ̶ cotlif
healdeþ. þat hi henon forð mid lande 7 mid lese heore alc mid his dele
beon on Sce Petres 'ge'wealde. 7 þam hirde of þam minstre hersumian 15
7 þeowian. And ic nelle nateswan geþafian þat anig man atbrede
oððer geutige mine gife 7 mine almesse þat ic habbe for minre saule
alesednesse into þare halegan stowe gegifan. oððer þat þer anig man
anig o[n]sting habbe on ænigne þingun. oþer on anigne timan butan
se abbod 7 þa gebroðera to þas minstres neode. And ic wille 7 20

fullice hate þat þes mundbirdnesse be strang 7 staþelfast into þare
halgen stowe a on ece yrfewerdnesse. Amen.

Folio heading : Scripta vacua nunc.   *Writ heading :* Carta sancti
Regis Edwardi de manerio de Eoueresle cum omnibus pertinentibus suis.
In margin in same hand : Suthamton' scir' Eoureslea.   3. anne *here*
and below MS. ; ann F.   4. Eoueres-] Eooueres- MS.   5. mid
mid milne MS.   6. and] at mid moren MS.   10. -kenninge]
-igge MS.   11. aspringeð] asprungeð MS.   12. fastlice] -icle MS.
12. Paþu mi meodes wrichte F ; Wlnoð min huscarl F, Wulþoð MS. ; Alfrice
Hort K. Hor *followed by* z *with a horizontal mark through,* MS.; Frebern F ;
min freosocne men F.   14. mid lande 7 mid lese MS. ; mid lande 7
mid loge F.   15. on þam minstre F, of MS.   17. oððer *here and*
below MS. ; oððe F.

Translation

King Edward sends friendly greetings to Archbishop Stigand and
Earl Harold and Eadnoth the staller, and all my thegns and my loyal
friends in Hampshire. And I inform you that I will and I grant
that St. Peter and the brethren at Westminster shall have the estate
of Eversley and everything lawfully pertaining thereto, with church
and with mill, with woodland and with open country, with pasture
and with heath, with waters and with moors, and with the meadow
which lies at Stratfield by the long bridge, and in all things as fully
and completely as ever I myself possessed it. And again I likewise
grant them that they have with it sake and soke, toll and team,
infangenetheof and flymenafyrmth and miskenning, and all other
rights in all matters that shall arise there. And I will and firmly
enjoin that Payn my ' mead-wright ', and Wulfnoth my housecarl,
and Alfric Hort(?) and Frebeorn, my free sokemen who hold the estate,
that they henceforth with land and with pasture, each of them with
his part, be in the power of St. Peter and obey and be subject to the
community of the monastery. And I will not on any consideration
permit that anyone set aside or alienate my gift and my pious
benefaction which I have given for the redemption of my soul to the
holy foundation, or that any one have any authority there in any
matter or at any time except the abbot and the brethren for the
needs of the monastery. And I will and give full command that
this protection of their rights remain firm and unshaken for the holy
foundation ever in perpetuity. Amen.

(86)

King Edward declares that he has given to Westminster Abbey
the land at Shepperton with judicial and financial rights, and
exemptions, as fully and completely as St. Dunstan bought it and

granted it by charter to the abbey. (1051–66, and probably 1057–66)

(Westm. Do. f. 154 b)

Edward cing gret Willem biscop 7 Leofwine eorl 7 Ælfgæt scirrefan   1
frendlice. 7 ic kiþe eow þ ic habbe gegifan Criste 7 Sc̄e Peter into
Westminstre þat land æt Scepertune mid all þ þer to herdet 7 mid
sace 7 mid socne scotfreo 7 gafulfreo on hundred 7 on scire swa full
7 swa forð swa Sc̄e Dunstan hit gebohte 7 into þam minstre Wulsi   5
abbode 7 þam broðeran gebocede. God 'eow' gehelde.

Folio heading : Midd'. Sheperton'.   *Writ heading :* Carta sancti
Regis Edwardi de terra de Sheperton'.   1. Ælfgæt] Ælfsæt MS.,
Alfget F.   3. herð F.

Translation

King Edward sends friendly greetings to Bishop William and Earl
Leofwine and Ælfgæt the sheriff. And I inform you that I have
given to Westminster, to Christ and to St. Peter, the land at Shepperton with everything belonging thereto, and with sake and with
soke, exempt from scot and tax in hundred and in shire, as fully
and as completely as St. Dunstan bought it and granted it by
charter to Abbot Wulfsi and the brethren for the monastery. God
keep you.

(87)

King Edward declares that he has given to Teinfrith his ' church-
wright ' the land at Shepperton with judicial and financial rights,
and exemptions. 1049–66, and probably 1057–66

(Westm. Do. f. 154 b)

Edward king gret Edwine abb̄ 7 Alfgæt scirrefa freondlice.   1
7 ic ciþe eow þat ic habbe gegifan Teinfriþe mine circwirhtan þ
land æt Scepertune mid sace 7 mid socne scotfreo 7 gafulfreo on
hundred 7 on scire. 7 ic nelle geþafian þ him ani man mid anigne
þinga misbeode. ac habbe he infangeneþeof 7 flimenefrimþe.   5

Heading : Carta eiusdem sancti Regis de eodem.

Translation

King Edward sends friendly greetings to Abbot Edwin and Ælfgæt
the sheriff. And I inform you that I have given to Teinfrith my

'church-wright' the land at Shepperton, with sake and with soke, exempt from scot and tax in hundred and in shire. And I will not permit anyone by any means to do him wrong. But let him have infangenetheof and flymenafirmth.

(88)

King Edward declares that with his full permission Ailric has granted the land at Greenford to Westminster Abbey in accordance with the agreement that the brethren and he have made. 1051–66, and probably 1057–66

(Cott Faust. A. iii, f. 105)

1 Edward king gret wel Willem biscop 7 Leofwine eorll 7 alle mine þeggnes onn Middelsex' frendlik. 7 ic kyþe eou þ it is min fulle unne þ Ailric hafet gegyfen þat land at Greneford Crist 7 Sainte Petre in to Westminstre for þare forewarde þe þase broðera 7 he 5 gemaked habbet. God eou gehealde.

Heading : Greneford. cap. ciiij.　　4. þase broðera, *a corruption of* þa gebroðera, g *being confused with* s.

Translation

King Edward sends cordial and friendly greetings to Bishop William and Earl Leofwine and all my thegns in Middlesex. And I inform you that it is with my full permission that Ailric has given the land at Greenford to Westminster, to Christ and to St. Peter, in accordance with the agreement that the brethren and he have made. God keep you.

(89)

King Edward declares that with his full permission Ailric has granted the land at Greenford to Westminster Abbey in accordance with the agreement that the brethren and he have made ; and he grants them judicial and financial rights. (1051–66, and probably 1057–66)

(Westm. Do. f. 129 b)

1 Edward king gret wel Willem biscop 7 Leofwyne eorl 7 alle mine þeyngnes on Middelsex' frendlice. 7 icc kyþe eou þat hit is min fulle unne þat Aylric hauet so gyfen þat land at Greneforde Crist ant Seinte Petre in to Westmenstre for þare forewarde þe þase broþera

7 he se maked habbað. 7 icc ann heom þar to saca 7 socna. toll 7 5
theam. infangeneþef. 7 alle þase rithe. þe to me belunged. God
eow so helde.

Folio heading : Midd'. Greneforde. *Writ heading :* Confirmacio
Sancti Edwardi Regis de terra in Greneforde quam Ailricus dedit ecclesie
Westm'. *In margin, in a different hand :* dupl'. Instances of
confusion of *g* and *s* have not been emended here : l. 3 so gyfen (gegyfen),
l. 4 þase broþera (þa gebroþera), l. 5 se maked (gemaked), l. 6 þase rithe (þa
gerihte), l. 7 so helde (gehelde).

Translation

King Edward sends cordial and friendly greetings to Bishop
William and Earl Leofwine and all my thegns in Middlesex. And
I inform you that it is with my full permission that Ailric has
given the land at Greenford to Westminster, to Christ and St. Peter,
in accordance with the agreement that the brethren and he have
made. And with this I grant them sake and soke, toll and team,
infangenetheof, and all the rights that belong to me. God keep you.

(90)

King Edward declares that Leofsi Duddesunu has given two and
a half hides of land at Wormley to Westminster Abbey with his
permission. 1053–66, and probably 1057–66

(Cott. Aug. ii. 81)

+ Eadward kyngc gret wel Wulfwi.ƀ.7 Leofwine eorl.7 ealle mine 1
þeignes on Heortfordscire freondlice. 7 íc kyþe eow þ Leofsi
Duddesunu hafað gegiuen Criste 7 Sc̄e Petre into Westmynstre
þridde healue hide landes æt Wurmeléa. be minre geleafan. 7 be
minre unnan. God eow geh*ealde*.   5

3. gegifan D, gifen F.   4. halfe D.   5. gehealde D, F.
Endorsed in hand of cent. xii : Wrmelea.

Translation

King Edward sends cordial and friendly greetings to Bishop
Wulfwig and Earl Leofwine and all my thegns in Hertfordshire.
And I inform you that Leofsi Duddesunu has given to Westminster, to Christ and to St. Peter, two and a half hides of land
at Wormley with my permission and consent. God keep you.

(91)

King Edward declares that the monks of Westminster are to have
the estate of Ayot and everything pertaining thereto, as fully and as
completely as ever Ælfwine Gottone and his wife held it and gave it
to the abbey; and he grants them judicial and financial rights.
(1053–66, and probably 1057–66)

(Westm. Do. f. 226 b)

1   Edward cingc gret Wulfwi ᛒ. 7 Leofwin eorl 7 Esgar stallere 7 alle
mine þeignas 7 mine holde freond on Hertfordscire freondlice. Ic
kiþe eow ꝥ ic wille 7 þat ic ann þat Sc̄e Peter 7 þa gebroðra on
Westminstre habben þat cotlif Ægate 7 alc þare þinga þe þar to mid
5 rihte gebireð. mid circe 7 mid milne mid wude 7 mid felde mid lese
7 mid mæde 7 on eallun þingun swa full 7 swa forð swa Ælwine
Gottone 7 his wif [hit] firmest ahten. 7 for here saule alesednesse into
þare halgen stowe gegafan. And ic ann hem 'eft' alswa ꝥ hi habben
þær to sace 7 socne toll 7 team. infangeneþeof 7 flemenesfrimthe
10 7 miskenninge 7 ealle oðere gerihte on allun þingun þe þar up
aspringeð. And ic nelle nateswon geþafian þat anig man hit
atbrede oððer geutie of þare halgan stowe. oððer þat enig man [þar]
anigne onstinge habbe on enigne þingan oððer on ænigne timan
butan se abbot 7 þa gebroðera to þas minstres neode. God eow
15 gehelde. 7 ealla þa þe sind holde into þam halgan stede. Amen.

> *Folio heading :* Hertford'. Aiegete.   *Writ heading :* Carta sancti
> Regis Edwardi de maner' de Aiegete.   1. Wlfsi F.   2. freondlice]
> frenond- MS.   5. gebireð] -ed MS.   6. Alfwine Gottune F.
> 7. hit *from* F (it).   7. for] four MS.   10. miskenninge] -igge
> MS.   11. aspringeð] asprungeð MS.   12. þar *from* F.   14. se
> abbot] ge MS.   15. gehealde F.

Translation

King Edward sends friendly greetings to Bishop Wulfwig and
Earl Leofwine and Esgar the staller and all my thegns and my loyal
friends in Hertfordshire. I inform you that I will and I grant that
St. Peter and the brethren at Westminster shall have the estate of
Ayot and everything lawfully pertaining thereto, with church and
with mill, with woodland and with open country, with pasture and
with meadow, and in all things as fully and as completely as ever
Ælfwine Gottone and his wife possessed it, and for the redemption
of their souls gave it to the holy foundation. And again I likewise
grant them that they have with it sake and soke, toll and team,
infangenetheof and flymenafyrmth and miskenning and all other

rights in all matters that shall arise there. And I will not on any consideration permit that anyone set it aside or alienate it from the holy foundation, or that anyone have any authority there in any matter or at any time except the abbot and the brethren for the needs of the monastery. God keep you and all those who are well-disposed towards the holy foundation. Amen.

(92)

King Edward declares that the monks of Westminster Abbey are to have the four hides of land at Tooting and everything lawfully pertaining thereto as fully and as completely as ever Swegen his kinsman held it of him and gave it to the abbey with his consent ; and he grants them judicial and financial rights. (1057-66)

(Westm. Do. f. 505)

Edward king gret Stigant biscop 7 Leofwine eorll 7 alle mine 1 þeygnas on Suðereie freondlice. 7 ic kiþe ow þ ic wille 7 þat ic ann þat Sce Peter 7 þa gebroðera on Westminstre habben þa feuwer hiden landes æt Totinges. 7 elc þare þinge þe þar to mid rihte gebirað. swa full 7 swa forð swa Swein myn may [hit] of me firmest 5 held. 7 into þare halgan stowe geaf. 7 ic þas fullice geuþe. 7 ic ann heom eft alswa þat hi habben þer ofer saca 7 socna toll. 7 team. infangeneþeof 7 flemenesfrimthe. 7 ealle oðre gerihtu on eallun þingun þe þer up aspringeð. 7 ic nelle geþafian þat ani mann habbe þer ofer anig onsting. buten se abbud 7 þa gebroðera. God eow 10 ealle gehealde.

Folio heading : Camer'.   *Writ heading :* Carta beati Regis Edwardi de quatuor hidis terre apud Toting' cum omnibus appendiciis.   *In margin :* Totinges.   5. gebirað] gebirad MS., geburað F.   5. hit formest of me F.   9. aspringeð] asprungeð MS.

Translation

King Edward sends friendly greetings to Bishop Stigand and Earl Leofwine and all my thegns in Surrey. And I inform you that I will and grant that St. Peter and the brethren at Westminster shall have the 4 hides of land at Tooting, and everything lawfully pertaining thereto, as fully and as completely as ever Swein my kinsman held (it) of me and gave it to the holy foundation ; and I gave my full consent to that. And again I likewise grant them that they have over it sake and soke, toll and team, infangenetheof and flymenafyrmth and all other rights in all matters that shall arise there. And I will not permit that anyone have any authority over it except the abbot and the brethren. God keep you all.

(93)

King Edward declares that the piece of land at Claygate and everything pertaining thereto is now henceforward to belong to Westminster Abbey as fully and as completely as ever Earl Tostig and
his wife Leofrun, the king's foster-mother, owned it and gave it
to the abbey with his consent ; and he grants to the monks judicial
and financial rights. (1058–66)

(Westminster Abbey Muniments xvii)

1   + Eadward kyng [gret. Stigand .ᵬ. on Winta]nceastre. 7 Wulfwold. aᵬᵬ. on Cyrteséiæ. 7 Leofwine e[orll. 7 Rodberd Wimarke sune
stallere.] 7 Tosti huskarll. 7 eal[le mine þeignes on] Suðreie. symle
ða ðe beoð to cumene. ealsǽ ða ðe nu synd [. freondlice.   7 ic kyþe
5 eow ꝥ ic wille] ðet ꝥ plótt landes æt Clæigate. l[i]gge nu heonon forð
ínn to Sce Petre æt Westmynstre. mid ælc ðere þing[a ꝥ þarto birð.
ðat sind] mid ðam þriddan treowwe on Kyngeswude ón Ditune. 7
mid ðam þriddan ǽcre. 7 mid ǽlc ðere þriddan ny[tþerflicre note.
ðe ðar of ariseð] on wúde. 7 ón felde. ón lǽse. 7 on ǽuesǽ. on merisce.
10 7 ón mǽduen. ón weren. 7 on wætere. scótfri 7 gafollfri of [scire.
7 hundrede. of gelde.] 7 of dǽnegelde. 7 of ealles cynnes ðingæ. swá
full. 7 swá forð. 7 swa fréo. swá Tosti eorll. 7 Leofrun his wíf min
fostermoder. hit [firmest ahten.] 7 ðider ínn becwæðen. on éce yrfðe.
7 íc ðes fullice geúðe. for minre saule. 7 for hiere. 7 for ealle cwiken.
15 7 for ealle deaden to alesen[nesse] 7 íc ánn heom ðer ofer sákæ.
7 sócne. tóll 7 teám. infangeneðeof. blodwite 7 wear[d]wite. hamsocne. 7 forsteall. 7 ealle ða oðre gerihte. ðe to me belimpað.   God
eow ealle gehealde. Sce Petres holde.

2. Cirteseye D.   12. wearwite MS., weardwite D.   *Endorsed :*
De cleigat[e]. Carta Sancti Regis Edwardi de manerio de Cleygate cum
libertatibus eiusdem prius concesso per Tostium comitem ecclesie Westm'.

Translation

King Edward sends friendly greetings to Stigand, bishop of
Winchester, and Wulfwold, abbot of Chertsey, and Earl Leofwine,
and Robert FitzWimarc the staller, and Tostig the housecarl, and
all my thegns in Surrey, those who are yet to come, as also those
who are now living.   And I inform you that my will is that the piece
of land at Claygate shall now henceforth belong to St. Peter's,
Westminster, with everything pertaining thereto, namely, with the
third tree in *Kingswood* at Ditton, and with the third acre, and with
a third of each of the profitable usages which shall arise there in
woodland and in open country, in pasture and in pannage, in marsh

and in meadow, in weirs and in water, exempt from scot and tax
in shire and in hundred, from geld and from Danegeld, and from
every kind of thing as fully and as completely and as freely as ever
Earl Tostig and Leofrun his wife, my foster-mother, owned it, and
bequeathed it to that foundation in perpetuity ; and I gave my full
consent to that, for (the good of) my soul, and for theirs and for the
redemption of all the living and all the dead. And I grant them
thereover sake and soke, toll and team, infangenetheof, blodwite,
and weardwite, hamsocn and foresteall and all the other rights
which belong to me. God keep you all, St. Peter's lieges.

(94)

King Edward declares that he has given to Westminster Abbey
Rutland and all that belongs to it, with judicial and financial rights,
as fully and as completely as he himself possessed it ; and
Queen Edith is to have it for her lifetime 1053–66, possibly
28 December 1065–5 January 1066

(Westminster Abbey Muniments xiv)

+ Eadward kyngc gret Wulfwi .ꝧ. 7 Norðman scirgerefan. 1
7 Ælfwine Merefinnes sunu. 7 ealle mine þeignes on Hamtunscire
frendlice.   7 ic kyþe eow ꝧ ic habbe gegifen Criste 7 Sce Petre into
Westmynstre Roteland 7 eall ꝧ þær to herð. mid saca. 7 mid socne.
mid tolle 7 mid teame. 7 on eallan ðingan. swa full. 7 swa forð swa 5
hit me silfan on handa stod.   7 ic ánn ꝧ Eadgiþ seo hlefdige hit on
hande habbe swa lange swa heo libbe 7 ælce gære ꝧ munster þær of
gegodige.   God eow gehealde.

3. freondlice F.   8. F *adds* Amen.   *Endorsed :* Roteland.
In different hand : Carta Sancti Edwardi Regis de Roteland cum pertinentibus
suis ecclesie Westm' concessis.   *In different hand :* Edwardus confessor.

Translation

King Edward sends friendly greetings to Bishop Wulfwig and
Northman the sheriff and Ælfwine, Merfinn's son, and all my thegns
in Northamptonshire. And I inform you that I have given to
Westminster, to Christ and to St. Peter, Rutland and everything
belonging to it, with sake and with soke, with toll and with team,
and in all things as fully and as completely as I myself possessed
it. And I grant that Queen Edith shall have it as long as she
shall live and annually enrich the monastery therefrom. God
keep you.

(95)

King Edward declares that he has given Launton to Westminster
Abbey with judicial and financial rights as fully and as completely
as he himself possessed it.   1057/58–1066, possibly 28 December
1065–5 January 1066

(Westm. Do. f. 275)

1   Eadward kyngc gret Wulwi .ƀ. 7 Gyrþ eorl 7 ealle mine þeignes
on Oxenfordescire freondlice.   7 ic kiþe eow ꝥ ic habbe gegifon
Langtun Criste 7 Seinte Petre into Westmun[s]tre mid saca 7 mid
socne mid tolle 7 mid teame 7 infangenan þeofe 7 [on] eallan þingan
5 swa full 7 swa forð. swa hit me silfan on hande stod.   7 ic nelle
geþafian ꝥ ænig man þær on ænig o[n]stingc habbe. buton se abƀ.
7 þæ gebroðra þær binnan.   God eow gehealde.

Folio heading : Oxon'. Langton'.   *Writ heading :* Carta beati Regis
Edwardi de Langton' cum libertatibus 7 omnibus pertinentibus suis.
4. on *from* F.   5. formest on hande F ; *see note on no.* 83.   6. se]
ge MS

Translation

King Edward sends friendly greetings to Bishop Wulfwig and Earl
Gyrth and all my thegns in Oxfordshire.   And I inform you that
I have given to Westminster, to Christ and to St. Peter, Launton,
with sake and soke, with toll and team and infangenetheof, and in all
things as fully and completely as I myself possessed it.   And I will
not permit that anyone have any authority therein except the
abbot and the brethren in the monastery.   God keep you.

(96)

King Edward declares that he has granted to Westminster Abbey
the land at Perton and everything belonging thereto with sake and
soke as fully and as completely as he himself held it.   1062–66,
possibly 28 December 1065–5 January 1066

(Westminster Abbey Muniments xii)

1   ✠ Eadweard cyngc gret Leofwine .ƀ. 7 Eadwine eorl. 7 ealle
mi[ne þe]gnas on Stæffordscire freondlice.   7 ic kyþe eow ꝥ ic habbe
gegifan Criste 7 Sc̄e Petre into W[es]tmynstre ꝥ land æt Pertune.
7 ælc þæra þinga þæs þe þær inn to herð on wuda 7 on felda mid
5 saca [7] mid socne swa full 7 swa forð swa hit me sylfan on handa
stod on eallan þingan. þan abbude [to] bigleofan 7 þam gebroþran

þe binnan þam mynstre wuniað. 7 ic nylle nane men geþafian ꝥ
þær geutige ænig þæra þinga þæs þe þær in to hyrð.

Letters in brackets from R.   1. Eadward R.   1. *traces of* c
under g *of* cyngc R.   2. þeignes R.   2. Stefford- R.   3. Westmunstre R.   4. herð R, F, herdeð D.   5. socna R.   6. eallen R.
7. nelle R.   7. nane men R, D, nanne men F.   8. God eow
ealle gehealde *added* R, D, F.   *Endorsed in later hand :* Pertuna.
8. *Several words expunged, under and following last 3 words of text, concluding
with* to gebyrað.

Translation

King Edward sends friendly greetings to Bishop Leofwine and
Earl Edwin and all my thegns in Staffordshire. And I inform you
that I have given to Westminster, to Christ and to St. Peter, the
land at Perton, and everything belonging thereto, in woodland and in
open country, with sake and with soke, as fully and as completely as
I myself possessed it in all things, for the sustenance of the abbot
and the brethren who dwell in the monastery. And I will not
permit anyone to alienate there any of the things that belong to
that foundation.

(97)

King Edward announces that he has given to Westminster Abbey
Windsor and Staines and everything belonging thereto with judicial
and financial rights as fully and as completely as he himself possessed
them. 1042–66, possibly 28 December 1065–5 January 1066

(Cott. Charter vii, 13)

+ Eadward kyngc gret alle mine bisceopes. 7 mine eorles. 7 mine 1
þegenes on Barrocscire. 7 on Middelsexen. freondlice. 7 íc kyþe
eow ꝥ íc habbe gegifan Criste 7 Sc̄e Petre into Westmynstre
Windlesóran. 7 Stáne. 7 eall ꝥ þær to herð. binnan burh. 7 butan.
mid sáca. 7 mid socne. mid tolle. 7 mid teame. 7 mid infangenum 5
þeofe. on wude. 7 on felde. be strande. 7 be lande. on stræte. 7 of
stræte. 7 on eallan þingan swa full. 7 swa forð swa hit me sylfan on
hande stod. 7 íc nelle geþafian ꝥ þær æni mann ænine onstync þær
ofer habbe [on] ænige þingan butan sé abð. 7 þa mynekas to Sc̄e
Petres neode. God eow gehealde.   10

1. *only faint traces of* alle, MS. *stained and rubbed* ; alle D, N, H, Hickes ;
wel F.   1. alle mine þegnes F.   7. formest on hande F. ; *see
note on no. 83.*   9. F *omits* þær ofer *before* habbe.   9. monekas
D ; þase broþran, *corruption of* þa gebroþran F.   *Endorsed in hand of
cent. xii :* Windlesores 7 Stanes.

Translation

King Edward sends friendly greetings to all my bishops and my earls and my thegns in Berkshire and in Middlesex. And I inform you that I have given to Westminster, to Christ and to St. Peter, Windsor and Staines, and everything belonging thereto, within borough and without, with sake and with soke, with toll and with team and with infangenetheof, in woodland and in open country, by strand and by land, on street and off street, and in all things as fully and as completely as I myself possessed it. And I will not permit that anyone have there any authority over it in any thing except the abbot and the monks for the needs of St. Peter. God keep you.

(98)

King Edward declares that the monks of Westminster Abbey are to have the estate of Staines with the land in London called *Stæningahaga* and the soke of 35 hides, with all the berewicks which he has granted to the abbey and with everything lawfully pertaining thereto as fully and as completely as they were assigned to the soke of Staines in olden times or were ever in his own hand ; and he also grants them judicial and financial rights. (1053–66, possibly 28 December 1065–5 January 1066)

(Westminster Abbey Muniments xvi)

1 + Eadward kincg grett Willelm biscop. 7 Harold eorl. 7 Esgar stealre. 7 ealle mine þegnas. 7 mine holde freond ón Middelsexan. freondlice.   Ic kyþe eow þ̵ icc wille. 7 icc ánn þ̵ Sc̄e Peter 7 þa gebroðra on Westmynstre habben to heora bileofan þ̵ cótlif Stana.
5 mid þam lande Stæningahaga wiðinnon Lundone. 7 fif 7 þrittig hida sokne þær tó. mid eallum þám berwican þe ícc habbe for minre sawle alesednysse in to þære halgan stowwe gegyfan. 7 ælcc þære þinga þe þær tó mid rihte gebyrað ón cyrcan 7 on mylnan. on wuda 7 on feldan. on læse 7 on hæðe. on mædum 7 on éitum. on wæterum
10 7 on werum. 7 on eallum þingum swa full 7 swa forð swa hy on ealdum timan in to Stana sokne geléd wæron. oððe me selfan fyrmest on handa stodan.   Ánd icc ánn heom eft ealswa þ̵ hy habben þær tó saka. 7 sokne. tóll. 7 téam. infangeneðeof. 7 flemenefyrmðe. griðbryce. 7 hamsokne. forsteall. 7 miskænninge. 7 ealle oþre gerihtu
15 on eallum þingum þe þær úpp aspringað. inne tíd. 7 ut óf tíde. binnan burh. 7 butan burhge. on stræte. 7 of stræte.   For þán ícc nelle nateshwón geþáfian. þ̵ ænig mán ætbréde oððe geútige mine gyfe 7 mine ælmesse swa mycel þ̵ sy an áker landes. þæs þe on æniges

mannes dægge in to þam cotlifan gebyrede. oððe þ þǽr ænig mán ænigne onstyng habbe on ænigum þingum. oððe on ænige timan. be 20 strande ne be lande. buton se abbod 7 þa gebroðra to þas mynstres neode. 7 ícc wille. 7 fæstlice bebeode. þ þeos mundbyrdnesse beo strang. 7 staþelfæst ín to þære halgan stowwe. á on éce erfeweardnesse. Amen. God eow ealle gehealda.

2. stallere F.   14. miskenninge D, F.   19. F *omits* þær *before* ænig.   *Endorsed :* Stanes.   In a later hand : *Stæningehage.*

Translation

King Edward sends friendly greetings to Bishop William and Earl Harold and Esgar the staller and all my thegns and my loyal friends in Middlesex. I inform you that I will and I grant that St. Peter and the brethren at Westminster shall have for their sustenance the estate of Staines, with the land *Stæningahaga* within London, and with it soke over 35 hides, with all the berewicks that I have given to the holy foundation for the redemption of my soul, and everything lawfully pertaining thereto in church and in mill, in woodland and in open country, in pasture and in heath, in meadows and in aits, in waters and in weirs, and in all things as fully and completely as they in olden times were assigned to the soke of Staines, or ever I myself possessed them. And again I likewise grant them that they have with them sake and soke, toll and team, infangenetheof and flymenafyrmth, grithbreach and hamsocn, foresteall and miskenning and all other rights in all matters that shall arise there, in festival season and outside it, within borough and without, on street and off street. Therefore I will not on any consideration permit that anyone set aside or alienate my gift and my pious benefaction (by) so much as an acre of land, in so far as it pertained in any man's day to the estates, or that anyone have any authority there in any matter or at any time, by strand or by land, except the abbot and the brethren for the needs of the monastery. And I will and firmly enjoin that this protection of their rights remain firm and unshaken for the holy foundation for ever in perpetuity. Amen. God keep you all.

(99)

King Edward declares that he has granted to Westminster Abbey Pershore and Deerhurst and everything belonging thereto with judicial and financial rights as fully and as completely as he himself possessed them. 1042-66, possibly 28 December 1065-5 January 1066

(Westm. Do. f. 316)

1   Eadward kingc gret mine biscopes 7 mine eorles 7 ealle mine
þegnas on Wigerccestresciren 7 on Gloucestrescire freondlice.
7 ic kiþe eow ꝥ ic habbe gegifan Criste 7 Sc̄e Petre into Westminstre
Perscoran 7 Deorhurst 7 eall ꝥ þerto birð. mid sace. 7 mid socne.
5 mid tolle. 7 mid teame. on stræte. 7 of stræte. on wuda. 7 on felda.
7 on eallan þingan. swa full 7 swa forð. swa hit me silfan on handa
stod.   7 ic nelle geþafian ꝥ þar anigne man ænigne onsting habbe
buton se abbut. 7 þa gebroðera to Seinte Petres neode.   God eow
geh*ealde*.

   Folio heading : Glouc'. Deorhurste.   *Writ heading :* Carti beati Regis
Edwardi de Persor' 7 Deorhurste.

Translation

   King Edward sends friendly greetings to my bishops and my earls
and all my thegns in Worcestershire and Gloucestershire.   And I
inform you that I have given to Westminster, to Christ and to St.
Peter, Pershore and Deerhurst and everything pertaining thereto,
with sake and with soke, with toll and with team, on street and
off street, in woodland and in open country, and in all things as
fully and completely as I myself possessed it.   And I will not
permit that anyone have any authority there except the abbot
and the brethren for the needs of St. Peter.   God keep you.

(100)

King Edward declares that he has given to Westminster Abbey
Pershore and Deerhurst and everything belonging thereto with
judicial and financial rights as fully and as completely as he himself
possessed them ; and commands that all the thegns of the lands be
henceforth subject to the abbot and monks.   (1042–66, possibly
28 December 1065–5 January 1066)

(Westm. Do. f. 278)

1   Eadward king gret mine biscopas 7 mine eorles 7 ealle mine
þeingnes on Wigercestrescire 7 on Glowercestrescire freondlice.   7 icc
kyþe eow ꝥ ic habbe gifen Criste 7 Sc̄e Petre into Westminstre
Periscoran 7 Deorhyrst 7 eall ꝥ þer to byreð mid sace. 7 mid socne.
5 mid tolle. and mid teame. 7 mid infangeneþeofe. on stræte. 7 of
stræte. on wude. 7 on felda. 7 on eallan þingan. swa full 7 swa forð
swa hit me silfan on handa stod.   7 ic hate 7 beode ꝥ ealle þa
þeignas of þam landen hynenforð understanden to þan abꝧ. 7 to

þam munecan into þan minstre. 7 ealle þa gerihte. 7 þa cnaulæcunga
þe to me belimpæð. don Criste 7 Sce Petre. 7 þam gebroðeran for ic 10
nelle geþafian ꝥ þer [ænig] man ænigne onstingc habbe buton se
abbod. 7 þa gebroðera. to Sce Petres niode.   God eow ealle gehealde.

Heading : Carta eiusdem beati Regis de manerio predicto cum omnibus
pertinentibus predictis.   3. gegifen F.   4. byreð MS., hirð F.
7. formest on hande F ; *see note on no. 83.*   7. alcc þa þegnes F.

Translation

King Edward sends friendly greetings to my bishops and my earls
and all my thegns in Worcestershire and Gloucestershire.   And I
inform you that I have given to Westminster, to Christ and to St.
Peter, Pershore and Deerhurst and everything pertaining thereto,
with sake and with soke, with toll and with team, and with
infangenetheof, on street and off street, in woodland and in open
country, and in all things as fully and completely as I myself
possessed it.   And I command and enjoin that all the thegns of the
lands be henceforth subject to the minster, to the abbot and to the
monks, and pay to Christ and St. Peter and the brethren all the
rights (*or* dues) and the recognition (of lordship) which belong to me,
for I will not permit that anyone have any authority there except the
abbot and the brethren for the needs of St. Peter.   God keep you
all.

(101)

King Edward declares that he has granted to Westminster Abbey
Pershore and Deerhurst and everything belonging thereto with
judicial and financial rights as fully and as completely as he himself
possessed them, and invokes a blessing on every man who shall be
loyal to the holy monastery.   (1042–66, possibly 28 December 1065–
5 January 1066)

(Westminster Abbey Muniments xv)

+ Eadweard cyngc gret wel mine. byscopes 7 abbedes. 7 ealle 1
mine þegenes. on Wigerceastrescire. 7 on Gleawcestrescire freondlice.
7 ic kyþe eow ꝥ ic habbe gegyfen Criste 7 Sce Petre into Westmynstre þa land Perscoran 7 Deorhyrsta. 7 eall ꝥ þær to herð mid
saca 7 mid socna. mid tolle 7 mid teame on stræte 7 of stræte. on 5
wude 7 on felde. 7 on eallan þingan. swa ful 7 swa forþ swa hit me
sylfan fyrþmest on handa stod.   7 ic nelle ꝥ þær æni mann ænig
onstyngc habbe. butan se abbod 7 þa gebroðra to Sce Petres niode.

7 Godes bletsunga syo mid ælc þara manna þe seo hold into þam
10 halgan mynstre.

4. birð D.   5. socne D.   7. firmest D.   *Endorsed :*
Perscora. Deorheorsta.

Translation

King Edward sends cordial and friendly greetings to my bishops
and abbots and all my thegns in Worcestershire and in Gloucestershire. And I inform you that I have given to Westminster, to Christ
and to St. Peter, the lands Pershore and Deerhurst, and everything
belonging thereto, with sake and with soke, with toll and with team,
on street and off street, in woodland and in open country, and
in all things as fully and completely as ever I myself possessed it.
And my will is that no one shall have any authority there except
the abbot and the brethren for the needs of St. Peter. And God's
blessing be with every man who is well-disposed towards the holy
monastery.

(102)

King Edward declares that the monks of Westminster Abbey are
to have the estates of Pershore and Deerhurst with all the land and
the berewicks which he has granted to the abbey and with everything lawfully pertaining thereto as fully and as completely as they
were assigned to the soke in olden times or were ever in his own hand ;
and he also grants them judicial and financial rights. (1062–66,
possibly 28 December 1065–5 January 1066)

(Westm. Do. f. 278)

1   Eadward kingc gret Eal[d]red ercebiscop. 7 Wulstan biscop
7 Wulfwi biscop. 7 ealle mine heafedmen. 7 mine þeingnes. 7 mine
sci[r]gerefan. 7 ealle mine holde freond on Wigercestrescire 7 on
Glowercestrescire. 7 on Oxonfordescire freondlice. Icc kiþe eow
5 þat icc wille 7 icc ann ꝥ Sc̄e Peter 7 þa gebroðera on Westminstre
habben to heora bileofan þa cotlif Perscoran. 7 Deorhirstan mid
eallum þan landum 7 mid eallum þan berwican þe ic habbe for minre
saule alesednesse into þare haalgum stowwe gifan 7 aelc þære þinga
þe þær to mid rihte gebirað mid circan. 7 mid milnan. mid wuda.
10 7 mid feldan. mid læse. 7 mid hæþe. mid mæden. 7 mid eʼiʼtum.
mid waterum. 7 mid werum. 7 mid eallum þingum swa full 7 swa
forð swa hi on ealdum dagum into þære socne geled weren oððe me
silfan fyrmest on handa stodan.   And ic anne hem eft alswa ꝥ hy

habben þar to saka. 7 soknæ. toll. 7 team infangenne þeof. 7 flemenes-
firmðe. griðbrice. 7 hamsocne. forsteall. 7 miskenninge. 7 ealle oðere 15
gerihtu on eallum þingum þe þær upp aspringað. inne tid. 7 ut of
tide. binnan burh. 7 butan burhge. on stræte. 7 of stræte. for þæn
icc nelle nateshwan geþafian. ꝥ anig man ætbrede oððe geutige mine
gife. 7 mine ælmesse. swa micell ꝥ sy an æker landes. þæs þe on
aeniges mannes dæge into þam cotlifan gebyrede. Ne eft ꝥ þær 20
ænig man aenigne onstingc habbe on ænigum þingan oððe on ænige
timan be strande. ne be lande. buton se abð. 7 þa gebroðera into
þa[m] minstre. 7 ic wille 7 fæstlice bebeode ꝥ þæs freodom 7 þeos
mundbirdnesse beo strang 7 staþelfast into þære halegan stowwe.
Gode to lofe. 7 Sꝍe Petre to wurðminte. 7 to gewealde a on ece 25
erfeweardnesse. Amen. God eow ealle gehealde.

Folio heading : Wygorn'. Persore cum hamelettis.   *Writ heading :*
Carta beati Regis Edwardi de Persora 7 omnibus appendiciis suis.   2. F
omits biscop *after* Wulfwi.   5. þat icc an F.   8. into þare
halagen stowe gegifan F.   12. on ealdum] in on ealdum MS.   14.
socne F.   16. aspringað] asprupgað MS.   22. buton] beton MS.
26. F *adds* Amen *at the end.*

Translation

King Edward sends friendly greetings to Archbishop Ealdred and
Bishop Wulfstan and Bishop Wulfwig and all my headmen and my
thegns and my sheriffs and all my loyal friends in Worcestershire
and in Gloucestershire and in Oxfordshire. I inform you that I will
and I grant that St. Peter and the brethren at Westminster shall
have for their sustenance the estates Pershore and Deerhurst, with
all the lands and all the berewicks that I have given to the holy
foundation for the redemption of my soul, and everything lawfully
pertaining thereto, with church and with mill, with woodland and
with open country, with pasture and with heath, with meadows and
with aits, with waters and with weirs, and with all things as fully
and completely as they in olden times were assigned to the soke or
ever I myself possessed them. And again I likewise grant them that
they have with them sake and soke, toll and team, infangenetheof
and flymenafyrmth, grithbreach and hamsocn, foresteall and miskenning and all other rights in all matters that shall arise there,
in festival season and outside it, within borough and without, on
street and off street. Therefore I will not on any consideration
permit that anyone set aside or alienate my gift and my pious
benefaction (by) so much as an acre of land, in so far as it pertained in any man's day to the estates : nor further that anyone
have any authority there in any matter or at any time, by strand
or by land, except the abbot and the brethren for the monastery.

And I will and firmly enjoin that this freedom and this protection of their rights remain firm and unshaken for the holy foundation to the praise of God and to the honour and authority of St. Peter for ever in perpetuity. Amen. God keep you all.

(103)

King Edward declares that he has given to Westminster Abbey Islip and a half-hide at Marston as fully and as completely as he himself possessed it, with sake and with soke. (28 December 1065–5 January 1066)

(Westm. Do. f. 270)

1 Eadward king gret Wulwi .℔. 7 Guyrð eorl 7 alle mine þeignes on Oxnefordscire. 7 ic kiþe eow þat ic habbe gegifen Criste 7 Sc̄e Petre into Westmunstre Gihtslepe. 7 ane healfe hide æt Mersce swa full 7 swa forð swa hit me silfan on hande stod. mid saca 7 mid socna.
5 7 on eallan þingan. God eow alle gehealde.

Heading : Carta eiusdem beati Regis de predicta villa de Istelepe 7 dimidia hida apud Mersce.

Translation

King Edward sends greetings to Bishop Wulfwig and Earl Gyrth and all my thegns in Oxfordshire. And I inform you that I have given to Westminster, to Christ and to St. Peter, Islip and a half-hide at Marston as fully and as completely as I myself possessed it, with sake and with soke, and in all things. God keep you all.

(104)

King Edward declares that he has given to Westminster Abbey the estate of Islip where he was born, and a half hide at Marston, with everything belonging thereto as fully and as completely and freely as he himself possessed it and as his mother Ælfgifu Emma gave it to him ; and he grants the monks judicial and financial rights. He directs his kinsman Wigod of Wallingford to transfer the land to the abbey on his behalf. (28 December 1065–5 January 1066)

(Westm. Do. f. 270)

1 Eadward king gret Wulsi biscop 7 Guirð eorll 7 alle mine þeingnes on Oxenfordescire freondlice. 7 ic kiþe eow þat ic habbe gegefen

Criste 7 Sc̄e Petre into Westmunstre ðet cotlif ic wæs geboran inne
be naman Gihtslepe. 7 ane healfe hide æt Mersce scotfre 7 gafolfreo
mid eallan ðam ðingan þæ ðer to belimpað on wude. 7 on felde. on 5
mæde 7 on watre mid ciricen. 7 mid ciricsocnen. swa full. 7 swa forð.
7 swa freo swa hit me siluan on hande stod. 7 swa swa Ælgyfu Imme
min moder on minre frumbirde dæiæge to forme gyfe hit me gæf.
7 to gecinde becwæð. 7 ic an heom þer ofer saca. 7 socna. toll. 7 team
7 infangeneþeof. 7 blodwite. 7 weardwite. 7 hamsocne. 7 forsteall. 10
griðbrice. 7 mundbrice. 7 ealle ða gerihte. þe to me belimpað.
Nu grete ic wel mine leofne mæi Wigod on Wallingeforde. 7 ic beode
ðe þat ðu on minre stede beride þas land þam hælge to hande. for ic
nelle nateshwon geðafian ᵽ þær ænig mann ænige onsting habbe on
ænigum þingum oððe on æn[i]gum timan butan se abᵬ. 7 þa gebroðra 15
to þæs munstres nitwur[ð]licre þearfe. 7 hwa se ðas ælmesse holdlice
healde. healde hine God. 7 Godes moder on ece blisse. 7 hwa swa
hio awende sieo he awænded fram Gode. to þare hellware stiþe
pinnesse. buton he hit on ðessere wrlde. þe stiðliker gebete. God
eow ealle gehealde. 7 Sc̄e Petres holde. 20

Folio heading : Oxoneford. Istelepe.   *Writ heading :* Carta beati
Regis Edwardi de Istele[pe].   1. Gyrð F.   2. Oxenforde]
Ouenforde MS.   4. ane hyde F.   8. firmbirde dawe F ; OE
frumbyrde dæge.   13. halge F.   19. wrlde Neufeldt] yrfþe MS.

Translation

King Edward sends friendly greetings to Bishop Wulfwig and Earl
Gyrth and all my thegns in Oxfordshire. And I inform you that
I have given to Westminster, to Christ and to St. Peter, the estate
where I was born, Islip by name, and a half-hide at Marston, exempt
from scot and tax, with everything belonging thereto, in woodland
and in open country, in meadow and in water, with church and with
church-soke, as fully and as completely and as freely as I myself
possessed it, and as Ælfgyfu Emma my mother gave it to me on the
day of my birth as a first gift, and assigned it as my heritage.
And I grant them over it sake and soke, toll and team and infangenetheof and blodwite and weardwite and hamsocn and foresteall,
grithbreach and mundbreach and all the rights that belong to me.
Now I cordially greet my dear kinsman Wigod of Wallingford, and
I command thee as my representative to bring these lands into the
possession of the saint, for I will not on any consideration permit that
anyone have any authority there in any matter or at any time
except the abbot and the brethren for the use and advantage of the
monastery. And whosoever shall loyally uphold this pious benefaction, may God and the Mother of God uphold him in everlasting

bliss, and whosoever shall turn it aside, may he be turned aside from God to the bitter torment of the dwellers in hell, unless he in this world make amends for it as stringently as possible. God keep you all and St. Peter's lieges.

(105)

King Edward declares that he has granted to St. Peter of West-minster full freedom upon all the lands belonging to the abbey with judicial and financial rights as fully and as completely as he himself possessed them ; and invokes a blessing on the man who shall increase the freedom of the abbey and the honour of the saint, and a curse on him who shall diminish them. (1051–66)

(Westm. Do. f. 96)

1 Edward king gret Willem biscop. 7 Leofstan. 7 Alfsi porterefen. 7 ealle mine burgþeygnes on Londone freondlice. 7 ic kyðe eow. þ ic habbe geunnen Sce Petre þam halegen apostle in to Westmunstre fulne fridom ofer ealle þa land þe lagon in to þene halgan stowe gefe 5 se þe hi gefe. 7 þar mide saca 7 socna. toll 7 team. 7 infangeneþeof. flymene fyrmðe 7 gryðbrice 7 hamsocne. 7 foresteall. 7 miskenninge 7 sceawinge. 7 alle oþere richte inne tid. 7 ut of tid. binnan burch 7 buten burch on strete 7 of strete swa full. 7 swa forð swa hi me sulfen formest an honden stodon. 7 gif eni man wille þa halegan 10 stowe heonen forð mid lande 7 mid loge godian. icc ann ealswa þ hit sig staþelfast. 7 ic nelle geþafian þ enig mann habbe enigne onsting ofer his land. ne ofer his menn ne be strandde ne be lannde. buton se abbot 7 þa gebroðera. to þas munstres neode. 7 se þe þeas munstres fridom 7 þas halges wurðscipe. ofer þis geeacnie. geeacnie God his lif 15 on þissere worlde. 7 þonne he heonon faren scule. God him selle ece myrhðe on heofnanrice. 7 se þe þes hallges wrðscipe 7 þes munstres fridom. 7 þene broðru note. gewani God. 7 Godes moder gewani his dawes her on werlde. 7 þanne he heonen faren scule. se is woniinge on helle grunde. buton he hit þe stiðliker wit[h] God gebete. 20 Amen.

Folio heading : Midd'. Londone.   *Writ heading :* Carta beati Edwardi Regis de libertatibus in Londone.   1. Alfsi] Alffis MS., Alfsy F.   3. geunnen] se unnen MS. ; gegifen 7 unnen Crist and Sainte Petre F.   4. lagon MS., longen F.   7. of] op MS. 10. hit] hut MS.   11. geþafian] se þafian MS.   11. enig] ening MS.   13. þa gebroðera] þase broderra MS.   16. wrðscipe] wrd- MS.   17. gewanye . . . gewani F ; so wann . . . se wann MS. 19. stiðliker] stilliker MS., stillikir F.   19. gebete] se bete MS. 19. F *adds :* God eou alle gehealde. Amen.

Translation

King Edward sends friendly greetings to Bishop William and Leofstan and Ælfsige the portreeves and all my *burhthegns* in London. And I inform you that I have granted to Westminster, to St. Peter the holy apostle, full freedom upon all the lands which belonged to the holy foundation, whosoever may have given them, and therewith sake and soke, toll and team and infangenetheof, flymenafyrmth and grithbreach and hamsocn and foresteall and miskenning and showing and all other rights, in festival season and outside it, within borough and without, on street and off street, as fully and as completely as ever I myself possessed them. And if anyone henceforth shall wish to enrich the holy foundation with land and with (? produce ? stock), I likewise grant that his benefaction remain unimpaired. And I will not permit that anyone have any authority over his land or over his men, by strand or by land, except the abbot and the brethren for the needs of the monastery. And whosoever shall increase the monastery's freedom and the honour of the saint over and above this, may God increase his life in this world and when he shall depart hence, may God grant him eternal joy in the heavenly kingdom ; and whosoever shall diminish the honour of the saint and the freedom of the monastery and the profit of the brethren, may God and the Mother of God diminish his days in this world, and when he shall depart hence, may his dwelling be in the abyss of hell, unless he make amends for it with God as stringently as possible. Amen. [F God keep you all. Amen.]

(106)

King Edward declares that he has granted to St. Peter of Westminster at the dedication of the church full freedom upon all the lands belonging to the abbey with judicial and financial rights as fully and as completely as he himself possessed them. (28 December 1065–5 January 1066)

(Westm. Do. f. 96)

Edward king [gret] Willem biscop 7 Leofstan. 7 Ealfsi porterefen 1
7 alle mine burchþeignes on Londone freondlice. 7 icc kiþe eou þat
ic habbe geunnen Sc̄e Petre into Westmunstre at þar kirkhaleginge
fulne fridom ofe[r] alle þe land þe lage into þare halagen stowe.
geafe se ðe his geafe. 7 þar mide. saka. 7 socna. toll. 7 team 5
infangeneþef. flimenesfirmðe 7 grit[h]brice. 7 hamsocne. 7 forestal.
7 miskenninge. 7 sceawinge. 7 alle oðere richte in tid. 7 ut of tid.
binnen burh 7 butan burh. on strate. 7 offe strate swa full 7 swa forð

swa hi me sulven firmest on hande stodan. 7 gif ani mann hennen
10 forð wille þa halegen stowe mid land 7 mid loge godian. icc ann
alswa þ hi[t] si staðelfast. 7 icc nelle geþafian þ eni mann habbe ani
onsting ofer his land ne ofer his men ne be strande ne be lande ne þat
ani man þas mundbirdnesse tobreke. God eow gehealde. Amen.

Heading : Item carta eiusdem Regis de libertatibus in Londone.
2. burhþegnes F.   3. geunnen] se unne MS.   6. -firmðe]
firmde MS.   7. oðere] odere MS.   11. geþafian] se þafian MS.
13. gehealde] se healde MS.

Translation

King Edward sends friendly greetings to Bishop William and
Leofstan and Ælfsige the portreeves and all my *burhthegns* in
London. And I inform you that I have granted to Westminster,
to St. Peter, at the dedication of the church, full freedom upon all the
land(s) which belonged to the holy foundation, whosoever may have
given them ; and therewith sake and soke, toll and team, infangenetheof, flymenafyrmth and grithbreach and hamsocn and foresteall and miskenning and showing and all other rights in festival
season or outside it, within borough and without, on street and
off street, as fully and as completely as ever I myself possessed
them. And if anyone henceforth shall wish to enrich the holy
foundation with land and with (? produce ? stock) I likewise grant
that his benefaction remain unimpaired. And I will not permit
that anyone have authority over his land or over his men, by
strand or by land, nor that anyone infringe this protection of their
rights. God keep you. Amen.

WINCHESTER

Seven writs, nos. 107–13, are printed here from Winchester sources,
six from those of Winchester Cathedral,[1] and one from a register of

[1] The building and consecration of the ' minster ' at Winchester (Winchester
Cathedral) is entered in the *Chronicle* F 648 ; see also A 643, B, C 642, E 641.
Its first dedication was in honour of the Holy Trinity and in memory of
St. Peter and St. Paul. At a later date the name of St. Swithun was added,
and by this name it was subsequently known. From the beginning of the
tenth century it was often called the Old Minster, to distinguish it from the
New Minster built at Winchester by King Edward the Elder. For the history
of this house, see *Mon. Angl.* i. 189 ff., VCH *Hampshire*, ii. 108 ff. ; A. W.
Goodman, *Chartulary of Winchester Cathedral* (Winchester, 1927), xliv ff.

New Minster (see p. 527). No. 107, which bears the name of King Æthelred II, is one of the two writs surviving—the other is no. 52— attributed to that king. No. 108 is an unquestionably authentic writ of his mother Queen Ælfthryth. The letter of the monk Edwin (no. 113) seems to be spurious. The Winchester writs of King Edward are of varying degrees of authenticity. No one of these texts has come down to us in contemporary form. The Codex Wintoniensis (B.M. Add. MS. 15350) is supposed to have been compiled in the time of Bishop Henry de Blois, 1130–50, but only no. 108 is copied in one of the main hands of the cartulary ; the others are in different hands of the twelfth century. The other Old Minster cartulary, B.M. Add. MS. 29436, was compiled for the most part in the thirteenth century. The character and date of the linguistic forms is an important factor in the criticism of these texts, and the relevant matter is considered in the discussion of the individual writ. There is reason to suppose that Anglo-Saxon was still being written at New Minster if not at Old Minster at any rate as late as the second half of the twelfth century (see p. 388).

CHILCOMB

No. 107, THE CHILCOMB WRIT in the name of King Æthelred II, relates to a large tract of country then called Chilcomb which lay round Winchester on each side of the town. Its boundaries are given in a charter of King Edward the Elder (B. 620–1), the authenticity of which is not certain. Within a boundary line on which were to be found (among other places) those now known as Swaythling, Crawley, Worthy, Alresford, Tichborne and Bishop's Waltham, many vills were enclosed. With these places were included the two outlying vills of Chilbolton near Andover, and Nursling near Southampton. In 1086, as in King Edward's time, the very extensive manor of the bishop of Winchester at Chilcomb, which was assigned to the support of the monks of Winchester Cathedral, was rated at one hide only.[1] There was land there for 68 ploughs. There were 12 ploughs in the demesne ; and there were 30 villeins and 115 bordars with 57 ploughs. There were 9 churches, and 20 serfs, and 4 mills worth 4 pounds, and 40 acres of meadow ; 23 shillings and 5 pence were paid for the pasture (*pro herbagio*), and there was woodland worth 30 pigs from the pannage. The whole manor was worth T.R.E. 73 pounds 10 shillings, afterwards the same sum, and in 1086 what the monks held was worth 80 pounds, and what was held by tenants, 24 pounds. The monks of Winchester

[1] DB i. 41, VCH *Hampshire*, i. 463 f.

Cathedral in their charters,[1] the authenticity of which as a series has frequently been questioned,[2] asserted that this great estate had come to them as a grant by the first Christian kings of the West Saxons, in the early days of Christianity in Wessex, in the seventh century, and they declared that king after king had confirmed this grant, which carried with it the privilege that the assessment of the estate should be reduced from 100 hides [3] to one hide.[4]   King Egbert, King Æthelwulf, King Alfred, King Edward the Elder, King Æthelstan, and King Edgar, are said to have confirmed this. The Chilcomb writ attributed to King Æthelred carries the story a stage further : King Æthelred is made to declare that Bishop Ælfheah sent him the charter (not now extant) granted by King Alfred concerning the land at Chilcomb ; this he had had read before him, and was greatly pleased with the ordinance and pious benefaction established by his ancestors and renewed by that king. His will now is that the land shall be assessed for all purposes at one hide, just as his ancestors established and freed it, whether there be more land there or whether there be less.   The privilege claimed by the monks of Winchester Cathedral is fully set out in the doubtful charter attributed to King Edward the Elder which has been mentioned above :—

' Seculares igitur episcoporum dicione subjecti intra ambitum hujus spatiosæ telluris (i.e. Chilcomb hundred) diversis in villis degentes censum episcopali sede

---

[1] The extant Winchester charters relating to Chilcomb are B. 493 (Æthel-wulf), B. 620-1 (Edward the Elder), B. 713 (Æthelstan), B. 1147 and 1148 (= Robertson no. 38), and B. 1159 (Edgar), B. 1160 (a memorandum concerning the hidage of Chilcomb discussed below).

[2] See Kemble, *The Saxons in England*, ed. 1876, ii. 487 ; Haddan and Stubbs, *Councils and Ecclesiastical Documents*, iii. 646 f. ; Earle, *Land-Charters*, cix ; W. H. Stevenson, *Asser's Life of King Alfred*, 322, n. 6 ; J. Armitage Robinson, *The Saxon Bishops of Wells*, 18.   It is sometimes asserted that the Chilcomb writ in the name of Æthelred which is under discussion was ' accepted ' by Kemble.   This means no more than that Kemble did not mark this writ with an asterisk as spurious.

[3] I am indebted to Dr. Cam for the suggestion that it is entirely probable that in the hundred hides belonging to Chilcomb is to be found the origin of the hundred of Fawley, one of the Winchester hundreds ; Easton, Avington, Ovington, Tichborne, Kilmeston, Bishopstoke, Owslebury, and Twyford (for which see p. 376 below) are in Fawley hundred.   For instances of hundreds annexed to an ecclesiastical estate see H. M. Cam, ' Manerium cum Hundredo ' in *Liberties and Communities*, pp. 64 ff. and F. M. Stenton, *The Early History of the Abbey of Abingdon*, 46-7.   The administration of the hundred must have ceased to be at Chilcomb, if it ever was there.   For the position of Fawley Down, where the hundred met, and for an account of Fawley hundred, see O. S. Anderson, *The English Hundred-Names*, ii. 185-6.

[4] It is now recognised that the ' hide ' was not a fixed area of land but a unit of assessment bearing no fixed relation either to area or to value.   See Maitland, *Domesday Book and Beyond*, 390 ff., VCH *Hampshire*, i. 402.

persolvant et expeditionem pontis arcisve restaurationem dum necessitas incubuerit incunctanter peragant et has .c. mansas omni obsequio defendant ita ut Ciltancumb cum suis appendiciis pro una tantummodo mansa ut olim constitutum fuerat reputetur ; moderno tempore uti antiquitus constitutum fuerat Hnutscillingc (Nursling) et Ceolboldingtun (Chilbolton) in quantitate horum .c. cassatorum persistant.' [1]

Other cases can be found of ' beneficial hidation ' in the Anglo-Saxon period, whereby an estate without being totally exempted by the crown from geld and other public burdens incumbent on all landowners, might have its assessment reduced to a lower figure. We learn for instance (DB i. 197) that the hidation of Chippenham, Cambs., had been reduced from 10 hides to 5 hides by permission of King Edward the Confessor, and that of a manor of 20 hides at Wenlock, Salop (DB i. 252 b), 4 hides were quit of geld in the time of King Cnut. Of Liskeard in Cornwall, a manor with land for 60 ploughs, we learn (DB i. 121 b) that Merleswein held it T.R.E. and paid geld for 2 hides : ' there are however 12 hides there '. In the case of Maugersbury the privilege is carried back to the time of King Æthelred ; at Maugersbury, which belonged to the abbey of Evesham, there were 8 hides T.R.E. ' and the ninth hide belongs to the church of St. Edward ; King Æthelred gave it quit (of geld) ' (DB i. 165 b). A further entry concerning a manor of Evesham Abbey (DB i. 175 b) provides with its reference to the charters of the abbey an interesting parallel to the claim concerning Chilcomb made in the Winchester charters :—

' Ipsa æcclesia [de Evesham] tenet Ambreslege. Hæc antiquitus pro iii hidis fuit libera sicut dicunt cartæ de æcclesia, sed T.R.E. fuit numerata pro xv hidis inter silvam et planum et iii hidæ ex eis sunt liberæ '.[2]

That the hidation of Chilcomb had been reduced may very well be true, though there does not seem to be any corroboration in other sources for the statements made in the Winchester charters. The argument put forward by W. H. Stevenson [3] against the authenticity of the Chilcomb charters as a whole, namely that ' we have no

---

[1] B. 620–1. For comments see Stevenson, *Asser*, 322, n. 6.

[2] J. H. Round remarks, ' Danegeld and the Finance of Domesday ', *Domesday Studies*, ed. P. E. Dove (London, 1888), i. 99 : ' Here the Abbey must have produced its title-deeds before the *legati*. The figures, however, would seem to suggest that while the exemption was only intended to free three hides out of the fifteen from geld, the Abbey must have endeavoured to represent it wrongfully as enacting that only three of the fifteen hides should be liable to the payment of geld.' Round takes ' numerata ' to mean that ' such was the assessed number on the rolls, which rolls, we must always remember, afforded the crown its indispensable check on the assertions and pretensions of its subject '. For further instances of ' beneficial hidation ', see Round *loc. cit.* 98–110, Maitland *op. cit.* 449, VCH *Hampshire*, i. 403 ff., App. iv, no. 13.

[3] *Asser's Life of King Alfred*, 322, n. 6.

indications that such reductions of hidation were known before the introduction of Danegeld, and no evidence beyond the Winchester charters that such reductions were made by royal charters ', was answered in part (by implication) by Maitland. Maitland declared (p. 450) that he could see nothing improbable in the supposition that Æthelred issued the writ ascribed to him and that what he said in it was substantially true ; that before Æthelred's day there may have been no impost known as a ' geld ', but there may have been other imposts to which land contributed at the rate of so much per hide ; and further ' we suspect that " beneficial hidation " had a long history before Domesday Book was made '. These other imposts included such burdens as the payment of the king's food-rent (*feorm*), the duty of entertaining his servants and persons seeking his court, the building of royal villages, and the cartage of goods.[1] From the three public burdens of service in the fyrd, and work on bridges and fortifications, exemption was rarely granted. Exemption from the general land-tax or ' geld ' which was levied to meet the tribute paid to the Danes in 991 and 994, and frequently in Æthelred's reign, and which was levied from 1012 to 1051 for the payment of a standing military force, was granted by King Edward to St. Edmund's Bury (no. 15).

Domesday records without comment that the great manor of Chilcomb with its nine churches was assessed at only one hide (DB i. 41). Several Winchester charters state that the number of hides originally attributed to Chilcomb was 100,[2] but the writ in the name of King Æthelred which is under discussion, makes no such statement. It is however accompanied in the cartulary by two memoranda, the first of which, since Kemble printed the texts continuously, was mistakenly supposed by Maitland to form an integral part of the writ. This memorandum raises difficulties ; it is printed as a footnote to no. 107. It begins : ' This is the extent (*or* amount) of the land belonging to Chilcomb, that is 100 hides in all with that which lies round about it.' It then continues with the names of eleven places, the modern villages of Easton, Avington, Ovington, Tichborne, Kilmeston, Bishopstoke, Brambridge (described in the VCH *Hampshire* iii. 334 as a hamlet in Twyford and Owslebury), together with Otterbourne and Twyford, to which are added the outlying villages of Chilbolton and Nursling. But as Maitland points out (*loc. cit.* p. 497), reference to the Domesday entries relating to these places reveals an important discrepancy. Of the eleven vills named in the memorandum (not counting Chilcomb) nine are separately assessed in Domesday among the other

---

[1] Stenton, *Anglo-Saxon England*, 284 ff., and p. 206 above.
[2] B. 620–1, 1147–8, 1161.

manors belonging to the bishop of Winchester. Two only are not mentioned there, Brambridge and Tichborne (concerning which the suggestion is made in the VCH *Hampshire,* iii. 337, that some at least perhaps was included in Twyford). If then the memorandum is directly contradicted by what Domesday tells us concerning these manors, can we suppose that it describes an earlier state of affairs, before the reduction of the hidation of Chilcomb had taken place ? Or did the compiler of the memorandum intend to make a distinction between ' the land belonging to Chilcomb ' and ' that which lies round about it ' ?   Or was he merely trying to account for the figure of 100 hides, which may have become traditional at Winchester ? Fortunately however, in whatever way the memorandum is interpreted, it does not, as Maitland supposed, form part of the writ, and the authenticity of the writ is not dependent on it.

Can we then accept the Chilcomb writ in the name of King Æthelred as authentic ?   That Æthelred did issue a writ, concerning some matter or another, for the monks of Winchester Cathedral seems certain, for it is difficult to believe that the address, with its reference to comparatively obscure persons such as Wulfmær and Æthelweard, is not authentic.   For the narrative style of the writ a parallel is at hand in the Christ Church writ of Cnut (no. 26).   For the phrase : *for ane hide werige,* parallels exist in the *werige his land(are),* of nos. 29 and 66, the one of Cnut, the other of Edward.   But is the document in question an unaltered copy of an authentic writ of Æthelred II ?   This is a question not easy to answer.   A remarkable feature of this text is the close resemblance of its phraseology to that of a text purporting to be a translation, made at King Edgar's command, of a Latin charter which he had granted for the Winchester monks.[1]   The Latin charter is undated, and has no list of witnesses.   In the English version, which is drawn up in the form of a declaration, and which has the appearance of a paraphrase rather than a literal translation of the Latin text, it is stated that Bishop Æthelwold (of Winchester) procured from King Edgar the renewal of the freedom of Chilcomb just as the king's ancestors had freed it, namely King Cynegils and his son King Cynewalh (Cenwalh), and afterwards Kings Egbert, Æthelwulf, Alfred, and Edward (the Elder).   King Edgar himself granted that the land should be assessed for all purposes at one hide as his ancestors had established and freed it, whether there were more land there or whether there were less.   He forbade the alienation of the land from that place, and the re-introduction of priests into the minster.   The amount of the estate was in all 100 hides but ' the good and wise kings one after the other freed it to the praise of God and for the use and

[1] B. 1147–8, Robertson (vernacular version), no. 38.

sustenance of his servants so that for all time it should be assessed at one hide '. The document concludes with a long and detailed anathema. With the phrase : *his yldran hit ær gefreodon . . . þe on angynne cristendomes hit sealdan* of the declaration associated with Edgar, compare : *minne yldran on angunne cristendomes . . . gesetten* in l. 5 of the writ attributed to Æthelred. With the phrases : *þæt man þæt land on eallum þingon for ane hide werode swa swa his yldran hit ær gesetton 7 gefreodon wære þær mare landes wære þær læsse* in the supposed charter of Edgar, compare : *þ hit man on eallum þingon for ane hide werige swa swa mine yldran hit ær gesetten 7 gefreodan sy þer mare landes sy þer lesse* in ll. 7–9 of the supposed writ of Æthelred. With the ' good and wise kings ' of the supposed charter of Edgar, compare ' the wise king ' Alfred, of the supposed writ of Æthelred. But the Chilcomb writ attributed to Æthelred which is under discussion says nothing of any charter of Edgar ; the charter that it mentions is a supposed charter of King Alfred, not now extant. How then are we to explain the resemblances between the two texts ? The place of the reputed charter of Edgar in English in the line of descent of this phraseology cannot be ascertained on the evidence now available. But it is at least a working hypothesis that the supposed charter of Alfred also contained these phrases, and that it was from this charter, which (so the writ informs us) was sent to King Æthelred by Bishop Ælfheah, and which, since it was read before the king, was probably in English, that the clerk of King Æthelred's writing-office, compiling the Chilcomb writ in the name of that king, took the phrases in question. If any rehandling of a writ of King Æthelred took place at Winchester, there are no direct indications of it in the text as it has come down to us. Bresslau however suggested [1] that the Chilcomb writ as we have it is possibly an interpolated copy of a writ of Æthelred II, a suggestion which one cannot help thinking may be due to a misunderstanding. Stevenson had remarked [2] that the writ is ' derived from the twelfth-century Codex Wintoniensis, a cartulary containing numerous forgeries ', and that ' even if the recapitulation of the estates is an addition due to the copyist of the charter, the text is still open to suspicion as it relates to the reduction of hidage of a hundred hides to one, a claim of the monks that necessitated a long series of twelfth-century forgeries '. These statements, says Bresslau, ' scheinen doch höchstens für eine Interpolation der Urkunde zu sprechen '. But there are no direct signs of interpolation of the text. Had Bresslau possibly misunderstood what Stevenson meant by ' the recapitulation of the estates '—

---

[1] *Archiv f. Urk.* vi (1918), 48, n. 3.
[2] *Eng. Hist. Rev.* xxvii (1912), 5, n. 16.

namely, the first memorandum which has been discussed above
(p. 376) and which I have printed as a footnote to no. 107—supposing this to be inserted in the writ ?   I find it difficult to follow
Bresslau's argument, for Stevenson regards the writ as ' open to
suspicion ', whereas Bresslau takes it without further argument as
genuine, but possibly interpolated.   Bresslau also quotes Maitland
as expressing no doubts as to the authenticity of the writ (*loc.
cit*. p. 264), while ignoring the comments of Maitland elsewhere
(*ibid*. p. 497) which are unfavourable to its authenticity.   Having
considered the whole series of Chilcomb charters, not excepting
the writ under discussion, and taking into account the discrepancy
between the Domesday statements and those of the Chilcomb
memorandum which has often been referred to, Maitland concluded (*loc. cit*. 497) that : ' It is to be feared that these charters
tell lies invented by those who wished to evade their share of
national burdens.'   To this conclusion Bresslau makes no reference.   As a further argument in favour of the authenticity of the
writ, he reports that in a communication made to him personally, Liebermann considered the writ genuine (' hält ihn für
echt ').

Having recorded these divergences of opinion, we must now look
at the writ itself.   If it is a fabrication, the forger—who may have
been at work before the Norman Conquest, or during that period
after the Norman Conquest till late in the twelfth century (no. 113)
when Anglo-Saxon was still being written at Winchester—has
succeeded remarkably well in giving to his text an appearance of
authenticity so far as the structure and style are concerned.   There
are however some peculiarities of form and spelling—more than there
are, for instance, in the copy of Ælfthryth's letter (no. 108),
undoubtedly a product of the late tenth century : *frunlice*, presumably for *frundlice*, which we find in the place of *freondlice* in the
Winchester Cathedral Chartulary copy of no. 111 ; *angunne* (in
the place of *angynne*, which appears in the supposed charter of
Edgar cited above) ; *ætforð* (of which I have found no other example)
for OE *ætforan* ; *minne*, a misspelling of *mine*.   These may be errors
of a transcriber or they may be mistakes of a forger.   It is not to be
denied that the Chilcomb writ has a highly dubious background, and
that its statements concerning the circumstances in which the reduction of the hidation of Chilcomb had taken place are uncorroborated
in any source except the other Chilcomb charters.   It is doubtful
whether it will ever be possible to speak positively on the question
of its authenticity.   But since Domesday tells us that Chilcomb was
assessed at one hide, and since it has not been proved that its
assessment at one hide was not renewed and confirmed by Kings

c c

Alfred and Æthelred, and since the only signs of later handling in the text could be explained on the supposition of a transcriber's errors, there is at least a chance that we have in this text a copy of an authentic writ of King Æthelred II.

ÆLFTHRYTH'S WRIT

There is no reason to doubt the authenticity of the WRIT (no. 108) ADDRESSED BY ÆLFTHRYTH to Archbishop Ælfric and Earl Æthelweard in the reign of her son King Æthelred II. Her testimony had evidently been sought in some enquiry concerning an estate at Ruishton in Somerset, a member of an immense estate at Taunton, which from early times had belonged to the bishopric of Winchester, but some part of which had by King Edgar's time come into the possession of the crown. King Edgar not only restored to Winchester the lands at Taunton, but also renewed its freedom ; and when on that occasion the king received in return gifts from Bishop Æthelwold, Ælfthryth herself received from the bishop a present of 50 mancuses in gold in return for her good offices.[1] As a result of the restoration of Taunton to the bishop of Winchester the thegns of the king who held land on the Taunton estate were informed by King Edgar that they must henceforth hold their land in conformity with the bishop's wishes, or else give it up. Among them was a certain Leofric, the holder of land at Ruishton, which was now, by the king's direction, transferred to the bishop. But by the efforts of Ælfthryth and of the sister of Leofric, Bishop Æthelwold was prevailed upon to grant to Leofric and his wife Wulfgyth [2] a lifetenancy of Ruishton, which on their death was to revert to Taunton. Ælfthryth was in a position to give first-hand information about this tenancy. She affirms that Leofric relinquished his title-deed (boc), that Bishop Æthelwold informed him that he could not be dispossessed by any of the bishop's successors, and that the bishop ordered two documents to be written, of which he himself retained one, the other he gave to Leofric.

[1] For other references to such payments made to the queen, see p. 480.

[2] That Leofric and Wulfgyth were husband and wife seems to be a legitimate inference from the text ; hi moston brucan . . . hyra dæg (l. 11) is in the plural. This does not seem to have been realised by H. Brunner, who describes this document as ' ein schwer verständlicher Brief ' (Zur Rechtsgeschichte der Römischen und Germanischen Urkunde (Berlin, 1880), 177 f.). Brunner takes Ælfthryth and Wulfgyth, both feminine names, to be masculine (' eines gewissen Ælfthryth ', ' dem Wulfgyth '), and supposes that it was Wulfgyth who was to hold Ruishton for life, and that Leofric was a previous tenant. This is a mistaken interpretation of the text.

THE BISHOPRIC

The two writs (nos. 109, 110) announcing that King Edward has granted to Bishop Ælfwine of Winchester the BISHOPRIC OF WIN-CHESTER (to which he had already been appointed in the reign of Cnut), as fully and completely as ever Cnut granted it to him, resemble each other closely. They differ mainly in their length. In no. 110 one finds qualifying the clause : ' as fully and completely as ever King Cnut granted it to him ', the additional passage : ' *binnan porte 7 butan, on lande 7 on strande, on wudan 7 on feldan 7 on læse* '. There is some justification for regarding this as a mere embellishment of the text. To the judicial and financial rights enumerated in no. 109, no. 110 adds *flymena fyrmðe on freolse 7 butan*. The linguistic differences between the two texts are of the most trifling description, far less considerable, for example, than those appearing in a Westminster group of somewhat similar texts (nos. 81, 82, 83) ; in both the Winchester texts the linguistic forms are those of late West Saxon, only very slightly modernised. The easiest way to account for the similarities and differences between the two documents is to suppose that the longer text (no. 110) is merely an improved and embellished version made at Winchester of the other. If the two texts were two writs separately issued the linguistic differences would probably have been more considerable. On these grounds it seems likely that the longer version no. 110 was not an independent writ of the Confessor, separately issued.

No. 109, the shorter of the two writs relating to Edward's grant to bishop Ælfwine of the bishopric of Winchester, as fully and com-pletely as ever Cnut granted it to him, may be authentic in substance in spite of what may be explained as careless copying. The *pe* in *pe land ligce* (to be corrected to *per* on the analogy of nos. 12, 47) ; the omission here, as in nos. 110, 112, of *freondlice* in the address, and similarly the omission in l. 10 of 110 of *pæra* in *for ealra pæra cyninga*—all these are doubtless merely scribal errors. There is nothing to excite suspicion in the list of judicial and financial rights to which the bishop, by the king's grant, is to be entitled. But one cannot help wondering whether the religious consideration (' to the praise of God, for my soul, and for the souls of all the kings who were before me and shall come after me ') is in place here ; if the religious consideration is authentic, so presumably is the anathema, on the principle that a penal clause may be introduced to safeguard a grant made for the donor's soul (see Introduction, p. 70). There is however no religious consideration and no anathema in nos. 64, 65, which offer a fair analogy, as they too confirm a bishop in rights already enjoyed by his predecessors ; nor is there anything of the sort in no. 50. The existence of no. 110 is in itself evidence of the working-over of these texts, and we cannot exclude the possibility that the religious consideration and the anathema may represent additions to an otherwise authentic writ of King Edward.

A close connection exists between no. 109 (the probably spurious no. 110, containing similar material, being left out of consideration here) and a declaration attributed to Cnut (K. 753), an earlier grant by whom no. 109 purports to confirm. Cnut's grant may be considered the original of all the charters of liberties to Winchester Cathedral ' so often confirmed by the Norman kings '.[1] Its form is irregular, but the framework (of Latin version and list of witnesses with dating clause) in which it appears, might possibly have been provided for it in Old Minster. It may or may not be authentic. The document begins : ' Cnut king by God's grace of all England and of all Danes informs [2] my bishops and my earls and all my thegns both Danish and English of what I grant to Old Minster at Winchester.' Besides the freedom from all secular dues save the *trimoda necessitas* enjoyed by this house in the time of his predecessors, Cnut grants them hamsocn, foresteall, mundbreach, which with sake and soke, toll, team, and infangenetheof, appear in Edward's writ, no. 109. He grants them every *wite* (' fine ') small and great (*ælces wites smales 7 greates*), and Edward's writ also includes *ælces wites læssan 7 maran*. The appearance of the religious consideration and the anathema in Edward's writ is perhaps to be explained by the appearance of similar features in Cnut's declaration : Cnut makes his grant to the praise of God and St. Peter and St. Paul and the saints who are buried in Old Minster, and his declaration concludes with an unusually long and elaborate penal clause. This text, whether authentic or not, may be in some way connected with the appearance in no. 109 of those features in which no. 109 differs from other writs of the same type. There seems no reason to doubt that no. 109 represents an authentic writ of Edward for Bishop Ælfwine, but whether the religious consideration and the anathema were included by the clerks of the king's secretariat, or whether they are later additions made at Old Minster, it is difficult to determine.

THE GOODBEGOT WRIT

No. 111, in which King Edward announces his confirmation of HIS MOTHER'S BEQUEST TO OLD MINSTER of the messuage (*haga*) known as ' Ælfrices *Godegebeaton* ', seems to be authentic, except for the final clause relating to Hayling. This writ, the main body

---

[1] V. H. Galbraith, *Eng. Hist. Rev.* xxxv (1920), 382.
[2] The printed text reads *cyðe*, to be corrected no doubt to *cyð*.

of which is free from suspicious features, provides an early reference
to the ' liberty of Goodbegot ', ' the manor of Goodbeat ', an enclave
of special jurisdiction in the heart of Winchester which remained
' independent of the city and independent of king or mayor
until 1541 '.[1] A court roll of the reign of Henry VIII [2] defines the
liberties of ' the manor of Goodbeat ' on the eve of their disappearance, and provides an interesting instance of continuity in the
exercise of privilege, in this case for nearly five hundred years.
Among the liberties of the prior and convent of St. Swithun (Winchester Cathedral) enumerated there, it is declared that :

' no mynyster of ye Kynge nether of none other lorde or franchese shall do any
execucion Wythyn the bounds of ye said Maner but alle only ye mynystours of
ye seid prior and his convent ', the prior and the convent having had possession
of these liberties from time immemorial.

It can scarcely be doubted that these liberties had their origin in
King Edward's declaration in the writ under discussion that : ' none
of my officers shall have any jurisdiction over those who dwell
therein, nor anyone in any matter, except the community and
those whom they appoint as their officers '.[3] The messuage in
Winchester to which King Edward's writ (no. 111) refers, as having
been bequeathed to Old Minster by his mother, Queen Ælfgifu
Emma, had come to her, as the writ asserts, by the gift of his father.
King Æthelred II in 1012 granted to her by a charter (K. 720) an
estate on which stood a church dedicated to St. Peter, within the
walls of Winchester on the north side of the city and near the
market-place. It was to be exempt from all services, even the
obligation of repairing walls and bridges and of military service,
and the queen was to have full liberty to dispose of this estate as
she herself should wish, ' whether she be still in health, or whether
she be dying '. The boundaries in English, which follow the Latin
text of the charter, have been worked out by Canon Goodman
(see n. 1, below) in relation to the topography of present-day
Winchester. Identifying the church of St. Peter with the no longer
existing church of St. Peter *in Macellis*, and taking the market-place
of Æthelred's charter to be the High Street, Canon Goodman concludes that the *haga* of Ælfric Goodsgetter (see p. 549) must have
extended between the High Street and St. George's Street, from
St. Peter's Street to what is now the George Hotel.

[1] VCH *Hampshire*, v. 34 ff.
[2] Printed A. W. Goodman, *The Manor of Goodbegot* (Winchester, 1923), 31.
[3] For other instances of the exclusion of royal officials, see p. 128. For
fourteenth- and early fifteenth-century references to this area of special
jurisdiction in the middle of Winchester, see J. S. Furley, *City Government of
Winchester* (Oxford, 1923), 91-2 ; VCH *Hampshire, ut supra* ; Goodman,
op. cit. 30-49.

Everything encourages the belief that no. III, in so far as it refers to the manor later called Goodbegot, is an authentic copy of a genuine writ of King Edward. But it seems more than doubtful whether the final clause, relating to the 10 hides at Hayling Island ever formed part of this writ when it was first issued.[1] According to Domesday there were several manors in Hayling Island. One was the undisputed possession of the monks of the bishopric of Winchester (i.e. Old Minster or St. Swithun's) ' who always held it '.[2] Another is entered under the lands of the abbey of Jumièges. Its previous holder had been Wulfward the White, who held it of Queen Edith *in alodium*.[3] But the Domesday entry informs us further that the monks of the bishopric of Winchester claimed this manor because Queen Emma gave it to their church, and at that time gave the monks seisin of one half; the other half she granted to Wulfward for his life only, on condition that on his death the monks should have his body for burial and the manor also; that Wulfward held his part of the manor on those terms until he died, in the time of King William; and that this was attested by Elsy (Æthelsige), abbot of Ramsey, and by the whole hundred.[4] Any claims however that the monks of Old Minster might have had to this manor were ignored by the Conqueror, who bestowed it on the

[1] According to a late tradition Hayling was one of the manors given by Queen Emma to the monks of the Old Minster in gratitude to St. Swithun for her success in the ordeal of the red-hot ploughshares, just as Portland (see no. 112) and other manors were by the same tradition said to have been given by her son King Edward. No contemporary corroboration appears to be forthcoming for this story of the queen's trial by ordeal, which may be fictitious. See *Historia Major Wintoniensis* in *Anglia Sacra* i. 233–5, and *Mon. Angl.* i. 190, 194, 210. On the spurious charter concerning Wargrave (Robertson no. 118), another manor supposed to have been given to the Old Minster in gratitude by the queen, see F. E. Harmer, *Bulletin of the John Rylands Library*, xxii (1938), 349–51.

[2] DB i. 43, VCH *Hampshire*, i. 468. This manor paid geld T.R.E. for 5 hides, in 1086 for 4 hides.

[3] On Wulfward the White, who held lands in many shires T.R.E., and who seems to have retained lands and royal favour after the Conquest, see VCH *Buckinghamshire*, i. 216–17, *Oxfordshire*, i. 379; for references in charters and elsewhere, see Tengvik, 319. Miss Robertson remarks (p. 463) that he seems to have had some special connection with Queen Edith.

[4] DB i. 43 b, VCH *Hampshire*, i. 473. See Robertson no. 114 for a charter (which the editor dates ' probably about 1053 '), preserved only in the Codex Wintoniensis, which purports to record an agreement between the monks of the Old Minster and Wulfward the White; he is to hold for his lifetime not only the 5 hides at Hayling bequeathed to him by Queen Ælfgifu Emma, but also the 5 hides bequeathed by her to the Old Minster, and on his death the whole 10 hides are to pass to Old Minster. Wulfward seems to have survived till 1084 (VCH *Somerset*, i. 533), but he was dead in 1086, as Domesday records.

monks of Jumièges, who still possessed it, as Domesday records, in 1086.[1] But at a later date the claims of the Westminster monks were recognised by William Rufus, according to a charter in his name enjoining that the monks of the bishopric of Winchester should have in peace the land at Hayling which Queen Emma gave them, *sicut liber regius hoc testatur*.[2] The dispute as to the ownership of Hayling dragged on for many years, and the matter was not finally settled till the reign of Stephen, when Henry, bishop of Winchester, and all the brethren of the church of Winchester, between 1139 and 1142, at the prayer of Pope Innocent, and in consideration of the poverty of the church of Jumièges, ceded to that church ' a portion of Hayling Island which the church of Jumièges had long possessed ', undertaking never again to stir up strife concerning it ; the monks of Jumièges for their part promising to pay to secure the undisturbed possession of the land a sum of 100 marks, of which 20 marks were remitted to them.[3] It would then have been greatly to the advantage of the Winchester monks to have documentary evidence of a bequest to them by Queen Emma of the disputed manor, and of its confirmation to them by her son. Two points in the short Hayling passage seem suspicious : the definite article *þe*, which indicates a date later than Edward's reign (see p. 393) ; and the verb *stande* in the sing., with ' the ten hides ' (cf. *habban* above). Then too the transition is clumsily managed by 7 and *ge*, both meaning ' and ' (unless the *ge* is emphatic —OE *gea*, ME *ge* in some texts, Mod. Eng. *yea* ; but this would be as odd in Old English as it is in Modern). The passage has the appearance of a later addition tacked on to an authentic writ in order to strengthen the claim of Old Minster to Hayling.

THE PORTLAND WRIT

The authenticity of no. 112, THE PORTLAND WRIT, in which King Edward declares that he has bequeathed Portland and everything belonging thereto to Old Minster, is not certain. We are no doubt safe in assuming that the bequest was to take effect after the king's death. The relevant Domesday entry (see p. 526) says that King Edward held Portland for the term of his life (*in vita sua*), but says nothing of any claim of the monks of Old Minster to its possession.

[1] The Conqueror's charter (*Calendar of documents preserved in France*, i. no. 1423) is dated ?1067 by J. H. Round.

[2] V. H. Galbraith, ' Royal Charters to Winchester ', *Eng. Hist. Rev.* xxxv (1920), 388, no. xii, dated by the editor 1096–1100.

[3] Round, *op. cit.* nos. 157–8, VCH *Hampshire*, i. 435.

If King Edward did in fact, as the writ announces, bequeath Portland to them, his intention was frustrated, for in 1086 Portland was held by King William. But on the other hand a claim of the monks of Winchester Cathedral (Old Minster) to Portland ' which King Edward gave them ', is admitted in a writ of Henry I : ' Facite ut monachi Sancti Swithuni de episcopatu Wintoniensi teneant bene et in pace *manerium de Porlande quod rex Edwardus eis dedit* et Wike et portum Waimuth et Melecumbe cum omnibus pertinentiis suis.' [1] In the thirteenth century they were in a position to grant to the bishop-elect of Winchester their manor of Portland, with the manor of Wyke, the vill of Weymouth, and the land of Helewell. [2] The possibility must then be admitted that Portland may actually have been bequeathed to Old Minster by King Edward, and the bequest announced by writ. But is the extant Portland writ a writ of the Confessor ? This is a difficult problem, for only here have we a writ purporting to announce a grant which was to take effect only after his death. In such a document features not normally found in Anglo-Saxon writs might not be out of place. The address to all the king's counsellors (*witan*, see Introduction, p. 53), ecclesiastical and lay, could be explained on the supposition that it was intended thereby to give to the document greater weight and wider publicity than an ordinary address to the local shire court could secure. Again reference to Miss Whitelock's *Anglo-Saxon Wills, passim*, will show that in many cases bequests to religious houses (and even grants notified in writs, see Introduction, p. 67) were made in the expectation of spiritual benefits, as in the Portland writ : ' for my soul and for the souls of all my kinsmen and for the souls of all the kings who shall rule this kingdom after me ' ; and the religious sanction : ' may he have to account for it with God ' is not out of place here (see Introduction, p. 69). Further, since the actual bequest would no doubt have been made orally before witnesses, it is not unnatural that names of (alleged) witnesses should be recorded in the writ (see Introduction, p. 73). The names, it should be noted, are names of only well-known persons. They may have formed part of the writ (if it is authentic) ; they may have been added at a later date. Incidentally the attribution of the style of *cancheler* here to Regenbald is questionable (see Introduction, p. 60). But it is hard to believe that this is an authentic copy of a writ of King Edward. *Freondlice*, normal in the address, and *wille* in l. 7, necessary to the syntax, may have been omitted carelessly ; the many late Old English and Middle English forms such as *Wyncheastre* and *Gealden* may be due to conscious or unconscious

---

[1] V. H. Galbraith, *loc. cit.* 390, no. xviii.
[2] VCH *Hampshire*, iii. 87.

modernisation by a transcriber.[1] But I cannot help thinking that the clause : *eall þ ðerto bilyð*, is suspicious. *Bilyð (to)*, with a dot over the *y* in the manuscript (as with nearly every other *y* in this text—*kyning* being an exception) may stand for *bilȳð*, in an earlier copy, i.e. *bilym(þ)ð*, as Dr. Kenneth Sisam has kindly pointed out to me. *Bilimpan* actually occurs in nos. 40, 74, 76, 93, 104, but not in this clause, where the verb normally employed is *hyran (heran)* or *gebyrian*, and moreover these particular texts are of doubtful value for determining the usages of the Confessor's scriptorium. Another possible way of explaining *bilyð* is to connect it with the rare verb ' belie ' (OE *belicgan, bilicgan*) ' to lie near ; to pertain or belong (to) ', see NED. Taken as a whole the Portland writ does not inspire confidence as a copy of an authentic writ, and it is easier to believe that its date of origin was in the late eleventh or early twelfth century. When the outline of the history of the manor which has been given above is considered, it is not difficult to imagine that circumstances may have arisen in which the fabrication of a text such as this may have been considered desirable if other evidence of a grant by the Confessor of Portland to Old Minster should not have been forthcoming.

EDWIN'S LETTER

The authenticity of no. 113, which purports to be A LETTER ADDRESSED TO HIS BISHOP BY EDWIN, A MONK of New Minster [2] at Winchester, seems more than doubtful. This text, ostensibly

---

[1] Compare *gealla* (' *eald-* '), ' of *þa gealla* minstre ', ' from the old minster ' (i.e. at Exeter), in a manumission of the second quarter of the twelfth century in the Exeter Book (Thorpe p. 647 = Earle p. 261). Compare also *geal (eall-)*, Thorpe p. 622 ; *gealra, gealle (eall-)*, Thorpe p. 632 = Earle p. 259. All these forms, whether printed by editors with *g-* or with *ȝ-*, represent a pronunciation with a *ȝ*-sound initially developing in late Old English or Middle English. See E. V. Gordon's note on the *gealgean* of *The Battle of Maldon*, l. 52 ; also Introd. to *The Exeter Book*, ed. Chambers, Förster and Flower, 45, n. 9. See also Sievers-Cook, and K. Brunner, § 212, n. 2 (but the usage is not confined to late Kentish).

[2] This monastery, called New Minster to distinguish it from the Old Minster or Cathedral at Winchester, was founded by King Edward the Elder, its consecration being recorded in the *Chronicle* F. 903. The clerks of Old Minster and New Minster were expelled and replaced by monks by Bishop Æthelwold after his accession to the see of Winchester in 963, the replacement of clerks by monks being a well-known feature of the monastic revival. In 1110 New Minster was transferred to Hyde, outside the north gate of the city, and the foundation was henceforth known as St. Peter's Abbey of Hyde, or Hyde Abbey. For the history of New Minster, see *Liber Vitae*, Register and Martyrology of New Minster and Hyde Abbey, ed. W. de Gray Birch (Hampshire Record Society, 1892), *passim* ; and for a list of manuscripts relating to New Minster, see *ibid.* p. lxxi ff. See further VCH *Hampshire*, ii. 116 ff.

recording the ratification of an agreement between Old Minster and New Minster at Winchester before A.D. 980 by the well-known Bishop Æthelwold of Winchester (afterwards canonised), has been preserved in the records of both the foundations concerned.   It was presumably written at New Minster, and it was copied into the *Liber Vitae* of that house in a handwriting of the twelfth century, probably of the latter part of the century.   Another copy, inferior from the linguistic point of view, but occasionally offering better readings, was copied into the Codex Wintoniensis of Old Minster in a handwriting of the end of the same century.   It is not unlikely that the document itself is a twelfth-century product.   In that case it would provide an interesting instance of the persistence in use of the characteristic writ protocol, though in a form, with the first person, rarely met with in surviving writs (see Introduction, p. 61).   And further it would indicate that at Winchester the knowledge of Anglo-Saxon still lived on at all events till the third quarter, or even the end, of the twelfth century, for the author of this text writes the language fluently and idiomatically, like a practised hand. The importance of this conclusion for the criticism of Anglo-Saxon writs at large, and particularly of Winchester writs, will be obvious.

There is nothing improbable in the terms of the agreement reported in this letter to have been made between Old and New Minster.   It was agreed that when a priest died the two communities should bury him and hold services for him jointly ; that each community should join in the celebration of the chief festival of the other ; and that if a member of either should misconduct himself, he should have recourse to the members of the other, and they would intercede for him.   The period assigned to this agreement in the letter under discussion is the time of King Edgar, the time also of St. Dunstan and St. Æthelwold, who were associated with him in the movement for monastic reform.   The occasion is a visit of Archbishop Dunstan and monks from New Minster and Old Minster—among them the poet and hagiographer Wulfstan—to Bishop Æthelwold, when he was lying sick, in the time of Abbot Æthelgar, who was the first abbot to rule over the New Minster after the replacement of the clerks by monks, and who was promoted to the see of Selsey in A.D. 980.   An impression of authenticity is given by the introduction, among the persons named as being present on this occasion, of Ælfwine, ' who is now abbot ', that is, of New Minster.   Is this fact, or is it fiction ?   It seems impossible to decide. The circumstantial details give an impression of veracity.   On the other hand the names of all the persons mentioned as being present when the agreement was ratified by Bishop Æthelwold appear in the lists which form a large part of the register of New Minster and

Hyde Abbey, into which this document has been copied. All the names, those of monks of New Minster and of Old Minster, could easily have been taken by the compiler of the document from these lists or from other such domestic records. Moreover an Edwine *sacerdos* who appears as thirty-sixth in a list of monks of New Minster, which is headed by the name of Abbot Æthelgar, bears the same name as the writer of the letter.[1] Abbot Æthelgar was famous in New Minster history; he subsequently became bishop of Selsey and archbishop of Canterbury, and Abbot Ælfwine too must have been long remembered at New Minster, for two volumes once belonging to him are still preserved.[2]

In the first paragraph the writer professes to tell us something of himself, and of an escapade of his three years previously which had led him to take advantage of one of the clauses in the agreement of which he subsequently gives an account—namely, that a monk misbehaving should be restored to the favour of his abbot by the mediation of the other community. He narrates how in consequence of a vision of St. Cuthbert he, a monk, child-master of New Minster, made his way to the saint's shrine (at Durham) in defiance of the prohibition of his abbot, Ælfwine, and how he was welcomed there by Bishop Æthelwine (of Durham). There, the writer says, he washed with his hands the body of the saint, ' and combed his head with a comb, and cut his hair with scissors, and clothed him all in new apparel, and took from him his old clothes ; some I left there, and some I have here '. This episode must have appeared the more worthy of credence at Winchester from the fact that the monks of New Minster included in a list of their relics : ' De barba Sancti Cuthberti et de uestimento eius '.[3] But the difficulties in the way of the acceptance of this narrative as veracious seem insuperable. In the first place the dates involved seem to be irreconcilable. The writer, Edwin, greets Bishop Ælfsige, who was bishop of Winchester

[1] A special mark has been placed against a few (e.g. Cedd *episcopus*, Asser *episcopus*) of the hundreds of names in these lists. It can scarcely be a coincidence that this mark appears in the lists against the names of Edwine *sacerdos* and of six of the names of persons mentioned in Edwin's letter ; i.e. Ealdwig *sacerdos*, Wulfstan *.i. cantor, sacerdos,* Godwine *.ii. decanus, sacerdos* in an Old Minster list, and in a New Minster list, Boia *sacerdos,* Ælfric *decanus, sacerdos,* Ælfnoð *pictor, sacerdos.* Birch conjectured (p. 15, n. 4) that the mark signifies ' buried here '. But whether this is so, or whether (as Professor M. D. Knowles suggested to me) the fourteenth-century investigator was checking the names in Edwin's letter, the fact remains that these were names which were readily at hand at New Minster.

[2] *Liber Vitae*, 47, note, 251 ff. ; see also Biographical Notes.

[3] *Ibid.* 147. This item comes third, immediately following : ' De uestimento Sancte Marie et de uestimento Sancti Petri '. There are other entries in the list relating to northern saints, including St. Acca, and St. Frithbert, both of Hexham, and St. Wilfrid.

1012/14–1032. Therefore at some time not later than 1029 (cf. l. 2, 'three years ago') he went to Durham, where (according to the writer) he met Bishop Æthelwine, who was not appointed to the see till 1056.[1] In the second place St. Cuthbert actually lay in his coffin robed in his pontificals. Reginald of Durham, writing not long after 1172, says that when the body of the saint was examined at the translation in 1104, it was clothed in an alb, amice, mitre, gold fillet, stole and fanon (maniple), tunic, dalmatic, and episcopal shoes.[2] When the tomb of St. Cuthbert was opened in 1827 there was found in it among many other treasures a magnificent stole and maniple which are still preserved,[3] made by order of one Ælfflæd (probably Queen Ælfflæd, the second wife of King Edward the Elder) for Frithestan, who was consecrated to the see of Winchester in A.D. 905, and who, incidentally, is mentioned in Edwin's letter (l. 29) as the first originator of the agreement, ratified later, made between Old Minster and New Minster. Queen Ælfflæd died before A.D. 916, Bishop Frithestan died in 931, and King Æthelstan a few years later gave to St. Cuthbert, among many other gifts, a stole with a maniple.[4] It is easy to imagine that the stole and maniple made by Ælfflæd's command for Bishop Frithestan may have come by some means after the death of both into the hands of King Æthelstan, to be presented at the coffin of St. Cuthbert by that king. The question is however raised by W. H. D. Longstaffe,[5] whether the statement in Edwin's letter, that the writer clad St. Cuthbert's body in new clothes, leaving some behind on his departure ('some I left there'), does not explain the appearance at Durham of 'Winchester vestments', namely the stole and maniple made for Frithestan. A similar suggestion is made in the *Dictionary of Christian Biography*, s. 'Cuthbert'. But this possibility seems remote. It is hard to imagine how such costly vestments as these could have come, a

[1] The date of appointment, c. 1032, of Abbot Ælfwine of New Minster (ll. 5, 6, 24) seems too uncertain to be brought into account here.

[2] *Reginaldi Monachi Dunelmensis Libellus de Admirandis Beati Cuthberti Miraculis* (Surtees Society, i, 1835), 84–90 ; B. Colgrave, *Two Lives of St. Cuthbert* (Cambridge, 1940), 130, 338. See also the anonymous account of the translation of 1104, Symeon of Durham, *Opera Omnia*, R.S. ed. Arnold, i. 247–61, especially 254–5, and, in general, J. Raine, *St. Cuthbert* (Durham, 1828). I am indebted for the Durham material here and for the references to Mr. Colgrave.

[3] Raine *op. cit.* 202 ff., and for a further description of the stole and maniple, C. F. Battiscombe, 'The Relics of St. Cuthbert', *Trans. Architect. and Archæolog. Soc. of Durham and Northumberland*, viii, pt. i (1937), 43–79 ; G. Baldwin Brown and Mrs. A. Christie, *Burlington Magazine*, xxiii (1913), 3 ff., 67 ff.

[4] Raine *op. cit.* 50.

[5] 'Unused Evidences relating to SS. Cuthbert and Bede', *Archaeologia Aeliana*, N.S. xiii (1889), 278–81.

century later, into the possession of a New Minster monk ; and in any case Edwin's story is probably, on other grounds, a fabrication. Moreover, as a third obstacle to the acceptance of Edwin's story as veracious, the vestments of St. Cuthbert were so greatly venerated as relics, that it is hardly credible that the writer of the letter would actually have been permitted to carry home with him to Winchester, as he claims to have done, some of the clothing of the saint (though, as has been said above, relics of St. Cuthbert are mentioned in the New Minster list of relics). C. F. Battiscombe (op. cit.) gives as an instance of the value attached to vestments of St. Cuthbert, the fact that the original chasuble of the saint, though removed from his tomb as long ago as A.D. 698, was still preserved at Durham in the fourteenth century.

But according to Durham writers of the twelfth century, Symeon of Durham, and Reginald of Durham, there was in the time of Bishop Edmund (1020–c. 1040), a sacrist at Durham called Ælfred Westou, who was notorious for the liberties which he took with the coffin and the corpse and the apparel of the saint.[1] The more developed account, whatever may have been its source, appears in the work of Reginald of Durham, a Durham monk, writing, as has been said above, not long after 1172. According to this story, Ælfred Westou, ' for the love which he bore to St. Cuthbert, was distinguished by peculiar privileges conceded to no one but himself, for, as often as it pleased him, he might freely and with impunity open the coffin of the saint, *might wrap him in such robes as he thought fit*, and he could obtain from him without delay whatever he requested ; whence it is recorded that he, from long familiarity, attained to such a degree of cordiality with the saint, that it was his custom *to cut the overgrowing hair of his venerable head*, to adjust it by *dividing and smoothing it with an ivory comb*, and to cut the nails of his fingers, tastefully reducing them to roundness '.[2] There was actually found in the tomb of St. Cuthbert in 1104 a comb and a

---

[1] See also H. H. E. Craster, ' Some Anglo-Saxon Records of the See of Durham ', *Archaeologia Aeliana*, 4th ser. i (1925), 190 ff.

[2] Reginald of Durham, *op. cit.* cap. xxvi (Surtees Society, 57) : English rendering from Raine *op. cit.* 59. We may compare what is recorded of the body of St. Edmund. It is said that Bishop Theodred having ventured to open the repository of the saint's body, washed the body and clothed it in *novis et optimis vestibus* and placed it in a wooden coffin (*locello*) ; see the *Passio Sancti Eadmundi* of Abbo of Fleury in *Memorials of St. Edmund's Abbey*, R.S. ed. Arnold, i. 22. The story is also told of the devout attendance at the tomb of St. Edmund of a woman who was wont yearly to clip and cut the hair and nails of the martyr, carefully collecting and placing in a small box the clippings, which at the time of the writer were still an object of veneration in the church ; see *Memorials*, i. 20, and also William of Malmesbury, *Gesta Regum*, R.S. i. 265.

pair of scissors.[1] Symeon of Durham also speaks of the devotion of Ælfred Westou to St. Cuthbert's relics and claims that the sacrist lived on until the days of Bishop Æthelwine (Egelwine).[2] The resemblance between the story of Ælfred Westou of Durham and Edwin of New Minster's supposed account of his own proceedings at the shrine of St. Cuthbert is striking. It is moreover to be observed that in several manuscripts of Symeon and Reginald of Durham the date A.D. 1022 is associated in the margin with Ælfred Westou. Mr. Colgrave has suggested to me that if the Winchester writer had seen the works of Reginald and Symeon of Durham, he might have taken the date A.D. 1022 from the margin, looked up the name of the appropriate bishop of Winchester (Ælfsige), and then, seeing Symeon's statement that Ælfred Westou lived on until the time of Bishop Æthelwine (of Durham), have brought into his text the name of Æthelwine. The apparent dates of the handwriting of the two texts in which this letter has come down to us do not preclude this possibility. And in fact the mention in Edwin's letter of Bishop Æthelwine (which involves a chronological disloca-tion) makes it more likely that the writer was using the work of Symeon of Durham, than that his account of Edwin's proceedings at the tomb of St. Cuthbert was composed independently. There was however actually a link between Winchester and Durham in the time of Ælfred Westou, for Edmund, who became bishop of Durham in 1020, was consecrated to this see at Winchester [3] by Archbishop Wulfstan of York, and Æthelric the brother, and pre-decessor in the bishopric, of Æthelwine, was his protégé.[4] But everything encourages the belief that this letter is spurious.

---

[1] Reginald of Durham *loc. cit.* Raine, 59, 198 ff., 216, Appendix 5–6. For a photograph of the comb, taken from the tomb when it was opened in 1827, and still preserved, see G. Baldwin Brown, *The Arts in Early England* (1930), vi, i. opposite p. 4 ; and R. H. Hodgkin, *History of the Anglo-Saxons*, ii. Plate 70. See also Battiscombe, *ut supra*.

[2] *Hist. Dun. Ecclesiæ*, R.S. ed. Arnold, i. 87.

[3] *Ibid.* i. 86.

[4] It is stated by Raine (*op. cit.* 53), on the authority of a manuscript of Prior Wessington of Durham, that in the time of Ælfsige, bishop of Chester-le-Street (968–90), Bishop Æthelwold of Winchester (cf. Edwin's letter, ll. 21 ff.) himself visited the shrine of St. Cuthbert, and that while there he ' raised the lid of St. Cuthbert's coffin, talked with the dead man as with a friend, and placed upon his body a pledge of his love '. But, as Mr. Colgrave has pointed out to me, the phraseology quoted by Raine with reference to a (supposed) visit of Bishop Æthelwold of Winchester is actually employed by William of Malmesbury (*Gesta Pontificum*, R.S. 180) with reference to a visit to St. Cuthbert's shrine of Bishop Ælfwold I of Sherborne (ob. 978), who had been once a monk of Winchester. There can be little doubt that the name of Bishop Æthelwold of Winchester has been wrongly substituted by Raine, or in his source, for that of Bishop Ælfwold of Sherborne, a less famous man.

A comparison will show that neither of the two extant manuscript texts of Edwin's letter is a copy of the other ; both must be derived from a common source. The transcriber of the Stowe MS. erased some words and particles which are to be found in Codex Wintoniensis, as if he were correcting his copy ; other small words are perhaps omitted in the Stowe MS. through carelessness. The copyist of Codex Wintoniensis makes some blunders, and also omits words here and there. Small differences in expression (noted in footnotes to text) also appear. There are also linguistic differences. Some words exhibiting late Old English and early Middle English sound- and spelling-changes in Codex Wintoniensis (e.g. *munkes* for *munekas*, *messedeie* for *mæssedæge*, *-cherf* for *-cearf*, *munstre* for *mynstre*) do not appear in these forms in the Stowe MS. For the most part the unetymological *æ* for which the Stowe MS. transscriber shows a fondness (e.g. *agænne*, *þidær*, *gæcearf*) does not appear in the text in Codex Wintoniensis, where there is only one instance, *gæwende*. But these are only changes such as might be expected from transcribers making in the early Middle English period copies of a text written (as it would seem) in an earlier form of the language, though not necessarily written at a much earlier date. The evidence suggests that the spellings of the text from which both are derived approached more nearly to the spellings of late West Saxon than do those of either of the existing manuscripts, and that the Stowe MS. text (printed here) reproduces the original text the more closely. But in all probability the original text, though written in something closely resembling late West Saxon, was not entirely devoid of forms denoting a later, twelfth-century, date of origin. In the first place the construction with *for* in line 22 (*for hine to geneosienne*) is characteristic of Middle English and not of the Old English period. And again, the frequent though not invariable use of the indeclinable definite article *þe* in both texts, if it was not merely the contribution of a copyist, favours the supposition that Edwin's letter was originally composed in the twelfth century, when this form appears.

A consideration of the material utilised by the writer combines with the linguistic and palaeographical evidence to support the conclusion that the letter was fabricated in the twelfth century, and probably in the latter part of the twelfth century if the writer had consulted the work of Reginald of Durham. Information kindly supplied to me by Professor M. D. Knowles enables us to ' place ' the letter in its twelfth-century background. There can be little doubt that in its description of an alleged agreement between the two Winchester monasteries, the letter represents one step in a notable movement, from c. 1170 to 1200, to assert and codify ' rights of exchange ' between black monk houses. This was one aspect of a notable tendency of the monastic ' chapter ' to assert its rights *vis à vis* the abbot—as a result partly of the abbot's growing independence as a feudal magnate, and partly of the tendency endemic in late twelfth-century Europe, to form *communitates* and *universitates*. Of such associations several instances are given by Professor Knowles in *The Monastic Order in England* (pp. 474-5 ; cf. 415-16). The movement petered out early in the next century, not only because it ran counter to the clear teaching of the Rule of St. Benedict [1] (and was even condemned by the Fourth Lateran Council), but also because the rivalry and particularism of individual monasteries soon came to be more powerful than the earlier feeling of solidarity. But the movement was there, c. 1170-1200, which is the period to which one would be disposed to assign Edwin's letter on other grounds. A remarkable parallel is cited by Professor Knowles (*op. cit.* p. 474) as having been drawn up c. 1200 between Evesham and Malmesbury. Among its provisions ' it gives full right of entry to choir, chapter and monastery, and enacts that a delinquent monk of one house may be sent to the other to live, not as a prisoner, but as a monk of the cloister, and that if a monk flees from one house to the other he is to be received there, and the abbot is to use his good offices to effect a reconciliation'. In this and other documents cited by Professor Knowles, as in Edwin's letter, the communities are asserting their own rights as against the abbot.

It is then unnecessary to seek for any particular occasion for the making of the alleged concordat between the two Winchester houses ; in the late twelfth century such agreements were being readily made elsewhere. And moreover the actual or fictitious ratification of such an agreement as is described in the letter as having been made at an earlier period by St. Æthelwold and the most important personages in their early history would in both houses add an additional sanction to its terms. But we need not necessarily suppose that the story of the writer's unauthorised pilgrimage to Durham is entirely devoid of any basis of fact. Miss Whitelock has suggested to me that Edwin's letter would the more easily have gained credence if there had existed at New Minster (as there well may have done) a tradition—connected possibly with the presence in their house of relics of St. Cuthbert, possibly with the presence at Durham of Bishop Frithestan's stole and maniple—of a journey from Winchester to Durham made in the early eleventh century by one of the brothers of their house.

---

[1] Cf. capitular decrees in W. A. Pantin, *Chapters of the Black Monks,* ii. 24-5.

And moreover, as has been said above (p. 392), there was actually in the early eleventh century a link between Winchester and Durham in the person of Bishop Edmund of Durham who in 1020 had come to Winchester for consecration to the see of Durham at the hands of his own archbishop, Wulfstan of York ; Edmund no doubt brought news from Durham to Winchester. But whatever degree of truth there may have been in any one of the statements in Edwin's letter, the chronological dislocation to which attention has been drawn above, in his account of his supposed visit to Durham, drives one to the conclusion that the letter itself is a fabrication. And the cumulative evidence suggests that this fabrication was composed in the latter part of the twelfth century by someone who had filled in the outlines of a story of a visit to . Durham by researches into the works of Durham writers and the records of his own house.

(107)

King Æthelred declares that the land at Chilcomb is now to be assessed for the discharge of all the obligations upon it at one hide, as had been established by his ancestors. (984–1001)

(Cod. Winton. f. 6)

Æþelred cynig gret Ælfric ealdorman 7 Wulmær. 7 Æþelweard 1
7 ealle þa þegenas on Hamtunscire. frunlice. 7 ic cyþe þe 7 eow
eallum þ Ælfheah biscop sende to me þæs landes boc æt Ciltancumbe.
7 ic hi let redan ætforan me. Þa licode me swyðe wel seo gesetnesse.
7 seo ælmesse þe minne yldran on angunne cristendomes into þere 5
halgan stowe gesetten. 7 se wisa cing Ælfred syððan geedniwode
on þære bec þe man ætforð me rædde. Nu wille ic þ hit man on
eallum þingon for ane hide werige swa swa mine yldran hit ær
gesetten. 7 gefreodan. sy þer mare landes sy þer lesse.

The writ ends at the foot of the page, but with space to continue. At top of second column of same page, in same hand : ' Ðus mycel is þæs landes into Ciltecumbe þ is ealles an hund hida. mid þam þe þer abutan lið. Æstuna .iiii. Æt Afintuna .v. 7 æt Ufintuna .v. Æt Ticceburnan .xxv. To Cylmestuna .v. To Stoce .v. To Brombrygce. 7 To Oterburnan .v. To Twyfyrde .xx. To Ceolbandingtune .xx. To Hnutscillingæ .v.'   *In margin in a later hand :* ' Nomina de pertinentibus ad Chyltecumb '.   *A second list follows in the same hand as the text :* ' An hund hida to Ciltancumba. To Hysseburnan. 7 To Hwitcyrcan. hun[d]endlyftig h.' etc.

Translation

King Æthelred sends friendly greetings to Earl Ælfric and Wulfmær and Æthelweard and all the thegns in Hampshire. And

D D

I inform thee, and all of you, that Bishop Ælfheah sent to me the charter of the land at Chilcomb, and I had it read before me. Then I was greatly pleased with the ordinance and the pious benefaction which my ancestors, when Christianity first began, established for the benefit of the holy foundation ; and the wise king Alfred afterwards renewed in the charter which was read before me. It is now my will that it shall be assessed for all purposes at one hide, just as my ancestors formerly established and freed it, whether there be more land there or whether there be less.

(108)

Ælfthryth gives testimony concerning an estate at Ruishton.
995–1002

(Cod. Winton. f. 26)

1   Alfðryð gret Ælfric arcebiscop 7 Eþelwerd ealdarman eadmodlice. 7 ic cyðe inc ðet íc eom to gewitnysse ꝥ Dunstan arcebiscop getehte Aþelwolde biscope Tantun eal swa hís béc specon. 7 Eadgar cyning hit agef ða, 7 bead ælcon his þegna þe enig land on þan
5 lande hafde, ꝥ hi hít ofeodon be þes biscopes gemedon oððe hit agefum. 7 se cyning cwæð þa þet he nahte nan land ut to syllanne, þa he ne dorste fram Godes ege him sylf ðet heafod habban ; 7 ma, gerad þa Risctun to þes biscopes handa. 7 Wulfgyþ rad þa to me to Cumbe 7 gesohte me. 7 íc ða for þan þe heo me gesib was,
10 7 Ælfswyð for þan þe he hyre broþor wás, abedon æt Aðelwold biscope ꝥ hi moston brucan þes landes hyra deg, 7 efter hyra dege eode þet lond into Tantune mid mete 7 mid mannum eal swa hit stode ; 7 wit hyt swiðe uneaðe to þan brocton. Nu cydde man me þæt Aðelwold bisceop 7 ic sceoldon ofneadian þa boc æt
15 Leofrice. Nu ne eom íc nanre neade gecnewe þe libbe, þe ma þe he wolde þeah he lyfode : ac Leofric hafde áne niwe boc ; þa agef he þa, þa cydde he mid þan þet he nolde nan fals þer on dón. Þa cydde Aðelwold bisceop hím ꝥ híne ne mihte nan his eftergenga bereafian ; hét þa gewritan twa gewritu, oðer him sulf hefde, oþer
20 he Leofrice sealde.

A large part of this text is left unpunctuated in the manuscript. It has therefore been punctuated here in full in accordance with modern usage.

Translation

Ælfthryth sends humble greetings to Archbishop Ælfric and Earl Æthelweard. And I inform you both that I bear witness that Archbishop Dunstan assigned Taunton to Bishop Æthelwold, in conformity with the bishop's charters. And King Edgar then relinquished it, and commanded every one of his thegns who had any land on the estate that they should hold it in conformity with the bishop's wish, or else give it up. And the king then said that he had no land to grant out, when he durst not, for fear of God, retain the headship himself ; and moreover he then put Ruishton under the bishop's control. And then Wulfgyth rode to me at Combe and sought me. And I then, because she was my kinswoman, and Ælfswyth because he (i.e. Leofric) was her brother, obtained from Bishop Æthelwold that they (i.e. Wulfgyth and Leofric) might enjoy the land for their lifetime, and after their death the land should go to Taunton, with produce and with men, just as it stood. And with great difficulty we two brought matters to this conclusion. Now I have been told that Bishop Æthelwold and I must have obtained the title-deed from Leofric by force. Now I, who am alive, am not aware of any force any more than he would be, if he were still alive. For Leofric had a new title-deed ; when he gave it up he thereby manifested that he would engage in no false dealings in the matter. Then Bishop Æthelwold told him that none of his successors could dispossess him. He then commanded two documents to be written, one he kept himself, the other he gave to Leofric.

(109)

King Edward declares that he has granted to Bishop Ælfwine the bishopric of Winchester as fully and as completely as ever King Cnut granted it to him, that is, with judicial and financial rights. (1042–47)

(Add. MS. 29436 f. 10)

Eadweard cýng gret ealle mine ƀ. 7 eorlas . 7 þegnas on ælcere 1
scire þe[r] land licge in to Ealdan Mynstre. 7 ic cyðe eow ꝥ ic
hæbbe geunnen Ælfwine ƀ þæs byscoprices. eall swa full 7 swa
forð swa Cnud cing hit him firmest geuðe. ꝥ is ꝥ ic geann Criste
7 Sɕe Petre 7 Sɕe Paule in to þan halgan stede 7 him ꝥ hig beon 5
heora sace wurðe 7 socne binnan port 7 butan. tolles wurðe 7
teames. forstealles 7 infangenes þeofes . hamsocne 7 mundbryces.
7 ælces wites læssan 7 maran. Gode to lofe for minre sawle. 7 for
ealra þæra cyninga þe ætforan me wæron. 7 æfter me cumað.
7 gif hwa þis awendan wylle. sy he fordemed mid Iudan Scariothe. 10
butan he ær his forðsiðe hit gebete.

Translation

King Edward sends friendly greetings to all my bishops and earls and thegns in every shire where there is land belonging to Old Minster. And I inform you that I have granted to Bishop Ælfwine the bishopric as fully and completely as ever King Cnut granted it to him ; that is to say, I grant to the holy place and to him, to Christ and St. Peter and St. Paul, that they be entitled to their sake and soke within town and without, to toll and team, foresteall and infangenetheof, hamsocn and mundbreach, and to every fine, smaller and greater, to the praise of God, for my soul, and for the souls of all the kings who were before me and shall come after me. And if anyone shall wish to alter this, may he be damned with Judas Iscariot, unless before his death he make amends for it.

(110)

King Edward declares that he has granted to Bishop Ælfwine the bishopric of Winchester as fully and completely as ever King Cnut granted it to him, and grants to Old Minster and to the bishop judicial and financial rights. (1042–47)

(Add. MS. 29436, f. 10)

1 Eadweard cing gret ealle mine ƀ. 7 eorlas 7 þegnas on ælcere
scire þe[r] land ligce in to Ealdan Mynstre. 7 ic cyðe eow ꝥ ic
hæbbe geunnen Ælfwine ƀ. þæs byscoprices. eall swa full 7 swa
forð swa Cnud cing hit him firmest geuðe. binnan porte 7 butan.
5 on lande 7 on strande. on wudan 7 on feldan. 7 on læse. 7 ic
geann Criste 7 Sc̄e Petre 7 Sc̄e Paule in to þan halgan stede. 7
him ꝥ hig beon heora sace wurðe 7 socne. binnan porte 7 butan.
tolles wurðe 7 teames. forstealles 7 infangenes þeofes. hamsocne
7 mundbrices. 7 flymene fyrmðe. on freolse 7 butan. 7 ælces wites
10 læssan 7 maran. Gode to lofe for minre sawle. 7 for ealra cyninga
þe ætforan me wæron. 7 æfter me cumað. 7 gif hwa þis awendan
wylle . sy he fordemed mid Iudan Scariothe. butan he ær his
forðsiðe hit gebete.

Heading : Carta Sancti Edwardi Regis de libertate ecclesie Winton.
4. forð] -d MS.

Translation

King Edward sends friendly greetings to all my bishops and earls and thegns in every shire where there is land belonging to

Old Minster. And I inform you that I have granted to Bishop Ælfwine the bishopric as fully and completely as ever King Cnut granted it to him within town and without, on land and on strand, in woodland and in open country and in pasture. And I grant to the holy place and to him, to Christ and St. Peter and St. Paul, that they be entitled to their sake and soke within town and without, to toll and team, foresteall and infangenetheof, hamsocn and mundbreach, and flymenafyrmth, in festival season and outside it, and to every fine, smaller and greater, to the praise of God, for my soul, and for the souls of all kings who were before me, and shall come after me. And if anyone shall wish to alter this, may he be damned with Judas Iscariot unless before his death he make amends for it.

(111)

King Edward declares that he has granted that his mother's bequest to the monks of Old Minster of the messuage in Winchester called 'Ælfric Goodsgetter's' shall stand, and that the ten hides at Hayling shall remain just as she bequeathed them to them. (1052–53)

(Add. MS. 29436, f. 10 b)

Eadward cing gret Stigand .b̄. 7 Godwine eorl. 7 ealle þa burhmen 1
on Wincestre. frondlice. 7 ic kyð̄e eow þ̄ ic hæbbe geunnen þ̄ se
cwyde stande þe min moder becwæð̄ Criste 7 Sc̄e Petre 7 Sc̄e
Swið̄une 7 þan hirede in to Ealdan Mynstre. þ̄ is se haga þe man
hæt Ælfrices Godebegeaton. þæne ic wille þ̄ hi habban eal swa 5
freo wið̄ ealle þa þing þe to me belimpoð̄. eal swa he hire æfter
mines fæder gyfe on handan stod. 7 non minra wicnera nane
socne nabbe uppon þa þe þær on uppon sittað̄. ne nan mann on
nanan þingan. butan se hired. 7 þa þe hi heom to wicneran settað̄.
7 ge þe tene hida æt Helinge stande al swa hi hi hem bicwað̄. 10

Heading : Carta Sancti Edwardi Regis de Godebiete.   3. becwæð̄]
-d MS.   3. R *omits* Sc̄e Petre.   6. wið̄] -d MS.   6. belimpoð̄]
belimwoð̄ MS. ; bilompeþ B ; belonggyed R ; belongged, -eþ S, P, M.
8. sittað̄] -d MS.   9. hired] -ð̄ MS.

Translation

King Edward sends friendly greetings to Bishop Stigand and Earl Godwine and all the citizens in Winchester. And I inform you that I have granted that the bequest shall stand which my mother made to Christ and St. Peter and St. Swithun and to the

community at Old Minster, namely, the messuage that is called
' Ælfric Goodsgetter's ', which I desire that they shall have just
as freely in respect of all the things that belong to me as she herself possessed it in accordance with my father's gift. And none
of my officers shall have any jurisdiction over those who dwell
therein, nor anyone in any matter, except the community and
those whom they appoint as their officers. And (and *or* ? yea)
the ten hides at Hayling shall remain just as she bequeathed them
to them.

(112)

King Edward declares that he has bequeathed Portland and
everything belonging thereto to Old Minster at Winchester.
(1053–66)

(Cod. Winton. f. 7)

1   Ædward kyning grett ælle mine wytan gehadode 7 lewede.
Ænd ic cyþe eow þ ic hebbe bicweðen Portland. 7 eall þ ðerto
bilyð ín to Gealden Mynstre on Wyncheastre Gode to lofe 7 Sc̄e
Petre. 7 Sc̄e Suuthune. þam monekan to scrudan 7 to fodan. for
5 mynre sawle. 7 for ealre mynra maga. 7 for ælre ðere kynga sawle.
þe æfter me þyse's' kynyngriches wældeð. La hwo ðisne cwidan
ondon [wille] . hebbe he wið Godd gemene on domes deig. Ðyss
sint þera manna naman þe ætt þysan cwidan weren. Eadgið. se
hlefdie. Stigand se archeb̄. Harold eorl. Rengebold cancheler.

In margin : De Portl'.   3. MS. bilyð, *with the customary dot over*
the y.   4. MS. Suuthune, *Old English* Swith(h)une.

Translation

King Edward sends friendly greetings to all my counsellors,
ecclesiastical and lay. And I inform you that I have bequeathed
Portland and everything belonging to it to Old Minster at Winchester, to the praise of God and St. Peter and St. Swithun, for
the clothing and food of the monks, for my soul, and for the souls
of all my kinsmen, and for the souls of all the kings who shall
rule this kingdom after me. Lo ! whosoever shall wish to undo
this bequest, may he have to account for it with God on the Day
of Judgment. These are the names of the persons who were at this
bequest : Queen Edith, Archbishop Stigand, Earl Harold, Regenbald
the chancellor.

(113)

The monk Edwin, child-master at New Minster, Winchester, informs Bishop Ælfsige of Winchester of his vision of St. Cuthbert, and of his visit to the shrine of the saint despite his abbot's prohibition. He tells how he was reconciled to his abbot through the mediation of the prior and community of Old Minster, in accordance with an agreement between Old and New Minster ratified long before by Bishop Æthelwold, and gives its terms and describes the circumstances in which the ratification took place.

(Stowe MS. no. 944, f. 40)

Ic Eadwine munuk cilda mæstere an Niwan mynstre grete þe wel 1
Ælfsige biscop. Ic kyþe [þe] laford ꝥ nu for þreon gearan ic læig
innan minan portice anbuton nontid. 7 me atewde þær þe halga
Cuthbert openlice. Ic þæs swiþe bliþe wæs. Ic eode to minan
abbode Ælfwine & bed hinæ ꝥ ic moste norþ faran to þan halgan 5
7 hine gesecan. Ac min abbod Ælfwine me þæs forwirnde 7 eac
forbead. Ic þa fæng on minne agænne ræd 7 eode me þidær norð.
7 [me] þær Ægelwine bisceop mid weorscipe underfeng. [7] me
geuþe God 7 þe halga ꝥ ic hine minan handan gewochs. 7 his
heafod mid kambe gekemde. 7 his hær mid scearan gæcearf. 7 hine 10
eall myd nywan scrude gescrydde. 7 his ealde claþas him fram
genam. sum ic þær let. 7 sum ic her habbe. Nu hlaford bæþohte
ic me ꝥ ic nefde mines abbodes leafe. 7 ic þær fore ham gæwende.
7 kom me into Ealdan Mynstre. 7 gesohte Crist 7 Sc̄e Peter. 7
Sc̄e Swiðun 7 þe wolde ac þu nære æt ham. Ac ic funde Leofwine 15
þone decanum 7 ealle þa gebroðra. 7 hi me weorþlice 7 bliþelice
underfengan. 7 me to minan abbode geþingodan. 7 he me bliþelice
underfeng. si Gode lof. Nu wille [ic] þæ kyþan hlaford Ælfsige
biscop hu þeos [ge]cwydrædene fyrmæst wæs [ge]staþelod betwyx
Ealdan Minstre. 7 Niwan Mynstre. ealswa ic self hi [ge]hyrde þa 20
þæ ic geong wæs. Hure hlaford Sc̄e Alwold læig seok 7 him kom
to þe haliga Dunstan of Cantwarabyrig for hine to geneosienne
7 ure ealder Æþælgar abbod þyder eode 7 munekas mid him. ꝥ
was Boia þe ealda 7 Ælfric decanus. 7 Ælfnoð þe metere. 7 Ælfwine
þæ nu abbod his. 7 þær coman munekas of Ealdan Minstre. ꝥ wæs 25
Ealdwig 7 Wlstan cantor 7 Godwine decanus 7 maniga oþre [mid
him]. þa aras Boia þæ ealda munuk 7 sæt a cneowan ætforan Sc̄e
Aþelwolde 7 bed hine ꝥ he scolde settan gode lagan betwyx þan
twam mynstran on muneca dagan. ealswa Friþestan biscop hæfde
geset a preosta dagan. ꝥ wæs ꝥ þa tweien hiredas weran eall to 30
anan. on eallan godcunnnesse. 7 ꝥ wæs gif ænig preost forferde
on aþere steda hi scolde ealle togædere kuman. 7 ꝥ lic bebirian.

7 eallne þeowdom don. þe to Gode belumpe. 7 a cirichalgamdeig
þe biþ binnan Ealdan Mynstre scoldan kuman þa preostas of
35 Niwan Mynstre to Ealdan Mynstre 7 þær beon to efensanga. 7 to
uhtsange 7 to mæssan 7 to gereorde. 7 þa preostas of Ealdan Mynstre
sceoldan kuman to Niwan Mynstre æt Sc̄e Iudoces mæssedæge eall
on þa ylce wisan. 7 gif ænigan preoste mistimode on aþran mynstre
ne fore he nahwider ac gesohte [he] his neahgeburas 7 hi him
40 þingadan. þa þis gehyrde Sc̄e Aþelwold. þa hæ rede ꝥ hit swa
wære [nu] on his timan 7 on þara muneka. 7 cwæþ Godes curs eallan
þan þe æfre [þis] undidan. 7 geaf to tacne ꝥ hit staþelfæst beon
sceolde twa brune mæssehakelan ane into Ealde Mynstre. 7 oðre
into Niwan Mynstre.

Letters in brackets and 3 necessary stops from W. *Except with* [þe] *in
l.* 2, [mid him] *in l.* 26, *and* [he], [nu], [þis], *in the last 6 lines, letters supplied
here in brackets have been erased in* MS., *as though the copyist were correcting his
copy.* 3. nontide W. 9. gewochs W] getwoch MS. 12. sume
(bis) W. 16. W *omits* 7 bliþelice. 18. willic W. 21. whu
se lafard W. 22. to gesydde W. 23. W *omits* ure *before* ealdor.
27. W *omits* þa aras *and reads* Boia þe ealde munuk set. 30. weron
altered to weran MS., weren W. 31. godcungnesse MS, godcunnesse W.
31. forðferde W. 32. aþere W] awere MS. 36. W *omits* to
uhtsange. 37. æt W] 7 Sc̄e Iudoces MS. 39. W *omits* hi.
41. munechen deie W. 43. W *ends with* Ealden Mynstre 7 ana . . .

Translation

I, Edwin, monk, master of the children at New Minster, greet
thee cordially, Bishop Ælfsige. I inform thee, lord, that three
years ago, I was lying in my cell about noon-tide, and there the
holy Cuthbert appeared to me plainly. I felt great joy at this.
I went to my abbot Ælfwine, and prayed him that I might go north
to the saint and visit him. But my abbot Ælfwine refused me
this, and also forbade it. Then I took my own course and made
my way north. And there Bishop Æthelwine received me with
honour ; and God and the saint granted me that I washed him
with my hands, and combed his head with a comb, and cut his
hair with scissors, and clothed him all in new apparel, and took
from him his old clothes. Some I left there, and some I have
here. Now, lord, I bethought myself that I had not my abbot's
leave, and therefore I turned home, and came into Old Minster
and sought Christ and St. Peter and St. Swithun, and would have
thee, but thou wert not at home. But I found Leofwine the prior
and all the brethren ; and they received me with honour and
gladness, and interceded for me to my abbot ; and he gladly
received me, God be praised ! Now I will tell thee lord, Bishop
Ælfsige, how this agreement was first established between Old

Minster and New Minster, as I myself heard it (i.e. the agreement) when I was young. Our lord St. Æthelwold was lying sick, and the holy Dunstan came to him from Canterbury to visit him. And our superior, Abbot Æthelgar, went there, and monks with him, namely, Boia the old, and Ælfric the prior, and Ælfnoth the painter, and Ælfwine who is now abbot. And there came monks from Old Minster, namely, Ealdwig, and Wulfstan the precentor, and God-wine the prior, and many others with him. Then Boia the old monk arose, and knelt before St. Æthelwold, and prayed him that he would establish good regulations between the two minsters in the monks' days, just as Bishop Frithestan had established in the priests' days : namely, that the two communities should be one in every divine service ; and that was to say, if any priest died in either foundation, they should come all together and bury the body and perform all the services that belong to God ; and on the day of the consecration of the church, in Old Minster, the priests from New Minster should come to Old Minster, and be present there at vespers and at nocturns and at mass and at refection ; and the priests from Old Minster should come to New Minster on St. Judoc's day just in the same way. And if there were mis-conduct on the part of any priest in either monastery, he should not go anywhere but he should seek his neighbours and they would intercede for him. When St. Æthelwold heard this, lo, he decreed that it should so be now in his time and in that of the monks ; and he pronounced the curse of God on all those who should ever undo this. And he gave as a token that the agreement should stand firm, two brown copes, one to Old Minster, and a second to New Minster.

WOLVERHAMPTON

Little is known of the church of St. Mary of Wolverhampton in the pre-Conquest period,[1] but the clue to the peculiarities of the alleged writ of King Edward—which cannot be authentic in its present form, and may be an entire fabrication—lies no doubt somewhere in its post-Conquest history. Between 1074 and 1085

[1] For the history of this foundation see Stebbing Shaw, *History and Antiquities of Staffordshire* (London, 1798), ii. 151 ff., and *Mon. Angl.*, vi. pt. 3, 1443.

William I granted the church of Wolverhampton, which had in 994 been richly endowed by the lady Wulfrun from whom Wolverhampton takes its name,[1] and the clergy of which consisted of a dean and canons, to his chaplain Samson, who had been a clerk of Bayeux Cathedral, and is styled in 1082 treasurer of Bayeux ; he was a brother of Thomas of Bayeux, archbishop of York.[2] In Domesday (DB. i, 247 b) the lands of the *canonici de Hantone*, and the lands of Samson, are entered under the same rubric. After his appointment in 1096 as bishop of Worcester, Samson gave the church of Wolverhampton to Worcester Cathedral, but it was afterwards attached to other religious foundations, until it was at length annexed by Edward IV to the chapel of Windsor, so that the dean of St. George's Chapel should be dean of the ' college or free chapel ' of Wolverhampton.[3] Some at any rate of the Wolverhampton records were transferred to Windsor, and one source of the Confessor's Wolverhampton writ (the one printed here) is an *inspeximus* charter of Edward III confirming this writ (and writs and a charter of William I, Henry II, and Henry, duke of Normandy and Aquitaine, and count of Anjou) which was in the possession of the Dean and Chapter of Windsor in 1640, and which, like the *inspeximus* charter of Edward IV, is now in the Harley collection.

The Confessor's Wolverhampton writ presents many peculiar features in spelling, accidence, syntax and vocabulary. Some of these may have been introduced by the fourteenth-century transcriber of Harley Charter 43. D. 29, but even if we admit this possibility, the writ is still much more idiosyncratic than any other text. Some forms are however recognisably those of King Edward's time, and others are merely later spellings (e.g. *frendliche, prestes*), such as appear in many later copies of authentic texts. Idiosyncrasies in this text are as follows : *Me treudam* is probably intended for *mine treuðan, fred'e* for *friðe, be heren* for 3rd pers. plur. of a verb *beheran* (not recorded in the dictionaries), *richeli* and *rich'* for *rihtlice* and *rihte* ; the last word *boed'* may stand for an earlier *beode* (compare p. 66 above). *Ic habben* and *ic hadden* have plural, not singular, endings. *Ic habben me treudam giuen ham* is not Old English syntax. It probably stands for : ' I have given them my

---

[1] On Wulfrun, and on her charter, endowing a religious house at the *heah tun* (dat. *into Heantune*), ' chief manor ', with large gifts of land, see D. Whitelock, *Anglo-Saxon Wills*, 152, 164, and the references there. In the Confessor's alleged writ the form (not contemporary) of the name is *Hampton*, in Domesday *Hantone* and *Handone*. But the name of Wulfrun came to be attached to the place. Until the thirteenth century the dedication of the church was to St. Mary, then to St. Peter and St. Paul, and then to St. Peter.

[2] Davis, *Regesta*, xx.   [3] Stebbing Shaw ii. 152, *Mon. Angl.* vi. 1443.

favour *or* protection' (see BT s.v. *treow*, f. 111) ; reference might
be intended to the king's *mund*, 'protection' (on which see p. 427).
Another possible meaning 'covenant, assurance of good faith'
(see BT *treowþ*, 111), seems less likely here. *Fred'e* and *frid'*, i.e.
freðe and *frið*, may mean 'in peace', or may mean 'free'. Evidence seems to be lacking for the existence in Old English legal
terminology of an uncompounded adjective *frið*, 'in peace, secure',
though the substantive *frið*, 'peace, security', is common. But
the existence in the legal terminology of the twelfth century of
pairs of words such as *frithborg* and *fri-(freo-)borg*, *frithsocn* and
frige-(fri-)soca (for which see NED s.v. frankpledge) seems to have
led to the supposition that *frith* and *freo*, 'free', were equivalent.
Liebermann supposed that the *friborgas* of the first edition of the
so-called Leges Edwardi Confessoris 20, 21, 28 (*temp*. Henry I)
were equivalent to the *frithborgas* of the second (c. 1160).[1] NED
states (*loc. cit.*) that the term 'frankpledge' was apparently a
Norman mis-translation of OE *friðborh* 'peace pledge', *frið* having
been supposed to be connected with 'free'. The occurrence of
freðe, frið, apparently in the sense of 'free' (or 'in peace') in
the Wolverhampton writ, cannot be explained by, or used as evidence for, the legal terminology of the Confessor's time ; in all
probability it reflects twelfth-century (or later) usage. Further,
beheren may be a word coined from OE *hyran* (*heran*), frequently
used in writs in the sense of 'belong (to)' ; here it seems to be
intended to mean 'ought', but the word is not recorded with this
meaning in the Anglo-Saxon dictionaries, and further the ending
-en is not that of Old English, which would have read *-að*. A
different rendering from mine is given for *here þing þer be heren
richeli to be frid*', by C. G. O. Bridgeman [2] ; he renders the passage :
'their possessions thereto rightly belonging also to be free'. This
may or may not have been the meaning of the compiler of the writ,
but *þer beheren* does not under normal conditions stand for 'thereto
belonging' ; what we find in authentic texts is : *þe þær to hyrað*.
I have not followed Bridgeman in his rendering of the remainder
of the writ : 'with sac and with soc, as full and as free as I first
had it in everything. And I will give them then whatever shall
rightfully belong to any of them.' But he may well be right in
supposing that to the compiler of this writ (as to the translator
of nos. 49, 50), *formest* meant 'first'. In later copies of authentic
texts however *formest* stands for OE *fyrmest*, 'to the furthest
extent, to the highest degree' ; see p. 63. The rendering in

[1] *Gesetze*, ii. 81, s.v. *friborg*.
[2] 'Staffordshire Pre-Conquest Charters', *Collections for a History of Staffordshire* (The William Salt Archæological Society), xxvi (1916), 125–6.

Dugdale's Latin version, for the final clause : *Et eis concedo quicquid eis ab aliquo recte concessum fuerit*, may express the intention of the compiler of the writ ; this clause in Edward's writ is impossible to translate as it stands, but, for a parallel, see no. 12 : *þat men hem ani unricht bede (beode)*. A further difficulty in the criticism of the Wolverhampton writ arises from the mention of two Leofwines in the address. If the address has any substantial basis of fact, the mention of Bishop Leofwine of Lichfield would limit the period of issue to 1053–66. ' Leuen *erles* (for *erle*) ' cannot then be Earl Leofwine, the father of Earl Leofric of Mercia, for Leofwine died before 1032, and possibly in 1023, and was succeeded by Leofric, who held the earldom till 1057 (see Biographical Notes). Leofric was succeeded by Ælfgar, and Ælfgar by Edwin, to whom no. 96, a Staffordshire writ, is addressed. Perhaps ' Leuen erle ' in the address is a mistake for ' Leofric eorl '. Bridgeman however suggests (*loc. cit.*) that Earl Godwine's son, Leofwine (see Biographical Notes), may have held the Mercian earldom or at least Staffordshire temporarily during one of Earl Ælfgar's periods of banishment ; but it must be noted that the sources make it clear that Ælfgar's periods of outlawry were of only short duration.

But if the writ is regarded as a whole it is evident that its structure is not irregular. The protocol is in the usual form of the Edwardian writ, and though *ic segge ou*, ' I say to you ', for the notification does not appear elsewhere, it is at all events intelligible. Again the passage : *mid sac and mid socne so ful and so ford* (for *forð*) *so ic formest it hadden (hadde) in alle þing*, is one which appears elsewhere in Anglo-Saxon writs. Several possibilities present themselves when one tries to account for the abnormal features of this writ. It may represent an attempt made after the Anglo-Saxon period to translate back into English a Latin version of a writ ; or again, an attempt to reconstruct a text which was damaged, or partly illegible. But it is at least equally probable that the text was composed after the Anglo-Saxon period by someone who was in some degree acquainted with the structure and formulas of the Anglo-Saxon writ, but was unpractised in the writing of Old English. William I had granted to Samson his chaplain the church of St. Mary of Wolverhampton ' cum terra et omnibus aliis rebus et consuetudinibus, *sicut melius predicta ecclesia habuit tempore regis Edwardi* '.[1] It is not unlikely that the Wolverhampton writ attributed to King Edward was composed at some period later than King William's time with the object of providing evidence of a grant made to the priests of this church by the Confessor.

---

[1] Davis, *Regesta*, no. 210, charter no. xxvi.

(114)

King Edward declares that he has granted his protection (*or* his pledge) to his priests at Wolverhampton, and that they and their minster and their things there shall be free (*or* in peace), with sake and with soke, as fully and completely as he ever had it.

(Harley Charter 43. D. 29)

Edward kyng gret Leuen bissop and Leuen erles and alle myne 1 þeignes on Staffordscire frendliche and ic segge ou þat myne prestes atte Hampton'. þat ic habben me treudam giuen ham. Nou wille ic þat he ben and here mynstre fred'e and here þing þer be heren richeli to be frid' mid sac and mid socne so ful and so ford so ic 5 formest it hadden in alle þing and ic wille giuen ham þan þat ham enyng man enyng on rich' boed'.

Translation

King Edward sends friendly greetings to Bishop Leofwine and Earl Leofwine and all my thegns in Staffordshire. And I say to you that my priests at Wolverhampton—that I have given them my pledge. Now it is my will that they and their minster be free (*or* in peace) ; and their things there ought rightly to be free (*or* in peace), with sake and with soke as fully and as completely as ever I had it in all things. And I will give them that which any man lawfully offers them (?) (*perhaps on a basis* (*cf. no. 12*) *of :* (' I will not permit) that anyone do them any wrong ').

WORCESTER

Everything encourages the belief that the three Worcester writs (nos. 115, 116, 117) are authentic. It is entirely probable that no. 115 in its existing form is an original writ written (and sealed) by the clerks of King Edward's secretariat. In this writ, addressed to the three shires within the diocese, which lay within Earl Ælfgar's earldom, and also to Earl Harold—probably because he had been present at the discussions which had preceded Wulfstan's appointment—King Edward announces THE APPOINTMENT OF WULFSTAN,

prior of the cathedral priory, TO THE SEE OF WORCESTER,[1] in succession to Bishop Ealdred, promoted to the see of York. On his
appointment as archbishop at Christmas 1060, Ealdred had hoped
to retain the bishopric of Worcester, holding it in plurality with
York as certain of his predecessors had done. But when he
arrived in Rome in 1061 to receive his pallium, Pope Nicholas
refused to grant to Ealdred this symbol of his office unless he surrendered Worcester—a condition which Ealdred refused to accept
until he was obliged to return to Rome, after having set out on
his journey home, in consequence of an attack by robbers by
whom he and his companions were stripped of their possessions.
The papal legates who had been sent to England, and who were
much impressed by Prior Wulfstan's mode of life when, at Ealdred's
suggestion, they spent the Lent of 1062 at the cathedral priory
at Worcester, recommended Wulfstan's election to the bishopric.
Their proposal was supported by the two archbishops Stigand and
Ealdred, and by Earls Ælfgar and Harold, and approved by King
Edward, and the election of Wulfstan, who was most reluctant
to undertake the office of bishop, was canonically confirmed on
29 August 1062 ; his consecration at York by Archbishop Ealdred
followed on 8 September.[2] The authenticity of the writ announcing
his appointment (no. 115) is beyond question. Its concluding
clauses, though similar clauses occur elsewhere (see Introduction,
p. 66), forbidding anyone to inflict any illegality on the bishop
or to deprive him of any thing which lawfully belonged to his
bishopric, would have been particularly appropriate to Wulfstan's
circumstances. It must have appeared more than probable that
the newly-appointed bishop would find himself obliged to take
steps to recover for his see, land and rights which might have come
into other hands, and in particular, to deal with claims on the
part of Archbishop Ealdred to lands and rights within the Worcester
diocese. It has been remarked by R. R. Darlington (op. cit. p.
xxvii) that Ealdred ' maintained to the end of his life a paramount
influence in Wulfstan's diocese ', and that for some time after his

[1] The bishopric of the Hwicce, later known as the bishopric of Worcester,
was founded towards the end of the seventh century. St. Peter's church at
Worcester seems to have been regarded as the cathedral church of the diocese
until the time of St. Oswald, who in 953 transferred the bishop's seat to a new
foundation dedicated to St. Mary. For the early history of the bishopric, see
VCH Worcestershire, iv. 376 ff., J. Armitage Robinson, St. Oswald and the
Church at Worcester (British Academy, Supplemental Papers, v, 1919), and
Atkins, ' The Church of Worcester from the Eighth to the Twelfth Century ',
The Antiquaries Journal, xvii (1937), 371–91, xx (1940), 1–38, 203–29 ; see also
D. Knowles, The Monastic Order in England (Cambridge, 1940), 75, n. 1.
[2] William of Malmesbury, Vita Wulfstani, ed. R. R. Darlington, xxv f. and
16–18.

consecration Wulfstan was left at York as Ealdred's deputy. On his return to Worcester Wulfstan received no more of the episcopal estates than seven villages, Ealdred retaining the rest, but he subsequently recovered the remaining lands of the bishopric either from Ealdred or from Ealdred's successor Archbishop Thomas.

WRIT FOR ÆLFSTAN

The second Worcester writ, no. 116, is an only slightly modernised copy of an authentic writ of King Edward, announcing A GRANT OF JUDICIAL AND FINANCIAL RIGHTS TO THE MONK ÆLFSTAN, Wulfstan's brother, appointed by Wulfstan to succeed him as prior of Worcester.[1] This writ bears a close resemblance to no. 11, a Bury writ in which King Edward announces that he has granted sake and soke to Abbot Leofstan and the community, a text which has come down to us in a contemporary hand, and the authenticity of which is also beyond suspicion. Ælfstan appears again in a writ of William I,[2] dated by Davis 1066–87, declaring that the king has granted to Ælfstan the prior[3] and to the monks of Worcester, all the 'customs' and dignities belonging to the priory in lands, churches, tithes and other ecclesiastical and secular possessions, as fully as they held them in the days of the king's predecessors, and he forbids any interference in the affairs of the monks except by leave of the prior.

TOLLS AT WORCESTER

The third Worcester writ, no. 117, in which King Edward announces that he has granted TO BISHOP WULFSTAN for his cathedral church A THIRD PART OF THE TOLLS known as seamtoln and as ceaptoln, enables one to carry a stage further the history of Worcester as a trading centre and of the revenue derived from it by the bishop. Though these compounds of 'toll' (toln, an alternative for toll) with OE seam, 'horse-load', and ceap, 'trading', do not seem to be entered in the Anglo-Saxon dictionaries, there is no reason to doubt that they were words in current use in Anglo-Saxon England.[4] The seamtoln, 'toll on the horse-load', formerly in the king's hand, but now granted as to one-third to Bishop Wulfstan, is no doubt to be identified with the seampending,

---

[1] Darlington, op. cit. xxxviii and footnote.
[2] Davis, Regesta, no. 252.
[3] On the use of decanus at Worcester in the eleventh and twelfth centuries in the sense of 'prior', see Sir Ivor Atkins, The Antiquaries Journal, xx (1940), 22, 24. See also Stubbs, Memorials of St. Dunstan, R.S. xiv ff.
[4] See F. E. Harmer, 'Chipping and Market' (for full reference see p. 78).

'penny on the horse-load ', one of the two tolls (the other was the *wægnscilling*, 'shilling on the wagon-load ') reserved to the king in a Worcester charter of the late ninth century, which gives the terms of an agreement made between 884 and 901 whereby the bishop of Worcester obtained from Earl Æthelred and his wife Æthelflæd, King Alfred's daughter, a grant of half the rights accruing to them at Worcester 'in market and in street '.[1] The penny on the horse-load, and the shilling on the wagon-load, of goods brought into the market at Worcester, as being royal rights, were not included among those rights, such as fines for fighting, fines for theft, fines for market offences, and other sources of profit, of which Bishop Werferth by this ninth-century agreement was to receive a half. Domesday records [2] that the bishop had the third penny of the borough at Worcester T.R.E. It has with much probability been suggested [3] that the bishop's claim to one-third of the burghal render was ultimately founded on the agreement made by the bishop with Æthelred and Æthelflæd in King Alfred's reign. But King Edward's writ for Wulfstan indicates that some part at any rate of his rights had been conferred by direct royal grant, the Confessor having given to Wulfstan one-third of the toll paid on every horse-load of produce and goods brought into Worcester market, and one-third of the toll paid by those buying and selling in the town. There is nothing in this document to excite suspicion. One formula has probably been altered at one stage or another, for we find here instead of *binnan burh* (*port*) 7 *butan* (see p. 428), or *wiðinnan burh* 7 *wiðutan* (see no. 61), a combination of the two, *wythynne porte* 7 *bouten*, the linguistic forms have been modernised, the definite article *þe* has been introduced in l. 3 (see p. 393), but all the evidence suggests that in no. 117 we have a later copy of an authentic writ of King Edward.

(115)

King Edward declares that he has granted to the monk Wulfstan the bishopric of Worcester with judicial and financial rights as fully and as completely as ever any of his predecessors had it.   1062

(Add. Charter 19802)

1   Eadward kyning gret Harold eorl 7 Ælfgar eorl 7 ealle þa ðegnas on Wigeraceastrescire 7 on Gleaweceastrescire 7 on Wæringwicscire

[1] F. E. Harmer, *English Historical Documents*, no. 13 = B. 579. On the historical importance of the charter, see VCH *Worcs.* iv. 376 ff., and James Tait, *The Medieval English Borough*, 19–23.
[2] DB i. 173 b, VCH *Worcs.* i. 294.   [3] VCH *Worcs.* i. 242, iv. 379.

freondlice. 7 ic cyðe eow ꝥ ic habbe geunnen Wulstane munuce
ꝥ .ɮ. rice into Wihgeraceastre mid sace 7 mid socne toll 7 team
binnan burhge 7 butan swa full 7 swa forð swa hit ænig his foregenga   5
fyrmæst on handa stode on eallan þingan for þan ic nylle geþafian
ꝥ him ænig mann æt ænigan þingan misbeode. oððe him of hande
drahge ænig þæra ðinga þe he mid rihte into his biseoprice ahge
to habbanne.

Endorsed in a hand of cent. early xiii : Edwardi regis.   8. biseop,
sic MS.

Translation

King Edward sends friendly greetings to Earl Harold and Earl
Ælfgar and all the thegns in Worcestershire and Gloucestershire
and Warwickshire. And I inform you that I have granted to the
monk Wulfstan the bishopric of Worcester with sake and with
soke, toll and team, within borough and without, as fully and as
completely in all things as ever any of his predecessors possessed
it. Therefore I will not permit anyone in any matter to do him
wrong, or to deprive him of any of the things that he ought lawfully
to have for his bishopric.

(116)

King Edward declares that he has granted to the monk Ælfstan
judicial and financial rights over his land and over his men.
Probably 1062

(Ch. R. 6 Edward II, m. 13)

+ Eadweard cyng gret Wulfstan ɮ . 7 Ælfgar eorl. 7 Ricard   1
minne huscarll 7 ealle mine þegnas . on Wigrecestrescire freondlice.
7 ic cyðe eow ꝥ ic habbe geunnen Alfstane munece ꝥ he beo his
sace weorðe 7 his socne . 7 tolles 7 teames ofer his land 7 ofer
his menn binnan porte 7 buton. 7 ic nelle geþafian ꝥ him ænig   5
man ænig unlage beode.

3. geunnen] geumen MS.   4. weorðe] weorde MS.

Translation

King Edward sends friendly greetings to Bishop Wulfstan and
Earl Ælfgar and Richard my housecarl and all my thegns in
Worcestershire. And I inform you that I have granted to the
monk Ælfstan that he be entitled to his sake and his soke, and
to toll and to team, over his land and over his men, within town
and without. And I will not permit anyone to do him any wrong.

E E

(117)

King Edward declares that he has granted to Bishop Wulfstan for St. Mary's minster (Worcester Cathedral) the third part of the 'seamtoll' and of the 'ceaptoll' as fully and as completely as he has (? had) the other thing. Probably 1062

(Liber Ruber f. 39 b)

1 Edward king gret Alfgar herl. 7 Richard. 7 alle myne þeynes on Wyrcestrechyre. wythynne porte 7 bouten frendlyche. 7 ich quyþe ou þat hy chulle þat Wolstan bissop be þe tridde deles wyrþe of semtolne 7 of chyptolne into Seynte Marie munstre so
5 ful 7 so forþh so he haued þat oþer þing.

In margin, in different hand : Carta super libertate tolonij. 5. þat oþer þing] yat oyer ying MS.

Translation

King Edward sends friendly greetings to Earl Ælfgar and Richard and all my thegns in Worcestershire, within town and without. And I inform you that my will is that Bishop Wulfstan be entitled to the third part of the 'seamtoll' and of the 'ceaptoll for St. Mary's minster as fully and as completely as he has (? had) the other thing.

YORK

Of the three York [1] writs, nos. 118–20, of King Edward, two announce grants of privileges to Archbishop Ealdred, while the third, no. 120, which seems to have escaped notice hitherto, relates to a grant by the king of the minster at Axminster in Devon to Ealdred, the 'deacon' of Archbishop Ealdred, for the canons of York Minster ; there can be little doubt that these three writs are authentic. The first, no. 118, announcing THE GRANT TO ARCHBISHOP EALDRED OF SAKE AND SOKE over his land and over all his men, is of a common type, belonging as it does to the writs employing the legal term *wyrðe* (see Introduction, pp. 63 f.),and its

[1] For the early history of the minster of St. Peter at York, see *Mon. Angl.* vi. 1172 ff. ; *Historians of the Church of York,* ed. J. Raine, R.S. 3 vols. ; VCH *Yorkshire,* iii. 375–83.

authenticity, as a (slightly modernised) copy of an authentic writ of King Edward, seems to be beyond question. In consequence of this and other grants to the archbishopric, in all the land of St. Peter of York (as in the lands of some other northern religious houses) neither the king nor the earl nor any one else had any 'custom' as Domesday Book bears witness.[1]

In no. 119, now extant only in Latin, King Edward declares that the archbishop is to have sake and soke over his men, and the right to exact toll from them on buying and selling, and to receive the profits arising from the process of 'vouching to warranty' in which they are involved (see Introduction, pp. 76 ff.), even when they reside on land over which the king himself exercises jurisdiction (*infra meam sacam et socam*), and that the archbishop is to enjoy these rights as fully and completely as he does on lands that are his own. We may compare the Ely writ, no. 47, in which King Edward announces that he has granted to Abbot Wulfric toll and team and other rights 'wherever his man may dwell, whatever he may do'. It is not difficult to imagine that circumstances may have arisen which caused Archbishop Ealdred to procure from the king a new writ safeguarding rights already granted him (if one is right in supposing that no. 118 was issued before no. 119). Domesday gives us information about York in King Edward's time and about the archbishop's rights there ; of the seven 'shires' (*scyre*), or wards, into which the city was divided, the archbishop had one, in which there were 189 inhabited dwellings.[2] In another survey the rights and legal dues of the archbishop are defined more closely.[3] He also held land in Yorkshire, Nottinghamshire, Gloucestershire, and other shires.[4] But because this writ is addressed to : *Tosti comiti et omnibus baronibus suis in Eboracensisira et in Nottinghamsira*, doubts were cast upon its authenticity by Farrer (i. 29). 'If this writ is genuine', says Farrer, 'it is difficult to see why the "barons" of Earl Tostig in Nottinghamshire should be addressed, for in that county his holding was very small.' But reference to no. 7, a Beverley writ similarly

---

[1] DB i. 298 b, VCH *Yorkshire*, ii. 194. The archbishop's liberties were confirmed by William I and his successors : see W. Farrer, *Early Yorkshire Charters*, i. nos. 12–18, 22. See also on the archbishop's jurisdiction, N. D. Hurnard, *Eng. Hist. Rev.* lxiv (1949), 315 f.

[2] DB i. 298, VCH *Yorks.* ii. 148–9, 191–5, and H. Lindkvist, 'A study on early medieval York', *Anglia*, Band 50 (1926), 349 f.

[3] F. Liebermann, *Archiv f. d. Stud. der neueren Sprachen*, cxi, 278 ; Mod. Eng. rendering of Liebermann's article, *Yorkshire Archæological Journal*, xviii. 412–16.

[4] DB i. 302–4, VCH *Yorks.* ii. 151, 209–16 ; and *Domesday Studies*, ed. P. E. Dove, ii. (1891), 407–9.

addressed, will show that in the York writ the translator was probably rendering : *Tostig eorl 7 ealle* mine *þegenas* ('Earl Tostig and all my thegns '), and that the inclusion of the thegns of Nottinghamshire in the address of the York writ was determined not by the fact that Earl Tostig held lands in Nottinghamshire, but that the archbishop did. The lands of the archbishop of York in Nottinghamshire described in Domesday ' still maintain their individuality as the Liberty of Southwell and Scrooby '.[1] The rendering *baro* for ' thegns ' (as we suppose) in the York writ is moreover an indication that the Latin version was made after the Norman Conquest (see p. 428). What is remarkable in this text is the phrase *infra meam sacam et socam.* *Infra* is frequently used in the Middle Ages for ' within ', but what we should expect here is *infra meam socam,* ' within the district over which I exercise jurisdiction '.[2] That the text in the vernacular which the translator was rendering read : *on mine socne* is made virtually certain by the appearance of *on mine socne* in the corresponding passage of a York writ of William I, fortunately written in English.[3] In this writ, dated 1066–69 by Davis, the king declares that Archbishop Ealdred shall be entitled to his bishopric and to his soke, to toll and team, within borough and without, *ofer his men 7 ofer his manna land on mine socne,* as fully and as completely in all things as ever he had them in King Edward's time. There is evidence to suggest that *socam* and *sacam et socam* were regarded as equivalent in the following passage from the Lincolnshire Domesday [4] : ' Archiepiscopus Thomas debet habere *socam* super terram Aschil quam habet episcopus Baiocensis in Vlingeham quia sicut testatur totus comitatus antecessor archiepiscopi habuit *sacam et socam* super eandem terram, et homines episcopi iniuste auferunt eidem archiepiscopo eandem *socam.*' In this passage *socam* and *sacam et socam* both mean ' jurisdiction ', but it may have been supposed that the two were interchangeable even when the meaning intended was not ' jurisdiction ' but ' district over which jurisdiction is exercised ' ; and this would seem to have been the case in the York writ, no. 118, under discussion here, translated possibly as late as about A.D. 1600. There is then nothing in this Latin version to cause one to doubt that it is a rendering of an authentic writ of King Edward.

[1] DB i. 283, VCH *Notts.* i. 255–7 ; on the charters by which these lands came to the archbishopric, VCH *Notts.* i. 217–20. Farrer adds as an afterthought : ' perhaps also *suis* should be *meis* '.

[2] For ' soke ' in this sense, see Introduction, p. 74.

[3] Davis, *Regesta,* no. 33, charter no. 2 *bis* ; Farrer, *op. cit.* no. 12.

[4] DB, i. 375, *The Lincolnshire Domesday,* ed. C. W. Foster and T. Longley (Lincoln Rec. Soc. 1924), 210.

THE MINSTER AT AXMINSTER

In no. 120 King Edward announces that he has granted the MINSTER AT AXMINSTER TO EALDRED, THE DEACON OF ARCHBISHOP EALDRED, as a pious benefaction for St. Peter's minster at York.[1] From the *Chronicle* s.a. 755 we learn that the minster at Axminster was in existence before the end of the eighth century.[2] What Edward's motive may have been in conferring this distant foundation on the priests at York is now unknown; but there was a route from Axminster to York by the highway known as the Fosse Way; this ran from Axminster through Bath and Leicester to Lincoln, where it met the highway known as Ermine Street, which ran from London to Lincoln and on into Yorkshire.[3] Or perhaps the route by sea and river would have been preferred. The clergy of York Minster for whom Edward's grant of the minster at Axminster was made, like those of the daughter churches at Ripon, Beverley and Southwell, lived a communal life and held their property in common. They had a refectory built for them by Archbishop Ealdred and probably a dormitory. Ealdred got rid of the *prisca rusticitas* of the church of York. He enjoined distinctive dress for the clergy at church and at synod, raised the standard of their services, and caused them to be more assiduous in almsgiving, in washing the feet of the poor, and in commemorating the faithful departed. The reforms which were instituted at this period are described by Folcard in the preface to the 'Vita S. Joannis' (of Beverley), which is dedicated to Archbishop Ealdred and was written at his suggestion.[4] In King Edward's time the canons at York were seven in number, but only three remained in 1070, on the arrival of Ealdred's successor, Archbishop Thomas. The rest had scattered in the troubles that followed the Conquest, at which time their records were also for the most part destroyed. The very extensive liberties of the canons of York Minster as men remembered them to have existed in the days of King Edward and of Archbishop Ealdred are however set out in a charter of confirmation of Henry I.[5] In their houses and lands, separated from those of the archbishop and devoted to their support, the

[1] The term *mynster* in early times (Lat. *monasterium*, OE *mynster*, was applied not only to monasteries of which the inmates were monks, but also to churches served by clergy living a communal life. See Stenton, *Anglo-Saxon England*, 148 ff.

[2] See further pp. 530 f. below.

[3] Robertson, *Laws*, 369. Merleswein, sheriff of Lincoln, held estates in Devon and Cornwall T.R.E.

[4] *Historians of the Church of York*, ed. Raine, R.S. i. 241.

[5] *Ibid.* iii. 34-6; A. F. Leach, *Visitations and Memorials of Southwell Minster* (Camden Society), 190-6.

canons had sake and soke, toll and team and infangenetheof, *intol* and *uttol*, and all the 'customs' of honour and liberty which the king himself had in his lands and which the archbishop himself held of God and the king.[1] The church at Axminster on the other hand may have been in decay at the time of the Confessor's grant. It was at all events believed at a later period that the performance of the offices of Axminster church (founded, or re-founded, so it was said, by King Æthelstan as a collegiate church for seven priests) had before the Conquest devolved upon a single incumbent, who was in enjoyment of the revenues.

The natural consequence of the Confessor's grant of the minster at Axminster to the canons of York Minster would have been a division of the revenues of the 'minster' or church at Axminster, unless of course, such a division had already been made under the (supposed) earlier priests mentioned in the Confessor's writ as having held the minster at Axminster before it was granted to Ealdred. The priest or priests who served the minster at Axminster would take a share, and Ealdred, the 'deacon', would take the rest for the York chapter. We learn from Domesday that the church at Axminster possessed in 1086 a half-hide of land, with land there for two ploughs ; its yearly value was 20 shillings (see p. 530). This half-hide of land is frequently identified with Prestaller (Priestaller) which, with the rectorial tithes of Axminster, was for centuries possessed by the prebendaries of Warthill and Grindall in York Minster.[2] The early records of Axminster church have not survived, but something is known of its history or supposed history from other sources. It is asserted for instance that in the twelfth century one of the priests who were then at Axminster was Queen Maud's confessor, and that on his appointment to a canonry at York, he stipulated with his successor to be allowed a pension of 8 marks a year for life. This amount is said to have been increased to 24 marks, and payment is said to have been claimed and received by York Minster until the early thirteenth century, when it was refused by Matthew de Apulia, vicar of

---

[1] For a list of their properties in 1086, see VCH *Yorkshire*, iii. 11. On *intol* and *uttol*, see p. 477.

[2] For a description of Prestaller and its history up to the third quarter of the nineteenth century, see James Davidson, *History of Axminster Church* (Exeter, 1835), 23 ff., G. P. R. Pulman, *The Book of the Axe* (4th ed. London, 1875), 671 ff. Prestaller was described by James B. Davidson, *The Athenæum*, 3 October 1885, 435, as ' an ancient manor, not strictly glebe, annexed to the church of Axminster : that is to say, the patron and rector of Axminster for the time being is lord of the manor, or reputed manor, and owner of Prestaller '. Davidson rightly adds that the identification of Prestaller with the half-hide of the church of Axminster in Domesday, is a matter of presumption only.

Axminster.[1] Some of the available information about Axminster comes from the records of Newenham Abbey, a Cistercian house founded near Axminster c. 1246, on which its founder conferred the manor of Axminster and everything belonging to it.[2] The claim of Newenham Abbey to the advowson of Axminster church led in the reigns of Edward I and III to protracted litigation, since this advowson was also claimed not only by the prebendaries of Warthill and Grindall in York Minster, but also by the Crown. As a result of the litigation the two York prebendaries were left in possession of Axminster church and its advowson. There is no evidence that the prebendaries knew of the Axminster writ of King Edward the Confessor, but in the course of the litigation they pleaded that ' King William the Conqueror by his charter granted to the church of St. Peter, York, to have and to hold to Robert and to Richard, then prebendaries of the same prebends [3] which the defendants now hold *pro indiviso*, to them and their successors for ever the church of Axminster, with sake and soke annexed to their prebends, by force of which charter they have held the church to their own use ', and they produced a confirmation of this charter by Edward III.[4] At a somewhat earlier date a writ of William Rufus had been entered on the Charter Roll. In this text the king is made to announce that he gives to St. Peter's, York, and to the two prebendaries of Warthill and Grindall in the said church, the church of Axminster with sake and soke and all rights and appurtenances ; and he declares that they are to have and hold the said church ' sicut aliquis alius melius et liberius, honorabilius et quietius primo ipsam tenuit tempore regis Edwardi et patris sui vel ante '.[5] This writ is marked spurious by Davis. But everything encourages the belief that the Axminster writ of King Edward (no. 120) is authentic.

---

[1] Davidson, *Axminster Church*, 10, Oliver, *Monasticon Dioecesis Exoniensis* (Exeter and London, 1846), 317–21. Oliver remarks : ' The pension of 24 marks was still paid, as I find in Bishop Bronescombe's register, by the vicar in October, 1259, as also in Bishop Stapeldon's register, in November,1320 '.

[2] For Newenham Abbey, see James Davidson, *History of Newenham Abbey* (London, 1843) ; Oliver *op. cit.* 357–71 ; *Mon. Angl.* v. 690.

[3] Archbishop Thomas, the successor of Ealdred at York, is credited with the institution of the prebendal system at York Minster ; see VCH *Yorkshire*, iii. 10.

[4] For the Conqueror's charter, see Oliver *op. cit.* 320, Davidson, *Axminster Church*, 9. See also *Cal. of Patent Rolls*, 7 Edward III, pt. i, m. 5 ; 8 Edward III, pt. ii, m. 4 ; 9 Edward III, pt. ii, m. 29 ; 13 Edward III, pt. i, m. 3 and 2.

[5] *Cal. of Charter Rolls*, 4 Edward III, m. 15 : Davis, *Regesta*, no. 487, and Charter no. lxxxiv. The text of the writ is copied in an *inspeximus* and confirmation of the same for the two prebendaries of the church of York.

There is nothing in its content, its phraseology, or its (modernised)
linguistic forms, to excite suspicion. We can confidently accept
it as a reasonably accurate copy of a writ of the Confessor.

(118)

King Edward declares that he has granted to Archbishop Ealdred
judicial and financial rights over his lands and over all his men.
Christmas 1060–66

(Reg. Magn. Alb. pt. i, f. 61 b)

1 Ead[ward] cynge gret mine b'es 7 mine eorlas an[d] ealle myne
þegenas on þam sciran þaer Ealdred aerceb' haefð land inne
freondlice 7 ic cyðe eow ꝥ ic wylle ꝥ he beo his saca [wurðe] 7
his socna ofer his land 7 ofer eallum his mannum tolles and teames
5 binnan porte 7 butan.

*Letters in brackets from B. Several representations of earlier 3 arising out of
(earlier) confusion with forms of s.* 1. B *wrongly expands* b'es (biscopes)
to beres; *cf. no. 52.* 2. haefð] haefd MS. 3. cyðe] cyde MS.
3. eow MS; nie or me B; inc *wrongly*) Farrer. 3. ꝥ] þ MS. (bis).
4. B *omits* eallum his.

Translation

King Edward sends friendly greetings to my bishops and my
earls and all my thegns in the shires in which Archbishop Ealdred
has land. And I inform you that my will is that he be entitled
to his sake and his soke, over his lands and over all his men, to
toll and to team, within town and without.

(119)

King Edward declares that he has granted to Archbishop Ealdred
judicial and financial rights over his men within the king's own soke
as fully and as completely as the archbishop has them in his own
lands. Christmas 1060–65

(Harley MS. 560, f. 23)

1 Edwardus rex Tosti comiti et omnibus baronibus suis in Eboracensisira et in Nottinghamsira salutem. Sciatis quod ego concessi
Aldredo archiepiscopo ut ipse habeat sacam et socam et toll et
team super suos homines infra meam sacam et socam ita plenarie
5 et principaliter sicut ipse habet in sua propria loca, et nolo ut
aliquis ei auferat quod ego ei concessi.

Heading : Aliud previlegium dedit idem Rex Edwardus archiepiscopo
Aldredo quod tale est. 5. nolo] volo MS.

(120)

King Edward announces that he has granted to Ealdred, the 'deacon' of Archbishop Ealdred, the minster at Axminster as a pious benefaction for St. Peter's minster at York (York Minster). Christmas 1060–66

(Reg. Magn. Alb. pt. i, f. 61 b)

Eadward cynge gret Leofric biscop 7 Harold eorl 7 Wada 7 alle   1
mine þegenas on Defenascire freondlice 7 ic cyðe eow þ ic habbe
geunnan Ealdrede þaes arcebiscopes dyacne Ealdredes þ mynster
at Axaminster 7 alc þaere þinge þaes þe þaer mid rithe to gebyrað
mid saca and mid socna swa full 7 swa forð swa hit aenig preost 5
toforan him firmest haefide into Peteres mynster on Euerwic to
almesse.

On forms of ꝣ here see note on no. 118.   2. cyðe] -de MS.   2. þ]
þ MS. (bis).   4. gebyrað] -ad MS.   5. saca *altered from* sace.
5. forð] -d MS.

Translation

King Edward sends friendly greetings to Bishop Leofric and Earl Harold and Wada and all my thegns in Devonshire. And I inform you that I have granted to Ealdred, the deacon of Archbishop Ealdred, the minster at Axminster, and all the things lawfully pertaining thereto, with sake and with soke, as fully and as completely as ever any priest before him had it, as a pious benefaction for St. Peter's minster at York.

GOSPATRIC'S WRIT

Of the history of the north-west of England in the eleventh century little is known, and the writ of Gospatric, lord of Allerdale and Dalston in Cumberland, thus becomes a historical source of considerable importance. The document is also of linguistic interest as exhibiting in its vocabulary something of that intermingling of peoples, Celtic, English, and Scandinavian, which is also reflected in the personal names and place-names appearing in the text. The personal name elements in particular, Celtic (Irish-Gaelic, Welsh), Scandinavian (prevailingly Norwegian, Danish), English (and Old German), are an indication of the history of this originally British region, colonised in part by English settlers, but also occupied in many places by Irish, Scandinavian, and partly Celticised Scandinavian, settlers from Ireland, the Hebrides, and the

Isle of Man.[1] The early history of the north-west of England has been traced, so far as the evidence allows, by Sir Frank Stenton.[2] Cumberland and Westmorland, which had formed part of the British kingdom known in later times as the kingdom of Cumbria or Strathclyde, passed into English hands about the beginning of the seventh century, and remained in English occupation for about three hundred years. But the appearance in Gospatric's writ of the clause ' the lands which were Cumbrian ', shows that these lands had been recovered by the kings of Strathclyde, in all probability in the early tenth century, and they were held by them for a considerable part of the next hundred and fifty years. Addressing his retainers (*wassenas*) and everyone dwelling in these lands (which according to Stenton ' may be roughly defined by the Derwent, the Eamont, the lakeland mountains, and the marshes at the head of the Solway ') Gospatric, a descendant of the ancient Bernician line of earls, and perhaps when the letter was written their heir (though not himself an earl)—who was to be murdered at Christmas 1064 at the court of the Confessor—speaking as of right, announces the conferment of various privileges. He declares that Thorfynn mac Thore shall be exempt from the payment of the dues and services accruing to himself from Allerdale, and that the men dwelling with Thorfynn at Cardew and Cumdivock shall be as fully exempt from the same dues as were Melmor and Thore (perhaps Thorfynn's father, but the name was a common one) and Sigulf in the days of Eadred (perhaps a predecessor of Gospatric in Allerdale. In a passage which is corrupt Gospatric associates himself with the well-known Earl Siward (' who fought against the Scots and put to flight the king Macbeth ', *Chron.* 1054 D), and appears to forbid that the peace (*grith*) which he and Siward have granted shall be broken ; one thinks of the crime of *grithbryce* mentioned from time to time in writs of the Confessor (see Introduction, p. 80). Unfortunately it cannot be discovered from the text, in its garbled state, whether Gospatric regards Earl Siward as his superior, or whether Siward is dead, and Gospatric is himself responsible for the maintenance of law and order in this region.[3] Further, on his own authority Gospatric declares that persons unnamed, seemingly those dwelling at Cardew and Cumdivock, shall be exempt from the payment of geld (*geyldfreo*, cf. pp. 513 f.), the national land tax, as he himself is free, and some other persons

---

[1] A. Bugge, *Trans. R. Hist. Soc.* 4th ser. iv (1921), 196 ff. ; Ekwall, Introd. xxi, *Dict. of English Place-Names.*

[2] *Royal Commission on Historical Monuments, Westmorland* (1936), pp. xlviii–liii.

[3] On the position of Gospatric, see H. W. C. Davis, *Eng. Hist. Rev.* xx (1905), 61–5.

named, and all his kinsmen and retainers (*wassenas*). This part
of Cumberland is unfortunately not described in Domesday Book.
We are driven to suppose that in a border district which had only
recently been detached from the kingdom of Strathclyde and
annexed to Northumbria, conditions as to the payment of geld,
from which only the king elsewhere could grant exemption (see
p. 376), may have been different from those existing in other parts
of the kingdom.[1] Again speaking in his own right, and with no
mention of any overlord, Gospatric grants to Thorfynn sake and
soke, toll and team, in the terms employed by English kings in
conferring these privileges upon their subjects, the legal processes
of the English kingdom having apparently been adopted ; though
Scandinavian custom was apparently followed when lands were
granted to Thorfynn's father Thore ' with *bode* and witnessman '.
There seems no reason to doubt that the document as it has come
down to us is derived from an authentic writ of Gospatric.

The text is preserved only in an imperfect transcript of the
thirteenth century, made seemingly by a man who had before him
a copy in Anglo-Saxon script, but was not accustomed to Anglo-
Saxon script or language.   In such circumstances the scribe would
keep the sense so far as he could understand it, or he might imitate
what he did not understand or understood only imperfectly ; but
the latest transcriber or one or more predecessors must also have
attempted to rewrite passages which were illegible, or to them
unintelligible, or they may have tried to improve upon what they
were copying.   Among the idiosyncrasies of the copyists of this
writ are the use of the termination *-un*, not only in the dative
plural (where it might be expected, among other forms) but in the
nominative and accusative (where it is highly irregular) ; the form
bydann, apparently for pres. part.   Some errors are merely mistakes in spelling : e.g. *neann* (*nan*), and the replacement of *w* by
y in *hyylkun* (*hwylk-*) and *eoy*, because the Anglo-Saxon letter
' wyn ' (= *w*) was unfamiliar. Disregarding a doubtful word
here and there, the following seem to represent authentic material :
(i) the protocol ; (ii) the passage following the notification (*ic
cyðe eow*) as far as *Caldebek* ; (iii) the passage *ic wille þ þeo mann
bydann* . . . *Eadread dagan* in its general outlines even if some
of the forms are strange ; (iv) *ne beo neann man swa ðeorif*, apart
from the spelling ; there is a parallel for this in no. 62 : *nan
man ne wurðe swa deorf* ; (v) the names in the *geyldfreo* passage

---

[1] On the origin of palatinate rights in the north, as a survival of the
independence of Northumbria, see W. Page, ' The Northumbrian Palatinates
and Regalities ' (*Archaeologia*, li (1888), 143–55 ; also R. Reid, *The King's
Council in the North* (1921), 12–39).

can hardly have been invented even if the exemption itself is not written in normal Anglo-Saxon; it may have been recast by a copyist; (vi) the final sentence from: *7 ic wille þ Thorfynn* to the end, even though the concluding phrases are obscure. The most difficult passage in the writ (discussed in notes below) is from: *ic heobbe gegyfen* to *welkynn ðeoronðer*. It undoubtedly contains some authentic matter, and its general tenor is intelligible, but the details seem to be irretrievably lost.

It is entirely probable that the writ of Gospatric, which here exhibits the form of protocol (address and salutation), and notification, frequently employed in letters and notably in royal writs, was originally written at any rate in part in the West Saxon literary dialect, as familiar then at York as it was at Westminster.[1] Forms characteristic of this West Saxon literary dialect are: *ealle*, *weald* (but there is also the non-West Saxon, or late, *ællun*, as well as *Calde*bek, *Wall*ðeof). The scribe also employed the West Saxon syncopated form *gret* (*greot*), and the West Saxon *gegyfen*. Other instances of Old English forms that have been preserved in this text are *freond-*, *cyðe*, *ænyg*, together with the ending (weor)*on*, and forms such as *ic*, *swa*. At what stage in the textual history of this writ Northumbrian forms entered in, cannot now be determined; we cannot exclude the possibility that some were to be found in the text when it was first issued. The most important of these are *leof* (WS *leaf*), *freals* (WS *freols*), *mið* (WS *mid*); the *i* in *ðeorif* (*deorf*) ought perhaps to be added.[2] Further, at some stage or stages in the history of the text a number of words would seem to have been respelt (in so far as they belonged to the original draft of the writ) in accordance with orthographical principles which did not come into operation in this country till after the Norman Conquest. These are exemplified by the frequent *eo* for OE *e* and for *e* which had developed in Middle English: e.g. *greot*, *þeo*, *weoron*, *he(o)bbe*; the spelling *ey* in *freyð* (*fyrhð*) and *geyld*; the *o*, *oo* for *u* in *onðer*, *woonnan*, *Sygoolf*. Again, it is virtually certain that the vocabulary, in the earliest form of the writ, included Celtic and Scandinavian words as well as English. Celtic words

---

[1] On the use of West Saxon as an official and literary dialect all over England in the early eleventh century, see K. Sisam, *Review of English Studies*, vii (1931), 12. For some Durham material, see H. H. E. Craster, ' Some Anglo-Saxon Records of the See of Durham ', *Archaeologia Aeliana*, 4th ser. i (1925), 189–98.

[2] Ragg in 1917 pointed out that the uninflected gen. sing. *Eadread, Moryn*, represent northern usage. Compare the inscription on the sundial of Pickering church, of A.D. 1055–65 (VCH *North Riding of Yorkshire*, facing p. 520): *in Eadward dagum cyng, in Tosti dagum eorl*. I am indebted for this reference to Professor Bruce Dickins.

are : *wassenas, mac,* and the intermingling of races in these regions is well illustrated by the Celtic *mac* joining the Scandinavian *Thorfynn* and *Thore* in the name of *Thorfynn mac Thore.* Scandinavian words are *drenge,* found in Old English as early as *The Battle of Maldon* (of the late tenth, or early eleventh, century) ; *heyninga* ; *mynna,* in form ON *minni,* in meaning, OE *myne*—if it is not OE *unna,* cf. no. 7 ; the Anglicised *wytnesmann,* and possibly *bode* ; *gyrth* for OE *grið,* a commonly-used loan-word from ON ; the present participle in *-and (-ann).* Foreign place-name elements have not been taken into consideration here. It is hard to say what is the origin of the strange construction : *þeo welkynn ðeoronðer* (see p. 534). There is no reason for accepting the conjecture of H. W. C. Davis [1] that the writ as it has come down to us was translated from Latin. The mixture of linguistic forms in this document is most easily accounted for by the supposition that it is a text composed in the vernacular in the Old English period which has undergone alteration at the hand of more than one transcriber.

(121)

Gospatric declares that Thorfynn mac Thore shall be free in respect of all things that are Gospatric's in Allerdale, and that the men dwelling with Thorfynn at Cardew and Cumdivock shall be free. He forbids that the peace granted to any man be broken. He declares that whosoever is dwelling there shall be exempt from geld as he and others are. He declares that Thorfynn is to have judicial and financial rights over certain lands in Cardew and Cumdivock. Probably 1041–64, possibly 1041–55

(MS. at Lowther Castle)

Gospatrik greot ealle mine wassenas 7 hyylkun mann freo 7 ðrenge 1
þeo woonnan on eallun þam landann þeo weoron Cōmbres 7 eallun
mine kynling freondlycc. 7 ic cyðe eoy þ̄ myne mynna is 7 full
leof þ̄ Thorfynn mac Thore beo swa freo on eallan ðynges þeo
beo myne on Alnerdall swa ænyg mann beo, oðer ic oðer ænyg 5
myne wassenas, on weald, on freyð, on heyninga, 7 æt ællun ðyngan
þeo bȳ eorðe bœnand 7 ðeoronðer, to Shauk, to Wafyr, to poll
Waðœn, to bek Troyte 7 þeo weald æt Caldebek. 7 ic wille þ̄ þeo
mann bydann mið Thorfynn æt Carðeú 7 Combeðeyfoch beo swa
freals myð hem swa Melmor 7 Thore 7 Sygoolf weoron on Eadread 10
dagan. 7 ne beo neann mann swa ðeorif þehat mið þ̄ ic heobbe
gegyfene to hem neghar brech seo gyrth ðyylc Eorl Syward 7 ic

[1] *Eng. Hist. Rev.* xx (1905), 61–5.

hebbe getyðet hem se frelycc swa ænyg mann leofand þeo welkynn ðeoronðer. 7 loc hyylkun bȳ þar byðann geyldfreo beo swa ic bȳ 15 7 swa Willann, Wallðeof 7 Wygande 7 Wyberth 7 Gamell 7 Kunyth 7 eallun mine kynling 7 wassenas. 7 ic wille þ̵ Thorfynn heobbe soc 7 sac, toll 7 theam, ofer eallun þam landan on Carðeu 7 on Combedeyfoch þ̵ weoron gyfene Thore on Moryn dagan freols myð bode 7 wytnesmann on þy ylk stow.

1. hyylkun MS., hwylkun L[iebermann].   1. ðrenge MS., drenge L.
2. *In* Cōmbres *a line in* MS. *over nearly the whole of* o *and the first two down-strokes of* m.   3. eoy MS., eow L.   3. mynna L] mynua MS.
But cf. no. 7, *l.* 2, unna, *translated here.*   11. ðeorif, *OE* deorf.
13. se frelycc] cefrelycc MS.   14. MS. enðer.   *For* onðer, *see* NED.
14. hyylkun MS., hwylkun L.   14. byðann *for* bydann.   15.
Willann *plain in* MS.; Willelmi, *emended to* Willelm, L.   19. on
þyylk MS., on þy ylke L.

Translation

Gospatric sends friendly greetings to all my *wassenas* and to every man, free man and dreng, dwelling in all the lands that were Cumbrian, and to all my kindred. And I inform you that I give my consent and full permission that Thorfynn mac Thore be as free in all things that are mine in Allerdale as any man may be, either I myself or any of my *wassenas*, in plain, in woodland, in enclosures, and in respect of all things that are above the earth and under it, as far as Chalk Beck as the Waver as the Wampool as Wiza Beck and the plain at Caldbeck. And it is my will that the men dwelling with Thorfynn at Cardew and Cumdivock shall be as free, along with him, as Melmor and Thore and Sigulf were in the days of Eadred. And let no man be so bold that— with what I have given to him (?)—anywhere break the peace which (?) Earl Siward and I have granted him as freely as to any man living under the sky. And whosoever is dwelling there is to be exempt from geld as I am, and as (are) Willann, Waltheof, and Wigand and Wiberht and Gamell and Kunyth and all my kindred and *wassenas*. And it is my will that Thorfynn shall have sake and soke, toll and team, over all the lands in Cardew and Cumdivock that were given to Thore in the days of Moryn, free from the obligation of providing messengers and witnesses, in the same place.

PART III
NOTES AND APPENDICES
NOTES
(1)

AUTHORITIES :—(R) P.R.O. Charter Roll 8 Edward II, m. 3, no. 5 (*Calendar of Charter Rolls*, iii. 274), printed here. Printed : Dugdale and Dodsworth, *Monasticon Anglicanum*, i (1655), 279 ; 1846 ed. iii. 56, no. iv ; K. 871 ; Thorpe p. 414 (from *Mon. Angl.*) ; Mod. Eng. rendering, Kemble, *Saxons in England*, ii. 67.

(M) Confirmation Roll 6–10 Henry VII, no. 1.

On the authenticity of this writ see p. 118.

DATE. Between Harold's appointment as earl of Wessex in 1053, and the death of Bishop Ælfwold of Sherborne in 1058.

l. 2. *Ic ciþe eow þæt Urk . . . habbe etc.* Cf. no. 5 : ' ic cyðe eow þæt Ordric abbud 7 eal þæt hired . . . habban 7 wealdan ' etc. One is naturally disposed to render this : ' I inform you that Urk is to have ' etc. The jussive use of the subjunctive is common in the Laws ; cf. II Cnut 73, ' Be wydewan ; þæt heo *sitte* xii monðas ceorl[l]æs ; and *sitte* ælc wuduwe werleas twelf monað 7 *ceose* heo syðð̄an þæt heo sylf wille ', (' Concerning widows : that she *is to remain* twelve months without a husband ; and every widow *is to remain* twelve months without a husband, and she *is* afterwards *to choose* what she herself wishes '). But the verb following *cyðan, gecyðan*, sometimes appears in the subjunctive even when a fact is stated ; see J. E. Wülfing, *Die Syntax in den Werken Alfreds des Grossen* (Bonn, 1894), ii. 91. We may compare : ' Scs Albanus cyþde 7 openade þæt he cristen *wære* ', (' St. Alban made known and declared that he *was* a Christian '), (*The Old English Version of Bede's Ecclesiastical History*, ed. Miller, E.T.T.S. i. 36, l. 9). If this is the construction in nos. 1 and 5, where there is in each case a passage referring to the king's ' command ', or ' grant and gift ', the translation would be : ' I inform you that Urk *has* his strand ', and ' I inform you that Abbot Ordric and all the community *have and possess* ' etc. For other writs where the king's consent or permission are referred to, see Introduction, p. 65.

l. 3. *Urk min huskarl.* Among the known members of the standing bodyguard of housecarls maintained by Cnut and his successors, the greater number bore, like Urk, a Scandinavian name. Royal housecarls are named from time to time in charters, occasionally as the recipients of grants of land from the king, and housecarls not only of King Edward but also of great lords are mentioned in Domesday as holders of land before the Conquest. See L. M. Larson, *The King's Household in England* (Madison, Wisconsin, 1904), 152–66 ; Hoops, *Reallexikon*, ii. 576, s.v. *huskarl* (Larson) ; F. M. Stenton, *The First Century of English Feudalism* (Oxford, 1932), 119–21 ; and for references in Domesday to housecarls holding land, G. Tengvik, *Old English Bynames* (Nomina Germanica no. 4, Uppsala, 1938), 255–6.

l. 3. *His strand.* The clause *on strande* often appears in writs when sources of profit are being enumerated ; e.g. no. 38, *on strande 7 on streame*, nos. 42, 61, 75, etc. *be lande 7 be strande* (and variations of this). See further Liebermann, ii. 639, s.v. ' Schiffbruch ', ii. 673, ' Strand ', iii. 152 (note 4, on II Æthelred 2, where the reference to Davis, *Regesta*, no. 108, should be corrected to no. 109).

l. 3. *Forn egen hys . . . land. Forn egen* no doubt represents OE *foran ongean* ' over against ', for instances of which see BT Suppt. s.v. *foran.*

l. 4. *Wel 7 freolslice.* This is the only occurrence in these writs of the adverb *freolslice*, for which see BT Suppt.; but there is no reason to doubt this form, which, though it is carelessly copied in the text of no. 1 printed here, is written quite plainly in another copy (for which see textual footnotes). For the substantive *freols*, see nos. 2, 8, 26 ; for the adjective *freols*, see nos. 6, 7, 121.

l. 5. *Eall þæt to hys strande gedryuen hys.* Little is known concerning the ownership of the sea and ' wreck ' during the Anglo-Saxon period. From this writ, the only document of those usually cited the authenticity of which is reasonably certain, we may infer that rights over the shore and over what was cast ashore by the sea were among the royal rights that the king was willing to grant to a subject. The Ramsey writ (no. 61) in which the king announces his grant to Ramsey Abbey of shipwreck (*scipbryce*) and what is cast up by the sea (*þa sæupwarp*) at Brancaster and Ringstead, with all the rights that he himself had by the sea coast anywhere in England, may contain pre-Conquest material, although it is unlikely to have taken shape in its present form before the Norman Conquest ; as may also a spurious Ramsey charter (K. 809) which purports to convey similar rights, and a spurious charter of St. Benet, Holme (K. 785), which purports to grant to that monastery *wrek in mari et in litore maris et in portibus maris.* A different ruling seems to have prevailed in the case of such miscellaneous valuables as were found on the Sandwich side of the wide channel running between the sea on the north coast of Kent and the sea on the east coast, and brought to Sandwich ; half of these, whether clothes, nets, weapons, iron, gold, or silver, were left to the finders, but the monks of Christ Church, Canterbury, claimed that King Cnut had granted them the right to the other half in a charter (*Crawford Charters*, no. 12, Robertson, *Anglo-Saxon Charters*, no. 82) the authenticity of which is not entirely above suspicion. Kemble argued (*Saxons in England*, ii. 65) that ' the recognized right of the king (to shipwreck) throughout the Norman times, and the total absence of any opposition to its exercise, are *prima facie* evidence of its having resided in the crown before the Conquest '.

The same rights as were granted to Urk by King Edward were granted by William I to the abbey of Abbotsbury into whose possession the lands of Urk and wife had come. In one writ King William mentions among the rights which he confirms to the abbey, everything pertaining to the abbey which is cast up by the sea on the shore. In another he declares that the abbot of Abbotsbury is to hold his land and everything belonging to his church in *wrec* and in all ' customs ' as he held them in King Edward's time, and that he is to have the ship broken on his land if he can justly prove that it belongs of right to his church (*Cal. of Charter Rolls*, ii. 131 (i) and (ii) ; the first also in Davis, *Regesta*, no. 109). It is recorded in the VCH *Dorset*, ii. 49, that at an inquisition made in 1268 it was stated that wreck of the sea had always belonged to the monks of Abbotsbury and that they had always enjoyed it ; that in 1315 Edward II confirmed afresh their right to wreck of the sea in connection with a *crassus piscis* (' fat fish ', whether sturgeon, porpoise, or whale) which had been cast ashore ; and that in 1388 the owner of a cargo complained that his merchandise had been seized by the abbot and others as though it had been a wreck, although thirteen of the crew had escaped (cf. Liebermann ii. 640, s.v. ' Schiffbruch ', 4, c : ' si unus de naufragio evaserit, navem et quod salvari poterit obtinebit ').

(2)

AUTHORITIES :—(R) as for no. 1, printed here. Printed : Dodsworth and Dugdale, *Mon. Angl.* i (1655), 279 ; 1846 ed. iii. 56, no. v ; Thorpe p. 426 (from *Mon. Angl.*), and p. 576, a slightly different text.

(M) as for no. 1.

On the authenticity of this writ see p. 118.

DATE. Between 1058, the date of the death of Bishop Ælfwold of Sherborne—Bishop Herman's predecessor, and 5 January 1066, the date of King Edward's death.

l. 2. *Ic cyðe eow þæt hit is min fulla unna þæt Tole . . . þæt heo becweðe* etc. For a parallel construction, see no. 7 : ' *ic cyðe eow þæt hit is min unna 7 min fulle leafe þæt Ealdred . . . þæt he dihte* ' etc. See also Introduction, p. 65.

l. 3. *Tole min mann.* Women tenants are occasionally described as *homo* in Domesday, as Tole is here described as *mann.* Instances are Ælueua (Ælfgifu) *homo* Aschil (DB i. 212) ; Godid (Godgyth) *homo* Asgari (DB i. 137, 137 b, 139 b, 140) ; Wluuen (Wulfwynn) *homo* regis E. (DB i. 150 b).

l. 3. *þæt heo becweðe hire land . . . æt Abbodesbyrig.* It is stated in the *Monasticon Anglicanum*, iii. 54, no. i, that the estates given by Tole and her husband to the abbey of Abbotsbury included Tolpuddle (a place formerly called *Pidele* which contains her name as its first element ; see A. Fägersten, *Place-Names of Dorset* (Uppsala Universitets Årsskrift, 1933) which she had purchased, Abbotsbury, Portisham, Hilton and *Anstie*. In Domesday the abbey appears (DB i. 78) as the holder of manors at these places, as well as at Wootton Abbas (which had been granted to Urk by the Confessor in a charter of 1044, K. 772), Shilvinghampton, Bourton, and (Stoke) Atram ; only *Anstie* is not specifically mentioned there.

l. 11. *Geheald 7 mund,* ' protector and guardian '. Cf. no. 7, ' geheald 7 mund '. For other instances of *mund* ' guardian, protector ', see Robertson, *Anglo-Saxon Charters*, no. 95, in which the Confessor declares that he is the *mund 7 upheald,* ' guardian and upholder ', of a monastery ; *ibid.* no. 113 ; *wit synd þisra landa hald 7 mund,* ' we (Earl Leofric and his wife) are protectors and guardians of these estates ' ; also D. Whitelock, *Anglo-Saxon Wills*, nos. 17, 29. For *mund* in the sense of ' protection, security, guardianship ', see notes on no. 26 ; and for *mundbryce*, ' violation of *mund* ', see Introduction, p. 80.

(3)

AUTHORITIES :—(C) Cott. Claud. C. ix, f. 128 b, cent. xiii, printed here.

(B) Cott. Claud. B. vi, f. 112, about 50 years later than C. Printed : *Chronicon Monasterii de Abingdon*, ed. J. Stevenson, R.S. i. 458 ; K. 948 ; Thorpe p. 378 ; H. Pierquin, *Chartes Anglo-Saxonnes* (Paris, 1912), p. 844, no. 82, from K.

On the authenticity of this writ see pp. 122 f.

DATE. The date A.D. 1052, entered by the editor in the margin of the *Chron. Abingdon*, i. 457, for the dispute concerning Leckhampstead, is only approximate. Brihtwine must have made his first agreement with Abbot Siward between Siward's appointment as abbot in 1030 and his promotion to the bishopric as coadjutor to Archbishop Eadsige in 1044. Siward's letter, printed here, which names Bishop Herman in the address, must have been written between the consecration of Herman as bishop of Ramsbury in 1045, and Siward's death on 23 October 1048. The settlement of the dispute in the time of Abbot Ordric (1052–66) was subsequent to the appointment of Harold as earl of Wessex in 1053. The erroneous date A.D. 1058 suggested for Siward's letter by the editor of the *Chron. Abingdon*, ii. 525, with a reference to the ' Saxon Chronicle under 1058 ', may be explained by confusion of this Siward with another Siward, who, after having been abbot of Chertsey (see *Chron.* D, E, 1058, Plummer ii. 248), was appointed to the see of Rochester in 1058. On these two Siwards and the confusion between them, see the articles under their names in DNB.

l. 3. *Terram de Lechamstede*. Leckhampstead, Berks. For the earlier history of this Abingdon estate, which the abbey continued to hold after the Conquest, see p. 122 above. In 1086 Reinbold, son-in-law of Abbot Rainald, held the 10 hides at Leckhampstead which Brihtwine (*Bricstuin*) had held of the abbot in King Edward's reign (DB i. 58 b, VCH *Berkshire*, i. 338). For the later history of Leckhampstead, see VCH *Berkshire*, iv. 61–2.

(4)

AUTHORITIES :—(C) as for no 3, f. 130, English and Latin, printed here.

(B) as for no. 3, f. 114, English and Latin. Printed : *Mon. Angl.* i. 517, no. xii (omitting Lat. version in manuscript) ; *Chron. Abingdon*, i. 464 ; K. 888 ; Lat. version only, Pierquin, p. 820, no. 52, from K.

(J) Bodleian Library MS. James 8, p. 80, a copy made c. 1632, Eng. and Lat., by Richard James, on whom, and on whose transcripts in the James MSS. see *Summary Catalogue of Western MSS. in the Bodleian Library*, 2, 2 (1937), 750 ff. and the references there ; see also pp. 235–7.

On the authenticity of this writ see pp. 123 ff., and on the legal terms employed see Introduction, pp. 73–81.

DATE. This writ, though probably not authentic as it stands, may have been based on an authentic writ, the date of issue of which would fall between 1052, the date of the appointment of Abbot Ordric, and 5 January 1066, the date of King Edward's death.

l. 2. *þeignas* ; Lat. version, *barones*. On *baro* as a rendering for OE *þegn*, ' thegn ', especially for the ' king's thegn ', see R. R. Reid, ' Barony and Thanage ', *Eng. Hist. Rev.* xxxv (1920), 161–99, especially 169–73. See also Liebermann, *Gesetze*, ii. 19, s.v. *baro*, and the references there ; also Stenton, *English Feudalism*, 83–113. For other instances in writs, see nos. 5, 12, 18 etc.

l. 4. *Binnan burgon 7 butan burgon*. The abbot is granted judicial and financial rights over his men ' within borough and without ', that is, wherever they may be. On the Anglo-Saxon *burh*, ' borough ', see F. M. Stenton's review in *History*, N.S. xviii (1933–34), 256–9, of Carl Stephenson, *Borough and Town* (The Medieval Academy of America, 1933) ; and James Tait, *The Medieval English Borough* (Manchester, 1936).

This formula more often appears as *binnan burh 7 butan* (*burh*), or with the dative, *binnan byrig 7 butan* (*byrig*) ; cf. nos. 28, 30, 38 etc. Is *burgan* here, as is suggested in BT Suppt. s.v. *burge* (with a query), the oblique case of a wk. nn. *burge* ? Or is it not, as Plummer suggested (*Two Saxon Chronicles*, i. 316), for *burgum*, i.e. dat. pl. ? The latter explanation is supported by plur. forms in some Latin versions ; e.g. *infra urbes 7 extra*, no. 34. In such cases the rendering should be : ' within boroughs and without '. For other instances, see Robertson, *Anglo-Saxon Charters*, p. 188 ; *Chron.* E 1116 ; Warner and Ellis, *Facs. of Royal and other Charters in the Brit. Mus.* (1903), i. 6 (a Christ Church writ of Henry I), and nos. 33, 34 below (both of these in later hands) ; also in no. 47.

On the formula : *binnan porte 7 butan,* ' within town and without ', see pp. 460 f.

(5)

AUTHORITIES :—(C) as for no. 3, f. 130, English and Latin, printed here. (B) as for no. 3, f. 114. Printed : *Mon. Angl.* i. 517, no. xiii (omitting Latin version) ; *Chron. Abingdon,* i. 465 ; K. 840 ; Earle p. 342 (with erroneous attribution of manuscripts to cent. xii) ; P. Vinogradoff, *English Society in the Eleventh Century* (Oxford, 1908), p. 107, n. 3 (omitting Latin). Lat. version, Pierquin, p. 817, no. 48, from K.

On the authenticity of this writ see pp. 125 ff., and on ' soke ' see Introduction, pp. 73-4.

DATE. This writ, though probably not authentic as it stands, may have been based on an authentic writ, the date of issue of which would fall between 1053, when Harold was appointed earl of Wessex, and 1055, when Bishop Herman relinquished the see of Ramsbury ; or as a second possibility, between 1058, when Herman received the sees of Ramsbury and Sherborne, and 1066, the date of King Edward's death.

l. 2. *Ic cyðe eow þæt Ordric abbud 7 eal þæt hired . . . habban 7 wealdan.* For this construction see note on no. 1.

l. 4. *Hornemeres hundred.* For the history of the hundred of Hormer, the northern corner of the county of Berkshire, and of its various parishes see VCH *Berkshire,* iv. 391–451. It is suggested by Sir Frank Stenton (*Early History of the Abbey of Abingdon,* 47 f.) that the hundred of Hormer represents the hundred hides attached to the royal estate in Abingdon, held by King Eadred in right of his office (*jure regali*), and said to have been bestowed by him on Bishop Æthelwold, to whom he had granted the *monasteriolum* at Abingdon ; compare the ' Vita S. Æthelwoldi ' in *Chron. Abingdon,* ii. 258 : ' dedit etiam rex possessionem regalem quam in Abendonia possederat (hoc est centum cassatos) cum optimis ædificiis, abbati et fratribus ad augmentum quotidiani victus.' He supposes the grant of the hundred hides to have been a grant of territory, which must have failed to become permanent, perhaps in consequence of the anti-monastic reaction, since the lands within the hundred were acquired by the abbey subsequently at different dates. All the land in Hormer hundred belonged to Abingdon in 1086.

l. 6. *Motgerefe.* There is no agreement as to the meaning of the compound *motgerefa,* not recorded as occurring elsewhere ; (*ge*)*mot-* stands here for *hundredgemot-*. Little is known concerning the officers of the hundred or of the hundred court before the Conquest ; for references to the relevant passages, see Liebermann, *Gesetze,* ii. 520, s.v. ' Hundred ', 25, 26. Liebermann supposes the *motgerefa* (*præpositus* in the Latin version) to be like the sheriff a government official, and suggests that he may be the same as the *præpositus* of the *Leges Henrici,* 92, 8, the officer of the hundred who is required to act when a case of *murdrum* (see p. 85) is discovered (*conueniat ibi hundretum cum preposito et uicinis*). Vinogradoff (*English Society in the Eleventh Century,* 107) supposes the *motgerefa* to be the *hundred(es)mann,* the *hundredes ealdor* ; for references see Liebermann *ut supra.* See also Morris, *The Medieval English Sheriff,* 25, for the judicial activity of the sheriff in the hundred.

(6)

AUTHORITIES :—Corpus Christi College Cambridge MS. 111, p. 92, cent. early xii. On this manuscript see M. R. James, *Cat. of the MSS. in the Library of Corpus Christi College, Cambridge,* i. 238. Printed : K. 821 ; W. Hunt, *Two Chartularies of the Priory of St. Peter at Bath,* Som. Rec. Soc. vii (1893), i. 35. On the authenticity of this writ see pp. 133 f.

DATE. The outside limits of dating are from 15 April 1061, the date of so's consecration as bishop of Wells, to 1082, the date given by William of Malmesbury for the appointment as abbot of Glastonbury of Æthelnoth's successor Thurstan (see Biographical Notes s. ' Æthelnoth, Abbot '). If the statement in the Exchequer Domesday be regarded as decisive (DB i. 89 b, VCH *Somerset,* i. 460), to the effect that Evesty and Ashwick and other land belonged to (*jacuit in*) Bath Abbey T.R.E. and could not be separated from it, then Wulfwold's grant will have taken effect before 5 January 1066, and the writ will have been issued between that date and 15 April 1061. But on the other hand a statement in the Exon Domesday (DB iv. 173), which says of Ashwick : ' valet pro anno xlii den. et quando abbas accepit valebit tantundem ', when taken in conjunction with a statement in the Exchequer Domesday that Abbot Wulfwold held the land on the day of King Edward's death, seems rather to suggest the contrary. Since Wulfwold was abbot both before and after the Conquest, and the grant passed from himself in his private capacity to himself as abbot, these passages seem to suggest that the abbot took seisin of the land for the abbey after the Conquest. In that case the writ will have been issued between 1066 and 1082. The absence of the name of Harold, as earl, in the address, may possibly imply that the letter was written in Harold's reign, or later (see Introduction, p. 48).

l. 3. *Eadweard cingc min hlaford geaf me þæt land æt Eofestige . . . and þa feowwer worðias æt Æscwican.* No charter appears to have survived relating to the Confessor's grant of Evesty to Wulfwold, but a charter concerning the king's grant of Ashwick still exists (K. 811, boundaries, vol. vi, p. 244 ; printed in full, Hunt i. 33). The king after a preamble states that he grants land at Ashwick ' cuidam abbati meo Wlfwoldo ', to hold for his lifetime, and when he feels his death approaching, to give it in perpetuity to whomsoever he pleases (' ut habeat uita comite quamdiu Deus uoluerit et cum dissolutionem sui corporis imminere sentierit cui uoluerit perpetualiter tribuendam '). He adds that it is to be free from all imposts except military service and the repair of fortifications and bridges. A statement in the charter to the effect that the charter was drawn up by Bishop Giso, might be considered to throw doubt on its authenticity. But it is altogether probable that the charter was, at the very least, founded on fact.

l. 4. *Æt Eofestige* ; rubric in cartulary, *Euestia.* Identified in the VCH *Somerset* i. 460, n. 3, with *Evesty,* the obsolete name of an estate in Wellow near Combe Hawey, Som. *Evestie* is mentioned in Domesday (DB i. 89 b) among the lands of St. Peter of Bath, immediately before Ashwick (see next note). According to the Exon Domesday (*Domesday Book,* ed. Ellis, iv. 73), both Evesty and Ashwick were held by Abbot Wulfwold on the day of King Edward's death. Evesty, like Ashwick, was a small estate, described in the Exon Domesday (Domesday Book iv. 173) as a *mansus.* There was land there T.R.E. for one plough, and there were three serfs, and four acres of meadow ; it was worth 20 shillings. It paid geld for one hide. For other references to Evesty, see VCH *Somerset loc. cit.* See also the *Calendar of the Manuscripts of the Dean and Chapter of Wells,* Hist. MSS. Comm. Report (1907), i. 440.

l. 4. *þa feowwer worðias æt Æscwican.* Ashwick, Som., three miles northeast of Shepton Mallet. It is remarked in BT that *worðig* (which remains in place-names in the form ' -worthy ', see further G. B. Grundy, *Dorset Nat. Hist. and F.C. Proc.* lv (1934), and lvi (1935), 110–30), in its simplest application seems to mean ' an enclosed homestead '. That the primary idea is that of an enclosure is to be deduced from statements in the Laws (Ine 40) concerning the necessity of a ceorl's putting a *tun* or hedge about his *worðig*. Although the word is used sometimes in connexion with land of considerable extent and places of some importance, it is also used as an equivalent to Latin *agellus, fundus, praedium,* the first of which is used to describe the land at Ashwick granted to Wulfwold in the charter of the Confessor referred to above : ' aliquantulam terrenæ possessionis partem . . . in illa possessione quae uulgo uocatur Æscwica ', and, ' haec autem suprascriptorum *agellorum* possessio '. According to the Exon Domesday (DB iv. 173), the abbot of Bath ' has a half-hide of land which is called Ashwick '. There was land there for half a plough, with two villeins paying annually 42 pence, and one serf, and 12 acres of meadow, and 3 acres of underwood. The meadow land is mentioned in a note appended to the boundaries in the Ashwick charter of the Confessor for Wulfwold : ' and besides this, twelve acres of meadow lying on the south side of the way, for the three homesteads (*into þam þreom worðigan*) for pasture for his cattle (*his orfe to læse*),' terms which appear again in Wulfwold's writ. According to Collinson (*History of the County of Somerset,* Bath, 1791, ii. 449), Bath Abbey had land at Ashwick up to the Dissolution.

l. 5. *Þa ækeras mæde.* It is tempting to suggest that a number (? twelve) has dropped out of the text before ' acres ' ; see the preceding note.

l. 5. *On wuda 7 on felda.* Feld either alone, or in the compound *feldlond,* denotes a stretch of open land, as opposed to woodland.

l. 8. *Innland,* i.e. ' demesne land ', land not held by any tenant but occupied by the owner or cultivated for his use. See further NED s.v. ' inland ', A ; and F. M. Stenton, *Anglo-Saxon England,* 477.

l. 8. *Ær dæge 7 æfter dæge.* Dæg in this context seems to mean not ' lifetime ' (as in *to syllanne on dæge 7 æfter dæge,* ' to grant in his lifetime and after it ', see BT Suppt), but ' day of one's death ' ; cf. Whitelock, *Wills,* p. 68, l. 17 : ' fremannen to note so he er deden *er daye 7 after daye* ', ' for freemen to use, as they did before, *both before my death and after* '. But in some contexts, and perhaps in those cited above, the phrase *ær dæg(e) 7 æfter (dæg)* seems to have developed the meaning ' at any time whatever, for ever, in perpetuity ' ; cf. no. 62 : ' scer 7 sacleas to fulle hwærfe wið æfric man *ær dæige 7 æfter dæige',* ' clear and undisputed in full exchange as regards every man *for ever* ' ; and ' sceolde þæt land gan inn to þam biscoprice æt Welle . . . on æcce yrfe *ær dæg 7 æfter* ', ' the land was to pass into the possession of the bishopric of Wells as an eternal inheritance *in perpetuity* ', (in a Wells charter in *Proc. of the Somerset Arch. and Nat. Hist. Soc.* xxii (1876), 106 ff.).

(7)

AUTHORITIES :—(R) Charter Roll 4 Edw. II, m. 20 (*Cal. of Ch. R.* iii. 140), printed here. Printed : W. Farrer, *Early Yorkshire Charters,* i (1914), no. 85.

(S) Ch. R. 4 Edw. III, no. 25 (*Cal. of Ch. R.* iv. 194).

(F) Ch. R. 1 Henry V, p. 1, no. 5 (*Cal. of Ch. R.* v. 457).

(P) Patent Roll 1 Ric. II, p. 3, m. 8 ; 5 Ric. II, p. 2, m. 13 ; 6 Henry VI, p. 2, m. 6 (*Cal. of P.R.* 1377–81, 120 ; 1381–85, 118 ; 1422–29, 490).

(M) Confirmation Roll 1 Hen. VIII, p. 2, no. 13.

(N) Conf. R. 3 and 4 Philip and Mary, m. 2, no. 15.

(L) Lansdowne MS. 446, f. 89, from the collections of Strype (1643–1737, see DNB). Printed : G. Poulson, *Beverlac* (London, 1829), i. 42 ; K. 1343 ; Thorpe p. 391.

(H) Harley MS. 560, f. 23, Latin version, in unidentified hand of cent.

xvi/xvii, not printed here; f. 40, an unsuccessful attempt (of the same period) to produce a copy of the writ in a script imitating Anglo-Saxon script. On the authenticity of this writ see pp. 135 ff.

DATE. After the appointment of Ealdred to the see of York at Christmas 1060, and before the expulsion of Tostig from his earldom in 1065. Compare no. 119.

l. 3. *Þæt he dihte priuilegium to þam landan þe ligcað innto Sče Iohannes mynstre æt Beferlicc.* For other instances of permission being given by Edward to an interested ecclesiastic for the drawing up of a *privilegium, freols, boc,* see nos. 26 (*freols settan*), 55 (*dihte boc*), 68 (*dichte priuilegium*) ; and for discussion see Introduction, pp. 35–41.

According to Bresslau, *Urkundenlehre,* i (1912), 4, *dictare* was used already in the late Roman period for ' to draw up, compose ' a charter. The term *privilegium* is explained (perhaps as a Latin loan-word) in an alleged charter of King Edgar to Ely (Robertson p. 100) as : ' a special honour or peculiar freedom ' (*sindorlice wyrðmynt oððe agen freodom*), and in a charter of St. Paul's, London (Thorpe p. 176) as : ' a special freedom ' (' þysne priuilege þæt is *synderlic freols* '). The term appears again in the Beverley writ procured from William I by Ealdred : *dictare privilegium* (Farrer i. 85, see p. 136). It is also used of a reputed diploma of William I for St. Martin's-le-Grand (Davis, *Regesta,* no. 22), where William is made to declare : ' I King William . . . ordered this *privilegium* to be drawn up ' (*het dihtan þæs priuileian*). See also A. Napier, *OE Glosses* (1909), 2589 etc.

The contents of the *privilegium* to be drawn up by Archbishop Ealdred for the lands belonging to St. John's minster at Beverley are nowhere stated. Domesday however states (DB i. 298 b, VCH *Yorks.* ii. 194) that in all the land of St. Peter (of York) and St. John (of Beverley) and of St. Wilfred (of Ripon) and of St. Cuthbert (of Durham) and of the Holy Trinity (of York), neither the king nor the earl nor any one else had any custom (*consuetudinem*). Moreover the writ (Farrer i. no. 88, 1066–69) obtained by Ealdred from William I, declaring that the king has granted Ealdred permission ' dictare privilegium ad omnes illas terras que adjacent ad ecclesiam Sancti Johannis de Beverlaco ', continues : ' et volo ut tota illa terra libera sit adversum me et adversum meos prepositos et adversum omnes homines preter archiepiscopum et presbiteros ejusdem ecclesie '. It is a reasonable assumption that such exemptions as these would have appeared in the *privilegium* drawn up by Archbishop Ealdred in the Confessor's time. Whether the *privilegium* would also have contained exemption from geld is uncertain. From a writ of Henry I (*Cal. of Ch. Rolls,* iii. 140) we learn that some of the lands of St. John of Beverley had been exempt from geld in the time of King Edward and King William I : ' Volo et precipio ut terra Sancti Johannis non geldet si ipsa non geldavit tempore regis Edwardi et patris mei, set sit quieta sicut homines comitatus inde portabunt ei testimonium '. Domesday also states (DB i. 304, VCH *Yorks.* ii. 215, iii. 11) that in Beverley the carucate of St. John was always quit from the king's geld, and that in King Edward's time it was worth 24 pounds to the archbishop and 20 pounds to the canons ; in 1086, while it still yielded 20 pounds to the canons, it yielded only 14 pounds to the archbishop. But other property of the canons is entered there as subject to geld. For the lands of St. John of Beverley, some of which were acquired after the Conquest, see DB i. 304 f., VCH *Yorks.* ii. 215 f. Details of Beverley privileges as reported at an enquiry held in 1106 were printed by Leach (p. 415, n. 5).

l. 7. *Geheald and mund.* For this formula, see no. 2.

l. 7. *Þæt þær nan mann nan þing on ne teo butan he.* Cf. II Cnut 70 : ' Ne *teo* se laford nan mare *on* his æhte butan his rihtan heregeate ', ' his lord shall *take* no more *from* his property than his legal heriot ' ; and for other instances of prohibition clauses with *teo*, see Introduction, p. 66. For *teon* used here and elsewhere in the sense ' to draw ' (to oneself), ' to take ', see BT and Suppt, s.v. *teon*, III, 3, 4. The passage is wrongly rendered by Thorpe : ' so that no man there . . . bring anything in '.

l. 12. *mynsterlif and samnung.* Thorpe's rendering ' monastery ' for *mynsterlif* is misleading, for this minster was served not by monks but by secular canons. The appearance in the vernacular writ of the Conqueror (see above p. 136, n. 2) of *mynsterlif 7 canonica samnung* suggests that *canonica* may have been at some stage omitted from the text of the writ printed here. *Samnung* glosses *synagoga, concilium, congregatio* (see BT and Suppt).

(8)

AUTHORITIES :—(F) Cambridge University Library MS. Ff. 2. 33 (the Sacrist's Register), f. 22 b, cent. late xiii or early xiv, English and Latin, printed here. Printed : K. 868 (inaccurately, omitting Latin).

(A) B.M. Add. MS. 14847 (Registrum Album), f. 30 b (*ol.* 34 b), roughly contemporary with F. English only. Here and in the following texts F and A (inferior to F) seem to be derived from the same source.

(G) C.U.L. MS. Gg. 4. 4 (Registrum Cellerarii), f. 162 b, cent. xv, Latin only.

See further on Bury MSS. pp. 152 ff. Copyists frequently place a stroke resembling an acute accent, and sometimes a curled stroke, over the letter *i* to distinguish it, in the neighbourhood of *n, m, u,* in words like *ic, it, is,* and sometimes when the *i* is final (e.g. in *biri*). In my opinion the device is purely calligraphic. Such strokes over *i* as appear in medieval cartularies of Bury and other houses, as also in Gospatric's writ (no. 121), are not reproduced here in printing the texts ; see notes on nos. 36, 40, 61, 64, 73, 74, 109, 121.

On the authenticity of this writ see pp. 139 ff. and on ' sake and soke ' see Introduction, pp. 73–6.

DATE. Between 1042, when Edward became king, and 1043, when Stigand succeeded Bishop Ælfric III in the see of Elmham. A note in a cent. xvi hand in G describes this as ' the first grant of King Edward Confessor (i.e. to Bury) made in the first year of his reign '.

l. 3. *Be þet minstres wirðe. Wyrðe beon* (with genitive case), ' to be worthy ' (of), is frequently used in Anglo-Saxon writs in the technical sense of ' to be entitled to ', ' to be privileged to have ', ' lawfully to possess ' ; see also note on pp. 475 f. and BT s.v. *weorðe.* For other instances see Introduction, p. 64.

l. 3. *At Seynt Eadmundes biri.* The old name for the place, Beadricesweorth (Beadoriceswyrth, and other spelling variants), was in the eleventh century being supplanted by *Sancte Eadmundes burh.* This name is frequently employed in eleventh-century wills (cf. Whitelock, pp. 68 and 76) and in the writs printed here ; in some of these writs the ' Saint ' is omitted. Miss Whitelock (p. 183) suggests that the will of Bishop Ælfric, dating from the reign of Harold Harefoot, provides the earliest instance of the use of *on Byrig* alone, for this place. It is remarked in *The Chief Elements in English Place-Names* (E.P.-N.S. 1924), 10, that it was only when the place had become a town of some importance that it came to be known as the *burh* of St. Edmund, and that *burh* would seem here to denote a ' town ' in contrast to the original small hamlet or village.

l. 5. *Se freols . . . þe Cnut king þider inne uthe.* The one extant Bury charter attributed to King Cnut (K. 735), a formal diploma in Latin with a long preamble and a list of witnesses, but no date, is followed in some sources (but not in all) by a vernacular charter, to much the same effect. One alleged original of the Latin charter is in the Muniment Room of the Corporation of King's Lynn (Ae. 34), and another at the British Museum (Cott. Aug. ii. 8), while a copy was entered in a late eleventh-century hand in a Bury Gospel Book (Harley MS. 76). A number of cartulary copies have also been preserved, as well as three copies entered on the Charter Rolls. The general tenor of the charter is as follows : King Cnut declares that the monastery called *Beadrichesworthe* shall always be inhabited by monks, and that it shall always be free from all domination of the bishops of that shire, and he confirms the freedom of election of the abbot formerly granted to that house by King Edmund. He enjoins that as often as the people pay *censum Danis*, either for ships or arms, the inhabitants of the place shall pay the same for the purposes that the brethren shall choose. Furthermore, he grants them the fish due to him annually *per thelonii lucrum*, and the fishery that Ulfketel had *in Wylle*, and all the rights from all pleas (*causarum*) in the vills which do now, and shall hereafter, pertain to the monastery. He confirms the queen's annual gift of 4000 eels to the monastery ; and finally pronounces an imprecation on any man attempting to deprive this house of its freedom or to bring back seculars (*clerici*) to this foundation.

The vernacular charter that follows (a good text of which is the copy at King's Lynn) is a summary or adaptation of the Latin diploma, thrown into a different form. Here the king declares to all men that he grants to the holy king St. Edmund, at the place where he is buried, freedom (*freodom*) in perpetuity, with all the rights that he ever possessed ; and this freedom is to remain unchanged and is never to become subject to the domination of any bishop of the shire. And as often as men pay heregeld or shipgeld the *tunscipe* are to pay as other men do, for the necessities of the monks. No man is to divert this foundation to men of another order (*to oðres hades mannum*). The king grants to the monks for the food all the fishery that Ulfketel had and the *gafol*-fish which accrue to the king himself ; and Queen Ælfgifu grants to the saint 4000 eels. Finally the king grants them all their *tunsocn* from all their lands, both those that they have now and those that they shall hereafter by God's favour acquire.

The authenticity of these two documents in their present form is at the least questionable (though an attempt to establish the authenticity of the Latin diploma in so far as the King's Lynn copy is concerned was made by C. W. Goodwin (*Norfolk Archaeology*, Norf. and Norw. Arch. Soc., iv (1855), 93–117)). Mrs. Lobel (*op. cit.* p. 5) has suggested that though the form of the Latin diploma may be dubious, ' there seems to be no reason to doubt its contents—grants which were confirmed by the Confessor (for this statement she gives a reference to the writ, no. 8, under discussion) and his immediate successors ' (see Douglas, *Feudal Documents*, pp. 50, 59, 62). A feature of the accompanying vernacular charter which does not appear to have been remarked upon, is its close correspondence in structure and phraseology with the English version of one of the dubious Bury charters attributed to the Confessor (K. 1346 ; see p. 141, n. 2 above) : the resemblances are so close that these two vernacular documents can hardly have been composed independently. But there are no such resemblances between the corresponding Latin charters. Further the style of the vernacular version of Cnut's charter is clumsy and its phraseology and syntax are in some respects peculiar. It is difficult to believe that it can be a copy of an authentic charter issued by King Cnut.

l. 7. *Sithen Hardcnut kyng mine brother.* The extant Bury charter attributed to Harthacnut (K. 761), generally acknowledged to be spurious, relates that at the petition of Archbishop Æthelnoth of Canterbury, Earl ' Ælfrid ', and the abbot of Bury, King Harthacnut confirms the charter of King Cnut to St. Edmund's, commands that the monastery shall be perpetually free from episcopal interference, and gives the abbot exclusive authority in the monastery and vill, forbidding any outsider to celebrate masses there except by the abbot's permission, and committing to the abbot the sole power of exercising justice unless he should decide in cases of homicide or adultery to commit any of his people to some other authority.   The charter concludes with an imprecation on any person who shall violate the king's decree, directing that the offender shall pay 30 talents of gold into the king's treasury.   This is probably the reputed charter of Harthacnut that was used to good effect in 1345–46 by the abbot of Bury, who successfully pleaded against the bishop of Norwich the total exemption of his house from all episcopal jurisdiction whatsoever (Mon. Ang. iii. 110).

(9)

AUTHORITIES :—(F) as for no. 8, f. 22.   Printed : K. 832.

(E) C.U.L. MS. Ee. 3. 60 (Album Registrum Vestiarii sive Registrum W. Pinchbeck), f. 127, cent. xiv.   Copy of inspeximus charter, 4 Edw. III, containing nos. 9, 15, 24, 25, in texts more closely related to those in F and A (no. 9 absent in A) than to those in S (below).   Printed (not always accurately): Lord Francis Hervey, The Pinchbeck Register (1925), i. 296.

(W) Harley MS. 638 (Registrum Werketon), f. 26 (ol. 14), cent. xiv, printed here.   Copy of inspeximus charter, 8 Edward II, containing nos. 9, 15, 24, 25 in texts superior on the whole to those on R (below).

(L) Harley MS. 743 (Registrum Lakenheath), f. 59 (ol. 8) cent. xiv.

(R) Charter Roll 8 Edw. II, m. 5 (Cal. of Ch. R. iii. 273).

(S) Ibid. 4 Edw. III, m. 24 (ibid. iv. 180).

(T) Ibid. 7–8 Rich. II, m. 28 (ibid. v. 295).

(U) Ibid. 1 Hen. IV, p. 2, m. 6 (ibid. v. 397).

(K) Ibid. 1 Hen. V, p. 2, no. 6 (ibid. v. 461).

(P) Patent Roll 2 Hen. VI, p. 2, m. 38 ; 2 Edw. IV, p. 6, m. 21 (Cal. of P.R. 1422–29, 175 ; 1461–67, 250).

(M) Confirmation Roll 2 Rich. III, p. 3, no. 9 ; 3 Hen. VII, p. 1, no. 10 ; 8 Hen. VIII, no. 5.

On the authenticity of the writ and on the ' sokes of the eight and a half hundreds ' see Introduction, pp. 145–7.

DATE.   The grant of Mildenhall and the sokes of the eight and a half hundreds to St. Edmund's Bury was traditionally associated with a visit of King Edward to the abbey in the first year of his reign ; see Hermann the archdeacon, ' Miracula Sancti Edmundi ', Mon. Angl. iii. 154, no. xxi, Arnold, i. 363, Liebermann, Ungedruckte Geschichtsquellen, 238, VCH Suffolk, ii. 58.

The same date of A.D. 1043–44 for the issue of this writ was arrived at on different grounds by H. W. C. Davis (Eng. Hist. Rev. xxiv (1909), 419). Davis conjectured that the sokes of the eight and a half hundreds which had belonged to Queen Ælfgifu Emma were forfeited by her on her disgrace (shortly after 16 November 1043, Chron. D), and were then made over to Bury by the king, her son.   He dated the writ under discussion 1043–44 on account of the mention in the address of Bishop Grimketel, who had held the East Anglian see for a short time after the ejection late in 1043 of Stigand.   According to the Chron. C 1043, Stigand, after Edward's coronation at Easter in that year, was

consecrated bishop of East Anglia (Elmham), but was soon afterwards
expelled from his bishopric, sharing the disgrace of the queen whose closest
adviser he is said to have been. The restoration of Stigand is recorded *Chron.*
E 1043 (to be corrected to 1044). We learn from Florence of Worcester s.a.
1038 that Grimketel, bishop of Selsey (Sussex) held the East Anglian see with
Selsey during the disgrace of Stigand, and although Florence's date, A.D. 1038,
for these events must be corrected to 1043–44, his account of the sequence of
bishops is probably correct. A similar account in C.U.L. MS. 4220 cited by
Miss Robertson (*Anglo-Saxon Charters*, 431), assigns to 1044 the death of
Ælfric III of Elmham, the appointment and ejection of Stigand, the appointment of Grimketel and his ejection for simony, and the reappointment of
Stigand ; but some of these events belong to 1043. Since an exact date
cannot be assigned to Grimketel's tenure of the East Anglian see, the writ
must be dated 1043–44, and more probably 1044 than 1043.

In a list of benefactors to the abbey (also found elsewhere) in Harley MS.
1005, f. 81, a fourteenth-century Bury register, to which another hand has
added notes and dates, the date 1046 is prefixed to the entries recording the
grant by Edward to Bury of Mildenhall and the eight and a half hundreds,
Coney Weston (no. 20), *Castre* and Pakenham (no. 14) and Ælfric Modercope's
grant of Loddon (no. 22). The basis of this dating, which is only approximately correct, is not known.

l. 3. *Æt Mildenhale.* Mildenhall, Suffolk. For later references to the
grant of Mildenhall to the abbey, see pp. 145 f. above. Domesday informs us
that ' King Edward gave Mildenhall (*Mitdenehalla*) to St. Edmund, and afterwards Stigand held under St. Edmund in the lifetime of King Edward
12 carucates of land as a manor ' (DB ii. 288 b, VCH *Suffolk*, i. 428). It was
later believed in the monastery that the monks had not dared to refuse the
request of Stigand, when he was bishop of East Anglia, that they would lend
him for the time being the vill of Mildenhall (' ut villam de Mildenhall ei ad
tempus accommodaremus '), and it was asserted that Stigand continued to
hold the manor of the monks (*de nobis*) during his tenure of the see of Canterbury, and that with all his other manors it came into the king's hand on his
ejection from his see in 1070 (*Mon. Angl.* iii. 154, no. xxi). The manor is
indeed entered in Domesday under the heading : ' Lands of Stigand which
William de Noers keeps in the king's hand '. Mildenhall was finally purchased
in 1189 from Richard I for the abbey by Abbot Samson for 1000 marks, ' quod
antiquo jure ad abbathiam suam ut dictum fuerat pertinebit ' (*Mon. Angl.*
iii. 104, note n.). The other Bury source mentioned above refers to the
recovery of ' manerium nostrum de Mildenhall quod postea rex Richardus
nobis per chartam suam reddidit tanquam jus Sancti Edmundi et confirmavit
et insuper chartæ Sancti Edwardi sigillum suum apposuit (*Mon. Angl.* iii. 154,
no. xxi).

l. 3. *Nigen half hundreda.* In this late copy ' nine ' (*nigen*) has been
substituted for the normal construction with the ordinal number, ' ninth ' ;
cf. no. 24, *healf nygoðe hundreda*, lit. ' half ninth hundreds ', i.e. eight and a half
hundreds. An apparently unnoticed form of the ordinal number ' ninth '
appears in the *nigend(e)* which is to be found in the F text of this writ, as also
in both texts (F, A) of no. 18, in no. 24 (F, A), and also in the spurious no. 10.
There is no reason to doubt that this form was at one time current. The
Middle English *Ayenbite of Inwyt* (in the Kentish dialect) has *neȝende*, ' ninth ',
zeuende, ' seventh ', *eȝtende*, ' eighth ', *tende*, ' tenth ' ; see J. K. Wallenberg,
The Vocabulary of Dan Michel's Ayenbite of Inwyt (Uppsala, 1923), s.v.
eȝtende. There is evidence for ordinals in -*nd*- of native origin in Old English
in the Mercian Rushworth [1] *siofund(a)*, Northumbrian Rushworth [2] *siofunda*,

Lindisfarne *seofunda, -onda* (K. Brunner, *Altenglische Grammatik* (1942), § 328). Similar forms appear in OFris *ni(u)gunda*, OSax *nigundo*, Gothic *niunda*, OIcel *niundi*. The ordinal *nigende* in these late Bury copies may then be a survival of an Old English form, reinforced perhaps by the Scandinavian form.

l. 4. *Into þinghogy*. *Into* is used here in the sense of 'pertaining to, centred at'; *þinghogy* is from ON *þing-haugr*, 'mound of the "þing" or assembly'. The centre of administration of the eight and a half hundreds was the court of the hundred of Thingoe (Bury itself lying outside these hundreds), held at that time on the 'thing-mound', a tumulus lying to the north-west of the town, in the vicinity of the East Anglian School of these days. For the topography, see the map of the Banleuca of St. Edmund printed by M. D. Lobel, *The Borough of Bury St. Edmunds*. On the hundred of Thingoe and on the other hundreds mentioned below, see O. S. Anderson, *The English Hundred-Names*, i (1934), 83 ff. The transfer of the sokes of these hundreds to the abbot would involve the subjection to his jurisdiction of all the men within these hundreds, no matter whose tenants they might be. For the jurisdiction of the abbot in the eight and a half hundreds, namely the hundreds of Thingoe, Thedwestrey, Blackbourn and Bradmere, Lackford, Risbridge, the double hundred of Babergh, and the half hundred of Cosford, see D. C. Douglas, *Feudal Documents*, pp. xlviii, n. i, clv, and 9. H. W. C. Davis (*Eng. Hist. Rev.* xxiv (1909), 418) pointed out that the franchise conveyed to the abbey included the whole of western Suffolk between the Little Ouse on the north and the Stour on the south, and that although the earliest mention of this district occurs here in connection with Queen Ælfgifu Emma, it seems unlikely that it was created for her benefit. He suggested that the district formed 'a miniature shire', and that Beadricesweorth, before it became the borough of St. Edmund, was the head of this liberty. Other writs of the Confessor (nos. 18, 24) and writs of William I and II (Douglas, Charters nos. 3, 17) inform us that the eight and a half hundreds had been administered on the queen's behalf by Ælfric, son of Wihtgar, and after him by a certain Ordgar (for whom see Robertson no. 92). See also on the Thingoe court, N. D. Hurnard, *Eng. Hist. Rev.* lxiv (1949), 319 f., and for its later history *ibid.* App. 324–7.

l. 5. *Minre meder*. Queen Ælfgifu Emma. See Biographical Notes.

(10)

AUTHORITIES :—(A) as for no. 8, f. 30 (*ol.* 34), printed here. Printed : K. 1342.

On the authenticity of this writ and on the 'sokes of the eight and a half hundreds', see Introduction, p. 147, and notes on no. 9.

DATE. Grimketel was bishop of East Anglia for a short time within the period 1043–44. Earl Ælfgar did not become earl of East Anglia till 1051 at the earliest. The address cannot be that of an authentic writ, and the writ, as spurious, is therefore not dated here.

(11)

AUTHORITIES :—(C) Cott. Aug. ii. 80, in a contemporary hand, printed here. Facsimile and text, *Facsimiles of Ancient Charters in the British Museum*, ed. E. A. Bond, pt. iv, no. 29. Printed : T. Madox, *Formulare Anglicanum* (London, 1702), 290, with Lat. version not printed here ; K. 894 (from this text, but with ref. to F below) ; K. Brandi, *Urkunden und Akten, für rechtsgeschichtliche und diplomatische Vorlesungen und Übungen* (3rd ed. Berlin and Leipzig, 1932) p. 46, no. 33. The text is written on an unusually wide piece of parchment, dimensions : 10″ broad, ⅞″ deep on left side, ¹¹⁄₁₆″ on right. No apparent signs of sealing. Lower edge cut after the text was written, so that the shafts of some letters have been cut through, as in no. 24. There is no direct indication that this is the original writ, written and sealed by the clerks of King Edward's secretariat. It may be the original writ or it may be a contemporary copy.

(F) as for no. 8, f. 22 b.

(A) as for no. 8, f. 30 b (*ol.* 34 b).

On the authenticity of this writ see p. 139, and on ' sake and soke ' see Introduction, pp. 73–6.

DATE. Between 1044, the date of Leofstan's appointment as abbot of Bury, and 1 August 1065, the date of his death.

(12)

AUTHORITIES :—(N) C.U.L. MS. Mm. 4. 19 (Registrum Nigrum), f. 105 b, not earlier than cent. late xii, English and Latin, printed here.

(F) as for no. 8, f. 22 b, English and Latin. Printed K. 892, English only.

(A) as for no. 8, f. 30 b (*ol.* 34 b), English and Latin. Printed K. 1345, Latin only.

On the authenticity of this writ see pp. 139 f., and on 'sake and soke' see Introduction, pp. 73–6.

DATE. As for no. 11.

(13)

AUTHORITIES :—(F) as for no. 8, f. 23, printed here. Printed : K. 852.

(A) as for no. 8, f. 31 (*ol.* 35).

On the authenticity of this writ see pp. 139 f.

DATE. Between 1044/5, the date of Harold's appointment to the earldom of East Anglia, and 1047, the date of the translation of Bishop Stigand of East Anglia (Elmham) to Winchester.

(14)

AUTHORITIES :—(F) as for no. 8, f. 23, printed here. Printed : K. 851.

(A) as for no. 8, f. 31 b (*ol.* 35 b).

On the authenticity of this writ see p. 148.

DATE. 1044/5–1047, as for no. 13. But if (as is probable) the Osgot of this writ is Osgot Clapa (see Biographical Notes), Pakenham may have come into the king's hands after Osgot's outlawry in 1046. In that case the date of the writ would be 1046–47.

l. 3. *þat lond at Pakenham.* Pakenham in Thedwestrey hundred, Suffolk. According to Domesday (DB ii. 361 b) St. Edmund of Bury in King Edward's time held as a manor seven carucates of land at Pakenham with sake and soke and all ' customs ' (including fold-soke) over the 44 villeins and the 23 bordars on the manor, and retained possession of the manor in 1086. There were also in the same vill 3 freemen with 30 acres of land, which they could give and sell, but soke and sake and commendation would remain in the saint's possession. Moreover, in King Edward's time the abbot of Bury had leased to a freeman half a carucate on condition that all his land, wherever it might be, should remain with the saint after his death, and of this freeman's land, at the time of the Survey, one carucate lay in Pakenham in demesne. Nothing is said in Domesday of the circumstances in which this land had come to the abbey. The manor is there stated to be 16 furlongs long and one league broad. Its value had increased from 10 pounds T.R.E. to 25 pounds in 1086, and it was rated for geld at 13½ pence.

(15)

AUTHORITIES :—(Q) P.R.O. Cartæ Antiquæ Roll P, no. 3, early cent. xiii. Copy in Harley MS. 84, f. 172 b, a transcript made before 1645 for Sir Simonds D'Ewes. For transcripts of the Cart. Antiq. Rolls, see *Cartæ Antiquæ*, Rolls 1–10, ed. L. Landon, Pipe Roll Society, New Series, xvii (1939), xii. Some writs printed here are mentioned in Landon's ed. This text is printed here.

(F) as for no. 8, f. 23. Printed : K. 879.

(A) as for no. 8, f. 31 (*ol.* 35).

(E) as for no 9, f. 127. Printed : Hervey, *Pinchbeck Register*, i. 296.

(W) as for no. 9, f. 26 (*ol.* 14).

(R) and other Ch., Pat., and Conf. R. copies as for no. 9.

On the authenticity of this writ see p. 139.

DATE. There seems no reason to reject the statement of the *Chron.* D 1052 (to be corrected to 1051) that King Edward in that year abolished the heregeld (which may or may not have been at this time an annual levy regularly imposed). The writ must have been issued after Ælfgar's first appointment to the East Anglian earldom, September 1051, and before the abolition of the tax. The *Estoire de Seint Aedward le Rei* (*Lives of Edward the Confessor,* R.S. p. 51), a late and untrustworthy source, states that Edward confirmed by charter the abolition of the tax ; it is not known in what circumstances he ceased to exact it. A dating for the writ of c. 1051 is probably correct.

l. 4. *Þæt Sc̄e Eadmundes inland sy scotfreo fram heregelde 7 fram eghwilc oðer gaful.* For *inland,* ' demesne land ', see p. 431. With *scotfreo,* ' exempt from payment of " scot " ', i.e. contribution, tax, compare nos. 76, 86, 87, 93, 104, *scotfreo 7 gafolfreo,* ' exempt from contribution and tax '. See also NED s.v. ' scot ' (where it is stated that although *scot* is ultimately identical with OE *sc(e)ot, gesc(e)ot* (compare no. 63, *scypgesceot*), its formal relation to this is somewhat uncertain, and that there can be little doubt that ME *scot* is partly of Scandinavian origin).

Heregeld (*-gyld, -gild*) was in the Confessor's time a land tax levied on the country as a whole to provide standing forces for the king's service. The chronicler recording (*Chron.* D 1052, to be corrected to 1051 ; see also Florence of Worcester s.a. 1051) the abolition by the Confessor of the oppressive heregeld, observes that the king abolished (*alede*) the heregeld which King Æthelred had instituted, ' in the 39th year from the time when he had begun it '. This takes one back to the years 1012–13, when *ful gyld* (' full payment ') and provisions were demanded not only by Swein and his *here,* but also by Thurkill and the *here* which lay at Greenwich, i.e. the 45 Danish ships which had entered King Æthelred's service (*Chron.* C, D, E, 1012, 1013). From that time onward heregeld was levied by Æthelred and his successors for the support of standing naval and military forces until its abolition by the Confessor ; as to whether it was levied annually or not see Liebermann, *Gesetze,* ii. 344–5, s.v. ' Dänengeld ' ; see also Hoops, *Reallexikon,* ii. 44 ff. s.v. ' Finanzwesen ' (Vinogradoff). Liebermann brings into opposition to the statement in the *Chronicle* that the tax was (in 1051) abolished by the Confessor a passage in Domesday (which, like one or two others of similar tenor, does not however seem to be decisive in the matter) : ' quando geldum dabatur tempore regis

Eadwardi communiter per totam Berchesciram '. It should be added that earlier in the reign of Æthelred, from 991 onward, large sums of money to pay off the Danes had been raised by taxation. See further *Chron.* C, D, E, F, 991, C, D, 1040, 1041, E, F, 1039, 1040, Plummer ii. 174–5, 218–19, 234 ; BT Suppt, s.v. *heregild* ; Liebermann *ut supra*. Compare also no. 93 below : *of gelde 7 of dænegelde*, and see note on pp. 513 f. See also Stenton, *Anglo-Saxon England*, 406.

For the various senses of *gafol* (among which ' tribute ', ' tax ', ' rent ', are common) see BT Suppt, and Hoops, *Reallexikon*, ii. 109, s.v. *gafol* (Vinogradoff). From the context the meaning here would seem to be ' tax ', possibly a tax laid directly on houses or holdings ; see Vinogradoff, *English Society in the Eleventh Century*, 143, Liebermann ii. 264, s.v. ' Abgabe '. The phrase *scotfreo 7 gafolfreo on scire 7 on hundrede* (with variants) in nos. 76, 86, 87, 93, suggests that in some cases at all events the gafol was collected by the officials of the shire or of the hundred. For *gafol* as rent, see no. 72.

(16)

AUTHORITIES :—(F) as for no. 8, f. 23 b, printed here. Printed : K. 876. (A) as for no. 8, f. 31 b (*ol.* 35 b). On the authenticity of this writ see pp. 148 f. DATE. Between the appointment of Ælfgar to the earldom of East Anglia after the banishment of Earl Godwine and his sons on 24 September 1051, and the death of Queen Ælfgifu Emma on 6, or 14, March 1052. l. 3. *At Kirkeby.* Kirby (Cane), Norfolk, a small manor held in 1086 by Rafridus of the abbot of Bury, and held by St. Edmund's in King Edward's time as two carucates of land. It was 9 furlongs in length and 5 in breadth, it rendered 10½ pence of geld, and its value had increased from 40 shillings to 6 pounds (DB ii. 212). l. 4. *Lefstan hire knyth.* ' Leofstan, her retainer '. OE *cniht* ' youth, follower, attendant, retainer ', has also in some contexts the meaning of ' military attendant, soldier ' ; and, at a later period, when associated with the idea of feudal tenure, that of ' knight '. In the Anglo-Saxon wills *cniht* is used, as it is here, with a possessive, in the sense of a retainer attached to the personal service of a nobleman ; see Whitelock, 127, Stenton, *English Feudalism*, 133 ff. For the development of the idea of military service in association with *cniht*, see Douglas, *Feudal Documents*, ci, n. 2.

(17)

AUTHORITIES :—(F) as for no. 8, f. 23, printed here. Printed : K. 878. (A) as for no. 8, f. 31 (*ol.* 35). On the authenticity of this writ see pp. 148 f., and on ' sake and soke ', pp. 73–6. DATE. Within one of Ælfgar's two periods of office as earl of East Anglia, and after the death of Queen Ælfgifu Emma ; either between March 1052 and September 1052 ; or between April 1053 and the autumn of 1057. The earlier date is to be preferred, for since no intermediate holder of Kirby is mentioned, the writ was probably issued not long after the queen's death. l. 2. *þat lond at Kirkeby.* See no. 16.

(18)

AUTHORITIES :—(F) as for no. 8, f. 22, English and Latin, printed here. Printed : K. 883, English only. (A) as for no. 8, f. 30 (*ol.* 34), English and Latin.

(G) as for no. 8, f. 163, Latin only.

(D) B.M. Add. MS. 5846, p. 33 (vol. 45 of the collections of the Rev. W. Cole (1714–82), made about the middle of cent. xviii). Latin only. Printed: *Mon. Angl.* iii. 137, no. vii (with a heading 'Mildenhall' which does not correspond with its contents); K. 905; Pierquin, *Chartes Anglo-Saxonnes*, p. 825, no. 58, from K.

For the authenticity of the writ see pp. 147 f., and for references to the 'sokes of the eight and a half hundreds', see pp. 145 ff. For the legal terms see Introduction, pp. 78 ff.

DATE. Within one of Ælfgar's two periods of office as earl of East Anglia, and after the death of Queen Emma; either between March 1052 and September 1052, or between April 1053 and the autumn of 1057.

l. 5. *So ful and so forth so mine moder it fermist aihte and it Alfrich Withgares sune hire to hande biwiste*, that is, the jurisdiction over the eight and a half hundreds was administered in her name by this Ælfric. See further no. 9, p. 437.

l. 7. *Ic ne am becnowe . . . ne hebberethef.* The occurrence of *becnowe* in this late copy (the only reference given for this word in BT Suppt) is not proof of the existence of an adjective *becnawe* in Old English. But may not an OE adjective *becnawe* have stood in the same relationship to the verb *becnawan*, as did *gecnawe* (cf. nos. 24, 39) to *gecnawan*? The ME phrase 'to be beknown', recorded from the *Cursor Mundi* of c. 1310 and four other texts (NED s.v. 'be-know' v. obs. 4) may be either a re-formation from a ME adjective *becnowe*, or a new formation from the verb 'becnow'. As an illustration of the uncertainty that might exist concerning the possession of rights of jurisdiction, see DB ii. 360 b (VCH *Suffolk*, i. 496), where it is recorded that in King Edward's time sake and soke and commendation over a number of freemen in the hundred of Stow in Suffolk belonged to St. Edmund (of Bury) 'of the gift of King Edward, as his writs and seals show, which the abbot has'; and that afterwards King William allowed the gift. But the king's reeve had received 4 shillings on account of the soke of one of these men 'whether it was rightly or wrongly neither the abbot nor his ministers knowing', while the hundred testified that 'they did not know St. Edmund at a later time to have been disseised of the soke after King Edward gave it'.

l. 8. *Hamsokne ne grithbreche* etc. The absence of *fyrdwite* from this list in all the extant texts is probably due to a copyist's omission at an earlier stage, for *fyrdwite* appears both in the Latin version here, and in the corresponding list in no. 24; it also appears in the corresponding list in writs of William I and II on the same subject (Douglas, *Feudal Documents*, 48, 60, Charters nos. 3, 18). These forfeitures (with the inclusion of fyrdwite) were no doubt the 'six forfeitures of St. Edmund' to which reference is made in Domesday Book. For further discussion and for references see Douglas, *ut supra*, clv ff.

l. 9. *Ne non þere rithte.* In Old English: 'ne nan þæra gerihta'. *Gerihta*, a term with many connotations, used often as an equivalent to *consuetudines* (for which see p. 451), is used in II Cnut 12–15, of royal *gerihta*, namely, the dues which the king has from all men in Wessex and in Mercia, and which he may grant away to a specially favoured subject; on these, namely mundbreach, hamsocn, foresteall and fyrdwite etc., see Introduction, pp. 79 ff. In some other writs *gerihta* is used, as it is here, to cover all other instances at the end of an enumeration of specific rights; e.g. no. 82, 'sake and soke, toll and team, infangenetheof . . . and all other rights; cf. also nos. 85, 91, 92 etc. Again, in nos. 28, 38, *gerihta* refers back to sake and soke, grithbreach etc., rights enumerated earlier in the text. Here, as elsewhere, 'rights' shades off into 'dues', as for instance in no. 100 : *ealle þa gerihte 7 þa cnaulæcunga*, 'all the rights (*or* dues) and the recognition of lordship '. Compare, for example, the account of the *gerihta* belonging after the Conquest, and probably before, to the church on the royal manor at Lambourn, Berks. (Robertson, 241). These *gerihta* included one hide of land free and quit, sake and soke, toll and team, and the tenth acre in the king's land, the produce of two acres at harvest, the tenth lamb and the tenth young pig ; at Michaelmas a wey of cheese, at Martinmas two sesters of corn and one pig, and at Easter fifteen pence. Pasture must be provided for the priest's oxen and cows, his sheep, his pigs and his horses ; every day wood must be brought for the priest's fire. Tithes must be paid to him and also church-tax (*cyricsceatt*). Compare also the term *Godes gerihta*, p. 487, and see further BT Suppt, s.v. *geriht*. See also the *gerihta* pertaining to Taunton (Robertson, 236 f., 485 ff.).

l. 9. *Be fullen wite*. In some contexts *be fullan wite* means ' under pain of the full penalty ', to be incurred if the prescribed course of action is not carried out ; compare II Edgar 3, ' every church-tax shall be rendered by Martinmas under pain of the full penalty which the written law prescribes ' (' be þam fullan wite þe seo domboc tæcð '). But in this writ the meaning seems to be ' at the full rate ', ' with the full penalty ', i.e. without any deduction ; compare BT Suppt, s.v. *be*, A, III, 23 (' marking measure, rate, degree '). The ' full penalty ' was sometimes 120 shillings ; see Liebermann ii. 247.

(19)

AUTHORITIES :—(F) as for no. 8, f. 22 b.   Printed : K. 884.

(A) as for no. 8, f. 30 b (*ol*. 34 b).

(L) as for no. 9, f. 59 b (*ol*. 8 b), printed here. This text is farther removed linguistically than A and F from the original writ, but preserves in l. 3 the *nou*, ' now ', which F and A omit.

On the authenticity of this writ see p. 139, and on ' soke ' see Introduction, pp. 73 f.

DATE. Within one of Ælfgar's two periods of office as earl of East Anglia ; either between September 1051 and September 1052, or between April 1053 and the autumn of 1057.

(20)

AUTHORITIES :—(F) as for no. 8, f. 23, printed here.   Printed : K. 880.

(A) as for no. 8, f. 31 b (*ol*. 35 b).

On the authenticity of this writ see p. 149, and on 'sake and soke' see Introduction, pp. 73–6.

DATE. As for no. 19.

l. 3. *Cunegestone*. Coney Weston in Blackbourn hundred, Suffolk. For the development of medial *w* in this name, compare *Canewdon*, Essex, which is discussed by P. H. Reaney, *The Place-Names of Essex* (E.P.-N.S.), 179. Domesday states (DB ii. 365, VCH *Suffolk*, i. 501) that in King Edward's time (and in 1086) St. Edmund held 2 carucates at Coney Weston (*Cunegestuna*) as a manor. There were 2 villeins there T.R.E., and then and in 1086 there were 3 bordars and 1 serf ; and 2 ploughs on the demesne, and half a plough belonging to the men. There were 2 acres of meadow, and woodland for 4 pigs. And there were 12 sokemen with half a carucate and 30 acres of land ; in King Edward's time there were 6 ploughs, in 1086, 4, and 2 acres of meadow. There was a church with 8 acres of free land in alms. The extent of the manor was 1 league in length and 6 furlongs in breadth, and its value had increased from 5 pounds in King Edward's time to 6 pounds in 1086. It paid in geld 17¼ pence.

(21)

AUTHORITIES :—(F) as for no. 8, f. 23, printed here.   Printed :   K. 877, Thorpe p. 416.

(A) as for no. 8, f. 31 b (ol. 35 b).

On the authenticity of this writ see pp. 149 ff.

DATE.   This writ and the following are dated by D. C. Douglas (*Feudal Documents*, cxi), 1047–65, the date 1047 being that of Æthelmær's appointment as bishop of East Anglia.   But it is possible to limit the dating to Ælfgar's two periods of office as earl of East Anglia, namely September 1051– September 1052, and April 1053 to the autumn of 1057.

l. 3.   *Mot bugan to þo tueyen abboten.*   On this instance of ' commendation ', see p. 149.

(22)

AUTHORITIES :—(F) as for no. 8, f. 22 b, printed here.   Printed :   K. 882.

(A) as for no. 8, f. 31 (ol. 35).

On the authenticity of the writ see pp. 149 ff., and on ' sake and soke ', see Introduction, pp. 73–6.

DATE.   As for no. 21.

l. 3.   *þat land at Lodne.*   Land at Loddon, Norfolk, was bequeathed to Bury by Ælfric Modercope in a will made in 1042 or 1043 (see p. 149 above). In 1086 Frodo held of the abbot of Bury, Loddon, which St. Edmund held T.R.E. for 3 carucates and 10 acres.   The Domesday entry (DB ii. 211 b, VCH *Norfolk*, ii. 133) states that the manor had increased in value from 40 shillings to 80 shillings, was 14 furlongs in length and 9 in breadth, and rendered 16 pence of geld.   Ælfric had granted his land to the abbey with sake and soke, and Domesday tells us that ' St. Edmund has the soke '.

(23)

AUTHORITIES :—(F) as for no. 8, f. 22 b, printed here.   Printed :   K. 881.

(A) as for no. 8, f. 30 b (ol. 34 b).

On the authenticity of the writ see p. 140, and on ' sake and soke ' see Introduction, pp. 73–6.

DATE.   After the appointment of Baldwine as abbot in succession to Leofstan who died on 1 August 1065, and before the death of King Edward on 5 January 1066.

(24)

AUTHORITIES :—(O) Cott. Aug. ii. 49, a contemporary copy, printed here. Facs. and text, *Facs. of Anc. Chart. in the Brit. Mus.* ed Bond, pt. iv, no. 40. Printed K. 874.   The text is written on a single piece of parchment, dimensions :   8¾″ broad, 2 11/16″ deep on left side, 2⅜″ on right.   Handwriting contemporary.   No apparent signs of sealing.   The top and lower edge cut after the text was written, so that the shafts of some letters have been cut through, as with no. 11.   The omission in l. 7 of *þinga*, which appears in all the later copies of this text, indicates that this is not the source from which these later copies were derived.   This is not the original writ written and sealed by the clerks of King Edward's secretariat, but a contemporary copy (carelessly omitting *þinga*) of the original writ.

(Q) Cartæ Antiquæ Roll P, no. 2. Copy in Harley MS. 84, f. 171 b. On these see p. 439.

(F) as for no. 8, f. 22 b.

(A) as for no. 8, f. 30 b (*ol.* 34 b).

(E) as for no. 9, f. 127. Printed: Hervey, *Pinchbeck Register,* i. 295 (incomplete, the last few lines being lightly scored through in E with horizontal lines in red ink).

(W) as for no. 9, f. 26 (*ol.* 14).

(R) and other Ch., Pat., and Conf. R. copies as for no. 9.

On the authenticity of this writ see pp. 147–8, and on the legal terms employed, see Introduction, pp. 73–81.

DATE. As for no. 23.

l. 10. *Þæt he mote beon ælc þæra gerihta wurðe.* For other instances of this construction, in which *wurðe* is accompanied by an uninflected *ælc,* cf. *Chron.* E 1046, Plummer i. 168 ; ' behet man him þæt he moste wurðe [beon] *ælc þæra þinga þe he ær ahte* ' ; *ibid.* 1052, Plummer i. 180 : ' gerndon to him þæt hi moston beon wurðe *ælc þæra þinga þe heom . . . of genumen wæs* '. The same construction occurs again in the Christ Church writ of Henry II printed by Joseph Hall, *Selections from Early Middle English,* i. no. iv, p. 12 : ' *þet hi beon ælc þare lande wurþa* þe hi eafdon en Edwardes kinges dege ', and in other charters of this series (on which see pp. 174–8 above). Hall's explanation, *ælc,* each of them, standing for the archbishop and the monks severally as well as jointly, must be erroneous, for the same construction is used in the first passage cited here where the pronoun to which *wurðe* refers is in the singular. On *gerihta,* see no. 18.

l. 15. *Mid his sweotelunge.* On the various senses of this term, see p. 449. I have adopted the rendering given for this passage in BT.

l. 16. *Þæt non oþer ne sy,* lit., ' that there be no other ', or ' that it be not otherwise '. For another instance in a writ of this rare formula, see no. 69, and also no. 80.

(25)

AUTHORITIES :—(Q) Cartæ Antiquæ Roll P, no. 4, printed here. Copy in Harley MS. 84, f. 172 b. On these, see p. 439 above.

(F) as for no. 8, f. 23. Printed: John Battely, *Antiquitates Sancti Edmundi Burgi* (Oxford, 1745), 134, with Lat. version which is not in manuscript ; *Mon. Angl.* iii. 138, no. viii ; Thorpe p. 415.

(A) as for no. 8, f. 31 (*ol.* 35).

(E) as for no. 9, f. 127. Printed: Hervey, *Pinchbeck Register,* i. 296.

(W) as for no 9, f. 26 (*ol.* 14). Printed K. 875.

(R) and other Ch., Pat., and Conf. R. copies as for no. 9.

On the authenticity of this writ see pp. 150 f.

DATE. As for no. 23.

l. 3. *Onne menetere wið inne Seint Eadmundes byrig.* For the English coinage of the tenth and eleventh centuries, see H. A. Grueber and C. F. Keary, *A Catalogue of English Coins in the British Museum,* vol. ii (Wessex and England to the Norman Conquest), London, 1893. Only three coins struck at Bury in the Confessor's reign appear (p. 356) in their lists. The moneyer was Morcere, and the coins bear King Edward's name. For a moneyer, Leofwine, at Bury temp. Harold Harefoot (1035–40), see G. C. Brooke, *English Coins* (2nd ed. 1942), 70. For instances of surviving coins issued by ecclesiastics before the Conquest, see G. C. Brooke, *ut supra*, 3, 11 ff., 18 ff., and Plates.

For the position of the moneyer during the Old English period (which is obscure), see G. C. Brooke, *A Catalogue of English Coins in the British Museum* : The Norman Kings (London, 1916) i. cxli–ii, and the references there. References to moneyers occur in the Laws and in Domesday Book, where the entry for Hereford gives the fullest information. At Hereford in King Edward's time there were seven moneyers, one of whom was the bishop's moneyer ; each of them paid certain fees, the king's moneyer to the king, the bishop's moneyer to the bishop, on receipt of dies after the introduction of a new type. When the king came to the city the moneyers made for him as many pennies as he required from the king's silver. The seven moneyers had sake and soke. On the death of any of the king's moneyers the king had 20 shillings for relief (*de relevamento*) but if he died intestate, his whole *censum* (' Bargeld ', Liebermann) went to the king. If the sheriff went into Wales with an army, the moneyers went with him under penalty of 40 shillings (DB i. 179, 189 b, VCH *Herefordshire*, i. 309–10). For further references to moneyers and mints in Domesday, see Brooke i. cxxxv and clx–clxxxviii ; see also Liebermann *Gesetze*, ii. 591 f. s.v. ' Münze '. For moneyers at Winchester T.R.E. see DB iv. 532–8.

l. 4. *Al swa me mine on hande stonden ower on enig minre burge alre freolukeost.* Kemble, giving references to Harley MS. 638 and MS. Ff. 2. 33, prints (omitting his accents) : *alswa me mine on hande stoden oðer on ænig minre burge alre freolikeost*, which (with *oðer* for MS. *oþer*, and *freolikeost* for MS. *-lukeost*) is the reading of the Harley MS. Thorpe (p. 415) gives the same references as Kemble, but does not print Kemble's text ; his text runs : *alswo me mine on hande stonden. ower on oni mire burge alre frelikest*, which (with *alswo* for MS. *also*, with a mark of punctuation (taken from Harley MS. 638) inserted after *stonden*, and with *mire* for *mine*) is the reading of MS. Ff. 2. 33. Nevertheless though Thorpe has the correct reading *stonden ower* (between which he inserts a stop), his translation is nearer to Kemble's text than to his own, for his rendering is : ' as freely as mine have stood in my service, or in any of my towns, most freely '. But the antithesis in Thorpe's translation between ' minters ' in the king's service, and the ' minters ' in any of the king's towns, is false. The Laws show that the minting of money was a royal prerogative, and it is improbable (as the references given in the next paragraph will show) that mintage rights could be acquired except as the result of a direct royal grant. The passage was correctly translated by Battely : ' tam libere in omni re habendum quam ego meos [monetarios] usquam in quovis meorum Burgorum habeo, omnium liberrime '. The form *ower*, ' anywhere ' (which Thorpe failed to recognise), occurs from time to time in Old English (e.g. in *Beowulf*, l. 2870) as a variant for *ahwær* ; for references, see BT Suppt.

Regulations concerning moneyers were issued by Æthelstan in an ordinance (II Æthelstan 14) declaring that there should be one coinage throughout the king's realm ; that no one should mint money except in a town (*port*) ; and that if a moneyer were found guilty of issuing base or light coins, the hand with which he committed the crime should be cut off and fastened up on the mint. If was moreover decreed that in Canterbury there should be seven moneyers (four for the king, two for the archbishop and one for the abbot (of St. Augustine's)), in Rochester two for the king and one for the bishop, the number of moneyers in London, Winchester, Lewes and some other boroughs (*burgum*) being determined at the same time. Grueber and Keary (*op. cit.* i. xxxii) remark that the right of bishops and abbots to use such mints

' was only a delegated right, for these archbishops and abbots never placed their names upon the coins ; and it need not have interfered with the royal prerogative to have the exclusive regulation of the coinage '. Æthelstan's ordinance that there should be one coinage throughout the country was re-enacted by Edgar, Æthelred II and Cnut (III Edgar 8, VI Æthelred 32, I, II Cnut 8). Æthelred II asserted the royal prerogative that no one except the king should have a moneyer (III Æthelred 8, 1) ; on this see Liebermann ii. 591, s.v. ' Münze ', 6. In a later code (IV Æthelred 9) he enacted that the number of moneyers should be reduced, so that in every principal town (*summo portu* there should be three, and in every other town there should be one. Another ordinance of the same king (III Æthelred 16 and IV Æthelred 5, 4) declared that moneyers who worked in woods or elsewhere (in secret) should forfeit their lives unless the king was willing to pardon them. Cnut also issued ordinances for the reform of the coinage, and in his reign and his predecessor's the old stringent penalties imposed on those who should debase the coinage were maintained and even increased (III Æthelred 8, IV Æthelred 5, 3, II Cnut 8–8, 2).

Evidence as to the mint-places in the reign of the Confessor is to be found in the inscriptions on coins and in Domesday entries. Brooke (*op. cit.* i. clx) remarks that seventy-three mints are known to have been in operation in the reign of the Confessor as against sixty-seven in the reign of William I. These statistics differ somewhat from those given by Liebermann, s.v. ' Münze ', where further information will be found.

(26)

AUTHORITIES :—B.M. Royal MS. I D. ix, f. 44 b, cent. late xi. Printed H. Wanley, *Antiquæ Litteraturæ Septentrionalis Liber Alter* (Oxford, 1705). p. 181 b (not quite accurately), and (following Wanley) K. 731, Thorpe p. 308. Also, with some inaccuracies, J. O. Westwood, *Palæographia Sacra Pictoria* (London, 1843–45), in section : ' The Latin Gospels of King Canute '. Manuscript described by Wanley, *ut supra*. See also on the manuscript, Warner and Gilson, *Catalogue of the Western MSS. in the Old Royal and King's Collections* (British Museum, 1921), 17–18 ; E. G. Millar, *English Illuminated Manuscripts from the xth to the xiiith century* (Paris and Brussels, 1926), 75, and the references there. Dr. Millar assigns this volume to cent. early xi, and suggests that it was executed for, and probably at, Christ Church, in the Winchester style. See also M. R. James, *The Ancient Libraries of Canterbury and Dover*, 524–30.

On the authenticity of the writ see pp. 168 ff.

DATE. Between the appointment of Thurkill as earl of East Anglia in 1017, and the death of Archbishop Lyfing on 12 June 1020.

l. 2. *Scirman.* Of the terms *scirman* and *scirgerefa*, both applied to Æthelwine (see Biographical Notes), the former falls into disuse. In the second half of the tenth century the title *scirigman* is used of an official, in this case a priest, presiding over a shire court (Robertson no. 41 = K. 1288) between c. 964 and 988. A little later, 995–1005, we hear of the *sciresman* Leofric (*ibid.* no. 69 = K. 929). The earliest appearance of the term *scirgerefa* belongs to the time of Cnut. On the *gerefa* associated with a *scir* already in the time of Æthelstan, see Stenton, *Anglo-Saxon England*, 540 ; and on the development of the title and the functions of the county sheriff, who ' does not come plainly into sight ' until the reign of Æthelred II, see the references given, p. 48, n. 2.

l. 2. *Twelfhynde 7 twihynde.* *Twelfhynde*, adj, ' having a wergeld of twelve hundred shillings '; similarly, *twihynde*, ' having a wergeld of two hundred shillings '. The *twihynde* man was of the rank of *ceorl*, the *twelfhynde* of the nobility ; compare the address of Cnut's Proclamation of 1020 (for references see p. 17, n. 1) : ' ealle his eorlas 7 ealne his þeodscype, *twelfhynde* 7 *twyhynde*, gehadode 7 lǣwede, on Englalande ', ' all his earls and all his subjects in England, *nobles and commoners*, ecclesiastics and laymen '. On the terms in question and for other references, see BT, and Liebermann, ii. 215 f. On the special meaning of these terms in this writ, see pp. 169 f.

l. 4. *Heo hǣfð nu lǣsse munde . . . ǣr hǣfde.* For *mund* used of persons, ' protector, guardian ', see no. 2. *Mund* also signifies ' protection, guardianship ', as it does here and in no. 74. On the king's *mund*, and the penalty for the violation of *mund*, see p. 80. In VI Æthelred 14, and I Cnut 2, 1–5 (and also in ' Edward and Guthrum ', 1) it is declared that the protection given by a church within its walls (*ælc cyricgrið binnan wagum*), and the protection granted by the king in person (*cyninges handgrið*) are to remain equally inviolate ; while the code of Cnut referred to declares that when homicide is committed within the walls of a church, compensation (in certain circumstances) shall be made for the violation of the protection of the church (*cyricgrið*) by the payment to the church in question of a sum equivalent to the breach of the king's own *mund* (*be cyninges fullan mundbryce*). But in VIII Æthelred 5 a distinction is made between the violation of the protection of a principal church (*heafodmynstres griðbryce*)—to which category Christ Church would undoubtedly belong—and that of churches of inferior status in civil law, where the compensation would be correspondingly less, according to their individual status, than the five pounds paid in districts under English law to churches of the highest rank. It seems clear that in Cnut's writ *mund* stands for the protection extended by Christ Church to those within its walls. In the tractate called *Grið* by Liebermann (i. 470 ff., rubric : *Be griðe and be munde*), we read : ' Hwilum wǣran heafodstedas and healice hadas micelre mǣðe and munde wyrðe and griðian mihton þa þe þæs beðorfton and þǣrto sohtan, aa be ðǣre mǣðe þe þǣrto gebyrede.' (' Chief places and exalted ranks were once entitled to great respect, and they were entitled to afford protection (*mund*), and could give sanctuary (*grið*) to those who needed it and repaired thereto, ever according to the dignity that belonged thereto '.) The *heafodstede* of this tractate, like the *heafodmynster* of Cnut's code, stands no doubt for ' cathedral ' or ' abbey ' (Liebermann iii. 265)—churches of the highest status. We may also compare a dubious charter of Chertsey Abbey (K. 844, on which see p. 205, n. 1), in which the Confessor is made to grant to the abbey 10 hides of land at (White) Waltham and the church of the same vill and other property, and to declare that the abbot and monks are to have and hold the vill as their right ' with as much *mund* ' as the king himself has (*mid alsua muchele munde alsua on meseluen stant*). Here again *mund* clearly stands for the protection extended by a religious house to other persons.

l. 5. *He moste niwne freols settan on minan naman.* *Freols* is used in Anglo-Saxon charters in the sense of : (i) Freedom, i.e. from the interference of other authorities, or from taxation or services or other burdens ; for a general discussion of the principle, see Hoops, *Reallexikon*, ii. 597 ff. s.v. ' Immunität '. (ii) A charter of freedom. For instances in charters see Robertson, *Anglo-Saxon Charters*, Index. *Niwan freols settan* is rendered in BT s.v. *freols*, 1, ' institute a new privilege '. But what does this mean ? What ' new privilege ' was the archbishop to institute, and why is this privilege not defined ? It seems much more likely that *freols* here means ' a charter of freedom ', and that *settan* means not ' institute ', but ' draw up '; compare

BT and Suppt, s.v. *settan*, XIII : ' to compose ' (a book). Compare Robertson no. 83 : *se cyng het þone arcebisceop þærto boc settan*, ' the king ordered the archbishop to draw up a charter about this '. See further Introduction, p. 35.

l. 9. *To ðan ylcan foreweardan þe hit Æpelbyrht cing gefreode . . . foregencgan.* No charters of kings earlier than Cnut purporting to grant privileges to Christ Church, Canterbury, appear to have survived. For references to the fire at Canterbury shortly after the Conquest, see p. 167.

l. 13. *Butan he hit þe stiðlicor gebete . . . be þæs arcebisceopes tæcincge.* On the first part of this passage, see Introduction, p. 69. For references in the legal codes to the prescription of compensation by a bishop, see VIII Æthelred 27 (= I Cnut, 5, 3), and also Cnut's Proclamation of 1020, § 9 ; for references in charters, compare Robertson no. 82. For extant penitential letters issued by Wulfstan as bishop of London and as archbishop, and by Archbishop Ælfric, see *Eng. Hist. Rev.* x (1895), 712 ff.

(27)

AUTHORITIES :—(Du) The Gospels of MacDurnan at Lambeth Palace, f. 69 b, cent. early xi, printed here. Hand probably fairly close in date to that of document. Printed, Earle p. 232. According to an entry in the volume these Gospels once belonged to Maelbright mac Durnan, abbot of Armagh and of Raphoe, and afterwards of Hy or Iona, who died in 927. The volume was acquired (perhaps after the abbot's death) by King Æthelstan, who gave it to Christ Church. There charters were copied into it, of which the latest that can be dated, an agreement between Archbishop Eadsige and a certain Toki (Robertson no. 90, see also *ibid.* no. 80), belongs to the period 1038–50. On this volume see E. G. Millar, *Les Principaux manuscrits à peintures du Lambeth Palace à Londres* (Paris, 1924), 7–15, and Plate I, an extract, printed separately, from the *Bulletin de 1924 de la Société française de reproductions de manuscrits à peintures* (Paris, 1924), and the references there. See also M. R. James and Claude Jenkins, *Catalogue of Manuscripts in Lambeth Palace* (Cambridge, 1930), 843–4 ; and for the Anglo-Saxon entries, the Appendix to the *Thirty-Fourth Report of the Deputy Keeper of the Public Records* (1873), 271–3. The difficult Latin inscription recording the association of the volume with Maelbright mac Durnan was elucidated by J. Armitage Robinson, *The Times of St. Dunstan* (Oxford, 1923), 55–9.

(Mo) B.M. Add. MS. 14907, pp. 6–7, copies by Lewis Morris (1700–65, see DNB). Printed : K. 1314, and *Saxons in England*, ii. 382, n. 2 ; Thorpe p. 313.

On the authenticity of this writ see p. 171.

DATE. Following the consecration of Æthelnoth on 13 November 1020.

l. 1. *þa hlæfdian.* For other instances of the style of ' Lady ' applied in accordance with contemporary usage to the king's wife, see nos. 70, 72, 79, 112. The witnessing clause of no. 61, in which the title ' cwen ' appears, applied to Edith, is not authentic. On the coronation of King Edgar in 973 and the *ordo* providing for the anointing of the queen and her investiture with crown and ring, see P. E. Schramm, *A History of the English Coronation*, trans. from German by L. G. Wickham Legg (Oxford, 1937), 22, where it is remarked that ' of course it was some time before the ideas underlying this ceremony were established among the Anglo-Saxons ', and that ' as late as the year 1000 it was not an understood thing that the queen should receive a crown at all '. The titles of the king's wife are also discussed by W. H. Stevenson, *Asser's*

Life of King Alfred, 200–2.   See also A. Campbell, *Encomium Emmæ* (Cam. Soc. 1949), 58 ff.

l. 2.   *Þæt we habbað gedon swa swa us swutelung fram eow com æt þam biscope. Æþelnope, þæt we habbað hine nu gebletsod.*   *Swutelung* (*sweotolung*), originally a vague word, ' manifestation ' ; cf. *swutelian*, ' to make clear, manifest, show, declare '.   The substantive is defined in BT s.v. *sweotolung*, in such contexts as the above, as ' evidence, testimony, declaration ', and (when written), ' testament, title-deed, certificate, prescript '.   In this passage it is rendered in BT ' evidence of your wish, mandate '.   Lingard (*History and Antiquities of the Anglo-Saxon Church* (1845), i. 94, n. 1) rendered the passage : ' that we have done to Bishop Æthelnoth as came to us in the *order* from you ; that we have consecrated him '.   I prefer on the whole Kemble's rendering (*Saxons in England*, ii. 302), ' notice ' ; or possibly ' declaration '.   It does not seem probable, from the indefiniteness of the reference, that Æthelnoth had received from King Cnut a *gewrit and insegel* ordering that the archbishop should consecrate him, as did Spearhafoc from King Edward in 1048 (see Appendix IV. 6).   Was this procedure unusual ?   The whole episode in which Spearhafoc was involved was remarkable, for Archbishop Robert refused to carry out the king's order ; see *Chron.* E 1048 and Stenton, *Anglo-Saxon England*, 461.   For other instances of the use of *swutelung* in writs, see nos. 24, 39.

Kemble rendered the passage : ' that we have done as notice came from you to us respecting bishop Æðelwold (a slip for Æðelnoth), namely that we have now consecrated him '.   This involves the consideration of the reference of the preposition *æt* in *æt þam biscope Æþelnope*.   BT Suppt, s.v. *æt*, 3 d, is probably right in taking this as an instance of *æt*, ' marking the object on which action takes effect ', i.e. ' done to ', and not ' done in respect of '.

l. 5.   *Ge witan on Gode þa mæþe.*   Kemble and Thorpe (wrongly) print as : *gewitan on Gode ðam æðe*, not recognising the expression *mæþe witan* ' show respect to '.   For another instance see the *Sermo Lupi ad Anglos* by this same Archbishop Wulfstan (ed. D. Whitelock, London, 1939), p. 33, l. 84 : *gif man on Godes griðe mæþe witan wolde* ; see also BT s.v. *mæþ*.

(28)

AUTHORITIES :—(Du) as for no. 27, f. 114 b, in an almost contemporary hand.   Facsimile and text (not quite accurate) : J. O. Westwood, *Palæographia Sacra Pictoria* (London, 1843–45), p. 12 and Plate 14.   Printed : Kemble, *Archæological Journal*, liii (1857), p. 61 ; Earle p. 232 ; F. Zinkeisen, *Die Anfänge der Lehnsgerichtsbarkeit in England* (Berlin, 1893), p. 6 (from Earle).   Not in Kemble's *Codex Diplomaticus*.   Modern English rendering: J. Goebel, Jr. *Felony and Misdemeanor*, i. 364, n. 96.
(Mo) as for no. 27, p. 9, two copies.

On the authenticity of this writ see p. 171, and for an explanation of the legal terms employed see Introduction, pp. 73–82.

DATE.   Shortly after Æthelnoth's consecration on 13 November 1020.   It seems natural to connect it with Wulfstan's request in no. 27.

l. 1.   *Mine gerefan.*   On the position and duties of the king's reeve, see Morris, *The Med. Eng. Sheriff* (the term ' king's reeve' and ' sheriff' not being synonymous) ; see also Liebermann, *Gesetze*, ii. 98, s.v. ' Gerefa ', ii. 481, s.v. ' Grafschaft ' ; and Introduction, pp. 48 ff.

l. 6.   *Ofer swa feala þegna swa ic him to lætan hæbbe.*   Cf. no. 38 (authentic) : *ofer swa feole þegna swa ic hiom habba to gelæten* ; and Latin version : *super omnes allodiarios quos eis habeo datos.*   For other instances, see nos. 33, 36. It was laid down in the third code of Æthelred II (III Æthelred 11) that ' no

one shall have jurisdiction over a thegn of the king except the king himself '
(nan man nage nane socne ofer cynges þegen buton cyng sylf). The idea
expressed in the clause under discussion is that the king has transferred
judicial and financial rights over certain of his thegns in the one case (no. 28)
to the archbishop, in the other (no. 38) to the abbot of St. Augustine's. Such
thegns are therefore said to have been 'granted' to them, (ge)læten, cf.
BT Suppt, s.v. læten, I (7), (8), ' to allow to have, to grant temporary possession
of ', and in the Latin version to have been ' given '. Further, from a long
passage on the customs of Kent on the first page of Domesday Book we learn
that the king had in 1086 (and undoubtedly in Anglo-Saxon times) certain
forfeitures over all the alodiarii of Kent and over their men, as well as a relief
on the death of an alodiarius, except on the land of Holy Trinity (Christ
Church, Canterbury), St. Augustine (of Canterbury), and St. Martin (? of
Dover), and the land of eight secular magnates (named). As the judicial and
financial rights named in these writs were granted by the king, the thegns of
the two great Canterbury churches could very well be described as ' those whom
I have granted them to have ', that is, ' those thegns the profits of whose
forfeitures I have transferred from myself to them '. For further information
about these alodiaries see Maitland, Domesday Book and Beyond, 153–4,
Vinogradoff, English Society in the Eleventh century, 236 f., 405, 412. They
seem to have been a special variety of the large and miscellaneous thegnly
class, and in Domesday occur only in Kent, Sussex, Hampshire and one or two
other counties. For post-Conquest writs employing the same phraseology, see
pp. 174–5. See also J. A. Jolliffe, ' Alod and Fee ', Camb. Hist. Journ. v
(1935–37), no. 3, 225 ff. ; Carl Stephenson, Eng. Hist. Rev. liv (1944), 295 f.

l. 10. Be minum freondscipe. On this see Introduction, p. 68, n. 1.

(29)

AUTHORITIES :—(T) Cott. Tib. B. iv (the so-called D (Worcester) text of the
Anglo-Saxon Chronicle), f. 87b, in an almost contemporary hand, which seems
to be identical with that of no. 30. Printed : G. Hickes, Linguarum Veterum
Septentrionalium Thesaurus (Oxford, 1705), i. 163, footnote ; K. 1323, Thorpe
p. 330 ; Earle p. 237 (the two latter from K.). On the possible origin of the
folio on which nos. 29, 30, are copied, see Wanley, Antiquæ Literaturæ
Septentrionalis Liber Alter (Oxford, 1705), 220, and M. R. James, The Ancient
Libraries of Canterbury and Dover (Cambridge, 1903), 524. Wanley suggested that the folio may originally have formed part of a volume of the
Gospels (MS. 194) at St. John's College, Oxford.

On the authenticity of this writ see pp. 171 f.

DATE. Between the appointment of Eadsige as bishop at St. Martin's in
1035, and the death of Cnut on 12 November in the same year.

l. 3. Werige his landare into his bisceoprice. Werige, from werian ' to
defend ' (cf. the Domesday phrase se defendere (pro)), with land, landare, and
words of similar meaning, is used in the technical sense of ' discharge the
obligations on, answer the claims on ', i.e. with regard to the payments and
services which might be exacted by the king from the holder of the land. For
these, see pp. 459 f.

(30)

AUTHORITIES :—(T) as for no. 29, f. 87. Printed : K. 1325 ; Earle p. 237
(from K.).

On the authenticity of this writ see p. 172.

DATE. As for no. 29.

(31)

AUTHORITIES :—(L) Lambeth MS. 1212, p. 16, a single parchment sheet tacked on to p. 17 of this manuscript. Text written in a hand of cent. xv. Unprinted. On this manuscript see M. R. James and Claude Jenkins, *Catalogue of the Manuscripts in the Library of Lambeth Palace*, pp. 828 ff. On the authenticity of this writ see p. 178, and on the legal terms employed see Introduction, pp. 73–82.

DATE. The date of an authentic writ with this address would be after Edward's accession in 1042 and within one of Eadsige's two periods of office as archbishop, namely, 1038–44, 1048–50. But the authenticity of this text is extremely doubtful.

l. 7. *On strande 7 on streame.* For *strand*, see nos. 1, 75, and the notes there given. For *on streame*, compare in App. IV, no. 5 : *ge on gafole ge on streame ge on strande ge on witun*, and also, in a charter (K. 726) attributed to King Edmund Ironside, which may or may not be authentic, *theolonium aquarum*. The king had a variety of rights on water and on waterways. At Southwark, for instance, King Edward had two parts of the dues of the stream (*de exitu aquæ*) and Earl Godwine the third (DB i. 32, VCH *Surrey*, i. 305). King Cnut possessed and granted to Christ Church, Canterbury (if the relevant charter is authentic), the haven at Sandwich and all the landing places, and the water dues from both sides of the river (*stream*) (Robertson no. 82). See further Liebermann ii. 730, s.v. ' Wasser ', and J. Hoops, *Reallexikon*, iv. 487, s.v. ' Wasserstrassen '.

l. 14. *Has consuetudines. Consuetudines*, ' customs ', i.e. things or matters customary, has many connotations ; for its various significations in the Laws, see Liebermann, *Gesetze*, ii. 40, s.v. *consuetudo*, and for its meanings in Domesday Book, Goebel, *Felony and Misdemeanor*, i. 379, n. 150. In the writ under discussion, as also in nos. 34, 36, *consuetudines* (like its equivalent *gerihta*, for which see p. 441) refers back to the judicial and financial rights enumerated earlier in the text ; for other instances of the use of *consuetudines* with reference to such royal *gerihta*, see *Cartæ Antiquæ*, Rolls 1-10, ed. L. Landon, Pipe Roll Society, N.S. xvii (1939), nos. 49, 50, 52, 64. *Consuetudines* is also used of customary rights ; e.g. *Chron. Abingdon*, ii. 1, in a writ of William I, *omnes consuetudines terrarum suarum* ; and like *gerihta* can stand for customary services and payments in money and in kind due from one person to another ; e.g. *ibid.* ii. 26, in a writ of William II, ' ecclesiam . . . cum terris et decimis et *consuetudinibus* ' ; *ibid.* ii. 95, in one of Henry I, ' *suas consuetudines* in navibus transeuntibus, scilicet in accipiendis allecibus et in mercatis faciendis '. Further, the term *consuetudinibus* may refer to taxes and other public burdens ; e.g. *Chron. Abingdon*, ii. 94, of Henry I : ' *de omnibus consuetudinibus meis*, scilicet de geldis et placitis et aliis rebus '. See further Maitland, *Domesday Book and Beyond*, 76 ff.

(32)

AUTHORITIES :—(L) as for no. 31, p. 332, of about the end of cent. xiii. Unprinted.
On the authenticity of this writ see pp. 178 ff.
DATE. As for no. 31.

(33)

AUTHORITIES :—(Ch) B.M. Campbell Charter xxi. 5, in two hands of cent. xi, printed here. A photograph is reproduced here as Plate 1. Facsimile and text : *Facs. of Anc. Chart. in the Brit. Mus.* ed. Bond, pt. iv, after no. 37. Printed : W. de Gray Birch, *Trans. R. Soc. Lit.* 2nd Series, x (1874), 146. Not in Kemble's *Codex.* The first hand, of the time of the Confessor, wrote up to and including *beon* in l. 4. The text after *beon* was washed out and written over by a hand not earlier in date than cent. late xi, which continued to the end of the text. The earlier text has been almost entirely expunged after *beon*, and although traces of letters are still visible, nothing can be recovered, even under ultra-violet rays. Dimensions of parchment : 7⅝" broad, 3¾" deep on left side, 3⅝" on right. Seal of hard yellowish-red wax, apparently varnished, very imperfect, with edges rubbed away, and outlines blurred, appended *sur simple queue* to the parchment ; there is also a wrapping tag. Seal described by Birch, *ut supra*, p. 145 (2), with two Plates ; see also *Cat. of Seals in the Brit. Mus.* i (1887), p. 3 (12), and Wyon's *Great Seals* (1887), p. 3 (7, 8), Plate 1 (7, 8). Everything encourages the belief that this is an original writ of King Edward which has been tampered with, and that the first three lines of the writ were written, and the seal appended, by the clerks of the Confessor's secretariat. A handwriting very similar to that of the new material in this writ and in C. 4 (see p. 173, n. 3) appears in the annals for 1031 and 1070 of *Chron.* A.

(I) D. and C. Lib. Canterbury, Reg. I, f. 58, cent. late xiii.

(Pa) Patent Roll 12 Henry VI, p. 2, m. 9. Printed : *Cal. of P.R.* 1429–36, 415.

(M) Conf. Roll 4 Henry VII, p. 1, m. 14.

(N) Conf. Roll 1 Henry VIII, p. 3, m. 9.

On the authenticity of the writ see pp. 173 ff., and on the legal terms employed see Introduction, pp. 73 ff.

DATE. The three opening lines up to and including *beon* belong to a writ issued between the flight of Robert of Jumièges, the predecessor of Stigand in the see of Canterbury, in September 1052, and the death of King Edward on 5 January 1066. But the writ as a whole is a composite document, and cannot therefore be dated.

(34)

AUTHORITIES :—

i. English :

(C) Dean and Chapter Library, Canterbury, C. 3, in a hand of c. 1100. The text is written on a single piece of parchment, dimensions : 11" by 3⅝" on left side, 2 11/16" on right. Facsimile : F. E. Harmer, *Bulletin of the John Rylands Library*, xxii (1938), and reprint, Manchester, 1938. No seal, but a deep ' step ' in the middle of the lower edge may indicate earlier sealing. Lower edge of parchment torn, and the broken edges drawn together with rough stitches. Right-hand edge of parchment worn and chipped, and words missing at the end of each line. The date of the hand forbids us to suppose that we have in this document an original writ written by the clerks of King Edward's secretariat, and the evidence of the linguistic forms—many of which indicate a later date than the Confessor's time—corroborates that of the date of the hand. Further there is internal evidence to suggest that this is not an authentic copy of an original writ of the Confessor ; see pp. 176 f. above. Owing to its lacunæ this text has not been printed here. N (below) resembles it closely, and, blunders apart (corrected in footnotes to text) differs from it only in about ten spellings : e.g. streame, stræme ; flæmene, flamene ; hæbbað, habbað ; dyrstig, dirstig. Text unprinted.

(D) D. and C. Lib. Canterbury, Roll C. 204, no. i, cent. xiii.

(I) as for no. 33, f. 58.

(E) D. and C. Lib. Reg. E, f. 53 b, c. 1300.

(A) *Ibid.* Reg. A, f. 158 b, cent. xiv.

(G) B.M. Add. MS. 6159, f. 7 (*ol.* 6), cent. xiv.

(Pa) as for no. 33.

(M) as for no. 33.

(N) as for no. 33, printed here.   See further above, under C.   This text is apparently an independent copy, and is not directly derived from M, above.

ii. Latin :

(Th) A copy in ' Evidentiæ ecclesiæ Christi Cant.' in the Thorne MS. in the Library of Corpus Christi College, Cambridge, this section being in a hand of cent. xii (M. R. James, *Cat. of the MSS. in the Library of Corpus Christi College, Cambridge* (1912), i. 451).   On Thorne, see p. 192, n. 2.   Printed : R. Twysden, *Historiae Anglicanae Scriptores*, x (London, 1652), col. 2224. The reference is MS. 189, f. 201.

(D) as for D above, no. xvii, printed here.

(A) as for A above, f. 90, no. 235.   Printed K. 909, with second reference to H below ; Pierquin, *Chartes Anglo-Saxonnes*, p. 828, no. 68, from K.

(P) Reg. P, f. 26, cent. xiv.

(L) Lambeth MS. 1212, p. 330, roughly contemporary with the register copies.

(G) as for G above, f. 10 (*ol.* 9).

(H) Harley MS. 1757, f. 172, second half of cent. xvi (before 1588).

(S) Cott. Cleop. E. i, f. 88, cent. xvii.

On the authenticity of this writ see pp. 175 ff. and on the legal terms employed see Introduction, pp. 73–82.

DATE.   The date of an authentic writ for Archbishop Stigand would be between 1052, the date of his appointment, and 1066, the date of Edward's death.   But the authenticity of this writ is more than dubious.

l. 7.   *Tolnes.*   For *toln*, from the same root as *toll*, see BT, and for other instances, see no. 117.

(35)

AUTHORITIES :—

i. English :

(Cd) Cott. Claud. A. iii, f. 5 b (*ol.* 4 b), cent. late xi, printed here.   Printed : *Mon. Angl.* i. 99, no. vi ; K. 847.   In both these printed texts the names of five witnesses have been wrongly affixed to this writ.   The witnesses belong in reality to a charter of Æthelred II.   The writ is copied in a space at the foot of the verso of a folio, the names of the five witnesses being written at the head of the recto of the following folio.   The mistake may have arisen from the fact that the name of Siward appears twice, first in Æthelred's charter, in proximity to the writ, and then in the writ itself.   The identity of the two Siwards is on chronological grounds improbable.   There is no real connection between the two texts.   The writ is written in a paler (or more faded ink), in a hand that is different from that of Æthelred's charter, though the two hands may be roughly contemporary.   Kemble, not observing this, and having attached the five names to the writ, (wrongly) omits them from the vernacular version of Æthelred's charter, but includes them in printing the Latin version.   See K. 715.   For a suggestion that the leaves on which this and other charters in Cd are copied, originally belonged to Cott. Tib. A. ii., a Gospel Book given by King Æthelstan to Christ Church, see N. R. Ker, *Brit. Mus. Quart.* xii (1938), 130 f.

ii. Latin :

(Th) as for no. 34.

(Cr) D. and C. Lib. Canterbury, Reg. C, no. 237, cent. xiii/xiv, printed here. Printed : Historical Manuscripts Commission, *Eighth Report*, App. p. 328.

(P) as for no. 34, f. 26 b.

(L) as for no. 31, p. 332, roughly contemporary with Cr.

(S) as for no. 34, f. 88 b.

On the authenticity of this writ see pp. 180 f., and on ' sake and soke ' see Introduction, pp. 73 ff.

DATE. After the appointment of Harold to the earldom, which included Kent, of his father Earl Godwine, who died on 15 April 1053 ; and before the death of Abbot Wulfric on 18 April 1061. The date of 1051 given in Cr to the Latin version of this writ cannot be correct. Was 1051 the date of the grant by Sigweard and his wife ?

l. 3. *Æt Merseham.* Mersham, Kent. The manor of. Mersham is described in the Exchequer Domesday (DB i. 3 b, VCH *Kent*, iii. 212) as a manor which the archbishop himself holds in demesne. In the time of King Edward it was assessed at 7 sulungs, in 1086 at 3 ; there was land for 12 ploughs. ' On the demesne are 3 ploughs and 39 villeins with 9 bordars who have 16 ploughs. A church is there and 2 mills worth 5 shillings, and 2 saltpans worth 5 shillings, and 13 acres of meadow, and woodland (to render) 30 pigs.' The value of the manor had increased from 10 pounds in King Edward's time and afterwards, to 20 pounds in 1086. For the account given of this manor in the Domesday Monachorum, see D. C. Douglas' edition, 91. In Latin versions of this writ (on which see p. 180) reference is made (as it is elsewhere, see Robertson no. 10 = B. 496) to the *pratis, siluis, marascis,* at Mersham, but these do not appear in the Anglo-Saxon text. Mersham appears in the list of estates appended to the Chartham charter attributed to the Confessor ; see p. 175, n. 5.

l. 6. *þæt se dom stande þe mine ðegenas gedemdan.* Compare no. 79 : *alswa swa hyo gedemde waron on þam nigon sciran on Wendelbury.* Nothing seems to be known concerning this judgment of the king's thegns, given presumably at a meeting of the shire court. In the shire court the judgment was given by the suitors, namely, those persons who were present by custom ; and this was so in the other Anglo-Saxon communal courts. On meetings of the shire court, see Introduction, pp. 46–53.

(36)

AUTHORITIES :—(Cl) Cott. Claud. D. x, f. 57, first half of cent. xiv, printed here. Printed : *Mon. Angl.* i. 139, no. xxxvi ; K. 756 ; Thorpe p. 336. Strokes resembling an acute accent placed in this manuscript over the letter *i*, chiefly in the neighbourhood of *n, m, u,* but also in other positions, have not been reproduced in the texts printed here ; compare note on p. 433.

(Ad) Add. MS. 29437, f. 90, a paper copy of mid. cent. xvii.

On the authenticity of the writ see pp. 190–1, and on the legal terms employed see Introduction, pp. 73–82.

DATE. Since there is no reason to suppose that this writ represents an authentic writ of Cnut it is not dated here.

l. 9. *Super omnes allodiarios quos eis habeo datos.* On this, see p. 450.

(37)

AUTHORITIES :—(B) Cott. Jul. D. ii, f. 85 b, cent. xiii, printed here. Printed : Dodsworth and Dugdale, *Monasticon Anglicanum,* i (1655), 84 ; 1846 ed. i. 449, no. ii (with a second reference to Q below).

(Q) Cartæ Antiquæ Roll I, no. 19 ; copy in Harley MS. 84, f. 101 b. On these see p. 439.

(O) Excheq. K.R. Misc. Bks. Series i, no. 27, f. 148 b, cent. late xiii/early xiv.

(Ed) D. and C. Lib. E. 19, f. 1 (*ol.* 13). According to a note in the manuscript the transcriber started transcribing the muniments of Minster (of which this writ is the first) in 1311.

(Cl) as for no. 36, f. 185, early cent. xiv.

(R) Ch. R. 20 Edw. II, m. 2, no. 6 (*Cal. of Ch. R.* iii. 492). Copy in Cl. above, f. 63, cent. xiv. Printed : K. 1326 ; H. Bresslau, *Diplomata Centum* (Berlin, 1872), no. 91, from K.

(W) Ch. R. 36 Edw. III, no. 3 (*Cal. of Ch. R.* v. 175).

(X) *Ibid.* 8 Hen. IV, no. 1 (*Cal. of Ch. R.* v. 433).

(Y) Pat. R. 2 Hen. VI, p. 3, m. 5 (*Cal. of P.R.* 1422–29, 215).

(Z) *Ibid.* 4 Edw. IV, p. 4, m. 29 (*ibid.* 1461–67, 403).

(Th) Copies in Thorne MS. (for which see no. 34), cent. xiv ; Twysden, col. 1783, without protocol and penal clause, col. 2127, in full, from W. Mod. Eng. rendering, A. H. Davis, *Wm. Thorne's Chron. of St. Aug. Cant.* (1934), 43, 571 ; see also *ibid.* xxix, on MS. A (inaccessible to me).

On the authenticity of this writ see pp. 191–7.

DATE. The date of Cnut's grant of the body of St. Mildred to St. Augustine's is given as 1027 by Thorne (col. 1783) and the other authorities of St. Augustine's, and that of 1030 for the translation of the relics to their church (Thorne *ibid.*). The actual journey of Cnut to Rome in 1027 is given its place between the two events in the chronicles of St. Augustine's ; on this journey see Liebermann's notes on Cnut's Proclamation of 1027 (*Gesetze,* iii. 189–92), and pp. 17, 101 above. On this evidence an authentic writ of Cnut notifying the grant would have been issued between 1027, the date of the grant in the traditions of St. Augustine's, and 1035, the date of Cnut's death. But the authenticity of this writ is uncertain. Thorne (a late authority) dates this actual writ in 1027.

l. 1. *Per Dei misericordiam basileus.* On *basileus*, which is frequently used in the styles of kings in charters, at any rate from the reign of Edmund onwards, see *Crawford Charters*, 110, 137. A charter (K. 750) in the name of Cnut copied in the Codex Wintoniensis, which may be genuine (see p. 552) employs the style *misericordia Dei basileus omnis Britanniæ regimen adeptus.* But reference to the vernacular writs of Cnut printed here (which begin : *Cnut cyng* etc.) shows that this style would not have been used in a close translation of an authentic writ of Cnut. The style ' basileus ' appears on seals of King Edward the Confessor. On the possibility that this style (as early as Æthelstan's reign) may be due to Byzantine influence, see R. S. Lopez, *Byzantion*, 18 (1946–48), 139 ff.

l. 4. *Sčo Augustino patrono meo.* Cnut's devotion to St. Augustine and to the monastery which he founded is enlarged upon by Goscelin, who in his ' Historia Major de Miraculis S. Augustini ' (see p. 191, n. 4) tells how Cnut on his voyage home from Rome escaped shipwreck by invoking St. Augustine, several of whose miracles, as Hardy remarks, relate to escape from shipwreck. The probable reasons for the king's devotion, as Goscelin conceived of them, are analysed in the Textus Translationis, cap. 6 : His veneration for the monastery itself, as one pre-eminent in his kingdom, his gratitude for the favours (*beneficia*) received from St. Augustine in the past, and his realisation that the abbey must have been under powerful protection when he considered that, while many other monasteries had suffered in the Danish invasions, it had remained unharmed. Cnut's particular regard for the monastery of St. Augustine was supposed to have been shown by his choice of bishops and heads of other houses from among its inmates (see Thorne col. 1782). But no contemporary evidence as to Cnut's special devotion to the saint seems to be forthcoming, and the description of St. Augustine as *patrono meo* in this writ, and the traditions of St. Augustine's as they appear for instance, in the writings of Goscelin, are not necessarily independent, the one of the other.

l. 4. *Corpus Sēe Mildriþe*. The body of St. Mildred, first buried in the church dedicated to St. Mary (on the site of or near the present parish church of Minster), built by her mother, the foundress of the nunnery, was afterwards reverently removed by Abbess Eadburh, the successor of St. Mildred, to a new church dedicated to St. Peter and St. Paul. On their translation in 1030 to the church of St. Augustine's, at Canterbury, her remains are supposed to have been enshrined in the choir, before the high altar, and to have been removed subsequently more than once (Thorne col. 1783–5, 1912). Her remains, or a portion of them, are said to have been taken at some unknown period to Holland, where a cult of St. Mildred of Thanet grew up in the diocese of Utrecht (for references see W. Levison, *England and the Continent in the Eighth Century*, 82, n. 2). The cult of St. Mildred has been revived in Thanet, and a small relic of the saint is said to have been brought there in 1882 when a convent dedicated in her name was founded at Minster (R. Stanton, *A Menology of England and Wales* (London, 1887) 333). The present Roman Catholic church of St. Mildred at Minster claims to possess a relic of the saint. On this see Dom Gregory Bish, O.S.B., *Minster Abbey* (1947), 17.

l. 5. *Cum tota terra sua infra insulam de Tenet 7 extra*. A number of charters have been preserved relating to alleged grants of land and privileges to the nunnery of Minster. Of these some purport to belong to the early days of the nunnery, beginning with a grant by Oswine, king of the Kentishmen (*Cantuariorum*) of land at Sturry (B. 35). Other charters attributed to early kings of Kent and to the Mercian kings Æthelbald and Offa, in favour of the abbesses Æbbe and Mildred and their successors, relate to grants of land, of the dues of ships, and of immunity from customs. The early Minster charters printed by John Lewis in a Supplement to his *History and Antiquities of the Isle of Tenet* (2nd ed. London, 1736), no. xxxii, 54–67, were headed by him *cartulæ fictitiæ*, and all those printed by Kemble were starred by him as spurious. It was however observed by Stubbs (*Dict. Christ. Biog.* iii. 914, s.n. Mildred) that although these charters are questionable, the nunnery may possibly have enjoyed the immunities supposed to have been guaranteed by them. In more recent years a plea for a careful reconsideration of Kemble's condemnation has been made by Mr. G. J. Turner and Dr. H. E. Salter, *The Register of St. Augustine's Abbey*, i. xvii–xxxix, where these charters are discussed in detail. Some of the possessions of the nunnery are said to have been lost at the end of the eighth century in the time of the fourth abbess Sigeburga (died 797), and the efforts of her successor to increase the number of the nuns and to recover some of the lands of her church were frustrated by the destruction of the nunnery by the Danes (Elmham, pp. 221–2). The nunnery may have been rebuilt but no records of subsequent grants to it appear to be forthcoming. According to the traditions of St. Augustine's one part of the lands of St. Mildred's was, at a time when the translation of her body was being proposed, in private hands, while the other part had come into the king's possession (Goscelin's 'Textus Translationis', cap. 6–9, Thorne col. 1909). Domesday, with reference to the Thanet hundred of St. Mildred (DB i. 12, VCH *Kent*, iii. 243), records that the abbot of St. Augustine's himself holds Thanet, a manor assessed at 48 sulungs. 'There is land there for 62 ploughs; on the demesne there are 2, and 150 villeins with 50 bordars have 63 ploughs. There is a church there and a priest who gives 20 shillings yearly. There are

1 salt-pan and 2 fisheries worth 3 pence, and 1 mill. . . . As much of the land of the villeins of this manor as is worth 9 pounds when there is peace in the country 3 knights (*milites*) hold, and there they have 3 ploughs '.

As to the Minster charters, Miss Whitelock has told me that in her opinion too much attention has been given above to opinions hostile to their authenticity, and that a large proportion (including B. 40, 41, 42, 44, 86, 88, 96, 141, 149) are probably authentic.   B. 35 may be authentic, but the date should be 690 (not 675).

l. 6. *Cum omnibus consuetudinibus ad suam ecclesiam pertinentibus.*   On *consuetudines*, a word of many connotations, see p. 451.   For the church at Minster, served after the destruction of the nunnery by two or three *clerici* as a *plebeia parrochia*, and mentioned with its priest in Domesday, see Thorne col. 1908, Elmham, p. 221.

(38)

AUTHORITIES :
i. English :

(Q) Cartæ Antiquæ Roll I, no. 12 ; copy in Harley MS. 84, f. 99 b, printed K. 831. On these manuscripts see p. 439. Besides inaccuracies of transcription the Harley MS. contains several bad blunders, which were corrected above the line by Sir Simonds D'Ewes. Two of the corrections thus made were disregarded by Kemble in printing his text, which has the unintelligible readings of the first version in Harley MS. 84 : *hæbbe on heora saca wurðe*, and *þienesse* (corrected by the reviser to *witnesse* from Q, where *witnesse* stands for *wicneras*).

(F) D. and C. Lib. Canterbury, F. 47, no. ii, cent. xv, badly defaced.

(X) as for no. 37.

(Y) as for no. 37, printed here.

(Z) as for no. 37.

ii. Latin :

(B) as for no. 37, f. 87.

(O) as for no. 37, f. 160 b.

(Ed) as for no. 37, f. 94, an incomplete copy.

(Cl) as for no. 36, f. 57, printed here. Printed : *Mon. Angl.* i. 139, no. xxxvii ; K. 902 ; Thorpe p. 420 ; Pierquin, *Chartes Anglo-Saxonnes*, p. 822, no. 55, from K.

(V) Abridged copies in ' Vitæ Abbatum ' (on which see p. 192, n. 1 above), Cott. Tib. A. ix, f. 119, and Lambeth MS. 419, f. 122 b, both cent. xiv. Printed : W. Somner, *A Treatise of Gavelkind* (London, 1660), 207.

(F) as for F. above, no. iii.

(J) Bodl. Lib. MS. James 22, p. 108, abridged copy written 1620–38. On James, see no. 4.

(Ad) as for no. 36.

On the authenticity of this writ see p. 197, and on the legal terms employed see Introduction, pp. 73–82.

DATE. After Edward's accession in 1042, and within one of Eadsige's two periods of office as archbishop, namely, 1038–44, 1048–50.

(39)

AUTHORITIES :—(Cl) as for no. 36, f. 177, printed here. Printed : *Mon. Angl.* i. 142, no. xlix ; K. 854 ; C. E. Woodruff, *A History of the Town and Port of Fordwich* (Canterbury, 1895) p. 25 (from K.).

(F) as for no. 38, no. i.

(R) as for no. 37. Copies, cent. xiv : (i) Cott. Claud. D. x (Cl. above), f. 63 b ; (ii) Cott. Faust. A. i, f. 84 b, printed G. J. Turner and H. E. Salter, *The Register of St. Augustine's Abbey*, i. 144.

(W) as for no. 37. Copy in Thorne MS. printed Twysden col. 2122. Mod. Eng. rendering, A. H. Davis, *Chronicle of St. Augustine's*, 573.

(X), (Y), (Z), as for no. 37.

(Ad) as for no. 36, f. 118 b.

The copies on the Charter and Patent Rolls and cartulary copies derived from them differ in many points of orthography from Cl and F ; they have to a considerable extent been modernised. In all of them the French loan-word *soffre* (in various spellings) replaces *geþafian* in l. 7.

On the authenticity of this writ see p. 197.

DATE. After Harold's appointment as earl of Wessex in 1053, and before King Edward's death on 5 January 1066. Thorne (col. 1784) and other chroniclers of this house date King Edward's grant of Fordwich in 1055 ; but there is no means of telling whether this refers to Edward's earlier grant of this estate, or to what is announced in the writ under discussion.

l. 3. *þan halgan þaer binnan.* The church of the monastery that he had founded had from the first been intended by St. Augustine to serve as a burial-place for himself and his successors in the see of Canterbury (nine of whom were buried there) and for the kings of Kent (Bede, *Hist. Eccles.* i. cap. 33, ed. Plummer, i. 70). William of Malmesbury (*Gesta Regum*, R.S. i. 267), writing in the early twelfth century, says that almost every corner of that monastery was filled with the bodies of saints of great name and merit. For details see R. U. Potts, ' The Tombs of the Kings and Archbishops in St. Austin's Abbey,' *Archæologia Cantiana*, xxxviii (1926), 97–112.

l. 4. *Sua micel landes binnan Fordwic . . . swa ic me sylf þer hafde.* Fordwich, Kent, two or three miles from Canterbury, on the R. Stour, and formerly a port for the passage of goods to Canterbury from the sea, and a place of commercial activity. The abbot of St. Augustine's was lord of the manor of Fordwich until the Dissolution. See further Woodruff, *A History of the Town and Port of Fordwich* ; *Mon. Angl.* i. 149 ; VCH *Kent*, iii. 244 ; *Archæologia Cantiana*, xviii (1889), 78 ff.

Domesday records (i. 12) that King Edward's part in Fordwich which he gave to St. Augustine's amounted to two-thirds : ' Ipse abbas (of St. Augustine's) tenet unum paruum burgum quod uocatur Forewic. Huius burgi duas partes dedit rex E. sancto Augustino'; and that in his day Fordwich contained 96 burgess tenements (*masuræ terræ*). A similar account is to be found in *An Eleventh Century Inquisition of St. Augustine's, Canterbury*, ed. A. Ballard (British Academy, 1920), p. 17. For the post-Conquest history of Fordwich see Davis, *Regesta*, nos. 98, 99, 100, and *Domesday Monachorum*, ed. Douglas, 32.

l. 9. *Þe mine swutelinge awaengnian wolde.* The verb *awægnian* (for which the form in the text is presumably a copyist's erroneous spelling) is not recorded in BT ; but it is not impossible that a verb of this form actually existed in Old English, and that it stood in the same relationship to *awægan* as does *gewægnian* to *gewægan*. Among the recorded meanings of *awægan* (for which see BT Suppt) are (i) ' to fail to perform,' (ii) ' to invalidate or nullify ' : such senses as these would be appropriate to *awægnian* in this context. The copies of this writ derived from the Charter Roll copies have *awemmen* (*-an*) (which may also have been the reading of F), recorded in BT Suppt only in the sense ' disfigure, defile '. But since other words from the same stem are used in legal language : cf. Robertson p. 42, ' *ure sylene* *gewemman*, ' impair our grant ', and I Cnut 2, 2, *handgrið stande æfre unwemme,* ' protection granted in person should always remain unviolate ', *awemman,* in the sense of ' impair ', may also have formed part of the legal vocabulary. *Swuteling* here stands no doubt for OE *swutelung*, one sense of which is ' declaration ' ; see p. 449 above.   The king had perhaps issued a declaration relating to his first grant of Fordwich beginning : ' Her swutelað on ðissum gewrite ', ' Here it is declared in this document ', etc.   There are many such declarations in Robertson, *Anglo-Saxon Charters.*

(40)

AUTHORITIES :—(V) Cott. Vitell. A. xiii, f. 50 b (*ol.* 49 b), second half of cent. xiii, printed here.   Printed : K. 848.   Strokes resembling an acute accent sometimes placed in this manuscript, and occasionally in the Chertsey texts on the Cartæ Antiquæ Roll (see nos. 41–3), over the letter *i* (chiefly in the neighbourhood of *n*, *m*, *u*, but also in other positions) have not been reproduced in the texts printed here ; see p. 433 above.

On the authenticity of this writ see pp. 205–8, and on the legal terms employed see Introduction, pp. 73–85.

DATE.   The date of an authentic writ with this address would fall between 1053, the date of Harold's appointment as earl of Wessex, and Edward's death on 5 January 1066.   But the authenticity of this writ is dubious.

l. 3.   *Seinte Petre into Cherteseye þane selue tun and Egeham and Þorpe and Chabbeham.*   The parish of Chertsey is closely adjacent to the other places named here, being bounded on the north-west by Egham and Thorpe, and on the south-west by Horsell and Chobham.   Chertsey, Egham, Thorpe, and Chobham, which were included in the original endowment said to have been made to the abbey by Frithuwald, and confirmed by later kings, are entered in Domesday under the land of the church of Chertsey (DB i. 32 b, VCH *Surrey*, i. 309–11).   For the history of these manors, which remained with the abbey until the Dissolution, see VCH *Surrey*, iii. 403–27, 437–40.

l. 4.   *Freo wið eche gescot and werc and ware*, ' free ' or ' exempt ' in regard to each contribution, work, and obligatory payment or service.   *Werc* (WS *weorc*) and *ware* (OE nom. *waru*) are mentioned in writs only in Chertsey texts (nos. 40, 41), and their appearance here is not evidence of an actual grant of them in so many words to Chertsey Abbey by the Confessor.   The exemption of the lands from these obligations meant that the king surrendered to the abbey everything accruing to him from these sources.

Gescot, ' payment, contribution ' (found also in the compounds *leohtgescot*, *Romgescot*, *sawolgescot*) occurs uncompounded in the Exeter guild statutes (Thorpe p. 614) ; for the more common word *scot*, see no. 15, and, for the related (*scyp*)*gesceot*, see no. 63.   By *werc* we are to understand the work done for their lord by his tenants.   *Waru* ' defence ', is related to the verb *werian* ' defend ', used in the special sense of ' discharge the obligations on, answer the claims on ' ; see note on no. 29.

Waru stands here for the obligations that lay upon, and the services that might be demanded from, the holders of land.   For the compounds *inware*, *utware*, see Robertson no. 81, and Liebermann, *Gesetze*, ii. p. 232, s.v. *utware*.

An indication of what these burdens might involve is given in a survey of the manor of Tidenham in Gloucestershire, printed by Miss Robertson, no. 109, and dated by Liebermann c. 1050 on the strength of its apparent relationship to the *Rectitudines*.   They include money-payments, the payment at every weir (on the Severn or the Wye) of every alternate fish and of every rare fish to the lord of the manor, and the obligation of informing the lord, when he was on the estate, whenever a fish was sold for money. As far as the *geneat* was concerned, the work demanded included, among many other things, riding and supplying carrying-service and transport, and driving herds. The *gebur's* work included ploughing (both for his lord and for church-tax), weir-building, fencing and digging, reaping and mowing; and the contributions exacted from him included 6 pence and half a sester of honey after Easter, 6 sesters of malt at Lammas, and a ball of good net yarn at Martinmas. From those who kept pigs, three out of the first seven were demanded, and after that always the tenth, and, in addition, payment for the right of having mast. But customs varied in different parts of the country and on different manors. At Hurstbourne Priors in Hampshire the *ceorlas* had many comparable obligations in money, kind, services and work; but on this estate, where there were no fisheries, the yearly dues included the payment at Easter of two ewes with two lambs, and the services included the washing and shearing of the sheep in the tenants' own time (Robertson, no. 110).

l. 7. *Inne freols 7 ut of freols. Freols,* ' festival ', a well-attested meaning of the word; cf. no. 110. The spurious writ of William I (mentioned above, p. 204, n. 2), confirming the rights and privileges possessed by Chertsey Abbey in the Confessor's time, has the corresponding phrase *in festo et sine festo.* In Anglo-Saxon writs *tid* is more common than *freols* : cf. no. 81, *inne tid 7 ut of tid.* But whatever the term employed there is evidence that penalties were increased when offences were committed on the days of church festivals; see further, note on no. 61.

(41)

AUTHORITIES :—(Q) Cartæ Antiquæ Roll D, no. 7, printed here. Mentioned, Landon's ed. no. 106. Copy in Harley MS. 84, f. 41. Printed : K. 850. On these manuscripts see p. 439 above.

(V) as for no. 40, f. 50 (*ol.* 49). Printed : *Mon. Angl.* i. 429, no. vii.

On the authenticity of the writ see pp. 205–8 and on the legal terms employed see Introduction, pp. 73–85.

DATE. As for no. 40. But the authenticity of this writ is in doubt.

l. 4. *Eggeham 7 Torp . . . mid þan hundrede of Goddelie.* Godley, Surrey. Chertsey, Egham, Thorpe and Chobham are in this hundred. For the early history of Godley hundred, see VCH *Surrey,* iii. 396–400, where it is stated that the (present) hundred or half hundred of Godley is made up of lands which, with the exception of Pyrford and Horsell, formed part of early grants to the monastery of Chertsey (see p. 202 above); and that Pyrford is the only manor in the hundred named in Domesday which was not held in 1086 by Chertsey Abbey.

(42)

AUTHORITIES :—(Q) Cartæ Antiquæ Roll D, no. 8, printed here. Mentioned, Landon's ed. no. 107. Copy in Harley MS 84, f. 41 b. On these manuscripts see p. 439.

(V) as for no 40, f. 50 (*ol.* 49). Printed : *Mon. Angl.* i. 429, no. vi ; K. 849.

On the authenticity of this writ see pp. 203–5, and on the legal terms employed see Introduction, pp. 73–82.

DATE. For an authentic writ, between 1058, when Wulfwold was appointed abbot of Chertsey, and 5 January 1066, the date of Edward's death. But the authenticity of this writ is not beyond question.

l. 8. *Binne porte 7 buten.* With this (normally spelt *binnan porte 7 butan*),

compare *binnan burh and butan* (see pp. 428 f.). Both *port* and *burh* are sometimes used of the same town in its different aspects, *port* as a trading centre
or market town, and *burh* as a place surrounded by a wall or an earthen
rampart : e.g. Worcester, nos. 115, 116. Compare NED port sb.² For other
instances of this formula see nos. 50 (Lat.), 64–5, 109–10, 116, 118.

(43)

AUTHORITIES :—(Q) Cartæ Antiquæ Roll D, no. 9. Mentioned, Landon's
ed. no. 108. Copy in Harley MS. 84, f. 41 b. On these manuscripts see
p. 439. This text is printed here.

(V) as for no. 40, f. 50 b. (*ol.* 49 b). Printed : *Mon. Angl.* i. 430, no. viii ;
K. 856.

On the authenticity of this writ see pp. 201 f., and on ' sake and soke '
see Introduction, pp. 73–6.

DATE. As for no. 42.

l. 3. *Ofer his hagan land her binnan.* Most probably ' over his own lands ' ;
see note on p. 201. *Her binnan,* ' here within ' (and not *þær binnan,* ' there
within '), if it is not an alteration made by a copyist, clearly indicates that the
writ was composed in London. No survey of London is to be found in
Domesday Book, so that the extent of the land held in the city by the abbot
of Chertsey cannot now be determined.

But the soke of the abbot of Chertsey in London (*socam suam de London*
in Chertsey writs of Henry I and II) was only one of a number of sokes,
that is, little pockets or islands of private jurisdiction, in Norman London.
On these see F. M. Stenton, *Norman London* (see p. 233, n. 1). For another
soke, lying in this case outside the city walls, see p. 233.

(44)

AUTHORITIES :—Cirencester Cartulary, p. 26, cent. early xiii. Printed
(incorrectly) : *Archæologia,* xxvi (1836), 256. The strokes in the manuscript
over the letter *i* have not been printed here ; see note on no. 8.

On the authenticity of this writ see pp. 211 ff., and on the legal terms employed see Introduction, pp. 73–8.

DATE. The writ cannot be dated more narrowly than the reign of the
Confessor, 1042–66.

l. 7. *His wite beo eall swa muchell swa þæt leodbiscopes æt ællan þingan,*
' the fine (*wite*) payable to him shall be equivalent to (lit. as great as) that
of a diocesan bishop in all things '. For the numerous offences for which
a *wite* was exacted, see Liebermann, ii. 671–3, ' Strafgeldfixum '. For *leod-
biscop,* ' diocesan bishop ', see Cnut's Proclamation of 1020 (for references to
which see p. 17, n. 1) in the address of which we find : ' his arcebiscopas
7 his *leodbiscopas* '. As early as the code of Æthelberht of Kent, of the early
years of the seventh century, it was enacted that in cases of theft a bishop's
property should be compensated eleven-fold, a priest's property nine-fold
(Æthelberht I). King Alfred, following Ine, decreed (Alfred 40) that the fine
for breaking into the fortified premises of the king (*cyninges burgbryce*) should
be 120 shillings, of an archbishop 90 shillings, of another bishop (i.e. not an
*arch*bishop) or of an ealdorman 60 shillings, and so down the scale until the
fine is reached of 5 shillings for breaking through a commoner's fence. From
this it follows that in Alfred's time the status of the diocesan bishop was
equivalent to that of an ealdorman.

(45)

AUTHORITIES :—(A) B.M. Add. Charter 28657, end of cent. xi, printed here. Autotype facsimile with Modern English rendering and notes : W. de Gray Birch, *The Anglo-Saxon Charter of King Edward the Confessor to Coventry Minster* (1889). Text copied on a single piece of parchment, dimensions : 6½″ broad, 9 7/16″ deep. A flap, 1″ deep, folded up along lower edge. Strands of faded yellow floss-silk, to which a seal (of which there is now no trace) may at one time have been appended, have been drawn through four incisions in the parchment. On the evidence of the date of the hand this is not an original writ of King Edward the Confessor. On internal evidence it is not an authentic copy of an original writ ; see pp. 216–18.

(J) Cott. Faust. A. viii, f. 75, copy of A by John Joscelin (1529–1603), with an interlinear Latin version in Joscelin's hand, apparently composed by him (not printed here).

(W) B.M. Add. MS. 32100, f. 115 b, cent. xvi, Latin version differing from the preceding, printed here. On this manuscript see no. 46.

On the authenticity of this writ see pp. 214 ff., and for an explanation of the legal terms employed see Introduction, pp. 73–85.

DATE. Since this writ is manifestly spurious it is not dated here.

l. 12. *On lande 7 on lóga.* Cf. *mid lande 7 mid loge*, nos. 77, 105, 106, also no. 85 (F), also *Mon. Angl.* i. 301, no. xl, a Westminster writ of William I relating to Pershore-Deerhurst (see nos. 99–102). All these are Westminster texts, and no. 45 (spurious) is linked in other ways with (doubtful) Westminster writs. The spelling *lóga* is apparently an instance of the late ending *-a* for *-e*. The derivation and meaning of *loge*, *lóga*, are unexplained. The scribe writes *lóga* here, but this does not indicate length of vowel for he also writes *Gód* (side by side with *God*). For a correction of the statement in Sievers-Cook, *Old English Grammar*, 3rd ed. § 8, 120, that length is indicated in manuscripts by an acute accent over the vowel, see K. Brunner, *Altenglische Grammatik* (1942), § 8, n. 1. The rendering ' water ' in BT Suppt, s.v. *log* (?), is partly based on the *cum terra et cum aqua* in Hickes's Latin rendering of no. 77 printed by Kemble ; it is also pointed out that the alliterative *land and lögr* is common in Icelandic ' so perhaps *loge* shows Scandinavian influence and is the same as English *lage* (from *lagu* " sea, water ") '. But reference to Cleasby-Vigfusson, *Icelandic-English Dictionary* (1874), s.v. *lögr*, shows that the alliterative *lands eða lagar* means ' on land or sea ', not ' on land or water '. The reference in BT Suppt, as an alternative to NED s.v. ' lough ', does not carry us much further, if this word represents ONorthumbrian *luh* ; for *luh* in the Lindisfarne Gospels renders *fretum*, *stagnum* (therefore not ' water '), and in any case the *loga* of this text of c. 1100 cannot stand for ONorthumbrian *luh*. Hickes' rendering, ' water ', is based on forms somewhat similar to those cited above. But ' water ' does not fit the context in no. 45 : ' land, *water*, gold, silver, treasure ', or in nos. 105–6.

It is worth noting that in no. 85 where the Faustina version reads : *mid lande 7 mid loge*, the Westminster Domesday version reads *mid lande 7 mid lese*, ' with land and with pasture '. Not much stress however can be laid on this in the absence of further evidence, for the variation between these phrases may be no more than the substitution of one alliterative phrase for another. But it is interesting to observe that the Latin version of no. 45 renders *on lande 7 on loga* by *in terris, in pascuis*. The Latin rendering was made after the Norman Conquest but it comes from the same source as no. 46, and is older than the hand of cent. xvi in which it is written. Nevertheless the rendering of *loga* by *pascuis* may be no more than a guess. One wonders whether *loge* could be connected with the adjective *fēa-lōg* of the Old English poem on St. Guthlac, line 217. BT and Suppt render this ' destitute ', but even if there is a connection between *loge* in the writs, and *fealog*, we still remain in ignorance of the meaning of *loge*. Could it mean ' produce ' ? Or could it (as Miss Whitelock has suggested to me) mean ' rents ' or ' buildings ' or ' stock ' ? The rare word *loh* appears in *Chron.* 693, where for *on his loh* in one text, two others have *on his steall*. Miss Whitelock has pointed out to me that one assumes that in this context the meaning is ' stead ', or else more definitely, ' see ', ' official position ' (cf. OE *gelogian*, ' put, place '), a meaning which would fit the *on þat ilke loh þe Aignoth was* in Miss Whitelock's *Wills*, p. 76. But there is no obvious connection between this *loh* and the term under discussion, and the *loge, loga*, of the writs remains unexplained.

l. 12. *On golde 7 on seolfre. on madmen 7 on oðre eallum þingum*. The extraordinary wealth of gold and silver and other treasure lavished on the monastery by Leofric and Godgifu is expatiated upon by William of Malmesbury (*Gest. Pont.* 309, *Gest. Reg.* i. 237), by Florence of Worcester (s.a. 1057), and by Ordericus Vitalis (*Hist. Eccles.* (ed. Le Prevost) ii. 183).

(46)

AUTHORITIES :—B.M. Add. MS. 32100, f. 115 b, cent. late xvi. Unprinted. This paper volume, not known to the edd. of *Mon. Angl.* or to Kemble, was purchased for the British Museum at Sotheby's in 1883. It contains extracts from cartularies and other monastic records made for Robert Beale, clerk to the Privy Council from 1572 till 1595 or later. For Beale see DNB. Notes in Beale's hand appear on many pages of this volume, frequently stating the source of individual entries. One important source was a paper book of Coventry Priory which was then in the custody of Mr. Fanshawe, Remembrancer of the Exchequer ; from this book the Coventry charters in *Mon. Angl.* iii. 190 ff. were derived. Another source was an ancient roll which has now disappeared, and which is associated by Beale with the name of William Walter. A Latin version (W) of no. 45, printed here, and the writ in Latin printed here as no. 46, were transcribed according to a note in the book in Beale's hand (Add. MS. 32100, f. 114) : ' out of an old parchement roole of Mr. William Walters '. The material transcribed there from the said roll (*ibid.* ff. 114–22 b) comprises a number of Coventry charters, some others of which are absent from the Coventry section of *Mon. Angl.* For references to what may or may not have been still another roll in Walter's possession (' an old roole which I borowed of Mr. William Walter of the Temple, written, as appered in the title, about the year of our Lord 1200 '), see Add. MS. 32100, f. 17 b, f. 78. The name of William Walter appears more than once in the early records of the Temple : see F. A. Inderwick, *A Calendar of the Inner Temple Records* (London, 1896 ff.) ; the admission is recorded on 12 February 1534–35 of a person of this name who was probably Beale's acquaintance.

On the authenticity of this writ see pp. 218 f., and on the legal terms employed see Introduction, pp. 73–8.

DATE. The presumed Anglo-Saxon writ of which this is a rendering, must have been issued between the foundation of the monastery c. 1043, and the appointment of Abbot Leofwine as bishop of Lichfield in succession to Wulfsige, who died in October 1053. According to Dugdale, *Antiquities of Warwickshire*, 105, the following appeared in the Chronicle of Geoffrey, prior of Coventry (A.D. 1216, see DNB) : ' Anno Domini MXLIII constructum fuit monasterium Coventrense a memorandæ recordationis duce Leurico et uxore ejus Godiva ; dedicatumque eodem anno ab archiepiscopo

Dorobernensi Edzio, quarto Non. Octob. post Pascha, Abbate Lefwino cum xxiiii monachis in eodem instituto '. The same date of 1043 appears in Edward's spurious foundation charter (see p. 215), and is no doubt correct.

l. 2. *In illis comitatibus ubi Leofwinus . . . habet terras intus.* The 23 or 24 vills which Earl Leofric is stated in the spurious foundation charters to have granted to Coventry minster were identified by Dugdale, *Antiquities of Warwickshire*, 105, as lying in the counties of Warwick, Gloucester, Worcester, Cheshire, Northampton and Leicester.

l. 7. *Ego nolo pati quod homo illi in aliqua re forisfaciat.* The emendation of the manuscript reading *satisfaciat* to *forisfaciat* ' do (him) an injury ' seems an obvious one. On *forisfacere* in this sense, see Stenton, *English Feudalism*, 250, n. 1. Stenton remarks that although in the Anglo-Norman law books *forisfacere* sometimes means ' to forfeit ', which is the usual later meaning of the word, it more often means ' to do injury to anyone ', a sense which is particularly evident in the so-called *Leges Edwardi Confessoris* ; for references see Liebermann, *Gesetze*, ii. 76. *Forisfacere* is used in the sense ' do wrong ' in K. 1317, a charter dated 1022, but preserved only in a cartulary copy. It is a reasonable conjecture that the reading of the (presumed) Anglo-Saxon writ of which this is a translation was some such phrase as : *ic nelle geþafian þæt him ænig man misbeode*, or, *þæt him ænig man ænig unlage (unriht, woh) beode*, for instances of which see Introduction, p. 66.

(47)

AUTHORITIES :—(C) Cott. Tib. A. vi, f. 102 b (*ol.* 121 b), cent. xii, English only, printed here. Printed : K. 885.

(O) Liber Eliensis, Trinity College Library, Cambridge, MS. O.2, 41, f. 104 b, no. 9, cent. xii, English only.

(T) Liber Eliensis, Trinity College, MS. O.2. 1, f. 79, no. 85, cent. late xii, Eng. with Latin version printed here. Printed : T. Gale, *Historiae Britannicae Scriptores XV* (1691), iii. 512.

(E) Liber Eliensis, Muniment Room of the Dean and Chapter at Ely, f. 77, no. 95, cent. early xiii, Eng. and Lat. Printed : D. J. Stewart, *Liber Eliensis* (Anglia Christiana Society, London, 1848), i. 215, no. 95 (from collations and not directly from manuscript).

(L) Liber Eliensis, Bodl. Lib. Laud Miscellany no. 647, f. 47 b, col. 2, cent. early xiv, English only.

(J) Bodl. Lib. MS. James, 10, p. 90, a copy of C, written by James about 1625–38. For James and the James MSS. see references on p. 428.

On the authenticity of this writ see pp. 222 ff., and on the legal terms employed see Introduction, pp. 76 ff.

DATE. Before Edward's death on 5 January 1066 and after the appointment of Wulfric as successor to Leofsige. On the date of Leofsige's death, whether 1045 or 1055, see p. 566.

(48)

AUTHORITIES :—Cott. Vesp. B. xxiv (Registrum Cartarum abbatiae de Evesham), f. 34 (*ol.* 30), c. 1200. Printed : K. 757.

On the authenticity of this writ see pp. 225 ff.

DATE. For an authentic writ, between 1017, the year of Cnut's accession, and 1030, the year of Earl Hakon's death. But the authenticity of this writ is not certain.

l. 4. *Illas quinque hidas apud Beningwurðe.* Bengeworth (Worcs.) lies opposite to Evesham on the left bank of the Severn, and was incorporated in

Evesham in 1605. For a detailed account of the complicated and disputed history of this estate, see J. H. Round in VCH *Worcs.* i. 252 ff. and ii. 397 ff., and for a criticism of the evidence, R. R. Darlington, *Eng. Hist. Rev.* xlviii (1933), 6, n. 3, and 187-90. One half of this ten-hide estate, said by Hemming (ed. Hearne, i. 269) to have been given by Bishop Brihtheah of Worcester during his episcopate (A.D. 1033-38) to his kinsman and chamberlain Atsere (Azor, DB i. 174, VCH *Worcs.* i. 297), and to have been appropriated after the Conquest by Urse, the sheriff of Worcestershire, seems to have been unconnected with Evesham. Of the other half, consisting of 5 hides, 4 hides were held in 1086 by the abbot of Evesham, the remaining hide having also been secured by Urse, who therefore held 6 hides at Bengeworth in 1086 (DB i. 175 b, VCH *Worcs.* i. 307). As to the manner in which the abbot of Evesham had secured this land, the monks of Worcester and of Evesham are at variance. Hemming (*ut supra*) gives us to understand that this estate had been held by a certain Ærngrim, who did service from his land to Worcester ; but that Ærngrim turned for protection to Abbot Æthelwig of Evesham (1058-77) to save his land from Urse the sheriff, and was subsequently deprived of it by sharp practice (*dolis et ingeniis*) on the part of the abbot (on whom see R. R. Darlington, *Eng. Hist. Rev.* xlviii (1933), Knowles, *Monastic Order in England,* 76). The estate was therefore lost to Worcester. The Evesham chronicler on the other hand says nothing of any dealings of the abbot with Ærngrim. He includes Bengeworth among the lands which Abbot Æthelwig secured for his church from King Edward and other good men, and names Bengeworth again among the estates which the bishops of Worcester had wrongfully held and which had been recovered for the abbey by Æthelwig (*Chron. Abbat. de Evesham,* 94-7). In the hope of reconciling the rival claims to Bengeworth and also to Hampton (see p. 226 above) a plea was held ' at Ildeberga in a court of 4 (? or 5) shires before the bishop of Bayeux and other barons of the king ' (DB i. 175 b, VCH *Worcs.* i. 307, and on the dating J. H. Le Patourel, *Eng. Hist. Rev.* lix (1944), 145), and there Æthelwig's successor Abbot Walter proved his right to Hampton and to 5 hides at Bengeworth, though he did not apparently succeed in recovering the one hide appropriated by Urse the sheriff. There were still however many matters outstanding between the bishop of Worcester and the abbot of Evesham, and an agreement was finally arrived at in the presence of the Domesday commissioners : the bishop abandoned certain of his claims, while the abbot of Evesham acknowledged that Hampton and Bengeworth were part of, and owed the usual services to, the bishop's hundred of Oswaldslow. For the texts, see M. M. Bigelow, *Placita Anglo-Normannica,* pp. 16-22, 287. It is difficult to find even in this long-protracted dispute any motive for the fabrication of an Evesham writ of Cnut.

(49)

AUTHORITIES :—(R) Bodl. Lib. MS. Rawlinson B. 329, f. 104 (*ol.* 118), Eng. and Lat., cent. xv. For a reference to the seal in the heading of the manuscript see p. 230. On the manuscript see *Cat. Cod. MSS. Bibl. Bodl.* ed. W. D. Macray, pt. v, fasc. i (1862), 598. Printed : K. 867 ; *Mon. Angl.* vi, pt. 3, p. 1212 (Lat. only). Lat. version, Pierquin, *Chartes Anglo-Saxonnes,* p. 820, no. 51, from K.

On the authenticity of this writ see pp. 228 f., and on ' sake and soke ' see Introduction, pp. 73-6.

DATE. During the period of the administration of the see of Hereford by Bishop Ealdred (wrongly called Alred *Eurl*), namely, 1056-60. Since Harold is addressed as earl the writ must have been issued after Earl Raulf's death on 21 December 1057. After Raulf's death Herefordshire was no longer administered as a separate earldom, but was merged in Harold's earldom of Wessex.

l. 4. *Alle heore men and alle heore londes.* For the numerous manors belonging to the canons of Hereford, see DB i. 181 b, VCH *Herefordshire*, i. 320 ff.

(50)

AUTHORITIES :—(R) as for no. 49, f. 104 b (*ol.* 118 b). Printed : K. 833 and *Saxons in England*, ii. 379 ; Thorpe p. 380 (with wrong ref. to R, f. 1646). Also Pierquin, *Chartes Anglo-Saxonnes*, p. 815, no. 44 (with erroneous references to Bury cartularies).

On the authenticity of this writ see pp. 229–30, and on ' sake and soke ' see Introduction, pp. 73–6.

DATE. Assuming that the style of ' bishop ' followed the name of Walter in the presumed Anglo-Saxon writ of which this is a rendering, that writ must have been issued after, but not long after, Walter's consecration on 15 April 1061, and before King Edward's death on 5 January 1066.

(51)

AUTHORITIES :—(U) Cartularium Prioratus Sanctæ Trinitatis infra Aldgate, Londini, MS. U. 2. 6, in the Library of the Hunterian Museum in the University of Glasgow, f. 149, printed here. The handwriting is a close imitation of Anglo-Saxon script. For particulars of this manuscript see R. R. Sharpe, *Calendar of Letter-Book C* (1901), pp. xvi, 216. J. Young and P. H. Aitken, *Cat. of the MSS. in the Lib. of the Hunterian Museum in the Univ. of Glasgow* (1908), p. 158, no. 215, assign this manuscript to cent. xiv–xv. This manuscript may or may not have been the register written in A.D. 1425 by Thomas de Axebrigge, a canon of the priory. In the copy of this writ a large crown in gold is set in the middle of a framework in the shape of a large capital E, most but not all of the characteristics of the E being thereby obscured. In the lower margin are emblazoned the arms of Westminster, described by Young and Aitken (*loc. cit.*) : ' on a shield (azure) five martlets (or) surrounding canton-wise a cross fleury (or) '.

(G) A transcript of the above, closely imitating the script and embellishments, in the Guildhall Library, London, MS. no. 122, vol. iv, p. 2, cent. xviii. Printed : A. Ballard, *British Borough Charters, 1042–1216* (1913), 127, Mod. Eng. rendering, 257. Ballard, apparently following Coote (see below) introduces into his text two serious errors : *ge eac mon* for *geeacnian*, line 7, *gefriðe* for *gesunde*, line 8.

(C) Letter-Book C of the City of London in the Guildhall Library, f. 134 b, c. 1291–1309, an inferior copy containing the erroneous reading *ge eac mon* mentioned above. Printed : R. R. Sharpe, *loc. cit.* 218.

(D) Liber Dunthorne in the Guildhall Records Office, f. 79, cent. xv, an inferior copy.

An attempt to reconstruct the text of the writ on the basis of C and D was made by H. C. Coote, *Trans. of the London and Middx. Archæol. Soc.* v (1881), 477–93, in an article now out-of-date. Coote was unacquainted with the excellent text printed here or with G.

On the authenticity of the writ see pp. 231 ff., and on ' sake and soke ' see Introduction, pp. 73–6.

DATE. Between the accession of Edward in 1042 and the death of Bishop Ælfweard on 25 July 1044.

l. 3. *On Ænglisce cnihte gilde.* The term ' English ' used here in the earliest surviving text concerning this gild is still applied to its members in the early twelfth century. In an agreement between the abbot of Ramsey and the priory of Holy Trinity, Aldgate, dated A.D. 1125–30 by J. H. Round, *Ancient Charters*, Pipe Roll Society, vol. x (1888), no. 14, the abbot of Ramsey relinquished his claim to land *de Anglica Cnithta gilda*, which *ipsi Anglici* had given to the church of Holy Trinity. See also p. 231, n. 1. For the membership of the gild, see pp. 233 f. above.

The question arises whether the use of ' English ' here implies some contrast with non-English *cnihtas*, and whether if the *cnihtas* are trading agents (as suggested above, p. 234), the use of the word ' English ' is an indication that Edward had already recognised some association of foreign merchants in London. I have not found any direct reference to non-English *cnihtas*, but there are indications of the existence of associations of foreign traders in London in the reign of King Edward the Confessor and earlier. It was suggested by Liebermann (*Gesetze*, ii. 491 ff. s.v. ' Handel ', 14 d) that the ' men of the Emperor ' (*homines imperatoris*) who, according to the regulations for trade at London known as IV Æthelred, were already in the reign of Æthelred II trading with London, were probably ' gegliedert in Genossenschaft '. The men of Rouen who in the same regulations are mentioned as trading with London in Æthelred's time had their own wharf at London in the reign of Edward the Confessor. Their rights are noted in a charter confirmed by Henry VI, 9 August 1445, and described as being of Henry, duke of Normandy, addressed to Hugh, archbishop of Rouen, and his lieges of Normandy, and said to be dated 1150–51 ; see C. H. Haskins, *Norman Institutions*, 48, where a reference is given to E. de Fréville, *Mémoire sur le commerce maritime de Rouen* (Rouen, 1857), i. 90, ii. 12 (which I have not seen), and to Round, *Calendar of Documents preserved in France*, no. 109. According to Round's summary of this charter the men of Rouen who are of the merchant gild shall be quit of all dues at London save for wine and ' fat fish ' (*crasso pisce*, on which see p. 426 above). They shall also be free to go through all the markets in England, saving the king's lawful dues. And the citizens of Rouen shall have at London the port of Dowgate (*Duuegate*) as they have had from the time of King Edward with the (customary) right (*consuetudo*) that if they find in that port a ship, whencesoever it be, they may order it to be removed, and shall [then] wait a flood and an ebb, and if the ship be not removed, the citizens of Rouen may, if they will, cut the ropes of that ship, and send her out, without [liability] to claim or penalty ; and if that ship be endangered by their action, they shall be responsible to no one. It would seem then that the Confessor had assigned to the citizens of Rouen in London the port of Dowgate, and had recognised their association. For the few references to foreigners trading in England in the pre-Conquest period, see W. Cunningham, *Growth of English Industry and Commerce* (5th ed. Cambridge, 1910), 130, 188, 194 ; Liebermann, *Gesetze*, ii. s.v. ' Fremde ', ' Handel ', ' Handschuh ' ; Sharpe, Introduction, p. ix.

The possibility that ' English ' in ' English Cnihtengild ' indicates not a contrast between English and foreign, but a provincial contrast, between Anglian and Saxon *cnihtas*, seems to me very unlikely. It is true that we hear of *Englum and Sæxum*, ' Angles and Saxons ', in a verse entry in the *Chronicle* s.v. 1065, but *Englisc* means ' English ' and not ' Anglian ' ; see BT Suppt, s.v. *Englisc*.

l. 5. *Ic wille þ heo beon swa godre lage wurðe swa heo wæron on Eadgares dæge cynges.* Compare no. 54, line 5 : *swa godera lagana wurðe* ; no. 113, line 28 : *settan gode lagan.* In the Cnihtengild writ *godre lage* probably stands for *godra laga,* plur., as *cnihte,* line 3, stands for *cnihta.* A weak gen. plur. *lagena* (spelt *lagana* above) was also current. Is the king in these passages confirming the legal rights and privileges of the gild or chapter ; or is he sanctioning the existing regulations of the gild or chapter ? The latter seems more likely. If the king had been announcing the confirmation of rights or privileges, it seems probable that he would have done so in some such phraseology as is employed by William I in his London writ (Liebermann, *Gesetze,* i. 486, Robertson, *Laws,* 230) : ' ic wylle þæt get beon *eallra þæra laga weorðe* þe gyt wæran on Eadwerdes dæge kynges ', ' My will is that both of you shall be *entitled to all the rights* to which you were (entitled) in the days of King Edward '. Among the various meanings current in the tenth and eleventh centuries for *lagu* (a loan-word from Old Norse which entered the language as plur., afterwards becoming fem. sing.), Miss Robertson (*Laws,* 307) cites ' legal conditions affecting a person or community (rights, privileges etc.) ', and ' regulations ' (for which see BT Suppt s.v. *lagu,* 1 c), and this is probably the meaning of the term here. For other instances of ' good ' used in conjunction with *lage,* see IV Edgar 2, 1, and 12. For Old English gild regulations, see Thorpe pp. 605–17, and C. Gross, *The Gild Merchant,* i. 181–8 ; to which should be added those among the ' Old English Entries in a Manuscript at Bern ', ed. H. Meritt, *Journal of English and Germanic Philology,* xxxiii (1934), 343–51 ; also edited, with corrections, by Max Förster, *Der Flussname Themse,* Appendix (for full reference see p. 266).

l. 6. *Ic wille eac hit mid gode geeacnian,* lit. ' augment it with good (things) '. For a parallel, see Thorpe p. 616, where the agreement for mutual prayer made between Bishop Wulfstan and the abbots of Evesham, Chertsey and other houses concludes with : ' God us gefultumige þæt we hit þus moten gelæstan 7 *mid suman gode geeacnian* ', ' May God give us his help that we may thus perform it, and *with some good augment it* '.

l. 7. *Þæt heom ænig man misbeode ac beon heo ealle gesunde.* The conjunction *ac,* ' but ', here introduces a phrase in strong opposition to the preceding. *Ac* stands for, ' on the contrary ', ' nay, rather '. For another instance see no. 87.

(52)

AUTHORITIES :—(J) Bodl. Lib. MS. James, 23, p. 32, written by James 1627–38 in a hand which imitates Anglo-Saxon script. Printed : *Early Charters of St. Paul's,* ed. M. Gibbs, Camden Society, Third Series, vol. lviii (1939), p. 2. On James and on the James MSS. see references on p. 428.

On the authenticity of this writ see pp. 235 ff., and on ' sake and soke ' see Introduction, pp. 73–6.

DATE. This writ (if authentic) cannot be more closely dated than the reign of King Æthelred II, 978–1016.

l. 4. *Swa godera laga wyrþe.* For *laga* in the sense of ' laws, regulations ', see no. 51.

(53)

AUTHORITIES :—(B) Liber B (now lost) of the Dean and Chapter of St. Paul's, f. 20 b. Printed, Dugdale, *History of St. Paul's* (1658), Appendix, p. 188, no. xi. B, and 2nd ed. 1716, Appendix, p. 13 ; 1818 ed. Appendix, p. 296 ; *Mon. Angl.* iii (1673), p. 304, xi. B ; K. 1319 ; Thorpe p. 319.

Text printed here from Dugdale, 1716 ed., described on the title-page as 'the Second Edition corrected and enlarged by the Author's own Hand'.

On the authenticity of this writ see pp. 239 f., and on the legal terms employed see Introduction, pp. 73–8.

DATE. Between the consecration of Duduc as bishop of Wells on 11 June 1033, and the death of Cnut on 12 November 1035.

l. 4. *Binnan tid 7 buton tid.* For this, see notes on no. 40, p. 460, and no. 61, pp. 477 f.

(54)

AUTHORITIES :—(B) Liber B (now lost) as for no. 53, f. 21 b. Printed, Dugdale, *History of St. Paul's* (1658), Appendix, p. 190, no. xii. B, and 2nd ed. 1716, Appendix, p. 14 ; 1818 ed. Appendix, p. 297, no. xvi ; *Mon. Angl.* iii (1673), p. 304, xii. B ; K. 887, Thorpe p. 416. Dugdale's text, superior on the whole to the others, and free from the misreadings *grete* and *misbedde* of P, is printed here from the second edition of 1716 (on which see no. 53, above).

(P) Liber A (Pilosus) of the D. and C., f. 1, copied 1241. Printed : *Early Charters of St. Paul's*, ed. M. Gibbs, p. 9.

(A) Roll A/69, no. 16, of the D. and C., cent. xiii. On this roll see Gibbs, p. xliii, n. 3.

(R) Charter Roll 9 Edw. II, m. 12, 12 Edw. III, m. 8 (*Cal. of Ch. R.* iii. 291, iv. 451). For other copies on Charter and Patent Rolls, see *Cal. of Ch. R.* vi. 24 ; *Cal. of P. R.* 1555–57, 544. For copies on Confirmation Rolls, see *Twenty-Ninth Report of the Deputy Keeper of the Public Records*, App. v, 31. See also W. Sparrow Simpson, *Registrum Statutorum et Consuetudinum Ecclesiæ Cathedralis S. Pauli Londinensis* (1873), 112, for transcripts in two registers of the *inspeximus* charter of 12 Edw. III.

(H) Harley Roll I. i, copy of an *inspeximus* by Hen. IV of various royal grants to St. Paul's, cent. late xv.

(J) Bodl. Lib. MS. James 25, p. 155, written by James about 1625–38. This text, in a rather cramped imitation of Anglo-Saxon script, bears a close resemblance to P. On James and on the James MSS. see p. 428 above.

(L) Lansdowne MS. 446, f. 91, as for no. 7.

(C) Cott. Jul. C. vii, f. 198 b, a copy closely imitating Anglo-Saxon script, with a drawing of both sides of a seal, by Nicholas Charles (d. 1613, see DNB). In spite of obvious spelling blunders, and in spite of a curious reversal of precedence in the address, which must be deliberate, whereby earls are made to precede bishops, and 'all' before 'my thegns' has dropped out, this text is clearly derived from a good source. A note accompanying the text in the manuscript runs : 'A Saxon charter of King Edward the Confessor | With this very seale broken just in this fashion'. The seal is imperfect in the drawing, the king's head, three of the insignia of majesty, and the inscription, being lacking. But though the backless throne and the king's posture are those customary on seals associated with King Edward (see p. 94), other details are different ; the king's sceptre is longer, the drapery is differently arranged, and the king's cloak has a patterned edge like that depicted on a seal attributed to William I on the same page. But one cannot help suspecting that these details may have been the draughtsman's own invention. It is not unlikely that the broken seal depicted here is also depicted—without the dubious details, and with less firm outlines of drapery and other details—in Add. MS. 5937, f. 56 b (*ol.* 96 b), with the description (but without the text) : 'A Saxon deed of Edward the Confessor'. The seal which Charles was depicting may have been blurred, and he may have filled in the details according to his taste. But since the writ itself has undergone interpolation, and C is in any case an altered copy of the text, it seems useless to speculate as to whether the seal that Charles was depicting was an authentic seal of the Confessor.

On the authenticity of the writ, see pp 237 ff., and on 'sake and soke' see Introduction, pp. 73–6.

DATE. Supposing this writ to represent an authentic writ of King Edward, and one that has possibly undergone interpolation, the authentic writ could not be more closely dated, on its contents, than 1042–66, the duration of the Confessor's reign. But its resemblance to no. 51 would suggest that it might have been issued at about the same time, 1042–44, a date which would be very appropriate to what is known of the conditions at St. Paul's; see p. 238.

(55)

AUTHORITIES :—Paris, Archives Nationales, Cartons des Rois, K. 19, no. 6, in a contemporary hand, printed here. A photograph is reproduced here as Plate 2. Printed : N. de Wailly, Éléments de Paléographie (Paris, 1838), i. 671, with Latin rendering not printed here ; J. Tardif, Archives de l'Empire, Monuments Historiques (Paris, 1866), pp. 171–2, no. 277 ; M. Bouquet, Recueil des Historiens des Gaules et de la France, xi (Paris, 1876), 656. Lat. version by W. Camden printed by J. Doublet, Histoire de l'Abbaye de S. Denys (Paris, 1625), 833, and from his text by Bouquet, not printed here. The text is written on a single piece of parchment, dimensions : 10″ broad, by 1¾″ on left side, 1¼″ on right. No seal is attached to the writ, but there are indications of former sealing. The writ is accompanied in the Archives Nationales by a Taynton diploma of King Edward copied in a hand of c. 1100 (see pp. 538 f.), to which a seal is attached ; described by Doublet ut supra ; and by M. Douët D'Arcq, Archives de l' Empire, Inventaires et Documents, Collection de Sceaux, iii (Paris, 1868), p. 261, no. 9997. Seal reproduced by Birch, Trans. R. Soc. Lit. (1874), p. 145, Plate, and by Wyon, Plate 1, 7 and 8. The seal (of the Second Type, see pp. 103 f.) is of dark fawn-coloured wax. The fact that the one-third of an inch, or so, of seal tag still remaining on the writ corresponds in width and texture with the tiny end of parchment projecting from the broken edge of the seal makes it virtually certain that this seal was once affixed to the writ, though it is now appended by a coarse seal tag to the lower edge of the diploma. Everything encourages the belief that this writ is the original Taynton writ written by the clerks of the royal secretariat, and that the seal in question was affixed to it by the royal clerks. For the seal see Plate 2 and p. 103.

On the authenticity of this writ, see pp. 243 f., and on 'sake and soke' see Introduction, pp. 73–6.

DATE. Between the appointment of Wulfwig to the see of Dorchester in 1053, and the death of Earl Raulf on 21 December 1057.

l. 4. þæt land æt Tengctune. Taynton, Oxon. On the grant of this land to the abbey of St. Denis, see p. 244. Its boundaries are given in the Taynton diploma of the Confessor for which see Appendix II, p. 538. A detailed account of this manor is given DB i. 157, VCH Oxon. i. 409. It was rated at 10 hides. There was land there for 15 ploughs. In 1086 there were in demesne 4 ploughs and 4 serfs ; and 17 villeins with 30 bordars had 17 ploughs. There were two mills rendering 32s. 6d. and 62s. 6d. for eels. There were 170 acres of meadow, pasture 1 league in length and half a league in breadth, and woodland 1 league in length and 4 furlongs in breadth. Between the quarry and the meadows and the pasture it rendered in 1086, 24s. 7d. In King Edward's time and afterwards it had been worth 10 pounds ; in 1086 it was worth altogether 15 pounds.

l. 7. *Wite he wið God.* ' Let him account for it with God ', is the rendering that suggests itself here ; cf. *wite*, ' punishment, fine ', and *witnian*, ' to punish '. ' To account for ' would seem to be a hitherto unrecorded sense of the verb *witan.* Compare *hæbbe he wið God gemæne,* 'may he have to account for it with God ', on which see Introduction, p. 69.

l. 8. *Þæt se biscop dihte boc þærto be minan fullan geleafan.* On this passage and on the Taynton diploma see Introduction, p. 36.

(56)

AUTHORITIES :—(A) Ramsey Chronicle in Bodleian Library, Rawlinson MS. B. 333, f. 19 b, cent. xiii, printed here. On this manuscript see *Cat. Cod. MSS. Bibl. Bodl.* ed. Macray, pt. v, fasc. i (1862), p. 602. Printed : Sir H. Spelman, *Glossarium Archaiologicum* (1664), 394.

(B) *Ibid.* f. 34 b, in the same hand.

(C) The same chronicle in Excheq. K.R. Misc. Bks. no. 28, f. 128, cent. xiv. Printed : T. Gale, *Historiae Britannicae Scriptores XV* (1691), ii. 449, cap. xcix ; K. 1331, from Gale ; *Chronicon Abbatiæ Rameseiensis*, ed. Macray, R.S. p. 152, no. 88.

For references to later transcripts of these manuscripts see *Chron. Abbat. Rames.*, pp. xii ff.

On the authenticity of the writ see p. 246. The usual legal terms are absent here.

DATE. Harthacnut reigned jointly with Harold Harefoot 1035–37 ; but it seems unlikely that this writ was issued until he had become sole king, after his return from Denmark. He reigned from June 1040 till his death on 8 June 1042.

l. 3. *Habeat mansum suum in Tedfordia.* Thetford, Norfolk. The Norfolk Domesday does not mention any holding of the abbot of Ramsey at Thetford. In 1086 the abbot of St. Edmund's Bury had one church and one house there, and the abbot of Ely three churches, a house and two messuages (*mansuras*) (DB ii. 119, VCH *Norfolk*, ii. 48). It is uncertain whether the *mansus* of the Latin translator of this text stands for ' house ', or ' messuage '. The heading has *mansio* ; see p. 256.

(57)

AUTHORITIES :—(A) as for no. 56, f. 19 b, printed here.

(B) *Ibid.* f. 34 b.

(C) as for no. 56, f. 127 b. Printed : Gale, ii. 449, cap. xcviii ; K. 1330, from Gale ; *Chron. Abbat. Rames.*, p. 151, no. 87 ; and Pierquin, *Chartes Anglo-Saxonnes*, p. 715, no. 52.

On the authenticity of this writ see p. 246.

DATE. As for no. 56.

l. 5. *Terram orientalem de Hemmingeforde.* Identified in the VCH *Huntingdon*, ii. 310, with Hemingford Grey, Hunts, an identification facilitated by the statement in the *Chron. Abbat. Rames.*, p. 152, that in the Conqueror's reign this manor was held by Alberic de Ver, who left it to his heirs. For the later history of this estate, which was confirmed to Ramsey by the Confessor see no. 58.

(58)

AUTHORITIES :—(A) as for no. 56, f. 21 b, printed here.

(C) as for no. 56, f. 130. Printed : Gale ii. 455, cap. cx ; K. 906 ; *Chron. Abbat. Rames.* p. 164, no. 99 ; Pierquin, *Chartes Anglo-Saxonnes*, p. 825, no. 59, from K.

On the authenticity of the writ see p. 246.

DATE. Assuming that the compiler of the *Chron. Abbat. Rames.* (p. 164) was right in saying that the grant of Hemingford to Ramsey was confirmed by Edward at the petition of Abbot Ælfwine, the writ must have been issued after Ælfwine's appointment as abbot in 1043, and before the death of Bishop Eadnoth of Dorchester in 1049.

l. 3. *Terram de Hemmingfordia.* This had been granted to Ramsey Abbey by King Harthacnut and his mother ; see no. 57 above. We learn from the *Chron. Abbat. Rames.* 152 that this estate at Hemingford, rated in 1086 at 11 hides, together with 5 hides at Yelling, which had been given to the abbey by the same donors, was leased by Abbot Ælfwine and the community to one Wulfwine for the term of his life, with reversion to Ramsey Abbey on his death. According to Domesday (DB i. 207, 208, VCH *Hunts.* i. 352, 354) the abbot resumed possession of (*recepit*) these manors after Ælfric (Aluric), to whom they had been granted subsequently on similar terms, had been killed at the battle of Hastings ; but the abbot was subsequently disseised of them by Alberic de Ver, who in 1086 held them directly of the king. Details regarding the manor are given in Domesday Book. For the subsequent history of the manor of Hemingford (Grey), see VCH *Hunts.* ii. 310 f. Both Hemingford and Yelling appear in the spurious Ramsey confirmation charter in the name of Edward the Confessor, on which see p. 473.

(59)

AUTHORITIES :—(A) as for no. 56, f. 21 b, printed here.

(C) as for no. 56, f. 130. Printed : Gale ii. 455, cap. cxi ; K. 903 ; *Chron. Abbat. Rames.*, p. 165, no. 100 ; Pierquin, *Chartes Anglo-Saxonnes*, p. 823, no. 56, from K.

On the authenticity of the writ see p. 246, and on ' sake and soke ' see Introduction, pp. 73–6.

DATE. 1050–52, Ulf's period of office as bishop of Dorchester.

l. 4. *Terram de Broctona quam egomet ibi habui cum saca 7 soca in omnibus.* Broughton, Hunts. Domesday throws further light on Edward's grant. In 1086 the abbot of Ramsey's estate at Broughton included 5 hides held by sokemen in King Edward's time, but King Edward ' gave the land and the soke over the men (*socam de eis*) to St. Benedict of Ramsey in return for a service which Abbot Ælfwine did for him in Saxony, and ever afterwards the saint held it '. These sokemen claimed that they had formerly received the penalties imposed in matters of incontinence, bloodshed (*blodewitam*), and larceny up to the sum of 4 pence, the abbot having the forfeiture for larceny above that sum (DB i. 204, 208, VCH *Hunts.* i. 342, 354). On *blodwite* see Introduction, pp. 83 f.

(60)

AUTHORITIES :—(A) as for no. 56, f. 21, printed here.

(C) as for no. 56, f. 130. Printed : Gale ii. 455, cap. cix ; *Chron. Abbat. Rames.*, p. 164, no. 98. Not in Kemble.

On the authenticity of the writ see pp. 246 ff., and on ' soke ' see Introduction, pp. 73 f.

DATE. Within one of Ælfgar's two periods of office as earl of East Anglia ; either between September 1051 and September 1052, or between April 1053 and the autumn of 1057. But the earlier period is ruled out if the appointment of Stigand to the see of Canterbury (after 14 September 1052) had already taken place (see p. 573) ; and the later date must be adopted. The statement in the *Chron. Abbat. Rames.* 163, that the writ was issued at the request of Abbot Ælfwine (1043–1079/80) in consequence of claims by other persons to possess this soke, already granted by King Edward to Ramsey Abbey, may have been based on the writ itself and not on any independent source.

l. 3. *Soca infra Bichamdich . . . eidem ecclesie data fuit.* Dr. O. K. Schram has informed me that *Bichamdic* is the great Devil's Dyke which runs north and south some seven miles east of Wimbotsham ; it forms the western boundary of the parish of Beechamwell (*ol. Bicham*, simply), so that this is the dyke at Beechamwell. Dr. Schram has also pointed out to me that ' within the dyke ', on the Ramsey side (the west), lies Barton Bendish, the second element of which is shown by medieval forms to be OE *binnan dice.* For the dykes of West Norfolk and North-West Suffolk see the sketch-map illustrating Sir Cyril Fox's *Archaeology of the Cambridge Region* (1923), 133. The soke *infra Bichamdic* was the soke of the hundred and a half of Clackclose, which was appendant to the Ramsey manor of Wimbotsham (*Cart. Mon. de Rames.* i. 241). The phraseology used in this writ : *sicut primo eidem ecclesie data fuit* is more vague than might have been expected, seeing that, according to no. 61, and according to Ramsey tradition incorporated in the spurious charter of the Confessor (K. 809 ; see also p. 256, n. 1), this soke was given to the abbey by King Edward himself. This charter purports to grant to Ramsey Abbey freedom from episcopal or lay authority and many other privileges ; and to confirm all previous grants of lands, liberties, or other things. That the profits of the abbot of Ramsey were considerable is to be seen from the Domesday entry concerning the hundred and a half of Clackclose : it is stated that ' of the soke of the hundred and a half St. Benedict has 70 shillings ' (DB ii. 215 b, VCH *Norfolk*, ii. 138). Numerous other Domesday entries show that both before and after the Conquest the abbot of Ramsey had jurisdiction over men in the hundred. On this hundred see further O. S. Anderson, *The English Hundred-Names*, i. 74. See also p. 475 below.

l. 7. *Ut Alfwinum abbatem . . . adiuuetis.* For other cases where the king requests that the beneficiaries of grants announced in writs shall be helped to maintain their rights see Introduction, p. 65.

(61)

AUTHORITIES :—

i. English :
   (R) Charter Roll 8 Edw. III, m. 13 (*Cal. of Ch. R.* iv. 308), printed here. Some letters of Anglo-Saxon script imitated in this copy. The curled stroke frequently placed over the letter *i* to distinguish it has not been reproduced here ; cf. note on no. 8.
   (P) Patent Roll 3 Ric. II, p. 2, m. 23 (*Cal. of P. R.* 1377–81, 441).
   (L) Patent Roll 4 Edw. IV, p. 4, m. 4 (*Cal. of P. R.* 1461–67, 409).
   (M) Confirmation Roll 3 Hen. VII, p. 5, no. 2, 1 Hen. VIII, p. 6, no. 4.
   (E) Ramsey Cartulary in Excheq. K.R. Misc. Bks. no. 28, f. 51 b, Eng.

and Lat., cent. xiv. Printed : *Cartularium Monasterii de Rameseia*, R.S. i. 218–21.

(T) *Ibid.* f. 141, Eng. only. Printed : *Cart. Mon. de Rames.* ii. 80–1. The linguistic forms of E and T differ considerably from those of R, and are further removed from Old English. E and T are identical except for insignificant variants.

(O) Cott. Otho B. xiv, f. 263 b (*ol.* 257 b), cent. xiv. This is of the same character as E, T, and may have been copied from one of them or from the same source.

(D) B.M. Add. MS. 4936, p. 179 b, a paper copy by F. Peck (1692–1743, see DNB), with many mistakes. Printed : *Mon. Angl.* ii. 560, no. x ; J. Wise and W. M. Noble, *Ramsey Abbey* (Huntingdon, 1881), 102–4, from the preceding, with an (inaccurate) Mod. Eng. rendering ; K. 853, a ' normalised ' text ; Thorpe pp. 421–3 ; Earle pp. 343–4. Peck's copy has a wrong ref. to 8 Edw. II (for III) ; this is adopted from Peck by edd. of *Mon. Angl.*, by K., and by edd. of *Cart. Mon. de Rames* (p. 218, n. 2). Although Thorpe gives a ref. to O, D, his text is almost identical with K.'s. Earle's text is identical with K.'s, though he gives a misleading reference to O, and a fallacious reference to the manuscript as ' of century xii '.

ii. Latin :

(A) as for no. 56, f. 21, printed here.

(C) as for no. 56, f. 129 b. Printed Gale ii. 454 ; K. 853 ; *Chron. Abbat. Rames.* 162–3 ; Thorpe p. 423 ; Earle p. 344 ; Pierquin, *Chartes Anglo-Saxonnes*, p. 818, no. 50, from K.

(E) as for E above, f. 52. Printed : *Cart. Mon. de Rames.* i. 221–2.

On the authenticity of this writ see pp. 249 ff., and on ' sake and soke ' and the other legal terms employed see Introduction, pp. 73 ff.

DATE. This writ is not authentic. The dates of the persons named in the address—which may have been taken from an authentic writ—do not agree with those indicated by the final dating and attesting clause. The address indicates a date after the appointment of Gyrth to an earldom in 1057/8 and before the death of Edward on 5 January 1066. The dates of the spurious attesting clause indicate a date between the marriage of Queen Edith in 1045 and the death of Earl Godwine on 15 April 1053. In a list of abbots of Ramsey (*Chron. Abbat. Rames.* 340, *Cart. Mon. de Rames.* iii. 173) the date 1047 is given to Edward's grant to Ramsey of Ringstead, Wimbotsham with the hundred and a half (of Clackclose), and the market at Downham ; there seems no reason why this date should not be correct. More than one writ relating to these grants may however have been issued.

l. 6. *Scipbryce 7 þa sæupwarp on eallan þingen æt Bramcæstre 7 æt Ringstyde swa . . . þær ahte. Scipbryce* is defined in NED (s.v. shipbreche) as ' the right to claim what is cast on the shore in a shipwreck ', with this reference and one other. For a note on rights over the shore and what was cast up by the sea, see no. 1. In the reign of Henry I, at a gathering of the men of nine hundreds, the abbot of Ramsey successfully laid claim to a cask of wine driven ashore (*wrecatum*) at Brancaster ; in the course of which suit it was declared that on two previous occasions predecessors of the abbot had proved their claim to the possession of a ' fat fish ' (*crassus piscis*, see p. 426) cast ashore at that place (*Chron. Abbat. Rames.* 266–8).

The spurious confirmation charter of the Confessor (for which see K. 809, p. 473) separates Brancaster from Ringstead (both in Norfolk). Brancaster is mentioned among estates which had come to the abbey before the Confessor's reign, while Ringstead is included among the grants made to the abbey by King Edward himself. According to Ramsey tradition (*Chron.*

Abbat. Rames. 160), Ringstead was given to the abbey at the request of Withman, who had formerly been abbot there. Domesday records (ii. 215 b, VCH *Norfolk*, ii. 139) that it was held by the abbey in 1086, as it had been before, and that St. Benedict had the soke ; but that 31 sokemen who had belonged to it in King Edward's time had been extracted from it. Ringstead was a manor one and a half leagues in length and one league in breadth, and it was worth 6 pounds in King Edward's time.

Land at Brancaster had been granted to Ramsey Abbey at an earlier date by Wulfgifu, the third wife of the founder, Earl Æthelwine of East Anglia (*Chron. Abbat. Rames.* 57, 192). In the first half of the twelfth century it was believed (perhaps mistakenly) that King Cnut had granted to the abbey Brancaster with everything belonging to it (*ibid.* p. 267, but cf. *ibid.* p. xxxix). The abbey was in possession of a manor there in 1086 (DB. ii. 215 b, VCH *Norfolk*, ii. 139) ; it was one league in length and a half in breadth, and in 1086 was worth 10 pounds.

In a writ in Latin issued, according to Davis, 1070–82, William I announced that he had granted to Ramsey Abbey sake and soke, toll and team and *latrocinium*, and *jacturam maris*, at Ringstead and Brancaster, and all the ' customs ' that the king could have ; he enjoined that wherever St. Benedict held land he should have all his ' customs ' as fully and as freely as the king himself had, and that the abbot should hold his abbey as fully (*pleniter*) as King Edward gave it to Abbot Ælfwine with everything pertaining to the abbey ; and commanded that if any one had taken land from the abbey since the king's coronation he was to restore it if he could not prove that it was given him by the chapter (*Cart. Mon. de Rames.* i. 233, Davis, *Regesta*, no. 177). For verbal resemblances between this document and the reputed writ of the Confessor under discussion, see p. 251 above. For confirmations to Ramsey Abbey of rights at Ringstead and Brancaster by later kings, see *Chron. Abbat. Rames.* pp. 209, 222–3, 228, 281, 323.

l. 10. *Seo socne wiðinnen Bicchamdic*, i.e. jurisdiction over the hundred and a half of Clackclose ; see p. 473 above. In the spurious Ramsey charter attributed to the Confessor (for which see also p. 473), and in other references to this donation (cf. *Chron. Abbat. Rames.* 160, K. 809) the Confessor's grant is described in some such terms as these : ' Ringstede . . . et Winebodesham cum hundredo et dimidio infra Bichamdic et cum sexaginta quatuor socamannis ad hundredum pertinentibus et cum foro de Dunham ad Winebodesham pertinente '. Were these ' sixty-four sokemen ', the men who were ' moot-worthy ', mentioned in line 13 below ? For references to confirmations of these grants purporting to have been made to the abbey by later kings and by Popes Innocent II and Alexander III, see *Cart. Mon. de Rames.* iii. 398.

l. 12. *Ealle þa gerihte þa æni king mæi ahen*. On this, see p. 251.

l. 12. *Ealle þa men þa beon motwurði ferdwurði 7 faldwurði in þæt oðer healfe hundred.*

Þæt oðer healfe hundred, ' the hundred and a half ', i.e. of Clackclose, the soke within *Bichamdic*, granted by the king to Ramsey Abbey ; see line 10, and cf. no. 60.

Motwurði, ' entitled to attend the *mot* '. Words compounded with OE *-weorð(e)*, *wyrðe*, fall into two groups. The first includes such words as *arweorðe*, *tælweorðe* (or *-wyrðe*), where the second element is to be rendered ' worthy of, deserving ' (honour, blame—whatever is named in the first element). To the second group belong such words as *aþweorðe*, *botweorðe*, *fyrdweorðe*, *motweorðe*, *faldweorðe* (or *-wyrðe*), of which the last two occur only in this text. Here the meaning must be ' entitled to have, privileged to have, qualified in respect of ', whatever is named in the first element. This is also the meaning of *weorð(e)*, *wyrðe* in legal contexts, not only in Anglo-Saxon writs (see Introduction, pp. 63 f.), but also in the legal codes; e.g. II Cnut 20, where *wyrðe* is used three times in the sense of ' having the right to, entitled to ', e.g. *he ne beo æniges freorihtes wyrðe*, ' he be not entitled to any of the rights of a freeman '. H. W. C. Davis pointed out (*Regesta*, p. xxix) that there is evidence that the right and duty of attending the shire or hundred court, rather than the manorial court, might be contingent on the tenure of a holding of a certain size. A writ of William II (Davis, *Regesta*, no. 393, Charter no. lxiv, and D. C. Douglas, *Feudal Documents of Bury St. Edmunds*, Charter no. 16), addressed to all the king's judges (*judicibus*), sheriffs and officials (*ministris*) of England, contains this precept : ' defendo etiam ut non cogatis homines Sancti ire ad schiras vel ad hundreda nisi illos qui tantum terre habent (Douglas, *tenent*) unde digni fuissent tempore regis Edwardi ire ad schiras vel ad hundreda '. To this evidence might be added that of the Domesday entry concerning Fersfield in Norfolk (DB. ii. 130 b) : ' In Feruella iacet soca et saca T.R.E. de omnibus qui minus habent quam xxx acras. De illis qui habent xxx acras iacet soca et saca in hundredo,' i.e. those persons with less than 30 acres were required to attend the manorial court of Fersfield, those with more, the court of the hundred.

In the same way, *ferdwurði* must surely mean (although BT Suppt translates it ' fit to serve in the fyrd ') ' qualified (or bound) to serve in the fyrd '. And it seems reasonable to suppose that *faldwurði* (rendered by the same authority, s.v. *faldweorþ*, *faldwyrþe*, ' bound to send sheep to the folds of the lord ') means in reality ' privileged or entitled to have his own fold '— the importance of having a supply of manure for the cultivation of the fields being a matter that needs no emphasising. For references in Domesday to persons privileged to have their own fold, see Maitland, *Domesday Book and Beyond*, 76 f., VCH *Norfolk*, ii. 31. It is, for instance, recorded of certain men at Risby in Thingoe hundred in Suffolk (DB ii. 356 b, VCH *Suffolk*, ii. 491) that St. Edmund of Bury had over them sake and soke and commendation and all customs, and they could not give or sell this land without leave of the abbot ; and further, *ad faldam etiam omnes excepto uno qui faldam habuit per se*, i.e. all had also to bring their sheep to the abbot's fold, except one who had a fold for himself, that is to say, he was *faldwurði*.

l. 14. *Swa hwilc man swa þa men ahe Sce Marie 7 Sce Benedictus 7 se abbod 7 þa gebroðra in to Ramesege habben þa socne on eallen þingen ofer heom.* The king directs that jurisdiction over the men who were ' mootworthy ', ' fyrd-worthy ' and ' fold-worthy ' be transferred from himself to the abbot and monks of Ramsey Abbey, although these men might voluntarily have put themselves under other lords, who are here described as ' owning ' the men, that is to say, they had their commendation. For an instance of commendation, see no. 21. For one case out of many where soke and commendation were in different hands, one might cite the Domesday entry concerning Tunstead in Norfolk (DB ii. 244, VCH *Norfolk*, ii. 168), which belonged to Roger of Poitou, and to which Earl R[alf] added 6 freemen with 1½ ploughlands. We are told that ' of these St. Benet (of Holme) has the soke, and the commendation of one of them '.

l. 16. *Þæt market æt Dunham bi waetere 7 bi lande. Dunham* is now Downham (Market) in Clackclose hundred, Norfolk. In this context *market* seems to stand for the right to receive the market revenues, this market having previously been, according to the text, in the king's hand. On the term *market*, and the date of its introduction into English (as a loan-word from the Continent), possibly by the Confessor's time, possibly later, see F. E. Harmer, ' *Chipping* and *Market* ; a lexicographical investigation ', in *Early Cultures of North-West Europe*, pp. 345 ff. The abbot of Ramsey does not seem to have held any land at Downham in 1086, only the commendation and the soke of nine *liberi homines* (DB ii. 160, VCH *Norfolk*, ii. 83), but at least four other tenants held land there. The abbot might well have possessed market rights without having any territorial rights at Downham. The clause *bi waetere* refers no doubt to waterborne traffic on the River Ouse, for references to which see my article, *ut supra*.

l. 16. *Mid inlade 7 mid utlade.* These terms stand no doubt for the toll on goods carried in, or out of, the market. The Latin rendering : *cum inductione et eductione* given in BT s.v. *inlad*, comes merely from the (later) Latin version of this text. We may compare the *intol* and *uttol* to which the canons of York Minster were entitled according to a confirmation charter of Henry I (for references see p. 415, n. 5), and the *seamtoln* of no. 117 (see p. 78).

l. 19. *In ælcer scire þær Scs Benedictus hafð land inne his saca 7 his socne, tol 7 team 7 infangenþeof, wiðinne burhe 7 wiðuten.* For grants of judicial and financial rights to Ramsey by post-Conquest kings, see *Chron. Abbat. Rames.* 205, 206, 208, 214 etc.

l. 24. *Ealle þa gyltes þa belimpeð to mine kinehelme.* This passage is the sole authority cited in BT Suppt for the use of OE *gylt* ' offence ', in the extended sense of ' penalty, payment on account of a crime ', and of OE *cynehelm* ' crown ' in the extended sense of ' kingship '. An examination of the other writs printed here will show that this formula does not occur there, and it is indeed doubtful whether it was in use in the Old English period. I have suggested elsewhere, *Bulletin of the John Rylands Library*, xxii (1938), 362, that the formula may represent an attempt by the compiler of this writ, in the early Norman period, to translate into English the Latin formulas of his day. For the use of the Latin equivalents *omnia placita ad coronam meam pertinentia*, and *omnia placita coronæ meæ pertinentia*, in two Ramsey charters attributed to Henry I inserted in the Ramsey Chronicle, see p. 251 above. See also a charter of John, *ibid.* 323, no. 405 ; *cum omnibus libertatibus et omnibus placitis quæ ad coronam nostram pertinent.*

l. 25. *Inne Iol 7 inne Easterne 7 inne þa hali wuca æt gangdagas on ealle þingan al swa ic heo me seolf ahe.*

Gangdagas, now known as Rogation Days, the three days before Ascension Day, were marked by the chanting of solemn supplications during procession (NED).

In the Old English period offences committed at certain holy seasons incurred a higher penalty than the normal payment. In Alfred 5, 5, double payment was exacted if a theft was committed on Sunday, or during Yule, or Easter, or on the holy Thursday (i.e. Ascension Day) in the Rogation Days, as was also exacted for thefts committed during Lent. See also II Cnut 47, imposing a double penalty for offences committed on a high festival. At Chester in the Confessor's time the fines for bloodshed and other offences were doubled at certain holy seasons, the twelve days of Christmas, Candlemas Day etc. ; see Liebermann, *Gesetze*, ii. 399, s.v. ' Feiertag ', J. Tait, *The Domesday Survey of Cheshire* (Chetham Society, 1916), 81. In the same way some writs contain the formula ' in festival season and outside it ' (e.g. nos. 53, 81–3). The extra payments for offences committed at holy seasons arose perhaps because the king's special peace had been imposed then, and these extra payments would naturally accrue to the king. It would seem then that the king grants to Ramsey Abbey this royal extra—if this passage in the Ramsey writ has a substantial basis of fact.

l. 26. *Tolfreo ofer ealle Engleland.* The term *tolfreo* does not seem to occur elsewhere in Anglo-Saxon texts, but it conforms to the same pattern as *scotfreo, gafolfreo, geldfreo,* ' exempt from scot, from gafol, from geld ', terms which occur in these writs ; see pp. 439, 535.

It may well have been current in Anglo-Saxon England. For a discussion of the term, see p. 252, and also Liebermann ii. 753, ' Zollabgabe ', 5.

l. 27. *Æt gæres cepinge,* lit. ' year's marketing ', i.e. ' fair ', *ceping, ciping* (*ceaping*), being a verbal substantive from *cepan* (and other spellings), ' to barter, buy and sell ' ; but *geares ceping* does not appear to be recorded in pre-Conquest texts. There is however good evidence for the existence of one fair in pre-Conquest England, and there were almost certainly more, the distinction between the ' market ' and the ' fair ' being that the market was held weekly or oftener for the exchange of local products, whilst the fair, held at longer intervals, generally annually, attracted buyers and sellers from distant parts who traded in luxuries as well as necessities. See further F. E. Harmer, ' *Chipping* and *Market* ', *ut supra.* The Latin rendering : *in omni foro et annuis nundinis,* ' in every market (place) and annual fair ', may be merely an expansion of the Old English text.

(62)

AUTHORITIES :—

i. English :

(R) as for no. 61, printed here.

(P), (L), and (M), as for no. 61.

(E) as for no. 61, f. 44 b, Eng. and Lat. Printed : *Cart. Mon. de Rames.* i. 188–91.

(T) *ibid.* f. 140, Eng. only. Printed : *Cart. Mon. de Rames.* ii. 79–80.

(O) as for no. 61, f. 263 (*ol.* 257). On the character of E, T, O, see no. 61. Printed : K. 904.

(D) as for no. 61, f. 179.

ii. Latin :

(A) as for no. 56, f. 21 b, printed here.

(C) as for no. 56, f. 130 b. Printed : Gale ii. 456 ; K. 904 ; *Chron. Abbat. Rames.* pp. 167–9 ; Pierquin, p. 823, no. 57, from K.

(E) as for E above, f. 45. Printed : *Cart. Mon. de Rames.* i. 191–3.

On the authenticity of this writ see pp. 252 ff.

DATE. This writ is not authentic but the address may have been taken from an authentic writ, issued 1055–65, the period of Tostig's tenure of the earldom of Northumbria.

The dating of the exchange and of the agreement between Ælfwine, abbot of Ramsey, and Leofric, abbot of Peterborough (the first of the transactions described in this document) involves a chronological difficulty, since Leofsige, here described as abbot of Ely, who is supposed to have died in 1045, is brought into the company of Leofric, whose appointment as abbot of Peterborough is said to have taken place in 1052, and of Wulfgeat, whose predecessor as abbot of Crowland seems to have been still living in 1053. The dating of the second transaction, the demarcation of the holdings in the fen of the abbeys of Ramsey and of Thorney, involves the same difficulty. For a suggestion that the date of Abbot Leofsige's death may have been put ten years too early, and that he actually died in 1055, see p. 566.

The dates of the persons named in the spurious dating and attesting clause, indicate the period between the appointment of Stigand as archbishop in 1052, and the death of the Confessor on 5 January 1066.

l. 4. *Of Burh.* This place, earlier called *Medehamstede,* and here called Burh, was afterwards called Peterborough, from the dedication of the monastery to St. Peter.

l. 5. *Heo habben gespeken.* Possibly ' agreed to, settled ', rather than ' spoken (of) ' ; cf. BT Suppt, s.v. *gesprecan,* IV.

l. 7. *Nigen gerde landes* ; Latin version *nouem virgatas.* If in this passage the *gerd* (WS *gierd*), or virgate, is reckoned, according to a common reckoning, at a fourth of a hide, then the hide of land called *Huntinges hide,* the two *gerde* of Godric, and the *gerd* each of Brand, Leofgar, and Ælfwine, added together make up the nine *gerde.*

l. 7. *Æt Ludintune,* Latin versions, *Lodingtone, Lodintonam.* Lutton, between Oundle and Stilton, Northants. For the early forms of Lutton, see *The Place-Names of Northamptonshire* (E.P.-N.S.), p. 204. An estate of 1½ hides at Lutton (*æt Lundingtune*) appears among the many estates acquired by an abbot of Peterborough for the abbey in the second half of the tenth century (Robertson no. 40). In 1086 the abbey of Ramsey held in *Luditone* half a hide of land ; and at the same date a tenant held of the abbot of Peterborough 2½ hides in *Lidintone,* presumably the same place (DB i. 221 b, 222, VCH *Northamptonshire,* i. 315, 318). For the later history of Lutton, see *The History and Antiquities of Northamptonshire of John Bridges,* ed. P. Whalley (Oxford, 1791), ii. 462 ff., and VCH *Northamptonshire,* ii. 584 f.

l. 8. *Of Scs Petrus socnelande of Burh,* i.e. the sokeland of St. Peter of Peterborough. The *terra de soca* or *soca* of Domesday was defined by Maitland, *Domesday Book and Beyond* (p. 115) as a territory in which the lord's rights are, or have been, of a judiciary rather than a proprietary kind, that is to say that the lord in such a case would receive the profits of justice without being entitled to ownership of the soil. For references to other definitions of this term see Carl Stephenson, *Eng. Hist. Rev.* lix (1944), 307–8.

l. 8. *Huntinges hide be name,* lit. ' *Huntinges hide* by name '. I have not succeeded in finding this estate in Lutton.

l. 10. *Scer 7 sacleas,* ' clear and undisputed '. *Scer,* a Scandinavian loan-word (ON *skærr,* ' pure, clear, serene '), is used in OE legal terminology in the sense ' unchallenged, undisputed, uncontested '. For other instances, see Robertson, p. 240 : ' an hyde landes *sker 7 sacleas* ', where the phrase is rendered by the editor ' free and quit ' ; and also a St. Paul's charter printed in the *Ninth Report of the Historical MSS. Commission,* Pt. i (1883), Appendix, 62 : ' heo habbað geunnen hyra land þam canonike *scær 7 saccleas.* For OE *sacleas* ' free from dispute, free from obligation, unmolested, secure ', see BT and Suppt and NED, s.v. ' sackless ', and the references there. For the variant *freo 7 sacleas,* see nos. 11, 17, 18, 22, and 25 in the records of legal transactions entered in the Exeter Book (Introd. to *The Exeter Book,* R. W. Chambers, Max Förster and Robin Flower, London, 1933, 44–54) ; for *sacleas and clæne,* see no. 69 below.

l. 10. *Ær dæige 7 æfter dæige,* ' at any time whatsoever, in perpetuity '. For a note on this formula, see no. 6.

l. 11. *Æt Mærham.* Marholm, Northants. According to the *Chron. Abbat. Rames.* 165, the land at Marholm, beautifully situated between Stamford and Peterborough in the midst of woods, had for a long time been possessed by Ramsey Abbey by a good title. Peterborough Abbey also owned land near, to which the abbot and monks of Peterborough wished to add the land at Marholm that they obtained from Ramsey *propter utilitatem vicinitatis.* Marholm is now a parish in the Soke of Peterborough.

For the history of Marholm, not mentioned in Domesday, nor directly in the description of the lands of Peterborough in the early twelfth century, see VCH *Northants*. ii. 499 f. For a grant of Marholm to Peterborough by Wulfric *cild*, see *Chron. of Hugh Candidus*, ed. Mellows (1949), 70.

l. 14. *Feower þusend æl inne lenten*. On the importance of the eel fisheries in the fenland, see H. C. Darby, *The Medieval Fenland* (1940), 22–32, with many references to the Ramsey cartulary.

l. 14. *To cariteð þon abbode*. *Cariteð*, 'voluntary payment'. For an instance of Latin *caritas* in this sense, see the Domesday entry for Conington, Hunts. (DB i. 206 b, VCH *Hunts*. i. 351), where a certain Turchil is stated to have held of the abbey of Thorney 6 hides at Conington, from which he used to render a voluntary payment (*karitatem*). For contexts where the rendering 'charitable gift' would be appropriate, see Robertson no. 104. For the form, a loan-word from French, cf. *Chron*.E 1137 (*carited*).

l. 16. *Wercstan æt Bernace*. Barnack, three and a half miles south-east of Stamford, Northants. According to *The Place-Names of Northampton-shire* (E.P.-N.S.), 230, a tract of broken ground at Barnack, called 'Hills and Holes', is the site of some of the former large quarries of 'Barnack Rag', which provided most of the building material for the abbeys of Peter-borough, Crowland, Thorney and Ramsey, and for most of the churches of Holland in Lincolnshire, and of the Marshland in Norfolk.

The right of the abbot of Ramsey to stone for his church is confirmed in a writ of Henry I to the abbot of Peterborough (*Chron. Abbat. Rames.* 229) : 'Præcipio quod abbas de Ramesia juste habeat petram ad opus ecclesiæ suæ faciendum et consuetudines suas sicut Alwinus abbas antecessor ejus habuit melius et super hoc inde non disturbetur.'

l. 21. *Of Crulande*. Crowland, Lincs. The traditions of the foundation, or re-foundation, of the Benedictine monastery at Crowland in the tenth century have been discussed by Miss D. Whitelock, 'The Conversion of the Eastern Danelaw', *Saga-Book of the Viking Society* (1941), 159–76. The founder is reputed to have been a certain Thurketel, abbot of Bedford ; but the exact date at which he established monks at Crowland is not known.

l. 22. *Ælfwine abbod hafð swa wið me gespeken 7 of his me igefen þæt ic habbe þis ilce forewarde igeated*. For another instance of the favour of the king (and of the queen) being secured by means of gifts, see *Chron. Abbat. Rames*. 170 : King Edward was induced to intervene in favour of Ramsey in a dispute concerning a bequest to the abbey by a gift of twenty marks of gold, five marks of gold being given to Queen Edith in order that she might employ her influence with the king. Another case is recorded by Hemming (Hearne i. 268 f.) : Bishop Wulfstan of Worcester obtained the Confessor's support for his claim to an estate which was due to revert to Worcester by means of a gift of a 'calicem aureum magni pretii'. See also p. 524 below, and Whitelock, *Wills*, no. 11. For references to 'Queen-gold' at a later date, see *Memoranda Roll 1 John* (Pipe Roll Soc. 1943), xix, xxxix, xcvj, and for numerous other references, see W. Prynne, *Aurum Reginæ* (London, 1668). See also B. 430 (a reference for which I am indebted to Miss Whitelock).

l. 30. *Þæt ilce mærke 7 mære æfter Cnutes delfe kinges ;* Latin version, *in Kingesdelf*. The *delf* mentioned here is a channel running north from near Ramsey Mere to the R. Nen at Peterborough. It is described by Dugdale, *The History of Imbanking and Draining of Divers Fens and Marshes* (2nd ed. London, 1772), 363 : 'About two miles distant from the north-east side of (Wittlesey Mere) there is a memorable channel cut through the body of the Fen, extending itself from near Ramsey to Peterborough, and is called King's delph. The common tradition is, that King Canutus, or his Queen, being in some peril, in their passage from Ramsey to Peterborough, by reason of the boisterousness of the waves upon Wittlesey Mere, caused this ditch to be first made.' For the tradition see the *Chronica Maiora* of Matthew Paris, R.S. i. 509. The editors of the *Place-Names of Bedfordshire and Huntingdonshire* (E.P.-N.S.), 185, remark that this tradition is confirmed by the form in this Ramsey text, which similarly identifies the king with Cnut ; and that in spite of the inconsistency (remarked on by Dugdale) of this tradition with the mention of the King's Delph in a Peterborough charter ascribed to King Edgar, ' we can keep Canute and believe him to have been the promoter of this piece of early fen-engineering ', in view of the fact that all these early Peterborough charters are notorious forgeries.

In course of time the name *King's Delf* (or *Delph*) came to be used not only for the channel but also for the neighbouring fen. The ' fen called Kyngesdelf ' is described by Dugdale (*op. cit.* 365) as belonging to the abbeys of Ramsey and Thorney and the priory of Ely. For an earlier instance see the rubric in the Ramsey cartulary (*Cart. Mon. de Rames.* i. 188) of the memorandum mentioned on pp. 253 f., which gives an account of the proceedings to which this writ refers : *Kyngesdelf. Prima divisio marisci de Kyngesdelf.* Hence the *in Kingesdelf* of the Latin version of the writ.

l. 31. *Ælfwine abbod of Ramesege hit betalde wið Siwarð abbod of Þornege ;* Latin version : *abbas Alfwinus eas diracionauit contra Siwardum abbatem.* For other instances of *betellan,* ' prove one's claim to ' (not recorded in BT or Suppt), see the memorandum quoted above (p. 253) from *Cart. Mon. de Rames.* i. 188, iii. 38. See also NED s.v. ' betell '.

l. 32. *Of Þornege.* Thorney Abbey, Cambs., first founded as a community of anchorites subordinate to Peterborough, refounded by Bishop Æthelwold in King Edgar's reign (*Mon. Angl.* ii. 592, Hugo Candidus in Sparke, *Historiae Anglicanae Scriptores Varii,* 27, and also ed. Mellows, 12, 42 f.).

l. 32. *Gangestyde.* This place is now lost. For other instances of the name (apparently an OScand compound, *gagnstaðr* ' meeting-place, place of opposition '—referring to the site of a fight—with later substitution of the cognate OE *stede* for ON *staðr*), see *The Place-Names of Cambridgeshire and the Isle of Ely* (E.P.-N.S.), 345, where this explanation is given.

l. 33. *Be Hyndelake.* This place is now lost. On Bodger's *Map of Whittlesea Mere* (1750) Hind Lake is marked at the north-east corner of the mere, the point which is approximately nearest to King's Delph. In *The Place-Names of Bedfordshire and Huntingdonshire* (E.P.-N.S.), 189, the name is explained as OE *hinda lacu,* ' hinds' stream ', that is, where they water. In the above-mentioned map several such ' lakes ' are marked on the edge of the mere—Long Lake, Barnsdale Lake, Henson's Lake.

l. 34. *Wendelesmere ;* Latin versions *Wenlesmere,* (A) *Witlesmere.* Similarly in the memorandum cited above (pp. 253–6), the Ramsey version reads *Wendlesmere,* the Thorney version *Witlesmere.*

The name *Wendlesmere* seems to be recorded in the Ramsey Chronicle and in the Ramsey Cartulary only in the several texts of this writ, and the closely-related memorandum mentioned on pp. 253 f., in which it occurs only in the Ramsey version. *Wendlesmere* may have been the name of one of the smaller meres connected by channels with Whittlesey Mere ; one might hazard the conjecture that the name may have fallen into disuse, and that *Witlesmere* may have been substituted for it. For the names of numerous meres in the fenland, see *Cart. Mon. de Rames.* i. 160. *Witlesmere,* later called Whittlesey Mere, was a large lake, now drained, situated in the north-east corner of Huntingdonshire, near to the Cambridgeshire boundary, and a little to the north-west of Ramsey. For the forms of the name see *The Place-Names of Bedfordshire and Huntingdonshire*, 191. For the boundaries of *Witlesmere*, see Robertson, 328, K. 733, and a Mod. Eng. rendering from another text in H. C. Darby, *The Medieval Fenland*, 25. For a reference to an agreement regarding rights there made between the abbot of Peterborough and the abbot of Thorney in King Edward's time see DB i. 205, VCH *Hunts.* i. 346.

l. 34. *Ragereholt*. In *The Place-Names of Bedfordshire and Huntingdonshire*, 186, s.v. 'Rawerholt', this name (now lost), which occurs in K. 733 in the form *Ragreholt*, is explained as a combination of OE *hragra* 'heron' and *holt* 'wood'. The wood lay between Whittlesey Mere and King's Delph.

l. 41. *Burðein* ; Latin version, *cubicularius*. For a discussion of the status and duties of the OE *burðegn* 'chamberlain', see L. M. Larson, *The King's Household in England*, 128–30. In Latin sources the corresponding terms are *camerarius, cubicularius*, titles which Larson is inclined to consider absolutely identical.

l. 81. *Ipsius lade*. *Lade* is OE *gelad*, 'lode', 'water-course'.

(63)

AUTHORITIES :—MS. Fonds latins 943 (Sherborne Pontifical), f. 170 b, in the Bibliothèque Nationale, Paris, in a contemporary hand, printed here from a photostat. Copied on the last leaf of the codex, the text is badly rubbed and in some places almost or wholly illegible. Punctuation marks, entirely lacking in the manuscript, have been supplied. For full description of the Sherborne Pontifical and of the section, ff. 163–70, perhaps not originally belonging to it, in which the text appears, see Brotanek and Förster (for full references to whom see p. 266). Printed : K. 708 (an inferior text) ; Brotanek, 29 ; Förster, *Themse*, 784. K., as is his wont, prints indifferently *ð* and *þ*, and adds accents (not in manuscript).

On the authenticity of this writ, see pp. 266 ff.

DATE. The outside limits of date for this writ are 1001/2–1009/12, the period of office of the writer, Bishop Æthelric of Sherborne. If, as is entirely probable, the Æthelmær of the letter is the ealdorman of that name who was ealdorman of the Western Provinces, the fact that he is here addressed without the style of 'ealdorman' may indicate that the letter was sent to him before his appointment to office. The most probable date for this is 1002 (see D. Whitelock *Anglo-Saxon Wills*, 141, 144 f.). This date of 1002 would also, on the above hypothesis, be the date of the letter, since Æthelric's appointment to the see of Sherborne took place in 1001/2. If we prefer to suppose that the immediate occasion of the letter was the ship levy of 1008, we shall have to suppose that Æthelmær was for some reason addressed without the style of 'ealdorman', and the letter will then be dated c. 1008. Miss Robertson has indeed pointed out (*Charters*, 387) that the fact that Æthelmær appears again simply as *minister* (after 1002) in charters of 1004 and 1005 (K. 710, 1301), suggests that after acting as ealdorman for a brief period in 1002 he resigned office, but took it up again some years later—in any case by 1007/12—when his signature as *ealdorman* appears in the Holcombe charter (see p. 268). Bishop Æthelric's letter must have been written before the agreement recorded in the Holcombe charter. This cannot be exactly dated ; it was made either between 1007 and 1012, or, on the supposition that the name of Bishop *Æthelsie* stands for Bishop *Ælfsie* II of Winchester (see p. 268, n. 1), in 1012,

l. 2. *Æt þam scypgesceote.* We can safely reject Brotanek's form *feogesceote*, suggested because this form appears elsewhere in the Paris MS. I am indebted to Mr. N. R. Ker for the information that Kemble read *scyp-* (the reading adopted here). This is also the reading of Förster and of Mr. Ker. Mr. Ker kindly informs me that a transcript of this text in Kemble's hand exists in a letter from Kemble to Charles Purton Cooper, secretary of the Record Commission, dated from Trinity College, Cambridge, 19 December 1834, and kept now in the 1834 volume of Cooper's correspondence in the library of Lincoln's Inn. In this transcript the word appears as *scyp-gesce[atte]* with (?*re*) written over the *-p* of *scyp*, and this suggests that it was because he did not understand the word that Kemble emended it to *scyr-gesceatte* when printing the text.

Förster explains *scypgesceot*, a word not recorded elsewhere in Anglo-Saxon texts, as 'contribution in sheep', taking *scyp* (also *scip*) as a form of OE *sceap* (*scep*), 'sheep', and citing the so-called *Leges Edwardi Confessoris*, 7, 4 (Liebermann i. 632, iii. 344) to show that the church claimed one lamb in ten. But I have not adopted this interpretation. In the first place, one would have, with Förster, to suppose that one or two words have been omitted after *Niwantune hæfdon*, and that a new subject began with : *an æt Bubbancumbe.* Secondly, a contribution in sheep, which could hardly have been more than a part of a composite render, seems too small a matter to account for the obvious importance attached to its loss by the sender of the letter. Thirdly, although, as Förster states, the forms *scip*, *scyp*, 'sheep', which are specially common in Northumbrian and in Mercian texts, do occur in the dialects of other areas (he cites two instances of each form), a much more obvious explanation of *scypgesceot* is available. In late West Saxon *scyp* is a common spelling for *scip*, 'ship', the compound *scypgesceot* is a natural one (cf. *leohtgesceot*, 'contribution for supplying lights' for a church), and the interpretation 'contribution to supply a ship', makes the whole letter coherent. In the Modern English rendering I have employed the term 'ship-scot', a term used for 'ship-money' in 1640 and 1643 (see NED s.v. 'ship', p. 706, col. i). 'Ship-scot' in the seventeenth century may have been preserved as a traditional term, or it may have been revived from documents when the controversy concerning the provision of ships for the navy arose. On the formal relations between *scot* and (*ge*)*sceot* see p. 439 above. See also NED s.v. 'shot', sb. 1 IV. For 'scot-free', see p. 439.

l. 2. *Mine foregengan on ealles folces gewitnysse æt Niwantune hæfdon.* Two interpretations seem possible here. The requirement that the bishopric of Sherborne should from its 300 hides supply a ship, in 1008, or at some earlier date, may have given rise to an enquiry as to which were the lands from which a contribution was due, and this enquiry may have been held at Newton. In that case we might translate : 'which my ancestors had by the testimony of the whole people, at Newton '. Or again, the contribution from the various estates of the bishop may have been paid at Newton, in which case we might translate : ' that my ancestors had at Newton by the testimony of the whole people '.

l. 3. *Æt Niwantune.* The place-names in this text have been identified by Brotanek and Förster in their editions, and also by A. Fägersten, *The Place-Names of Dorset* (Uppsala Universitets Årsskrift, 1933) ; also by Ekwall, *Oxford Dictionary of English Place-Names.* Brotanek and Förster suggest as possible identifications for this very common name, Maiden Newton, 5 miles from Cerne Abbas, or Sturminster Newton, 11 miles from Sherborne. But neither of these appears in the lists given in *Feudal Aids*, vol. ii, for dates ranging from 1285 to 1431, of vills and hamlets in the Salisbury (Sherborne) hundreds of Sherborne, Yetminster and Beaminster (see p. 267, n. 2 above), in which, as Dr. Cam has pointed out to me, a number of the places named by Bishop Æthelric are to be found. For other Dorset places of this name, see Fägersten, *ut supra*.

l. 3. *Æt Bubbancumbe.* Bubbancumb, Bubba's *cumb*, 'coomb, deep hollow or valley', was presumably in the neighbourhood of Melbury Bubb, situated on the slope of Bubb Down Hill (in Yetminster hundred). *Bubba* was presumably an early owner. On the OE name *Bubba*, see F. M. Stenton, 'Lindsey and its Kings' in *Essays in History presented to R. Lane Poole*, 138, n. 2, and for instances of its use in place-names, see Förster, *Themse*, 785. William Bubb was tenant at Melbury Bubb in 1212. *Bubbeton* (in Yetminster hundred) appears in 1431 (*Feudal Aids*, ii. 108). For further details see Fägersten, 224.

l. 4. *Æt Awultune.* Alton Pancras, 2 miles from Cerne Abbas (Fägersten, 193).

l. 4. *Æt Upcerle.* Brotanek equates this with *Upcernle* (*n* disappearing between two consonants) and identifies it with Up Cerne, a village about a mile north of Cerne Abbas. On *Cernel*, see Fägersten, 196.

l. 4. *Æt Cliftune.* Clifton Maybank, 5 miles from Sherborne; see Fägersten, 222.

l. 5. *Æt Hiwisce.* Förster observes that there are three places in Dorset named *Hewish* or *Huish*. He suggests that Hewish (Farm) in Milton Abbas (Fägersten, 192) may be referred to here. Another possibility is Huish (Farm) in Sydling St. Nicholas (*ibid.* 202), which is in Sydling Liberty, adjoining the Up Cerne fragment of Sherborne hundred. Unfortunately no early names for either of these places seem to be recorded. There is another Huish in Winterbourne Zelstone (*ibid.* 73). Förster remarks that Huish Episcopi, Somerset, 15 miles north of Sherborne (for which the form *Hiwisc* occurs in 973) belonged to the bishop of Wells. Brotanek found in K. 730 (from the Shaftesbury cartulary) a hill called *Hiwiscbergh*, named with *Holancumb* and other places in the boundaries of Cheselbourne, 6½ miles from Up Cerne, and for that reason suggested that the text should read *Hiwiscbeorge*. There does not however seem to be room for this in the manuscript; see textual variants.

l. 5. *Æt Tril.* Identified by Förster with Trill (Farm) near Sherborne (Fägersten, 210).

l. 5. *Æt Wyllon.* Brotanek's suggestion that this is Wells in Somerset seems rightly to be rejected by Förster. It is identified, perhaps correctly, by Ekwall, *Dict. of English Place-Names*, with Wool, Dorset, DB *Wille, Welle*, but this place appears elsewhere than in the Salisbury (Sherborne) hundreds in *Feudal Aids* (cf. ii. 10, 24). It is not impossible that the place named in the text is to be identified with one of the many places in Dorset with names compounded with 'well'. Of those suggested by Förster, Woolcombe Mautravers (DB *Wellecome*) in Melbury Bubb, and Stallen (1285 *Stawell*), both appearing in the Salisbury (Sherborne) hundreds in Dorset (*Feud. Aids*, ii. 5, 41, 58, 75, 108), might be considered among other possibilities.

l. 5. *Æt Buchæmatune.* Identified by Fägersten (p. 184) with Bockhampton in south Dorset, 3 miles from Dorchester, DB *Bochehamtone*; this was however, as Dr. Cam has pointed out to me, in St. George hundred, a royal hundred, in 1285 (*Feud. Aids*, ii. 17, *Bochamtone*). Another suggestion was made by Förster, namely Buckham, near Dibberford, DB *Bochenham* (compare Fägersten p. 263), but forms in -*tune* seem to be lacking. Buckham is reckoned sometimes in Sherborne hundred, sometimes in Beaminster hundred, at various dates from 1285 to 1431 (*Feud. Aids*, ii. 8, 59, 75, 107), and appears in the spellings *Bukeham, Boucham, Bocham, Boukham*.

l. 6. *Æt Dibberwurðe*. Identified by Fägersten, 267, and Förster, with Dibberford, near Broadwindsor, Dorset, about 16 miles from Sherborne.

l. 6. *Æt Peder*[...] *þære abbuddyssan an*. More than one possibility suggests itself here. It is not inconceivable that *Peder*[ ] stands for a personal name, that of the abbess holding one hide of land which formerly contributed to the ship-scot of the bishopric of Sherborne. In that case the rendering would be : ' one with the abbess Peder[ ] '. On general grounds this interpretation seems somewhat improbable. And moreover names in *Ped-* are in Anglo-Saxon excessively rare. Searle in his *Onomasticon* cites instances of *Peada, Peda,* and *Pede,* all seemingly masculine ; and *Pedwardine,* Herefordshire, and *Pedwell,* Somerset, are explained by Ekwall in the *Dictionary of English Place-Names* as containing the (presumably masculine) personal name *Peoda*. But no name *Peder-* seems to be recorded in Anglo-Saxon sources. Another possibility is that *Peder*[ ] stands for the name of a place. Can we suppose that the construction runs : ' one at *Peder*[ ] of the abbess '—in distinction to another place of the same name ? Or, as seems on the whole less probable, should a preposition (possibly *æt* ; cf. Bosworth Toller Suppt s.v. *æt*, 1, e, f) be inserted before *þære abbuddyssan* ? The meaning in that case would be : ' one at *Peder*[ ] with (*or* from) the abbess '. It seems in any case doubtful whether *Peder*[ ] could stand for an early form of the name of the R. Parret, or perhaps of Perrott, in Dorset. Brotanek indeed on the strength of the occurrence of the form (*juxta*) *Pedridun* in an ancient list of the possessions of the bishopric of Sherborne (*Mon. Angl.* i. 337), prints here *æt ped*[*ridun*]::, the two colons standing for other letters. Brotanek's *Pedridun* would be an oblique case of the name of the R. Parret, for which Ekwall cites the forms *Pedredistrem,* (*oþ*) *Pedridan,* (*be eastan*) *Pedredan*— or perhaps of Perrott in Dorset, which takes its name from the stream and appears in Domesday Book as *Pedret, Peret* (Fägersten, 280). But Brotanek's reading *æt Ped*[*ridun*]:: does not seem to be that of the manuscript. Is it possible that *Peder*[ ] in this text stands for the old name of a district including North Petherwin in Devon and South Petherwin in Cornwall ? These two places are some miles apart, and since they have no natural features in common it is suggested in *The Place-Names of Devon* (E.P.-N.S.) i. 158, that the name *Petherwin* was originally that of a district or large area, and that this is rendered probable by the fact that there is a Cornish hundred called *Pyder*. *Petherwin* would in that case be a compound name, the additional element being British **vindo,* Welsh *gwyn,* Cornish *gwin,* ' white '. Unfortunately no pre-Conquest forms of these names seem to have been recorded, forms with *Pidre-, Pydre-, Pider-, Pither-* being most numerous among those recorded, from the twelfth century onwards, in *The Place-Names of Devon,* and by Ekwall. In the fourteenth and fifteenth centuries the form (North) *Pederwyn* is recorded, but the form with *-e-* may possibly not be ancient.

l. 10. *Æt Holancumbe*. There are several places named Holcombe in the south-west. Among the possessions of the bishopric of Sherborne enumerated in a Sherborne charter attributed to King Æthelred II, dated 998 (K. 701), are 9 *cassati* at *Holancumb*. Although this charter is not authentic, the bishopric of Sherborne may have possessed land at this place. The number 9 here is noteworthy, for 9 is the number of hides at Holcombe required to make up, together with the 33 hides already mentioned in Bishop Æthelric's letter, the full total of 42 hides to which he refers. On this evidence it is probable that the *Holancumb* of the charter attributed to Æthelred is identical with the place of the same name which appears in the letter under discussion, and which also formed the subject of the agreement of the monks of Sherborne Cathedral with Edmund the Ætheling which has been discussed above (Robertson no. 74, see p. 268 above). Fägersten's identification (*op. cit.* 194) of this place with Holcombe (Farm) near Alton Pancras in Dorset—one of the places mentioned in the bishop of Sherborne's letter—may be correct, since, as he says, this is the only Holcombe in Dorset. The number 9 appears again in Exon Domesday (DB iv. 277, VCH *Devon*, i. 455) in connection with the Devonshire manor of Holcombe (Rogus), which is stated to have paid geld for 9 hides. This may have been the *Holacumb* which was the subject of an agreement made by the bishop of Sherborne in the reign of the Confessor, in 1045 or 1046 (Robertson no. 105) ; that this Holcombe was in Devon seems probable from the fact that the agreement concerning it was made at Exeter before Earl Godwine and the whole shire. There are several other places of the same name in Devon : for instance, Holcombe Burnell, which, as Mr. Joseph Fowler has pointed out to me, is described as ' late belonging to the monastery of Shurbourne, Dorset ', in Letters and Papers of Henry VIII, 4 January 1539–40, no. 282 (39). But neither Holcombe Burnell nor Holcombe Rogus appear among the possessions of the bishopric of Salisbury (the successor of Sherborne) in Domesday, where the holders of these manors before and after the Conquest are named. Nor is it possible from Domesday to ascertain anything about Holcombe near Alton Pancras, Dorset. It seems likely that before the Survey was taken, the Sherborne estate at Holcombe, wherever it may have been, had passed out of the possession of the bishop and community.

(64)

Authorities :—(A) Liber Albus I (Register I) of the Dean and Chapter of Wells, f. 14, 14 b, Eng. and Lat., cent. xiii, printed here. See further *Calendar of the MSS. of the Dean and Chapter of Wells*, Hist. MSS. Comm., vol. i (1907), p. ix, where Liber Albus I is dated A.D. 1240 or shortly after. Printed : Hickes, *Thesaurus* (1705), i. 160 ; *Mon. Angl.* ii. 286, no. iv, from Hickes and B (below). Hickes printed his Wells texts from copies supplied to him by the archdeacon and the ' seneschallus ' of Wells. They are characterised by numerous misspellings and occasional omissions. Further, though B below is named as a source by Kemble and Thorpe, their texts are influenced in some degree by Hickes' texts. The texts printed in this edition are the first to be printed directly from A.

The hand of A frequently embellishes the round *d* (*ð*) by drawing one or more strokes through it, and is also inclined to draw a stroke through the round *d* as a mark of abbreviation. These letters in the manuscript are easily confused with ð. Strokes placed in this manuscript over the letter *i* to distinguish it are not reproduced in the texts printed here; compare note on p. 433.

(B) Harley MS. 6968, f. 7, English only, a transcript of A made c. 1686 by the Rev. Matthew Hutton (1639–1711, see DNB), an acquaintance of Hickes. Hickes (*op. cit.* p. 145) speaks in complimentary terms of Hutton, who had procured for him a manuscript of Ælfric's Latin Grammar. Latin versions omitted by Hutton. No. 65 omitted, and nos. 69, 70 incomplete. No. 67 is not in A, and therefore does not appear in B. No. 64 is printed : K. 835 and *Sax. in England*, ii. 380 ; Thorpe, 387. Lat. vers. from Hickes or *Mon. Angl.*

On the authenticity of this writ see p. 272, and on ' sake and soke ' see Introduction, pp. 73–6.

DATE. After the appointment of Giso to the see of Wells in 1060, and before his consecration at Rome on 15 April 1061.

l. 9. *Other þ man hit ofgo on his gemode swo man with him hit finde mage.* The manuscript reading is *gemoð*, where the stroke through the *ð* indicates no doubt abbreviation. Thorpe prints *gemoð*, and renders the passage : 'or that it be settled at his gemot, as may be best for him ', supposing, as did Hickes, that *gemoð* stood for OE *gemot*. There is not however, to my knowledge, any instance in these Wells writs of substitution of *ð* for *t*. There can be little doubt that the manuscript reading stands for *gemode*. In BT Suppt the passage is entered s.v. *gemede, nn.* ' that which is agreeable to one, or in conformity with one's will, pleasure ' ; see also the related adjectives *gemod, gemodsum,* and the verb *gemodsumian* in BT and Suppt. *On his gemode* will then mean ' as may be agreeable to him, in conformity with his will, according to his pleasure '. For *ofgan,* ' to hold by allowance of another ', see BT *ofgan* III, and compare no. 108 here : *hi hit ofeodon be þes biscopes gemedon* (plur.) ; see also Robertson, p. 188, ll. 20–5 : 'butan sum heora freonda þa land furþor *on þæs arcebisceopes gemede* ofgan mage to rihtan gafole oððe to oþran forewyrdan swa hit man þænne findan mage wið þone arcebisceop ', ' unless one of their friends can continue to hold the estates, *agreeably to the archbishop,* at a fair rent or on such other terms as can be devised at the time with the archbishop '.

l. 10. *þat ge him fulstan to driuan Godes gerichte.* Compare no. 71, *Godes yerichtten.* The term *Godes gerihta* is used sometimes in a wide, sometimes in a narrower sense. A striking parallel to the passage under discussion here, where the phrase is probably used in the wider sense, appears in Cnut's Proclamation of 1020 (Liebermann, *Gesetze,* i. 273–5, Robertson, *Laws,* 140–5). In article 8, the king, after praying his archbishops and all his diocesan bishops to be zealous with regard to the rights of the church (*ymbe Godes gerihta*), each in the district entrusted to him, enjoins upon his ealdormen (*ealdormannum*) to support the bishops in furthering the rights of the church (*þæt hy fylstan þam biscopum to Godes gerihtum*), and his royal authority, and the well-being of the whole nation. See also article 2, where *to Godes gerihtum,* ' the rights of the church ', and *to rihte woroldlage,* ' just secular law ', stand in conjunction. *Godes gerihta,* in the narrower sense of ' God's dues ', namely, payments to the church, are defined in the fifth and sixth codes of King Æthelred II (V Æthelred 11 = VI Æthelred 16 ff.) as plough-alms, tithe of young livestock, tithe of the fruits of the earth, Peter's pence, light-dues, and payment for the souls of the dead. For other references see Robertson, *Laws,* 393, s.v. *Godes gerihta* ; see also *Sermo Lupi ad Anglos,* ed. Whitelock, ll. 25, 28, 37.

(65)

AUTHORITIES :—(A) as for no 64, f. 14, Eng. and Lat., printed here. Printed : Hickes i. 144 (engraved plate to show the character of the script), i. 161 (text) ; the two do not always agree. The script in the plate is larger than that of the manuscript, and the plate contains three errors : *frendlich* for MS. *-liche* ; *sy hit londe* for MS. *sy hit on londe* ; *hat richt sy* for MS. *hit richt sy.* Also printed *Mon. Angl.* ii. 287, no. v ; K. 838 ; *Sax. in Eng.* ii. 380. Lat. version, Pierquin, *Chartes Anglo-Saxonnes,* p. 816, no. 46, from K.

On the authenticity of this writ see pp. 272 f., and on ' sake and soke ' see Introduction, pp. 73–6.

DATE. After, but probably not long after, Giso's consecration to the see of Wells on 15 April 1061, and before King Edward's death on 5 January 1066.

l. 7. *Cristendom to spekene*. Compare no. 71, *at þys cristendome*. *Cristendom to spekene*, lit. ' to speak Christianity ', was understood (perhaps rightly) by the compiler of the later Latin version to mean : *ad fidem predicandam 7 Christianitatem sustinendam*. But *cristendom*, like *Godes gerihta* (on which see note on no. 64, l. 10), was used both in a wide and in a narrow sense ; it may already have acquired in the reign of the Confessor the sense of ' the rights of the bishop ', ' spiritual jurisdiction ' which it had in the time of William I. Compare DB i. 298 b, VCH *Yorkshire*, ii. 194 : *quod pertinet ad christianitatem*, ' what belongs to the spiritual jurisdiction ' (of the archbishop) ; and also a writ of William I for St. Paul's (*Early Charters of St. Paul's*, ed. M. Gibbs, p. 13) : *ealle þa gerithte þe in to tham cristendome gebyrað on morðspreche 7 on unrichthæmed 7 on unrichtweorc*, ' all the rights pertaining to spiritual (or episcopal) jurisdiction in morðspræc and in unrihthæmed and in unrihtweorc '. See also NED s.v. ' Christianity ', 4.

l. 8. *Eal swo ich getrowwen to eow habben*. For another instance of this phrase with OE *getruwa*, see no. 71.

(66)

AUTHORITIES :—(A) as for no. 64, f. 17 b, 18, Eng. and Lat., printed here. Printed : Hickes i. 162 f. ; *Mon. Angl.* ii. 287, no. ix.

(B) as for no. 64, Eng. only, f. 9.   Printed : K. 836, with Lat. vers. from Hickes or *Mon. Angl.*

On the authenticity of this writ see pp. 272 f.

DATE.   After Giso's consecration on 15 April 1061, and before Edward's death on 5 January 1066.

l. 3.   *Weryge nu his land æt Chyw*.   Chew (Magna), Som.   For *werian* in the sense of ' discharge the obligations on ', see nos. 29, 107.

According to this writ the manor of Chew had belonged to Giso's predecessor in the see of Wells ; but it is not known how it came to the bishopric. This large manor, in which there was land for 50 ploughs, is entered in the Somerset Domesday (DB i. 89 b, VCH *Somerset*, i. 457) under the land of the bishop of Wells, who is said to have held it T.R.E. and to have paid geld for 30 hides.   In a spurious confirmation charter of the Confessor (K. 816, and with different spellings and a list of witnesses, calendared in the *Calendar of the MSS. of the Dean and Chapter of Wells*, Hist. MSS. Comm. (1907–14), i. 428) an estate of 50 hides at Chew is included among the possessions of the bishopric of Wells confirmed by the king.   The history of Chew Magna has been traced by F. A. Wood, *Collections for a Parochial History of Chew Magna* (Bristol, 1903).

(67)

AUTHORITIES :—(F) Liber Fuscus (Reg. IV) of the D. and C. of Wells, f. 14, Eng. only, cent. early xiv, printed here.   An inferior text with a line of descent differing from that of other Wells writs.   On the manuscript see the *First Report*, Hist. MSS. Comm. (1874), i. 93, col. i, where it is described among the manuscripts in the Bishop's Registry, Wells : it is now in the Library of the Dean and Chapter.   See also Holtzmann, *Papsturkunden* (1930–35), ii. 54.   Printed : Hickes, i. 162, n., K. 834.

(R) Liber Albus II (Reg. III), f. 21 b, a copy of F, of c. 1500.   See *Cal. of the MSS. of the D. and C. of Wells*, i. x.

On the authenticity of this writ see p. 273.

DATE.   This writ is spurious and is therefore not dated here.

(68)

AUTHORITIES :—(A) as for no. 64, f. 17 b, Eng. and Lat., printed here. Printed : Hickes i. 161 ; *Mon. Angl.* ii. 287, no. vi.

(H) as for no. 64, Eng. only, f. 8. Printed : K. 837 with Lat. vers. from Hickes or *Mon. Angl.* ; Earle p. 341 (from K.). Lat. vers., Pierquin, p. 816, no. 45, from K.

On the authenticity of this writ see pp. 273 f., and on ' sake and soke ' see Introduction pp. 73 ff.

DATE. As for no 66.

l. 3. *þæt land æt Weodmor.* Wedmore, Som. For the earlier history of Wedmore, see p. 273 above. Lands held by Giso at Wedmore appear twice in Domesday. But this was probably the land held by Giso as a ' member ' of the royal manor of Cheddar, and held by him of King Edward T.R.E. The sheriff at the time of the Survey reckoned 12 pounds for it annually in the king's farm (DB i. 86, 89 b, VCH *Somerset*, i. 435, 458). The Exon Domesday adds (*Domesday Book*, iv. 90) that the bishop held this manor of King Edward ' long before ' the king's death. In the spurious confirmation charter of the Confessor to Giso (K. 816, *Hist. MSS. Comm. Report* (1907–14), i. 428) Wedmore is reckoned at 4 hides ; and to it three *villulæ* are said to belong, one of them being *Mercern* (Mark), on which see no. 72 below.

l. 6. *Mid eallon þam forwyrhtan þe me oþer minon æftergengan to honda begon wyllen.* This passage is not noticed in BT but the Suppt gives for *forwyrht* (which has a derivative *manforwyrht*) the rendering ' evildoing, sin, crime ', with one reference : *buton forwyrhtum*, from the so-called *Poenitentiale Ecgberti, Archiepiscopi Eboracensis*, edited by B. Thorpe, *Ancient Laws and Institutes of England* (Record Commission, 1840), ii. 238, and rendered by Thorpe *sine malefactis*. It is strange that *forwyrht* in this sense should be so rarely recorded in OE, seeing that the verb *forwyrcan* is not uncommon. In the passage under discussion the *forwyrhtan* in question are perhaps the offences for which the penalty was paid to the king, *þa gerihta þe se cingc ah* of II Cnut 12, 14, 15 : these were mundbryce, hamsocn, foresteall, flymena-fyrmth, and fyrdwite (see further, Introduction pp. 79 ff.). This rendering of *forwyrhtan* involves the adoption into the text of the interlineated *begon*, presumably from OE *began* ' to fall to one's lot ' ; cf. BT Suppt, *began* I, a (2). And *wyllen* must then denote simple futurity. The whole clause would mean ' with all the offences that shall fall to me or to my successors '.

A less satisfactory interpretation would be to render *forwyrhtan* ' evildoers ' (cf. BT Suppt, *forwyrcan* II) and to adopt the reading *bogen*, ' submitted ' (OE *bugon*). The clause was not understood by the (thirteenth-century) compiler of the Latin version of this writ who writes in its place *aut alicui predecessorum*.

l. 11. *þæt se biscop dichte priuilegium þær to bi minon fullan gelifan.* See Introduction, p. 39.

(69)

AUTHORITIES :—(A) as for no. 64, f. 14, 14 b, Eng. and Lat., printed here. Printed : Hickes i. 136 (incomplete), 160, with a second Latin version composed by himself before the text of the cartulary Latin version reached him (not printed here) ; *Mon. Angl.* ii. 286, no. iii ; K. 839 ; Lat. version, Pierquin, *Chartes Anglo-Saxonnes*, p. 817, no. 47, from K.

(B) as for no. 64, Eng. only, f. 6 (incomplete).

On the authenticity of this writ see p. 274, and on ' sake and soke ' see Introduction, pp. 73–6.

DATE. As for no. 66.

l. 3. *His land æt Hlytton.* Litton, Som. This estate appears as *Hlittun* in the spurious charter of the Confessor confirming his possessions to Bishop Giso (K. 816, *Hist. MSS. Comm. Report* (1907–14), i. 428). In Domesday this manor is entered under the land of the bishop of Wells, and it is stated that the canons of St. Andrew (of Wells) hold *Litune* (DB i. 89 b, VCH *Somerset*, i. 458). They held it T.R.E. and paid geld for 8½ hides. There was land there for 7 ploughs and in 1086 it was worth 100 shillings; there were 3 mills and 60 acres of meadow and 1000 acres of pasture and 3 furlongs of woodland in length and breadth. There were in demesne 6½ hides with 2 ploughs and 6 serfs, and there were 8 villeins and 7 bordars with 4 ploughs.

l. 3. *Sacleas and clane,* ' undisputed and unburdened '. For *sacleas,* ' free from dispute ', and for the phrases : *scer 7 sacleas, freo 7 sacleas,* see no. 62 above. For *clæne* in the technical sense of ' free from burdens or obligations incurred by the previous owner ', see Robertson, p. 331.

l. 4. *Æt Peddredan,* Latin version, *apud Perret.* Identified by Ekwall (*Dict. of English Place-Names,* s.n. Perrott) with (North) Perrott, Somerset, which appears in Domesday as *Peret*; see further note on p. 485 above.

(70)

AUTHORITIES :—(A) as for no. 64, f. 18, Eng. and Lat., printed here. Printed : Hickes i. 163, with a second Latin version composed by himself before the cartulary Latin version reached him (not printed here) ; *Mon. Angl.* ii. 288, no. x ; K. 917 ; Lat. vers., Pierquin, p. 836, no. 70, from K.

(B) as for no. 64, Eng. only, p. 9 (incomplete).

On the authenticity of this writ see p. 274.

DATE. As for no. 66.

l. 1. *Se hlauedige.* For other instances of ' Lady ' employed, according to common usage, in the sense of ' Queen ', see nos. 27, 72, 79, 112, and p. 448.

l. 3. *Þaes londes æt Milferton.* Milverton, Som. Milverton appears twice in Domesday ; once as a manor held by Giso T.R.E. on which he paid geld for one virgate of land. It was held in 1086 by King William. Milverton appears again (with many details) among the lands of Queen Edith held in 1086 by King William. See DB i. 87, 89 b, VCH *Somerset*, i. 440, 458. See further p. 274. Milverton is not mentioned in the spurious confirmation charter of the Confessor (K. 816).

l. 5. *Habbe hut biridan.* For *ut* (here written *hut*) in the sense of ' away from this estate ', cf. no. 18, l. 8, no. 24, l. 12. For OE *beridan,* ' seize ', cf. no. 104.

l. 7. *Spece se mann wið þone mann þe him ær land sealde. Sp(r)ecan wið,* followed by a noun or pronoun in the accusative case, is frequently used of friendly relations in the sense of ' converse with, discuss ' ; cf. BT, s.v. *wið,* III (7). This sense seems more probable than the sense ' speak against ', also recorded in BT, *ibid.* III (14). But in the context of this writ one cannot exclude the possibility that *specan wið* means ' to bring a claim against ', though *sp(r)ecan* in this sense is usually accompanied by *on* ; cf. BT, p. 905, s.v. *sprecan,* the final paragraph.

(71)

AUTHORITIES :—(A) as for no. 64, f. 14, 14 b, Eng. and Lat., printed here. Printed : Hickes i. 162 : *Mon. Angl.* ii. 287, no. viii.

(B) as for no. 64, Eng. only, f. 8. Printed : K. 976, with Lat. vers. from Hickes or *Mon. Angl.* Lat. vers., Pierquin, p. 853, no. 96, from K.

On the authenticity of this writ see pp. 275 f., and on ' sake and soke ' and other legal terms employed see Introduction, pp. 73 ff.

DATE. After Harold's accession on 6 January 1066 and before his death on 14 October 1066.

l. 6. *At þys cristendome Godes yerichtten for to setten 7 to driuen.* For *cristendom*, see note on no. 65, and for *Godes gerichte*, see note on no. 64.

(72)

AUTHORITIES :—(A) as for no. 64, f. 17 b, Eng. and Lat., printed here. Printed : Hickes i. 162 ; *Mon. Angl.* ii. 287, no. vii.

(B) as for no. 64, Eng. only, p. 9. Printed : K. 918 ; Thorpe p. 427.

On the authenticity of this writ see pp. 274 f., and on ' sake and soke ' see Introduction, pp. 73–6.

DATE. After King Edward's death on 5 January 1066 and before Queen Edith's death on 18 December 1075.

l. 1. *Al þat hundred at Wedmore.* Dr. H. M. Cam has kindly suggested to me that this may be the hundred court of Bempstone hundred, Somerset, in which the parishes of Wedmore and Mark now lie. This hundred was once held by the see of Wells. According to Collinson the place of meeting was at a large stone in the parish of Allerton, and from this stone the hundred of Bempstone took its name, but the court may have been held at other centres, especially at a Wells manor ; for references, see O. S. Anderson, *The English Hundred Names*, ii. 49. See also H. M. Cam, *Liberties and Communities*, 108 f.

l. 3. *þat land at Merkerun* ; Latin version *Merke*. Mark, Som. The form *Merkerun* with final -*er(u)n* is supported by *Mercern* in King Edward's spurious confirmation charter (K. 816, *Hist. MSS. Comm. Report,* (1907–14), i. 429), and *Merken* in Giso's *Historiola*. Ekwall (*Dictionary of English Place-Names,* s. ' Mark ') suggests as its origin OE *mearc-ærn* ' boundary house '. The form *Merketun* in Hickes (adopted by *Mon. Angl.*, Kemble, Thorpe), is not that of Liber Albus I, and must be due either to miscopying or to deliberate alteration. This estate is not mentioned in Domesday as an independent manor, perhaps, as R. W. Eyton suggested (*Domesday Studies, Somerset,* i, 38, n. 1), because it was regarded as a mere member of Wedmore. King Edward's spurious confirmation charter (see above) names Mercern as a *villula* belonging to Wedmore.

l. 7. *Mi gauel haueð ofhealden six gear eiðer ge hunig 7 eac feoch.* For *gafol*, generally, see p. 440 and references given there. For *gafol*, ' rent ', payments in money, in kind, and in services, due from the peasant to the lord of the estate, see Liebermann, *Gesetze*, ii. 264, s.v. *Abgabe*, 7, and the references there given. See also the survey of the manor of Tidenham, and the account of the services and dues rendered at Hurstbourne Priors (Robertson nos. 109, 110). From the *Rectitudines Singularum Personarum* (Liebermann i. 444–53) we learn that there were due from the *gebur*, among many dues and services, at Michaelmas 10 *gafol*-pence, at Martinmas 23 (or more probably 24) sesters of barley and 2 hens, at Easter a young sheep or 2 pence. We hear also of the *gafolyrth* of the *gebur* (i.e. his *gafol*-ploughing, rendered *Pachtpflügen* by Liebermann ; see further BT Suppt, s.v. *gafolirþ*). Further, on one estate a *gebur* would pay *gafol* in honey, on another in food (*metegafol*), on another in ale (*ealugafol*). For honey, and payments in honey, in the Old English period, see Liebermann ii. 311, s.v. *Bienen*. See also note on no. 40 above.

K K

(73)

AUTHORITIES :—(M) ' Ex Autogr. in archiv. S. Petri Westmon.', now lost,
a writ thus described and printed by Madox, *Formulare Anglicanum* (1702),
p. 36, no. lx. The text printed here is taken from Madox's text. A footnote by Madox states that : ' Upon a Strip of Parchment cut from the
bottom hangs a Round Seal of Red Wax, three inches Large ', and that it is
delineated in Speed's *Hist. of Great Britaine* (1632 ed., 393). Assuming
that Madox has represented his exemplar accurately, the linguistic evidence
suggests that this is a text of the eleventh century, but the intrusive 7
(7, ' and ') in the valediction (see p. 72 above) and two late spellings, forbid
us to suppose that Madox had before him an original writ of King Edward
the Confessor. The ' round seal of red wax ' recalls the seals of nos. 76,
93, 94, all later copies. On the authenticity of these seals, see pp. 102 ff.
above. Madox gives a Latin version, not printed here.

(F) Cott. Faust. A. iii, f. 108 (*ol.* 97), cent. late xiii. See further on this
manuscript pp. 296 f. above. Strokes resembling an acute accent placed in this
manuscript over the letter *i* chiefly in the neighbourhood of *n*, *m*, *u*, but also
in other positions, have not been reproduced in the texts printed here ;
compare note on p. 433. Printed : *Mon. Angl.* i. 299, no. xxi ; K. 870
(with reference to both M and F) ; E. Neufeldt, *Zur Sprache des Urkundenbuches von Westminster* (1907), no. 15.

On the authenticity of this writ see p. 301, and on the legal terms employed,
see Introduction, pp. 73–8.

DATE. This writ may represent an authentic writ of Edward issued after his
accession in ? June 1042, and before the death of Bishop Ælfweard of London on
25 July 1044, but it is doubtful whether it is fully authentic in its present form.

l. 3. *Se byrig æt Winintune 7 feower hidan landes þær to.* No *burh* in
the sense of a prehistoric or Roman or Anglo-Saxon earthwork is known to
have existed at Wennington, and it seems entirely probable that this is a
survival of the early application of the term *burh* to a fortified dwelling or
defensible house. A well-known instance is the *burh* at *Merantun* mentioned
in the *Chronicle* s.a. 755. On instances in London, e.g. Aldermanbury and
Bucklersbury, see F. M. Stenton, *Norman London*, 15. After the Conquest
the term is used in the place-names of Hertfordshire, Essex, Middlesex, and
in some degree in Buckinghamshire, in the sense of ' manor-house ', ' manor '.
See further *The Chief Elements Used in English Place-Names* (E.P.-N.S.),
i, Pt. ii, 10 ; *The Place-Names of Hertfordshire* (E.P.-N.S.), 243.

l. 3. *Æt Winintune.* Identified in the VCH *Essex*, i. 445 with the
Wemtuna (for *Wenituna*) of DB ii. 15, and with Wennington, Essex. The
abbey of Westminster held here before the Conquest a manor assessed at
2½ hides, and continued to hold it in 1086. But a half-hide of land here which
had been granted to the abbey by a *liber homo* was lost to them in 1086.
This manor may possibly represent the 4 hides of the Wennington writ, if
this writ records an actual grant by King Edward to Westminster. The
half-hide lost by the abbey may or may not have been the land ' at the lea '.
The traditions relating to Wennington and to Ætsere Swearte are confused in
the spurious Westminster charters. The First Charter of King Edward (see
pp. 289–90, above) makes Ætsere Swearte the donor of Leyton, Essex, and
includes 4 hides at Wennington among the lands which had formed part of the
ancient endowment of the abbey.

As to the land *æt þære lea* (' open ground ', whether meadow, pasture, or
arable land) mentioned here as an appendage to Wennington, its situation
is not known.

One would naturally infer that this outlying parcel of land was in the neighbourhood of Wennington ; and the early forms of the name of the neighbouring parish of Aveley are compounded of OE *leah* and of OE *Ælfgyth*, which was the name of the wife of the Ætsere Swearte of this writ ; cf. DB *Aluitheleam*, and P. H. Reaney, *The Place-Names of Essex* (E.P.-N.S.), 120. There is no mention in the Domesday entries for the three manors at Aveley either of Ætsere Swearte or of his wife Ælfgyth, and the land at Aveley is not there assigned to Westminster Abbey either before or after the Conquest. But the grant, if it is authentic, belongs to the first years of King Edward's reign, and an outlying parcel of land, even if it actually came into the possession of the abbey, may well have been lost later. But the identification suggested above is not certain ; OE *leah* is a common element in Essex place-names, and uncompounded forms are also to be found ; see *The Place-Names of Essex*, 568, 585.

I have not noticed any other charter referring to the land ' at the lea ' except a charter attributed to William I in Cott. Faust. A. iii. f. 60b (not apparently noticed by Davis), on the authenticity of which see p. 301 :

' Willelmus rex Anglie Willelmo episcopo London' 7 Gaufrido de Magna Villa 7 vicecomiti 7 omnibus ministris 7 fidelibus suis Francis 7 Anglis de Essexa salutem. Volo ut sciatis quod ego concedo et firmiter precipio ut ecclesia Sancti Petri Westm' 7 Vitalis abbas et monachi eiusdem ecclesie habeant manerium de Winiton' et ecclesiam suam in eadem villa cum terra et cum socna de Lea que ad predictum manerium 7 ad ecclesiam pertinent quiete 7 honorifice in omnibus rebus 7 consuetudinibus 7 legibus 7 cum omnimoda libertate sicut Adserus 7 Aluida uxor sua pro salute anime sue ea Sancto Petro dederunt 7 sicut rex Edwardus melius 7 plenius 7 liberius illa predicto sancto concessit. Et defendo super hoc ne ullus eis aliquam iniuriam faciat quia nolo ut aliquis ullam intromissionem de illis ullo tempore habeat nisi abbas 7 monachi ad usum monasterii. Teste W. episcopo Dunelm' 7 Walcelino episcopo Winton', R. comite Mell.'

In this writ Bishop William of London, who died in 1075, is brought into conjunction with Abbot Vitalis, who was appointed in 1076 (*Crawford Charters*, 93). If the W. bishop of Durham was intended to stand for Bishop Walcher of Durham, Walcher was a possible witness at the time ; but in the corresponding Kelvedon writ (see p. 494) the bishop of Durham's name is given as William. Bishop William died in 1080, and could not have witnessed a charter with William, bishop of London.

l. 3. *Mid þære cyrice.* Cf. no. 104. For later reference to the abbot of Westminster's church at Wennington, see a writ of Henry I (Armitage Robinson, *Gilbert Crispin*, p. 149, no. 31). Throughout Domesday Book a church is regarded as a piece of property to be included among the sources of profit on a manor. See the Domesday record of the sale and giving in pledge of the church of St. Mary of the borough at Huntingdon, and the comments of F. M. Stenton (DB i. 208, VCH *Hunts.* i. 325, 354). See also on the legal position of the parish church in England at this time, H. Boehmer, ' Das Eigenkirchentum in England ', in *Festgabe für Felix Liebermann*, 1921, 301–53 ; and on the church as a piece of property, Hoops, *Reallexikon*, i. 527 ff., s.v. ' Eigenkirche '. The Huntingdon episode above is Appendix IV, 14.

l. 4. *Mid þære cyricsocne.* Cf. no. 104. ' Church-soke ' here and in no. 104 seems to mean ' the soke over the church ', i.e. the profits of justice over the land with which the church is endowed and possibly also the penalties for offences committed in and immediately around the church. Compare DB i. 375 : ' Ilbert de Laci has two parts of the soke over the church and the land which belongs to it '. See also F. M. Stenton, Introduction,

p. xxxviii, in *The Lincolnshire Domesday*, ed. C. W. Foster and T. Longley (Lincoln Record Society, xix, 1924). It seems less likely that 'church-soke' here means : 'the territory subjected to the jurisdiction of the church', as the term is defined by Stephenson and Marcham, *Sources of English Constitutional History*, 31.

l. 12. *Ænig mann ænigne onstyng habbe.* For other instances of this formula, see Introduction, p. 66. OE *onsting* is rendered in BT and Suppt, 'authority, the right to intervene, or thrust oneself into, the affairs of others'. The uncompounded verb *stingan*, 'to thrust (something into)' is used figuratively in the sense 'to thrust oneself into the affairs of another, to exercise authority'; cf. BT *stingan* I a, where a similar usage in Icelandic is cited : Þu hefir mjök *stungizk* til þessa mals, 'thou hast meddled much with this case'.

l. 14. *To ðes mynstres nytþærflicre neode.* For another instance of the compound *nytþearflic* (*nyt*[*t*], 'use, advantage, profit', and *þearflic*, 'useful, profitable, advantageous'), not apparently recorded in BT or Suppt, see no. 93. In nos. 76, 84, 104, we find *nytweorðlic* ; *nytweorðlic þearf* is rendered 'useful requirements' in BT.

(74)

AUTHORITIES :—(F) as for no. 73, f. 107 (*ol.* 96), printed here. Printed : *Mon. Angl.* i. 299, no. xix ; K. 869 ; Neufeldt no. 13.

(D) Westminster Domesday f. 269, cent. early xiv. See further on this cartulary, pp. 295 f. This text is incomplete. The lower half of the folio is cut or torn away after the first *ic*, and only the upper parts of the words remain as far as *Kylewenduna*, at the end of the line. Then after *þar* . . . *þ*, in line 3 the rest of the folio is missing. Some letters of Anglo-Saxon script imitated in no. 74 as in other texts in D. An indication concerning this is given under individual texts when D is printed here as there are exceptions. See further on this manuscript p. 292 above. Strokes resembling an acute accent placed in this manuscript over the letter *i* chiefly in the neighbourhood of *n, m, u,* but also in other positions, have not been reproduced in the texts printed here ; compare note on p. 433.

On the authenticity of this writ see pp. 301 ff., and on the legal terms employed see Introduction, pp. 74–8.

DATE. Since the writ is probably spurious it is not dated here. The address is identical with that of no. 73.

l. 3. *At Killeuendun.* Kelvedon Hatch, Essex. For the identification see P. H. Reaney, *Place-Names of Essex*, 58–9. In 1086 Westminster Abbey held Kelvedon ; in King Edward's time Ailricus had held it as a manor and as 2 hides (DB ii. 14 b, VCH *Essex*, i. 445). A Kelvedon writ in the name of William I (not apparently noticed by Davis) appears in Cott. Faust. A. iii, f. 60 :

'Willelmus rex Anglie Willelmo episcopo London' 7 Gaufrido vicecomiti 7 omnibus ministris 7 fidelibus suis Francis 7 Anglis de Essex' salutem. Sciatis quia volo 7 firmiter precipio ut Sanctus Petrus 7 monachi Westm' habeant manerium Killeuenduna' cum omnibus appendiciis suis sicut Ailricus pro anima sua predicto sancto donavit 7 sicut Edwardus rex melius 7 liberius concessit cum saca 7 soca cum toll 7 theam 7 latrone 7 cum omnibus rebus 7 consuetudinibus 7 legibus. Et nolo ut aliquis de illo aliquid auferat aut diminuat nec ullus aliquam omnino habeat intromissionem aliquo tempore nisi abbas 7 monachi ad utilitatem monasterii. T. Willelmo episcopo Dunel', Walcelino episcopo Winton', Yvone Taillebosc 7 Rodberto de Oleyo, apud Winlesor'.'

Because of the conjunction here of William of London, died 1075, and William of Durham, nominated 1080, this writ is not authentic ; see pp. 302–3.

l. 5. *It formest hauchten, 7 þider inne beqwað.* For other instances of the same formula (*hauchten,* OE *ahton*), see nos. 76, 84, *ahte 7 becwæð,* 93, *ahton 7 becwædon.* No. 73 has *ahten 7 gefon*; see also no. 75.

l. 12. *Þæt minstre is on minen munde.* For *mund,* see no. 26.

(75)

AUTHORITIES :—(F) as for no. 73, f. 111 (*ol.* 100). Printed : *Mon. Angl.* i. 300, no. xxx; K. 872; Neufeldt no. 24.

(D) as for no. 74, f. 506, printed here. Printed : Thorpe p. 361. On Thorpe's misleading reference to 'Nig. Quat. Westm.', see p. 296 above. Thorpe's text is not a close copy of D. Anglo-Saxon script in some degree imitated here.

On the authenticity of this writ see pp. 307 f. The usual legal terms are absent from this writ.

DATE. This writ may represent an authentic writ of Edward, but it may not be a close copy of such a writ. An authentic writ with this address would have the same dating as no. 73 q.v.

l. 3. *þat land 7 þane wearf.* No further mention of this grant seems to be forthcoming among the Westminster records. For an account of the wharfs and quays of London in the eleventh century, see W. R. Lethaby, *London before the Conquest* (London, 1902), 90 ff. Other grants of wharfs are mentioned in Westminster charters; e.g. the First Charter of William I (see p. 337) mentions the gift of a wharf to Westminster Abbey by a certain citizen of London called Alwoldus *Cockesfot*; see also Davis, *Reesta,* no. 217.

l. 7. *Be lande 7 be strande.* For *strand* in the sense ' (sea) shore ', see nos. 1, 31. The strand in this case is the land bordering the Thames; the king transfers to the monks of Westminster the rights that the donors had themselves possessed there. Compare the Domesday entry relating to Southwark, held by King Edward on the day of his death : ' The men of Southwark testify that in the time of King Edward no one took toll on the strand or in the water street (*vico aquæ*) except the king; and if anyone committing a trespass there should be questioned, he paid the fine (*emendebat*) to the king. If, however, he should escape unquestioned to the jurisdiction of him who had sake and soke, he (the lord) was to have the fine from the accused ' (DB i. 32, VCH *Surrey,* i. 305).

(76)

AUTHORITIES :—(W) Westminster Abbey Muniments xi, end of cent. xi, printed here. Facsimile and text : *Ordnance Survey Facsimiles of Anglo-Saxon Manuscripts,* ed. W. B. Sanders, pt. ii, Westminster, no. 9. Printed : W. de Gray Birch, *Trans. R. Soc. Lit.* 2nd Series x (1874), pp. 142 f.; Neufeldt no. 8 (O). The text is copied on a single piece of parchment, dimensions : 9½″ broad, 3″ on left side, 2⅛″ on right. Seal of reddish-white wax, very imperfect, similar to those of nos. 93, 94, but in paler wax, appended *sur simple queue.* Described by Birch *loc. cit.* 142 (9). There is a very narrow wrapping tag. The date of the hand forbids us to suppose that this is an original writ written and sealed by the clerks of the Confessor's secretariat. Other evidence suggests that this is not an authentic copy of such a writ; see pp. 297–9. It is perhaps worth mentioning that, as with nos. 80, 94, the seal is affixed upside-down.

(F) as for no. 73, f. 105 b (*ol.* 94 b). Printed : *Mon. Angl.* i. 298, no. xiv; K. 828; Neufeldt 8 (F).

(D) as for no. 74, f. 647.

On the authenticity of this writ see p. 299, and on the legal terms employed see Introduction, pp. 73–8.

DATE. Any authentic writ of Edward addressed to Archbishop Eadsige would have been issued between 1042 and Eadsige's death in 1050 ; but there is a possibility that this writ as a whole is spurious.

l. 4. *Cotlif.* This term is used in the *Chron.* A 1001 in connection with *ham,* ' residence ' : *ðone ham æt Wealtham 7 oðra cotlifa fela.* See also nos. 84, 85, 91, 98, 102, 104, all Westminster texts. Since no one of these writs has come down to us in a contemporary copy, the appearance in them of *cotlif* is not evidence that this word formed part of the vocabulary used in authentic writs. In BT Suppt the editor remarks (s.v. *cotlif*) that in ' the charters of Edward the Confessor ' (namely, the writs enumerated above) the word seems used in the sense of ' manor ', but, as Dr. Cam has kindly pointed out to me, this term is strictly speaking not applicable to pre-Norman institutions. ' Manor ' implies the economic organisation of labour bound to the land, and the feudal conception of tenure. *Cotlif* has therefore been rendered 'estate ' here ; but no single English term is an exact equivalent. Max Förster suggests that from c. 1000 ' Kossätendorf ' would be appropriate ; see *Reliquienkultus in Altengland* (Munich, 1943), 66, n. 3.

l. 4. *Leosne.* Lessness, near Erith, Kent. For the history of this estate see pp. 299 f. There was land there for 17 ploughs ; on the demesne was 1 ; and 60 villeins with 3 bordars had 15 ploughs. There were 2 serfs and 3 cottars and 3 fisheries worth 4 shillings and 30 acres of meadow and woodland (to render) 20 pigs. We learn further from Domesday (DB i. 6 b, VCH *Kent,* iii. 222) that the holder of the manor in King Edward's time had been Asor, doubtless the Atsere of this writ. The manor had been assessed at 10 sulungs T.R.E. ; in 1086 it was assessed at 4 sulungs.

l. 7. *Scotfreo 7 gafolfreo on scire 7 on hundrede,* ' free from payment of scot (i.e. contribution, tax) and of gafol (i.e. tribute, tax, rent) in shire and in hundred ': cf. no. 15 : *scotfreo fram heregelde 7 fram eghwilc oðer gaful,* and the notes there. The words *scot* and *gafol* taken together probably cover all rents and taxes. For other instances (with variants) of this clause, see nos. 86, 87, 93, and with omission of the second part, no. 104.

(77)

AUTHORITIES :—(A) Cotton Charter vii. 6, cent. late xi, or cent. early xii, more probably the latter. Facs. and text : *Facs. of Anc. Chart. in the Brit. Mus.* ed. Bond, pt. iv, no. 34. Printed : Hickes, *Thesaurus,* i. 158, with a Latin version not printed here ; K. 843, with Hickes's Lat. version ; Neufeldt no. 17 (O). Lat. version, Pierquin, *Chartes Anglo-Saxonnes,* p. 817, no. 49, from K. Text copied on a single piece of parchment, dimensions : 6 $\frac{9}{16}$" broad, 4$\frac{1}{8}$" deep on left side, 4$\frac{3}{16}$" on right. The parchment has been damaged and is defaced by open cracks. No trace of sealing, but a seal was appended in the time of Hickes, who describes it as follows : ' Charta . . . cera sigillo impressa et ligamine serico, pro more Normannorum, pendente firmata est, cujus in prima fronte extat effigies regis dextra crucem, sinistra orbem tenens ; in aversa autem, eadem effigies, dextra hastam, cui supereminet columba, et sinistra gladium gestans. Inscriptio autem in utraque facie est, Sigillum Eadwardi Anglorum Basilei.' A ' rough tricking ' of the reverse of the seal of this writ (the first few clauses of which accompany the drawing) appears in Lansdowne MS. 860, f. 304 (*ol.* 366), temp. Queen Elizabeth. A note states that the writ was then ' in custodia Gulielmi Camden '. The seal as described by Hickes, and as depicted in the Lansdowne MS., resembles seals of King Edward the Confessor. The ' crux ' appearing in Hickes's description above was no doubt the trefoil depicted on the Confessor's seals. The date of the hand forbids us to suppose that this is an original writ written and sealed by the clerks of the Confessor's secretariat ; and if this text is based upon such a writ, it has probably undergone alterations of various kinds. On Wanley's condemnation of this writ, see p. 328.

(F) as for no. 73, f. 108 b (*ol.* 97 b). Printed : *Mon. Angl.* i. 299, no. xxiii ; Neufeldt no. 17 (F).

(D) as for no. 74, f. 114 b.

On the authenticity of this writ see pp. 308-9, and on the legal terms employed see Introduction, pp. 73-8.

DATE. This may possibly represent an authentic writ of Edward, probably embellished and enlarged. The date of an authentic writ with this address would have been after the appointment of Robert of Jumièges to the see of London in August 1044, and before his promotion to that of Canterbury at mid-Lent in 1051. The name of Osgod Clapa (mentioned in the address) has not been found in lists of witnesses to charters after 1046, the year in which he was banished. He appeared in 1049 with a naval force off the coast of Flanders but soon afterwards went back to Denmark. It is not known when he returned to England or whether he was restored to the royal favour. On this evidence the date of the hypothetical original would be 1044-46, but the outside limits would be 1044-51.

l. 4. *Æt Cealchylle.* The name survives in Chalkhill House, in Gore Hundred, Middx., on the road from Neasden to Kingsbury Green, south-west of Hendon ; see *The Place-Names of Middlesex* (E.P.-N.S.), 62.

From an early date however this name was confused by the compilers and rubricators of the cartularies and histories of Westminster Abbey with early forms of the name ' Chelsea '. The rubricator of Westminster Domesday of cent. xiv has headed the page on which this writ is entered : *Midd.' Chelhchuth'* (an early form of Chelsea). A hand of cent. xv has drawn attention to his mistake by a note in Latin showing the connection that existed at that time between Chalkhill and Westminster Abbey : ' See : The servant of the Infirmary receives a stipend from Chalkhill which is near Eggesware (Edgeware, Middx.) on the day of St. Peter ad Vincula (1 August), five shillings '. This confusion of Chalkhill and Chelsea has crept into the printed text of a writ of William I in Davis, *Regesta*, no. 89, and charter no. xii, where, although the manuscript has quite plainly *Cealchille*, Davis prints *Cealchithe*. In this writ King William declares that the monks of Westminster are to have *ad subsidium victuale* the land called *Cealchille*, with everything pertaining thereto, with sake and soke, toll and team, *latro* and *emissio* and all other things and ' customs ' with which Turstan, King Edward's housecarl, held it of that king *in alodium*, and gave it to the aforesaid holy place, and as King Edward conceded it, and confirmed the grant *per cartas privilegii sui* ; and he forbids on pain of a fine of 10 pounds, that anyone shall take from Westminster Abbey a single acre in woodland or in open country, or inflict upon the abbey any injustice or wrong, or dare to intervene at any time or in any way. This writ in the name of William is probably spurious, for Bishop William of London, who died in 1075, appears in the address, while Bishop William of Durham, who was not nominated till 1080, appears among the witnesses. Davis suggested that the original may have read *W[alcher] episcopus Dunelm.*, and that this may have been expanded by a transcriber to *Willelm* ; but compare the Wennington and Kelvedon writs of William I for Westminster (pp. 493-4), which have a similar chronological dislocation, and may indeed have been fabricated by the same hand. There is indeed reason to suppose that the abbey did not long retain Chalkhill. So far as I have observed, the folio on which these two Chalkhill writs are written, the one in the name of King Edward, the other in that of King William, is the only one devoted to this manor in the Westminster Domesday cartulary, where the texts relating to individual estates are grouped together. But cf. the note of cent. xv, above.

l. 5. *Mid lande 7 mid loge.* For this formula see note on no. 45.

l. 6. *Mid mæste 7 mid æuesan*; cf. also l. 13 below, *þæt þridde swiin of æuesan*; and no. 93, l. 9, *on æuesæ.* OE *mæst* ' mast ' is of course a collective name for the fruit of the oak, beech, chestnut, and other forest trees, especially for feeding pigs. OE *æfesa, æfesn,* with a Latin equivalent *pasnagium,* ' pannage ', is the term used for the pasturing of pigs in woodland ; also for the right or privilege of so doing ; also for the payment made to the owner of the woodland for this right ; and also for the profits accruing therefrom to the owner of the woodland (see NED). The payments rendered for mast and for pannage varied from time to time and from place to place : the payment for pannage was frequently rendered in kind. We read of pannage being paid for in kind in the code of Ine : every third pig being taken when the bacon was 3 fingers thick, every fourth when the bacon was 2 fingers thick, every fifth when it was a thumb thick (Ine 49, 3). From a survey of the manor of Tidenham in Glouc. (dated c. 1050 by Liebermann) we learn that it was the rule that he who had 7 pigs should give 3, and thereafter always the tenth, and, in spite of this, pay for the right of having mast when there was mast (Robertson, *Charters,* p. 207). In Domesday (for references see VCH *Sussex,* i. 365, *Surrey,* i. 291) we hear of manors on which 1 pig in 7, or 1 pig in 10, had to be paid to the lord for the right of pasturing. The total number of pigs paid for this right is frequently recorded in Domesday, where the extent of woodland was frequently estimated by the number of pigs that it could feed, or by the number of pigs paid to the owner by way of rent. For instance, on Archbishop Lanfranc's manor at Malling in Sussex there was woodland yielding 300 pigs from the pannage (*silva ccc porcorum de pasnagio*). By *þæt þridde swiin of æuesan* in line 13 of this writ is meant 1 pig in every 3 of the pigs rendered for pannage.

The reference given for the rendering ' the produce of woods on which swine might be fed ' in BT Suppt, s.v. *æfesa,* is the Latin version of this writ printed by Kemble. This version (not to be found in the Westminster cartularies) seems to have been composed by Hickes (*loc. cit.* i. 159 note), who has misunderstood the passage, explaining *swiin* as an error for *suum,* which he takes to be OE *seam,* ' horse-load '. He (erroneously) renders the passage in the Chalkhill writ : ' tertiam quamque sarcinam iumentariam fructuum (qui nascuntur in sylua proxime ad Kyngesbyrig sita) '.

l. 13. *Þæt þridde treow,* i.e. one tree in every three. Compare no. 93 : *mid ðam þriddan treowwe* on Kyngeswude on Ditune. For other grants of one tree in every three see B. 757 : ' the third tree in *Monnespol* grove ' ; Robertson p. 80 : ' in the wood every third tree '. See also the Domesday entry concerning *Hauocumbe* in Dorset, where Earl Edwin had the right to the third oak (*tercia quercus*) in the royal wood (DB i. 75).

l. 13. *Þæs nextan wudes þe lið to Kyngesbyrig.* Kingsbury, Middx. The editors of *The Place-Names of Middlesex* observe (p. 61) that ' the association of the place with a king ' (' the king's manor or stronghold ') goes back at least to A.D. 957. *Licgan to,* ' pertain to '. The Domesday entry for Kingsbury (DB i. 128 b) mentions a wood there ' worth ' 200 pigs (*silva cc porc* ') ; see note on line 6. In King Edward's time the manor of Kingsbury, rated at 2½ hides, had been held by Alwin Horne, to whom it had been mortgaged by a certain ' man ' of the abbot of Westminster ; in 1086 it was held under the abbot of Westminster by William *camerarius* (for whom see Armitage Robinson, *Gilbert Crispin*, 130), who, according to a tradition preserved in the spurious Telligraphus of William I (see p. 337 above), gave to Westminster Abbey 3 hides in Kingsbury.

l. 14. *Se is gemæne . . . gelegd wæs.* It seems natural to take the phrase *swa he onn ældum timum gelegd wæs* with *gemæne* ' common ', i.e. held in common (by individuals to whom the trees and the pannage of the wood that they owned in common were assigned by ancient custom). For other instances of *gemæne* see K. 1163 : ' se wudu benorðan ðam and seo læs and ðæt mæsten is *gemæne* to ðam an and twentigum hidum ' ; B. 994 : ' se wuda *gemæne* þe into Loceresleage hyrð ' ; and BT Suppt, s.v. *gemæne*. For an early lawsuit concerning wood pasture (*wudulæs*) in Worcestershire, which was settled on the basis of arrangements made perhaps a century before, see Robertson no. 5.

(78)

AUTHORITIES :—(F) as for no. 73, f. 106 (*ol.* 95). Printed : *Mon. Angl.* i. 298, no. xv ; K. 827 ; Neufeldt no. 9.

(D) as for no. 74, f. 185 b, printed here. Anglo-Saxon script in some degree imitated in this copy.

On the authenticity of this writ see pp. 313–15, and on the legal terms employed see Introduction, pp. 73–8.

DATE. Beorn appears as earl in 1045, and Bishop Eadnoth and Earl Beorn died in 1049. An authentic writ with this address would therefore date from 1045–49. But it seems likely that this writ has at any rate undergone interpolation or alteration, if indeed it is not a fabrication.

l. 3. *Ældenham.* Aldenham, Herts. Two manors at Aldenham are mentioned in Domesday. The abbot of Westminster held in 1086 a manor in the hundred of Dacorum, rated at 9 hides, which had belonged to the abbey in King Edward's reign. Another manor, rated at 1 hide, in the hundred of *Albanestou*, was held in 1086 by a tenant under the abbot of St. Albans (DB i. 135, 136, VCH *Herts.* i. 312, 315). But the abbot of St. Albans at some date unknown put forward a claim to rights in the Westminster manor at Aldenham. The early history of the dispute between the two houses is obscure, but some details are available for the thirteenth century, when the abbot of Westminster's manor of Aldenham lay in the abbot of St. Albans' hundred of Cashio, formerly *Albanestou*. Dr. Cam has pointed out to me that the disputes in the thirteenth century were largely due to the fact that nearly all the land in Cashio hundred (the earlier hundred of *Albanestou*), except Aldenham, belonged to the abbot of St. Albans, that it was a conflict of two great franchise-holders as to whether the privileges of the abbey of Westminster could override those of St. Albans, and that the settlements are almost entirely concerned with matters of administration and jurisdiction. See further, the article by H. M. Cam in *Studies in Manorial History* by A. E. Levett (Oxford, 1938), 129–31. It is there stated that ' in 1201 a jury found that the hundred bailiff held view of frankpledge in Aldenham ; that Aldenham men who wished to purge themselves by the ordeal of water had to go to St. Albans ; that Aldenham men who waged battle had to fight in the St. Albans hundred court ; and that Aldenham men who were to be hanged must be hanged on the gallows of St. Albans '. The results of further disputes between the two abbots were more favourable to the abbot of Westminster. In a final accord in 1256 statements were made as to the distribution of the perquisites of justice arising in Aldenham between the two abbots. It was laid down ' that the township of Aldenham should do suit to the hundred of Cashio, wherever it should be held, every three weeks, with a penalty of four shillings for every default in attendance. The tenants of the abbot of Westminster were to be kept in his prison, if arrested for crime, and tried at Aldenham before the bailiff of St. Albans by other free men of the hundred and manor, and thieves condemned at Aldenham were to be hanged on a gallows common to both abbots '. Once a year the bailiff of the hundred was to hold the view of frankpledge at Aldenham. Other matters on which the two houses were at variance were also decided on this occasion.

At the Dissolution Westminster Abbey held the manor and rectory of Aldenham. According to the VCH *Hertfordshire* ii. 151, the grant of Aldenham to the abbey of Westminster by the Confessor was on record at an even later date, for it is there stated that on 12 February 1555 there was confirmed to Ralph Stepneth and his wife, to whom the manor, the rectory and the advowson of the church were granted in 1546 by Henry VIII, ' freedom from toll for all their goods ', as Edward the Confessor had granted to the abbots of Westminster and their men.

l. 5. *þiowlice*. Two instances of the adjective *þeowlic* ' servile ' are recorded in BT and Suppt, but no corresponding adverb. The appearance of the adverb here is not evidence that it was in use in the time of the Confessor.

l. 5. *Ætforen gewitnesse mid halra tunge Ælfrice þam abbode 7 þam gebroðran up betæhte*. *Mid halra tunge*, lit. ' with whole tongue ', i.e., in plain unequivocal language ; cf. BT and Suppt, s.v. *hal*. A close parallel to the passage cited above is to be found in another Westminster charter (Robertson, p. 92) : ' þa betæhte Ecgferð *on halre tungan* land 7 boc on cynges gewitnesse Dunstane arcebisceope '. Miss Robertson renders the phrase ' unequivocally ' but remarks (p. 338) that it seems possible that in its context the phrase here) and perhaps elsewhere) corresponds to Latin *viva voce*. But Miss Whitelock has suggested to me that *mid halra tunge* might possibly mean ' distinctly ', in view of the use in *Ælfric's Saints' Lives*, ed. Skeat, ii (1900), xxxi, line 1118. A dumb maiden is healed, ' 7 hæfde hire spræce *mid halre tungan* ', i.e. she was able to speak properly and distinctly.

l. 7. *Into þam minstre be'o' Offie 7 be Cenwulfes cinges dagum* (Westminster Domesday) ; *into þan minstre behoue 7 be Kenwlfes kinges dagen* (Cott. Faust. A iii). This passage presents difficulties which can scarcely be solved in the absence of any earlier version. In most cases the texts of the writs in Westminster Domesday preserve earlier forms more faithfully than do those in Cott. Faust. A. iii ; but it is difficult to account for the interlinear *o* above *be* and for the spelling *Offie* for *Offa*, unless we suppose that they originated at a time when the correct forms (*be Offan*) were not known. But there are even now at Westminster two copies on single pieces of parchment of an Aldenham charter attributed to Offa, a copy of which immediately precedes this writ in the Westminster Domesday cartulary. On the other hand it is difficult to accept the Faustina version (above). As it stands it is ungrammatical : ' for the benefit of the minster (with *minstre*, apparently for genitive *minstres*) and in King Coenwulf's days '. If we amend the syntax by removing *and*, there remains the difficulty that it is with Offa and not with Coenwulf that Abbot Ordbriht is associated in the Aldenham charter mentioned above. It is easier on the whole to suppose that the Faustina *behoue* (OE *behof*, Mod. Eng. ' behoof ') is a scribal substitution for *be Offan*.

J. Armitage Robinson (*The Saxon Bishops of Wells*, 67) remarks that the early history of Westminster may be said to begin with King Offa, towards the end of the eighth century, and that the Westminster historian Sulcard (see

p. 287) says that Offa had intended to place monks there, but that his purpose was not carried out. The authenticity as a product of Offa's reign of the Aldenham charter attributed to Offa, in its two extant forms (*Ordnance Survey Facsimiles*, pt. ii, Westminster, p. 2, nos. i and 2 ; K. 149, B. 245), is doubtful ; but, as Armitage Robinson remarks, the grant that the charter describes may very well have been made by Offa to the monastery. In this charter (in Latin, with bounds in English), dated 785, King Offa makes to Westminster a grant of 10 *cassates* of land at Aldenham in perpetuity, Abbot Ordbriht having paid for it 100 mancuses of pure gold in an armlet. Flete (ed. Armitage Robinson, 34) mentions as evidence of the dignity and freedom of Westminster Abbey, charters and deeds of Offa, Coenwulf, Edgar, Æthelred, St. Edward, William I, and their successors up to the time of Henry VI. Nothing is known, from any early source, of benefactions of King Coenwulf of Mercia to Westminster Abbey. The editors of the *Crawford Charters* suggest (p. 93) that his name was probably inserted into the so-called Great Charter of King Edgar to Westminster (see p. 338) because he was known as a benefactor of monasteries, but we cannot of course exclude the possibility that he may have made grants to Westminster of which no records are now extant. Offa was also the reputed founder of the abbey of St. Albans, Coenwulf of Winchcombe.

l. 8. *Swa swa Ædgar cinge on his gewrite . . . gefestnode.* No genuine charter of King Edgar confirming this estate to Westminster is now known to be extant, but Aldenham is mentioned in the spurious Great Charter of King Edgar in a list of estates bestowed on the monastery by earlier kings. This charter (on which see p. 338) states that the monastery had been enriched with gifts and privileges by Offa and Coenwulf *regibus celeberrimis*, a point of some interest in view of the inclusion of these names in the Aldenham writ. The spurious Great Charter of Dunstan (B. 1050) probably compiled about the same time as the charter attributed to Edgar (see *Crawford Charters*, 92) adds to the names of reputed benefactors of Westminster those of Edgar and of Alfred. Another spurious charter, the so-called First Charter of the Confessor (see pp. 289 f.) confirms to the monastery 10 hides at Aldenham among the grants of earlier kings.

(79)

AUTHORITIES :—(F) as for no. 73, f. 107 (*ol*. 96). Printed : *Mon. Angl.* i. 298, no. xvii ; K. 826 ; Neufeldt no. 11.

(D) as for no. 74, f. 227, printed here. Anglo-Saxon script in some degree imitated here.

On the authenticity of this writ see pp. 315 f., and on the legal terms employed see Introduction, pp. 73–8.

DATE. Any authentic writ naming Eadnoth of Dorchester in the address would have been issued before the bishop's death in 1049. The authenticity of the present writ in its extant form is not certain, and it would appear at the least to have undergone interpolation. But assuming that King Edward did actually issue a Datchworth-Watton writ in favour of Westminster Abbey naming Eadnoth in the address, and that the mention of the transaction between Ælfwynn and Abbot Eadwine and the community formed part of it when it was first issued, then the only possible date for the issue of such a writ would be 1049, after the appointment of Edwin as abbot of Westminster (in succession to Wulfnoth, who, according to Flete, died on 19 October 1049) and before the death of Bishop Eadnoth in the same year. It is to be noted that *Chronicle* C records (correctly) under the year 1049 the death of Eadnoth and that of Wulfnoth, Edwin's predecessor, and also the death of Earl Beorn.

l. 3. *Deceswrþe 7 Wattune.* Datchworth and Watton, Herts. Watton is identified in the *Crawford Charters* (p. 98) with Watton-at-Stone, Hertford. In the spurious First Charter of the Confessor (see pp. 289f.), in which the king is made to confirm the grant of these estates to the abbey, the land at Datchworth is said to comprise 4 hides and 1 virgate ; that at Watton 4½ hides. The abbot of Westminster is said in Domesday to have held T.R.E. at Datchworth 3 hides and 1 virgate, and to have had in addition the overlordship of 1 hide held by Aluric Blac. At Watton the abbot had T.R.E. 1 hide, Aluric Blac held of the abbot 2 hides and Godwine held of the abbot 1½ hides. But by 1086 the abbot of Westminster had sustained losses both at Datchworth and at Watton. At Datchworth he still held 3 hides and 1 virgate, and at Watton 1 hide. But the holdings of Aluric Blac—although according to Domesday they could not be alienated from the church (of Westminster)— had both at Datchworth and at Watton been lost to the abbey and had passed into the hands of the archbishop of Canterbury, together with a half-hide at Watton held by Almar, a man of Aluric ; Aluric Blac having been the man of Archbishop Stigand in respect of other estates, Stigand's successor Lanfranc made this a pretext for seizing the lands that Aluric held of the abbot of Westminster. The archbishop still retained possession of them in 1086, and had granted the lands to his tenant Anschitil de Ros (DB i. 133, 135 ; VCH *Herts.* i. 305, 312, iii. 78).

Still another loss sustained by the abbot of Westminster at Watton is recorded in Domesday Book. The estate of 1½ hides at Watton which Godwine had held of the abbey T.R.E. was to have reverted to the abbey at his death. But his wife illegally transferred the lordship to Eddeva Pulchra, apparently during the lifetime of her husband and before the death of the Confessor. This estate seems to have been granted by William I to Count Alan, though Godwine still held part of the land of him at the time of the Survey, 16 acres having been abstracted from it after the Conquest to form an additional holding for Anschitil de Ros, who held it under the Archbishop (DB i. 136 b, VCH *Herts.*, i. 319, iii. 161 ; Freeman, i. 397, v. 525).

The abbot of Westminster's desire to establish his claim to these estates, which were perhaps already being broken up, is seen in a writ that he secured from William I which immediately follows the present one in Westminster Domesday (Davis, *Regesta*, no. 16). This writ instructs Edmund the sheriff (of Hertfordshire), Alfwine Gottune (see p. 552), and Leofwine Scufe, that they are on the king's behalf to put St. Peter's, Westminster, into full possession of the estates at Watton and at Datchworth (' þæt ge geridan þa land æt Watton 7 æt Daccewurðe Sce Petre to handa '), and to investigate the king's own rights there. It seems likely that this writ belongs to the early years of the Conqueror's reign (Davis dates it ? 1067), and there seems no reason to doubt its authenticity. According to the VCH *Herts.* iii. 78, 161, the one hide remaining to the abbot of Westminster at Watton was afterwards united to the Westminster manor of Stevenage, while the overlordship of Datchworth remained with the abbots of Westminster until the sixteenth century. When in 1540 the abbey was converted into the seat of a bishopric, Datchworth was confirmed to the see, but in 1554 granted to the bishopric of London.

l. 5. *Alwunn si nunne hit heold of þam minstre 7 atforen Ædiðe þaire hlafdie Æadwine abbyde 7 þam monecan up hyo betehte.* Nothing further is known of Ælfwynn or of the circumstances in which this transaction took place. The phraseology used closely resembles that used in lines 5–7 of the Aldenham writ (no. 78), and it seems natural to interpret these lines in the same way. In that case *hyo* in the phrase *up hyo betehte* will be neut. accus. plur. ' them ' (referring to the two estates), and *hit* in the phrase *hit heold* will either be a scribal error for *hio* (*hie*) or else will refer to the two estates collectively. The same verb *betæcan* (without *up*) is used in a Westminster charter of high repute (Robertson p. 92) : ' þa *betæhte* Ecgferð on halre tungan land 7 boc on cynges gewitnesse Dunstane arcebisceope ', ' then Ecgferth unequivocally committed both the estate and the title-deeds with the cognisance of the king to archbishop Dunstan ' ; for an alternative rendering for *on halre tungan*, see p. 550. Incidentally we learn from this charter that Ecgferth held this estate till the end of his life and that it was then (supposedly when his death was approaching) that he made over the land and the title-deeds to Dunstan (' in order that he might act as guardian to his widow and child '). For another instance of a nun holding land, see DB i. 173 b, VCH *Worcs.* i. 295 : a hide of land had been leased to the nun Eadgyth for as long as the monks of Worcester Cathedral were willing and could dispense with it ; but their number increasing in King William's time, she restored it to them.

l. 7. *Æadgar cingc in to þam minstre hyo geuuþe*. *Decewrthe* and *Wattune* are named in the spurious Great Charter of King Edgar (K. 483 = 555, *Crawford Charters* no. vi ; see p. 338 above) among the estates which were granted to Westminster by the King himself. On the mention of King Edgar in this writ, see pp. 315 f.

l. 8. *Swa hyo gedemde waron on þam nigon sciran on Wendelbury*. Lit. ' in the nine shires ', i.e. ' in (a court of) the nine shires '. The rendering ' in ' for *on* in the text receives support from the phraseology of Domesday in an entry which refers to a court of four shires : ' Has v hidas (at Bengeworth) diratiocinauit Walter Abbod ad Ildebergam *in iiii sciris* coram episcopo baiocensi 7 aliis baronibus regis ' (DB i. 175 b, VCH *Worcs.* i. 307). For a reference to a judgment given in a shire court see no. 35.

Nothing is known from other sources of this assembly of representatives of nine shires in which judgment was given in the suit concerning Datchworth and Watton, and there is no indication as to its date, whether in the reign of the Confessor or before his time. Occasionally in the pre-Conquest period, and frequently after the Conquest, we hear of the holding of assemblies of the magnates from several contiguous shires in which matters at issue concerning lands were settled. The *micel gemot* at Alderbury in Wiltshire late in the tenth century which was informed of a purchase of land by Osgar, Abbot of Abingdon, was attended by magnates from at least three shires (Robertson no. 51). In the post-Conquest period we hear of courts of five and of seven shires presided over by Bishop Odo of Bayeux (Bigelow, *Placita Anglo-Normannica*, 20, 22) of one of four ' sheriffdoms ' at which Queen Matilda was present (DB i. 238 b, VCH *Warwick*, i. 303), and of another of four shires at Kentford (Bigelow p. 22). The claim of Bishop Arfast against Abbot Baldwine of Bury (see pp. 141 ff.) was at one stage investigated in a court of nine shires (*novem comitatum cetu*) at Bury, presided over by Archbishop Lanfranc (Arnold, *Memorials of Bury St. Edmunds*, R.S. i. 65).

Is the *Wendelbury* of the text, Wellingborough, Northants ? This appears in Domesday as *Wendle(s)berie* and *Wedlingeberie*, and as *Wendelburg*, among many other spellings, in the thirteenth century ; see *The Place-Names of Northamptonshire* (E.P.-N.S.), 140, where the name is interpreted to mean ' *burh* of Wændel's people '. Another possibility is Wendlebury near Bicester, Oxon., which appears in Domesday as *Wandesberie* and in other sources has as its first element *Wendel-, Wendle-* ; see Ekwall, *Dictionary of Place-Names*. A Vandlebury outside Cambridge appears as *Wendelbiri* in the thirteenth century ; this form contains the same personal name *Wændel* as Wellingborough and Wendlebury ; see *The Place-Names of Cambridgeshire and of the Isle of Ely* (E.P.-N.S.), 88. Vandlebury was indeed the meeting-place of 9 hundreds (not shires) in the reign of Stephen (*Anglia Sacra*, i. 619) : **apud**

Wyndilbyry . . . coram novem hundredis. But the possibility that Vandle-bury is the *Wendelbury* of Edward's writ seems remote, for neither Datchworth nor Watton is in Cambridgeshire. Of these possibilities Wellingborough seems on the whole the most likely.

(80)

AUTHORITIES :—(S) B.M. Sloane Charter xxxiv. 1, printed here, a spurious writ. The hand has the appearance of a contemporary hand. Facs. and text : *Facs. of Anc. Chart. in the Brit. Mus.* ed. Bond, pt. iv, no. 35 (but with erroneous reference to Cotton Charter xxxiv. 1). Printed : Birch, *Trans. R. Soc. Lit.* 2nd ser. x, 140, inaccurately ; Neufeldt no. 18 (O). The writ is written on a single piece of parchment, dimensions : 8″ broad, 2½″ on left side, 1⅝″ on right. Text in poor condition and very faint in places ; letters no longer visible have been supplied in my text from Bond's transcript. A seal of reddish-brown substance, with main features well preserved, but bent and twisted, appended upside-down *sur simple queue* to seal tag. A ' step ' may indicate the former presence of a wrapping tag. Seal described : Birch, *Trans. ut supra*, 139 (1), and *Cat. of Seals in the Brit. Mus.* i. 2 (5) ; Wyon, *Great Seals*, 3 (5). On internal evidence (see pp. 316 f.) this is not a product of the clerks of King Edward's secretariat. On Wanley's condemnation of this writ see p. 328.

(F) as for no. 73, f. 109 (*ol.* 98). Printed : *Mon. Angl.* i. 299, no. xxiv ; K. 873 ; Neufeldt no. 18 (F).

(D) as for no. 74, f. 648.

On the authenticity of the writ see pp. 316 ff.

DATE. This writ in so far as it relates to the Westminster claim to Ickworth cannot be dated. If the protocol is that of an authentic writ, that writ must have been issued between the appointment of Æthelmær to the bishopric of East Anglia in 1047, and the death of Abbot Leofstan of Bury on 1 August 1065. The conjunction (which may be authentic) of Harold and Gyrth in the address makes it difficult to date it more closely, since Gyrth may here have been acting in a subordinate capacity to Harold, or he may have succeeded to the earldom. See further Biographical Notes.

l. 3. *Æt Iccawurðe.* Ickworth, Suffolk, in Thingoe hundred (see p. 437), about 3 miles from Bury St. Edmunds. The history of Ickworth is obscure. In 1086 and T.R.E. St. Edmund of Bury held Ickworth (*Kkwortha*), rated at 3 carucates (DB ii. 375 b), and the fact that the Ickworth writ is addressed among others to Abbot Leofstan of Bury indicates that Bury had some interest in the estate to which this writ refers. Land at Ickworth and other places had been bequeathed to Bury by Theodred, bishop of London, in a will dating from 942–c. 951 (Whitelock p. 4), but a document in the *Pinch-beck Register,* ed. Hervey, ii. 283, 380, says that the monks ' after the expulsion of the clerks ' exchanged Ickworth with a certain *miles* for *Elveden.* For the reputed grant of Ickworth to Westminster by one of the Confessor's *milites*, and on a lease by Abbot Vitalis of Westminster of land at Ickworth, see pp. 317 f. On the exchange, mentioned above, and on the subsequent history of Ickworth, see John Gage, *Hist. and Antiq. of Suffolk ; Thingoe Hundred* (London, 1838), 275 ff. Gage says nothing of any connection between Ickworth and Westminster Abbey.

l. 6. *Swa hraðe swa þis gewrit her nu gerædd beo.* For another reference to the reading of a writ (presumably in the shire court) see a writ of William I enjoining that any of the things which may have been alienated from two Westminster manors are to be restored within seven nights from the time the writ is read : ' þat itt cume ongean binnen sefen nihten þas (MS. þar) þe þis gewritt geræd bið ' (Davis, *Regesta*, no. 87, text in Neufeldt no. 31, and *Mon. Angl.* i. 301, no. xxxvii). Similarly another writ of William I enjoins that the things alienated from the land at Marston are to be restored within seven nights ' from the day on which this letter shall come to you ' (cume ongean in þas dages binnen sefen nihte þe þis gewritt to eow comþ) (Davis, no. 18, Text in Neufeldt no. 28 and *Mon. Angl.* i. 301, no. xxxiv).

(81)

AUTHORITIES :—(E) Westminster Abbey Muniments xviii, second half of cent. xi, printed here, Facs. and text : *Ordnance Survey Facsimiles*, ed. Sanders, pt. ii, Westminster, no. 17. Printed : R. Widmore, *Enquiry into the Time of the First Foundation of Westminster Abbey* (1743) Appendix no. 1, with Lat. version by Widmore not printed here. Text copied on a single piece of parchment, dimensions : 5⅞″ broad, 1¾″ deep on left side, 1¼″ on right. The hand might be contemporary (with a writ issued 1049–66), but it seems more likely that it is a little later ; it is a square hand more characteristic of the later than of the earlier cent. xi. No seal, but two tags. The upper tag broken away perhaps through the weight of a seal. It is difficult to decide on palæographical grounds whether this is or is not an original writ written (and sealed) by the clerks of King Edward the Confessor's secretariat, but taking into account the linguistic evidence, one is inclined to think that it is a slightly later copy of an original writ.

(D) as for no. 74, f. 46.

Not in F.

On the authenticity of the writ see p. 318, and on the legal terms employed see Introduction, pp. 73–81.

DATE. After the appointment as abbot of Edwin in succession to Wulfnoth (who according to Flete died on 19 October 1049), and before Edward's death on 5 January 1066.

(82)

AUTHORITIES :—(T) Westminster Abbey Muniments xix, second half of cent. xi, printed here. Facs. and text : *Ordn. Surv. Facs.* pt. ii, Westminster, no. 16. Printed : Birch, *Trans. R. Soc. Lit.* 2nd ser. x. 143 ; Neufeldt no. 22 (O). Text written in dark ink on a single piece of parchment with dark patches. Dimensions : 6⅞″ broad, 1 11/16″ deep, right side, 1 5/16″ left. A small semicircular gap in the top edge extends from the first line of the text into the second. A small fragment of seal now vanished, but described by Birch, *ut supra*, 143 (10), as ' a small white flaky fragment of the centre of the seal ' is shown in the *Ord. Surv. Facs.* appended *sur simple queue* to a seal tag. A ' step ' may indicate the former existence of a wrapping tag. The evidence of the linguistic forms combines with palæographical evidence to suggest that this text is probably a copy made after the Confessor's time, possibly from an authentic writ of that king.

(F) as for no. 73, f. 110 (*ol.* 89). Printed : *Mon. Angl.* i. 300, no. xxviii ; Neufeldt no. 22 (F). K. 889 is a combination of nos. 81, 82.

(D) as for no. 74, f. 46.

On the authenticity of this writ see pp. 318 f., and on the legal terms employed see Introduction, pp. 73–81.

DATE. This writ cannot be more narrowly dated than Edward's reign, 1042–66.

l. 6. *On stræte 7 of stræte.* Cf. nos. 83, 97–101, 105, 106 (all Westminster texts, and some dubious, but nos. 97 and 99 are authentic). Information as to the king's prerogative over the highway is much more abundant after the Norman Conquest than before ; see Liebermann ii. 673–5, s.v. ' Strasse ', and also J. Goebel, *Felony and Misdemeanor*, 431, n. 345. In the so-called *Leis Willelme*, 26 (compiled 1090–1135), we read : ' If anyone slays or assaults anyone who is travelling through the country on any of the four highways, namely, Watling Street, Ermine Street, the Fosse Way, the Icknield Way, he violates the king's peace ' (Liebermann i. 510, Robertson, *Laws*, 267). See also IV Æthelred 4 (extant only in the Quadripartitus), Liebermann i. 234, Robertson, *Laws*, 74 : ' He who assaults an innocent person on the king's highway, if he is slain, shall lie in an unhonoured grave.' Compare also DB i. 280, VCH *Nottinghamshire*, i. 248 : ' In Nottingham the water of Trent and the Fosse(way) and the road toward York are so guarded that if anyone impedes the passage of boats or if anyone ploughs or makes a ditch within two perches of the king's road he has to pay a fine of (*emendare per*) 8 pounds.' See also in the A version of the Penenden trial (J. Le Patourel in *Studies . . . presented to F. M. Powicke*, 24) the king's *consuetudines* throughout all the lands of Christ Church. The king had the amends if a man of the archbishop dug up the king's highway, or if a tree was felled across it, or if bloodshed or homicide or other crime was committed upon it (provided in the last case that the offender was detained at once ; otherwise the king could not lawfully demand anything).

(83)

AUTHORITIES :—(F) as for no. 73, f. 111 b (*ol.* 100 b). Printed *Mon. Angl.* i. 300, no. xxxi ; Neufeldt no. 26.

(D) as for no. 74, f. 46, printed here. Anglo-Saxon script is in some degree imitated in this copy.

On the authenticity of this writ see pp. 318 f., and on the legal terms employed see Introduction, pp. 73–81.

DATE. As for no. 82.

(84)

AUTHORITIES :—(F) as for no. 73, f. 107 b (*ol.* 96 b), printed here. Printed : *Mon. Angl.* i. 299, no. xx ; K. 859 ; Neufeldt no. 14.

Not in D.

On the authenticity of this writ see p. 299, and on the legal terms employed see Introduction, pp. 73–82.

DATE. If in its extant form this writ is a copy of an authentic writ of King Edward or based on such a writ, that writ must have been issued after the appointment of William to the see of London in 1051. Since Essex formed part of Harold's earldom when he was earl of East Anglia, the writ must have been issued before he relinquished that earldom after the death of Earl Godwine on 15 April 1053. But it can be dated still more closely, for the only time when Bishop William could have been addressed in a writ in conjunction with Harold, as earl of Essex, was in the last months of 1052 or in the early months of 1053. When William was appointed to the see of London after the deposition (before consecration) of Spearhafoc in the autumn of 1051, Earl Godwine and his family were in exile. When on 14 September 1052 negotiations were begun for their return, Bishop William fled oversea with Archbishop Robert. But Florence of Worcester tells us s.a. 1052 that William was shortly afterwards (*parvo post tempore*) recalled and reinstated. The writ must have been issued after his return, and during the few remaining months in which Harold held the earldom of Essex.

l. 3. *Molesham*. Moulsham, Essex. This is probably the manor of *Molesham* held by Westminster Abbey both in King Edward's time and in 1086 as 5 hides less 30 acres. In King Edward's time there were 8 villeins and 4 bordars there. Then, as in 1086, there were 3 ploughs on the demesne and 4 ploughs belonging to the men. There was woodland for 400 swine, and 30 acres of meadow (DB ii. 15, VCH *Essex*, i. 445). The spurious Telligraphus of King Edward (for which see p. 290) preserves a tradition (which may be authentic) that Moulsham was granted by Leofcild to the abbey *cum terra bruerii* ('heathland') *appendice sua*. This no doubt is the *terra de Brom* ('broom, heath') mentioned in two other Westminster writs. The first of these (Cott. Faust. A iii f. 60, not noticed by Davis) runs as follows :

'Willelmus rex Anglie omnibus ministris 7 fidelibus suis de Essexa salutem. Sciatis quia uolo 7 concedo ut Sanctus Petrus 7 Gillebertus abbas habeant manerium Mulesham cum omnibus appendiciis suis 7 cum terra de Brom quam Wlmarus de eodem sancto tenuit cum saca 7 soca cum toll 7 theam 7 latrone 7 cum omnibus rebus 7 consuetudinibus 7 legibus sicut rex Edwardus melius 7 liberius predicto sancto concessit. Et nolo ut aliquis ullam intromissionem de illis ullo tempore habeat nisi abbas 7 monachi ad usum monasterii. T. W. episcopo Dunel. 7 R. comit. de Mellent.'

A writ of William II referring to the same manor follows on the next folio :

'Willelmus rex Anglie P. de Valoniis 7 vicecomiti 7 omnibus ministris suis de Essex salutem. Precipio uobis ut resaisiatis ecclesiam Sancti Petri Westm. de terra de Brom quam Wlmarus tenuit de predicto sancto 7 quam Thuroldus dapifer episcopi Baioc. iniuste 7 per vim ei abstulit. Et uolo 7 concedo ut ita habeat manerium de Mulesham ad quod terra illa pertinet sicut rex Edwardus melius 7 plenius eidem sancto concessit 7 sicut pater meus per breve suum precepit. Et defendo ne aliquis super hoc illi aliquam torturam faciat. T. R. Bloet 7 R. Bigot. Apud Windlesores.'

The Wlmarus (OE Wulfmær) of these two writs was no doubt the Vlmarus, a *liber homo*, who held T.R.E. what is described in DB ii. 25 b (VCH *Essex*, i. 459) as 'the other Molesham' (in an entry following one relating to *Molesham*, held T.R.E. by a certain Godric) ; the name of this manor, which Vlmarus held as 1 hide and 40 acres, is preserved in Moulsham Hall in Great Leighs, Essex (Reaney, *Place-Names of Essex*, 257). In 1086 Wulfmær's manor at Moulsham was held of the bishop of Bayeux by a certain R, identified by Round (VCH *Essex*, i. 459 b) with Ralf, the son of Turold 'of Rochester'. This Turold, described by Round (*ibid.* i. 342) as a 'great land-grabber', was no doubt the Thurold of William II's writ. *Brom* is too common an Essex place-name element for it to be possible to identify the *Brom* of the two post-Conquest writs.

(85)

AUTHORITIES :—(F) as for no. 73, f. 105 (*ol*. 94). Printed : *Mon. Angl.* i. 298, no. xiii ; K. 845 ; Neufeldt no. 7.

(D) as for no. 74, f. 647 b, printed here. Anglo-Saxon script in some degree imitated in this copy.

On the authenticity of this writ see pp. 309–10, and on the legal terms employed see Introduction, pp. 73–83.

DATE. If this writ, as seems probable, represents an authentic writ of Edward, probably altered and expanded, it must have been issued after Harold's appointment as earl of Wessex after the death of his father Earl Godwine on 15 April 1053, and before the Confessor's death on 5 January 1066.

l. 4. *Þat cotlif Eouereslea.* Eversley, Hants. Westminster Abbey held Eversley in 1086, but four *liberi homines* had held it T.R.E. as 4 manors of King Edward *in alodium*. It was then assessed at 5 hides, but in 1086 at 4 hides. In 1086 there were 10 villeins and 4 bordars with 3 ploughs, and 2 mills worth 105 pence. There was woodland worth 30 shillings, and a messuage (*haga*) in Winchester worth 7 pence, and 12 acres of meadow. In King Edward's time Eversley was worth 100 shillings, and afterwards 4 pounds 10 shillings ; in 1086 it was worth 4 pounds (DB i. 43 b, VCH *Hants*, i. 472). King Edward's grant of Eversley is mentioned in the spurious Telligraphus of that king (see p. 290) in terms which are not independent of the Eversley writ : ' Euereslea quod tenuerunt de me quattuor ministri mei videlicet Painus Wlnothus Frebern' 7 Ælfric' pro .iiii. maneriis 7 pro .v. hid' cum prato quod est ad Stratfelde iuxta longem pontem 7 cum omnibus que sibi pertinent.' Full details of the history of this manor are given in VCH *Hants.*, iv. 33–5. The overlordship of Eversley is there stated to have continued with Westminster Abbey at least as late as the end of the fifteenth century, the manor being held by the annual payment of a yearling sparrowhawk.

l. 5. *Mid milne.* On mills as a source of profits in the late eleventh century, see Ellis, *General Introduction to Domesday Book* (1833), i. 122–6 ; also VCH *Sussex*, i. 366. The profits of the numerous mills mentioned in Domesday are sometimes reckoned in money, sometimes partly in money and partly in grain, occasionally in eels from the mill stream, and occasionally in other commodities. See also on Domesday water-mills, M. T. Hodgen, *Antiquity*, xiii (1939), 261 ff.

l. 7. *Mid þare maed þat lið at Stratfelde with þare lange brigge.* There are several villages of this name in the neighbourhood of Eversley. The ' long bridge ' was probably a bridge over the R. Loddon, possibly one now represented by Stone Bridge in Stratfield Saye Park, or by another of the existing bridges.

l. 12. *Min medwrihte.* The compound *medu-wyrhta*, ' mead-wright ', i.e. ' brewer ', does not seem to be recorded in BT or Suppt, but other compounds of OE *medu* appear there, and compounds with *wyrhta* are common. There is no reason for doubting that this is a genuine Old English word. On the royal mead-brewer, *medyt*, in early Welsh sources, see Larson, *King's Household*, 197, where it is suggested that English influence in this matter is probable.

l. 13. *Mine fre socne men þe þæt cotlif healdeþ.* OE *socnmann* does not seem to be recorded in the Anglo-Saxon dictionaries, but its Latin equivalent *sochemannus* is frequent in Domesday. In Domesday however the four men who held Eversley of King Edward are called *liberi homines*, and are said to have held their land *in alodium* (for reference see note on no. 28, l. 6 above). For passages showing that the same person might be called both ' sokeman ' and *liber homo*, see Carl Stephenson, ' Commendation and Related Problems in Domesday ', *Eng. Hist. Rev.* lix (1944), 306, n. 2, where references are also given to writings on the difficult problem of the interpretation of these terms. For a description of *sochemanni* as ' men under a lord's jurisdiction ', see Stenton, *Anglo-Saxon England*, 470 ; see also *ibid.* 508. But other definitions have been propounded. Liebermann ii. 455, s.v. ' Gerichtsbarkeit ', prints the passage under discussion *min freosocne men*, which is the reading of the Faustina text (in Kemble), and draws the conclusion, in my opinion unwarranted, that ' Bereich der Gerichtsbarkeit heisst *freosocn* '.

l. 14. *Mid lande 7 mid lese.* The pair *land—læs*, ' cultivated land—

pasture ', appears in ' Hit Becwæð ', in the passage cited in Introduction, p. 88. For *mid lande and mid loge,* in the Faustina text, see p. 462.

(86)

AUTHORITIES :—(F) as for no. 73, f. 108 (*ol.* 97). Printed : *Mon. Angl·* i. 299, no. xxii ; K. 858 ; Neufeldt no. 16.

(D) as for no. 74, f. 154 b, printed here. Anglo-Saxon script is in some degree imitated in this copy.

On the authenticity of this writ see pp. 319–20 and on ' sake and soke ' see Introduction, pp. 73–6.

DATE. The authenticity of this writ is not certain. An authentic writ with this address would be dated 1051–66, after the appointment of William to the see of London in 1051, and before the Confessor's death, 5 January 1066 ; a narrower dating would be 1057–66, on the probability that Leofwine was appointed to an earldom in 1057.

l. 3. *Æt Scepertune.* Shepperton, Middx. This manor was held T.R.E. and in 1086 by the abbot of Westminster and was rated at 8 hides ; it was then, and had been in King Edward's time, in demesne (DB i. 128 b). According to the tradition incorporated in the spurious Great Charter of Dunstan (B. 1050, see p. 338), fabricated c. 1100 according to *Crawford Charters,* p. 92), Dunstan had bought the land at Shepperton which he gave to Westminster from a widow named Ealfleda (Æthelflæd) for 60 bezants. The spurious Telligraphus of King Æthelred (Thorpe p. 298) states that the land at Shepperton was to revert to Westminster after the death of Æthelflæd to whom it had apparently been granted for life, together with an estate at Sunbury which was to revert to the abbey under the same conditions. But in the spurious First Charter and Telligraphus of King Edward (pp. 289 f.) a different tradition appears ; no mention is made of Dunstan, and the 8 hides at Shepperton are confirmed to the abbey among the grants of earlier kings.

l. 4. *Scotfreo 7 gafulfreo on hundred 7 on scire.* For these formulas see no. 15 ; see also note on no. 76.

l. 5. *Swa See Dunstan hit gebohte 7 into þam minstre Wulsi abbode 7 þam broðeran gebocede.* There is no need to regard as an interpolation the title of ' Saint ' assigned here to Dunstan. Stubbs (*Memorials of St. Dunstan*), R.S., ix) remarks that Dunstan ' was canonized in popular regard almost from the day he died, and that he was the favourite saint of the mother church of England for more than a century and a half '. Of Lives of St. Dunstan edited by Stubbs one was written within sixteen, another within twenty-three, years of his death. In the reign of Cnut Dunstan's name was inserted in the Kalendar by direction of the witan (I Cnut, 17, 1).

According to Westminster tradition the monastery was re-founded by Dunstan when bishop of London with King Edgar's co-operation. William of Malmesbury (*Gesta Pontificum,* 178) states that Dunstan established at Westminster a small monastery for 12 monks and made Wulsinus (see Biographical Notes s.n. Wulfsige) their abbot. The spurious Greàt Charter of Dunstan for the abbey (see p. 338) gives details of the lands provided by Dunstan for its endowment.

(87)

AUTHORITIES :—(D) as for no. 74,. f. 154 b, printed here. Printed : F. E. Harmer, *Eng. Hist. Rev.* li (1936), 97–103. Anglo-Saxon script in some degree imitated in this copy.

Not in F.

On the authenticity of this writ see pp. 319–20, and on the legal terms employed see Introduction, pp. 73–82.

DATE. This writ must have been issued after the appointment of Edwin as abbot of Westminster in succession to Wulfnoth (who according to Flete died on 19 October 1049) ; and before the death of the Confessor in 1066. It is a natural inference that the grant of land at Shepperton to Teinfrith was subsequent to the grant of Shepperton to Westminster Abbey, probably between 1057 and 1066 (no. 87), so that this writ also should probably be dated 1057–66.

l. 2. *Mine circwirhtan.* There seems no reason to doubt that this, like ' mead-wright ' (no. 85), is a genuine, though apparently otherwise unrecorded, Old English term. The term ' mason ' (from French) was current in Middle English. The first instance of ' architect ' (' master-builder ') recorded in NED is dated 1563. For the Confessor's church at Westminster Abbey, see p. 292.

l. 3. *Æt Scepertune.* Shepperton, Middx. Domesday says nothing of Teinfrith as a holder of land there ; see no. 86.

l. 5. *Ac habbe he.* On the force of *ac* here, see p. 468.

(88)

AUTHORITIES :—(F) as for no. 74, f. 105 (*ol.* 94), printed here. Printed : *Mon. Ang.* i. 298, no. xi ; K. 860 ; Neufeldt no. 5.

On the authenticity of this writ see pp. 320 ff.

DATE. On the assumption that this form of the Greenford writ is authentic, it must be dated 1051–66, between William's appointment to the see of London in 1051, and the Confessor's death on 5 January 1066 ; a narrower dating would be 1057–66, on the probability that Leofwine was appointed to an earldom in 1057.

l. 3. *Greneford,* Greenford, Middx. According to Domesday Book (DB i. 128 b, 129 b) there were two manors at Greenford, one rated at 3 hides was held by Ernulf of Geoffrey de Mandeville, having been held T.R.E. by 2 sokemen ; the other, rated at 11½ hides, was held in 1086 by the abbot of Westminster as it had also been held T.R.E. Nothing is said of Ailric as a former holder of land there, nor is he mentioned in the later Westminster charters, so that it is not possible to determine whether land granted by him formed part of the Westminster manor of Greenford. Indeed, the spurious First Charter and the spurious Telligraphus of the Confessor (p. 289) state (whether correctly or not) that the king confirmed to the abbey, among other gifts made to that house by earlier kings, an estate of 12 hides and 1 virgate at Greenford.

(89)

AUTHORITIES :—(D) as for no. 74, f. 129 b. Unprinted. Copied by the same hand as nos. 105, 106.

On the authenticity of this writ see pp. 320 ff., and on the legal terms employed see Introduction, pp. 73–8.

DATE. It is improbable that this writ is authentic as it stands, but an authentic writ with this address would have the dating of no. 88 q.v.

(90)

AUTHORITIES :—(L) Cott. Aug. ii, 81, cent. late xi, printed here. Facs. and text : *Facs. of Anc. Chart. in the Brit. Mus.* ed. Bond, pt. iv. no. 41. Printed : Madox, *Formulare Anglicanum*, p. 1, no. 1 ; K. 866 ; Sweet, *Anglo-Saxon Reader*, 10th ed. no. xii. D ; Neufeldt no. 12 (O) ; H. Hall, *Formula Book of Diplomatic Documents* (1908), p. 52. The text is written on a single piece of parchment, dimensions : 7″ broad, 1⅛″ deep. The lower edge is straight, and there is no direct indication of former sealing. The date of the hand forbids us to suppose that this is an original writ, written (and sealed) by the clerks of King Edward the Confessor's secretariat. It is entirely probable that it is a later copy of the original Wormley writ.

(F) as for no. 73, f. 107 (*ol.* 96). Printed : *Mon. Angl.* i. 297, no. xviii ; Neufeldt no. 12 (F).

(D) as for no. 74, f. 647.

On the authenticity of this writ see pp. 322 f.

DATE. After Wulfwig's appointment to the see of Dorchester in 1053 and before King Edward's death on 5 January 1066 ; a narrower dating would be 1057–66, on the probability that Leofwine was appointed to an earldom in 1057.

l. 4. *þridde healue hide landes æt Wurmelea.* Wormley, Herts. The land at Wormley granted to the monks of Westminster by Leofsi Duddesunu was not in their possession in 1086. Of the three manors at Wormley in 1086, one had been held in King Edward's time by the canons of Waltham, who still retained it, another by Alsi, a man of Eddeva. The third, a manor of 2½ hides (which may reasonably be identified with the 2½ hides of the Wormley writ, was in 1086 held of the king by Alwin Dodesone (DB i. 136 b, 137, 142 ; VCH *Herts.*, i. 317, 320, 342). See further p. 322 above. There was land there for 2 ploughs and these were there in 1086, with 6 villeins and a serf. There was meadow sufficient for 2 ploughteams, pasture sufficient for the livestock, woodland to feed 150 pigs. The total value of the manor in 1086 was 40 shillings, when received 50 shillings, in King Edward's time 60 shillings.

(91)

AUTHORITIES :—(F) as for no. 73, f. 105 b (*ol.* 95 b). Printed : *Mon. Angl.* i. 298, no. xvi ; K. 864 ; Neufeldt no. 10.

(D) as for no. 74, f. 226 b, printed here. Anglo-Saxon script is in some degree imitated in this copy.

On the authenticity of this writ see pp. 310–11, and on the legal terms employed see Introduction, pp. 73–83.

DATE. This writ may possibly represent an authentic writ of King Edward, but if so the text has been embellished and 'improved'. An authentic writ with this address would have been issued 1053–66, between Wulfwi's appointment to the see of Dorchester in 1053 and the Confessor's death on 5 January 1066 ; a narrower dating would be 1057–66, on the probability that Leofwine was appointed to an earldom in 1057.

l. 4. *Ægate.* Ayot, Herts. Of the 3 manors at *Aiete* in 1086 this is no doubt the one rated at 2½ hides then held by Geoffrey of Westminster Abbey, and held in King Edward's time by Aluuinus, a thegn of King Edward (DB i. 135, VCH *Herts.* i. 313), whom we may confidently identify with the Ælwine Gottone of this writ. The manor is identified by J. H. Round in VCH *Herts.* i. 313 with Ayot St. Lawrence, and the Geoffrey of the Domesday entry with Geoffrey de Mandeville, since the manor is found in posses-

sion of his heirs at a later date. For further details see VCH *Herts.* iii. 59
where it is stated that the overlordship of Westminster apparently lapsed.
For comment on the Domesday statement (DB i. 135) that with regard to
this manor the abbot claims that King William conceded to him, see p. 310
above.

(92)

AUTHORITIES :—(F) as for no. 73, f. 105 (*ol.* 94). Printed : *Mon. Angl.*
i. 298, no. xii ; K. 846 ; Neufeldt no. 6.

(D) as for no. 74, f. 505, printed here. Anglo-Saxon script in some degree
imitated in this copy.

On the authenticity of this writ see pp. 311–13, and on the legal terms
employed see Introduction, pp. 73–82.

DATE. If this writ is authentic, it must have been issued between the
appointment of Leofwine to an earldom probably in 1057, and the death
of the Confessor on 5 January 1066, Stigand having retained the see of
Winchester in plurality after his promotion to Canterbury. But its authenticity is doubtful.

l. 4. *Æt Totinges.* Tooting, Surrey. According to Domesday (DB i. 32,
VCH *Surrey*, i. 306) the Westminster manor at Tooting was a small manor
with land for 1½ ploughs valued T.R.E. and in 1086 at 40s, and when the
abbot received it at 20s. There were 2 villeins with half a plough and
3 acres of meadow. In King Edward's time it was assessed at 4 hides, the
figure which appears in the present writ and in the texts quoted on p. 312,
where the history of the manor is discussed. In 1086 it was held of Westminster Abbey by Odbert who had ' paid nothing for geld '. There were
two other manors at Tooting in 1086.

(93)

AUTHORITIES :—(Y) Westminster Abbey Muniments xvii, c. 1100. Facs.
and text : *Ordn. Surv. Facs.* ed. Sanders, pt. ii, Westminster, no. 15. Printed :
Birch, *Trans. R. Soc. Lit.* 2nd ser. x. 141. The text is copied very clearly
on a single piece of parchment, dimensions : 10⅛″ broad, 3⅜″ deep, left side,
right side defective. There is a large gap in the upper edge extending into
the third line, and the right-hand edge has broken or torn away ; there is
also a small hole in the parchment. The gaps in the text have been filled
from D. D is a good copy (with little modernisation) either of Y or of a
parallel text. A seal of red wax, similar to those of nos. 76, 94, is attached
sur simple queue to a seal tag, below which there is a narrower wrapping
tag. Seal, imperfect, described by Birch, *ut supra*, p. 141 (7) and Wyon,
Great Seals, p. 3 (5, 6) ; but Birch's description of this writ as a ' fine original
Anglo-Saxon charter of the king ' is erroneous. The date of the handwriting
forbids us to suppose that this is an original writ written and sealed by the
clerks of the royal secretariat ; and further there is reason to believe that
the writ is not authentic ; see p. 305.

(D) As for no. 74, f. 465.

Not in F.

On the authenticity of this writ see pp. 303–6, and on the legal terms
employed see Introduction, pp. 73–85.

DATE. Although the writ is not authentic, its address or part of it may
have been derived from an authentic writ issued between the appointment
of Wulfwold as abbot of Chertsey, probably in 1058, and the death of the

Confessor on 5 January 1066. Stigand retained the see of Winchester even after his promotion to the archbishopric of Canterbury.

l. 5. *Þæt plott landes æt Clæigate.* Claygate in Thames Ditton, Surrey. This manor, in Kingston hundred, is entered in Domesday (DB i. 32) as a manor of Westminster Abbey, but Tostig is not mentioned as a former holder of land there. In King Edward's time the manor had been assessed at 2½ hides, and in 1086 it was assessed at a half-hide. The land was for 2 ploughs ; in demesne there was one, and there were 3 villeins and 2 bordars with one plough. There were 5 acres of meadow, and a wood 'worth' one pig (see p. 498). In King Edward's time it was worth 40 shillings, in 1086, 50 shillings. I have rendered *plott landes* as 'piece of land' because the details given in Domesday of the Westminster manor at Claygate make the Mod. Eng. 'plot' inappropriate. For the subsequent history of Claygate, see pp. 305 f. and O. Manning and W. Bray, *History and Antiquities of the County of Surrey* (London, 1804–14), i. *460.

l. 7. *Mid ðam þriddan treowwe on Kyngeswude on Ditune.* For grants of one tree in every three, see no. 77 and the references there given. It is distinctly possible that the wood in question was the 'wood worth 15 pigs' in the manor at Ditton (DB i. 35, identified in the VCH *Surrey*, i. 317 with Long Ditton), which Almar had held of King Edward before the Conquest, though Domesday says nothing of any rights of Westminster Abbey there. The phrase corresponding to *on Kyngeswude* in the Claygate writ attributed to the Conqueror (see p. 305) is *in silva mea*, but in 1086 the manor was no longer in the king's hand.

l. 8. *Mid ðam þriddan æcre.* That is, with one acre-strip in three of ploughed land. In the Claygate writ attributed to William I (see p. 305) the corresponding clause is : *cum tertia acra si nemus defecerit.*

l. 8. *Mid ælc ðere þridde nytþerflicre note ðe ðar of ariseð on wude 7 on felde* etc. For *nytþearflic* see no. 73. The phrase corresponding to this in the spurious Claygate writ of William I (see p. 305 above) is : *cum tertia utilitate ejusdem ville de Ditona in bosco et plano* etc. The literal meaning of the OE phrase is 'with each of the third profitable usage etc.', i.e. 'with a third of each of the profitable usages (which shall arise there in woodland and in open country)'. Davis renders the Latin phrase 'the third of all valuable rights'. Dr. Cam has observed to me that this appears to offer a fair analogy to the third penny of the shire (court) or of the borough (court) often enjoyed by the earl.

l. 9. *On æuesæ.* For OE *æfesn, æfesa* (of which *æuesæ* is a late form of an oblique case) 'the pasturing of pigs in woodland, pannage', see no. 77.

l. 10. *On weren.* For weirs, composed of fences or enclosures of stakes in a river or other water for taking or preserving fish, or of eel pots for catching eels, see Robertson, pp. 46, 256, BT s.v. *wer* and NED s.v. 'weir'. In a survey of Tidenham, Glouc., dated by Liebermann c. 1050 (Robertson no. 109), mention is made of weirs in the Wye and in the Severn, and it is stated that at every weir within the 30 hides (in Tidenham) every alternate fish belongs to the lord of the manor, and every rare fish which is of value ; and that no one has the right of selling any fish for money when the lord is on the estate, without informing him about it.

l. 10. *Scotfri 7 gafollfri of scire 7 hundrede.* On these formulas, see no. 76.

l. 11. *Of gelde 7 of dænegelde.* 'Geld' is the national land tax paid by landowners to the king both before the Conquest and after ; 'Danegeld' may be no more than an equivalent term, arising out of some confusion with earlier levies raised to pay off the Danes. Sometimes the two are given as equivalent in post-Conquest documents : e.g. Davis, *Regesta*, p. 120, charter no. 10 : ' quietos . . . ab omni mea consuetudine et censu pecunie que *geld et danegeld* anglice vocatur ' ; *ibid.* p. 125, charter no. 25 : ' quietas de murdro et *geldo vel danegeldo* ' ; similarly, *Chron. Abbat. Rames.* 224 : ' ab omni collectione census qui *geld vel scot vel Denegeld* anglice nominatur '. The term was in common use from the latter part of the eleventh century onwards : cf. the Domesday entry for Stamford (DB i. 336 b, *Lincolnshire Domesday*, ed. Foster and Longley, 8) : ' Stanford burgum regis dedit geldum T.R.E. pro xii hundrez 7 dimidio in exercitu 7 nauigio 7 *in Danegeld* ', ' the royal borough of Stamford gave geld T.R.E. for 12½ hundreds for army service and boat service and *for Danegeld* '. See further Liebermann ii. 344–5, s.v. ' Dänengeld ' ; and also note on *heregeld*, p. 439 above. The appearance of ' Danegeld ' in this writ cannot be regarded as evidence that the term was in use in the Confessor's time.

(94)

AUTHORITIES :—(R) Westminster Abbey Muniments xiv, cent. late xi, printed here. Facs. and text : *Ordn. Surv. Facs.* ed. Sanders, pt. ii, Westminster, no. 13. Printed : R. Widmore, *An History of the Church of St. Peter, Westminster* (1751), Appendix, no. 1, with Lat. version by Widmore, not printed here ; K. 863 ; Birch, *Trans. R. Soc. Lit.* 2nd ser. x. 142 ; Neufeldt no. 19 (O). The text is written on a single piece of parchment, dimensions : 8⅞″ broad, 2¼″ left side, 1½″ right side. A seal of red wax, broken and imperfect, on which however the upper part of the king's figure, and insignia, and part of the inscription, are still visible, and which resembles those of nos. 76, 93, is appended *sur simple queue* to a seal tag. A slight ' step ' may indicate the former presence of a wrapping tag. Seal described by Birch, *ut supra*, p. 142 (8). The date of the hand prevents us from supposing that this is an original writ written and sealed by the clerks of King Edward's secretariat, but there is no obstacle to the belief that it is a copy of an original writ, into which a few later forms have crept ; *þeignes, frendlice, hlefdige, gære* and probably *munster*. Incidentally, the seal is affixed upside-down.

(F) as for no. 73, f. 109 (*ol.* 98). Printed : *Mon. Angl.* i. 299, no. xxv ; Neufeldt no. 19 (F).

(D) as for no. 74, f. 594.

On the authenticity of this writ see pp. 323–4, and for an explanation of the legal terms employed see Introduction, pp. 73–8.

DATE. The writ must have been issued between the appointment of Wulfwig to the see of Dorchester in 1053 and Edward's death on 5 January 1066. For the probability that the grant of Rutland may have been made after the dedication of the church on 28 December 1065, see p. 291.

l. 4. *Roteland.* It has been remarked by F. M. Stenton (VCH *Rutland*, i. 135) that the fact that this writ is addressed to the county authorities of Northamptonshire indicates that the part of present-day Rutland to which the writ refers was, for the time being at least, under their jurisdiction. Though the ' Roteland ' here granted to Queen Edith with the provision that it should revert to Westminster Abbey after her death probably meant the wapentake of Martinsley—which in 1086 was united with the wapentake of Alstoe under the name ' Roteland '—the wording of the writ suggests that she may have possessed some rights over the whole. In 1086 the whole of Martinsley wapentake (made up of the 3 manors of Oakham, Hambleton and Ridlington), with their dependent berewicks, was possessed outright by King William, with the exception of a manor of 1 carucate held in 1066 by a certain Leofnoth (Leuenot) (DB i. 293 b, VCH *Rutland*, 139–40), but in King Edward's time it had been held by Queen Edith and it is a natural inference that she continued to hold these lands until her death in 1075. Stenton has also shown that there is ground for believing that in granting Rutland to his wife, Queen Edith, the Confessor was only following the example of his father King Æthelred II who, according to Gaimar (*L'Estorie des Engles*, R.S. l. 4139), had granted Rutland with other lands to his queen, Emma, on her marriage to him in 1002 ; and has suggested that ' it is at least a working hypothesis that in the successive possession of Rutland, first by Emma and then by Edith, we have the real cause which originally separated this district from the local shire organisation and thus made possible the gradual development of the modern county '. The connection of Rutland with the queens of England may have begun at an even earlier date. Gaimar adds ' ke Elstruet aueit eu deuant '. This Elstruet has been identified with Ælfthryth, the second wife of King Edgar and the mother of King Æthelred, and it is distinctly probable that this vast estate was given to Ælfthryth by her husband (VCH *Rutland*, pp. 132, 135, 166). For Ælfthryth, see Biographical Notes. For a late fourteenth-century reference to this soke, see *Piers Plowman*, B text, Passus II, line 110 : ' Rainolde the reue of Rotland sokene.'

(95)

AUTHORITIES :—(F) as for no. 73, f. 103 b (*ol.* 92 b). Printed : *Mon. Angl.* i. 297, no. viii : J. Dunkin, *Oxfordshire, The History and Antiquities of the Hundreds of Bullington and Ploughley* (London, 1823), i. 313 : K. 865 ; Neufeldt no. 2.

(D) as for no. 74, f. 275. Anglo-Saxon script in some degree imitated in this copy.

On the authenticity of this writ see p. 324, and on the legal terms employed see Introduction, .pp. 73–8.

DATE. On the probability that Gyrth was appointed to the earldom of Oxfordshire in 1057/8 (see Biographical Notes) the writ can be dated between that time and Edward's death in 1066. For the possibility that the grant of Launton was made after the dedication of the church on 28 December 1065 see p. 291.

l. 3. *Langtun.* Launton, near Bicester, Oxon. King Edward's grant to Westminster of land at Launton is noted in the Oxfordshire Domesday (DB i. 154 b), where it is stated that the king holds *Cherielintone* (for *Chertelintone* = Kirtlington), and that the soke of 2½ hundreds belongs to the manor except for 2½ hides in *Lantone* which formerly belonged (*jacuerunt*) there. The king gave these to St. Peter of Westminster and to Baldwine his god-son (*filiolo*). It was conjectured by Ellis (*A General Introduction to Domesday Book*, i. 204) that the land was given to Westminster for the education and support as a novice of Baldwine (who is otherwise unknown), or for his maintenance as a monk. In the spurious Telligraphus of the Confessor (see p. 290), which may not be independent of the Domesday entry, King Edward is made to confirm to the abbey : ' Langetune cum omnibus que sibi pertinent 7 cum terra Baldewyni filioli mei que est in eadem villa ' among his own grants.

(96)

AUTHORITIES :—(P) Westminster Abbey Muniments xii, in a contemporary hand, printed here. Facs. and text : *Ordn. Surv. Facs.* ed. Sanders, pt. ii, Westminster, no. 12. Printed : Birch, *Trans. R. Soc. Lit.* 2nd ser. x. 146 ; Neufeldt no. 20 b. Text written on a single piece of parchment, dimensions ; 7 3/16″ broad, 2″ deep, left side, 1 1/4″, right. The parchment has broken away leaving gaps in the first four lines ; the last line is complete, but the parchment is deeply creased. A small white flaky fragment of a wax seal— apparently the central portion—is appended *sur simple queue* to a seal tag, with a narrow wrapping tag beneath. Seal described Birch, *ut supra*, 146 (3). There is a distinct probability that this is the original Perton writ written and sealed by the clerks of King Edward's secretariat.

(R) Westminster Abbey Muniments xiii, second half of cent. xi. Facs. and text as above, no 11. Printed : Neufeldt no. 20 a. Text written on a single piece of parchment, dimensions : 7 1/2″ broad, 3″ deep, left side, 2 1/2″, right. In a larger hand than P, and in somewhat paler ink. The spacing suggests that it is a copy. No seal and no wrapping tag, but a deep ' step ' may indicate the former existence of these. The date of the hand prevents us from supposing that this is an original writ of King Edward the Confessor, written (and sealed) by the clerks of the royal secretariat. Its contents are identical with those of P, but there are some orthographical variants (in footnotes).

(F) as for no. 73, f. 109 b (*ol.* 98 b). Printed : *Mon. Angl.* i. 300, no. xxvi ; K. 842 ; Neufeldt no. 20 (F).

(D) as for no. 74, f. 648.

On the authenticity of this writ see pp. 324 ff., and on 'sake and soke' see Introduction, pp. 73–6.

DATE. Between the appointment of Edwin as earl of Mercia between 1062 and 1066, and the death of the Confessor on 5 January 1066. For the probability that the grant of Perton was made after the dedication of the church on 28 December 1065, see p. 291.

l. 3. *Æt Pertune.* Perton (or Purton), a hamlet in the parish of Tettenhall, Staffs. Domesday says nothing of any former holder of the manor at Perton, rated at 3 hides, held by Westminster Abbey in 1086 (DB i. 247 b). There was land there for 6 ploughs ; there was 1 plough in the demesne, and 13 villeins and 2 bordars and 1 *liber homo* with 5 ploughs. There were 8 acres of meadow and a wood half a league in length and in breadth. It was worth in 1086 and previously, 40 shillings.

(97)

AUTHORITIES :—(O) Cott. Charter vii. 13, cent. late xi, printed here. Facs. and text : *Facs. of Anc. Charters in the Brit. Mus.* ed. Bond, pt. iv, no. 36. Printed : Hickes, *Thesaurus*, i. 141 ; K. 886 ; Thorpe p. 414 ; Neufeldt no. 4 (O). These last four give an erroneous ref. : ' Aut. Arch. Ecc. Wig.' ; but there is no copy of this writ at Worcester Cathedral. Hickes's text differs from that printed here, but his variants are probably merely errors of transcription. Text written on a single piece of parchment, dimensions : 7 1/4″ broad, 2 3/16″ left side, 2 1/8″ right. Parchment badly rubbed and stained and blackened along six open cracks in lower edge. There is now no trace of the seal described by Hickes : ' Chartæ huic membranaceæ appendet, lemnisco ex ipsa membrana exciso, sigillum, in cujus altera facie Rex in solio sedens dextrâ crucem, sinistrâ orbem tenet ; in altera vero, solio insidens dextrâ hastam, cui columba supereminet, tenet, et sinistrâ gladium vibrat. Inscriptio circa limbum in utraque facie : Sigillum Eadwardi Anglorum Basilei.' The seal here described resembles seals attributed to the Confessor ; it seems reasonable to suppose that the *crux* of Hickes's description is the trefoil (as with no. 77). The date of the hand forbids us to suppose that this is an original writ of King Edward the Confessor written and sealed by the clerks of the royal secretariat, but it seems altogether likely that it is a copy of an original writ.

(F) as for no. 73, f. 104 b (*ol.* 93 b). Printed : *Mon. Angl.* i, 298, no. x ; Neufeldt no. 4.

(D) as for no. 74, f. 133.

(N) Liber Niger Quarternus of the D. and C. of Westminster, f. 12, written towards the end of cent. xv, copied either from D or from a common source.

(H) a duplicate or transcript of the above in the Liber Niger Quaternus belonging to the College of Arms, f. 13 b. See further on N and H p. 295 above.

On the authenticity of this writ see pp. 327–8, and on the legal terms employed see Introduction, pp. 73–8.

DATE. In the absence of personal names this writ cannot be dated more closely than Edward's reign, 1042–66. For the possibility that the grant of Windsor and Staines was made after the dedication of the church on 28 December 1065, see p. 291.

l. 4. *Windlesovan.* Windsor, Berks. Domesday informs us (DB i. 56 b, VCH *Berks.* i. 327) that King William holds Windsor in demesne, and that King Edward held it. There were 20 hides there, including besides the vill, in which there were 95 messuages (*hagæ*), arable land, meadow and woodland, and a fishery. Nothing is said here of any claim of the monks of Westminster to Windsor ; but from the Surrey Domesday (DB i. 32, VCH *Surrey,* i. 305) we learn that King William gave the manor of Battersea to Westminster Abbey in exchange for (Old) Windsor. To the land at Windsor thus taken from the abbey King William added a half-hide which he took from the manor of Clewer, and it was on this half-hide that Windsor Castle was built (DB i. 62 b, VCH *Berks.* i. 362). The spurious First Charter of William I (see p. 337) preserves the tradition that it was because of its advantages for hunting that King William wished to have Windsor. From writs of William I it is apparent that not only Battersea but also Ockendon and Feering were granted by him to the monks of Westminster in exchange for their manor of Windsor ; see Davis, *Regesta,* nos. 45, 86–7, 163. In the third of these (*ibid.* no. 87, dated by Davis 1066–75) he declares that Feering and Ockendon, which he has granted to Westminster Abbey in exchange for Windsor, are now to belong to the abbey as fully and completely as he himself has granted them, and that Swegen the sheriff is to ensure that the abbey has possession.

l. 4. *Stane.* Staines, Middx. ; see note on no. 98.

(98)

AUTHORITIES :—(G) Westminster Abbey Muniments xvi, end of cent. xi, printed here. Facs. and text : *Ordn. Surv. Facs.* pt. ii, Westminster, no. 10. Printed : Earle p. 302, Neufeldt no. 3 (O). The text is written very clearly in dark ink on a single piece of parchment, dimensions : 6″ broad, 3½″ left side, 3¾″ right. There is no indication of sealing ; a slight ' step ' on the left side may be due to warping of parchment. This document does not look like a writ ; and in any case the date of the hand forbids us to suppose that it is an original writ of the Confessor written and sealed by the clerks of the king's secretariat. Further there are grounds for believing that it is not an authentic copy of an original writ ; see further pp. 328–30.

(F) as for no. 73, f. 104 (ol. 93). Printed Mon. Ang. i. 297, no. ix ; K. 855 ; Neufeldt no. 3 (F).

(D) as for no. 74, f. 133.

(N) as for no. 97, f. 12.

(H) as for no. 97, f. 13 b.

On the authenticity of this writ see pp. 313, 328 ff. ; on the legal terms employed see Introduction, pp. 73–83.

DATE. This writ may represent an authentic writ of Edward issued between Harold's appointment as earl of Wessex in 1053, and the Confessor's death on 5 January 1066 ; but if so it has at the least been altered and expanded. For the possibility that Staines may have been granted to the abbey after the dedication of the church on 28 December 1065, see p. 291.

l. 4. *þæt cotlif Stana mid þam lande Stæningahaga wiðinnon Lundone.* The manor of Staines, rated at 19 hides, is entered in Domesday (DB i. 128) among the possessions of Westminster Abbey, but the statement in Domesday : *valet 35 librae. Quando receperunt similiter. T.R.E. xl librae*, implies that the abbey was not seised of this manor until after the Conquest. There were 6 mills there, two weirs, meadow and pasture, woodland worth 30 pigs, and 2 arpents of vineyard. Four berewicks belonged to the manor as they had before the Conquest. Besides the villeins, bordars, cotters, and serfs of Staines, the Domesday entry mentions 46 burgesses, who rendered 40 shillings per annum. The suggestion was made by Maitland (*Domesday Book and Beyond*, 181) that these were burgesses appurtenant to the manor of Staines but living in London, and that this passage should be taken in connection with the Confessor's grant to Westminster of the land *Stæningahaga* (i.e. *haga* of the men of Staines, OE *haga*, originally ' hedge ', being subsequently used for an enclosed area, a dwelling-place, a messuage, an urban tenement) in London. Maitland's guess that ' Staining Lane in the City of London, wherein stood ' until the Great Fire ' the church of St. Mary, Staining, was so called . . . because it once contained the haws of the men of Staines,' can be accepted. A reference to the *ecclesia de Stanninge-hage* in the cartulary of St. Mary Clerkenwell (MS. Cott. Faust. B ii f. 9) makes the identification of this church with St. Mary's, Staining Lane, virtually certain, since it is known that the nunnery of Clerkenwell to which the *ecclesia de Stanningehage* is there confirmed, held the patronage of St. Mary's, Staining Lane, continuously henceforth until the Dissolution. Miss M. B. Honeybourne has kindly pointed out to me that the only other possible church (other than St. Mary's, Staining Lane) with which the *ecclesia de Stanningehage* could be identified is that of All Hallows, Staining. This church was however regularly known, from early times, as ' Stainingchurch ', i.e. Stone Church, a name never used for St. Mary's—for which St. Mary, Staining Lane, was the usual description. Furthermore All Hallows, Staining, is known to have been in lay patronage much later than the date of the grant of the *ecclesia de Stanningehage* to the nunnery of Clerkenwell (cf. R. Newcourt, *Repertorium Ecclesiasticum Parochiale Londinense* (London, 1708–10), i. 256, and the City's *Liber Custumarum*, ed. H. T. Riley (in *Munimenta Gildhallæ Londoniensis*, R.S.), i. 238). For these reasons the identification by H. A. Harben, *Dictionary of London* (1918), 18, of the *ecclesia de Stanningehage* with All Hallows, Staining, must be rejected. The cartulary of St. Mary Clerkenwell has now been edited by W. O. Hassall, Camden Society, 1949.

1. 5. *Fif 7 þrittig hida sokne þær to.* On ' soke ' see p. 74. The possession of property did not imply any right to receive the profits of justice arising in it, and King Edward here grants to the monks of Westminster rights of jurisdiction over lands owned by other persons. From the Middlesex Domesday we learn that the soke over other lands had belonged to Staines in King Edward's time. Of one hide at Ashford (*Exeforde*) which had been held in King Edward's time by a man of the abbot of Chertsey, we are told (DB i. 129) that the soke belonged to Staines (*soca unde jacebat in Stanes*). Similar statements are made concerning 8 hides in Laleham, held T.R.E. by a housecarl of King Edward ; and concerning land at Charlton (*Cerdentone*) assessed at 5 hides, held T.R.E. by two brothers, one a man of Archbishop Stigand, the other a man of Earl Leofwine (*ibid.* 130 b). All these were no doubt counted among the 35 hides over which the monks of Westminster were to have the soke.

1. 6. *Mid eallum þam berwican.* The berewick in the eleventh century was normally an outlying estate attached to a central manor. The soil of the berewick was considered to belong to the lord of the manor of which it formed a part. Four unnamed berewicks of the manor of Staines are mentioned in the Middlesex Domesday (DB i. 128 b). Of these one may have been the 2 hides at Laleham held before the Conquest under the abbot of Westminster by the reeve (*prefectus*) of Staines, who could not give or sell his land out of Staines (*non potuit dare uel uendere extra Stanes*) without the abbot's permission (DB i. 129). The spurious Telligraphus of King Edward (for which see p. 290) names among the *territoriis 7 berewicis 7 omnibus appendiciis* belonging to Staines, Yeoveney, Laleham, Ashford, Halliford and Teddington, without however stating which of these were to be counted among the berewicks.

1. 9. *On eitum,* cf. no. 102. Mod. Eng. ' ait, eyot, aight, eight ', islet, commonly used of islets in the Thames and in some other rivers. For the etymology of the word see NED s.v. *ait,* and *The Place-Names of Hertfordshire* (E.P.-N.S.), 119.

(99)

Authorities :—(D) as for no. 74, f. 316. Printed : F. E. Harmer, *Eng. Hist. Rev.* li (1936), 97–103. Anglo-Saxon script in some degree imitated in this copy.

Not in F.

On the authenticity of this writ see p. 330, and on the legal terms employed see Introduction, pp. 73–8.

Date. In the absence of personal names this writ cannot be dated within narrower limits than the reign of Edward, 1042–66. For the possibility that the grant of Pershore and Deerhurst was made after the dedication of the church on 28 December 1065, see p. 291.

1. 4. *Perscoran.* Pershore, Worcs. Domesday Book speaks of two manors at Pershore (DB i. 174 b–175, VCH *Worcs.* i. 299 ff.). Of the Westminster manor there we learn that : ' The church of Westminster holds Pershore. King Edward held this manor and gave it to that church as quit and free of all claims as he was holding it in his demesne, the whole county (court) being witness.' Of the 200 hides of this vast manor, 2 hides (identified in *The Place-Names of Worcestershire* (E.P.-N.S.), 217, with the part of the town called Portsmouth, *ol.* Portmote), which were in Pershore itself, never paid geld in King Edward's time. Besides villeins, serfs, and 1 bondwoman, there were in 1086 28 burgesses rendering 30 shillings. The

toll rendered 12 shillings. There were in 1086 3 mills, meadow and wood-land, and a church which rendered 16 shillings. The whole manor in King Edward's time rendered 83 pounds and 50 sestiers of honey ' with all (the profits of) the pleas of the free (*francorum*) men '. The details given in Domesday of other lands and of their holders are followed by the statement that ' all these above-said lands belonged and belong (*jacuerunt et jacent*) to Pershore '. But Domesday also records that the abbey of Pershore ' held and holds the manor itself of Pershore ', and that there were 26 hides that paid geld. That rights of the abbeys of Westminster and of Pershore con-flicted is evident from the Domesday statement concerning the payment of *circset*, i.e. one horse-load of grain at Martinmas. The county (court) said that Pershore Abbey ought to have this from all 300 hides, that is, not only on its own 100 hides, but also on the 200 hides held by Westminster Abbey. The only right accruing to the abbot of Westminster from this payment on his own lands arose in the case of default. Then the abbot of Westminster received the penalty to which the offender was liable, and the abbot of Pershore the full discharge of the debt. See further pp. 331 f. above.

l. 4. *Deorhurst*. Deerhurst, Glos. This manor of 59 hides is entered in Domesday (DB i. 166) among the possessions of Westminster Abbey, to which it had also belonged in King Edward's time. There were then 5 hides in the head of the manor (*in capite manerii*). In 1086 there were 3 ploughs there, and 20 villeins, 8 bordars with 10 ploughs, and 6 serfs. There were 60 acres of meadow and a wood 2 leagues long and half a league wide. To the manor belonged 4 berewicks. The whole manor (of which many further details are given) rendered in King Edward's time *de firma* 41 pounds, and 8 sestiers of honey. In 1086 it was worth 40 pounds. On the history of the church of Deerhurst see p. 293. For the boundaries of the manor, see Westm. Do. f. 316.

(100)

AUTHORITIES :—(F) as for no. 73, f. 112 (*ol.* 101). Printed : *Mon. Angl.* i. 300, no. xxxiii ; K. 830 ; Neufeldt no 27 (F).

(D) as for no. 74, f. 278, printed here. Anglo-Saxon script in some degree imitated in this copy and in the other writs on this folio.

On the authenticity of this writ see pp. 330–1, and on the legal terms employed see Introduction, pp. 73–8.

DATE. See no. 99. But it is not certain that this represents a writ of King Edward independently issued.

l. 9. *þa cnaulæcunga*, i.e. ' the recognition ' of lordship, the term being equivalent to *recognitio* in the *pro recognitione* of Domesday ; e.g. ' *pro recognitione* dabat in anno monachis unam firmam aut xx solidos ' (DB i. 175, VCH *Worcs.* i. 304). But it is distinctly probable that the word is used here in the plural. We may compare *recognitiones*, ' acknowledgements ', in D. and C. Lib. Cant., C. 8.

(101)

AUTHORITIES :—(U) Westminster Abbey Muniments xv, second half of cent. xi (not at end of century). Facs. and text : *Ordn. Surv. Facs.* pt. ii, Westminster, no. xiv. Printed : Birch, *Trans. R. Soc. Lit.* 2nd ser. x. 147 ; Neufeldt no. 27 (O). Text written on a single piece of parchment, dimen-sions : 9″ broad, 1¾″ left side, 1½″ right. A small flaky white wax fragment containing the centre of a seal is appended *sur simple queue* to a seal tag. There is no indication of a wrapping tag. Seal described, Birch, *ut supra*, 146 (111), with Plate ; Birch, *Cat. of Seals*, i. 3 (14), from a plaster cast of this seal in the British Museum ; Wyon, *Great Seals*, 4 (9, 10), and Plate II (9, 10). Birch and Wyon take this to be a Third Seal of King Edward the Confessor, the only specimen known. But there is no evidence either way as to the authenticity of this Third type. Linguistic forms within the text (for which see p. 332) make it probable that the text as it has come down to us was not a product of the clerks of the Confessor's secretariat. It seems likely that this is a slightly altered copy of an original writ of King Edward. In that case this seal cannot be an authentic seal of King Edward affixed to the writ by the royal clerks.

(D) as for no. 74, f. 278.

Not in F.

On the authenticity of the writ see pp. 331 f., and on the legal terms employed see Introduction, pp. 73–8.

DATE. See no. 99.

(102)

AUTHORITIES :—(F) as for no. 73, f. 109 b (*ol.* 98 b). Printed : *Mon. Angl.* i. 300, no. xxvii ; K. 829 ; Earle p. 340 (from K. with erroneous attribution of the manuscript to cent. xii) ; Neufeldt no. 21.

(D) as for no. 74, f. 278, printed here. Anglo-Saxon script in some degree imitated in this copy.

On the authenticity of this writ see pp. 313, 328 ff.; on the legal terms employed see Introduction, pp. 73–83.

DATE. If, as seems possible, this text is based on an authentic writ of Edward, the date of that writ would fall between Wulfstan's appointment to the see of Worcester on 8 September 1062 and the Confessor's death on 5 January 1066. For the possibility that the grant of Pershore and Deerhurst may have been made after the dedication of the church on 28 December 1065, see p. 291.

l. 6. *Mid eallum þan landum 7 mid eallum þan berwican.* For the term ' berewick ' see p. 519 above. For the berewicks of Deerhurst see DB i. 166 : *ad hoc manerium pertinent hæ berewicæ Herdeuuic v hid. Bortune viii hid. Teodeham vii hid. Sudtune v hid.* The extensive ' lands ' of Pershore, amounting to 200 hides, or one-third of the shire, are set out in DB i. 174 b ff. For its berewicks see the entry concerning Peopleton (*Piplintune*) in DB i. 175 : ' in the same berewick Godric held 3 hides etc.' ; on which Round remarked (VCH *Worcestershire*, i. 303 note) that ' Peopleton is treated as a mere Berewick (dependency) of Pershore, which seems, therefore, to be the status of the other places among which it occurs '.

(103)

AUTHORITIES :—(D) as for no. 74, f. 270. Printed : F. E. Harmer, *Eng. Hist. Rev.* li (1936), 97–103. Anglo-Saxon script in some degree imitated in this copy.

Not in F.

On the authenticity of this writ see pp. 334–6, and on ' sake and soke ' see Introduction, pp. 73–6.

DATE. If this is a copy of an independent writ of Edward, that writ must have been issued after Wulfwig's appointment to the see of Dorchester in 1053. According to a writ of William I (see p. 335) the grant of Islip to the abbey was made by Edward *ad dedicacionem illius ecclesie*, that is on 28 December 1065. The same tradition is preserved in Widmore's charter (see p. 291), and there seems no reason to reject it.

l. 3. *Gihtslepe*. Islip, Oxon. According to Domesday (DB i. 160, VCH *Oxfordshire*, i. 422) in 1086 the wife of Roger d'Ivry held of the king 5 hides in *Ietelape*, of which 3 hides had never paid geld. There was land there for 15 ploughs. In 1086 there were in demesne 3 ploughs and 2 serfs ; and 10 villeins with 5 bordars had 3 ploughs. There was a mill rendering 20 shillings, and 30 acres of meadow, pasture 3 furlongs in length and 2 in breadth, woodland 1 league in length and half a league in breadth. It was worth 7 pounds in King Edward's time ; when received, 8 pounds ; in 1086, 10 pounds. ' Godric and Alwin held it freely.' We learn further that the wife of Roger d'Ivry held this land, as well as land in Oddington, of the king *in commendatione* ; on this see p. 335 above. Nothing is said in Domesday of any rights of Westminster Abbey at Islip, either before the Conquest or after. The subsequent history of the estate is given in outline by J. Dunkin, *Oxfordshire, Bullington and Ploughley*, i. 274 ff. But owing to the existence of evidence unknown to Dunkin, his statements require correction on some points. Miss Barbara Harvey has kindly informed me that Islip did not remain in the possession of either the Ivrys or the Grente-mesnils (the family to which Roger d'Ivry's wife belonged, see p. 335, n. 1) ; and that whether or not Westminster Abbey recovered Islip before the death of Adeline d'Ivry, this manor, between 1165 and 1204, and probably from the reign of Henry I, was in the possession of the Norman branch of the de Curci family. The right of Westminster Abbey to Islip was finally recognised in 1204, when the abbot and convent of Westminster successfully laid claim to it on the ground that the vill and liberties of Islip had been bestowed on them by King Edward the Confessor. They apparently remained in possession of the manor until the Dissolution, when the abbey and all its possessions were surrendered to the king. On the formation shortly afterwards of the new bishopric of Westminster the manor and rectory of Islip were assigned to its endowment, and on the disappearance of the bishopric ten years later the manor and advowson were granted to its successors, the Dean and Chapter of Westminster, who retained both until the nineteenth century, and still retain the advowson of Islip.

l. 3. *Æt Mersce*. Marston, Oxon., two or three miles from Islip. In the spurious Telligraphus of King Edward (see p. 290), which has probably on this matter preserved a genuine tradition, it is stated that this small estate of a half-hide of land had belonged to the king's chamberlain Weodet : ' Gihtslepe villam in qua natus fui cum omnibus sibi pertinentibus et cum dimid. hyda Weodis chamerarii mei que est in Mersche '. See further p. 335. The identification of *Mersc* with Marston is rendered certain by the name *Mersctun* given to the estate bequeathed to Westminster by Weodet in a writ of William I cited on p. 335.

(104)

AUTHORITIES :—(F) as for no. 73, f. 103 (*ol.* 92). Printed : *Mon. Angl.* i. 297, no. vii ; Dunkin, *Oxfordshire, Bullington and Ploughley*, i. 290 ; K. 862 ; Thorpe p. 368 (a conflate or ' normalised ' text ; see also under no. 75) ; Neufeldt no. 1.

(D) as for no. 74, f. 270, printed here. Anglo-Saxon script in some degree imitated in this copy.

(J) as for no. 4, James MS. 24, p. 54, a copy of F, as far as *biquath*, made about 1625-38. On James MSS. and on James, see references under no. 4. Printed : White Kennett, *Parochial Antiquities* (Oxford, 1818), i. 68, but with incorrect reference (p. 75) to James's MS.

On the authenticity of this writ see pp. 336 f. ; on the legal terms employed see pp. 73-85. On Islip and Marston (*Gihtslepe* and *Mersc*), see no. 103.

DATE. See no. 103.

l. 4. *Scotfre 7 gafolfreo*. On this formula see no. 76.

l. 6. *Mid ciricen 7 mid ciricsocnen*. On this, see note on no. 73.

l. 13. *On minre stede*, lit. ' in my place ', i.e. as my deputy or representative ; see NED, where the earliest reference given dates from c. 1400. It is to be noted that *stede* is given an adjective *minre* with feminine termination, whereas it is marked masculine in BT. For parallel cases see no. 75 (Chalkhill) *be fulre wite*, no. 90, *be minre geleafan 7 be minre unnan* ; see also p. 127, n. 2.

(105)

AUTHORITIES :—(F) as for no. 73, f. 110 b (*ol.* 99 b). Printed : *Mon. Angl.* i. 300, no. xxix ; K. 861 ; Neufeldt no. 23.

(D) as for no. 74, f. 96, printed here. Copied by the same hand as nos. 89 and 106.

On the authenticity of the writ see pp. 332-4, and on the legal terms employed see Introduction, pp. 73-85.

DATE. It is doubtful whether this represents an independent writ of Edward separately issued, but the address indicates a date between William's appointment to the see of London in 1051 and Edward's death on 5 January 1066.

(106)

AUTHORITIES :—(F) as for no. 73, f. 111 b (*ol.* 100 b). Printed : *Mon. Angl.* i. 300, no. xxxii ; Neufeldt no. 25.

(D) as for no. 74, f. 96, printed here. Copied by the same hand as nos. 89 and 105.

On the authenticity of the writ see pp. 332-4 ; on the legal terms employed see Introduction, pp. 73-85.

DATE. This text probably represents an authentic writ of Edward which has not come down to us in unaltered form. If the reference in the text to the *kirkhaleging* is authentic, the grant must have been made after the dedication of the church on 28 December 1065, and the writ issued before King Edward's death on 5 January 1066.

(107)

AUTHORITIES :—(W) Codex Wintoniensis, B.M. Add. MS. 15350, f. 6 (*ol.* 4), cent. xii, printed here. Printed K. 642. The Codex Wintoniensis is a cartulary of the church of St. Swithun, Winchester (Winchester Cathedral), supposed to have been compiled in the time of Bishop Henry de Blois, between 1130 and 1150, with some later entries.

On the authenticity of this writ see pp. 373 ff.

DATE. This writ, if it is authentic, must have been issued between the appointment of Ælfheah to the see of Winchester in 984, and the death of Æthelweard in battle on 23 May 1001 (assuming that the Æthelweard

M M

of the address is rightly identified with the king's high-reeve of that name ;
see Biographical Notes).

l. 3. *þæs landes boc æt Ciltancumbe* . . . *se wisa cing Ælfred syððan
geedniwode on þære bec.* The reference must be to a charter concerning
Chilcomb granted by Alfred which is not now known to exist. For the
Chilcomb charters, see pp. 374–5 above.

l. 8. *For ane hide werige.* For *werige*, lit. ' defend itself ', i.e. ' discharge
the obligations on, answer the claims on ', see p. 450 and the references
there. *For ane hide*, ' at the rate of one hide '.

(108)

AUTHORITIES :—(W) as for no. 107 above, f. 26 (*ol.* 24), cent. xii, printed
here. This text is written in one of the main hands of the cartulary, of
1130–50. Printed : K. 717 ; Thorpe p. 295.
On the authenticity of this writ see p. 380.

DATE. Between the appointment of Ælfric to the see of Canterbury in
995, and the death of Ælfthryth, which took place before the end of 1002.
The transactions regarding Ruishton described in the latter must have
taken place between the appointment of Æthelwold to the see of Winchester
in 963, and before the death of Edgar in 975.

l. 2. *Dunstan arcebiscop getehte Apelwolde biscope Tantun eal swa his bec
specon.* Taunton, Som. *His bec*, i.e. the title-deeds of the estate. Winchester charters attribute the first grant of land at Taunton to Winchester
Cathedral to Frithegyth, wife of Æthelheard, king of the West Saxons,
who is said himself to have increased the estate there by the grant of other
land, at his wife's request, in 737 (B. 158). Other kings associated with
grants to Winchester of land or rights at Taunton in charters, some of which
may not be authentic, are : Æthelwulf (B. 475, 476), Edward the Elder
(B. 612), Æthelstan (B. 727), and Eadred (B. 831) ; see also B. 611. In the
time of King Edward the Confessor Archbishop Stigand, who was also bishop
of Winchester, held at Taunton an immense manor where there was land
in 1086 for 100 ploughs, ' and besides this the bishop has in demesne land
for 20 ploughs which never paid geld '. He paid geld for 54 hides, 2½ virgates
(DB i. 87 b, VCH *Somerset*, i. 442).

Two Taunton charters are attributed to King Edgar. In one which has
come down to us without date or list of witnesses (B. 1149) King Edgar
is represented as restoring to Winchester 100 hides at Taunton. In the other,
extant both in Latin (B. 1219) and in English (B. 1220 = Robertson no. 45),
King Edgar is said to have renewed the freedom of Taunton for the episcopal
see at Winchester exactly as King Edward the Elder had freed it ; in return
for this Bishop Æthelwold is said to have given to the king 200 mancuses
of gold and a silver cup worth five pounds, and to Ælfthryth his wife—no
doubt the sender of the letter under discussion—50 mancuses of gold, ' in
return for her help in his just mission '. This charter attributed to King
Edgar can hardly be authentic as it stands. Although it is drawn up in
the form of a declaration, it is provided with a dating clause and a list of
witnesses, with crosses, and phrases (in Latin) signifying their consent,
such as are proper only to the solemn royal diploma. Further, there is in
the dating clause a chronological dislocation, for it gives the year as 978,
and also as ' the tenth year ' of King Edgar ; but Edgar became sole king
in 959, and further the year 978 is impossible for some of the persons named
as witnesses. There are two copies of the Anglo-Saxon text, dating clause,
and list of witnesses, in the same hand, in the twelfth-century Codex Wintoni-

ensis, one accompanied by a Latin text which is not an exact equivalent (B. 1219), the other without the Latin text. Can we suppose that the dating clause, the list of witnesses, and the Latin text, were added by the monks of Winchester to a (possibly authentic) Anglo-Saxon charter ? In any case it seems improbable that this charter is devoid of any substantial basis of fact.

l. 8. *Risctun.* Ruishton, Som., a village about 2½ miles east of Taunton, of which it was a member. A charter attributed to King Æthelwulf (B. 476) records a grant to Winchester of an immense area in which Ruishton was included. Another charter attributed to the same king (B. 475) records a grant to Winchester of 8 *manentes* at Ruishton as well as land elsewhere, and gives the boundaries ; for these see G. B. Grundy, *Som. Arch. and Nat. Hist. Soc. Proc.*, lxxiii (1928), 1–32. Another Ruishton charter is B. 549, which records a grant by King Alfred to Winchester of 8 *manentes* at Ruishton.

l. 9. *To Cumbe.* OE *cumb* ' a coomb, a deep hollow or valley ', is frequently found as a place-name, particularly in the south-west ; it appears in Modern English as *Comb, Combe, Coombe.* There is nothing in the text to enable one to identify this place.

(109)

AUTHORITIES :—(A) B.M. Add. MS. 29436, f. 10, cent. xiii, printed here. Printed : V. H. Galbraith, *Eng. Hist. Rev.* xxxv (1920), 385, no. i. The manuscript is a cartulary, of St. Swithun, Winchester (Winchester Cathedral), of cent. xiii, except for some later entries. The strokes frequently placed in this manuscript over the letter *i* to distinguish it mainly in the neighbourhood of *n, m, u,* have not been reproduced in the texts printed here ; compare note on no. 8.

On the authenticity of this writ, see pp. 381 ff., and on the legal terms employed see Introduction, pp. 73–81.

DATE. Between Edward's accession in 1042 and the death of Bishop Ælfwine of Winchester on 29 August 1047.

l. 8. *Ælces wites læssan 7 maran.* For a similar phrase in a closely-related charter in the name of Cnut, see p. 382. The specific forfeitures (*fihtwite, fyrdwite,* see Introduction, pp. 81 ff.) appear in a few writs, but only here (and in the closely-linked no. 110) and in no. 44 do we find *wite,* ' fine ', uncompounded in Anglo-Saxon writs. But see also App. IV, no. 5.

(110)

AUTHORITIES :—(A) as for no. 109, f. 10, printed here.

(R) Charter Roll 10 Edw. II, m. 6. Printed : *Cal. of Ch. R.* iii. 347.

(S) Ch. R. 9 Edw. III, m. 10 ; 4 Ric. II, m. 13 ; 1 Hen. IV, p. 2, m. 24 ; 2 Hen. V, p. 1, m. 39 ; *Cal. of Ch. R.* iv. 340, v. 271, 394, 468).

(L) Winchester Cathedral Library Records, vol. i, nos. 121, 122, *inspeximus* charter 4 Ric. II (see S), and duplicate copy (imperfect). Also *inspeximus* charter 1 Hen. IV (see S).

(P) Pat. R. 2 Hen. VI, p. 2, m. 11 ; 2 Edw. IV, p. 6, m. 9 (*Cal. of P.R.* 1422–29, 191 ; 1461–67, 252).

(M) Conf. R. 4 Hen. VII, p. 2, m. 17 ; 2 Hen. VIII, p. 2, m. 22 ; 2 Hen. VIII, p. 3, m. 3.

On the authenticity of this writ see pp. 381 ff., and on the legal terms employed see Introduction, pp. 73–82.

DATE. As for no. 109 if the writ is authentic. But it is probably merely an enlarged and improved version of no. 109.

(111)

AUTHORITIES :—(A) as for no. 109, f. 10 b, printed here.   Printed : A. W.
Goodman, *The Manor of Goodbegot* (Winchester, 1923), p. 6.

(B) Winchester Cathedral Chartulary, no. 31, cent. xiii, an inferior text.
Calendared : A. W. Goodman, *Chartulary of Winchester Cathedral* (Winchester 1927), p. 14, no. 31.

(R) as for no. 110.

(S), (P), (M), as for no. 110.

(L) as for no. 110.

The texts of the group R, S, P, M, preserve some Old English spellings
more faithfully than A. But because they read *belonggyed* (*belongged*) (for
an earlier *belimpað*), and also insert ' and ' after this word, destroying the
syntax, A has been printed here.

On the authenticity of this writ see pp. 382 ff.

DATE.   Between the death of Queen Ælfgifu Emma on 6, or 14, March
1052, and the death of Earl Godwine on 15 April 1053, in so far as the writ
is authentic.

l. 5. *Swa freo wið ealle þa þing* etc. For the privileges of the estate
granted to Ælfgifu in King Æthelred's charter, see p. 383 above. In 1096
William II granted and confirmed to the monks of Old Minster all the houses
and lands which they held in Winchester ; the house of Aluric Godebegete
was to be held by them free and quit of all customs and services, as free
and quit as ever they held it in the time of King Edward and of the king's
father King William (*Eng. Hist. Rev.* xxxv (1920), 388, no. xi). In the
Winchester survey of 1103–15 (or 1107–15, see *ibid.* p. 383) we are told
that ' the house of Godebiete was free in the time of King Edward and it is
now free ' ; and in the survey of 1148 : ' The land of Godebieta was always
free and is free ' (see the Winton Domesday in DB iv. 532 b, 543 b ;
see also Goodman, *The Manor of Goodbegot,* 7 ff.).

l. 10. *Æt Helinge.* Hayling Island, off the coast of Hampshire.   For
its connection with Winchester Cathedral, see pp. 384–5 above.

(112)

AUTHORITIES :—(W) as for no. 107, f. 7 (*ol.* 5), printed here.   Copied in
a blank space in MS. in a handwriting of c. 1200.   Printed : K. 891.

On the authenticity of this writ see pp. 385 ff.

DATE.   The authenticity of this writ is not certain, but any genuine
writ of Edward with these contents witnessed by Harold would have been
issued after the appointment of Harold as earl of Wessex after Godwine's
death on 15 April 1053, and before Edward's death on 5 January 1066.

l. 2. *Portland.* Portland, Dorset. *Chron.* E 1052 records that, in the
interval between his banishment in September 1051 and his reconciliation
with the king in September 1052, Earl Godwine and his forces, on leaving
the Isle of Wight, ' went westwards until they came to Portland and went
ashore and did as much harm as they could do '. It is distinctly probable
that this treatment was inflicted on the place because it was a royal manor.
We learn from Domesday that King William held ' the island which is called
Porland ', and that King Edward held it during his lifetime (*in vita sua*).
In 1086 the king had 3 ploughs on the demesne, and 5 serfs, and there was
1 villein there ; 90 bordars had 23 ploughs ; there was meadow there and
pasture ; and the manor with its appurtenances rendered 65 *libras albas*
(DB i. 75).   For the history of the manor of Portland, see VCH *Hants.* iii. 87.

(113)

AUTHORITIES :—(S) B.M. Stowe MS. no. 944 (the Hyde Register), f. 40–40 b, in a hand which is definitely of cent. xii, and probably of the latter part of the century. Printed : *Liber Vitae ; Register and Martyrology of New Minster and Hyde Abbey, Winchester,* ed. W. de Gray Birch (Hampshire Record Society, 1892), pp. 96–100, with erroneous description of manuscript as Stowe MS. no. 960. The handwriting seems to be that of a man accustomed to writing Anglo-Saxon. The Stowe MS. is printed here.

(W) as for no. 107, f. 116 b–117 (*ol.* 114 b–115). The text is copied between a text in one of the main hands of the cartulary (of 1130–50) and another in a hand of c. 1300. The consensus of British Museum opinion is that the hand of this text probably dates from the end of cent. xii. Printed : K. 922 ; Thorpe pp. 321–4 ; Birch *ut supra.*

On the authenticity of this letter, see pp. 387 ff.

DATE. If there is any substantial basis of fact for the agreement described in the letter, the ratification must have taken place before the promotion of Abbot Æthelgar to the see of Selsey in A.D. 984. The letter itself involves chronological difficulties and cannot be dated. As it stands, it is probably a product of about the last quarter of cent. xii.

l. 1. *Cilda mæstere.* (W) *meistre.* The form *mæstere, meistre,* is of course the Middle English form (from French), the Old English form being *magister, mægester*; see NED. On the life of oblate children in religious houses, see *Ælfric's Colloquy,* ed. G. N. Garmonsway (London, 1939), 44 ff. and the references there.

l. 28. *Settan gode lagan.* For other instances of *gode lagan* see no. 51, and pp. 467 f. In the above phrase *lagan* stands for the regulations determining the relations between the two communities.

l. 37. *Sancte Iudoces mæssedæge.* 13 December, but see p. 564.

(114)

AUTHORITIES :—(H) Harley Charter 43. D. 29, *inspeximus* charter 2 Edward III, of 7 May 1328, with Great Seal appended. Printed : *Mon. Angl.* vi. 1446, with erroneous ascription to Edward I, alterations in spelling, and introduction of letters from Anglo-Saxon script (not justifiable from the existing manuscript). In the manuscript there is a long *r*. The distinction between the letters standing for Anglo-Saxon þ, and *y,* whereby a dot is put over the *y,* is not made consistently in the manuscript or in the other copies below ; and since the various copies do not agree on this point, I have printed þ or *y* at my own discretion. Anglo-Saxon ð is represented by *d* with a stroke beside it. This text is printed here.

(F) Harley Charter 43. E. 51, *inspeximus* charter 1 Edward IV, of 21 November 1461, with Great Seal appended. No long *r* in this copy.

(R) Charter Roll 2 Edw. III, m. 17, no. 67 (*Cal. of Ch. R.* iv. 83).

(P) Patent Roll 2 Ric. II, p. 2, m. 19, 1 Edw. IV, p. 2, m. 4 (*Cal. of P.R.* 1377–81, 336 ; 1461–67, 61). R and P resemble each other closely.

On the authenticity of this writ see pp. 403 ff.

DATE. On the limit of dating imposed by the inclusion in the address of Bishop Leofwine (of Lichfield), see p. 406. But the writ is spurious, and is not therefore dated here.

(115)

AUTHORITIES :—B.M. Add. Charter 19802, in a contemporary hand. Facs. and text : *Facs. of Anc. Chart. in the Brit. Mus.* ed. Bond, pt. iv, no. 39 (placed after no. 41) ; frontispiece of *Saint Wulstan,* J. W. Lamb (S.P.C.K. 1933). Text written on a single piece of parchment, dimensions : 7½″ broad, 1⅓″ deep, left side, 1⅝″, right. A deep ' step ' appears to indicate former sealing, and there appear to be remains of a wrapping tag. It is entirely probable that we have here an original writ written (and sealed) by the clerks of King Edward's secretariat. But attention must be drawn to the absence of an initial + (which may or may not have been customary), and to the mis-spelling *biseoprice* (for *biscop-* or *bisceop*) in the last line.

On the authenticity of this writ see pp. 407 f., and on the legal terms employed see Introduction, pp. 73-8.

DATE. Between the election of Wulfstan to the see of Worcester in the spring or summer of 1062 (his election being canonically confirmed on 29 August), and his consecration on 8 September 1062.

(116)

AUTHORITIES :—(R) Ch. R. 6 Edw. II, m. 13, printed here. Some letters of Anglo-Saxon script imitated in this copy. Printed : *Cal. of Ch. R.* iii. 206.

(S) Ch. R. 3 Edw. III, m. 10, 9 Edw. III, m. 13, 15–17 Ric. II, no. 2 (*Cal. of Ch. R.* iv. 128, 336, v. 346).

(P) Pat. R. 10 Edw. I, m. 10, 1 Edw. IV, p. 6, m. 23, 4 Edw. IV, p. 3, m. 3 (*Cal. of P.R.* 1281–92, 26 (with text), 1461–67, 159, 401).

(M) Conf. R. 3 Hen. VII, p. 2, no. 15, 2 Hen. VIII, p. 5, no. 6.

(B) Worcester Cathedral Library B. 1600, a copy of *inspeximus* charter 6 Edw. II (cf. R) of cent. xiv. Printed : J. H. Bloom. *Original Charters relating to the City of Worcester* (Worcester Historical Society, 1909), 169. There are a very few orthographical differences between this and R, of no significance.

On the authenticity of this writ see p. 409, and on the legal terms employed see Introduction, pp. 73-8.

DATE. After the consecration of Wulfstan to the see of Worcester on 8 September 1062, and before the death of Earl Ælfgar, probably in the same year (see Biographical Notes).

(117)

AUTHORITIES :—Liber Ruber in the Diocesan Registry at Worcester, f. 39 b, cent. late xiii or early xiv, printed here. This writ has hitherto been known only from the text printed by Dr. William Thomas (1670–1738, see DNB) in *An Account of the Bishops of Worcester,* 76, bound up with *A Survey of the Cathedral Church of Worcester* (London, 1736) from a manuscript to which he frequently refers as ' Liber Albus, sive Extenta et Chartæ ', and which subsequently disappeared. The numerous references to his source given by Thomas in this manuscript enable it to be identified with a manuscript recently discovered in the Diocesan Registry at Worcester by Sir Ivor Atkins, Librarian of Worcester Cathedral, to whom I am greatly indebted for informing me of his discovery and for making it possible for me to consult the manuscript. Sir Ivor Atkins has pointed out to me that since the pagination of the two manuscripts is the same, the fact that one is called ' Liber Albus ', and the other marked ' Liber Ruber ' on the inside of an old cover in an eighteenth- or nineteenth-century hand, need not be an obstacle to this identification. Careless copying or deliberate alteration, or both, may be responsible for the differences to be observed between Thomas's text of this writ and that in the Liber Ruber, printed here. Thomas gives a reference to f. 39 b as his source for the text, and there seems no reason for doubting that he had what is now called Liber Ruber before him. There is at any rate no evidence for the existence of a duplicate copy of the newly-discovered Liber Ruber at Worcester, such as we have for the Liber Niger Quaternus of Westminster Abbey (see p. 295 above). Thomas's practices in copying a 'modernised' text cannot be investigated, for lack of material for comparison. For *-chyre* Thomas prints *-shyre*; for *wythynne, withynne*; for *bouten*, he prints *witouten*; for *ich, iche*; for *hy chulle* (a form common in Middle English) he prints *hy wulle*; for *tridde deles, triddeles*; and in the last line of the text he prints *forth* and *oþer*. But since his readings have no manuscript authority they have not been printed on p. 407 as textual variants.

On the authenticity of the writ see pp. 409 f., and on the terms *semtoln* and *chyptoln*, see p. 78.

DATE. As for no. 116.

l. 3. *Þe tridde deles wyrþe. Tridde* is for OE *þridda*, 'third', in the sense of 'one in three'; see note on *þæt þridde treow*, p. 498 above.

l. 5. *So he haued þat oþer þing. Haued* could stand for OE *hæfde* past tense, or for *hæfð* present. Does 'the other thing' refer to the general grant of sake and soke to Wulfstan announced in no. 112? Or was it understood as plur., 'other things'? Or did the original writ read: *þær oþer þing*, 'other things there'?

(118)

AUTHORITIES :—(A) Registrum Magnum Album, Dean and Chapter Library, York Minster, pt. i, f. 61 b, cent. xiv, printed here. Printed: K. 893 (with erroneous ref. to MS. Cott. Aug. ii. 80).

(B) *Ibid.* f. 62 b, with slightly different spellings, possibly in same hand. Printed in 'normalised' spellings, W. Farrer, *Early Yorkshire Charters* i. (1914) 29, no. 10.

On the authenticity of this writ see pp. 412 f., and on the legal terms employed see Introduction, pp. 73–8.

DATE. After the appointment of Ealdred to the see of York at Christmas 1060, and before King Edward's death on 5 January 1066.

(119)

AUTHORITIES :—(H) Harley MS. 560, f. 23, a modern transcript in an unidentified hand of cent. xvi or xvii, printed here. Printed: Farrer, *Early Yorkshire Charters*, i. 29, no. 11.

On the authenticity of this writ see pp. 413 f., and on the legal terms employed see Introduction, pp. 73–8.

DATE. After the appointment of Ealdred to the see of York at Christmas 1060, and before the expulsion of Tostig from his earldom in 1065. Compare no. 7.

(120)

AUTHORITIES :—(A) as for no. 118, pt. i, f. 61 b. Unprinted.

On the authenticity of the writ see pp. 415 ff., and on 'sake and soke' see Introduction, pp. 73–6.

DATE. As for no. 118.

l. 3. *Ealdrede þaes arcebiscopes dyacne Ealdredes.* Since Axminster was given to the archbishop's ' deacon ' for the benefit of the chapter of York Minster, it seems reasonable to suppose that in this context the archbishop's ' deacon ' was the official elsewhere called the ' archdeacon ' (i.e. originally the chief deacon, of those attendant on a bishop). Among the functions of the archdeacon were the administration of the finances of the diocese, and the supervision of the clergy. On the archdeacon, and on the multiplication of archdeacons in Kent in the ninth century, see M. Deanesly, *Eng. Hist. Rev.* xlii (1927), 1–11, and the references there given; see also W. H. Frere, *Visitation Articles and Injunctions*, vol. i (Alcuin Club Collections xiv, 1910), 41–7, and A. Hamilton Thompson, *Diocesan Organization in the Middle Ages : Archdeacons and Rural Deans* (British Academy, 1943, from Proceedings, vol. xxix). There is some evidence (though none of it is contemporary) for archdeacons in Kent before the Conquest, in the early eleventh century. A certain Brinstan is mentioned by Leland (*Collectanea*, ed. Hearne (2nd ed. London, 1770), iv, 7), who quotes with the heading: *E veteri quodam codice monasterii S. Augustini, Cant.* a statement : *S. Brinstanus, archidiaconus S. Ælphegi, in hac ecclesia* (i.e. a church in Thanet) *jacet in porticu aquilonari* ; it seems probable that Brinstan was constituted archdeacon of Canterbury by Archbishop Ælfheah (and not archdeacon of Winchester, Ælfheah's former see). An ecclesiastic of Ælfheah's time, the Ælfmær who betrayed Canterbury to the Danes in the attack on the city in which Ælfheah himself was captured, is styled *archidiaconus* by Florence of Worcester (see Biographical Notes, s. Ælfmær, Abbot). A third name ought possibly to be added to this list, though the evidence is again late and unsatisfactory, that of Haymo (Haimo), supposed to have been alive in the reign of the Confessor, named by the fifteenth-century bibliographer John Boston of Bury, and mentioned among the archdeacons of Canterbury at all events from the time of Nicholas Harpsfield's *Historia Anglicana Ecclesiastica* (p. 242 in the Douai edition of 1622) ; see also W. Somner, *The Antiquities of Canterbury*, 2nd ed. by Battely (London, 1703), Part ii, 145–60, and also J. Dart, *History and Antiquities of the Cathedral Church of Canterbury* (London, 1726), 191 ff. For Haymo, and for a criticism of statements made concerning him, see DNB. Evidence of the existence of an archdeacon in the diocese of York in the eleventh century, before the Conquest, appears in the Northumbrian Priests' Law (dated by Liebermann 1027–c. 1060, that is, rather before, than in, the time of Archbishop Ealdred), in which fines are imposed on priests who disregard the summons of the archdeacon or continue to say mass despite his prohibition (Liebermann, *Gesetze*, i. 380, iii. 220–1 ; see also R. R. Darlington, *Eng. Hist. Rev.* li (1936), 413, n. 1).

l. 3. *þ mynster at Axaminster.* The estate in Devon which took its name from Axminster, i.e. the ' minster ' by the R. Axe, seems to have been from early times a possession of the West Saxon royal house, and it is entirely probable that the minster was an ancient royal foundation. After describing the royal manor at Axminster (*Alseministra*) Domesday records (Exon Domesday in *Domesday Book* (Rec. Comm.) iv. 77 and VCH *Devon*, i. 404) : ' To the church of Axminster a half-hide of the land of this manor belongs. This two ploughs can till and they are there ; and there are 12 bordars there. It is worth 20 shillings a year.' Nothing is known of the minster before 786, when Cyneheard, the brother of Sigeberht, king of Wessex, was buried at Axminster after his celebrated fight with Cynewulf, Sigeberht's successor, recorded in *Chron.* 755. A charter of King Edward the Elder dated 901 (B. 588) is stated to have been written *in loco celebri qui dicitur*

Axemunster. In histories of Axminster church (Oliver, *Mon. Dioec. Exon.* 317, Davidson, *Axminster Church*, 7, Pulman, *Book of the Axe*, 599), it is stated that King Æthelstan gave the church of Axminster to seven priests who should there for ever serve God for the souls of seven earls and many others who were killed in a battle which he had fought against foreigners (*aliens*), ' which fight began at Calix Down, in the parish of Colyton, and extended to Colecroft, below Axminster, on which spot they were slain, A.D. 937 '. It has frequently been assumed that the battle in question was the battle of Brunanburh. For arguments in support of this assumption, see H. Norris, *The Athenæum*, 12 September 1885 ; and to the contrary, James B. Davidson, *ibid.* 3 October 1885. For a review of writings concerning the site of Brunanburh, see A. Campbell, *The Battle of Brunanburh* (London, 1938). The chief sources for the history of Axminster church are B.M. MS. Arundel 17, and the Newenham Register (formerly in the Phillipps Collection), acquired in 1947 by the Bodleian Library (MS. Top. Devon, d. 5).

(121)

AUTHORITIES :—Manuscript in muniment room at Lowther Castle, Westmorland, copied in a hand of cent. xiii on an almost rectangular piece of parchment, dimensions : 10″ by 3¾″. Text printed here from a photograph of the manuscript, kindly supplied to me by Miss A. M. Armstrong. Punctuation, lacking in the manuscript, has been supplied. The text represents a mixture of forms of writing. The copyist copied as nearly as he could most of the letters, in a script to which he was unaccustomed, but he forms some of the capitals and other letters in the fashion of his own time. He imitates to the best of his ability Anglo-Saxon ȝ, ð, þ, long *r*, and the letter ' wyn ' (the Anglo-Saxon form of *w*), but sometimes writes *y* (with a dot over it) for the latter. He sometimes writes ð when *d* would have been expected, but his *mið*, *myð* (for *mid*) is a recognised Northumbrian form. The stroke placed by the copyist over *i* before *n*, and in the word *ic* has not been reproduced here (see note on p. 433), nor has the dot or stroke placed over *y*. Facs. and text : F. Liebermann, *Archiv für das Studium der neueren Sprachen und Literaturen*, cxi (1903), 275–84 ; F. W. Ragg, *Trans. Cumb. and Westmor. Antiq. and Archæol. Soc.* N.S. xvii (1917), 198–218. Printed : F. W. Ragg, *The Ancestor*, vii (Oct. 1903), 246–7 ; also *Trans. Cumb. and Westmor. Antiq. and Archæol. Soc.* N.S. v (1905), 71–84 ; James Wilson, *Scottish Historical Review*, i (1904), 62–9, VCH *Cumberland*, ii. 231–4, and also *Register of the Priory of St. Bee's* (Surtees Society, no. 126), 1915, 526–7 ; W. Greenwell in *History of Northumberland* (Northumberland County History Committee, Newcastle and London), vii (1904), 25–6 ; H. B. Hinckley, ' The Riddle of *The Ormulum* ', *Philological Quarterly*, xiv, no. 2 (April 1935), 211. On the authenticity of this writ see pp. 419 ff., on the legal terms, pp. 73–8

DATE. The writ from which the existing text is derived must have been issued before the death of Gospatric on 28 December 1064. If, as is not certain, since the passage in question is corrupt, the terms in which Earl Siward is referred to can be taken to imply as H. W. C. Davis supposed (see Biographical Notes s.n. Gospatric), that Earl Siward was alive when the writ was issued, then the date of the writ will fall before 1055, the year of Earl Siward's death. It seems unlikely that the writ was issued until after the murder of Earl Eadwulf in 1041, when Gospatric became the heir of the ancient Bernician line of earls, and when Siward himself became the immediate ruler of the whole of Northumbria. The writ is probably therefore to be assigned to the period 1041–64, possibly 1041–55.

l. 1. *Wassenas.* A term of Celtic origin : OBrit *wass,* OWelsh **uas,* Middle and Modern Welsh *gwas,* also in OBret and in OGaul (**uassos,* Latinised as *vassus,* from which is derived, through French and Med. Lat., English *vassal*). The same element appears in ' *Gos*patric ' ; see Biographical Notes. The form *wassenas* in the writs contains the *-en-* which is not only used as a diminutive ending added to nouns, but is also used in abstract and collective nouns ; see Morris Jones, *Welsh Grammar, Hist. and Compar.* (1913), 229 f. (a reference for which I am indebted to Professor Max Förster). The form **gwasan* must have existed in older Welsh on the evidence of Welsh *gwasan-aeth,* ' service ', and other derivatives. The word has been given the OE plur. ending *-as.*

The meaning of the word in the Celtic languages has (according to Professor Förster) a fairly wide range : lad, youth ; servant, rogue, rascal ; husband ; vassal. It is not known to occur elsewhere in English, and one can only guess at the meaning of the term in the three passages in which it is employed in this writ. Suggestions that have been made are ' dependents ', ' retainers ', ' vassals '. H. W. C. Davis supposed that *wassenas* = thegns, but it seems improbable that the basis for this was anything more solid than an unfortunate suggestion reported by J. Wilson (*Scot. Hist. Rev.* i. 66, n. 2) to have been made by Liebermann, but not to be found in Liebermann's own edition of the writ, where the rendering given is ' Vasallen '.

l. 1. *Hyylkun mann freo 7 ðrenge.* The appearance in line 14 below of *loc hyylkun* (OE *loc hwylc*) suggests that the form intended in both cases is *hwylk,* the Anglo-Saxon letter ' wyn ' (*w*) having been miscopied as *y*. But the sense required here is ' every ', whereas OE *hwilc,* when used as an indefinite adjective or pronoun means ' any ', as does also ME *whilk* (a northern form), when used in a generalised sense ; see NED, s.v. ' which ', 12. Could *hyylkun* stand here for an earlier *gehwylcne,* ' every ', with northern omission of *ge-* ? A. Brandl suggested (in Liebermann's edition of the writ) that MS. *hyylk-* stands for *ilk-,* the northern and north-midland form of *ilche,* southern *ælch(e),* ' each, every ' ; see NED s.v. ' ilk ', a.

The fact that the free man and the dreng are brought together in a conjunction which may have become traditional in the northern English poem *Cursor Mundi* (c. 1300), line 16022 (Cottonian version) : *All þai gadird oþe tun, bath freman and dring,* combines with other evidence to suggest that *freo* in Gospatric's writ was a technical term, as was also *liber* in the Domesday phrase *liber homo.* Allerdale is not surveyed in Domesday, but *liberi homines* and *drengs* are mentioned among the holders of land in that part of modern Lancashire which lies between the Ribble and the Mersey (DB i. 269 b–270). It was remarked by Vinogradoff, *Growth of the Manor* (1905), 342, that although no single term can be named as the Old English equivalent of the Latin *liber homo,* Latin versions of later Saxon documents sometimes translate ' thegn ' by *liber homo,* and it is therefore at least suggestive that Ranulf Flambard, bishop of Durham, addressed all his thegns and drengs in the Durham enclave of Islandshire and Norhamshire in a writ issued between 1106 and 1128 (Liebermann, *loc. cit.* 283). The *dreng* (the word in Old English is a Scandinavian loan-word) held his land by military and other services. Stenton has explained (*English Feudalism,* 146) that the *dreng* of the eleventh century was the Scandinavian equivalent of the English *cniht* (on which see p. 440 above), and that though he was associated more closely than his English equivalent with the administration of his lord's estates, he belonged to the same social class. On the drengage tenures of the north at a later period, see J. E. A. Jolliffe, *Eng. Hist. Rev.* xli (1926), 1–42. And on the *liber homo,* see note on no. 85, line 13, above.

l. 2. *On eallun þam landann þeo weoron Cōmbres.* With *Cōmbres,* 'Cumbrian', cf. the Scottish surname *Ingles* (*Inglis*), 'English', the ending *-es* in both cases representing OE *-isc,* Mod. Eng. *-ish.* 'Which were Cumbrian', i.e. which had belonged to the British kingdom of Strathclyde; see further p. 420. Stenton (*Roy. Comm. Hist. Mon. Westmorland,* lii) observes that the phrase implies that at the time when it was used these lands were English, and suggests that the reconquest may have taken place in Cnut's reign.

l. 3. *Mine kynling.* The rare word *kynling* does not seem to be recorded in BT, but many other words formed with *-ling* are recorded there : cf. OE *cyðling,* glossing Lat. *cognatus,* and OE *sibling* 'relative'. *Kinling* appears in a riming charter attributed to King Edward (K. 899), which is not of course authentic in its present form : ' Iche Edouard kingc haue geuen of my forreste the keepinge . . . to Randolfe Peperkinge and to his kinling.' The meaning of the term, a derivative of OE *cynn* 'kindred, family, kin', is 'kindred'.

l. 5. *On Alnerdall . . . to Shauk, to Wafyr, to poll Waðæn, to bek Troyte 7 þeo weald æt Caldebek.* These names are nearly all to be found in Ekwall's *Dictionary of English Place-Names. Alnerdall,* a district in west Cumberland, is Mod. Eng. *Allerdale.* The name in this writ is Scandinavian in form, ON *Alnardalr,* the valley of the R. Alen, later Ellen. The other names indicate the northern and eastern boundaries of Allerdale. *Shauk,* a British river-name, is identified by Professor Ekwall with Chalk Beck, which flows into the R. Wampool near Thursby. *Wafyr* is the R. Waver, which flows into Solway Firth. *Poll Waðæn* is the R. Wampool, which flows into Solway Firth a little to the north of the R. Waver ; Dr. Ekwall remarks that in the form *poll Waðæn,* i.e. ' pool' or ' stream' and (probably) ON *vaðill* ' ford', the order of the elements has been reversed in Celtic fashion. On ' inversion compounds', see Ekwall, *Scandinavians and Celts in the North-West of England* (Lund, 1918). *Bek Troyte,* which also presents the same inverted order, was identified by Ekwall, *ibid.* 18, with Wiza Beck, which enters the Wampool near Wigton. *Caldebek* is Caldbeck, the most southerly place of those named here, which takes its name from the stream (' cold brook ') at the place.

l. 6. *On weald, on freyð, on heyninga. Weald,* ' plain', with sense of ON *völlr. Freyð* is OE *fyrhð* ' woodland' ; see NED s.v. ' frith', sb. [2]. *Heyninga* ' enclosures' is described in *The Chief Elements in English Place-Names* (E.P.-N.S.), 31, as a loan-word in Middle English from Dan. *hegning,* used of enclosed as opposed to common land, and there defined as ' the preserving of grass for cattle, protected grass, any fenced field or enclosure'. We cannot however exclude the possibility that the word was derived in the Old English period from ON *hegna* ' hedge, fence, enclose'. See also NED s.v. ' hain', v., and ' haining', verb. substant., and *English Dialect Dictionary,* s.v. ' haining'. The word survives also in place-names : e.g. *Haining* (Durham and Northumberland), *Heynings* (Lincs.), *Hyning* (Lancs.) ; see further for references E. Ekwall, *The Place-Names of Lancashire* (Manchester, 1922), 188.

The formula : *on weald, on freyð, on heyninga,* obviously represents an adaptation to local conditions of such formulæ as *on wuda, on felda, on strande, on streame* etc. in King Edward's writs.

l. 6. *Æt ællun ðyngan þeo bȳ eorðe bænand 7 ðeoronðer.* Possibly ' in respect of all things that are above the earth and under it '. The original text cannot be recovered here with any certainty, and this passage may have reached its present shape by progressive misreading ; e.g. *bufan,* ' above ', written *buuan*, then *bunan*, and then confused with present participle, and so on. Or possibly the transcriber may have been trying to supply something illegible. There is no OE word *bœnand* which will fit in, and the meaning 'pray, request' of ONorse *bœna* will not do here. The first part of the clause presumably includes such things as produce. By the second, 'under it', the donor may have envisaged such possibilities as mining for metals (iron, lead and others), quarrying for stone or slate, digging for clay.

l. 9. *Æt Carðeu 7 Combeðeyfoch.* Cardew and Cumdivock, two hamlets in the parish of Dalston, south of Carlisle and north of Caldbeck, in the neighbourhood of Chalk Beck (*Shauk*). The etymology of *Cardew* is obscure ; see Ekwall, *Scandinavians and Celts*, 106. For *Cumdivock*, explained by him as a British name, see *Dict. of English Place-Names*. On the later history of Cardew, see Ragg, *Trans. Cumb. and Westmor. Antiq. and Archæol. Soc.* N.S. xvii (1917), 198 f. : ' The barony or manor of Dalston under which Cardew was held had been in the immediate tenure of the Crown and was given by Henry III to William Mauclerk, bishop of Carlisle, to be held by the bishops as superior lords '. See also on these and other place-names, the forthcoming *Place-Names of Cumberland* (E.P.-N.S.).

l. 11. *Þehat mið Þ ic heobbe gegyfene to hem neghar brech seo gyrth ðyylc Eorl Syward 7 ic hebbe getyðet hem se frelycc swa ænyg man leofand þeo welkynn ðeoronðer.* This passage exhibits a number of remarkable features, and if it is ultimately derived from an Old English text, it has been greatly altered in transmission. *Þehat* is possibly merely a mistake in spelling ; or it may have arisen from a copyist's attempt to expand the common *Þ* (*þæt*). Old English usage requires that the dative pronoun ' him ' after the verb ' to give ' should be unaccompanied by ' to ' ; *gegyfen to hem* is therefore irregular. *Neghar* may go back ultimately to an OE *nahwær* ' nowhere ', or possibly to ' neither '. Wilson takes *ghar brech* as ' cause to break ', with *ne* as the negative, but one would expect the offence of *grithbreach* (p. 80) to be committed at first hand. Again, *seo* (*gyrth*) is the feminine nominative of the definite article ; what is required here with *gyrth* (for OE *grið*, *gryð*, a loanword from Scandinavian) is the accusative neuter *þæt*. For *ðyylc*, see the note on line 19 below. Presumably because OE *ðylc* ' such ', and ME *thilk* ' that, that same ' are not used as relative pronouns, Liebermann proposed to emend to *swyylk* ' such as ' (see BT s.v. *swilc*, IV), but this construction seems somewhat forced. For the MS. *cefrelycc*, Liebermann emends to *æfrelyce*, which does not seem to be recorded elsewhere. This cannot be accepted because ' as ' before *ænyg man* requires another ' as ' to complete the sense. An obvious emendation is to *se frelycc*, *se* being used in OE (and ME) as well as *swa*, for ' so, as ' ; see BT, s.v. *se*, ' so ', and Stratmann-Bradley, *Middle-English Dictionary*, s.v. *swá*. Further, what is the reference of the clause : *se frelycc swa ænyg mann leofand* etc. ? If *ænyg* is in the nom. case, then it runs : ' Earl Siward and I have granted . . . as freely as any man ' etc. ; but *ænyg* is no doubt to be construed as dat. : ' as freely as *to* any man ' etc. Finally, no construction is to be found in normal Old English parallel to the clause *þeo welkynn ðeoronðer*, ' the skies thereunder '. This expression is as peculiar in Old English as it is in Modern English, and the form *welkynn* strongly suggests a Middle English date of origin ; the OE form was *wolcnu* (*weolcnu*). In fact the difficulties presented by this passage are such that W. H. Stevenson is reported by Wilson to have considered that the text was hopelessly corrupt, and to have suggested that a copyist must have omitted a line or a clause. It is however doubtful whether the recovery of a lost line or clause would be sufficient to enable one to restore the original sense underlying this passage, supposing it to have formed part of an authentic writ. It seems distinctly probable that something having been omitted at an earlier stage of the history of the text, or some part of it having become illegible, a copyist (perhaps the copyist responsible for the existing text, or a predecessor) may have attempted to rewrite the passage, but unsuccessfully, owing to an imperfect knowledge of Anglo-Saxon. Liebermann translates as follows, but unfortunately makes no comment : ' dass er bezüglich dessen was ich jenem gegeben habe irgendwo den Frieden breche, solchen wie Graf Siward und ich jenem ewiglich verliehen habe, wie irgend jemand dort lebend unter dem Himmel '.

l. 14. *Geyldfreo.* For parallel forms, cf. *scotfreo, gafolfreo,* see p. 439. On the *geld,* see pp. 513 f.

l. 19. *Myð bode 7 wytnesmann.* This is a formula appearing in records relating to Lancs., Westm., Cumb., and Durham, in the thirteenth and fourteenth centuries, where the provision of *bode* and ' witnessman ' appears among the services exacted from holders of land ; for references, see NED s.v. ' witnessman '. Among the passages cited there we may compare : quieti de secta facienda ad curiam meam . . . *et de Bode et de Wyttenesman* . . . que seruicia quondam petii de predictis Abbati et Conuentu. Other instances are given by R. Stewart-Brown, *The Serjeants of the Peace* (Manchester, 1936) ; for references, see Index. It is there explained (p. 82 ff.) that the duty was laid upon certain holdings, to go with the serjeants of the peace to assist in and to attest the service of summons, and the arrest of criminals and seizure of their goods ; to be present when offenders were placed under sureties ; and to attend at court to give testimony of such proceedings. In such contexts ' witnessman ' then means acting as a witness and giving testimony of what has been seen. ' Bode ' is to be explained as the obligation of acting as a messenger. What then is the meaning of the clause as it appears in Gospatric's writ (assuming that the clause goes back to the Anglo-Saxon period) ?

There can scarcely be any doubt that ' witnessman ' is an anglicised form of ON *vitnismaðr,* ' witnessman ', but *bode* in this context is susceptible of more than one interpretation. In Gospatric's writ it is declared that the grantee is to have judicial and financial rights over lands which had formerly been given to another person *freols myd bode and wytnesmann.* The reference of *freols* in this context is unfortunately not clear. Is the passage to be interpreted : ' freely, with (the right to claim) *bode* and witnessman ' ; or ' free from (the obligation of providing) *bode* and witnessman ' ?

In view of the later contexts in which the phrase is used, cited above, it seems likely that ' *bode* and witnessman ' stands for the duty of providing men to carry messages and to act as witnesses ; *bode* would then stand for ON *boði* or OE *boda,* ' announcer, messenger '. On the importance given to the witness in Anglo-Saxon law, and on the provision of messengers, see Stewart-Brown, *loc. cit.* 85–6. It seems less probable that *bode* stands here for ON *boð,* ' summons ', i.e. to a public assembly where, before witnesses, the lands given to Thore would (on this interpretation) have been declared free from payments and services. The *boð* or ' summons ' was in Old Norse an ordinary term of law, and it denoted the arrow or axe or other object sent to call people to battle or council ; see Cleasby-Vigfusson, *Icelandic-English Dictionary,* s.v. *boð,* 4 β. On the whole, the least likely explanation is that given by H. W. C. Davis, ' with proclamation and witnesses ', following a suggestion of Ragg that *bode* meant ' proclamation '. Although *bodian* can mean ' to proclaim ', this rendering of *bode* seems to lack support elsewhere ; see BT s.v. *bod.* On this interpretation ' *bode* and witnessman ' would ' refer to the ceremony of livery of seisin, and mean that the grant had been made with public proclamation (*bode*) and before witnesses ' ; see Stewart-Brown, 84. But this interpretation cannot be accepted.

l. 19. *On þy ylk stow.* Supposing this phrase to have stood in the original draft of the writ, it would presumably have appeared in the form *on þy ylcan stowe*. In the rendering ' in that place ', adopted by Ragg for the reading *on þyylk stow*, *þyylk* is used in a sense which seems to have developed in or before the thirteenth century ; see NED s.v. ' thilk ', dem. adj. and pron. But however it is translated the reference of the above clause in this context is far from clear.

APPENDICES

APPENDIX I

J. T. Fowler, *Memorials of Ripon*, i (Surtees Society, 74), 89–90 [1]

In nomine Sanctæ et Individuæ Trinitatis, Atelstanus Rex Angliæ omnibus hominibus suis de Eboratura (*sic*) per totam Angliam salutem. Sciatis quod ego confirmo ecclesiæ et capitulo Rypon' pacem suam, et omnes libertates et consuetudines suas, et concedo eis curiam suam de omnibus querelis et in omnibus curiis de hominibus Sancti Wilfridi, ipsis et hominibus suis vel contra ipsos vel intra se ad invicem, vel quæ fieri possunt, et judicium suum per frodmortele, et quod homines sui sint credendi per suum *ya* et per suum *na*, et omnes terras habitas et habendas, et homines suos, ita liberos quod nec rex Angliæ nec ministri ejus nec archiepiscopus Eboracensis nec ministri ejus aliquod faciant vel habeant quod est ad terras suas vel ad sokam capituli. Testibus T. archiepiscopo Ebor. et P. præposito Beverlaci.

[1] See p. 14, n. 1.

APPENDIX II

In nomine summi Dei viventis. et videntis. Trinitatis essentia.
uereque Deus est. nichil mutabile. nec in eternitate. nec in ueritate.
nec in uoluntate habet. que uere initium initio carens. finisque fine
carens. ambiguitate cunctimoda penitus abjecta. ueraciter credenda
est. In qua siquidem personarum Trinitate Patris. uidelicet et
Filii et Spiritus Sancti substantie unitatis. ineffabilis. incompre-
hensibilis. incircumscriptibilis. omnique sensui humano etiam et
angelico inscrutabilis. et inuestigalibilis. impenetrabilisque semper
predicanda. laudanda. preconiisque infatigabiliter attolenda est
immensis.   Quam ob causam ego Edvvardus rex Anglorum. cum
essem in pace. in gloria regni mei. pro salute anime mee. patrumque
meorum. qui ante me regnauerunt. cum consultu et decreto pri-
matum. fideliumque meorum. dedi Sancto Dyonisio qui celebris
memorie apud nos quidem nominatur. apud Francos autem. et
colitur et habetur. uillam quandam nominatam Teintuna. in
territorio et comitatu urbis que Oxenaforda dicitur. cum omnibus
appendiciis eius. id est terris. siluis. pascuis. aquis. pratis. cultis.
et incultis.   Sit autem terra hec immunis et libera. ab omni negotio.
excepta expeditione. et pontis. uel arcis instauratione. Quod si
qui uiolauerint. sit pars eorum decreto Dei et meo. omniumque
episcoporum quorum nomina hic habentur. cum Juda traditore.
cum Dathan et Abiron in ignem eternum ubi uermis eorum non
moritur. et ignis non extinguitur. nisi reatum suum coram Deo et
Sancto Dyonisio emendauerint.

Þis syndan þa landgemære into Tængtune. þ is ærest of þam
readan clife on Ælfredes denn. 7 of þam denne. on þone háran
stán. 7 of þam stane on Mægnhilde beorh. 7 'óf' þam beorge on
riscwille. 7 of þære wylle. on þa ruga ðyrna. 7 of þara ðyrne on
þon holan broch. 7 of þam bróche on hæselford. 7 of þam forde
andlangc weges on þone stapel. 7 of þam stapele on dryge pytt.
7 of þam pytte. on fulla wille. 7 of þære wylle. on cobbanhyll.
7 of þære hylle. on cobbanbróc. 7 of þam broche andlang streames
inne wenric. 7 swa to þam readan clyfe.   Þis is þ gemære to þam
more þe þider innto ligð. þ is of díclace a wilstede. 7 of wilstede
on ryðera ford. 7 of þam forde on wireneges þorn. 7 of þam
þorne. andlang wenric on beafolces ears. 7 of beafolces earse
andlang Témese be healfan stréame eft inne díclace. Þis is þ
gemære to þam wuda þider inn. þ is ærest of friðeles stane on þone

[1] See Introduction, pp. 35 ff., and for printed texts see p. 36, n. 1.

538

stanian weigg. 7 of þam wege on fæste gráf. 7 of þam grafe andlang
weges on wiðilea. 7 of þære lea swa eft on þone stan.

.Nono.

Anno dominice incarnationis. M. L. IX. scripta est hec cartula
his testibus consentientibus quorum nomina inferius carraxari
uidentur.

+ Ego Edvvardus rex totius Britthannie telluris. hanc meam
  donationem Sancto Dyonisio concessi. et signo agie crucis
  munitam condonaui.

+ Ego Eadgyð conlaterana eiusdem regis hoc mihi placere cum
  beniuolentia professa sum.

+ Ego Stigandus metropolitanus Christi ecclesie archiepiscopus.
  necne Wintoniensis ecclesie donum regis cum tropheo
  sancte crucis libentissimo animo confirmaui.

+ Ego Kynsinus. Eboracensis ecclesie archiepiscopus. prefatum
  munus consolidaui.

+ Ego Wlfwinus Dorcacastrensis ecclesie episcopus predictum
  hoc regis donum benignissima manu conscripsi.

+ Ego Dodico episcopus conclusi.

+ Ego Herimannus episcopus consignaui.

+ Ego Aldredus episcopus consensum prebui.   ·

+ Ego Willelmus episcopus consensi.

+ Ego Ægelmærus episcopus corroboraui.

+ Ego Haroldus dux.

+ Ego Ælfgar dux.

+ Ego Tostig dux.

+ Ego Leofwine dux.

+ Ego Gyrð dux.

+ Ego Swegen m'.

+ Ego Eadric m'.

+ Ego Godric m'.

+ Ego Atsor m'.

+ Ego Esgar m'.

+ Ego Raulf m'.

+ Ego Rotbert m'.

+ Ego Brihtric m'.

+ Ego Vlf m'.

Et ego Balduinus Sancti Dyonisii monachus. sub regimine abbatis
mei Hugonis constitutus. tunc temporis Anglorum Regis Edvvardy
medicus. omnibus quorum hic adnotata sunt nomina sine cuiuslibet
calumpnia scriptum huius donationis confirmantibus de manu
eiusdem regis et scriptum. et donum. imperpetuum Sancto Dyonisio
habendum suscepi.

APPENDIX III

¶ Extracta de testamento Sc̄i Eadwardi Regis. Volo quod omnia que donaui monasterio beati Apostolorum principis Petri peculiaris patroni nostri sint stabilita et confirmata imperpetuum et quod nullus successorum nostrorum Regum ex hiis subtrahere aut diminuere uel disperdere qualibet occasione iudicio uel potestate presumat ne pace terrena priuetur.

¶ Volo quod post mortem Edgithe Regine conjugis mee Roteland cum omnibus ad se pertinentibus detur monasterio meo beatissimi Petri et reddatur sine tardicione abbati et monachis ibidem Deo seruientibus imperpetuum.

¶ Volo quod si locus meus religiosus de Deorhirste cuius regimen dedi monasterio Sc̄i Dionisii prope Parisius (*sic*) contigerit ut futuris temporibus alienetur a monasterio Sc̄i Dionisii quod ex tunc monasterium beatissimi beati Petri habeat et possideat dictum locum meum de Deorhirste et eius regimen imperpetuum.

¶ Volo quod Eldredus archiepiscopus Leofricus et Godwinus episcopi Rodbertus capellanus Edwinus et Leoffwinus comites ultime voluntatis mee testes et perimpletores faciant et perficiant omnia scripta et dicta mea ut possint euadere eternam dampnacionem et ut regnum meum et reges successores mei habeant pacem temporalem.

[1] See pp. 292 ff. above.

APPENDIX IV

LOST WRITS AND NEGATIVE STATEMENTS [1]

1. KING ÆTHELRED II

K. 693, Thorpe p. 288, A. J. Robertson, *Anglo-Saxon Charters*, no. 66, A.D. 990–92.

' þa sende se cyning be Æluere abbude *his insegel* to þam gemote æt Cwicelmeshlæwe 7 *grette* ealle þa witan þe þær gesomnode wæron, þ̄ wæs Æþelsige biscop 7 Æscwig biscop 7 Ælfric abbud 7 eal sio scir, 7 bæd 7 het þ̄ hi scioldon Wynflæde 7 Leofwine swa rihtlice geseman swa him æfre rihtlicost þuhte ' (' Then the king sent *his seal* to the meeting at Cuckamsley by Abbot Ælfhere and *greeted* all the witan who were assembled there, namely Bishop Æthelsige and Bishop Æscwig and Abbot Ælfric and the whole shire, and prayed and commanded them to settle the case between Wynflæd and Leofwine as justly as they could ').

2. KING ÆTHELRED II

K. 929, Thorpe p. 301, Robertson, no. 69, A.D. 995–1005/6.

' þa ða him seo talu cuð wæs, þa sende he *gewrit* 7 *his insegl* to þam arcebisceope Ælfrice, 7 bead him þ̄ he 7 hys þegenas on East Cent 7 on West Cent hy on riht gesemdon be ontale 7 be oftale ' (' When the claim was known to him, he (King Æthelred II) sent *a letter and his seal* to archbishop Ælfric, and gave him orders that he and his thegns in East Kent and West Kent should settle the dispute between them justly, weighing both claim and counterclaim ').

3. KING ÆTHELRED II

Anglo-Saxon Chronicle C, D, E, F, 1014, ed. Thorpe, i. 272, Plummer, i. 145 :—

' þa sende se cyning his sunu Eadweard hider mid his ærendracum 7 *het gretan ealne his leodscype*, 7 cwæð þ̄ he him hold hlaford beon wolde, 7 ælc þæra ðinga betan þe hi ealle ascunudon 7 ælc þara ðinga forgyfen beon sceolde þe him gedon oþþe gecweden wære, wið þam ðe hi ealle anrædlice butan swicdome to him gecyrdon ' (' Then the king sent his son Edward hither with his messengers,

---

[1] This list is not intended to be exhaustive. It indicates the circumstances in which writs now lost were issued by Anglo-Saxon kings, or in which the issue of writs was considered by contemporaries to be appropriate. Writs mentioned in Domesday which are not definitely attributed to King Edward, or undoubtedly to be assigned to him, are not included here.

and *bade greet all his people*, and said that he would be to them a gracious lord, and would remedy all the things which they all hated and everything should be forgiven that had been done or said against him, on condition that they all unanimously without treachery submitted to him'). Compare Fl. Wig. *Chronicon ex Chronicis*, ed. Thorpe, i. 169 : 'Quibus auditis Eadwardum filium suum cum legatis suis ad eos dirigens, *majores minoresque gentis suæ amicabiliter salutavit* promittens se illis mitem devotumque dominum futurum.'

4. KING CNUT

Goscelin's Text. Transl. Beatæ Mildrethæ, cap. xii (Cott. Vesp. B. xx, f. 174 b) ; Thorne col. 1910.

Abbot Ælfstan petitions Cnut for leave to translate the relics of St. Mildred to his own church ; '. . . et in illo sancto sabbato (before Whit Sunday) regis donum regina Emma simul fauente totum desiderium suum *cum regis litteris* (i.e. with a writ, or writs) Deo aspirante optinuit. Similarly Thorne : the abbot obtained ' *regias litteras* translationem prædictam adhuc faciendam fermiter confirmantes '.

For the background see p. 193 above.

5. KING HAROLD HAREFOOT

Bond, *Facsimiles of Ancient Charters in the British Museum*, pt. iv, no. 20 ; K. 758, Thorpe p. 338, Earle p. 297, Robertson no. 91, A.D. C. 1037–40.

' Þa sende Harold king Ælfgar munuc agen to þam arcebiscope Eadsige 7 to eallon Cristes cyrcean munecan, *7 grette hig ealle Godes gretincge 7 his*, 7 het Þ hig sceoldan habban Sandwic into Cristes cyrcean *swa full 7 swa forð swa hig hit æfre hæfdon on ænies kinges dæge, ge on gafole, ge on streame, ge on strande, ge on witun, ge on eallon þam þingan þe hit æfre ænig king fyrmest hæfde ætforan him* ' (' Then King Harold sent the monk Ælfgar back to Archbishop Eadsige and to all the monks of Christ Church, and *greeted them all with God's greeting and his own, and ordered that they should have Sandwich for Christ Church as fully and as completely as ever they had it in any king's day, both in rent and in stream and on strand and in fines and in all the things [with] which any king ever had had it before him* '.

6. KING EDWARD THE CONFESSOR

Anglo-Saxon Chronicle, E 1048 (to be corrected to 1051) ; ed. Thorpe i. 313, Plummer i. 172. See p. 449 above.

' Ða com Sparhafoc abbod be wege to him *mid þæs cynges gewrite*

7 *insegle* to þan þet he hine hadian sceolde to biscope into Lundene '
(' Then Abbot Spearhafoc came to him on the way *with the king's
letter and seal* to the effect that he should consecrate him as bishop
of London ').

7. KING EDWARD THE CONFESSOR

For reference see p. 249, n. 2 above.

Abbot Ælfwine of Ramsey successfully prayed King Edward
' quousque supradictas donationes suas *litteris Anglicis regiæ suæ
imaginis impressione roboratis* (i.e. letters with seals) ad futuræ
posteritatis malitiam refellendam communiret '.

8. KING EDWARD THE CONFESSOR

DB i. 50, VCH *Hants.* i. 507.   Rockbourn, Hants.

Concerning the liability to geld of land at Rockbourn, which
was held by Aluui, ' dicit hundredum quod T.R.E. quieta et soluta
fuit et *inde habet Aluui sigillum regis E* '.

9. KING EDWARD THE CONFESSOR

DB i. 50, VCH *Hants.* i. 507.   Rockbourn, Hants.

Sawin holds of the king a half-hide in Rockbourn.   He himself
held it of King Edward *in alodium*.   The sheriff's officers say that
the half-hide belongs to the king's farm ; ' sed hundredum et scira
dicunt quod rex E. dedit huic et *inde habet sigillum ejus* '.

10. KING EDWARD THE CONFESSOR

DB i. 59, VCH *Berks.* i. 341.   Sparsholt, Berks.

The shire court attests concerning this manor that Edric, who
used to hold it, gave it over to his son who was a monk at Abingdon,
to hold it at farm and to provide himself (*sibi*, i.e. the donor)
therefrom with the necessaries of life, and after his death to have
the manor.   And therefore the men of the shire court do not know
how far it belongs to the abbey, for they have seen neither king's
writ nor seal concerning it.   ' Abbas uero testatur quod in T.R.E.
misit ille manerium ad ecclesiam unde erat et *inde habet breuem
et sigillum R.E.* attestantibus omnibus monachis suis.'

11. KING EDWARD THE CONFESSOR

DB i. 60 b, VCH *Berks.* i. 350.   Woolhampton, Berks.

' Hanc terram dedit rex E. de sua firma Godrico et *inde uiderunt
sigillum ejus homines de comitatu*.   Praeter istas hidas accepit ipse
Godricus de firma regis unam virgatam terræ de qua non uiderunt
sigillum regis.'

For comment see VCH *Berks.* i. 293, 350.

12. KING EDWARD THE CONFESSOR

DB i. 78 b, Cheselbourne, Dorset, and Shaftesbury Abbey.

' Istum manerium et Sture abstulerat Heraldus 'comes' S. Mariæ T.R.E. sed W. rex eam fecit resaisiri quia in ipsa æcclesia inuentus est *breuis cum sigillo R. E.* precipiens ut æcclesiæ restituerentur cum Melecome quem rex adhuc tenet.'

13. KING EDWARD THE CONFESSOR

DB i. 169. Henry de Ferrers' manor of Lechlade, Glouc.

' Ibi xv hidæ geldantes. Sed ipse rex concessit vi hidas quietas a geldo. Hoc testatur omnis comitatus et ipse qui *sigillum regis detulit.*'

For comment on ' beneficial hidation ' see p. 375 above. Also mentioned by J. H. Round in *Domesday Studies*, ed. Dove, i. 98.

14. KING EDWARD THE CONFESSOR

DB i. 208, VCH *Hunts.* i. 354. *Clamores.*

The jurors of Huntingdon say that the church of St. Mary of the borough and the land annexed to it belonged to the church of Thorney, but the abbot gave it in pledge to the burgesses. But King Edward gave it to Vitalis and Bernard his priests, and they sold it to Hugh the king's chamberlain. ' Hugo uero uendidit eam ii presbyteris de Huntedune et *habent inde sigillum regis E.* Eustachius modo habet eam sine liberatore et sine breui et sine saisitore.'

For comment see VCH *Hunts.* i. 325.

15. KING EDWARD THE CONFESSOR

DB i. 208 b, VCH *Hunts.* i. 355. ' Ovretone ', not mentioned here, but identified with the land in question by F. M. Stenton, VCH *Hunts.* i. 327.

' De terra Leuric dicunt quod fuit in soca regis sed Remigius episcopus ostendit *breuem regis Edw.* per quem Leuricum cum omni terra dederit in episcopatum Lincoliæ cum saca et soca.'

For comment see Stenton *ut supra.*

16. KING EDWARD THE CONFESSOR

DB i. 374, VCH *Yorkshire*, ii. 295.

All the land which Drogo claimed upon St. John (of Beverley) is affirmed to the use of the same St. John by the men of the Riding and by the gift of King William which he gave to St. John in the time of Archbishop Ealdred. ' *De hoc habent canonici sigillum regis Edw. et regis Willi.*'

17. KING EDWARD THE CONFESSOR

DB ii. 310 b, VCH *Suffolk*, i. 450. Fordley, Suffolk.
The land of which Edric of Laxfield had been deprived by King
Edward when he was outlawed was restored to him on his reconciliation with the king. ' Dedit etiam *breuem et sigillum* ut qui-
cumque de suis liberis commendatis hominibus ad eum uellent
redire suo concessu redirent.'
For comment, see Carl Stephenson, *Eng. Hist. Rev.* lix (1944), 303.

18. KING EDWARD THE CONFESSOR

DB ii. 360 b, VCH *Suffolk*, i. 496. Freemen in Stow hundred,
under *Anhus* (' Onehouse '), with reference to the abbey of
Bury. See p. 441 above.
' Et fuit soca et saca (soca MS.) et commendatio de istis omnibus
Sancti Edmundi ex dono regis E. *sicut breuia et sigillum demonstrant
que abbas habet.'*

19. KING EDWARD THE CONFESSOR

DB ii. 379, VCH *Suffolk*, i. 516. Wangford Hundred.
Over the ' ferling ' of Elmham Bishop William has soke and
sake except over Bishop Stigand's men, ' et B[aldwine] abbas per
testimonium hundredi *habuit breuem de R.E.* quod ipse habere
debuit socam et sacam super terram Sancti Edmundi et suos (sui
MS.) homines '.

20. KING EDWARD THE CONFESSOR. Negative statement.

DB i. 197, VCH *Cambs.* i. 383. Chippenham, Cambs.
Orgar the sheriff himself had 3 hides of this land and could give
it to whom he would. Orgar put this land in pledge for 7 marks
of gold and 2 ounces, as Geoffrey's men say, ' sed homines de
hundredo neque *breue aliquid* neque legatum R.E. inde uiderunt
neque testimonium perhibent '.

21. KING EDWARD THE CONFESSOR. Negative statement.

DB i. 208, VCH *Hunts.* i. 355. Keystone, Hunts.
They say that Keystone was and is of the farm of King Edward
and although Aluric the sheriff resided in that vill, he nevertheless
always paid the king's farm therefrom, and his sons after him until
Eustace assumed (*accepit*) the sheriffdom, ' nec unquam uiderunt
uel audierunt *sigillum regis E.* quod eam foris misisset de firma sua '.

PART IV

BIOGRAPHICAL NOTES
ON PERSONS NAMED IN ANGLO-SAXON WRITS

The Biographical Notes on persons named in the texts of Anglo-Saxon Writs, and on these alone, have been brought together here in one section to facilitate reference, since many of the names appear in more than one document. The purpose of the Notes is to identify the person, and to supply dates for his or her career. In the case of well-known figures it has seemed desirable to give only the salient facts or dates (for the benefit of readers who are not specialists) ; further information will be found in the standard works on the period. In the case of less-known persons who do not figure in such works, or who appear in texts hitherto unprinted, an attempt has been made to bring together here all the information possible. In every case emphasis has been laid upon such dates as are available, since Anglo-Saxon writs can be dated only from the dates of the persons whose names appear in them ; this consideration explains the amount of space given to the discussion of dates which are uncertain or disputed. The evidence for the dates of bishops given in well-known authorities such as Stubbs' *Registrum Sacrum Anglicanum*, and in Searle's two books, has been carefully re-examined. Since in the compilation of the *Handbook of British Chronology* (R. Hist. Soc. 1939) use was made for episcopal dates of the lists in Stubbs and Searle (see Preface, viii), the *Handbook* itself has not been cited for these dates as an independent authority. The evidence for the dates of Anglo-Saxon rulers has also been re-examined.

To avoid printing large numbers of variant forms of names, names are entered in this list in the form which they have been given in the headings to the writs and in the translation which accompanies each writ in Old English. With writs extant only in Latin (and not translated), the name is entered under the form which it is given in the writ heading ; if it does not appear in the heading then it will be given in the form in which it appears in the text (with a reference). For the most part the spelling of names adopted here is that of F. M. Stenton's *Anglo-Saxon England*.

ABBREVIATIONS

Ashdown : M. Ashdown, *English and Norse Documents* (Cambridge), 1930.
Fl. Wig. : Florence of Worcester, *Chronicon ex Chronicis*, ed. Thorpe.
Wm. Malmesbury, *G.P.* : William of Malmesbury, *Gesta Pontificum*, R.S.
Plummer : Plummer, *Two Saxon Chronicles Parallel*.
Searle, *Bishops* : *Anglo-Saxon Bishops, Kings and Nobles* (Cambridge), 1899.
Stubbs : *Registrum Sacrum Anglicanum*, 2nd ed. 1897.

See also the list of Abbreviations at the beginning of the book.

Ædnotho, nos. 57, 58, see **Eadnoth.**
Ægelnodo, no. 37, see **Æthelnoth.**
Ælfgæt the sheriff, nos. 86, 87. Sheriff of Middlesex. Otherwise unknown.
Ælfgar, Earl, nos. 10, 15–22, 60, 115–17. Earl of East Anglia 1051–52 and 1053–57 ; earl of Mercia 1057–62. Ælfgar was the son of Earl Leofric (q.v.) and his wife Godgifu (Godiva) (q.v.). During the exile of Earl Godwine

and his family, which lasted from 24 September 1051 to 14 September 1052, Ælfgar held the earldom of East Anglia which Harold had had (*Chron.* E, 1048, to be corrected to 1051), but relinquished it on Harold's reinstatement. In 1053 he was re-appointed to the same earldom, now vacated by Harold on his appointment to the earldom of Mercia after his father's death on 15 April 1053 (*Chron.* C, D, E, 1053). Having been outlawed at a meeting of the witan in 1055 (on an accusation of treachery, according to *Chron.* E, 1055, though C and D adopt a more favourable attitude), Ælfgar obtained the help of Gruffydd ap Llywelyn, king of Gwynned and Powys, and of a force of Norsemen from Ireland, with whom he attacked and put to flight an English force, and ravaged the town of Hereford, sacking and burning the minster. He was shortly afterwards restored to his earldom. In 1057 he was appointed earl of Mercia after the death of his father, Earl Leofric, on 31 August (or 30 September) 1057 (*Chron.* D, E). In 1058 he was again banished, and again won back his position with the help of Gruffydd and of a fleet from Norway. Ælfgar took part in the discussions in the spring or summer of 1062 concerning the appointment of Wulfstan (q.v.) to the see of Worcester ; this appointment was canonically confirmed on 29 August of that year. Ælfgar is not heard of again, and the date of his death is not known. We infer from Domesday that Ælfgar had died before the date of King Edward's death on 5 January 1066. No weight is to be attached to the fact that Ælgarus *dux* attests a charter dated 1065 (K. 815), for in Kemble's copy the date and the regnal year do not agree. In another copy of the same text dated 1062 the signature of Ælfgar does not occur. But the charter is in any case spurious : see R. R. Darlington, *Vita Wulfstani* (Royal Historical Society, London, 1928), xxvi, n. 2.

Ælfgifu Emma, Queen, nos. 9, 10, 16–18, 24, 27, 57, 58, 104, 111. Ælfgifu was the English name adopted by Emma (Imma, Ymma), daughter of Richard I (the Fearless) duke of the Normans, on her marriage in the spring of 1002 to King Æthelred II. In these writs only the name Ælfgifu occurs ; in several she is referred to but not named. By her first marriage, she had two sons, Edward (the Confessor) and Alfred. By her second marriage in 1017 to King Cnut, Æthelred's successor, she was the mother of Harthacnut (q.v.). After the death of Cnut she was deprived by Harold Harefoot of all King Cnut's ' best treasures ' (*Chron.* C, D, 1035), and when Harold was in 1037 formally recognised as king, she was driven into exile ; on her stay in Bruges see P. Grierson, *Trans. R. Hist. Soc.* 4th ser. xxiii (1941), 96 f. She returned to England with Harthacnut in 1040. Shortly after 16 November 1043, she was deprived by her son King Edward (who had succeeded Harthacnut), and the great earls, of the immense treasure that she had accumulated, on the charge (*Chron.* D 1043) that ' she had been very harsh to the king her son in that she had done less for him than he wished, before he became king and also after ' (see also C, E (misdated 1042)) ; and at the same time Bishop Stigand, her closest adviser, was also disgraced. After this Ælfgifu was allowed to reside at Winchester, her house there being mentioned in the Winton Domesday (DB iv. 535). She attested charters after her disgrace ; her last datable signature seems to occur between 26 December 1045, and 1047 (Robertson no. 101). Her death is recorded in *Chron.* C 1051 ; but as C begins the year on March 25, the correct date of the queen's death seems to be 1052 (14 March in C, 6 March in D), the year under which it is entered in D and E. She was buried in Old Minster at Winchester by the side of her husband Cnut. For full details of her career, see A. Campbell, *Encomium Emmae Reginae* (R. Hist. Soc., Camden Third Series, lxxii, 1949).

Ælfgyth, no. 73. Otherwise unknown.

Ælfheah, Bishop, no. 107. Bishop of Winchester 984–1006, then arch-bishop of Canterbury till his murder by the Danes on 19 April 1012. Under the name of St. Alphege he is venerated as a saint and martyr. On the date of 1005 given by Stubbs for Ælfheah's translation to the see of Canterbury, see Plummer ii. 183, where the evidence is discussed. The death of his pre-decessor Ælfric (q.v.) is dated 1005 and 1006 in the various texts of the *Chronicle.* For further details of the career of Ælfheah, and for references, see Ashdown, 296.

Ælfið, see **Ælfgyth.**

Ælfmær, Abbot, no. 26. Abbot of St. Augustine's, 1006–23/7. Ælfmær's promotion to the see of Sherborne is dated in 1022 by Thorne, col. 1782. He attests as abbot K. 734, dated 1022, and also Robertson no. 82, *Crawford Charters,* no. xii, dated 1023, and with a list of witnesses possible for that year. So that if this charter is authentic and correctly dated, Ælfmær's appointment to Sherborne cannot have taken place before 1023. The dates of Ælfmær's tenure of the see of Sherborne, and the appointment of his successor Bishop Brihtwine II, are unfortunately merely a matter of inference, but Ælfmær must have ceased to be abbot of St. Augustine's by 1027, the date traditionally assigned to the grant of the body of St. Mildred by Cnut to his successor Ælfstan (q.v.). It should be noted that Stubbs, p. 33, has (mistakenly) accepted for Ælfmær's appointment as bishop the date of 1017, given in another passage, col. 1783, by Thorne, where a *v* has probably been substituted for *x* in writing the date. In view of Ælfmær's promotion to the episcopate, and the encomium pronounced upon him by Thorne, col. 1783, it is unlikely that he was (as has sometimes been suggested) the Ælfmær (without a title) who betrayed Canterbury to the Danes in 1011, on which occasion Abbot Ælfmær escaped (*Chron.* C, D, E, 1011). Fl. Wig. i. 164 supposes these two Ælfmærs to be different persons, styling the betrayer of Canterbury *archi-diaconus* (see p. 530), and the Ælfmær who escaped, abbot of St. Augustine's.

Ælfmær, no. 30. There is nothing to connect this Ælfmær with any contemporary bearer of this common name ; see p. 172 above.

Ælfnoth þe metere, 'painter', no. 113. See further p. 389, n. 1.

Ælfred, see **Alfred.**

Ælfric, Abbot, no. 78. Possibly the Abbot Ælfric whose death is dated 956 in a Westminster list of abbots (VCH *London,* i. 454 f. ; see also *Flete's Hist. of Westminster Abbey,* ed. Armitage Robinson, 78, where Ælfric is mentioned, but it is mistakenly supposed by Flete that this Ælfric became bishop of Crediton) ; but no Earl Sihtric is known to have been living at this time. Miss Whitelock has suggested to me that since an Earl Sihtric (q.v.) attests charters dated 1026 and 1031, the name *Ælfric* in the Aldenham charter may have been a mistake for *Ælfwig* II. Ælfwig II's period of office at West-minster is dated in the Westminster list of abbots mentioned above 1004–17, but according to Flete he was abbot for twenty years, which would fit in with his appearance in 997 as witness to a charter of Æthelred II (K. 698), if the charter is authentic and correctly dated. But this dating may not be right. Armitage Robinson (*Flete's History of Westminster Abbey,* 140) observes that Flete's dating is often 'demonstrably wrong' for the eleventh and twelfth centuries, and himself attempts 'a provisional chronology', dating Ælfwig's period of office (*ibid.* 139), 1005–19 March 1025, but taking 'no responsibility' for this dating. In his opinion the first secure date is the death of Abbot Wulfnoth, the predecessor of Abbot Edwin (q.v.), in 1049.

Ælfric, Archbishop, nos. 30, 108. Appointed archbishop of Canter-bury on 21 April 995 (*Chron.* F), having been previously bishop of Ramsbury. His death is entered in *Chron.* A 1005, C, D, E, F, and Fl. Wig. 1006. The date of his death was 16 November. For Ælfric's Will and for his career, see Whitelock no. 18. His predecessor, Archbishop Sigeric, died on 28 October (or thereabouts) 994 ; see K. Sisam, *Rev. Eng. Stud.* vii (1931), 16.

Ælfric, Archbishop, no. 53. Called Ælfric Puttoc, appointed archbishop of York in 1023, died on 22 January 1051. For details of his career see DNB.

Ælfric, Bishop, no. 8. Ælfric III, bishop of Elmham 1038/9–1042/3. According to a Bury list of benefactors (*Pinchbeck Register*, ed. Hervey, ii. 287), there were three bishops of Elmham (East Anglia) of this name : *unus bonus, alter niger, et tercius paruus, ob differencia uocati.* Ælfric I lived in the time of Edgar. Ælfric II died about Christmas 1038 (*Chron.* C, E, 1038). In a list of East Anglian bishops in Wm. Malmesbury *G.P.* 150 (*Alfuuinus, duo Elfrici, Stigandus*), and Fl. Wig. i. 233, Ælfric II is followed by another bishop named Ælfric, and this succession should be accepted. This involves the rejection of the conflicting statement in Fl. Wig. i. 193, that Ælfric II was immediately followed by Stigand as bishop of East Anglia in 1038. Ælfric III must have died in 1042/3 ; the consecration of his successor Stigand is recorded in *Chron.* C 1043 as having taken place after the coronation of King Edward on 3 April 1043.

Ælfric, decanus, no. 113. See further p. 389, n. 1.

Ælfric, Ealdorman, no. 107. Probably the ealdorman of Hampshire, of the reign of Æthelred II, and probably the ealdorman of this name killed in 1016 at the battle of Ashingdon (*Chron.* C, D, E, 1016). On the problem of the contemporary Ælfrics, see *Crawford Charters,* 120–1, and Ashdown, 297. Ælfric of Hampshire acquired an evil reputation as a traitor ; cf. *Chron.* C, D, E, 992, 1003.

Ælfric Godebegeata, no. 111. Otherwise unknown. This is phonologically the earliest form recorded of the by-name given to Ælfric, explained by A. W. Goodman (*The Manor of Goodbegot* (Winchester, 1923), 10 f.) on the authority of W. H. Stevenson and H. M. Chadwick as a compound of *goda,* gen. plur. of ' goods, property ', and *begeaton* (*begeatan*), gen. sing. of an unrecorded, but regularly formed, *begeata,* ' one who acquires or possesses ', cf. the verb *begietan.* The original nom. form of the by-name would be *goda begeata.* Canon Goodman gives a list of forms illustrating the phonological development of the compound in Winchester sources until about 1801, when it dropped almost entirely out of use, to be revived in modern times as ' Godbegot ', when the Tudor mansion on the estate, at the corner of St. Peter's Street and High Street, Winchester, was turned into a hotel under the sign of ' Ye Olde Hostel of Godbegot '. The history of the Winchester manor is traced in detail by Canon Goodman. For references to the *domus Godebiete* in the Winton Domesday, see note on no. 111 ; and for other information on this subject not given there, see DB iv. 532, 543.

Ælfric Hort (?), no. 85. *Hort* is the form of the by-name printed by Kemble and by Neufeldt as from the Faustina text. But this reading may not be correct, for in Faustina, and even more clearly in Westm. Do., there are indications of uncertainty or possibly of abbreviation. Could the by-name in the exemplars they were copying have been OE *horh, horu,* ' phlegm ; dirt, filth ' ? E. Ekwall (*Early London Personal Names,* Lund, 1947, 154) cites, as coming from these roots, Alfred *Hore,* Alfred *Horeh,* 1170–87 ; and gives as a parallel Nicholas *Smud* (i.e. ' a dirty speck or mark, a stain ').

Ælfric Modercope, nos. 21, 22. For Ælfric's will and for comments on his bequest of Loddon to Bury, and on his commendation of himself to the abbots of Bury and of Ely, see pp. 149 ff. Concerning his social status, Miss Whitelock remarks (p. 186) that although his heriot of one mark of gold (mentioned in his will) is less than that of a king's thegn (who according to the code of

Cnut (II Cnut 71) should pay, in addition, horses and weapons), it is three times as much as that of the lesser thegn. The Bury lists of benefactors (*The Pinchbeck Register*, ed. Hervey, ii. 290) give to Ælfricus *Modercoppe* the style of *nobilis heros*, which, if it is not a conventional epithet (it is applied to another benefactor), may imply some military status. Ælfric's by-name *Modercop(e)* does not seem to be recorded elsewhere than in Bury documents. Tengvik suggests (p. 223) that *Modercope* may possibly be derived from OWScand *Móðir-Kópi* (derived from *kópa* ' to stare, gape ', with a prefixed by-name *Móðir* ' mother ').

Ælfric, vicecomes, no. 59. Sheriff of Huntingdonshire, mentioned as *vicecomes* T.R.E. in Domesday. In the borough of Huntingdon he held T.R.E. one messuage afterwards given by William I to Ælfric's wife and sons, and he is also mentioned in connection with the vill of Keystone (DB i. 203, 208, VCH *Hunts.* i. 337, 355) ; see Morris, *Medieval English Sheriff*, 24, n. 52.

Ælfric, Wihtgar's son, nos. 18, 24. Attests a grant in reversion to Bury (Robertson no. 92 = K. 978), Thurstan's bequest to Christ Church (Whitelock no. 30 = K. 788), and a grant to St. Albans by his kinsman Æthelwine the Black (*Niger*) (K. 962). He may be the *Ælfric* of Writ no. 9, and of Robertson no. 97 ; see s. Ælfwine, no. 9. He disputed Æthelwine the Black's will in favour of Ramsey Abbey (*Chron. Abbat. Rames.* 169). A kinswoman bequeathed him land in Suffolk 1035–44 (Whitelock no. 29 = K. 931). He appears in Domesday as having held T.R.E. at Clare, Suffolk, 24 carucates of land as a manor (DB ii. 389 b, VCH *Suffolk*, i. 527). A Bury list of benefactors (*Pinchbeck Register*, ii. 290), which records his grant of Melford to the abbey, and his foundation of a house of secular canons at Clare (on which see VCH *Suffolk*, i. 398), says that he lived in the reigns of Æthelred, Cnut, Harold, Harthacnut, and Edward.

Ælfric, no 9. Possibly Ælfric, Wihtgar's son, q.v.

Ælfsige, Bishop, no. 113. Bishop of Winchester 1012/14–1032. The Ælfsige III, placed by Searle, *Bishops*, etc. p. 74, with a query, between Stigand (deposed 1070) and Walkelin (consecrated 1070) can be deleted, for there is no reason to believe in his existence. The only source for him given there is no. 113. See further pp. 389 f.

Ælfsige the portreeve, nos. 105, 106. Portreeve of London, conjointly with Leofstan, on the authority of these two texts. Otherwise unknown.

Ælfstan, Abbot, nos. 29, 30, 37. Abbot of St. Augustine's, in succession to Ælfmær (q.v.) and associated in the traditions of his house with the grant of the body of St. Mildred by Cnut to St. Augustine's in 1027, and its translation to his church at Whitsun, 1030. The latest probably authentic charter attested by him as abbot appears to be K. 776, but he is also wrongly described as *dux* in K. 780, both of these being dated 1045. Since Bishop Herman of Ramsbury appears among the witnesses, these charters must have been issued later than 22 April 1045, the date of the death of Herman's predecessor, Bishop Brihtwold. Ælfstan ceased, not long after, to hold office because of his ' great infirmity ', and was succeeded by Wulfric (q.v.). Ælfstan died on 5 July 1046 (*Chron.* E 1044, to be corrected to 1046). See further Thorne, col. 1783 f.

Ælfstan the monk, no. 116. Ælfstan, brother of Wulfstan II, bishop of Worcester, succeeded Wulfstan as prior of the cathedral priory at Worcester after the promotion of Wulfstan to the bishopric. It is no doubt as prior that Ælfstan is addressed in no. 116. Ælfstan is described as *decanus* i.e. prior (see p. 409, n. 1) in the writ of the Conqueror in his favour (see p. 409), and in the record of the bond of confraternity drawn up c. 1077 between Wulfstan and other ecclesiastics (Thorpe p. 615). Ælfstan acquired for the monks of the cathedral priory land at Lench, Dunhampstead and Peachley, Worcs. Between 1077 and 1080 he was succeeded in office by a certain Thomas. For further references to Ælfstan see Sir I. Atkins, *The Antiquaries Journal*, xx (1940), pp. 19 ff.

Ælfswyth, no. 108. Otherwise unknown.

Ælfthryth, no. 108. It is a reasonable presumption that this is Ælfthryth, second wife of King Edgar and mother of King Æthelred II. The marriage is entered in *Chron.* D 965, but it may have taken place as early as 964 (the date to which Florence of Worcester (i. 140) assigns it), on the evidence of a charter dated 964 (B. 1143) in which King Edgar makes a grant to her as his consort. She was the daughter of Ordgar, ealdorman of Devon, and according to Florence of Worcester, the widow of Æthelwold, ealdorman of East Anglia, the son of Æthelstan 'Half-King'. She is mentioned in wills as a legatee, and her grandson Æthelstan the Ætheling refers to her as 'Ælfthryth my grandmother, who brought me up' (Whitelock nos. 9, 15, 20). Ælfthryth's testimony was utilised in a lawsuit in King Æthelred's reign (Robertson no. 66). For the story that she was responsible for the murder in 978 of her stepson King Edward the Martyr, and for other stories current about her, see *Crawford Charters*, p. 85, Whitelock p. 123, and, more fully, C. E. Wright, *The Cultivation of Saga in Anglo-Saxon England* (Edinburgh, 1939), 146–53, 157–71. Ælfthryth attests charters till 999. She must have died before the end of 1002, for in that year her son King Æthelred II gave lands to the nunnery of Wherwell for her soul (K. 707).

Ælfweard, Bishop, nos. 51, 73, 74, 75. Bishop of London 1035–44. Ælfweard, who is described in the *Chronicon Abbatiæ de Evesham*, R.S. 83, as a kinsman of Cnut, had been appointed abbot of Evesham in 1014, and retained this office after his promotion to the bishopric. He resigned his offices, apparently in 1044, owing to an illness which is said to have been leprosy, and having been refused admittance to his monastery of Evesham, he retired to Ramsey, where in his early days he had been a monk, and died there in the same year (*ibid.* 85 ; *Chron. Abbat. Rames.*, R.S. 157–8 ; Fl. Wig. 1044). The date of his death is given as viii kal. Aug. (i.e. 25 July) in *Chron.* D 1045 (to be corrected to 1044) ; the statement in Fl. Wig. that the day was Wednesday, which is correct for 1044, has no independent authority. But the editor of the *Chron. Abbat. de Eves.* 85 gives the date (from MS. Cott. Vesp. B. xv. f. 17 b) as 27 July, and this is accepted by Stubbs, p. 35, and by DNB.

Ælfwig, Bishop, no. 53. Bishop of London 1014–c. 1035, consecrated at York on 16 February 1014 (*Chron.* D). Stubbs observes (p. 33) that Ælfwig attests charters till 1035, a statement apparently based on the appearance of the name of Ælfwius, bishop of London, in a list of witnesses appended to K. 753, a Winchester charter dated 1035. The charter was marked spurious by Kemble, but the list of witnesses may be genuine and may belong to that year. The date of the death of Ælfwig does not seem to have been recorded, but the appointment of his successor Ælfweard (q.v.) is placed in the *Chron. Abbat. Rames.* 148, before the death of Cnut (on 12 November 1035).

Ælfwine, Abbot, no. 113. Abbot of New Minster, Winchester, from c. 1032 (the date of his first signature, K. 746) till his death on 24 November 1057. For further details see the *Liber Vitæ* of New Minster and Hyde Abbey, ed. Birch, xxxi etc.

Ælfwine, Abbot, nos. 59–62. Abbot of Ramsey 1043–1079/80. He was one of the English churchmen (the others being Bishop Duduc (q.v.) of Wells, and Abbot Wulfric (q.v.) of St. Augustine's) sent by King Edward to attend the Council of Rheims on 3 October 1049. He is said to have given up the charge of all external business owing to ill-health contracted chiefly through a journey to Rome which he made within the last few years of the Confessor's life, on a mission from the king. For a reference in Domesday to a service which he did for King Edward ' in Saxony ', see p. 472 ; and for a reference to a time ' when the abbot was in Denmark ', see DB i. 208, VCH *Huntingdonshire*, i. 354. For further details concerning Ælfwine, see *Chron. Abbat. Rames.* pp. 127, 156–77, 340, Liebermann, *Ungedruckte Anglo-Normannische Geschichtsquellen*, 205, n. 13.

Ælfwine, Bishop, nos. 53, 109, 110. Bishop of Winchester 1032–47. Ælfwine, a ' king's priest ', was appointed to the see in succession to Ælfsige, whose death is recorded, together with Ælfwine's accession, in *Chron.* E 1032. But an *Ælfsinus episcopus* attests a charter of Cnut dated 1033, preserved in the Codex Wintoniensis (K. 750). Supposing that the charter is authentic and correctly dated, the discrepancy could be accounted for by the use of different dates for beginning the year, or on the other hand *Ælfsinus* may have been mis-written for *Ælfwinus*. Ælfwine died on 29 August 1047.

Ælfwine þe Blace, no. 62. Possibly to be identified with the Aluuinus '*Blach*' who appears in Domesday as the former holder of one hide at Hemingford, Hunts. (DB i. 207, VCH *Huntingdonshire*, i. 353). On the by-name *Blace* (*se Blaca*) see Tengvik, 292.

Ælfwine Gottone, no. 91. Alleged donor of Ayot to Westminster Abbey, to be identified with Aluuinus, a thegn of King Edward, who held Ayot (St. Lawrence) T.R.E. ' and could sell it ' (see p. 310), and with Aluuinus of Godtone, a Hertfordshire landowner T.R.E. (DB i. 135 b, 138 b, 143, VCH *Herts*. i. 314, 326, 344), who also held land in Essex (DB ii. 36, VCH *Essex*, i. 474). On the position of Ælfwine see J. H. Round in VCH *Herts*. i. 277–8. His local prominence is indicated by a writ of William I (Neufeldt no. 30, Davis, *Regesta*, no. 16, where it is dated ?1067) addressed to Edmund, sheriff (of Hertfordshire), Alfwine Gottune and Leofwine Scufe, requiring them on the king's behalf to bring the estates at Watton and at Datchworth (see no. 79) into the possession of Westminster Abbey. Ælfwine must have died before 1086, for by that time all his estates had passed into other hands. No evidence is forthcoming to support Davis's identification (*loc. cit.*) of this Ælfwine with the Alwin Dodesone who in 1086 held Wormley (see no. 90) of the king. The by-name Godtone (for variants see Tengvik, pp. 43, 125) is perhaps derived as Feilitzen suggests (p. 181) from an unidentified place in Hertfordshire.

Ælfwine, Merefinn's son, no. 94. Otherwise unknown.

Ælfwine, no. 9. If the *Ælfric* that follows is for Ælfric, Wihtgar's son (q.v.), then this Ælfwine may be Ælfwine *filius Wulfredi* who attests K. 962, 788, with him. These two may be the *Ælfwine* and *Ælfric* (without patronymics) who attest Robertson no. 97. But there is also an Ælfwine *Wluardes sune* attesting Robertson no. 92 (= K. 978), with Ælfric, Wihtgar's son, and his father's name may have been *Wulfweard*, and not *Wulfred*.

Ælfwold, Bishop, no. 1. Bishop of Sherborne from 1045/46 till his death in 1058. He was renowned among his contemporaries for his asceticism and strictness of life ; see Wm. Malmesbury, *G.P.* 179.

Ælfwynn, the nun, no. 79. Otherwise unknown.

Ælred, Earl (Hereford), see **Ealdred, Bishop**.

Ælwi, see **Ælfwig**.

Æthelberht, King, no. 26. King of Kent. He received Augustine and his monks on their arrival in Kent, and was baptised by Augustine in 597. Æthelberht gave Augustine a dwelling-place in Canterbury, where Augustine founded the monastery afterwards called Christ Church (Canterbury Cathedral). He died on 24 February, probably in 616.

Æthelberht (Ethelbert), St., no. 49. King of East Anglia, beheaded in 794 at the command of Offa, king of Mercia. He was and is the patron saint of the see of Hereford. His day in the Kalendar is 20 May. For Lives of the saint, see M. R. James, *Eng. Hist. Rev.* xxxii (1917), 214–44.

Ætheldred, see **Æthelthryth.**

Æthelgar, Abbot, no. 113. Pupil of Bishop Æthelwold of Winchester (q.v.), appointed abbot of New Minster in 964, after the expulsion of the canons and their replacement by monks (*Chron.* A 964). In 980 he was promoted to the see of Selsey, and in 988 translated to Canterbury, in succession to Dunstan. He died on 13 February 990. See further *Liber Vitae,* New Minster and Hyde Abbey, ed. Birch, xxvi ff. etc. and DNB.

Æthelmær, Bishop, nos. 15–25, 60, 61, 80. Bishop of Elmham (East Anglia) from 1047 until his deposition in 1070. He succeeded his brother Stigand as bishop of Elmham on the translation of the latter to Winchester in 1047, and retained his see till 1070, when he was deprived of his office on the deposition of Stigand, then archbishop of Canterbury (Fl. Wig. ii. 5). For a bequest by Æthelmær of a portion of his landed property and 'half a hundred marks of silver ' to St. Edmund's Bury, see Whitelock no. 35. The date of his death is not known. For Domesday references to Æthelmær, see Freeman iv. 333, Feilitzen 184–5. The fact that Æthelmær had a wife (DB ii. 195) may, as Freeman suggests, have contributed to his deposition.

Æthelmær, no. 63. Identified by Brotanek and Förster with Æthelmær, the son of the ealdorman Æthelweard (q.v.). The supposition that Æthelmær succeeded his father in office as ealdorman of the Western Provinces is not accepted by the editors of the *Crawford Charters* (pp. 87 f.), and their hesitation to accept the identification of the Æthelmær who was the son of the ealdorman Æthelweard, with the ealdorman named Æthelmær who submitted to Swein in 1013 together with the western thegns (*Chron.* C, D, E, 1013), is re-echoed by R. Flower in *The Exeter Book of Old English Poetry,* p. 87. There is however evidence overlooked by them in favour of the supposition that Æthelmær, the son of the ealdorman Æthelweard, the founder of the monasteries at Cerne and at Eynsham, and, like his father, a patron of Ælfric the homilist, succeeded his father in the office of ealdorman, apparently in 1002 ; for this evidence, and for further details concerning these persons, see D. Whitelock, pp. 144–5, A. J. Robertson, pp. 386–7. There can be little doubt that the Æthelmær addressed in this writ is the Æthelmær *ealdorman* who witnessed in 1012 the lease of land at Holcombe to Edmund the Ætheling by the community at Sherborne (Robertson, no. 74 ; see also p. 268 above), and the Æthelmær *dux* who witnessed a grant of King Æthelred to Sherborne in 1014 (K. 1309). See also p. 9. For the literary importance of Æthelmær, see pp. 20 f. above.

Æthelnoth, Abbot, nos. 6, 64–8, 71. Abbot of Glastonbury. We learn from *Chron.* D that Æthelnoth was appointed in 1053, and that he was among those who accompanied William on his visit (in 1067) to Normandy. His deposition at a council held in London is recorded in the Latin ' Acts of Lanfranc ' (Plummer i. 289) as having taken place in Lanfranc's eighth year (August 1077–August 1078). But doubt was cast on this by Freeman (iv. 389, n. 2) on the ground that Wm. Malmesbury, ' De Antiquitate Glastoniensis Ecclesiæ ' (Gale, *Historiae Britannicae Scriptores XV,* ii. 330) dates the appointment of Thurstan as abbot of Glastonbury in 1082, without any mention of the deposition of Æthelnoth, and that ' it is hardly like the policy of Lanfranc to leave the abbey vacant for five years '. There is some slight evidence that Æthelnoth was believed to have been still in office in 1081, in the fact that he is made to attest two charters, of Bury and of Westminster, with lists of witnesses strikingly similar though not identical, to which that date is given

(Davis, *Regesta*, nos. 137, 144). But not much weight can be attached to this, for the authenticity of the Bury charter has been doubted (see pp. 143-4 above), and the Westminster charter is marked as spurious by Davis. After his deposition Æthelnoth lived some time at Canterbury (Stubbs, *Memorials of Saint Dunstan*, 420).

Æthelnoth, Archbishop, nos. 27-30, 36, 37, 53. Archbishop of Canterbury, 1020-38. Æthelnoth, at the time of his appointment a monk and *decanus* (i.e. prior) at Christ Church (*Chron.* D, E, 1020), was consecrated on 13 November (*Chron.* D) by Archbishop Wulfstan of York (*Chron.* F). Wulfstan's letter to the king and queen announcing that Æthelnoth's consecration has taken place is still extant as no. 27. Fl. Wig. 1038 says that Æthelnoth died on October 29, and this is his day in the Kalendar. But *Chron.* E 1038 dates his death November 1 (*on kal. Nov.*, perhaps omitting *iiii* after *on*). *Chron.* C, D, 1038 and Fl. Wig. call Æthelnoth ' the Good ', and D speaks movingly of the devotion to him of Bishop Æthelric of Sussex (Selsey). For details of Æthelnoth's career, see DNB.

Æthelred II, King, nos. 52, 68, 107, 111. King of England March 978 (crowned 14 April 978) to autumn 1013, when King Swein Forkbeard of Denmark was recognised as king of England. Æthelred was in exile in Normandy from January 1014 until after the death of Swein on 3 February 1014. After giving an undertaking to rule his people more justly than he had done before, he returned to England, and ruled as king till his death on 23 April 1016. In the spring of 1002 he married Ælfgifu Emma (q.v.). The evidence as to the date of his accession is conflicting, and this date is given in some sources as 979. See further Plummer ii. 166. His epithet ' Unready ' must have arisen from a bitter play on the king's name : Æthelred Unræd, i.e. ' noble counsel ', ' no counsel '.

Æthelric, Bishop, no. 63. Bishop of Sherborne 1001/2–1009/12. Æthelric attests charters in 1002 (K. 707, 1295, 1297) and in 1009 (K. 1306). No dated charters of 1010 or 1011 seem to have survived, but his successor Æthelsige attests a charter of 1012 (K. 719).

Æthelric (Ailhre), the chamberlain, no. 74. The *Ægelricus* who gave Kelvedon to Westminster Abbey; of the spurious First Charter of King Edward (see pp. 289 f.) ; and the *Ailricus* of Domesday (on whom see pp. 302 f. above).

Æthelric, nos. 26, 29, 30. Æthelric in the address is probably the Æthelric who was reeve in 1035 (no. 29). But the name Æthelric is a common one at this time. An Æthelric Bigga was a landowner in Kent and a benefactor of Christ Church and St. Augustine's in Canterbury (see Robertson p. 409 for references), but there is nothing to connect him with any Æthelric in these writs.

Æthelric the reeve, no. 29. See the preceding note.

Æthelstan, Abbot, no. 56. Abbot of Ramsey from 1020 or 1021 to 1043. He was murdered in church by an Irish dependent whom he had saved from starvation and maintained for many years, on Michaelmas Eve 1043. See further *Chron. Abbat. Rames.* 124-5, 155-6, 340. I have refrained from emending the manuscript form *Æthestanus* (where the other text reads *Æthelstanus*) on the chance that this may be, not a scribal error, but an instance of loss of -*l*- through dissimilation. Max Förster, *Der Flussname Themse* (for full reference see p. 266), 769, cites for this, Borowski, *Lautdubletten im Altenglischen* (Halle, 1924), 67, which I have not seen.

Æthelstan, King, Appendix. Crowned king at Kingston on 4 September 925, having been previously recognised first as king of the West Saxons and then king of Mercia as well. In 934 he led an expedition into Scotland, and on his journey north made gifts to the churches of Beverley, Ripon, and Chester-le-Street. He died on 27 October 939. On the conflicting evidence for the death of his father, King Edward the Elder (for which on the whole the date 17 July 924 is to be preferred), see Plummer ii. 132 ff.

Æthelthryth, St., no. 21. Æthelthryth (Etheldreda), daughter of Anna, king of the East Angles, married first to Tondberht, who bestowed on her the isle of Ely, and then to Ecgfrith, king of Northumbria. She retired to Ely and founded there in 673 a religious house of which she became the first abbess. She died in 679. See *Venerabilis Baedae Opera Historica*, ed. Plummer, i. 243 ff. For the monastery at Ely, see no. 47.

Æthelweard, Ealdorman, no. 108. Ealdorman of the Western Provinces (i.e. of Wessex west of Selwood). He attests charters as *dux* from 975 to 998. The exact date of his death is unknown, but he was alive in the episcopate of Burhwold, bishop of Cornwall, whose predecessor attests a charter of 1002 (K. 981, 1297 ; cf. Whitelock, 145). He was succeeded by his son Æthelmær (q.v.). Ealdorman Æthelweard has with great probability been identified with the chronicler of that name, who was a descendant of King Æthelred I, an elder brother of King Alfred. The homilist Ælfric addressed to Æthelweard his translation of the Pentateuch and his Lives of the Saints (see p. 23). For further details of his career, see *Crawford Charters*, 118 ff. See also pp. 9 f., 21.

Æthelweard, no. 107. For the numerous Æthelweards of this period, when the name is particularly common, see *Crawford Charters*, 118–20, where the Æthelweard of no. 107 is identified with the king's high-reeve of that name who was slain with 80 others in a battle at *Æpelinga dene*, in which the local forces of Hampshire were defeated by the Danes (*Chron.* A 1001). Two high-reeves, of whom Æthelweard was one, took part in this battle. For the suggestion that the southern high-reeve was the reeve of a large borough-district, see H. M. Chadwick, *Anglo-Saxon Institutions*, 237 ; and for passages in which this term occurs, see Larson, *King's Household in England*, 113–16. Evidence has been brought forward by Professor Bruce Dickins (*Leeds Studies in English*, vi. 1937, 25–7), which makes probable an identification of the Æthelweard of this writ, who was also the king's high-reeve, with a *minister* of the same name who appears in the list of friends and benefactors in the Hyde Register, and also with an Æthelweard whose name appears in one of the obits in an eleventh-century calendar from New Minster, Winchester (later Hyde Abbey). From this evidence we may conjecture that the battle in which Æthelweard was slain took place on 23 May 1001—a date which gives us an (approximate) *terminus ad quem* for the Chilcomb writ.

Æthelwig, of Thetford, no. 56. To be identified with Ailwi (Ailuuinus) de Tedfort, whose name occurs (in several other spellings) in Domesday entries relating to Norfolk and Suffolk, sometimes without the place-name ; see Feilitzen, 189–90. Feilitzen observes that in a spurious charter of the abbey of St. Benet of Holme (K. 785), with the ostensible date c. 1044–47, Ægelwinus *ealderman* appears as the former owner of a number of estates ; and that in another charter (*Register of St. Benet of Holme*, ed. J. R. West (Norfolk Record Society), i. 169) he is referred to as Egelwy *pater* Stannardi, i.e. Stanheard, who appears in Domesday in several places as his successor. The meaning of *ealderman* in the spurious Holme charter cited above is uncertain ; but from the Thetford writ it is clear that in King Edward's time Æthelwig held some official position in Thetford. On the position of Æthelwig after the Conquest, see F. M. Stenton (*Eng. Hist. Rev.* xxxvii (1922), 227, n. 6, and 233), who observes that Æthelwig, one of the wealthiest *antecessores* of Roger Bigod in Norfolk, had undoubtedly filled some official position in that county in the years immediately following the Norman Conquest, and that the Norfolk Domesday contains several passages which suggest that he may · once have been sheriff, though he is never addressed in that capacity in any writ of William I. See also Freeman, v. Appendix, Note P (where his name is wrongly given as OE *Ælfwig* or *Ælfwine*).

Æthelwine, Bishop, no. 113. Bishop of Durham 1056–71. Æthelwine succeeded his brother Æthelric (on whose episcopate see Plummer ii. 220). Æthelwine was outlawed in 1068 or 1069 (*Chron.* D 1068, E 1069). He joined the insurgents at Ely, but submitted to William. He was deposed (in 1071) and sent to Abingdon, where he died (*Chron.* D 1072, E 1071; see also Plummer, ii. 267). Thorpe, however, was probably right in suggesting that this part of *Chron.* D 1068 (above) ought really to be dated 1069.

Æthelwine the sheriff, no. 26. The *scirman* Æthelwine of this writ is no doubt the Æthelwine *sciregerefa* who was present at a Kentish marriage agreement (Robertson no. 77) drawn up between 1016 and 1020 in the presence of King Cnut, and also attested by Archbishop Lyfing, and the community at Christ Church, and Abbot Ælfmær, and the community at St. Augustine's. Both Lyfing and Ælfmær are addressed in no. 26, in which Æthelwine's name occurs.

Æthelwold, Bishop, St., nos. 108, 113. Bishop of Winchester from 963 until his death on 1 August 984. Æthelwold was, with Dunstan, one of the leaders in the monastic revival. In his time the canons were driven out and monks were established at Old Minster and New Minster at Winchester. He was afterwards canonised. For further details see Plummer, ii. 155 and the references there given; J. Armitage Robinson, *The Times of St. Dunstan*, ch. v; also the 'Vita Æthelwoldi' by Abbot Ælfric the homilist in the *Chron. Mon. de Abingdon*, ii. 255–66 (Mod. Eng. rendering by S. H. Gem, *An Anglo-Saxon Abbot* (1912), 166–80); see also D. Knowles, *The Monastic Order in England* (Cambridge, 1940), 39 ff.

Ætsere, of Lessness, no. 76. The position of Ætsere of Lessness is established in Domesday, which in a list of men in two Kentish lathes who had sake and soke, names Azor of *Lesneis*; and in the entry concerning Lessness names him as the former holder under the name Asor (DB i. 1 b, 6 b). The name Ætsere (the Anglicised form of ODan and OSwed *Azur*, ON *Ǫzurr*) was not uncommon in England at this time; for numerous instances in Domesday, see Feilitzen, 170. The final -e is explained by Miss Whitelock (*Saga-Book of the Viking Society*, xii, Part II (1940), 142) as due to analogy with English names in -(*h*)*ere*. A certain Atsur *Roda* ('the Red') witnesses 1045–47 an agreement made by Archbishop Eadsige (Robertson no. 101), and appears in Domesday as tenant of land in Kent (DB i. 13, VCH *Kent*, iii. 248). An Ætsere *Swearte* ('the Black') gave Wennington in Essex to Westminster Abbey (no. 73 above). No evidence seems to be forthcoming to enable one to identify Ætsere of Lessness with either of these, or with any of the other bearers of this name. Miss Whitelock has suggested to me that Atsur *Roda* was probably the *Azorvot* who held land T.R.E. in *Bilec* (*Domesday Monachorum* ed. Douglas, 103).

Ætsere Swearte, no. 73. On the name Ætsere, see preceding note. It is not known whether Ætsere Swearte is to be identified with any of the known bearers of this name. For *Swearte* 'black' as a by-name, see Tengvik, 338.

Agelwinus, no. 56, see **Æthelwig.**

Ailhre burthein, no. 74, see **Æthelric the chamberlain.**

Ailmarus episcopus, no. 60, see **Æthelmær.**

Ailric, of Greenford, nos. 88, 89. Otherwise unknown. He does not appear in the spurious Westminster charters.

Alfgarus, comes, no. 60, see **Ælfgar.**

Alfred, King, no. 107. King of Wessex from 871 till his death on 26 October 899 (W. H. Stevenson, *Eng. Hist. Rev.* xiii (1898), 71–7).

Alfred, of Litton, no. 69. Otherwise unknown.

Alfred, the sheriff, no. 1. Sheriff of Dorset. He is named in DB i. 83 as the holder T.R.E. of the manor of Lulworth (*Luluorde*) in Dorset.

Alfricus, Alfwinus, no. 59, see **Ælfric, Ælfwine.**

Alred, Eurl, no. 49. This must be a copyist's error for *Al[d]red biscop*, correctly given in the Latin version as *Aldredum episcopum*. This was Ealdred (q.v.), later archbishop of York, who administered the see of Hereford from 1056 to 1060, while holding the sees of Worcester and Ramsbury from c. 1055 to 1058, and the see of Worcester from 1058 to 1060. There is no record of any earl named Alred (for Ealdred or Æthelred) at this period.

Augustine, St., nos. 36, 37, 38, 39. Sent as a missionary to England in 597 with a band of about 40 monks, he was received by King Æthelberht of Kent, who was subsequently baptised. In the same year Augustine was consecrated bishop. He founded the cathedral (later called Christ Church) in Canterbury, and also founded a monastery afterwards called by his name, outside the east wall of the city, to serve as a burial-place for himself and his successors, and for the kings of Kent. On the date of Augustine's death, probably 26 May 604, see *Baedae Opera Historica*, ed. Plummer, ii. 81.

Baldwine, Abbot, nos. 23–5, Abbot of St. Edmund's Bury 1065–1097 or 1098 (see Douglas, *Feudal Documents*, xlviii). On Baldwine's career, first as monk of St. Denis, then as prior of a dependent cell of the abbey, then (before 1065) as doctor to the Confessor, who appointed him abbot of Bury in succession to Leofstan (q.v.), and later in the service of the Conqueror, see Douglas, *op. cit., passim*. For his connection with the abbey of St. Denis, see Appendix II and pp. 244, 293.

Benedict, St., nos. 45, 58–62. St. Benedict of Nursia (died c. 547), abbot of Monte Cassino, the author of the famous *Rule of St. Benedict*, on which see D. Knowles, *The Monastic Order in England*, 3 ff., and the references there given.

Beorn, Earl, nos. 78, 79. Son of Jarl Ulf and Estrith, the sister of King Cnut, and Earl Godwine's nephew by marriage. Beorn attests charters as earl in 1045 and 1049 (K. 778, 787). On the evidence of these two writs (which may not be independent, see p. 315), Hertfordshire lay within his earldom. On Beorn's treacherous murder by Earl Swein in 1049, and the events which led up to it, see Plummer ii. 229–31, and the references there.

Boia þe ealda, no. 113. See further p. 389, n. 1. On the name see Feilitzen, 205 ; and also E. J. Dobson, ' The Etymology and Meaning of *Boy* ', *Medium Ævum*, 1940, 121 ff. On the by-name, see Tengvik, 311.

Brand, no. 62. This (Scandinavian) name is rare, but there is no link between this Brand, and Brand, a housecarl of King Edward, mentioned in the Hertfordshire Domesday (DB i. 138 b). An identification with Brand, successively monk, provost, and abbot (1066–69) of Peterborough appears improbable.

Brihtnoth, no. 3. Otherwise unknown.

Brihtwine, of Bengeworth, no. 48. Otherwise unknown.

Brihtwine, of Leckhampstead, no. 3. Son of Brihtmund, and brother of Brihtnoth, and rightly identified by Round (VCH *Berks.* i. 298) with the ' Bricstuin ' of whom Domesday records (DB i. 58 b, VCH *Berks.* i. 338) that he held Leckhampstead of the abbot of Abingdon T.R.E. adding with reference to Brihtwine and two other tenants of the abbot, that ' they could not go to another lord ' (*non potuerunt recedere*).

Cnut, King, nos. 3, 8, 26–30, 33, 36–8, 44, 48, 51, 53, 56–7, 62, 109–10.

King of England November 1016 to 12 November 1035 (having secured Mercia and the Danelaw by agreement in the summer of 1016). In July 1017 he married Queen Ælfgifu Emma (q.v.), widow of his predecessor Æthelred. Between 1019 and 1029 Cnut, who was king of Denmark, and also conquered Norway, was absent for long periods from England (for details see *Handbook of British Chronology*, 32) ; but his periods of absence have no bearing on the dating of extant writs. In March and April 1027 he was in Rome, and was present at the coronation of the Emperor Conrad II. For full details of his career, see L. M. Larson, *Canute the Great* (New York and London, 1912).

Coenwulf, no. 78. King of Mercia 796–821. In his time London still belonged to Mercia, as it had done in Offa's time.

Cuthbert, St., no. 113. The famous saint, bishop of Lindisfarne 685–6, died 687. See further *Two Lives of St. Cuthbert*, ed. B. Colgrave (Cambridge, 1940). The coffin containing St. Cuthbert's body accompanied the monks of Lindisfarne on their wanderings after their flight before the Danes in 875. It subsequently, after 883, rested at Chester-le-Street, from whence it was moved in 995 to Ripon and thence to Durham, where a church and shrine for it were completed in 998.

Cynegyth, no. 75. Otherwise unknown.

Cyneric, nos. 57, 58. Otherwise unknown.

Cyneweard, no. 3. Otherwise unknown.

Dionisius, St., no. 55. St. Denis, patron of the abbey near Paris named after him. See further S. M. Crosby, *The Abbey of St. Denis*, 475–1122, i (Yale Historical Publications, 1942). Crosby concludes that St. Denis, bishop of Paris, was beheaded as a Christian martyr, between 249 and 251, in a village to be identified with the St. Denis of the present day. About 475 a church was built over his tomb, and his cult grew rapidly in the sixth and following centuries.

Dudde, no. 90. ? masculine or feminine. In the spurious Telligraphus of William I (see p. 337), Leofsige is described as *filius Duddi*, supposedly masculine. *Dudde*, fem. and *Dudda*, masc. appear in K. 1354. See further on these names and their variants, Feilitzen, 223, Tengvik, 154, 179, 216 etc. and also M. Redin, *Studies on uncompounded personal names in Old English* (1919).

Duduc, Bishop, nos. 53, 64. Bishop of Wells, consecrated on 11 June 1033, died on 18 January 1060. By birth either a Lotharingian (Fl. Wig. 1060), or a Saxon (*Historiola*, ed. Hunter, 15). He is probably to be identified with the Duduc *presbyter* who attests a charter of 1033 (K. 1318).

Dunstan, St., nos. 27, 86, 108, 113. Appointed bishop of Worcester 957, of London 959, archbishop of Canterbury 960, died on 19 May 988. He was the leader of the movement for monastic reform. For his connection with Westminster Abbey, see pp. 286–338. See further Plummer, ii. 144–5, 153–4, and especially Stubbs, *Memorials of Saint Dunstan*, and J. Armitage Robinson, *The Times of St. Dunstan*. See also W. Levison, *Das Werden der Ursula-Legende* (Cologne, 1928, Bonner Jahrbücher cxxxii), 64 ff. (a reference given me by the late Wilhelm Levison, which I have not seen), D. Knowles, *Monastic Order*, 36 ff.

Eadnoth, Bishop, nos. 57–8, 78–9. Bishop of Dorchester 1034–49. *Chron.* C 1049, recording his death calls him ' the good bishop of Oxfordshire '.

Eadnoth, the staller, no. 85. Eadnoth, staller (on which see pp. 50 ff.) under King Edward, held office under Kings Harold and William I. He is addressed as Eadnoth the staller in a writ of William for Bath Abbey (Davis, *Regesta*, no. 7) and described as staller in *Chron.* D 1067, Fl. Wig. 1068 (' staller of King Harold '), where his death whilst leading the militia of Somerset against the sons of King Harold is recorded. There is no evidence for Kemble's assumption (endorsed by Morris, *Med. Eng. Sheriff*, 37, n. 164) that he held the office of sheriff; see pp. 51 f. He is identified by Round (VCH *Berks.* i. 295) with the Ednod *dapifer* of the Wiltshire Domesday (DB i. 69), and the Eadnotus *constabulus* of the Abingdon Chronicle (*Chron. Mon. Abingdon*, ii. 19). For lands held by Eadnoth T.R.E. see Feilitzen, 233. Details of his holdings are collected by Freeman iv. Appendix, Note N.

Eadread, no. 121. Ragg's suggestion that this might be a misspelling of the name of Ealdred, earl of Northumbria c. 1019-38, half-brother of Gospatric (q.v.), and father-in-law of Earl Siward, was accepted by H. W. C. Davis. But since the name Eadred was current, there seems to be no reason for rejecting the manuscript reading. This Eadred is however otherwise unknown; but the *Moryn* of l. 18 (*on Moryn dagan*) is also obscure.

Eadsige, Archbishop, nos. 29-32, 38, 45, 76. Bishop at St. Martin's 1035-38, archbishop of Canterbury 1038 to 1044 and 1048 to 29 October 1050. Eadsige, a priest, and one of Cnut's chaplains, later became a monk at Christ Church (*Chron. F. and Fl. Wig.* 1038; Robertson nos. 85 (not authentic in its present form), 86), before his promotion to the episcopate. At Easter 1043 Eadsige crowned Edward as king. In 1044 he resigned his office because of ill-health (*Chron.* C 1044, E 1043), and Siward (q.v.) was appointed as his deputy. But Eadsige resumed office again in 1048 on the retirement of Siward (*Chron.* C 1048), and held it till his death in 1050.

Ealdred, Archbishop, nos. 7, 49 (Lat.), 102, 118-20. Bishop of Worcester 1046-62, bishop of Worcester and archbishop of York Christmas 1060-62, archbishop of York alone, 1062-69. He administered the see of Ramsbury from c. 1055 to 1058, after the resignation of Herman (q.v.), and held the see of Hereford, ' donec antistes constitueretur ', actually 1056-60. On his journeys to Rome, see pp. 288-9. He went to Germany in 1054 to arrange for the return to England of Edward, the son of Edmund Ironside, and stayed there a year (*Chron.* C, D, and Fl. Wig. 1054); and in 1058 went on a pilgrimage to Jerusalem by way of Hungary (*Chron.* D and Fl. Wig. 1058). He is described as ' a man of cosmopolitan tastes with a natural gift for diplomacy ' by R. R. Darlington, *Eng. Hist. Rev.* xlviii (1933), 4, n. 2. On Ealdred's activities, see also pp. 136, 415. Ealdred died on 11 September 1069.

Ealdred, the ' deacon ', no. 120. Otherwise unknown.

Ealdwig, no. 113. See further p. 389, n. 1.

Edgar, King, nos. 51, 78-9, 108. King of Mercia and the Danelaw 957-59, King of England 959-8 July 975. He married Ælfthryth (q.v.).

Edith (Eadgyth), the Lady, nos. 61 (' queen '), 69, 70, 72, 79, 94, 112. Daughter of Earl Godwine, married to King Edward on 23 January 1045. She was disgraced after the outlawry of her father and brothers in September 1051, and sent to the nunnery at Wherwell, but was restored to the king's favour on their reinstatement a year later. She died at Winchester on 18 December 1075. On the title ' Lady ', see p. 448.

Edmund, St., nos. 8-11, 13-15, 17-25. King of East Anglia, killed by the Danes on 20 November 869. By the early years of the tenth century he had come to be honoured as a saint in East Anglia. On the cult of St. Edmund see W. H. Stevenson, *Asser's Life of King Alfred*, 231 f., Stenton, *Anglo-Saxon England*, 246; see also C. E. Wright, *The Cultivation of Saga in Anglo-Saxon England*, 172-4.

Edward, King, nos. 1, 2, 4, 5, etc. King of England 1042-66. Edward, son of Æthelred II and Ælfgifu Emma, was elected, *or* received as, king (see Plummer, ii. 221), after the death of his half-brother Harthacnut on 8 June 1042, and before the burial of the latter (*Chron.* E 1041), and crowned on 3 April 1043. He married Edith (q.v.), daughter of Earl Godwine. The date generally accepted for Edward's death is 5 January 1066, and that is the date that I have adopted here ; but Westminster tradition gives January 4 as the day of his death. For the Westminster tradition see *pridie nonas Ianuarii* in the *Vita Æduuardi* (ed. Luard, *Lives of Edward the Confessor*), p. 434, Osbert of Clare (ed. Bloch, p. 111), Ailred of Rievaulx (*Life of St. Edward*, in Twysden, *Scriptores X*, col. 402). Armitage Robinson (*Archaeologia*, lxii, 81–100) adopts the date 4 January, and observes that the feast of the Depositio S. Edwardi was kept on 5 January. But Ailred of Rievaulx was also acquainted with the other tradition, for in the *Genealogia Regum* (ed. Twysden, col. 366) he gives for Edward's death the date *in vigilia Epiphaniæ*, i.e. 5 January, as does also Flete (ed. Armitage Robinson, 82). See also *Chron.* C, D, E : 'he forðferde (died) *on twelftan æfen* 7 hyne man bebyrigde (buried) *on twelftan dæig*'. Similarly Fl. Wig. (i. 224), Ordericus Vitalis (ed. Le Prevost, ii. 118), Hermann the archdeacon, *Miracula S. Eadmundi* (Arnold, *Memorials*, i. 57). Wm. Malmesbury (*G.R.* i. 280) says that Edward was buried on the day of the Epiphany, i.e. 6 January. Symeon of Durham (erroneously) combines both dates : *pridie nonas Ianuarii, Epiphaniæ Domini vigilia* (*Opera Omnia*, ed. Arnold, ii. 179). On the title 'Confessor' given to Edward, see *Camb. Med. Hist.* iii (1922), 399, and on his canonization in 1161 by Pope Alexander III, see E. W. Kemp, 'Pope Alexander III and the Canonization of Saints', *Trans. R. Hist. Soc.* 4th ser. xxvii (1945), 16–17, and the references there. See also Kemp, *Canonization and Authority in the Western Church* (Oxford, 1948), 76 ff.

Edwin (Eadwine), Abbot, nos. 62, 79, 81, 87. Appointed abbot of Westminster in succession to Wulfnoth who died according to *Chron.* C in 1049 (D 1050), and according to Flete (ed. Armitage Robinson, 82) on 19 October of that year. Flete, who records that Edwin owed his election to the influence of the Confessor ('mediante beato rege Edwardo'), gives as the date of his death, 12 June 1068. Armitage Robinson (*op. cit.* 140) argues however that unless we reject the evidence of three writs attributed to William I, it is not likely that Edwin died before 12 June 1071. The value of these three writs of William (Davis, *Regesta*, nos. 52, 53, 237) for dating purposes seems very doubtful ; see above p. 314 (Aldenham), p. 334 (Islip), p. 305 (Claygate).

Edwin (Eadwine), Earl, no. 96. Succeeded his father Earl Ælfgar as earl of Mercia, on his death, at some unknown date between 1062 and 1066. On the defeat in September 1066 of Edwin and his brother Morcar (who had succeeded Tostig as earl of Northumbria), by the combined forces of Tostig and King Harold Hardrada of Norway, and the events leading up to this, see *Chron.* C, D, 1065, 1066 : and on Edwin's death at the hands of his own followers in 1071, see *ibid.* E 1071, D 1072, Fl. Wig. 1071.

Edwin (Eadwine), no. 113. Otherwise unknown.

Esgar, the staller, nos. 62, 75, 76, 91, 98. Grandson of (the well-known) Tofi the Proud, and addressed here in writs of which the one most likely to be authentic is no. 75 ; the attesting clause of no. 62 is certainly spurious. His name (ONorse *Ásgeirr*, ODan *Esger*) appears in various spellings (on which see Feilitzen, 164) as attesting charters, not all authentic, purporting to have been issued by the Confessor. He appears as *minister* in K. 806, 824–5 (both spurious), also as *minister* in Appendix II ; as staller in K. 771 (spurious) ; as *regis dapifer* in K. 808 ; as *regiae procurator aulae* in the spurious Waltham charter (K. 813, see p. 59). Æsgarus *quidam stallere* is said in the *Liber Eliensis* (ed. Stewart, p. 217) to have seized by force lands belonging to the monastery of Ely. He is no doubt the *Ansgardus* represented by Guy of Amiens as entering into negotiations with William which led to the submission of London to the Conqueror (*Carmen de Hastingae Proelio*, line 687 ff., ed. Giles, *Script. Rer. Gest. Will. Conquest.* (1845), 46 ff. ; see also Freeman, iii. 544 ff.). There is little or no evidence for Round's assumption (accepted by Morris, *Med. Eng. Sheriff*, 37, n. 164) that Esgar was portreeve of London and sheriff of Middlesex ; see p. 51. On his lands see Feilitzen, 166. See also p. 51, n. 6. For a suggestion that Esgar may have given his name to East Garston, Berks. see F. M. Stenton, *Place-Names of Berkshire* (Reading, 1911), 26–8.

Ethelbert, St., see Æthelberht.

Frebeorn, no. 85. Otherwise unknown.

Frithestan, Bishop, no. 113. Bishop of Winchester 909–31. See further Plummer ii. 136.

Gamell, no. 121. Otherwise unknown. The name *Gamel* (ON *Gamall*, ODan and OSw *Gamal*) was very common in this country, as a loan-name from Scandinavian.

Giso, Bishop, nos. 6, 64–72. Bishop of Wells, appointed 1060, consecrated at Rome (with Walter, bishop of Hereford) on 15 April 1061, died 1088. Giso was a native of St. Trond, in the diocese of Liége. *Chron.* D 1060 recording his appointment calls him ' priest ' (cf. no. 64), and Fl. Wig. i. 218 styles him *regis capellanus*. For the autobiography of Giso, see pp. 271–6.

Gode, no. 74. An identification is chronologically possible of this Gode with Gode, daughter of Ælfwine and Wulfgyth, and sister of Ketel Alder, whose family held lands in Essex, Suffolk and Norfolk (Whitelock nos. 32, 34). But no definite link between them is known to exist, and Gode may in either case be merely the shortened form of the feminine name Godgifu.

Godgifu, no. 45. Wife of Earl Leofric of Mercia, and mother of Earl Ælfgar. Godgifu survived her husband (who died in 1057), and lived on into the reign of William I, but died before 1086. She was associated with her husband not only in the foundation and endowment of the monastery at Coventry (see note on p. 216), but also in the endowment between 1053 and 1055 of St. Mary's at Stow (Robertson no. 115). According to Fl. Wig. 1057, Leofric and Godgifu also ' enriched with valuable ornaments ' the monasteries at Leominster and Wenlock, and the two monasteries at Chester, namely, those dedicated to St. John the Baptist and to St. Werburg ; gave lands to Worcester ; and added to the buildings, ornaments and endowments of the abbey of Evesham.

Godric þe Densce, no. 62. Otherwise unknown. *þe Densce* is OE *se Denisca*, ' the Danish '. On this by-name, see Tengvik 135.

Godric, no. 5. Possibly Godric, sheriff of Berkshire (and Buckinghamshire), who was killed at Hastings in 1066 (*Chron. Mon. de Abingdon*, i. 491). On the numerous complaints recorded against Godric the sheriff, and his encroachments on the royal demesne, see Morris, *Medieval English Sheriff*, 29, 36 ; see also Freeman, iv. Appendix, Note B, VCH *Berks.* i, 293.

Godwine, Bishop, nos. 26, 76. Bishop of Rochester, attests charters from 995 to 1046, and there is no mention of another bishop of Rochester until the appointment of Siward in 1058. It has often been suggested that there may have been two bishops of Rochester named Godwine in succession.

Godwine decanus, no. 113. See further p. 389, n. 1.

Godwine, Earl, nos. 3, 38, 53, 61, 111. The famous earl of Wessex, first appointed to this office by Cnut, and attesting as *dux* in 1018 (K. 728). Kent also lay within Godwine's earldom (*Chron.* D 1052, and no. 38). Godwine took a leading part in national affairs. In 1045 his daughter Edith was married to King Edward, and his sons were in course of time provided with earldoms. On the events leading to the banishment of Godwine and his family on 24 September 1051, and their reinstatement on 14/15 September 1052, see Plummer, ii. 234 ff. and the references there. Earl Godwine died at Winchester on 15 April 1053, and was buried in Old Minster.

Godwine, the sheriff, nos. 64–7. Sheriff of Somerset (addressed in no. 65 without his style), identified by Feilitzen, p. 271, with Godwine the *præpositus regis* who held T.R.E. the manor of Eastham in Somerset with the king's manor of Crewkerne (DB i. 92, VCH *Somerset*, i. 477).

Gospatric, no. 121. Identified with great probability by H. W. C. Davis (*Eng. Hist. Rev.* xx (1905), 61–5) with Gospatric, a son of Uhtred, earl of Northumbria. From Fl. Wig. 1065 we learn that Gospatric was treacherously murdered in the court of King Edward on 28 December 1064, and that the deed was done by order of Queen Edith, in the interest of her brother Earl Tostig, to whom Gospatric, the heir of the native earls of Bernicia, may well have appeared a dangerous rival. The murder of Gospatric, together with that of two other persons, slain by Earl Tostig's order, and included by Florence with him under the description of *nobilium Northhymbrensium ministrorum,* is given by Florence as one of the causes of the revolt of the Northumbrians against Earl Tostig in 1065. For Gospatric's descent, see Davis, *loc. cit.* and Searle, *Bishops,* p. 371. A less probable identification is with Gospatric, earl of Northumberland, 1067–72 (Searle p. 375). The name *Gospatric* (OWelsh *Guas-,* ' servant ', with the second element remodelled on English, ' servant of Patric ') was not uncommon in the north ; see further Feilitzen, 274. It was in fact borne by several other descendants of Earl Uhtred.

Grimketel, Bishop, nos. 9, 10. Bishop of Selsey 1039–47. He held for a short time the see of East Anglia (Elmham) in conjunction with that of Selsey, his appointment to Elmham having followed the ejection of Stigand (q.v.) from that see in 1043–44. Wm. Malmesbury (*G.P.* 150) and Fl. Wig. i. 193 state that Grimketel bought his appointment to Elmham (*pro auro est electus*). On his ejection from the East Anglian see on the return of Stigand, Grimketel retained that of Selsey, and witnessed a charter as bishop (of Selsey) in 1046 (K. 784). He died in the following year.

Gyrth, Earl, nos. 23–5, 61, 80, 95, 103–4. Fourth son of Earl Godwine, appointed to the earldom of East Anglia probably after Earl Ælfgar received the earldom of Mercia in succession to his father in the autumn of 1057. Gyrth also received, possibly in 1057/8, possibly at a later date (see Freeman ii. 566), the earldom of Oxfordshire held by Earl Raulf till his death on 21 December 1057. For his journey to Rome with his brother Tostig in 1061, see the *Vita Æduuardi* (ed. Luard, *Lives of the Confessor,* p. 410), and for his presence at the battle of Stamford Bridge on 25 September 1066, see the *Foundation of Waltham Abbey,* ed. Stubbs, c. 20. Gyrth was killed at Hastings on 14 October 1066. For references to the lands held by him, see Feilitzen p. 280.

Hakon (Hacun), Earl, no. 48. Hakon, son of the Norwegian Earl Eric of Northumbria, and nephew of Cnut, came to England about 1017, having been driven out of Norway by Olaf Haroldsson (St. Olaf), and was appointed by Cnut to an earldom by 1019, when he attests K. 729 as *dux.* Evidence that Hakon's earldom was Worcestershire appears not only in writ no. 48, but also in Robertson nos. 81, 83, two charters of c. 1023 dealing with Worcestershire affairs, in which Hakon appears. Hakon, who married Cnut's niece Gunhild, was made viceroy of Norway in 1028, but was drowned in the Pentland Firth two years later on his return from a visit to England.

On the Norse evidence concerning his career, see *Crawford Charters*, 147–8, Ashdown, 282.

Harold, Earl, and King, nos. 1, 2, 5, 13, 14, 35, 39, 40–2, 49, 50, 61, 62, 64–71, 80, 84, 85, 98, 112, 115, 120. Second son of Earl Godwine, appointed earl of East Anglia in 1044/5. Miss Robertson has pointed out (*op. cit.* p. 463) that he attests a charter of 1044 (*Journal of the British Archaeological Association*, xxxix (1883), p. 294) with the title *nobilis*, and two charters of 1045 (K. 776, 780), with identical lists of witnesses, with the title *minister*; and that two charters with earlier dates, one dated 1043 (K. 916), and one dated 1044 (K. 771), both of which he is made to attest as *dux*, are highly suspicious. The earliest dated and authentic royal charter in which he appears as *dux* (K. 781) belongs to 1045. He appears however with the title of earl as witness to a will (Whitelock no. 31) which cannot be dated later than 1044, since Leofstan, who is there styled ' dean ', was probably the Leofstan who was appointed abbot of Bury in 1044. The easiest way of bringing these dates into harmony is to suppose that where they appear to conflict, the year was reckoned as beginning at different dates. Harold was banished with his father and brothers on 24 September 1051, and went, accompanied by Leofwine, to Ireland. He was reinstated with them in September 1052. On the death of Earl Godwine in April 1053 Harold relinquished the earldom of East Anglia and succeeded to his father's earldom of Wessex (and Kent), whilst the earldom of Herefordshire was merged with Harold's earldom on the death in 1057 of Earl Raulf. In 1056 Harold made a visit to Flanders (P. Grierson, *Eng. Hist. Rev.* li (1936), 90–7). He succeeded King Edward as king of England on 6 January 1066. On 25 September of the same year he defeated his brother Earl Tostig and King Harold Hardrada of Norway at Stamford Bridge, but was killed at the battle of Hastings on 14 October 1066.

Harthacnut, King, nos. 8, 56, 57, 58. Son of Cnut and Ælfgifu Emma, acted as joint king of England with Harold Harefoot from late 1035 to early 1037, and sole king of England from June 1040 till his death on 8 June 1042. On the death of Cnut in 1035 Harthacnut was ruling Denmark with the title of king. The rival claimant to the English throne was his half-brother Harold Harefoot. At a meeting of the witan at Oxford it was decided that Harold should rule England as regent, and that Queen Ælfgifu Emma should reside at Winchester with a body of her son Harthacnut's housecarls, and maintain his interests in Wessex (*Chron.* E 1036, Plummer, ii. 208 ff., 218). But Harthacnut was at that time unable to leave Denmark, and Harold was in the following year recognised formally as king of England. On the death of Harold on 17 March 1040 Harthacnut was invited to return to England, and he arrived on 17 June 1040, and was crowned by the arch-bishop of Canterbury (Grierson, *Trans. R. Hist. Soc.* 1941, 97). *Chron.* C, D, 1040 speaks of the heavy tax that he imposed, and says that ' he did nothing kingly during his reign '; yet he made grants to monasteries and gave to the poor ; William of Poitiers observes that *ob morbos etiam quos frequenter patiebatur, plus Deum in oculis habebat et vitæ humanæ brevitatem* (ed. J. A. Giles (London, 1845), 79). Harthacnut died ' as he stood at his drink ' (*Chron.* C, D, 1042) at the marriage feast of the daughter of Osgod Clapa and Tofi the Proud, on 8 June 1042. On the derivation of his name, see Campbell, *Encomium Emmae*, 97–8.

Herman, Bishop, nos. 2, 3, 5. Bishop of Ramsbury 1045–55, bishop of Ramsbury and Sherborne 1058. The name is OGer *Her(e)man*. Wm. Malmesbury *G.P.* 182 describes him as ' natione Flandrensi ', Fl. Wig. 1045 as ' de Lotharingia oriundus ' ; on which see A. Wilmart, *Revue Bénédictine,*

1 (1938), 48, and P. Grierson, *loc. cit.* (in preceding note), 101. Herman had been a ' king's priest ' (*Chron.* E 1043²). In 1055 he resigned the poorly endowed see of Ramsbury, having been frustrated in his attempt to transfer his episcopal seat to the wealthy abbey of Malmesbury, and became a monk at St. Bertin's. But when in 1058 the see of Sherborne became vacant, he returned to England and received this see in addition to Ramsbury, which during his absence, or part of it, had been administered by Ealdred, then bishop of Worcester. In 1075 Herman transferred the see of Ramsbury and Sherborne to Old Sarum. He died in 1078.

Hugelin, the burthegn, no. 62. This was no doubt Hugo *camerarius, camerarius regis Edwardi,* whose name appears in Domesday as the former holder of land in Berkshire, Oxfordshire, Huntingdonshire and Warwickshire (DB i. 63, 157, 208, 239). Hugelinus *camerarius* appears in the list of witnesses to a spurious charter of the Confessor (K. 771), and the same person, under the name of Hugo *regis camerarius,* is made to attest a doubtful charter of the same king (K. 810). He may have been the Huhgelin *minister* who attests a charter of Archbishop Ealdred (K. 823). In Ramsey records he is styled *cubicularius,* the term used by the translator of the Ramsey writ, no. 62, to render OE *burðegn.* In the *Chron. Abbat. Rames.* 171, Hugelinus, the king's *cubicularius,* is said to have been entrusted with the keeping of the charters deposited in the king's treasury (*gazophylacium*) ; for arguments in support of this statement, see Larson, *op. cit.,* 133. In Flete's *History of Westminster Abbey* (ed. Armitage Robinson, 83) Hugelin (described there as ' Hugolinus nobilis principalis sancti regis Edwardi cubicularius semper Deo devotus et praedicto regi inter omnes hujus regni proceres miles fidelissimus ') is said to have been buried in Westminster Abbey, and the words inscribed over his tomb after the removal of his body to the new chapter house, subsequent to the rebuilding of the abbey by Henry III, are given. See also Appendix IV, no. 14.

Hunting, no. 62. Otherwise unknown.

John of Beverley, St., no. 7. Bishop of Hexham, and afterwards of York, died on 7 May 721, and was canonized in 1037.

Iudoc, St., no. 113. A seventh-century Breton saint, whose relics were translated to New Minster at Winchester (see *Chron.* F 903). See further, Plummer, ii. 123, and *Dictionary of Christian Biography* ; and for more recent studies, Jost Trier, ' Der Heilige Jodocus ; sein Leben und seine Verehrung ' (*Germanistische Abhandlungen,* lvi. Breslau, 1924), and W. Levison, ' Eine Predigt des Lupus von Ferrières ' (*Kultur- und Universalgeschichte, Walter Goetz dargebracht,* Leipzig, 1927, 3–14). St. Judoc's day is usually given as 13 December, but the day of his translation (9 January) was also celebrated at Winchester ; see Trier, *ut supra,* pp. 152 f.

Kineward, no. 3, see **Cyneweard.**

Kinric, nos. 57, 58, see **Cyneric.**

Kunyth, no. 121. Otherwise unknown. In the opinion of Professor Max Förster this is the Mod. Eng. *Kenneth* (Withycombe, *Oxf. Dict. Christ. Names,* 83), derived from Welsh *Cennydd,* the name of a sixth-century saint. The *Cynoht* of Symeon of Durham (*Op.* ed. Arnold, ii. 45) seems to be a misspelling for **Cynoth.* OIr *Cinaed* is too remote in form to be relevant here.

Leofcild of Moulsham, no. 84. It is not known whether Leofcild of Moulsham (in Essex) is to be identified with Leofcild, sheriff of Essex (see next note) or with any person of this name mentioned in charters or in Domesday Book.

Leofcild, the sheriff, nos. 73, 74. Sheriff of Essex. He witnessed as sheriff Thurstan's bequest of Wimbish to Christ Church in 1042 or 1043

(Whitelock, no. 30). He may have been the Leofcild who witnessed, 1043–45, Thurstan's Will (Whitelock no. 31). He may or may not have been the Leofcild who gave Moulsham, Essex, to Westminster Abbey (no. 84). For other instances of the name Leofcild in charters of about this time, see Whitelock no. 29, and K. 769 (Leofcild *minister*). For some eight Domesday references to tenants in Essex and Suffolk T.R.E. named Leofcild, see Feilitzen p. 311. Wheatley, held T.R.E. by Leuecilt *tegnus regis* (DB ii. 43), was held in 1086 by Swein 'of Essex', whose father Robert fitz Wimarch had also been sheriff of Essex ; but the connection may be illusory. Feilitzen however suggests that all the references given above concern one and the same person.

Leofgar, no. 62. Otherwise unknown.

Leofric, Abbot (of Peterborough), no. 62. Nephew of Earl Leofric of Mercia, appointed abbot of Peterborough 1052, according to a Peterborough insertion in *Chron.* E 1052. He died on 31 October 1066, after his return to Peterborough from Hastings, where he had accompanied Harold on his campaign, and where he had fallen sick. For Leofric's enrichment of the abbey of Peterborough, see *Chron.* E 1052, 1066 ; in the latter it is stated that the king gave to Leofric the abbeys of Burton, Coventry (founded by Leofric's uncle, Earl Leofric), Crowland, and Thorney. For comments on the pluralism of Leofric, see R. R. Darlington, *Eng. Hist. Rev.* li (1936), p. 403, n. 1, where it is suggested that the other abbeys would have gained by being under the nominal rule and protection of Abbot Leofric, a member of a rich and powerful family. For corroboration of the chronicler's statement, so far as Thorney is concerned, see the memorandum referred to on p. 254 above. A different date, 1057, is given for Leofric's appointment to Peterborough by Hugo Candidus (ed. Sparke, *Historiæ Anglicanæ Scriptores Varii* (London, 1723), 41, and in the so-called *Chron. Johannis Abbatis S. Petri de Burgo* (Sparke, 44). See also W. T. Mellows, *Chron. of Hugh Candidus* (Oxford, 1949), 161 (new edition).

Leofric, Bishop, no. 120. Appointed in 1046 bishop of the united sees of Cornwall and of Devon, his episcopal seat being at Crediton ; but this he removed in 1050, for greater security, to Exeter. Leofric had been a 'king's priest' before his promotion to the episcopate (*Chron.* E 1044). For further details of the origin and career of Leofric, who gave the Exeter Book to the cathedral chapter at Exeter, see *The Exeter Book of Old English Poetry*, R. W. Chambers, M. Förster and R. Flower (London, 1933). Leofric died on 10 February 1072.

Leofric, Earl, nos. 45, 46, 53. Son of Earl Leofwine (ealdorman of the Hwicce under Æthelred II, who died possibly in 1023), husband of Godgifu, appointed earl of Mercia by Cnut between 1023 and 1032, and probably in the earlier part of this period. Although Leofric's first signature as *dux* in a dated charter occurs in 1032 (K. 746), he also attests as *dux* an undated charter (K. 1324) which, if genuine, should probably be dated 1023–24. Leofric may have held some subordinate earldom as early as 1017, since Florence of Worcester records that in 1017 he was appointed *dux* by Cnut, in place of his brother Northman, slain by Cnut's orders at the same time as Eadric Streona. For a suggestion that Leofric may have succeeded to the position of Earl Eilaf, who seems to have had authority over some part of western Mercia, and who signs as *dux* 1018–24, see D. Whitelock, *Saga-Book of the Viking Society*, xii (1940), 135. On Leofric's gifts to monasteries see s.n. Godgifu ; but see also R. R. Darlington, *Vita Wulfstani*, p. xxiv, on the part played by him in the despoilment of Worcester. Leofric played a leading part in the Confessor's reign, and is praised for his wisdom in *Chron.*

D 1057. He died in the autumn of 1057, either on 30 September (*Chron.* D) or on 31 August (Fl. Wig.), and was buried in the monastery at Coventry.

Leofric, of Ruishton, no. 107. Otherwise unknown.

Leofric, Vicecomes, no. 48. Probably sheriff of Worcestershire, mentioned with Hakon ' and all the shire ' in two charters of c. 1023, Robertson nos. 81, 83, dealing with estates in Worcestershire.

Leofrun, no. 93. Otherwise unknown.

Leofsige, Abbot (of Ely), no. 62. Date of appointment uncertain. Death dated 1045 in the *Liber Eliensis*, but Leofsige may have died in 1055. Two abbots named Leofsige attest a charter of 1053–55 (Robertson no. 115 = K. 956), and one of them may have been abbot of Ely. This evidence combines with that of Writ no. 62, where Leofsige of Ely is brought into conjunction with Leofric of Peterborough, probably appointed to office in 1052 (see p. 255), to suggest that the death of Leofsige has been placed ten years too early in the *Liber Eliensis*. The same suggestion is made on other grounds by Miss Robertson p. 467. She supposes that Wulfric, Leofsige's successor, could not have been blessed as abbot (as he is stated to have been in the *Liber Eliensis*, ii. c. 94) by Archbishop Stigand in 1045, since Stigand did not become archbishop of Canterbury till 1052. But on the other hand (as Miss Whitelock has reminded me) Stigand could have blessed Wulfric as abbot (if Wulfric had in fact been appointed) while he was bishop of Elmham 1043/4–47, and it would be natural for a later writer to refer to him by his later title. In view of the existence of two abbots called Leofsige at the time, the two charters, K. 800, 801, ostensibly dated 1054, 1055, cited as an additional argument by Miss Robertson, do not seem to bear upon this question, since they do not name the house over which the Abbot Leofsige named in them presided. Moreover K. 800, dated 1054, is also attested by Eadsige, archbishop of Canterbury, who died in 1050, and K. 801, dated 1055, is attested by Ealdred, archbishop of York, not appointed to York till 1061. They are therefore useless for dating purposes. Nevertheless Miss Robertson may well be right, on the other grounds given above, in suggesting that the *Liber Eliensis* has put Leofsige's death ten years too early.

Leofsige, Bishop, no. 48. Bishop of Worcester 1016, till his death on 19 August 1033. Described by Fl. Wig. i. 189 as ' magnæ religionis et modestiæ vir '.

Leofsi Duddesunu, no. 90. Called Leofsi de Lundonia in the spurious First Charter of the Confessor (for which see pp. 289 f.). In the spurious Telligraphus of William I (for which see p. 337), which may preserve a genuine tradition, he is described as ' Leofsinus filius Duddi qui preerat illius ecclesie cementariis ', i.e. master-mason. This Leofsi cannot be identified with certainty with any bearer of this name mentioned in Domesday : for references see Feilitzen p. 315.

Leofstan, Abbot, nos. 11, 12, 23, 80. Abbot of St. Edmund's Bury from 1044 till his death on 1 August 1065. He had accompanied Ufi, whom he succeeded, on his migration to Bury from St. Benet, Holme. He is probably Leofstan the ' dean ' (*decan*) of Bury who was a beneficiary under the will of Bishop Ælfric II of Elmham, and who witnessed Thurstan's Will in 1043 or 1044 (Whitelock nos. 26, 31). It was to cure Leofstan of a chronic malady that Baldwine (q.v.), who eventually succeeded him, was sent to Bury by the Confessor (Wm. Malmesbury, *G.P.* 156 ; see also Douglas, *Feudal Documents*, lxi, n. 5).

Leofstan the portreeve, nos. 105, 106. To be identified no doubt with the Lyefstan *portireue* (of London) who, with the bishop, and with many thegns 'both within borough and without', attested c. 1054 a grant to Christ Church, Canterbury, of a homestead and the church of All Hallows, in London (Robertson no. 116). For a list of portreeves, see Tengvik, 265.

Leofstan, Queen Ælfgifu Emma's retainer, no. 16. Otherwise unknown.

Leofwine, Abbot, Bishop, nos. 45, 46, 96, 114 (*Leuen*). Appointed abbot of Coventry on the foundation of the monastery c. 1043, and bishop of Lichfield in 1053 (*Chron.* C, D, and Fl. Wig.). The date of his death is given by Stubbs and Searle as 1067. For a suggestion that Leofwine was the unnamed bishop of Lichfield, who in 1069 was excommunicated, and in April 1070 surrendered his bishopric to the king, and who was still alive in the latter part of 1070, see James Tait, *Essays in History presented to R. Lane Poole,* 155 f. See also Helene Tillmann, *Die päpstlichen Legaten in England bis* . . . 1218, Dissertation, Bonn, 1926, 13 f.

Leofwine, decanus, no. 113. Otherwise unknown.

Leofwine, Earl, nos. 76, 86, 88, 89, 90, 91, 92, 93. Fifth son of Earl Godwine, supposed by Freeman (ii. 419) to have been appointed to an earldom in 1057, on the redistribution of earldoms necessitated by the death of Earl Leofric and Earl Raulf. On the evidence of nos. 88–89, 90, Leofwine's earldom included Middlesex and Hertfordshire ; nos. 76, 92, 93, in which he appears as earl of Kent and of Surrey, are doubtful or spurious. Leofwine was killed at Hastings on 14 October 1066. For references in Domesday to the numerous manors held by Leofwine T.R.E. see Feilitzen, 317–19.

Leuen erles, no. 114. For suggestions as to his identity, see p. 406.

Lyfing, Archbishop, no. 26. Archbishop of Canterbury 1013, till his death on 12 June 1020. He had from 999 to 1013 been bishop of Wells. For a reference in Cnut's Proclamation of 1020 to letters and messages from Rome from the pope brought to him by Lyfing, see Liebermann i. 273, Robertson, *Laws,* p. 141. *Chron.* D 1019 (to be corrected to 1020) recording Lyfing's death, calls him ' a very sagacious (*rædfæst*) man, both in spiritual and worldly affairs '.

Mahthildis, Matildis, no. 35 (Latin version). See further pp. 180 f. The name is OG *Mahthild.*

Melmor, no. 121. Otherwise unknown. The name is either OIr *Máel-Mór,* or *Máel-Muire* ' servant of St. Mary ', as Dr. M. A. O'Brien has kindly pointed out to me, the latter being a much more frequent name. For a discussion of the name *Máelmuire,* see W. H. Stevenson, *Eng. Hist. Rev.* xxvii (1912), 9, n. 31. The name appears in *Melmerby* (Cumberland and North Riding of Yorkshire).

Merefinn, no. 94. This may be the Merefin who held ' freely ' T.R.E. land in Foxley, Northants, valued in 1086 at 5 shillings (DB i. 223 b, VCH *Northants.* i. 324). The only other instance of the name in Searle's *Onomasticon* is St. Merefin (Fl. Wig. i. 33), brother of St. Mildred (q.v.), whose family traditions (though they may be of early origin) were apparently written down much later than the seventh century. For the name, see F. Liebermann, *Die Heiligen Englands* (Hanover, 1889), p. 3, line 7 : ' Merefynn '; cf. pp. iv ff. ` Feilitzen, 327, cites a twelfth-century *Merafin* from the Durham *Liber Vitae.* See also Ekwall, *Early London Pers. Names,* 54, for instances in twelfth-century London.

Mildred (OE Mildðryð), St., no. 37. Best known as abbess of a nunnery at Minster in Thanet. She was the daughter of Merewalh, one of a line of under-kings who ruled over the Magesæte in the seventh and eighth centuries. Her mother Eormenborg was a member of the Kentish royal house, and her two sisters, like herself, attained eminence in the religious life.

A treatise on the saints buried in England of which the earliest extant version was copied in the early eleventh century, gives the descent of the family of St. Mildred, and the story of the foundation of the nunnery at Minster in Thanet, on land that had been given to Eormenbeorg by the king of Kent as wergeld for the murder of her two brothers. We are told that, after the return of Mildred from a nunnery overseas where she had been sent for training, her mother gave her the nunnery at Minster when it was established (gestaðolad), and that she, and 70 maidens with her, received the veil from Archbishop Theodore (died 690). The foundation of the nunnery is dated 670 in the Chronologia Augustinensis, which may be approximately correct. Mildred appears as abbess in a charter of 696 (B. 88), and attests (with four other abbesses) a privilege (B. 91) granted 696–716 to churches and monasteries in Kent. She appears as the recipient of royal grants of lands and privileges in charters, B. 141, 149, 150, 846, of which the first two are probably authentic, the others based on authentic material; their ostensible dates range from 724 to 732 or 733. The exact date of her death is not known; her festival is celebrated on 13 July. For the treatise on the saints buried in England from which our knowledge of St. Mildred is largely derived, see F. Liebermann, Die Heiligen Englands (as in preceding note, pp. 3–5), Birch, Liber Vitae of New Minster and Hyde Abbey, 83–94. See also the fragmentary Anglo-Saxon tractate, ' Natale Sanctæ Mildrethæ Virginis ', in Cockayne, Leechdoms, R.S. iii. 422. For other lives of St. Mildred, including Goscelin's, which contains much legendary matter, and has been the basis of subsequent biographies, see Hardy, Cat. of Materials, R.S. i. pp. 376–84. Some of the materials for a life of St. Mildred are discussed by Stubbs, Dict. Christ. Biog. s.n. ' Mildred '. See also Bibliotheca Hagiographica Latina, ii (Brussels, 1900–1), nos. 5960–64 ; also Alfons M. Zimmermann, Kalendarium Benedictinum, ii (Metten, 1934), pp. 446 f., F. Wormald, English Kalendars before A.D. 1100 (Henry Bradshaw Society, col. lxxii), London, 1934, for her place in the calendar.

Moryn, no. 121. Otherwise unknown. According to the VCH Cumberland, ii. 233, the name is found elsewhere : Dalston is said to have been forfeited at a later date by a certain Hervey, son of Morin. Dr. M. A. O'Brien has suggested to me that the name may be OIr Morand > Morann ; or possibly OIr Mórfind (pronounced Mórinn c. 1050). Another possibility (suggested to me by Professor Förster) is that the word is a diminutive form of OIr mor, ' great '.

Northman, the sheriff, nos. 62, 94. On the evidence of these two writs, sheriff of Northamptonshire. Morris (Med. Eng. Sheriff, 35, n. 148, 43, n. 21) suggests that he may be Northman (Norman), sheriff of Suffolk in King William's reign (see Round, Feudal England, 428, Davis, Regesta, no. 41). But the name Northman, Norman, was not uncommon from the tenth century onwards, and the identification may be erroneous. For Domesday instances, see Feilitzen, 331.

Offa, no. 78. King of Mercia 757–96. London and the surrounding country lay within the realm of Offa, who was overlord of all the southern kingdoms.

Ordbriht, Abbot, no. 78. Associated as abbot of Westminster, in a charter attributed to King Offa (see p. 501), dated 785, and in the Aldenham writ (no. 78), with a grant of land at Aldenham by Offa to Westminster Abbey. Flete's statement (ed. Armitage Robinson, 78) that Ordbriht became bishop of Selsey may have been due to confusion with Ordbriht, abbot of Chertsey, probably the Ordbriht who was bishop of Selsey from 988/989 to 1009 (Plummer, ii. 158). Ordbriht appears in the ancient list of abbots of Westminster printed in the VCH *London*, i. 454, and is there said to have died in 797 (a date which may or may not be correct).

Ordric, Abbot, nos. 4, 5. Abbot of Abingdon 1052–22 January 1066. See further, *Chron. Abingdon*, i. 464–82, ii. 119, 281–2.

Osbern (Osebarnus), no. 50. Lands in Herefordshire, Worcestershire, and Shropshire, were held T.R.E. and in 1086 by Osbern, son of Richard fitz Scrob. For Osbern, see Feilitzen p. 338 (where the name spelt *Osbern* in Domesday, is explained as the Normanised or Anglicised form of ON *Ásbiǫrn*, or else OLG *Osbern*) ; Round, *Feudal England*, 322 ff. ; DNB xlviii. 185–6. It is a reasonable conjecture that this is the Osbern addressed in the Hereford writ. Freeman's view (ii. 345, n. 3) that Osbern was sheriff of Herefordshire, since ' the position in the writ in which his name occurs is one which generally belongs to the sheriff ', is merely an assumption, and may be erroneous ; see p. 52.

Osgot (Osgod), Osgot Clapa, nos. 14, 53, 77. A Dane (the name is ON *Ásgautr*, ODan *Asgot*), and probably the Osgod *minister* who attests charters of Cnut and Edward from 1026 (K. 743) to 1046 (K. 783, 1335). In charters and the *Chronicle* he appears sometimes with, sometimes without, the by-name *Clapa* (on which see Tengvik, 303 f.). Osgot was staller to King Edward but was outlawed in 1046 (*Chron.* C 1046, D 1047), and possibly went to Flanders. On the events of the year 1049, when Osgot appeared with a force of ships off Wulpen, not far from Bruges, see Freeman, ii. 89–90, 108, and for a slightly different interpretation of an obscure episode, P. Grierson, *Trans. R. Hist. Soc.* 4th ser. xxiii, 99. *Chron.* C, D, 1054 records that Osgot died ' suddenly as he lay in his bed '—presumably in England, but nothing is known of the date or circumstances of his return. For an anecdote concerning the arrogance of Osgot Clapa (there called *quidam major domus*), see Hermann the archdeacon's *Miracula Sancti Eadmundi* (Arnold, *Memorials*, i. 54 f.). See also Arnold i. 135.

The Osgot of no. 14, the Pakenham writ, of 1044/5–1047, is however identified by D. Whitelock, *Anglo-Saxon Wills*, 102, with Osgot, son of Eadulf, to whom his kinsman, Bishop Theodred of London, bequeathed 942–c. 951, certain estates, including land at Pakenham—an identification difficult to accept without corroboration, since the writ seems to imply that Osgot was the previous owner, and if Osgot had been Osgot, son of Eadulf, he would have had an extraordinarily long life. The Osgot of the Pakenham writ may have been descended from Osgot, son of Eadulf. There seems no reason for rejecting the Bury tradition which makes Osgot Clapa the former owner : compare for instance a passage in the *Pinchbeck Register*, ed. Hervey, ii. 289 : ' Idem (rex sanctus) dedit Sancto Edmundo *Pakenham quod ante habuit Osgothus Claf* '. Pakenham may have come into the king's hand as a sequel to Osgot's outlawry in 1046.

Osweard, vicecomes, nos. 35, 39. Styled *vicecomes* in Lat. version of no. 35, sheriff of Kent. On losses to the king's manor of Dartford through acts of Osweard ' then sheriff ', who had lost his office before the Confessor's death, see DB i. 2 b, VCH *Kent*, iii. 208 (cited by Morris, *Medieval English Sheriff*, 36). There is no clear link between this Osweard, and Osweard of Harrietsham, Osweard of Norton, or others named in Kentish charters or in Domesday, for whom see Robertson, 423, Feilitzen, 340. Nor is any connection known between this Osweard and the Osuuardus, who according to the Domesday Monachorum ff. 85, 86 (ed. Douglas), held T.R.E. Erith of the archbishop of Canterbury, and also one *sullinc* in Sheppey ; and who is not named by the Exchequer Domesday in relation to these places. I am indebted for this reference to Miss Whitelock.

Payn, the king's 'mead-wright ', no. 85. His name appears as *Painus* in the Westm. Do. copy of the spurious Telligraphus of King Edward (see p. 290). *Payn* must be the Middle English form of a name twice written *Pagen* (Lat. *Paganus*, Med. French *Païen*, *Payen*, see Feilitzen, 343, Tengvik, 193) in the Hampshire entries in Domesday (DB i. 51 b, VCH *Hants.* i. 513–14 ; ' Pagen holds of the king 1 hide and 1 virgate in Buckholt (*Bocolt*) ' ; ' Pagen held two manors called Boldre (*Bovre*) '. But there is no definite link between these entries—which may not both refer to the same person— and the *Payn* of the writ relating to Eversley (which also is in Hampshire).

Raulf, Earl, no. 55. Nephew of King Edward, whose sister Godgifu had been married to Drogo, count of the Vexin (Stenton, *Anglo-Saxon England,* 552). Raulf accompanied his uncle to England in 1041 (*Chron. Abbat. Rames.* 171). His signatures as *dux* begin in 1050 (K. 792–3), but the locality of his earldom, in which he raised forces in the king's support in 1051, and which is unnamed in *Chron.* D 1052, is not known. At a later date Raulf is found to be acting as earl of Herefordshire, and the Taynton writ, no. 55, is evidence that he was earl of Oxfordshire. It is entirely probable that he received these two shires when the earldom held by Earl Swein was divided c. 1053 after his death (Stenton, *op. cit.* 561). For Earl Raulf's failure to defend Herefordshire in 1055 against the forces of Earl Ælfgar and King Gruffydd, see *Chron.* C, D, E, 1055. Fl. Wig. 1055 calls him *timidus dux Radulfus*. For a more favourable view of his activities, see Stenton, *loc. cit.* Raulf died on 21 December 1057, and was buried at Peterborough (*Chron.* D 1057), of which abbey (as Miss Whitelock has pointed out to me) he had been a benefactor (Mellows, *Chron. Hugh Candidus,* 69).

Regenbald (Reinbold, Rengebold cancheler), nos. 44, 112. Priest first of the Confessor (no. 44), afterwards of William I (see p. 212). Of foreign descent on the evidence of his name, OG *Rain-*, *Reinbald* (Feilitzen p. 347). The form *Reinbold* of the Confessor's writ occurs also in a writ of William I (Davis, *Regesta*, no. 9), and in Domesday (for references see Feilitzen *ut supra*). The spelling *Regenbald*, an Anglicised form (cf. OE *Swegen*, *Swegn*, for *Swein*, from ON *Sveinn* (with diphthong), ODan, OSwed *Sven*) now used generally by historians, appears in the spurious Waltham charter of the Confessor (K. 813), and in the other writ of William I for him (*Regesta* no. 19). On the status of Regenbald and on his connection with Cirencester, see pp. 211 ff. ; on the possibility that he may have been styled *cancellarius* before the Conquest, see Introduction, pp. 60 f. On Regenbald and on his possessions, see J. H. Round, *Feudal England,* 421–6, and DNB s.n. ' Regenbald ' ; Davis, *Regesta*, xv.

Ricard, ' my housecarl ', Richard, nos. 116, 117. To be identified no doubt with Richard fitz Scrob, a Norman who, according to Fl. Wig. i. 210, was allowed to remain in England as one of the king's favourites, when the Normans were banished in 1052, after the reconciliation of Earl Godwine with the king. Richard fitz Scrob settled in Herefordshire, and gave his name to Richard's Castle. For references to lands in Herefordshire and Shropshire held T.R.E. by Ricard, no doubt the same person, see Feilitzen 349. His son was Osbern, q.v.

Robert (Rodberd), Bishop, no. 77. Bishop of London 1044–51, archbishop of Canterbury 1051 (mid-Lent)–14 September 1052. Robert (Champart), a Norman, abbot of Jumièges, stood high in the favour of King Edward, who gave him the bishopric of London, and later promoted him to the see of Canterbury, setting aside the choice of the monks of Christ Church (*Vita*

Æduuardi, ed. Luard, 399 f.).   On the opening of negotiations for the reconciliation of Earl Godwine and his family with the king on 14 September 1052, Robert who had opposed Godwine's party, fled overseas, abandoning his pallium, and was declared an outlaw (*Chron.* E, F, 1052).   He is said (Wm. Malmesbury, *G.P.* 35) to have gone to Rome and to have secured from the pope letters ordering his reinstatement, but did not return to this country.   His see of Canterbury was filled not long after, during his lifetime, by the appointment of Stigand, then bishop of Winchester.   The date of his death is given as 1070 by Stubbs p. 35 ; but see on this dating, R. R. Darlington, *Eng. Hist. Rev.* li (1936), 420, n. 2, where it is observed that the date 1070 is given without any authority being cited, that Wm. Malmesbury (*ut supra*) uses language which implies that he did not long survive his return to Jumièges, and that he may have been dead in 1058.   It is to be noted that Robert was appointed to the see of London in August 1044 (Fl. Wig. 1044, Freeman ii. 69).   He was appointed to Canterbury at mid-Lent 1051 (*Chron.* C 1050), went to Rome for his pallium, and on his return was enthroned at Christ Church on St. Peter's day, i.e. 29 June (*Chron.* E 1048, to be corrected to 1051).

Robert fitz Wimarch, the staller, nos. 76, 84, 93.   His mother bore a Breton name (q.v.).   Described in the *Vita Æduuardi* (ed. Luard, 431), which says he was present at the Confessor's deathbed, as 'regalis palatii stabilitor et ejusdem regis propinquus ', he may have been the Robert ' regis consanguineus ' of the spurious Waltham charter (K. 813, see p. 59).   Of the writs in which he appears the most likely to be authentic is no. 84 ; K. 771, ostensibly dated 1044, cannot be authentic, for it is attested by Abbot Edwin of Westminster, not appointed till 1049.   Robert, said to have sent to Duke William, ' domino suo atque consanguineo ', news of the battle of Stamford Bridge (Wm. of Poitiers, *Gesta Willelmi Ducis*, ed. Giles, 128), was sheriff of Essex under William, but there is no evidence for Kemble's assumption (see pp. 51 f.), endorsed by Morris, *Med. Eng. Sheriff,* 37, n. 164, that he held that office under the Confessor.   Robert was dead by 1086 (DB ii. 98, 47 b, VCH *Essex,* i. 564, 490).   His son was Swein ' of Essex ' ; see s. ' Swein, the king's kinsman '.   On lands held by Robert before and after the Conquest, see Feilitzen, 349 f.   See Freeman, iv, Appendix, Note D ; DNB s. ' Robert the Staller ' (Round) ; see also pp. 51 f.

Semer, no. 17.   Otherwise unknown.   The name is OE Sæmær.

Sigulf (Sygoolf), no. 121.   Otherwise unknown.

Sigweard, no. 35.   There is no definite link between this Siward (Sigeweard) and contemporary bearers of this name in Kent.   A Siward of Chilham (on whose family connections see Robertson p. 419) attests a grant of land by Cnut to Christ Church (Robertson no. 85, not in its present form authentic), and a Siward appears in Domesday as holding land of King Edward (DB i. 6, VCH *Kent*, iii. 221).

Sihtric, Earl, no. 78.   Possibly the Sihtric *dux* who attests charters of Cnut of 1026 (K. 743), and 1031 (K. 743)—on the supposition that the latter is authentic, although the names of the archbishops of Canterbury and York have been confused.   But this identification cannot be accepted unless we suppose, as has been tentatively suggested above, that the name of *Ælfric* (q.v.) as abbot of Westminster has been mis-written for *Ælfwig*.

Siward, Bishop, no. 3.   Appointed abbot of Abingdon in 1030.   In 1044 he was appointed to administer the see of Canterbury when Archbishop Eadsige (q.v.) resigned owing to ill-health.   Fl. Wig. 1049 calls Siward *chorepiscopus* of Eadsige, archbishop of Canterbury ; on this office in England, see Levison, *England and the Continent in the Eighth Century,* 66, n. 4, and the references there. Siward, too, retired in 1048, through ill-health, returned to Abingdon, and died within two months, on 23 October 1048 (*Chron.* C 1048).

Siward, Earl, nos. 59, 121. A Dane (ODan *Sigwarth*), appointed earl of Northumbria by Cnut, his first signature as *dux* appearing in a charter dated 1033 (K. 749). For the first few years of Siward's rule the northern region, between the Tees and the Scottish border, continued to be ruled by native earls of the ancient Bernician line. But after the murder in 1041 by order of Harthacnut of Earl Eadwulf, the last of these to hold power in the extreme north, Siward became the immediate ruler of the whole of Northumbria. Symeon of Durham (*Opera*, R.S. ii. 198) indeed declares that Eadwulf was killed by Siward himself (*interfectus est a Siwardo*). In 1043 Earl Siwarth was present at the confiscation by the king of the property of Queen Ælfgifu Emma (*Chron.* D 1043). In 1051, at King Edward's summons, he took the king's part against Earl Godwine, in the struggle which ended in Godwine's banishment. On the evidence of no. 59 Siward was for a time earl of Huntingdonshire, and he held land there T.R.E. (DB i. 203, 208). In Gospatric's writ (no. 121) Siward appears as lord over lands which had formerly belonged to the British kingdom of Strathclyde, and it is entirely probable that this extension of his earldom was due to Siward himself. The most famous episode in his career is his expedition to Scotland and his defeat of Macbeth and his forces (*Chron.* C, D, 1054). Siward died in 1055, and was buried at York in the *mynster* at *Galmanho* which he himself had built and consecrated in the name of God and St. Olave (*Chron.* C, D, 1055) ; for Siward's *mynster*, see B. Dickins, *Saga-Book of the Viking Society*, xii (1939), 56–7). Siward was nicknamed *Digera*, i.e. OWScand *Digri < digr* ' big ', ' stout ' ; see Tengvik, 310. Earl Siward married the daughter of Earl Ealdred of Northumbria, and Earl Waltheof was their son.

Siwarth, Abbot (of Thorney), no. 62. Abbot of Thorney here, but described in the memorandum discussed on p. 254 as provost of Thorney (when the abbey was in the charge of Abbot Leofric of Peterborough), and as having later become abbot. But there is reason to believe that Siwarth was never actually blessed as abbot of Thorney, though he himself may have used that title. Miss Whitelock has pointed out to me that the compiler of the fifteenth-century list of abbots of Thorney in B.M. Add. MS. 40,000, f. 11, remarks that Siwarth was *nacione Danus*, and says : *nulla facta professione nec episcopali benedictione recepta, quasi prepositus secularis hoc monasterium* circiter decem annos *inuasit et occupauit*. Further a twelfth-century list of names of abbots of Thorney, from Godeman to Gunther, does not mention Siwarth, though it does include Fulcard, whose position was also irregular, whom Lanfranc deposed, and whom it places without title, after the abbots (Whitelock, *Saga-Book of the Viking Society*, xii, Part II (1940), 131).

Stigand, Stigande, Stigant, Bishop, Archbishop, nos. 13, 14, 33–5, 39–42, 60–2, 85, 92, 93, 111, 112. Bishop of East Anglia (Elmham) from 3 April 1043 to late November 1043, and 1044–47 ; bishop of Winchester 1047–70 ; archbishop of Canterbury in plurality with Winchester 1052–70. Deposed 11 April 1070. Died 22 February 1072. The name is ONorse *Stigandr*, with a weak form *Stigandi*. Stigand, no doubt the priest of Cnut, to whom Cnut committed the newly-founded minster at Ashingdon (*Chron.* F 1020), was consecrated bishop of Elmham after the coronation of King Edward on Easter-Day 1043 (*Chron.* C 1043), but was deprived of his see late in the same year, in consequence of the disgrace of Queen Ælfgifu Emma (q.v.) shortly after 16 November 1043. He was reinstated not long after (*Chron.* E 1043, to be corrected to 1044), and Grimketel, who had taken his place at Elmham, was ejected. The early events of Stigand's career have however been involved in a good deal of confusion; see Wharton, *Anglia Sacra*, i. 406, where Stigand's ejection from Elmham is put in 1040 instead of 1043; and Freeman's story (i. 501), for which there is no real evidence, that Stigand was ejected from a bishopric 'seemingly before consecration'. See also the incompatible statements in Searle's *Bishops*, p. 51, that Stigand was consecrated to Elmham c. 1040 but deposed in 1042, ? before consecration, and his suggestion (p. 52) that the statement in *Chron.* C 1043, that Stigand was consecrated on 3 April 1043, may be a mistake. In 1047 Stigand was translated to Winchester, retaining this see even after his translation to Canterbury (Fl. Wig. 1070, Wm. Malmesbury, *G.R.* ii. 244). When Archbishop Robert (q.v.) fled overseas in September 1052, his place was filled by the appointment of Stigand. Freeman, ii. 340, assumes that the appointment was made either in September 1052 or at the following Christmas. But this appointment was not recognised by the reforming party in the Roman curia, and Stigand was not granted the pallium until 1058, when he at last received it from Pope Benedict X. Although Stigand was accorded in England the dignity and revenues of an archbishop, his position was regarded as anomalous, and between 1052 and 1066 no English bishop came to him for consecration except in the months immediately following his recognition by Pope Benedict; and when Benedict was deposed in January 1059, Stigand incurred the odium of having received the pallium from a pope who was regarded as a usurper. See further R. R. Darlington, *Eng. Hist. Rev.* li (1936), 420, and for the (inconclusive) evidence relating to the style accorded to Stigand, whether 'bishop' or 'archbishop' after his appointment to Canterbury, see pp. 247 f. above. After the Conquest Stigand continued to hold the sees of Canterbury and Winchester, and indeed consecrated Remigius as bishop of Dorchester in 1067, but in 1070 he was deposed. For the immense possessions of Stigand T.R.E. as they are recorded in Domesday, see Feilitzen p. 374. For Stigand's relations with the papacy, see Stenton, *Anglo-Saxon England*, 459, and Tillmann, *ut supra*, 11 ff.

Swein, the king's kinsman, no. 92. The possibility (suggested by Armitage Robinson, *Gilbert Crispin*, p. 128) that this is Swein 'of Essex', son of Robert fitz Wimarch the staller (q.v.), is increased by the fact that Swein is described as the king's kinsman in the writ, as is also Robert fitz Wimarch elsewhere. Swein 'of Essex' had succeeded his father as sheriff of Essex by 1075 (see Davis, *Regesta*, nos. 84–7), and appears in Domesday as holding land in Essex (DB ii. 42 ff., VCH *Essex*, i: 482 ff.), though no longer sheriff (DB ii. 2 b, VCH *Essex*, i. 429). Neufeldt's identification of the Swein of the Tooting writ with Earl Swein, son of Earl Godwine, must be rejected, since Earl Swein's death is mentioned *Chron.* C and Fl. Wig. 1052, whereas the Swein who held Tooting was, according to Domesday (see pp. 311 f.), still alive after the Conquest. See further on Swein, VCH *Essex*, i. 345–6.

Swetman the portreeve, no. 43. Otherwise unknown.

Swithun, St., nos. 111, 112, 113. Bishop of Winchester, consecrated 30 October 852, died 2 July 862. Swithun was said to have performed miracles after the translation of his relics, and was canonised in popular tradition. See further Plummer, ii. 83. For Lives of St. Swithun see *Bibliotheca Hagiographica Latina*, ii (Brussels, 1900–01), nos. 7943–9.

Sygoolf, see **Sigulf**.

Teinfrith, 'my church-wright', no. 87. Otherwise unknown. For a discussion of his name, whether an eleventh-century, or later, Anglo-Norman spelling of Old English *Thegn-*, or an Anglicised form of a Continental Germanic name (as seems on the whole more probable), see F. E. Harmer, *Eng. Hist. Rev.* li (1936), 98, n. 1.

Thore, no. 121. This common Scandinavian loan-name occurs three times in the writ : (1) for the father of Thorfynn ; (2) for the person mentioned with Melmor and Sigulf ; (3) for the former owner of lands at Cardew and Cumdivock. It cannot be determined whether any one of these was identical with any other.

Thored, no. 53. There is no clear link between this Thored and bearers of this not uncommon Norse name, appearing in charters of varying degrees of authenticity of Cnut, Harthacnut, and Edward. Two *ministri* of this name, for instance, sign together in 1023 and 1024 (K. 739, 741). A Thored the staller appears in a spurious Christ Church charter (Robertson, no. 85, on which see *Bull. of the John Rylands Library*, xxii (1938), 353 ff.), together with Osgod Clapa, Bishop Ælfwig of London, and Archbishop Æthelnoth, all of whom are mentioned in Cnut's writ, no. 53. On the name *Thor(e)d, Thorth,* see Björkman, *Nordische Personennamen in England* (Halle, 1910), 149–50 ; and on contemporary bearers of the name see *Crawford Charters,* 148.

Thorfynn mac Thore, no. 121. Otherwise unknown. For references to one or more bearers of this name (ON *Þorfinnr*) in Yorkshire T.R.E. (spelt *Torfin,* once *Turfin*), see Feilitzen, 392. *Mac* ' son of ' is Gaelic.

Thuri (Turi), comes, nos. 57, 58. To be identified no doubt with Thuri, *comes Mediterraneorum,* mentioned in Fl. Wig. 1041 as having taken part with Earls Leofric of Mercia, Godwine of Wessex, Siward of Northumbria, and Hrani of the Magesæte, and the other earls, in a punitive expedition sent by Harthacnut in 1041 against Worcester. Turi attests as Thuri(g) *dux,* signing after Godwine, Leofric, and Siward, charters of Harthacnut and Edward of 1042 (K. 763) and 1044–51 (K. 797), and a St. Albans charter of 1042–49 (K. 962), signing after Earl Siward. He is no doubt the *Thuni,* for *Thuri,* of a Worcester charter attested by Earls Godwine and Leofric dated 1038 (K. 760). He also appears in a spurious charter of Harthacnut (K. 761). His earldom, whether subordinate or independent, lay no doubt in the midlands, and on the evidence of the two Ramsey writs, included Huntingdonshire. Its extent is not known, but Freeman conjectured (ii. 557) that it took in the whole eastern part of Mercia. On this name, whether for ONorse *Þórir,* or as a shortened form for compounds in *Thur-* (e.g. *Thurstan*), see D. Whitelock, *Saga-Book of the Viking Soc.* xii (1940), 145, n. 3.

Thurkill, Earl, no. 26. Thurkill the Tall, a Dane, whose brother was the chief of the Vikings of Jómsborg, appeared in England with a large force in 1009 (*Chron.* C), but after fighting several battles against the English, and harrying and burning in various parts, took service three years later with King Æthelred with 45 ships (*Chron.* E 1012). About two years later he again changed sides, and was in 1017 appointed earl of East Anglia by Cnut. For the next four years Thurkill occupied a prominent position in this country. His name as *dux* comes first among laymen attesting charters of Cnut of 1018–19 (K. 728–30), and he alone is mentioned by name in the address of Cnut's Proclamation of 1020 (for which see p. 17, n. 1), a circumstance which suggests that he may have acted as regent during Cnut's absence abroad. In 1021 Thurkill was outlawed, but *Chron.* C 1023 records that he and Cnut were reconciled two years later, and that he was entrusted with the government of Denmark. He is said to have died not long afterwards. For further details, see *Crawford Charters,* 139–41, Ashdown, pp. 293 f., Robertson, *Laws,* pp. 343 f.

Thurstan, the king's housecarl, no. 77. This may be the Turstinus *teignus regis* E. who in the Confessor's reign held Cranford, Middlesex (DB i. 130 b), but no definite connection between the two has been established. For a Thurstan who in 1042 or 1043 made a bequest to Christ Church, and whose will is also extant, see Whitelock nos. 30, 31. But the name, an Anglicised form, cf. ONorse *Þorsteinn*, was not uncommon in the eleventh century; for Domesday instances see Feilitzen, 396.

Tofig, Touid, the sheriff, nos. 6, 68–71. Sheriff of Somerset, probably in succession to Godwine (q.v.) who was in office as late as 1061. He appears as sheriff of Somerset after the Conquest in a Wells Writ (*Regesta*, no. 160, dated by Davis, 1066–82), and in a Bath writ (*Regesta*, no. 7, dated by Davis, 1067). He may have been the Tou[i]g *minister* of the Banwell charter (*Regesta*, no. 23, dated by Freeman and Davis, 1068, Earle p. 431). For his lands in Somerset, see VCH *Somerset*, i. 419, Feilitzen, 384; see also Feilitzen for the Scandinavian name *Tofi, Toui*. On the -*id* in *Touid*, see Feilitzen § 133, n. 3.

Tole, no. 2. The frequently-repeated assertion that Tole was a native of Rouen is seemingly based on a statement in *Mon. Angl.* iii. 54, which cannot be corroborated since the early Abbotsbury records are lost. The name is ODan *Tola*. A fragment of a charter of Tole is printed in *Ord. Surv. Facs.* part ii, Ilchester, no. 5.

Toli, the sheriff, nos. 10, 18, 20, 23–5, 61. Toli, the sheriff of Norfolk and Suffolk of no. 61, is no doubt the Toli addressed without a title in the other writs. He appears as *vicecomes* T.R.E. in Norfolk and Suffolk entries in Domesday (for references see Feilitzen, 386). Morris's statement (*Medieval English Sheriff*, 23, n. 47) that Toli is mentioned in a writ along with Bishop Grimketel, is based on no. 10, which is spurious. Morris points out (*ut supra*, 36) that Toli gave land to St. Edmund's (DB ii. 211 b).

Tostig, Earl, nos. 7, 62, 119. Third son of Earl Godwine, succeeded Siward as earl of Northumbria in 1055. In or before 1051 (*Vita Æduuardi*, ed. Luard, 404) Tostig had married Judith, daughter of Baldwine IV of Flanders (see p. 303), and went to Bruges with his father Earl Godwine and other members of his family on their banishment in September 1051. On the misadventures of Tostig and his party on their journey home from Rome, see *Chron.* D 1061, Freeman ii. 452 ff. In November 1065 Tostig was ejected by the Northumbrians from his earldom (see p. 562), went with his wife to Bruges, and was living at St. Omer at the time of the Confessor's death (*Chron.* C 1065). On the evidence of no. 119 the earldom of Northampton had also been given to Tostig, a fact which explains the occupation of Northampton by the Northumbrian rebels when they moved south in 1065, and their ravaging the country round about (*Chron.* D, E). Returning to England with a naval force after King Edward's death, Tostig, after ravaging the coast, went to Scotland, and joined King Harold Hardrada in his invasion of Yorkshire. He was killed at the battle of Stamford Bridge, 25 September 1066. Miss Whitelock has observed to me that the address of no. 119 affords additional proof to hints elsewhere that Nottinghamshire was part of the Northumbrian earldom in the latter part of Edward's reign. The -*ig* in the common form of this name, *Tostig*, that I have used here (as also in such spellings as *Tofig, Tolig*) is of course an inverted spelling for -*i* (cf. Feilitzen § 134).

Tostig, Earl, no. 93. This can scarcely be Earl Godwine's son Tostig; see p. 304, where reference is made to a semi-legendary Tostig, earl of Huntingdon, said to have been killed by Earl Siward, father of Earl Waltheof, while on a visit to King Edward at Westminster; see the *Vita et Passio Waldevi*, text (in a manuscript of cent. xiii) and translation in C. E. Wright's *Cultivation of Saga in Anglo-Saxon England*, 131 f., 268 ff. One cannot help suspecting that the Tostig who succeeded Siward (q.v.) in the earldom of Northumbria has been confused in the saga which underlies the *Vita Waldevi*, with the Eadwulf who was Siward's predecessor, and whom Siward is said by Symeon of Durham to have slain. Further, as Freeman suggested (ii. 559), some confused tradition of the actual succession of Siward, Tostig, son of Godwine, and Waltheof, to the earldom of Huntingdon, may possibly have formed an element in the legend of Tostig, earl of Huntingdon. On Domesday evidence for Tostig, son of Godwine's, tenure of the earldom of Huntingdon, see F. M. Stenton in VCH *Hunts.* i. 334-5. In the *Vita Waldevi* Tostig is said to have married Earl Godwine's daughter, the queen's sister. This looks like a hopelessly confused reminiscence of the actual family relationships of the real Earl Tostig, son of Earl Godwine, and brother of Queen Edith. There is no charter evidence for a Tostig, earl of Huntingdon ; K. 742, with the ostensible date of 1026, attested by Tostig *dux* (who on this dating could not be Earl Godwine's son), has an impossible list of witnesses for that date. There is in any case no room here for the Leofrun, wife of Tostig, foster-mother of King Edward, of the Claygate writ, no. 93. For these reasons it seems more probable, as has been suggested above (p. 304), that the ' Earl ' which precedes Tostig's name, is merely a later addition to the text.

Tostig, the housecarl, no. 93. Otherwise unknown.

Touid the sheriff, see **Tofig.**

Turi, comes, nos. 57, 58, see **Thuri.**

Ufi (Vui), Abbot, no. 8. Appointed abbot of Bury in 1020, died in 1044. He had been prior of St. Benet, Holme, and went to Bury with a colony of monks from Holme.

Ulf, Bishop, no. 59. A Norman, bishop of Dorchester from 1050 until 14 September 1052, when he fled overseas with his fellow countrymen Archbishop Robert (q.v.) and Bishop William (q.v.), and was included with the other Frenchmen in the sentence of outlawry. Ulf had been a *regis capellanus* before his appointment (Fl. Wig. 1049). For comments on his unfitness for office, see *Chron.* C 1049, D 1050, E 1047. His successor Wulfwig was appointed in his lifetime.

Ulf the portreeve, the sheriff, nos. 75, 77. Portreeve of London and sheriff of Middlesex. Otherwise unknown.

Urk, the king's housecarl, nos. 1, 2. Received from Cnut in 1024 a grant of land at Portisham, near Abbotsbury, Dorset (K. 741, *Ord. Surv. Facs.* pt. ii, Ilchester, no. 2), and attests as *minister* Cnut's charter (K. 1318) for his housecarl Bovi. The Confessor granted him land at (Abbott's) Wootton in Dorset as *meo fideli ministro* in 1044 (K. 772, *Ord. Surv. Facs.*, *ut supra*, no. 3). For the statutes of the gild founded by Urk at Abbotsbury, see K. 942 = Thorpe p. 605. That he was not of English birth is indicated by the words introducing his name in K. 772 : ' qui juxta sue proprie gentis consuetudinem ab infantili etate nomen accepit Orc '. The name is probably Scandinavian, and the same as the *Orcus* which occurs once in Domesday (see Feilitzen, 335).

Wada, no. 120. A Wado appears as the holder of land T.R.E. in Devon at Modbury, *Tori*, Bolbery, Shilston, and Honicknowle, and in Somerset at Ashbrittle (*Aisse*) (DB i. 105, 105 b, 92, Exon Domesday 221, 219 b, 220 b, 222 (*Wadel*), 269, 513 b). The name is comparatively rare (for other Domesday instances see Feilitzen p. 407), and it is distinctly possible that the Wada of the writ was identical with the holder of land at some, if not all, of these places.

Walter, Bishop, no. 50. Bishop of Hereford 1060-79. Walter, a Lotharingian, who had been chaplain to Queen Edith (Fl. Wig. 1060), was appointed bishop of Hereford on the resignation in 1060 of Ealdred (q.v.), who had administered the see since the death of Bishop Leofgar on 16 June

1056. He was consecrated at Rome (with Giso of Wells) on 15 April 1061.

Waltheof (Wall-), no. 121. Otherwise unknown.

Wiberht (Wyberth), no. 121. Otherwise unknown. The name is probably OE *Wigbeorht* (if it is not OG *Wigbert*).

Wigand (Wygande), no. 121. Otherwise unknown. The name is OG *Wigand.*

Wigod of Wallingford, no. 104. Described here as the king's kinsman, and probably to be identified with the Wigod *minister* who attests a grant of Bishop Lyfing of Worcester in 1042 (K. 764), and with the Wigodus *regis pincerna* in the list of witnesses appended to the spurious Waltham charter (K. 813, see p. 59). He is also made to attest two spurious Westminster charters (K. 824, 825, on which see pp. 289 f.). For the name *Wigod* or *Wigot* (ODan and OSwed (runic) *Vigot*), and for Domesday references to Wigod, see Feilitzen, 404. See also Freeman, iv. Appendix, Note C.

Wihtgar, nos. 18, 24. The name *Wihtgar (Wisgar, Witgar, Withgar)* occurs frequently in the Domesday entries relating to Suffolk and Essex. Many of these refer to the younger Wihtgar, the son of Ælfric, Wihtgar's son, and the predecessor of Richard fitz Gilbert of Clare; see VCH *Essex,* i. 348, *Suffolk,* i. 398. Feilitzen, 414, identifies the elder Wihtgar, of the writs, with the Wihtgar, described in three of the entries as a *liber homo,* who held T.R.E. land in Essex at Epping, and in Suffolk at Kembrook, Creeting and Ousden (DB ii. 35, 343, 411, 445 b).

Willann, no. 121. *Willann* in the manuscript seems clear, though Liebermann preferred *Willelmi.* The name *Willann* may have been familiar to the copyist, but its occurrence here should not, unless corroborated by other evidence, be taken to prove that this name was current in this region in the Old English period. Ragg observes that a personal or family name *Willan* occurs in Westmorland documents much later. It is also current at the present time in the North Riding of Yorkshire. But Ragg's suggestion that *Willann* has replaced an earlier *Weland* (OG, see Feilitzen, 411) seems not unlikely.

William (Willelm), Bishop, nos. 43, 84, 86, 88, 89, 98, 105, 106. Bishop of London 1051–75. William, a Norman, who had been a 'king's priest' (*Chron.* E 1048), was appointed to the see of London in the autumn of 1051, after the deposition (before consecration) of Spearhafoc, following the fall of Earl Godwine and his family, and was consecrated by Archbishop Robert. On 14 September 1052, William fled overseas with Archbishop Robert (q.v.) and Bishop Ulf of Dorchester (q.v.), but was recalled shortly after, and reinstated *propter suam bonitatem* (Fl. Wig. 1052). He died in 1075.

Wimarch, nos. 76, 93. Mother of Robert the staller (q.v.), called *nobilis mulier* by William of Poitiers (ed. Giles, p. 128). There is no direct link between this Wimarch and the Wimarcha of a Christ Church obituary: '16 Kal. Oct. Obiit Wimarcha soror nostra' (John Dart, *Hist. and Antiq. of the Cath. Church of Canterbury* (1726), Appendix, no. xii, p. xxxvii). On the Breton name *Wimarch,* OBret *Wiuhomarch,* see Feilitzen, 415, Tengvik, 231, and references. For later instances see *Hist. et Cart. Mon. S. Petri Glouc.* R.S. i. 354, *Liber Vitae,* New Minster and Hyde Abbey, ed. Birch, 145, *Trans. R. Hist. Soc.* 4th ser. iv (1921), 184.

Wudumann, no. 72. Otherwise unknown. No Somerset instances of this rare name seem to be recorded in Domesday; see Feilitzen, 418.

Wulfgar, portreeve of London, no. 51. Otherwise unknown.

Wulfgeat, Abbot, no. 62. Abbot of Crowland and formerly abbot of Peakirk. Ordericus Vitalis, *Hist. Eccles.* (ed. Le Prevost), ii. 284, and the

Successio Abbatum (ed. R. Gough, *Hist. of Croyland Abbey* (London, 1784), 137–44) merely state that Wulfgeat, then abbot of Peakirk, obtained from King Edward permission to unite the communities of Peakirk and of Crowland, and to preside over them both. A different version of the story appears in the pseudo-Ingulf (ed. W. Fulman, *Rev. Angl. Script. Vet.* (1684), i. 62–4), and in the so-called *Chron. Johannis Abbatis S. Petri de Burgo* s.a. 1048 (in Sparke's *Hist. Angl. Script. Varii*, 41), where Wulfgeat is supposed to have lost his monastery and all its lands in consequence of a lawsuit with Peterborough, and King Edward is said to have taken him and his monks under his protection, appointing Wulfgeat to the office of abbot of Crowland which had just become vacant through the death of Abbot Brihtmær. The writer of the pseudo-Ingulf moreover inserts a Latin letter (which there is no reason to believe to be authentic), supposed to have been addressed by the Confessor to the subprior and convent of Crowland, announcing the appointment of Wulfgeat as ' prelate ' over them. There is great uncertainty regarding the dates of the abbots of Crowland at this period. But Miss Robertson has shown (*Charters*, 468) that Wulfgeat's predecessor Brihtmær was probably still alive at any rate as late as 1053, and that his successor Ulfketel may have been appointed to the abbacy in 1061 or 1062. The dates : 1053–61 or 1062, for Wulfgeat's tenure of office, are to be preferred to those of 1048–52 adopted in the *Monasticon Anglicanum*, for the latter dating cannot be reconciled with other evidence, namely the charter (Robertson no. 115) in which Wulfgeat's predecessor Brihtmær appears in company with Bishop Leofwine of Lichfield (q.v.), not appointed till after October 1053.

Wulfgyth, no. 108. Otherwise unknown.

Wulfmær, no. 107. Possibly to be identified with the Wulfmær to whom a hide of land at Barton, Hants, was leased in King Æthelred's reign by the abbot and community of New Minster, Winchester, according to a charter (Robertson no. 70) attested (among others) by Bishop Ælfheah and Earl Ælfric and Æthelweard, all mentioned in King Æthelred's writ. He may have been the Wulfmær *minister* who attests charters of King Æthelred from 986 to 1005 (K. 654, 687, 692, 714), but there is no direct evidence for these identifications.

Wulfnoth, the king's housecarl, no. 85. Otherwise unknown.

Wulfric, Abbot, no. 35. Abbot of St. Augustine's, 1045–61. *Chron.* E (at this stage a Canterbury text, cf. Plummer, ii, Introduction p. l) records s.a. 1043 [2], to be corrected to 1045, that Wulfric received the episcopal benediction as abbot on 26 December 1045, during the lifetime of his predecessor Ælfstan (q.v.). *Chron.* E 1061, recording Wulfric's death on 14 kal. May (18 April), adds a further detail, based no doubt on special knowledge, that Wulfric died ' within Easter week ', which is correct for 18 April 1061. The different dating of *Chron.* D 1061, which dates his death on 14 kal. April (19 March) must therefore be rejected. The dates of *Chron.* E—which is an earlier authority—also conflict with those given by Thorne, col. 1784, and Elmham, p. 26, which must be rejected. They date Wulfric's appointment in 1047 and his death in 1059. See further on Abbot Wulfric, Thorne col. 1784 f.

Wulfric, Abbot of Ely, no. 47. For a suggestion that the date of Wulfric's appointment in succession to Leofsige, said in the *Liber Eliensis* to have been made in 1045, has been dated ten years too early, see s. ' Leofsige, Abbot of Ely '. In that case, Wulfric, a kinsman of the Confessor, will have succeeded Leofsige in 1055. Wulfric seems to have died shortly before the Confessor's death, for his successor Thurstan was appointed to Ely by King Harold soon after his accession to the throne (*Liber Eliensis*, ii. cap. 98, 100).

Wulfsige, Abbot, no. 86. Appointed by Dunstan (when bishop of London) to rule over the newly-constituted abbey of Westminster, a *cenobiolum* for 12 monks (Wm. Malmesbury, *G.P.* 178). Since Dunstan was probably appointed to the see of London in 959, that will be the earliest date for Wulfsige's appointment (and not 958, as in *Flete*, ed. Armitage Robinson, 79). He may have been appointed abbot at this time (Malmesbury *loc. cit.*), or his appointment as abbot may have followed many years later (*Flete*, ed. Armitage Robinson, 79). He attended as abbot (of Westminster) a witenage-mot in 989 or 990 (Robertson no. 63). In 992 he was appointed bishop of Sherborne, retaining his office as abbot (*Flete*, *loc. cit.*). But he must (if the relevant charter is authentic and correctly dated) have relinquished the abbacy by 997, for he attests a charter of Æthelred II (K. 698), dated 997, as bishop of Sherborne, in conjunction with Ælfwig, abbot of Westminster (discussed above under ' Ælfric, Abbot '). Wulfsige died, not in 1005 (as in Armitage Robinson's ' Dates of the Abbots ' in *Flete*, 139), but in 1001/2 (cf. K. 706, dated 1001, attested by Wulfsige as bishop of Sherborne, and K. 707, dated 1002, attested by Bishop Æthelric, probably Wulfsige's successor). Wulfsige was canonised, being known as St. Wulsin.

Wulfstan, Archbishop, no. 27. Archbishop of York from 1002 till his death on 28 May 1023. Wulfstan held the see of London from 996 to 1002, when he was translated to the combined sees of Worcester and York. He relinquished the see of Worcester in 1016, and held that of York alone until his death. Wulfstan is well-known as the writer of homilies, more particularly the famous *Sermo Lupi ad Anglos*. He seems to have taken an active part in drafting the later laws of Æthelred II, which contain many phrases and constructions characteristic of works known to be by Wulfstan. For his career as ecclesiastic, statesman, and homilist, see D. Whitelock, *Eng. Hist. Rev.* lii (1937), 460 ff., lvi (1941), i. ff., lxiii (1948), 433 ff. ; *Sermo Lupi ad Anglos* (London, 1939) ; *Trans. R. Hist. Soc.* xxiv (1942), 25 ff.

Wulfstan, Bishop, nos. 102, 115 (monk), 116, 117. Wulfstan II, bishop of Worcester 1062–95. For the life of Wulfstan, see the *Vita Wulfstani* of William of Malmesbury, ed. R. R. Darlington (Royal Historical Society, 1928), and Sir Ivor Atkins, ' The Church of Worcester ', *The Antiquaries Journal*, vol. xx (1940), 1–38, 203–29. Wulfstan, a priest, afterwards took monastic vows, and entered the cathedral priory at Worcester where he filled in turn the office of school-master, precentor and sacristan. On the death of Æthelwine he was elected prior. He was subsequently appointed to the see of Worcester in circumstances which are described on pp. 407–9 above ; his election was canonically confirmed on 29 August 1062, and he was consecrated on 8 September. From 1075 Wulfstan occupied a unique position as the only surviving prelate of English birth. The date of his death is given by Fl. Wig. as 18 January 1095, but R. R. Darlington has shown (*loc. cit.* p. xliii) that the correct date must be 20 January. Wulfstan was formally canonised in 1203.

Wulfstan, cantor, no. 113. Precentor of Winchester, and according to Wm. Malmesbury (*G.R.* ed. Stubbs, i. 167), an attendant and pupil of Bishop Æthelwold, and his biographer. On his literary works, which (according to Malmesbury) included a treatise *De Tonorum Harmonia*, and which also included, besides a Life of St. Æthelwold, the versification of an account of the life and miracles of St. Swithun (ed. M. Huber, *Beilage zum Jahresbericht des humanistischen Gymnasiums Metten*, 1905–06), see T. Wright, *Biographia Britannica Literaria* (1842–46), i. 471–4, and DNB. See also p. 389, n. 1.

Wulfwig, Bishop, nos. 55, 62, 90, 91, 94, 95, 102, 103, 104 (*Wulsi*). Bishop of Dorchester 1053–67, appointed to the see in the lifetime of his predecessor Ulf (q.v.). He went abroad for his consecration (*Chron.* C 1053). Wulfwig died in 1067.

Wulfwold, Abbot, no. 6, Abbot of Bath ; nos. 42, 43, 93, Abbot of Chertsey (an identification rightly made by Mr. Philip Grierson, ' Les Livres de l'Abbé Seiwold de Bath ', *Revue Bénédictine,* lii (1940), 96–116. Mr. Grierson points out that Wulfwold was a pluralist ; Chertsey, richer and more important than Bath, he governed in person, whereas at Bath, from 1061 to 1084, Wulfwold and another abbot held office conjointly. Wulfwold was probably appointed abbot of Chertsey on Siward's promotion to the see of Rochester in 1058 (*Chron.* D, E, Plummer, ii. 248) ; there is no mention of any other abbot of Chertsey at this time. For an alleged charter of Edward the Confessor in favour of Wulfwold as abbot of Chertsey (K. 812), see pp. 202 f. above. Wulfwold was abbot of Bath in 1061, in which year King Edward gave him land at Ashwick (see no. 6 ; and on the Ashwick charter, K. 811, see p. 430), his colleague at this time being Ælfwig, succeeded by Sæwold, who was succeeded by Ælfsige, Wulfwold retaining all this time his office of abbot (VCH *Somerset,* ii. 70). It is suggested in the VCH *Somerset* (*loc. cit.*) that the phrase in the Confessor's charter : *cuidam abbati meo Wlfwoldo,* may indicate a special relationship to the king. Wulfwold appears as abbot of Bath in two writs of William I (Davis, *Regesta,* nos. 7 and 241, dated by the editor 1067 and 1066–87 respectively). Wulfwold's signature is attached to the document regarding the dispute heard before William I in 1072 in which Lanfranc claimed the primacy (Raine, *Hist. of the Church of York,* R.S. iii. 13). He was one of the six abbots who between 1072 and 1077 entered into a bond of association with Wulfstan, bishop of Worcester, and pledged themselves with Wulfstan to observe the rule of St. Benedict, to be loyal to their own bishop and to the king and queen, and to perform certain religious observances for their own mutual benefit and that of the inmates of their houses (Thorpe pp. 615–17 ; for comment see VCH *Surrey,* ii. 58, n. 10) ; in this association Wulfwold acted for Chertsey, his colleague Ælfsige for Bath. Wulfwold was present at the plea at Kentford (*Lib. Eliensis,* p. 251 ; see p. 223 above). Wulfwold died on 19 April 1084 (*Chron.* E).

Wulsi, Bishop, no 104, see **Wulfwig.**

Wy-, see **Wi-.**

INDEX

Persons who are the subjects of Biographical Notes (pp. 546-80) do not appear in this Index unless additional information (amounting to more than an incidental reference) can be provided.

Among the abbreviations used in the Index the following should be noted:—

abb	abbot	cha	charter	emp	emperor
abp	archbishop	ct	court	gt	grant
auth	authentic	e.	earl	mon	monastery
bp	bishop	eald	ealdorman	sher	sheriff

Figures in bold type stand for the numbers of the writs.

exclusionary clauses, 29 n. 1, 66, 169 ; sher & *motgerefa*, **5**, 127–30 ; bp, **8**, 140–5 ; sher, **41**, 205–7 ; royal officials, **111**, 383 & n. 3, *see also* **54**, 238–9

excommunication, 68–9, 123, 275, 567

exemption, monastic, 140 & n. 3, 141 & n. 2, 142, 144 ; *see also* monastery

Exeter : ' The Exeter Book of Old English Poetry ', 9 & n. 1, 2, 21 n. 1, 479, 553, 565 ; port-reeves at, 50 n. 4

Extracta de Testamento Sancti Eadwardi Regis, 292–4, App. III

Eynsham, abbey of, *see* Ælfric

fabrication of writs : discussed, 105–7 ; lists, 117–18

fair, *see* geares ceping

Fanton, Ess, 105 & n. 1, 295, 306, 338

faldwurthi, *see* fold-

Fawley hundred, 374 n. 3

Fécamp, cha (K. 890), 16 n. 1

feld, ' open land ' in formula with ' woodland ', *see* wudu

Felix, Frankish secretary of K. Æthelwulf, 33 & n. 2

fenland disputes, 252–5

feoh, ' money ', **72**

festival season, *see* freols, tid

fideles in writs, 54 ; in Frankish dipls, 29

fihtwite : meaning of, 81 ; **18, 24, 45, 47, 61,** 73–4, 79, 84, 147, 223

fine, 46, 74, 79–85, 126, 212, 319, 495 ; *see also* wite

First Charter : Edw Conf (K. 824), 289 n. 3, 288–91, & *passim* in Westm material ; Wm I, 312 n. 2, 337, 517

First Seal, Edw Conf : discussed, 102–3

fish, fishery, 305, 434, 451, 457, 459–60, 496, 513, 517 ; *crassus piscis*, 426, 467, 474

flymenafyrmth : meaning of, 81–2 ; **28, 33, 34, 38, 40–42** *and fq.*, 73–4, 79, 204–8, 299, 307, 311, 381

fold-soke, 438

fold-worthy, **61,** 249, 475–6

Folkestone, Kent, cha (K. 1327), 51 n. 3, 239

Fonthill, Wilts, 12, 16

food-rent, 376

for, conj., ME, 331, 336

Fordwich, Kent, 458 ; writ, **39**, 197

foreign : ? influence on writ development, 2, 28–34 ; imitation of writ, 3–5 ; priests at St. Paul's,

238 & n. 2, in royal scriptorium, 29 n. 1 ; traders, 83, 467

foreshore, rights, *see* strand

foresteall : meaning of, 81 ; 73–4, 79 ; in formula, ' grithbreach and hamsocn and foresteall ', *see* grithbreach ; in DB, 319

forfeiture, *forisfactura* : as offence, 79–82, 125, 173, n. 1, 223, 319 ; as punishment (forfeiture), 77–82, 225–6, 310, 319 ; **48**, *forisfacta* ; *see also* gylt, forwyrhtan

forger, 61, 106 n. 1, 144, 295, 298, 316, 338–9

forisfacere, ' do injury to ', 464

formest, *see* fyrmest

formulas : of writ, discussed, 61–73 ; patterns of, 85–92 ; after Cq, 43 n. 3 ; continuity in, 14, 57, 61, 65 ; of dipl, 8 ; of papal chancery, 26 n. 1

Förster M., 266 & n. 2, 483, 496, 564

forwyrhtan, **68**, 273–4, 489 ; *see also* forfeiture

Fosse Way, 415, 506

France : wax seal in, 93–8 ; charters, *see* Capetian, Carolingian, Frankish ; traders from, 83 ; Frenchman, 85, 115

Frankish, Franks : diplomas, 2, 29–30, 32 n. 1, 72, 91 n. 1, 128 n. 1, 305 ; mandates, 29–34, 73 n. 1 ; methods of sealing, 92–3 ; art of government, 33 ; *see also* Felix, foreign, *indiculus*

frankpledge, 206, 405

fraternity, *see* confraternity

free : ' freely ', **111** ; free (from gafol, geld, scot, toll, etc.), *note*, 496, 526 ; *see also* freeman

freedom, **61**, 249, 337, 432–4 ; full freedom, **45, 73, 75, 77, 105, 106**

freely, **42, 61,** 203, 206

freeman : freeman and dreng, **121**, 532 ; commended freemen, 19, App. IV no. 17 ; as technical term, *see* liber homo ; free sokemen, *see* sokemen

Freeman, E. A., 51–2, 275, 553, 573

freols, ' festival ', *note*, 460 ; **40, 41, 110**, 207 ; *see also* tid

freols : nn., ' freedom ', ' cha of freedom ', 35, 39, 140, 168–70, 432–4 ; *note*, 426, 447–8 ; *freols*, adj., ' free ', *freolslice*, adv. ' freely ', 426

freondlice : discussed, 62–3

friendship, loss of king's : meaning of, 67–8 & n. 1 ; 212, 329

frith, and cpds, **114**, 405

INDEX

591

Green, J. R., 275

Greenford, Middx, 321, 510 ; writs, **88, 89,** 298, 312, 320–2

greeting formula ; discussed, 1, 61–3 ; in papal letters, 26 n. 1 ; *sende gretan, hateð gretan,* 10–11 ; *hælo eow wyscað,* 11 ; in Frankish mandate, 31 ; *see also* salutemformula

Grentemesnil : Hugh de, 335 n. 1 ; 522

Grimbald of St. Bertin's, 32

Grimketel, bp, 146–7, 435–6, 562, 572, 575

grith, ' peace ', ' protection ', **121,** 80, 420, 423, 534 ; ' God's grith and mine ', **62,** ' God's grith and St. Mary's and mine ', **45** ; sanctuary, 447

grithbreach, *grithbryce* : meaning of, 80 ; 73–4, 79 ; in formula, ' grithbreach, and hamsocn and foresteall ', with some differences in order, **4, 18, 24,** & *passim* ; first appearance in authent writ of formula, **28,** 171 ; formula, 123–5, 204–8, 307, 329, 336, 441 ; ref in DB, 319 ; grithbreach with mundbreach, 336

guard, *see* weardwite

gylt, ' offence ', **61,** 477 ; *see also* forfeiture

Gyrth, e., 316, 474, 562

haga, ' messuage ', **111,** 382–3, 508, 517–18

hagan land, ' own lands ', 201–2

Hakon K. of Norway, gt by, 4

halra tunge, mid, note, 500

Hampshire, **85, 107** ; sher, 52 ; local forces, 555

Hampton, Worcs, 37 & n. 1, 38, 226, 465

hamsocn : meaning of, 79–80 ; in formula, ' grithbreach, and hamsocn and foresteall ', *see* grithbreach ; *see also* heimfare

hand over landbook and land, to, 40–1 ; *see also* scriptum et donum suscepi

handwriting as criterion of date, 113–14, 318, 325, 328, 332

hanging wax seal : Engl innovation, 92–3 ; imitated abroad, 93

Harold I, K., Harefoot : 547 ; coins of, 151 n. 2 ; burial-place, 287 ; lost writ, abstract of, 4, 16–19, 62, 71, App. IV no. 5

Harold II, e., K., 103, 123, 203 n. 3, 228, 271, 300–2, 407–8, App. IV

no. 12, 559, 563, 578 ; earldoms, 48, 246, 316, 506–7, 547, 563 ; Wells writ, 19, 63, 270–1, 275–6

Harrow, Middx, hunting rights at, 179

Harthacnut (Harda-), K., 17–18, 563 : Ramsey writs, 18, 63, 67, 69–70, 246 : Bury cha, 140–1 & n. 2, 142, 434–5

Haskins, C. H., 49 n. 2, 98, 467

Hastings, B. of, 472, 561–3, 567

Hayling Island, Hants, 384 & n. 1, 526 : writ, **111,** 382–5 ; cha, Wm I, II, 385

headmen, **102,** 48

heimfare, heinfara, 167, 319

Helmstan of Fonthill, 12–13

help for beneficiary requested : discussed, 65

Hemingford, Hunts, 471–2 ; writs, **57, 58,** 246 ; 552

Henry de Blois bp of Winchester, 373, 385, 523

Henry I, K. ; writs, writ-cha, cha, Abingd, 125, 128–30 ; Ch Ch, 168, 174–7 ; Chertsey, 203 n. 4, 206–8 ; Cirenc, 212–13 ; Cnihtengild, 231 n. 1, 232 & n. 1 ; Ely, 223 ; Lond, 179 ; Ramsey, 251 ; Westm, 306, 312 n. 3 ; Winch, 386 ; York, 415 ; *Dei gratia* style, 176, 177 n. 1

Henry II, K., writs, etc., Abingd, 129 n. 1 ; Ch Ch, 44, 168, 174–9 ; Chertsey, 203 n. 4, 206–8 ; Cnihtengild, 231 n. 1 ; Westm, 306 ; *Dei gratia* style, *see* Henry I, above

Henry III, K., writs, etc., St. Aug, 190 ; Chertsey, 202–6

Henry I, K. of France, seal of, 95, 98 & n. 5

Henry II, K., emp, seal of, 96

Henry III, emp, 99, 100 n. 4 ; seal of, 96, 101

Henry IV, emp, seal, 96, 101

Hereford, 84, 227–8, 547 ; bpric, 227 n. 3 ; bps, *see* Æthelstan, Leofgar, Walter ; cath (St. Ethelbert's), canons, 227 n. 3, 228 & n. 1, 547 ; moneyers, 151, 445 ; writs, **49, 50,** 57, 64, 116, 227–30, 405 ; seal, 105, 229–30 ; cartulary, 465

Herefordshire, **49, 50,** 569 ; shire ct, 46 ; sher, 52, 228 ; earldom, 466, 563, 570

heregeld : *note,* 439–40 ; writ, **15,** 376, 434

Herfast, *see* Arfast

heriot, 549

Printed in Great Britain by Butler & Tanner Ltd., Frome and London

A Bromfield and a Coventry Writ of King Edward the Confessor

ABBREVIATIONS

AS Writs *Anglo-Saxon Writs*, ed. F. E. Harmer (Manchester, 1952).
DB Domesday Book.

DNB *Dictionary of National Biography*.
VCH *Shropshire Victoria County History of Shropshire*.

IN the introduction to his valuable Short Catalogue of *Medieval Cartularies of Great Britain* (London, 1957) Mr G. R. C. Davis remarks that in the survival to our own day of individual cartularies (i.e. registers of charters or muniments) much has been due to chance—to the good fortune whereby some texts have remained undisturbed, and often unnoticed, among the archives or other places of safe-keeping, where they were placed in the past by those who made them, often centuries ago. Others, treasured as title-deeds, have passed from owner to owner with the estates with which they are concerned. But not all the charters in these collections, or the individual charters copied on single pieces of parchment which still survive in large numbers, can be taken at their face-value. Charters indeed might prove to be of value as evidence of claims in some dispute and be preserved as evidence of title irrespective of their genuineness. In his interesting paper on 'The Nature and Use of the Westminster Abbey Muniments'[1] Mr L. E. Tanner pointed out that the Offa charter at Westminster Abbey is 'at least a century later than the date it bears'. The impressive charter of Archbishop Dunstan, 'with its seal whereon Dunstan is described as Bishop of Worcester on one side and Bishop of London on the other', Mr Tanner describes as 'a work of imagination dating from the early part of the twelfth century'. 'It did excellent work for us,' he continues, 'for

[1] *Transactions of the Royal Historical Society*, 4th ser., XIX (1936), 43-78.

it entirely convinced Archbishop Stephen Langton in 1222 that the claim of the Bishop of London to jurisdiction over the Abbey could not be substantiated and that claim has not since been renewed.' And other instances of the fabrication of evidence could easily be found, as for example in the Coventry material which will be discussed below (p. 98 ff.). The Coventry writ printed here in English for the first time is, however, a late-thirteenth- or early-fourteenth-century copy[1] of an authentic writ of King Edward the Confessor (below, p. 102 f.). One potential source of charter material which has only rarely been drawn upon consists of the documents laid up in episcopal registries or copied into the registers themselves. The writ concerning Bromfield, in Shropshire, printed and discussed below, was copied in the early fourteenth century into the Register of Richard de Swinfield, bishop of Hereford (1283-1317), probably from a copy found in the archives of the priory which took the place of the former Bromfield Minster.[2] Garbled as is its text, it yet preserves the main outlines and the characteristic details of a typical Edwardian writ; and although W. W. Capes, who printed it (see below, p. 101), treated it with caution, there can scarcely be any doubt of its fundamental authenticity.[3]

The Bromfield writ (below, p. 101 f.) was issued by King Edward the Confessor for the twelve canons of Bromfield, a village between Ludlow and Shrewsbury, situated near the confluence of the Rivers Teme and Onny, about two and a half miles north-west

[1] Consulted verbally, Mr G. R. C. Davis kindly informed me that he would date to the early fourteenth century the handwriting of the Coventry cartulary quire (*Medieval Cartularies*, no. 275) in which the writ appears; the quire being written as a single compilation. Miss Joan C. Lancaster, to whom the recent discovery of the writ is due (see below, p. 98 f.), kindly informed me verbally that, on grounds of content and of handwriting, she would date the quire in question to the late thirteenth century.

[2] I am greatly indebted to the bishop of Hereford for his kind permission, with the concurrence of Prebendary Moir, to print this writ preserved in the Hereford Diocesan Registry. I also owe thanks to the Diocesan Registrar and his secretary for giving me access to it. The above suggestion as to its provenance was made by W. W. Capes.

[3] I owe the opportunity of editing it here to the generosity of Professor Bruce Dickins, who relinquished the writ to me after discovering it in Capes' editions published by the Cantilupe Society.

of Ludlow.[1] Apart from the writ under discussion, no information appears to be available as to the pre-Conquest history of this community of secular clerks, save for an episode which forms a highlight in the somewhat monotonous Shropshire section of Domesday Book, and which adds a few facts to what is known from other sources of the happenings of the last few weeks, or days, of the Confessor's life. The date of the foundation of the 'minster' which the clerks served at Bromfield, dedicated to St Mary, is unknown. But there can be little doubt that it was an 'old minster',[2] one of those ancient establishments, sometimes of royal, sometimes of episcopal, foundation, in which, although the term *monasterium* might be applied to them, the members of the community were not monks but secular clerks—'my clerks', as the Confessor describes them in his writ; *canonici* as they are termed in Domesday Book. Sir Frank Stenton has observed[3] that in the eighth century and even later the term 'minster' was often applied to a church served by a group of clergy sharing a communal life, and that it is through this usage that the greater parish church came to be called a minster, a term which often remained for centuries to distinguish such foundations. D. H. S. Cranage observed[4] that the Saxon parish of Bromfield was very extensive, including Ludford and Halford, and very possibly several other places and even Ludlow itself. Does the king's description of the beneficiaries in the Bromfield writ as 'my clerks' imply that this was a royal foundation? Or does it imply the existence of bonds of friendship and affection between the king

---

[1] I am indebted for valuable information concerning Bromfield and its minster and later priory to the guide to *Bromfield Priory and Church in Shropshire* (Chester, 1947) by Prebendary A. L. Moir, M.A., F.R.Hist.Soc., formerly vicar of Bromfield, who has printed not only the Bromfield writ (from Capes' text) but also a number of later Bromfield charters and references. My text and my translation differ in some respects from Prebendary Moir's.

[2] cf. II Edgar, 1, i, *Die Gesetze der Angelsachsen*, ed. F. Liebermann (Halle, 1903-16), 1, 196, and *The Laws of the Kings of England from Edmund to Henry I*, ed. A. J. Robertson (Cambridge, 1925), p. 20: 'All payment of tithe is to be made to the old minster (*ad matrem ecclesiam*) to which the parish belongs.' Here the 'old minster' is distinguished from later churches which might be built within its parish.

[3] *Anglo-Saxon England*, 2nd ed. (Oxford, 1947), pp. 148-9, 152 and 660.

[4] *An Architectural Account of the Churches of Shropshire*, I (Wellington, 1894), 70-6; R. W. Eyton, *Antiquities of Shropshire*, v (London, 1857), 207-24.

and the canons, perhaps of close acquaintance? The two possibilities are not of course mutually exclusive. King Edward may well have visited their minster when journeying to and from his numerous Shropshire manors, or when visiting Shrewsbury, where special provision in the way of guards and beaters was made for him when he went hunting.[1] That there were some dealings between them is evident from the episode referred to above (p. 91), which in Eyton's view displayed King Edward as 'injudicious in his choice of favourites, zealously pious in his intentions, dilatory and irresolute in his actions'.[2] We learn from Domesday Book[3] that in the manor of St Mary at Bromfield there were in King Edward's time twenty hides, and that twelve canons of this church had the whole. One of their number, named Spirtes,[4] alone held ten hides (of the twenty), but when he was banished from England (for a reason not stated) King Edward gave his ten hides to Robert fitz Wimarch[5] as to a canon (*sicut canonico*). Robert however gave them to his son-in-law. When the canons pointed this out to the king, he forthwith ordered that the land should revert to the church, 'only delaying (to enforce this order) till at the Court of the then approaching Christmas he should be able to order Robert (personally) to provide other land for his son-in-law'.[6] But the king himself died, says Domesday Book, at the very time of that feast (*in ipsis festis diebus*).[7] And

---

[1] DB, I, 252; *VCH Shropshire*, I, 309.   [2] *op. cit.*, v, 208.

[3] DB, I, 252b; *VCH Shropshire*, I, 313.

[4] For the distinctive name *Spirtes, Spirites*, see O. von Feilitzen, *The Pre-Conquest Personal Names of Domesday Book* (Uppsala, 1937), p. 207 and n. 3. On 'Spirtes the canon' see Eyton, *op. cit.*, v, 208-9. Spirtes is said to have been a favourite of two kings, Harold Harefoot and Harthacnut. Could his banishment have been due to possible pro-Danish sympathies, as Prebendary Moir suggests?

[5] On this well-known figure, see *DNB*. See also *AS Writs*, p. 571.

[6] This is Eyton's rendering of the Latin *tantum inducians donec ad curiam instantis natalis Domini Roberto iuberet ut genero suo terram aliam prouideret*. James Tait, however (*VCH Shropshire*, I, 292), interprets it to mean that the king postponed execution (of his order) until the Christmas Court of 1065, to give Robert time to provide his son-in-law with land elsewhere.

[7] It is known that at Christmas 1065 King Edward was taken ill so that he was unable to be present at the dedication on 28 December of the new church at Westminster which he had built for the abbey. He died on 5 January 1066. The *Vita Ædwardi*, ed. H. R. Luard, *Lives of Edward the Confessor* (Rolls Series, 1858), p. 431, which describes Robert fitz Wimarch as *regalis palatii stabilitor et ejusdem regis propinquus*, says he was present at the Confessor's death-bed.

from that time till now (1086) the church has lost the land. This land Robert now holds under Earl Roger, and it is waste, and was found waste—an allusion to devastation suffered by the western and southern parts of the shire through Welsh inroads (or possibly after the Norman Conquest). In all, concludes Domesday Book, there is land (sufficient) for fifty-four ploughs. But in the early twelfth century the constitution of this minster of twelve secular canons was altered, and it became a community of Benedictine monks, which later, in 1155, became a cell of St Peter's, Gloucester.[1]

The Bromfield writ appears to date from the years 1056-61, when the see of Hereford was vacant, and most probably from the last of those years, and to have been issued a little later than a writ (1057-60) of the Confessor for the priests of Hereford Cathedral.[2] It is addressed to Archbishop Ealdred of York (1060-69), Bishop Begard, Earl Harold—to whose earldom of Wessex Herefordshire had been annexed after the death in 1057 of Earl Ralf—and 'all my thegns in Herefordshire and in Shropshire':[3] the adverb *freondlice*, which by custom concluded the clause, has no doubt been lost in transmission. Its date must be subsequent to 25 December 1060, the date of Ealdred's election to the see of York. But for four years previously, from 1056—when on 16 June the martial Bishop Leofgar of Hereford, having occupied the see only eleven weeks and four days, fell in battle against the Welsh[4]—Ealdred, bishop of the neighbouring see of Worcester, had administered the see of Hereford during a vacancy *donec antistes constitueretur*. The new bishop of Hereford, Walter, a Lotharingian, was consecrated by Pope Nicolas II at Rome on 15 April (Easter Day) in 1061. The issue of the writ

---

[1] For its subsequent history, see W. Dugdale, *Monasticon Anglicanum* (London, 1846), IV, 154 ff.; Moir, *op. cit.*, and the charters there printed.

[2] *AS Writs*, no. 49.

[3] The words 'and of Saloppshire' entered above the line were previously omitted, no doubt through inadvertence. The form *Saloppshire* was not in use in the Confessor's time. It represents an Anglo-Norman alteration of the OE *Scrobbesbyrigscir*, namely the shire attached to Shrewsbury, OE *Scrobbesbyrig, Scrobesbyrig*, which gave it its name, and which is itself derived from the OE personal name *Scrob(b)*. For other forms see E. Ekwall, *The Concise Oxford Dictionary of English Place-Names*, 3rd ed. (Oxford, 1947); these include *Salopescira* 1094-8, from which ModE *Salop* is derived, and DB *Sciropescire*, ModE *Shropshire*.

[4] ASC 1056 C, D.

would seem then to fall between these dates, namely Christmas 1060 and Easter 1061. As for Bishop Begard, also addressed in the writ, his name does not appear in the lists of Anglo-Saxon bishops, and our knowledge of the occupants of sees elsewhere is imperfect. Could the name Begard represent the alteration of the name of a Welsh bishop, and in particular (as Professor Bruce Dickins has suggested to me) that of Bleiddud, bishop of St David's, who might conceivably have followed a precedent established by a predecessor, called Tremerin or Tramerin in English sources,[1] and have acted in a temporary capacity as bishop of Hereford after Ealdred's promotion in 1060 and before the arrival in 1061 of Walter?[2] W. W. Capes, however, when he printed the writ, hazarded the conjecture that the name Begard 'may have been altered by the transcriber from that of Bedreu, a bishop of Llandaff at this time' (whom I have been unable to trace); but he did not offer any evidence. The contemporary bishop 'of Llandaff' would seem, however, to have been a certain Herewald.[3] On the other hand, in view of the constant coming and going of ecclesiastics between England and the Continent at this period, we cannot dismiss the possibility that Begard had come to England from overseas.

In the late Old English period the royal writ was employed to inform those concerned, namely, in most cases, the officers and suitors of a public court (most often a shire court), that the king

[1] Tramerin (who died in 1055) had assisted Bishop Athelstan of Hereford as coadjutor after Athelstan had been incapacitated by blindness; see ASC 1055 C, D; Florence of Worcester, *Chronicon ex Chronicis*, ed. B. Thorpe (London, 1848-9), I, 214.

[2] The death of Bleiddud (Bledud), bishop of St David's, is dated to 1071 in H. Wharton, *Anglia Sacra* (London, 1691), II, 649, and that of his predecessor Joseph to 1061. If this dating is correct, and if Bleiddud was Begard (as is by no means certain), he might conceivably have been addressed as bishop in this writ (before Easter 1061). W. Stubbs does not include these bishops of St David's in his lists in *Registrum Sacrum Anglicanum*, 2nd ed. (Oxford, 1897), save that he cites (p. 37) a statement by R. de Diceto that Bleduc of St David's was consecrated at Canterbury by Æthelnoth (1020-38). But it is difficult to feel any confidence in R. de Diceto's dating, though if Bleduc was Bleiddud, he might originally have been consecrated first as bishop of some other see, but have been associated by R. de Diceto with a later appointment to St David's. It is fortunate that the dating of the writ does not rest on these uncertainties.

[3] On the diocese of Llandaff see Christopher Brooke, 'The Archbishops of St David's, Llandaff and Caerleon-on-Usk', *Studies in the Early British Church*, ed. N. K. Chadwick (Cambridge, 1958), pp. 201-42.

had made (or confirmed) a grant of office, privileges, land or other such matters to an individual or a community. In the Bromfield writ, as in many others, the king is notifying a grant (very probably in return for a heavy payment) of rights which will increase the prestige of the Bromfield canons, augment their revenues, and safeguard them from interference—rights which the king himself possessed and which only he could grant away.[1] The grant of *sake and soke* gave them the right to take the profits of jurisdiction arising from offences committed upon their lands. The grant of *infangenetheof* gave them the right of doing justice on a thief taken within the estate in possession of stolen property. As for the grants of *grithbreach, hamsocn* and *forsteall* (or *foresteall*)— these have reference to serious crimes which were normally reserved to the king's own jurisdiction, unless, as in this writ, he granted away the proceeds of the penalties imposed to some specially favoured person or community. We learn from Domesday Book[2] that at Shrewsbury and no doubt elsewhere in the shire, in King Edward's time, the very heavy penalty of 100 shillings was imposed on those guilty of ambush (*forsteall*), or of forcible entry into people's houses (*hamsocn* or *heinfare*). The same heavy fine had to be paid by the man who knowingly committed the crime called *grithbreach*, that is infringed the king's peace, namely, the protection extended by the king to certain persons, places, times and seasons. This penalty of 100 shillings was incurred if the king's peace had been imposed by the king's officer, the sheriff. If however the peace so violated had been imposed by the king's own hand, then the offender was condemned to outlawry. Moreover, in addition to these 'forfeitures', the king grants to the Bromfield canons every fine (*ylces wites*), that is to say every fine which was exacted as punishment for a large number of offences (in addition to the compensation which had to be paid to the injured party) 'within borough and without', that is in every place upon their lands. The king does not however grant them the heavy penalty paid for harbouring fugitives(*flymenafyrmth*), one of the category of more serious crimes which was however granted away to many religious houses.

The grant of *toll and team*, which still remains for mention, denotes, so far as *toll* is concerned, the right to take toll on the sale

---

[1] On these see Stenton, *op. cit.*, pp. 488-95.
[2] I, 252; *VCH Shropshire*, I, 309.

of cattle or other goods within an estate. *Team* stands for the right to take the profits and perhaps to hold the legal procedure in a case of 'vouching to warranty', whereby a person accused of the unlawful possession of goods, could 'vouch his warrantor', that is, pass on the charge to the person from whom he had acquired the property in dispute. But with this grant to the canons of Bromfield, as also in a very similar writ in favour of the monks of St Augustine's, Canterbury,[1] local conditions are taken into account. Both these communities had property adjacent to rivers and streams, with river-banks, strands, landing-places, markets, mills, mill-ponds, bridges, ferries and so on, where all kinds of trading and trafficking giving rise to *toll* and to *team* went on. St Augustine's, for instance, had its port at Fordwich on the R. Stour near Canterbury, whilst rivers and streams flowed through the Bromfield canons' lands and their minster itself was situated on a peninsula. 'On strand and in stream' appears then in these and other grants of the Confessor, so that the beneficiaries succeeded to whatever rights of toll the king by custom had formerly enjoyed upon their property.

The protection extended in the latter part of the Bromfield writ, safe-guarding the canons from appropriation and interference, especially episcopal interference, may well have appeared to be a necessary precaution in view of the impending arrival of the new bishop. But writ after writ of the Confessor expresses similar prohibitions, in different terms, as does, for example, the writ, referred to above (p. 93), secured by the priests of Hereford Cathedral. The exception that is made, 'save whomsoever they may themselves desire', is no doubt to be interpreted in the light of similar exceptions elsewhere, that is, 'except themselves and their officers (*wicneras*)'. And, as in other writs, so in this one, a sanction is mentioned, namely, 'on pain of losing my friendship'—a threat which is no doubt to be interpreted in a positive sense, that the offender will incur the king's enmity.

A few further points invite comment:

(*a*) Reference to the 'common form' of Edwardian writs suggests that in the clause *ich coupe ow þat ich habbe ʒeuen*, etc., the verb *ʒeuen* has replaced *geunnen*, normally used in a clause which is

---

[1] *AS Writs*, no. 38.

followed by the construction 'that they be worthy of, i.e. shall be entitled to, shall legally possess, such and such a privilege'.[1]

(*b*) The grant is represented as being made to *Seynte Marie moder Cristes munstres*—obviously a corruption of the text. Until evidence to the contrary is forthcoming, it seems reasonable to suppose that *moder Cristes* is an interpolation in this context. Did the original text include *minster* in this passage? In that case the construction would probably have been 'I have granted *into Sēe Marian mynstre*',[2] i.e. 'for the benefit of, to, St Mary's minster'. But grants are not infrequently represented as being made to a saint in person, as, for example, 'I have granted to my kinsman St Edmund' (*AS Writs*, no. 14), 'I have granted to St Augustine' (*AS Writs*, no. 38), and in the Bromfield writ, as a possibility, 'I have granted *Sēe Marie*'. I have included both these possibilities in my amended text.

(*c*) There is no close parallel known to me for the valedictory clause, *sound ow ʒe holden*. On the analogy of the closely parallel St Augustine's writ referred to above, the Bromfield writ may well have concluded with *God eow gehealde*, 'God keep you'—a valediction, which, with the variant *God eow ealle gehealde*, forms the conclusion of about twenty Anglo-Saxon writs. On the other hand, the Cnihtengild writ (*AS Writs*, no. 51) concludes with 'I will not permit anyone to do them wrong, but (on the contrary) may they all prosper (*beon heo ealle gesunde*). And God keep you all (*God eow ealle gehealde*).' I have therefore, with this possible precedent in view, ventured in my amended text to read *Beoð gesunde*.[3] *God eow gehealde*. ('Farewell. God keep you.')

The interest of the Bromfield writ extends then in several directions. It enlarges our knowledge of the history of this community of secular priests by providing evidence of its existence which is independent of Domesday Book. Not only that, it is the only writ relating to Shropshire which has come down to us, though two Hereford writs are extant, one for the priests of Hereford Cathedral (1057-60) (see above, p. 93), the other for Bishop Walter (1061-66), whose arrival the Bromfield canons and

---

[1] See *AS Writs*, p. 64.
[2] cf. *AS Writs*, no. 4.
[3] See Bosworth-Toller, s.v. *gesund*, where *beoþ gesunde* corresponds to *avete*, *salvete*.

G

the Hereford priests must have been expecting between Christmas 1060 and Easter 1061, when the Bromfield writ was issued. It provides a further instance of large and comprehensive grants to religious communities. And although it has been preserved only in garbled form, it conforms in every respect to the pattern of other authentic writs of King Edward the Confessor.

An entirely favourable judgement can likewise be pronounced on the authentic Coventry writ here printed in English for the first time.[1] This straightforward and unassuming text stands in almost ludicrous contrast to the mass of forged charters and writs in the names of Earl Leofric, King Edward the Confessor, and William I, put forward by the monks of Coventry from the late eleventh century onwards in pursuance of their claims to lands and privileges. Among these fabrications is the impressive writ in the name of Edward the Confessor purporting to confirm the munificent gifts made to the monastery at Coventry, which they had founded, by Earl Leofric of Mercia and his wife Godgifu (Lady Godiva), which is commonly cited in histories of Coventry, but which is none the less a forgery of the twelfth century.[2] But there can be no doubt that authentic charters and writs which have now disappeared were issued for this house, at the time of its foundation and consecration in 1043, and subsequently, as they were for other houses. The authentic writ under discussion must have been issued between 1043 and 1053, that is after the foundation and consecration of the monastery and before the appointment of Abbot Leofwine of Coventry to the see of Lichfield in 1053. The recovery of this text affords an excellent example of how large a part is played by chance in these matters. The fragmentary Coventry cartulary in which it has been preserved was bound at some time between wooden boards in company with, among other matters, a sixteenth-century register of the Gregory family, afterwards Gregory-Hood.[3] This manuscript was recently deposited by its owner, Major A. M. H. Gregory-Hood, M.C., in the Shakespeare Birthplace Library at Stratford-upon-Avon. Investigating the material in this manuscript, Miss Joan C. Lancaster, to

[1] A Latin translation, all that was then available, is printed and edited as *AS Writs*, no. 46.
[2] *AS Writs*, no. 45.
[3] Davis, *op. cit.*, no. 275.

whom I am greatly indebted, noticed the Anglo-Saxon writ under discussion and communicated her discovery to me.[1]

The foundation in 1043 of the monastery of St Mary at Coventry has rightly been associated since that time with Earl Leofric, who was appointed earl of Mercia by Cnut, and who played a leading part in the Confessor's reign; the compiler of the D version of the Anglo-Saxon Chronicle, recording Leofric's death, and burial at Coventry, in 1057, praises him for his wisdom. His wife Godgifu (Godiva) was associated with her husband not only in the foundation of Coventry, but also in the endowment of St Mary's at Stow, and the enrichment of the monasteries at Leominster, Wenlock and Chester. They made grants of land to Worcester, and munificent gifts to the abbey of Evesham. On Coventry too Leofric and Godgifu are said to have lavished much treasure as well as lands and many other gifts.[2]

The accepted account of the foundation of the monastery of St Mary at Coventry, as it appears for instance in Dugdale's *Antiquities of Warwickshire* (1765) and in his *Monasticon Anglicanum* (vol. III), has been based upon the forged charters, taken in combination with the Coventry chronicles. These charters have recently been critically examined by Miss Lancaster in an important article to which I am greatly indebted.[3] Rightly attributing to Earl Leofric (and Godgifu) the foundation at Coventry of a monastery of Benedictine monks, the charters attribute to him, as an endowment for his foundation, the grant of half Coventry (later known as 'the prior's half'), and, in addition to this, twenty-four vills in Warwickshire and elsewhere, as well as extensive judicial and financial rights. In the authentic writ of the Confessor printed here, the king confirms to Abbot Leofwine *sake and soke, toll and team* (see above, p. 95 f.) over his lands and over

---

[1] I am deeply obliged to Major A. M. H. Gregory-Hood, of Loxley Hall, Warwickshire, for very kindly agreeing to the publication of this writ. I am at the same time indebted to the Shakespeare Birthplace Trustees, as custodians of the document, for their permission. I also owe grateful thanks to Levi Fox, Esq., M.A., Director, for his good offices in kindly making the writ available to me, and for permission to print.

[2] For the oldest forms of the legend of Lady Godiva riding naked through Coventry to secure for the people of Coventry freedom from toll, see *DNB*, s.v. *Godiva*; see also Dugdale, *op. cit.*, vol. III, p.177, n. K.

[3] 'The Coventry Forged Charters: a Reconsideration', *Bulletin of the Institute of Historical Research*, XXVII (1954), 113-40.

his men as fully and completely as ever Earl Leofric had. And in this connexion it is reasonable to enquire: what grants of land did Leofric actually make to the monastery? Did he in fact grant half Coventry and the twenty-four vills?

These are among the problems discussed by Miss Lancaster in her very able investigation of the Coventry charters. After a long and detailed examination of the evidence, she is led to the conclusion that in Domesday Book 'the prior's half' of Coventry does not appear among the monastery's lands, and that in 1086 the monastery had not yet put forward its claims to half Coventry and the twenty-four vills. She suggests as a possible inference that the monastery was built on land which belonged to Godgifu in her own right; that Coventry was actually hers, not Earl Leofric's; and that Godgifu is therefore rightly included by the chroniclers as co-founder of this monastery; whilst Leofric granted them not half Coventry and the twenty-four vills,[1] but other lands and those judicial and financial rights to which reference is made in the authentic writ of the Confessor under discussion—a list of privileges which is inflated to greater length in the forged charters and writs of this house.

Miss Lancaster points out that this authentic writ of the Confessor and a (mutilated) confirmation of it by William I were disregarded when the forgeries, which had been manufactured, had served their purpose; not once does either of these genuine texts appear in a charter of confirmation or in the many lawsuits in which the priory was involved in the thirteenth and fourteenth centuries. It is indeed surprising that the Confessor's writ and the Latin translation should have survived at all, and that it should have been thought worth while to copy these texts into a Coventry cartulary. It is unfortunate that this, the only English version, should have come down to us only in a 'modernized' text, the orthography of which has been altered in transmission. The scribal alterations to be noted here do not however necessitate the presentation (as with the Bromfield writ) of an amended version of the text. But it is worth noting that the French loan-word *suffre* has been substituted for the *gepafian*, 'allow, permit', which is common form in writs of King Edward the Confessor.

---

[1] The reference in my *AS Writs*, p. 464, to the twenty-four vills, which Earl Leofric is stated in the spurious foundation charters to have granted to Coventry minster, should therefore be withdrawn.

A Bromfield and a Coventry Writ

BROMFIELD

King Edward declares that he has granted to his clerks at Bromfield judicial and financial rights over their lands. Date: Christmas 1060–Easter 1061.

Authorities

(R) Registrum Ricardi de Swinfield, Episcopi Herefordensis, A.D. 1283-1317, in the custody of the Diocesan Registrar, Hereford, fol. 152 (*olim* 153), in an early-fourteenth-century hand, printed here. I have made myself responsible for capital letters, but otherwise the spelling and punctuation of the manuscript have been preserved, except that the *punctus elevatus*, when it occurs, is indicated by a stop.

An amended text with modern punctuation is provided below. The main purpose of this is to restore the (conjectural) Edwardian formulas which have been garbled in transmission, rather than to supply examples of contemporary orthography (though I have of course endeavoured to avoid anachronisms).

Printed: W. W. Capes, *The Register of Richard de Swinfield*, Bishop of Hereford (1283-1317) (Cantilupe Society, Hereford, 1909), p. 425, with small inaccuracies. This volume was also issued, with Latin title, by the Canterbury and York Society (London, 1909).

(L) A copy of the same writ, now lost, formerly 'in the archives of the Dean and Chapter of Hereford'.

Printed: (*a*) W. W. Capes, *Charters and Records of Hereford Cathedral* (Cantilupe Society, Hereford, 1908), p. 2, with very slight differences from the preceding text. (*b*) A. L. Moir (following Capes), *Bromfield Priory and Church in Shropshire* (Chester, 1947), p. 39.

TEXT IN THE BISHOP'S REGISTER

Edward kynge gret Eldred Erchebissop and Begard Bíssop and Harald eorl and alle myne þeynes of Herefordshíre 'and of Saloppshíre' and ich coupe ow þat ich habbe ȝeuen Seynte Marie moder Crístes munstres and myne clerkes of Bromfelde þat in þoen munstre wonyeth on Cristes þewedome þat hoe boe on hore sake worþe and hore sokene of hore lond an gryþes bruches and homesokene and forstalles and ínfonggeneþeues and ulkes wytes worthe bynne burch and wít outentolles and teames of stronde and of streme. and ich nulle þolyen þat enyman enyþyng ouersoe nouþer Bíssop ne nan oþer man boten lokewo ysself wolle and ich nulle ȝe þawyen þat enyman þys abreke by myne froshype. sound ow ȝe holden.

AMENDED TEXT

Eadward kyngc gret Ealdred ærcebiscop and Begard biscop and
Harold eorl and ealle mine þegnas on Herefordscire and on
Scrobbesbyrigscire [freondlice]. And ic cyðe eow þæt ic hæbbe
geunnen into Sc̄e Marian mynstre (*or* Sc̄e Marie) and minum
clericum æt Bromfelde þe in þæm mynstre wuniað on Cristes
þeowdome, þæt hie beon heora saca wurðe and heora socne ofer
heora land, and griþes bryces and hamsocne and forstealles and
infangeneþeofes, and ylces wites wurðe binnan burh and butan,
tolles and teames on strande and on streame. And ich nylle
geþolian þæt ænig man ænig þing þær on teo, nawþer biscop ne
nan oþer man, butan lochwa hy selfe wyllen. And ic nylle geþafian
þæt ænig man þis abrece be minum freondscipe. [? Beoð]
gesunde. [God] eow gehealde.

MODERN ENGLISH RENDERING

King Edward sends friendly greetings to Archbishop Ealdred
and Bishop Begard and Earl Harold and all my thegns in Herefordshire and in Shropshire. And I inform you that I have granted
to St Mary's minster (*or* to St Mary) and to my clerks at Bromfield
who dwell in the minster in the service of Christ, that they be
entitled to (*lit.* worthy of) their sake and their soke (i.e. jurisdiction)
over their lands, and to payments made as penalty for breach of the
peace (*grithbryce*) and for forcible entry into people's houses
(*hamsocn*) and for committing ambush (*forsteall*) and to the right
of doing justice on a thief taken within the estate in possession of
stolen property (*infangenetheof*), and (that they be) entitled to
every fine within borough and without, to toll and to 'vouching
to warranty' (*team*) on strand and in stream. And I will not
suffer anyone to take anything therefrom, neither bishop nor any
other person, save whomsoever they may themselves desire. And
I will not permit anyone to violate this on pain of losing my friendship. [?Fare] well. [God] keep you.

COVENTRY

King Edward declares that he has granted to Abbot Leofwine
judicial and financial rights over his lands and over his men as
fully and as completely as ever Earl Leofric had. Date: 1043-53.

Authority

(G) Gregory Leger Book (otherwise, Stivichall Leger Book) in Shakespeare Birthplace Library, Stratford-upon-Avon, pp. 23-4, in a late-thirteenth- or early-fourteenth-century hand, printed here. The spelling and punctuation of the manuscript have been preserved, except that an ordinary letter *y* has been substituted for the *y* with a dot over it which is invariable in the manuscript, and which stands for both *y* and *þ*. In ʒe in l. 1 and ʒer in l. 2, ʒ also stands for *þ*. The symbol 7, employed here for 'and', has a stroke through it.

Unprinted. But for Latin versions see *AS Writs*, no. 46, where a Latin translation is edited with commentary.

TEXT

[E]dward ʒe kynge gret myne Busshopes 7 myne Erles 7 alle myne theygnes ín ye shíre ʒer ʒer Leouwyn Abbot ín Couentr' habbet lond ínne freondliche.   7 ich chuthe ou yat ich wille yat he boe hís sace 7 ys socene wurth.   tolles 7 temes ouer hys lond 7 ou*er* hys meyn bynnen borough 7 bouten so foul 7 so forth so so Leofríc Erl fírmest hauede.   7 ich nulle suffren yat mon hym ín any thyng mysbede. [Latin translation follows immediately.]

MODERN ENGLISH RENDERING

King Edward sends friendly greetings to my bishops and my earls and all my thegns in the shires in which Abbot Leofwine of Coventry has lands. And I inform you that it is my will that he be entitled to (*lit.* worthy of) his sake and his soke (i.e. jurisdiction), to toll and to 'vouching to warranty' (*team*) over his lands and over his men within borough and without as fully and as completely as ever Earl Leofric had. And I will not permit anyone to do him wrong in any matter.

FLORENCE E. HARMER